READINGS IN AMERICAN PUBLIC POLICY

Edited by
DENNIS PATTERSON
Department of Political Science
Texas Tech University

Cover image © Shutterstock, Inc.

Kendall Hunt
publishing company

www.kendallhunt.com
Send all inquiries to:
4050 Westmark Drive
Dubuque, IA 52004-1840

Copyright © 2010 by Kendall Hunt Publishing Company

ISBN 978-0-7575-7680-5

All rights reserved. No part of this publication may be reproduced,
stored in a retrieval system, or transmitted, in any form or by any means,
electronic, mechanical, photocopying, recording, or otherwise,
without the prior written permission of the copyright owner.

Printed in the United States of America
10 9 8 7 6 5 4 3 2 1

Contents

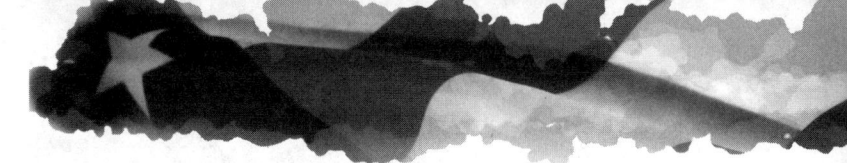

Chapter 1 — 1
Politics and the Policy Process

"Models of Politics: Some Help in Thinking About Public Policy"
Thomas Dye

"The Science of Muddling Through"
Charles E. Lindbloom

Chapter 2 — 27
Economic Policy

"The Market and the Polis"
Deborah Stone

"Economic Policy: Translating Theory into Practice"
Charles L. Cochran and Eloise F. Malone

"Budgeting for Recovery: The Need to Increase the Federal Deficit to Revive a Weak Economy"
Josh Bivens

"Economic Stimulus Pushed by Flawed Job Analysis"
Curtis Dubay, Karen Campbell and Paul Winfree

"Economic Recovery: How Best to End the Recession"
J.D. Foster and William Beach

Chapter 3 — 89
Health Care Policy

"Health Care Policy"
Carter A. Wilson

The President's Proposal

"Yes, Mr. President A Free Market can Fix Health Care"
Michael F. Cannon

Chapter 4 — 133
Education Policy

"Education Policy"
Jay M. Shafritz and Christopher P. Borick

Brown vs. Board of Education: About the Case

Lemmon vs. Kurtzman, 403 U.S. 602 (1971)

Chapter 5 — 187
Energy and Environment

"Environmental Problems and Politics"
Michael E. Kraft

Climate Change 2007 Synthesis Report: Summary for Policy Makers

"Resolving the impasse in American energy policy: The case for a transformational R&D strategy at the U.S. Department of Energy"
Benjamin K. Sovacool

"Water conservation policy alternatives for the Ogallala Aquifer in Texas"
Jeff Johnson, Phillip N. Johnson, Eduardo Segarra and David Willis

Chapter 6 — 271
Criminal Justice Policy

"Criminal Justice Policy"
Christopher A. Simon

"The Most Dangerous Right"
Dennis A. Henigan

District of Columbia vs. Heller

Chapter 7 — 371
WELFARE POLICY

"The Politics and Economics of Inequality"
Charles L. Cochran and Eloise F. Malone

The Personal Responsibility and Work Reconciliation Act: Summary of Provisions
National Association of Social Workers

"Inside the Middle Class: Bad Times Hit the Good Life"
Paul Taylor

Chapter 8 — 395
FOREIGN POLICY

"Models of International Relations and Foreign Policy"
Oli Holsti

"A Moral Core for U.S. Foreign Policy: Is Idealism Dead?"
Derek Chollet and Tod Lindberg

"What Should This Fight Be Called? Metaphors of Counterterrorism and Their Implications"
Arie W. Kruglanski, Martha Crenshaw, Jerrold M. Post and Jeff Victoroff

Introduction

Public policy is a collective outcome that results from some type of government action. In this definition, *government action* refers to the entire range of decisions that all levels of government (local, state, and national) can possibly make, including a decision not to act in a certain situation; *collective outcome* refers to a result that affects all in the deciding government's area of authority. Government decisions that lead to collective outcomes are thus the essence of public policy, and they can be the result of both formal and informal processes and may take many forms, including, but not limited to, laws, regulations, administrative actions, decisions by courts, and executive orders. Given these characteristics, we can easily conclude that public policy is important in the lives of everyone—the young and old, males and females, students and workers, voters and nonvoters, and so on. As a result, it is wise for everyone to study it and understand it as best as we can.

The purpose of this course is to provide such an opportunity, and it will accomplish this by offering students an introduction to public policy that will help them better understand the many ways it affects their lives. This will involve focusing on two aspects of public policy: (1) the content of the various substantive areas of public policy and (2) the processes through which specific policy items are considered, passed, and implemented. Concerning the content of public policy, this course will show students what is involved in the areas of economic policy and the different approaches the government has taken to address the problems it has presented, such as health care policy; K-12 and higher education policy; energy and environment policy and how they are related to each other; criminal justice policy and the different subareas it has involved; welfare policy, especially how it has changed in the past two decades; and foreign policy. In addition to the content of public policy, this course will also introduce students to the processes through which specific problems are taken up by one or more levels of government and considered through specific public policy actions to address that problem in some way. This aspect of the course will then help students understand why, for better or worse, we have the public policy outcomes that we witness in the various policy areas covered.

This then leads us to the purpose of this supplemental reader in this introductory public policy course. Most important is the fact that the content and processes of public policy are dynamic and thus what is important in one period of time may be supplanted by something else in another period. This is true in terms of the principal players involved in the policy processes, specifically the elected and appointed officials who hold the various legislative, executive, and judicial offices that consider the problems faced by individuals in their respective areas of authority and then take some action to address these problems. It is also true of the substantive areas themselves, which vary in terms of the challenges they present to individuals who will be affected by policy outcomes and the players who will produce these outcomes. As a result, it is important for students to be provided with the most up-to-date information possible on public policy, something that is difficult to do in the standard textbook format. This supplemental reader offers students the most up-to-date treatment of the various policy areas. For example, we all know that health care, a long-standing policy problem in the United States, went through a recent reform. To better understand that reform in its most contemporary aspects, this reader supplements the overview students will receive in this course's text with readings that cover President Obama's actual proposal and criticisms of that proposal.

In addition to this, public policy is such a broad area of study that the average textbook cannot cover all that it involves, both substantively and procedurally, and at the level of depth necessary to give students the understanding they need for the goals of this course to be realized. Indeed, most texts are forced to cover the various substantive areas of public policy in summary fashion. This is not problematic in and of itself because it allows for a breath of treatment that gives students a broadly gauged overview of public policy. On the other hand, summary treatments that are the hallmark of most textbooks are not useful for depth of treatment, which is a necessary component of a sincere attempt to convey to students the complexities and nuances that are often involved in the substance and processes of public policy studies. This reader remedies this problem by supplementing course texts with in-depth readings on selected policy topics. Consider, for example, the gun control area of criminal justice policy, which has been driven in large part by constitutional considerations and thus by decisions made by the U.S. Supreme Court. Most public policy texts treat this policy area by summarizing relevant legislative acts and important court cases. This is an adequate approach if one's purpose is simply to give students a flavor of related court cases and legislative efforts, but it is are not adequate if students are to emerge from their studies with a truly deep appreciation of the intricate issues involved in this difficult area of public policy. For this reason, we include in this reader the text of the most recent Supreme Court case dealing with gun control, *District of Columbia vs. Heller*.

These are the goals of this course in public policy and the manner in which the Department of Political Science at Texas Tech University will use this reader to accomplish them. We hope that students find this information provided in this reader useful, both as students completing this course in public policy and as young citizens in the state of Texas and the United States.

Models of Politics: Some Help in Thinking About Public Policy

Thomas Dye

Models for Policy Analysis

A model is a simplified representation of some aspect of the real world. It may be an actual physical representation—a model airplane, for example, or the tabletop buildings that planners and architects use to show how things will look when proposed projects are completed. Or a model may be a diagram—a road map, for example, or a flow chart that political scientists use to show how a bill becomes law.

Uses of Models

The models we shall use in studying policy are *conceptual models*. These are word models that try to

- Simplify and clarify our thinking about politics and public policy.
- Identify important aspects of policy problems.
- Help us to communicate with each other by focusing on essential features of political life.
- Direct our efforts to understand public policy better by suggesting what is important and what is unimportant.
- Suggest explanations for public policy and predict its consequences.

Selected Policy Models

Over the years, political science, like other scientific disciplines, has developed a number of models to help us understand political life. Throughout this volume we will try to see whether these models have any utility in the study of public policy. Specifically, we want to examine public policy from the perspective of the following models:

- Institutional model
- Process model
- Rational model
- Incremental model
- Group model
- Elite model
- Public choice model
- Game theory model

Each of these terms identifies a major conceptual model that can be found in the literature of political science. None of these models was derived especially to study public policy, yet each offers a separate way of thinking about policy and even suggests some of the general causes and consequences of public policy.

These models are not competitive in the sense that any one of them could be judged "best." Each one provides a separate focus on political life, and each can help us to understand different things about public policy. Although some policies appear at first glance to lend themselves to explanation by one particular model, most policies are a combination of rational planning, incrementalism, interest group activity, elite preferences, game playing, public choice, political processes, and institutional influences. In later chapters these models will be employed, singularly and in combination, to describe and explain specific policies. Following is a brief description of each model, with particular attention to the separate ways in which public policy can be viewed.

Institutionalism: Policy as Institutional Output

Government institutions have long been a central focus of political science. Traditionally, political science was defined as the study of government institutions. Political activities generally center around particular government institutions—Congress, the presidency, courts, bureaucracies, states, municipalities, and so on. Public policy is authoritatively determined, implemented, and enforced by these institutions.

The relationship between public policy and government institutions is very close. Strictly speaking, a policy does not become a *public* policy

"Models of Politics: Some Help in Thinking about Public Policy," from *Understanding Public Policy, 13th ed.*, by Thomas R. Dye, pp. 11-27. Copyright © 2011 by Pearson Education, Inc. Reprinted by permission.

until it is adopted, implemented, and enforced by some government institution. Government institutions give public policy three distinctive characteristics. First, government lends *legitimacy* to policies. Government policies are generally regarded as legal obligations that command the loyalty of citizens. People may regard the policies of other groups and associations in society—corporations, churches, professional organizations, civic associations, and so forth—as important and even binding. But only government policies involve legal obligations. Second, government policies involve *universality*. Only government policies extend to all people in a society; the policies of other groups or organizations reach only a part of the society. Finally, government monopolizes *coercion* in society—only government can legitimately imprison violators of its policies. The sanctions that can be imposed by other groups or organizations in society are more limited. It is precisely this ability of government to command the loyalty of all its citizens, to enact policies governing the whole society, and to monopolize the legitimate use of force that encourages individuals and groups to work for enactment of their preferences into policy.

The Constitution of the United States establishes the fundamental institutional structure for policymaking. It is "the supreme Law of the Land" (Article VI). Its key structural components—separation of powers and checks and balances among the legislative, executive, and judicial branches of the national government—together with federalism—dividing power between the nation and the states—were designed by the Founders in part "to form a more perfect Union." These institutional arrangements have changed significantly over more than two centuries, yet no other written constitution in the world has remained in place for so long. Throughout this volume we will be concerned with the effect of these institutional arrangements on public policy. And in Chapter 12 we shall explore in some detail the effect of federalism.

Federalism recognizes that both the national government and the state governments derive independent legal authority from their own citizens: both can pass their own laws, levy their own taxes, and maintain their own courts. The states also have important roles in the selection of national officeholders—in the apportionment of congressional seats, in the allocation of two U.S. senators to each state, and in the allocation of electoral votes for president. Most important, perhaps, both the Congress and three-quarters of states must consent to any changes in the Constitution itself.

Process: Policy as Political Activity

Today political processes and behaviors are a central focus of political science. Since World War II, modern "behavioral" political science has studied the activities of voters, interest groups, legislators, presidents, bureaucrats, judges, and other political actors. One of the main purposes has been to discover patterns of activities—or "processes." Political scientists with an interest in policy have grouped various activities according to their relationship with public policy. The result is a set of *policy processes*, which usually follow the general outline in Table 1–1. In short, one can view the policy process as a series of political activities—problem identification, agenda setting, formulation, legitimation, implementation, and evaluation.

The process model is useful in helping us to understand the various activities involved in policymaking. We want to keep in mind that *policymaking* involves agenda setting (capturing the attention of policymakers), formulating proposals (devising and selecting policy options), legitimating policy

---

INSTITUTIONALISM: APPLYING THE MODEL

In Chapter 12, "American Federalism: Institutional Arrangements and Public Policy," we shall examine some of the problems of American federalism—the distribution of money and power among federal, state, and local governments.

PROCESSES: APPLYING THE MODEL

Political processes and behaviors are considered in each of the policy areas studied in this book. Additional commentary on the impact of political activity on public policy is found in Chapter 3, "The Policymaking Process: Decision-Making Activities."

TABLE 1.1

The Policy Process

- *Problem Identification.* The identification of policy problems through demand from individuals and groups for government action.
- *Agenda Setting.* Focusing the attention of the mass media and public officials on specific public problems to decide what will be decided.
- *Policy Formulation.* The development of policy proposals by interest groups, White House staff, congressional committees, and think tanks.
- *Policy Legitimation.* The selection and enactment of policies through actions by Congress, the president, and the courts.
- *Policy Implementation.* The implementation of policies through government bureaucracies, public expenditures, regulations, and other activities of executive agencies.
- *Policy Evaluation.* The evaluation of policies by government agencies themselves, outside consultants, the media, and the general public.

(developing political support; winning congressional, presidential, or court approval), implementing policy (creating bureaucracies, spending money, enforcing laws), and evaluating policy (finding out whether policies work, whether they are popular).

RATIONALISM: POLICY AS MAXIMUM SOCIAL GAIN

A rational policy is one that achieves "maximum social gain"; that is, governments should choose policies resulting in gains to society that exceed costs by the greatest amount, and governments should refrain from policies if costs exceed gains.

Note that there are really two important guidelines in this definition of maximum social gain. First, no policy should be adopted if its costs exceed its benefits. Second, among policy alternatives, decision makers should choose the policy that produces the greatest benefit over cost. In other words, a policy is rational when the difference between the values it achieves and the values it sacrifices is positive and greater than any other policy alternative. One should *not* view rationalism in a narrow dollars-and-cents framework, in which basic social values are sacrificed for dollar savings. Rationalism involves the calculation of *all* social, political, and economic values sacrificed or achieved by a public policy, not just those that can be measured in dollars.

To select a rational policy, policymakers must (1) know all the society's value preferences and their relative weights, (2) know all the policy alternatives available, (3) know all the consequences of each policy alternative, (4) calculate the ratio of benefits to costs for each policy alternative, and (5) select the most efficient policy alternative. This rationality assumes that the value preferences of *society as a whole* can be known and weighted. It is not enough to know and weigh the values of some groups and not others. There must be a complete understanding of societal values. Rational policymaking also requires *information* about alternative policies, the *predictive capacity* to foresee accurately the consequences of alternate policies, and the *intelligence* to calculate correctly the ratio of costs to benefits. Finally, rational policymaking requires a *decision-making system* that facilitates rationality in policy formation. A diagram of such a system is shown in Figure 1.1.

RATIONALISM: APPLYING THE MODEL

Chapter 4, "Criminal Justice: Rationality and Irrationality in Public Policy," shows that rational policies to deter crime—policies ensuring certainty, swiftness, and severity of punishment—have seldom been implemented. The problems of achieving rationality in public policy are also discussed in Chapter 5, "Health and Welfare: The Search for Rational Strategies." We will consider the general design of alternative strategies in dealing with poverty, health, and welfare. We will observe how these strategies are implemented in public policy, and we will analyze some of the obstacles to the achievement of rationality in public policy.

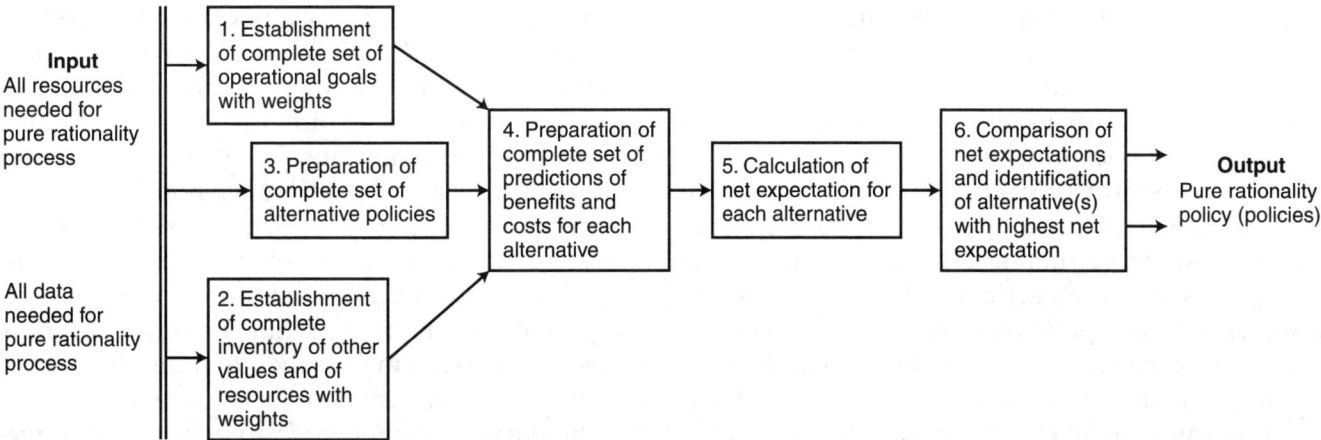

FIGURE 1.1 A Rational Model of a Decision System The rational model assumes complete agreement on goals, knowledge of alternative policies, and the ability to calculate and select the policies with the greatest benefits and least costs.

However, there are many barriers to rational decision making, so many, in fact, that it rarely takes place at all in government. Yet the model remains important for analytic purposes because it helps to identify barriers to rationality. It assists in posing the question, Why is policymaking *not* a more rational process? At the outset we can hypothesize several important *obstacles to rational policymaking*:

- Many conflicting benefits and costs cannot be compared or weighted; for example, it is difficult to compare or weigh the value of individual life against the costs of regulation.
- Policymakers may not be motivated to make decisions on the basis of societal goals but instead try to maximize, their own rewards—power, status, reelection, and money.
- Policymakers may not be motivated to maximize net social gain but merely to satisfy demands for progress; they do not search until they find "the one best way"; instead they halt their search when they find an alternative that will work.
- Large investments in existing programs and policies (sunk costs) prevent policymakers from reconsidering alternatives foreclosed by previous decisions.
- There are innumerable barriers to collecting all the information required to know all possible policy alternatives and the consequences of each, including the cost of information gathering, the availability of the information, and the time involved in its collection.
- Neither the predictive capacities of the social and behavioral sciences nor those of the physical and biological sciences are sufficiently advanced to enable policymakers to understand the full benefits or costs of each policy alternative.
- Policymakers, even with the most advanced computerized analytical techniques, do not have sufficient intelligence to calculate accurately costs and benefits when a large number of diverse political, social, economic, and cultural values are at stake.
- Uncertainty about the consequences of various policy alternatives compels policymakers to stick as closely as possible to previous policies to reduce the likelihood of unanticipated negative consequences.
- The segmentalized nature of policymaking in large bureaucracies makes it difficult to coordinate decision making so that the input of all the various specialists is brought to bear at the point of decision.

INCREMENTALISM: POLICY AS VARIATIONS ON THE PAST

Incrementalism views public policy as a continuation of past government activities with only incremental modifications. Political scientist Charles E. Lindblom first presented the incremental model in the course of a critique of the rational model of decision making.[1] According to Lindblom, decision makers do *not* annually review the whole range of existing and proposed policies, identify societal goals, research the benefits and costs of alternative policies in achieving these goals, rank order of preferences for each policy alternative in terms of the maximum net benefits, and then make a selection on the basis of all relevant information. On the contrary, constraints of time, information, and cost prevent policymakers from identifying the full range of policy alternatives and their consequences. Constraints of politics prevent the establishment of clear-cut societal goals and the accurate calculation of costs and benefits. The incremental model recognizes the impractical nature of "rational-comprehensive" policymaking, and describes a more conservative process of decision making.

Incrementalism is conservative in that existing programs, policies, and expenditures are considered as a *base*, and attention is concentrated on new programs and policies and on increases, decreases, or modifications of current programs. (For example, budgetary policy for any government activity or program for 2012 might be viewed incrementally, as shown in Figure 1.2.) Policymakers generally accept the legitimacy of established programs and tacitly agree to continue previous policies.

They do this because they do not have the time, information, or money to investigate all the alternatives to existing policy. The cost of collecting all this information is too great. Policymakers do not have sufficient predictive capacities to know what all the consequences of each alternative will be. Nor are they able to calculate cost–benefit ratios for alternative policies when many diverse political, social, economic, and cultural values are at stake. Thus completely "rational" policy may turn out to be "inefficient" (despite the contradiction in terms) if the time and cost of developing a rational policy are excessive.

Moreover, incrementalism is politically expedient. Agreement comes easier in policymaking when the items in dispute are only increases or decreases in budgets or modifications to existing programs. Conflict is heightened when decision making focuses on major policy shifts involving great gains or losses, or "all-or-nothing," "yes-or-no" policy decisions. Because the political tension involved in getting new programs or policies passed every year would be very great, past policy victories are continued into future years unless there is a substantial political realignment. Thus, incrementalism is important in reducing conflict, maintaining stability, and preserving the political system itself.

But *the incremental model may fail when policymakers are confronted with crises*. When faced with potential collapse of the nation's financial markets in 2008, the president, Congress, the Treasury Department, and the Federal Reserve Board came together to agree on an unprecedented, *nonincremental* expansion of federal power (see Chapter 7, "Economic Policy: Incremental and Nonincremental Policymaking"). Overall, federal spending and deficits increased dramatically, well beyond any levels that might have been predicted by the incremental model. The Treasury Department was given unprecedented authority and $700 billion to "bail out" the nation's major financial institutions. The Federal Reserve Board reduced interest rates to their lowest in history and provided unprecedented amounts of credit to the financial system. Congress itself passed a "stimulus package," the largest single spending bill in the nation's history. Incrementalism was abandoned.

Group Theory: Policy as Equilibrium in the Group Struggle

Group theory begins with the proposition that interaction among groups is the central fact of politics.[2] Individuals with common interests band together formally or informally to press their

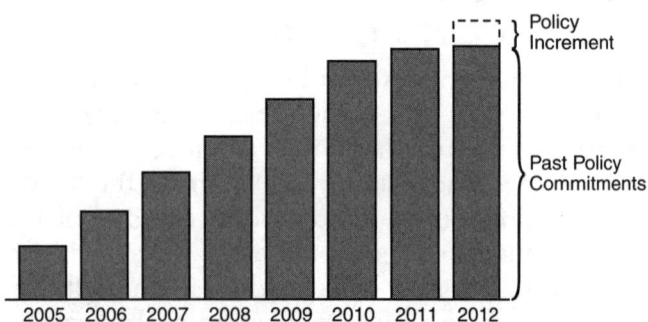

Figure 1.2 The Incremental Model The incremental model assumes that policymakers rarely examine past policy commitments, but rather focus their attention on changes in policies and expenditures.

INCREMENTALISM: APPLYING THE MODEL

Special attention to incrementalism is given in the discussion of government budgeting in Chapter 7, "Economic Policy: Incremental and Nonincremental Policymaking."

demands on government. According to political scientist David Truman, an interest group is "a shared-attitude group that makes certain claims upon other groups in the society"; such a group becomes political "if and when it makes a claim through or upon any of the institutions of government."[3] Individuals are important in politics only when they act as part of, or on behalf of, group interests. The group becomes the essential bridge between the individual and the government. Politics is really the struggle among groups to influence public policy. The task of the political system is to *manage group conflict* by (1) establishing rules of the game in the group struggle, (2) arranging compromises and balancing interests, (3) enacting compromises in the form of public policy, and (4) enforcing these compromises.

According to group theorists, public policy at any given time is the equilibrium reached in the group struggle (see Figure 1.3). This equilibrium is determined by the relative influence of various interest groups. Changes in the relative influence of any interest groups can be expected to result in changes in public policy; policy will move in the direction desired by the groups gaining influence and away from the desires of groups losing influence. The influence of groups is determined by their numbers, wealth, organizational strength, leadership, access to decision makers, and internal cohesion.[4]

GROUP THEORY: APPLYING THE MODEL

Throughout this volume we will describe struggles over public policy. In Chapter 6, "Education; Group Struggles," we will examine group conflict over public policy in the discussions of education and school issues. In Chapter 8, "Tax Policy: Battling the Special Interests," we will observe the power of interest groups in obtaining special treatments in the tax code and obstructing efforts to reform the nation's tax laws.

The whole interest group system—the political system itself—is held together in equilibrium by several forces. First, there is a large, nearly universal, *latent group* in American society that supports the constitutional system and prevailing rules of the game. This group is not always visible but can be activated to administer overwhelming rebuke to any group that attacks the system and threatens to destroy the equilibrium.

Second, *overlapping group membership* helps to maintain the equilibrium by preventing any one group from moving too far from prevailing values. Individuals who belong to any one group also belong to other groups, and this fact moderates the

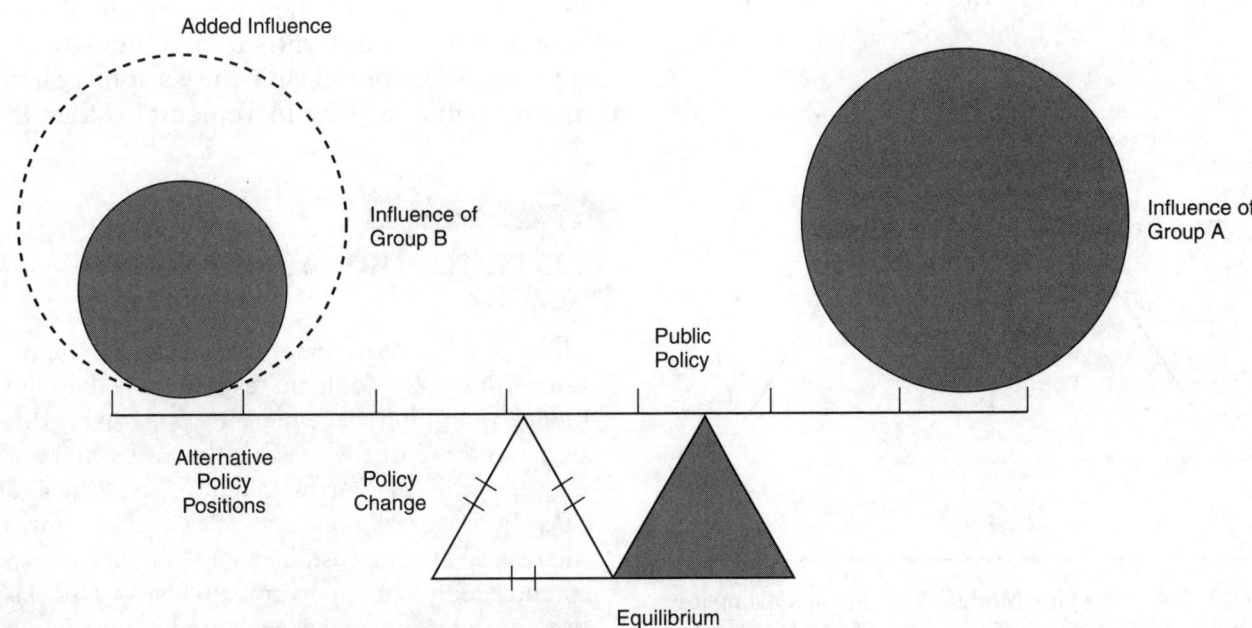

FIGURE 1.3 The Group Model The group model assumes that public policy is a balance of interest group influence; policies change when particular interest groups gain or lose influence.

demands of groups who must avoid offending their members who have other group affiliations.

Finally, the *checking and balancing resulting from group competition* also helps to maintain equilibrium in the system. No single group constitutes a majority in American society. The power of each group is checked by the power of competing groups. "Countervailing" centers of power function to check the influence of any single group and protect the individual from exploitation.

ELITE THEORY: POLICY AS ELITE PREFERENCE

Public policy may also be viewed as the preferences and values of a governing elite.[5] Although it is often asserted that public policy reflects the demands of "the people," this may express the myth rather than the reality of American democracy. Elite theory suggests that the people are apathetic and ill informed about public policy, that elites actually shape mass opinion on policy questions more than masses shape elite opinion. Thus, public policy really turns out to be the preferences of elites. Public officials and administrators merely carry out the policies decided on by the elite. Policies flow downward from elites to masses; they do not arise from mass demands (see Figure 1.4).

Elite theory can be summarized briefly as follows:

- Society is divided into the few who have power and the many who do not. Only a small number of persons allocate values for society; the masses do not decide public policy.
- The few who govern are not typical of the masses who are governed. Elites are drawn disproportionately from the upper socioeconomic strata of society.
- The movement of nonelites to elite positions must be slow and continuous to maintain stability and avoid revolution. Only nonelites who have accepted the basic elite consensus can be admitted to governing circles.
- Elites share consensus in behalf of the basic values of the social system and the preservation of the system. In America, the bases of elite consensus are the sanctity of private property, limited government, and individual liberty.
- Public policy does not reflect the demands of masses but rather the prevailing values of the elite. Changes in public policy will be incremental rather than revolutionary.
- Active elites are subject to relatively little direct influence from apathetic masses. Elites influence masses more than masses influence elites.

What are the implications of elite theory for policy analysis? Elitism implies that public policy does not reflect the demands of the people so much as it does the interests, values, and preferences of elites. Therefore, change and innovations in public policy come about as a result of redefinitions by elites of their own values. Because of the general conservatism of elites—that is, their interest in preserving the system—change in public policy will be incremental rather than

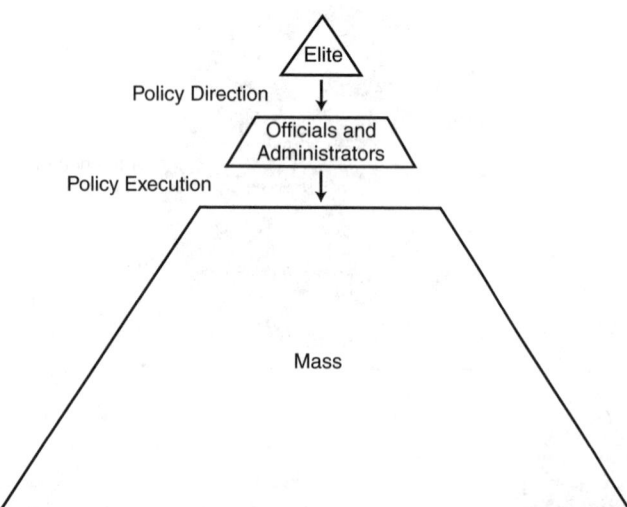

FIGURE 1.4 The Elite Model The elite model implies that public policy does not flow upward from demands by the people, but rather downward from the interests, values, and preferences of elites.

ELITE THEORY: APPLYING THE MODEL

Chapter 9, "International Trade and Immigration: Elite-Mass Conflict," expands on the elite model by arguing that when elite preferences differ from those of the masses, the preferences of elites prevail. Chapter 11, "Civil Rights: Elite and Mass Interaction," portrays the civil rights movement as an effort by established national elites to extend equality of opportunity to blacks. Opposition to civil rights policies is found among white masses in the states.

revolutionary. Changes in the political system occur when events threaten the system, and elites, acting on the basis of enlightened self-interest, institute reforms to preserve the system and their place in it. The values of elites may be very "public regarding." A sense of *noblesse oblige* may permeate elite values, and the welfare of the masses may be an important element in elite decision making. Elitism does not necessarily mean that public policy will be hostile toward mass welfare but only that the responsibility for mass welfare rests on the shoulders of elites, not masses.

PUBLIC CHOICE THEORY: POLICY AS COLLECTIVE DECISION MAKING BY SELF-INTERESTED INDIVIDUALS

Public choice is the economic study of nonmarket decision making, especially the application of economic analyses to public policymaking. Traditionally, economics studied behavior in the marketplace and assumed that individuals pursued their private interests; political science studied behavior in the public arena and assumed that individuals pursued their own notion of the public interest. Thus, separate versions of human motivation developed in economics and political science: the idea of *homo economicus* assumed a self-interested actor seeking to maximize personal benefits; that of *homo politicus* assumed a public-spirited actor seeking to maximize societal welfare.

But public choice theory challenges the notion that individuals act differently in politics than they do in the marketplace. This theory assumes that all political actors—voters, taxpayers, candidates, legislators, bureaucrats, interest groups, parties, and governments—*seek to maximize their personal benefits in politics as well as in the marketplace*. James Buchanan, the Nobel Prize–winning economist and leading scholar in modern public choice theory, argues that individuals come together in politics for their own mutual benefit, just as they come together in the marketplace; and by agreement (contract) among themselves they can enhance their own well-being, in the same way as by trading in the marketplace.[6] In short, people pursue their self-interest in both politics and the marketplace, but even with selfish motives they can mutually benefit through collective decision making.

Government itself arises from a *social contract* among individuals who agree for their mutual benefit to obey laws and support the government in exchange for protection of their own lives, liberties, and property. Thus, public choice theorists claim to be intellectual heirs to the English political philosopher John Locke, as well as to Thomas Jefferson, who incorporated this social contract notion into the American Declaration of Independence. Enlightened self-interest leads individuals to a constitutional contract establishing a government to protect life, liberty, and property.

Public choice theory recognizes that government must perform certain functions that the marketplace is unable to handle, that is, it must remedy certain "market failures." First, government must provide *public goods*—goods and services that must be supplied to everyone if they are supplied to anyone. The market cannot provide public goods because their costs exceed their value to any single buyer, and a single buyer would not be in a position to keep nonbuyers from using it. National defense is the most common example: protection from foreign invasion is too expensive for a single person to buy, and once it is provided no one can be excluded from its benefits. So people must act collectively through government to provide for the common defense. Second, *externalities* are another recognized market failure and justification for government intervention. An externality occurs when an activity of one individual, firm, or local government imposes uncompensated costs on others. The most common examples are air and water pollution: the discharge of air and water pollutants imposes costs on others. Governments respond by either regulating the activities that produce externalities or imposing penalties (fines)

PUBLIC CHOICE: APPLYING THE MODEL

The public choice theory is employed in Chapter 10, "Energy and Environmental Policy: Externalities and Interests," to aid in recognizing environmental pollution as a problem in the control of externalities in human activity. Public choice theory also helps us to understand the behavior of environmental interest groups in dramatizing and publicizing their cause.

on these activities to compensate for their costs to society.

Public choice theory helps to explain why political parties and candidates generally fail to offer clear policy alternatives in election campaigns. Parties and candidates are not interested in advancing principles but rather in winning elections. They formulate their policy positions to win elections; they do not win elections to formulate policy. Thus each party and candidate seeks policy positions that will attract the greatest number of voters.[7] *Given a unimodal distribution of opinion on any policy question* (see Figure 1.5), *parties and candidates will move toward the center to maximize votes*. Only "ideologues" (irrational, ideologically motivated people) ignore the vote-maximizing centrist strategy.

Game Theory: Policy as Rational Choice in Competitive Situations

Game theory is the study of decisions in situations in which two or more *rational* participants have choices to make and the outcome depends on the choices made by each. It is applied to areas in policymaking in which there is no independently "best" choice that one can make—in which the "best" outcomes depend upon what others do.

The idea of "game" is that rational decision makers are involved in choices that are interdependent. "Players" must adjust their conduct to reflect not only their own desires and abilities but also their expectations about what others will do. Perhaps the connotation of a "game" is unfortunate, suggesting that game theory is not really appropriate for serious conflict situations. But just the opposite is true: game theory can be applied to decisions about war and peace, the use of nuclear weapons, international diplomacy, bargaining and coalition building in Congress or the United Nations, and a variety of other important political situations. A "player" may be an individual, a group, or a national government—indeed, anybody with well-defined goals who is capable of rational action.

Consider the game of "chicken." Two adolescents drive their cars toward each other at a high speed, each with one set of wheels on the center line of the highway. If neither veers off course they will crash. Whoever veers is "chicken." Both drivers prefer to avoid death, but they also want to avoid the "dishonor" of being "chicken." The outcome depends on what both drivers do, and each driver must try to predict how the other will behave. This form of "brinkmanship" is common in international relations (see Figure 1.6). Inspection of the payoff matrix suggests that it would be better for both drivers to veer in order to minimize the possibility of a great loss (−10). But the matrix is too simple. One or both players may place a different value on the outcomes than is suggested by the numbers. For example, one player may prefer death to dishonor in the game. Each player must try to calculate the values of the other, and neither has complete information about the values of the opponent. Moreover, bluffing or the deliberate misrepresentation of one's values or resources to an opponent is always a possibility. For example, a possible strategy in the game of chicken is to allow your opponent to see you drink heavily before the game, stumble drunkenly toward your car, and mumble something about having lived long enough in this rotten world. The effect of this communication on your opponent may increase his or her estimate of your likelihood of staying on course, and hence provide incentive for your opponent to veer and allow you to win.

An important component of game theory is the notion of *deterrence*. Deterrence is the effort to prevent an opponent from undertaking an action by inspiring fear of the consequences of the action. Players engage in deterrence when they

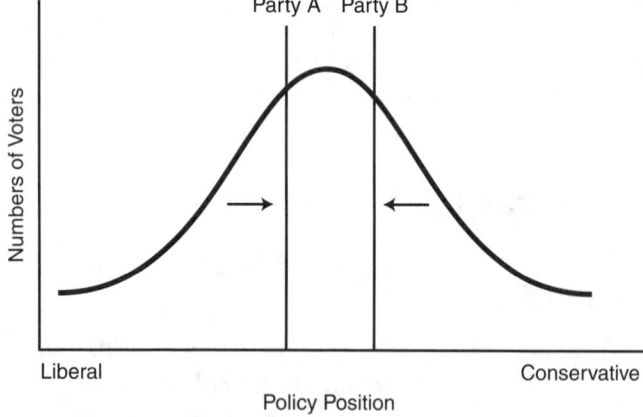

Figure 1.5 Public Choice: A Vote-Maximizing Model of Party Competition Public choice theory assumes that individuals and organizations seek to maximize their own benefits in politics; for example, parties and candidates whose policy views may be distinctly liberal or conservative move to the center at election time to win the most votes.

The game theorist himself or herself supplies the numerical values to the payoffs. If Driver A chooses to stay on course and Driver B chooses to stay on course also, the result might be scored as −10 for both players, who wreck their cars. But if Driver A chooses to stay on course and Driver B veers, then Driver A might get +5 ("courage") and Driver B−5 ("dishonor"). If Driver A veers but Driver B stays on course, the results would be reversed. If both veer, each is dishonored slightly (−1), but not as much as when one or the other stayed on course.

		DRIVER A'S CHOICES	
		Stay on Course	Veer
DRIVER B'S CHOICES	Stay on course	A:−10 B:−10	A:−5 B:+5
	Veer	A:+5 B:−5	A:−1 B:−1

FIGURE 1.6   A Game-Theoretic Matrix for the Game of Chicken   Game theory suggests that policymakers, or "players," adjust their conduct to reflect not only their own preferences but also the likely choices of opponents.

GAME THEORY: APPLYING THE MODEL

Game theory is frequently applied in international conflicts. We will explore the utility of game theory, especially the notion of deterrence, in Chapter 13, "Defense Policy: Strategies for Serious Games." We will also explore the weakness of deterrence in defending against terrorism in Chapter 14, "Homeland Security: Terrorism and Nondeterrable Threats."

threaten their opponents with retaliatory actions that promise to impose costs on their opponents that are far in excess of any benefits their opponents might envision by taking these actions. *Deterrence is really a psychological defense: it tries to prevent opponents from undertaking a particular action by creating in their minds the fear of costly retaliation.*

The success of deterrence depends on the credibility of the retaliatory threat and on the rationality of the opponent. Opponents must truly believe that their actions will result in retaliatory responses that inflict unacceptable costs on themselves, their people, or their nation. Opponents who do not really believe a retaliatory attack will occur are not deterred. Moreover, opponents must be *rational*—opponents must weigh the potential costs and benefits of their actions and choose a course of action that does not result in costs that exceed gains. Opponents who are irrational—who do not consider the costs of their actions to themselves, or their people, or their nation—are not deterred.

MODELS: HOW TO TELL IF THEY ARE HELPING OR NOT

A model is merely an abstraction or representation of political life. When we think of political systems or elites or groups or rational decision making or incrementalism or games, we are abstracting from the real world in an attempt to simplify, clarify, and understand what is really important about politics. Before we begin our study of public policy, let us set forth some general criteria for evaluating the usefulness of concepts and models.

ORDER AND SIMPLIFY REALITY

Certainly the utility of a model lies in its ability to order and simplify political life so that we can think about it more clearly and understand the relationships we find in the real world. Yet too much simplification can lead to inaccuracies in our thinking about reality. On the one hand, if a concept is too narrow or identifies only superficial phenomena, we may not be able to use it to explain public policy. On the other hand, if a concept is too broad and suggests overly complex relationships, it may become so complicated and unmanageable that it is not really an aid to understanding. In other words, some theories of politics may be too complex to be helpful, while others may be too simplistic.

Identify What Is Significant

A model should also identify the really significant aspects of public policy. It should direct attention away from irrelevant variables or circumstances and focus on the real causes and significant consequences of public policy. Of course, what is "real," "relevant," or "significant" is to some extent a function of an individual's personal values. But we can all agree that the utility of a concept is related to its ability to identify what it is that is really important about politics.

Be Congruent with Reality

Generally, a model should be congruent with reality—that is, it ought to have real empirical referents. We would expect to have difficulty with a concept that identifies a process that does not really occur or symbolizes phenomena that do not exist in the real world. However, we must not be too quick to dismiss unrealistic concepts *if* they succeed in directing our attention to why they are unrealistic. For example, no one contends that government decision making is completely rational—public officials do not always act to maximize societal values and minimize societal costs. Yet the concept of rational decision making may still be useful, albeit unrealistic, if it makes us realize how irrational government decision making really is and prompts us to inquire why.

Provide Meaningful Communication

A concept or model should also communicate something meaningful. If too many people disagree over the meaning of a concept, its utility in communication is diminished. For example, if no one really agrees on what constitutes an elite, the concept of an elite does not mean the same thing to everyone. If one defines an elite as a group of democratically elected public officials who are representative of the general public, one is communicating a different idea in using the term than one who defines an elite as an unrepresentative minority that makes decisions for society based on its own interests.

Direct Inquiry and Research

A model should help to direct inquiry and research into public policy. A concept should be operational—that is, it should refer directly to real-world phenomena that can be observed, measured, and verified. A concept, or a series of interrelated concepts (which we refer to as a model), should suggest relationships in the real world that can be tested and verified. If there is no way to prove or disprove the ideas suggested by a concept, the concept is not really useful in developing a science of politics.

Suggest Explanations

Finally, a model should suggest an explanation of public policy. It should suggest hypotheses about the causes and consequences of public policy—hypotheses that can be tested against real-world data. A model that merely describes public policy is not as useful as one that explains public policy, or at least suggests some possible explanations.

The Science of "Muddling Through"

By Charles E. Lindblom
Associate Professor of Economics Yale University

Suppose an administrator is given responsibility for formulating policy with respect to inflation. He might start by trying to list all related values in order of importance, e.g., full employment, reasonable business profit, protection of small savings, prevention of a stock market crash. Then all possible policy outcomes could be rated as more or less efficient in attaining a maximum of these values. This would of course require a prodigious inquiry into values held by members of society and an equally prodigious set of calculations on how much of each value is equal to how much of each other value. He could then proceed to outline all possible policy alternatives. In a third step, he would undertake systematic comparison of his multitude of alternatives to determine which attains the greatest amount of values.

In comparing policies, he would take advantage of any theory available that generalized about classes of policies. In considering inflation, for example, he would compare all policies in the light of the theory of prices. Since no alternatives are beyond his investigation, he would consider strict central control and the abolition of all prices and markets on the one hand and elimination of all public controls with reliance completely on the free market on the other, both in the light of whatever theoretical generalizations he could find on such hypothetical economies.

Finally, he would try to make the choice that would in fact maximize his values.

An alternative line of attack would be to set as his principal objective, either explicitly or without conscious thought, the relatively simple goal of keeping prices level. This objective might be compromised or complicated by only a few other goals, such as full employment. He would in fact disregard most other social values as beyond his present interest, and he would for the moment not even attempt to rank the few values that he regarded as immediately relevant. Were he pressed, he would quickly admit that he was ignoring many related values and many possible important consequences of his policies.

As a second step, he would outline those relatively few policy alternatives that occurred to him. He would then compare them. In comparing his limited number of alternatives, most of them familiar from past controversies, he would not ordinarily find a body of theory precise enough to carry him through a comparison of their respective consequences. Instead he would rely heavily on the record of past experience with small policy steps to predict the consequences of similar steps extended into the future.

Moreover, he would find that the policy alternatives combined objectives or values in different ways. For example, one policy might offer price level stability at the cost of some risk of unemployment; another might offer less price stability but also less risk of unemployment. Hence, the next step in his approach—the final selection—would combine into one the choice among values and the choice among instruments for reaching values. It would not, as in the first method of policymaking, approximate a more mechanical process of choosing the means that best satisfied goals that were previously clarified and ranked. Because practitioners of the second approach expect to achieve their goals only partially, they would expect to repeat endlessly the sequence just described, as conditions and aspirations changed and as accuracy of prediction improved.

By Root or by Branch

For complex problems, the first of these two approaches is of course impossible. Although such an approach can be described, it cannot be practiced except for relatively simple problems and even then

"The Science of Muddling Through," by Charles E. Lindblom, from *Public Administration Review*, Vol. 19, No. 2, pp. 79-88. Copyright © 1959 American Society for Public Administration. Reproduced by permission of Blackwell Publishing Ltd.

only in a somewhat modified form. It assumes intellectual capacities and sources of information that men simply do not possess, and it is even more absurd as an approach to policy when the time and money that can be allocated to a policy problem is limited, as is always the case. Of particular importance to public administrators is the fact that public agencies are in effect usually instructed not to practice the first method. That is to say, their prescribed functions and constraints—the politically or legally possible—restrict their attention to relatively few values and relatively few alternative policies among the countless alternatives that might be imagined. It is the second method that is practiced.

Curiously, however, the literatures of decision-making, policy formulation, planning, and public administration formalize the first approach rather than the second, leaving public administrators who handle complex decisions in the position of practicing what few preach. For emphasis I run some risk of overstatement. True enough, the literature is well aware of limits on man's capacities and of the inevitability that policies will be approached in some such style as the second. But attempts to formalize rational policy formulation—to lay out explicitly the necessary steps in the process—usually describe the first approach and not the second.[1]

The common tendency to describe policy formulation even for complex problems as though it followed the first approach has been strengthened by the attention given to, and successes enjoyed by, operations research, statistical decision theory, and systems analysis. The hallmarks of these procedures, typical of the first approach, are clarity of objective, explicitness of evaluation, a high degree of comprehensiveness of overview, and, wherever possible, quantification of values for mathematical analysis. But these advanced procedures remain largely the appropriate techniques of relatively small-scale problem-solving where the total number of variables to be considered is small and value problems restricted. Charles Hitch, head of the Economics Division of RAND Corporation, one of the leading centers for application of these techniques, has written:

❝ I would make the empirical generalization from my experience at RAND and elsewhere that operations research is the art of sub-optimizing, i.e., of solving some lower-level problems, and that difficulties increase and our special competence diminishes by an order of magnitude with every level of decision making we attempt to ascend. The sort of simple explicit model which operations researchers are so proficient in using can certainly reflect most of the significant factors influencing traffic control on the George Washington Bridge, but the proportion of the relevant reality which we can represent by any such model or models in studying, say, a major foreign-policy decision, appears to be almost trivial.[2]

Accordingly, I propose in this paper to clarify and formalize the second method, much neglected in the literature. This might be described as the method of *successive limited comparisons*. I will contrast it with the first approach, which might be called the rational-comprehensive method.[3] More impressionistically and briefly—and therefore generally used in this article—they could be characterized as the branch method and root method, the former continually building out from the current situation, step-by-step and by small degrees; the latter starting from fundamentals anew each time, building on the past only as experience is embodied in a theory, and always prepared to start completely from the ground up.

Let us put the characteristics of the two methods side by side in simplest terms.

Assuming that the root method is familiar and understandable, we proceed directly to clarification of its alternative by contrast. In explaining the second, we shall be describing how most

---

[1]James G. March and Herbert A. Simon similarly characterize the literature. They also take some important steps, as have Simon's recent articles, to describe a less heroic model of policy-making. See *Organizations* (John Wiley and Sons, 1958), p. 137.

[2]"Operations Research and National Planning—A Dissent," 5 *Operations Research* 718 (October, 1957). Hitch's dissent is from particular points made in the article to which his paper is a reply; his claim that operations research is for low-level problems is widely accepted.

For examples of the kind of problems to which operations research is applied, see C. W. Churchman, R. L. Ackoff and E. L. Arnoff, *Introduction to Operations Research* (John Wiley and Sons, 1957); and J. F. McCloskey and J. M. Coppinger (eds.), *Operations Research for Management*, Vol. II, (The Johns Hopkins Press, 1956).

[3]I am assuming that administrators often make policy and advise in the making of policy and am treating decision-making and policy-making as synonymous for purposes of this paper.

administrators do in fact approach complex questions, for the root method, the "best" way as a blueprint or model, is in fact not workable for complex policy questions, and administrators are forced to use the method of successive limited comparisons.

INTERTWINING EVALUATION AND EMPIRICAL ANALYSIS (1B)

The quickest way to understand how values are handled in the method of successive limited comparisons is to see how the root method often breaks down in *its* handling of values or objectives. The idea that values should be clarified, and in advance of the examination of alternative policies, is appealing. But what happens when we attempt it for complex social problems? The first difficulty is that on many critical values or objectives, citizens disagree, congressmen disagree, and public administrators disagree. Even where a fairly specific objective is prescribed for the administrator, there remains considerable room for disagreement on sub-objectives. Consider, for example, the conflict with respect to locating public housing, described in Meyerson and Banfield's study of the Chicago Housing Authority[4]—disagreement which occurred despite the clear objective of providing a certain number of public housing units in the city. Similarly conflicting are objectives in highway location, traffic control, minimum wage administration, development of tourist facilities in national parks, or insect control.

Administrators cannot escape these conflicts by ascertaining the majority's preference, for preferences have not been registered on most issues; indeed, there often *are* no preferences in the absence of public discussion sufficient to bring an issue to the attention of the electorate. Furthermore, there is a question of whether intensity of feeling should be considered as well as the number of persons preferring each alternative. By the impossibility of doing otherwise, administrators often are reduced to deciding policy without clarifying objectives first.

Even when an administrator resolves to follow his own values as a criterion for decisions, he

---

[4]Martin Meyers and Edward C. Banfield, *Politics, Planning and the Public Interest* (The Free Press, 1955).

Rational-Comprehensive (Root)	**Successive Limited Comparisons (Branch)**
1a. Clarification of values or objectives distinct from and usually prerequisite to empirical analysis of alternative policies.	1b. Selection of value goals and empirical analysis of the needed action are not distinct from one other but are closely intertwined.
2a. Policy-formulation is therefore approached through means-end analysis: First the ends are isolated, then the means to achieve them are sought.	2b. Since means and ends are not distinct, means-end analysis is often inappropriate or limited.
3a. The test of a "good" policy is that it can be shown to be the most appropriate means to desired ends.	3b. The test of a "good" policy is typically that various analysts find themselves directly agreeing on a policy (without their agreeing that it is the most appropriate means to an agreed objective).

4a. Analysis is comprehensive; every important relevant factor is taken into account.	4b. Analysis is drastically limited:
	  i) Important possible outcomes are neglected.
	  ii) Important alternative potential policies are neglected.
	  iii) Important affected values are neglected.

5a. Theory is often heavily relied upon.	5b. A succession of comparisons greatly reduces or eliminates reliance on theory.

often will not know how to rank them when they conflict with one another, as they usually do. Suppose, for example, that an administrator must relocate tenants living in tenements scheduled for destruction. One objective is to empty the buildings fairly promptly, another is to find suitable accommodation for persons displaced, another is to avoid friction with residents in other areas in which a large influx would be unwelcome, another is to deal with all concerned through persuasion if possible, and so on.

How does one state even to himself the relative importance of these partially conflicting values? A simple ranking of them is not enough; one needs ideally to know how much of one value is worth sacrificing for some of another value. The answer is that typically the administrator chooses—and must choose—directly among policies in which these values are combined in different ways. He cannot first clarify his values and then choose among policies.

A more subtle third point underlies both the first two. Social objectives do not always have the same relative values. One objective may be highly prized in one circumstance, another in another circumstance. If, for example, an administrator values highly both the dispatch with which his agency can carry through its projects *and* good public relations, it matters little which of the two possibly conflicting values he favors in some abstract or general sense. Policy questions arise in forms which put to administrators such a question as: Given the degree to which we are or are not already achieving the values of dispatch and the values of good public relations, is it worth sacrificing a little speed for a happier clientele, or is it better to risk offending the clientele so that we can get on with our work? The answer to such a question varies with circumstances.

The value problem is, as the example shows, always a problem of adjustments at a margin. But there is no practicable way to state marginal objectives or values except in terms of particular policies. That one value is preferred to another in one decision situation does not mean that it will be preferred in another decision situation in which it can be had only at great sacrifice of another value. Attempts to rank or order values in general and abstract terms so that they do not shift from decision to decision end up by ignoring the relevant marginal preferences. The significance of this third point thus goes very far. Even if all administrators had at hand an agreed set of values, objectives, and constraints, and an agreed ranking of these values, objectives, and constraints, their marginal values in actual choice situations would be impossible to formulate.

Unable consequently to formulate the relevant values first and then choose among policies to achieve them, administrators must choose directly among alternative policies that offer different marginal combinations of values. Somewhat paradoxically, the only practicable way to disclose one's relevant marginal values even to oneself is to describe the policy one chooses to achieve them. Except roughly and vaguely, I know of no way to describe—or even to understand—what my relative evaluations are for, say, freedom and security, speed and accuracy in governmental decisions, or low taxes and better schools than to describe my preferences among specific policy choices that might be made between the alternatives in each of the pairs.

In summary, two aspects of the process by which values are actually handled can be distinguished. The first is clear: evaluation and empirical analysis are intertwined; that is, one chooses among values and among policies at one and the same time. Put a little more elaborately, one simultaneously chooses a policy to attain certain objectives and chooses the objectives themselves. The second aspect is related but distinct: the administrator focuses his attention on marginal or incremental values. Whether he is aware of it or not, he does not find general formulations of objectives very helpful and in fact makes specific marginal or incremental comparisons. Two policies, X and Y, confront him. Both promise the same degree of attainment of objectives *a*, *b*, *c*, *d*, and *e*. But X promises him somewhat more of *f* than does Y, while Y promises him somewhat more of *g* than does X. In choosing between them, he is in fact offered the alternative of a marginal or incremental amount of *f* at the expense of a marginal or incremental amount of *g*. The only values that are relevant to his choice are these increments by which the two policies differ; and, when he finally chooses between the two marginal values, he does so by making a choice between policies.[5]

---

[5] The line of argument is, of course, an extension of the theory of market choice, especially the theory of consumer choice, to public policy choices.

As to whether the attempt to clarify objectives in advance of policy selection is more or less rational than the close intertwining of marginal evaluation and empirical analysis, the principal difference established is that for complex problems the first is impossible and irrelevant, and the second is both possible and relevant. The second is possible because the administrator need not try to analyze any values except the values by which alternative policies differ and need not be concerned with them except as they differ marginally. His need for information on values or objectives is drastically reduced as compared with the root method; and his capacity for grasping, comprehending, and relating values to one another is not strained beyond the breaking point.

Relations Between Means and Ends (2b)

Decision-making is ordinarily formalized as a means-ends relationship: means are conceived to be evaluated and chosen in the light of ends finally selected independently of and prior to the choice of means. This is the means-ends relationship of the root method. But it follows from all that has just been said that such a means-ends relationship is possible only to the extent that values are agreed upon, are reconcilable, and are stable at the margin. Typically, therefore, such a mean-sends relationship is absent from the branch method, where means and ends are simultaneously chosen.

Yet any departure from the means-ends relationship of the root method will strike some readers as inconceivable. For it will appear to them that only in such a relationship is it possible to determine whether one policy choice is better or worse than another. How can an administrator know whether he has made a wise or foolish decision if he is without prior values or objectives by which to judge his decisions? The answer to this question calls up the third distinctive difference between root and branch methods: how to decide the best policy.

The Test of "Good" Policy (3b)

In the root method, a decision is "correct," "good," or "rational" if it can be shown to attain some specified objective, where the objective can be specified without simply describing the decision itself. Where objectives are defined only through the marginal or incremental approach to values described above, it is still sometimes possible to test whether a policy does in fact attain the desired objectives; but a precise statement of the objectives takes the form of a description of the policy chosen or some alternative to it. To show that a policy is mistaken one cannot offer an abstract argument that important objectives are not achieved; one must instead argue that another policy is more to be preferred.

So far, the departure from customary ways of looking at problem-solving is not troublesome, for many administrators will be quick to agree that the most effective discussion of the correctness of policy does take the form of comparison with other policies that might have been chosen. But what of the situation in which administrators cannot agree on values or objectives, either abstractly or in marginal terms? What then is the test of "good" policy? For the root method, there is no test. Agreement on objectives failing, there is no standard of "correctness." For the method of successive limited comparisons, the test is agreement on policy itself, which remains possible even when agreement on values is not.

It has been suggested that continuing agreement in Congress on the desirability of extending old age insurance stems from liberal desires to strengthen the welfare programs of the federal government and from conservative desires to reduce union demands for private pension plans. If so, this is an excellent demonstration of the ease with which individuals of different ideologies often can agree on concrete policy. Labor mediators report a similar phenomenon: the contestants cannot agree on criteria for settling their disputes but can agree on specific proposals. Similarly, when one administrator's objective turns out to be another's means, they often can agree on policy.

Agreement on policy thus becomes the only practicable test of the policy's correctness. And for one administrator to seek to win the other over to agreement on ends as well would accomplish nothing and create quite unnecessary controversy.

If agreement directly on policy as a test for "best" policy seems a poor substitute for testing the policy against its objectives, it ought to be remembered that objectives themselves have no ultimate validity other than they are agreed upon. Hence agreement is the test of "best" policy in both methods. But where the root method requires agreement on what elements in the decision constitute objectives and on which of these objectives should be sought, the branch method falls back on agreement wherever it can be found.

In an important sense, therefore, it is not irrational for an administrator to defend a policy as good without being able to specify what it is good for.

Non-Comprehensive Analysis (4b)

Ideally, rational-comprehensive analysis leaves out nothing important. But it is impossible to take everything important into consideration unless 'important" is so narrowly defined that analysis is in fact quite limited. Limits on human intellectual capacities and on available information set definite limits to man's capacity to be comprehensive. In actual fact, therefore, no one can practice the rational-comprehensive method for really complex problems, and every administrator faced with a sufficiently complex problem must find ways drastically to simplify.

An administrator assisting in the formulation of agricultural economic policy cannot in the first place be competent on all possible policies. He cannot even comprehend one policy entirely. In planning a soil bank program, he cannot successfully anticipate the impact of higher or lower farm income on, say, urbanization—the possible consequent loosening of family ties, possible consequent eventual need for revisions in social security and further implications for tax problems arising out of new federal responsibilities for social security and municipal responsibilities for urban services. Nor, to follow another line of repercussions, can he work through the soil bank program's effects on prices for agricultural products in foreign markets and consequent implications for foreign relations, including those arising out of economic rivalry between the United States and the U.S.S.R.

In the method of successive limited comparisons, simplification is systematically achieved in two principal ways. First, it is achieved through limitation of policy comparisons to those policies that differ in relatively small degree from policies presently in effect. Such a limitation immediately reduces the number of alternatives to be investigated and also drastically simplifies the character of the investigation of each. For it is not necessary to undertake fundamental inquiry into an alternative and its consequences; it is necessary only to study those respects in which the proposed alternative and its consequences differ from the status quo. The empirical comparison of marginal differences among alternative policies that differ only marginally is, of course, a counterpart to the incremental or marginal comparison of values discussed above.[6]

Relevance as Well as Realism

It is a matter of common observation that in Western democracies public administrators and policy analysts in general do largely limit their analyses to incremental or marginal differences in policies that are chosen to differ only incrementally. They do not do so, however, solely because they desperately need some way to simplify their problems; they also do so in order to be relevant. Democracies change their policies almost entirely through incremental adjustments. Policy does not move in leaps and bounds.

The incremental character of political change in the United States has often been remarked. The two major political parties agree on fundamentals; they offer alternative policies to the voters only on relatively small points of difference. Both parties favor full employment, but they define it somewhat differently; both favor the development of water power resources, but in slightly different ways; and both favor unemployment compensation, but not the same level of benefits. Similarly, shifts of policy within a party take place largely through a series of relatively small changes, as can be seen in their only gradual acceptance of the idea of governmental responsibility for support of the unemployed, a change in party positions beginning in the early 30's and culminating in a sense in the Employment Act of 1946.

Party behavior is in turn rooted in public attitudes, and political theorists cannot conceive of democracy's surviving in the United States in the absence of fundamental agreement on potentially disruptive issues, with consequent limitation of policy debates to relatively small differences in policy.

Since the policies ignored by the administrator are politically impossible and so irrelevant, the

---

[6]A more precise definition of incremental policies and a discussion of whether a change that appears "small" to one observer might be seen differently by another is to be found in my "Policy Analysis," 48 *American Economic Review* 298 (June, 1958).

simplification of analysis achieved by concentrating on policies that differ only incrementally is not a capricious kind of simplification. In addition, it can be argued that, given the limits on knowledge within which policy-makers are confined, simplifying by limiting the focus to small variations from present policy makes the most of available knowledge. Because policies being considered are like present and past policies, the administrator can obtain information and claim some insight. Non-incremental policy proposals are therefore typically not only politically irrelevant but also unpredictable in their consequences.

The second method of simplification of analysis is the practice of ignoring important possible consequences of possible policies, as well as the values attached to the neglected consequences. If this appears to disclose a shocking shortcoming of successive limited comparisons, it can be replied that, even if the exclusions are random, policies may nevertheless be more intelligently formulated than through futile attempts to achieve a comprehensiveness beyond human capacity. Actually, however, the exclusions, seeming arbitrary or random from one point of view, need be neither.

Achieving a Degree of Comprehensiveness

Suppose that each value neglected by one policy-making agency were a major concern of at least one other agency. In that case, a helpful division of labor would be achieved, and no agency need find its task beyond its capacities. The shortcomings of such a system would be that one agency might destroy a value either before another agency could be activated to safeguard it or in spite of another agency's efforts. But the possibility that important values may be lost is present in any form of organization, even where agencies attempt to comprehend in planning more than is humanly possible.

The virtue of such a hypothetical division of labor is that every important interest or value has its watchdog. And these watchdogs can protect the interests in their jurisdiction in two quite different ways: first, by redressing damages done by other agencies; and, second, by anticipating and heading off injury before it occurs.

In a society like that of the United States in which individuals are free to combine to pursue almost any possible common interest they might have and in which government agencies are sensitive to the pressures of these groups, the system described is approximated. Almost every interest has its watchdog. Without claiming that every interest has a sufficiently powerful watchdog, it can be argued that our system often can assure a more comprehensive regard for the values of the whole society than any attempt at intellectual comprehensiveness.

In the United States, for example, no part of government attempts a comprehensive overview of policy on income distribution. A policy nevertheless evolves, and one responding to a wide variety of interests. A process of mutual adjustment among farm groups, labor unions, municipalities and school boards, tax authorities, and government agencies with responsibilities in the fields of housing, health, highways, national parks, fire, and police accomplishes a distribution of income in which particular income problems neglected at one point in the decision processes become central at another point.

Mutual adjustment is more pervasive than the explicit forms it takes in negotiation between groups; it persists through the mutual impacts of groups upon each other even where they are not in communication. For all the imperfections and latent dangers in this ubiquitous process of mutual adjustment, it will often accomplish an adaptation of policies to a wider range of interests than could be done by one group centrally.

Note, too, how the incremental pattern of policy-making fits with the multiple pressure pattern. For when decisions are only incremental—closely related to known policies, it is easier for one group to anticipate the kind of moves another might make and easier too for it to make correction for injury already accomplished.[7]

Even partisanship and narrowness, to use pejorative terms, will sometimes be assets to rational decision-making, for they can doubly insure that what one agency neglects, another will not; they specialize personnel to distinct points of view. The claim is valid that effective rational coordination of the federal administration, if possible to achieve at all, would require an agreed set of values[8]—if "rational" is defined as the practice of the root method of decision-making. But a high

---

[7] The link between the practice of the method of successive limited comparisons and mutual adjustment of interests in a highly fragmented decision-making process adds a new facet to pluralist theories of government and administration.

[8] Herbert Simon, Donald W. Smithburg, and Victor A. Thompson, *Public Administration* (Alfred A. Knopf, 1950). P. 434.

degree of administrative coordination occurs as each agency adjusts its policies to the concerns of the other agencies in the process of fragmented decision-making I have just described.

For all the apparent shortcomings of the incremental approach to policy alternatives with its arbitrary exclusion coupled with fragmentation, when compared to the root method, the branch method often looks far superior. In the root method, the inevitable exclusion of factors is accidental, unsystematic, and not defensible by any argument so far developed, while in the branch method the exclusions are deliberate, systematic, and defensible. Ideally, of course, the root method does not exclude; in practice it must.

Nor does the branch method necessarily neglect long-run considerations and objectives. It is clear that important values must be omitted in considering policy, and sometimes the only way long-run objectives can be given adequate attention is through the neglect of short-run considerations. But the values omitted can be either long-run or short-run.

SUCCESSION OF COMPARISONS (5B)

The final distinctive element in the branch method is that the comparisons, together with the policy choice, proceed in a chronological series. Policy is not made once and for all; it is made and remade endlessly. Policy-making is a process of successive approximation to some desired objectives in which what is desired itself continues to change under reconsideration.

Making policy is at best a very rough process. Neither social scientists, nor politicians, nor public administrators yet know enough about the social world to avoid repeated error in predicting the consequences of policy moves. A wise policy-maker consequently expects that his policies will achieve only part of what he hopes and at the same time will produce unanticipated consequences he would have preferred to avoid. If he proceeds through a *succession* of incremental changes, he avoids serious lasting mistakes in several ways.

In the first place, past sequences of policy steps have given him knowledge about the probable consequences of further similar steps. Second, he need not attempt big jumps toward his goals that would require predictions beyond his or anyone else's knowledge, because he never expects his policy to be a final resolution of a problem. His decision is only one step, one that if successful can quickly be followed by another. Third, he is in effect able to test his previous predictions as he moves on to each further step. Lastly, he often can remedy a past error fairly quickly—more quickly than if policy proceeded through more distinct steps widely spaced in time.

Compare this comparative analysis of incremental changes with the aspiration to employ theory in the root method. Man cannot think without classifying, without subsuming one experience under a more general category of experiences. The attempt to push categorization as far as possible and to find general propositions which can be applied to specific situations is what I refer to with the word "theory." Where root analysis often leans heavily on theory in this sense, the branch method does not.

The assumption of root analysts is that theory is the most systematic and economical way to bring relevant knowledge to bear on a specific problem. Granting the assumption, an unhappy fact is that we do not have adequate theory to apply to problems in any policy area, although theory is more adequate in some areas—monetary policy, for example—than in others. Comparative analysis, as in the branch method, is sometimes a systematic alternative to theory.

Suppose an administrator must choose among a small group of policies that differ only incrementally from each other and from present policy. He might aspire to "understand" each of the alternatives—for example, to know all the consequences of each aspect of each policy. If so, he would indeed require theory. In fact, however, he would usually decide that, *for policy-making purposes*, he need know, as explained above, only the consequences of each of those aspects of the policies in which they differed from one another. For this much more modest aspiration, he requires no theory (although it might be helpful, if available), for he can proceed to isolate probable differences by examining the differences in consequences associated with past differences in policies, a feasible program because he can take his observations from a long sequence of incremental changes.

For example, without a more comprehensive social theory about juvenile delinquency than scholars have yet produced, one cannot possibly understand the ways in which a variety of public policies—say on education, housing, recreation, employment, race relations, and policing—might encourage or discourage delinquency. And one needs such an understanding if he undertakes the comprehensive overview of the problem prescribed in the models of the root method. If, however, one merely wants to mobilize knowledge sufficient to assist in a choice among a small group of similar policies—alternative policies on juvenile court procedures, for example—he can do so by comparative analysis of the results of similar past policy moves.

THEORISTS AND PRACTITIONERS

This difference explains—in some cases at least—why the administrator often feels that the outside expert or academic problem-solver is sometimes not helpful and why they in turn often urge more theory on him. And it explains why an administrator often feels more confident when "flying by the seat of his pants" than when following the advice of theorists. Theorists often ask the administrator to go the long way round to the solution of his problems, in effect ask him to follow the best canons of the scientific method, when the administrator knows that the best available theory will work less well than more modest incremental comparisons. Theorists do not realize that the administrator is often in fact practicing a systematic method. It would be foolish to push this explanation too far, for sometimes practical decision-makers are pursuing neither a theoretical approach nor successive comparisons, nor any other systematic method.

It may be worth emphasizing that theory is sometimes of extremely limited helpfulness in policy-making for at least two rather different reasons. It is greedy for facts; it can be constructed only through a great collection of observations. And it is typically insufficiently precise for application to a policy process that moves through small changes. In contrast, the comparative method both economizes on the need for facts and directs the analyst's attention to just those facts that are relevant to the fine choices faced by the decision-maker.

With respect to precision of theory, economic theory serves as an example. It predicts that an economy without money or prices would in certain specified ways misallocate resources, but this finding pertains to an alternative far removed from the kind of policies on which administrators need help. On the other hand, it is not precise enough to predict the consequences of policies restricting business mergers, and this is the kind of issue on which the administrators need help. Only in relatively restricted areas does economic theory achieve sufficient precision to go far in resolving policy questions; its helpfulness in policy-making is always so limited that it requires supplementation through comparative analysis.

SUCCESSIVE COMPARISON AS A SYSTEM

Successive limited comparisons is, then, indeed a method or system; it is not a failure of method for which administrators ought to apologize. None the less, its imperfections, which have not been explored in this paper, are many. For example, the method is without a built-in safeguard for all relevant values, and it also may lead the decision-maker to overlook excellent policies for no other reason than that they are not suggested by the chain of successive policy steps leading up to the present. Hence, it ought to be said that under this method, as well as under some of the most sophisticated variants of the root method—operations research, for example—policies will continue to be as foolish as they are wise.

Why then bother to describe the method in all the above detail? Because it is in fact a common method of policy formulation, and is, for complex problems, the principal reliance of administrators as well as of other policy analysts.[9] And because it will be superior to any other decision-making method available for complex

---

[9] Elsewhere I have explored this same method of policy formulation as practiced by academic analysts of policy ("Policy Analysis," 48 *American Economic* Review 298 [June, 1958]). Although it has been here presented as a method for public administrators, it is no less necessary to analysts more removed from immediate policy questions, despite their tendencies to describe their own analytical efforts as though they were the rational-comprehensive method with an especially heavy use of theory. Similarly, this same method is inevitably resorted to in personal problem-solving, where means and ends are sometimes impossible to separate, where aspirations or objectives undergo constant development, and where drastic simplification of the complexity of the real world is urgent if problems are to be solved in the time that can be given to them. To an economist accustomed to dealing with the marginal or incremental concept in market processes, the central idea in the method is that both evaluation and empirical analysis are incremental. Accordingly I have referred to the method elsewhere as "the incremental method."

problems in many circumstances, certainly superior to a futile attempt at superhuman comprehensiveness. The reaction of the public administrator to the exposition of method doubtless will be less a discovery of a new method than a better acquaintance with an old. But by becoming more conscious of their practice of this method, administrators might practice it with more skill and know when to extend or constrict its use. (That they sometimes practice it effectively and sometimes not may explain the extremes of opinion on "muddling through," which is both praised as a highly sophisticated form of problem-solving and denounced as no method at all. For I suspect that in so far as there is a system in what is known as "muddling through," this method is it.)

One of the noteworthy incidental consequences of clarification of the method is the light it throws on the suspicion an administrator sometimes entertains that a consultant or adviser is not speaking relevantly and responsibly when in fact by all ordinary objective evidence he is. The trouble lies in the fact that most of us approach policy problems within a framework given by our view of a chain of successive policy choices made up to the present. One's thinking about appropriate policies with respect, say, to urban traffic control is greatly influenced by one's knowledge of the incremental steps taken up to the present. An administrator enjoys an intimate knowledge of his past sequences that "outsiders" do not share, and his thinking and that of the "outsider" will consequently be different in ways that may puzzle both. Both may appear to be talking intelligently, yet each may find the other unsatisfactory. The relevance of the policy chain of succession is even more clear when an American tries to discuss, say, antitrust policy with a Swiss, for the chains of policy in the two countries are strikingly different and the two individuals consequently have organized their knowledge in quite different ways.

If this phenomenon is a barrier to communication, an understanding of it promises an enrichment of intellectual interaction in policy formulation. Once the source of difference is understood, it will sometimes be stimulating for an administrator to seek out a policy analyst whose recent experience is with a policy chain different from his own.

This raises again a question only briefly discussed above on the merits of like-mindedness among government administrators. While much of organization theory argues the virtues of common values and agreed organizational objectives, for complex problems in which the root method is inapplicable, agencies will want among their own personnel two types of diversification: administrators whose thinking is organized by reference to policy chains other than those familiar to most members of the organization and, even more commonly, administrators whose professional or personal values or interests create diversity of view (perhaps coming from different specialties, social classes, geographical areas) so that, even within a single agency, decision-making can be fragmented and parts of the agency can serve as watchdogs for other parts.

Notes

1. See Charles E. Lindblom,"The Science of Muddling Through," *Public Administration Review*, 19 (Spring 1959), 79–88; Aaron Wildavsky, *The Politics of the Budgetary Process* (Boston: Little, Brown, 1964).
2. The classic statement on group theory is David B. Truman, *The Governmental Process* (New York: Knopf, 1951).
3. Ibid., p. 37.
4. Earl Latham,"The Group Basis of Politics," in *Political Behavior*, ed. Heinz Eulau, Samuel J. Eldersveld, and Morris Janowitz (New York: Free Press, 1956), p. 239.
5. Elite theory is explained at length in Thomas R. Dye and Harmon Zeigler, *The Irony of Democracy*, 14th ed. (Belmont, CA: Wadsworth, 2009).
6. James M. Buchanan and Gordon Tullock, *The Calculus of Consent* (Ann Arbor: University of Michigan Press, 1962).
7. Anthony Downs, *An Economic Theory of Democracy* (New York: Harper & Row, 1957).

Bibliography

Bickers, Kenneth N., and John T. Williams. *Public Policy Analysis: A Political Economy Approach.* Boston: Houghton Mifflin, 2001.

Buchanan, James M., and Gordon Tullock. *The Calculus of Consent.* Ann Arbor: University of Michigan Press, 1962.

Dahl, Robert A., and Bruce Stinebrickner. *Modern Political Analysis*, 6th ed. New York: Longman 2003.

Downs, Anthony. *An Economic Theory of Democracy.* New York: Harper & Row, 1957.

Dye, Thomas R. *Top Down Policymaking.* Washington, DC: CQ Press, 2000.

Lindblom, Charles E., and Edward J. Woodhouse. *The Policy-Making Process*, 3rd ed. New York: Longman, 1993.

Truman, David B. *The Government Process.* New York: Knopf, 1954.

Watson, Joel. *Strategy: An Introduction to Game Theory.* New York: W. W. Norton, 2001.

Wildavsky, Aaron. *The New Politics of the Budgetary Process*, 2nd ed. New York: HarperCollins, 1992.

Web Sites

American Political Science Association. Home page of academic political scientists' professional organization. *www.apsanet.org*

Public Agenda Online. Brief guide to a variety of policy issues, including public opinion surveys on these issues. *www.publicagenda.org*

Almanac of Policy Issues. Background information on a variety of issues with links to sources. *www.policyalmanac.org*

Public Opinion Online. Compilation of recent public opinion polls on policy issues, political actors, government Institutions, etc. *www.pollingreport.com*

The Gallup Organization. Home page of the Gallup public opinion organization. *www.gallup.com*

National Center for Policy Research. Conservative policy research organization, with studies on a variety of policy issues. *www.nationalcenter.org*

Progressive Policy Institute. Liberal policy research organization, with policy briefs on a variety of issues. *www.ppionline.org*

National Issues. Collection of current articles on a variety of policy issues. *www.nationalissues.com*

Economic Policy

chapter 2

The Market and the Polis

Deborah Stone

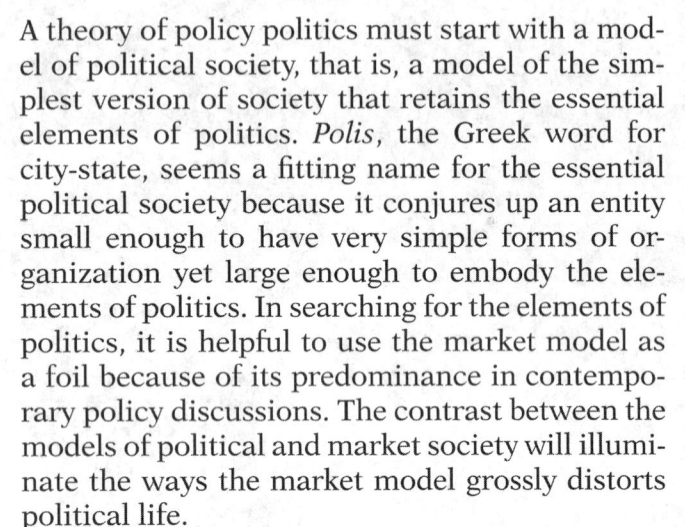

A theory of policy politics must start with a model of political society, that is, a model of the simplest version of society that retains the essential elements of politics. *Polis*, the Greek word for city-state, seems a fitting name for the essential political society because it conjures up an entity small enough to have very simple forms of organization yet large enough to embody the elements of politics. In searching for the elements of politics, it is helpful to use the market model as a foil because of its predominance in contemporary policy discussions. The contrast between the models of political and market society will illuminate the ways the market model grossly distorts political life.

A market can be simply defined as a social system in which individuals pursue their own welfare by exchanging things with others whenever trades are mutually beneficial. Economists often begin their discussions of the market by conjuring up the Robinson Crusoe society, where two people on a lush tropical island swap coconuts and small game animals. They trade to make each person better off, but since each person always has the option of producing everything for himself, trading is never an absolute necessity for either one. (Economists usually neglect to mention that the "real" Crusoe was able to salvage a veritable microcosm of industrial society from his shipwrecked vessel—from gunpowder and muskets to cables and nails.) Participants in the market are in competition with each other for scarce resources; each person tries to acquire things at the least possible cost, and to convert raw materials into more valuable things that can be sold at the highest possible price.

In the market model, individuals act only to maximize their own self-interest. Here "self-interest" means their own welfare, however they define that for themselves. It does not mean that they act "selfishly"; their self-interest might include, for example, the well-being of their family and friends. The competitive drive to maximize one's own welfare stimulates people to be very resourceful, creative, clever, and productive, and ultimately raises the level of economic well-being of society as a whole. With this description of the essence of the market model, we can start to build an alternative model of the polis by contrasting more detailed features of the market model and a political community.

COMMUNITY

A model purporting to capture the essence of political life would have to be far more complex than the Robinson Crusoe society, with or without its industrial artifacts. Because politics and policy can happen only in communities, community must be the starting point of our polis. Public policy is about communities trying to achieve something as communities. This is true even though there is almost always conflict within a community over what its goals should be and who its members are, and even though every communal goal ultimately must be achieved through the behavior of individuals. Unlike the market, which starts with individuals and assumes no goals, preferences, or intentions other than those held by individuals, a model of the polis must assume both collective will and collective effort.

Untold volumes of political philosophy have tried to define and explain this phenomenon of collective intention. But even without being able to define it, we know intuitively that societies behave as if they had one. We can scarcely speak about societies without using the language of collective will ("Democrats want . . ."; "Farmers seek . . ."; "The administration is trying . . ."). Every child knows the feeling of being in a group and reaching consensus. We can argue about whether consensus implies unanimity or only

---

"The Market and the Polis" from *Policy Paradox: The Art of Political Decision Making, Revised Edition* by Deborah Stone. Copyright © 2002, 1997, 1988 by Deborah Stone. Used by permission of W.W. Norton & Company, Inc.

majority, or whether apparent consensus masks suppressed dissension. But we know that consensus is a feeling of collective will, and we know when it exists and when it does not, just as surely (and sometimes mistakenly) as we know when we are hungry and when we are not.

A community must have a membership, and some way of defining who is a member of the community and who is not. Membership is in some sense the primary political issue, for membership definitions and rules determine who is allowed to participate in community activities, and who is governed by community rules and authority. Nation-states have rules for citizenship. Private clubs have qualifications for members and procedures by which people can join. Churches have formal rituals for new members to join. Neighborhoods may have no formal rules limiting who may become a member, but informal practices such as restrictive covenants on property deeds, bank redlining in mortgage lending, and sheer harassment may accomplish racial exclusion when formal rules cannot.

The most highly contested and passionate political fights are about membership. Mere physical residence in a place is not always the same thing as political membership. Proposition 187 in California, a provision that prohibits undocumented aliens from using public schools, Medicaid, and other social programs, is one of many immigration backlash movements that differentiates among residents, giving political benefits to some but not others. The distinction between residence and citizenship is only the beginning of conflicts over membership. In the United States, we have had a long tradition of multiple civic statuses among people who were nominally citizens: female and black citizens were not allowed to vote, own property, or serve on juries, for example, and Chinese-American citizens were subject to unique restrictions, such as having to carry proof of citizenship and being subject to deportation.[1]

A model of the polis must also include a distinction between political community and cultural community. A political community is a group of people who live under the same political rules and structure of governance and share status as citizens. A cultural community is a group of people who share a culture and draw their identities from a common language, history, and traditions.[2] In many nations, including the United States, the political community includes diverse cultural communities, and policy politics entails a profound dilemma: how to integrate several cultural communities into a single political community without destroying or sacrificing their identity and integrity. Issues such as bilingual education or interracial adoption simply cannot be understood in terms of individuals pursuing their self-interests. The arguments for permitting or encouraging bilingual education, or for prohibiting adoption of black and Native American children by parents of a different cultural community, are about defense of communities, and about the pitting of community interests against individual interests.

Membership in a community defines social and economic rights as well as political rights. What makes a collection of individuals a community is not only some definitional principles specifying who's in and who's out, but also mutual aid among members. Sharing burdens and bounty is the glue that holds people together. When immigrant groups have come to the United States (or elsewhere), they have tended to stick together in ethnic neighborhoods, and one of the first things they do is establish mutual aid societies to pool their resources. Through these associations, they provide each other with money for culturally acceptable funerals, for sickness and life insurance, and for credit to establish new businesses.[3] Pooling resources for redistribution to the needy is the essence of insurance, and in this sense of sharing and caring for each other, insurance is a characteristic feature of community.

In the market model, insurance is another financial product that firms sell in order to make a profit, and buyers buy in order to protect themselves against economic losses due to various risks,

---

[1] The concept and practice of multiple civic statuses is developed and documented by Rogers Smith, "Beyond Tocqueville, Myrdal, and Hartz: The Multiple Traditions in America," *American Political Science Review* 87, no. 3 (Sept. 1993): 549–66. An excellent meditation on membership is Chapter 2 of Michael Walzer's *Spheres of Justice* (Cambridge, Mass.: Harvard University Press, 1983).

[2] This distinction, as well as the whole issue of cultural pluralism within political communities, is clearly and richly explored in Will Kymlicka, *Liberalism, Community and Culture* (Oxford: Clarendon Press, 1989).

[3] See Lizabeth Cohen, *Making a New Deal: Industrial Workers in Chicago* (Cambridge, England: Cambridge University Press, 1991); and Scott Cummings, ed., *Self-Help in Urban America: Patterns of Minority Business Enterprise* (Port Washington, N.Y.: Kennikat Press, 1980).

such as the risk of becoming unable to work. In the polis, mutual aid is a good in itself that people create, collectively, in order to foster and protect a community. Mutual aid is one bond among individuals that holds them together as a community. And in a larger sense, sharing, caring, and maintaining relationships is at least as strong a motivator of human behavior as competition, separation, and promotion of one's separate self-interests.

Public Interest

In the polis, there is a public interest. "Public interest" might mean any of several things. It could be individual interests held in common, things everyone wants for themselves, such as a high standard of living. It could be individual goals for the community. Often people want things for their community that conflict with what they want for themselves. They want good schools and clean air, perhaps, but also lower taxes and the right to burn their trash. Citizens in this view have two sides: a private, rather self-interested side and a more public-spirited side, and we might think of the public interest as those things desired by the public-spirited side of citizens.

Yet another interpretation of public interest is those goals on which there is a consensus. Programs and policies favored by a majority of citizens, for example, would comprise the public interest. In this interpretation, the public interest is not necessarily enduring. It is whatever most people want at the moment, and so it changes over time. And of course, this notion of public interest raises questions of what counts as consensus and how we would know whether true consensus exists.

Finally, the public interest could mean things that are good for a community as a community. Even the most minimally organized community has some stake in preserving its own sense of order and fair play, whatever form that takes. All communities have a general interest in having some governing processes and some means for resolving disputes without violence. The members of a community almost always have an interest in its survival, and therefore in its perpetuation and its defense against outsiders. This question of community survival is at the heart of the debate over nuclear weapons. One side argues that nuclear weapons are essential for survival because only they can provide sufficient national defense. The other side argues that nuclear weapons are antithetical to survival because, if used, they will destroy society and possibly annihilate mankind. Both sides agree that community survival is what is at stake.

There is virtually never full agreement on the public interest, yet we need to make it a defining characteristic of the polis because so much of politics is people fighting over what the public interest is and trying to realize their own definitions of it. Let it be an empty box, but no matter; in the polis, people expend a lot of energy trying to fill up that box. The concept of public interest is to the polis what self-interest is to the market. They are both abstractions whose specific contents we do not need to know in order to use them to explain and predict people's behavior. We simply assume that people behave as if they were trying to realize the public interest or maximize their self-interest.

This is not to deny that politics also includes people pursuing their self-interest. But there is no society on earth in which people are allowed to do that blatantly and exclusively, so that even if we only want to understand how people pursue their self-interest, we need to understand how conceptions of the public interest shape and constrain people's strategies for pursuing their own interests.

It would be as much a mistake to think that the market has no concept of public interest as to believe that the polis has no room for self-interest. But there is a world of difference between public interest in a market and a polis. In theory, the public interest or general welfare in a market society is the net result of all individuals pursuing their self-interest. In economic theory, given a well-functioning market and a fair initial income distribution, whatever happens is by definition the best result for society as a whole. In a market, in short, the empty box of public interest is filled as an afterthought with the side effects of other activities. In the polis, by contrast, people fill the box intentionally, with forethought, planning, and conscious effort.

Commons Problems

Because people often pursue a conception of public interest that is different from their conception of self-interest, the polis is characterized by a special problem: how to combine self-interest and public interest, or, to put it another way, how to have both private benefits and collective benefits. Situations where self-interest and public interest work against each other are known as commons problems, and in the polis, commons problems are common. There are two types of commons problems. In one, actions with private benefits entail social costs; for example, discharging industrial wastes into a lake is a cheap method of disposal for a factory owner but ruins the water for everyone else. In the other, social benefits necessitate private sacrifices; for example, maintaining a school system requires individual tax payments. But note that any situation can be described both ways: clean lakes are a social benefit entailing the private costs of nonpolluting waste disposal, and a poor school system is the social cost of high private consumption. Whether we label a situation as "social benefits and private costs," or as "social costs and private benefits" is a matter of point of view. Commons problems are also called collective action problems because it is hard to motivate people to undertake private costs or forgo private benefits for the collective good.

In market theory, commons problems are thought to be the exception rather than the rule. Most actions in the market model do not have social consequences. In the polis, by contrast, commons problems are everything. Not only do they crop up frequently, but most significant policy problems are commons problems. It is rare in the polis that the benefits and costs of an action are entirely self-contained, affecting only one or two individuals. Actions have not only immediate effects, but side effects, unanticipated consequences, second- and third-order effects, long-term effects, and ripple effects. The language of policy is full of such metaphors recognizing the broad social consequences of individual actions. The major dilemma of policy in the polis is how to get people to give primacy to these broader consequences in their private calculus of choices, especially in an era when the dominant culture celebrates private consumption and personal gain.

INFLUENCE

Fortunately, the vast gap between self-interest and public interest is bridged in the polis by some potent forces: influence, cooperation, and loyalty. Influence is inherent in communities, even communities of two. People are not freewheeling, freethinking atoms whose desires arise from spontaneous generation. Our ideas about what we want and the choices we make are shaped by education, persuasion, and the general process of socialization. (Chapter 3 goes into more detail about how people's desires, or what economists call "preferences," are shaped by influences outside themselves.) Several studies of inner-city youths, for example, have shown how the desire for gold chains, expensive sneakers, and luxury cars is nothing but a reflection of mainstream consumer culture in which these things are heavily promoted as desirable. Yet according to some views, poor kids are supposed to ignore and resist the powerful messages around them, because they don't have enough (legitimately earned) money to afford these items.

Actions, no less than ideas, are influenced by others—by the choices other people have made and the ones we expect them to make, by what they want us to do, and by what we think they expect us to do. More often than not, our choices are conditional. A worker will go out on strike only if she thinks that enough of her fellow workers will join her. A citizen will complain about postal service only if he believes that the post office will take some action in response.

Influence works not simply by putting one individual under a figurative spell of another, but also in ways that lead to curious phenomena of collective behavior. "Bandwagon effects" in elections happen when a candidate's initial lead causes people to support him or her because they want to be on board with a winner. Panics happen when people fear an economic collapse, rush to cash out their bank accounts, and in so doing bring about the collapse they feared. Mobs often act with a peculiar sense of direction and purpose, as if coordinated by a leader, when in fact there is none. Fads for hula hoops or backward baseball caps are frivolous examples of collective behavior; prison riots and "white flight" from urban neighborhoods are more serious. Such things can happen only because people's choices are conditional. They want to do something only if most people will do it (say, go on strike), or to do something before most people do it (say, get their money out of the bank).

Influence sometimes spills over into coercion, and the line between them is fuzzy at best. In fact, one big difference between traditional conservatives and liberals is where they place that line. Liberals tend to see coercion in economic necessity, and the far Left is wont to see it in any kind of need, even that born of desire to "keep up with the Joneses." Conservatives have a more restricted view of coercion, seeing it only in physical force and commands backed up by the threat of force; but the far Right is wont to see coercion in any government rule or regulation, because all laws are backed by the government's monopoly on the legitimate use of force. There is no correct place to draw the line, because coercion is an idea about behavior, a label and an interpretation, rather than the behavior itself. In all its fuzziness, the influence-coercion boundary will be an aspect of many of the dilemmas developed in this book. For now, it is important to state that influence—in all its varieties and degrees of strength—is one of the central elements in politics.

COOPERATION

In the polis, cooperation is every bit as important as competition. This is true for two reasons. First, politics involves seeking allies and organizing cooperation in order to compete with opponents. Whenever there are two sides to an issue and more than two people involved, there must be alliances among the people on one side. Children usually learn this lesson when they play in threesomes. Every conflict unites some people as it divides others, and politics has as much to do with how alliances are made and held together as with how people are divided.[4] For this reason, the two-person models so prominent in the field of economics are politically empty: they have no possibility for strategic coalitions and shifting alliances, nor do they allow for joint effort, leadership, or coordination. For example, in one of the most popular textbooks on policy analysis, the chapter on "Public Choice," which deals with questions of the nature of society, how we should evaluate social welfare, and how we should make social choices, is developed entirely around a two-person model called "Bill-John City."[5]

The second reason cooperation must be central to a model of politics is that it is essential to power. Cooperation is often a more effective form of subordination than coercion. Authority that depends solely on coercion cannot extend very far. Even prison guards, with seemingly all the resources stacked on their side, need the cooperation of inmates to keep order in the prison. Despite bars, locks, and the guards' monopoly on weapons, prisoners outnumber the guards. So guards bargain with prisoners, offering them favors and privileges to gain their cooperation.[6] One of the most chilling aspects of accounts of Nazi concentration camps is how the camp commanders obtained the cooperation and participation of inmates in running the camps. Under threat of imminent death, prisoners were willing to conduct massacres and handle the bodies, while Nazi soldiers had often balked at the same tasks.[7] Accounts of extreme terrorism such as this illustrate another way that cooperation and coercion can become intertwined.

In the ideal market of textbooks, there is nothing but pure competition, which means no cooperation among either buyers or sellers. Sellers compete with each other to obtain raw materials at the lowest prices and to sell their products at the highest profit. They compete with perspicacious buyers, who shop around for the best deals and thereby force the sellers to offer lower prices. Cooperation, when it occurs, is a deviation from the well-functioning market and most words to describe it in the market model are pejorative—collusion, oligarchy, price-fixing, insider trading. In the polis, cooperation is the norm. It is the inseparable other side of competition and a necessary ingredient of power. The words to describe it are decidedly more positive—coalition, alliance, union, party, support.

LOYALTY

Related to cooperation is loyalty. Cooperation entails alliances, and alliances are at least somewhat enduring. In the ideal market, a buyer will switch suppliers in response to a price or quality change, rather than stick with the previous supplier. There is no "glue" in buyer-seller relations. In politics, relationships are not so fluid. They involve gifts, favors, support, and, most of all, future obligations. Political alliances bind people over time. To

---

[4] A wonderful treatise on this aspect of politics is E. E. Schattschneider, *The Semisovereign People* (Hinsdale, Ill.: Dryden Press, 1970), especially chap. 4.

[5] Edith Stokey and Richard Zeckhauser, *A Primer of Policy Analysis* (New York: Norton, 1978), chap. 9.

[6] Gresham Sykes, *Society of Captives* (Princeton, N.J.: Princeton University Press, 1958), chap. 5.

[7] Jean-Francois Steiner, *Treblinka* (New York: Simon and Schuster, 1967), especially pp. 55–75.

[8] Schattschneider, op. cit. (note 4), p. 66.

paraphrase E. E. Schattschneider, politics is more like choosing a spouse than shopping in a five-and-ten-cent store.[8]

The differing views of loyalty in the market and polis models are evident from our language, also. In the market, people are "buyers" and "sellers." In politics, they are "enemies" and "friends." It is characteristic of friendships that we stick with our friends, even when they hurt us or do things not much to our liking. We honor friends more for what we have shared in the past than for what we expect them to do for us now and in the future. Friendships are forgiving in a way that pure commercial relationships are not (or should not be). The idea of a "pure" commercial relationship is precisely one not tainted by loyalty or sentiment. In the polis, history counts for a lot; in the market, it counts for nothing.

This does not mean that political alliances are perfectly stable or that people never abandon friends and join hands with former enemies. Children learn this lesson from their threesomes, too. But it does mean that in the polis there is a presumption of loyalty. The expectation is that people will normally stick by their friends and allies, and that it takes a major event—something that triggers a deep fear or offers a vast opportunity—to get them to switch their loyalties. There is risk to breaking old alliances, and people do not do it lightly.

GROUPS

Influence, cooperation, and loyalty are powerful forces, and the result is that groups and organizations, rather than individuals, are the building blocks of the polis.[9] Groups are important in three ways. First, people belong to institutions and organizations, even when they are not formal members. They are participants in organizations as citizens, employees, customers, students, taxpayers, voters, and potential recruits, if not as staff, managers, or leaders. Their opinions are shaped by organizations, their interests are profoundly affected by the behavior of organizations, and they depend on organizations to represent their interests.

Second, policy making is not only about solving public problems, but about how groups are formed, split, and re-formed to achieve public purposes. On policy issues of any significance, it is groups that confront each other, using individuals only as their spokesmen. Groups coalesce and divide over policy proposals, depending on how they expect the proposal to affect them. Injured war veterans are glad to have the support of the retarded citizen groups when they are trying to establish a National Institute of Handicapped Research, but eager to dissociate themselves when job rights for the handicapped are at issue.

Third, groups are important because decisions of the polis are collective. They are explicitly collective, through formal procedures such as voting, administrative rule-making, and bargaining, and through public bodies, such as courts, juries, legislatures, committees, or agencies. Beyond this formal sense, public decisions are implicitly collective in that even when officials have "sole authority," they are influenced by outside opinion and pressure. Policy decisions are not made by abstract people, but by people in social roles and organizations, addressing audiences of people in social roles and organizations, and using procedures that have been collectively approved. The roles, settings, procedures, and audiences exert their own influence, even on the most strong-willed and independent minds.

INFORMATION

In the ideal market, information is "perfect," meaning it is accurate, complete, and available to everyone at no cost. In the polis, by contrast, information is interpretive, incomplete, and strategically withheld. Of course, it would be silly to say there is no such thing as correct information. Surely, when the newspaper reports that a share of IBM stock sold yesterday for $118, or that Senator Kennedy voted for a gun control bill, or that a police officer used the word "nigger" forty-one times in tape-recorded interviews, we are quite confident that the information is accurate and that it makes sense to think of that kind of information as being correct or incorrect. But in politics, the important

---

[9] To make groups the building block of the polis is not to espouse a pluralist theory of politics. Central to pluralist theory is the belief that all important interests become organized in groups and thus are represented in the give-and-take of pressure group politics. Equally important is the belief that no group can consistently dominate politics. I insist on groups not to show that a political system is fair or representative or balanced, but rather to point out that politics is necessarily a system of alliances. If we look at people only as individuals, we will miss facets of their motivation and action essential to an understanding of policy; even worse, we will miss aspects of politics that cannot be captured simply by adding up individual actions.

thing is what people make of such reports. People act on what they believe to be the financial health of a company, whether they think their senator represents their interests, or what they think a policeman's use of racial epithets means for the possibility of fair trials for black citizens. Interpretations are more powerful than facts.

Much of what we "know" is what we believe to be true. And what we believe about information depends on who tells us (the source) and how it is presented (the medium, the choice of language, the context). Some people are more likely to believe medical information from a doctor than from a friend, whereas others are more likely to believe a friend than a doctor. Some people find print more convincing than television, and vice versa. The words, pictures, and imagery of information affect its very message as well as its persuasiveness. Both the timing of information with respect to related events and the juxtaposition of one set of ideas with another can change the way information is perceived.

Because politics is driven by how people interpret information, much political activity is an effort to control interpretations. Political candidates and their campaign advisors are notorious for their creative presentation of information, or "spin control." But strategic manipulation of information is by no means the preserve of shady politicians. We all do it, have done it, and will continue to do it. (Think about the last time you told your professor why your paper was late, your students why the exams weren't graded yet, your friendly IRS agent what your earnings were, or even yourself about your honesty.) Information in the polis is different from information in the market model, both because it depends so much on interpretation and because it is itself the object of strategic manipulation. Part III of this book is centrally concerned with how information about policy is strategically created in politics.

In the polis, information is never complete. We can never know all the possible means for achieving a goal or all the possible effects of an action, especially since all actions have side effects, unanticipated consequences, and long-term effects. Nor can we know for sure what other people will do in response to our actions, yet often we choose to act on the basis of what we expect others to do. If people act at all, they must necessarily act on guesses, hunches, expectations, hopes, and faith, as well as on facts.

Information is never fully and equally available to all participants in politics. There is a cost to acquiring information, if only the cost of spending one's own time. To the extent that information is complicated, sophisticated, or technical, it requires education to be understood, and education is not uniformly distributed. These are by now standard critiques of the market model.

But even more important for a model of the polis is that crucial information is very often *deliberately* kept secret. The ideas of inventors, the business plans of entrepreneurs, the decision of a government to devalue its currency, the number of seats American Airlines reserves for "Super Saver" fares, whether a putative candidate will in fact run for election, where the town fathers are thinking of locating a sewage treatment plant—every one of these things is kept secret because someone expects someone else to behave differently once the information is made public. Secrecy and revelation are tools of political strategy, and we would grossly misunderstand the character of information in politics if we thought of it as neutral facts, readily disclosed.

PASSION

In the market, economic resources are governed by the laws of matter. Resources are finite, scarce, and consumed upon use. Whatever is used for making guns cannot be used for making butter (a textbook example conceived by someone who surely never made either). People can do only one thing at a time (produce guns or butter) and material can be only one thing at a time (a gun or a stick of butter).

In the polis, there is another set of laws operating alongside the laws of matter that might be called laws of paradox if the phrase weren't paradoxical itself. Instead I'll call them the laws of passion, because they describe phenomena that behave more like emotions than like physical matter. One of these laws is that passion feeds on itself. Like passion, political resources are often enlarged or enhanced through use, rather than diminished. Channels of influence and political connections, for example, grow by being used. The more people work together and help each other, the more committed they become to each other and to their nominal goal. The more something is done—say, a regulatory agency consults with industry leaders on its proposals, or a school board negotiates with teachers on salaries—the more valuable the personal connections and organizational ties become, and the more people's expectations of "doing things the way they have always been done" grow.

Political skills and authority also grow with use, and it is no accident that we often use the metaphor of "exercise" when talking about them. That skills should grow with practice is not so surprising, but it is worth exploring why authority should work the same way. Precedent is important in authority. The more one makes certain types of decisions, the easier it is to continue in the same path, in part because repeated decisions require no new thought, and in part because people are less likely to resist or even question orders and requests they have obeyed before. How often have we justified our own begrudging compliance by telling ourselves, "I've never protested all the other times I've been asked to do this, so how can I refuse now?" Or, on the other side, "I've let them get away with it many times before, so it is hardly fair to punish them now." In short, the more often an order is issued and obeyed, the stronger the presumption of compliance.

This phenomenon of resource expansion through exercise, use, practice, and expression is ignored in the market model. A distinguished former chairman of the Council of Economic Advisors once wrote that market-like arrangements are good because they "reduce the need for compassion, patriotism, brotherly love and cultural solidarity as motivating forces behind social improvement.... However vital [these things] may be to a civilized society, [they] are in *too short supply* to serve as substitutes" for the more plentiful motive of self-interest.[10] To make such an analogy between compassion and widgets, to see them both as items with fixed quantities that are diminished by use, is to be blinded by the market model. Who but a die-hard economist would believe that people are born with a limited stockpile of sentiments and passions, to be hoarded through life lest they be spent too quickly? More often than not, waving the flag increases the feeling of patriotism, just as comforting a frightened child increases one's sense of compassion.

Some other laws of passion governing the polis can be mentioned briefly here and will be explored more fully in the rest of the book. One is that *the whole is greater than the sum of its parts.* A protest march, for example, means something more than a few thousand people walking down a street; the repeated refusal to sell houses to blacks in a neighborhood means something more than a series of unrelated seller decisions. Widgets may simply get cheaper through mass production—economists call that economies of scale—but most human actions change their meaning and impact when done in concert or in quantity.

Another law of passion is that *things can mean (and therefore be) more than one thing at once.* Conviction of white-collar criminals with nominal fines means both that the government condemns the activity and that it does not. Any expenditure is a debit to the spender, but income to somebody else. Thus, the growth of health care expenditures bemoaned by employers and taxpayers also means new professional opportunities and job growth, especially for women and minorities. Chapter 6 focuses on the role of ambiguity in politics. Here it is enough to note that ambiguity and symbolic meanings find no home in the market model of society, where everything has its precise value or cost.

POWER

Up to this point I have defined the polis by contrasting it with a market model of society. It is worth summarizing the characteristics here, emphasizing what the polis is instead of what it is not:

1. It is a community, or perhaps multiple communities, with ideas, images, will, and effort quite apart from individual goals and behavior.
2. It has a public interest, if only as an idea about which people fight.
3. Most of its policy problems are commons problems.
4. Influence is pervasive, and the boundary between influence and coercion is always contested.
5. Cooperation is as important as competition.
6. Loyalty is the norm.
7. Groups and organizations are the building blocks.
8. Information is interpretive, incomplete, and strategic.
9. It is governed by the laws of passion as well as the laws of matter.

---

[10] Charles L. Schultze, *The Public Use of Private Interest* (Washington, D.C.: Brookings Institution, 1977), pp. 17–18, emphasis added.

By now, my readers must surely be wondering how a reputable political scientist could build a model of political society without making power a defining characteristic, let alone the primary one. I save power for last because it is derived from all the other elements. Power cannot be defined without reference to them. It is a phenomenon of communities. Its purpose is always to subordinate individual self-interest to other interests—sometimes to other individual or group interests, sometimes to the public interest. It operates through influence, cooperation, and loyalty. It is based also on the strategic control of information. And finally, it is a resource that obeys the laws of passion rather than the laws of matter.

Any model of society must specify its source of energy, the force or forces that drive change. In the market model, change is driven by exchange, which is in turn motivated by the individual quest to improve one's own welfare. Through exchanges, the use and distribution of resources is changed.

In the polis, change occurs through the interaction of mutually defining ideas and alliances. Ideas about politics shape political alliances, and strategic considerations of building and maintaining alliances in turn shape the ideas people espouse and seek to implement. In my model of the polis, I emphasize ideas and portrayals as key forms of power in policy making. This book is not so much about how people collect and deploy the "traditional" resources of power—money, votes, and offices—but how they use ideas to gather political support and diminish the support of opponents, all in order to control policy.

Ideas are the very stuff of politics. People fight about ideas, fight for them, and fight against them.

CONCEPTS OF SOCIETY

	Market Model	*Polis Model*
1. Unit of analysis	individual	community
2. Motivations	self-interest	public interest (as well as self-interest)
3. Chief conflict	self-interest vs. self-interest	self-interest vs. public interest (commons problems)
4. Source of people's ideas and preferences	self-generation within the individual	influences from outside
5. Nature of collective activity	competition	cooperation and competition
6. Criteria for individual decision making	maximizing self-interest, minimizing cost	loyalty (to people, places, organizations, products), maximize self-interest, promote public interest
7. Building blocks of social action	individuals	groups and organizations
8. Nature of information	accurate, complete, fully available	ambiguous, interpretive, incomplete, strategically manipulated
9. How things work	laws of matter (e.g., material resources are finite and diminish with use)	laws of passion (e.g., human resources are renewable and expand with use)
10. Sources of change	material exchange	ideas, persuasion, alliances
	quest to maximize own welfare	pursuit of power, pursuit of own welfare, pursuit of public interest

Political conflict is never simply over material conditions and choices, but over what is legitimate. The passion in politics comes from conflicting senses of fairness, justice, rightness, and goodness. Moreover, people fight *with* ideas as well as about them. The different sides in a conflict create different portrayals of the battle—who is affected, how they are affected, and what is at stake. Political fights are conducted with money, with rules, with votes, and with favors, to be sure, but they are conducted above all with words and ideas.

Every idea about policy draws boundaries. It tells what or who is included or excluded in a category. These boundaries are more than intellectual—they define people in and out of a conflict or place them on different sides. In politics, the representation of issues is strategically designed to attract support to one's side, to forge some alliances and break others. Ideas and alliances are intimately connected.

Finally, the interaction between ideas and alliances is ever-changing and never-ending. Problems in the polis are never "solved" in the way that economic needs are met in the market model. It is not as though we can place an order for justice, and once the order is filled, the job is done. (Indeed, modern economists have had to wrestle with the problem of why even material needs seem to grow even as they are fulfilled.) As Plutarch wrote:

> They are wrong who think that politics is like an ocean voyage or a military campaign, something to be done with some end in view, or something which levels off as soon as that end is reached. It is not a public chore, to be got over with; it is a way of life.[11]

---

[11] Plutarch, cited in Jonathan Schell, *The Fate of the Earth* (New York: Avon Books, 1982), p. 109.

Economic Policy: Translating Theory into Practice

Charles L. Cochran and Eloise F. Malone

As Chapter 5 indicated, prior to the 1930s most policy analysts accepted the economic theory of the time, which held that a market economy would achieve the macroeconomic goals of full employment, price stability, and productivity growth without government intervention. The Great Depression shattered such complacent beliefs: John Maynard Keynes's theories demonstrated how achieving macroeconomic goals required government intervention through monetary and fiscal policies. This was officially endorsed in the United States by the Employment Act of 1946 and reinforced by the Full Employment and Balanced Growth Act of 1978, which committed the federal government to specific policy goals for unemployment inflation, and economic growth.

Those acts recognize the responsibility of the state for creating the economic conditions that will result in full employment and otherwise provide for the social welfare of citizens. Economic policies are the primary means by which a government provides or guarantees a range of services to protect people in circumstances such as childhood, sickness, and old age.

Promoting the General Welfare in Practice

The obligation of democratic government to "promote the general welfare" is embedded in the Constitution. As democratic revolutions spread throughout Europe after the American Revolution, they embraced this notion of government as the servant of the people in contrast to monarchial or authoritarian governments where the people were the servants of the state. The idea of the welfare state has evolved to mean different things in different countries. Most countries of the European Union and Canada use the term *welfare state* to indicate the state's responsibility for providing comprehensive and universal welfare for its citizens. In welfare economics, welfare is thought of in terms of the utility provided by the things people choose to have. This may include social services such as health care, access to nationally guaranteed education, and even a guarantee of a minimum income. Welfare may also refer to the services designed to protect people against social problems such as crime, unemployment, learning disabilities, and social insecurity. The European Union notes that it is the obligation of the state to provide "social protection" to its citizens at the highest level possible. The European Union accepts an institutional model of welfare in which the state is to provide social protection and welfare as an individual right.

In the United States, social welfare policy is often understood to refer to "welfare provided by the state." The United States burst upon the scene in a revolution against King George III's mercantilist meddling, proclaiming the virtues of laissez-faire. Americans embraced the myth that they were the chosen people delivered from bondage and destined to be free of tyrannical government. Thomas Malthus's view of poverty as deserved punishment for moral failings was widely accepted. This perspective demanding "workfare" for recipients of welfare, and ending welfare as we have known it, was promoted by the Clinton administration.

In the United States, federalism has divided the responsibility for welfare. States are responsible for the administration of public assistance and health care programs even when most of the funding comes from the national government. When compared to other developed nations, the federal government has played a very limited role in providing social welfare policies. The national government's major foray into national social welfare was during the administration of Franklin Roosevelt in the 1930s, which provided for Social Security and most federally financed

"Economic Policy: Translating Theory into Practice" from *Public Policy: Perspectives and Choices, 3rd edition* by Charles L. Cochran and Eloise F. Malone. Copyright © 2005 by Lynne Rienner Publishers, Inc. Used with permission of the publisher.

welfare programs, and the administration of Lyndon Johnson in the 1960s, which provided for Medicaid and Medicare and engaged in a wide variety of other projects at the local level such as "Operation Head Start" in the "War on Poverty." But these programs have been suspect by social and political conservatives whose goal is to dismantle the New Deal and the War on Poverty by limiting government's financial support for those programs. Social welfare systems in the United States are dependent not only on federal and state support, but also on private, religious, and corporate assistance. The resulting systems tend to be complex, inefficient, and expensive.

Several economic policy goals are generally accepted by all governments. They include full employment, price stability (low levels of inflation), and economic growth. The role of the policy analyst is to design policies that will best achieve these goals. In the United States, Congress and the president, along with a host of policy advisers, try to formulate policies to achieve the goals through the political process.

Evolution of Political-Economic Thinking

The Great Depression was the catalyst for the development and application of the Keynesian approach to economic policy. Franklin Roosevelt scrambled to turn the economy around and instinctively engaged in many policies consistent with Keynesian theory when he launched the New Deal. The New Deal signified a fundamental change in the role of government in U.S. society. For the first time, the government tried to change certain market structures to provide more socially acceptable outcomes for an economy in severe distress. The recognition that government may alter market outcomes is a significant change in political philosophy. A laissez-faire view of society no longer described the perfect model of the relationship between government and the economy. It is now widely accepted that Keynes's conclusion that, because the level of aggregate demand will not usually add up to just the right amount to achieve price stability and full employment, fiscal policy is required to achieve those goals.

The government's effort to guide the economy to maintain high levels of employment and nudge it toward growth whenever it shows signs of weakening is not a radical change to capitalism. But to business leaders and ideological conservatives, government spending is inherently wasteful. For those who believe in a social Darwinist, laissez-faire view of society, there is always a suspicion that government spending is a thinly disguised entering wedge for socialism. The debate lasted until World War II brought the unprecedented rise in expenditure, and a corresponding decline in unemployment. The federal government mobilized the nation for war, and the years of massive output led to a new attitude toward government involvement in the economy.

The new environment resulted in passage of the Employment Act of 1946, which held the government responsible for providing "maximum employment, production, and purchasing power." Most important, the law moved the debate from *whether* the government should be involved in directing the economy, to *how* to best achieve a robust economy.

The Employment Act also created the Council of Economic Advisers (CEA), to be responsible for preparing an annual economic report of the president. Although the Bureau of the Budget was completely under the control of the president, Senate confirmation of the CEA indicated that responsibility for the macro-economic health of the nation would not be under the exclusive control of the president. The act also created the Joint Economic Committee in Congress to have legislative oversight in the area of economic affairs, which further limited the power of the president.

Differing Perspectives

Political economic policy is concerned with the interaction of political and economic forces and the way that governmental authority influences economic activity. The policy that results is the outcome of the competition between coalitions and elite demands, as constrained by institutional capacities and previous policy decisions.

Two models are generally used by officials in contemplating appropriate economic policies. The first is a variation on the classical model referred to as the neoclassical model. The classical model held that labor markets perform like other competitive markets. It assumed that there was a wage at which everyone could find employment. As the price of labor fell, demand for the cheaper labor would rise and unemployment would disappear. Ultimately it held that all unemployment was temporary or voluntary, because anyone unable to find work must be asking too high a wage. During the Great Depression the continuation of high unemployment despite falling wages was an undeniable failure of classical theory concerning labor markets finding equilibrium at full employment. The neoclassical model concedes that the state is justified in intervening only in situations of clear market failure. However, there is a presumption in favor of free market forces as being efficient and therefore legitimate.

The second model relies on the insights provided by John Maynard Keynes that, left to itself, the economy might not tend toward equilibrium at full employment. However, if policymakers were to use monetary and fiscal policies correctly, these policies could increase economic activity and reduce unemployment. According to his theory, monetary and fiscal policy could be employed throughout the business cycle to maintain low inflation and high employment. For example, the **full-employment budget,** based on calculations of what government tax revenues would be at a hypothetical state of full employment, is one fiscal policy that could be used to maintain high employment. Government expenditures would be based on the projected level of revenues at full employment. The additional spending at the level as if there were full employment would provide a measured additional demand to the economy that would stimulate job creation. Keynesian theory provided some hope that economic policy could insulate society from the wildly fluctuating business cycles of the past. More important, Keynesian theory provided an intellectual justification for active involvement by the state and social spending.

It would be difficult to overstate the importance that Keynes's economic theory had as a political doctrine. Keynesian theory provided an intellectual framework that justified state activism and social spending for policymakers. Previously, policymakers who increased spending during economic downturns were charged with being fiscally irresponsible and threatening to bankrupt the nation. Now the spending could be justified as stabilizing the economy. In fact, programs could be designed to automatically stabilize the economy by programming spending increases precisely when the economy was contracting, to limit the depth of the business cycle. When the economy begins expanding, social welfare expenditures automatically contract, reducing the potential for growth that would result in excessive inflation. This theory provided the justification for the welfare state.

Crude Policy Instruments

As noted previously, there are at least two major problems with using these fiscal and monetary instruments effectively. The first problem is that even if the goals of full employment and price stability are accepted, there is considerable debate about the best way to achieve them. Nowhere is the disagreement regarding how to achieve non-controversial goals more apparent than in the schools of thought regarding market failure. If unregulated markets generated full employment, price stability, economic growth, and an equitable distribution of income as classical economic theory suggests, there would be no need for government intervention. However, markets do fail and governments are called on to intervene. Does government intervention accomplish its goal of economic growth and reduced unemployment and inflation? If not, government interventions also fail. In the real world, of course, nothing is perfect, so the real choice is between imperfect markets and imperfect policy interventions.

A second major problem for economic policy is that governments may be unable to achieve full employment, prevent inflation, or stimulate economic expansion, because those responsible for economic policy are either unable or unwilling to take the action required. The separation of powers fragments the responsibility for economic policy and weakens the government's ability to control the economy. While the president is by far the single most important player in economic policy, his ability to control events or policy is often overestimated. Taxing and spending is largely determined by the performance of the economy at the time the budget is introduced to Congress, and the forecast during the period of the budget. Much of the budget includes programs over which a president has little control, such as debt refinancing and various entitlement programs.

The President

The executive branch itself contains different departments at the cabinet level, such as the Departments of Commerce, Treasury, and Labor, each with different goals. In addition, the Office of Management and Budget (OMB) assists the president in preparing the budget and submitting it to Congress. The OMB tries to submit a budget that reflects the priorities of the president. But federal agencies submitting their budget requests usually believe in the value of their own programs and press for expanded funding. If the OMB reduces the budget requests of the agencies they may appeal directly to the president or seek informal support from the Congress.

Since Article 1 of the Constitution provides that Congress alone has the power to "appropriate" money, it ensures the budgetary process will involve partisan maneuvering for political advantage. Not surprisingly, politicians often design budget projections to win support for their agendas. The most flagrant examples of predicting unrealistically low projections of inflation and optimistic projections of economic performance occurred during the first two years of the Reagan administration. Ronald Reagan began his presidency promising to eliminate the deficit, increase defense spending, cut taxes, and reduce what he perceived to be the excesses of the welfare state.[1] During a presidential election, challengers are anxious to place the blame for any economic failures on the incumbent when offering their own solutions to economic problems.

Monetary policy as a tool to control the money supply is primarily centered on the Federal Reserve banking system. By loosening or tightening the reserve requirements that banks have to maintain on their deposits, the Federal Reserve (the "Fed") is able to encourage or discourage lending money, which is the source of much economic activity. The theory also suggested that it should make more money available to the banking system to lend at low interest rates when funds were needed, and reduce the amount available when money seemed in excess supply by buying or selling bonds. The Federal Reserve did not take this action early in the Great Depression.

Presidential influence on monetary policy is based on the power to appoint individuals to the Federal Reserve's board of governors. The president's subsequent influence after appointment is largely informal, although the relationship is often much closer than press accounts would indicate. The president often works the good cop/bad cop routine with the Fed for public consumption when the latter makes a politically difficult decision. The president complains to the press that soft economic conditions are caused by a recalcitrant Fed that refuses to lower interest rates sufficiently. Or conversely, that inflation could be brought under control if the Fed would only tighten the money supply. Blame is directed toward the Fed, since its members do not run for election, while the president presents himself as a nice guy without sufficient clout to implement his more compassionate goals.

THE POLICYMAKERS

Policymakers do not prefer high unemployment to full employment, inflation to price stability, or economic recessions to economic growth. But political entrepreneurs have short time horizons and may not find it in their interest to take the action required to reduce inflation, or to get a vigorous economic expansion under way. The may agree with the notion that there is no free lunch, but they are also aware that the price of lunch may be deferred. Elected officials prefer policies that provide short-term benefits before election day and bills that will not come due until after voters have cast their retrospective votes. Thus, in the U.S. political process, there is a bias in favor of policies with short-term benefits and long-term costs. This fact has profound implications for the conduct of long-term economic growth and stabilization policies as opposed to near-term policies.

In practical terms, suppose that the government increases its expenditures by borrowing rather than raising taxes. The result will be an increase in aggregate demand—the total demand for an economy's goods and services. The distributional benefits of increased output and employment will be felt almost immediately. The costs of this expansion, reflected in higher prices, will manifest themselves only months later, hopefully after an election. So from a politician's perspective, the political "goods" arrive first: an increase in employment and a rise in real gross domestic product (GDP). The political "bads" arrive later: higher debt servicing and higher inflation. Every member of the House of Representatives is never more than two years away from election and averages only one year. Every president is never more than four years from an election and averages only two years. Politicians have a very strong incentive to pursue the near-term political "goods" and put off worrying about the "bads" as long as they are in office.

To the extent that presidents do engage in economic tightening, they have a strong incentive to pursue such policies early in their terms and pursue expansionist policies as elections draw near. And to the degree that voters have short memories and limited sophistication of economic policies, they are likely to reward the political entrepreneur who engages in economic expansion just before the election.[2] Survival being a basic instinct among all politicians, these facts of political life also lead to short-term thinking.

Many recent economic problems have required the spending of more money by the government, but the string of massive federal deficits in recent years has precluded increased spending. A conspicuous solution to increased spending needs and huge deficits is large tax increases. But such increases would cause pain to taxpayers and threaten a reduction in consumer demand that could lead to greater unemployment long before a reduction in the deficit would reduce inflation or free up new government monies. In this case the political "bads" arrive rather promptly, while the "goods" would likely arrive much later and be felt only gradually. Not surprisingly, the three presidential elections in the 1980s were won by the candidate who took the hardest line against raising taxes. In 1992, presidential candidate Bill Clinton was able to neutralize the appeal of President George H.W. Bush, who had broken his pledge of "no new taxes," by indicating that he himself was a "new kind of Democrat" committed to reducing the deficit by reducing expenditures, and also to cutting taxes for middle-income taxpayers. Once in office, though, President Clinton faced pressure to initiate spending cuts but increase taxes, and to do both quickly. If the process were delayed, the fear was that it would be impossible to do either as the 1994 elections approached. Clinton barely achieved the tax increases without one Republican vote, by limiting the increases to wealthier Americans who had received steep tax decreases during the Reagan-Bush years. The political costs were enormous, however, as Republicans gained control of the House of Representatives. George W. Bush campaigned in 2000 and 2004 on the platform of cutting taxes. However, with Republicans in control of both houses of Congress and the presidency, there was considerable reluctance to directly cut expenditures also desired by other constituents.

Political entrepreneurs thus have a bias toward expansionary fiscal and monetary policies, since lower taxes and increased expenditures for special interest groups provide strong support for an incumbent's bid for reelection. Policies to reduce spending and increase taxes cause unrest among voters. Even though the optimal policy often requires long-term strategies, the political incentives for incumbents may not reflect the long-term economic interests of the nation. Political entrepreneurs find it extremely difficult to continue unpleasant policies as the exigencies of elections threaten their futures.

There is considerable irony in the fact that voters deplore the deficits and rail against the inability of governments, yet threaten to retaliate against candidates who support the painful economic measures needed to end them. The result is a built-in bias favoring lower rather than higher taxes and higher rather than lower expenditures. But cutting government spending inevitably means reducing benefits to someone who is currently receiving them. Voters who are hurt by government policies and lose benefits are thought to have long memories at election time, a notion that definitely has long-term effects on politicians' voting behavior.

Taxes as an Instrument of Policy

Through its ability to adjust taxes, especially income taxes, the government can guide the economy. The idea of monetary policy was not entirely new in the 1930s, but the idea regarding the use of taxes and national budgets as management tools of economic policy to counter economic cycles of boom and bust *was* new. Although the government borrows money to finance its operations, taxes collected from a variety of sources are the main reservoir of government expenditures.

But the question of who pays is inextricably linked to several other questions regarding tax policy. What is a fair distribution of income? What are the major issues involved in deciding who should bear the burden of taxes? What do political scientists and policy analysts take into consideration when they talk about a fair tax system? Does the U.S. tax system meet the criteria for fairness while promoting the general welfare?

Government intervention is a conscious decision not to leave the provision of certain goods or services to the marketplace. It is a determination that political, not economic considerations will prescribe which services the government will provide. Taxes are required to finance these goods and services. Therefore, the main purpose of taxation is to move purchasing power from the private to the public sector. But in order to understand and judge these economic policies, their distributional consequences must be understood.

Antitax sentiment has always run high in the

United States. Recall that the American Revolution began as a tax revolt with the dumping of tea into the Boston Harbor, because the colonists objected to the taxes levied on the tea. After the adoption of the Constitution, the government relied primarily on customs duties to fund the limited national budget. Congress enacted an income tax during the Civil War, but it expired at that war's end. In 1894 Congress passed another income tax bill. That tax was declared unconstitutional in 1895 in *Pollock v. Farmers' Loan and Trust Co*. As a result, the Sixteenth Amendment to the Constitution was passed, which was ratified in 1916 and gave Congress the power "to lay and collect taxes on incomes, from whatever source derived."

Although the personal income tax soon became the primary source of revenue for the government, the portion of income paid in taxes in the United States is still well below the percentage of income paid as taxes by workers in other countries. Figure 2.1 illustrate this fact. The data in the figure support the evidence that Americans are not overtaxed. Taxes from all levels of government are expressed as a percentage of each country's GDP, or output. This is the best measure of relative taxation, because it includes not only the tax burden, but also an indication of the ability to pay the taxes levied.

The Organization for Economic Cooperation and Development (OECD), one of the most reliable sources of data for international comparisons, found that of thirty countries examined (mostly Western, industrialized nations), only Mexico collects a smaller share of revenues as a percentage of GDP than the United States.[3] After falling in most OECD countries between 2000 and 2002, tax revenues as a percentage of GDP leveled out in 2003 and in some cases began to rise again. However, the United States experienced particularly large reductions in tax-to-GDP ratios between 2000 and 2003, from 29.9 percent to 25.4 percent.

Even though Americans are among the least-taxed people in the industrialized world, aversion to taxes runs high and politicians are usually rewarded for a vigorous and righteous defense of constituents against rapacious tax collectors. This is often accompanied by an indignant opposition to any increase in social welfare spending, since any increased public expenditures would entail higher taxes.

The reality is that when compared to most industrialized nations, the United States is a tax haven. Overall, government expenditures as a share of GDP remain consistently lower than in any other OECD country.

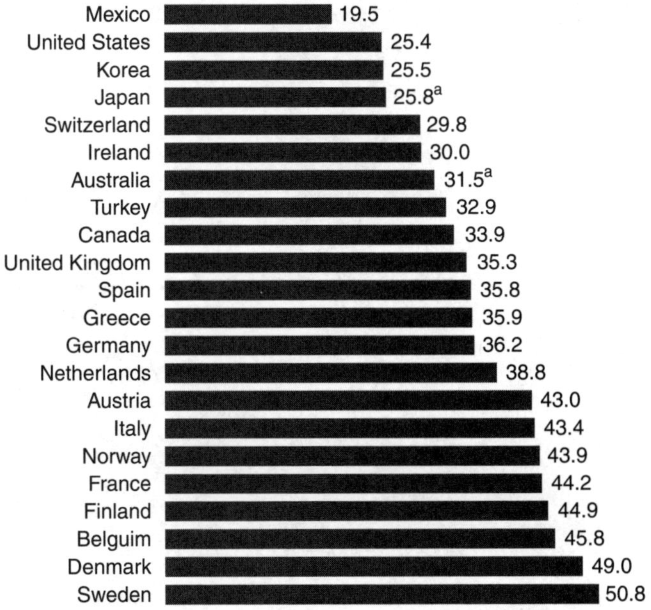

Country	%
Mexico	19.5
United States	25.4
Korea	25.5
Japan	25.8[a]
Switzerland	29.8
Ireland	30.0
Australia	31.5[a]
Turkey	32.9
Canada	33.9
United Kingdom	35.3
Spain	35.8
Greece	35.9
Germany	36.2
Netherlands	38.8
Austria	43.0
Italy	43.4
Norway	43.9
France	44.2
Finland	44.9
Belguim	45.8
Denmark	49.0
Sweden	50.8

Source: Organization for Economic Cooperation Development (OECD), *Revenue Statistics 1965–2003* (Paris: OECD, 2004), p. 18.
Note: a 2002 data.

FIGURE 2.1 Total Tax Revenue as a Percentage of GDP, 2003 (includes national and local taxes and social security contributions)

TAXATION IN THE UNITED STATES

Federal, state, and local governments obtain revenue to finance programs from taxing three basic sources: income, consumption, and wealth. The largest single source of revenue for the federal government is the **personal income tax,** followed by **social insurance tax** and **corporate income tax.** Most state governments use taxes on income and consumption. Local governments rely almost entirely on taxing property and wealth.

TAXES ON INCOME

Figure 2.2 presents a breakdown of the sources of revenue for the national government. In addition to income taxes, wages are subject to sa **payroll tax,** which is levied on a company's payroll (half of which is deducted from an employee's paycheck) to finance the Social Security and Medicare programs. Payroll taxes are now the second major source of revenue.

Workers transfer part of their earnings to retired workers through mandatory payroll deductions that in 2005 amounted to 6.2 percent

Federal Government Receipts, 2004

- Individual income taxes, 42%
- Social insurance, 41%
- Corporate income taxes, 9%
- Excise taxes, 4%
- Other sources, 4%

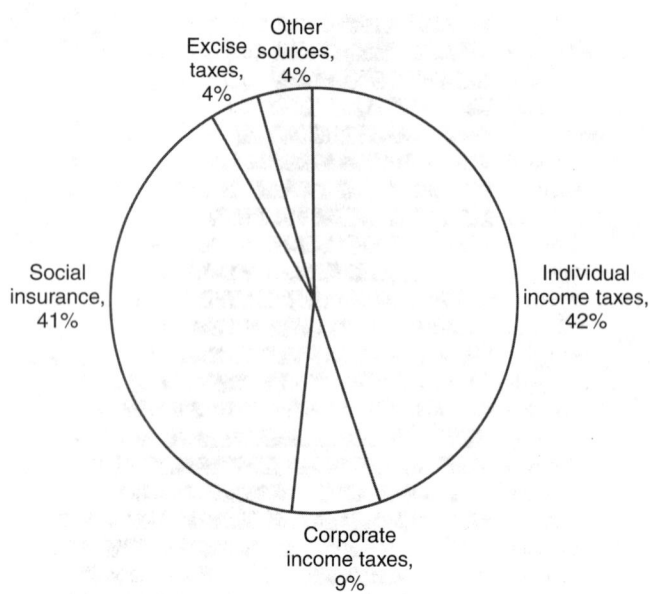

Source: U.S. Census Bureau, *Statistical Abstract* 2004–2005 (Washington D.C., U.S. Government Printing Office 2004), p. 311.

FIGURE 2.2 Federal Government Receipts, 2004

of wages on income up to $90,000. Employers contribute an equal amount. Over the past five years, payroll tax revenues have increased from 36 to 41 percent and individual income tax revenues have decreased from 44 to 42 percent, while corporate tax revenues have declined from 12 to 9 percent.

TAXES ON CONSUMPTION

The most important taxes on consumption are the **sales tax** and the **excise tax.** Sales taxes are a major source of revenue for most states and many major cities. Most states raise the majority of their revenue from a combination of income taxes and sales taxes imposed on the purchase of a wide variety of goods and services (although many states exclude some essential items such as food from their sales taxes).

Excise taxes, which are taxes on specific products, are a source of revenue for state and local governments, as well as for the national government. Some items subject to federal excise taxes include gasoline, airline tickets, alcohol, cigarettes and firearms. A tax levied on the sale of tobacco products or alcohol is often referred to as a **sin tax,** based on the idea that use of these products imposes externalities on nonusers in the form of air pollution, litter, health hazards, and increases in the cost of medical care. Some excise taxes are targeted at purchasers of certain goods who will eventually benefit when the money is spent by the government Gasoline taxes, for example, are used to finance highway construction. An excise tax that is levied on buyers of expensive nonessential items such as yachts or expensive jewelry is referred to as a **luxury tax,** as the incomes of these people are assumed to be high enough to absorb the costs.

Most excise taxes are levied on goods with a relatively **inelastic demand.** If the demand were highly elastic, the tax would push sales down significantly, resulting in only small government revenues.[4] Politicians find that raising taxes usually costs some voter support. Therefore, they prefer that taxes be borne by as small a group as possible, or by such a large group that it is a minimal burden on each payer. Politicians find it easier to impose excise taxes than any other form of tax, because they can raise a significant amount of revenue while affecting a relatively small number of voters. Nevertheless, excise taxes have declined in importance as a source of federal revenue. Their share of federal tax revenues fell from 13 percent in 1960 to 3 percent in 2003.

TAXES ON PROPERTY AND WEALTH

The **property tax** has traditionally been the main source of revenue for state and local governments. Many local governments tax private homes, land, and business property based on its assessed market value. Some states and local governments impose taxes on the value of specific types personal property such as cars, boats, and occasionally livestock. Property taxes account for over 75 percent of the revenue raised through taxes on wealth.[5] Other taxes imposed on wealth include inheritance, estate, and gift taxes.

PRINCIPLES OF TAXATION: EFFICIENCY AND FAIRNESS

Although no one likes to transfer control over part of their income to the government, most people grudgingly comply. The primary purpose of taxation is to raise revenues to carry out government policy goals, although there are other goals as well, such as discouraging the consumption of certain goods. Voluntary compliance is related to the perceived **tax efficiency** (or neutrality) and **tax fairness** of the system.

TAX EFFICIENCY

Efficiency, or neutrality, suggests that unless there is adequate justification, we should try to interfere as little as possible with the market allocation. The freest movement of goods and services maximizes economic efficiency and therefore overall economic well-being. Unfortunately, every tax invites concerted efforts to avoid it and influences economic activity and the allocation of resources, even in cases where the market process works well and needs no outside regulation. For example, the preferential treatment that allows individuals to deduct from income taxes the cost of mortgage interest and property taxes on their homes, distorts the market by increasing the demand for homeownership over rental units. Similarly, tax laws allow child care payments to be deducted from taxes owed. Such preferential treatment, referred to as a **tax expenditure** or "loophole," represents a loss in government revenue just as though the government wrote a check for the amount of the deduction.

Special interest groups that receive preferential treatment are vigorous defenders of their tax subsidies, and thus subsidies are very difficult to eliminate. This raises the issue of fairness.

Tax Fairness

Political scientists, economists, and philosophers have wrestled for hundreds of years with the concept of what constitutes a just and equitable tax system. If the system is perceived as unfair, people are more likely to evade taxes, if possible, or pressure political entrepreneurs more aggressively to reduce their tax burden. There are two main principles of fairness.

Benefit Principle

The **benefit principle** holds that people should pay taxes in proportion to the benefits they receive. This principle tries to make public goods similar to private goods in that payment for services is commensurate with the amount of goods or services received. If the purpose of taxes is to pay for government services, then those who gain from those services should pay. A toll bridge is justified using the benefit principle. Tolls collected are used to pay the bonds used for bridge construction and to maintain the bridge. Because those who pay the toll are the same people who use the bridge, the toll is viewed as a fair way to pay for the government service. The more they use the bridge, the more they will pay. Those who do not pay can be excluded. The major disadvantage of this principle is that it will not work for public goods from which nonpayers cannot be excluded, or where it is difficult to determine who benefits or by what amount. For

---

CASE STUDY: TAX EXPENDITURES

A tax expenditure is defined as the reduction in tax revenue that results when government programs or benefits are provided through the tax system rather than reported as budgetary expenditures. The reductions are usually made by offering special tax rates, exemptions, or tax credits to programs' beneficiaries. Governments introduce tax expenditures primarily to achieve social policy objectives such as wealth transfers to lower-income families or to promote economic development and job creation.

The federal government "spends" hundreds of billions of dollars on tax expenditures each year. The largest tax expenditure—the exclusion for employer contributions for health insurance (see Table 2.1)—is also the fastest growing. The main reason the government reports tax expenditures is to improve accountability by providing a more complete picture of its spending.

Governments use the tax system to deliver programs to reduce their own administrative costs and reduce compliance costs for recipients. There are several negative aspects to tax expenditures. Their overall cost receives less public scrutiny than is the case for spending programs, because it need not be formally approved every year. The benefits of the major tax expenditures tend to go to high-income earners to an even greater degree than do entitlements. This can run counter to the objective of incorporating progressiveness into the tax system. Tax expenditures are big and automatic, and costs are often hard to control as many of the benefits tend to be more open-ended and enforcement is often more difficult than for spending programs.

---

example, who benefits most from law enforcement and the judicial system, the rich or the poor Figure 2.3 indicates where the federal dollar is spent.

The benefit principle is often used to argue that the more affluent citizens should have a higher tax burden than poorer citizens, because they benefit more from public services. For example, the wealthy receive more benefit from a police force than do poor citizens because they have more wealth to protect and their losses would be much greater in the event of theft. Therefore, since police protection is more beneficial to the affluent, they should contribute more.

TABLE 2.1

Largest Tax Expenditures, 2005

Rank	Tax Expenditure	Cost to Treasury (in $ billions)
1.	Exclusion for employer contributions for medical insurance	109.4
2.	Exclusion of employer pension plan contribution and earnings	99.3
3.	Reduced rates of tax on dividends and long-term capital gains	76.8
4.	Deduction for mortgage interest on owner-occupied residences	69.9
5.	Deduction of state and local government income and personal property taxes	40.9
6.	Exclusion of capital gains at death	37.7
7.	Tax credit for children under age seventeen	35.7
8.	Earned Income Credit	35.4
9.	Deduction for charitable contributions other than for education and health	28.8
10.	Exclusion of Social Security benefits for retired workers	20.8
11.	Exclusion of interest on life insurance savings	25.4
12.	Deferral of capital gains on sales of principal residence	18.0

Source: Estimates of Federal Tax Expenditures for Fiscal Years 2004–2008, prepared for the Committee on Ways and Means by the Staff of the Joint Committee on Taxation (Washington, D.C: U.S. Government Printing Office; 2003)

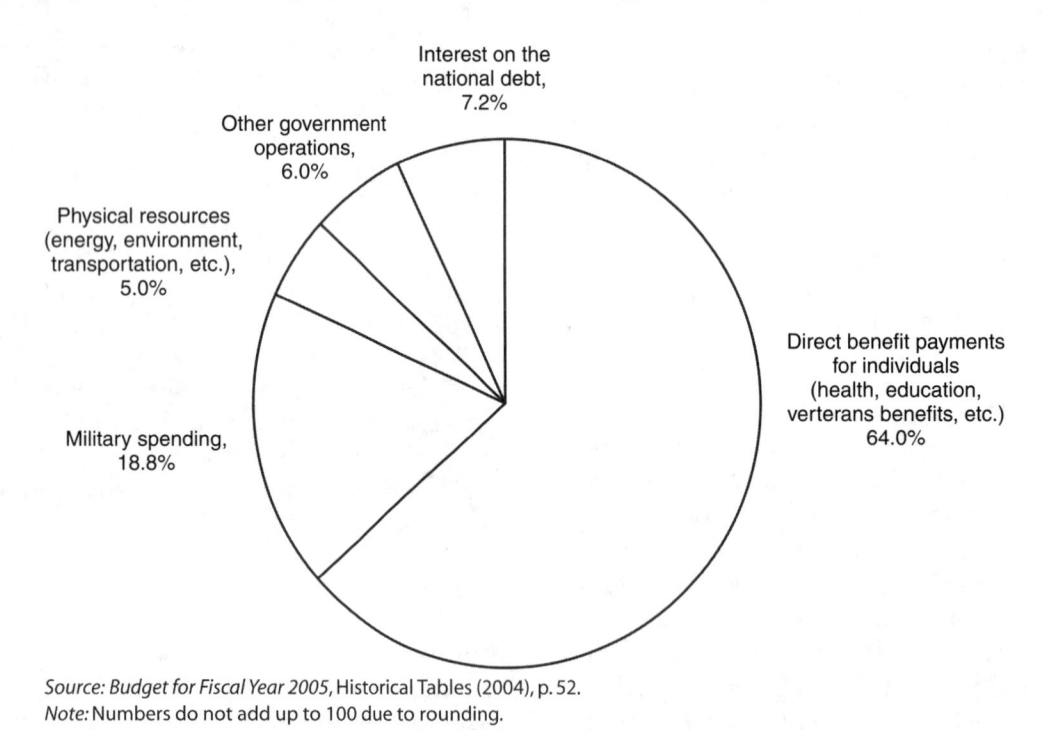

Pie chart:
- Interest on the national debt, 7.2%
- Other government operations, 6.0%
- Physical resources (energy, environment, transportation, etc.), 5.0%
- Military spending, 18.8%
- Direct benefit payments for individuals (health, education, verterans benefits, etc.) 64.0%

Source: Budget for Fiscal Year 2005, Historical Tables (2004), p. 52.
Note: Numbers do not add up to 100 due to rounding.

FIGURE 2.3 How the Federal Budget Dollar Is Spent, Fiscal Year 2005

The welfare of the wealthy is best served by the Securities and Exchange Commission, the Federal Reserve system, national security, or by the judicial system. If there was agreement on who benefits and by how much, then taxes could be allocated accordingly. Allocating taxes by this principle provides an incentive to insist that someone else is the main beneficiary. If these taxes could be allocated accurately, there would be no income redistribution.

ABILITY-TO-PAY PRINCIPLE

The **ability-to-pay principle** claims that fairness requires that taxes be allocated according to the incomes and/or wealth of taxpayers, regardless of how much or how little they benefit. According to this principle, the wealthy may benefit more than the poor from some government expenditures and less than the poor from others. But since they are better able to pay than the poor, they should pay more in taxes. This principle is justified by the argument that all citizens should make an "equal sacrifice." Fairness in this system requires both horizontal and vertical equity.

Horizontal equity means that individuals who have nearly equal incomes should have nearly equal tax burdens. This is the concept Plato had in mind when he wrote in Book One of *The Republic*, "When there is an income tax, the just man will pay more and the unjust less on the same amount of income." Horizontal equity is lacking when those with equal abilities to pay are treated differently because of tax deductions, credits, or preferences not available to all taxpayers equal terms.

Vertical equity means that those with higher ability to pay should pay more taxes than those with less ability to pay. There is less agreement on how much more the rich should pay. In fact, taxes are generally classified according to their incidence. **Tax incidence** is the actual distribution of the tax burden on different levels of income. Tax systems are classified as progressive, proportional (some-times referred to as a "flat"), and regressive, as illustrated in Figure 2.4.

A **progressive tax** is one in which the tax rate rises as income rises. Wealthier taxpayers pay a larger percentage of their income in taxes than do low-income tax payers. A progressive tax redistributes wealth from the more affluent to the less affluent. Keynesian economic theory supports a progressive income tax. Most Americans support progressive taxes on the ground that ability to pay rises more than proportionately with income.

A **proportional tax** is one in which the tax is the same through all income levels. Ordinarily called a flat tax, a proportional tax is often praised by its supporters for its efficiency. By assessing a tax as a fixed percentage of income, a wage earner's decisions do not affect the amount of tax owed nor distort incentives. Since theoretically there are no deductions, everyone can easily compute the amount of taxes owed and there is little need to hire accountants or tax lawyers. Because the proportional tax is so efficient and imposes only a slight administrative burden on taxpayers, many argue that we should adopt it. But efficiency is only one goal of the tax system. Although some think that a system in which everyone pays the same percentage of their income is fair, others argue that is not equitable. A proportional tax is neutral in regard to income distribution.

Under a **regressive tax,** the average rate declines as income rises. It is called "regressive" because high-income taxpayers pay a smaller percentage of their income than do low-income taxpayers, even though they may still pay a higher amount in absolute dollars. A regressive tax redistributes income from the poor to the wealthy. Regressive tax systems are so manifestly unfair that few openly advocate them. A notable exception is George Gilder, a conservative writer with refreshing frankness but doubtful logic who wrote that "regressive taxes help the poor."[6] Gilder, whose work was widely and approvingly read by supply-siders of the early 1980s, also declared that "to help the poor and middle classes, one must cut the taxes on the rich."[7]

Because state and local governments often rely on sales and property taxes these tend to be regressive. State and local sales taxes increased during the 1980s along with local property taxes. A sales tax is often confused with a flat tax because two individuals with vastly different incomes will pay the same sales tax on the purchase of ten gallons of gas. Sales and property taxes are regressive because poorer people must spend a higher percentage of their income for goods and services, as well as housing costs, than do the affluent.

In theory, the federal income tax supports the principle of vertical equity by being very mildly

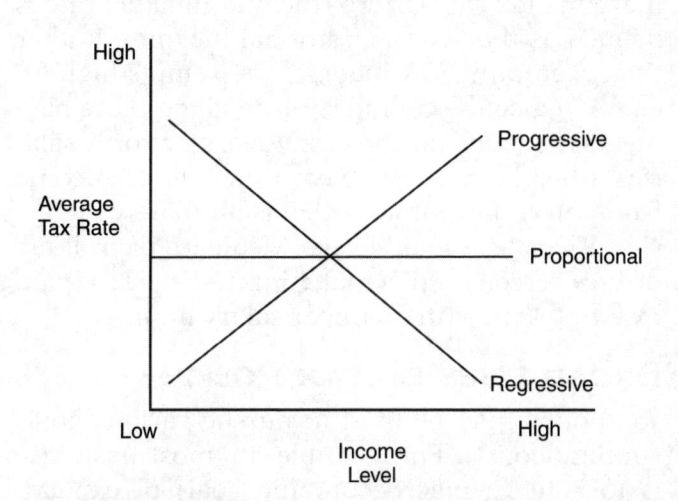

FIGURE 2.4 Tax incidence: Progress, Proportional, and Regressive

progressive. The tax cuts in 2001, 2002, and 2003 have significantly reduced the progressivity of the federal income tax. There is no agreement on how progressive the tax code should be, or even on how the ability to pay should be measured. For example, should adjustments be made for catastrophic medical expenses? What about families who may have several children in college at once?

Federal tax progressivity has been declining for over two decades. When taxes paid by individuals to federal, state, and local levels of government are combined, the mildly progressive features at the national level are offset by regressive taxes at the local level, resulting in a roughly proportional tax system. The trend toward inequality is attributable to the increased influence of those who argue in favor of tax neutrality (proportional tax). The avowed purpose of the tax cuts in the first term of George W. Bush was to reduce the progressive nature of the federal tax system and make it more "neutral." By primarily reducing the taxes of those in the highest brackets and cutting government funding for social welfare programs, it intended to reduce the redistributive effect of transferring wealth to the poor. Tax deductions and exemptions, often referred to as loopholes, are subtracted from personal income to determine the taxable income. All tax loopholes encourage taxpayers to engage in certain types of behavior to avoid taxes. Most loopholes primarily benefit the more affluent and therefore they erode the progressivity of the income tax. This effectively reduces the tax rate if certain conditions are met.[8]

One policy analyst, William Gale, proposes tax reform that would be revenue neutral while broadening the tax base, reducing effective tax rates (rates paid after deductions are factored in), and simplifying the process.[9] Briefly, he contends that itemized deductions are at the heart of any serious effort at tax reform. Although they are popular and subsidize various activities thought of as "good," they create many problems. He argues that deductions largely subsidize activity that would have occurred anyway. By eroding the tax base, they require higher tax rates than would otherwise be necessary.

It may be argued that deductions under the current system are also unfair. Why should a high-income household save 38¢ on a dollar of mortgage interest while a low-income household saves 15¢? Why should homeowners with a large mortgage be able to use a tax-deductible home equity loan to buy a car, when renters with similar incomes cannot? Other deductions for state and local taxes are often justified on ability-to-pay grounds, since the taxes directly reduce household income. However, state and local taxes largely pay for services that households consume, such as schools, roads, and parks. But if taxes buy services, they should be part of the taxable income. For instance, a household that paid $30 a month for garbage collection to a private company would not expect a deduction. Why should a household that pays the same amount in local taxes for trash removal get a deduction?[10]

Many who support the neutrality of the tax system argue that efforts to redistribute wealth through tax transfers are not very effective. They maintain that a progressive income tax reduces the incentives for the more affluent to work and save. By encouraging the affluent to invest their wealth, the size of the total economic pie will be increased so that the benefits that trickle down to the poor will exceed any benefits from redistribution through tax transfers. They insist that the fact that some entrepreneurs become extraordinarily wealthy is irrelevant, because their actions have improved society.

Social Security tax (the payroll tax) is an example of a tax that is proportional in the lower ranges, but regressive for those receiving income in excess of the maximum wage for which taxes are withheld. As mentioned above, this payroll tax requires individuals and employers to pay the same rate (6.2 percent, 12.4 percent total) on wages up to $90,000 (in 2005). Above $90,000 the marginal tax rate is zero (the marginal tax rate is defined as the tax on additional income). Rather than exempting low incomes, it exempts high incomes. Once the ceiling is reached, no more payments are made for the year. Also, since only salaries are subject to the payroll tax, while income from interest is untouched, it is ultimately regressive. There is an additional Medicare payroll tax of 1.45 percent with a matching 1.45 percent paid by employers with no upper salary limit.

Broad Uses of Tax Policy

Tax policy may be used to pursue various goals simultaneously. For example, its most basic use is to achieve macroeconomic goals of expanding the economy and employment. Taxes may be used as an economic policy to provide income

CASE STUDY: LOTTERIES AS A REGRESSIVE TAX

Gambling generates enormous amounts of revenue for governments and the gaming industry. But its enchanting promises of significant benefits for the general welfare frequently do not live up to expectations.

A study by Alicia Hansen found that in 2002 the average American spent more on lotteries than on reading materials or movies. In 2003, total spending on lotteries was almost $45 billion, or $155 for every man, woman, and child in the United States. About $14 billion of that money went into state coffers.

The fact that playing the lottery, is voluntary does not make the "profit" any less of a tax. It is analogous to states raising revenue from an excise tax on alcohol. The purchaser of alcohol does so voluntarily, but no one denies that it is a tax. Some then concede that it is a tax, but that a tax of choice is preferable to a tax that is paid reluctantly, and presumably the purchaser of alcohol or a lottery ticket is willing to pay the tax.

Political entrepreneurs have discovered that the average voter does not think of the lottery as a tax, which removes a major barrier to taxation. The transfer of lottery revenues to state treasuries is an implicit tax on lottery bettors. There is a consensus among researchers that state lotteries a decidedly regressive form of taxation in that average lottery sales are highest in low-income areas and lower in areas of higher economic and educational levels.

Sponsored gambling allows many state governments to use lotteries to minimize taxes that would otherwise have to be paid by middle- and upper-income groups. The result is that states have increasingly resorted to lotteries to increase revenues as a way of side-stepping opposition to tax increases. New Hampshire started the first modern state lottery in 1964. In 2005, forty-one states and the District of Columbia sponsored lotteries.

Per capita lottery ticket sales were three times higher in inner-city Detroit than in the suburbs in 1988. Of $104 million contributed to Michigan's school aid fund by Detroit lottery ticket purchasers, inner-city schools received only $80 million. The remaining $24 million was transferred to more affluent suburban school districts. A 1988 study of the Florida lottery, which also earmarks profits from sales to go into the general education fund, found that when one includes the tax incidence (who pays) and the benefit incidence (who receives the funds,) the tax was regressive for those with incomes below $40,000. The benefits of the net tax are proportionally distributed at incomes between $40,000 and $70,000 and become progressive at incomes above $70,000. Congress commissioned a National Impact Study, which found that gambling had not improved Florida's education or health services. Prior to the introduction of the state lottery, Florida allocated 60 percent of its budget for school improvement. Five-years after the introduction of gambling, only 51 percent of its budget was allocated to education. The study noted that "the problem with a lottery is that lottery profits are used as a substitute for tax dollars, not as a supplement to them."

Lotteries violate the tax principles of both neutrality and equity. There is also the ethical question of exploiting human desire to extract a regressive tax on the poor.

Sources: Alicia Hansen, "Lotteries and State Fiscal Policy," Tax Foundation Background Paper no. 46 (Washington, D.C.: Tax Foundation October 2004); Mary Borg, Paul Mason, and Stephen Shapiro, *The Economic Consequence of State Lotteries* (New York: Praeger, 1991).

security, to increase investment spending, and to stimulate aggregate spending.

President John Kennedy announced his intention to provide a tax cut aimed primarily at middle- and low-income families in order to stimulate a lethargic economy. Lyndon Johnson, upon succeeding Kennedy, agreed with Kennedy's logic and shifted the emphasis from expanding federal spending to boosting private consumer demand and business investment. He cut personal and corporate taxes by $11 billion, and economic activity increased exactly as the model had predicted.

Much larger tax cuts were implemented by Ronald Reagan in 1981. These cuts were directed primarily at reducing the tax burden of the affluent rather than that of middle- and lower-income workers. The top tax rate was cut from 70 to 28 percent. All told, personal taxes were cut by $250 billion over a three-year period and corporate taxes were cut by $70 billion. The deficit spending and increased consumer demand that resulted did get the economy out of its deepest recession, in 1981–1982, since the Great Depression.

President Bill Clinton won election by campaigning against policies that kept the economy lagging behind its potential, using the slogan "it's the economy, stupid." He cited the need for more fiscal stimulus during the campaign and suggested the need for middle-income tax cuts. Upon his election, however, he recognized that the economy had hit the bottom of the recession and was starting to expand. He was aware of the Keynesian multiplier at work and decided that additional stimulus might create the problem of inflation.

Instead he decided to tackle the difficult and politically risky strategy of dealing with the long-term problem of the deficit and its drag on the economy. He raised taxes on the top 2 percent of income earners over the unanimous opposition of Republicans, who predicted economic catastrophe. He also cut government spending while providing tax credits for investments to stimulate economic expansion. His actions set in motion the longest uninterrupted economic expansion since World War II. (See Figure 2.5.)

President George W. Bush proposed the largest tax cuts in history. He proposed a $1.6 *trillion* cut over a ten-year period. He argued that with the government surpluses from 1998 through 2001, the nation could afford the tax cuts.[11] He argued at the same time that, because the economy was slowing down, although unemployment was

Source: Congressional Budget Office, 2005.

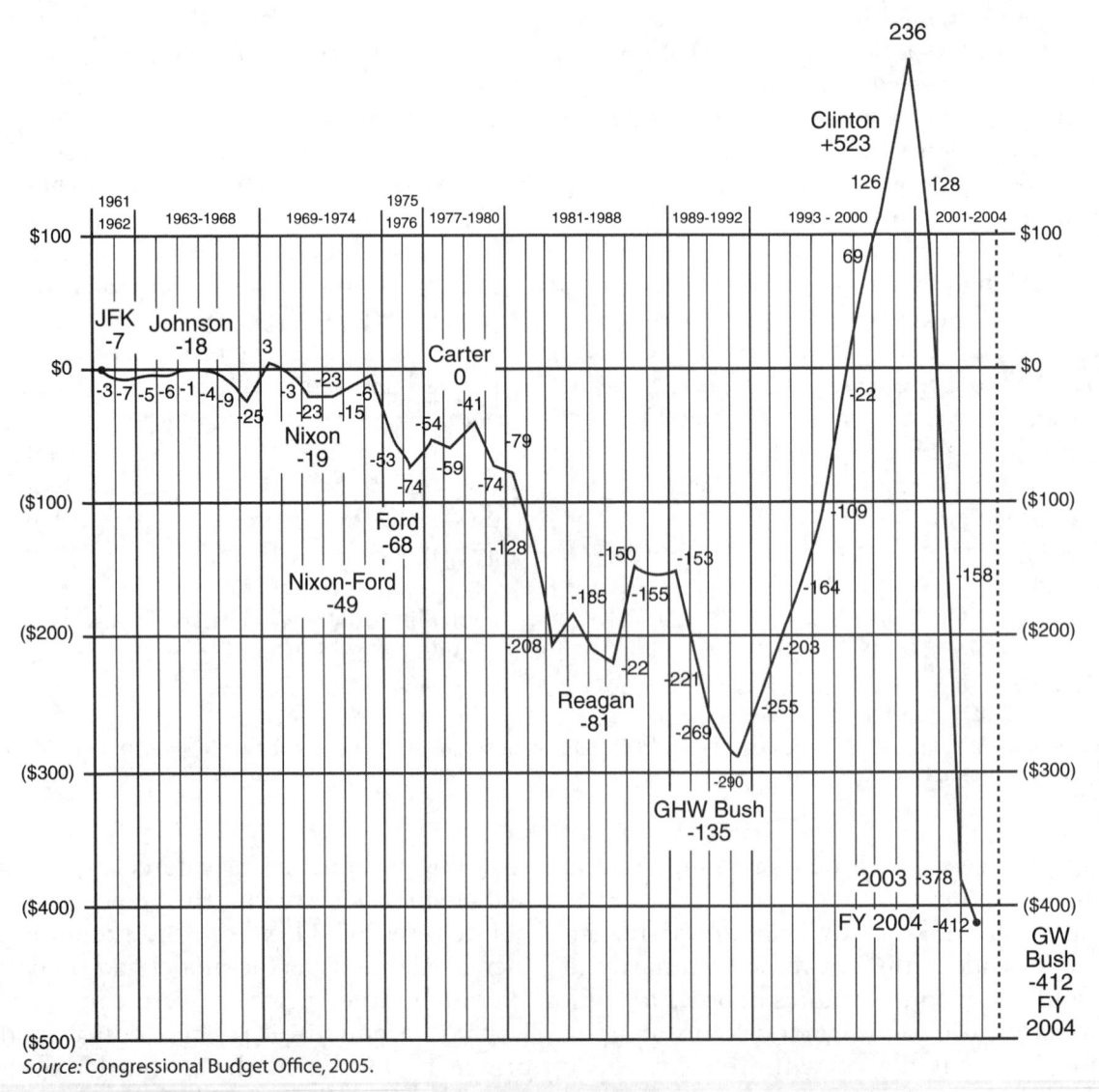

FIGURE 2.5 Yearly U.S. Budget Deficit or Surplus, 1961–2004 (in U.S.$ billions)

hovering around 4 percent, a tax cut was needed to stimulate the economy. Finally, he argued that taxes in the United States were oppressive and people needed relief. Indeed, the 2001 tax bill was titled "The Economic Growth and Tax Relief Reconciliation Act." Congress agreed and ultimately passed a $1.35 trillion dollar tax cut over ten years. Additional tax cuts were passed in 2002 to "stimulate the economy." Tax cuts were passed again in 2003 and 2004.

The 2001–2004 tax cuts have already affected the U.S. economy in a variety of ways and will have an even larger impact in the future. The cuts have been in place long enough for analysis to provide a clearer picture of how they are affecting the economy and different income groups, and how they will influence future budgetary decisions. The Congressional Budget Office (CBO), which provides Congress with analysis of legislative action and is currently headed by a Republican, released a study that found that the Bush tax cuts will increase income inequality by raising the after-tax income of the most affluent far more than it will raise the after-tax income of middle- and low-income households.[12] Table 2.2 indicates who benefits the most from the Bush tax cuts.

Bear in mind that these calculations, based on CBO data, exclude the effects of the corporate tax cuts and the effects of the estate tax cuts. Nevertheless, those, in the bottom fifth, with an average income of $16,600, received an average tax cut of $230 in 2004, while the top fifth, with an average income of $203,700, received tax reductions averaging $4,890, and the top 1 percent, with an average income of $1,171,000, received an average tax cut of $40,990.

A more salient measurement in examining the effect of tax cuts is to assess after-tax income at different levels, since this indicates how much households have available to spend and save. This measurement also shows that the tax cuts disproportionately benefit those who are already the most affluent. According to the CBO data, the top 1 percent saw its after-tax income grow by an average of 5.3 percent, more than three and a half times the percentage increase received by the bottom quintile. Therefore, even if all households receive a tax cut, there is an increase in inequality, since after-tax income will rise by a larger percentage for more affluent than for less well-off households.

Since additional tax cuts that almost exclusively benefit affluent households, such as the elimination of the estate tax and the removal of the limitation on itemized deductions, will be phased in over the next several years, the ultimate effect will be even more unequal. Some defenders of the tax cuts have argued that everyone is a "winner" since everyone received a tax cut. However, the tax

TABLE 2.2

Who Benefits from the 2001–2004 Bush Tax Cuts?

	Average Income ($)	Average Tax Cut ($)	Share of the Tax Cut (%)	Change in After Tax Income (%)
All	80,100	1,680	100.0	2.7
Bottom quintile	16,600	230	2.8	1.5
Second quintile	38,100	720	8.3	2.2
Middle quintile	57,400	980	11.5	2.0
Fourth quintile	84,300	1,520	17.7	2.3
Top quintile	203,700	4,890	59.9	3.3
81–90 percent	116,600	2,210	13.4	2.5
91–95 percent	115,000	3,180	9.8	2.7
96–99 percent	243,100	4,830	12.0	2.8
Top 1 percent	1,171,000	40,990	24.6	5.3

Source: David Kamin and Isaac Shapiro, *Studies Shed New Light on Effects of Administration's Tax Cuts* (Washington, D.C.: Center on Budget and Policy Priorities, September 13, 2004), p. 4.
Note: Percentages may not sum to 100 due to rounding.

cuts have thus far been financed through growing deficits. The tax cuts must eventually be financed through either tax increases or spending cuts, because the economy cannot sustain such large and persistent deficits. In all likelihood, since the administration has ruled out raising taxes to reduce the deficit, cuts in spending will target programs that benefit middle- and lower-income households. Although advocates of the tax cuts routinely describe them as designed to be in favor of family and small business, a study by William Gale and Peter Orszag at the Brookings Institution shows, in a distributional analysis of the tax cuts, that "most families (that is, tax units with children) and most tax units with small business income will be worse off once the financing is included."[13] Since the tax cuts disproportionately benefited the wealthy, middle- and low-income households will suffer corresponding benefit losses.

The tax cuts were poorly designed to achieve their stated goal of stimulating the economy. They disproportionately benefited those with the highest incomes the very households that were more likely to save than to spend their tax cuts. A different tax cut package that targeted middle- and low-income households would have resulted in more money flowing into the economy in the form of an increase in consumer demand, creating the stimulus sought by the administration. Lower taxes can stimulate growth by improving incentives to work, save, and invest However, by targeting the affluent, the tax cuts created income effects that reduced the need to engage in productive economic activity. The current policy subsidizes old capital, providing windfall gains to asset holders, and undermines incentives for new activity; and by raising the budget deficit, it reduces national savings and raises interest rates. Jobs created following the tax cuts fell well below the administration's own predictions.[14] In fact, Mark Zandi, chief economist at Economy.com, points out that most Americans experienced a decline in real household incomes between 2001 and 2004. He notes that "no other President since World War II has suffered out-right job declines during their term."[15] The conclusion is inescapable that the tax cuts were poorly designed to stimulate economic growth.[16]

Data by the administration's 2004 Mid-Session Budget Review indicates that the tax cuts have played a larger role than all other legislation or policy in raising the budget deficit. That review showed that, until mid-2004, the tax cuts accounted for 57 percent of the worsening fiscal picture, more than all other policies combined.[17]

Some defenders have argued that the administration's tax cuts have actually made the tax system more progressive. They maintain that high-income taxpayers are generally paying a significantly greater percentage of federal income taxes because of the 2001–2003 tax cuts. They argue that high-income taxpayers only had a "comparable reduction" in their tax burden relative to middle-income taxpayers. This ignores taxes other than the income tax. Unlike the income tax, which is mildly progressive, other federal taxes, such as the payroll tax, are regressive with middle- and low-income households paying a greater share of their income to these taxes than do the wealthiest taxpayers. CBO data show that 75 percent of all taxpayers pay more in payroll taxes than they do in income taxes. Analyzing tax burdens by focusing solely on the income tax and ignoring other taxes produces misleading results, as the CBO pointed out. Noting that the upper-income groups pay a higher share of taxes only tells us that the upper-income group is paying a larger share of the *much smaller amount of federal income taxes* being collected after the tax cuts. It is possible to increase the share of taxes paid by the affluent at the same time that the law makes after-tax income more unequal. Focusing on changes in the share of taxes paid misses the more meaningful after-tax income, which determines what households have at their disposal.[18]

At the beginning of the second term of George W. Bush, the effect of the changes in tax policy will be of increasing importance. By any reasonable measure, making the tax cuts permanent will be unaffordable. The tax cuts are regressive and will transfer more resources away from the poor toward the affluent. As a result, most households will be worse off. Another suggested goal of the recent tax cuts was to pave the way for a more fundamental tax reform. Many observers find that the changes may actually make reform more difficult to achieve. Some tax cut supporters justify the tax policy as an effort to reduce government spending.[19] This view claims that the cuts are justified in an effort to "starve the beast" of excessive social welfare spending. Essentially, this is an argument that reducing revenues is the best way to control spending, that the structure of the Bush tax cuts was justified by the goal of controlling spending.

However, it is not clear that tax cuts are effective in cutting spending. Nor does the effort to reduce spending justify regressive tax cuts. It could be argued that since most spending cuts would be regressive (hurting the least well off the most), a tax cut aimed at reducing spending should, on fairness grounds, be progressive (that is, give greater tax cuts to households as one moves down the income ladder). Instead, the social welfare structure for those less well off is being severely curtailed. The tax cuts have not been effective in reducing spending, since spending has increased in all budget categories of defense, nondefense discretionary, and entitlement spending. Finally, even if "starving the beast" was legitimate as an original justification in 2001, when there were government surpluses, making the tax cuts permanent will create a **structural deficit** even if the economy arrives at full employment. A structural deficit occurs when government expenditures would still exceed tax revenues even if tax receipts were calculated assuming full employment.

The administration has stressed the need to make the tax cuts permanent in every budget it has presented, which will result in significantly rising costs after 2010 due to the elimination of the estate tax and the removal of the limitation on itemized deductions and the use of personal exemptions for high-income households. The baby boomers will also begin retiring at this time, putting increasing strains on health care costs. Therefore, meeting the administration's goal of cutting the deficit in half by 2009 ignores the main effect of making the cuts Permanent Since the Bush administration has ruled out any tax increase to reduce the deficit the only remaining options are to cut spending and to grow the economy. Since the cuts are not well designed to encourage robust economic growth, spending cuts are likely to appear as the most attractive tool. The result will be that distributional issues in social welfare policies will continue to be important throughout the second term of the Bush administration.

SOCIAL SECURITY AND REDUCING POVERTY AMONG THE ELDERLY

Until the twentieth century, few Americans could look forward to a retirement period at the end of their working lives. In 1900 the life expectancy for males was about forty-four years. Nevertheless, about two-thirds of men aged sixty-five and older were still in the labor force.[20] With insufficient savings and without a pension program, most were forced to work as long as they were physically able. By 2002, with a life expectancy of over seventy-seven years, the average age of retirement for males was just over sixty-three years.[21] Americans tend to stay in the labor force longer than the citizens of many OECD countries.[22] Advances in life expectancy and an extended retirement are clear advances in the general welfare of society. They also presents challenging public policy issues.

Since the administration of Franklin Roosevelt, the government has developed programs and, through legislation, encouraged policies to ensure that the elderly have sufficient income to provide for their needs during retirement. Social Security was initiated in 1935 to provide elderly Americans with a basic safety net. It was never intended to completely meet retirement needs. Nevertheless, this New Deal system has become the nation's main retirement program.

For most families, their primary savings for their retirement years consists of pensions and savings plans that are encouraged by tax incentives, Legislation providing tax incentives for employer-based pensions was passed in 1921. Legislation establishing Keogh accounts (1962) and individual retirement accounts (1974) expanded the eligibility for workers to participate in tax-sheltered savings plans. Nevertheless, only about half of all workers are covered by any form of a pension plan, with higher-income workers much more likely to be covered than low-income workers. The result is that for the average worker, Social Security makes up a larger part of their retirement income than private pensions, as indicated in Figure 2.6.

Currently, about 95 percent of married couples, one of whom is sixty-five or older, receive Social Security benefits. Social Security is the only form of pension income for about half of these households. Many financial planners suggest that most families need about 70 percent of their preretirement income in order to maintain their standard of living. Currently, Social Security accounts for about 42 percent of the preretirement earnings of an average wage earner who retires at sixty-five.[23] This percentage is expected to decline, to 36 percent, until 2027, when the

Figure 2.6 Average Income by Source for the Elderly, 2000

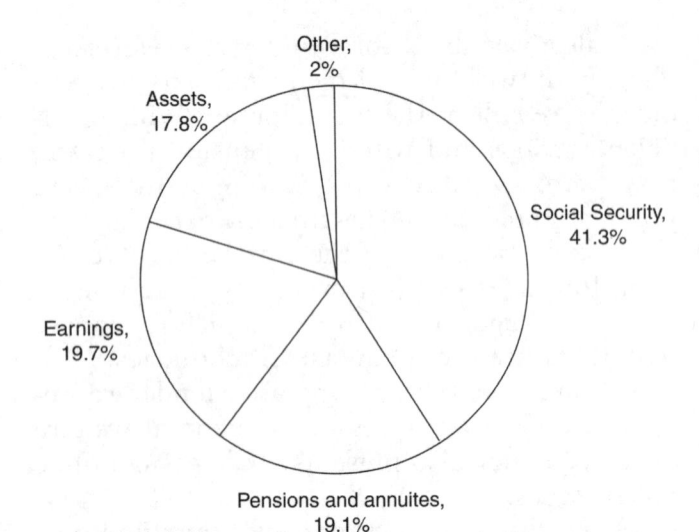

- Social Security, 41.3%
- Pensions and annuites, 19.1%
- Earnings, 19.7%
- Assets, 17.8%
- Other, 2%

Source: Employee Benefit Research Institute, tabulations of data from the March 2001 Current Population Survey, June 2002.
Note: 100% = $20,851. Numbers do not add up to 100 due to rounding.

"normal retirement age" will reach sixty-seven. It is expected to remain at 36 percent after that.

In fact, in 2003 Social Security lifted close to 15 million above the poverty line and millions more from near-poverty. This was not always the case. In 1959 the average monthly Social Security check was $70, providing an annual income of under $1,000 per year at a time when the Census Bureau found that it would take $3,000 to provide an adequate budget for an elderly couple. In 1961 a White House conference on aging found that over half of elderly couples could not afford decent housing, proper nutrition, or adequate medical care. John Kennedy and Lyndon Johnson subsequently pushed to expand Social Security and establish Medicare Since 1959, poverty rates among the elderly have declined, from 35 percent to 10 percent in 2003, compared to the national poverty rate of 12.4 percent. The major events that have contributed to this change in the lives of the elderly in the United States are the significant increases in Social Security benefits enacted in the 1960s and 1970s, and the indexing of those benefits to average wage increases. In the first decade of the twenty-first century, the war on poverty of the elderly stands as an unqualified social welfare success story. Without Social Security, about half the elderly would fall below the poverty line.

The system has a deliberate redistributive slant to reduce poverty. Retirees who earn lower wages during their working careers get higher returns. The Social Security benefit schedule is progressive, and although some benefits are subject to partial taxation, the benefits are not means-tested. This allows many people to add other sources of income, such as pension benefits, to their Social Security benefits to achieve a level of income in retirement close to the level achieved during them working years. Social Security lifts more elderly people out of poverty—nine our of ten—than all other transfer programs combined.

Social Security also works as a national group insurance plan to provide payments to roughly 5 million disabled adults and 3 million children every month About half the children who receive benefits have lost one or both parents. In short, Social Security is a valuable program that replaces income in the event of retirement, disability, or death, serving to reduce the income inequality across certain groups.

The Social Security system quit being a "pay as you go" program in the 1980s In order to strengthen the system in 1983, the Reagan administration accepted recommendation from a commission headed by Alan Greenspan to sharply raise payroll taxes to prefund Social Security's future obligations. The administration also accepted the recommendation to increase the age of full retirement to offset increased life expectancy, from sixty-five to sixty-seven, which, as mentioned above, will be fully implemented in 2027. Penalties will be correspondingly adjusted upward for early retirement at age sixty-two as well. The surplus payroll fax-receipts are used to buy government bonds to be held in the Social Security trust fund. The money, and the bonds, do not belong to the government or the general public. They belong to the Social Security trust fund and to the workers whose payroll tax contributions created the Social Security surplus.[24] In essence, those who have paid Social Security payroll taxes from 1983 onward have been funding their own retirement.

The government has used the money from those bonds to fund other operations. Without the Social Security surplus, the government would have been forced to cut other programs, raise taxes, or increase the deficit. In 2019, retiree benefits will begin to exceed payroll tax receipts. At that time, Social Security tax receipts will be supplemented by redeeming some of the bonds purchased since 1983. Bonds are one of the world's safest investments. The government must pay the interest on the bonds and redeem them, because the alternative of defaulting on them would be catastrophic to its ability to sell bonds to finance its deficit.

In 2003 the Social Security Trust Fund Administration stated that the bonds would allow full funding until 2042. In the summer of 2004, using more recent data, the Congressional Budget Office projected that Social Security will be self-funding until 2052, when its bonds are to be cashed in. At that point, projected benefits would begin to exceed revenue by just 19 percent.[25] Thus "if nothing is done to the Social Security system, the average annual benefit per person would fall in the future but would remain higher in inflation-adjusted dollars than [it is] today."[26]

BUSH'S PROPOSALS TO REFORM SOCIAL SECURITY

President Bush has made the restructuring of Social Security the centerpiece of his second term. His Social Security Commission has put forward a plan to dramatically shrink Social Security benefits, replacing a much smaller share of pre-retirement wages for workers who retire in the future. While many policy analysts agree that adjustments must be made to the system, others suggest that the administration is trying to create an artificial sense of crisis that requires immediate and decisive action the administration.[27]

Claims of a crisis in Social Security are viewed by the system's supporters as scare tactics and spin to create momentum to destroy the program in order to save it. The administration has undertaken a major public relations campaign to sell the nation on Bush's Social Security changes, because "that is where the momentum is."[28] The administration has suggested that Social Security will run out of funds in 2019, ignoring the continued worker contributions and the ability to redeem bonds. Dean Baker and Mark Weisbrot dubbed Social Security "the phony crisis" in their book by that title, wherein they maintain that Congress intends to use the money lent by buying bonds to fund the deficit and has a moral burden to redeem them, just as it does for all other bonds.[29] It would be outrageous for the government to use the money and then cut it from Social Security when it comes time to redeem the bonds. Charles Blahous, the White House's point person on Social Security, argues that that is "not much consolation to the worker of 2025 that there was an understanding in 1983 that he foot the bill."[30]

THE SOCIAL SECURITY COMMISSION PLAN

Bush has indicated that the commission's plan is a good starting point, but has not committed his administration to it at this point. This plan, which has been referred to as "privatization," would allow workers to divert up to 4 percent of the 12.4 percent payroll tax (roughly a third), up to $1,000, into a personal investment accounts Proponents claim this would bring more Americans into the 'ownership" soeren as they would own part of their retirement. Guaranteed benefits would be cut by the amount contributed to personal accounts.

The commission's proposal would also change the benefit structure from what is referred to as "wage indexing" to "price indexing." Wages typically rise faster than prices. Over time, a household's standard of living increases, because its wages rise faster than prices. The plan's proponents frequently try to portray the change as not representing a benefit reduction but as merely curbing excessive growth in Social Security benefits.[31] The benefit formula, which would be implemented beginning in 2009, would gradually reduce benefits, which over time would be substantial. A CBO analysis found that the proposed change would save significantly more than is needed to close Social Security's long-term financing gap.[32]

Under the current formula, as mentioned above, an average wage earner when retires in 2027, when the full retirement age will be sixty-seven, will receive. Social Security benefits that replace 36 percent of his or her preretirement earnings (as opposed to 42 percent for an average wage earner at age sixty-five me 2004). Under the proposal to lower replacement rates by adopting a "price indexing" rather than the current "wage indexing" formula, Social Security would only replace 27 percent of the income of the average wage earner who retires in 2042 and just 20 percent of the income of the average wage earner who retires in 2075. The result is that the standard-of-living support that Social Security would provide for retirees will decline appreciably, relative to the standard of living the worker had before retiring and relative to the standard of living the rest of society enjoys.[33]

The government would have to borrow about $2 trillion to offset the reduction in payroll taxes, in order to prevent a shortfall in payments owed to current retirees. Proponents of the plan have suggested that the $2 trillion is a necessary "bailout" of the system. However, it is the individual accounts that would create a cash flow shortfall by diverting funds away from Social Security long before benefits will be reduced. In fact, it is the private accounts that would push the Social Security trust fund into insolvency and threaten its financial condition.

Another major objection to this plan is that the stock market goes down as well as up. Obviously, as a retirement system, the stock market cannot offer the security that Social Security provides. Moreover, the less a wage earner makes, the less he or she has to invest and the smaller his or her return will be. It would be especially shortsighted to make retirement benefits more risky for those who earn low wages In contrast, under the current system, Social Security deliberately distributes benefits to provide a slightly more generous annuity to those recipients whose incomes were low during their wage-earning years. There is also the obvious problem, especially for those less well off, of preretirement withdrawals to pay for family health or other emergencies, as well as for education. The result is that these funds would not actually provide retirement security.

The problem of achieving retirement security is compounded by the fact that the proposed shift to the stock market for Social Security corresponds to a shift in employer-provided retirement plans. In 1980, almost two out of five households (39 percent) had defined-benefit pension plans; in 2005, only about one in five (21 percent) do. Increasingly, workers in 401(k) investment plans are dependent on the vagaries of the stock market in the primary pension plan. It would make more sense to permit wage earners to add to the basic Social Security contribution with tax-deferred investment contributions, not reduce it.

The administration's view appears to be driven largely by ideology. It holds the view that private markets are more efficient. Despite the fact that over 99 percent of Social Security's current revenues go toward benefits and less than 1 percent to overhead, the administration suggests that the private sector would be more efficient. However, the CBO's own analysis shows that the administrative costs of private accounts in Social Security will incur overhead charges that would result in benefit of about 20 percent.[34] And Paul Krugman has observed that the risks of privatization may make the problem worse. He notes that the government of Chile is often cited as the model for privatization; however, after more than twenty years the Chilean government must pour in additional money because it must "provide subsidies for workers failing to accumulate enough capital to provide a minimum pension."[35]

More Modest Proposals

Most scholarly opinion holds that the basic structure of Social Security is sound and does not justify a complete overhaul. If no changes are made to Social Security, it will not run out of money before 2052, allowing time to make adjustment to guarantee the program's long-term health. To put the "crisis" in perspective, a study by the Center on Budget and Policy Priorities found that the deficit in Social Security over the next seventy-five years will equal 0.4 percent of GDP, according to the CBO. By comparison, the cost over the next seventy-five years of the tax cuts enacted from 2001 to 2003 will be roughly 2 percent of GDP. If the tax cuts are made permanent, their cost will be five times larger, over the next seventy-five years, than the amount of the Social Security shortfall. Furthermore, just the cost of the tax cuts for the top 1 percent of the population, a group whose annual average income exceeds $1 million, is half again as large as the Social Security shortfall (0.4 versus 0.6 percent of GDP).[36]

Peter Orszag, a senior fellow at the Brookings Institution, and Peter Diamond, a leading scholar on Social Security at the Massachusetts Institute of Technology, propose progressive reforms. Under their plan, the payroll tax would be increased gradually from 12.4 to 13.7 percent over forty years. They propose trimming benefits by about 4 percent in 2032 and 12 percent in 2052. The increase in life expectancy has made Social Security less progressive, since those who earn higher wages tend to live longer than those who earn lower wages. To address this issue, Orszag proposes to reduce benefits to the top 15 percent of beneficiaries.[37]

Also, the proportion of earnings that go untaxed has accelerated in the past two decades, as income for the already affluent has increased rapidly while that for middle- and low-income workers has stagnated. The maximum taxable earnings base could be gradually raised about 15 percent above the current $90,000 maximum and indexed to inflation. Orszag and Diamond would also require mandatory coverage for newly hired state and local workers, which would also widen the base of workers paying into the system.

Conclusion

The theory of John Maynard Keynes provided the intellectual framework of welfare capitalism, to justify government's role in guiding the economy when it failed to live up to society's expectations. In the United States, the New Deal under Franklin Roosevelt tried to correct the weaknesses in the economy and to strengthen its workings. During the New Deal, government stepped in to manage the economy to a greater extent than had ever been done before. By the end of World War II, there was an acceptance of the idea that government had a responsibility to manage the economy to create the conditions that would provide for employment opportunities.

The experience of the war showed that economic policy could bring about high levels of employment and resulted in the Employment Act of 1946. The government is even more fully committed to these goals by the Full Employment and Balanced Growth Act of 1978, which established specific goals for unemployment (4 percent), inflation (3 percent), and economic growth (4 percent). The government has rarely attained all these goals, however. Achieving them would go a long way toward creating the conditions to promote the general welfare through various social policies. There was hope at the end of the Clinton administration that, with full employment, low inflation, and a growing economy, new programs could be undertaken to extend social welfare programs.

There are many reasons why these goals may be difficult to attain, including problems of measurement, design, and policy implementation. Perhaps even more important in the failure to achieve the economic goals that are necessary to effectively pursue social welfare policies is the increasing ideological dimension in politics. The economic theory is fairly settled, even if coordinating monetary and fiscal policies to achieve the basic goals is far from foolproof. Ideology not only provides different perspectives regarding sound social welfare policy, but it also elevates ideological commitment over pragmatic problem solving. Ideology frequently trumps practical politics. Years of conservative marketing have convinced many Americans that government programs always create inefficient, bloated bureaucracies, while private markets are always more efficient despite evidence to the contrary, as in the case of Social Security and Medicare administration. Government is seen as a "necessary evil" rather than as a "necessary good" that can improve the social welfare of the nation's citizens.

For example, the political consensus that government should take action to generally reduce great inequalities has broken down over the past several decades. The consensus of using the tools of monetary and fiscal policy to encourage a long trend of greater equalization in U.S. society receded. It is clear that the same tools can be used to increase inequality, as supply-side economics and the tax cuts from 2001 to 2003 illustrate. Considerable disagreement has arisen over what the role of government *should be* in using the power of taxation to redistribute income. And the social safety net is weakened when policies such as raising the minimum wage or expanding the Earned Income Tax Credit for the working poor are ignored.

Social Security has become the nation's greatest retirement program and is of particular importance to lower-income workers when they reach retirement. Oppponents of Social Security have put forward proposals that would severely weaken its ability to provide needed support, especially for lower-income workers, who frequently are not covered by a pension. A change is of course necessary to ensure that workers reaching retirement will have sufficient assets to maintain a reasonable standard of living. Political consensus may be lacking in this crucial area of social welfare policy, as it is elsewhere in public policy. Policies proposed by the Republican majority, who currently control the White House and both houses of Congress, may unfortunately exacerbate the problems of the most needy.

Budgeting for Recovery: The Need to Increase the Federal Deficit to Revive a Weak Economy

By Josh Bivens

With 8 million jobs lost since December 2007 and the unemployment rate at its highest level in 26 years, the need to address the profound weakness in the job market persists even as many economists are predicting that an end to the recession is near or even past.

A large hurdle standing in the way of strong action on jobs is the point of view that federal deficits must always be strictly avoided. While this belief may respond to our ingrained notions about thriftiness and "living within our means," it is entirely wrong from the standpoint of basic economics. To abet a strong economy, sometimes the federal budget needs to have a surplus, sometimes it needs to be balanced, and sometimes it needs to be in deficit. When workers and plants are idle and offices are empty, and when investment funds are begging to be borrowed, this is the time for deficits. The federal government can foster economic recovery by incurring them. In fact, they are a pre-condition to a robust recovery. In short, the obstacle to strong action on creating jobs posed by deficits is strictly political, not economic.

This paper examines the relationships between federal deficits, interest rates, inflation, international indebtedness and generational equity. Its single most important point is that our conventional notions of thrift turn upside-down when the nation confronts a recession.

- As long as there are idle resources in labor and capital markets and interest rates controlled by the Federal Reserve are at or near zero, *none* of the negative outcomes feared from running larger deficits will come to pass. For the next year or two at least, the biggest threat regarding deficits is that they will not be large enough to support the public relief and investments needed to pull the economy into a sustained recovery and provide the 10 million-plus jobs necessary to restore the U.S. labor market to its pre-recession strength.
- Supporters of the American Recovery and Reinvestment Act (ARRA), enacted in February 2009, argue that it was necessary for pulling the economy out of its downward spiral. Critics of the Recovery Act argue that it contributes too much to rising federal deficits, and that these deficits will prove disastrous to the American economy. But the Recovery Act will have only a small impact on the overall budget deficit, even in the short run. In the longer run (over the next decade or more), when the economy will have presumably recovered and concerns about budget deficits may be legitimate, the Recovery Act has no effect at all.
- Deficits in the long run are driven almost entirely by spending on Medicare and Medicaid. Without these programs, the federal budget (excluding interest payments) would be in surplus indefinitely. Since the rise in Medicare and Medicaid spending is driven by the economy-wide rise in health costs, fundamental health reform that reduces the cost of health care is the key to long-run budget balance.
- The United States has not had to rely on foreigners to finance the rise in government deficits in the past year-and-a-half. Private domestic savings in the United States have expanded *faster* than government borrowing in the past year. In other words, there is no shortage of domestic residents willing to hold government debt right now.

The Arithmetic of Budget Deficits

In fiscal year 2009, which ended on September 30, the Congressional Budget Office (CBO) estimates that the federal deficit will total $1.6 trillion, or

"Budgeting for Recovery: The Need to Increase the Federal Deficit to Revive a Weak Economy" by Josh Bivens, from *EPI Briefing Paper*, No. 253, January 6, 2010, pp. 1-24. Copyright © 2010 Economic Policy Institute. Reprinted with permission.

11.2% of GDP. In 2010, the deficit is forecast to total $1.38 trillion, or 9.6% of GDP. These will be the two largest annual deficits on record since World War II.

Budget Deficits Defined

A deficit occurs when the federal government's spending exceeds its revenues in a given year. To finance the difference, the government borrows from the public by selling Treasury bonds, notes, and bills.

Federal spending is dominated by Social Security and other non-health-related entitlements, Medicare and Medicaid, defense spending, and interest payments on the federal debt (**Figure 2.7**). All other spending (so-called non-defense domestic discretionary spending) accounts for only 15% of the overall budget.

Federal revenues are dominated by federal income taxes and social insurance taxes, the bulk of which are the FICA taxes that fund Social Security and Medicare (**Figure 2.8**). Payroll taxes have grown in importance in recent years and now provide more than a third of all federal government revenues.

Causes of Current Deficits

On the most salient political question—*how much of these deficits are due to the policies of the Obama administration*—the answer is, very little. Auerbach and Gale (2009) and Irons, Edwards, and Turner (2009) have provided useful analyses of the deficit over the past decade, and the following section draws on them. It is important to note that changes in the budget deficit can occur for two reasons: policy changes and changes in economic conditions. Policy changes affect the budget balance in obvious ways—cutting tax rates, for example, will increase the deficit. However, economic conditions can also affect the deficit. For example, as the economy slows or enters a recession, tax collections will mechanically fall and social spending may rise, tending to increase deficits. A key theme that emerges out of these reviews is that *most* of the deterioration in the budget balance that occurred between 2001 and 2008 is due to policy changes undertaken during the Bush administration and *not* changes in economic conditions. In 2009, by contrast, the deteriorating economy dominates in explaining the large increase in that year's deficit.

The Economic Expansion of 2001-07

The CBO forecast in 2001 that the federal budget balance would improve by roughly $300 billion between 2001 and 2007 (the years of economic expansion in the last business cycle), reaching a surplus of $573 billion in 2007. Instead, the budget was in constant deficit during those years, with the 2007 deficit reaching $161 billion. While this deficit was small relative to the size of the

Source: CBO.

Figure 2.8 Federal revenue by source, 2008

Source: CBO.

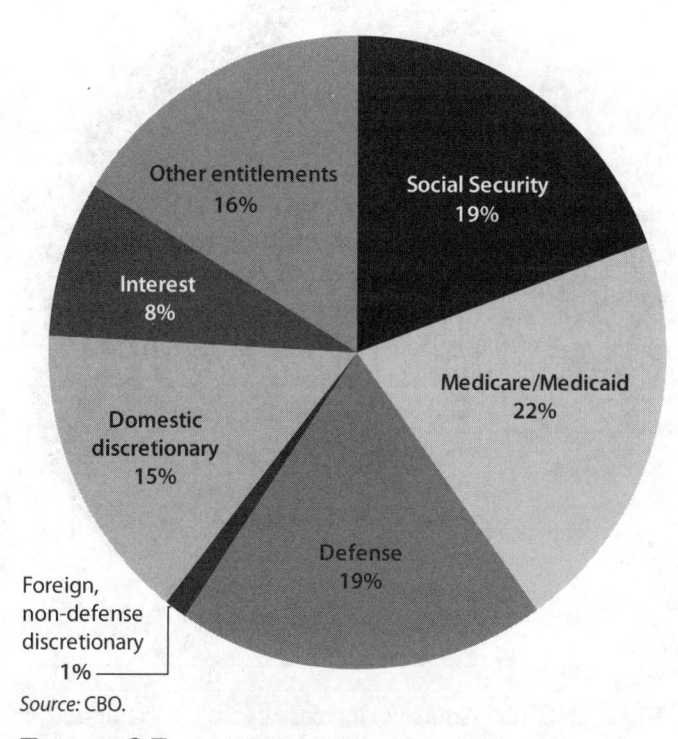

Figure 2.7 Federal expenditures by type, 2008

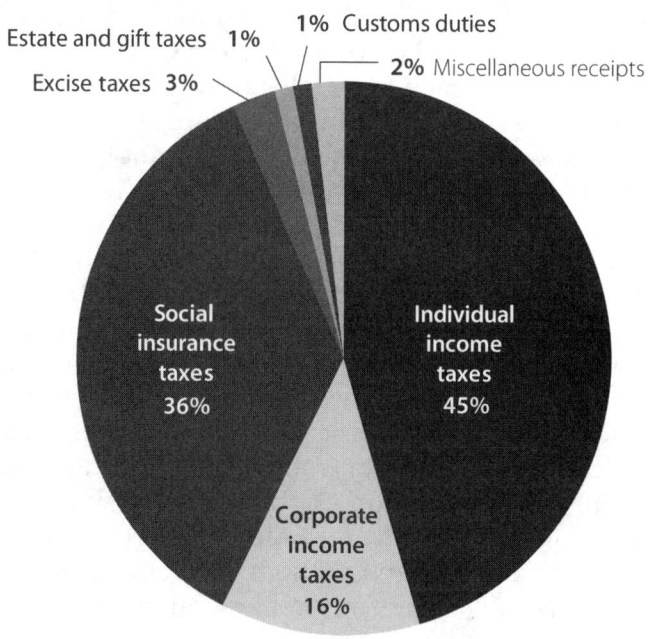

economy (1.2% of GDP), it represented a $736 billion *decline* relative to what the CBO forecast in 2001. Auerbach and Gale (2009) estimate that 98% of this decline can be explained by policy changes undertaken since 2001 and not by unexpectedly slow economic growth.

The Center on Budget and Policy Priorities has identified the biggest specific policies behind the rise in deficits since 2001 (**Figure 2.9**). The single biggest policy change was the string of tax cuts passed over this time, which explain almost *half* of the policy-driven declines in budget balance. Increased defense and security spending (including the wars in Iraq and Afghanistan) explains roughly a third of this increase, with the rest consumed by the new Medicare prescription drug benefit (created without a revenue source) and other miscellaneous policy changes.

2008: First Year of Recession

In 2008 the deficit hit $459 billion, a jump of $298 billion from the year before. Roughly $160 billion of this increase could be accounted for by the first stimulus package, which comprised roughly $100 billion in tax cuts to households and $60 billion in tax cuts for businesses. Many interventions that ended up in the Recovery Act (especially the infrastructure investments) were rejected by policy makers crafting this first stimulus package because they were not "timely" enough—the worry being that the recession would be over before infrastructure projects could get underway. Of course, if major infrastructure investments had been part of the early 2008 stimulus package, they would have been fully online and paying large dividends when the economy began its freefall later that year.

Even in this first full year of recession, less than a quarter ($71 billion) of the $298 billion increase in the deficit from 2007 to 2008 was attributed by the CBO to overall economic weakness. By the end of 2008 the difference between the actual deficit and the CBO's 2001 forecast had climbed to $1,091 billion, and even after a year of recession only $83 billion could be laid to the decline in the economy.

2009: The Economy Implodes

Between January 2008 and August 2009, the baseline CBO deficit projection rose by a staggering $1,380 billion. Well over a half ($778 billion) of this increase is forecast to stem from changing economic conditions and not from policy changes. Of the remaining $600 billion, less than a third is attributable to ARRA spending. **Figure 2.10** displays the main drivers of the change in the CBO baseline between these two dates.

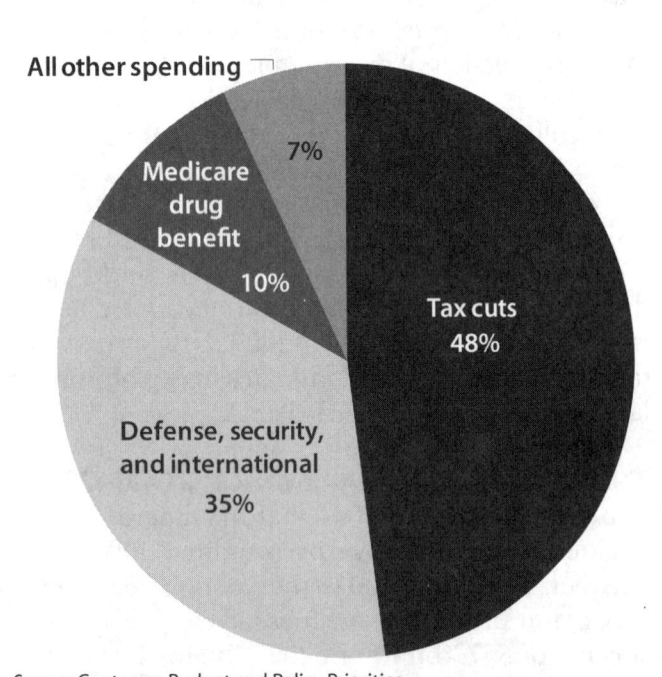

Figure 2.9 Contribution of policy changes to growth in deficit since 2001

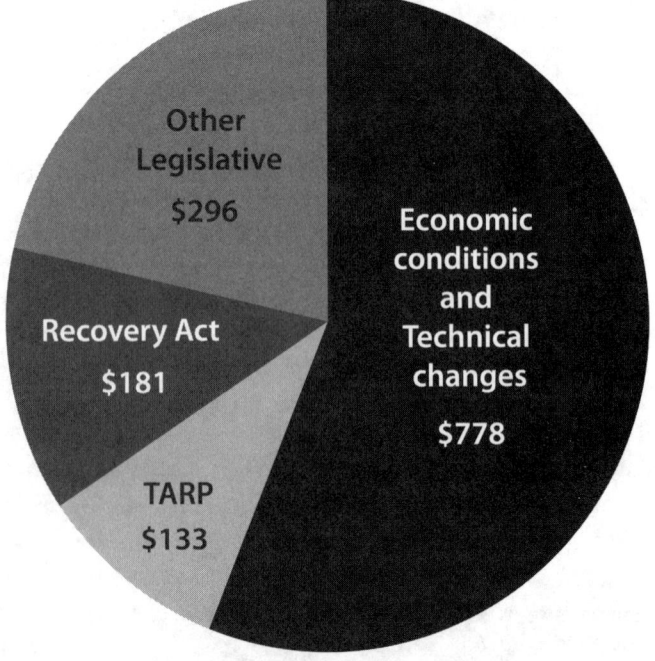

- Tax cuts 48%
- Defense, security, and international 35%
- Medicare drug benefit 10%
- All other spending 7%

Source: Center on Budget and Policy Priorities.

Figure 2.10 Source of increase in projected budget deficits, January 2008–August 2009 (billions)

- Economic conditions and Technical changes $778
- Other Legislative $296
- Recovery Act $181
- TARP $133

Source: CBO.

While the imploding economy can explain the lion's share of the year-over-year increase in the deficit, it is important to remember that the $2.3 trillion difference between the large surplus projected in 2001 by the CBO for 2009 and the large deficit that has come to pass this year is still mostly a function of policy changes undertaken over that time period; they contributed $1.4 trillion to this change. While the economy is clearly having a huge impact on the deficit in 2009, the fiscal policy undertaken to address the worst downturn since the Great Depression and the loss in government revenue due to the downturn together total less than half the rise in the deficit stemming from policy actions undertaken during the Bush years. In short, policy makers could have fought the current recession just as aggressively through fiscal policy and yet maintained a deficit *half* as large as it is today *were it not for these policy changes*.

THE ROLE OF THE RECOVERY ACT IN RISING DEFICITS

The rise in the deficit in 2009 caused by ARRA ($181 billion) is less than a quarter of the decline caused by the worsening economy itself (just under $800 billion). For the near term, then, anyone concerned about large deficits should support policies to boost the ailing economy to stem the mechanical hemorrhaging of tax revenue and the rise in safety net spending that has accompanied it.

Further, given that the Recovery Act is specifically designed to wind down quickly after 2011, ARRA is not an issue over the longer run in which concerns about the deficit have some merit.

THE IMPACT OF BAILOUTS ON THE BUDGET AND THE DEFICIT

The federal government's rescue of insured and non-insured financial institutions and assets and its loans and support for automakers affect the budget, the deficit, and the debt in complicated ways.

For example, the CBO expects a large portion of the $700 billion authorized for the Troubled Assets Relief Program (TARP) to be returned to taxpayers, and the agency includes only the expected net cost of these TARP loans (the portion the CBO deems unlikely to be paid back) in a given year's deficit. However, the full gross cost of the TARP interventions is reflected in the rise of the public *debt*. Disbursing this money forced greater debt to be taken on, and any payback will come from returns on private debt or equity now owned by the government.

Conversely, the nationalization of Fannie Mae and Freddie Mac adds more to annual deficits than to the national debt. The government issued no new debt to acquire these companies; rather, it declared them insolvent and took them into conservatorship. Now that they are government entities, however, the cost of guaranteeing the liabilities of the bonds that Fannie and Freddie issue to finance their purchase of mortgages will add to the annual deficit.

These bailouts have provided valuable subsidies to those receiving them (the CBO, for example, has estimated that over a third of TARP outlays will be a pure subsidy to the financial institutions receiving them), and they have added significantly to the short-term budget deficit. Further, the benefits of these bailouts to the economy are less clear than those provided by the Recovery Act. But the bottom line for the deficit is that these interventions are not expected to be ongoing outlays of the federal government and should have little impact on the long-run budget.

FEDERAL DEBT DEFINED AND MEASURED

The federal debt is the total amount owed on the accumulation of past budget deficits offset by past budget surpluses. At the end of fiscal year 2008, the federal debt owed to entities outside the federal government was valued at 41% of gross domestic product (GDP).[1] Expressing the outstanding federal debt held by the public as a share of overall GDP is a common convention that is useful because it indicates the burden a given dollar value of debt actually imposes on the overall economy. Generally, the way that the United States (as well as other advanced economies) has worked off the burden of debt in the post–World War II era is simply by having the overall economy grow faster than the debt. Only in the years between 1997 and 2000 was the actual value of the outstanding debt reduced, and even in that period most of the decline in the debt-to-GDP ratio was driven by economic growth, not the retiring of outstanding debt.

Over the past 45 years (the period tracked by the CBO) the debt-to-GDP ratio has varied greatly around its average of 36%. This average, however,

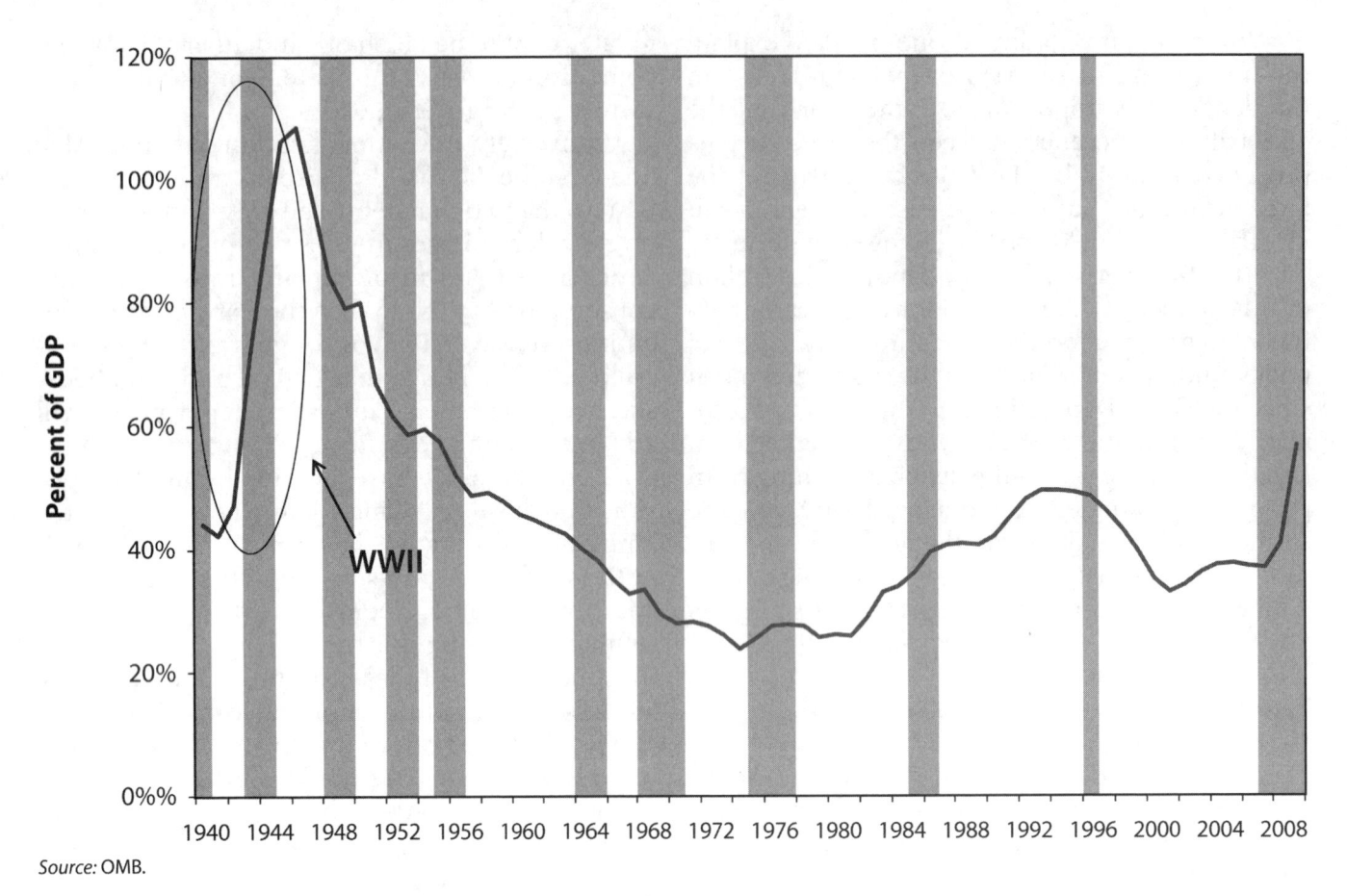

FIGURE 2.11 Federal debt held by the public as share of GDP

Source: OMB.

masks lots of variation: between 1979 and 1995 it rose by more than 23 percentage points, from 26% to 49%. Then between 1995 and 2001 it fell by almost 16 percentage points (**Figure 2.11**). In short, fluctuations in the debt-to-GDP ratio should not be cause for great alarm; policy changes and/or small changes in the rate of GDP growth can quickly reverse its trend.

Generally, sharp increases in the debt-to-GDP ratio are driven by wars and recessions, while (generally steadier) declines occur during economic expansions. An important exception to this pattern, however, occurred in the 1980s and early 1990s, a period of economic expansion that coincided with a sharp run-up in the debt-to-GDP ratio. This divergence from the general pattern was driven by large budget deficits that were driven by large tax cuts for affluent taxpayers and a sharp increase in defense spending.

Lastly, it is worth noting that the debt-to-GDP ratio in the United States remains well below that of many other industrialized countries, which have maintained higher debt levels for decades while still managing to close the gap between their living standards and those in the United States. (**Figure 2.12**).

DEFICITS AND DEBT OVER THE NEXT 10 YEARS

Figure 2.13 shows the CBO projections of debt-to-GDP ratios after: (1) extending policies of the Bush administration, (2) enacting policies proposed by the Obama administration, (3) enacting the Obama administration policies without the Recovery Act, and (4) enacting Obama policies without the costs of the Recovery Act and TARP. Both the Recovery Act and TARP lead to one-time increases in the debt-to-GDP ratio, but the longer-run trends are dominated by other factors. In each of the four scenarios, the debt-to-GDP ratio rises rapidly and by almost identical amounts (between 53.7% and 56.0%).

With regard to the Obama policies specifically, only about four of the projected 41 percentage-point change in the debt-to-GDP ratio from 2008 to 2019 are associated with the Recovery Act, and its entire effect is felt by 2012; it leaves no imprint

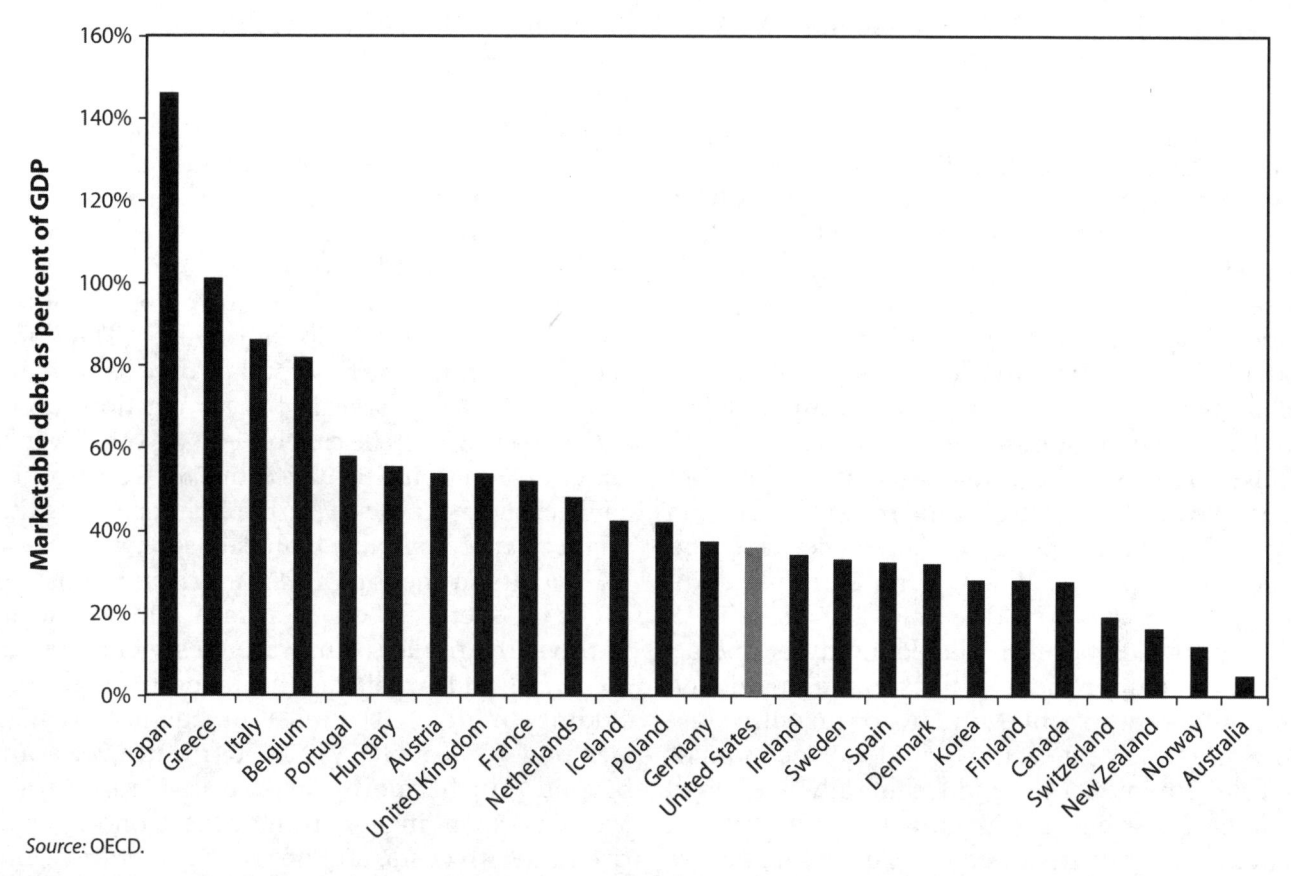

FIGURE 2.12 Debt to GDP ratios, various countries, 2008

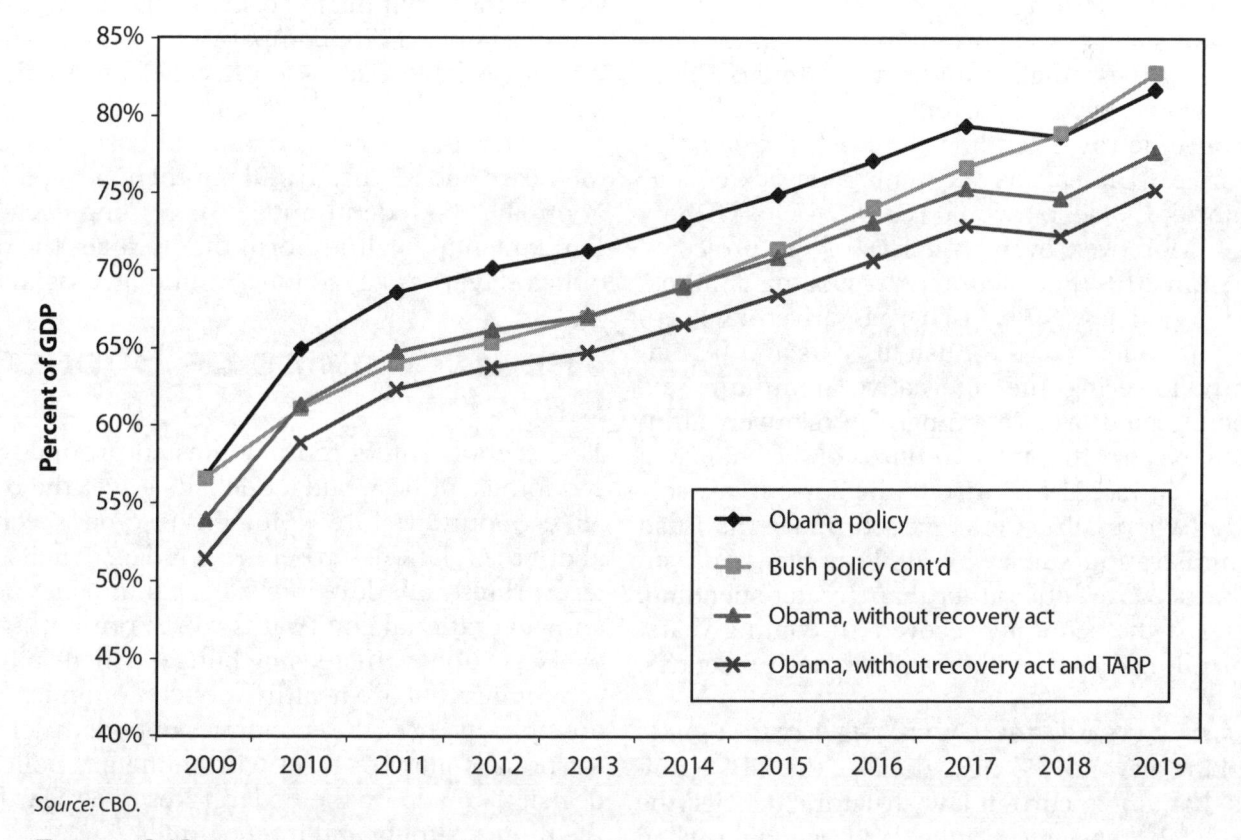

Source: OECD.

FIGURE 2.13 Debt-to-GDP ratio under four scenarios

Source: CBO.

thereafter. In other words, the recovery package is not a significant factor in the future trajectory of federal debt.

It is important to note that the rise in the federal debt that is associated with the purchase of private-sector assets will be offset at least partially by the value of these new assets. The Office of Management and Budget (OMB) forecasts that this offset will be roughly 9 percentage points in 2019, almost a quarter of the gross in crease in federal indebtedness, leaving the actual rise in federal indebtedness quite a bit less than even the publicly held federal debt numbers would indicate.

Nevertheless, these forecasts predict budget deficits by 2019 that leave little room for error on the part of future policy makers. Auerbach and Gale (2009) project that Obama administration budget proposals would lead to deficits in 2019 of 5.5% of GDP even if the economy is operating at full employment. This is too high a deficit for a full-employment economy to run with equanimity. As the next section will detail, economies at full employment should generally see small deficits that trend downward. Large and rising deficits during times of economic downturns are useful, but large deficits during times of full employment (when there are no idle resources) have the potential to drag down economic growth.

That said, it is important to note that the deficit in 2019 is smaller under this scenario than what would occur if current policy were allowed to continue (by extending the Bush tax cuts, for example). Under this "current policy extended" scenario, the deficit would reach 6.4% of GDP by 2019. Moreover, over a quarter of the projected deficit in 2019 that occurs under Obama administration policies (5.5% of GDP) is driven by keeping components of the Bush tax cuts and permanently lowering the alternative minimum tax, which is paid overwhelmingly by relatively affluent taxpayers. In total, two-thirds of the change in the deficit in 2019 relative to the current law scenario (where all tax cuts passed under the Bush administration sunset by 2011) policy is driven by reduced revenue rather than greater spending. Thus, as the economy recovers in coming years, controlling deficits will mean looking at revenues.

Deficits and Debt Over the Long Term

Looking beyond the next decade, the CBO projects that, under current law, structural deficits (the mismatch between revenues and spending when the economy is otherwise healthy) are projected to rise to almost 10% of GDP in 2050 and then grow steadily higher. An economy at full employment should not run deficits like these seen currently in a depressed economy, so policy makers should strive to change this projection. Among other problems, deficits of this size would require interest payments on the federal debt by 2050 that consume almost a third of all federal spending. Currently, 8% of federal spending goes to service the debt. The difference between the current level of debt service and that which would prevail if the projections above came to pass would be roughly equal to having to finance an additional Pentagon by 2050. Clearly, this could crowd out other types of public spending that might be more valuable than debt service.

Deficits in the long run are driven almost entirely by spending on Medicare and Medicaid. Without the outlays (and revenues) generated by Medicare and Medicaid the federal budget (excluding interest) is almost in balance (deficits well under 2% of GDP) in 2050 (**Figure 2.14**) and beyond. Furthermore, the rise in Medicare and Medicaid spending is driven by the economy-wide rise in health costs, and not by any factor specific to the federal health rograms. And even though Medicare has been more successful than the private sector in reining in costs for the past quarter-century (since 1970, comparable costs in private insurance have risen 48% faster than Medicare payments; see **Figure 2.15**). However, even these slower-than-private-sector rates of cost growth in Medicare and Medicaid still put them on a path to dominate the federal budget in coming decades. Fundamental health reform that reduces the cost of health care is key to long-run budget, balance.

The Economics of Budget Deficits

This section enters more contested ground—the economics of how budget deficits affect the overall economy. Before going into some specifics about the relationship between budget deficits, interest rates, inflation, international indebtedness, and generational equity, it is worth presenting an overview of how increasing budget deficits affects economies that are healthy versus economies that are sick, and how the economics of budget deficits (or fiscal policy) interact with monetary policy—decisions made by the Federal Reserve regarding the money supply and interest rates.

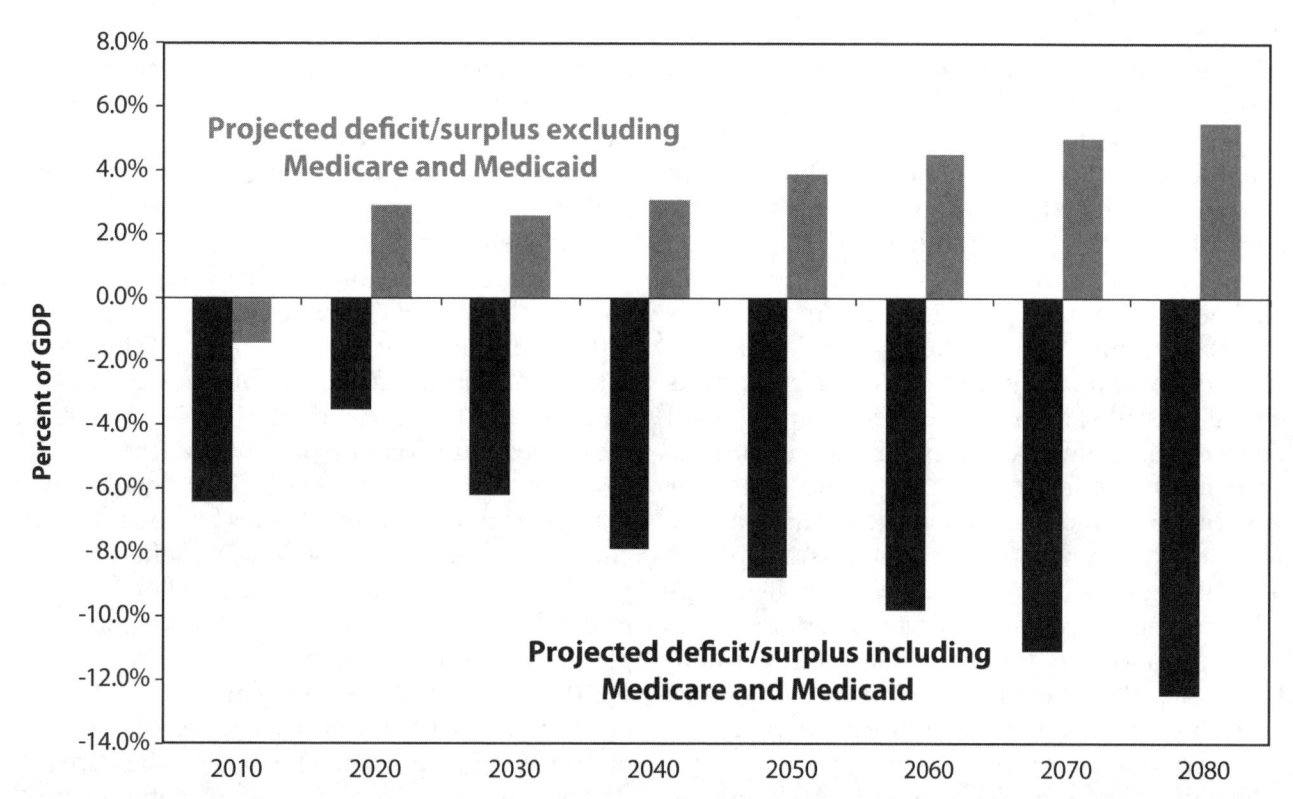

Note: Interest payments on debt are excluded from both scenarios. Scenario without Medicare/Medicaid also excludes their associated revenues.
Source: CBO.

FIGURE 2.14 Projected budget deficit or surplus, including and excluding Medicare and Medicaid

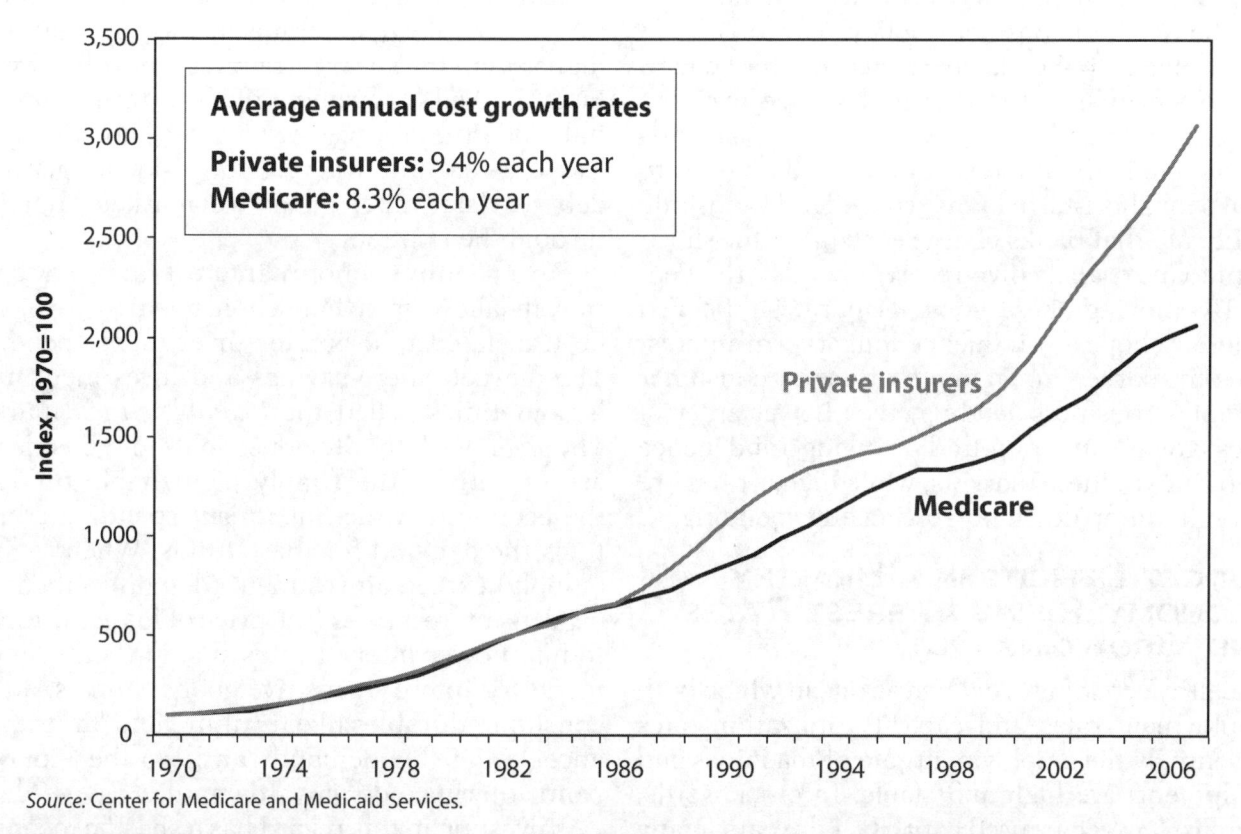

Source: Center for Medicare and Medicaid Services.

FIGURE 2.15 Cumulative growth in per-enrollee payments for personal health care, Medicare, and private insurers, 1970–2007

Fiscal policy is conducted by Congress and the president in their design of the federal budget. A rising budget deficit (the result of either increased spending or lower taxes, or both) spurs economic activity whenever there is excess capacity in labor and capital markets—that is, when unemployment is high or capacity utilization low. The government is demanding more goods and services and transferring more income to households than it is collecting in revenue, thus causing overall spending in the economy to rise, all else equal. Conversely, a rising budget surplus (the result of either reduced spending or higher taxes, or both) reduces economic activity as the government removes more purchasing power from the economy through taxes than it pumps back in through spending and transfers.

Policy decisions that increase a budget deficit are generally labeled *expansionary* while those that reduce a deficit (or increase a surplus) are labeled *contractionary*.

Fiscal balance can rise or fall even with no explicit change in policy. A weakening economy causes tax revenues to fall and spending on safety net programs to rise even with no change in tax or spending policy. But fiscal *policy* generally refers to those changes in the debt and deficit that are the result of conscious policy decisions.

Monetary policy is conducted by the Federal Reserve primarily through its leverage over the discount rate and the federal funds rate. The discount rate is the interest rate the Fed charges to banks for short-term loans. The federal funds rate is the rate that banks charge each other for short-term loans of their own reserves held by the Fed.

By moving these short-term rates, the Fed generally hopes to influence longer-term interest rates in markets for home mortgages, consumer durables, business lending, etc. Lower interest rates are meant to spur borrowing (and hence spending) in these markets, while higher rates are meant to tamp down borrowing and spending.

Budget Deficits in a Healthy Economy: Rising Interest Rates and 'Crowding Out'

A healthy economy is defined as one in which both employment rates and capacity utilization rates (essentially the employment rate of machines and equipment) are high and stable. In other words, there isn't much unused capacity. For years, many economists assumed that economies could be kept healthy entirely through changes to monetary policy. If the economy began to slow, the Federal Reserve could cut short-term interest rates and thereby boost demand for business investment and interest-sensitive consumer items like autos and household durables.

But the limitation of the Fed's leverage to short-term interest rates reduces its capacity to influence spending or investment. The interest rates that matter most for businesses and consumers are those on debt that is longer term than overnight loans from the Fed, riskier than reserves at the Fed, and subject to erosion by inflation. And these interest rates can be affected by changes in the size of the budget deficit.

Take interest rates in the market for corporate debt, for example. Firms that wish to expand plant and equipment may decide to borrow (issue bonds) to finance this investment. These bonds are long term, with maturity dates of three, five, or 10 years or even longer. Further, they are risky, i.e., not immune from the risk of default. Finally, they are exposed to the risk that a burst of inflation will degrade their value.

Because of the commitment required and the risks involved in long-term instruments, real (inflation-adjusted) interest rates in the market for the long term are almost always substantially higher than the short-term rates controlled by the Fed. The Fed's movement of short-term rates can influence these longer-term rates, but nevertheless the real interest rate for risky, longer-term debt is determined in active markets, not just through Fed policy.

In a healthy economy, interest rates play a key role in allowing a household's extra savings to be translated into greater investment spending. The market where savings and investment meet is sometimes called the *loanable funds* market. The *savings* of private households and businesses are essentially the supply of loanable funds in the economy, while *investment* spending constitutes the demand for these funds. When savings (supply) exceeds investment (demand), then one expects interest rates (the price of loanable funds) to fall. Lower interest rates should then spur demand for interest-sensitive goods (homes, autos, consumer durables like furniture and large appliances), and this demand can keep the economy from entering a downward spiral.

Investing in this regard has a specific meaning: building new plants and equipment or building new residential housing. Buying a share of stock on an exchange is not investing—it's just transferring ownership. Investment in this definition must be something that increases the physical capital stock of the economy.[2] The translation of greater savings into more investment demand (facilitated by falling interest rates) provided by the market for loanable funds is what theoretically keeps falling consumption (the flip-side of rising savings) from triggering a recession when households decide to start saving more.

How Budget Deficits Affect Interest Rates in a Healthy Economy

An increase in the federal budget deficit means that the government increases its demand for loanable funds from its own citizens as well as international investors. In a healthy economy, this means that the government begins competing with private borrowers for a fixed supply of savings, and this competition drives up interest rates. This increase in interest rates may reduce private-sector investments in plants and equipment, and this decline in investment means that the overall economy has a smaller capital stock with which to work.

The size of a nation's capital stock is a key driver of productivity growth, and oductivity growth defines how fast living standards can rise. The crowding out of private-sector investment that occurs when governments increase budget deficits in a healthy economy is the prime argument for a hawkish view against rising budget deficits when the economy is healthy.

Budget Deficits in a Weak Economy: Shock Absorbers that 'Crowd in' Investment

However, this deficit hawkishness is profoundly destructive if practiced when an economy is sick. When employment and capacity utilization rates are low and falling even as the interest rates controlled by the Federal Reserve are at or near zero, there is no reason to fear that rising deficits will crowd out private investment. So long as there are idle resources in the economy, deficits will tend to increase *both* savings and investment in roughly equal measure, leading to no sustained upward pressure on rates.

The current recession became a catastrophe because American consumers rapidly pulled back on their consumption spending in the wake of the bursting housing bubble. The personal savings rate has jumped from essentially zero at the beginning of the recession to almost 7% today, representing an extraordinary pullback in consumer spending. Hatzius (2009) estimates that this spending pullback was even larger than the one that precipitated the Great Depression.

In the simple loanable funds scenario, the rise in savings enabled by this pullback in private spending by households should have led to a sharp decline in interest rates and a rise in investment by businesses, and this swap of increased business investment for reduced consumer spending should have kept the economy from entering a prolonged recession. However, instead the recession has led private businesses to sharply decrease their own investment spending even as interest rates have fallen. After all, when a large portion of existing plant and equipment is standing idle, building more does not make a lot of sense, even if the cost of financing is low.

This highlights a key problem with the naïve version of the loanable funds theory of investment—*both savings and investment depend on overall national income*. In a healthy economy with high and stable employment rates, national income is generally stable and the loanable funds model works relatively well at predicting what will happen to interest rates. However, when overall national income is changing rapidly (say because of a steep recession), the model becomes an unsuitable guide for predicting interest rate changes.

The rapid increase in idle capacity since the recession began has dampened demand for business investment so severely that desired saving exceeds this demand for new investments even when the interest rates controlled by the Fed sit at zero—that is, even when borrowing is essentially free. At present, the economy needs these rates to be *negative* to bring investment demand in line with savings. Since the Fed cannot engineer negative interest rates through its conventional policy tools, it is essentially out of ammunition, making alternative policy responses—expansionary fiscal policy in particular—that much more necessary.

With the extra supply of loanable funds going begging in the private sector, critics of additional federal spending have no cause to worry about interest rate increases stemming from rising deficits.

In essence, by looking at only *one slice* (government, not private) of *one side* (the demand-side, not the supply-side) of the loanable funds markets that determine interest rates they miss the fact that the private sector is simultaneously reducing its own demand for loanable funds (business spending falls) as well as increasing the supply (private savings rising) of these funds. Both of these private influences on the loanable funds market have put severe *downward* pressure on interest rates.

Rather than crowding out private-sector investment through higher interest rates, government demand is only partially filling the gap caused by the private-sector pullback.

How Soon do we need to Worry About Rising Interest Rates?

If the economy recovers and savings start to translate into investment spending at non-zero interest rates, all while labor and capital resources are near-fully utilized, then continuing to run large budget deficits could indeed start bidding up interest rates and crowding out private investment. In this case, deficits would add to overall economic activity but would instead displace private activity with public activity.

The economy is nowhere near this point. Private demand for loans has plummeted, and idle resources abound. Further, most economic studies of private investment decisions find that current GDP growth has a greater impact on investment than do interest rates. So, a stimulus package that adds to GDP will substantially *crowd in* private investment through this so-called "accelerator" effect (rising GDP leading to rising investment spending).

Moreover, economic recovery in and of itself provides its own moderating pressure on interest rates. As national income begins growing again, so too will total national savings, since they are a relatively stable fraction of national income. This increase in national savings will increase the supply of loanable funds, which will put downward pressure on interest rates.

The current economy will not experience sustained upward pressure on interest rates caused by fiscal deficits until it nears full employment. Almost all projections show that the economy is several years away from that goal.

The economics notwithstanding, opponents of stimulus and the country's age-old community of deficit hawks will point to any uptick in interest rates or even any suggestion of one to generate fear that deficits are threatening to choke off growth (numerous news stories in summer 2009 raised alarms about rising long-term interest rates and the role of deficits). **Figure 2.16** shows just how odd these fears are—since the fall of 2008 and throughout the enactment of Recovery Act spending, long-term rates have wobbled up and down within a range that is the lowest in the last half-century.

In regard to these short-term wobbles in interest rates, it is important to note that interest rates on government debt have many determinants besides the level of the federal deficit. The most important determinant over the past year has been the perceived level of risk of private alternatives to government debt as stores of wealth; the financial crisis and the widespread threat of bankruptcy in almost all major financial institutions made investors around the world afraid of almost all private debt instruments. They flocked to government bonds (this is sometimes labeled a "flight to safety"), thereby driving up their prices and driving down their interest rates. As fears of widespread financial institution bankruptcy abate, investors will likely be willing to exchange public for private debt instruments, and this switch would lead to an uptick in the interest rates on public debt. When that happens, it's a sign not of a problem but rather a sign of economic recovery and stabilization.

Budget Deficits and Inflation

Deficits this year and next will not spur accelerating inflation. Moreover, deficits in these two years may save the economy from rapid disinflation or even deflation, which is a worse problem than inflation.

When an economy is operating at full employment, with no idle workers or plants, then a rise in the federal budget deficit could generate inflationary pressures. Specifically, if the government began demanding more goods and services, and if the Federal Reserve accommodated these demands by not raising interest rates, then the extra demand for output when no further output could be produced (remember, this is an example where all workers and factories are already fully employed) could lead to higher prices instead of more economic activity.

However, nothing about the current situation suggests that this worry is plausible. For one,

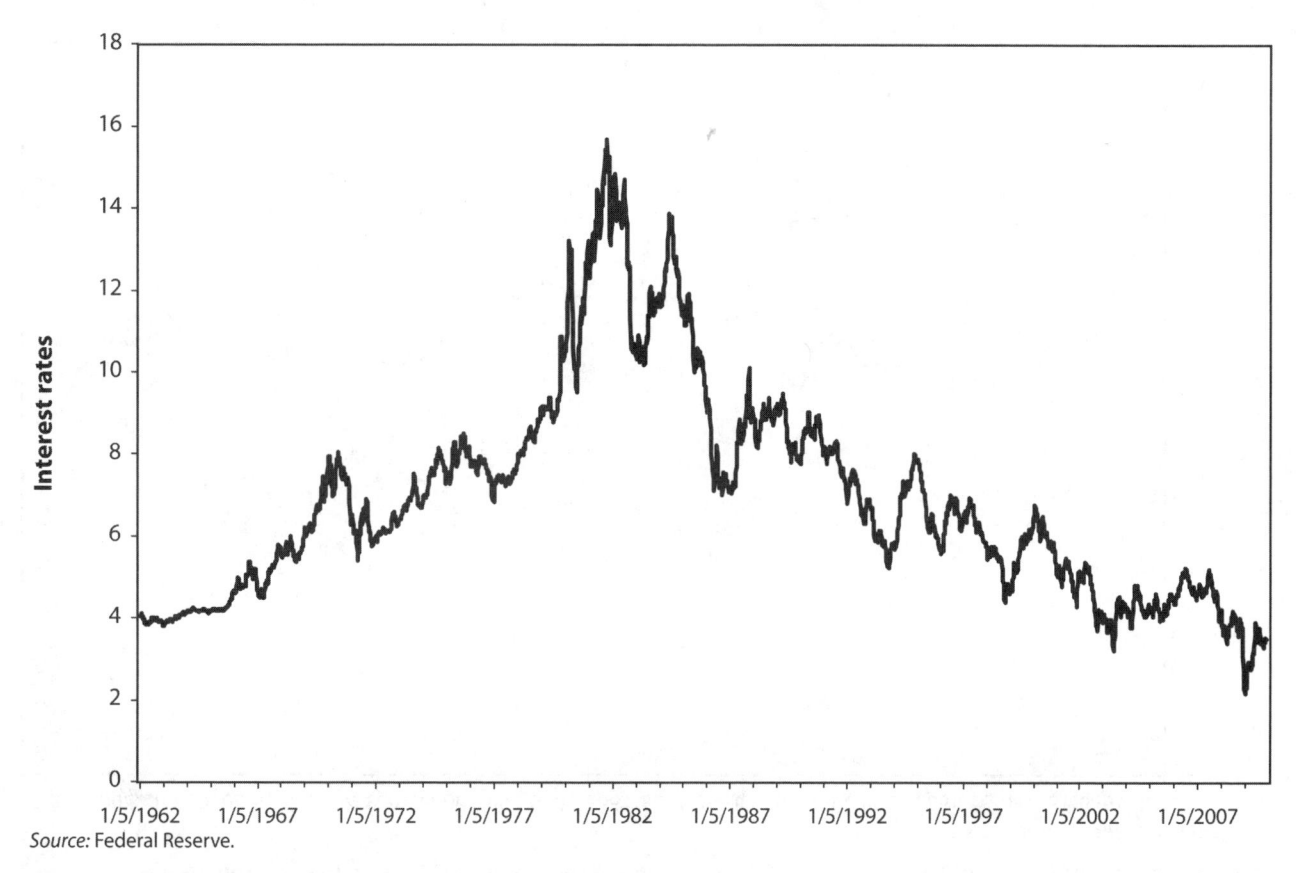

FIGURE 2.16 Interest rates on 10-year Treasury securities

Source: Federal Reserve.

workers and factories are idle in record numbers. Until the unemployment rate falls and the capacity utilization rate rises to levels that prevailed before the recession, there is no reason to think that federal budget deficits will cause prices, rather than overall economic activity, to increase. In fact, even the pre-recession capacity rates are weak markers of economic strength: the unemployment and capacity utilization rates were too high and too low, respectively, to indicate that the economy was at full employment in December 2007, when the recession began. Family income never recovered the level it attained in the prior business cycle (which ended in 2001), wage growth for typical workers was lackluster in the 2000s, and some measures of labor market strength (the employment-to-population ratio, for example) did not rise at all even during the expansion phase of the last business cycle (**Figure 2.17** shows the capacity utilization rate and the employment-to-population ratio over the last 20-year period).

To forestall the risk of inflation brought on by too much demand relative to supply in the overall economy, the Federal Reserve can tamp down demand through interest rate increases. Unlike the zero-bound on interest rate cutting, there is no limit as to how high interest rates can be set by the Fed.

A Bigger Danger than Inflation: Deflation

The real danger with worries about inflation is that they will distract from legitimate concerns about disinflation, or even deflation. In 2009 there were eight outright declines in the year-over-year consumer price index (**Figure 2.18**). The last time this happened was in 1955, on the heels of a recession that saw the single-largest half-year economic contraction since the Great Depression. The first quarter of 2009 marked the end of the second-largest half-year contraction since the Depression.

Deflation is dangerous for three reasons. First, as prices fall consumers put off purchases of big-ticket items. If you think a refrigerator will be cheaper in six months, why buy it today? Deferred consumption spending is just what the economy does not need today.

Second, falling prices lead to rising real (that is, inflation-adjusted) interest rates. If the interest

70 CHAPTER 2 Economic Policy

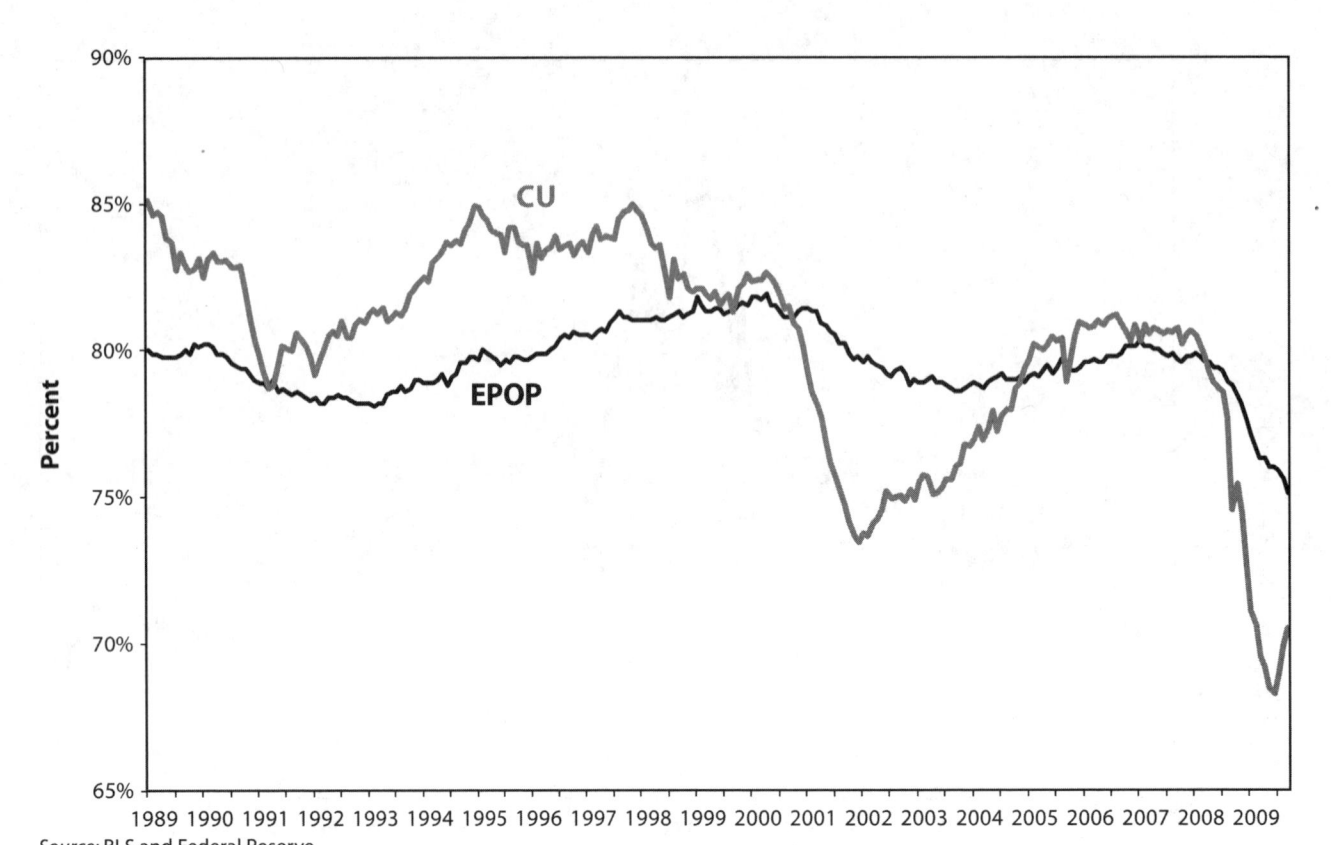

Source: BLS and Federal Reserve.

FIGURE 2.17 Capacity utilization rate and employment-to-population ratio (ages 25 to 54), 1989-present

Source: BLS.

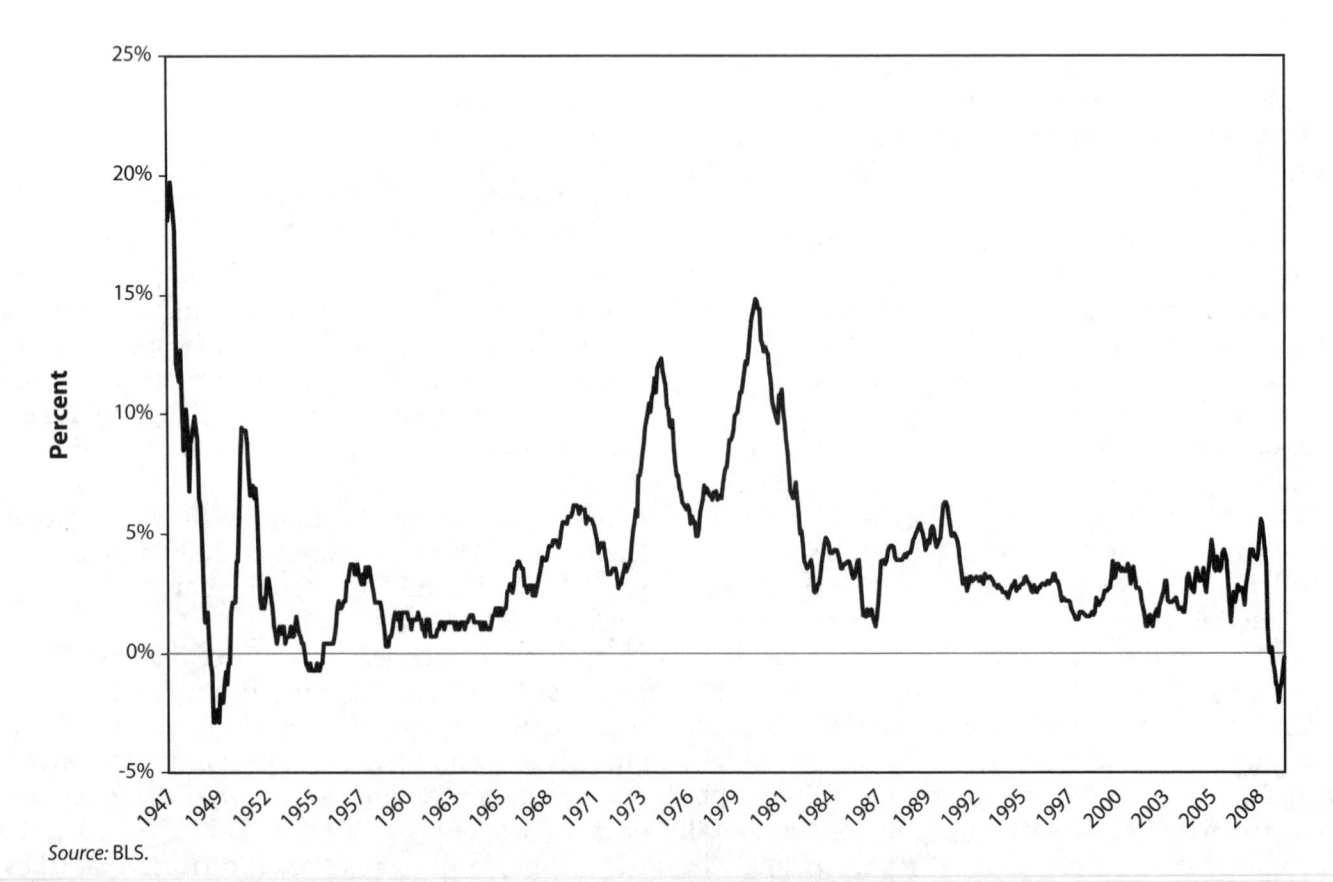

FIGURE 2.18 Year-over-year change in consumer price index, 1947 to present

rate I owe on my mortgage is fixed at 5%, and inflation is 5%, then I'm paying 0% *real* (inflation-adjusted) interest on my loan. If instead I have a mortgage with a 5% rate and prices are falling by 5%, then my mortgage is actually costing 10% in terms of the purchasing power relative to other goods and services I am surrendering to service the loan.

Rising real interest rates are something else that the economy does not need right now. They may be attractive to savers, but they squeeze borrowers. Given that borrowing is a key source of financing for much business investment and that tens of millions of American households are now net debtors, higher rates would threaten to choke off new spending.

Currently the nominal rate controlled by the Fed is stuck at zero. But the economy needs real rates that are substantially less than zero right now to spur borrowing and spending. That is, households and businesses are so reluctant to borrow and spend, and so determined to save, that only negative interest rates (which would make borrowing attractive and saving a bad bargain) will convince them to do otherwise. Deflation pushes real rates up and, since the Fed is at the zero bound on nominal rates, it can't do anything about deflation driving real rates up and possibly choking off demand for borrowing and spending.

Third, falling prices lead to a rise in the effective burden of many kinds of debt. Much debt (say mortgages) is denominated in fixed dollars. When inflation leads to a rise in the overall price level (including wages and salaries, which are just one kind of price in the economy), fixed-dollar debts become smaller relative to other prices (including salaries). Conversely, deflation in overall prices (including wages and salaries) will increase the burden of fixed debt and will lead to a crowding out of other types of spending. Again, the economy needs spending right now, so crowding out of spending through the debt-deflation effect is dangerous.

Given the dangers posed by deflation, the small possibility that aggressive recession-fighting policies (like another stimulus package, for example) may generate a bit of inflation is worth the risk. In fact, there are reasons why moderate inflation in the next three to five years could be a good thing for the U.S. economy. For one, a problem in the economy at the moment is that both households and firms remain stuck under prior debt. As inflation erodes the effective burden of debt, balance sheets improve. For another, researchers at the Federal Reserve have estimated that the U.S. economy needs real interest rates of roughly *minus* 5% to bring the economy back to full employment. Given that nominal rates cannot go below zero, moderate inflation is needed to pull down real rates close to this level. Since it is *expectations about future inflation* as much as current inflation rates that determine real interest rates, instilling economic expectations about moderate inflation in the next few years could be a great benefit to the U.S. economy.

BUDGET DEFICITS AND "GENERATIONAL FAIRNESS"

A common question asked in the past year regarding deficits is whether or not they have any direct link to conceptions of "generational fairness." The short answer to this question is simply 'no'. The longer answer is that to assess the effect of taking on debt today for living standards tomorrow, one must know the *health* of the economy when this debt was incurred as well as to what use the debt was put.

The textbook economic argument that government deficits can make our kids poorer is the straightforward case made before about the effect of rising deficits in a healthy economy. To recap, in a full-employment economy, rising deficits mean that the government competes with private borrowers for available savings in the market for loanable funds. This competition causes interest rates to rise and crowds out private investments. Since investments yield a larger capital stock for the economy, and since a larger capital stock leads to higher productivity, this crowding out carries the potential to hurt future generations by bequeathing to them a smaller capital stock and slower productivity growth. Because productivity provides the ceiling on how fast living standards can rise, budget deficits in a full-employment economy carry the potential to make our children poorer.

However, when resources are sitting idle there is no one to crowd out. Government debt incurred when the economy is in a severe recession is unlikely to spur interest rate increases and is likely to crowd in private investment by giving firms a reason (i.e., more consumers with spending power) to invest. Our children will be richer as a result of expansionary fiscal policy.

Yet even if the public debt did crowd out private investment, it's far from clear that our children will be poorer in the future. If the increase in public debt funded productive public investments (universal pre-kindergarten, for example, or mass transit systems that cut down greenhouse gas emissions and reduce the cost of commuting to work), then replacing private investment with public investment can create a more productive capital stock for our children. In any case, the new government borrowing over the past year and for the near future is not competing with private investors for scarce savings.

TODAY'S DEFICITS AND TOMORROW'S TAXES

Another angle of the generational fairness argument, besides the one that we're spending our children's inheritance, is that our spending will burden our children with taxes. It is true indeed that today's children will pay taxes as adults to service this debt. Yet they will also inherit the Treasury bonds and receive the interest payments financed by these higher taxes. And the increase in taxes on tomorrow's generation needed to finance this debt will be exactly offset by the increase in interest income that these taxes pay for. Of course, not everyone will own Treasury bills—they are a form of wealth that is held disproportionately by a select slice of households—yet everyone will have to pay taxes to finance paying off Treasury bill holders. If we find this objectionable, however, this is a strictly *intra*-generational issue.

BUDGET DEFICITS AND FOREIGN INDEBTEDNESS

Heard often over the past year is some variant of "who is paying for all of this stimulus?" The answer is, we are. The government is borrowing what the U.S. private sector is saving.

Private domestic savings in the United States have expanded *faster* than government borrowing in the past year. **Figure 2.19**, which charts borrowing as a share of GDP for the last half century, shows private-sector borrowing to be at a historic low—in fact, it's negative, meaning that people are saving—while federal government borrowing is at a historic high. There is no shortage of people

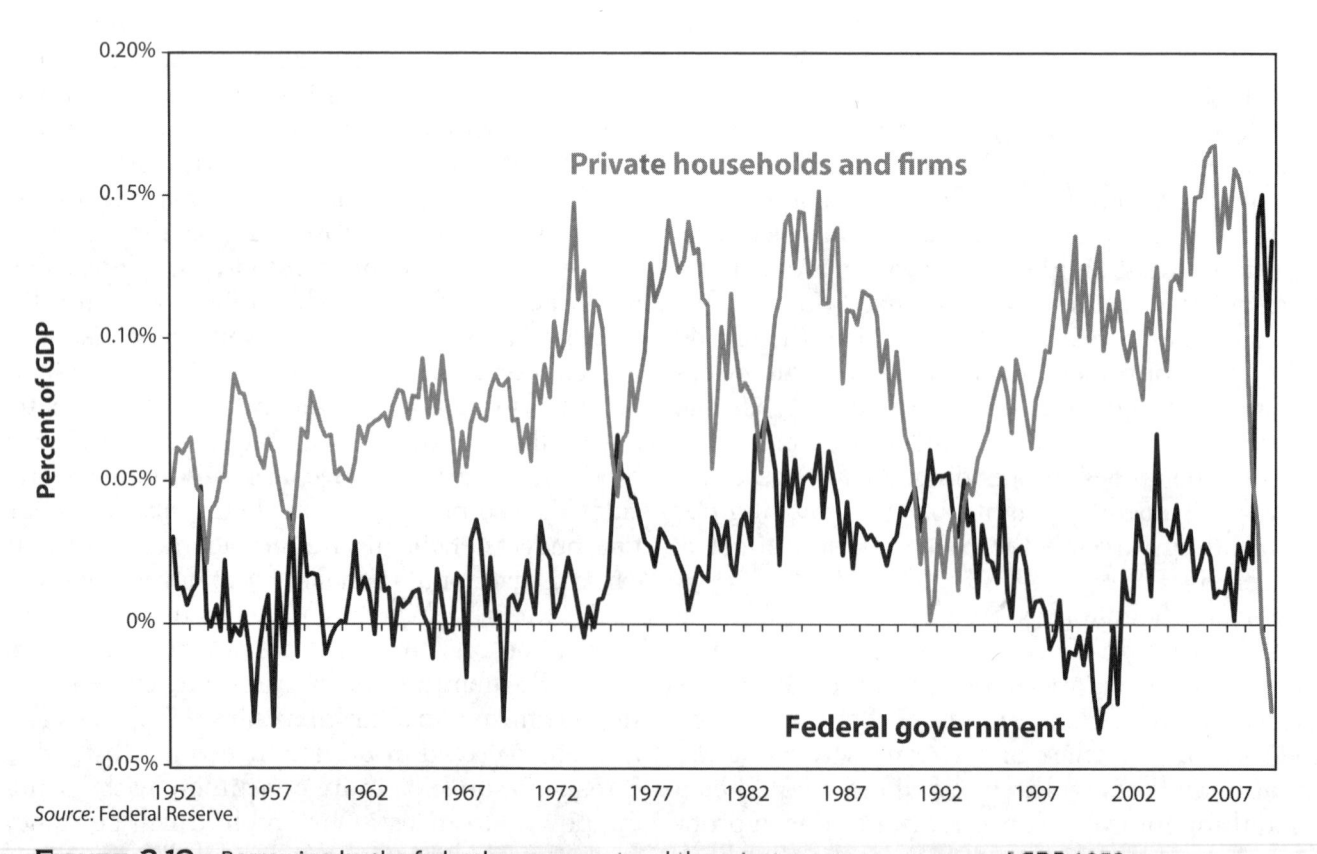

FIGURE 2.19 Borrowing by the federal government and the private sector, as percent of GDP, 1952-present

willing to hold government debt; rather, the problem is the shortage of people who want to incur debt in order to undertake spending. The problem that the stimulus package is trying to solve is that American households and businesses are *saving too much relative to investment demand*. In this situation, the deficits associated with the Recovery Act will find ready domestic financing in the near term.

A REAL CONCERN FOR GENERATIONAL FAIRNESS: THE TRADE DEFICIT

While domestic savings have been sufficient to finance new government borrowing over the past year, the outstanding stock of government bonds issued to cover past deficits is tradeable in global financial markets, and currently about half of this stock is held by foreigners. Interest payments on debt held by foreign investors leak out of the domestic economy and reduce national income.

However, the problem of international indebtedness is not a problem of the budget deficit, and those worried that deficits today mean foregone claims to income tomorrow need to focus on the another deficit: the trade deficit.

To illustrate this issue, take as an example the case where a government runs a large budget deficit but exactly balances its trade flows (the United States in 1991 had a budget deficit of 4.5% of GDP and a trade deficit of 0.45%, not far from this case), and assume that the entire federal budget deficit is financed by domestic residents. Taxes to service the addition to debt will fall on domestic residents, but they'll also receive the interest payments made with these higher taxes. In short, there is no effect on international indebtedness (the debt is wholly owned by domestic residents) and no effect on generational equity (in every generation the net effect of higher taxes and increased interest income will completely cancel out).

Now, take as an example a country with a balanced federal budget, or even a surplus, and a large trade deficit—the United States in the late 1990s, for example. In this case, because the country is importing more than it is exporting and because imports (like every other economic good or service) must be paid for, the difference between imports and exports must be made up by transferring ownership of U.S.-based assets to foreign investors. These assets can be the stock of currently outstanding Treasury bills (i.e., the debt of the federal government), equity stakes or debt of private companies, or a mix of the two. But, in this case, because something of value *today* was enjoyed by U.S. residents (the excess of imports over exports), these residents have given up claims on income generated *tomorrow* (the return to the assets whose ownership was transferred abroad).

In short, running a trade deficit (unlike a budget deficit) means that current generations are supporting their living standards at the expense of future generations. For those troubled by generational equity, it is the trade deficit, not the budget deficit, that should be the target.

ARE BUDGET DEFICITS AND TRADE DEFICITS RELATED?

In the early 1980s, a concurrent increase in both the trade and federal budget deficits led to much talk about the "twin deficits" of the U.S. economy. A simple story of causality was formulated which held that large federal budget deficits lead directly to large trade deficits. The theory behind this story was that budget deficits in an economy with no idle resources lead to a rise in interest rates as governments compete with private borrowers for loanable funds. These higher interest rates make dollar-denominated assets a better investment than assets denominated in other currencies, and foreign investors will hence shift more of their purchases toward these dollar-denominated assets. This subsequently bids up the price for dollars, causing the value of the U.S. dollar to rise. A rising dollar makes U.S. exports more expensive on global markets and makes foreign imports into the U.S. market cheap. As we export less and import more as a result, the trade deficit rises.

This story, however, is nor persuasive as an explanation of why the United States has been running sustained trade deficits for almost the past two decades. Between 1996 and 2001, the federal budget balance as a share of GDP actually improved by almost 2 percentage points (it rose from deficit to surplus) while the trade deficit deteriorated by more than 2 percentage points (**Figure 2.20**). And since the beginning of 2006 the federal budget deficit has grown by over 5 percentage points of GDP while the trade balance improved by almost 4 percentage points.

So, since the early and mid-1990s the movement of trade and federal budget deficits do not coincide nearly enough to make much of a causal

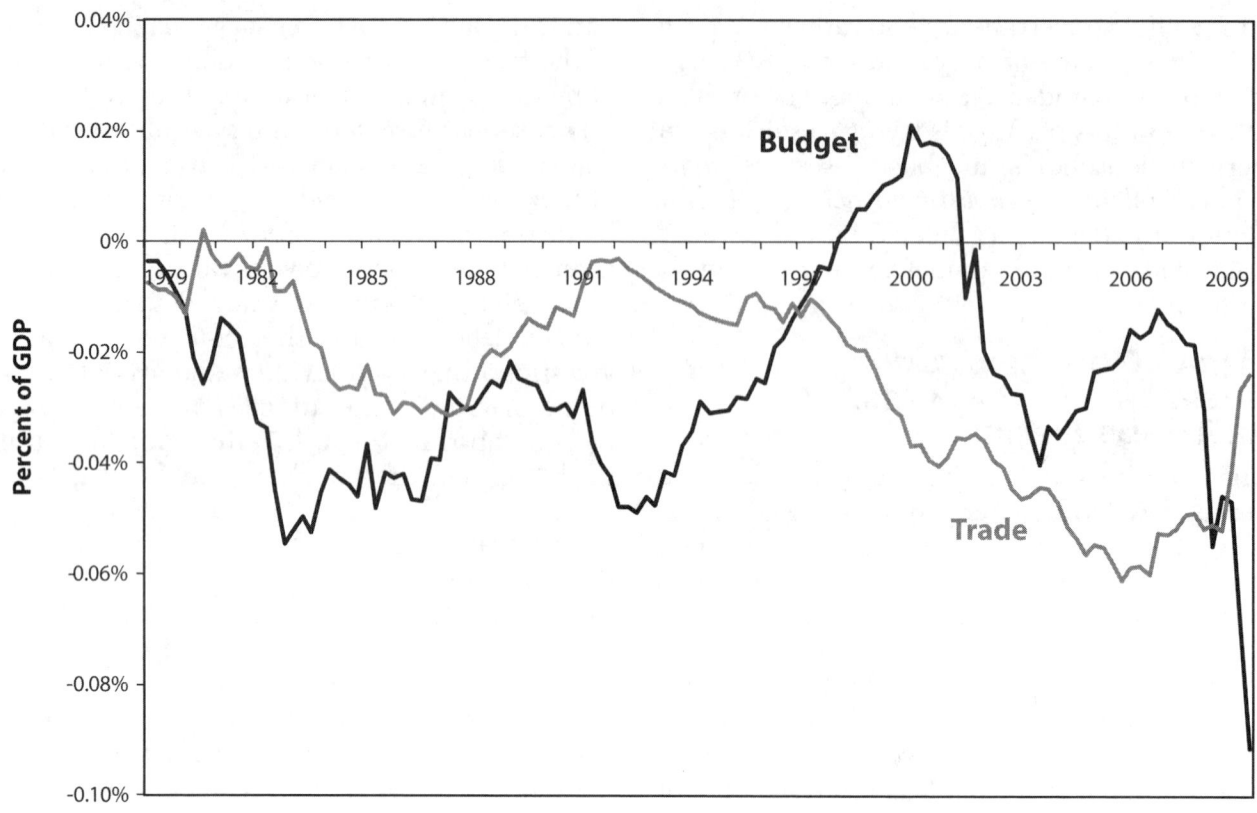

FIGURE 2.20 Trade and federal budget deficits as percent of GDP, 1979-present

Source: Bureau of Economic Analysis.

THE ROLE OF BORROWING IN CAUSING THE RECESSION AND IMPLICATIONS FOR DEFICITS

link between budget deficits and trade deficits.[3] It's past time to retire the twin deficits story.

While excessive private-sector borrowing (and lending, it needs to be remembered) played a role in generating the recession, it does not follow that boosting public debt is the wrong thing to do in response.

The problem facing the U.S. economy right now is deficient private demand: spending on consumption goods, investment goods, and foreign spending on U.S. exports all cratered in the past year, fallout from the bursting housing bubble and the resulting global economic slowdown. As households and businesses pull back on spending, private demand for goods and services is insufficient to sustain the number of jobs the economy had before the recession. The result has been the massive job loss of the past year-and-a-half.

When private-sector demand growth (either consumption spending, business investment, or exports) is too weak to sustain employment, public demand can and should be increased through expansionary fiscal policy. Expansionary fiscal policy is, by definition, *increasing* government borrowing, either by cutting taxes or increasing government spending, or both. This increase in borrowing injects demand into the economy (either directly through government spending or indirectly by raising private purchasing power through tax cuts and/or transfer payments) and helps offset the employment loss caused by the pullback in private demand.

When the federal government undertakes expansionary fiscal policy during a recession, it is borrowing at precisely the time when it is not competing with households and businesses for loanable funds (and both household and business demands for new borrowing have plummeted in recent years, as seen earlier in Figure 2.19). A rough rule of thumb is that the federal government should try to offset what the private sector is doing in regards to building up or running down debt. When private-sector borrowing is rising rapidly, federal government borrowing should decline. Growing private-sector borrowing generally means private spending is increasing, so demand from the government is less necessary to sustain a full-employment economy. Falling private-sector borrowing generally means that private spending is contracting, so demand from the government is necessary to forestall (or shorten) an economic slowdown.

When the private sector began excessive borrowing during the housing bubble of the early and mid-2000s, the government should not have responded with the 2001 and 2003 tax cuts that massively increased deficits (that these tax cuts were regressive and poorly designed even for short-run purposes are extra reasons why they should not have been passed). However, just because this rough rule of thumb was not followed under the Bush administration doesn't mean that it should be thrown out the window. As private-sector borrowing and spending plummeted over the past year-and-a-half, it was good policy for the government to step up its borrowing and spending to avert (or at least shorten) the resulting recession and rise in unemployment.

Of course, there are many other tools besides government borrowing and saving that can be used to target economic stability. For example, when the private sector (mostly banks and other financial institutions, but private households too) borrowed too much and became over-leveraged during the 2000s expansion, the fault of policy makers was both failing to stem the growth of private-sector borrowing and failing to offset it with borrowing and spending policies. For example, caps on leverage at financial institutions would have inhibited risky lending, and households could have been clearly warned by policy makers about the imminent danger of a collapse in housing prices.

In any case, regardless of what causes a recession, even if it is excessive borrowing, it is almost always proper for fiscal policy to become *more* expansionary during the downturn.

Recovering from Earlier Recessions without 'Stimulus Packages'

The quickest lever than can be pulled when fighting recessions is the Fed's lowering of the short-term interest rates it controls; fiscal policy demands full congressional debate and presidential support and hence takes longer to implement. But the impact of lowered rates has a long lag time (12-18 months), even in a healthy economy. And in today's particularly weak economy interest rate cuts even to zero have had little effect, since one of the primary transmission mechanisms through which cuts usually spur economic activity is increased home sales and home building (the other key transmission mechanism is rising business investment). After the deflation of the housing bubble, the housing sector is unlikely to be an engine of growth anytime soon, regardless of what happens to interest rates.

This situation is in stark contrast to the early 1980s and early 1990s recessions, both of which were caused at least in part by the Fed *raising* interest rates. Given that the economy entered these recessions with relatively high and rising interest rates, the Fed had lots of room to cut rates to try to spur recovery (in the early 1980s, the federal funds rate reached 20%). This time, the economy has entered the recession with rates already pressed down to zero (**Figure 2.21**).

Accidental Stimuli

However, though there were no explicit stimulus policies in these earlier period, policy-driven increases in federal deficits amounted to de facto stimulus packages during both the 1980s and 2000s recessions. In both cases they took the form of large, regressive tax cuts and increased military spending. And in both cases the policies were advocated before recessions hit—they were ideologically driven tax cuts that happened to coincide with recessions, or accidental stimuli that provided economic stimulus nevertheless. The 1981 and 2001 tax cuts reduced federal revenues by an amount equal to 3.6% and 1.4% of GDP, respectively, in the two years after their enactment. This is a substantial fiscal impulse—the Recovery Act will add roughly 1.4% to the economy in 2009.

The tax cuts of the early 1980s and 2000s created slightly smaller deficits during the recession and immediate after-math than will likely be created by ARRA. Further, neither of these tax cut packages were constructed in a good way if short-run recovery was the goal. For stimulus spending to be most effective, government should spend money directly on public investments and relief, or enact tax cuts and transfers directed to the households that are the most cash-strapped and therefore the most likely to spend the money quickly. (**Figure 2.22** uses data from Moody's Economy.com to illustrate the economic

CHAPTER 2 Economic Policy

SOURCE: Federal Reserve.

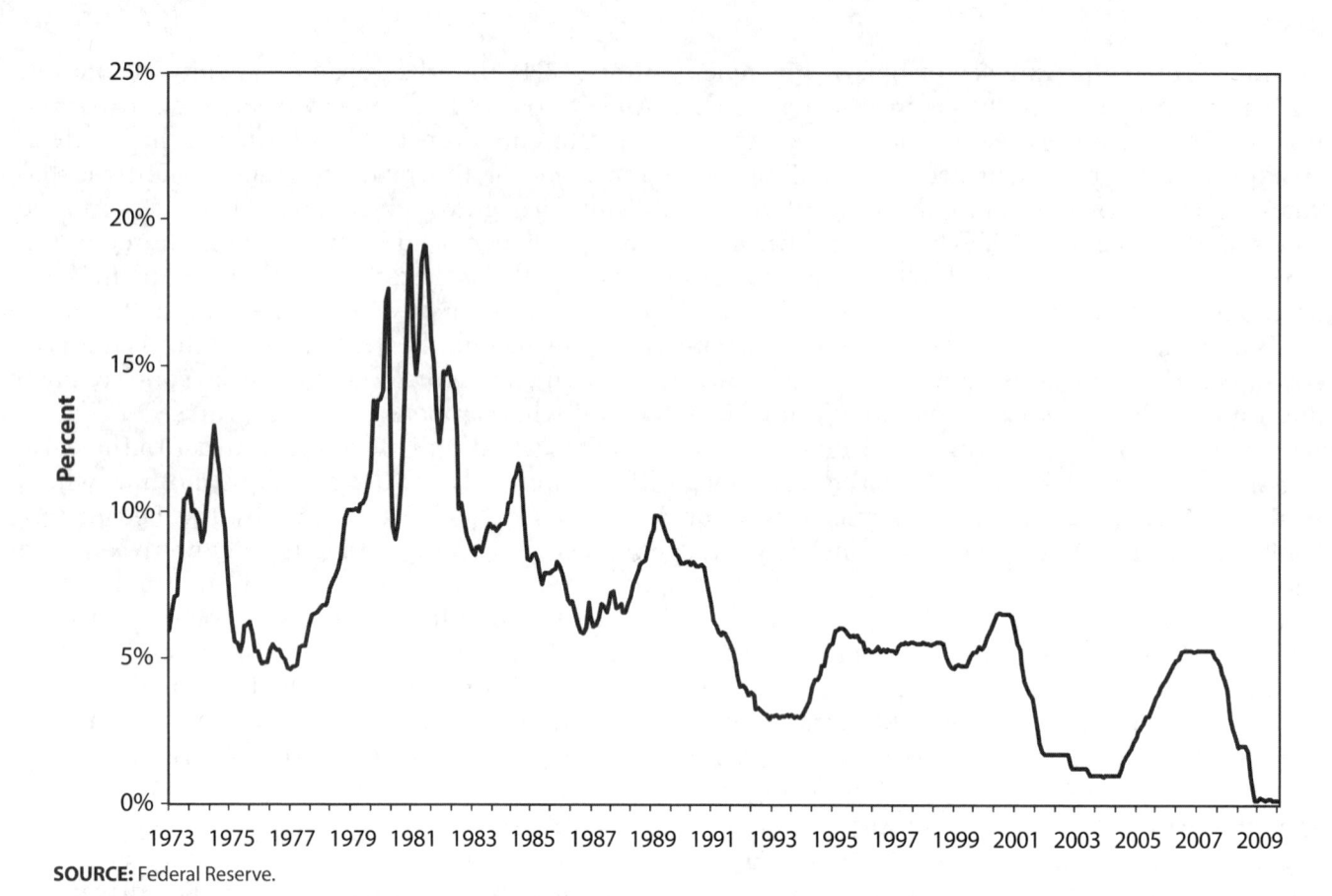

FIGURE 2.21 Federal funds rate, 1973-present

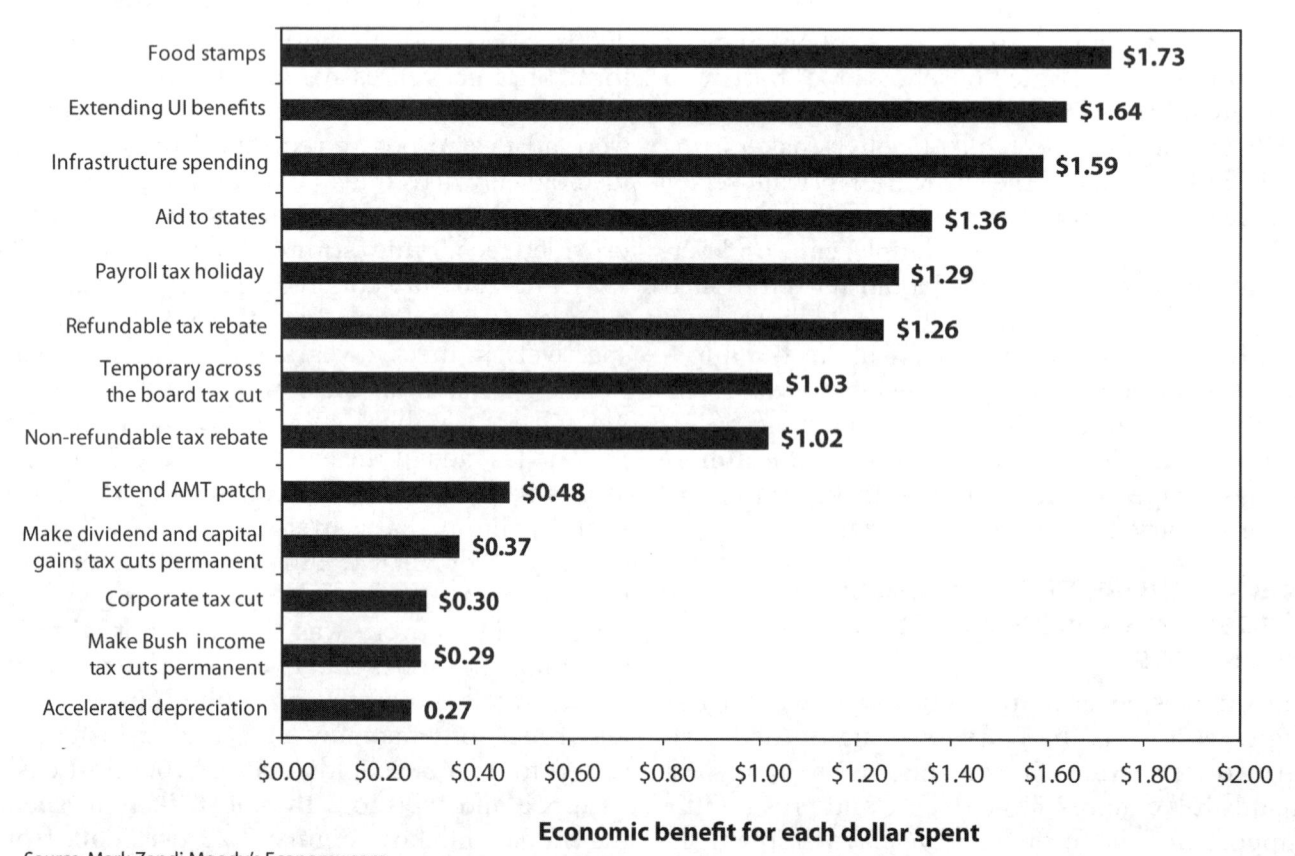

Category	Economic benefit
Food stamps	$1.73
Extending UI benefits	$1.64
Infrastructure spending	$1.59
Aid to states	$1.36
Payroll tax holiday	$1.29
Refundable tax rebate	$1.26
Temporary across the board tax cut	$1.03
Non-refundable tax rebate	$1.02
Extend AMT patch	$0.48
Make dividend and capital gains tax cuts permanent	$0.37
Corporate tax cut	$0.30
Make Bush income tax cuts permanent	$0.29
Accelerated depreciation	0.27

Economic benefit for each dollar spent

Source: Mark Zandi Moody's Economy.com.

FIGURE 2.22 Economic benefits of $1 of stimulus spending

stimulus created from $1 of government spending in various areas.) Neither the 1980s nor the 2000s tax cuts followed this rule. Further, the tax cuts in the 1980s were enacted while the Federal Reserve was raising interest rates, and so much of the beneficial impact of tax cuts was neutralized by the Fed.

Finally, because the 1980s and 2000s tax cuts were poorly designed as stimulus, they did little for the economy but still continued to add to federal budget deficits well after the recession was over—in other words, they were not temporary responses to a crisis. By contrast, the Recovery Act's direct draw on revenues will have almost entirely wound down by the end of 2011. This may be too short a lifespan for the stimulus package, since labor markets may still be slack by the end of 2011. The CBO projects that unemployment at the end of 2011 will be 9.1%, nearly twice the 4.9% rate that prevailed before the recession.

Conclusion

Worries about deficit spending, misplaced when the economy is weak, usually peak at precisely the wrong time.

In 2001 the Congressional Budget Office projected that in fiscal year 2008 the federal government would have a $635 billion surplus. Instead it had a $459 billion deficit. The $1 trillion-plus difference between projection and reality was almost entirely the result of policy decisions to enact tax cuts, fight two wars, and provide a Medicare prescription drug benefit. Yet at no time were there any serious calls, as there are today during the worst financial crisis in most of our lifetimes, to impanel a deficit commission to look at the budget problem.

The Obama administration is not doing anything radical in using policy-driven increases in the deficit to fight the recession. When the economy is weak and capacity is sitting idle, hawkish opposition to deficits holds the nation's prosperity hostage to ideology that has no grounding in basic, common-sense economics. Besides not being particularly radical, enacting large policy-driven increases in the deficit as the economy enters recession is common—both the Reagan and the second Bush administrations undertook large expansionary fiscal policy changes. The true danger that current stimulus policies pose to the economy in coming years is that they will be too small to fund the public relief and investments that are necessary to ensure a sustained recovery.

Economic Stimulus Pushed by Flawed Jobs Analysis

Curtis Dubay, Karen Campbell, Ph.D., and Paul Winfree

A recently released report by Christina Romer, chair of the President's Council of Economic Advisers, and Jared Bernstein, the Vice President's chief economist, is being widely cited by Administration officials (including the President) and Members of Congress as proof that the stimulus package currently being debated in Congress—especially the spending portion—will actually stimulate the economy.

The Romer–Bernstein report finds that the stimulus plan will create about 3.7 million jobs and reduce the unemployment rate by about two percentage points from where it would have been without the stimulus by the fourth quarter of 2010.[1] The report is supposed to lend academic creditability to a plan based on political considerations, but the estimates created are founded on loose assumptions that lack academic rigor. The report should not be relied upon as an accurate measure of the impact of the Obama fiscal stimulus plan because it relies on rules of thumb and other back-of-the envelope calculations rather than sound economic analysis.

Wrong Multipliers

Romer and Bernstein estimate how much government spending and tax cuts will increase production, or gross domestic product (GDP). To do so, they use what economists refer to as a multiplier. The multiplier is the amount that a change in government spending or tax cuts will increase GDP. For instance, a multiplier of one means that a $1 increase in government spending results in a $1 increase in GDP. A multiplier greater than one means that a spending increase or tax cut has secondary effects that further boost GDP. The secondary effects occur as the original money makes its way though the economy and businesses hire more employees or increase their pay, buy new inventory, or invest to expand operations.

The Romer and Bernstein multipliers for government spending and tax cuts were estimated by the Federal Reserve's FRB/US model and a leading private forecasting firm.[2] They settle on a multiplier of approximately 1.5 for government spending and about 0.99 for tax cuts.[3] This would suggest that for every dollar the government spends, GDP increases $1.50, while every dollar in lower government taxes increases GDP by just under a dollar. Romer and Bernstein, however, are uncertain of the multipliers and note as much in the report: "We confess to considerable uncertainty about our choice of multipliers for this element of the package."[4]

Romer and Bernstein are right to be uncertain of the multiplier they use, especially the spending multiplier. Economists generally estimate the size of the spending multiplier in their analyses by looking at historically *similar* experiences. Romer and Bernstein, however, rely on a model based on historical data that is not comparable to current economic conditions, because an increase in government spending as large as this one has never been tried as a stimulus before.

---

1. Christina Romer and Jared Bernstein, "The job Impact of the American Recovery and Reinvestment Plan," Office of the President-elect, p. 4, January 9, 2009, at *http://otrans.3cdn.net/45593e8ecbd339d074_l3m6bt1te.pdf* (January 13, 2008).

2. *Ibid.*, p. 12.

3. Large U.S. economic structural forecasting models are based on estimated econometric relationships. For these models to work, demand and supply must equilibrate. For analytical traction, models in the Keynesian tradition typically adjust supply to demand, effectively assuming that demand creates its own supply. Therefore any direct increased spending will pull output up, thus overestimating the implied multiplier by ignoring some of the negative effects this would have on supply variables.

4. Romer and Bernstein, "The job Impact of the American Recovery and Reinvestment Plan," p. 12.

"Economic Stimulus Pushed by Flawed Jobs Analysis" by Curtis Dubay, Karen Campbell, Ph.D., and Paul Winfree, from *WebMemo*, No. 2252, January 28, 2009, pp. 1-3, www.heritage.org/Research/Economy/wm252.cfm. Copyright © 2009 by The Heritage Foundation. Reprinted by permission.

Rather than take the time to estimate a more accurate multiplier, Romer and Bernstein use one estimated for much lower levels of spending and assume it applies to the massive spending program under analysis.

They then apply the spending multiplier to the proposed total spending in the stimulus package. They ignore the fact that the stimulus package contains spending on a variety of items—everything from money for the National Endowment for the Arts and new sod for national monuments to infrastructure spending. Romer and Bernstein, therefore, assume that all spending affects the economy equally.

A better back-of-the-envelope calculation would at least consider estimated multipliers from a range of different models and assumptions. Many economists have used a variety of methods and assumptions to estimate the size of multipliers for government spending and found them to be lower than those used by Romer and Bernstein.[5]

RULE OF THUMB

To estimate the number of jobs created by increased government spending, Romer and Bernstein multiply the amount of government spending in the stimulus plan by the multiplier discussed above. The outcome is the increase in GDP resulting from the increased spending. They then apply a "rule of thumb" that a 1 percent increase in GDP results in the creation of 1 million jobs.[6] They do not justify this rule by citing any empirical or theoretical research.

The "rule of thumb" is misused because it assumes that increases in GDP create jobs. In fact, the relationship is actually the other way around. Production and work create GDP, so it is more accurate to say that 1 million more jobs produce 1 percent more GDP.

AUTHORS UNCERTAIN

Romer and Bernstein's analysis is based on loose assumptions about the multiplier effects and inexact rules of thumb about job creation. It is no wonder they are uncertain of the results of their report:

It should be understood that all of the estimates presented in this memo are subject to significant margins of error. . . . Our estimates of economic relationships and rules of thumb are derived from historical experience and so will not apply exactly in any given episode. Furthermore, the uncertainty is surely higher than normal now because the current recession is unusual both in its fundamental causes and its severity.[7]

Romer and Bernstein are admitting that their methods are likely to lead to inaccurate results. The informal manner in which the analysis was conducted should give pause to anyone using the results of the report to support passage of the stimulus plan.

NOT TO BE TRUSTED

The Obama Administration and Members of Congress are relying on a flawed report as evidence of the effectiveness of the stimulus plan. The report should not be trusted. It is based on faulty assumptions that even the authors admit create significant margins of error. More rigorous research has shown that tax rate cuts will create millions of jobs and cost less than the Obama plan.[8] Taxpayers deserve better information before their money is spent on things that will not offer the return they were promised.

—*Curtis S. Dubay is a Senior Analyst in Tax Policy in the Thomas A. Roe Institute for Economic Policy Studies, Karen A. Campbell, Ph.D., is Policy Analyst in Macroeconomics, and Paul L. Winfree is a Policy Analyst in the Center for Data Analysis at The Heritage Foundation.*

---

5. Andrew Mountford and Harald Uhlig, in "What Are the Effects of Fiscal Policy Shocks?" (NBER Working Paper No. 14551, December 2008), have estimated the effects and compare these with other studies of various spending impacts. The competing multipliers are all less than one; see also Valerie A. Ramey, "Identifying Government Spending Shocks: It's All in the Timing," at *http://econ.ucsd.edu/~vramey/research/Identifying-Govt.pdf* (January 27, 2009); Christina D. Romer and David H. Romer, "The Macroeconomic Effects of Tax Changes: Estimates Based on a New Measure of Fiscal Shocks," NBER Working Paper No. 13264, July 2007; Robert Hall and Susan Woodward, "Measuring the Effect of Infrastructure Spending on GDP," Financial Crisis and Recession, December 11, 2008, at *http://woodwardhall.wordpress.com/2008/12/11/measuring-the-effect-of-infrastructure-spending-on-gdp* (January 27, 2009).

6. Romer and Bernstein, "The Job Impact of the American Recovery and Reinvestment Plan," p. 3.

7. *Ibid.*, p. 2.

8. See J. D. Foster and William W. Beach, "Economic Recovery: How Best to End the Recession," Heritage Foundation Web-Memo No. 2191, January 7, 2009, at *http://www.heritage.org/Research/Economy/wm2191.cfm.*

Economic Recovery: How Best to End the Recession

J. D. Foster, Ph.D., and William W. Beach

The economy has been in recession for over a year, contracted rapidly toward the end of 2008, and is likely to continue to contract through the first half of 2009 and possibly beyond. The new Administration and new Congress are developing a stimulus program to soften the recession and accelerate the recovery.

Given the high level of economic pain, policymakers need to pursue stimulus policies that work. The centerpiece of an effective stimulus policy should involve two elements:

1. Extend the 2001 and 2003 tax reductions for as long as possible—certainly through at least 2013 to prevent a tax increase. Better yet, make the tax reductions permanent; and
2. Reduce tax rates on individuals, small businesses, and corporations through 2013 by lowering the top rate by 10 percentage points and reducing rates by similar amounts for lower income level taxpayers.

According to analysis using The Heritage Foundation's mainstream model of the U.S. economy, relative to current law, these policies would:

- Soften the recession in 2009 and speed the economic recovery through 2010 and beyond;
- Increase employment by a half million jobs in 2009 and by 1.3 million jobs in 2010 and create 4.8 million jobs from 2009 through 2012; and
- Reduce federal tax receipts during the critical fiscal years of 2009 and 2011 by $636 billion.

The aggressive tax policy changes of Heritage's plan, plus the intensive activities of the Federal Reserve, are the best combination of federal policies to end or shorten recessions.[1] Further, whereas the Heritage tax plan would strengthen the economy, the types of tax proposals mentioned as part of the Obama stimulus would have almost no effect on the economy, the proposed increase in spending would have no effect on the overall economy whatsoever, and the resulting deficits would be of such unprecedented magnitudes as likely to trigger a recovery-stifling rise in interest rates. Thus, rather than increasing spending, Congress should reduce spending now and over the long-term through entitlement reform to reduce the upward pressure on interest rates.[2]

Focusing on What Works

The current recession is likely to be deep and may be more severe than any economic downturn since the Great Depression of the 1930s—call today's economic mess the "Great Recession." Fortunately, the economy and financial markets are working through their difficulties and will, eventually, stabilize and strengthen on their own. The economy will recover even absent an effective federal fiscal policy response. However, an effective tax policy response can meaningfully soften the recession and speed the recovery, which is no small feat to an individual looking for work.

Much of official Washington is focused on a big stimulus plan based predominantly on increased spending, possibly including an expanded infrastructure program plus aid to the states and to low-income families. Whatever the merits of these programs on other policy grounds might be, they would not stimulate—

---

1. Christina Romer and David Romer, "What Ends Recessions?" NBER *Working Paper* No. 4765, June 1994.

2. For related discussions on effective stimulus policies, see Nicola Moore, "Economic Stimulus: Dos and Don'ts," Heritage Foundation *WebMemo* No. 2187, January 6, 2009, at *http://www.heritage.org/Research/Economy/wm2187.cfm*; Ronald D. Utt, "Learning from Japan: Infrastructure Spending Won't Boost the Economy," Heritage Foundation *Backgrounder* No. 2222, December 16, 2008, at *http://www.heritage.org/Research/Economy/bg2222.cfm*;, Brian Riedl, "Why Government Spending Doesn't Stimulate Economic Growth," Heritage Foundation *Backgrounder* No. 2208, November 8, 2008, at *http://www.heritage.org/Research/Budget/bg2208.cfm*.

"Economic Recovery: How Best to End the Recession" by J.D. Foster, Ph.D., and William W. Beach, from *WebMemo*, No. 2191, January 7, 2009, revised and updated January 26, 2009, pp. 1-3, www.heritage.org/Research/Economy/wm2191.cfm. Copyright © 2009 by The Heritage Foundation. Reprinted by permission.

and indeed are likely to weaken—the economy in the near term.

The American economy does not rise and fall with the level of aggregate demand or deficit spending. Further, government cannot simply pump up total demand through deficit spending. The deficit for 2009 is already projected to exceed $1 trillion, so if deficit spending were effective, the economy should already be poised to take off.

Yet the economy is contracting despite these unprecedented deficits because government spending in excess of tax revenues will be financed by borrowing from the private sector, which deprives the private sector of a like amount of purchasing power. In short, deficit-financed government spending goes up and private spending goes down, changing the composition of demand but not the total.

Focusing on demand in this way is like focusing on the sound of one hand clapping. The other hand is supply, and that is where the economic action really is. There are normal processes that launch a recovery and drive an economy. These processes involve individuals and businesses responding to opportunities and incentives. When they respond, these individuals and businesses produce more goods and services valued in the marketplace, simultaneously increasing production, demand, and income. An effective stimulus policy recognizes these economic processes and seeks to accelerate them. Lower marginal tax rates stimulate the economy because they improve the incentives facing individuals and businesses to work, invest, take risks, and seize opportunities.

Step One: Extend the 2001 and 2003 Tax Cuts at Least through 2013

The economy faces a massive tax hike in 2011 when the tax relief enacted in 2001 and 2003 expires. President Obama has suggested he would prevent most of this tax hike but not the increase in top marginal tax rates, the increase in the dividend and capital gains tax rates, and the return of the death tax. That policy view is highly unfortunate: It is difficult for the economy to gain its footing when facing the threat of a punitive tax hike. There will be time enough to debate the progressivity of tax policy when the economy recovers fully. The focus now must be on speeding the recovery itself, and extending current policy in its entirety is the first step. It is, however, a policy of avoiding harm, and so it is only a necessary first step.

Step Two: Reduce Marginal Tax Rates for Individuals and Businesses

Reduce the top tax rates on individuals, small businesses, and corporations by 10 percentage points through 2013, and reduce the individual income tax rates to three levels: 10, 15, and 25 percent. In addition, as part of this second step:

- The Alternative Minimum Tax should be repealed; and
- The death tax rate reduced to 15 percent with a $5 million individual exclusion.

President Obama and Congress may want to consider additional tax elements to build on this foundation, such as expanding bonus depreciation for small businesses, but these additional elements cannot match rate reductions as sound and effective tax policy.

According to analysis performed at the Center for Data Analysis at The Heritage Foundation using the widely respected Global Insight U.S. Macroeconomic Model,[3] these policy changes would strengthen the economy significantly this year. Compared to the economy's trajectory absent a stimulus policy adopting the Heritage tax proposal would mean that 493,000 more Americans have jobs by the end of 2009, and, by the end of 2010, employment would increase by 1.3 million jobs. Over this same two-year period, these tax policy changes would add an additional $187 billion in GDP and increase the economy's otherwise sluggish growth rate by six-tenths of a percentage point.

This two-step tax policy would reduce tax receipts relative to current policy by about $640 billion over three years. This figure results from the fact that new growth in jobs and output would expand the tax base for personal income taxes by an average of $204 billion and corporate income taxes by an average of $51 billion per year over this critical three-year period, thereby significantly reducing the net tax loss to the Treasury.

---

3. For information about the details and operation of the Global Insight U.S. Macroeconomic Model, see "Description of the Global Insight Short-Term US Macroeconomic Model," at *http://www.heritage.org/cda/upload/globalinsightmodel.pdf*.

Economic recovery does not come from Washington, but Washington can help. Economic recovery is achieved by the economy itself, and Washington's effective help moves that process along at a swifter pace. By far the most effective means of helping the economy recover is to improve the incentives that drive economic activity, and that means reducing tax rates on work, saving, investment, risk taking, and entrepreneurial activity.

—*J. D. Foster, Ph.D., is Norman B. Ture Senior Fellow in the Economics of Fiscal Policy in the Thomas A. Roe Institute for Economic Policy Studies, and William W. Beach is Director of the Center for Data Analysis, at The Heritage Foundation.*

QUESTIONS FOR DISCUSSION

1. In what way has history provided a test for Keynes and a theory of government spending? Was it conclusive?
2. What kinds of problems do large budget deficits pose for the nation's economy? What are the different problems in the short run as opposed to the long run?
3. "Budgets are a serious problem." What additional information does a policy analyst need to make an assessment of this statement?
4. Why are investments critical in determining the level of prosperity?
5. Is a balanced-budget amendment a wise policy? Why or why not?
6. What alternative tax policies are available to the government? What are the positives and negatives associated with each?
7. What are the characteristics of a "good" tax system? Why are vertical and horizontal equity important?

USEFUL WEBSITES

American Enterprise Institute, http://www.aei.org.

Center on Budget and Policy Priorities, http://www.cbpp.org.

Congressional Budget Office, http://www.cbo.gov.

Brookings Institution, http://www.brookings.edu.

Economic Policy Institute, http://www.epinet.org.

Heritage Foundation, http://www.heritage.org.

National Bureau of Economic Research, http//:www.nber.org.

Office of Management and Budget, http://www.access.gpo.gov/usbudget.

Office of Tax Policy, U.S. Treasury, http://www.ustreas.gov/taxpolicy.

Organization for Economic Cooperation and Development (OECD), http://www.oecd.org.

Social Security Administration, http://www.sss.gov.

SUGGESTED READINGS

Auerbach, Alan J., and William G. Gale. "Tax Cuts and the Budget." *Tax Notes* 90 (2001).

Auerbach, Alan J., and Kevin A. Hassett. "Uncertainty and Design of Long-Run Fiscal Policy." In Alan J. Auerbach and Ronald D. Lee, eds., *Demographic Change and Fiscal Policy*. Cambridge: Cambridge University Press, 2001.

Burman, Leonard E., William G. Gale, Jeffrey Rohaly, and Benjamin H. Harris. *The Individual AMT: Problems and Potential Solutions*. Urban-Brookings Tax Policy. Center Discussion Paper no. 5. Washington, D.C.: Brookings Institution, September 2002.

Congressional Budget Office. *The Budget and Economic Outlook: Fiscal Years 2003–2010*. Washington, D.C.: U.S. Government Printing Office, 2002.

Gale, William, and Peter Orszag. *The Economic Effects of Long-Term Fiscal Discipline*. Urban-Brookings Tax Policy Center Discussion Paper no. 100. Washington, D.C. Brookings Institution, December 2002.

Kamin, David, and Isaac Shapiro. *Studies Shed New Light on Effects of Administration Tax Cuts*. Washington, D.C.: Center on Budget and Policy Priorities, 2004.

Kogan, Richard. *How to Avoid Over-Committing the Available Surplus: Would a Tax-Cut. "Trigger" Be*

Effective or Is There a Better Way? Washington, D.C.: Center on Budget and Policy Priorities, 2001.

Shoven, John B. "The Impact of Major Life Expectancy Improvements on the Financing of Social Security, Medicare, and Medicaid." In Henry J. Aaron and William B. Schwartz eds., *Creating Methuselah: Molecular Medicine and the Problems of an Aging Society*. Washington, D.C.: Brookings Institution, 2003.

Notes

1. Reagan held that his agenda would stimulate such economic growth that enough tax revenues would be created to balance the budget by 1984. Starting with Reagan's assumption and working backward, former' budget director David Stockman hastily put together a five-year plan openly referred to as the "Rosy Scenario." Stockman and his colleagues' secret calculations showed the deficit rising dramatically, but in public he insisted that his Rosy Scenario projections were valid. Later in his memoirs, Stockman stated that he "out-and-out cooked the books," inventing spurious cuts to make the deficit appear smaller. See David Stockman, *The Triumph of Politics* (New York: Harper and Row, 1986), p.383.
2. Thomas Willett and King Banaian, "Models of the Political Process and Their Implications for Stagflation: A Public Choice Perspective," in Thomas D. Willett, ed., *Political Business Cycles: The Political Economy of Money, Inflation, and Unemployment* (Durham, N.C.: Duke University Press, 1988).
3. Organization for Economic Cooperation and Development, *Revenue Statistics 1965–2003* (OECD), *p. 18.*
4. The decline in sales resulting from the tax that is not offset by the tax revenue generated is referred to as a "deadweight loss," in that no one gets the money. Since a small number of voters buy cigarettes and alcohol, the price increase will not significantly affect sales. A much larger number of voters buy gas, but the political cost to an elected official of a tax on petroleum is acceptable because the deadweight losses are minimal and because the tax burden on each voter is relatively small.
5. See http://www.treas.gov/education/fact-sheets/taxes/economics.shtml, p. 3.
6. George Gilder, *Wealth and Poverty* (New York: Basic Books, 1981), p. 188.
7. Ibid.
8. An interesting tax loophole is the federal tax-exempt status of state and municipal bonds. Tax-exempt bonds are a curiosity peculiar to the United States. They are a remnant of the doctrine of state sovereignty, which originally held that the salaries of state employees must be free from federal tax. States fiercely resist any suggestion of elimination of the tax-free status because of the resulting increase in the cost of their borrowing.
9. William G. Gale, *Tax Reform Is Dead, Long Live Tax Reform*, Brookings Policy Brief no. 12 (Washington, D.C.: Brookings Institution, 2004).
10. Ibid.
11. Budget deficits declined each year of the Clinton administration and turned a surplus in 1998. In 1998 through 2001, tax revenues as a percentage of GDP were 20 percent, 20 percent, 20.9 percent, and 19.8 percent respectively. Outlays as a percentage of GDP for the same years were 19.2 percent, 18.6 percent, 18.4 percent, and 18.6 percent respectively. See *The Budget and Economic Outlook: Fiscal Years 2005–2014* (Washington, D.C.: U.S. Government Printing Office, January 26, 2004), Historic Budget Data, app. F, tab. 2.
12. Congressional Budget Office, *Effective Federal Tax Rates Under Current Law: 2001–2004* (Washington, D.C.: U.S. Government Printing Office, August 2004).
13. William G. Gale and Peter R. Orszag, "Tax Notes," in William G. Gale and Peter R. Orszag, *Bush Administration Tax Policy: Summary and Outlook* (Washington, D.C.: Brookings Institution, November 29, 2004), p. 1280. Gale and Orszag produced eight papers analyzing and evaluating different aspects of the Bush administration's tax policy during his first term. They are an excellent resource for anyone interested in the ramifications of tax policy.
14. The Economic Policy Institute found that by September 2004, the number of jobs created after the tax cuts fell 2,668,000 short of administration predictions made in 2003. The 1.6 million jobs created constituted just 38 percent of the administration's projection. See Economic Policy Institute, "Job Watch: Tracking Jobs and Wages," http://www.job watch.org. Also referenced in David Kamin and Isaac Shapiro, *Studies Shed New Light on Effects of Administration's Tax Cuts* (Washington, D.C.: Center on Budget and Policy. Priorities, 2004), p. 2.

15. Mark M. Zandi, "Assessing President Bush's Fiscal Policies," http://www.economy.com, July 2004. Also referenced in Kamin and Shapiro, *Studies*, p. 6.
16. Gale and Orszag, "Tax Notes," p. 1281.
17. Kamin and Shapiro, *Studies*, p. 2.
18. Ibid., p.11.
19. Gale and Orszag, "Tax Notes," p. 1282.
20. Dan McGill, Kyle Brown, John Haley, and Sylvester Schieber, *Fundamentals of Private Pensions*, 7th ed. (Philadelphia: University of Pennsylvania Press, 1996), p.5.
21. U.S. Census Bureau, *Statistical Abstract 2003* (Washington, D.C.: U.S. Government Printing Office, 2003), pp. 847, 857. See also *Current Population Survey for 2000*. The participation rate for women in the labor force has increased dramatically. The average age of withdrawal from the labor force for women is 63.4 years, with a life expectancy of an additional 20.4 years.
22. U.S. Census Bureau, *Statistical Abstract 2003*, p. 857.
23. *OASDI Trustees Report 2004*, tab. VI.F.
24. On this point, see Allen W. Smith, *The Looting of Social Security* (New York Carroll and Graf, 2003).
25. Congressional Budget Office, *The Outlook for Social Security* (Washington, D.C.: U.S. Government Printing Office, June 2004).
26. Jonathan Weisman, "Revamping Social Security," *Washington Post*, January 2005, p. A8.
27. Ibid.
28. Edmund L. Andrew, "Bush Puts Social Security at Top of Economic Conference. *New York Times*, December 16, 2004.
29. Dean Baker and Mark Weisbrot, *Social Security: The Phony Crisis* (Chicago University of Chicago Press, 1999).
30. Quoted in Weisman, "Revamping Social Security," p. A8.
31. Robert Greenstein, *So-Called "Price Indexing" Proposal Would Result in Deep Reductions over Time in Social Security Benefits* (Washington, D.C.: Center on Budget and Policy Priorities, December 21, 2004), p. 2.
32. Ibid., p. 4. See also Congressional Budget Office, *Long-Term Analysis of Plan 2 of the President's Commission to Strengthen Social Security* (Washington, D.C.: U.S. Government Printing Office, July 21, 2004; updated September 30, 2004), tab. 2. Under the current formula the worker's annual earnings for each of his or her thirty-five highest-earning years are averaged and divided by twelve. The result is the worker's "average indexed monthly earnings." The individual's benefit is then determined essentially as (at full retirement age): 90 percent of the worker's first $612 of average indexed monthly earnings, plus 32 percent of average monthly earnings between $623 and $3,689 (if the worker's earnings were that high), and 15 percent of any average monthly earnings covered above that. The worker's benefit level is determined at the time the worker retires. And the worker's benefit is then adjusted in each succeeding year in accordance with the annual change in the CPI (the measure of the average change in consumer prices over a period of time in a fixed market basket of goods and services).

In the proposed price-indexing method, the 90, 32, and 15 percent factors would be multiplied by the ratio of the percentage change in the CPI to the percentage change in average wages over the previous twelve months (wages usually rise faster than prices). The result is that if prices rise by 3 percent and wages rise by 4 percent in a year, the worker's standard of living rises by 1 percent. Under this formula the ratio would be 1.03 divided by 1.04, or 0.99 percent. See Greenstein, *So-Called "Price Indexing,"* p. 4.
33. Greenstein, *So-Called "Price Indexing,"* p. 4.
34. Congressional Budget Office, *Administrative Costs of Private Accounts in Social Security* (Washington, D.C.: U.S. Government Printing Office, March 2004).
35. Paul Krugman, "Buying into Failure," *New York Times*, December 17, 2004, p. A35.
36. Jason Furman, William G. Gale, and Peter R. Orszag, *Would Borrowing $2 Trillion for Individual Accounts Eliminate $10 Trillion in Social Security Liabilities?* (Washington, D.C.: Center on Budget and Policy Priorities, December 13, 2004).
37. Event Summary, *Saving Social Security: Which Way to Reform?* (Washington, D.C.: Brookings Institution, December 10, 2003).

REFERENCES

Auerbach, Alan, and William Gale. 2009. "An Update on the Economic and Fiscal Crises: 2009 and Beyond." Washington, D.C.: Brookings Institution.

Blecker, Robert. 1991. *Beyond the Twin Deficits*. Washington, D.C.: Economic Policy Institute.

Center on Budget and Policy Priorities. 2009. "How Legislation Enacted Since 2001 Contributed to Deficits Over 2001-2008." Washington, D.C.: CBPP. http://www.cbpp.org/research/index.cfm?fa=topic&id=29

Hatzius, Jan. 2009. Goldman Sachs daily research note, July 15.

Irons, John, Kathryn Edwards, and Anna Turner. 2009. "The 2009 Budget Deficit: How Did We Get Here?" Issue Brief No. 262. Washington, D.C.: Economic Policy Institute.

ENDNOTES

1. Much federal debt is actually owed to the government itself—most notably in the form of the Social Security Trust Fund.
2. Spending to augment human capital is also a productive investment, but in the macroeconomic statistical aggregates only investments in physical capital are measured and tracked.
3. Blecker (1991) noted that the simple twin deficits story was almost surely wrong even in the early 1980s, a time when the simple correlations held together.

chapter 3

Health Care Policy

Health Care Policy

Carter A. Wilson

Health care policy involves promoting public health and providing medical assistance to people who are injured, ill, or infirm. This policy had moved from the distributive to the redistributive policy category, as it shifted from one policy regime to the other. There were two major health care policy regimes of the 20th century: the solo doctor or Progressive regime and the Medicaid/Medicare regime. The solo doctor regime was characterized by public health, municipal and private nonprofit hospitals, and solo doctors. Local governments established public health departments to prevent epidemics and to promote public health. This was a distributive policy, as public health benefits the entire population.

The Medicare/Medicaid policy regime emerged out of the social movements of the 1960s. Medicaid is primarily for Temporary Assistance for Needy Families (TANF), Supplemental Security Income (SSI), and nursing home clients. Medicare is primarily for Social Security recipients. These programs fall into the redistributive policy category as they shift resources from the advantaged to the disadvantaged and involve ideological disputes and political conflicts. This regime has remained in place since 1965, although there have been significant changes in national health care policies over the past 45 years.

The Medicare/Medicaid policy regime addressed problems of providing health care coverage for the poor and the elderly, but avoided the issue of universal health care coverage. Health care policy changed incrementally. These changes included the expansion of Medicaid to include children from families just above the poverty level, the creation of cost controls, the use of private health maintenance organizations (HMOs) to assist in delivering Medicaid and Medicare services, and the establishment of pharmaceutical drug coverage for Medicare recipients.

The Solo Doctor Policy Regime

The independent family doctor and local health departments characterized health care during the late 19th and early 20th century, the period of the solo doctor policy regime. Most doctors were in family practice and operated independent of hospitals. Doctors made house calls and treated most people in their homes. Doctors controlled their own profession and dominated health care politics. The **American Medical Association (AMA),** formed in 1847, represented medical doctors and dominated the political arena at least until the last third of the 20th century.

The number of hospitals increased "twenty fold between 1860 and 1910" (Klebanow et al. 1977, 203). Many military hospitals were built during the Civil War, such as the Armory Square Union hospital shown on the opening page of this chapter. Most hospitals built during this period were private and nonprofit. By the first decade of the 20th century, most cities had established health departments and built municipal hospitals. Local spending for public health increased exponentially in this period. With thousands of people living in close proximity to each other—a product of urbanization—epidemics could spread rapidly with devastating consequences. With the discovery of bacteria, viruses, and sterilization, health departments emerged to help prevent and manage the spread of diseases in large cities. Local health departments provided public health services such as immunizations, tests for communicable diseases, the regulation of local restaurants and private establishments, the monitoring of local diseases, and the collection of health records and statistics.

With the exception of military hospitals and land grants for medical colleges, federal health care was practically nonexistent. National health care proposals were introduced

---

"Health Care Policy" from *Public Policy: Continuity and Change* by Carter A. Wilson, pp. 128-151. Copyright © 2006. Published by McGraw-Hill Humanities/Social Sciences/Languages. Reproduced with permission of The McGraw-Hill Companies

to Congress during the Progressive period and the New Deal era. However, the American Medical Association (AMA) played a key role in pushing the issue of national health care off the federal agenda.

There were two federal programs before 1965. Congress passed the *Hill-Burton Act of 1946* (officially, the *Hospital Survey and Construction Act*) and the *Kerr-Mills Act of 1960*. The Hill-Burton Act provided assistance for the construction of hospitals, with the expectation that hospitals would provide some charity for poor people in need of emergency hospital care. To assist in providing health care for the poor and the elderly, the Kerr-Mills Act set aside federal money to be matched by state funds.

For the most part, health care before 1965 remained a private affair, involving a close relationship between the family doctor and the individual patient. There were some local public health programs and some state or local support for hospitals.

The dominant idea of the solo doctor was that local governments promoted public health, but the unregulated private market provided health care. The market consisted of the doctors, who were the providers, and the patients, who were the consumers. The AMA, fearing government control of the medical profession, vigorously opposed federal health insurance programs which it branded as socialized medicine.

Explaining Policy Regime Change

The solo doctor policy regime lasted until about 1965, with the birth of the new Medicare/Medicaid regime. Three factors contributed to the big change in health care policy and the new policy regime.

Technology and Medical Specialization

First, technological and specialization changes in the medical profession impacted the health care market and the role of doctors. Medical knowledge and technology advanced tremendously throughout the 20th century. X rays, discovered in the late 1890s, emerged as an indispensable diagnostic tool during the 1930s. Sonar, discovered in the early 20th century, emerged as ultrasound in the mid-1950s, an important diagnostic tool for gynecologists. By the 1950s advancements in medical technology had produced new fields of medical specialization—cardiology, dermatology, gynecology, pediatrics, and many others—and new support technicians such as X-ray technicians and laboratory technicians. Because of the cost and complexity of modern medicine, doctors were constrained to become part of a larger medical complex, which included hospitals, technicians, and specialists. By the 1960s most doctors were tied to a medical complex. Advances in medical technology had ended the era of the solo doctor who made regular house calls.

Rise of New Medical Organizations

The second factor that contributed to the changes in health care policy was the rise of new organizations. Many health insurance companies like Blue Cross and Blue Shield emerged in the 1930s. They were controlled by doctors or by hospitals. It was not until the rise of **health maintenance organizations (HMOs)** in the 1970s that doctors began to lose some control over their own profession. However, health insurance had a subtle impact on the rise of the Medicare and Medicaid programs. By the 1960s the high cost of medical care made private health insurance coverage essential for health care. Other organizations such as the American Hospital Association (AHA) and the American Association of Medical Schools (AAMS) emerged during the 1950s. The rise of these organizations meant that the AMA now shared power in the health policy area.

The Antipoverty Movement

The third factor that contributed to the big policy change was the antipoverty movement of the 1960s. As noted in Chapter 5, the discovery in America during the 1960s of diseases associated with poverty, diseases afflicting children and the elderly, and diseases as severe as those in the poorest underdeveloped countries precipitated changes in the dominant way of thinking about health care policy. These health care issues among children and the elderly were well publicized by the Physician Task Force, Senate hearings, and popular books. The problem of nutrition and disease was aggravated by the lack of health care insurance and access to medical care, except for state or county hospitals, among most of the poor and the elderly. The publicity of the problems of the elderly and poor combined with the antipoverty social movement of the 1960s to create strong pressures for the establishment of some sort of federally funded health care program for the poor and the elderly.

MEDICARE/MEDICAID POLICY REGIME

In response to these pressures, President Lyndon B. Johnson and Congress passed in 1965 Title XVIII and Title XIX of the Social Security Act, creating the Medicare and the Medicaid programs, respectively. These new policies initiated a major change in federal health care policy and introduced the Medicare/Medicaid policy regime.

Medicare is a national program, financed exclusively by the federal government. It is associated with the Social Security program and is primarily for Social Security recipients. It was expanded in 1972 to include people suffering from kidney disease and, more recently, a subsidy and discount for prescription drugs.

Medicare has evolved into a complex program with several parts. **Medicare Part A** covers most medical costs associated with hospitalization: the cost of surgery, intensive care, hospital-related diagnostic tests, medical treatment, prescription drugs, other hospital-related medical services, and a semiprivate room. Part A does not cover physician care.

Medicare Part B is optional. It operates like physician care insurance, with copayments and deductibles. The federal government pays a large share of the premium. The recipient pays the balance. Part B covers visits to the doctor's office, outpatient hospital services, laboratory and diagnostic tests, and ambulance services.

Medicare Part C, sometimes called Medicare Plus Choice, was introduced in 1997. It gives Medicare recipients the option of joining an HMO or another insurance option in lieu of the fee-for-service plan provided by Medicare.

The *Medicare Modernization Act of 2003* established **Medicare Part D**. It allowed Medicare recipients to purchase a discount drug card in the spring of 2004, but the major provisions of this part will not go into effect until 2006. This bill will be discussed in more detail later. Medicare Part A covers prescription drugs associated with hospital care and Part B covers them as part of outpatient care, but otherwise Medicare beneficiaries had to pay out of pocket for prescription drugs, at least up to 2006. Medicare does not cover long-term care. A few Medicare recipients purchased additional private insurance to cover services not covered by Part A or B. This additional private insurance was called **Medigap,** as it was purported to cover gaps in Medicare.

Medicaid has been associated with the poor, with the idea that it would be primarily for AFDC, and SSI recipients. Like the AFDC/TANF program, Medicaid funding was split between the federal government and the state governments, with the federal government contributing the larger share. The program expanded rapidly throughout the late 1960s and early 1970s, especially as the number of AFDC and SSI recipients increased.

A significant proportion of Medicaid recipients are children. Other recipients include the low-income elderly, blind, physically and mentally disabled, and other adults. Freund and McGuire claimed:

> Children constitute 49 percent of Medicaid recipients, but consume only about 16 percent of Medicaid funds; the elderly used 31 percent of Medicaid dollars, representing only 11.5 percent of those eligible.... Thus, Medicaid has *not* functioned primarily as a source of health care for lower-class persons, especially children, among whom poverty rates are at a 30-year high. Rather, its main recipients appear to be those who were made poor by the costs of health care in disability and old age. (1999, 293)

Most of the Medicaid funds go to the blind and disabled, as health care programs serving this population tend to be more intense, long term, and costly. At one time more than 50 percent of Medicaid funds went to long-term care (Coughlin, Ku, and Holahan 1194). Today the figure is around 35 percent (Burwell, Eiken and Sredl 2002). Eligibility for longterm Medicaid assistance is determined by financial and medical need.

Medicaid coverage is comprehensive. It covers most services associated with hospital care: surgery, recovery, intensive care, radiology, and laboratory and diagnostic tests. It also covers physician care: prescription drugs, prosthetic devices, dental service, home health care, and nursing facilities.

CHANGES IN MEDICAID AND MEDICARE

After cutting social welfare programs in 1981, Congress expanded Medicaid eligibility standards to cover more low-income children and pregnant women. Three years later Congress expanded Medicaid coverage to include all children meeting state AFDC/TANF eligibility standards and pregnant women who would qualify for AFDC/TANF after giving birth.

In 1988 Congress passed the *Medicare Catastrophic Coverage Act (MCCA)*, which expanded Medicaid coverage to include all pregnant women and infant children whose family income was below the federal poverty line. It also expanded Medicaid eligibility because some state eligibility standards for TANF and Medicaid were below the federal Poverty line MCCA did many other things.

- Assisted low-income Medicare recipients in paying Part B premiums.
- Created special health care surtaxes and provided coverage for sudden and catastrophic illnesses that bankrupted families.
- Most important, it expanded Medicare coverage, but Medicare recipients were required to pay an increased premium for the additional benefits. Part B premiums were scheduled to increase in 1989 and Part A enrollees would pay a supplemental premium. The rate of this premium would depend on the Medicare recipients' income or federal income tax liability.

Kart added:

" For the first time, older people alone (and really only those with annual income tax liability) were being asked to underwrite an expansion in the Medicare benefits. Faced with pressure from politically active older adults and their organizational representatives, who were upset about the funding mechanisms for these expanded benefits, Congress passed the Medicare Catastrophic Coverage Repeal Act of 1989 and repealed the Medicare catastrophic benefits legislated in 1988. (2001, 500)

Thus, the MCCA was repealed and most provisions were terminated, except for the expansion of coverage to low-income children and pregnant women.

Insurance and Health Maintenance Organizations

Health care policy involves both the public and the private sectors. Medicaid and Medicare cover about one-third of the population. Most people are covered by private insurance. Today the health insurance industry is dominated by health maintenance organizations.

Health insurance emerged in the early 20th century, but the industry did not begin to grow until the 1930s, with the formation of hospital and physician insurance formed by organizations of hospitals and doctors. Hospitals created the hospital insurance called Blue Cross. The American Medical Association formed Blue Shield, a physician insurance. With this insurance, the client would pay the insurance organization an annual fee or premium. In exchange for the fee, the insurance organization would promise to cover most, but not all, of the clients hospital and doctors' expenses. Until the late 1960s, Blue Cross/Blue Shield dominated the private health insurance market. Other large commercial insurance companies such as Metropolitan Life, Prudential, and others competed with Blue Cross/Blue Shield.

In 1973 Congress passed the *Health Maintenance Organization Act* in response to escalating health care costs and to calls for national health care for people who were not poor or elderly. The act offered federal financial assistance to develop health maintenance organizations.

The problem with escalating health care costs was that health insurance companies paid the physicians and hospitals whatever they charged. Neither the patient nor the insurance company looked for cheaper rates and there was little competition. The costs of physician and hospital services increased much faster than the rate of inflation. Health insurance companies did little to control costs and there were no market mechanisms to do so. The plan was to get HMOs to compete among themselves to reduce health care costs and provide cheaper health care coverage. There are about four different types of HMOs:

1. The staff type of HMO hires individual physicians to work for the organization in a facility it either owns or leases. The HMO pays the doctors a fixed salary, generally regardless of the number of patients. Sometimes the HMO pays a bonus for efficiency in service delivery.
2. The group type of HMO owns or leases the facility, but contracts with a group of physicians to provide medical services, with a set limit for doctor fees.
3. With the individual practice association, the HMO pays physicians a set fee for service.
4. The network type involves a few groups of physicians leasing their own facilities and contracting with the HMO.

In addition to the HMO arrangement, physicians have organized their own insurance groups called **preferred provider organizations (PPOs)**.

HMOs dominate the private health care market. Because of recent changes in federal policies, a few HMOs have begun covering some Medicare and Medicaid recipients. The HMO would provide health care coverage for the Medicare or Medicaid recipient, and Medicaid or Medicare would pay the HMO. This connection between HMOs and federal health care programs represented an important change in the Medicare/Medicaid policy regime.

In 1974 Congress passed the *Employee Retirement Income Security Act (ERISA)*, largely to protect the retirement funds of people employed in private companies. It also allowed employers with large numbers of employees to pool resources and to provide their own employee health care program. The law prohibits state governments from taxing the premiums employers pay on health insurance policies and restricts the ability of states to regulate the self-insured health program.

HEALTH CARE CRISIS

Despite the emergence of HMOs, current health care policy is in crisis. There are three dimensions of this crisis: a crisis of costs, a crisis of access, and a crisis of quality. The cost of health care has been increasing geometrically over the past two decades. More Americans are now without health care insurance than there were 10 or 20 years ago. Although Americans spend more on health care than most other developed countries, life expectancy is lower and infant mortality higher in the United States compared to those developed countries.

THE COST PROBLEM

Health care costs have risen in terms of total spending and in terms of spending as a percent of GNP (gross national product), the total amount spent in the nation on goods and services. In 1960 total health care costs annually represented a little more than 5 percent of GNP, or about $27.0 billion. It had increased to 7 percent of GNP and $73 billion by 1970, and to about 9 percent of GNP and $246 billion by 1980. Today it hovers around 18 percent of GNP, or over $1.9 trillion. (See Table 3.1.) Summarizing the magnitude of the increases in health care costs, health policy analyst Mark Peterson wrote:

> Health care expenditures emerged as a major concern in the 1970s, but by the early 1990s many business leaders, citizen group advocates, and policy makers had concluded that nothing short of government intervention would stem the tide. Medical inflation was 12 percent or higher each year, typically twice the overall consumer price index. Between 1970 and 1989, employer spending on wages and salaries, controlling for inflation, went up just 1 percent, but for health benefits, it rose 163 percent. (1998, 183)

There are several explanations for the escalating health care costs. Whereas inflation in the general economy is a major factor, health care costs have increased well beyond what is explained by inflation. The other factors include demographics, medical technology, third-party payers, Medicare/Medicaid, and perverse market incentives.

DEMOGRAPHIC FACTORS

Two demographic factors contributed to the increase in health care costs: the aging of the general population and the rise of costly epidemics. More people are living past age 65 than ever before. More people living longer means more diseases related to old age: heart disease, strokes, Alzheimer's, dementia, and others. These diseases often require long-term care and contribute substantially to rising health care costs.

TABLE 3.1

Health Care Costs from 1960 to 2005

Category	1960	1970	1980	1990	2000	2005
Total expenditures (In billions of dollars)	27	73	246	696	1,310	1,907

* Projected figure.
SOURCE: U.S. Census Bureau, *Statistical Abstract of the United States*, 2003.

Epidemics of the late 1990s have driven up health care costs even more than old age. For example, the rise of the AIDS (acquired immunodeficiency syndrome) epidemic has drive up health care costs. Full-blown AIDS patients require expensive drugs and long-term hospital care.

Medical Technology

Another explanation for the increase in health care costs is the growth in investment in medical technology. There are two major areas of medical technology: diagnostic and treatment. Diagnostic technology includes the development of such devices as computerized axial tomography, better know as the CAT scan. Recent technological developments have been in the area of high-resolution computer tomography and magnetic resonance imaging (MRI), that is, more sophisticated scanning with more detailed and colorful images for the diagnosis of disease. Other developments have included the use of computers in laboratory work.

Treatment technology includes the development of laser surgery, pacemakers, organ transplants, and artificial body parts such as knee joints, hips, and others. These technological developments required the investment of billions of dollars in medical research. A single transplant alone can cost hundreds of thousands of dollars.

In some cases, new technology initially lowers costs. For example, the CAT scan lowers costs because its use avoids expensive and invasive exploratory surgery. However, once in place, its use has become routine and frequent. Moreover, it has generated a whole new category of health care specialists, just as the invention of the X ray contributed to the rise of the X-ray technician profession. For another example, the creation of devices to improve breathing contributed to the rise of the inhalation therapy profession. The increased use of the technology and the growth in the number of new specialists associated with it add to health care costs.

Third-Party Payers: HMOs and Private Insurance

HMOs and private insurance have operated to control costs. The federal government had supported the growth of HMOs, particularly to control health care costs. HMOs have been successful in controlling costs in some areas, but they have been unsuccessful in others as their expenses, particularly administrative costs, have risen. Summarizing their assessment of private insurance and HMOs, Freund and McGuire reached the following conclusion:

> The U.S. system of private insurance is structurally inefficient and expensive to administer because it is based on the exclusion and discrimination of denying coverage to precisely those who need the most health care. . . . To screen all claims by insured patients to enforce these exclusions and other restrictive terms, commercial insurance companies spend 33.5 cents for each dollar of benefits provided. These administrative costs are 14 times those of Medicare (2.3 cents per dollar) because all persons covered by Medicare have the same coverage and terms. (1999, 289)

HMOs have tried to control costs, but they have reduced costs by decreasing some services.

Increases in Medicare/Medicaid

Medicaid and Medicare costs have soared over the past 20 years. The federal government's share of Medicaid in 1988 was $30 billion. It rose to $82 billion six years later. In the same period Medicare rose from $86 billion to $159.5 billion (McKenna 1998, 628). Spending for Medicare increased from $197.4 billion in 2000 to about $270.5 billion in 2004 (Statistical Abstract 2004). Federal spending for Medicaid increased from $117.9 billion in 2000 to $160.7 billion in 2003 (U.S. Congressional Budget Office 2004).

The increase in Medicaid was due to two factors: the increase in the number of recipients and the increase in health care costs, especially hospitalization and long-term care, such as nursing homes.

Both programs, combined with the growth of private insurance, expanded the health care market. The rapid expansion of public spending in this field, without cost controls, has encouraged price increases beyond the rate of inflation (Coughlin, Ku, and Holahan 1994).

Perverse Market Incentives

Robert LeBow, president of the Physicians for a National Health Program, suggested that the high cost of American health care is partially the result of perverse market incentives and a religious faith in the market.

> With respect to the financing of health care, "the market" has been an abject failure. The market may work well with automobiles, housing, and

fast food. But buying health care is a far cry from buying a hamburger. The much-vaunted advantage of market "competition" in health care has only resulted in increased woes for providers and patients. With competition being almost exclusively based on cost, the result has been the creation of oligopolies, the control of the market by large corporations. (2003, 18)

LeBow argued that although managed care temporarily controlled inflation in health care prices, "the effect was short lived" (2003, 18). He suggested that HMOs tried to control costs through cutting back on the length of stay in hospitals, cutting back on reimbursements, and denying some services. He added:

Managed-care organizations underpriced their products to gain market share and, as a result, half of them lost money in the late '90s. Many continue to lose money today. Moreover, the popular backlash to the abuses of managed care forced managed-care organizations to abandon many of their rationing mechanisms. Maybe the forces of competition could lead to better outcomes if quality were the issue, but with cost and profits as the motivators, "the market" in health care has lead to . . . a marked decrease in choice . . . increased diversion of resources to administration, marketing, and profits, with less money left for patient care . . . decrease in quality care, expansion of for profit HMOs . . . [and] frustrated physicians because administrative demands have limited the amount of time they are able to spend with patients. (2003, 19–20)

Compared with other countries, including those with universal health care, the United States pays a substantially higher percentage of administrative costs.

The Impact of Costs

The increase of health care costs has had three major impacts. First, it has impacted the economy; a greater share of GNP now goes to health care. This increase has also impacted the cost of production and the profits of major corporations. Corporations had to spend more money on health care, as insurance premiums increased. In *Health of Nations: An International Perspective on U.S. Health Care Reform*, Laurene Graig argued that health care costs impact American businesses much more than they impact businesses in other countries. Private businesses in the United States pay for health care as part of their benefit packages for their employees. In contrast, the national government pays for these costs in other developed countries. The high cost of U.S. health care leaves American businesses at a competitive disadvantage compared to their foreign competitors.

The burden of health care costs in other nations is spread across the entire population, and no one industry or sector is overburdened. In the United States, on the other hand, industries with older work forces, such as steel and autos, do pay significantly higher health care costs. Indeed, in industries such as automobile manufacturing, health benefits costs are the largest nonwage factor in production costs. (Graig 1993, 23)

The second impact has been on state governments, which have been hard hit by increases in Medicaid costs, driven up by the increasing cost of nursing homes, hospital care, and more recipients.

The third impact has been on individuals and families. Many companies have begun shifting health care costs to their employees. This shift has meant that employee medical benefits have declined and that employees pay more money out of pocket for the health care they do get.

Bonser, McGregor, and Oster (1996) discussed several cases that illustrate the impacts of health care costs on families and individuals. One involved a family in which two sons, three and six years old, were diagnosed with cystic fibrosis. The family paid $1,500 a month for the medicine to treat the disease. Fortunately, their insurance covered the cost of the drugs.

Another case involved a 39-year-old married woman who had a stroke and required constant care. The couple's private health insurance did not cover long-term care at home or a nursing home. The husband's income disqualified her for Medicaid and she was too young for Medicare. The family attorney advised the husband to divorce his wife so that she might qualify for Medicaid and go into a nursing home.

Another case involved a married couple priced out of insurance. The wife was 59 years old and the husband 63. They were not eligible for Medicare or Medicaid. In 1988 their insurance cost $3,578 annually, with a $500 deductible for hospital coverage. By 1992 it cost $10,500 with a $2,000 deductible.

COST CONTROLS

Both the private sector HMOs and the public sector Medicaid and Medicare programs have been successful in controlling health care costs in a number of areas. They have set limits on the number of hospital days they would pay for. This practice has provided incentives to shift patients from the more expensive hospital care facilities to the less expensive outpatient care facilities. HMOs have used family or primary care physicians to regulate costs. For example, HMOs have refused to pay for the services of medical specialists unless authorized by the primary care physician. Furthermore, some HMO arrangements require the primary care physician to get authorization from the HMO before recommending specialists or special forms of treatment.

In 1983 Medicare replaced the fee-for-service system of reimbursement with a new prospective payment system. Under the fee-for-service system, Medicare paid hospitals whatever they charged. Under the prospective payment system (PPS) rather than paying hospitals whatever they charged, Medicare established set prices for specific medical services. These prices involved diagnostic-related group (DRGs), a list of specific ailments with a corresponding list of the price of treatment. The government would pay out the set rate for the specific diagnosis. If physicians generally charged more, they would still get the established rate, and suffer loss. If the physicians generally charged less, they would get the higher amount and enjoy the gain. The use of DRGs provided incentives to control costs.

Despite these efforts, health care costs have continued to rise even though the rate of increase had slowed. High health care costs remained a problem.

THE ACCESS PROBLEM

The crisis in health care costs has contributed to another crisis: a crisis in access to health care. Most people find health care too expensive to pay for out of pocket. Despite the range of people covered by private insurance, Medicare, and Medicaid, the number of people without any health care coverage—private or public—has increased. Table 3.2 lists the groups covered by Medicaid and Medicare.

THE UNINSURED

As Table 3.3 shows, more people are without any health care coverage today than 15 years ago.

TABLE 3.2

Groups Covered

By Medicaid	By Medicare
TANE recipients*	Elderly
SSI recipients*	Low-income elderly
Pregnant women qualified for TANF after giving birth*	End Stage Renal Disease
Children age six and under at 133 percent of poverty level qualified	
Children age 18 and under below the poverty level*	

*Low-income Medicare beneficiaries.

TABLE 3.3

People with No Health Insurance

Year	Not Covered (In millions)	Percent
1990	34.7	13.9
1994	39.7	15.2
1996	40.6	15.4
1997	41.7	15.6
1998	43.4	15.6
2001	41.2	14.6
2002	43.6	15.2
2003	45.0	15.6

SOURCE: U.S. Census Bureau, *Statistical Abstract of the United States*, 2003.

Moreover, the numbers and percentages are still increasing.

The number of people without any health care covered increased from 34.7 million in 1990 to 45.0 million by 2003. The proportion of the uninsured increased from 13.9 percent in 1990 to 15.6 percent by 2003.

Several reasons explain the recent growth of the uninsured. One reason has to do with the area in which people are employed. Most adults without health care insurance do have jobs. An estimated 75 percent of the uninsured population consists of employed persons and their dependents (Freund and McGuire 1999, 295). The uninsured just happen to work in occupations unlikely to provide health care insurance: the self-employed, part-time workers, small businesses, the service sector, and others. The self-employed include independent truckers, mechanics, or contractors. The owners of these businesses have to purchase their own health insurance or manage without it. Many do without. Neighborhood stores, restaurants, and other small businesses have too few employees to get the type of health insurance discounts given to large companies with well over a hundred employees.

Another reason for the rising number of the uninsured is the shift of jobs from the industrial sector to the service sector. Many people who have lost jobs with benefits in the unionized industrial sector—steel, automobiles—have obtained jobs without health care benefits in the service sector. Service sector jobs include security guards, maintenance workers, restaurant workers, or the retail clerks—jobs that come with lower pay and no benefits.

Health care policy analyst Vicente Navarro provides several examples illustrating the increase in the uninsured, resulting from the contraction in the industrial sector. All of Navarro's examples are from Baltimore, Maryland. In 1990 John Dunlop was laid off from the Bethlehem Steel mill where he had worked for over 20 years. Not only had he lost his job, but he lost his health insurance as well.

> He could no longer receive the care he needed for a heart condition because he could not afford the insurance. He died in May 1993 from a stroke. He was one of the 100,000 people who die in the United States each year because they cannot afford medical care.

Many underemployed workers have no health care insurance. The underemployed are those with part-time jobs, but prefer full-time work. More businesses have employed people part-time, usually 35 hours a week, in order to avoid having to pay health care benefits. This practice has increased the ranks of the uninsured.

Anne Lorraine is an example of an underemployed worker with no health insurance. She is a single, African-American woman with three children. She has two jobs, one of which is as a custodial worker at Johns-Hopkins Hospital. Neither of her two employers pays health benefits for her or her family and Lorraine cannot afford to pay the premiums on her own. About 32 percent of all health care workers in the United States have no health insurance (Navarro 1993, 10).

THE UNINSURED

The problem of the uninsured has been aggravated by the underinsurance problem. The Congressional Budget Office defines the *underinsured* as those who pay more than 10 percent of their annual income on health care (Calkins, Fernandopulle, and Marino 1995, 179). Several factors contribute to this problem. Probably the number one factor is the absence of coverage for long-term care. Few private policies cover long-term care. Medicare does not Medicaid covers it, but only for the medically needy who meet financial eligibility requirements. Another factor producing underinsurance has been the practice of shifting health care costs from the employer to the employee. This practice generally results in employees with higher premiums, fewer benefits, and greater deductibles. One example sited earlier is the case of a family with a $500 deductible in 1988 which rose to a $2,000 deductible in 1992. A deduction of $2,000 constitutes underinsurance for those with incomes of $20,000 or lower. It can be a serious financial burden even for middle-class families.

Mary McCormick of Baltimore illustrates the problem of the underinsured. Mrs. McCormick was an administrator at the Maryland National Bank where she had full health care coverage for physician and hospital care.

> On January 27, 1992, she had a stroke that left her so seriously handicapped that she needed long-term care. But her health insurance did not include this benefit. She had to sell almost everything she owned to make herself eligible for government assistance. And in order to protect her husband's assets—their home and car—she had to divorce him. In March 1993 Mary killed herself. She was one of the 202 million people in the United States whose health benefits do not include long-term care. (Navarro 1993, 10)

HOLES IN MEDICAID AND MEDICARE

Medicaid and Medicare operate to some degree as a safety net to catch the poor and elderly who ordinarily would not have any health care at all. However, there are several holes in the Medicaid and Medicare safety net.

1. Medicaid does not cover the working poor. It does not cover adults without children whose

incomes fall below the poverty line. It does not cover childless adults who are unemployed or who work but earn less than the poverty level.
2. Medicaid does not cover children ages 7 to 18 whose family incomes are just above the poverty level.
3. Medicaid does not work as effectively as private insurance. Since it usually pays only 60 percent of doctor fees, many doctors will not accept Medicaid patients. Many Medicaid beneficiaries do not have primary care physicians and use Medicaid primarily for emergency care. This problem impacts the quality of health care received by Medicaid recipients.
4. Finally, recent studies of poor children indicate that many families eligible for Medicaid do not even apply for benefits. In some cases, parents are not aware that they and their children are eligible for Medicaid; in other cases, the difficulty in obtaining coverage discourages families from applying.

Medicare has one main hole in its coverage. It does not cover long-term nursing care.

Underinsurance also affects Medicare recipients. Freund and McGuire provided examples to illustrate this problem. Dorothy and Frank are a married couple in their 70s with a monthly income of $1,400 in Social Security benefits.

> They have Medicare coverage, but noncovered health care expenditures consume about 50 percent of their entire family budget, leaving them scrimping to pay for food, utilities, and other basic needs. Their monthly costs include modest Medigap insurance policy, $200; Medicare premiums, $85; prescriptions and other medicine, $250; deductibles and other charges not covered by Medicare or Medigap, $50; long-term care insurance (for Dorothy; Frank is not eligible because of preexisting health conditions), $200.... (1999, 291)

Another example is that of an 85-year-old widow, Clarissa, who lives alone on Social Security payments of $650 per month.

> Her health care needs not covered by Medicare consume 40 percent of her fixed income. They include Medicare premium, $42; prescriptions and other medicine, $120 (but she spends only $80, because she can't afford prescription painkillers for her arthritis); Medigap insurance, $80 (for a minimal policy); other charges not covered, $20. (1999, 291)

THE QUALITY ISSUE

Political leaders have debated the issue of whether access to health care impacts health status or health outcomes. On one side of the argument, political leaders insist that health status is a function of lifestyles. Lifestyles include eating habits, exercise, smoking, and drug and alcohol abuse. They say that poor health has little to do with access to health care, as the poorest uninsured person has access to emergency care. They contend that if Americans have a lower life expectancy than people in other countries, it may be that Americans eat more red meat, consume more high-fat foods, smoke more, and exercise less. High-fat diets and the lack of exercise contribute to obesity and related health problems such as diabetes, high blood pressure, and heart disease. High rates of disease are often attributable to alcohol and drug abuse. These factors affect the health status of Americans regardless of the high quality of health care in the United States.

On the other side of the argument, critics of the U.S. health care system insist that public policy makes a difference in health status. For example, Patel and Rushefsky (1995) argued that the uninsured suffering from an acute illness are less likely to seek medical attention than those with private insurance. "For example, uninsured and Medicaid patients suffering from appendicitis are more likely to experience a ruptured appendix than privately insured patients" (p. 111). Also babies from uninsured families and Medicaid-insured babies "are likely to be discharged from hospitals sooner than privately insured babies" (Patel and Rushefsky 1995, 112).

Other critics maintain that the United States has the most expensive and technologically advanced health care system in the world, yet Americans have unimpressive health indicators. Table 3.4 compares the per capita spending, life expectancy, and infant mortality of the United States and a number of industrialized countries. Americans spend more on health care than any other country in the world. In terms of per capita spending—the amount spent per person—the United States spends three times what Great Britain spends; more than twice what Japan, Austria, and the Netherlands spend; and almost double what Germany, Norway, France, Sweden,

TABLE 3.4

Health Status Spending and Outcomes in Selected Industrialized Nations

Nation	Per Capita Spending 1997 ($)	Life Expectancy 1996 (Years) Female	Male	Infant Mortality 1996 (%)
Australia	1,805	81.1	75.2	5.8
Austria	1,793	80.2	73.9	5.1
Belgium	1,747	81.0	74.3	6.0
Canada	2,095	81.5	75.4	6.0
Czech Republic	904	77.2	70.5	6.0
Denmark	1,848	78.0	72.8	5.2
Finland	1,447	80.5	73.0	4.0
France	2,051	82.0	74.1	4.9
Germany	2,339	79.9	73.6	5.0
Greece	974	80.4	75.1	7.3
Iceland	1,374	78.5	73.2	3.7
Italy	1,589	81.3	74.9	5.8
Japan	1,741	83.6	77.0	3.8
Luxembourg	2,340	80.0	73.0	4.9
Netherlands	1,838	80.4	74.7	5.2
New Zealand	1,352	79.8	74.3	7.4
Norway	1,814	81.1	75.4	4.0
Spain	1,168	81.6	74.4	5.0
Sweden	1,728	81.5	76.5	4.0
Switzerland	2,547	81.9	75.7	4.7
United kingdom	1,347	79.3	74.4	6.1
Unites States	3,925	79.4	72.7	7.8

* Per 1,000 live births.
SOURCE: Anderson and Poullier. "Health Spending, Access, and Outcomes: Trends in Industrialized Countries," *Health Affairs* 18(3), 1999.

and Switzerland spend. The only country that comes close to U.S. spending levels is Switzerland, but the United States outspends this country by $1,300 in per capita health care costs.

The higher U.S. spending levels do not translate into better health indicators. Out of 22 developed countries, the United States ranks 18th in female life expectancy and 21st in male life expectancy. Only the Czech Republic has a lower male life expectancy than the United States. It should be noted that the Czech Republic also has the lowest per capita health care spending.

The United States has the highest infant mortality rate among the other 21 developed countries: 7.8 per 1,000 live births. The United Kingdom is ranked 21st with an infant mortality rate of 6.1 (see Table 3.4).

Infant mortality rates are higher in American cities than in the country at large. These rates are higher among African Americans than those of some Third World countries. For example, the infant mortality rate for Mexico is 17.0 per 1,000 live births (Anderson and Poullier 1999). Table 3.5 shows that the rate for African Americans is 17.5 for Washington, D.C., 17.6 for Buffalo and Chicago, 17.8 for Cincinnati and Detroit, 18.0 for St. Louis, and 18.8 for Memphis.

White Americans have infant mortality rates lower than blacks in select cities, but substantially higher than those found in developed countries. For example, the infant mortality rate for whites is high in cities like Buffalo, Detroit, Cincinnati, and Norfolk. These rates for whites are no doubt associated with low incomes, which may be related to poor diet and adequate access to medical care (see Tables 3.5 and 3.6).

IMPROVEMENTS IN HEALTH STATUS OVER TIME

Despite the poorer health outcomes for the United States compared with other developed

TABLE 3.5

Infant Mortality Rates in Select U.S. Cities, 1995–1998 (Per 1,000 Live Births)

City	Total	White	Black
Atlanta	11.7	6.7	14.6
Boston	6.7	4.8	10.0
Buffalo	12.0	8.1	17.6
Chicago	11.5	7.0	17.6
Cincinnati	12.9	8.4	17.8
Dallas	6.4	5.4	2.6
Detroit	14.4	8.2	17.8
Indianapolis	9.2	7.5	14.0
Membhis	15.4	7.2	18.8
Milwaukee	8.9	6.3	12.0
New Orleans	9.4	6.4	10.4
New York	7.4	4.5	12.1
Norfolk	14.0	11.6	16.5
Philadelphia	12.0	6.7	16.6
St. Louis	8.9	7.5	18.0
San Francisco	4.6	2.6	12.3
Tampa	7.4	5.4	15.8
Toledo	7.5	5.6	12.2
Washington, DC	—	—	17.5
Wichita	8.3	7.6	14.7

SOURCE: Centers for Disease Control and Prevention 2002.

TABLE 3.6

Infant Mortality Rates in Select Years (Per 1,000 Live Births)

Year	Rate(%)
1950	29.2
1960	26.0
1970	20.2
1980	12.6
1990	8.6
1995	7.6
1998	7.2
1999	7.1
2000	6.9
2001	6.8

SOURCE: U.S. Census Bureau, *Statistical Abstract of the United States*, 2002.

countries, the health status of Americans has improved substantially throughout the 20th century. Infant mortality rates have declined substantially over the past 30 years and life expectancy rates have increased throughout the past century. Infant mortality rates have declined from 20 per 1,000 in 1970 to about 6.8 today (see Table 3.6). Life expectancy rates increased from 47.3 years in 1900 to 68.2 years in 1950. They have continued to increase and today they are around 76.7, about 74 for men and 79.4 for women (U.S. Census Bureau 2002).

Several factors have contributed to improved health over the years, most of which are related to improved standards of living. Some of these factors are economic such as increased wages and purchasing power. Some have to do with the expansion of public amenities and modern facilities: electricity, refrigeration, indoor bathrooms, gas stoves, running water, and sewer and sanitation services. Others are related to public policies such as workplace safety the minimum wage, maximum working hours, child labor, and other related policies. Public health policies such as immunization and disease control also have contributed to higher life expectancy.

As you have read, the debate over whether lifestyles or public policies are responsible for health status continues. Lifestyles indeed impact health conditions. At the same time, public policies such as food stamps, nutrition programs for women and children, and Medicaid and Medicare have contributed to declines in infant mortality rates and possibly to a marginal increase in life expectancy.

HEALTH CARE POLICY INITIATIVES OF THE LATE 20TH CENTURY

There were three major health policy initiatives of the late 1990s: the failed Health Security Act of 1993, the Health Insurance Act of 1996, and the health care rights movement.

THE HEALTH SECURITY ACT OF 1993

The defeated *Health Security Act of 1993* was one of the most important health care policy initiatives of the late 20th century. President Bill Clinton, who had campaigned on a promise of providing national health care, introduced it. The idea was that this bill would be the social security act for health care. It was designed to address the problems of costs and access. It was an ambitious piece of legislation, over 1,300 pages long. It underscored six principles: security, savings, quality, choice, simplicity, and responsibility.

The first principle, security, was designed to provide health insurance coverage for every American. It proposed to cover people through existing private health insurance organizations such as HMOs. It prohibited private insurance companies from refusing to cover people because of preexisting conditions. It would guarantee continuous coverage for those who lost their jobs, switched jobs, or started a small business. The bill covered the following:

- Preventive care (i.e., screenings, physicals, immunizations, mammograms, prenatal care)
- Doctor visits
- Prescription drugs
- Hospital services
- Emergency/ambulance services
- Laboratory and diagnostic services
- Mental health and substance abuse treatment
- Expanded home health care

The second principle, savings, was designed to control health care costs. It limited how much insurance companies could raise premiums. States would be required to create health alliances to oversee competition among HMOs or private insurance companies and to provide consumers with information on costs and quality. The goal was that health alliances would facilitate competition among the insurance companies in ways that would encourage lower prices.

The third principle, quality, was expected to improve quality by emphasizing preventive care and guaranteeing a wide range of benefits. The Health Security Act would enhance the fourth principle, choice, by preserving the right to choose one's own physician. The Executive Summary of the Health Security Act said this about choice:

> The proposal ensures that you can follow your doctor and his or her team to any plan they might join. Today, more and more employers are forcing their employees into plans that restrict your choice of doctor. After reform, your boss or insurance company won't choose your doctor or health plan—you will.

Simplicity involved reducing paperwork, requiring insurance companies to use a single claim form, streamlining billings, and others. Responsibility, the last principle, entailed making health care everyone's business and producing health care cards for everyone.

Most Americans favored the ideal of national health insurance. Most expected the federal government to solve the cost, access, and quality problem of health care. Most initially supported the Health Security Act, yet the bill was defeated. Three factors contributed to its demise: (1) interest group opposition and support, (2) a divided Congress, and (3) the complexity of the bill.

INTEREST GROUP OPPOSITION

By 1990 the political landscape involving national health care politics and traditional interest groups had changed. The American Medical Association was not as influential as it had been in the past. Fewer physicians were members. New organizations of physicians had emerged to challenge its leadership. Moreover, the rise of HMOs had changed the medical profession in ways that reduced the power of doctors. In the interest of controlling costs, HMOs challenged more of the decisions made by doctors. Summing up the situation with the AMA, Peterson wrote:

> The previous alliance of medical, business, and insurance interests that had always prevented the federal government from enacting comprehensive reform was split in every conceivable way. For example, the membership of the American Medical Association (AMA) declined from an estimated 90 percent of physicians in private practice to over two-thirds of all physicians as recently as the 1960s to 41 percent in the 1990s. Scores of specialty organizations with an invigorated Washington presence, including the American College of Surgeons and American Academy of Family Physicians, challenged the AMAs position on health care reform and its role as medicine's voice. (1998, 184)

The AMA, joined by insurance and business organizations, initially supported the Health Security Act. A new organization, the Physicians for a National Health Program (PNHP), was formed to support universal health care. It appeared that the Medicaid/Medicare policy regime was going to collapse and give way to a new national health care regime.

Nevertheless, the old regime held together. A few interest groups opposed to national health care policy mobilized. They initiated a three-pronged attack on the new policy: They attacked the policy directly in the media, mobilized to rebuild the coalition of the old regime, and lobbied directly to defeat the bill.

The political organization that first attacked the Health Security Act was the National Federation of Independent Business (NFIB). "With 600,000 members scattered across every state and congressional district, and with millions of dollars committed to its two-stage campaign of grassroots mobilization and heavy inside lobbying against the president's proposal, the NFIB alone was a formidable source of opposition" (Peterson 1998, 194).

The NFIB worked with several other organizations to create a coalition opposing the Health Security Act. These included the National Restaurant Association, the Independent Insurance Agents of America, and the Christian Coalition. Television and lobbying campaigns hostile to the act were launched. The coalition opposed to the Health Security Act was called the No Name Coalition. Its leaders conducted focus group interviews and discovered that although Americans favored national health care, they were worried about big government and the competence of the federal government. "Bombarded with the message that Clinton proposed a government takeover of medical care that even threatened doctors and patients with jail terms if they violated the rules, the public grew increasingly worried about the ramifications of reform" (Peterson 1998, 195). Congressional leaders opposed to the bill contacted leaders in the AMA and the U.S. Chamber of Commerce and succeeded in persuading them to change their position and join the opposition. A powerful coalition emerged to oppose the bill.

Organized support for the bill was weak. The organizations expected to support the bill included consumer interest, organized labor groups, and senior citizen groups. There were three problems with this support. First, organized labor was weak and divided. The AFL-CIO leadership supported the bill, but they had some difficulty in getting support among local and affiliated labor unions, The length and complexity of the bill created problems in generating support. Also, more liberal groups favored more government support and less involvement of private insurance companies. The bill failed precisely because it had strong interest group opposition and weak interest group support.

DIVIDED CONGRESS

The second reason the bill was defeated is that opposition to the bill in Congress was united and support was divided. Republican Party leader Newt Gingrich, Speaker of the House at the time, was a very organized and influential leader and mobilized House Republicans to defeat the bill.

Democrats were divided over the bill. Liberal Democrats, such as consumer interest groups, wanted a bill with more federal involvement and more federal subsidies. "The pivotal point in the debate came in the spring of 1994, when John Dingell, the powerhouse chairman of the House Energy and Commerce Committee and long-time advocate of health care reform, could not overcome the opposition of key moderate Democrats to muster the majority needed to report a bill" (Peterson 1998, 196).

COMPLEXITY OF THE BILL

The complexity of the Health Security Act contributed to its demise. Leaders of political organizations that supported the bill first had to read it and understand it, then explain it to their constituents before they could build support. They had difficulties countering the opposition because the bill was so complex.

Clinton had introduced the bill in 1993. It was stalled in the House Energy and Commerce Committee in 1994. When the Republicans took control of the House and Senate after the 1994 election, the bill was dead by the end of the year. The submission of the bill to multiple committees also contributed to its death, a point noted in Chapter 4. The bill was submitted to about 10 different congressional committees.

KENNEDY-KESSEBAUM ACT OF 1996

A year after the demise of the Health Security Act, senators Edward Kennedy and Nancy Kessebaum introduced the Health Insurance Portability and Accountability Act, perhaps better known as the *Kennedy-Kessebaum Act of 1996*. This act attempted to address the twin problems of portability and accountability. The portability problem has to do with workers who are offered a new job, but are faced with the possibility of losing their current health care coverage. The new law required the health care insurer to continue coverage for workers changing jobs. The accountability problem refers to a new health care provider refusing to cover previously existing health conditions. The law prohibited employers from refusing to cover preexisting conditions for new employees who had been covered elsewhere within 63 days of starting the new job.

Several amendments to the Kennedy-Kessebaum Act were proposed, but only a few were approved. One major amendment allowed the establishment of tax-exempt medical savings accounts (MCAs). Only a limited number of MCAs would be approved for Medicare recipients and they would operate like retirement accounts. The MCAs were strongly supported by the Republicans, who had a narrow majority. Kennedy and Kessebaum accepted the MCA provision as a compromise to ensure the passage of the bill. Senate Majority Leader Bob Dole played a key role in forging the compromise, producing bipartisan support and getting the bill through the Senate.

THE MEDICARE MODERNIZATION ACT OF 2003

President George W. Bush introduced the Medicare Modernization Act of 2003, another complicated bill that added drug coverage and introduced changes in Medicare. The bill had five noteworthy aspects.

1. The bill provides a drug discount card, which seniors can purchase for $30 a year. It provides discounts of 10 percent to 25 percent for prescription drugs.
2. The bill provides a drug coverage option to Medicare recipients under Medicare Part D. Recipients would pay a premium of $35 a month. After a $250 deductible, Medicare would pay 75 percent of the costs of drugs up to $2,250. There is no coverage for the cost of drugs between $2,250 and $5,000. Medicare will pay. 95 percent of the cost of drugs costing more than $5,100.
3. The bill provides a sliding scale of benefits for low-income recipients. Medicare recipients whose income falls below the poverty line and who qualify for Medicaid would be exempt from paying premiums and deductibles. They would pay a one dollar co-pay for the drugs. Medicare recipients with incomes below 135 percent, but above 100 percent of the poverty line and with assets below $6,000 would also be exempt from premiums and deductibles, but would have to pay a $2 co-pay for drugs. As income and assets increase, premiums, deductibles, and co-pays would also increase.
4. The bill offers subsidies of up to $86 billion to employers who provide prescription drug benefits to retirees who are over 65 and eligible for Medicare.
5. Finally, the bill encourages Medicare recipients to move into HMOs. In this sense, it expands on the Medicare changes of 1996, which established Medicare Part C.

There was a great deal of conflict over the Medicare Modernization Act, not just between liberals and conservatives but also within each group. The American Association of Retired Persons supported the bill; although the bill was not what they wanted, it was a beginning. They had fought a long time for prescription drug benefits. The Alliance for Retired Americans opposed the bill and issued a press release stating, "Under the proposed bill, Medicare as we know it will cease to exits." They were especially concerned with the privatization of Medicare or the shifting of a fee-for-service program into HMOs. They also complained that the bill does not control the cost of drugs and precludes seniors from getting cheaper drugs from Canada.

Some conservatives were divided over the bill, primarily because of its projected costs: about $400 billion over a 10-year period. President Bush emphasized the privatization provision to obtain support from conservatives and the prescription drug coverage to obtain support from liberals. Corporate leaders supported the bill because of its allocation of $86 billion in subsidies to industries that provide prescription drug coverage for their retired workers.

Bush persuaded most Republicans, a majority in Congress, to support his bill. A few Democrats joined the Republicans, guaranteeing its passage.

SUMMARY

The 20th century saw two major health care policy regimes: the solo doctor or Progressive regime and the Medicare/Medicaid regime. The solo doctor policy regime was characterized by local public health programs designed to prevent epidemics and reduce the spread of diseases, by local public and private nonprofit hospitals, and by solo doctors. Health care policy had changed little up to 1965. National health care proposals were introduced during the Progressive era and again during the New Deal, but they failed. Health care remained a private affair between doctor and patient. State and local governments, with some federal support, assisted in the construction of hospitals and provided a little assistance to poor people for emergency hospital care. The American Medical Association had fought bitterly against any proposal for a national health care system which it characterized as socialized medicine, a violation of the free market, and a dangerous interference with the private relationship between doctor and patient.

In 1965 the passage of Title XVIII and XIX of the Social Security Act, which established Medicare and Medicaid, marked a policy regime change. Several factors stressed the old Progressive policy regime and facilitated the change. First, technological and organizational changes in medical practice impacted the world of the physician, transforming the solo doctor into an associate of a large medical complex with hospitals, expensive medical machines, and a host of medical specialists. These changes contributed to substantial increases in health care costs. Second, the rise of health care insurance and later health maintenance organizations (HMOs) provided coverage for upper- and middle-class families, but left the poor and elderly without health care. Third, the antipoverty movement of the 1960s focused public attention on the health care issues of the poor and elderly people. These changes helped to produce the Medicare/Medicaid policy regime.

Medicare provided health care coverage for the elderly. Medicaid provided coverage for the disabled, for poor families with children, and for poor people needing long-term nursing home care. Medicare and Medicaid changed incrementally from 1965 to the present.

The Clinton administration added some minor protections for people covered by private insurance. The Kennedy-Kessebaum Act prohibited employers from refusing to cover preexisting conditions for new employees who had previous coverage. The Bush administration added a seminal prescription drug program. The Medicare/Medicaid policy regimes remain intact.

Efforts to establish a national universal health care system failed in the 1990s. Although powerful organizations like the AARP and the AFL-CIO supported such a system, other powerful organizations were opposed to it. These organizations included the National Federation of Independent Business, the National Association of Manufacturers, the Pharmaceutical Manufacturers Association, and the Health Insurance Association of America. Nevertheless, the cost and access crises in health care will continue to exert strong pressures for substantial policy changes. A few states have already moved in the direction of universal health care coverage.

The President's Proposal February 22, 2010

The President's Proposal puts American families and small business owners in control of their own health care.

- It makes insurance more <u>affordable</u> by providing the largest middle class tax cut for health care in history, reducing premium costs for tens of millions of families and small business owners who are priced out of coverage today. This helps over 31 million Americans afford health care who do not get it today – and makes coverage more affordable for many more.
- It sets up a <u>new competitive health insurance market</u> giving tens of millions of Americans the exact same insurance choices that members of Congress will have.
- It brings <u>greater accountability</u> to health care by laying out commonsense rules of the road to keep premiums down and prevent insurance industry abuses and denial of care.
- It will <u>end discrimination</u> against Americans with pre-existing conditions.
- It puts our <u>budget and economy on a more stable path</u> by reducing the deficit by $100 billion over the next ten years – and about $1 trillion over the second decade – by cutting government overspending and reining in waste, fraud and abuse.

The President's Proposal bridges the gap between the House and Senate bills and includes new provisions to crack down on waste, fraud and abuse.

It includes a targeted set of changes to the Patient Protection and Affordable Care Act, the Senate-passed health insurance reform bill. The President's Proposal reflects policies from the House-passed bill and the President's priorities. Key changes include:

- Eliminating the Nebraska FMAP provision and providing significant additional Federal financing to all States for the expansion of Medicaid;
- Closing the Medicare prescription drug "donut hole" coverage gap;
- Strengthening the Senate bill's provisions that make insurance affordable for individuals and families;
- Strengthening the provisions to fight fraud, waste, and abuse in Medicare and Medicaid;
- Increasing the threshold for the excise tax on the most expensive health plans from $23,000 for a family plan to $27,500 and starting it in 2018 for all plans;
- Improving insurance protections for consumers and creating a new Health Insurance Rate Authority to provide Federal assistance and oversight to States in conducting reviews of unreasonable rate increases and other unfair practices of insurance plans.

A detailed summary of the provisions included in the President's Plan is set forth below:

POLICIES TO IMPROVE THE AFFORDABILITY AND ACCOUNTABILITY

INCREASE TAX CREDITS FOR HEALTH INSURANCE PREMIUMS

Health insurance today often costs too much and covers too little. Lack of affordability leads people to delay care, skip care, rack up large medical bills, or become uninsured. The House and Senate health insurance bills lower premiums through increased competition, oversight, and new accountability standards set by insurance exchanges. The bills also provide tax credits and reduced cost sharing for families with modest income. The President's Proposal improves the affordability of health care by increasing the tax credits for families. Relative to the Senate bill, the President's Proposal lowers premiums for families with income below $44,000 and above $66,000. Relative to the House bill, the proposal makes premiums less expensive for families with income between roughly $55,000 and $88,000.

The President's Proposal also improves the cost sharing assistance for individuals and families relative to the Senate bill. Families with

Tax Credits: Maximum Percent of Income Paid for Premiums

Income for a Family of Four		House	Senate	President's Proposal
From:	To:			
$22,000	$29,000	1.5%	2.0%	2.0 – 3.0%
$29,000	$33,000	1.5 – 3.0%	4.0 – 4.6%	3.0 – 4.0%
$33,000	$44,000	3.0 – 5.5%	4.6 – 6.3%	4.0 – 6.3%
$44,000	$55,000	5.5 – 8.0%	6.3 – 8.1%	6.3 – 8.1%
$55,000	$66,000	8.0 – 10.0%	8.1 – 9.8%	8.1 – 9.5%
$66,000	$77,000	10.0 – 11.0%	9.8%	9.5%
$77,000	$88,000	11.0 – 12.0%	9.8%	9.5%

Ranges from 133-150% of poverty, then 150-400% of poverty in 50% increments, rounded to the nearest $1,000

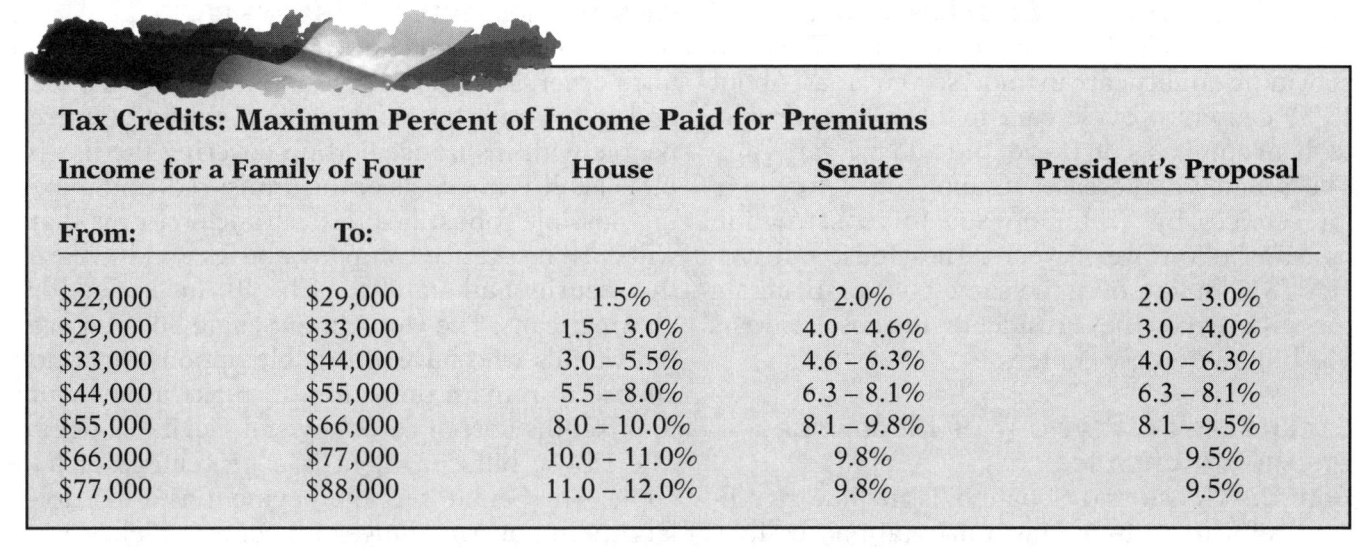

income below $55,000 will get extra assistance; the additional funding to insurers will cover between 73 and 94% of their health care costs. It provides the same cost-sharing assistance as the Senate bill for higher-income families and the same assistance as the House bill for families with income from $77,000 to $88,000.

CLOSE THE MEDICARE PRESCRIPTION DRUG "DONUT HOLE"

The Medicare drug benefit provides vital help to seniors who take prescription drugs, but under current law, it leaves many beneficiaries without assistance when they need it most. Medicare stops paying for prescriptions after the plan and beneficiary have spent $2,830 on prescription drugs, and only starts paying again after out-of-pocket spending hits $4,550. This "donut hole" leaves seniors paying the full cost of expensive medicines, causing many to skip doses or not fill prescriptions at all – harming their health and raising other types of health costs. The Senate bill provides a 50% discount for certain drugs in the donut hole. The House bill fully phases out the donut hole over 10 years. Both bills raise the dollar amount before the donut hole begins by $500 in 2010.

Relative to the Senate bill, the President's Proposal fills the "donut hole" entirely. It begins by replacing the $500 increase in the initial coverage limit with a $250 rebate to Medicare beneficiaries who hit the donut hole in 2010. It also closes the donut hole completely by phasing down the coinsurance so it is the standard 25% by 2020 throughout the coverage gap.

Reduced Cost Sharing: Percent of Costs Paid for by Health Insurance Plan

Income for a Family of Four		House	Senate	President's Proposal
From:	To:			
$29,000	$33,000	97%	90%	94%
$33,000	$44,000	93%	80%	85%
$44,000	$55,000	85%	70%	73%
$55,000	$66,000	78%	70%	70%
$66,000	$77,000	72%	70%	70%
$77,000	$88,000	70%	70%	70%

Ranges from 133-150% of poverty, then 150-400% of poverty in 50% increments, rounded to the nearest $1,000

Invest in Community Health Centers

Community health centers play a critical role in providing quality care in underserved areas. About 1,250 centers provide care to 20 million people, with an emphasis on preventive and primary care. The Senate bill increases funding to these centers for services by $7 billion and for construction by $1.5 billion over 5 years. The House bill provides $12 billion over the same 5 years. Bridging the difference, the President's Proposal invests $11 billion in these centers.

Strengthen Oversight of Insurance Premium Increases

Both the House and Senate bills include significant reforms to make insurance fair, accessible, and affordable to all people, regardless of pre-existing conditions. One essential policy is "rate review" meaning that health insurers must submit their proposed premium increases to the State authority or Secretary for review. The President's Proposal strengthens this policy by ensuring that, if a rate increase is unreasonable and unjustified, health insurers must lower premiums, provide rebates, or take other actions to make premiums affordable. A new Health Insurance Rate Authority will be created to provide needed oversight at the Federal level and help States determine how rate review will be enforced and monitor insurance market behavior.

Extend Consumer Protections against Health Insurer Practices

The Senate bill includes a "grandfather" policy that allows people who like their current coverage, to keep it. The President's Proposal adds certain important consumer protections to these "grandfathered" plans. Within months of legislation being enacted, it requires plans to cover adult dependents up to age 26, prohibits rescissions, mandates that plans have a stronger appeals process, and requires State insurance authorities to conduct annual rate review, backed up by the oversight of the HHS Secretary. When the exchanges begin in 2014, the President's Proposal adds new protections that prohibit all annual and lifetime limits, ban pre-existing condition exclusions, and prohibit discrimination in favor of highly compensated individuals. Beginning in 2018, the President's Proposal requires "grandfathered" plans to cover proven preventive services with no cost sharing.

Improve Individual Responsibility

All Americans should have affordable health insurance coverage. This helps everyone, both insured and uninsured, by reducing cost shifting, where people with insurance end up covering the inevitable health care costs of the uninsured, and making possible robust health insurance reforms that will curb insurance company abuses and increase the security and stability of health insurance for all Americans. The House and Senate bills require individuals who have affordable options but who choose to remain uninsured to make a payment to offset the cost of care they will inevitably need. The House bill's payment is a percentage of income. The Senate sets the payment as a flat dollar amount or percentage of income, whichever is higher (although not higher than the lowest premium in the area). Both the House and Senate bill provide a low-income exemption, for those individuals with incomes below the tax filing threshold (House) or below the poverty threshold (Senate). The Senate also includes a "hardship" exemption for people who cannot afford insurance, included in the President's Proposal. It protects those who would face premiums of more than 8 percent of their income from having to pay any assessment and they can purchase a low-cost catastrophic plan in the exchange if they choose.

The President's Proposal adopts the Senate approach but lowers the flat dollar assessments, and raises the percent of income assessment that individuals pay if they choose not to become insured. Specifically, it lowers the flat dollar amounts from $495 to $325 in 2015 and $750 to $695 in 2016. Subsequent years are indexed to $695 rather than $750, so the flat dollar amounts in later years are lower than the Senate bill as well. The President's Proposal raises the percent of income that is an alternative payment amount from 0.5 to 1.0% in 2014, 1.0 to 2.0% in 2015, and 2.0 to 2.5% for 2016 and subsequent years – the same percent of income as in the House bill, which makes the assessment more progressive. For ease of administration, the President's Proposal changes the payment exemption from the Senate policy (individuals with income below the poverty threshold) to individuals with income below the tax filing threshold (the House policy). In other words, a married couple with income below $18,700 will not have to pay the assessment. The President's Proposal also adopts the Senate's "hardship" exemption.

STRENGTHEN EMPLOYER RESPONSIBILITY

Businesses are strained by the current health insurance system. Health costs eat into their ability to hire workers, invest in and expand their businesses, and compete locally and globally. Like individuals, larger employers should share in the responsibility for finding the solution. Under the Senate bill, there is no mandate for employers to provide health insurance. But as a matter of fairness, the Senate bill requires large employers (i.e., those with more than 50 workers) to make payments only if taxpayers are supporting the health insurance for their workers. The assessment on the employer is $3,000 per full-time worker obtaining tax credits in the exchange if that employer's coverage is unaffordable, or $750 per full-time worker if the employer has a worker obtaining tax credits in the exchange but doesn't offer coverage in the first place. The House bill requires a payroll tax for insurers that do not offer health insurance that meets minimum standards. The tax is 8% generally and phases in for employers with annual payrolls from $500,000 to $750,000; according to the Congressional Budget Office (CBO), the assessment for a firm with average wages of $40,000 would be $3,200 per worker.

Under the President's Proposal, small businesses will receive $40 billion in tax credits to support coverage for their workers beginning this year. Consistent with the Senate bill, small businesses with fewer than 50 workers would be exempt from any employer responsibility policies.

The President's Proposal is consistent with the Senate bill in that it does not impose a mandate on employers to offer or provide health insurance, but does require them to help defray the cost if taxpayers are footing the bill for their workers. The President's Proposal improves the transition to the employer responsibility policy for employers with 50 or more workers by subtracting out the first 30 workers from the payment calculation (e.g., a firm with 51 workers that does not offer coverage will pay an amount equal to 51 minus 30, or 21 times the applicable per employee payment amount). It changes the applicable payment amount for firms with more than 50 employees that do not offer coverage to $2,000 – an amount that is one-third less than the average House assessment for a typical firm and less than half of the average employer contribution to health insurance in 2009. It applies the same firm-size threshold across the board to all industries. It fully eliminates the assessment for workers in a waiting period, while maintaining the 90-day limit on the length of any waiting period beginning in 2014.

POLICIES TO CRACK DOWN ON WASTE, FRAUD AND ABUSE

The House and Senate health reform bills contain an unprecedented array of aggressive new authorities to fight waste, fraud and abuse. The President's Proposal builds on those provisions by incorporating a number of additional proposals that are either part of the Administration's FY 2011 Budget Proposal or were included in Republican plans.

COMPREHENSIVE SANCTIONS DATABASE

The President's Proposal establishes a comprehensive Medicare and Medicaid sanctions database, overseen by the HHS Inspector General. This database will provide a central storage location, allowing for law enforcement access to information related to past sanctions on health care providers, suppliers and related entities. (Source: H.R. 3400, "Empowering Patients First Act" (Republican Study Committee bill))

REGISTRATION AND BACKGROUND CHECKS OF BILLING AGENCIES AND INDIVIDUALS

In an effort to decrease dishonest billing practices in the Medicare program, the President's Proposal will assist in reducing the number of individuals and agencies with a history of fraudulent activities participating in Federal health care programs. It ensures that entities that bill for Medicare on behalf of providers are in good standing. It also strengthens the Secretary's ability to exclude from Medicare individuals who knowingly submit false or fraudulent claims. (Source: H.R. 3970, "Medical Rights & Reform Act" (Kirk bill))

EXPANDED ACCESS TO THE HEALTHCARE INTEGRITY AND PROTECTION DATA BANK

Increasing access to the health care integrity data bank will improve coordination and information sharing in anti-fraud efforts. The President's Proposal broadens access to the data bank to quality control and peer review organizations and private plans that are involved in furnishing items or services reimbursed by Federal health care program. It includes criminal penalties for misuse. (Source: H.R. 3970, "Medical Rights & Reform Act" (Kirk bill))

LIABILITY OF MEDICARE ADMINISTRATIVE CONTRACTORS FOR CLAIMS SUBMITTED BY EXCLUDED PROVIDERS

In attacking fraud, it is critical to ensure the contractors that are paying claims are doing their utmost to ensure excluded providers do not receive Medicare payments. Therefore, the President's Proposal provision holds Medicare Administrative Contractors accountable for Federal payment for individuals or entities excluded from the Federal programs or items or services for which payment is denied. (Source: H.R. 3970, "Medical Rights & Reform Act" (Kirk bill))

COMMUNITY MENTAL HEALTH CENTERS

The President's Proposal ensures that individuals have access to comprehensive mental health services in the community setting, but strengthens standards for facilities that seek reimbursement as community mental health centers by ensuring these facilities are not taking advantage of Medicare patients or the taxpayers. (Source: H.R. 3970, "Medical Rights & Reform Act" (Kirk bill))

LIMITING DEBT DISCHARGE IN BANKRUPTCIES OF FRAUDULENT HEALTH CARE PROVIDERS OR SUPPLIERS

The President's Proposal will assist in recovering overpayments made to providers and suppliers and return such funds to the Medicare Trust Fund. It prevents fraudulent health care providers from discharging through bankruptcy amounts due to the Secretary from overpayments. (Source: H.R. 3970, "Medical Rights & Reform Act" (Kirk bill))

USE OF TECHNOLOGY FOR REAL-TIME DATA REVIEW

The President's Proposal speeds access to claims data to identify potentially fraudulent payments more quickly. It establishes a system for using technology to provide real-time data analysis of claim and payments under public programs to identify and stop waste, fraud and abuse. (Source: Roskam Amendment offered in House Ways & Means Committee markup)

ILLEGAL DISTRIBUTION OF A MEDICARE OR MEDICAID BENEFICIARY IDENTIFICATION OR BILLING PRIVILEGES

Fraudulent billing to Medicare and Medicaid programs costs taxpayers millions of dollars each year. Individuals looking to gain access to a beneficiary's personal information approach Medicare and Medicaid beneficiaries with false incentives. Many beneficiaries unwittingly give over this personal information without ever receiving promised services. The President's Proposal adds strong sanctions, including jail time, for individuals who purchase, sell or distribute Medicare beneficiary identification numbers or billing privileges under Medicare or Medicaid – if done knowingly, intentionally, and with intent to defraud. (Source: H.R. 3970, "Medical Rights & Reform Act" (Kirk bill))

STUDY OF UNIVERSAL PRODUCT NUMBERS CLAIMS FORMS FOR SELECTED ITEMS AND SERVICES UNDER THE MEDICARE PROGRAM

The President's Proposal requires HHS to study and issue a report to Congress that examines the costs and benefits of assigning universal product numbers (UPNs) to selected items and services reimbursed under Medicare. The report must examine whether UPNs could help improve the efficient operation of Medicare and its ability to detect fraud and abuse. (Source: H.R. 3970, "Medical Rights & Reform Act" (Kirk bill), Roskam Amendment offered in House Ways & Means Committee markup)

MEDICAID PRESCRIPTION DRUG PROFILING

The President's Proposal requires States to monitor and remediate high-risk billing activity, not limited to prescription drug classes involving a high volume of claims, to improve Medicaid integrity and beneficiary quality of care. States may choose one or more drug classes and must develop or review and update their care plan to reduce utilization and remediate any preventable episodes of care where possible. Requiring States to monitor high-risk billing activity to identify prescribing and utilization patterns that may indicate abuse or excessive prescription drug utilization will assist in improving Medicaid program integrity and save taxpayer dollars. (Source: President's FY 2011 Budget)

MEDICARE ADVANTAGE RISK ADJUSTMENT ERRORS

The President's Proposal requires in statute that the HHS Secretary extrapolate the error rate found in the risk adjustment data validation (RADV) audits to the entire Medicare Advantage contract payment for a given year when recouping overpayments. Extrapolating risk score errors in MA plans is consistent with the methodology used in the Medicare fee-for-service program and enables Medicare to recover risk adjustment overpayments. MA plans have an incentive to report more severe beneficiary diagnoses than are justified because they receive higher payments for higher risk scores.(Source: President's FY 2011 Budget)

Modify Certain Medicare Medical Review Limitations

The Medicare Modernization Act of 2003 placed certain limitations on the type of review that could be conducted by Medicare Administrative Contractors prior to the payment of Medicare Part A and B claims. The President's Proposal modifies these statutory provisions that currently limit random medical review and place statutory limitations on the application of Medicare prepayment review. Modifying certain medical review limitations will give Medicare contractors better and more efficient access to medical records and claims, which helps to reduce waste, fraud and abuse. (Source: President's FY 2011 Budget)

Establish a CMS-IRS Data Match to Identify Fraudulent Providers

The President's Proposal authorizes the Centers for Medicare & Medicaid Services (CMS) to work collaboratively with the Internal Revenue Service (IRS) to determine which providers have seriously delinquent tax debt to help identify potentially fraudulent providers sooner. The data match will primarily target certain high-risk provider types in high-vulnerability areas. This proposal also enables both IRS and Medicare to recoup any monies owed to the Federal government through this program. By requiring the Internal Revenue Service (IRS) to disclose to CMS those entities that have evaded filing taxes and matching the data against provider billing data, this proposal will enable CMS to better detect fraudulent providers billing the Medicare program. (Source: President's FY 2011 Budget)

Preventing Delays in Access to Generic Drugs

Currently, brand-name pharmaceutical companies can delay generic competition through agreements whereby they pay the generic company to keep its drug off the market for a period of time, called "pay-for-delay." This hurts consumers by delaying their access to generic drugs, which are usually less expensive than their branded counterparts. The Federal Trade Commission (FTC) recently estimated that this could cost consumers $35 billion over 10 years. The President's proposal adopts a provision from the bipartisan legislation that gives the FTC enforcement authority to address this problem. Specifically, it makes anti-competitive and unlawful any agreement in which a generic drug manufacturer receives anything of value from a brand-name drug manufacturer that contains a provision in which the generic drug manufacturer agrees to limit or forego research, development, marketing, manufacturing or sales of the generic drug. This presumption can only be overcome if the parties to such an agreement demonstrate by clear and convincing evidence that the pro-competitive benefits of the agreement outweigh the anti-competitive effects of the agreement. The proposal also requires the Chief Executive Officer of the branded pharmaceutical company to certify to the accuracy and completeness of any agreements required to be filed with the FTC.

Policies to Contain Costs and Ensure Fiscal Sustainability

Improve Medicare Advantage Payments

Medicare currently overpays private plans by 14 percent on average to provide the same benefits as the traditional program – and much more in some areas of the country. The Medicare Advantage program has also done little to reward quality. Moreover, plans have gamed the payment system in ways drive up the public cost of the program. All of this is why Medicare Advantage has become a very profitable line of business for some of the nation's largest health insurers. The Senate bill creates a bidding model for payment rates and phases in changes to limit potential disruptions for beneficiaries. The House proposal phases payments down based on local fee-for-service costs.

The President's Proposal represents a compromise between the House and Senate bills, blending elements of both bills, while providing greater certainty of cost savings by linking to current fee-for-service costs. Specifically, the President's Proposal creates a set of benchmark payments at different percentages of the current average fee-for-service costs in an area. It phases these benchmarks in gradually in order to avoid disruption to beneficiaries, taking into account the relative payments to fee-for-service costs in an area. It provides bonuses for quality and enrollee satisfaction. It adjusts rebates of savings between the benchmark payment and actual plan bid to take into account the transition as well as a plan's quality rating: plans with low quality scores receive lower rebates (i.e., can keep less of any savings they generate). Finally, the President's Proposal requires a payment adjustment for unjustified coding patterns in Medicare Advantage plans that have raised payments more rapidly than the evidence of their enrollees' health status and costs suggests is warranted, based on actuarial analysis. This is the primary source of additional savings compared to the Senate proposal.

DELAY AND REFORM THE HIGH-COST PLAN EXCISE TAX

Part of the reason for high and rising insurance costs is that insurers have little incentive to lower their premiums. The Senate bill includes a tax on high-cost health insurance plans. CBO has estimated that this policy will reduce premiums as well as contribute to long-run deficit reduction. The President's Proposal changes the effective date of the Senate policy from 2013 to 2018 to provide additional transition time for high-cost plans to become more efficient. It also raises the amount of premiums that are exempt from the assessment from $8,500 for singles to $10,200 and from $23,000 for families to $27,500 and indexes these amounts for subsequent years at general inflation plus 1 percent. To the degree that health costs rise unexpectedly quickly between now and 2018, the initial threshold would be adjusted upwards automatically. To ensure that the tax affects firms equitably, the President's Proposal reforms it by including an adjustment for firms whose health costs are higher due to the age or gender of their workers, and by no longer counting dental and vision benefits as potentially taxable benefits. The President's Proposal maintains the Senate bill's permanent adjustment in favor of high-risk occupations such as "first responders."

BROADEN THE MEDICARE HOSPITAL INSURANCE (HI) TAX BASE FOR HIGH-INCOME TAXPAYERS

Under current law, people who earn a salary pay the Medicare HI tax on their earned income, but those who have substantial unearned income do not, raising issues of fairness. The House bill includes a 5.4% surcharge on high-income households to improve the fairness of the tax system and to support health reform. The Senate bill includes an increase in the HI tax for high-income households for similar reasons, an increase of 0.9% on earnings above a specific threshold for a total employee assessment of 2.35% on these amounts. The President's Proposal adopts the Senate bill approach and adds a 2.9 percent assessment (equal to the combined employer and employee share of the existing HI tax) on income from interest, dividends, annuities, royalties and rents, other than such income which is derived in the ordinary course of a trade or business which is not a passive activity (e.g., income from active participation in S corporations) on taxpayers with respect to income above $200,000 for singles and $250,000 for married couples filing jointly. The additional revenues from the tax on earned income would be credited to the HI trust fund and the revenues from the tax on unearned income would be credited to the Supplemental Medical Insurance (SMI) trust fund.

INCREASE IN FEES ON BRAND NAME PHARMACEUTICALS

As more Americans gain health insurance, more will be able to pay for prescription drugs. Moreover, the President's plan closes the Medicare "donut hole," ensuring that seniors do not skip or cut back on needed prescriptions. Both policies will result in new revenue for the pharmaceutical industry. The President's Proposal increases the revenue from the assessment on this industry which is $23 billion in the Senate bill by $10 billion over 10 years. It also delays the implementation of these fees by one year, until 2011, and makes changes to facilitate administration by the IRS.

CLOSE TAX LOOPHOLES

Adopts two House proposals to close tax loopholes: (1) Current law provides a tax credit for the production of cellulosic biofuels. The credit was designed to promote the production and use of renewable fuels. Certain liquid byproducts derived from processing paper or pulp (known as "black liquor" when derived from the kraft process) were not intended to be covered by this credit. The President's Proposal adopts the House bill's policy to clarify that they are not eligible for the tax credit. (2) The President's Proposal helps prevent unjustified tax shelters by clarifying the circumstances under which transactions have "economic substance" (as opposed to being undertaken solely to obtain tax benefits) and raises the penalties for transactions that lack economic substance. In so doing, it adopts the House's policy, with minor technical changes.

OTHER POLICY IMPROVEMENTS

IMPROVE THE FAIRNESS OF FEDERAL FUNDING FOR STATES

States have been partners with the Federal government in creating a health care safety net for low-income and vulnerable populations. They administer and share in the cost of Medicaid and the Children's Health Insurance Program (CHIP). The Senate bill creates a nationwide Medicaid eligibility floor as a foundation for exchanges at $29,000 for a family of 4 (133% of poverty) – and provides financial support that varies by State to do so.

Relative to the Senate bill, the President's Proposal replaces the variable State support in the Senate bill with uniform 100% Federal support for all States for newly eligible individuals from 2014 through 2017, 95% support for 2018 and 2019, and 90% for 2020 and subsequent years. This approach resembles that in the House bill, which provided full support for all States for the first two years, and then 91% support thereafter. The President's Proposal also recognizes the early investment that some States have made in helping the uninsured by expanding Medicaid to adults with income below 100% of poverty by increasing those States' matching rate on certain health care services by 8 percentage points beginning in 2014. The President's Proposal also provides additional assistance to the Territories, raising the Medicaid funding cap by 35% rather than the Senate bill's 30%.

SIMPLIFY INCOME DEFINITIONS

The President's Proposal seeks to simplify eligibility rules for various existing programs as well as for the new tax credits. Consistent with some of the policies in the House bill, the President's Proposal will conform income definitions to make the system simpler for beneficiaries to navigate and States and the Federal government to administer by: changing the definition of income used for assistance from modified gross income to modified adjusted gross income, which is easier to implement; creating a 5% income disregard for certain Medicaid eligibility determinations to ease the transition from States' current use of income disregards; streamlining the income reconciliation process for determining tax credits and reduced cost sharing; and clarifying the tax treatment of employer contributions for adultdependent coverage.

DELAY AND REFORM OF FEES ON HEALTH INSURANCE PROVIDERS

Like the drug industry, the health insurance industry stands to gain as more Americans get coverage. The Senate bill includes a $67 billion assessment on health insurers over 10 years to offset some of the cost of enrolling millions of Americans in their plans. The President's Proposal delays the assessment until 2014 to coincide with broader coverage provisions which will substantially expand the market for health insurance providers. It provides limited exemptions for plans that serve critical purposes for the community, including non-profits that receive more than 80 percent of their income from government programs targeting low-income or elderly populations, or those with disabilities, as well as for voluntary employees' beneficiary associations (VEBAs) that are not established by employers.

DELAY AND CONVERT FEE ON MEDICAL DEVICE MANUFACTURERS TO EXCISE TAX

The medical device industry also stands to gain from expanding health insurance coverage. Both the House and Senate bills raise $20 billion in revenue from this industry over 10 years. The President's Proposal replaces the medical device fee with an excise tax (yielding the same revenue) that starts in 2013 to facilitate administration by the IRS.

STRENGTHEN THE CLASS ACT

The House and Senate health insurance reform proposals include the Community Living Assistance Services and Supports (CLASS) Program, a voluntary, privately-funded long-term services insurance program. The CLASS Program offers workers an optional payroll deduction for an insurance program that provides a cash benefit if they become disabled. The President's Proposal makes a series of changes to the Senate bill to improve the CLASS program's financial stability and ensure its long-run solvency.

PROTECT THE SOCIAL SECURITY TRUST FUNDS

The President's Proposal provides that, if necessary, funds will be transferred to the Social Security Trust Funds to ensure that they are held harmless by the Proposal.

ENSURE EFFECTIVE IMPLEMENTATION

The policy changes in health insurance reform will require careful, effective, deliberate, and transparent implementation. The President's Proposal appropriates $1 billion for the Administration to implement health insurance reform policies. It also delays several of the policies to ensure effective implementation and improve transitions: the therapeutic discovery credit, elimination of the deduction for expenses allocable to the Medicare Part D subsidy, the pharmaceutical and medical device industry fees, and the health insurance industry fee.

Learn more about the President's Proposal at http:www.whitehouse.gov/health-care-meeting

Yes, Mr. President A Free Market Can Fix Health Care

Michael F. Cannon

EXECUTIVE SUMMARY

In March 2009, President Barack Obama said, "If there is a way of getting this done where we're driving down costs and people are getting health insurance at an affordable rate, and have choice of doctor, have flexibility in terms of their plans, and we could do that entirely through the market, I'd be happy to do it that way." This paper explains how letting workers control their health care dollars and tearing down regulatory barriers to competition would control costs, expand choice, improve health care quality, and make health coverage more secure.

First, Congress should give Medicare enrolees a voucher and the freedom to choose any health plan on the market. Vouchers would be means-tested, would contain Medicare spending, and are the only way to protect seniors from government rationing.

Second, to give workers control over their health care dollars, Congress should reform the tax treatment of health care with "large" health savings accounts. Large HSAs would reduce the number of uninsured Americans, would free workers to purchase secure health coverage from any source, and would effectively give workers a $9.7 trillion tax cut without increasing the federal budget deficit.

Third, Congress should break up state monopolies on insurance and clinician licensing. Allowing consumers to purchase health insurance licensed by other states could cover one-third of the uninsured without any new taxes or government subsidies.

Finally, Congress should reform Medicaid and the State Children's Health Insurance Program the way it reformed welfare in 1996. Block-granting those programs would reduce the deficit and encourage states to target resources to the truly needy.

The great advantage of a free market is that innovation and more prudent decisionmaking means that fewer patients will fall through the cracks.

> Whereas President Obama attempts to pour more resources into health care, a free market would get more out of America's health care sector.

INTRODUCTION

In March 2009, at the outset of his effort to overhaul America's health care sector, President Barack Obama told a White House summit:

> If there is a way of getting this done where we're driving down costs and people are getting health insurance at an affordable rate, and have choice of doctor, have flexibility in terms of their plans, and we could do that entirely through the market, I'd be happy to do it that way.[1]

This paper explains how a free market can and would control costs, expand choice, improve health care quality, and make health coverage more secure. The key steps that would move America toward a free health care market are Medicare, tax, and regulatory reforms that give consumers control over their health care dollars and free them to choose from a wide variety of providers and health plans.

At present, America's health care sector is far from a free market. Government directly controls nearly half of all health care spending, and indirectly controls most of the remainder.[2] Government controls more than half of the nation's health *insurance* dollars (through Medicare, Medicaid, and other public programs), and delegates control over another third to employers through the preferential tax treatment granted to employer-sponsored

---

Michael F. Cannon is director of health policy studies at the Cato Institute and coauthor of Healthy Competition: What's Holding Back Health Care and How to Free It.

"Yes, Mr. President: A Free Market Can Fix Health Care" by Michael F. Cannon, from *Policy Analysis*, No. 650. Copyright © 2009 by Cato Institute. Reproduced with permission of Cato Institute in the format Textbook via Copyright Clearance Center.

health insurance.[3] The federal government imposes an average tax penalty of more than 40 percent on the one market that offers a wide range of health plans and seamless coverage between jobs: the "individual" market, where consumers purchase coverage directly from insurers. (Indeed, that tax penalty may explain much public dissatisfaction with the individual market.[4]) More than half of U.S. health care spending takes place under government price and exchange controls. As President Obama's economic adviser Larry Summers reminds us, "Price and exchange controls inevitably create harmful economic distortions. Both the distortions and the economic damage get worse with time."[5] That is to say nothing of the countless counterproductive regulations that government imposes on clinicians, insurance, medical products, and health care facilities.[6]

As health economist Victor Fuchs explains, most leading health care reforms "aim at cost shifting rather than cost reduction."[7] Whereas the legislation that President Obama is shepherding through Congress attempts to cover the uninsured by pouring more resources into health care, a free market would get more out of America's health care sector. Letting Americans control their health care dollars and breaking up the states' monopolies on insurance and clinician licensing (with "regulatory federalism") would put access to health care within reach of millions of Americans by putting downward pressure on health care prices and health insurance premiums. Those reforms would also dramatically improve quality by allowing various health plans, with various payment systems and delivery systems, to compete on a level playing field.

Controlling Costs

Health care spending is growing unsustainably. Over the past 30 years, health care spending has grown more than 2 percentage points faster than the economy overall,[8] and now stands at 18 percent of GDP.[9]

That would not be a problem if we were getting our money's worth. The most credible estimates, however, suggest an alarming one-third of health care spending does nothing to make patients healthier or happier.[10] In 2009, Americans will waste more than $800 billion—about 6 percent of U.S. GDP—on medical care that provides zero benefit to patients. Americans will waste additional billions on services whose benefits are not worth the cost. That wasteful spending results in higher taxes, higher health insurance premiums, and more uninsured Americans.

Government Failure

Government is largely incapable of eliminating wasteful health care spending, because nobody spends other people's money as carefully as they spend their own. Government tax and entitlement policy denies patients ownership of their health care dollars, and thereby strips them of any incentive to control costs. Due to federal tax policy, for example, Stanford University health economist Alain Enthoven estimates that "less than 5 percent of the insured workforce can both choose a health plan and reap the full savings from choosing economically."[11] Indeed, consumers resist efforts to eliminate wasteful spending, and with good reason. Since they are enjoying health insurance that is effectively purchased with other people's money, consumers receive no direct financial benefit from eliminating wasteful spending, whether through cost-sharing or care management. When Medicare tries to eliminate coverage of low-value services or to reduce excessive provider payments, seniors experience nothing but pain. Workers perceive increased cost-sharing or managed-care controls as cuts in their compensation. Even though these steps should ultimately lead to higher wages and lower taxes, those benefits are not salient to seniors and workers.[12]

That lack of cost-consciousness creates what author David Goldhill describes as "an accidental collusion between providers benefiting from higher costs and patients who don't fully bear them."[13] Former Senate Majority Leader Tom Daschle writes that this results in a politically powerful "patient-provider pincer movement" that blocks efforts to reduce wasteful spending.[14] The patient-provider pincer movement prevents Medicare from considering cost-effectiveness when deciding whether to cover particular services; repeatedly eliminates funding for federal agencies that conduct comparative-effectiveness research;[15] preserves excessive Medicare payments for specialists, insurers, and procedures; blocks competitive bidding for durable medical equipment in Medicare; has made a joke out of the scheduled "sustainable-growth-rate" cuts to Medicare physician payments; and even curtails private-sector efforts to eliminate wasteful spending with managed-care controls.

The end result is that both government-and employer-sponsored insurance waste money in ways that consumers spending their own money never would. If the health reform legislation currently before Congress becomes law, politicians and employers will continue to control Americans' health care dollars, and this government failure will persist.[16]

THE FREE-MARKET ALTERNATIVE

A free market, in contrast, would eliminate wasteful health care spending. Individuals would control their own health care dollars and would therefore benefit directly from reducing waste. A less-regulated market would also free Americans to choose from a wide variety of health plans and providers.

When consumers own and control their health care dollars—in particular, the money that purchases their health insurance—the self-interest of hundreds of millions of Americans will lead them to choose health plans that eliminate wasteful spending, whether through cost-sharing or care management, in exchange for lower premiums. Peter Orszag, President Obama's director of the Office of Management and Budget, testified before Congress on the promise of individual ownership:

> Government is largely incapable of eliminating wasteful health care spending, because nobody spends other people's money as carefully as they spend their own.

" Workers may demand less efficiency from the health system than they would if they knew the full cost that they pay via forgone wages for coverage or if they knew the actual cost of the services being provided.[17]

[I]magine what the world would be like if workers [understood] that today it was costing them $10,000 a year in take-home pay for their employer-spon-sored insurance, and that could be $7,000 and they could have $3,000 more in their pockets today if we could relieve these inefficiencies out of the health system. Making those costs more transparent may generate demand for efficiency.[18]

Consumers who *own* the money they are spending are a cornerstone of free and functional markets. A free market would reduce wasteful spending with minimal harm because, unlike price controls and other tools of government rationing,[19] markets allocate resources according to consumer preferences, rather than the preferences of politicians, government bureaucrats, or special-interest lobbyists.

Restoring individual ownership to health care will require a two-pronged strategy.

MEDICARE REFORM

For Americans covered by Medicare, Congress should give enrollees a voucher and let them choose any health plan available on the market.[20] To ensure that all beneficiaries can afford a basic health plan, Medicare should give larger vouchers to poorer and sicker seniors and smaller vouchers to healthy and wealthy seniors, using current health-risk-adjustment mechanisms[21] and Social Security data on lifetime earnings.[22]

The amount of each individual's voucher must be fixed, so that enrollees who want to purchase comprehensive coverage would have to pay more for it. Likewise, if a Medicare enrollee chooses an economical policy, she could save the balance of her voucher in an account dedicated to out-of-pocket medical expenses. When enrollees bear the added cost of comprehensive coverage, and reap the savings from more economical coverage, their self-interest will lead them to select health plans that curb wasteful spending. Letting seniors make their own rationing decisions is the only way to protect seniors from government rationing.[23]

> Medicare vouchers are the only way to protect seniors from government rationing.

TAX REFORM

In the film *Sicko*, director Michael Moore took five Ground Zero rescue workers to Cuba, where they received "free" treatment for the ailments they contracted during the 9/11 rescue effort. All five had employer-sponsored insurance on September 11, 2001, but lost their coverage when they subsequently lost those jobs.[24] Had they been free to purchase coverage directly from an insurance company without penalty, Moore would have had more difficulty finding sick, uninsured Americans.

To give people under age 65 the freedom to control their health care dollars without penalty, Congress must reform the tax code. Employer-provided health insurance currently receives favorable tax treatment compared to health insurance that consumers purchase directly. That tax preference reduces the after-tax price of employer-sponsored insurance by 30 percent on average, which is the equivalent of imposing a 42-percent tax penalty on coverage purchased directly from an insurance company. As a result, some 163 million non-elderly Americans obtain coverage through an employer, while only 18 million purchase coverage directly from an insurance company.[25] The "tax exclusion" for employer-sponsored insurance encourages wasteful health spending by also distorting the after-tax price of medical services relative to other uses of income.[26]

This supposed tax "break" for employer-sponsored health insurance actually operates more like a tax hike, because it denies workers control over a large portion of their earnings as well as their health care decisions. To obtain this tax break in 2009, workers with self-only coverage sacrificed control over more than $4,000 of their earnings to their employers, while those with family coverage sacrificed control of nearly $10,000, on average.[27] Analysts typically call those amounts the "employer contribution" to the cost of health benefits, yet economists agree that employers fund those contributions by reducing workers' wages.[28] In other words, that money is part of each worker's earnings, but the worker does not and cannot control it. This tax break also largely confines workers' coverage choices to the few (if any) options their employer offers. In 2008, 80 percent of covered workers had at most two health insurance options; 47 percent had only one option.[29]

The tax preference for employer-sponsored insurance therefore creates a health insurance "market" that largely resembles a government program. Much like a tax, it denies workers control over their earnings. Much like a government program, it empowers agents—that is, employers—to determine whether consumers will have a choice of health plans, and what those choices will be. As with government programs, federal nondiscrimination rules effectively impose price controls that prohibit insurance premiums from varying according to risk.

Returning those earnings to the workers requires reforming the tax code so that all health insurance—whether purchased through an employer or directly from an insurer—receives the same tax treatment. For example, replacing the current tax exclusion with either health-insurance tax credits,[30] a standard deduction for health insurance,[31] or large health savings accounts[32] would level the playing field between employment-based coverage and other sources of health insurance. Absent any tax preference for employer-sponsored coverage, workers could demand that employers give them their $4,000 or $10,000 as cash, and could use those funds to purchase coverage from any source. A competitive labor market would force employers to comply.[33]

All of which means that eliminating the tax preference for job-based insurance would be an enormous tax *cut*. First and most obvious, the above-mentioned tax reforms would provide tax breaks to all individuals, regardless of where they purchase health insurance. Those reforms would therefore deliver tax relief to individuals who purchase insurance outside an employment setting, and who currently receive no tax break.

Second, and less obvious, eliminating the tax preference for employer-sponsored insurance would result in a massive tax cut for workers with employer-sponsored insurance, because each insured worker would gain control over $4,000 or $10,000 of her earnings that she currently does not control. In 2007, employers contributed more than $532 billion to employee health benefits. In the prior 10 years, aggregate employer contributions grew at an average rate of 8 percent. Assuming that they continue to grow at that rate through 2019, employer contributions to employee health benefits will total $9.7 trillion over the next 10 years.[34]

> Eliminating the tax preference for job-based insurance would be an enormous tax *cut* totaling $9.7 trillion over the next 10 years.

Eliminating the tax preference for employer-sponsored insurance would therefore shift control over more than $532 billion each year, and $9.7 trillion over the next 10 years, from employers to workers. That effective $9.7 trillion tax cut would not increase the federal budget deficit, and it would more than swamp any small, explicit tax increases that altering the existing tax treatment of employer-sponsored insurance would impose on some insured workers.[35] Unlike other tax reforms, Large HSAs would deliver that tax cut immediately and with greater transparency.

Workers would receive that tax cut even if employers immediately dropped their health benefits. An employer who did not cash out its workers would lose those workers to competing firms who either continue to offer health benefits, or who pay workers the cash equivalent of those health benefits. The CBO writes:

> To be sure, workers' cash compensation might not increase immediately by the full amount of any reduction in employers' payments for health insurance. For that reason, firms that currently contribute toward the costs of their workers' health benefits could temporarily reap some savings in labor costs.[36]

But those savings would not be permanent, because a competitive labor market would force those firms to pay workers the full value of those cancelled health benefits. Again, Large HSAs would make that tax cut immediate and transparent, and all but eliminate the incentive for employers to capture that short-term gain.

Eliminating the tax preference for employer-sponsored insurance would also expand consumers' health plan choices. Workers would be free to remain with their company's health plan. Yet they would no longer be confined to the few (if any) choices their employer offers. They could choose any health plan available on the market; including plans with varying benefits, cost-sharing structures, delivery systems, and payment systems. Consumers who value greater physician choice, but who are currendy locked into closed-panel managed-care plans, could select a fee-for-service plan. Consumers who value lower premiums more than physician choice could do the reverse.

In the process, consumers' self-interest would eliminate wasteful spending. The Congressional Budget Office writes that "with a fixed-dollar tax credit or deduction . . . employees would capture more of the savings from choosing a cheaper plan. As a result, the CBO estimates that people would ultimately select plans with premiums that are between 15 percent and 20 percent lower than the premiums they would pay under current law."[37] Unlike government efforts to ration medical care, consumers would curb spending in ways that fit their individual preferences.

Medicare reform and tax reform would further reduce costs by spurring greater competition between health plans and providers. With seniors choosing from a menu of private health plans, the market would no longer operate under the stranglehold of Medicare's fee-for-service price and exchange controls. Greater competition would put downward pressure on prices for medical services. Provider competition would also grow as cost-conscious consumers make greater use of mid-level clinicians for basic care, such as through retail clinics and other settings.[38]

ANSWERING THE CRITICS

Few dispute that letting consumers control their health care dollars would reduce wasteful health care spending. The most common criticism of individual ownership is that consumers would restrain spending too much; that many consumers would skimp on care, leading to higher costs down the road. Research suggests that is not the case. The RAND Health Insurance Experiment showed that either cost-sharing or care management can reduce wasteful health care spending without harming overall health.[39] Individual ownership and greater competition could even improve health by expanding access to health plans that emphasize preventive care, coordinated care, information technologies (including electronic medical records), medical-error reduction, and comparative-effectiveness research.[40]

Critics also fear that, in the transition from the current tax preference for employer-sponsored insurance to a level playing field, some workers with high-cost illnesses would be unable to obtain coverage. If enough workers leave an employer's health plan for the individual market, the employer may have to drop its health benefits. The sickest people in those pools would then have difficulty purchasing coverage on their own.

For several reasons, this serious concern should not be an obstacle to letting workers control their own money. First, thousands of workers are already losing their employer-sponsored insurance with every passing day, because employers are either dropping coverage or eliminating jobs.[41] Many have expensive illnesses and are subsequently unable to purchase coverage. They generally receive no tax breaks to help them purchase private health insurance. Tax reform would assist those workers by reducing the after-tax

> The individual market provides coverage as secure as, or more secure than, job-based coverage.

cost of coverage for everyone who purchases insurance on the individual market.

Second, the freedom to purchase health insurance directly from an insurance company—coverage that stays with consumers between jobs—will guarantee that fewer Americans would find themselves in such dire straits. Economists Mark Pauly and Robert Lieberthal found that, for people with high-cost illnesses, the individual market provides coverage as secure as, or more secure than, job-based coverage: "a young male high risk who initially had small-[employer] coverage faces a 44 percent chance of becoming uninsured . . . a risk nearly twice as great as it would be if he initially had individual insurance."[42]

Third, the individual market does a better job of providing health insurance to the sick than conventional wisdom suggests. Pauly, Susan Marquis of the RAND Corporation, and their respective colleagues find that there is significant subsidization of the sick by the healthy in the individual market, and that such pooling increases over time.[43] Contrary to the conventional wisdom, Marquis and colleagues find that in California's individual market, "a large number of people with health problems do obtain coverage."[44]

Fourth, the above-mentioned tax reforms would put relatively more money in the hands of workers with higher medical costs. Economists consistently find that cash wages adjust downward to account for the higher costs that older,[45] obese,[46] and female[47] employees impose on an employer's health plan. Put differently, workers with costly medical conditions accept lower wages than they could otherwise command, in order to obtain health benefits.

Those workers would therefore receive the biggest tax cuts after eliminating the tax preference for employer-sponsored insurance. The fact that those workers currently accept lower wages than they could otherwise command means that they would generally receive more than the average $4,000 or $10,000 annual cash-out. A free market would therefore do exactly what so-called "risk-adjustment" schemes attempt to do: target resources to the people who need them most.

Whereas President Obama and congressional Democrats have proposed taxing high-cost health plans, which would hit older, unionized, and female workers the hardest, eliminating the tax preference for employer-sponsored insurance would give those workers the most tax *relief*. Unlike other tax reforms, which would delay that tax cut, Large HSAs would deliver those resources to sick workers immediately. To the extent that those workers are at a higher risk of losing their jobs and their coverage because they fall ill, the freedom to purchase secure, portable coverage is likewise more valuable to them than to other workers.

Finally, Large HSAs would go even further by extending the same tax relief to the uninsurable as to those who purchase insurance-something that no other tax reform proposal would do.

Affordable Coverage and a Choice of Doctors and Health Plans

Making health insurance more affordable requires more than giving consumers control over their health care dollars. Government regulations drive health care costs higher by blocking competition from more-efficient providers, insurance plans, delivery systems—and even more-efficient regulators. Reforming insurance and clinician regulation with "regulatory federalism" would make health insurance more affordable, as well as expand the freedom to choose one's own doctor and health plan.

Monopolistic Insurance Licensing

State health-insurance licensing is a prime example of costly regulation. Each state requires insurers to obtain a license from that state's government in order to sell insurance within that state's borders. Those laws effectively give each state a monopoly over providing consumer protections to insurance purchasers because they prevent employers and individuals from purchasing health insurance licensed and regulated by other states.[49]

Some form of regulation is necessary to ensure that health insurers keep their commitments to their enrollees. Yet monopolistic insurance-licensing laws may be more harmful than helpful. Those laws give government the power to dictate the terms of every health insurance policy sold in the state—a power that is inevitably captured by the health care industry.

> Some form of regulation is necessary. Yet monopolistic insurance-licensing laws may be more harmful than helpful.

As a result, state insurance-licensing laws require consumers to purchase coverage for an average of 42 specific types of health services—whether the consumer wants that coverage or not.[50] Some states also use insurance-licensing laws to enact price controls that tax healthy consumers to subsidize the sick. Those price-control laws typically do little to increase risk pooling,[51] but they do create perverse incentives for insurers to avoid the sick[52] and can cause insurance markets to unravel.[53] Physicians have used insurance-licensing laws to protect their incomes from market forces that would otherwise make health care more affordable.[54] The Congressional Budget Office estimates that state health insurance regulations increase health insurance premiums by 15 percent on average.[55] Eliminating just half of that burden could save families $1,000 or more on their premiums.[56]

> Like all monopolies, the monopolies that state governments hold over licensing clinicians and insurers produce high-cost, low-quality consumer protections.

Monopolistic Clinician Licensing

Regulation increases health care costs by blocking competition between clinicians as well.[57] As with insurance, each state requires clinicians to obtain a license from that state's government in order to practice within its borders. Those clinician-licensing laws define a "scope of practice" for each type of mid-level clinician, such as nurse practitioners and physician assistants. Those laws give government the power to decide what tasks each type of clinician may perform. Again, that power is inevitably captured by the health care industry—in this case, by competing clinicians, especially physicians.

Clinicians' scopes of practice are a perennial battleground for clinician groups who try to block competition for their members by narrowing the range of services that competing clinicians perform, or the settings in which they practice. Ophthalmologists use licensing laws to prevent optometrists from performing surgical procedures. Anesthesiologists use licensing laws to block competition from nurse anesthetists. Physicians use licensing laws to prevent podiatrists from treating the ankle,[58] as well as to restrict nurse practitioners' ability to prescribe drugs and operate retail clinics.[59] Physicians have even used clinician-licensing laws to block competition from health insurers that contain costs by making more extensive use of mid-level clinicians (e.g., physician assistants, nurse practitioners).[60] There is ample evidence that clinician-licensing laws have increased costs by blocking competition, yet there is little or no evidence that such laws have made patients any healthier.[61]

Some type of regulation is necessary to prevent clinicians (including physicians) from practicing beyond their competence. Like monopolistic insurance licensing, however, monopolistic clinician licensing appears to be an inadequate and even counterproductive form of regulation.

Break up Regulatory Monopolies

Consumer protections are ultimately a product. Like all monopolies, the monopolies that state governments hold over licensing clinicians and insurers produce high-cost, low-quality consumer protections. The most promising way to spur cost-saving competition between clinicians and insurers is to break up those monopolies and force regulators to compete to provide the best set of consumer protections.

With regard to insurance, that means preventing states from using their insurance-licensing laws as a barrier to entry for insurance products licensed by other states. An employer or consumer in Michigan, for example, should be allowed to purchase an insurance policy licensed in Connecticut or any other state, so that the only insurance regulations that would govern that relationship would be Connecticut's. Those regulations could be incorporated into the insurance contract, so that the purchaser could enforce Connecticut's consumer protections in Michigan courts, even with the help of Michigan's insurance commissioner.[62] (States courts frequently enforce other states' laws already.[63])

Allowing state-issued insurance licenses to cross state lines would make insurance more affordable. It would give employers and individual purchasers the freedom to choose only the coverage and regulatory protections they want, and to avoid unwanted regulatory costs. A study by Stephen Parente and colleagues at the University of Minnesota estimated that ending those regulatory monopolies could cover an additional 17 million Americans, or one-third of the most commonly cited estimate of the uninsured.[64] Moreover, it would do so without creating any new taxes or new government subsidies, and would likely reduce the federal deficit.[65]

With regard to clinicians, breaking up regulatory monopolies means preventing state governments from barring entry to clinicians licensed by other states. Physicians and other clinicians licensed by Virginia should be able to practice in Maryland or Maine or Montana under the terms of their Virginia license, while still subject to local malpractice rules. That change would give physicians and mid-level clinicians more freedom to live and practice where they wish.

The primary benefit of ending this regulatory monopoly, however, would likely come from encouraging competition by corporate providers of care,[66] such as retail clinics and health plans like Kaiser Permanente and Group Health Cooperative. Such providers operate their own facilities and employ their own staff of clinicians. Health plans like Kaiser and Group Health strive to make medical care more affordable, in part by using mid-level clinicians to their full competence. Making state-issued clinician licenses portable would enable such organizations to compete nationwide without facing different regulatory obstacles in each state.

Eliminating both types of regulatory monopoly would force states to compete to provide the protections that consumers demand, while avoiding unwanted regulatory costs. States that want to collect licensing fees and premium taxes would face powerful incentives to find the "right" amount of regulation—not too much and not too little—much like Delaware has made itself the go-to state in the market for corporate chartering laws.

Ideally, state legislatures would take the lead by recognizing the clinician and insurance licenses issued by other states. Yet Congress can act as well, using its powers under the Commerce Clause to tear down these barriers to trade between the states.[67]

"Regulatory federalism," as it is called, would expand the array of health-insurance and medical-delivery choices available to consumers—particularly by allowing competition from more efficient providers and health plans that states' regulatory monopolies hold at bay.

ANSWERING THE CRITICS

Critics fear that breaking up states' regulatory monopolies would spur states to gut essential consumer protections in an effort to capture health insurance premium taxes and clinician licensing fees. The result would be a "race to the bottom" where fly-by-night insurance companies and incompetent clinicians do harm to patients.

Yet political factors and competitive market forces would prevent a race to the bottom by restoring vital consumer protections. Suppose that Delaware gutted its consumer protections and began issuing licenses to sketchy insurers and clinicians, in the hope of collecting lots of premium taxes and licensing fees. Could Delaware get away with it? Not likely. First, some of those insurers and clinicians would inevitably harm Delaware residents, who would demand that their politicians restore those essential consumer protections. Second, competitors would discipline the low-quality clinicians and health plans licensed by Delaware. Higher-quality insurers and clinicians would advertise their credentials, including the fact that they comply with the stronger consumer protections demanded by other states. Third, courts in other states would deter Delaware-licensed insurers and clinicians from bad behavior by enforcing contracts and punishing medical negligence. Regulatory federalism would still allow each state to set its own medical malpractice rules, which provide additional (and perhaps superior) protections against incompetent clinicians. Finally, consumers themselves would discipline low-quality insurers and clinicians after learning of Delaware's reputation through the news, *Consume Reports*, and other

"Regulatory federalism" would allow competition from more efficient providers and health plans that states' regulatory monopolies hold at bay.

media. Whether Delaware eliminated vital consumer protections deliberately or inadvertently, these self-correcting mechanisms would restore those essential consumer protections.

Critics likewise fear that allowing consumers to avoid state-imposed price controls on health insurance would lead health insurers to dump patients because they need expensive care. Yet markets offer protections against such behavior. First, Mark Pauly and Johns Hopkins University economist Bradley Herring find that absent price controls, insurers set premiums so as to eliminate any incentive for low-risk consumers to avoid pooling with high-risk consumers.[68] Second, the controversy over rescissions in California's individual market demonstrates both that insurers may shirk their commitments to the sick, but also that the courts, media scrutiny, and the forces of reputation and competition check such behavior.[69] If Americans were free to choose their own health plan, the forces of reputation and competition would be even stronger (while administrative costs in the individual market would fall).[70] Third, University of Chicago economist John H. Cochrane explains that a free market would further discipline insurers by offering products that give even sick patients the freedom to flee a disreputable insurer.[71] Indeed, Cochrane explains, it is government price controls—not market forces—that encourage insurers to avoid sick people, because price controls prevent insurers from charging enrollees a premium that covers their cost to the plan.

Monopoly—not competition—produces a race to the bottom. Regulatory federalism will drive a race to equilibrium by finding the best balance between too little, regulation and too much regulation.

Helping the Needy

A free market would provide better and. more affordable health insurance to more Americans, but it would not provide health insurance to every last person. Many would require subsidized health care, either because they did not purchase health insurance when they could have, or because health insurance was never within their grasp.

The first contribution, that a free market would make to alleviate the suffering of the needy would be to reduce the number of Americans who find themselves unable to afford medical care. Through greater price competition and innovation, a free market would put health insurance and medical care within the reach for more low- and middle-income Americans. It would also provide more seamless and secure health insurance coverage, so that fewer Americans would find themselves sick and uninsured.

Moreover, subsidizing the needy need not disrupt the crucial progress that markets can make on reducing costs and improving quality. For example, considerable evidence suggests that government programs like Medicaid and the State Children's Health Insurance Program enroll many non-needy people who could obtain coverage on their own.[72] Better management of those programs would make more resources available for the truly needy.

Congress should build on the success of welfare reform by reforming those programs the same way it reformed the Aid to Families with Dependent Children program in 1996: with block grants that give states the ability and the incentive to target those resources to the truly needy.[73] As markets make health insurance more secure and medical care more affordable, fewer people will fall into this vulnerable situation, and it will be easier to care for those who do.

> Congress should reform Medicaid and the State Children's Health Insurance Program with block grants that give states the ability and the incentive to target those resources to the truly needy.

Conclusion

When President Obama said, "We've got to admit that the free market has not worked perfectly when it comes to health care," he was doubly correct. The free market hasn't worked perfectly, because it hasn't been given a chance to work at all.

But he was also correct in the sense that a free market would fall short of perfection. Contrary to former Vermont governor Howard Dean's assessment that Obama's reform plan is "perfect," perfection is not an option.[75] Former Senate majority leader Tom Daschle more sensibly observes, "Even if we achieve 'universal' coverage, there will be some percentage of people who still fall through the cracks."[76]

The risk of health care reforms that expand government control over health care—including a new "government option,"[77] mandates,[78] and price and exchange controls—is that they would further reduce innovation and lead to even less-prudent resource decisions, both of which will cause those cracks to widen.

The great advantage of a free market is that it encourages innovation and more prudent resource allocations, which fills those cracks in over time. Many believe health care reform should include a government guarantee of "universal coverage," which even supporters often admit isn't universal in reality. If a free market were to save even more people from falling through the cracks, who would hesitate to support it?

At his March 2009 health care summit, Obama also said, "In this effort, every voice has to be heard. Every idea must be considered."[79] At a town hall meeting in June 2009, he said, "I'm very open-minded. And if people can show me here's a good idea and here's how we can get it done and it's not something I've thought of, I'm happy to steal people's ideas. You know, I'm not ideologically driven one way or another about it."[80]

Letting consumers control their health care dollars and choose from a wide array of competing health plans and providers would make health care better, more affordable, safer, and more secure. Medicare reform, tax reform, and regulatory federalism stand ready to put those cornerstones of a free health care market in place.

They await their champion.

REVIEW QUESTIONS

1. How does health care at the beginning of the 21st century differ from health care at the beginning of the 20th century?
2. What factors contributed to the health care crises of cost and access?
3. How does the cost and quality of health care in the United States compare with the cost and quality in other developed nations?
4. What is Medicaid? Medicare? Who are the recipients of each?
5. What is the Health Security Act? What did it propose? Why was it defeated?
6. Discuss the Medicare Modernization Act of 2003. Why was this policy so controversial?

SELECT WEBSITES

This is the Medicaid homepage.
http://www.cms.gov/medicaid/

This is the Medicare Website.
http://www.medicare.org

KEY TERMS

American Medical Association
health maintenance organizations (HMOs)
Medicaid
Medicare Part A
Medicare Part B

Medicare Part C
Medicare Part D
Medigap
preferred provider organizations (PPOs)

NOTES

1. White House Office of the Press Secretary, "Closing Remarks by the President at White House Forum on Health Reform," March 5, 2009, http://www.whitehouse.gov/the_press_office/Closing Remarks-by-the-President-at-White-House-Forum-on-Health-Reform/.
2. Michael F. Cannon, "Does Barack Obama Support Socialized Medicine?" Cato Institute Briefing Paper no. 108, October 7, 2008, http://www.cato.org/pubs/bp/bp108.pdf.
3. Michael F. Cannon, "A Better Way to Generate and Use Comparative-Effectiveness Research," Cato Institute Policy Analysis no. 632, February 2, 2009, http://www.cato.org/pubs/pas/pa632.pdf.
4. See, for example, Mark V. Pauly and Robert D. Lieberthal, "How Risky Is Individual Health Insurance?" *Health Affairs* Web Exclusive, May 6, 2008, p. w248, http://content.healthaffairs.org/cgi/content/abstract/hlthaff.27.3.w242vl.

5. Lawrence H. Summers, "No Short-cuts to Development" (remarks by the Deputy Secretary of the Treasury to the IDB Conference on Development Thinking and Practice, U.S. Department of the Treasury press release, September 4, 1996), http://www.treas.gov/press/releases/rr1247.htm.

6. See Christopher J. Conover, "Health Care Regulation: A $169 Billion Hidden Tax," Cato Institute Policy Analysis no. 527, October 4, 2004, http://www.cato.org/pubs/pas/pa527.pdf. See also James C. Robinson, "The End of Asymmetric Information," *Journal of Health Politics, Policy and Law* 26 no. 5 (October 2001): 1045–53. ("To some within the health care community, the uniqueness doctrine is self-evident and needs no justification. After all, health care is essential to health. That food and shelter are even more vital and seem to be produced without professional licensure, nonprofit organization, compulsory insurance, class action lawsuits, and 133,000 pages of regulatory prescription in the *Federal Register* does not shake the faith of the orthodox.")

7. Victor Fuchs, "Cost Shifting Does Not Reduce the Cost of Health Care," *Journal of the American Medical Association* 302, no. 9 (September 2, 2009): 999–1000, http://jama.ama-assn.org/cgi/content/short/302/9/999.

8. U.S. Congressional Budget Office, "The Long-Term Outlook for Health Care Spending," November 2007, p. 8, http://www.cbo.gov/ftpdocs/87xx/doc8758/MainText.3.1.shtml.

9. U.S. Centers for Medicare & Medicaid Services, "National Health Expenditure Projections 2008–2018," http://wwwcms.hhs.gov/NationalHealthExpendData/downloads/proj2008.pdf. Were that trend to persist, the United States would spend 100 percent of its GDP on health care by 2082. Peter R. Orszag (testimony before Senate Committee on the Budget, U.S. Congressional Budget Office, January 31, 2008, p. 11), http://www.cbo.gov/ftpdocs/89xx/doc8948/01-31-HealthTestimony.pdf.

10. Elliott S. Fisher, "Expert Voices: More Care Is Not Better Care," *National Institute for Health Care Management* no. 7, January 2005, http://www.nihcm.org/~nihcmor/pdf/ExpertV7.pdf.

11. Alain C. Enthoven, "Open the Markets and Level the Playing Field," in *Toward a 21st Century Health System: The Contributions and Promise of Prepaid Group Practice*, ed. Alain C. Enthoven and Laura A. Tollen (San Francisco: Jossey-Bass, 2004), p. 232.

12. See, for example, Peter R. Orszag, "Health Care and Behavioral Economics; A Presentation to the National Academy of Social Insurance," p. 6, http://www.cbo.gov/ftpdocs/93xx/doc9317/05-29-NASI_Speech.pdf.

13. David Goldhill, "How American Health Care Killed My Father," *Atlantic*, September 2009, http://www.theatlantic.com/doc/print/200909/health-care.

14. Tom Daschle, Scott S. Greenberger, and Jeanne M. Lambrew, *Critical: What We Can Do about the Health-Care Crisis* (New York: Thomas Dunne Books, 2008), p. 114.

15. Cannon, "A Better Way to Generate and Use Comparative-Effectiveness Research."

16. See, for example, Michael F. Cannon, "Fannie Med: Why a "Public Option" Is Hazardous to Your Health," Cato Institute Policy Analysis no. 642, August 6, 2009, http://www.cato.org/pubs/pas/pa642.pdf; Michael F. Cannon, "All the President's Mandates: Compulsory Health Insurance Is a Government Takeover," Cato Institute Briefing Paper no. 114, September 23, 2009, http://www.cato.org/pubs/bp/bpl14.pdf; Michael Tanner, "Halfway to Where? Answering the Key Questions of Health Care Reform," Cato Institute Policy Analysis no. 643, September 9, 2009, http://www.cato.org/pubs/pas/pa643.pdf; and Michael Tanner, "Obama-Care to Come: Seven Bad Ideas for Health Care Reform," Cato Institute Policy Analysis no. 638, May 21, 2009, http://www.cato.org/pubs/pas/pa 638.pdf.

17. Peter R. Orszag, "The Long-Term Budget Outlook and Options for Slowing the Growth of Health Care Costs" (testimony before the Committee on Finance United States Senate, U.S. Congressional Budget Office, June 17, 2008), http://www.cbo.gov/ftpdocs/93xx/doc9385/MainText.2.1.shtml.

18. Quoted in U.S. Senate Republican Policy Committee, "Health Care Costs and Their Impact on Middle-Class Wages," *RPC Bulletin*, October 1, 2008, p. 6, http://rpc.senate.gov/public/_files/BulletinImpactofHealthCostsonMiddleClass100108.pdf.

19. Michael F. Cannon, "How Can I Ration Your Medical Care? Let Me Count the Ways," *Townhall Magazine*, September 2009, p. 51, http://www.cato.org/pubs/articles/cannon-obamacare-townhall-magazine.pdf.

20. See, for example Mark V. Pauly, *Markets without Magic: How Competition Might Save Medicare* (Washington: AEI Press, 2008).

21. See, for example, Melvin J. Ingber, "Implementation of Risk Adjustment for Medicare," *Health Care Financing Review* 21, no 3 (Spring, 2000): 119, http://www.cms.hhs.gov/HealthCareFinancingReview/Downloads/00springpg119.pdf; Gregory C.

Pope et al., "Risk Adjustment of Medicare Capitation Payments Using the CMS-HCC Model," *Health Care Financing Review* 25, no. 4 (Summer 2004): 119, http://www.cms.hhs.gov/HealthCareFinancing Review/Downloads/04Summerpg119.pdf; and John Kautter et al., "Medicare Risk Adjustment for the Frail Elderly," *Health Care Financing Review* 30, no 2 (Winter 2008): 83, http://findarticles.com/p/articles/mi_m0795/is_2_30/ai_n31440029/.

22. See, for example, Andrew Samwick, "Means-Testing Medicare," *Vox Baby*, September 11, 2006, http://voxbaby.blogspot.com/2006/09/means-testing-medicare.html; and C. Eugene Steuerle, "Taxing the Elderly on Their Medicare Benefits," *Tax Analysts*, July 21, 1997, http://www.urban.org/url.cfm?ID=1000109.

23. Michael F. Cannon, "How Can I Ration Your Medical Care?"

24. Personal conversations with Reggie Cervantes, John Graham, and Bill Maher, Washington, DC, June 20, 2007.

25. Paul Fronstin, "Sources of Health Insurance and Characteristics of the Uninsured: Analysis of the March 2008 Current Population Survey," Employee Benefit Research Institute Issue Brief no. 321, September 2008, p. 5, http://www.ebri.org/pdf/briefspdf/EBRI-IB_09a-2008.pdf. Data are for 2007.

26. Michael F. Cannon, "Large Health Savings Accounts: A Step toward Tax Neutrality for Health Care," *Forum for Health Economics & Policy* 11, no. 2 (Health Care Reform), Article 3 (2008), http://www.bepress.com/fhep/11/2/3/.

27. Gary Claxton et al., "Employer Health Benefits: 2009 Annual Survey," Kaiser Family Foundation/Health Research and Educational Trust, September 15, 2009, pp. 79–80, http://dehbs.kff.org/pdf/2009/7936.pdf.

28. Michael A. Morrissey and John Cawley, "Health Economists' Views of Health Policy," *Journal of Health, Politics, Policy, and Law* 33, no. 4 (August 2008): 712.

29. Claxton et al.

30. For an example of a health-insurance tax credits proposal, see Len Burman et al., "An Updated Analysis of the 2008 Presidential Candidates' Tax Plans: Revised August 15, 2008," Tax Policy Center, updated September 12, 2008, http://www.taxpolicycenter.org/UploadedPDF/411749_updated_candidates.pdf.

31. For an example of a proposal to create a standard deduction for health insurance, see Leonard E. Burman et al., "The President's Proposed Standard Deduction for Health Insurance: An Evaluation," Tax Policy Center, February 15, 2007, http://www.taxpolicycenter.org/publications/url.cfm?ID=411423.

32. Cannon, "Large Health Savings Accounts: A Step toward Tax Neutrality for Health Care."

33. See, for example, Jason Furman, "Reforming the Tax Treatment of Health Care: Right Ways and Wrong Ways," Brookings Institution, February 24, 2008, p. 8, http://www.taxpolicycenter.org/tpccontent/healthconference_furman.pdf. ("Most labor market models have the feature that firms that drop coverage will ultimately pay their workers more, money they could put towards purchasing insurance in the individual market.")

34. The $534 billion figure represents total "employer contributions" toward employee health benefits. "Sponsors of Health Care Costs: Businesses, Households, and Governments, 1987–2007," U.S. Centers for Medicare & Medicaid Services, p. 5, Table 1, http://www.cms.hhs.gov/NationalHealthExpendData/downloads/bhg07.pdf; and author's calculations. If the annual growth in employer "contributions" gradually declines to 3 percent over that period, the 10-year figure would still be more than $8 trillion.

35. Typically, those would be workers with the most expensive employer-sponsored insurance plans and/or those who are in the highest tax brackets.

36. U.S. Congressional Budget Office, "Effects of Changes to the Health Insurance System on Labor Markets," CBO Economic and Budget Issue Brief, July 13, 2009, p. 8, http://www.cbo.gov/ftpdocs/104xx/doc10435/07-13-HealthCareAndLaborMarkets.pdf.

37. U.S. Congressional Budget Office, *Key Issues in Analyzing Major Health Insurance Proposals*, December 2008, p. xvii, http://www.cbo.gov/ftpdocs/99xx/doc9924/12-18-KeyIssues.pdf.

38. See, for example, Ateev Mehrotra et al., "Retail Clinics, Primary Care Physicians, and Emergency Departments: A Comparison Of Patients' Visits," *Health Affairs* 27, no. 5 (2008): 1272–82, http://content.healthaffairs.org/cgi/content/abstract/27/5/1272.

39. See generally, Joseph P. Newhouse et al., *Free for All? Lessons from the RAND Health Insurance Experiment* (Cambridge, MA: Harvard University Press, 1996).

40. Cannon, "A Better Way to Generate and Use Comparative-Effectiveness Research."

41. There are more than 50 million job "separations" in the United States each year. U.S. Bureau of Labor Statistics, "Job Openings and Labor

Turnover: January 2009" (press release, March 10, 2009), http://www.bls.gov/news.release/archives/jolts_03102009.pdf. A recent study by the Center for American Progress suggested that during the recent economic downturn, 14,000 U.S. workers joined the ranks of the uninsured each day. That paper relied on two particularly bad months for job losses (December 2008 and January 2009). Applying the paper's methodology to a broader period of rising unemployment (January 2008 through August 2009) produces a figure below 9,000. Center for American Progress Action Fund, "Health Care in Crisis: 14,000 Losing Coverage a Day," February 2009, http://www.americanprogressaction.org/issues/2009/02/pdf/health_care_crisis.pdf; U.S. Bureau of Labor Statistics, "Labor Force Statistics from the Current Population Survey," September 30, 2009, http://data.bls.gov/PDQ/servlet/SurveyOutputServlet?data_tool=latest_numbers&series_id=LNS14000000;and author's calculations. Among those 9,000 workers, many are healthy, and many will regain coverage after a number of months. Nevertheless, the problem of workers with high-cost conditions losing their health insurance and then being unable to afford coverage is very real. See Jonathan Cohn, *Sick: The Untold Story of America's Health Care Crisis—and the People Who Pay the Price* (New York: HarperCollins, 2007).
42. Mark V. Pauly and Robert D. Lieberthal, "How Risky Is Individual Health Insurance?"
43. Mark Pauly, "How Private Health Insurance Pools Risk," NBER Reporter: Research Summary (Summer 2005), http://www.nber.org/reporter/summer05/pauly.html; and M. Susan Marquis et al., "Consumer Decision Making in the Individual Health Insurance Market," *Health Affairs* Web Exclusive (May 2, 2006): w226, http://content.healthaffairs.org/cgi/content/short/hlthaff.25.w2 26vl.
44. Marquis et al.
45. Mark Pauly and Bradley Herring, *Pooling Health Insurance Risks* (Washington: AEI Press, 1999), pp. 69–70.
46. Jay Bhattacharya and M. Kate Bundorf, "The Incidence of the Healthcare Costs of Obesity," *Journal of Health Economics* 28, no. 3 (May 2009): 649–58, http://healthpolicy.stanford.edu/publications/the_incidence_of_the_healthcare_costs_of_obesity/.
47. Jonathan Gruber, "The Incidence of Mandated. Maternity Benefits,' *The American Economic Review* 84, no. 3 (june 1994): 622–41, http://aysps.gsu.edu/isp/files/isp_summer_school_2008_erard_incidence_of_mandated_maternity_benefits.pdf.
48. Elise Gould and Alexandra Minicozzi, "Who is Adversely Affected by Limiting the Tax Exclusion of Employment-Based Premiums?" Economic Policy Institute Working Paper no. 281 (March 2009), http://www.epi.org/page/-/pdf/wp281.pdf.
49. Michael F. Cannon, "Health Insurance Regulation," in *Cato Handbook for Policymakers*, 7th ed., ed. David Boaz (Washington: Cato Institute, 2009), p. 167, http://www.cato.org/pubs/handbook/hb111/hb111-16.pdf.
50. Victoria Craig Bunce and J. P. Wieske, "Health Insurance Mandates in the States 2009," Council for Affordable Health Insurance, 2009, http://www.cahi.org/cahi_contents/resources/pdf/HealthInsuranceMandates2009.pdf.
51. Pauly, "How Private Health Insurance Pools Risk."
52. John H. Cochrane, "Health-Status Insurance: How Markets Can Provide Health Security," Cato Institute Policy Analysis no. 633, February 18, 2009, http://www.cato.org/pubs/pas/pa-633.pdf.
53. Pauly, "How Private Health Insurance Pools Risk."
54. See, generally. Paul Starr, *The Social Transformation of American Medicine* (New York: Basic Books, 1982 [actually published in January 1983]); and Michael A. Morrissey, "State Health Care Reform: Protecting the Provider," in *American Health Care: Government, Market Processes and the Public Interest*, ed. Roger D. Feldman (Oakland, CA: Independent Institute, 2000), http://www.independent.org/store/book_detail.asp?bookID=33.
55. U.S. Congressional Budget Office, "Increasing Small-Firm Health Insurance Coverage through Association Health Plans and HealthMarts," CBO Paper, January 2000, p. 3, http://www.cbo.gov/ftpdocs/18xx/docl815/healthins.pdf; and author's calculations.
56. A typical employer-provided family plan cost $13,375 in 2009. Gary Claxton et al., "Employer Health Benefits: 2009 Annual Survey," Kaiser Family Foundation/Health Research and Educational Trust, September 15, 2009, p. 14, http://ehbs.kff.org/pdf/2009/7936.pdf. If a family plan with that premium could avoid half of the average regulatory burden, the savings would be more than $1,000.
57. Clinicians include physicians; physician assistants; nurse practitioners and other advanced-practice nurses; physical therapists; optometrists; and other medical practitioners.
58. See generally Shirley V. Svorny, "Medical Licensing: An Obstacle to Affordable, Quality Care," Cato

Institute Policy Analysis no. 621, September 17, 2008, http://www.cato.org/pubs/pas/pa-621.pdf.

59. See, for example, Illinois State Medical Society, "Doctor's [sic] Seek Retail Health Clinic Oversight to Ensure Patient Safety, Adequate Follow-Up Care" (news release, February 19, 2008), http://www.isms.org/NewsRoom/newsreleases/Pages/nr2008_0218.aspx; and U.S. Federal Trade Commission (letter to Hon. Elaine Nekritz, May 29, 2008), http://www.ftc.gov/os/2008/06/V080013letter.pdf.

60. Cannon, "A Better Way to Generate and Use Comparative-Effectiveness Research."

61. Svorny, "Medical Licensing: An Obstacle to Affordable, Quality Care."

62. See Henry Butler and Larry Ribstein, "The Single-License Solution," *Regulation* 31, no. 4 (Winter 2008–2009): 36–42.

63. See, for example, Erin A. O'Hara and Larry E. Ribstein, *The Law Market* (Oxford: Oxford University Press, 2009).

64. Stephen T. Parente et al., "Consumer Response to a National Marketplace for Individual Insurance," Carlson School of Management working paper, June 28, 2008, p. 8, http://www.aei.org/docLib/20080730_National_Marketpla.pdf.

65. U.S. Congressional Budget Office, "H.R. 2355: Health Care Choice Act of 2005" (cost estimate, September 12, 2005), http://www.cbo.gov/ftp docs/66xx/doc6639/hr2355.pdf. (As more workers opt for individual-market coverage over employer-sponsored insurance, more of workers' overall compensation would become subject to income and payroll taxes, resulting in an incidental increase in federal revenues.)

66. See Arnold Kling and Michael F. Cannon, "Does the Doctor Need a Boss?" Cato Institute Briefing Paper no. 111, January 13, 2009, http:// www.cato.org/pubs/bp/bp111.pdf.

67. U.S. Constitution, Article I, section 8.

68. Bradley Herring and Mark V. Pauly, "Incentive-Compatible Guaranteed-Renewable Health Insurance Premiums," *Journal of Health Economics* 25 (2005): 395–417, http://www.sciencedirect.com/science?_ob=ArticleURL&_udi=B6V8K-4JP9FP6-1&_user=10&_rdoc=1&_fmt=&_orig=search&_sort=d&_docanchor=&view=c&_searchStrId=1030484307&_rerunOrigin=google&_acct=C000050221&_version=1&_urlVersion=0&_userid=10&md5=652644515e80a777202cf2a6e3c279b2.

69. See, for example, Lisa Girion, "Blue Cross Makes Policy About-Face," *Los Angeles Times*, May 11, 2007, http://www.latimes.com/business/la-fi-insure11may11,1,1299206.story.

70. Mark Pauly, Allison Percy, and Bradley Herring, 'Individual versus Job-Based Health Insurance: Weighing the Pros and Cons," *Health Affairs* 18, no. 6 (November/December 1999): 28–44, http://content.healthaffairs.org/cgi/content/abstract/18/6/28.

71. Cochrane explains how disease-specific pay-outs, whose use is legally limited to purchasing health insurance, would enable sick patients to afford whatever premiums the market would charge and thereby free the sick to flee a substandard health plan. John H. Cochrane, "Health-Status Insurance: How Markets Can Provide Health Security," Cato Institute Policy Analysis no. 633, February 18, 2009, http://www.cato.org/pubs/pas /pa-633.pdf.

72. See, for example, Jonathan Gruber and Kosali Simon, "Crowd-out 10 Years Later: Have Recent Public Insurance Expansions Crowded out Private Health Insurance?" *Journal of Health Economics* 27, no. 2, (March 2008): 201–17; Michael F. Cannon, "Medicaid's Unseen Costs," Cato Institute Policy Analysis no. 548, August 18, 2005, http://www.cato.org/pub_display.php?pub_id=4049; Michael F. Cannon, "Sinking SCHIP: A First Step toward Stopping the Growth of Government Health Programs," Cato Institute Briefing Paper no. 99, September 13, 2007, http://www.cato.org/pub_display.php?pub_id= 8697; and Stephen A. Moses, "Aging America's Achilles Heel: Medicaid Long-Term Care," Cato Institute Policy Analysis no. 549, September 1, 2005, http://www.cato.org/pubs/pas/pa549.pdf

73. See Cannon, "Medicaid's Unseen Costs," and Cannon, "Sinking SCHIP."

74. White House Office of the Press Secretary, "Remarks by the President in Town Hall Meeting on Health Care: Southwest High School, Green Bay, Wisconsin," June 11, 2009, http://www.whitehouse.gov/the_press_office/Remarks-by-the-President-in-Town-Hall-Meeting-on-Health-Care-in-Green-Bay-Wisconsin/.

75. Christina Bellantoni, "Dean Says 'Enough' on Limbaugh," *Washington Times*, March 10, 2009, http://www.washingtontimes.com/news/2009/mar/10/dean-touts-perfect-obama-health-plan/. See also Harold Demsetz, "Information and Efficiency: Another Viewpoint," *Journal of Law and Economics* 12, no. 1 (April 1969): 1, http://www.scribd.com/doc/19623869/Demsetz-H-1969-Information-and-Efficiency-Another-Viewpoint. ("The view that now pervades much public policy economics

implicitly presents the relevant choice as between an ideal norm and an existing 'imperfect' institutional arrangement. This nirvana approach differs considerably from a *comparative institution* approach in which the relevant choice is between alternative real institutional arrangements.")

76. Tom Daschle, Scott S. Greenberger, and Jeanne M. Lambrew, *Critical: What We Can Do about the Health-Care Crisis* (New York: Thomas Dunne Books, 2008), p. 164.

77. Michael F. Cannon, "Fannie Med."

78. Michael F. Cannon, "All the President's Mandates."

79. "President Obama Speaks at Healthcare Summit," *CQ Transcripts Wire/Washington Post*, March 5, 2009, http://www.washingtonpost.com/wp-dyn/content/article/2009/03/05/AR2009030501850.html.

80. Mara Liasson, "Obama Pitches Health Care Overhaul in Wisconsin," NPR.org, June 12, 2009, http://www.npr.org/templates/story/story.php?storyId=105285850.

EDUCATION POLICY

chapter
4

EDUCATION POLICY

Jay M. Shafritz and Christopher P. Borick

KEYNOTE: HOW *BROWN* CHANGED *PLESSY*'S DOCTRINE

In June 1967, President Lyndon Johnson had a Supreme Court vacancy` to fill. This president, who did more for the civil rights of minorities than any other in the twentieth century, had decided to appoint the first African American to the court. He had asked Nicholas Katzenbach, his former attorney general, a professor at the Yale Law School, to prepare a list of possible appointees. As they reviewed the candidates, they came to **Thurgood Marshall**. Juan Williams, in his biography of Marshall, quotes the president as saying: "Marshall's not the best—he's not the most outstanding black lawyer in the country." Katzenbach replied: "Mr. President, if you appoint anybody, any black to that court but Thurgood Marshall, you are insulting every black in the country. Thurgood is *the* black lawyer as far as blacks are concerned—I mean there can't be any doubt about that." Marshall, who was made a federal judge by President John F. Kennedy in 1961 and made **solicitor general** by Johnson in 1964, was to be elevated once again. On June 13, President Johnson announced that Marshall was his nominee. Despite strong opposition by some senators from southern states, Marshall was confirmed by a vote of 69 to 11 and joined the Court on October 2.

But why was Marshall "*the* black lawyer"? Because he had spent most of his career (1939-1961) as the director of the Legal Defense and Education Fund of the National Association for the Advancement of Colored People (NAACP). In that role he won 29 of the 32 civil rights cases he argued before the U.S. Supreme Court. His overall legal strategy was to whittle down bit by bit the **Jim Crow** laws that sanctioned the segregation then prevalent in the American South. This culminated in one of the true landmarks of Supreme Court history, the case of *Brown v. Board of Education of Topeka, Kansas* (1954).

The essence of the *Brown* decision was whether black and white children should attend the same schools. Prior to *Brown*, the prevailing doctrine on civil rights was "separate but equal." This meant that blacks did not suffer an infringement of their constitutional rights as citizens if they were not allowed to use the same facilities as whites as long as "separate but equal" facilities were provided. Although this may have sounded fair on the surface, there were two insurmountable arguments against it. First, there was the simple reality that what was provided separately was hardly ever equal. Second, there was the inherent stigma of being treated differently. How could you be equal if you were not treated equally? There was no doubt that this made second-class citizens of African Americans.

What made this doctrine particularly insidious was the fact that it derived not just from custom and the Jim Crow laws of the South but was famously promulgated by the U.S. Supreme Court. In *Plessy v. Ferguson* (1896), the Court held that segregated railroad facilities for African Americans, facilities that were considered equal in quality to those provided for whites, were legal. This case didn't just happen. Homer Plessy, at the time a 30-year old shoemaker from New Orleans, volunteered to test an 1890 Louisiana law providing for "equal but separate accommodations for the white and colored races" on railroads. So on June 7,

---

Thurgood Marshall (1908–1993) The civil rights lawyer who was the first black justice of the U.S. Supreme Court (1967-1991).

solicitor general The official of the Department of Justice who is the actual attorney representing the federal government before the U.S. Supreme Court and any other courts.

Jim Crow A name given to any law requiring the segregation of the races. All such statutes are now unconstitutional. But prior to the Civil Rights Act of 1964, many southern states had laws requiring separate drinking fountains, separate rest rooms, separate sections of theaters, and so on for blacks and whites. The name "Jim Crow" comes from a nineteenth-century vaudeville character who was called Jim (a common name) Crow (for a black-colored bird). Thus the name was applied to things having to do with blacks.

"Education Policy" from *Introducing Public Policy*, by Jay M. Shafritz and Christopher P. Borick, pp. 181-210. Copyright © 2008 by Pearson Education, Inc. Reprinted by permission.

1892, Plessy bought a first class ticket on the East Louisiana Railway. Plessy was so white looking (he only had one black great-grandparent) that he had to inform the train conductor that he was "a colored man." As expected the conductor then asked him to transfer to the "colored" car. When Plessy refused, in one of American history's first sit-ins, he was duly arrested for crimes "against the peace and dignity of the state."

Four years later Plessy's case reached the Supreme Court. His lawyers urged the Court to reject the "equal but separate" law because it violated the equal protection clause of the **Fourteenth Amendment**. But the Court saw no such violation. The majority opinion stated that "the object of the [Fourteenth] amendment was undoubtedly to enforce the absolute equality of the two races before the law, but in the nature of things it could not have been intended to abolish distinctions based upon color, or to enforce social, as distinguished from political, equality."

The Court felt that reasonableness was the essence of the case: "The case reduces itself to the question whether the statute of Louisiana is a reasonable regulation. . . . Gauged by this standard, we cannot say that a law which authorizes or even requires the separation of the two races in public conveyances is unreasonable, or more obnoxious to the fourteenth amendment than the Acts of Congress requiring separate schools for colored children in the District of Columbia, the constitutionality of which does not seem to have been questioned."

The Court even denied the plaintiff's "assumption that the enforced separation of the two races stamps the colored race with a badge of inferiority. If this be so, it is not by reason of anything found in the act, but solely because the colored race chooses to put that construction upon it." The *Plessy* case was a disaster for civil rights. Instead of striking down a Jim Crow law in one state, it allowed the Supreme Court to formally sanction the doctrine. This made it easier for race-based legislation to be expanded and sustained.

Plessy put the stamp of inferiority on every American of African descent. One justice saw this clearly. In his lone dissenting opinion, Justice John Marshall Harlan (1833-1911), ironically a former slave owner from Kentucky, wrote:

"We boast of the freedom enjoyed by our people. . . . But it is difficult to reconcile that boast with a state of the law which, practically, puts the brand of servitude and degradation upon a large class of our fellow citizens, our equals before the law. The thin disguise of 'equal' accommodations for passengers in the railroad coaches will not mislead anyone, or atone for the wrong this day done."

More than half a century later, Thurgood Marshall of the NAACP led the legal team that urged the Court to overturn the "wrong this day done" in the *Plessy* decision and nullify this doctrine, asserting that separate was "inherently unequal." Linda Brown was a seven-year-old girl in Topeka, Kansas, when her famous case started winding its way to the high court. She lived just a few blocks from a local elementary school. But since that was for whites only, she had to attend a "colored" school on the other side of town. This required that she cross railroad tracks to then take a long bus ride. Her father, Oliver, joined a group of African Americans who sought for three years to get Topeka to improve the "colored" schools. Finally they filed a lawsuit and Brown found his name as the first of the plaintiffs.

In *Brown*, the Court decided that the separation of children by race and according to law in public schools "generates a feeling of inferiority as to their [the minority group's] status in the community that may affect their hearts and minds in a way unlikely ever to be undone." Consequently, it held that "separate educational facilities are inherently unequal" and therefore violate the equal protection clause of the Fourteenth Amendment. Chief Justice **Earl Warren**, in delivering the unanimous opinion of the Court, stated that public education "is the very foundation of good citizenship." It was so important to the nation that considerations of

---

Fourteenth Amendment The post–Civil War amendment to the U.S. Constitution that defines citizenship and mandates due process as well as equal protection of the law for all citizens.

Earl Warren (1891–1974) The chief justice of the United States from 1953 to 1969, who became the symbol of judicial activism and led the Court to many landmark decisions on desegregation, civil rights, First Amendment freedoms, and the rights of criminal defendants. President Dwight D. Eisenhower, who appointed Warren to the Supreme Court, isagreed with the activist approach of the Warren Court and was quoted as saying that Warren's appointment was the "Biggest damfool mistake I ever made." *New York Times Magazine*, July 28, 1968.

original intent What the 1789 framers of the U.S. Constitution really meant; what they really intended, by their words, phrases, and sentences used in the document. The original intent of the framers is often a debatable issue, often espoused by strict constructionists, and often a code word (or phrase) for conservative attempts to reverse Supreme Court decisions on social policy and individual rights.

the **original intent** of the Fourteenth Amendment were less important than remedying the present situation. So the Court effectively brushed aside the question of whether the Fourteenth Amendment was ever intended to cover public education. Warren stated: "In approaching this problem we cannot turn the clock back to 1868 when the Amendment was adopted, or even to 1896 when *Plessy v. Ferguson* was written. We must consider public education in the light of its full development and present place in American life."

Then Warren proceeded to dismantle the doctrine of separate but equal. "We come then to the question presented: does segregation of children in public schools solely on the basis of race, even though the physical facilities and other 'tangible' factors may be equal, deprive the children of the minority group of equal educational opportunities? We believe that it does."

Warren acknowledged that the Court accepted the validity of various psychologists that segregated schools damaged minority students by creating "a feeling of inferiority." Finally he concluded that "in the field of public education the doctrine of 'separate but equal' has no place."

Carved in stone on the front of the U.S. Supreme Court building are the words "equal justice under law." Those words epitomize the philosophic foundation of American government. Yet they once sustained a doctrine that some citizens were less equal than others. Figure 4.1 illustrates this using our doctrinal template.

The *Brown* decision kept the philosophy but revised the doctrine, so that a new policy of integration emerged, as illustrated in Figure 4.2.

The man at the forefront of the legal fight to change the doctrine of separate but equal was Thurgood Marshall. Martin Luther King, Jr., marched in the streets to demand civil rights and became the personification of the civil rights movement. But Marshall marched into federal court and, far more often than not, when he marched out the civil rights of all Americans had

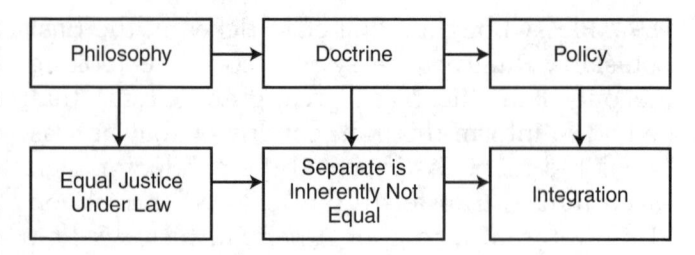

FIGURE 4.2

been expanded. This is why by 1967 Marshall was considered "*the* black lawyer" in America and the obvious choice for the first black seat on the U.S. Supreme Court.

For Discussion: Why is the *Brown* decision generally considered to be the legal foundation of the modern civil rights movement? Was Chief Justice Earl Warren right to delay the *Brown* decision until he could get a unanimous vote on it in order to make it more acceptable to the American public?

WHO MAKES EDUCATION POLICY

You might logically think that education policy is mostly made by educators—teachers and school administrators. But you would be wrong. As the keynote has shown, larger societal issues often take precedence. Just as war policy has long been considered too important to be left just to the generals, so too, education policy is too important to be left to educators.

The schools are often the battlefield for fights over policy issues that have wider impact. The *Brown* decision was not just about segregation in education. It was an invaluable precedent in the subsequent fostering of integration in employment and housing by both legislative and judicial means. To further illustrate this point, here are two other major examples of the larger society using the Supreme Court to dictate education policy. In *School District of Abington Township v. Schemp* (1963), the

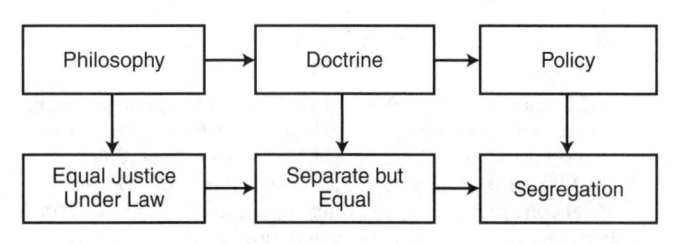

FIGURE 4.1

establishment clause The first part of the First Amendment, which asserts that "Congress shall make no law respecting an establishment of religion." The clause is the basis for the separation of church and state in the United States. Yet the Supreme Court has held, in *Everson v. Board of Education* (1947), that it is not a violation of the establishment clause for the government to pay for the cost of busing children to religious schools; nor was the tax-exempt status of religious property—at issue in *Walz v. Tax Commission of the City of New York* (1970)—a violation. Increasingly, the Court is taking an attitude of "benevolent neutrality" toward religion.

Supreme Court held that school prayers or other religious exercises violated the **establishment clause** of the **First Amendment**. This is the present legal basis for the absence of prayers at governmental meetings and the placement of secular seasonal decorations on public property instead of religiously focused displays such as nativity scenes. In *Lau v. Nichols* (1974), the Court ruled that students of Chinese ancestry in San Francisco who did not understand English were "effectively foreclosed from any meaningful education." In mandating bilingual education in public schools, the Court also provided the precedent for an increasingly multilingual nation with bi- or multilingual social workers, police officers, public defenders, and ballots.

The big issues of education policy hardly ever stay in the classroom—even when they start there. Arguments over the specifics of curriculum frequently break through school walls. For example:

- Should sex education be taught in the public schools? If so, at what age? Should abstinence be advocated or condoms distributed?
- How should human evolution be treated? Should it be taught as scientific truth or as the alternative to creationism?
- Should the reading of literature by "dead white European males" (William Shakespeare, Charles Dickens, George Bernard Shaw, etc.) be replaced by more politically correct works by women and minority group authors?
- Should private corporations be allowed to take over low-performing schools in the hope that they will be able to enhance student performance?
- Should illegal aliens who graduate from state high schools be allowed to pay in-state resident tuition (instead of the higher out-of-state rate) to attend state universities?

These are the kinds of issues that generate strong feelings on both sides and encourage parents to attend school board meetings, file lawsuits, and sometimes, in despair, move themselves and their children out of the school district.

A Short History of American Education Policy

Religion was the prime motivator for the creation of educational institutions in the American colonies. Initially children were taught the traditional "three Rs" (reading, 'riting, and 'rithmetic) at home by their parents or tutors. The Pilgrims, who first settled in Massachusetts in 1620, had created the first secondary school, Boston Public Latin Grammar School, by 1635. It was designed to prepare elite young males for positions of political and/or religious leadership. The term "public" did not connote public support but implied that the school was open to anyone who could afford the fees necessary for enrollment. By 1647, the Colony passed a law requiring that every town with 50 or more families had to hire a teacher—so even the poor could learn to read the Bible.

Because of similar developments in the other American colonies, by the time of the Revolutionary War in 1776, basic literacy was commonplace if not universal. Indeed, a strong case can be made that American literacy was a major factor in creating popular sentiment for independence from England. Remember that the revolution was formented by **committees of correspondence**, by countless newspapers, and by polemicists such as **Thomas Paine**. The colonial government's goal was to educate citizens well enough to read the Bible and hymn books. But they soon found that those trained to read scripture often preferred to read the pamphlets advocating sedition written by religious skeptics like Paine.

Although there has often been heated debate about what should be taught, the continuing importance of educating the young has long been acknowledged. The reason for this was best summarized in this couplet by English poet Alexander Pope (1688–1744).

First Amendment The amendment to the U.S. Constitution asserting that "Congress shall make no law respecting an establishment of religion, or prohibiting the free exercise thereof; or abridging the freedom of speech, or of the press; or the right of the people peaceably to assemble, and to petition the government for a redress of grievances." This, the first part—and backbone—of the Bill of Rights, originally applied only to the federal government but has been extended to the states through the due process and equal protection clauses of the Fourteenth Amendment.

committees of correspondence Citizens' committees created in the American colonies after 1772 to exchange information and arouse resistance to English rule.

Thomas Paine (1737–1809) The Revolutionary War pamphleteer whose Common Sense (1776) became a sensational "best seller" and helped crystallize sentiment for a total break with England. sedition Advocating resistance to or rebellion against a legally established government.

> *'Tis education forms the common mind:*
> *Just as the twig is bent, the tree's inclin'd.*

By the 1830s, a "common school" movement was increasingly pushing the United States toward free, meaning tax-supported, elementary school for all children. It was argued by reformers such as **Horace Mann** that only free basic education in which children of all segments of society commingled would create the mutual respect essential for the functioning of a democracy. By the time of the Civil War, over half of school-age children attended school. The common school movement also substantially encouraged higher education. In order to meet the increasing demand for teachers, the states created teacher-training or "normal schools"—most of which have now evolved into state colleges and universities.

Once primary school education became a given, there arose a parallel demand for mass-based secondary education. High schools, the public sector counterpart to the traditional preparatory (or prep) school, became common in major population centers by the latter part of the nineteenth century. However, these public institutions, designed to acculturate a vast immigrant population and train workers for industry at first focused more on vocational education than academic preparation. As the movement toward progressive education spearheaded by **John Dewey** took hold in the early twentieth century, today's comprehensive high school emerged with a curriculum that offered academic, workplace, and practical life skills, all within an egalitarian context.

It was this vast expansion of public high schools that made possible the explosive growth of American higher education in the mid-twentieth century. First these schools provided a vast new pool of recruits to supplement the prep school graduates. Then they created a pool of millions of high school graduates able to take advantage of the **G.I. Bill** after World War II. This greatly enhanced higher education, as old colleges expanded and new ones were created. Then the children of all those highly educated veterans—the baby boomers—by their sheer numbers forced an even greater expansion of American colleges and universities beginning in the 1960s.

These historical trends in education have been pushed by economic forces. The needs of an increasingly sophisticated industrial and **postindustrial society** for an increasingly educated and technologically skilled workforce have driven American educational policies in many ways. From creating basic literacy, as with the common schools, to developing marketable skills through vocational education, public education has provided fundamental human resources for the nation's economy. While education in itself is desirable because it leads to better citizens leading **the good life** in ever more fulfilling ways, the reality is that education policy is driven at least as much by **economic determinism** as other factors.

Governmental Machinery for Education Policymaking

A special district is a unit of local government typically performing a single function and overlapping traditional political boundaries. Examples include

---

Horace Mann (1796–1859) An early educational leader and politician who espoused such reforms as universal education for girls as well as boys, the establishment of state normal schools for teacher training, and a practical curriculum. He asserted that education was "the great equalizer of the condition of men, the balance wheel of the social machinery."

John Dewey (1859–1952) An educational reformer who contended that learning and schooling should focus on the individual and include all life experiences rather than focusing narrowly on academic subject matter. Dewey was one of the primary forces behind the Progressive Movement in education.

G.I. Bill The American Servicemen's Readjustment Act of 1944. It provided low-interest, no-down-payment home mortgages and education benefits that allowed a whole generation of working-class veterans to go to college and advance into the middle class.

postindustrial society A phrase coined by Daniel Bell in *The Coming of Post-Industrial Society* (1973) to describe the new social structures evolving in modern societies in the second half of the twentieth century. Bell holds that the "axial principle" of postindustrial society is the centrality of theoretical knowledge as the source of innovation and policy formation for the society. Hallmarks of postindustrial society include a change from a goods-producing to a service economy, the preeminence of a professional and technical class, and the creation of a new intellectual technology.

the good life The end or goal of political community. This notion goes back to Aristotle, who wrote in his *Politics* (4th century B.C.): "When several villages are united in a single complete community, large enough to be nearly or quite self-sufficing, the state comes into existence, originating in the bare needs of life, and continuing in existence for the sake of a good life."

economic determinism The doctrine holding that economic concerns are the primary motivating factors of human behavior and historical development, and that all social, political, or moral justifications for action can be traced to conscious or unconscious economic motives.

transportation districts, fire protection districts, library districts, water districts, sewer districts, and so on. Because special districts are such useful devices, they have been multiplying rapidly. In 1942 there were only 8,299 of them in the entire United States. In 2005, there were 35,052—not including school districts. They constitute more than one-third of all American government entities.

A school district is a special district for the provision of local public education. The total number of school districts has been constantly shrinking because of mergers. There were more than 108,000 school districts in 1942; today there are fewer than 14,000.

School districts are typically managed by a school board, which is usually chosen by **nonpartisan elections**. It functions much like a public-sector counterpart to a corporate board of directors. Thus the school board usually appoints a chief executive officer called a superintendent to run the school system. The school board, with the professional advice provided by the superintendent and his or her staff, makes policy—usually at regularly scheduled meetings open to the public.

Within any of the 50 states, final authority over educational policy rests with the state government. Nevertheless, for much of the nation's public school history, state governments with the exception of Hawaii's have delegated most of their school authority to local, separate, and independent school districts. However, in recent years, the role of the states in public school education has increased as a result of demands from local governments for large amounts of financial aid and a growing demand from a number of quarters—parents, businesspersons, educational associations, etc.—to improve the quality of public school education.

Despite all their problems, the public schools on the whole have been the greatest antipoverty program in the nation's history. For generations, poor and immigrant students have gone into school and come out as employable citizens. Good schools are part of the essential infrastructure of industrial societies. If students don't graduate with employable skills at government expense, they will be have to be trained at corporate expense.

Education policy covers an almost infinite variety of issues, from **busing** to fostering racial integration to **zoning** to keep "adult"—meaning pornographic—bookstores an appropriate distance from school grounds. Since the creation of the Department of Education in 1979, the federal government's role in education policy has become more significant. For example, the No Child Left Behind Act of 2002 has attempted to make public schools more accountable for their performance through varied economic incentives from the federal government. Even though this somewhat controversial act creates new levels of accountability by mandating standardized testing, the federal role, while increasingly visible, is inherently a tiny part of the nation's overall effort to educate its children.

Public education is overwhelmingly the responsibility of the states and their local school districts. Consequently, the rest of this chapter will focus on three of the most contentious problems in contemporary local public education: school financing, the unionization of public school teachers, and school vouchers. Just as in the keynote, our doctrinal template will be used to illustrate the evolving nature of each of these issues.

FINANCING THE PUBLIC SCHOOLS

A central issue arising in the governance of public school education and one that has commanded the attention of reformers and state leaders in recent years is the fiscal disparity among individual school districts—a situation that contributes to educational inequalities among the districts. Much of the problem of school finance can be

---

nonpartisan election A local election in which a candidate runs for office without formally indicating political party affiliation.

busing The transporting of children to schools at a greater distance from their homes than those they would otherwise attend in order to achieve racial desegregation. Busing has often been mandated by the federal courts as a remedy for past practices of discrimination. Parents who want their children to attend neighborhood schools have strongly objected to it and it has, in consequence, been a major factor in white flight from central cities. Busing is often used as an example of government by the judiciary, because even though it has been one of the most controversial domestic policies in the history of the United States, it has never been specifically sanctioned by Congress.

zoning The process by which local government can designate the types of structures and activities for a particular area. Zoning began in the 1920s to protect neighborhoods from the encroachments of business and industry and to preserve their economic and social integrity. It involves a highly complex legal process, which is often effected by local politics.

traced to the reliance of a local school district on local property taxes. This means simply that school districts that do not have much taxable property cannot finance their schools as well as those containing large **tax bases**.

A property tax is any tax on land and its improvements, such as buildings (or on personal property such as automobiles and jewelry). This tax is the mainstay of most local governments; it provides nearly half of the revenues that local governments get from their own sources. To administer a property tax, the tax base must first be defined—that is, as housing and land, automobiles, other assets, whatever. An evaluation of the value of the tax base must then be made—this is the assessment. Finally, a tax rate usually an amount to be paid per $100 value of the tax base, is levied. Since the value of the tax base will appreciate or depreciate substantially over time, continuing assessments must be made.

Arguments for the property tax resemble a good news/bad news joke. The good news is that the property tax provides a stable revenue source and has a good track record as a strong revenue raiser. The bad news is that its stability can also be considered inflexibility, as it does not keep pace with income growth. The good news is that, since property is generally unmovable, it is hard to miss, and therefore provides a visible tax base for relatively unskilled local tax officers to administer. The bad news is that the administration and assessment of property tax is at best erratic and at worst a horrendous mess. The result is that the property tax base tends to erode over time; the property of the wealthy and the politically influential may be undervalued; there is a strong incidence effect on newcomers; and the elderly are being increasingly pressed to meet property tax burdens.

A school tax is a local real-property tax imposed by a school district. Because school taxes are largely dependent upon the value of housing, rich districts have always tended to have more revenue, and better overall educational programs,

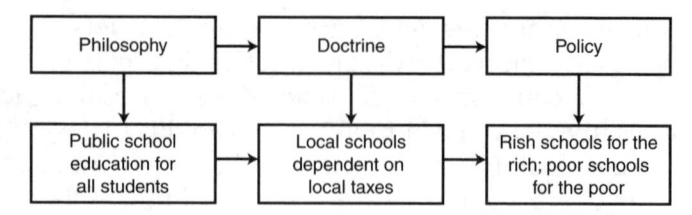

FIGURE 4.3

than poor districts. This situation is summarized by our doctrinal template in Figure 4.3.

EFFORTS TO EQUALIZE SCHOOL FUNDING

As a result of inequalities in per-pupil expenditures among school districts in the same state, the charge has been made that students in poor districts were being denied equal protection of the law as guaranteed by the Fourteenth Amendment. This issue was addressed by the U.S. Supreme Court in *San Antonio Independent School District v. Rodriguez* (1973). In this case the Court overturned a federal district court ruling holding that the Texas system of school finance violated the equal protection clause of the Fourteenth Amendment because it discriminated against poor school districts.

Although the Supreme Court in *San Antonio* refused to strike down as unconstitutional the school district local property tax for the financing of public schools, many state courts have held state school finance systems to be unconstitutional because they discriminate against children in low-wealth school districts. Between 1971 and 2005, state supreme courts in 25 states (including Texas) ruled that property tax financing methods needed to be reformed to provide equal protection to students. States whose courts have required changes in the financing of schools are found throughout the nation, as can be seen in Table 4.1.

The first state to require changes to the dominance of local property tax financing of schools was California. In 1976, the California Supreme Court reaffirmed its groundbreaking 1971 decision in the case of *Serrano v. Priest*. The decision in this case held that California's constitution makes wealth-related inequalities in education expenditures unconstitutional and rejected the principle of "local control" as justifying discrimination against children in low-wealth school districts. According to the California Supreme Court in *Serrano*, the public school "funding scheme invidiously discriminates against the poor because

---

tax base The thing or value on the basis of which taxes are levied. Some of the more common tax bases include individual income, corporate income, real property, motor vehicles, sales of commodities and services, utilities, events, imports, estates, and gifts. The rate of a tax to be imposed against a given tax base may be either specific or ad valorem. Specific taxes raise a specific, nonvariable amount of revenue from each unit of the tax base (e.g., 10 cents per gallon of gasoline). Ad valorem taxes are expressed as a percentage, and the revenue yield varies according to the value of the tax base.

TABLE 4.1

States with Laws That Limit the Use of Property Tax to Finance Public Education

State	Year of First Court Decision Requiring Reform of Educational Finance System
Alabama	1993
Alaska	1999
Arizona	1973
Arkansas	1985
California	1971
Connecticut	1977
Idaho	1998
New Mexico	1998
Kentucky	1989
Massachusetts	1993
Maryland	2000
Missouri	1993
Montana	1974
New Hampshire	1993
New Jersey	1973
New Mexico	1998
North Carolina	2000
Ohio	1997
South Carolina	2005
Tennessee	1993
Texas	1989
Vermont	1997
Washington	1978
West Virginia	1979
Wyoming	1980

SOURCE: National Access Network, Teachers College, Columbia University.

it makes the quality of the child's education a function of the wealth of his parents and neighbors."

Many state courts have not only done what the U.S. Supreme Court failed to do but have also enacted legislation designed to bring the level of educational resources in low-wealth districts on a par with the educational tasks the districts must perform.

Nevertheless, a number of state courts and legislatures have used the *Rodriguez* decision to allow inequalities resulting from differential school district wealth to continue. And with inflation, some poor school districts have fallen even further behind the wealthier ones.

In his highly recognized book *Savage Inequalities*, Jonathan Kozol called public attention to these disparities, noting extreme differences in per-pupil spending within many states. For example, while the Philadelphia public school system spent $9,050 per student in 2003, the average per pupil expenditures in nearby Montgomery County was $13,575. Again, without federal requirement or state court edict, property taxes continue to be the primary financing mechanisms for schools in many places.

SINCE RODRIGUEZ

As we have noted, many state courts have often found statewide school finance systems discriminatory and unconstitutional because such systems base the allocation of educational resources among school districts on factors having nothing to do with education. Thus state courts have taken the lead in doing something about the fact that educational opportunities had become a function of whether a youngster lives in a high-wealth (high local property tax) or a low-wealth (low property tax) school district.

Yet in many states, legal challenges against property tax financing of public education have not been successful. In the 1990s alone, challenges against unequal methods of educational financing were rejected in 20 different states. According to David G. Long, the major reason for courts' sustaining inequitable financing systems that stem from unequal tax bases has been the preservation of "local control." But school financing reforms in many states have shown that methods do exist for eliminating discriminatory funding while maintaining local control. Overall, the legitimacy of inequitable school financing systems has now been considerably undermined, with continued legal challenges mounting in many states.

The totality of all this state court activity to equalize school spending has led to the newly emerging doctrinal template summarized by Figure 4.4. Just as with racial integration, we are not there yet and may never get there completely. But it is increasingly recognized that spending less to educate the poor than the rich is not only a counterproductive policy but one that is hardly defensible in a democratic society.

Although many states have long sought to equalize the resources of their local schools, two decisions in 1990 will continue to affect local education financing: (1) New Jersey decided not to provide state aid to its wealthiest school districts so that more revenue could be given to the

ALTERNATIVE THEORIES

Localized Versus Equalized Educational Finance

In an area of public policy that is crowded with controversy, school finance stands out as a perpetual point of contention in the area of public education. For decades the nation's legislative and judicial institutions have served as battlegrounds where forces struggled over the way Americans pay for their schools. At the heart of these battles has been the conflict between two potent forces in the nation's political traditions—local control and equality.

Throughout the past two centuries the control of public education, including its finance, has rested largely at the local level. However, disparities in school performance and facilities raised concerns that the provision of public education was unequal in nature. Dozens of court cases and many pieces of legislation have attempted to address the controversies over school finance, but the end result has been a patchwork of policies that seem to have only exacerbated the conflicts. With the decision in *San Antonio v. Rodriguez* (1973) the Supreme Court found the Constitution does not require equality in educational finance, the states have been left to resolve the matter on their own. From California to New Jersey states continue to serve as the venue for emotional battles that inevitably pit two valued aspects of America's political system against each other. As with any conflict between two cherished traditions, it's hard to imagine resolutions that will please everyone. But if one tradition is to trump another, how should we decide which value is more important?

poorest and (2) the U.S. Supreme Court in *Missouri v. Jenkins* (1990) held that a federal judge had the authority to order a school district to raise taxes—in this instance to pay for a **magnet school** plan designed to remedy the past practice of school segregation. Justice Byron White, in the opinion of the Court, said, "A court order directing a local government body to levy its own taxes is plainly a judicial act within the power of a Federal Court." Nevertheless, Justice Anthony M. Kennedy, in a dissent, said, "Today's casual embrace of taxation imposed by the unelected, life-tenured federal judiciary disregards fundamental precepts for the democratic control of public institutions."

LABOR POLICY CONFRONTS EDUCATION POLICY

Unions are formal organizations created by groups of employees to represent their interests before management. "Labor relations" is the term for all of the interactions between the union leaders and management. The importance of labor relations in the public schools is evident by the fact that practically every public school teacher is also a member of one of two unions: the National Education Association with 2.8 million members in 2006 or the American Federation of Teachers with over 1.3 million members in 2006.

These **AFL-CIO**-affiliated unions with close to 4 million members (in AFL-CIO) are extraordinarily influential in state, local, and national politics

---

magnet school A school within the public school system that offers a unique and/or specialized program for the purpose of attracting students voluntarily from throughout the school district who will represent a racial and ethnic mix—i.e., voluntary desegregation. Generally a magnet school will emphasize either a specific curricular area (e.g., arts or sciences) or a particular education philosophy (e.g., 'open' concept or fundamentalist orientation).

AFL-CIO The American Federation of Labor-Congress of Industrial Organizations, a voluntary federation of over a hundred national and international labor unions representing over 13 million workers. The AFL-CIO is not itself a union; it does no bargaining. It is perhaps best thought of as a union of unions. The affiliated unions created the AFL-CIO in 1955 to coordinate a wide range of joint activities. Each member union remains autonomous, conducting its own affairs in the manner determined by its own members. Each has its own headquarters, officers, and staff. Each decides its own economic policies, carries on its own contract negotiations, sets its own dues, and provides its own membership services. Each is free to withdraw at any time. But through such voluntary participation, the AFL-CIO, based in Washington, plays a role in establishing overall policies for the U.S. labor movement, which in turn advances the interests of every union.

Philosophy → Doctrine → Policy

Public school education for all students → Local school revenues are equalized → Same education spending for both rich and poor students

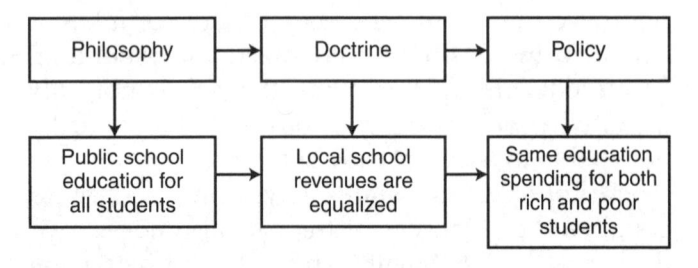

FIGURE 4.4

and in the making of education policy. Their electoral clout overwhelmingly favors the Democratic Party and is unabashedly used to influence school board elections whether partisan or not. According to Sol Stern, these unions collect $2 billion in annual dues, many millions of which go into the campaign coffers or the **political action committees** of favored politicians at every level of government. These perfectly legal bribes allow the union to dominate education policymaking. While such financial contributions are quite legal, critics of public education quality have argued that meaningful education reform is being blocked by teachers' unions unwilling to accept any change that would damage their position in any way. Therefore it is important that we examine the workings of unions more closely to understand their impact on education policy in the United States.

How Unions Work

Unions work to protect the interests of all of their members—from the least competent to the most competent. Indeed, the union officers have a **fiduciary** responsibility to treat all members equally. So if you are a member in good standing (meaning you pay your union dues), the union is formally obligated to protect you from such workplace hazards as overdemanding supervisors, poor performance evaluations, and all adverse actions up to and including attempts at dismissal. Unions obtain the power to do these things by means of collective bargaining.

Collective Bargaining

Collective bargaining is negotiating on behalf of a group of employees as opposed to individual bargaining where each worker represents only himself or herself. "Collective bargaining" is a comprehensive term that encompasses the negotiating process leading to a contract between labor and management on wages, hours, and other conditions of employment as well as the subsequent administration and interpretation of the signed contract. Collective bargaining is, in effect, the continuous relations between union representatives and employers.

Overall, the public sector is incredibly fragmented in terms of collective bargaining. Because there is no national law on the subject, states and cities vary widely in their practices. The law differs from one place to another, placing substantial burdens on national labor unions and dispute resolution personnel who work in different jurisdictions. While the opportunity to experiment and to adapt to **local union** conditions is valuable, such fragmentation makes it hard to speak of "public-sector collective bargaining" without engaging in overgeneralization.

Impasse Resolution

An impasse is a condition that exists during labor-management negotiations when either party feels that no further progress can be made toward a settlement. The most common techniques used to break the impasse are mediation, fact finding, and arbitration.

Mediation or conciliation is any attempt by an impartial third party to help settle disputes. A mediator has no power but that of persuasion; the mediator's suggestions are advisory and may be rejected by both parties. Mediation and conciliation tend to be used interchangeably to denote the entrance of an impartial third party into a labor dispute. However, there is a distinction. Conciliation is the less active term. It technically refers simply to efforts to bring the parties together so that they may resolve their problems themselves. Mediation, in contrast, is a more active term. It implies that an active effort will be made to help the parties reach agreement by clarifying issues, asking questions, and making specific proposals.

Fact finding is an impartial review of the issues in a labor dispute by a specially appointed third party, whether it be a single individual, panel, or board. The fact finder holds formal or informal hearings and submits a report to the

---

political action committee (PAC) An organization whose purpose is to raise and then distribute campaign funds to candidates for political office. Because federal law restricts the amount of money a corporation, union, trade association, or individual can give to a candidate, PACs have evolved as the major means by which significant contributions can influence an election. The PACs were developed by labor unions during and after World War II to acknowledge and encourage the new, potentially significant political power of the American labor movement and to separate specific labor interests from larger public interests in the effort to blunt public criticism of "big labor's" political influence.

fiduciary A relationship where one person acts for another in a formal and legally binding position of trust usually in overseeing the property or affairs of another.

local union A regional organization of union members chartered by the national union with which it is affiliated. For example, the National Education Association charters local unions in thousands of school districts.

administrative agency and/or the parties involved. The fact finder's report, usually advisory, may contain specific recommendations. Fact finding is rare in the public sector because the facts, being a matter of public record, are seldom in dispute. It is the interpretation of the facts that is at issue. For example, management may view a budget surplus as an opportunity to reduce taxes. But labor unions may view the same surplus as an opportunity to raise wages.

Arbitration is the means of settling a dispute by having an impartial third party (the arbitrator) hold a formal hearing and render a decision that may or may not be binding on both sides. The arbitrator may be a single individual or a board of three, five, or more (usually an uneven number). When boards are used, they may include impartial members and representatives from both of the disputants. In the context of labor relations, arbitrators are selected jointly by labor and management, recommended by the Federal **Mediation and Conciliation Service**, by a state or local agency offering similar referrals, or by the private **American Arbitration Association**.

Compulsory arbitration is a negotiating process whereby the parties are required by law to arbitrate their dispute. Some state statutes concerning collective bargaining impasses in the public sector mandate that parties who have exhausted all other means of achieving a settlement must submit their dispute to an arbitrator. The intent of such requirements for compulsory arbitration is to induce the parties to reach agreement by presenting them with an alternative that is certain, even though in some respects it may be unpleasant to everyone involved.

Arbitration inherently undercuts the bargaining process itself. If both sides are convinced a dispute will go to arbitration, they will tend to spend most of their time posturing rather than negotiating or compromising. Moreover, arbitration cannot resolve the concern that the sovereign—the state and not its employees—makes public policy. And arbitrators' decisions are not automatically sensible or in the public interest. Sometimes, they may even disregard a jurisdiction's ability to pay for the awards they authorize.

SCHOOL'S OUT WHEN THEY STRIKE OUT

A strike is a mutual agreement among workers (whether members of a union or not) to a temporary work stoppage to obtain—or to resist—a change in their working conditions. The term is thought to have nautical origins, because sailors would stop work by striking or taking down their sails. A strike or potential strike is considered an essential element of the collective bargaining process. Many labor leaders claim that collective bargaining can never be more than a charade without the right to strike. Major strikes have been declining in frequency in recent years, as unions in both the public and private sectors have lost a large measure of economic clout and political support. Public employee strikes have been declining for another reason as well. A great percentage of public sector strikes in the 1960s and early 1970s were over one issue: recognition of the union for purposes of collective bargaining. Because recognition strikes tend to be one-time issues and many states have in the last three decades passed comprehensive public employee relations laws, public-sector labor strife has been less prevalent than it once was.

Nevertheless, strikes do occur. In at least 13 states they are perfectly legal for teachers: Alaska, California, Hawaii, Idaho, Illinois, Minnesota, Montana, Ohio, Oregon, Pennsylvania, Rhode Island, Vermont, and Wisconsin. It is often the case that workers will not work after a contract has

---

administrative agency An administrative agency is any impartial private or government organization that oversees or facilitates the labor relations process. While generally headed by a board of three to five members, these agencies make rulings on unfair labor practices, on the appropriateness of bargaining units, and sometimes on the proper interpretation of a contract or the legitimacy of a scope of bargaining. They also oversee authorization elections and certify the winners as the exclusive bargaining agents for the employees in a bargaining unit. The National Labor Relations Board (NLRB), created in 1935 by an act of Congress, is the prototype of administrative agencies dealing with labor relations. The equivalent agency for federal employees is the Federal Labor Relations Authority, created by the Civil Service Reform Act of 1978 to oversee the creation of bargaining units, supervise elections, and otherwise deal with labor-management issues in federal agencies. In the states such agencies are generally called public employment relations boards (or PERBs).

Federal Mediation and Conciliation Service (FMCS) The labor-management mediation agency created by the Labor-Management Relations (Taft-Hartley) Act of 1947 as an independent agency of the federal government.

American Arbitration Association An organization that supplies arbitrators who help settle labor and other disputes through arbitration, mediation, and other voluntary methods. The association's National Panel of Arbitrators consists of thousands of men and women, each an expert in some field or profession, who have been nominated for their knowledge and reputation for impartiality.

expired. "No contract, no work" remains fundamental to collective bargaining, since the purpose of negotiations is to arrive at agreements to govern the workplace. Sometimes, as negotiations reach the hour for the termination of the existing contract, the "clock is stopped" and marathon, all night/all day, bargaining sessions take place. There is no doubt that "no contract, no work" places a great deal of pressure on both sides to arrive at an agreement.

The union leader is often in a complicated political position. A strike and the **solidarity** it promotes may be necessary for the leader to maintain his or her position. Union leaders tend to oversell their ability to dictate conditions to management. In order to justify their leadership and the exclusive representative position of the union, they tend to generate very high expectations. Eventually, the gap between these expectations and reality leads the membership to think it has been "sold out" by the union leader. Subsequent contract rejection by the membership can be viewed as a technique to compel management to further concessions.

THE CONTRACT

As Figure 4.5 shows, the whole reason for collective bargaining is to arrive at a contract that unambiguously delineates the wages, **fringe benefits,** and obligations of employees as well as the **reserved rights** of management. These contracts make the teachers' unions extraordinarily powerful for two reasons: (1) they tend to protect the rights of teachers at the expense of management and (2) they show how involved the unions are in making education policy.

THE RIGHTS OF TEACHERS

It is to be expected that the contract will provide for wages and fringe benefits. But all contracts also provide for elaborate grievance procedures—the specific means by which complaints by or about teachers are channeled for adjustment

---

solidarity Labor union unitedness; the common responsibilities and interests of union members.

fringe benefits Nonwage or supplemental benefits (such as insurance, pensions, vacations, sick leave, etc.) that employees receive in addition to their regular pay.

reserved rights Those work-related prerogatives that a labor contract assigns to management; rights that are intrinsic to effective management and thus not subject to collective bargaining.

SOLIDARITY FOREVER

The union movement encouraged the singing of stirring "message" songs as a way of building morale and gaining membership. Some unions even issued official song books designed to fit into an overall pocket. Perhaps the most famous of all union songs (many of which were parodies of well-known hymns) is *Solidarity Forever*, which should be sung to the tune of *The Battle Hymn of the Republic*.

It is we who plowed the prairies, built the cities where they trade,
Dug the mines and built the workshops, endless miles of railroad laid;
Now we stand outcast and starving mid the wonders we have made But the union makes us strong!

Solidarity forever!
Solidarity forever!
Solidarity forever!
For the union makes us strong!

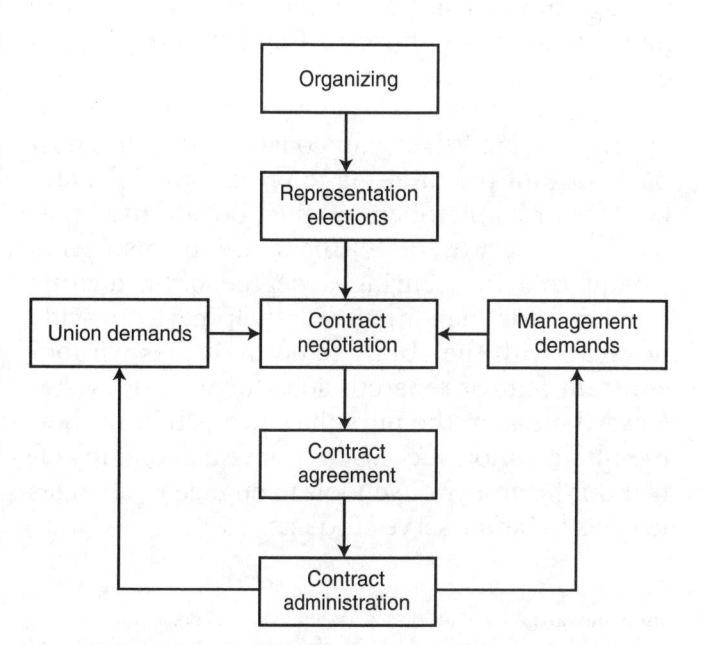

FIGURE 4.5 An Overview of the Collective Bargaining Cycle

through progressively higher levels of authority in both the employing organization and the union. These means in their totality are referred to as the "grievance machinery." This ranges from relatively informal consultations between **shop stewards** and first-level supervisors to formal grievance arbitration. Under the **Weingarten Rule**, any union member who suspects that he or she is being investigated for misconduct has the right to the presence of a union representative while being interrogated by management investigators. This means that teachers cannot be chastised, reprimanded, disciplined, or otherwise held to account for poor performance without a union representative providing a rebuttal in order to protect the interests—meaning the job—of the errant teacher. Thus strong unions make it virtually impossible to take action against teachers who are not doing their job well. Only the grossest violators of professional conduct are ever dismissed. According to Matthew Miller, over a recent five-year period, only 62 of the 220,000 tenured teachers in California were dismissed. That is less than 13 a year.

And to add insult to injury, principals generally lack the ability to "punish" marginal teachers by paying them less. The typical contract provides for a "lock-step" pay scale. Thus teachers with degrees in physics and math (difficult to recruit) are paid the same as those in English and physical education. Pay for performance—paying more to the better teachers—is also generally opposed by the unions. When you consider that the most basic task of the union is to protect the jobs and benefits of its members, it must be admitted that they do it very well. Teachers' unions also serve a vital role in securing a degree of "academic freedom" for their members, helping to provide teachers with the ability to do their jobs without constant fear of repercussions for what they say. Nevertheless, in the pursuit of protection of their members, union success may have a damaging effect on the ability of schools to engage in changes needed to better serve students.

Union-Made Policy

The typical contract also contains many elements that bear directly upon education policy. As the unions have grown large and more politically powerful they have sought to expand the scope of bargaining to include a wide variety of policy issues. Examples include:

How many students should be in each classroom? Should new teaching assignments be decided by school principals or be made a function of **seniority**?

Should the school calendar be decided by the school board alone or jointly with the union?

Should teachers have a veto over the type and frequency of standardized testing used to evaluate student performance?

Should teachers be able to prevent a school district from allowing private corporations to take over troubled schools?

How much discretion should individual teachers have regarding student discipline?

And should higher salaries or signing bonuses be given to attract more teachers of math and science?

The problem with teachers and their unions getting involved with the making of education policy is that it creates a classic **conflict of interest**. The classic statement on conflict of interest was made by Charles E. Wilson during his January 15, 1953, confirmation hearing to be secretary of defense in the Eisenhower Administration. Wilson, who had just resigned as president of General Motors, was asked if he could make a decision in the interests of the United States if that decision was adverse to the interests of General Motors, a corporation in which he held considerable stock. Wilson replied: "For years I thought what was good for our country was good for General Motors, and vice versa. The difference did not exist." This is the attitude taken by many teachers: what's good for the union is good for the students and vice versa. But is it? This is the central question of education policy today.

---

shop steward A local union's most immediate representative in a department, usually elected by fellow employees. Typically the steward continues with a regular job and handles union matters on a part-time basis.

Weingarten Rule So called because the right of an employee under investigation to have union representation was upheld by the U.S. Supreme Court in *National Labor Relations Board v. J. Weingarten* (1975).

seniority The priority given to individuals in an organization who are the most senior, have the longest service. Seniority is often used to determine who will be promoted, subjected to layoff, or given/denied other employment advantages.

conflict of interest Any situation in which the personal interest of an officeholder may influence or appear to influence that officeholder's decision on a matter of public interest.

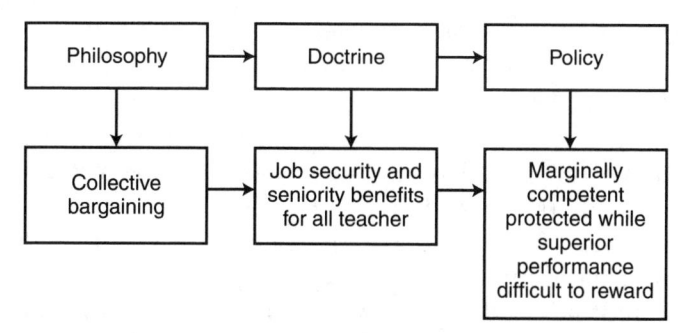

FIGURE 4.6 The Doctrinal Template Applied to Public School Unions

SCHOOL CHOICE

There are two basic kinds of school choice programs: (1) those within the public schools and (2) those that allow students to attend public or private schools—at public expense.

PUBLIC SCHOOL CHOICE

There are two major categories of arguments for public school choice. The first Bella Rosenberg calls the *principled argument*, which asserts that our society has a public interest in maintaining a public school system but that there is no concomitant public interest requiring children to attend one public school over another. Accordingly, this argument states parents should be allowed to choose the public school their children will attend.

The second call for public school choice is the *instrumental argument*. This view sees choice as the means to achieve educational diversity, student achievement, and parent satisfaction. It assumes that competition promulgated through public school choice would increase educational opportunity and consumer satisfaction the same as in a market economy. But schools cannot easily work like a free-market economy. For the most part, gaining or losing students under choice plans would not result in making or losing profit for a school and therefore would not be a stimulus to its improvement. Wealthy districts hardly want to attract students who will raise their costs of education, while low-income school districts have no capacity to attract students from wealthy districts.

Before we decide to rush ahead with public school choice, we should sort out the various models of choice and their respective costs, benefits, and trade-offs. The first and most common model of choice is the *interdistrict model*, which allows urban students to attend suburban schools and vice versa. Typically, interdistrict choice plans have been a one-way ticket from the cities to the suburbs. Importantly, the suburban schools that participate in choice plans act just like private schools: to wit, they keep out "undesirable" urban students. So while the urban students who enter the choice programs have usually been successful, left behind are the majority of urban-school students with no role model students and fewer parents to push for the betterment of their schools.

Statewide choice is another model of public school choice. Such plans permit students to attend school in any district in the state as long as the nonresident school district is willing, has space, and the transfer does not imperil racial balance. State aid follows the student, thus reducing the financial excuses for districts not to accept nonresident students. However, statewide choice does not really accomplish as much as it implies: the reason is that very few parents are going to send their children to anything but their own school district or to a nearby adjacent one.

Controlled-choice programs are another form of choice. Such programs "compel" parents and students to choose a school anywhere in the district or within some zones within a district, subject to the maintenance of racial balance. Accordingly, racial balance is the factor determining whether students get their first, second, or third choices, On balance, controlled-choice plans encourage improvement in school attendance, student achievement, and racial diversity. However, transportation costs are greatly increased.

SCHOOL VOUCHERS

Voucher programs are a pure public choice in that the public gets to choose among alternative sources for services. Citizens who meet eligibility

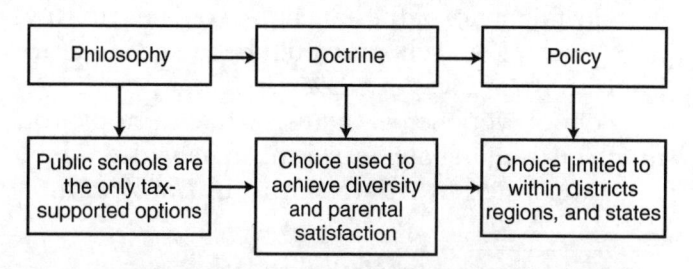

FIGURE 4.7 The Doctrinal Template Applied to Public School Choice

MILTON FRIEDMAN'S CORE ARGUMENT IN FAVOR OF SCHOOL VOUCHERS

If one were to seek deliberately to devise a system of recruiting and paying teachers calculated to repel the imaginative and daring and self-confident and to attract the dull and mediocre and uninspiring, he could hardly do better than imitate the system of requiring teaching certificates and enforcing standard salary structures that has developed in the larger city and state-wide systems. It is perhaps surprising that the level of ability in elementary and secondary school teaching is as high as it is under these circumstances. The alternative [voucher] system would resolve these problems and permit competition to be effective in rewarding merit and attracting ability to teaching.

SOURCE: Milton Friedman (1962). *Capitalism and Freedom*. Chicago: University of Chicago Press.

criteria are given a voucher with which they can purchase goods or services on the open market. Thus government buys something but gets the benefits of free-market competition as the public selects among competing options. Two long-standing, successful, and now noncontroversial voucher programs are food stamps and the higher education benefits available to military veterans since World War II.

Vouchers for primary and secondary education, popularly known as school vouchers, have been far more controversial. The core idea behind school vouchers is parental choice. Parents in participating school districts would be given a voucher to spend on the school of their choosing. Theoretically, a voucher system would encourage competition among schools, since no school would be guaranteed students or funds. Each school would have to earn its fair share of the education vouchers to stay in business. Poor schools would be forced either to improve themselves or close.

School voucher systems, while a topic of much current debate, are hardly a new idea. They were suggested by **Adam Smith** in *The Wealth of Nations* (1776), by Thomas Paine in *The Rights of Man* (1792), and by **John Stuart Mill** in *Our Liberty* (1859). But contemporary analysis of the utility of school vouchers begins with the work of **Milton Friedman**. As early as 1955, he argued that all parents should be provided with unrestricted vouchers that would allow them to send their students to either public or private schools. Friedman's advocacy of school vouchers follows in the tradition of Hayek's (see Chapter 7 Keynote) aversion to state planning. And as with Hayek's notions, Friedman's ideas on education were met with heavy skepticism. He was proposing nothing less than the abolition of the public schools as we knew them. However, as the public schools, faced with the related problems of busing and **white flight**, seemed to deteriorate beyond redemption, his ideas became newly appealing.

THE PROS AND CONS OF SCHOOL VOUCHERS

By the beginning of the twenty-first century, to voucher or not to voucher had become a major issue in many school districts. As with all significant policy issues, there are political forces in favor as well as those opposed.

In favor are:

1. The ideological privatizers of the Hayek-Friedman intellectual heritage and the **Reagan revolution**

Adam Smith (1723–1790) The Scottish economist who provided the first systematic analysis of economic phenomena and the intellectual foundation for laissez-faire capitalism.

John Stuart Mill (1806–1873) The English political reformer and philosopher best known for his classic argument in defense of civil liberties for those with diverse political opinions.

Milton Friedman (1912–2006) The conservative economist who is a leading proponent of a return to laissez-faire economics. A 1976 Nobel Prize winner, he has been a major influence on thinking about monetary policy, consumption, and government regulation. Friedman is generally considered to be the intellectual godfather to the movement toward government deregulation.

white flight The movement of white residents from central cities. It was a common response to public school busing to achieve school racial integration. If they could afford it, whites would tend to move out of the central city and into the suburbs so that their children could attend neighborhood schools. White flight most often occurred when the school population became overwhelmingly black and when bus rides were deemed excessively long.

Reagan revolution The radical changes in the nation's fiscal and tax policies under the Reagan administration, which redefined domestic priorities and curtailed federal programs designed to solve social problems. As Reagan often said: "Government is not the solution to our problems. Government is the problem."

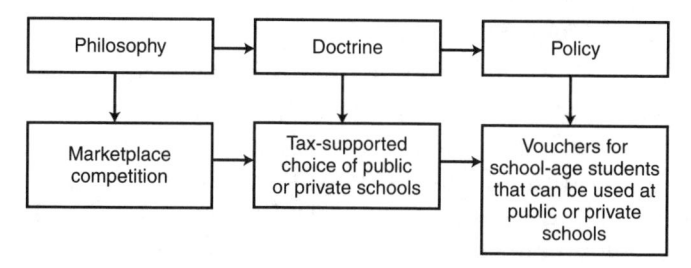

FIGURE 4.8 The Doctrinal Template Applied to School Voucher Programs

2. Inner city residents—often minority—who want a better deal for their children than the frequently dangerous and academically unchallenging local public schools
3. Private schools, especially those with religious affiliations that want to expand their enrollment

Opposed are:

1. Local public school districts that fear losing their effective monopoly on education from kindergarten through high school
2. Public-sector unions representing the teachers who fear losing jobs and the draining of resources from the public school system
3. Supporters of the establishment clause of the First Amendment who fear a breakdown in separation of church and state
4. Affluent white suburban voters who are quite happy with their local public schools and don't want large numbers of minority students from the inner city using vouchers to attend their schools

THE POLITICS OF VOUCHERS

The political dynamics of the voucher proposal have kept and will keep the issue in virtual paralysis, at least for the foreseeable future. This is because the two major political parties are each divided on the issue. The Republicans are ideologically very much in favor but will not be able to marshal enough support for widespread enactment so long as their core constituency—affluent white suburban voters—oppose it. And they oppose it with even greater intensity when it is suggested that voucher programs should have a **means test**. The Democrats, strongly supported by the teachers' unions, tend to oppose vouchers

means test An income criterion used to determine if someone is eligible for government welfare or other benefits.

except that many of their inner-city constituents favor having a choice of educational options for their children. Terry M. Neal of the *Washington Post* quotes David Bositis of the Joint Center for Political and Economic Studies, a black think tank in Washington, on why vouchers will be a long time coming: "White suburbanites are cool to school vouchers. And young blacks and Hispanics under 35 are very hot on vouchers. . . . Since when in American politics have the things that young African Americans wanted ever been something that is likely to be achieved?"

Those who already send their children to private or religious schools favor vouchers as a financial windfall, but they are balanced by those concerned by the church-state separation issue. In 2002 the Supreme Court directly addressed this concern. In *Zelman v. Simmons-Harris*, it held that a Cleveland, Ohio, experimental "pilot" school voucher program, which effectively underwrote tuition at religious schools, was constitutional as long as parents could choose from among a variety of both secular and religious schools. According to Chief Justice William H. Rehnquist, writing the majority opinion, "In sum, the Ohio program is entirely neutral with respect to religion. It provides benefits directly to a wide spectrum of individuals, defined only by financial need and residence in a particular school district. It permits such individuals to exercise genuine choice among options public and private, secular and religious." But this 5-to-4 decision had considerable dissent. For example, Associate Justice John Paul Stevens called the ruling "profoundly misguided" and wrote: "Whenever we remove a brick from the wall that was designed to separate religion and government, we increase the risk of religious strife and weaken the foundation of our democracy."

Milton Friedman, from his perch as a fellow at the Hoover Institution in California, greeted the Supreme Court's decision with enthusiasm and wrote that the "decision clears the way for a major expansion of parental school choice." But consider that in 2000 the states of California and Michigan had ballot initiatives on school vouchers defeated by overwhelming margins. In 2001, President George W. Bush, who campaigned with promises to push school vouchers, signed into law major education reform legislation with no mention of vouchers. There is simply scant support for vouchers in Congress. According to Terry M. Moe (quoted by Adam Nagourney), coauthor of one of the most

ALTERNATIVE THEORIES

School Voucher Systems Versus Traditional Public Schools

with school voucher system	with traditional schools
parents choose school	governments choose school
schools compete for students	schools assigned students
free market competition	government monopoly
vouchers provided by government	students attend at no charge
vouchers good in public or private schools	private schools are not an option

Note that school voucher programs, because they present a viable alternative, are a direct threat to the traditional public school. Would you want the children in your family to have the options offered by voucher systems?

influential books on school choice, the Court's decision is "going to add legitimacy to vouchers, but it's not going to change the basic power alignment, because unions are extraordinarily powerful in the politics of education, and they are dedicated to defeating vouchers everywhere."

Washington Post columnist **George Will** sums up the reasons why school vouchers will not break out of their experimental and "pilot" program nature anytime soon: 'The opposition to school choice for the poor is the starkest immorality in contemporary politics. It is the defense of the strong (teachers' unions) and comfortable (the middle class, content with its public schools and fretful that school choice might diminish their schools' resources and admit poor children to their schools) against the weak and suffering—inner-city children."

George Will (1941–) The nationally syndicated conservative political columnist noted for being one of President Ronald Reagan's major informal advisors and for his constant comparisons of politics to baseball.

SUMMARY

The schools are often the battlefield for fights over policy issues that have wider impact. For example, the *Brown* decision was not just about segregation in education. It was an invaluable precedent in the subsequent fostering of integration in employment and housing by both legislative and judicial means. The big issues of education policy hardly ever stay in the classroom, even when they start there.

The historical trends in education have been pushed by economic forces. The needs of an increasingly sophisticated industrial and postindustrial society for an educated and technologically skilled work force led to public policies creating basic literacy (as with the common schools) and vocational education (offered by high schools) and finally a higher education complex that offers both a traditional liberal education as well as technical studies in every imaginable field. Whereas education in itself is desirable because it leads to better citizens leading the good life in ever more fulfilling ways, the reality is that education policy is driven by the economic needs of a society.

Within any of the 50 states, final authority over educational policy rests with the state government. Nevertheless, for much of the nation's public school history, state governments with the exception of Hawaii's have delegated most of their school authority to local, separate, and independent school districts. A central issue arising in the governance of public school education is the fiscal disparity among individual school districts—a situation that contributes to inequalities among the districts.

The importance of labor relations in the public schools is evident by the fact that practically every public school teacher is also a member of one of two unions: the National Education Association or the American Federation of Teachers. With close to 4 million members, these unions are extraordinarily influential in state, local, and national politics and in the making of education policy.

There are two kinds of school choice programs: (1) those within the public schools and (2) those that allow students to attend either public or private schools—at public expense by means of vouchers. The core idea behind school vouchers is parental choice. Parents in participating school districts would be given a voucher to spend on the school of their choosing. Theoretically, a voucher system would encourage competition among schools, since no school would be guaranteed students or funds. Each school would have to earn its fair share of the education vouchers to stay in business. Poor schools would be forced to either improve at close.

Brown v. Board of Education About The Case

The 1954 United States Supreme Court decision in *Oliver L. Brown et.al. v. the Board of Education of Topeka (KS) et.al.* is among the most significant judicial turning points in the development of our country. Originally led by Charles H. Houston, and later Thurgood Marshall and a formidable legal team, it dismantled the legal basis for racial segregation in schools and other public facilities.

By declaring that the discriminatory nature of racial segregation ... "violates the 14th amendment to the U.S. Constitution, which guarantees all citizens equal protection of the laws," *Brown v. Board of Education* laid the foundation for shaping future national and international policies regarding human rights.

Brown v. Board of Education was not simply about children and education. The laws and policies struck down by this court decision were products of the human tendencies to prejudge, discriminate against, and stereotype other people by their ethnic, religious, physical, or cultural characteristics. Ending this behavior as a legal practice caused far reaching social and ideological implications, which continue to be felt throughout our country. The *Brown* decision inspired and galvanized human rights struggles across the country and around the world.

What this legal challenge represents is at the core of United States history and the freedoms we enjoy. The U.S. Supreme Court decision in *Brown* began a critical chapter in the maturation of our democracy. It reaffirmed the sovereign power of the people of the United States in the protection of their natural rights from arbitrary limits and restrictions imposed by state and local governments. These rights are recognized in the Declaration of Independence and guaranteed by the U.S. Constitution.

While this case was an important historic milestone, it is often misunderstood. Over the years, the facts pertaining to the *Brown* case have been overshadowed by myths and mischaracterizations:

- *Brown v. Board of Education* was not the first challenge to school segregation. As early as 1849, African Americans filed suit against an educational system that mandated racial segregation, in the case of Roberts v. City of Boston.
- Oliver Brown, the case namesake, was just one of the nearly 200 plaintiffs from five states who were part of the NAACP cases brought before the Supreme Court in 1951. The Kansas case was named for Oliver *Brown* as a legal strategy to have a man head the plaintiff roster.

The *Brown* decision initiated educational and social reform throughout the United States and was a catalyst in launching the modern Civil Rights Movement. Bringing about change in the years since the *Brown* case continues to be difficult. But the *Brown v. Board of Education* victory brought this country one step closer to living up to its democratic ideas.

This document tells the story of *Brown v. Board of Education* and the history makers involved in the case.

The Case

The Supreme Court combined five cases under the heading of *Brown* v. Board of Education, because each sought the same legal remedy. The combined cases emanated from Delaware, Kansas, South Carolina, Virginia and Washington, DC. The following describes those cases:

Delaware - Belton v. Gebhart (Bulah v. Gebhart)

First petitioned in 1951, these local cases challenged the inferior conditions of two black schools designated for African American children. In the suburb of Claymont, African American children were prohibited from attending the area's local high school. Instead, they had to ride a school bus for nearly an hour to attend Howard High School

From The *Brown* Foundation website, http://www.brownvboard.org, "Brown vs. Board of Education: About the Case," written by Cheryl Brown Henderson, President and daughter of case namesake Oliver Brown. Copyright © 1996-2008. Reprinted by permission.

in Wilmington. Located in an industrial area of the state's capital city, Howard High School also suffered from a deficient curriculum, pupil-teacher ratio, teacher training, extra curricular activities program, and physical plant. In the rural community of Hockessin, African American students were forced to attend a dilapidated one-room school house and were not provided transportation to the school, while white children in the area were provided transportation and a better school facility. In both cases, Louis Redding, a local NAACP attorney, represented the plaintiffs, African American parents. Although the State Supreme Court ruled in favor of the plaintiffs, the decision did not apply to all schools in Delaware. These class action cases were named for Ethel Belton and Shirley Bulah.

KANSAS - *BROWN* V. BOARD OF EDUCATION

In 1950 the Topeka NAACP, led by McKinley Burnett, set out to organize a legal challenge to an 1879 State law that permitted racially segregated elementary schools in certain cities based on population. For Kansas this would become the 12th case filed in the state focused on ending segregation in public schools. The local NAACP assembled a group of 13 parents who agreed to be plaintiffs on behalf of their 20 children. Following direction from legal counsel they attempted to enroll their children in segregated white schools and all were denied. Topeka operated eighteen neighborhood schools for white children, while African American children had access to only four schools. In February of 1951 the Topeka NAACP filed a case on their behalf. Although this was a class action it was named for one of the plaintiffs Oliver Brown.

SOUTH CAROLINA - BRIGGS V. ELLIOT

In Claredon County, the State NAACP first attempted, unsuccessfully and with a single plaintiff, to take legal action in 1947 against the inferior conditions African American students experienced under South Carolina's racially segregated school system. By 1951, community activist Rev. J.A. DeLaine, convinced African American parents to join the NAACP efforts to file a class action suit in U.S. District Court. The Court found that the schools designated for African Americans were grossly inadequate in terms of buildings, transportation and teacher's salaries when compared to the schools provided for whites. An order to equalize the facilities was virtually ignored by school officials and the schools were never made equal. This class action case was named for Harry Briggs, Sr.

VIRGINIA - DAVIS V. COUNTY SCHOOL BOARD OF PRINCE EDWARD COUNTY

One of the few public high schools available to African Americans in the state was Robert Moton High School in Prince Edward County. Built in 1943, it was never large enough to accommodate its student population. Eventually hastily constructed tar paper covered buildings were added as classrooms. The gross inadequacies of these classrooms sparked a student strike in 1951. Organized by sixteen year old Barbara Johns, the students initially sought to acquire a new building with indoor plumbing. The NAACP soon joined their struggles and challenged the inferior quality of their school facilities in court. Although the U.S. District Court ordered that the plaintiffs be provided with equal school facilities, they were denied access to the white schools in their area. This class action case was named for Dorothy Davis.

WASHINGTON, DC - BOLLING V. C. MELVIN SHARPE

Eleven African American junior High School students were taken on a field trip to the cities new modern John Phillip Sousa school for whites only. Accompanied by local activist Gardner Bishop, who requested admittance for the students and was denied, the African American students were ordered to return to their grossly inadequate school. A suit was filed on their behalf in 1951. After review with the *Brown* case in 1954, the Supreme Court ruled "segregation in the District of Columbia public schools...is a denial of the due process of law guaranteed by the Fifth Amendment..." This class action case was named for Spottswood Bolling.

Lemon v. Kurtzman, 403 U. S. 602 (1971)

U.S. Supreme Court
Lemon v. Kurtzman
No. 89
Argued March 3, 1971
Decided June 28, 1971*
403 U.S. 602

Appeal from the United States District Court for the Eastern District of Pennsylvania

Syllabus

Rhode Island's 1969 Salary Supplement Act provides for a 15% salary supplement to be paid to teachers in nonpublic schools at which the average per-pupil expenditure on secular education is below the average in public schools. Eligible teachers must teach only courses offered in the public schools, using only materials used in the public schools, and must agree not to teach courses in religion. A three-judge court found that about 25% of the State's elementary students attended nonpublic schools, about 95% of whom attended Roman Catholic affiliated schools, and that to date about 250 teachers at Roman Catholic schools are the sole beneficiaries under the Act. The court found that the parochial school system was "an integral part of the religious mission of the Catholic Church," and held that the Act fostered "excessive entanglement" between government and religion, thus violating the Establishment Clause. Pennsylvania's Nonpublic Elementary and Secondary Education Act, passed in 1968, authorizes the state Superintendent of Public Instruction to "purchase" certain "secular educational services" from nonpublic schools, directly reimbursing those schools solely for teachers' salaries, textbooks, and instructional materials. Reimbursement is restricted to courses in specific secular subjects, the textbooks and materials must be approved by the Superintendent, and no payment is to be made for any course containing "any subject matter expressing religious teaching, or the morals or forms of worship of any sect." Contracts were made with schools that have more than 20% of all the students in the State, most of which were affiliated with the Roman Catholic Church. The complaint challenging the constitutionality of

Page 403 U. S. 603

the Act alleged that the church-affiliated schools are controlled by religious organizations, have the purpose of propagating and promoting a particular religious faith, and conduct their operations to fulfill that purpose. A three-judge court granted the State's motion to dismiss the complaint for failure to state a claim for relief, finding no violation of the Establishment or Free Exercise Clause.

Held: Both statutes are unconstitutional under the Religion Clauses of the First Amendment, as the cumulative impact of the entire relationship arising under the statutes involves excessive entanglement between government and religion. Pp. 403 U. S. 611-625.

(a) The entanglement in the Rhode Island program arises because of the religious activity and purpose of the church-affiliated schools, especially with respect to children of impressionable age in the primary grades, and the dangers that a teacher under religious control and discipline poses to the separation of religious from purely secular aspects of elementary education in such schools. These factors require continuing state surveillance to ensure that the statutory restrictions are obeyed and the First Amendment otherwise respected. Furthermore, under the Act, the government must inspect school records to determine what part of the expenditures is attributable to secular education, as opposed to religious activity, in the event a nonpublic school's expenditures per pupil exceed the comparable figures for public schools. Pp. 403 U. S. 615-620.

(b) The entanglement in the Pennsylvania program also arises from the restrictions and surveillance necessary to ensure that teachers play a strictly nonideological role and the state supervision of nonpublic school accounting procedures required to establish the cost of secular, as distinguished from religious, education. In addition, the Pennsylvania statute has the further defect of providing continuing financial aid directly to the church-related schools. Historically, governmental control and surveillance measures tend to follow cash grant programs, and here the government's post-audit power to inspect the financial records of church-related schools creates an intimate and continuing relationship between church and state. Pp. 403 U. S. 620-622.

(c) Political division along religious lines was one of the evils at which the First Amendment aimed, and in these programs, where successive and probably permanent annual appropriations that benefit relatively few religious groups are involved, political

Page 403 U. S. 604

fragmentation and divisiveness on religious lines are likely to be intensified. Pp. 403 U. S. 622-624.

(d) Unlike the tax exemption for places of religious worship, upheld in *Walz v. Tax Commission*, 397 U. S. 664, which was based on a practice of 200 years, these innovative programs have self-perpetuating and self-expanding propensities which provide a warning signal against entanglement between government and religion. Pp. 624-625.

No. 89, 310 F.Supp. 35, reversed and remanded; Nos. 569 and 570, 316 F.Supp. 112, affirmed.

BURGER, C.J., delivered the opinion of the Court, in which BLACK, DOUGLAS, HARLAN, STEWART, MARSHALL (as to Nos. 569 and 570), and BLACKMUN, JJ., joined. DOUGLAS, J., filed a concurring opinion, *post*, p. 403 U. S. 625, in which BLACK, J., joined, and in which MARSHALL, J. (as to Nos. 569 and 570), joined, filing a separate statement, *post*, p. 403 U. S. 642. BRENNAN, J., filed a concurring opinion, *post*, p. 403 U. S. 642. WHITE, J., filed an opinion concurring in the judgment in No. 89 and dissenting in Nos. 569 and 570, *post*, p. 403 U. S. 661. MARSHALL, J., took no part in the consideration or decision of No. 89.

Page 403 U. S. 606

MR. CHIEF JUSTICE BURGER delivered the opinion of the Court.

These two appeals raise questions as to Pennsylvania and Rhode Island statutes providing state aid to church-related elementary and secondary schools. Both statutes are challenged as violative of the Establishment and Free Exercise Clauses of the First Amendment and the Due Process Clause of the Fourteenth Amendment.

Pennsylvania has adopted a statutory program that provides financial support to nonpublic elementary and

Page 403 U. S. 607

secondary schools by way of reimbursement for the cost of teachers' salaries, textbooks, and instructional materials in specified secular subjects. Rhode Island has adopted a statute under which the State pays directly to teachers in nonpublic elementary schools a supplement of 15% of their annual salary. Under each statute, state aid has been given to church-related educational institutions. We hold that both statutes are unconstitutional.

I
THE RHODE ISLAND STATUTE

The Rhode Island Salary Supplement Act[1] was enacted in 1969. It rests on the legislative finding that the quality of education available in nonpublic elementary schools has been jeopardized by the rapidly rising salaries needed to attract competent and dedicated teachers. The Act authorizes state officials to supplement the salaries of teachers of secular subjects in nonpublic elementary schools by paying directly to a teacher an amount not in excess of 15% of his current annual salary. As supplemented, however, a nonpublic school teacher's salary cannot exceed the maximum paid to teachers in the State's public schools, and the recipient must be certified by the state board of education in substantially the same manner as public school teachers.

In order to be eligible for the Rhode Island salary supplement, the recipient must teach in a nonpublic school at which the average per-pupil expenditure on secular education is less than the average in the State's public schools during a specified period. Appellant State Commissioner of Education also requires eligible schools to submit financial data. If this information indicates a per-pupil expenditure in excess of the statutory limitation,

Page 403 U. S. 608

the records of the school in question must be examined in order to assess how much of the expenditure is attributable to secular education and how much to religious activity.[2]

The Act also requires that teachers eligible for salary supplements must teach only those subjects that are offered in the State's public schools. They must use "only teaching materials which are used in the public schools." Finally, any teacher applying for a salary supplement must first agree in writing "not to teach a course in religion for so long as or during such time as he or she receives any salary supplements" under the Act.

Appellees are citizens and taxpayers of Rhode Island. They brought this suit to have the Rhode Island Salary Supplement Act declared unconstitutional and its operation enjoined on the ground that it violates the Establishment and Free Exercise Clauses of the First Amendment. Appellants are state officials charged with administration of the Act, teachers eligible for salary supplements under the Act, and parents of children in church-related elementary schools whose teachers would receive state salary assistance.

A three-judge federal court was convened pursuant to 28 U.S.C. §§ 2281, 2284. It found that Rhode Island's nonpublic elementary schools accommodated approximately 25% of the State's pupils. About 95% of these pupils attended schools affiliated with the Roman Catholic church. To date, some 250 teachers have applied for benefits under the Act. All of them are employed by Roman Catholic schools.

Page 403 U. S. 609

The court held a hearing at which extensive evidence was introduced concerning the nature of the secular instruction offered in the Roman Catholic schools whose teachers would be eligible for salary assistance under the Act. Although the court found that concern for religious values does not necessarily affect the content of secular subjects, it also found that the parochial school system was "an integral part of the religious mission of the Catholic Church."

The District Court concluded that the Act violated the Establishment Clause, holding that it fostered "excessive entanglement" between government and religion. In addition, two judges thought that the Act had the impermissible effect of giving "significant aid to a religious enterprise." 316 F.Supp. 112. We affirm.

THE PENNSYLVANIA STATUTE

Pennsylvania has adopted a program that has some, but not all, of the features of the Rhode Island program. The Pennsylvania Nonpublic Elementary and Secondary Education Act[3] was passed in 1968 in response to a crisis that the Pennsylvania Legislature found existed in the State's nonpublic schools due to rapidly rising costs. The statute affirmatively reflects the legislative conclusion that the State's educational goals could appropriately be fulfilled by government support of "those purely secular educational objectives achieved through nonpublic education. . . ."

The statute authorizes appellee state Superintendent of Public Instruction to "purchase" specified "secular educational services" from nonpublic schools. Under the "contracts" authorized by the statute, the State directly reimburses nonpublic schools solely for their actual expenditures for teachers' salaries, textbooks, and instructional materials. A school seeking reimbursement must

Page 403 U. S. 610

maintain prescribed accounting procedures that identify the "separate" cost of the "secular educational service." These accounts are subject to state audit. The funds for this program were originally derived from a new tax on horse and harness racing, but the Act is now financed by a portion of the state tax on cigarettes.

There are several significant statutory restrictions on state aid. Reimbursement is limited to courses "presented in the curricula of the public schools." It is further limited "solely" to courses in the following "secular" subjects: mathematics, modern foreign languages,[4] physical science, and physical education. Textbooks and instructional materials included in the program must be approved by the state Superintendent of Public Instruction. Finally, the statute prohibits reimbursement for any course that contains "any subject matter expressing religious teaching, or the morals or forms of worship of any sect."

The Act went into effect on July 1, 1968, and the first reimbursement payments to schools were made on September 2, 1969. It appears that some $5 million has been expended annually under the Act. The State has now entered into contracts with some 1,181 nonpublic elementary and secondary schools with a student population of some 535,215 pupils — more than 20% of the total number of students in the State. More than 96% of these pupils attend church-related schools, and most of these schools are affiliated with the Roman Catholic church.

Appellants brought this action in the District Court to challenge the constitutionality of the

Pennsylvania statute. The organizational plaintiffs appellants are associations of persons resident in Pennsylvania declaring

Page 403 U. S. 611

belief in the separation of church and state; individual plaintiffs appellants are citizens and taxpayers of Pennsylvania. Appellant Lemon, in addition to being a citizen and a taxpayer, is a parent of a child attending public school in Pennsylvania. Lemon also alleges that he purchased a ticket at a race track, and thus had paid the specific tax that supports the expenditures under the Act. Appellees are state officials who have the responsibility for administering the Act. In addition seven church-related schools are defendants appellees.

A three-judge federal court was convened pursuant to 28 U.S.C. §§ 2281, 2284. The District Court held that the individual plaintiffs appellants had standing to challenge the Act, 310 F.Supp. 42. The organizational plaintiffs appellants were denied standing under *Flast v. Cohen*, 392 U. S. 83, 392 U. S. 99, 101 (1968).

The court granted appellees' motion to dismiss the complaint for failure to state a claim for relief.[5] 310 F.Supp. 35. It held that the Act violated neither the Establishment nor the Free Exercise Clause, Chief Judge Hastie dissenting. We reverse.

II

In *Everson v. Board of Education*, 330 U. S. 1 (1947), this Court upheld a state statute that reimbursed the parents of parochial school children for bus transportation

Page 403 U. S. 612

expenses. There, MR. JUSTICE BLACK, writing for the majority, suggested that the decision carried to "the verge" of forbidden territory under the Religion Clauses. Id. at 330 U. S. 16. Candor compels acknowledgment, moreover, that we can only dimly perceive the lines of demarcation in this extraordinarily sensitive area of constitutional law.

The language of the Religion Clauses of the First Amendment is, at best, opaque, particularly when compared with other portions of the Amendment. Its authors did not simply prohibit the establishment of a state church or a state religion, an area history shows they regarded as very important and fraught with great dangers. Instead, they commanded that there should be "no law respecting an establishment of religion."

A law may be one "respecting" the forbidden objective while falling short of its total realization. A law "respecting" the proscribed result, that is, the establishment of religion, is not always easily identifiable as one violative of the Clause. A given law might not establish a state religion, but nevertheless be one "respecting" that end in the sense of being a step that could lead to such establishment, and hence offend the First Amendment.

In the absence of precisely stated constitutional prohibitions, we must draw lines with reference to the three main evils against which the Establishment Clause was intended to afford protection: "sponsorship, financial support, and active involvement of the sovereign in religious activity." Walz v. Tax Commission, 397 U. S. 664, 397 U. S. 668 (1970).

Every analysis in this area must begin with consideration of the cumulative criteria developed by the Court over many years. Three such tests may be gleaned from our cases. First, the statute must have a secular legislative purpose; second, its principal or primary effect must be one that neither advances nor inhibits religion, *Board of Education v. Allen*, 392 U. S. 236, 392 U. S. 243 (1968);

Page 403 U. S. 613

finally, the statute must not foster "an excessive government entanglement with religion." *Walz, supra*, at 397 U. S. 674.

Inquiry into the legislative purposes of the Pennsylvania and Rhode Island statutes affords no basis for a conclusion that the legislative intent was to advance religion. On the contrary, the statutes themselves clearly state that they are intended to enhance the quality of the secular education in all schools covered by the compulsory attendance laws. There is no reason to believe the legislatures meant anything else. A State always has a legitimate concern for maintaining minimum standards in all schools it allows to operate. As in *Allen*, we find nothing here that undermines the stated legislative intent; it must therefore be accorded appropriate deference.

In *Allen*, the Court acknowledged that secular and religious teachings were not necessarily so intertwined that secular textbooks furnished to students by the State were, in fact, instrumental in the teaching of religion. 392 U.S. at 392 U. S. 248. The legislatures of Rhode Island and Pennsylvania have concluded that secular and religious education are identifiable and separable. In the abstract, we have no quarrel with this conclusion.

The two legislatures, however, have also recognized that church-related elementary and secondary schools have a significant religious mission, and that a substantial portion of their activities is religiously oriented. They have therefore sought to create statutory restrictions designed to guarantee the separation between secular and religious educational functions, and to ensure that State financial aid supports only the former. All these provisions are precautions taken in candid recognition that these programs approached, even if they did not intrude upon, the forbidden areas under the Religion Clauses. We need not decide whether these legislative precautions restrict the principal or primary effect of the programs to the point where they do not offend the Religion

Page 403 U. S. 614

Clauses, for we conclude that the cumulative impact of the entire relationship arising under the statutes in each State involves excessive entanglement between government and religion.

III

In *Walz v. Tax Commission, supra,* the Court upheld state tax exemptions for real property owned by religious organizations and used for religious worship. That holding, however, tended to confine, rather than enlarge, the area of permissible state involvement with religious institutions by calling for close scrutiny of the degree of entanglement involved in the relationship. The objective is to prevent, as far as possible, the intrusion of either into the precincts of the other.

Our prior holdings do not call for total separation between church and state; total separation is not possible in an absolute sense. Some relationship between government and religious organizations is inevitable. *Zorach v. Clauson,* 343 U. S. 306, 343 U. S. 312 (1952); *Sherbert v. Verner,* 374 U. S. 398, 374 U. S. 422 (1963) (HARLAN, J., dissenting). Fire inspections, building and zoning regulations, and state requirements under compulsory school attendance laws are examples of necessary and permissible contacts. Indeed, under the statutory exemption before us in *Walz,* the State had a continuing burden to ascertain that the exempt property was, in fact, being used for religious worship. Judicial caveats against entanglement must recognize that the line of separation, far from being a "wall," is a blurred, indistinct, and variable barrier depending on all the circumstances of a particular relationship.

This is not to suggest, however, that we are to engage in a legalistic minuet in which precise rules and forms must govern. A true minuet is a matter of pure form and style, the observance of which is itself the substantive end. Here we examine the form of the relationship for the light that it casts on the substance.

Page 403 U. S. 615

In order to determine whether the government entanglement with religion is excessive, we must examine the character and purposes of the institutions that are benefited, the nature of the aid that the State provides, and the resulting relationship between the government and the religious authority. MR. JUSTICE HARLAN, in a separate opinion in *Walz, supra,* echoed the classic warning as to "programs, whose very nature is apt to entangle the state in details of administration. . . ." *Id.* at 397 U. S. 695. Here we find that both statutes foster an impermissible degree of entanglement.

(A) RHODE ISLAND PROGRAM

The District Court made extensive findings on the grave potential for excessive entanglement that inheres in the religious character and purpose of the Roman Catholic elementary schools of Rhode Island, to date the sole beneficiaries of the Rhode Island Salary Supplement Act.

The church schools involved in the program are located close to parish churches. This understandably permits convenient access for religious exercises, since instruction in faith and morals is part of the total educational process. The school buildings contain identifying religious symbols such as crosses on the exterior and crucifixes, and religious paintings and statues either in the classrooms or hallways. Although only approximately 30 minutes a day are devoted to direct religious instruction, there are religiously oriented extracurricular activities. Approximately two-thirds of the teachers in these schools are nuns of various religious orders. Their dedicated efforts provide an atmosphere in which religious instruction and religious vocations are natural and proper parts of life in such schools. Indeed, as the District Court found, the role of teaching nuns in enhancing the religious atmosphere has led the parochial school authorities

Page 403 U. S. 616

to attempt to maintain a one-to-one ratio between nuns and lay teachers in all schools, rather than to permit some to be staffed almost entirely by lay teachers.

On the basis of these findings, the District Court concluded that the parochial schools constituted "an integral part of the religious mission of the Catholic Church." The various characteristics of the schools make them "a powerful vehicle for transmitting the Catholic faith to the next generation." This process of inculcating religious doctrine is, of course, enhanced by the impressionable age of the pupils, in primary schools particularly. In short, parochial schools involve substantial religious activity and purpose.[6]

The substantial religious character of these church-related schools gives rise to entangling church-state relationships of the kind the Religion Clauses sought to avoid. Although the District Court found that concern for religious values did not inevitably or necessarily intrude into the content of secular subjects, the considerable religious activities of these schools led the legislature to provide for careful governmental controls and surveillance by state authorities in order to ensure that state aid supports only secular education.

The dangers and corresponding entanglements are enhanced by the particular form of aid that the Rhode Island Act provides. Our decisions from *Everson* to *Allen* have permitted the States to provide church-related schools with secular, neutral, or nonideological services, facilities, or materials. Bus transportation, school lunches, public health services, and secular textbooks supplied in common to all students were not

Page 403 U. S. 617

thought to offend the Establishment Clause. We note that the dissenters in *Allen* seemed chiefly concerned with the pragmatic difficulties involved in ensuring the truly secular content of the textbooks provided at state expense.

In *Allen*, the Court refused to make assumptions, on a meager record, about the religious content of the textbooks that the State would be asked to provide. We cannot, however, refuse here to recognize that teachers have a substantially different ideological character from books. In terms of potential for involving some aspect of faith or morals in secular subjects, a textbook's content is ascertainable, but a teacher's handling of a subject is not. We cannot ignore the danger that a teacher under religious control and discipline poses to the separation of the religious from the purely secular aspects of pre-college education. The conflict of functions inheres in the situation.

In our view, the record shows these dangers are present to a substantial degree. The Rhode Island Roman Catholic elementary schools are under the general supervision of the Bishop of Providence and his appointed representative, the Diocesan Superintendent of Schools. In most cases, each individual parish, however, assumes the ultimate financial responsibility for the school, with the parish priest authorizing the allocation of parish funds. With only two exceptions, school principals are nuns appointed either by the Superintendent or the Mother Provincial of the order whose members staff the school. By 1969, lay teachers constituted more than a third of all teachers in the parochial elementary schools, and their number is growing. They are first interviewed by the superintendent's office and then by the school principal. The contracts are signed by the parish priest, and he retains some discretion in negotiating salary levels. Religious authority necessarily pervades the school system.

Page 403 U. S. 618

The schools are governed by the standards set forth in a "Handbook of School Regulations," which has the force of synodal law in the diocese. It emphasizes the role and importance of the teacher in parochial schools:

"The prime factor for the success or the failure of the school is the spirit and personality, as well as the professional competency, of the teacher. . . ."

The Handbook also states that: "Religious formation is not confined to formal courses; nor is it restricted to a single subject area." Finally, the Handbook advises teachers to stimulate interest in religious vocations and missionary work. Given the mission of the church school, these instructions are consistent and logical.

Several teachers testified, however, that they did not inject religion into their secular classes. And the District Court found that religious values did not necessarily affect the content of the secular instruction. But what has been recounted suggests the potential, if not actual, hazards of this form of state aid. The teacher is employed by a religious organization, subject to the direction and discipline of religious authorities, and works in a system dedicated to rearing children in a particular faith. These controls are not lessened by the fact that most of the lay teachers are of the Catholic faith. Inevitably, some of a teacher's responsibilities hover on the border between secular and religious orientation.

We need not and do not assume that teachers in parochial schools will be guilty of bad faith or any conscious design to evade the limitations imposed by the statute and the First Amendment. We simply recognize that a dedicated religious person, teaching in a school affiliated with his or her faith and operated to inculcate its tenets, will inevitably experience great difficulty in remaining religiously neutral. Doctrines and faith are not inculcated or advanced by neutrals. With the best of intentions, such a teacher would find it hard to make

Page 403 U. S. 619

a total separation between secular teaching and religious doctrine. What would appear to some to be essential to good citizenship might well for others border on or constitute instruction in religion. Further difficulties are inherent in the combination of religious discipline and the possibility of disagreement between teacher and religious authorities over the meaning of the statutory restrictions.

We do not assume, however, that parochial school teachers will be unsuccessful in their attempts to segregate their religious belief from their secular educational responsibilities. But the potential for impermissible fostering of religion is present. The Rhode Island Legislature has not, and could not, provide state aid on the basis of a mere assumption that secular teachers under religious discipline can avoid conflicts. The State must be certain, given the Religion Clauses, that subsidized teachers do not inculcate religion — indeed, the State here has undertaken to do so. To ensure that no trespass occurs, the State has therefore carefully conditioned its aid with pervasive restrictions. An eligible recipient must teach only those courses that are offered in the public schools and use only those texts and materials that are found in the public schools. In addition, the teacher must not engage in teaching any course in religion.

A comprehensive, discriminating, and continuing state surveillance will inevitably be required to ensure that these restrictions are obeyed and the First Amendment otherwise respected. Unlike a book, a teacher cannot be inspected once so as to determine the extent and intent of his or her personal beliefs and subjective acceptance of the limitations imposed by the First Amendment. These prophylactic contacts will involve excessive and enduring entanglement between state and church.

Page 403 U. S. 620

There is another area of entanglement in the Rhode Island program that gives concern. The statute excludes teachers employed by nonpublic schools whose average per-pupil expenditures on secular education equal or exceed the comparable figures for public schools. In the event that the total expenditures of an otherwise eligible school exceed this norm, the program requires the government to examine the school's records in order to determine how much of the total expenditures is attributable to secular education and how much to religious activity. This kind of state inspection and evaluation of the religious content of a religious organization is fraught with the sort of entanglement that the Constitution forbids. It is a relationship pregnant with dangers of excessive government direction of church schools, and hence of churches. The Court noted "the hazards of government supporting churches" in *Walz v. Tax Commission, supra,* at 397 U. S. 675, and we cannot ignore here the danger that pervasive modern governmental power will ultimately intrude on religion and thus conflict with the Religion Clauses.

(B) PENNSYLVANIA PROGRAM

The Pennsylvania statute also provides state aid to church-related schools for teachers' salaries. The complaint describes an educational system that is very similar to the one existing in Rhode Island. According to the allegations, the church-related elementary and secondary schools are controlled by religious organizations, have the purpose of propagating and promoting a particular religious faith, and conduct their operations to fulfill that purpose. Since this complaint was dismissed for failure to state a claim for relief, we must accept these allegations as true for purposes of our review.

As we noted earlier, the very restrictions and surveillance necessary to ensure that teachers play a strictly nonideological role give rise to entanglements between

Page 403 U. S. 621

church and state. The Pennsylvania statute, like that of Rhode Island, fosters this kind of relationship. Reimbursement is not only limited to courses offered in the public schools and materials approved by state officials, but the statute excludes "any subject matter expressing religious teaching, or the morals or forms of worship of any sect." In addition, schools seeking reimbursement must maintain accounting procedures that require the State to establish the cost of the secular, as distinguished from the religious, instruction.

The Pennsylvania statute, moreover, has the further defect of providing state financial aid directly to the church-related school. This factor distinguishes both *Everson* and *Allen*, for, in both those cases, the Court was careful to point out that state aid was provided to the student and his parents — not to the church-related school. *Board of Education v. Allen, supra,* at 392 U. S. 243-244; *Everson v. Board of Education, supra,* at 330 U. S. 18. In *Walz v. Tax Commission, supra,* at 397 U. S. 675, the Court warned of the dangers of direct payments to religious organizations:

"Obviously a direct money subsidy would be a relationship pregnant with involvement and, as with most governmental grant programs, could encompass sustained and detailed administrative relationships for enforcement of statutory or administrative standards...."

The history of government grants of a continuing cash subsidy indicates that such programs have almost always been accompanied by varying measures of control and surveillance. The government cash grants before us now provide no basis for predicting that comprehensive measures of surveillance and controls will not follow. In particular, the government's post-audit power to inspect and evaluate a church-related school's financial records and to determine which expenditures are religious and

Page 403 U. S. 622

which are secular creates an intimate and continuing relationship between church and state.

IV

A broader base of entanglement of yet a different character is presented by the divisive political potential of these state programs. In a community where such a large number of pupils are served by church-related schools, it can be assumed that state assistance will entail considerable political activity. Partisans of parochial schools, understandably concerned with rising costs and sincerely dedicated to both the religious and secular educational missions of their schools, will inevitably champion this cause and promote political action to achieve their goals. Those who oppose state aid, whether for constitutional, religious, or fiscal reasons, will inevitably respond and employ all of the usual political campaign techniques to prevail. Candidates will be forced to declare, and voters to choose. It would be unrealistic to ignore the fact that many people confronted with issues of this kind will find their votes aligned with their faith.

Ordinarily, political debate and division, however vigorous or even partisan, are normal and healthy manifestations of our democratic system of government, but political division along religious lines was one of the principal evils against which the First Amendment was intended to protect. Freund, Comment, Public Aid to Parochial Schools, 82 Harv.L.Rev. 1680, 1692 (1969). The potential divisiveness of such conflict is a threat to the normal political process. *Walz v. Tax Commission, supra,* at 397 U. S. 695 (separate opinion of HARLAN, J.). *See also Board of Education v. Allen,* 392 U.S. at 392 U. S. 249 (HARLAN, J., concurring); *Abington School District v. Schempp,* 374 U. S. 203, 374 U. S. 307 (1963) (Goldberg, J., concurring). To have States or communities divide on the issues presented by state aid to parochial schools would tend to confuse

Page 403 U. S. 623

and obscure other issues of great urgency. We have an expanding array of vexing issues, local and national, domestic and international, to debate and divide on. It conflicts with our whole history and tradition to permit questions of the Religion Clauses to assume such importance in our legislatures and in our elections that they could divert attention from the myriad issues and problems that confront every level of government. The highways of church and state relationships are not likely to be one-way streets, and the Constitution's authors sought to protect religious worship from the pervasive power of government. The history of many countries attests to the hazards of religion's intruding into the political arena or of political power intruding into the legitimate and free exercise of religious belief.

Of course, as the Court noted in *Walz*, "[a]dherents of particular faiths and individual churches frequently take strong positions on public issues." *Walz v. Tax Commission, supra,* at 397 U. S. 670. We could not expect otherwise, for religious values pervade the fabric of our national life. But, in *Walz*, we dealt with a status under state tax laws for the benefit of all religious groups. Here we are confronted with successive and very likely permanent annual appropriations that benefit relatively few religious groups. Political fragmentation and divisiveness on religious lines are thus likely to be intensified.

The potential for political divisiveness related to religious belief and practice is aggravated in these two statutory programs by the need for continuing annual appropriations and the likelihood of larger and larger demands as costs and populations grow. The Rhode Island District Court found that the parochial school system's "monumental and deepening financial crisis" would "inescapably" require larger annual appropriations subsidizing greater percentages of the salaries of lay teachers. Although no facts have been developed in this respect

Page 403 U. S. 624

in the Pennsylvania case, it appears that such pressures for expanding aid have already required the state legislature to include a portion of the state revenues from cigarette taxes in the program.

V

In *Walz*, it was argued that a tax exemption for places of religious worship would prove to be the first step in an inevitable progression leading to the establishment of state churches and state religion. That claim could not stand up against more than 200 years of virtually universal practice imbedded in our colonial experience and continuing into the present.

The progression argument, however, is more persuasive here. We have no long history of state aid to church-related educational institutions comparable to 200 years of tax exemption for churches. Indeed, the state programs before us today represent something of an innovation. We have already noted that modern governmental programs have self-perpetuating and self-expanding propensities. These internal pressures are only enhanced when the schemes involve institutions whose legitimate needs are growing and whose interests have substantial political support. Nor can we fail to see that, in constitutional adjudication, some steps which, when taken, were thought to approach "the verge" have become the platform for yet further steps. A certain momentum develops in constitutional theory, and it can be a "downhill thrust" easily set in motion but difficult to retard or stop. Development by momentum is not invariably bad; indeed, it is the way the common law has grown, but it is a force to be recognized and reckoned with. The dangers are increased by the difficulty of perceiving in advance exactly where the "verge" of the precipice lies. As well as constituting an independent evil against which the Religion Clauses were intended to protect, involvement

Page 403 U. S. 625

or entanglement between government and religion serves as a warning signal.

Finally, nothing we have said can be construed to disparage the role of church-related elementary and secondary schools in our national life. Their contribution has been and is enormous. Nor do we ignore their economic plight in a period of rising costs and expanding need. Taxpayers generally have been spared vast sums by the maintenance of these educational institutions by religious organizations, largely by the gifts of faithful adherents.

The merit and benefits of these schools, however, are not the issue before us in these cases. The sole question is whether state aid to these schools can be squared with the dictates of the Religion Clauses. Under our system, the choice has been made that government is to be entirely excluded from the area of religious instruction, and churches excluded from the affairs of government. The Constitution decrees that religion must be a private matter for the individual, the family, and the institutions of private choice, and that, while some involvement and entanglement are inevitable, lines must be drawn.

The judgment of the Rhode Island District Court in No. 569 and No. 570 is affirmed. The judgment of the Pennsylvania District Court in No. 89 is reversed, and the case is remanded for further proceedings consistent with this opinion.

MR. JUSTICE MARSHALL took no part in the consideration or decision of No. 89.

* Together with No. 569, *Earley et al. v. DiCenso et al.*, and No. 570, *Robinson, Commissioner of Education of Rhode Island, et al. v. DiCenso et al.*, on appeal from the United States District Court for the District of Rhode Island.

MR. JUSTICE DOUGLAS, whom MR. JUSTICE BLACK joins, concurring.

While I join the opinion of the Court, I have expressed at some length my views as to the rationale of today's decision in these three cases.

Page 403 U. S. 626

They involve two different statutory schemes for providing aid to parochial schools. *Lemon* deals with the Pennsylvania Nonpublic Elementary and Secondary Education Act, Laws 1968, Act No. 109. By its terms, the Pennsylvania Act allows the State to provide funds directly to private schools to purchase "secular educational service" such as teachers' salaries, textbooks, and educational materials. Pa.Stat.Ann., Tit. 24, § 5604 (Supp. 1971). Reimbursement for these services may be made only for courses in mathematics, modern foreign languages, physical science, and physical education. Reimbursement is prohibited for any course containing subject matter "expressing religious teaching, or the morals or forms of worship of any sect." § 5603 (Supp. 1971). To qualify, a school must demonstrate that its pupils achieve a satisfactory level of performance in standardized tests approved by the Superintendent of Public Instruction, and that the textbooks and other instructional materials used in these courses have been approved by the Superintendent of Public Instruction. The three-judge District Court below upheld this statute against the argument that it violates the Establishment Clause. We noted probable jurisdiction. 397 U.S. 1034.

The *DiCenso* cases involve the Rhode Island Salary Supplement Act, Laws 1969, c. 246. The Rhode Island Act authorizes supplementing the salaries of teachers of secular subjects in nonprofit private schools. The supplement is not more than 15% of an eligible teacher's current salary, but cannot exceed the maximum salary paid to teachers in the State's public schools. To be eligible, a teacher must teach only those subjects offered in public schools in the State, must be certified in substantially the same manner as teachers in public schools, and may use only teaching materials which are used in the public schools. Also the teacher must agree in writing

Page 403 U. S. 627

"not to teach a course in religion for so long as or during such time as he or she receives any salary supplements." R.I.Gen.Laws Ann. § 16-51-3 (Supp. 1970). The schools themselves must not be operated for profit, must meet state educational standards, and the annual per-student expenditure for secular education must not equal or exceed "the average annual per student expenditure in the public schools in the state at the same grade level in the second preceding fiscal year." § 16-51-2 (Supp. 1970). While the Rhode Island Act, unlike the Pennsylvania Act, provides for direct payments to the teacher, the three-judge District Court below found it unconstitutional because it "results in excessive government entanglement with religion." Probable jurisdiction was noted, and the cases were set for oral argument with the other school cases. 400 U.S. 901.

In *Walz v. Tax Commission,* 397 U. S. 664, 397 U. S. 674, the Court in approving a tax exemption for church property said:

"Determining that the legislative purpose of tax exemption is not aimed at establishing, sponsoring, or supporting religion does not end the inquiry, however. We must also be sure that the end result — the effect — is not an excessive government entanglement with religion."

There is, in my view, such an entanglement here. The surveillance or supervision of the States needed to police grants involved in these three cases, if performed, puts a public investigator into every classroom and entails a pervasive monitoring of these church agencies by the secular authorities. Yet if that surveillance or supervision does not occur, the zeal of religious proselytizers promises to carry the day and make a shambles of the Establishment Clause. Moreover, when taxpayers of

Page 403 U. S. 628

many faiths are required to contribute money for the propagation of one faith, the Free Exercise Clause is infringed.

The analysis of the constitutional objections to these two state systems of grants to parochial or sectarian schools must start with the admitted and obvious fact that the *raison d'etre* of parochial schools is the propagation of a religious faith. They also teach secular subjects, but they came into existence in this country because Protestant groups were perverting the public schools by using them to propagate their faith. The Catholics naturally rebelled. If schools were to be used to propagate a particular creed or religion, then Catholic ideals should also be served. Hence, the advent of parochial schools.

By 1840, there were 200 Catholic parish schools in the United States.[2.1] By 1964, there were 60 times as many.[2.2] Today, 57% of the

9,000 Catholic parishes in the country have their church schools. "[E]very diocesan chancery has its school department, and enjoys a primacy of status."[2.3] The parish schools indeed consume 40% to 65% of the parish's total income.[2.4] The parish is so "school-centered" that "[t]he school almost becomes the very reason for being."[2.5]

Early in the 19th century, the Protestants obtained control of the New York school system and used it to promote reading and teaching of the Scriptures as revealed in the King James version of the Bible.[2.6] The contests

Page 403 U. S. 629

between Protestants and Catholics, often erupting into violence including the burning of Catholic churches, are a twice-told tale;[2.7] the Know-Nothing Party, which included in its platform "daily Bible reading in the schools,"[2.8] carried three States in 1854 — Massachusetts, Pennsylvania, and Delaware.[2.9] Parochial schools grew, but not Catholic schools alone. Other dissenting sects established their own schools — Lutherans, Methodists, Presbyterians, and others.[2.10] But the major force in shaping the pattern of education in this country was the conflict between Protestants and Catholics. The Catholics logically argued that a public school was sectarian when it taught the King James version of the Bible. They therefore wanted it removed from the public schools, and, in time, they tried to get public funds for their own parochial schools.[2.11]

The constitutional right of dissenters to substitute their parochial schools for public schools was sustained by the Court in *Pierce v. Society of Sisters,* 268 U. S. 510.

The story of conflict and dissension is long and well known. The result was a state of so-called equilibrium, where religious instruction was eliminated from public schools and the use of public funds to support religious schools was deemed to be banned.[2.12]

But the hydraulic pressures created by political forces and by economic stress were great, and they began to

Page 403 U. S. 630

change the situation. Laws were passed — state and federal — that dispensed public funds to sustain religious schools and the plea was always in the educational frame of reference: education in all sectors was needed, from languages to calculus to nuclear physics. And it was forcefully argued that a linguist or mathematician or physicist trained in religious schools was just as competent as one trained in secular schools.

And so we have gradually edged into a situation where vast amounts of public funds are supplied each year to sectarian schools.[2.13]

And the argument is made that the private parochial school system takes about $9 billion a year off the back of government[2.14] — as if that were enough to justify violating the Establishment Clause.

While the evolution of the public school system in this country marked an escape from denominational control, and was therefore admirable as seen through the eyes of those who think like Madison and Jefferson, it has disadvantages. The main one is that a state system may attempt to mold all students alike according to the views of the dominant group, and to discourage the emergence of individual idiosyncrasies.

Sectarian education, however, does not remedy that condition. The advantages of sectarian education relate solely to religious or doctrinal matters. They give the

Page 403 U. S. 631

church the opportunity to indoctrinate its creed delicately and indirectly, or massively through doctrinal courses.

Many nations follow that course: Moslem nations teach the Koran in their schools; Sweden vests its elementary education in the parish; Newfoundland puts its school system under three superintendents — one from the Church of England, one from the Catholic church, one from the United Church. In Ireland, the public schools are under denominational managership— Catholic, Episcopalian, Presbyterian, and Hebrew.

England puts sectarian schools under the umbrella of its school system. It finances sectarian education; it exerts control by prescribing standards; it requires some free scholarships; it provides nondenominational membership on the board of directors.[2.15]

The British system is, in other words, one of surveillance over sectarian schools. We too have surveillance over sectarian schools, but only to the extent of making sure that minimum educational standards are met, *viz.*, competent teachers, accreditation of the school for diplomas, the number of hours of work and credits allowed, and so on.

But we have never faced, until recently, the problem of policing sectarian schools. Any surveillance to date has been minor, and has related only to the consistently unchallenged matters of accreditation of the sectarian school in the State's school system.[2.16]

The Rhode Island Act allows a supplementary salary to a teacher in a sectarian school if he or she "does not teach a course in religion."

Page 403 U. S. 632

The Pennsylvania Act provides for state financing of instruction in mathematics, modern foreign languages, physical science, and physical education, provided that the instruction in those courses "shall not include any subject matter expressing religious teaching, or the morals or forms of worship of any sect."

Public financial support of parochial schools puts those schools under disabilities with which they were not previously burdened. For, as we held in *Cooper v. Aaron,* 358 U. S. 1, 358 U. S. 19, governmental activities relating to schools "must be exercised consistently with federal constitutional requirements." There we were concerned with equal protection; here we are faced with issues of Establishment of religion and its Free Exercise as those concepts are used in the First Amendment.

Where the governmental activity is the financing of the private school, the various limitations or restraints imposed by the Constitution on state governments come into play. Thus, Arkansas, as part of its attempt to avoid the consequences of *Brown v. Board of Education,* 347 U. S. 483, 347 U. S. 349 U.S. 294, withdrew its financial support from some public schools and sent the funds instead to private schools. That state action was held to violate the Equal Protection Clause. *Aaron v. McKinley,* 173 F.Supp. 944, 952. We affirmed, *sub nom. Faubus v. Aaron,* 361 U. S. 197. Louisiana tried a like tactic, and it too was invalidated. *Poindexter v. Louisiana Financial Assistance Commission,* 296 F.Supp. 686. Again we affirmed. 393 U. S. 17. Whatever might be the result in case of grants to students,[2.17] it is clear that, once

Page 403 U. S. 633

one of the States finances a private school, it is duty-bound to make certain that the school stays within secular bounds and does not use the public funds to promote sectarian causes.

The government may, of course, finance a hospital though it is run by a religious order, provided it is open to people of all races and creeds. *Bradfield v. Roberts,* 175 U. S. 291. The government itself could enter the hospital business, and it would, of course, make no difference if its agents who ran its hospitals were Catholics, Methodists, agnostics, or whatnot. For the hospital is not indulging in religious instruction or guidance or indoctrination. As Mr. Justice Jackson said in *Everson v. Board of Education,* 330 U. S. 1, 330 U. S. 26 (dissenting):

"[Each State has] great latitude in deciding for itself, in the light of its own conditions, what shall be public purposes in its scheme of things. It may socialize utilities and economic enterprises and make taxpayers' business out of what conventionally had been private business. It may make public business of individual welfare, health, education, entertainment or security. But it cannot make public business of religious worship or instruction, or of attendance at religious institutions of any character."

The reason is that given by Madison in his Remonstrance:[2.18]

"[T]he same authority which can force a citizen to contribute three pence only of his property for

Page 403 U. S. 634

the support of any one establishment, may force him to conform to any other establishment. . . ."

When Madison, in his Remonstrance, attacked a taxing measure to support religious activities, he advanced a series of reasons for opposing it. One that is extremely relevant here was phrased as follows:[2.19]

"[I]t will destroy that moderation and harmony which the forbearance of our laws to intermeddle with Religion, has produced amongst its several sects."

Intermeddling, to use Madison's word, or "entanglement," to use what was said in *Walz,* has two aspects. The intrusion of government into religious schools through grants, supervision, or surveillance may result in establishment of religion in the constitutional sense when what the State does enthrones a particular sect for overt or subtle propagation of its faith. Those activities of the State may also intrude on the Free Exercise Clause by depriving a teacher, under threats of reprisals, of the right to give sectarian construction or interpretation of, say, history and literature, or to use the teaching of such subjects to inculcate a religious creed or dogma.

Under these laws, there will be vast governmental suppression, surveillance, or meddling in church affairs. As I indicated in *Tilton v. Richardson, post,* p. 403 U. S. 689, decided this day, school prayers, the daily routine of parochial schools, must go if our decision in *Engel v. Vitale,* 370 U. S. 421, is honored. If it is not honored, then the state has established a religious sect. Elimination of prayers is only part of the problem. The curriculum presents subtle and difficult problems. The constitutional mandate can in part be carried out by censoring the curricula. What is palpably a sectarian course can be marked for

Page 403 U. S. 635

deletion. But the problem only starts there. Sectarian instruction, in which, of course, a State may not indulge, can take place in a course on Shakespeare or in one on mathematics. No matter what the curriculum offers, the question is, what is *taught?* We deal not with evil teachers, but with zealous ones who may use any opportunity to indoctrinate a class.[2,20]

It is well known that everything taught in most parochial schools is taught with the ultimate goal of religious education in mind. Rev. Joseph H. Fichter, S.J., stated in Parochial School: A Sociological Study 86 (1958):

"It is a commonplace observation that, in the parochial school, religion permeates the whole curriculum, and is not confined to a single half-hour period of the day. Even arithmetic can be used as an instrument of pious thoughts, as in the case of the teacher who gave this problem to her class:"

"If it takes forty thousand priests and a hundred and forty thousand sisters to care for forty million Catholics in the United States, how many more priests and sisters will be needed to convert and care for the hundred million non-Catholics in the United States?"

One can imagine what a religious zealot, as contrasted to a civil libertarian, can do with the Reformation

Page 403 U. S. 636

or with the Inquisition. Much history can be given the gloss of a particular religion. I would think that policing these grants to detect sectarian instruction would be insufferable to religious partisans, and would breed division and dissension between church and state.

This problem looms large where the church controls the hiring and firing of teachers:

"[I]n the public school, the selection of a faculty and the administration of the school usually rests with a school board, which is subject to election and recall by the voters, but in the parochial school, the selection of a faculty and the administration of the school is in the hands of the bishop alone, and usually is administered through the local priest. If a faculty member in the public school believes that he has been treated unjustly in being disciplined or dismissed, he can seek redress through the civil court, and he is guaranteed a hearing. But if a faculty member in a parochial school is disciplined or dismissed, he has no recourse whatsoever. The word of the bishop or priest is final, even without explanation if he so chooses. The tax payers have a voice in the way their money is used in the public school, but the people who support a parochial school have no voice at all in such affairs."

L. Boettner, Roman Catholicism 375 (1962).

Board of Education v. Allen, 392 U. S. 236, dealt only with textbooks. Even so, some had difficulty giving approval. Yet books can be easily examined independently of other aspects of the teaching process. In the present cases, we deal with the totality of instruction destined to be sectarian, at least in part, if the religious character of the school is to be maintained. A school which operates to commingle religion with other instruction plainly cannot completely secularize its instruction.

Page 403 U. S. 637

Parochial schools, in large measure, do not accept the assumption that secular subjects should be unrelated to religious teaching.

Lemon involves a state statute that prescribes that courses in mathematics, modern foreign languages, physical science, and physical education "shall not include any subject matter expressing religious teaching, or the morals or forms of worship of any sect." The subtleties involved in applying this standard are obvious. It places the State astride a sectarian school and gives it power to dictate what is or is not secular, what is or is not religious. I can think of no more disrupting influence apt to promote rancor and ill-will between church and state than this kind of surveillance and control. They are the very opposite of the "moderation and harmony" between church and state which Madison thought was the aim and purpose of the Establishment Clause.

The *DiCenso* cases have all the vices which are in *Lemon,* because the supplementary salary payable to the teacher is conditioned on his or her not teaching "a course in religion."

Moreover, the *DiCenso* cases reveal another, but related, knotty problem presented when church and state launch one of these educational programs. The Bishop of Rhode Island has a Handbook of School Regulations for the Diocese of Providence.[2.21]

The school board supervises "the education, both spiritual and secular, in the parochial schools and diocesan high schools."

The superintendent is an agent of the bishop, and he interprets and makes "effective state and diocesan educational directives."

Page 403 U. S. 638

The pastors visit the schools and "give their assistance in promoting spiritual and intellectual discipline."

Community supervisors "assist the teacher in the problems of instruction," and these duties are:

"I. To become well enough acquainted with the teachers of their communities so as to be able to advise the community superiors on matters of placement and reassignment."

"II. To act as liaison between the provincialate and the religious teacher in the school."

"III. To cooperate with the superintendent by studying the diocesan school regulations and to encourage the teachers of their community to observe these regulations."

"IV. To avoid giving any orders or directions to the teachers of their community that may be in conflict with diocesan regulations or policy regarding curriculum, testing, textbooks, method, or administrative matters."

"V. To refer questions concerning school administration beyond the scope of their own authority to the proper diocesan school authorities, namely, the superintendent of schools or the pastor."

The length of the school day includes Mass:
"A full day session for Catholic schools at the elementary level consists of five and one-half hours, exclusive of lunch and Mass,[2.22] but inclusive of recess for pupils in grades 1-3."

A course of study or syllabus prescribed for an elementary or secondary school is "mandatory."

Page 403 U. S. 639

Religious instruction is provided as follows:

"A. Systematic religious instructions must be provided in all schools of the diocese."

"B. Modern catechetics requires a teacher with unusual aptitudes, specialized training, and such function of the spirit that his words possess the force of a personal call. He should be so filled with his subject that he can freely improvise in discussion, dramatization, drawing, song, and prayer. A teacher so gifted and so permeated by the message of the Gospel is rare. Perhaps no teacher in a given school attains that ideal. But some teachers come nearer it than others. If our pupils are to hear the Good News so that their minds are enlightened and their hearts respond to the love of God and His Christ, if they are to be formed into vital, twentieth-century Christians, they should receive their religious instructions only from the very best teachers."

"C. Inasmuch as the textbooks employed in religious instruction above the fifth grade require a high degree of catechetical preparation, religion should be a departmentalized subject in grade six through twelve."

Religious activities are provided, through observance of specified holy days and participation in Mass.

"Religious formation' is not restricted to courses, but is achieved 'through the example of the faculty, the tone of the school . . . and religious activities."

No unauthorized priest may address the students.

"Retreats and days of recollection form an integral part of our religious program in the Catholic schools."

Religious factors are used in the selection of students:

"Although wealth should never serve as a criterion for accepting a pupil into a Catholic school, all other

Page 403 U. S. 640

things being equal, it would seem fair to give preference to a child whose parents support the parish. Regular use of the budget, rather than the size of the contributions, would appear equitable. It indicates whether parents regularly attend Mass."

These are only highlights of the handbook. But they indicate how pervasive is the religious control over the school, and how remote this type of school is from the secular school. Public funds supporting that structure are used to perpetuate a doctrine and creed in innumerable and in pervasive ways. Those who man these schools are good people, zealous people, dedicated people. But they are dedicated to ideas that the Framers of our Constitution placed beyond the reach of government.

If the government closed its eyes to the manner in which these grants are actually used, it would be allowing public funds to promote sectarian education. If it did not close its eyes, but undertook the surveillance needed, it would, I fear, intermeddle in parochial affairs in a way that would breed only rancor and dissension.

We have announced over and over again that the use of taxpayers' money to support parochial schools violates the First Amendment, applicable to the States by virtue of the Fourteenth.

We said in unequivocal words in *Everson v. Board of Education*, 330 U. S. 1, 330 U. S. 16,

"No tax in any amount, large or small, can be levied to support any religious activities or institutions, whatever they may be called, or whatever form they may adopt to teach or practice religion."

We reiterated the same idea in *Zorach v. Clauson*, 343 U. S. 306, 343 U. S. 314, and in *McGowan v. Maryland*, 366 U. S. 420, 366 U. S. 443, and in *Torcaso v. Watkins*, 367 U. S. 488, 367 U. S. 493. We repeated the same idea in *McCollum v. Board of Education*, 333 U. S. 203, 333 U. S. 210, and added that a State's

Page 403 U. S. 641

tax-supported public schools could not be used "for the dissemination of religious doctrines," nor could a State provide the church "pupils for their religious classes through use of the State's compulsory public school machinery." *Id.* at 333 U. S. 212.

Yet, in spite of this long and consistent history, there are those who have the courage to announce that a State may nonetheless finance the secular part of a sectarian school's educational program. That, however, makes a grave constitutional decision turn merely on cost accounting and bookkeeping entries. A history class, a literature class, or a science class in a parochial school is not a separate institute; it is part of the organic whole which the State subsidizes. The funds are used in these cases to pay or help pay the salaries of teachers in parochial schools; and the presence of teachers is critical to the essential purpose of the parochial school, *viz.*, to advance the religious endeavors of the particular church. It matters not that the teacher receiving taxpayers' money only teaches religion a fraction of the time. Nor does it matter that he or she teaches no religion. The school is an organism living on one budget. What the taxpayers give for salaries of those who teach only the humanities or science without any trace of proselytizing enables the school to use all of its own funds for religious training. As Judge Coffin said, 316 F.Supp. 112, 120, we would be blind to realities if we let "sophisticated bookkeeping" sanction "almost total subsidy of a religious institution by assigning the bulk of the institution's expenses to *secular'* activities." *And sophisticated attempts to avoid the Constitution are just as invalid as simple-minded ones. Lane v. Wilson,* 307 U. S. 268, 307 U. S. 275.

In my view, the taxpayers' forced contribution to the

Page 403 U. S. 642

parochial schools in the present cases violates the First Amendment.

MR. JUSTICE MARSHALL, who took no part in the consideration or decision of No. 89, *see ante,* p. 403 U. S. 625, while intimating no view as to the continuing vitality of *Everson v. Board of Education,* 330 U. S. 1 (1947), concurs in MR. JUSTICE DOUGLAS' opinion covering Nos. 569 and 570.

MR. JUSTICE BRENNAN. *

I agree that the judgments in Nos. 569 and 570 must be affirmed. In my view, the judgment in No. 89 must be reversed outright. I dissent in No. 153 insofar as the plurality opinion and the opinion of my Brother WHITE sustain the constitutionality, as applied to sectarian institutions, of the Federal Higher Education Facilities Act of 1963, as amended, 77 Stat. 363, 20 U.S.C. § 711 *et seq.* (1964 ed. and Supp. V). In my view, that Act is unconstitutional insofar as it authorizes grants of federal tax monies to sectarian institutions, but is unconstitutional only to that extent. I therefore think that our remand of the case should be limited to the direction of a hearing to determine whether the four institutional appellees here are sectarian institutions.

I continue to adhere to the view that, to give concrete meaning to the Establishment Clause,

"the line we must draw between the permissible and the impermissible is one which accords with history and faithfully reflects the understanding of the Founding Fathers. It is a line which the Court has consistently sought to mark in its decisions expounding the religious guarantees of the First

Page 403 U. S. 643

Amendment. What the Framers meant to foreclose, and what our decisions under the Establishment Clause have forbidden, are those involvements of religious with secular institutions which (a) serve the essentially religious activities of religious institutions; (b) employ the organs of government for essentially religious purposes; or (c) use essentially religious means to serve governmental ends, where secular means would suffice. When the secular and religious institutions become involved in such a manner, there inhere in the relationship precisely those dangers — as much to church as to state — which the Framers feared would subvert religious liberty and the strength of a system of secular government."

Abington School District v. Schempp, 374 U. S. 203, 374 U. S. 294-295 (1963) (concurring opinion); *Walz v. Tax Commission,* 397 U. S. 664, 397 U. S. 680-681 (1970) (concurring opinion).

The common feature of all three statutes before us is the provision of a direct subsidy from public funds for activities carried on by sectarian educational institutions. We have sustained the reimbursement of parents for bus fares of students under a scheme applicable to both public and nonpublic schools, *Everson v. Board of Education,* 330 U. S. 1 (1947). We have also sustained the loan of textbooks in secular subjects to students of both public and nonpublic schools, *Board of Education v. Allen,* 392 U. S. 236 (1968). See also *Bradfield v. Roberts,* 175 U. S. 291 (1899).

The statutory schemes before us, however, have features not present in either the *Everson* or *Allen* schemes. For example, the reimbursement or the loan of books ended government involvement in *Everson* and *Allen.* In contrast, each of the schemes here exacts a promise in some form that the subsidy will not be used to finance

Page 403 U. S. 644

courses in religious subjects — promises that must be and are policed to assure compliance. Again, although the federal subsidy, similar to the *Everson* and *Allen* subsidies, is available to both public and nonpublic colleges and universities, the Rhode Island and Pennsylvania subsidies are restricted to nonpublic schools, and, for practical purposes, to Roman Catholic parochial schools.[3.1] These and other features I shall mention mean for me that *Everson* and *Allen* do not control these cases. Rather, the history of public subsidy of sectarian schools, and the purposes and operation of these particular statutes, must be examined to determine whether the statutes breach the Establishment Clause. *Walz v. Tax Commission, supra,* at 397 U. S. 681 (concurring opinion).

Page 403 U. S. 645

I

In sharp contrast to the "undeviating acceptance given religious tax exemptions from our earliest days as a Nation," *ibid.*, subsidy of sectarian educational institutions became embroiled in bitter controversies very soon after the Nation was formed. Public education was, of course, virtually nonexistent when the Constitution was adopted. Colonial Massachusetts in 1647 had directed towns to establish schools, Benjamin Franklin in 1749 proposed a Philadelphia Academy, and Jefferson labored to establish a public school system in Virginia.[3.2] But these were the exceptions. Education in the Colonies was overwhelmingly a private enterprise, usually carried on as a denominational activity by the dominant Protestant sects. In point of fact, government generally looked to the church to provide education, and often contributed support through donations of land and money. E. Cubberley, Public Education in the United States 171 (1919).

Nor was there substantial change in the years immediately following ratification of the Constitution and the Bill of Rights. Schools continued to be local and, in the main, denominational institutions.[3.3] But the demand for public education soon emerged. The evolution of the struggle in New York City is illustrative.[3.4] In 1786, the first New York State Legislature ordered that one section in each township be set aside for the "gospel and schools." With no public schools, various private agencies and churches operated "charity schools" for the poor of New

Page 403 U. S. 646

York City and received money from the state common school fund. The forerunner of the city's public schools was organized in 1805 when DeWitt Clinton founded

"The Society for Establishment of a Free School in the City of New York for the Education of such poor Children as do not belong to or are not provided for by any Religious Society."

The State and city aided the society, and it built many schools. Gradually, however, competition and bickering among the Free School Society and the various church schools developed over the apportionment of state school funds. As a result, in 1825, the legislature transferred to the city council the responsibility for distributing New York City's share of the state funds. The council stopped funding religious societies which operated 16 sectarian schools, but continued supporting schools connected with the Protestant Orphan Asylum Society. Thereafter, in 1831, the Catholic Orphan Asylum Society demanded and received public funds to operate its schools, but a request of Methodists for funds for the same purpose was denied. Nine years later, the Catholics enlarged their request for public monies to include all parochial schools, contending that the council was subsidizing sectarian books and instruction of the Public School Society, which Clinton's Free School Society had become. The city's Scotch Presbyterian and Jewish communities immediately followed with requests for funds to finance their schools. Although the Public School Society undertook to revise its texts to meet the objections, in 1842, the state legislature closed the bitter controversy by enacting a law that established a City Board of Education to set up free public schools, prohibited the distribution of public funds to sectarian schools, and prohibited the teaching of sectarian doctrine in any public school.

The Nation's rapidly developing religious heterogeneity, the tide of Jacksonian democracy, and growing

Page 403 U. S. 647

urbanization soon led to widespread demands throughout the States for secular public education. At the same time, strong opposition developed to use of the States' taxing powers to support private sectarian schools.[3.5] Although the controversy over religious exercises in the public schools continued into this century, *Schempp*, 374 U.S. at 374 U. S. 268-277 (BRENNAN, J., concurring), the opponents of subsidy to sectarian schools had largely won their fight by 1900. In fact, after 1840, no efforts of sectarian schools to obtain a share of public school funds succeeded. Cubberley, *supra*, at 179. Between 1840 and 1875, 19 States added provisions to their constitutions prohibiting the use of public school funds to aid sectarian schools, *id.* at 180, and by 1900, 16 more States had added similar provisions. In fact, no State admitted to the Union after 1858, except West Virginia, omitted such provision from its first constitution. *Ibid.* Today, fewer than a half-dozen States omit such provisions from their constitutions.[3.6]

Page 403 U. S. 648

And, in 1897, Congress included in its appropriation act for the District of Columbia a statement declaring it

"to be the policy of the Government of the United States to make no appropriation of money or property for the purpose of founding, maintaining, or aiding by payment for services, expenses, or otherwise, any church or religious denomination, or any institution or society which is under sectarian or ecclesiastical control."

29 Stat. 411.

Thus, for more than a century, the consensus, enforced by legislatures and courts with substantial consistency, has been that public subsidy of sectarian schools constitutes an impermissible involvement of secular with

Page 403 U. S. 649

religious institutions.[3.7] If this history is not itself compelling against the validity of the three subsidy statutes, in the sense we found in *Walz* that "undeviating acceptance" was highly significant in favor of the validity of religious tax exemption, other forms of governmental involvement that each of the three statutes requires tip the scales, in my view, against the validity of each of them. These are involvements that threaten

"danger as much to church as to state which the Framers feared would subvert religious liberty and the strength of a system of secular government."

Schempp, 374 U.S. at 374 U. S. 295 (BRENNAN, J., concurring).

"[G]overnment and religion have discrete interests which are mutually best served when each avoids too close a proximity to the other. It is not only the nonbeliever who fears the injection of sectarian doctrines and controversies into the civil polity, but, in as high degree, it is the devout believer who fears the secularization of a creed which becomes too deeply involved with and dependent upon the government."

Id. at 374 U. S. 259 (BRENNAN, J., concurring). All three of these statutes require "too close a proximity" of government to the subsidized sectarian institutions and, in my view, create real dangers of "the secularization of a creed."

Page 403 U. S. 650

II

The Rhode Island statute requires Roman Catholic teachers to surrender their right to teach religion courses and to promise not to "inject" religious teaching into their secular courses. This has led at least one teacher to stop praying with his classes,[3.8] a concrete testimonial to the self-censorship that inevitably accompanies state regulation of delicate First Amendment freedoms. *Cf. Smith v. California*, 361 U. S. 147 (1959); *Speer v. Randall*, 357 U. S. 513, 357 U. S. 526 (1958). Both the Rhode Island and Pennsylvania statutes prescribe extensive standardization of the content of secular courses, and of the teaching materials and textbooks to be used in teaching the courses. And the regulations to implement those requirements necessarily require policing of instruction in the schools. The picture of state inspectors prowling the halls of parochial schools and auditing classroom instruction surely raises more than an imagined specter of governmental "secularization of a creed."

The same dangers attend the federal subsidy, even if less obviously. The Federal Government exacts a promise that no "sectarian instruction" or "religious worship" will take place in a subsidized building. The Office of Education polices the promise.[3.9] In one instance, federal

Page 403 U. S. 651

officials demanded that a college cease teaching a course entitled "The History of Methodism" in a federally assisted building, although the Establishment Clause

"plainly does not foreclose teaching about the Holy Scriptures or about the differences between religious sects in classes in literature or history."

Schempp, 374 U.S. at 374 U. S. 300 (BRENNAN, J., concurring). These examples illustrate the complete incompatibility of such surveillance with the restraints barring interference with religious freedom.[3.10]

Policing the content of courses, the specific textbooks used, and indeed the words of teachers is far different from the legitimate policing carried on under state compulsory attendance laws or laws regulating minimum levels of educational achievement. Government's legitimate interest in ensuring certain minimum skill levels and the acquisition of certain knowledge does not carry with it power to prescribe what shall not be taught, or what methods of instruction shall be used, or what opinions the teacher may offer in the course of teaching.

Moreover, when a sectarian institution accepts state financial aid, it becomes obligated, under the Equal Protection Clause of the Fourteenth Amendment, not to discriminate in admissions policies and faculty selection.

Page 403 U. S. 652

The District Court in the Rhode Island case pinpointed the dilemma:

"Applying these standards to parochial schools might well restrict their ability to discriminate in admissions policies and in the hiring and firing of teachers. At some point, the school becomes 'public' for more purposes than the Church could wish. At that point, the Church may justifiably feel that its victory on the Establishment Clause has meant abandonment of the Free Exercise Clause."

316 F.Supp. at 121-122 (citations omitted).

III

In any event, I do not believe that elimination of these aspects of "too close a proximity" would save these three statutes. I expressed the view in *Walz* that "[g]eneral subsidies of religious activities would, of course, constitute impermissible state involvement with religion." 397 U.S. at 397 U. S. 690 (concurring opinion). I do not think the subsidies under these statutes fall outside "[g]eneral subsidies of religious activities" merely because they are restricted to support of the teaching of secular subjects. In *Walz*, the passive aspect of the benefits conferred by a tax exemption, particularly since cessation of the exemptions might easily lead to impermissible involvements and conflicts, led me to conclude that exemptions were consistent with the First Amendment values. However, I contrasted direct government subsidies:

"Tax exemptions and general subsidies, however, are qualitatively different. Though both provide economic assistance, they do so in fundamentally different ways. A subsidy involves the direct transfer of public monies to the subsidized enterprise, and uses resources exacted from taxpayers as a whole. An exemption, on the other hand, involves no such

Page 403 U. S. 653

transfer. It assists the exempted enterprise only passively, by relieving a privately funded venture of the burden of paying taxes. In other words, '[i]n the case of direct subsidy, the state forcibly diverts the income of both believers and nonbelievers to churches,' while,"

"[i]n the case of an exemption, the state merely refrains from diverting to its own uses income independently generated by the churches through voluntary contributions."

"Thus," "the symbolism of tax exemption is significant as a manifestation that organized religion is not expected to support the state; by the same token the state is not expected to support the church."

397 U.S. at 397 U. S. 690-691 (footnotes and citations omitted) (concurring opinion).

Pennsylvania, Rhode Island, and the Federal Government argue strenuously that the government monies in all these cases are not "[g]eneral subsidies of religious activities," because they are paid specifically and solely for the secular education that the sectarian institutions provide.[3.11]

Before turning to the decisions of this Court on which this argument is based, it is important to recall again the history of subsidies to sectarian schools. See 403 U. S. 6 and 403 U. S. 7, supra. The recurrent argument, consistently rejected in the past, has been that government grants to sectarian schools ought not be viewed as impermissible subsidies

"because [the schools] relieve the State of a burden, which it would otherwise be itself required to bear. . . . they will render a service to the state by performing for it its duty of educating the children of the people."

Cook County v. Chicago Industrial School, 125 Ill. 540, 571, 18 N.E. 183, 197 (1888).

Nonetheless, it is argued once again in these cases that sectarian schools and universities perform two separable functions. First, they provide secular education, and second, they teach the tenets of a particular sect. Since the State has determined that the secular education provided in sectarian schools serves the legitimate state interest in the education of its citizens, it is contended that state aid solely to the secular education function does not involve the State in aid to religion. *Pierce v. Society of Sisters,* 268 U. S. 510 (1925), and *Board of Education v. Allen, supra,* are relied on as support for the argument. Our opinion in *Allen* recognized that sectarian schools provide both a secular and a sectarian education:

"[T]his Court has long recognized that religious schools pursue two goals, religious instruction and secular education. In the leading case of *Pierce v. Society of Sisters,* 268 U. S. 510 (1925), the Court held that . . . Oregon had not shown that its interest in secular education required that all children attend publicly operated schools. A premise of this

Page 403 U. S. 655

holding was the view that the State's interest in education would be served sufficiently by reliance on the secular teaching that accompanied religious training in the schools maintained by the Society of Sisters."

"* * * *"

[T]he continued willingness to rely on private school systems, including parochial systems, strongly suggests that a wide segment of informed opinion, legislative and otherwise, has found that those schools do an acceptable job of providing secular education to their students. This judgment is further evidence that parochial schools are performing, in addition to their sectarian function, the task of secular education.

Board of Education v. Allen, 392 U.S. at 392 U. S. 245, 392 U. S. 247-248 (footnote omitted). But I do not read *Pierce* or *Allen* as supporting the proposition that public subsidy of a sectarian institution's secular training is permissible state involvement. I read them as supporting the proposition that, as an identifiable set of skills and an identifiable quantum of knowledge, secular education may be effectively provided either in the religious context of parochial schools or outside the context of religion in public schools. The State's interest in secular education may be defined broadly as an interest in ensuring that all children within its boundaries acquire a minimum level of competency in certain skills, such as reading, writing, and arithmetic, as well as a minimum amount of information and knowledge in certain subjects such as history, geography, science, literature, and law. Without such skills and knowledge, an individual will be at a severe disadvantage both in participating in democratic self-government and in earning a living in a modern industrial economy. But the State has no proper interest in prescribing the precise forum in which such skills and knowledge are learned, since acquisition of this

Page 403 U. S. 656

secular education is neither incompatible with religious learning, nor is it inconsistent with or inimical to religious precepts.

When the same secular educational process occurs in both public and sectarian schools, *Allen* held that the State could provide secular textbooks for use in that process to students in both public and sectarian schools. Of course, the State could not provide textbooks giving religious instruction. But since the textbooks involved in *Allen* would, at least in theory, be limited to secular education, no aid to sectarian instruction was involved.

More important, since the textbooks in *Allen* had been previously provided by the parents, and not the schools, 392 U.S. at 392 U. S. 244 n. 6, no aid to the institution was involved. Rather, as in the case of the bus transportation in *Everson*, the general program of providing all children in the State with free secular textbooks assisted all parents in schooling their children. And as in *Everson*, there was undoubtedly the possibility that some parents might not have been able to exercise their constitutional right to send their children to parochial school if the parents were compelled themselves to pay for textbooks. However, as my Brother BLACK wrote for the Court in *Everson*,

"[C]utting off church schools from these [general] services, so separate and so indisputably marked off from the religious function, would make it far more difficult for the schools to operate. But such is obviously not the purpose of the First Amendment. That Amendment requires the state to be a neutral in its relations with groups of religious believers and non-believers; it does not require the state to be their adversary. State power is no more to be used so as to handicap religions than it is to favor them."

330 U.S. at 330 U. S. 18.

Page 403 U. S. 657

Allen, in my view, simply sustained a statute in which the State was "neutral in its relations with groups of religious believers and nonbelievers." The only context in which the Court in *Allen* employed the distinction between secular and religious in a parochial school was to reach its conclusion that the textbooks that the State was providing could and would be secular.[3.12] The present cases, however, involve direct subsidies of tax monies to the schools themselves, and we cannot blink the fact that the secular education those schools provide goes hand in hand with the religious mission that is the only reason for the schools' existence. Within the institution, the two are inextricably intertwined.

The District Court in the *DiCenso* case found that all the varied aspects of the parochial school's program — the nature of its faculty, its supervision, decor, program, extracurricular activities, assemblies, courses, etc. — produced an "intangible *religious atmosphere,*'" since the "*diocesan school system is an integral part of the religious mission of the Catholic Church,*" and "*a powerful vehicle for transmitting the Catholic faith to the next generation.*" 316 F.Supp. at 117. *Quality teaching in secular subjects is an integral part of this religious enterprise. "Good secular teaching is as essential to the religious mission of the parochial schools as a roof for the school or desks for the classrooms." 316 F.Supp. at 117-118. That teaching cannot be separated from the environment in which it occurs, for its integration with the religious mission is both the theory and the strength of the religious school.*

The common ingredient of the three prongs of the test

Page 403 U. S. 658

set forth at the outset of this opinion is whether the statutes involve government in the "essentially religious activities" of religious institutions. My analysis of the operation, purposes, and effects of these statutes leads me inescapably to the conclusion that they do impermissibly involve the States and the Federal Government with the "essentially religious activities" of sectarian educational institutions. More specifically, for the reasons stated, I think each government uses "essentially religious means to serve governmental ends, where secular means would suffice." This Nation long ago committed itself to primary reliance upon publicly supported public education to serve its important goals in secular education. Our religious diversity gave strong impetus to that commitment.

"[T]he American experiment in free public education available to all children has been guided in large measure by the dramatic evolution of the religious diversity among the population which our public schools serve. . . . The public schools are supported entirely, in most communities, by public funds — funds exacted not only from parents, nor alone from those who hold particular religious views, nor indeed from those who subscribe to any creed at all. It is implicit in the history and character of American public education that the public schools serve a uniquely public function: the training of American citizens in an atmosphere free of parochial, divisive, or separatist influences of any sort — an atmosphere in which children may assimilate a heritage common to all American groups and religions. This is a heritage neither theistic nor atheistic, but simply civic and patriotic."

Schempp, 374 U.S. at 374 U. S. 241-242 (citation omitted) (BRENNAN, J., concurring).

Page 403 U. S. 659

I conclude that, in using sectarian institutions to further goals in secular education, the three statutes do violence to the principle that

"government may not employ religious means to serve secular interests, however legitimate they may be, at least without the clearest demonstration that nonreligious means will not suffice."

Schempp, supra, at 374 U. S. 265 (BRENNAN, J., concurring).

IV

The plurality's treatment of the issues in *Tilton*, No. 153, diverges so substantially from my own that I add these further comments. I believe that the Establishment Clause forbids the Federal Government to provide funds to sectarian universities in which the propagation and advancement of a particular religion are a function or purpose of the institution. Since the District Court made no findings whether the four institutional appellees here are sectarian, I would remand the case to the District Court with directions to determine whether the institutional appellees are "sectarian" institutions.

I reach this conclusion for the reasons I have stated: the necessarily deep involvement of government in the religious activities of such an institution through the policing of restrictions, and the fact that subsidies of tax monies directly to a sectarian institution necessarily aid the proselytizing function of the institution. The plurality argues that neither of these dangers is present.[3,13]

At the risk of repetition, I emphasize that a sectarian university is the equivalent in the realm of higher education of the Catholic elementary schools in Rhode Island; it is an educational institution in which the propagation

Page 403 U. S. 660

and advancement of a particular religion are a primary function of the institution. I do not believe that construction grants to such a sectarian institution are permissible. The reason is not that religion "permeates" the secular education that is provided. Rather, it is that the secular education is provided within the environment of religion; the institution is dedicated to two goals, secular education and religious instruction. When aid flows directly to the institution, both functions benefit. The plurality would examine only the activities that occur within the federally assisted building, and ignore the religious nature of the school of which it is a part. The "religious enterprise" aided by the construction grants involves the maintenance of an educational environment — which includes high-quality, purely secular educational courses — within which religious instruction occurs in a variety of ways.

The plurality also argues that no impermissible entanglement exists here. My Brother WHITE cogently comments upon that argument:

"Why the federal program in the *Tilton* case is not embroiled in the same difficulties [as the Rhode Island program] is never adequately explained."

Post at 403 U. S. 668. I do not see any significant difference in the Federal Government's telling the sectarian university not to teach any nonsecular subjects in a certain building, and Rhode Island's telling the Catholic school teacher not to teach religion. The vice is the creation through subsidy of a relationship in which the government polices the teaching practices of a religious school or university. The plurality suggests that the facts that college students are less impressionable and that college courses are less susceptible to religious permeation may lessen the need for federal policing. But the record shows that such policing has occurred, and occurred in a heavy-handed way. Given the dangers of self-censorship in such a situation, I cannot agree that the dangers of

Page 403 U. S. 661

entanglement are insubstantial. Finally, the plurality suggests that the "nonideological" nature of a building, as contrasted with a teacher, reduces the need for policing. But the Federal Government imposes restrictions on every class taught in the federally assisted building. It is therefore not the "nonideological" building that is policed; rather, it is the courses given there, and the teachers who teach them. Thus, the policing is precisely the same as under the state statutes, and that is what offends the Constitution.

V

I therefore agree that the two state statutes that focus primarily on providing public funds to sectarian schools are unconstitutional. However, the federal statute in No. 153 is a general program of construction grants to all colleges and universities, including sectarian institutions. Since I believe the statute's extension of eligibility to sectarian institutions is severable for the broad general program authorized, I would hold the Higher Education Facilities Act unconstitutional only insofar as it authorized grants of federal tax monies to sectarian institutions — institutions that have a purpose or function to propagate or advance a particular religion. Therefore, if the District Court determines that any of the four institutional appellees here are "sectarian," that court, in my view, should enjoin the other appellees from making grants to it.

* This opinion also applies to No. 153, *Tilton et al. v. Richardson, Secretary of Health, Education, and Welfare, et al.,* post, p. 403 U. S. 672.

MR. JUSTICE WHITE, concurring in the judgments in No. 153 (*post*, p. 403 U. S. 672) and No. 90 and dissenting in Nos. 560 and 570.

It is our good fortune that the States of this country long ago recognized that instruction of the young and old ranks high on the scale of proper governmental functions,

Page 403 U. S. 662

and not only undertook secular education as a public responsibility, but also required compulsory attendance at school by their young. Having recognized the value of educated citizens and assumed the task of educating them, the States now before us assert a right to provide for the secular education of children whether they attend public schools or choose to enter private institutions, even when those institutions are church-related. The Federal Government also asserts that it is entitled, where requested, to contribute to the cost of secular education by furnishing buildings and facilities to all institutions of higher learning, public and private alike. Both the United States and the States urge that, if parents choose to have their children receive instruction in the required secular subjects in a school where religion is also taught and a religious atmosphere may prevail, part or all of the cost of such secular instruction may be paid for by governmental grants to the religious institution conducting the school and seeking the grant. Those who challenge this position would bar official contributions to secular education where the family prefers the parochial to both the public and nonsectarian private school.

The issue is fairly joined. It is precisely the kind of issue the Constitution contemplates this Court must ultimately decide. This is true although neither affirmance nor reversal of any of these cases follows automatically from the spare language of the First Amendment, from its history, or from the cases of this Court construing it, and even though reasonable men can very easily and sensibly differ over the import of that language.

But, while the decision of the Court is legitimate, it is surely quite wrong in overturning the Pennsylvania and Rhode Island statutes on the ground that they amount to an establishment of religion forbidden by the First Amendment.

Page 403 U. S. 663

No one in these cases questions the constitutional right of parents to satisfy their state-imposed obligation to educate their children by sending them to private schools, sectarian or otherwise, as long as those schools meet minimum standards established for secular instruction. The States are not only permitted, but required by the Constitution, to free students attending private schools from any public school attendance obligation. *Pierce v. Society of Sisters,* 268 U. S. 510 (1925). The States may also furnish transportation for students, *Everson v. Board of Education,* 330 U. S. 1 (1947), and books for teaching secular subjects to students attending parochial and other private as well as public schools, *Board of Education v. Allen,* 392 U. S. 236 (1968); we have also upheld arrangements whereby students are released from public school classes so that they may attend religious instruction. *Zorach v. Clauson,* 343 U. S. 306 (1952). Outside the field of education, we have upheld Sunday closing laws, *McGowan v. Maryland,* 366 U. S. 420 (1961), state and federal laws exempting church property and church activity from taxation, *Walz v. Tax Commission,* 397 U. S. 664 (1970), and governmental grants to religious organizations for the purpose of financing improvements in the facilities of hospitals managed and controlled by religious orders. *Bradfield v. Roberts,* 175 U. S. 291 (1899).

Our prior cases have recognized the dual role of parochial schools in American society: they perform both religious and secular functions. *See Board of Education v. Allen, supra,* at 392 U. S. 248. Our cases also recognize that legislation having a secular purpose and extending governmental assistance to sectarian schools in the performance of their secular functions does not constitute "law[s] respecting an establishment of religion" forbidden by the First Amendment merely because a secular program may incidentally benefit a church in fulfilling its religious mission.

Page 403 U. S. 664

That religion may indirectly benefit from governmental aid to the secular activities of churches does not convert that aid into an impermissible establishment of religion.

This much the Court squarely holds in the *Tilton* case, where it also expressly rejects the notion that payments made directly to a religious institution are, without more, forbidden by the First Amendment. In *Tilton,* the Court decides that the Federal Government may finance the separate function of secular education carried on in a parochial setting. It reaches this result although sectarian institutions undeniably will obtain substantial benefit from federal aid; without federal funding to provide adequate facilities for secular education, the student bodies of those institutions might remain stationary, or even decrease in size, and the institutions might ultimately have to close their doors.

It is enough for me that the States and the Federal Government are financing a separable secular function of overriding importance in order to sustain the legislation here challenged. That religion and private interests other than education may substantially benefit does not convert these laws into impermissible establishments of religion.

It is unnecessary, therefore, to urge that the Free Exercise Clause of the First Amendment at least permits government, in some respects, to modify and mold its secular programs out of express concern for free-exercise values. *See Walz v. Tax Commission, supra,* at 397 U. S. 673 (tax exemption for religious properties; "[t]he limits of permissible state accommodation to religion are by no means coextensive with the noninterference mandated by the Free Exercise Clause. To equate the two would be to deny a national heritage with roots in the Revolution itself"); *Sherbert v. Verner,* 374 U. S. 398 (1963) (exemption of Seventh Day Adventist from eligibility requirements for

Page 403 U. S. 665

unemployment insurance not only permitted, but required, by the Free Exercise Clause); *Zorach v. Clauson, supra,* at 343 U. S. 313-314 (students excused from regular public school routine to obtain religious instruction; "[w]hen the state encourages religious instruction . . . , it follows the best of our traditions. For it then respects the religious nature of our people, and accommodates the public service to their spiritual needs"). *See also Abington School District v. Schempp,* 374 U. S. 203, 374 U. S. 308 (1963) (STEWART, J., dissenting); *Welsh v. United States,* 398 U. S. 333, 398 U. S. 367 (1970) (WHITE, J., dissenting). The Establishment Clause, however, coexists in the First Amendment with the Free Exercise Clause, and the latter is surely relevant in cases such as these. Where a state program seeks to ensure the proper education of its young, in private as well as public schools, free exercise considerations at least counsel against refusing support for students attending parochial schools simply because, in that setting, they are also being instructed in the tenets of the faith they are constitutionally free to practice.

I would sustain both the federal and the Rhode Island programs at issue in these cases, and I therefore concur in the judgment in No. 153[4.1] and dissent from the judgments in Nos. 569 and 570. Although I would also reject the facial challenge to the Pennsylvania statute, I concur in the judgment in No. 89 for the reasons given below.

The Court strikes down the Rhode Island statute on its face. No fault is found with the secular purpose of the program; there is no suggestion that the purpose of the program was aid to religion disguised in secular attire. Nor does the Court find that the primary effect of the program is to aid religion, rather than to implement secular goals. The Court nevertheless finds

Page 403 U. S. 666

that impermissible "entanglement" will result from administration of the program. The reasoning is a curious and mystifying blend, but a critical factor appears to be an unwillingness to accept the District Court's express findings that, on the evidence before it, none of the teachers here involved mixed religious and secular instruction. Rather, the District Court struck down the Rhode Island statute because it concluded that activities outside the secular classroom would probably have a religious content. and that support for religious education therefore necessarily resulted from the financial aid to the secular programs, since that aid generally strengthened the parochial schools and increased the number of their students. In view of the decision in *Tilton*, however, where these same factors were found insufficient to invalidate the federal plan, the Court is forced to other considerations. Accepting the District Court's observation in *DiCenso* that education is an integral part of the religious mission of the Catholic church — an observation that should neither surprise nor alarm anyone, especially judges who have already approved substantial aid to parochial schools in various forms — the majority then interposes findings and conclusions that the District Court expressly abjured, namely, that nuns, clerics, and dedicated Catholic laymen unavoidably pose a grave risk in that they might not be able to put aside their religion in the secular classroom. Although stopping short of considering them untrustworthy, the Court concludes that, for them, the difficulties of avoiding teaching religion along with secular subjects would pose intolerable risks, and would, in any event, entail an unacceptable enforcement regime. Thus, the potential for impermissible fostering of religion in secular classrooms — an untested assumption of the Court — paradoxically renders unacceptable the State's efforts at insuring that secular teachers under religious discipline successfully avoid conflicts between the religious mission

Page 403 U. S. 667

of the school and the secular purpose of the State's education program.

The difficulty with this is twofold. In the first place, it is contrary to the evidence and the District Court's findings in *DiCenso*. The Court points to nothing in this record indicating that any participating teacher had inserted religion into his secular teaching, or had had any difficulty in avoiding doing so. The testimony of the teachers was quite the contrary. The District Court expressly found that

"[t]his concern for religious values does not necessarily affect the content of secular subjects in diocesan schools. On the contrary, several teachers testified at trial that they did not inject religion into their secular classes, and one teacher deposed that he taught exactly as he had while employed in a public school. This testimony gains added credibility from the fact that several of the teachers were non-Catholics. Moreover, because of the restrictions of Rhode Island's textbook loan law . . . and the explicit requirement of the Salary Supplement Act, teaching materials used by applicants for aid must be approved for use in the public schools."

DiCenso v. Robinson, 316 F.Supp. 112, 117 (RI 1970). Elsewhere, the District Court reiterated that the defect of the Rhode Island statute was "not that religious doctrine overtly intrudes into all instruction," *ibid.*, but factors aside from secular courses, plus the fact that good secular teaching was itself essential for implementing the religious mission of the parochial school.

Secondly, the Court accepts the model for the Catholic elementary and secondary schools that was rejected for the Catholic universities or colleges in the *Tilton* case. There, it was urged that the Catholic condition of higher learning was an integral part of the religious mission of the church, and that these institutions did everything they could to foster the faith. The Court's response was that, on the record before it, none of

Page 403 U. S. 668

the involved institutions was shown to have complied with the model, and that it would not purport to pass on cases not before it. Here, however, the Court strikes down this Rhode Island statute based primarily on its own model and its own suppositions and unsupported views of what is likely to happen in Rhode Island parochial school classrooms, although, on this record, there is no indication that entanglement difficulties will accompany the salary supplement program.

The Court thus creates an insoluble paradox for the State and the parochial schools. The State cannot finance secular instruction if it permits religion to be taught in the same classroom; but if it exacts a promise that religion not be so taught — a promise the school and its teachers are quite willing and, on this record, able, to give — and enforces it, it is then entangled in the "no entanglement" aspect of the Court's Establishment Clause jurisprudence.

Why the federal program in the *Tilton* case is not embroiled in the same difficulties is never adequately explained. Surely the notion that college students are more mature and resistant to indoctrination is a makeweight, for, in *Tilton*, there is careful note of the federal condition on funding and the enforcement mechanism available. If religious teaching in federally financed buildings was permitted, the powers of resistance of college students would in no way save the federal scheme. Nor can I imagine the basis for finding college clerics more reliable in keeping promises than their counterparts in elementary and secondary schools — particularly those in the Rhode Island case, since, within five years, the majority of teachers in Rhode Island parochial schools will be lay persons, many of them non-Catholic.

Both the District Court and this Court in *DiCenso* have seized on the Rhode Island formula for supplementing

Page 403 U. S. 669

teachers' salaries since it requires the State to verify the amount of school money spent for secular, as distinguished from religious, purposes. Only teachers in those schools having per-pupil expenditures for secular subjects below the state average qualify under the system, an aspect of the state scheme which is said to provoke serious "entanglement." But this is also a slender reed on which to strike down this law, for, as the District Court found, only once since the inception of the program has it been necessary to segregate expenditures in this manner.

The District Court also focused on the recurring nature of payments by the State of Rhode Island; salaries must be supplemented and money appropriated every year, and hence the opportunity for controversy and friction over state aid to religious schools will constantly remain before the State. The Court, in *DiCenso*, adopts this theme, and makes much of the fact that, under the federal scheme, the grant to a religious institution is a one-time matter. But this argument is without real force. It is apparent that federal interest in any grant will be a continuing one, since the conditions attached to the grant must be enforced. More important, the federal grant program is an ongoing one. The same grant will not be repeated, but new ones to the same or different schools will be made year after year. Thus, the same potential for recurring political controversy accompanies the federal program. Rhode Island may have the problem of appropriating money each year to supplement the salaries of teachers, but the United States must each year seek financing for the new grants it desires to make and must supervise the ones already on the record.

With respect to Pennsylvania, the Court, accepting as true the factual allegations of the complaint, as it must for purposes of a motion to dismiss, would reverse the dismissal of the complaint and invalidate the legislation.

Page 403 U. S. 670

The critical allegations, as paraphrased by the Court, are that

"the church-related elementary and secondary schools are controlled by religious organizations, have the purpose of propagating and promoting a particular religious faith, and conduct their operations to fulfill that purpose."

Ante at 403 U. S. 620. From these allegations, the Court concludes that forbidden entanglements would follow from enforcing compliance with the secular purpose for which the state money is being paid.

I disagree. There is no specific allegation in the complaint that sectarian teaching does or would invade secular classes supported by state funds. That the schools are operated to promote a particular religion is quite consistent with the view that secular teaching devoid of religious instruction can successfully be maintained, for good secular instruction is, as Judge Coffin wrote for the District Court in the Rhode Island case, essential to the success of the religious mission of the parochial school. I would no more here than in the Rhode Island case substitute presumption for proof that religion is or would be taught in state-financed secular courses or assume that enforcement measures would be so extensive as to border on a free exercise violation. We should not forget that the Pennsylvania statute does not compel church schools to accept state funds. I cannot hold that the First Amendment forbids an agreement between the school and the State that the state funds would be used only to teach secular subjects.

I do agree, however, that the complaint should not have been dismissed for failure to state a cause of action. Although it did not specifically allege that the schools involved mixed religious teaching with secular subjects, the complaint did allege that the schools were operated to fulfill religious purposes. and one of the legal theories stated in the complaint was that the Pennsylvania Act "finances and participates in the blending of sectarian

Page 403 U. S. 671

and secular instruction." At trial under this complaint, evidence showing such a blend in a course supported by state funds would appear to be admissible and, if credited, would establish financing of religious instruction by the State. Hence, I would reverse the judgment of the District Court and remand the case for trial, thereby holding the Pennsylvania legislation valid on its face but leaving open the question of its validity as applied to the particular facts of this case.

I find it very difficult to follow the distinction between the federal and state programs in terms of their First Amendment acceptability. My difficulty is not surprising, since there is frank acknowledgment that "we can only dimly perceive the boundaries of permissible government activity in this sensitive area of constitutional adjudication," *Tilton v. Richardson, post* at 403 U. S. 678, and that "[j]udicial caveats against entanglement" are a "blurred, indistinct and variable barrier." *Ante* at 403 U. S. 614. I find it even more difficult, with these acknowledgments in mind, to understand how the Court can accept the considered judgment of Congress that its program is constitutional, and yet reject the equally considered decisions of the Rhode Island and Pennsylvania legislatures that their programs represent a constitutionally acceptable accommodation between church and state.[4.2]

KEY CONCEPTS

collective bargaining Bargaining on behalf of a group of employees, as opposed to individual bargaining where each worker represents only himself or herself.

Common School Movement The nineteenth-century reforms that created tax-supported elementary education for all children.

impasse A situation that exists during labor-management negotiations when either party feels that no further progress can be made toward a settlement unless the process of negotiating changes. The most common techniques used to break an impasse are mediation, fact finding, and arbitration.

inequitable school financing The situation existing when educational opportunities are a function of whether a youngster lives in a high-wealth (high local property tax) or low-wealth (low property tax) school district.

school board The usually elected managers of a school district who make school policies and hire a superintendent to implement them.

school district A special district for the provision of local public education.

school tax A local real-property tax imposed by a school district.

school voucher program The government provision of primary and secondary education by giving the parents of school-age children a redeemable voucher with which to purchase educational services on the open market.

strike A mutual agreement among workers (whether members of a union or not) to a temporary work stoppage to obtain or resist a change in their working conditions.

unions Groups of employees who create a formal organization (the union) to represent their interests before management.

REVIEW QUESTIONS

1. What kinds of tools have governments used to equalize funding for public school systems?
2. What are the various forms of school choice plans that have been implemented in the United States?
3. What are the major arguments for the adoption of school choice plans?
4. Why have teachers' unions developed into one of the strongest forms of organized labor in the United States?
5. What parts of the U.S. Constitution have had the greatest impact on education policy?

BIBLIOGRAPHY

Brimelow, Peter (2003). *The Worm in the Apple*. New York: HarperCollins.

Chubb, John E., and Terry M. Moe (1990). *Politics, Markets and America's Schools*. Washington D.C.: The Brookings Institution.

Friedman, Milton (1955). "The Role of Government in Education." In: *Economics and the Public Interest*, ed. Robert A. Solo. New Brunswick, NJ: Rutgers University Press.

───── (1962). *Capitalism and Freedom*. Chicago: University of Chicago Press.

───── (2002). "The Market Can Transform Our Schools." *New York Times* (July 2).

Gill, Brian P., and others (2001). *Rhetoric Versus Reality: What We Know and What We Need to Know About Vouchers and Charter Schools*. Santa Monica, CA: RAND Corporation.

Hayek, Friederich A. (1988). "Our Poisoned Language." In: *The Fatal Conceit: The Errors of Socialism*. Chicago: University of Chicago Press.

Kearny, Richard (2000). *Labor Relations in the Public Sector*, 3rd ed. New York: Marcel Dekker.

Kendall, James (1955). *Michael Faraday*. London: Farber and Farber.

Kluger, Richard (1976). *Simple Justice: The History of Brown v. Board of Education and Black America's Struggle for Equality*. New York: Knopf.

Long, David C. (1983). "Rodriguez: The State Courts Respond." *Phi Delta Kappan* 64 (March).

McPherson, Stephanie Sammartino (2000). *Lau v. Nichols: Bilingual Education in the Public Schools*. Berkeley Heights, NJ: Enslow Publishers.

Miller, Matthew (2003). *The Two Percent Solution: Fixing America's Problems in Ways Liberals and Conservatives Can Love*. New York: Public Affairs Press.

Mosher, Frederick (1982). *Democracy and the Public Service*, 2nd ed. New York: Oxford University Press.

Nagourney, Adam (2002). "The Battleground Shifts." *New York Times* (June 28).

Neal, Terry M. (2002). "School Vouchers—Where Is the Constituency?" *Washington Post* (July 3).

Odden, Allan, and Larry Picus (1999). *School Finance: A Policy Perspective*, 2nd ed. New York: McGraw-Hill.

Rosenberg, Bella (1989). "Public School Choice: Can We Find the Right Balance?" *American Educator* (Summer).

Rosenbloom, David H., and Jay M. Shafritz (1985). *Essentials of Labor Relations*. Reston, VA: Reston Publishing.

Sammartino, Stephanie (2000). *Lau v. Nichols: Bilingual Education in the Public Schools*. Berkeley Heights, NJ: Enslow Publishers.

Shafritz, Jay M., Norma Riccucci, David H. Rosenbloom, Katherine Naff, and Al Hyde (2001). *Personnel Management in Government*, 5th ed. New York: Marcel Dekker.

Stern, Sol (2003). *Breaking Free: Public School Lessons and the Imperative of School Choice*. New York; Encounter Books.

Will, George F. (2002). "Implacable Enemies of Choice." *Washington Post* (June 28).

Williams, Juan (1998). *Thurgood Marshall: American Revolutionary*. New York: Times Books/Random House.

Woodward, C. Vann (1974). *The Strange Career of Jim Crow*. New York: Oxford University Press.

RECOMMENDED BOOKS

Bolick, Clint (2003). *Vouchers Wars: Waging the Legal Battle over School Choice*. Washington, D.C.: Cato Institute. The history of the efforts to make education vouchers a viable option for parents.

Kearney, Richard (2000). *Labor Relations in the Public Sector*, 3rd ed. New York: Marcel Dekker. The rules of the game in governmental collective bargaining at all levels of government.

Mosher, Frederick (1982). *Democracy and the Public Service*, 2nd ed. New York: Oxford University Press. The classic short history of the U.S. public service and the impact that an ever-increasing professionalism has had upon it.

Ravitch, Diane (2001). *Left Bank: A Century of Battles Over School Reform*. New York: Simon & Schuster. A history of American educational reform efforts written for a popular audience.

Steverle, C. Eugene, and others, eds. (2000). *Vouchers and the Provision of Public Services*. Washington, D.C.: Brookings Institution Press. A comparative analysis of how vouchers are used for education, child care, job training, housing, and health care.

Related Web Sites

American Federation of State, County and Municipal Employees **www.afscme.org**

American Federation of Teachers **www.aft.org**

Department of Education **www.ed.gov**

Federal Mediation and Conciliation Service **www.fmcs.gov**

International Personnel Management Association **www.ipma-hr.org**

National Education Association **www.nea.org**

National Labor-Management Association **www.nlma.org**

U.S. National Labor Relations Board **www.nlrb.gov**

Voucher Home Page **http://www.aft.org/research/vouchers/**

Endnotes

1. R.I.Gen.Laws Ann. § 16-51-1 *et seq.* (Supp. 1970).
2. The District Court found only one instance in which this breakdown between religious and secular expenses was necessary. The school in question was not affiliated with the Catholic church. The court found it unlikely that such determinations would be necessary with respect to Catholic schools, because their heavy reliance on nuns kept their wage costs substantially below those of the public schools.
3. Pa.Stat.Ann., Tit. 24, §§ 5601-5609 (Supp. 1971).
4. Latin, Hebrew, and classical Greek are excluded.
5. Plaintiffs appellants also claimed that the Act violated the Equal Protection Clause of the Fourteenth Amendment by providing state assistance to private institutions that discriminated on racial and religious grounds in their admissions and hiring policies. The court unanimously held that no plaintiff had standing to raise this claim because the complaint did not allege that the child of any plaintiff had been denied admission to any nonpublic school on racial or religious grounds. Our decision makes it unnecessary for us to reach this issue.
6. *See, e.g.,* J. Fichter, Parochial School: A Sociological Study 77-108 (1958); Giannella, Religious Liberty, Nonestablishment, and Doctrinal Development, pt. II, The Nonestablishment Principle, 81 Harv.L.Rev. 513, 574 (1968).

2.1. A. Stokes & L. Pfeffer, Church and State in the United States 229 (1964).

2.2. *Ibid.*

2.3. Deedy, Should Catholic Schools Survive?, New Republic, Mar. 13, 1971, pp. 15, 16.

2.4. *Id.* at 17.

2.5. *Ibid.*

2.6. Stokes & Pfeffer, *supra*, 403 U. S. 1, at 231.

2.7. *Id.* at 231-239.

2.8. *Id.* at 237.

2.9. *Ibid.*

2.10. R. Butts, The American Tradition in Religion and Education 115 (1950).

2.11. *Id.* at 118. *And see* R. Finney, A Brief History of the American Public School 44-45 (1924).

2.12. *See* E. Knight, Education in the United States 3, 314 (3d rev. ed.1951); E. Cubberley, Public Education in the United States 164 *et seq.* (1919).

2.13. In 1960, the Federal Government provided $500 million to private colleges and universities. Amounts contributed by state and local governments to private schools at any level were negligible. Just one decade later, federal aid to private colleges and universities had grown to $2.1 billion. State aid had begun and reached $100 million. Statistical Abstract of the United States 105 (1970). As the present cases demonstrate, we are now reaching a point where state aid is being given to private elementary and secondary school as well as colleges and universities.

2.14. Deedy, *supra*, 403 U. S. 3, at 16.

2.15. S. Curtis, History of Education in Great Britain 316-383 (5th ed.1963); W. Alexander, Education in England, c. II (2d ed.1964).

2.16. *See Pierce v. Society of Sisters,* 268 U. S. 510, 268 U. S. 534; *Meyer v. Nebraska,* 262 U. S. 390, 262 U. S. 402.

2.17. Grants to students in the context of the problems of desegregated public schools have without exception been stricken down as tools of the forbidden discrimination. *See Griffin v. School Bd. of Prince Edward County,* 377

U. S. 218; *Hall v. St. Helena Parish School Bd.,* 197 F.Supp. 649, *aff'd,* 368 U. S. 515; *Lee v. Macon County Bd.,* 267 F.Supp. 458, *aff'd sub nom. Wallace v. United States,* 389 U. S. 215; *Poindexter v. Louisiana Financial Assistance Commission,* 275 F. Supp. 833, *aff'd,* 389 U. S. 571; *Brown v. South Carolina State Bd.,* 296 F.Supp. 199, *aff'd,* 393 U. S. 222; *Coffey v. State Educ. Finance Commission,* 296 F.Supp. 1389; *Lee v. Macon County Bd.,* 31 F.Supp. 743.

2.18. Remonstrance ❑ 3. The Memorial and Remonstrance Against Religious Assessments has been reproduced in appendices to the opinion of Rutledge, J., in *Everson,* 330 U.S. at 330 U. S. 63, and to that of DOUGLAS, J., in *Walz,* 397 U.S. at 397 U. S. 719.

2.19. Remonstrance ❑ 11.

2.20. "In the parochial schools, Roman Catholic indoctrination is included in every subject. History, literature, geography, civics, and science are given a Roman Catholic slant. The whole education of the child is filled with propaganda. That, of course, is the very purpose of such schools, the very reason for going to all of the work and expense of maintaining a dual school system. Their purpose is not so much to educate, but to indoctrinate and train, not to teach Scripture truths and Americanism, but to make loyal Roman Catholics. The children are regimented, and are told what to wear, what to do, and what to think."

L. Boettner, Roman Catholicism 360 (1962).

2.21. It was said on oral argument that the handbook shown as an exhibit in the record had been superseded. The provisions hereinafter quoted are from the handbook as it reads after all the deletions to which we were referred.

2.22. "The use of school time to participate in the Holy Sacrifice of the Mass on the feasts of All Saints, Ascension, and the patronal saint of the parish or school, as well as during the 40 Hours Devotion, is proper and commendable."

3.1. At the time of trial, 95% of the elementary school children in private schools in Rhode Island attended Roman Catholic schools. Only nonpublic school teachers could receive the subsidy, and then only if they taught in schools in which the average per-pupil expenditure on secular education did not equal or exceed the average for the State's public schools. Some 250 of the 342 lay teachers employed in Rhode Island Roman Catholic schools had applied for and been declared eligible for the subsidy. To receive it, the teacher must (1) have a state teaching certificate; (2) teach exclusively secular subjects taught in the State's public schools; (3) use only teaching materials approved for use in the public schools; (4) not teach religion; and (5) promise in writing not to teach a course in religion while receiving the salary supplement.

Unlike the Rhode Island case, the Pennsylvania case lacks a factual record, since the complaint was dismissed on motion. We must therefore decide the constitutional challenge as addressed to the face of the Pennsylvania statute. Appellants allege that the nonpublic schools are segregated in Pennsylvania by race and religion, and that the Act perpetrates and promotes the segregation of races "with the ultimate result of promoting two school systems in Pennsylvania — a public school system predominantly black, poor and inferior and a private, subsidized school system predominantly white, affluent and superior." Brief for Appellants Lemon *et al.* 9. The District Court held that appellants lacked standing to assert this equal protection claim. In my view, this was plain error.

3.2. E. Cubberley, Public Education in the United States 17 (1919); *Abington School District v. Schempp,* 374 U. S. 203, 374 U. S. 238 n. 7 and authorities cited therein (BRENNAN, J., concurring).

3.3. C. Antieau, A. Downey, E. Roberts, Freedom from Federal Establishment 174 (1964).

3.4. B. Confrey, Secularism in American Education: Its History 127-129 (1931).

3.5. *See generally* R. Butts, The American Tradition in Religion and Education 111-145 (1950); 2 A. Stokes, Church and State in the United States 47-72 (1950); Cubberley, *supra,* 403 U. S. 2, at 155-181.

3.6. *See* Ala.Const., Art. XIV, § 263; Alaska Const., Art. VII, § 1; Ariz.Const., Art. II, § 12, Art. XI, §§ 7, 8; Ark.Const., Art. XIV, § 2; Calif.Const., Art. IX, § 8; Colo.Const., Art. IX, § 7; Conn. Const., Art. VIII, § 4; Del.Const., Art. X, § 3; Fla. Const., Decl. of Rights, Art. I, § 3; Ga.Const., Art. VIII, § 12, par. 1; Hawaii Const., Art. IX, § 1; Idaho Const., Art. IX, § 5; Ill.Const., Art. VIII, § 3; Ind.Const., Art. 8, § 3; Kan.Const., Art. 6, § 6(c); Ky.Const., § 189; La.Const., Art. XII, § 13; Mass.Const., Amend. Art. XLVI, § 2; Mich.

Const., Art. I, § 4; Minn.Const., Art. VIII, § 2; Miss.Const., Art. 8, § 208; Mo.Const., Art. IX, § 8; Mont.Const., Art. XI, § 8; Neb.Const., Art. VII, § 11; Nev.Const., Art. 11, § 10; N.H.Const., Pt. II, Art. 83; N.J.Const., Art. VIII, § 4, par. 2; N.Mex.Const., Art. XII, § 3; N.Y.Const., Art. XI, § 3; N.Car.Const., Art. IX, §§ 4, 12; N.Dak. Const., Art. VIII, § 152; Ohio Const., Art. VI, § 2; Okla.Const., Art. II, § 5; Ore.Const., Art. VIII, § 2; Penn.Const., Art. 3, § 15; R.I.Const., Art. XII, § 4; S.C.Const., Art. XI, § 9; S. Dak.Const., Art. VIII, § 16; Tenn.Const., Art. XI, § 12; Tex. Const., Art. VII, § 5; Utah Const., Art. X, § 13; Va.Const., Art. IX, § 141; Wash.Const., Art. IX, § 4; W.Va.Const., Art. XII, § 4; Wis.Const., Art. I, § 18, Art. X, § 2; Wyo.Const., Art. 7, § 8. The overwhelming majority of these constitutional provisions either prohibit expenditures of public funds on sectarian schools or prohibit the expenditure of public school funds for any purpose other than support of public schools. For a discussion and categorization of the various constitutional formulations, see Note, Catholic Schools and Public Money, 50 Yale L.J. 917 (1941). Many of the constitutional provisions are collected in B. Confrey, Secularism in American Education: Its History 47-125 (1931). Many state constitutions explicitly apply the prohibition to aid to sectarian colleges and universities. See, e.g., Colo.Const., Art. IX, § 7; Idaho Const., Art. IX, § 5; Ill.Const., Art. VIII, § 3; Kan.Const., Art. 6, § 6(c); Mass.Const., Amend. Art. XLVI, § 2; Mo.Const., Art. IX, § 8; Mont. Const., Art. XI, § 8; Neb.Const., Art. VII, § 11; N.Mex.Const., Art. XII, § 3; S.C.Const., Art. XI, § 9; Utah Const., Art. X, § 13; Wyo.Const., Art. 7, § 8. At least one judicial decision construing the word "schools" held that the word does not include colleges and universities, Opinion of the Justice, 214 Mass. 599, 102 N.E. 464 (1913), but that decision was overruled by constitutional amendment. Mass.Const., Amend. Art. XLVI, § 2.

3.7. See, e.g., *Wright v. School Dist.*, 151 Kan. 485, 99 P.2d 737 (1940); *Atchison, T. & S. F. R. Co. v. City of Atchison*, 47 Kan. 712, 28 P. 1000 (1892); *Williams v. Board of Trustees*, 173 Ky. 708, 191 S.W. 507 (1917); *Opinion of the Justices*, 214 Mass. 599, 102 N.E. 464 (1913); *Jenkins v. Andover*, 103 Mass. 94 (1869); *Otken v. Lamkin*, 56 Miss. 758 (1879); *Harfst v. Hoegen*, 349 Mo. 808, 163 S.W.2d 609 (1942); *State ex rel. Public School Dist. v. Taylor*, 122 Neb. 454, 240 N.W. 573 (1932); *State ex rel. Nevada Orphan Asylum v. Hallock*, 16 Nev. 373 (1882); *Synod of Dakota v. State*, 2 S.D. 366, 50 N.W. 632 (1891).

3.8. "Already, the Act has restricted the role of teachers. The evidence before us indicates that some otherwise qualified teachers have stopped teaching courses in religion in order to qualify for aid under the Act. One teacher, in fact, testified that he no longer prays with his class, lest he endanger his subsidy."
316 F.Supp. at 121.

3.9. The Office of Education stipulated as follows: "The Office of Education is now engaged in making a series of on-site reviews of completed projects to verify that conditions under which Federal assistance was provided are being implemented. During these visits, class schedules and course descriptions contained in the school catalog are analyzed to ascertain that nothing in the nature of sectarian instruction is scheduled in any area constructed with the use of Federal funds. If there is found to be an indication that a portion of academic facilities constructed with Federal assistance is used in any way for sectarian purposes, *either the questionable practice must be terminated* or the institution must assume full responsibility for the cost of constructing the area involved."
App. in No. 153, p. 82 (emphasis added).

3.10. The plurality opinion in No. 153 would strike down the 20-year "period of Federal interest," 20 U.S.C. § 754(a), upon the ground that "[t]he restrictive obligations of a recipient institution under § 751(a)(2) cannot, compatibly with the Religion Clauses, expire while the building has substantial value." *Post* at 403 U. S. 683. Thus, the surveillance constituting the "too close a proximity" which for me offends the Establishment Clause continues for the life of the building.

3.11. The Pennsylvania statute differs from Rhode Island's in providing the subsidy without regard to whether the sectarian school's average per-pupil expenditure on secular education equals or exceeds the average of the State's public schools. Nor is there any limitation of the subsidy to nonpublic schools that are financially embarrassed. Thus, the statute, on its face, permits use of the state subsidy for the purpose of maintaining or attracting an audience for religious education, and also permits sectarian schools not needing the aid to apply it to exceed the quality of secular education provided in public schools. These features of the Pennsylvania scheme seem to me to invalidate it under the Establishment Clause as granting preferences to sectarian schools.

3.12. The three dissenters in *Allen* focused primarily on their disagreement with the Court that the textbooks provided would be secular. *See* 392 U.S. at 392 U. S. 252-253 (BLACK, J., dissenting); *id.* at 392 U. S. 257 (DOUGLAS, J., dissenting); *id.* at 392 U. S. 270 (Fortas, J., dissenting).

3.13. Much of the plurality's argument is directed at establishing that the specific institutional appellees here, as well as most church-related colleges, are not sectarian in that they do not have a purpose or function to advance or propagate a specific religion. Those questions must await hearings and findings by the District Court.

4.1. I accept the Court's invalidation of the provision in the federal legislation whereby the restriction on the use of buildings constructed with federal funds terminates after 20 years.

4.2. As a postscript, I should note that both the federal and state cases are decided on specified Establishment Clause considerations, without reaching the questions that would be presented if the evidence in any of these cases showed that any of the involved schools restricted entry on racial or religious grounds or required all students gaining admission to receive instruction in the tenets of a particular faith. For myself, if such proof were made, the legislation would, to that extent, be unconstitutional.

chapter 5

ENERGY AND ENVIRONMENT

Environmental Problems and Politics

Michael E. Kraft

In 2008, gasoline prices in the United States soared to record highs of over $4 a gallon on average, reflecting strong economic growth around the world that consumes vast quantities of oil and other fossil fuels. Politicians responded to public outcries over the high prices by searching for ways to ease the pain. Many sought to increase domestic oil supplies (which they argued would reduce prices) in part by renewing oil and gas exploration in off-shore public lands long closed to such drilling for fear of the environmental impacts. Republicans found the off-shore drilling issue to be a political winner, and they hammered the point home all summer, leading to the memorable chant at their early September presidential nominating convention: "drill, baby, drill." The Democrats had largely conceded the argument well before that time, and Congress formally ended the off-shore drilling prohibition in a largely symbolic move; the conditions Congress set made drilling unlikely to occur to any extent.

The new visibility of energy issues in the midst of a presidential campaign also led to remarkable calls for a federal gas tax "holiday" for the summer months of peak driving. That position was favored by Hilary Clinton, then a leading candidate for the Democratic nomination, and Senator John McCain, R-Ariz., the eventual Republican nominee. For his part, candidate Barrack Obama dismissed the idea as mere pandering to the public. He was joined in that view by nearly all economists, who agreed that lowering gas taxes was the wrong action to take. Some added that the nation ought to be encouraging *less* use of gasoline and other fossil-fuel energy sources whereas lowering the gas tax would likely *increase* its use. Others noted that most of the oil we use is imported and imposes both economic and national security risks on the nation. In addition, of course, burning gasoline contributes to climate change.[1] To students of environmental policy, the underlying cause of rising energy costs was no puzzle. Americans have had an insatiable appetite for energy to power their cars, heat and cool their homes, and enjoy the many conveniences of modern life. With a surging global demand for oil and natural gas and short-term constraints on supplies, higher prices were a given. Whatever the merit of short-term arguments, the long-term solution lies more in reducing demand than increasing supply.

High oil prices in this case came with a silver lining. People can change their behavior if they believe prices will remain high, and the American public did just that in 2008. Their love affair with trucks and SUVs was seemingly over as they scrambled to find fuel-efficient vehicles. Automobile manufacturers responded by beginning to tout their most fuel-efficient, but long-neglected, models. Even when gas prices plummeted later in the year as a global recession took hold and sharply cut into demand for oil, people were reluctant to return to their old vehicle preferences, a message that the auto industry finally seemed to grasp as all of the major manufacturers tried to expedite production of a new generation of fuel-efficient cars. General Motors, which was forced to file for bankruptcy to emerge as a new and leaner corporation, was heavily dependent on its SUV and truck sales, and it pinned its hopes in part on the Chevrolet Volt, likely to be the first plug-in hybrid to hit the market in late 2010.[2] Another sign of the times was growing demand for mass transit as an alternative to driving. It shot up so quickly that many cities found themselves unable to keep up; a number reluctantly began raising prices and planned for buying new rail cars.[3]

The furor over high gasoline and other energy prices in 2008 and the political and economic responses to them tell us much about environmental policy and politics in the twenty-first century. Problems often are hard to identify, and taking

"Environmental Problems and Politics" from *Environmental Policy and Politics*, 5th ed., by Michael E. Kraft, pp. 1-25. Copyright © 2011 by Pearson Education, Inc. Reprinted by permission.

action on them is not always easy because it requires policymakers to resolve sometimes deep conflicts over what government ought to do and what should be left to individual choice in the marketplace. For example, should government provide subsidies for oil and gas companies to encourage greater energy production, as it has for years? Should it impose mandatory energy efficiency requirements to reduce demand, as Congress did in 2007 by raising the federal fuel efficiency standards for vehicles, or provide an economic incentive to achieve the same end, for example, through a hike in the gasoline tax (as European nations have done)? Should it fund scientific and technological research that could help develop new sources of energy, as President Obama did both in the economic stimulus measures that Congress approved in February 2009 and in his first presidential budget recommendations? Each strategy has its backers among scientists, policy analysts, interest groups, and policymakers, and each group is convinced that its approach is the right thing to do. Sometimes, as was the case on energy issues and climate change in early 2009, scientific evidence and public support reach a "tipping point" that facilitates agreement on the need to take action if not always on the details of public policy (Guber and Bosso 2010; Vig and Kraft 2010).

These kinds of policy disagreements might suggest that no consensus at all exists about environmental problems or their solutions today. Yet nearly all serious students of environmental policy recognize the abundant cause for concern and that environmental threats, if anything, are more pervasive and ominous today than they were when the modern environmental movement began in the late 1960s.

The problems are familiar to most people, if not always easy to understand. They include air and water pollution, public exposure to toxic chemicals and hazardous wastes, the production of large quantities of solid wastes (including new electronic waste) that wind up in landfills, heavy reliance worldwide on use of fossil fuels that contribute to the risk of climate change, and the destruction of ecologically critical lands and forests, which in turn hastens the loss of biological diversity. To these problems we can add continuing growth of the human population and high levels of consumption of energy and natural resources; these two patterns can exacerbate all other environmental problems. Many would also put on the list the deterioration of the quality of life in increasingly congested cities around the world.

Reports on these and related issues fill the airwaves and newspapers every year and are covered and debated intensely on thousands of Web sites and blogs. Not surprisingly, they provoke public apprehension over apparently unceasing environmental degradation. Individuals can see the evidence in their own neighborhoods, communities, and regions, and it clearly affects them. Not only in the United States, but worldwide, people have long believed that the environment is in serious decline and they have strongly supported efforts to reverse the trend even when environmental and energy issues have not been as salient as many other issues, such as the economy (Dunlap and York 2008; Global Strategy Group 2004; Guber and Bosso 2010; Leiserowitz, Maibach, and Roser-Renouf 2009). Their fears have been shared by many of the world's policymakers, who helped set the agenda for the historic Earth Summit, the United Nations Conference on Environment and Development, held in 1992 in Rio de Janeiro, Brazil; the follow-up World Summit on Sustainable Development held in Johannesburg, South Africa, in 2002; and more recent international conferences.

The Earth Summit was the largest international diplomatic conference ever held, attracting representatives from 179 nations (including 118 heads of state). More than 8,000 journalists covered the event. In addition, representatives from more than 7,000 nongovernmental organizations (NGOs) attended a concurrent Global Forum at a nearby site in Rio. The "Rio-Plus-10" summit in Johannesburg received much less attention, but it also attracted a large number of official delegates, NGO representatives, and members of the press (Speth 2003). These kinds of meetings may be seen by most people as nothing more than a brief news story at best, yet they have been instrumental in setting the global environmental agenda and building political consensus for action (O'Neill 2009).

For example, in the presummit planning sessions for the 1992 Earth Summit and at the conference itself, one could detect a palpable sense of urgency over worsening environmental problems and their implications for economic development, especially in poor nations. Yet, there was also much evidence of public determination to deal with the problems. In a postsummit UN publication containing that conference's Agenda 21 action program, the meeting's organizer, Maurice Strong, spoke optimistically about what he termed "a wildfire of interest and support" that the Earth Summit had ignited throughout the world and that he hoped would stimulate a global movement toward sustainable paths of development (United Nations 1993, 1). Five years earlier, the report of the World Commission on Environment and Development (the Brundtland Commission), **Our Common Future** (1987), had similar effects. It sold 1 million copies in 30 languages and spurred extensive policy changes in both the government and private sectors.

Sadly, neither the Brundtland Commission report nor the Earth Summit fundamentally altered political priorities around the world (Tobin 2010), but they clearly did provide some clarity to the inherently vague concept of sustainable development. The Brundtland Commission defined it as "development that meets the needs of the present without compromising the ability of future generations to meet their own needs" (World Commission 1987, 43). What does this mean? Scholars and policymakers have noted that needs can be defined and met in many ways, and there have been proposals for "strong" and "weak" versions of sustainability, with differing expectations for societal responses, whether the actions take place in international agencies, local governments, or on college and university campuses (Hempel 2009; Portney 2003, 2009; Mazmanian and Kraft 2009). But at a practical level, the implications are clear enough: that many societal trends, such as use of fossil fuels, simply cannot continue because they are not sustainable on a finite planet. Consider this summary and appraisal from one prominent report released a year before the 1992 summit that underscored astonishing world trends in population and economic growth in the twentieth century:

> Since 1900, the world's population has multiplied more than three times. Its economy has grown twentyfold. The consumption of fossil fuels has grown by a factor of 30, and industrial production by a factor of 50. Most of that growth, about four-fifths of it, has occurred since 1950. Much of it is unsustainable. Earth's basic life-supporting capital of forests, species, and soils is being depleted and its fresh waters and oceans are being degraded at an accelerating rate. (MacNeill, Winsemius, and Yakushiji 1991, 3)

At the time the authors were looking back to social, economic, and environmental changes earlier in the twentieth century. What lies ahead in the rest of the twenty-first century is equally striking and worrisome. For example, the United Nations estimates that the world's 2009 population of 6.8 billion people will grow to about 9.4 billion by 2050, with virtually all of that growth occurring in the developing nations. To feed, house, and otherwise provide for people's needs and aspirations will tax natural resources and ecological systems throughout the world. This is particularly so given the high level of economic growth that is also expected over the next half century. China, for example, has long expected its economic output to quadruple over the next 15 years, although the recession of 2008-2009 clearly slowed its growth rate somewhat. By 2006, every week to ten days China was opening a coal-fired power plant large enough to serve the energy needs of every household in Dallas or San Diego. By 2008, the press was reporting estimates of two new power plants per week in China, with India rapidly increasing its own use of coal for similar purposes, though at least China was ahead of the United States in the transition to cleaner coal-fired plants and was rapidly advancing in solar power technology.[4] Automobile sales in China were soaring as well, growing ninefold from 2000 to 2009 despite extensive construction of mass transit lines to handle growing demand for transportation.[5] This kind of economic growth is important for increasing opportunities for billions of people around the world and advancing social justice (Friedman 2005), yet it must also be compatible with the limits of natural systems. It is difficult for most of us to understand these historic trends and their effects. Yet, as biologist Jane Lubchenco noted over a decade ago in her 1997 presidential address to the American Association for the Advancement of Science (AAAS), over the last several decades "humans have emerged as a new force of nature." We are, she argued, "modifying physical, chemical, and biological systems in new ways, at faster rates, and over larger spatial scales than ever recorded on Earth." The result of these modifications is that humans have "unwittingly embarked upon a grand experiment with our planet," with "profound implications for all of life on Earth" (Lubchenco 1998, 492).[6]

These remarkable transformations raise fundamental issues for the study of environmental policy and politics. Will the Earth be able to accommodate the kind of growth widely anticipated over the next century? If so, what will be the likely human and ecological cost? How well equipped are the world's nations to respond to the many needs created by such social, economic, and ecological trends? Will political systems around the world prove able and willing to tackle these problems, and will they act soon enough? For example, will they be able to design, adopt, and implement effective policies to protect public health, and to do so before millions of people face dire consequences? Will they be able to do the same to promote sustainable use of natural resources before ecological systems are pushed to the breaking point?

This book tries to address these questions, although it can only scratch the surface. For that reason I provide extensive references and Web sites throughout to encourage you to explore many topics in more detail. In the chapters that follow I review policy actions of the U.S. federal government, but I also pay attention to state and local policy developments within the United States and to international environmental policy.

Environmental Policy and Politics

Put most simply, politics is about the collective choices we make as a society. It concerns policy goals and the means we use to achieve them as well as the way we organize and govern ourselves, for example, through the governmental institutions on which we rely and the political processes we use to make decisions. Over the next several decades, the United States and other nations face important choices. They can maintain current policies and practices or they can envision a better future and design the institutions and policies necessary to help bring the needed change. They can rely on an unregulated marketplace where individual choice reigns or they can try to accelerate and consciously direct a transition to that future in other ways. Such decisions are at least as important in the United States as they are in other nations, and the ecological consequences are probably greater here than in any other nation in the world. The National Commission on the Environment captured the choices well in a report from the early 1990s that is equally pertinent today:

> If America continues down its current path, primarily reacting to environmental injuries and trying to repair them, the quality of our environment will continue to deteriorate, and eventually our economy will decline as well. If, however, our country pioneers new technologies, shifts its policies, makes bold economic changes, and embraces a new ethic of environmentally responsible behavior, it is far more likely that the coming years will bring a higher quality of life, a healthier environment, and a more vibrant economy for all Americans. (1993, xi)

The commission concluded that "natural processes that support life on Earth are increasingly at risk," and as a solution it endorsed sustainable development. Such development could serve, the commission said, as a "central guiding principle for national environmental and economic policy making," which it saw as inextricably linked, and thereby restore environmental quality, create broad-based economic progress, and brighten prospects for future generations. Consistent with its bipartisan composition, the commission observed that such a strategy would involve a combination of market forces, government regulations, and private and individual initiatives. These comments were made nearly two decades ago and yet they are equally if not more appropriate today, as evident in many of the proposals put forth by the Obama administration and Congress to act on energy and climate change.

The nearly universal embrace of the idea of "sustainable development" is an important signpost for the early twenty-first century, even if it remains a somewhat vague term that can mask serious economic and political conflicts. It was evident in the name given to the 2002 Johannesburg conference (the World Summit on Sustainable Development) and in a major, but largely neglected, report by the Clinton administration's President's Council on Sustainable Development (1996). Such widespread endorsement of the principle of sustainability would have been inconceivable a generation ago. In the early 1970s, books describing the "environmental crisis" and proposing ways to deal with "limits to growth" and "ecological scarcity" may have won over some college audiences and urged on nascent environmental organizations, but they had little discernible effect on the higher reaches of government and corporate officialdom in the United States and most other nations. In the early twenty-first century, the language of sustainability not only penetrates to that level but has also kindled promising grassroots activity and corporate commitment both across the nation and around the world, including on many college and university campuses that now have a sustainability director or coordinator (Axelrod, Downie, and Vig 2005; Mazmanian and Kraft 2009; Starke 2008).[7] Moreover, bestselling authors such as Thomas Friedman have done much to popularize both the need for and the difficulty of achieving sustainable development in a world that increasingly is, in Friedman's terms, "hot, flat, and crowded"—where climate change, rapidly growing populations, and an expanding middle class brought on by globalization threaten the planet (Friedman 2006, 2008).

These developments signal fundamental changes that have occurred in both U.S. and global environmental policy and politics over the past four decades. The initial environmental agenda of the late 1960s and 1970s focused on air and water pollution control and the preservation of natural resources such as parks, wilderness, and wildlife. This is often called the first generation of environmental policy. In this period, the problems were thought to be simple and the solutions obvious and relatively easy to put into effect. Public and congressional enthusiasm for environmental protection policy supported the adoption of innovative and stringent federal programs that would force offending industries to clean up. That was true even where policy goals appeared to exceed both available technical knowledge and the capacity of administrative agencies to take on the new responsibilities mandated by law (Jones 1975). In such a political climate, the costs of achieving new environmental standards were rarely a major consideration.

As new policies were implemented in the 1970s and 1980s, their ambitious goals proved to be far more difficult to achieve than anticipated and much more costly. By the late 1970s and early 1980s, policymakers and environmentalists became increasingly frustrated with the slow pace of progress, and complaints from regulated industry and state and local governments mounted steadily (Durant 1992; Vig and Kraft 1984). These concerns, particularly on the part of business groups, economists, and conservatives, led to a second generation of environmental policy efforts that began around 1980 in Ronald Reagan's administration, with an emphasis on more efficient regulation and promotion of alternatives to regulation, such as use of market incentives, voluntary pollution control initiatives, public-private partnerships, and collaboration among various stakeholders (Fiorino 2006; Mazmanian and Kraft 2009).

For the most part, the initial environmental laws remain in force today despite three decades of criticism and experimentation with such alternatives at both national and state levels. The reasons are largely political. There has been no agreement on how to reform the core environmental statutes, despite some limited success with modification of the Clean Air Act in 1990, the Safe Drinking Water Act in 1996, and pesticide control policy in 1996 through the Food Quality Protection Act. Democrats and Republicans, and environmentalists and business groups, have fought for much of this time, with some of the fiercest battles taking place during the Clinton administration in the 1990s and the Bush administration in the 2000s (Eisner 2007; Klyza and Sousa 2008; Vig and Kraft 2010). As we will see in the chapters that follow, the challenges today involve not only how best to modernize U.S. environmental policy but how to grapple with a new and complex array of third-generation problems and policy actions that have emerged, from dealing with global climate change to local sustainability initiatives. In this sense, we can detect continuities with the old environmental politics even as a new era is unfolding that is rich in hope and possibilities.

PERSPECTIVES ON ENVIRONMENTAL PROBLEMS

Even a casual review of commentary on the environment over the past decade reveals widely disparate views of ecological problems and what ought to be done about them (Huber 2000; Lomborg 2001; Vig and Kraft 2010). That should not be surprising. Definitions and understanding of any public problem are affected by political ideologies and values, education and professional training, and work or community experience. They vary greatly across society and among scientists, policymakers, and the public.

This book is about the role of politics and government in identifying, understanding, and responding to the world's environmental problems. It argues that policy choices are inescapably political in the sense that they seek to resolve conflicts inherent in the balancing of environmental protection and other social and economic goals. That is, such a process involves a struggle over whose definition of the public interest should prevail and precisely how we should reconcile environmental goals with other competing values such as economic well-being, individual rights, and social justice. It also serves as a reminder of the important role that government plays in dealing with environmental problems. Before turning directly to that role, however, several other leading perspectives on environmental problems, their causes, and their solution should be noted. These are (1) science and technology, (2) economics and incentive structures, and (3) values and ethics. These differing perspectives are usually discussed to some extent at various points in the policymaking process, but it is nonetheless worth highlighting the differences in the way environmental problems are seen and acted on.

Scientific Knowledge and Its Use

Many scientists (and business leaders as well) believe that environmental problems can be traced chiefly to a lack of scientific knowledge about the dynamics of natural systems or the use of technology. They may also point to a failure to put such knowledge to good use in both the government and the private sector (Keller 2009). That is, they have a great deal of confidence in science and engineering for solving environmental problems. For example, ecologists believe that improving our knowledge of biological diversity will highlight existing and anticipated threats; thus it may contribute to the strengthening of public policy to protect endangered species and their habitats. Better knowledge of the risks to human health posed by toxic chemicals could facilitate formulation of pollution control strategies. Knowledge of new production technologies could lead industry likewise to adopt so-called green business practices, as many have done. Or businesses may choose to market greener products, such as plug-in hybrid automobiles, because advances in battery technology allow them to do so (Press and Mazmanian 2010).

Not surprisingly, scientists and engineers urge increased research on environmental and energy issues, more extensive and reliable monitoring of environmental conditions and trends over time, better use of science (and scientists) in policymaking, and the development of new technologies with fewer negative environmental impacts. Government policymakers also may share this view, which explains why the federal government has invested billions of dollars a year in research on global climate change, and several billion dollars more on other environmental research. There has been no shortage of recommendations for additional spending or for scientists playing a far more active role in communicating scientific knowledge to the public and policymakers, as Jane Lubchenco (1998) urged in her AAAS address mentioned earlier.[8]

The Obama administration's willingness to invest billions on energy research, particularly for renewable sources on which spending had been minimal during much of the 2000s, speaks to the power of these kinds of recommendations, as does Obama's statements that science will play a more prominent role in his administration than was the case during the Bush administration. His selection of John Holdren, a Harvard physicist and noted environmental policy scholar, as his science adviser and of Steven Chu, a Nobel Prize laureate and strong advocate for action on climate change, as secretary of energy, suggests he is likely to keep these promises. Indeed, early in his presidency a speech he made at the National Academy of Sciences confirming his support for scientific research was exceptionally well received; said one academy member: "the days of science taking a back seat to ideology are over."[9] The reference was clearly to a number of decisions in the Bush administration that scientists inside and outside of government thought were made without sufficient regard for scientific evidence. The disputes ranged from the appropriate standards for mercury emissions from power plants to issues of climate change and protection of biological diversity (Andrews 2006b; Ascher, Steelman, and Healy 2010; Rosenbaum 2010).[10]

In recent years, many environmental scientists also have argued for a novel approach to setting research priorities by emphasizing the need for an interdisciplinary "sustainability science" that "seeks to understand the fundamental character of interactions between nature and society" (Kates et al. 2001, 641). Other scientists have called for a new federal body, an independent Earth Systems Science Agency, which might transcend bureaucratic boundaries and promote innovative solutions to environmental problems (Schaefer et al. 2008). Advocates of these kinds of scientific research and agency realignment believe that a much closer affiliation between environmental science and the world of public policy is needed. At least one of the reasons they take this position is their concern that scientific work may not be properly appreciated or understood by the public and policymakers. There are good reasons for such concern. As we will see in Chapter 4, the public's understanding of environmental issues is quite limited, and many continue to hold views directly at odds with current scientific evidence, for example on climate change. Such findings have led scientists to call for programs to improve the public's scientific and environmental literacy.[11] A further benefit of any financial investment in environmental science and technology might be to make the nation more competitive in a global economy heavily dependent on scientific and technological advances.

Economics and Incentives

Another group of commentators, particularly economists, finds the major causes of environmental ills to be less a deficiency of scientific knowledge or available technologies than an unfortunate imbalance of incentives. We misuse natural resources, especially common-pool resources such as the atmosphere, surface waters, and public lands, or we fail to adopt promising new technologies such as solar power because we think we gain economically from current practices or we do not suffer an economic loss (Ostrom 1990, 1999). In his classic essay on the "tragedy of the commons," Garrett Hardin (1968) illustrated how individuals may be led to exploit to the point of depletion those resources they hold in common. Sometimes natural resource policies have the perverse effect of encouraging the very degradation they are designed to prevent by setting artificially low market prices (e.g., for irrigation water or use of public lands for timber harvesting, mining, or grazing) through government subsidies to resource users (Burger and Gochfeld 1998; Myers and Kent 2001; Roodman 1997).

We regularly see evidence of this general phenomenon of short-sighted action. In 1994, faced with a fishery on the verge of collapse, an industry-dominated fishery management council in New England recommended a drastic cutback in allowable fishing in the Georges Bank area off Cape Cod. Previous limitations on fishing proved insufficient to prevent the exhaustion of the principal species that had supported commercial fishing in the area for generations.[12] Similar behavior is evident in urban areas. Individuals resist using mass transit and insist on driving their automobiles to work in congested and polluted cities even when they can plainly see the environmental degradation their behavior causes.

Because of such behavioral patterns, economists, planners, and policy analysts propose that we redesign the economic and behavioral incentives that current unrealistic market prices create (Freeman 2006; Keohane and Olmstead 2007; Ostrom 2008). These prices send inaccurate and inappropriate signals to consumers and businesses and thus encourage behavior that may be environmentally destructive. We need, such analysts say, to internalize the external costs of individual and collective decision making and establish something closer to full social cost accounting that reflects real environmental gains and losses. It might be done, for example, with public tax policies. As we saw at the chapter's beginning, a tax on the use of gasoline and other fossil fuels could discourage their use and build demand for energy-efficient technologies; in 2009, Congress was seriously considering imposing such a tax as one element in a proposed climate change policy. Similarly, a tax credit for use of energy-efficient appliances such as refrigerators and air conditioners or for hybrid or other fuel-efficient vehicles could encourage individuals to make such purchases, which could save them money over time as well as reduce the use of fossil fuels. Such a credit could also give manufacturers more reason to make products of this kind. The popularity of such action could also be seen in legislation approved by Congress in 2009 to offer federally funded vouchers in return for trading in and scraping older cars with poor fuel efficiency (often termed "cash for clunkers"); the vouchers (as high as $4,500) could be used to reduce the cost of buying new, more efficient vehicles. Half a dozen states have tried similar, though less generous, programs. The Car Allowance Rebate System became so popular with auto dealers and buyers that the $1 billion that Congress had set aside for it was exhausted in one week and had to be supplemented with $2 billion in additional funds to extend the program for a few additional weeks.[13]

This argument extends to reform of the usual measures of economic accounting, such as the gross national product (GNP). Critics, such as the organization Redefining Progress (www.rprogress.org), complain that such measures fail to consider the value of environmental damage, such as loss of forest or wetland habitats. Some even call for a new paradigm of ecological economics and a fair valuing of "nature's services" to humans (Cobb, Halstead, and Rowe 1995; Costanza 1991; Daily 1997). For example, one widely discussed report in 1997 estimated the economic value of the services of all global ecological systems and the natural capital stocks that produce them at an astonishing $33 trillion a year. In comparison, the global GNP at the time was $18 trillion a year (Costanza et al. 1997). On a more concrete level, in 1997 New York City decided to spend $660 million to preserve a watershed in the Catskill Mountains north of the city because the water supply could be purified by microorganisms as it percolated through the soil. The city's alternative was to construct a water treatment plant that could have cost $6 billion or more.[14] Many other cases of this kind could be cited. With increased attention to climate change, for example, environmental and other organizations, and some businesses, are beginning to calculate the carbon footprints of foods and many other products. It seems evident that only with accurate price signals and revised accounting mechanisms can individual and market choices steer the nation and the world in the direction of environmental sustainability.

ENVIRONMENTAL VALUES AND ETHICS

Philosophers and environmentalists offer a third perspective. The environmental crisis, they believe, is at heart a consequence of our belief systems and values, which they see as seriously deficient in the face of contemporary ecological threats, whatever their other virtues may be. For example, William Catton and Riley Dunlap (1980) have defined a dominant social paradigm (DSP), or worldview, of Western industrial societies that includes a number of core beliefs: humans are fundamentally different from all other species on Earth over which they have dominion, the world is vast and provides unlimited opportunities for humans, and human history is one of progress in which all major problems can be solved. Other premises and values follow from these beliefs: the primacy of economic well-being; the acceptability of risks associated with technologies that produce wealth; a low valuation of nature; and the absence of any real limits to economic growth (summarized in Milbrath 1989, 189).

Environmentalists argue that the values represented by the DSP strongly affect our personal behavior and institutional priorities and constitute one of the most fundamental causes of natural resource depletion and environmental degradation (Kempton, Boster, and Hartley 1996; Milbrath 1984, 1989; Paehlke 1989), and also a major limitation on what any public policies realistically can achieve. Environmentalists thus contend that the DSP and the values related to it must change if human behavior is to be made more consonant with sustainable use of the biosphere. Such ideas are not new even if they are more prominent today than in earlier periods. For example, Aldo Leopold, one of the most celebrated advocates of an environmental ethic, wrote in his prophetic **A Sand County Almanac** (originally published in 1949) that society would gain from adoption of an environmental ethic, which he termed a **land ethic**: "A thing is right when it tends to preserve the integrity, stability, and beauty of the biotic community. It is wrong when it tends otherwise" (Leopold 1970, 262).

Contemporary accounts reflect Leopold's view. Robert Paehlke, for example, derived a list of 13 values that constitute the "essential core of an environmental perspective." He further distilled these into three key goals: (1) protection of ecological systems, wilderness, and biodiversity; (2) minimization of negative impacts on human health; and (3) establishment of sustainable patterns of resource use (Paehlke 2000). Much environmental writing espouses similar values to achieve these broad ends, and environmental organizations often urge their members to change their behavior in these ways, such as reducing their use of energy and water and seeking sources of food with minimal environmental impact (e.g., Durning 1992; Leiserowitz and Fernandez 2008; Princen, Maniates, and Conca 2002; Starke 2008).

The implication is that merely reforming environmental policies to improve short-term governmental actions is not enough. Instead, changes in political, social, cultural, and economic institutions may be needed as well even if environmental writers continue to debate precisely what kinds of changes are necessary. For example, political philosophers disagree about key political values and institutions, including such fundamental issues as the structure and authority of government and the role of the public in decision making (Dryzek and Lester 1995; Eckersley 2004; Lewis 1994; Luke 1997; Ophuls and Boyan 1992).

The Role of Government and Politics

Each of these three perspectives offers distinctive insights into environmental problems and their solutions. All make sense, although none alone offers a complete understanding or a sufficient agenda for action. Few would question that society needs better scientific knowledge, a shift to environmentally benign and more productive technologies, or more comprehensive policy analysis and planning. Nor would many deny the need for greater economic and personal incentives to conserve energy, water, and other resources or a stronger and more widely shared commitment to environmental values in our personal lives.

Moreover, few would disagree that diverse actions by individuals and institutions at all levels of society, in the public as well as the private sector, will be essential to the long-term goals of environmental protection and sustainable development. People may choose to live close to where they work and walk or commute on bicycles or use mass transit rather than private automobiles, or they may at least use fuel-efficient vehicles. They may also seek durable, energy-efficient, and environmentally safe consumer goods and use fewer of them, recycle or compost wastes, and adjust their air-conditioning and heating systems to conserve energy. Similarly, businesses can do much to improve energy efficiency, prevent pollution, and promote other sustainable practices, and many are trying to do so today (Esty and Winston 2006; Press and Mazmanian 2010).

Government nonetheless has an essential role to play in resolving environmental problems. Public policies shape the kind of scientific research that is supported and thus the pace and character of scientific and technological developments. Governmental policies also affect the design and use of economic incentives (think gasoline taxes) and changes in society's environmental values (e.g., through educational programs). We look to government for such policies because environmental threats represent public or collective goods problems that *cannot* be solved through private action alone. The costs may simply be too great for private initiatives, and certain activities may require the legal authority or political legitimacy that only governments possess. Examples include setting aside large areas of public lands for national parks, wilderness, and wildlife preserves, and establishment of a range of international environmental, development, and population assistance programs.

Much the same is true of national or state regulatory and taxation policies. Such policies are adopted largely because society concludes that market forces by themselves do not produce the desired outcomes, a message strongly reinforced by the deep recession of 2008–2009 that many attributed to decisions not to regulate highly speculative financial activities on Wall Street. Even free-market enthusiasts admit that "imperfections" in markets (such as inadequate information, lack of competitiveness, and externalities such as pollution) may justify government regulation. In all these cases, private sector activity may well contribute to desired social ends. Yet, the scope and magnitude of environmental problems, the level of resources needed to address them, and urgent public pressures for action may push the issues onto governmental agendas.

In these ways, the resultant public policies help fill the gaps created when millions of individuals and thousands of corporations make independent choices in a market economy (Ophuls and Boyan 1992; Ostrom 1990; Ostrom et al. 2002). However rational such choices are from the individual or corporate viewpoint, they are almost always guided by greater concern for personal gain and short-term corporate profits than for the long-term social goals of a clean and safe environment or for sustainable development. Hence, there is a need for establishing some limits on those choices or providing incentives to help ensure that individuals and organizations make them in a socially responsible manner. Those are the preeminent purposes of environmental policy.

The goals of environmental policies and the means chosen to achieve them are set by a variety of political processes, from the local to the international level. They are also a product of the interaction of thousands of individuals and groups that participate actively in those processes. Environmentalists are well represented in decision making at most levels of government today, if not quite on a par with business and industry groups (Bosso 2005; Duffy 2003; Kraft and Kamieniecki 2007). The presence of a multiplicity of interest groups and the visibility of environmental policies usually guarantees that policy goals and instruments are subject to intense political debate, with particular scrutiny given to their costs and effectiveness today.

Democracy, Politics, and Environmental Policy

Most of this text presents an overview of U.S. environmental policies and their evolution over four decades. But there is a theme to this description as well. It is that democratic decision making and public support are crucial to successful environmental politics. They are especially important if environmental policy is to be socially acceptable as well as technically sound. Democratic politics is rarely easy, and it is made especially difficult when individuals and groups hold sharply divergent perspectives on the issues and are reluctant or unable to compromise on their views. Conflict over environmental policy has been common during the past four decades and it continues today, as evident in disputes over energy policy and climate change, among many other issues. At the same time, there are prominent examples at all levels of government that demonstrate how conflicts can be resolved through collaborative processes and how broadly supported environmental policies can be adopted and put into effect (Layzer 2008; Lubell, Leach, and Sabatier 2009; Mazmanian and Kraft 2009; Sabatier et al. 2005).

It should be said, however, that not all appraisals of environmental politics are so positive about the potential for democratic solutions. Critics have argued that public involvement or civic environmentalism (John 1994, 2004) can be problematic when citizens lack the capacity to understand often-complex environmental issues or are adamantly opposed to actions that they believe may threaten their way of life. As the next generation of environmental policies does indeed begin to take on questions of lifestyle (e.g., consumption of energy), such critics wonder if democratic processes might not make it very difficult for governments to take essential action and to do so expeditiously (Heilbroner 1991; Ophuls and Boyan 1992).

On the other side of this argument, scholars have found that public concern about the environment and support for environmental protection efforts have been relatively high and persistent over time even if most people are not very well informed on the issues (Dunlap 1995; Guber and Bosso 2010). Others maintain that the public can deal reasonably well with difficult technical issues if given the opportunity to learn about and discuss them with others. It is also possible to design public policies to make it easier for people to participate in decision making and thus increase the responsiveness of government to citizen needs (Baber and Bartlett 2005; Daley 2007; Ingram and Smith 1993; Kraft 2000). Whatever one's appraisal of governmental capabilities and the potential for democratic politics, obviously environmental policies adopted since the 1960s will have real and important effects in the United States and around the world. Some may be positive and some negative. It makes sense to try to understand their origins, current forms, achievements, and deficiencies. I try to do that throughout the text.

Defining Environmental Policy

Public policy can be defined as a course of government action in response to social problems; it is what governments choose to do about those problems. Environmental policy refers to governmental actions that affect or attempt to affect environmental quality or the use of natural resources. It represents society's collective decision to pursue certain environmental goals and objectives and to use particular tools to achieve them. Environmental policy is not found in any single statute or administrative decision. Rather, it is set by a diverse collection of statutes, regulations, and court precedents that govern the nation, and it is affected by the attitudes and behavior of the officials who are responsible for implementing and enforcing the law. Environmental policy includes not only what governments choose to do to protect environmental quality and natural resources but what they decide *not* to do; a decision not to act means that governments allow other forces to shape the environment. For example, by choosing not to have a comprehensive energy policy in the last several decades, the nation in effect left the decisions about how much and what kind of energy we use to individuals and corporations. That choice is now being seriously reconsidered as we come to appreciate the consequences of the nation's heavy reliance on fossil fuels, including importation of nearly 60 percent of the oil we use.

Public policy scholars also remind us that policies may be tangible, with real consequences, or largely symbolic (Anderson 2006). That is, not all environmental policies are intended to solve problems. Some are mainly expressive in nature. They articulate environmental values and goals that are intensely held by the public and especially by key interest groups, such as environmentalists. Such statements may have little direct relationship to legally specified policy goals and objectives, although they may nevertheless bring about important environmental changes over time by influencing public beliefs and organizational values and decision making (Bartlett 1994; Cantrill and Oravec 1996). A good example at the international level is the Kyoto Protocol on climate change, which is set to expire in 2012 and will be replaced by a newly negotiated treaty. Signing or not signing the protocol sent an important message during the 1990s and 2000s about a nation's position on the issue, and adoption of the protocol itself signaled that nations around the world took climate change seriously. Yet agreeing to the protocol said little about what nations actually did regarding their policies and practices that contributed to emissions of greenhouse gases (Harrison and Sundstrom 2010).

Policy Typologies

Political scientists have found it useful to distinguish among several basic types of policies, such as regulatory, distributive, and redistributive policies. Each is associated with different patterns of policymaking (Anderson 2006; Lowi 1979). Most environmental policies fall into one category or the other, although as is the case with most typologies, the fit is imperfect.

Regulatory policies attempt to reduce or expand the choices available to citizens and corporations to achieve a social goal. They may raise the cost of, prohibit, or compel certain actions through provision of sanctions and incentives. The most common approach is the setting and enforcement of standards such as the amount of pollutants that a factory or utility may emit into the air or water. Most environmental protection policies such as the Clean Air Act and the Clean Water Act are regulatory. The politics associated with regulatory policy tend to pit environmental and public health group against industry. The former seeks benefits for the general population (such as reduced exposure to toxic chemicals), whereas the latter tries to minimize the costs and burdens imposed by government regulators. When the issues are highly visible and the public is supportive, government may impose a tough policy. If the issues are not very prominent or the public is less united, however, industry does better in getting its way (Kraft and Kamieniecki 2007; Wilson 1980).

In contrast to environmental protection efforts like this, most natural resources and conservation policies historically have been distributive. They have allocated or distributed public resources, often in the form of financial subsidies or comparable specific benefits to clientele groups. The purpose has been to achieve social goals such as providing access to public lands for mining, grazing, forestry, or recreation; protecting biological diversity; or fostering the development of energy resources such as oil, coal, or nuclear power (Clarke and McCool 1996; Duffy 1997; McConnell 1966). The U.S. Congress traditionally has favored such distributive (critics call them "pork-barrel") policies, which convey highly visible benefits to politically important constituencies for whom the issues are highly salient. The general public usually has little interest in the issues, so its political influence is often minimal. Not surprisingly, such policies often are criticized for fostering inequitable and inefficient uses of public resources and often environmentally destructive practices (Lowry 2006; Lubell and Segee 2010; Myers and Kent 2001).

The Breadth of Environmental Policy

As might be expected, environmental policy choices are affected by a diversity of social, political, and economic forces that vary from year to year and from one locality to another. As a result, the United States has a disparate and uncoordinated collection of environmental policies that were enacted in different historical periods and for quite different purposes. For example, policies regulating gold mining on public lands that were first approved in the nineteenth century were still in effect in 2009 and are at odds with more contemporary views on what kinds of mining serve the public interest. President Obama's secretary of the interior, Ken Salazar, promised to try to reform the policy and in 2009 the Senate was actively considering such changes. Generous subsidies for nuclear power development approved in the 1950s and 1960s also continue today, despite public skepticism about the acceptability of nuclear power.

Taken together, this collection of environmental, energy, and resource policies seems to defy common sense. Certainly it falls shorts of an integrated approach to solving environmental problems. As Dean Mann put it long ago, environmental policy 'is rather a jerry-built structure in which innumerable individuals, private groups, bureaucrats, politicians, agencies, courts, political parties, and circumstances have laid down the planks, hammered the nails, plastered over the cracks, made sometimes unsightly additions and deletions, and generally defied 'holistic' or 'ecological' principles of policy design' (1986, 4). Political commitments like these made decades ago make it difficult for policymakers to start all over. Thus normally they consider incremental adjustments to the present mix of policies rather than wholesale or radical policy change.

Environmental policy today also has an exceedingly broad scope. Traditionally, it was considered to involve the conservation or protection of natural resources such as public lands and waters, wilderness, and wildlife, and thus was concerned with recreational opportunities and aesthetic values in addition to ecological preservation. Since the late 1960s, the term has been more often used to refer to environmental protection efforts of government, such as air and water pollution control, which are grounded in a concern for human health. In industrialized nations, these policies have sought to reverse trends of environmental degradation affecting the land, air, and water, and to work toward achievement of acceptable levels of environmental quality (Desai 2002; Steinberg and VanDeveer 2010).

However, environmental policy extends well beyond environmental protection and natural resource conservation. It includes, more often implicitly than explicitly, governmental actions affecting human health and safety; energy use; transportation; urban design and building standards; agriculture and food production; human population growth; national and international security; and the protection of vital global ecological, chemical, and geophysical systems (Deudney and Matthew 1999; Matthew 2010; Mazmanian and Kraft 2009; O'Neill 2009; Starke 2008).

Hence, environmental policy cuts an exceptionally wide swath and has a pervasive and growing effect on modern human affairs. It embraces both long-term and global as well as short-term and local actions.

ENVIRONMENTAL PROBLEMS AND PUBLIC POLICY

As the preceding discussion suggests, identifying the nature of environmental problems and the solutions that may be needed to address them is rarely an easy task. Since the late 1960s, we have been bombarded with news about a multitude of threats to public health and the environment, with varying hints about the degree of scientific consensus or the extent of disagreement between environmentalists and their opponents. Sometimes the dangers are highly visible, as they are to residents of neighborhoods near heavily polluting industries. Usually, however, they are not, and citizens are left puzzled about the severity of the problems, whom to believe, and what they ought to do.

Increasingly, it seems, environmental problems of the third generation, such asglobal climate change and loss of biodiversity, are even more difficult to recognize and solve than the more familiar issues of the first generation of environmental concerns of the early 1970s (e.g., air and water pollution). Solutions may be very costly, and the benefits to society are long term and may be difficult to measure (Daily 1997). Thus third-generation environmental problems tend to be more politically controversial and more difficult to address than the environmental problems of earlier eras.

For all these reasons, students of environmental policy need to develop a robust capacity to sort through the partial and often-biased information that is available so as to make sense of the world and the public policy choices we face. Policymakers and the public need the same skills. There is no great puzzle about the pertinent questions to ask about any public policy controversy, including those associated with the environment. They concern the nature and causes of the problems that are faced (including who or what is affected by them and in what ways), what might be done about them, and if government intervention is called for, what kind of policy tools (such as regulation, public education, or use of market incentives) are most appropriate.

Defining the Problems: The Nature of Environmental Risks

One set of concerns focuses on the nature of environmental problems, their causes, and their consequences. An enormous amount of information is available on the state of the environment and new research findings appear continually. Much of that information is easily available on the Internet, particularly at government agency Web sites and at sites maintained by environmental organizations, many of which are discussed throughout the text. Whatever the source of data, some interpretation and assessment are almost always essential, and some sites and their reports reflect more credible scientific and professional analysis than do others.

Forecasting Environmental Conditions

Some of the most difficult estimates about environmental problems involve forecasts of future environmental conditions. What will the human population be in 2050 or how much energy will the United States use in 2025, and how much of it will likely come from fossil fuel sources? All such forecasts involve making assumptions about economic, social, and technological change, which may not be fully understood. The best studies carefully set out the assumptions that underlie their projections and describe the forecasting methods they use. Even so, uncertainty and controversy are common, and some of it centers on what critics may charge are unwarranted assumptions and faulty methods.

A current illustration of the kind of challenge involved with forecasting is climate change. The Intergovernmental Panel on Climate Change (IPCC), a UN-sponsored body, has reflected overwhelming scientific consensus in its projections of anticipated climate change in the twenty-first century. Such changes could raise global mean temperatures over the next 100 years as well as lead to a variety of potentially devastating environmental and economic effects (IPCC 2007). Yet, scientific and political debate continues over the validity of such projections and their policy implications. Part of the reason is that questions remain about the precise relationship between greenhouse gas concentration in the atmosphere and temperature increases, the probability that temperatures will rise by a certain amount, and the location and timing of climate disturbances such as increased rainfall and the severity of storms. The complex computer models that scientists use to make these projections cannot provide all the answers, and even where the forecasts agree on environmental effects, economists and policymakers may reach very different conclusions about the costs and benefits of possible policy actions (DiMento and Doughman 2007; Nordhaus 2008; Selin and VanDeveer 2009, 2010; Stern 2007).[15]

In cases like this, some participants in the debates may exploit the inevitable scientific and economic uncertainties to bolster their arguments. Highly vocal critics of environmentalists, such as conservative talk show host Rush Limbaugh, find much with which they heatedly disagree, and they rail against what they see as exaggerated threats and extreme positions. As entertaining as such attacks may be, they rarely are helpful in understanding either the scientific or policy issues involved. In 2004, for example, the late novelist Michael Crichton published *State of Fear*, a best-selling thriller that featured environmentalists as the villains and included extensive attacks on the scientific consensus regarding climate change; scientists responded with predictable outrage at the misleading characterization of their work.[16] Contemporary politics, of course, has created a demand for simple ideas expressed in news conference or talk radio sound bites, or prominently featured on popular blog sites. Those who contribute to or turn to these sources of information often are not inclined to work through complex scientific issues and consider tough policy choices. These tendencies are especially great when an environmental problem first becomes visible and is judged quickly and superficially. With experience, debate, and learning, ideology may give way to more thoughtful appraisals of problems and solutions.

Assessing Risks: Social and Technical Issues

As the climate change example indicates, we always need to ask some critical questions about the nature of the environmental problems at issue. A common way to do that is to use the language of risk assessment or risk analysis. Analysts try to estimate the magnitude of risks that are posed to public health or to the environment, say from toxic chemicals or a warming planet. The information from such analysis often becomes central to public policy debates.

Yet, risk assessment involves use of a relatively new and evolving set of methods for estimating both human health and ecosystem risks, and there is considerable disagreement over how to apply these methods and what to do with the information they produce. Environmentalists often have been opposed to its use for fear that it will diminish the urgency of the problems (Andrews 2006b). Industry representatives and many political conservatives have their own doubts about how the Environmental Protection Agency (EPA) and other agencies use risk assessment, but they are supportive of the methods because they see them as one way to avoid excessive regulation of small risks that can drive up costs (Huber 2000; Lichter and Rothman 1999; Wildavsky 1995).

Supporters of risk assessment argue that it can be a useful, if imperfect, tool for systematic evaluation of many, though not all, environmental problems. It also can help establish a formal process that brings into the open for public debate many of the otherwise hidden biases and assumptions that shape environmental policy (Davies 1996; National Research Council 1996; Presidential/Congressional Commission on Risk Assessment and Risk Management 1997). But they also note that risks are seen very differently by professionals than they are seen by the general public.

The technical community (e.g., scientists, engineers, and EPA professional staff) tends to define risk as a product of the probability of an event or exposure and the consequences, such as health or environmental effects that follow. This is expressed in the formula $R = P \times C$, where R is the risk level, P is the probability, and C is a measure of the consequences. For risk assessors, the task is to identify and measure a risk (such as the health effects of fine particulates or mercury in the air) and then evaluate the level or magnitude of the risk to judge how acceptable it is. Those risks that are viewed as unacceptably high are candidates for regulation.

The public tends to see risks in a very different way. Ordinary citizens give a greater weight to qualities such as the degree to which risks are uncertain, uncontrollable, inequitable, involuntary, dreaded, or potentially fatal or catastrophic (Slovic 1987). On those bases, the public perceptions of risk may differ dramatically from those of government scientists, as they do most notably in the case of nuclear power and nuclear waste disposal. In these cases, experts believe the risks are small and the public thinks they are large. Hence people tend to oppose nuclear waste repositories that are located nearby (Dunlap, Kraft, and Rosa 1993; U.S. EPA 1990b).[17]

Scholars describe these differences in terms of two conflicting concepts of rationality, and they argue that both are valid. Susan Hadden captures the differences well:

"Technical rationality" is a mindset that trusts evidence and the scientific method, appeals to expertise for justification, values universality and consistency, and considers unspecifiable impacts to be irrelevant to present decision-making. "Cultural rationality," in contrast, appeals to traditional and peer groups rather than to experts, focuses on personal and family risks rather than the depersonalized, statistical approach, holds unanticipated risks to be fully relevant to near-term decision-making, and trusts process rather than evidence. (Hadden 1991, 49)[18]

These differences in understanding environmental and health risks can greatly complicate the conduct, communication, and use of risk assessments in environmental policy decisions. That is particularly so when government agencies lose public trust, a recurring problem, for example, in hazardous waste and nuclear waste policy actions (Kraft 2000; Munton 1996; Slovic 1993). Yet such different perspectives on risk do not eliminate the genuine need to provide credible risk assessments to try to get a useful fix on the severity of various environmental problems (such as air pollution, drinking water contamination, or risk of exposure to toxic chemicals) and to decide what might be done about them, that is, how best to reduce the risks.

Even without such disparities in risk perception between technical experts and the public, assessing the severity of environmental problems must take place amid much uncertainty. Consider the challenge of dealing with indoor air pollutants such as radon, a naturally occurring, short-lived radioactive gas formed by the decay of uranium found in small quantities in soil and rocks. Colorless and odorless, it enters homes through walls and foundations (and sometimes in drinking water), and its decay products may be inhaled along with dust particles in the air to which they become attached, posing a risk of lung damage and cancer. In 1987 the EPA declared that radon was "the most deadly environmental hazard in the U.S.," and by 2009 the agency's Web page described it as the second leading cause of lung cancer in the United States, second only to smoking, and the leading cause among nonsmokers. The EPA says that radon is responsible for some 21,000 lung cancer deaths a year, of which 2,900 are among people who have never smoked. Not surprisingly, the agency urges people to test their homes for radon.[19]

The best evidence of radon's effects on human health is based on high-dose exposure of uranium miners. Yet extrapolation from mines to homes is difficult. Moreover, although radon experts agree that the gas is a substantial risk at levels that are two to four times the EPA's "action level" for home exposure, it is more difficult to confirm a significant cause-and-effect relationship at the lower levels found in the typical home. EPA and other scientists believe that the indirect evidence is strong enough to take action to reduce exposure to radon in individuals' homes. But critics question how aggressively the nation should attempt to reduce radon levels, in part because they think that doing so could be quite costly (Cole 1993).

Coping with Environmental Risks

As the radon example shows, another set of important questions concerns what, if anything, to do about environmental problems once we recognize them. Are they serious enough to require action? If so, is governmental intervention necessary, or might we address the problem better through alternative approaches, such as private or voluntary action? Such decisions are affected by judgments about public needs and the effects on society and the economy. For example, the Clinton administration tended to favor mandatory government regulation of many environmental risks, whereas George W. Bush's administration favored voluntary action and market incentives. President Obama is likely to be much closer to Clinton's example than to Bush's.

What Is an Acceptable Risk?

For the public and its political representatives, two difficult issues are how to determine a so-called acceptable level of risk and how to set environmental policy priorities. For environmental policy, the question is often phrased as "How clean is clean enough?" or "How safe is safe enough?" in light of available technology or the costs involved in reducing or eliminating such risks and competing demands in other sectors of society (e.g., education and health care) for the resources involved. Should drinking water standards be set at a level that ensures essentially no risk of cancer from contaminants, as the Safe Drinking Water Act required prior to 1996? Or should the EPA be permitted to weigh health risks and the costs of reducing those risks within reasonable limits? In 1996 Congress adopted the latter position. Equally important are the questions of who should make such judgments and on what basis should judgments be made. Countless decisions of this kind are made every year in the process of implementing environmental policies. Over the last few years, for example, the EPA has struggled with standards on arsenic in drinking water, mercury emissions from power plants, and pesticide residues allowed in food (Andrews 2006b; Rosenbaum 2010).

These judgments about acceptable risk involve chiefly policy (some would say political), not technical, decisions. That is, they call for a judgment about what is acceptable to society or what might survive a legal challenge to the agency making the decision. Even when the science is firm, such decisions are difficult to make in the adversarial context in which they are debated. Moreover, the seemingly straightforward task of setting priorities will naturally pit one community or set of interests against another. That so much is at stake is another reason to rely on the democratic political process to make these choices, or at a minimum to provide for sufficient accountability when decisions are delegated to bureaucratic officials.

Remediation of hazardous waste sites illustrates the dilemma of making risk decisions. Estimates of the costs for cleaning up the tens of thousands of sites in the United States, including heavily contaminated federal facilities such as the Hanford Nuclear Reservation in the state of Washington, have ranged from $500 billion to more than $1 trillion, depending on the cleanup standard used (Russell, Colglazier, and Tonn 1992). In 2009, the U.S. Department of Energy (DOE) estimated the costs just for its own former nuclear weapons production facilities at $265 to $305 billion over the next 30 years, and it characterized the task as one of the most technically challenging and complex cleanup efforts in the world (National Research Council 2009).[20] At the 570-square-mile Hanford site, among the worst in the nation, the DOE and its predecessor agencies allowed 127 million gallons of toxic liquid waste to leak into the ground. Between 750,000 and 1 million gallons of high-level nuclear waste have leaked from single-shell storage tanks, and they have contaminated more than 200 square miles of groundwater. Cleanup of the Hanford site alone could cost $45 billion and take many decades to complete.

Yet are all these sites equally important for public health and environmental quality? Should all be cleaned up to the same standard regardless of their future use, cleanup costs, and disputed estimates of the benefits that will result? How do we consider the needs of future generations in making such judgments so that the present society does not simply pass along hidden risks to them? Is the nation prepared to commit massive societal resources to such a cleanup program? We've done a poor job historically of answering these difficult questions, but Congress did address many of them throughout the past decade as it considered renewal of the Superfund toxic waste program. That Congress could not agree on a course of action indicates the extent of the controversy.

COMPARING RISKS AND SETTING PRIORITIES

Governments have limited budgetary II resources, a situation made much worse by the recession of 2008–2009 and the federal government's massive economic stimulus spending that followed. The public also has little appetite for tax increases. These conditions force policymakers and the public to face real choices. If we cannot do everything, which programs and activities merit spending and which do not?

The federal EPA has issued several reports ranking environmental problems according to their estimated seriousness. They include a 1987 report, *Unfinished Business: A Comparative Assessment of Environmental Problems*, and a 1990 report, *Reducing Risk: Setting Priorities and Strategies for Environmental Protection*. One Striking finding is that the American public worries a great deal about some environmental problems, such as hazardous waste sites and groundwater contamination, which the EPA accords a relatively low rating of severity. The public also exhibits much less concern about other problems, such as the loss of natural habitats and biodiversity, ozone depletion, climate change, and indoor air pollution (including radon), which are given high ratings by EPA staff and the agency's Science Advisory Board. Historically, the U.S. Congress has tended to reflect the public's views and has set EPA priorities and budgets in a way that conflicts with the ostensible risks posed the nation (Andrews 2006b; U.S. EPA 1987, 1990b).

Critics charge, with good justification, that such legislative decisions promotecostly and inefficient environmental policies. Thus they suggest that we need to find ways to compare environmental and health risks and to distinguish the more serious risks from the less important. Such efforts will likely play an increasingly important role in the future to help frame environmental policy issues, promote public involvement and debate over them, and assist both the public and policymakers in making critical policy choices.

PUBLIC POLICY RESPONSES

Finally, if governmental intervention is thought to be essential, what public policies are most appropriate, and at which level of government (international, national, state, or local) should they be put into effect? Governments have a diversified set of tools in their policy repertoires. Among others they include regulation, taxation, use of subsidies and market incentives, funding for research, provision of information, education, and purchase of goods and services. Policy analysts ask which approaches are most suitable in a given situation, either alone or in combination with others (Kraft and Furlong 2010; Weimer and Vining 2005).

A lively debate has arisen in recent years over the relative advantages and disadvantages of the widely used regulatory approach ("command and control") as well as such competing or supplementary devices as market-based incentives, information disclosure, and public-private partnerships (Eisner 2007; Fiorino 2006; Press and Mazmanian 2010). Such newer approaches have been incorporated into both federal and state environmental policies, from the Clean Air Act to measures for reducing the use of toxic chemicals. Both the federal and state governments also have helped spur technological developments through their power in the marketplace. Governments buy large quantities of certain products such as computers and other office equipment and motor vehicles. Even without regulation, they can alter production processes by buying only those products that meet, say, stringent energy efficiency or fuel economy standards. Analysts typically weigh such policy alternatives according to various criteria, including likely effectiveness, technical feasibility, economic efficiency, and political and social acceptability. None of that is easy to do, but the exercise brings useful information to the table to be debated.

To address questions of equity or social justice, analysts and policymakers also need to ask about the distribution of environmental costs, benefits, and risks across society, as well as internationally and across generations. Numerous studies suggest that many environmental risks, such as those posed by industrial facilities, disproportionately affect poor and minority citizens, who are more likely than others to live in heavily industrialized areas with oil refineries, chemical plants, and similar facilities or in inner cities with high levels of air pollutants (Ringquist 2006). Similarly, risks associated with anticipated climate changes are far more likely to affect poor nations than affluent, industrialized nations that can better afford to adapt to a new climate regime, even at the low to middle range of climate change scenarios (IPCC 2007; Selin and VanDeveer 2010).

For programs already in existence, we need to ask many of the same questions. Which policy approaches are now used, and how successful are they? Would other approaches work better? Would they be more effective? Would they cost less? (Morgenstern and Portney 2004). Some programs might be made more effective through higher funding levels, better implementation, institutional reforms, and similar adjustments. But some programs may be so poorly designed or so badly implemented that they should be ended

Conclusions

A simple idea lies behind all these questions about the nature of environmental problems and strategies for dealing with them. Improving society's response to these problems, particularly in the form of environmental policy, requires a careful appraisal and a serious effort to determine what kinds of solutions hold the greatest promise We will never have enough information to be certain of all the risks posed, the effects that present policies may have, and the likely effectiveness of proposed courses of action. As citizens, however, we can deal better with the welter of data and arguments by focusing on the core issues outlined in the preceding sections and acknowledging that disagreements are at least as much about different political values and policy goals as they are about how to interpret limited and ambiguous scientific information (Stone 2002). If citizens demand that policymakers do the same, we can move a lot closer to a defensible set of environmental policies that offer genuine promise for addressing the many challenges that the nation faces.

Chapter 2 focuses on an overview of contemporary environmental problems, from pollution control and energy use to loss of biological diversity and the consequences of human population growth. The intention is to ask the kinds of questions posed in the previous sections related to each of the major areas of environmental concern and thus to lay out a diverse range of contemporary environmental problems, the progress being made to date in dealing with them, and the challenges that lie ahead.

Climate Change 2007: Synthesis Report Summary for Policymakers

Based on a draft prepared By"

Lenny Bernstein, Peter Bosch, Osvaldo Canziani, Zhenlin Chen, Renate Christ, Ogunlade Davidson, William Hare, Saleemul Huq, David Karoly, Vladimir Kattsov, Zbigniew Kundzewicz, Jian Liu, Ulrike Lohmann, Martin Manning, Taroh Matsuno, Bettina Menne, Bert Metz, Monirul Mirza, Neville Nicholls, Leonard Nurse, Rajendra Pachauri, Jean Palutikof, Martin Parry, Dahe Qin, Nijavalli Ravindranath, Andy Reisinger, Jiawen Ren, Keywan Riahi, Cynthia Rosenzweig, Matilde Rusticucci, Stephen Schneider, Youba Sokona, Susan Solomon, Peter Stott, Ronald Stouffer, Taishi Sugiyama, Rob Swart, Dennis Tirpak, Coleen Vogel, Gary Yohe

An Assessment of the Intergovernmental Panel on Climate Change

This summary, approved in detail at IPCC Plenary XXVII (Valencia, Spain, 12-17 November 2007), represents the formally agreed statement of the IPCC concerning key findings and uncertainties contained in the Working Group contributions to the Fourth Assessment Report.

Introduction

This Synthesis Report is based on the assessment carried out by the three Working Groups of the Intergovernmental Panel on Climate Change (IPCC). It provides an integrated view of climate change as the final part of the IPCC's Fourth Assessment Report (AR4).

A complete elaboration of the Topics covered in this summary can be found in this Synthesis Report and in the underlying reports of the three Working Groups.

1. Observed Changes in Climate and Their Effects

Warming of the climate system is unequivocal, as is now evident from observations of increases in global average air and ocean temperatures, widespread melting of snow and ice and rising global average sea level (Figure 5.1). {1.1}

Eleven of the last twelve years (1995-2006) rank among the twelve warmest years in the instrumental record of global surface temperature (since 1850). The 100-year linear trend (1906-2005) of 0.74 [0.56 to 0.92]°C[1] is larger than the corresponding trend of 0.6 [0.4 to 0.8]°C (1901-2000) given in the Third Assessment Report (TAR) (Figure 5.1). The temperature increase is widespread over the globe and is greater at higher northern latitudes. Land regions have warmed faster than the oceans (Figures 5.2, 5.4). {1.1, 1.2}

Rising sea level is consistent with warming (Figure 5.l). Global average sea level has risen since 1961 at an average rate of 1.8 [1.3 to 2.3] mm/yr and since 1993 at 3.1 [2.4 to 3.8] mm/yr, with contributions from thermal expansion, melting glaciers and ice caps, and the polar ice sheets. Whether the faster rate for 1993 to 2003 reflects decadal variation or an increase in the longer-term trend is unclear. {1.1}

Observed decreases in snow and ice extent are also consistent with warming (Figure 5. 1). Satellite data since 1978 show that annual average Arctic sea ice extent has shrunk by 2.7 [2.1 to 3.3]% per decade, with larger decreases in

"Summary for Policy Makers" from *Climate Change 2007: Synthesis Report*. Contribution of Working Groups I, II and III to the Fourth Assessment Report of the Intergovernmental Panel on Climate Change, pp. 1-22. IPCC, Geneva, Switzerland. Reprinted by permission.

Changes in temperature, sea level and Northern Hemisphere snow cover

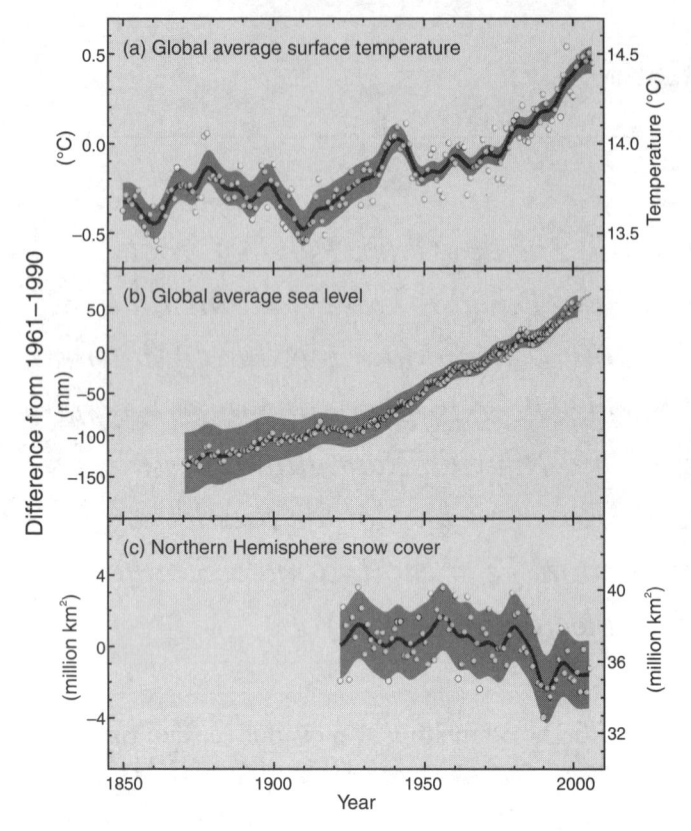

FIGURE 5.1 Observed changes in (a) global average surface temperature; (b) global average sea level from tide gauge (blue) and satellite (red) data and (c) Northern Hemisphere snow cover for March-April. All differences are relative to corresponding averages for the period 1961-1990. Smoothed curves represent decadal averaged values while circles show yearly values. The shaded areas are the uncertainty intervals estimated from a comprehensive analysis of known uncertainties (a and b) and from the time series (c). {Figure 1.1}

summer of 7.4 [5.0 to 9.8]% per decade. Mountain glaciers and snow cover on average have declined in both hemispheres. *{1.1}*

From 1900 to 2005, precipitation increased significantly in eastern parts of North and South America, northern Europe and northern and central Asia but declined in the Sahel, the Mediterranean, southern Africa and parts of southern Asia. Globally, the area affected by drought has *likely*[2] increased since the 1970s. *{1.1}*

It is *very likely* that over the past 50 years: cold days, cold nights and frosts have become less frequent over most land areas, and hot days and hot nights have become more frequent. It is *likely* that: heat waves have become more frequent over most land areas, the frequency of heavy precipitation events has increased over most areas, and since 1975 the incidence of extreme high sea level[3] has increased worldwide. *{1.1}*

There is observational evidence of an increase in intense tropical cyclone activity in the North Atlantic since about 1970, with limited evidence of increases elsewhere. There is no clear trend in the annual numbers of tropical cyclones. It is difficult to ascertain longer-term trends in cyclone activity, particularly prior to 1970. *{1.1}*

Average Northern Hemisphere temperatures during the second half of the 20th century were *very likely* higher than during any other 50-year period in the last 500 years and *likely* the highest in at least the past 1300 years. *{1.1}*

> Observational evidence[4] from all continents and most oceans shows that many natural systems are being affected by regional climate changes, particularly temperature increases. *{1.2}*

Changes in snow, ice and frozen ground have with *high confidence* increased the number and size of glacial lakes, increased ground instability in mountain and other permafrost regions and led to changes in some Arctic and Antarctic ecosystems. *{1.2}*

There is *high confidence* that some hydrological systems have also been affected through increased runoff and earlier spring peak discharge in many glacier- and snow-fed rivers and through effects on thermal structure and water quality of warming rivers and lakes. *{1.2}*

In terrestrial ecosystems, earlier timing of spring events and poleward and upward shifts in plant and animal ranges are with *very high confidence* linked to recent warming. In some

---

[1] Numbers in square brackets indicate a 90% uncertainty interval around a best estimate, i.e. there is an estimated 5% likelihood that the value could be above the range given in square brackets and 5% likelihood that the value could be below that range. Uncertainty intervals are not necessarily symmetric around the corresponding best estimate.

[2] Words in italics represent calibrated expressions of uncertainty and confidence. Relevant terms are explained in the Box 'Treatment of uncertainty' in the Introduction of this Synthesis Report.

[3] Excluding tsunamis, which are not due to climate change. Extreme high sea level depends on average sea level and on regional weather systems. It is defined here as the highest 1% of hourly values of observed sea level at a station for a given reference period.

[4] Based largely on data sets that cover the period since 1970.

CHAPTER 5 Energy and Environment   207

Changes in physical and biological systems and surface temperature 1970-2004

	NAM		LA		EUR	28,115	AFR		AS		ANZ		PR*		TER	28,586	MFW**		GLO	28,671
	355	455	53	5	119		5	2	106	8	6	0	120	24	764		1	85	765	
	94%	92%	98%	100%	94%	89%	100%	100%	96%	100%	100%	—	91%	100%	94%	90%	100%	99%	94%	90%

Observed data series
○ Physical systems (snow, ice and frozen ground; hydrology; coastal processes)
◉ Biological systems (terrestrial, marine, and freshwater)

Europe ***
○ 1-30
○ 31-100
○ 101-800
○ 801-1,200
○ 1,201-7500

Temperature change °C
1970-2004
-1.0 -0.2 0.2 1.0 2.0 3.5

Physical	Biological
Number of significant observed changes	Number of significant observed changes
Percentage of significant changes consistent with warming	Percentage of significant changes consistent with warming

* Polar regions include also observed changes in marine and freshwater biological systems.
** Marine and freshwater includes observed changes at sites and large areas in oceans, small islands and continents. Locations of large-area marine changes are not shown on the map.
*** Circles in Europe represent 1 to 7,500 data series.

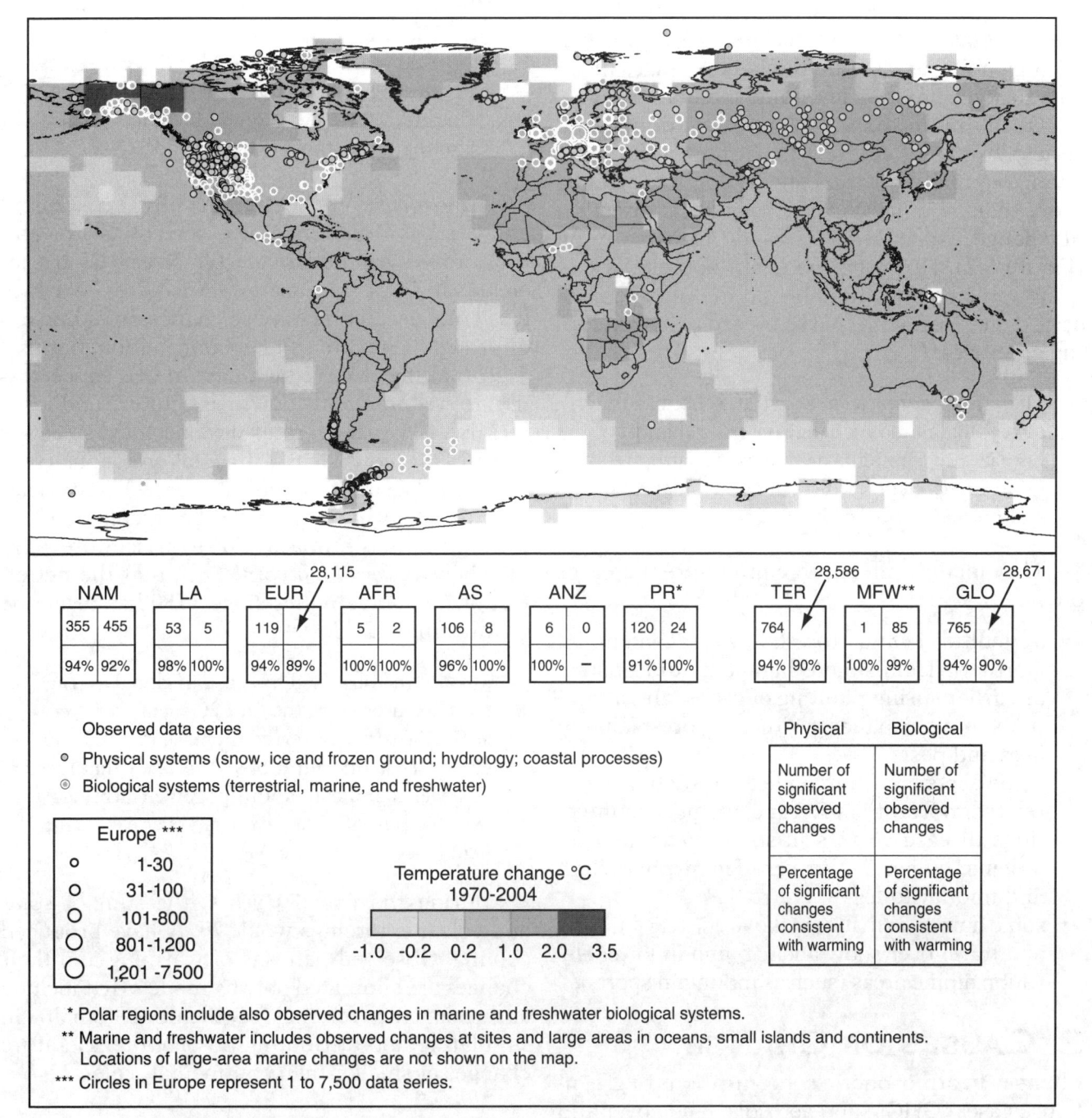

FIGURE 5.2 Locations of significant changes in data series of physical systems (snow, ice and frozen ground; hydrology; and coastal processes) and biological systems (terrestrial, marine and freshwater biological systems), are shown together with surface air temperature changes over the period 1970-2004. A subset of about 29,000 data series was selected from about 80,000 data series from 577 studies. These met the following criteria: (1) ending in 1990 or later; (2) spanning a period of at least 20 years; and (3) showing a significant change in either direction, as assessed in individual studies. These data series are from about 75 studies (of which about 70 are new since the TAR) and contain about 29,000 data series, of which about 28,000 are from European studies. White areas do not contain sufficient observational climate data to estimate a temperature trend. The 2 × 2 boxes show the total number of data series with significant changes (top row) and the percentage of those consistent with warming (bottom row) for (i) continental regions: North America (NAM), Latin America (LA), Europe (EUR), Africa (AFR), Asia (AS), Australia and New Zealand (ANZ), and Polar Regions (PR) and (ii) global-scale: Terrestrial (TER), Marine and Freshwater (MFW), and Global (GLO). The numbers of studies from the seven regional boxes (NAM, EUR, AFR, AS, ANZ, PR) do not add up to the global (GLO) totals because numbers from regions except Polar do not include the numbers related to Marine and Freshwater (MFW) systems. Locations of large-area marine changes are not shown on the map. {Figure 1.2}

marine and freshwater systems, shifts in ranges and changes in algal, plankton and fish abundance are with *high confidence* associated with rising water temperatures, as well as related changes in ice cover, salinity, oxygen levels and circulation. *{1.2}*

Of the more than 29,000 observational data series, from 75 studies, that show significant change in many physical and biological systems, more than 89% are consistent with the direction of change expected as a response to warming (Figure 5.2). However, there is a notable lack of geographic balance in data and literature on observed changes, with marked scarcity in developing countries. *{1.2, 1.3}*

> There is *medium confidence* that other effects of regional climate change on natural and human environments are emerging, although many are difficult to discern due to adaptation and non-climatic drivers. *{1.2}*

They include effects of temperature increases on: *{1.2}*

- agricultural and forestry management at Northern Hemisphere higher latitudes, such as earlier spring planting of crops, and alterations in disturbance regimes of forests due to fires and pests
- some aspects of human health, such as heat-related mortality in Europe, changes in infectious disease vectors in some areas, and allergenic pollen in Northern Hemisphere high and mid-latitudes
- some human activities in the Arctic (e.g. hunting and travel over snow and ice) and in lower-elevation alpine areas (such as mountain sports).

2. Causes of Change

Changes in atmospheric concentrations of greenhouse gases (GHGs) and aerosols, land cover and solar radiation alter the energy balance of the climate system. *{2.2}*

> Global GHG emissions due to human activities have grown since pre-industrial times, with an increase of 70% between 1970 and 2004 (Figure 5.3).[5] *{2.1}*

Carbon dioxide (CO_2) is the most important anthropogenic GHG Its annual emissions grew by about 80% between 1970 and 2004. The long-term trend of declining CO_2 emissions per unit of energy supplied reversed after 2000. *{2.1}*

> Global atmospheric concentrations of CO_2, methane (CH_4) and nitrous oxide (N_2O) have increased markedly as a result of human activities since 1750 and now far exceed pre-industrial values determined from ice cores spanning many thousands of years. *{2.2}*

Atmospheric concentrations of CO_2 (379ppm) and CH_4 (1774ppb) in 2005 exceed by far the natural range over the last 650,000 years. Global increases in CO_2 concentrations are due primarily to fossil fuel use, with land-use change providing another significant but smaller contribution. It is *very likely* that the observed increase in CH_4 concentration is predominantly due to agriculture and fossil fuel use. CH_4 growth rates have declined since the early 1990s, consistent with total emissions (sum of anthropogenic and natural sources) being nearly constant during this period. The increase in N_2O concentration is primarily due to agriculture. *{2.2}*

There is *very high confidence* that the net effect of human activities since 1750 has been one of warming.[6] *{2.2}*

> Most of the observed increase in global average temperatures since the mid-20th century is *very likely* due to the observed increase in anthropogenic GHG concentrations.[7] It is *likely* that there has been significant anthropogenic warming over the past 50 years averaged over each continent (except Antarctica) (Figure 5.4). *{2.4}*

During the past 50 years, the sum of solar and volcanic forcings would *likely* have produced cooling. Observed patterns of warming and their changes are simulated only by models that include anthropogenic forcings. Difficulties remain in simulating and attributing observed temperature changes at smaller than continental scales. *{2.4}*

---

[5] Includes only carbon dioxide (CO_2), methane (CH_4), nitrous oxide (N_2O), hydrofluorocarbons (HFCs), perfluorocarbons (PFCs) and sulphurhexafluoride (SF_6), whose emissions are covered by the United Nations Framework Convention on Climate Change (UNFCCC). These GHGs are weighted by their 100-year Global Warming Potentials, using values consistent with reporting under the UNFCCC.

[6] Increases in GHGs tend to warm the surface while the net effect of increases in aerosols tends to cool it. The net effect due to human activities since the pre-industrial era is one of warming (+1.6 [+0.6 to +2.4] W/m²). In comparison, changes in solar irradiance are estimated to have caused a small warming effect (+0.12 [+0.06 to +0.30] W/m²).

[7] Consideration of remaining uncertainty is based on current methodologies.

CHAPTER 5 Energy and Environment   209

Global anthropogenic GHG emissions

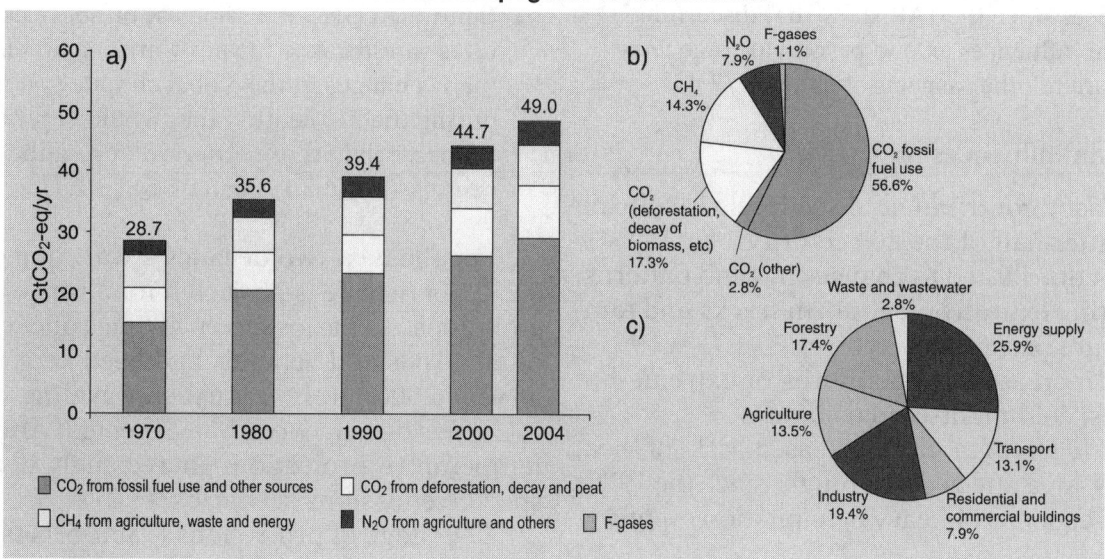

FIGURE 5.3 (a) Global annual emissions of anthropogenic GHGs from 1970 to 2004.[5] (b) Share of different anthropogenic GHGs in total emissions in 2004 in terms of carbon dioxide equivalents. (CO_2-eq). (c) Share of different sectors in total anthropogenic GHG emissions in 2004 in terms of CO_2-eq. (Forestry includes deforestation.) {Figure 2.1}

Global and continental temperature change

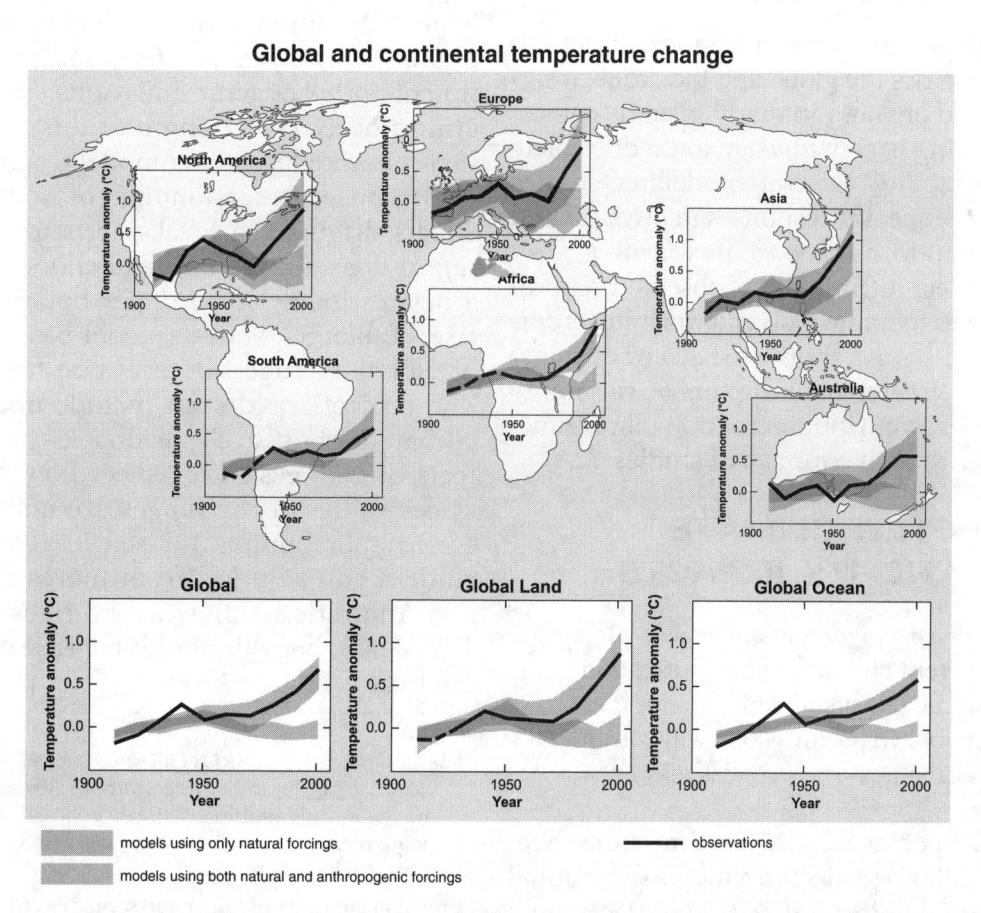

FIGURE 5.4 Comparison of observed continental- and global-scale changes in surface temperature with results simulated by climate models using either natural or both natural and anthropogenic forcings. Decadal averages of observations are shown for the period 1906-2005 (black line) plotted against the centre of the decade and relative to the corresponding average for the period 1901-1950. Lines are dashed where spatial coverage is less than 50%. Blue shaded bands show the 5 to 95% range for 19 simulations from five climate models using only the natural forcings due to solar activity and volcanoes. Red shaded bands show the 5 to 95% range for 58 simulations from 14 climate models using both natural and anthropogenic forcings. {Figure 2.5}

"Advances since the TAR show that discernible human influences extend beyond average temperature to other aspects of climate. *{2.4}*

Human influences have: *{2.4}*

- *very likely* contributed to sea level rise during the latter half of the 20th century
- *likely* contributed to changes in wind patterns, affecting extra-tropical storm tracks and temperature patterns
- *likely* increased temperatures of extreme hot nights, cold nights and cold days
- *more likely than not* increased risk of heat waves, area affected by drought since the 1970s and frequency of heavy precipitation events.

"Anthropogenic warming over the last three decades has likely had a discernible influence at the global scale on observed changes in many physical and biological systems. *{2.4}*

Spatial agreement between regions of significant warming across the globe and locations of significant observed changes in many systems consistent with warming is *very unlikely* to be due solely to natural variability. Several modelling studies have linked some specific responses in physical and biological systems to anthropogenic warming. *{2.4}*

More complete attribution of observed natural system responses to anthropogenic warming is currently prevented by the short time scales of many impact studies, greater natural climate variability at regional scales, contributions of non-climate factors and limited spatial coverage of studies. *{2.4}*

3. Projected climate change and its impacts

"There is *high agreement* and *much evidence* that with current climate change mitigation policies and related sustainable development practices, global GHG emissions will continue to grow over the next few decades. *{3.1}*

The IPCC Special Report on Emissions Scenarios (SRES, 2000) projects an increase of global GHG emissions by 25 to 90% (CO_2-eq) between 2000 and 2030 (Figure 5.5), with fossil fuels maintaining their dominant position in the global energy mix to 2030 and beyond. More recent scenarios without additional emissions mitigation are comparable in range.[8,9] *{3.1}*

"Continued GHG emissions at or above current rates would cause further warming and induce many changes in the global climate system during the 21st century that would very *likely* be larger than those observed during the 20th century (Table 5.1, Figure 5.5). *{3.2.1}*

For the next two decades a warming of about 0.2°C per decade is projected for a range of SRES emissions scenarios. Even if the concentrations of all GHGs and aerosols had been kept constant at year 2000 levels, a further warming of about 0.1°C per decade would be expected. Afterwards, temperature projections increasingly depend on specific emissions scenarios. *{3.2}*

The range of projections (Table 5.1) is broadly consistent with the TAR, but uncertainties and upper ranges for temperature are larger mainly because the broader range of available models suggests stronger climate-carbon cycle feedbacks. Warming reduces terrestrial and ocean uptake of atmospheric CO_2, increasing the fraction of anthropogenic emissions remaining in the atmosphere. The strength of this feedback effect varies markedly among models. *{2.3, 3.2.1}*

Because understanding of some important effects driving sea level rise is too limited, this report does not assess the likelihood, nor provide a best estimate or an upper bound for sea level rise. Table 5.1 shows model-based projections of global average sea level rise for 2090-2099.[10] The projections do not include uncertainties in climate-carbon cycle feedbacks nor the full effects of changes in ice sheet flow, therefore the upper values of the ranges are not to be considered upper bounds for sea level rise. They include a contribution from increased Greenland and Antarctic ice flow at the rates observed for 1993-2003, but this could increase or decrease in the future.[11] *{3.2.1}*

---

[8] For an explanation of SRES emissions scenarios, see Box 'SRES scenarios' in Topic 3 of this Synthesis Report. These scenarios do not include additional climate policies above current ones; more recent studies differ with respect to UNFCCC and Kyoto Protocol inclusion.

[9] Emission pathways of mitigation scenarios are discussed in Section 5.

[10] TAR projections were made for 2100, whereas the projections for this report are for 2090-2099. The TAR would have had similar ranges to those in Table 5.1 if it had treated uncertainties in the same way.

[11] For discussion of the longer term, see material below.

Scenarios for GHG emissions from 2000 to 2100 (in the absence of additional climate policies) and projections of surface temperatures

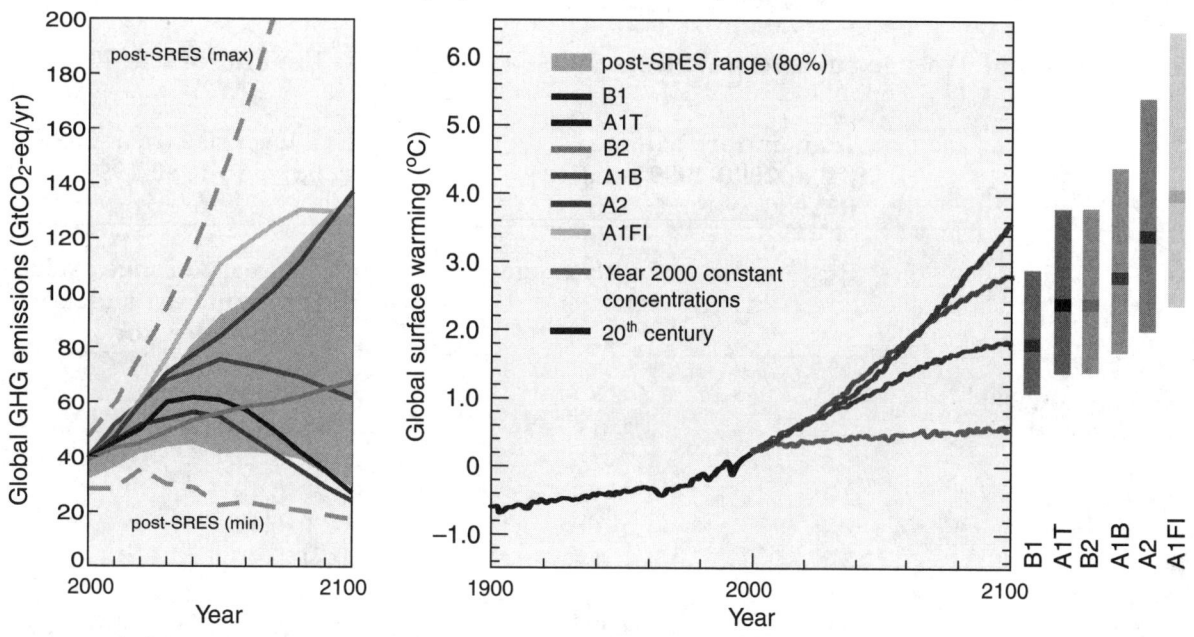

FIGURE 5.5 Left Panel: Global GHG emissions (in GtCO$_2$-eq) in the absence of climate policies: six illustrative SRES marker scenarios (coloured lines) and the 80th percentile range of recent scenarios published since SRES (post-SRES) (gray shaded area). Dashed lines show the full range of post-SRES scenarios. The emissions include CO$_2$, CH$_4$, N$_2$O and F-gases.
Right Panel: Solid lines are multi-model global averages of surface warming for scenarios A2, A1B and B1, shown as continuations of the 20th-century simulations. These projections also take into account emissions of short-lived GHGs and aerosols. The pink line is not a scenario, but is for Atmosphere-Ocean General Circulation Model (AOGCM) simulations where atmospheric concentrations are held constant at year 2000 values. The bars at the right of the figure indicate the best estimate (solid line within each bar) and the likely range assessed for the six SRES marker scenarios at 2090-2099. All temperatures are relative to the period 1980-1999. {Figures 3.1 and 3.2}

"There is now higher confidence than in the TAR in projected patterns of warming and other regional-scale features, including changes in wind patterns, precipitation and some aspects of extremes and sea ice. *[3.2.2]*

Regional-scale changes include: *[3.2.2]*

- warming greatest over land and at most high northern latitudes and least over Southern Ocean and parts of the North Atlantic Ocean, continuing recent observed trends (Figure 5.6)
- contraction of snow cover area, increases in thaw depth over most permafrost regions and decrease in sea ice extent; in some projections using SRES scenarios, Arctic late-summer sea ice disappears almost entirely by the latter part of the 21st century
- *very likely* increase in frequency of hot extremes, heat waves and heavy precipitation
- *likely* increase in tropical cyclone intensity; less confidence in global decrease of tropical cyclone numbers
- poleward shift of extra-tropical storm tracks with consequent changes in wind, precipitation and temperature patterns
- *very likely* precipitation increases in high latitudes and *likely* decreases in most subtropical land regions, continuing observed recent trends.

There is *high confidence* that by mid-century, annual river runoff and water availability are projected to increase at high latitudes (and in some tropical wet areas) and decrease in some dry regions in the mid-latitudes and tropics. There is also *high confidence* that many semi-arid areas (e.g. Mediterranean Basin, western United States, southern Africa and north-eastern Brazil) will suffer a decrease in water resources due to climate change. *[3.3.1, Figure 3.5]*

"Studies since the TAR have enabled more systematic understanding of the timing and magnitude of impacts related to differing amounts and rates of climate change. *[3.3.1, 3.3.2]*

TABLE 5.1

Projected global average surface warming and sea level rise at the end of the 21st century. {Table 3.1}

Case	Temperature change (°C at 2090-2099 relative to 1980-1999)[a,d] Best estimate	*Likely* range	Sea level rise (m at 2090-2099 relative to 1980-1999) Model-based range excluding future rapid dynamical changes in ice flow
Constant year 2000 concentrations[b]	0.6	0.3–0.9	Not available
B1 scenario	1.8	1.1–2.9	0.18–0.38
A1T scenario	2.4	1.4–3.8	0.20–0.45
B2 scenario	2.4	1.4–3.8	0.20–0.43
A1B scenario	2.8	1.7–4.4	0.21–0.48
A2 scenario	3.4	2.0–5.4	0.23–0.51
A1F1 scenario	4.0	2.4–6.4	0.26–0.59

Notes:
a) Temperatures are assessed best estimates and *likely* uncertainty ranges from a hierarchy of models of varying complexity as well as observational constraints.
b) Year 2000 constant composition is derived from Atmosphere-Ocean General Circulation Models (AOGCMs) only.
c) All scenarios above are six SRES marker scenarios. Approximate CO_2-eq concentrations corresponding to the computed radiative forcing due to anthropogenic GHGs and aerosols in 2100 (see p. 823 of the Working Group I TAR) for the SRES B1, AIT, B2, A1B, A2 and A1FI illustrative marker scenarios are about 600, 700, 800, 850, 1250 and 1550ppm, respectively.
d) Temperature changes are expressed as the difference from the period 1980-1999. To express the change relative to the period 1850-1899 add 0.5°C.

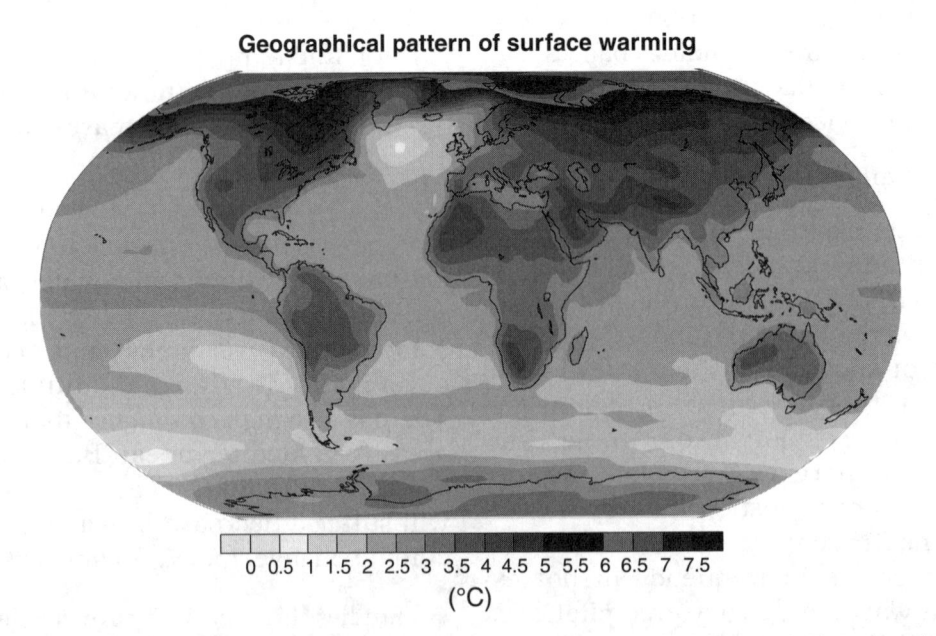

Geographical pattern of surface warming

FIGURE 5.6 Projected surface temperature changes for the late 21st century (2090-2099). The map shows the multi-AOGCM average project for the A1B SRES scenario. Temperatures are relative to the period 1980-1999. *{Figure 3.2}*

Figure 5.7 presents examples of this new information for systems and sectors. The top panel shows impacts increasing with increasing temperature change. Their estimated magnitude and timing is also affected by development pathway (lower panel). {3.3.1}

Examples of some projected impacts for different regions are given in Table 5.2.

Some systems, sectors and regions are *likely* to be especially affected by climate change.[12] {3.3.3}

Systems and sectors: {3.3.3}

- particular ecosystems:
  - terrestrial: tundra, boreal forest and mountain regions because of sensitivity to warming; mediterranean-type ecosystems because of reduction in rainfall; and tropical rainforests where precipitation declines
  - coastal: mangroves and salt marshes, due to multiple stresses
  - marine: coral reefs due to multiple stresses; the sea ice biome because of sensitivity to warming
- water resources in some dry regions at mid-latitudes[13] and in the dry tropics, due to changes in rainfall and evapotranspiration, and in areas dependent on snow and ice melt
- agriculture in low latitudes, due to reduced water availability
- low-lying coastal systems, due to threat of sea level rise and increased risk from extreme weather events
- human health in populations with low adaptive capacity.

Regions: {3.3.3}

- the Arctic, because of the impacts of high rates of projected warming on natural systems and human communities
- Africa, because of low adaptive capacity and projected climate change impacts
- small islands, where there is high exposure of population and infrastructure to projected climate change impacts
- Asian and African megadeltas, due to large populations and high exposure to sea level rise, storm surges and river flooding.

---

[12] Identified on the basis of expert judgement of the assessed literature and considering the magnitude, timing and projected rate of climate change, sensitivity and adaptive capacity.

[13] Including arid and semi-arid regions.

Within other areas, even those with high incomes, some people (such as the poor, young children and the elderly) can be particularly at risk, and also some areas and some activities. {3.3.3}

OCEAN ACIDIFICATION

The uptake of anthropogenic carbon since 1750 has led to the ocean becoming more acidic with an average decrease in pH of 0.1 units. Increasing atmospheric CO_2 concentrations lead to further acidification. Projections based on SRES scenarios give a reduction in average global surface ocean pH of between 0.14 and 0.35 units over the 21st century. While the effects of observed ocean acidification on the marine biosphere are as yet undocumented, the progressive acidification of oceans is expected to have negative impacts on marine shell-forming organisms (e.g. corals) and their dependent species. {3.3.4}

> Altered frequencies and intensities of extreme weather, together with sea level rise, are expected to have mostly adverse effects on natural and human systems. {3.3.5}

Examples for selected extremes and sectors are shown in Table 5.3.

> Anthropogenic warming and sea level rise would continue for centuries due to the time scales associated with climate processes and feedbacks, even if GHG concentrations were to be stabilised. {3.2.3}

Estimated long-term (multi-century) warming corresponding to the six AR4 Working Group III stabilisation categories is shown in Figure 5.8.

Contraction of the Greenland ice sheet is projected to continue to contribute to sea level rise after 2100. Current models suggest virtually complete elimination of the Greenland ice sheet and a resulting contribution to sea level rise of about 7m if global average warming were sustained for millennia in excess of 1.9 to 4.6°C relative to pre-industrial values. The corresponding future temperatures in Greenland are comparable to those inferred for the last interglacial period 125,000 years ago, when palaeoclimatic information suggests reductions of polar land ice extent and 4 to 6m of sea level rise. {3.2.3}

Current global model studies project that the Antarctic ice sheet will remain too cold for widespread surface melting and gain mass due to

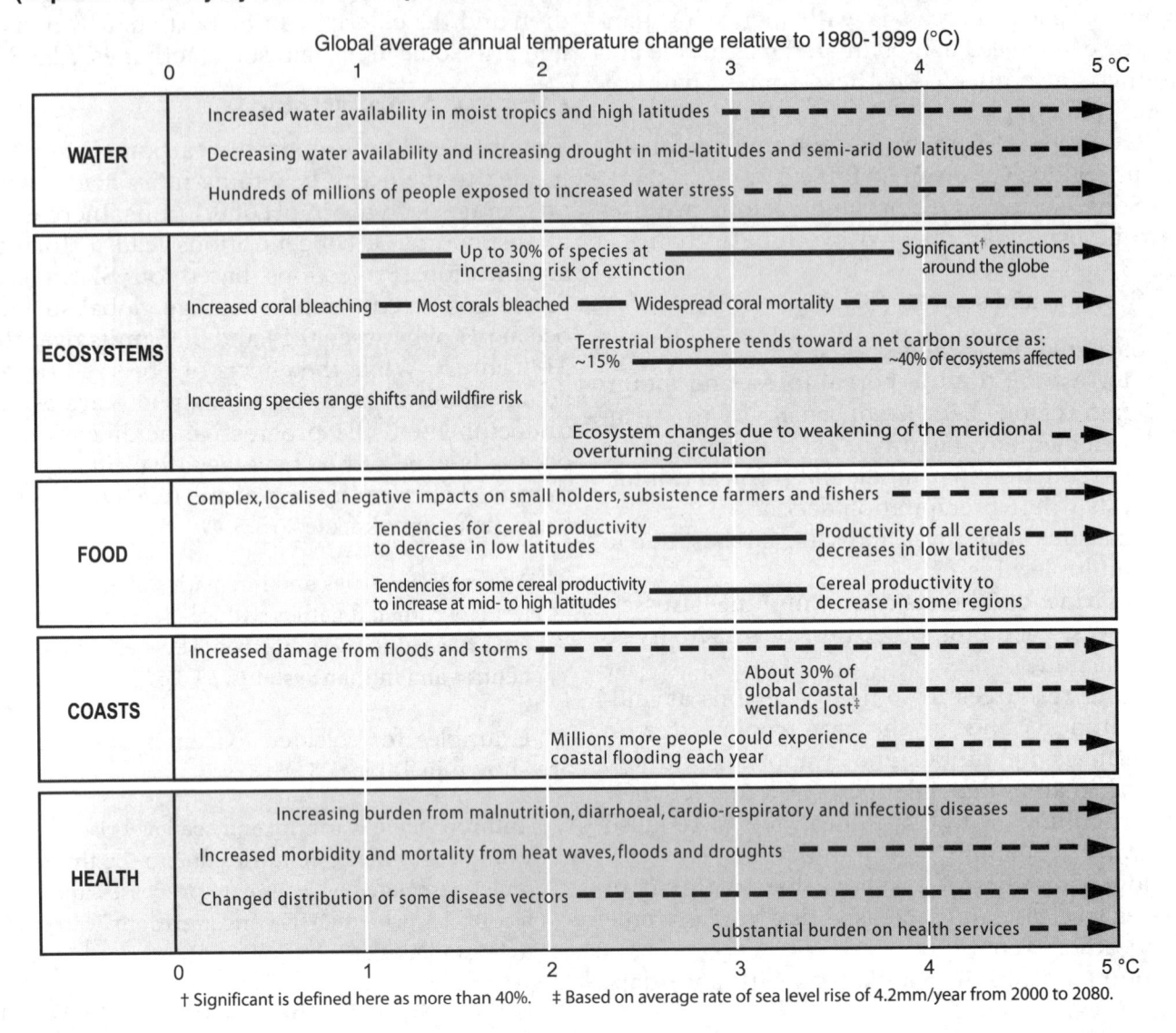

Examples of impacts associated with global average temperature change
(Impacts will vary by extent of adaptation, rate of temperature change and socio-economic pathway)

Global average annual temperature change relative to 1980-1999 (°C)

	0 — 1 — 2 — 3 — 4 — 5 °C
WATER	Increased water availability in moist tropics and high latitudes → Decreasing water availability and increasing drought in mid-latitudes and semi-arid low latitudes → Hundreds of millions of people exposed to increased water stress →
ECOSYSTEMS	Up to 30% of species at increasing risk of extinction — Significant† extinctions around the globe → Increased coral bleaching — Most corals bleached — Widespread coral mortality → Terrestrial biosphere tends toward a net carbon source as: ~15% — ~40% of ecosystems affected → Increasing species range shifts and wildfire risk Ecosystem changes due to weakening of the meridional overturning circulation →
FOOD	Complex, localised negative impacts on small holders, subsistence farmers and fishers → Tendencies for cereal productivity to decrease in low latitudes — Productivity of all cereals decreases in low latitudes → Tendencies for some cereal productivity to increase at mid- to high latitudes — Cereal productivity to decrease in some regions
COASTS	Increased damage from floods and storms → About 30% of global coastal wetlands lost‡ → Millions more people could experience coastal flooding each year →
HEALTH	Increasing burden from malnutrition, diarrhoeal, cardio-respiratory and infectious diseases → Increased morbidity and mortality from heat waves, floods and droughts → Changed distribution of some disease vectors → Substantial burden on health services →

0 — 1 — 2 — 3 — 4 — 5 °C

† Significant is defined here as more than 40%.   ‡ Based on average rate of sea level rise of 4.2mm/year from 2000 to 2080.

Warming by 2090-2099 relative to 1980-1999 for non-mitigation scenarios

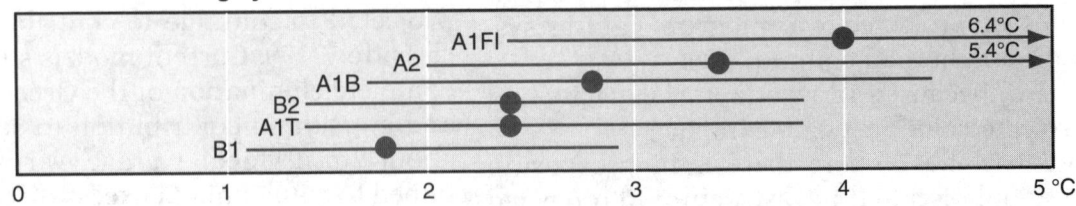

A1FI — 6.4°C
A2 — 5.4°C
A1B
B2
A1T
B1

0 — 1 — 2 — 3 — 4 — 5 °C

FIGURE 5.7 Examples of impacts associated with projected global average surface warming. **Upper panel:** Illustrative examples of global impacts projected for climate changes (and sea level and atmospheric CO_2 where relevant) associated with different amounts of increase in global average surface temperature in the 21st century. The black lines link impacts; broken-line arrows indicate impacts continuing with increasing temperature. Entries are placed so that the left-hand side of text indicates the approximate level of warming that is associated with the onset of a given impact. Quantitative entries for water scarcity and flooding represent the additional impacts of climate change relative to the conditions projected across the range of SRES scenarios A1FI, A2, B1 and B2. Adaptation to climate change is not included in these estimations. Confidence levels for all statements are high. **Lower panel:** Dots and bars indicate the best estimate and likely ranges of warming assessed for the six SRES marker scenarios for 2090-2099 relative to 1980-1999. {Figure 3.6}

TABLE 5.2

Examples of some projected regional impacts. {3.3.2}

Africa	• By 2020, between 75 and 250 million of people are projected to be exposed to increased water stress due to climate change. • By 2020, in some countries, yields from rain-fed agriculture could be reduced by up to 50%. Agricultural production, including access to food, in many African countries is projected to be severely compromised. This would further adversely affect food security and exacerbate malnutrition. • Towards the end of the 21st century, projected sea level rise will affect low-lying coastal areas with large populations. The cost of adaptation could amount to at least 5 to 10% of Gross Domestic Product (GDP). • By 2080, an increase of 5 to 8% of arid and semi-arid land in Africa is projected under a range of climate scenarios (TS).
Asia	• By the 2050s, freshwater availability in Central, South, East and South-East Asia, particularly in large river basins, is projected to decrease. • Coastal areas, especially heavily populated megadelta regions in South, East and South-East Asia, will be at greatest risk due to increased flooding from the sea and, in some megadeltas, flooding from the rivers. • Climate change is projected to compound the pressures on natural resources and the environment associated with rapid urbanisation, industrialisation and economic development. • Endemic morbidity and mortality due to diarrhoeal disease primarily associated with floods and droughts are expected to rise in East, South and South-East Asia due to projected changes in the hydrological cycle.
Austrial and New Zealand	• By 2020, significant loss of biodiversity is projected to occur in some ecologically rich sites, including the Great Barrier Reef and Queensland Wet Tropics. • By 2030, water security problems are projected to intensify in southern and eastern Australia and, in New Zealand, in Northland and some eastern regions. • By 2030, production from agriculture and forestry is projected to decline over much of southern and eastern Australia, and over parts of eastern New Zealand, due to increased drought and fire. However, in New Zealand, initial benefits are projected in some other regions. • By 2050, ongoing coastal development and population growth in some areas of Australia and New Zealand are projected to exacerbate risks from sea level rise and increases in the severity and frequency of storms and coastal flooding.
Europe	• Climate change is expected to magnify regional differences in Europe's natural resources and assets. Negative impacts will include increased risk of inland flash floods and more frequent coastal flooding and increased erosion (due to storminess and sea level rise). • Mountainous areas will face glacier retreat, reduced snow cover and winter tourism, and extensive species losses (in some areas up to 60% under high emissions scenarios by 2080). • In southern Europe, climate change is projected to worsen conditions (high temperatures and drought) in a region already vulnerable to climate variability, and to reduce water availability, hydropower potential, summer tourism and, in general, crop productivity. • Climate change is also projected to increase the health risks due to heat waves and the frequency of wildfires.
Latin America	• By mid-century, increases in temperature and associated decreases in soil water are projected to lead to gradual replacement of tropical forest by savanna in eastern Amazonia. Semi-arid vegetation will tend to be replaced by arid-land vegetation.

continued

TABLE 5.2

Examples of some projected regional impacts. {3.3.2}—cont'd

	• There is a risk of significant biodiversity loss through species extinction in many areas of tropical Latin America.
	• Productivity of some important crops is projected to decrease and livestock productivity to decline, with adverse consequences for food security. In temperate zones, soybean yields are projected to increase. Overall, the number of people at risk of hunger is projected to increase (TS; *medium confidence*).
	• Changes in precipitation patterns and the disappearance of glaciers are projected to significantly affect water availability for human consumption, agriculture and energy generation.
North America	• Warming in western mountains is projected to cause decreased snowpack, more winter flooding and reduced summer flows, exacerbating competition for over-allocated water resources.
	• In the early decades of the century, moderate climate change is projected to increase aggregate yields of rain-fed agriculture by 5 to 20%, but with important variability among regions. Major challenges are projected for crops that are near the warm end of their suitable range or which depend on highly utilised water resources.
	• Cities that currently experience heat waves are expected to be further challenged by an increased number, intensity and duration of heat waves during the course of the century, with potential for adverse health impacts.
	• Coastal communities and habitats will be increasingly stressed by climate change impacts interacting with development and pollution.
Polar Regions	• The main projected biophysical effects are reductions in thickness and extent of glaciers, ice sheets and sea ice, and changes in natural ecosystems with detrimental effects on many organisms including migratory birds, mammals and higher predators.
	• For human communities in the Arctic, impacts, particularly those resulting from changing snow and ice conditions, are projected to be mixed.
	• Detrimental impacts would include those on infrastructure and traditional indigenous ways of life.
	• In both polar regions, specific ecosystems and habitats are projected to be vulnerable, as climatic barriers to species invasions are lowered.
Small Islands	• Sea level rise is expected to exacerbate inundation, storm surge, erosion and other coastal hazards, thus threatening vital infrastructure, settlements and facilities that support the livelihood of island communities.
	• Deterioration in coastal conditions, for example through erosion of beaches and coral bleaching, is expected to affect local resources.
	• By mid-century, climate change is expected to reduce water resources in many small islands, e.g. in the Caribbean and Pacific, to the point where they become insufficient to meet demand during low-rainfall periods.
	• With higher temperatures, increased invasion by non-native species is expected to occur, particularly on mid- and high-latitude islands.

Note:
Unless stated explicitly, all entries are from Working Group II 5 text, and are either *very high confidence* or *high confidence* statements, reflecting different sectors (agriculture, ecosystems, water, coasts, health, industry and settlements). The Working Group II SPM refers to the source of the statements, timelines and temperatures. The magnitude and timing of impacts that will ultimately be realised will vary with the amount and rate of climate change, emissions scenarios, development pathways and adaptation.

Estimated multi-century warming relative to 1980-1999 for AR4 stabilisation categories

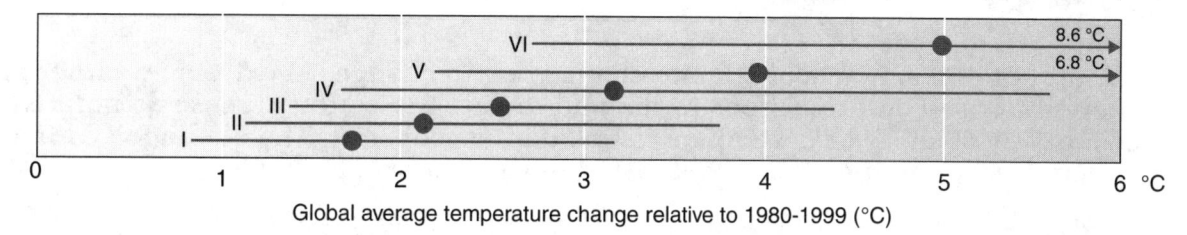

FIGURE 5.8 Estimated long-term (multi-century) warming corresponding to the six AR4 Working Group III stabilisation categories (Table 5.6). The temperature scale has been shifted by -0.5°C compared to Table 5.6 to account approximately for the warming between pre-industrial and 1980–1999. For most stabilisation levels global average temperature is approaching the equilibrium level over a few centuries. For GHG emissions scenarios that lead to stabilisation at levels comparable to SRES B1 and A1B by 2100 (600 and 850ppm CO_2-eq; category IV and V), assessed models project that about 65 to 70% of the estimated global equilibrium temperature increase, assuming a climate sensitivity of 3°C, would be realised at the time of stabilisation. For the much lower stabilisation scenarios (category I and II, Figure 5.11), the equilibrium temperature may be reached earlier. {Figure 3.4}

increased snowfall. However, net loss of ice mass could occur if dynamical ice discharge dominates the ice sheet mass balance. {3.2.3}

> Anthropogenic warming could lead to some impacts that are abrupt or irreversible, depending upon the rate and magnitude of the climate change. {3.4}

Partial loss of ice sheets on polar land could imply metres of sea level rise, major changes in coastlines and inundation of low-lying areas, with greatest effects in river deltas and low-lying islands. Such changes are projected to occur over millennial time scales, but more rapid sea level rise on century time scales cannot be excluded. {3.4}

Climate change is *likely* to lead to some irreversible impacts. There is *medium confidence* that approximately 20 to 30% of species assessed so far are *likely* to be at increased risk of extinction if increases in global average warming exceed 1.5 to 2.5°C (relative to 1980–1999). As global average temperature increase exceeds about 3.5°C, model projections suggest significant extinctions (40 to 70% of species assessed) around the globe. {3.4}

Based on current model simulations, the meridional overturning circulation (MOC) of the Atlantic Ocean will *very likely* slow down during the 21st century; nevertheless temperatures over the Atlantic and Europe are projected to increase. The MOC is *very unlikely* to undergo a large abrupt transition during the 21st century.

Longer-term MOC changes cannot be assessed with confidence. Impacts of large-scale and persistent changes in the MOC are *likely* to include changes in marine ecosystem productivity, fisheries, ocean CO_2 uptake, oceanic oxygen concentrations and terrestrial vegetation. Changes in terrestrial and ocean CO_2 uptake may feed back on the climate system. {3.4}

4. ADAPTATION AND MITIGATION OPTIONS[14]

> A wide array of adaptation options is available, but more extensive adaptation than is currently occurring is required to reduce vulnerability to climate change. There are barriers, limits and costs, which are not fully understood. {4.2}

Societies have a long record of managing the impacts of weather- and climate-related events. Nevertheless, additional adaptation measures will be required to reduce the adverse impacts of projected climate change and variability, regardless of the scale of mitigation undertaken over the next two to three decades. Moreover, vulnerability to climate change can be exacerbated by other stresses. These arise from, for example, current climate hazards, poverty and unequal access to

---

[14] While this Section deals with adaptation and mitigation separately, these responses can be complementary. This theme is discussed in Section 5.

TABLE 5.3

Examples of possible impacts of climate change due to changes in extreme weather and climate events, based on projections to the mid- to late 21st century. These do not take into account any changes or developments in adaptive capacity. The likelihood estimates in column two relate to the phenomena listed in column one. {Table 3.2}

Phenomenon[a] and direction of trend	Likelihood of future trends based on projections for 21st century using SRES scenarios	Examples of major projected impacts by sector			
		Agriculture, forestry and ecosystems	Water resources	Human health	Industry, settlement and society
Over most land areas, warmer and fewer cold days and nights, warmer and more frequent hot days and nights	*Virtually certain*[b]	Increased yields in colder environments; decreased yields in warmer environments; increased insect outbreaks	Effects on water resources relying on snowmelt; effects on some water supplies	Reduced human mortality from decreased cold exposure	Reduced energy demand for heating; increased demand for cooling; declining air quality in cities; reduced disruption to transport due to snow, ice; effects on winter tourism
Warm spells/ heat waves. Frequency increases over most land areas	*Very likely*	Reduced yields in warmer regions due to heat stress; increased danger of wildfire	Increased water demand; water quality problems, e.g. algal blooms	Increased risk of heat-related mortality, especially for the elderly, chronically sick, very young and socially isolated	Reduction in quality of life for people in warm areas without appropriate housing; impacts on the elderly, very young and poor
Heavy precipitation events. Frequency increases over most areas	*Very likely*	Damage to crops; soil erosion, inability to cultivate land due to waterlogging of soils	Adverse effects on quality of surface and groundwater; contamination of water supply; water scarcity may be relieved	Increased risk of deaths, injuries and infectious, respiratory and skin diseases	Disruption of settlements, commerce, transport and societies due to flooding: pressures on urban and rural infrastructures; loss of property
Area affected by drought increases	*Likely*	Land degradation; lower yields/ crop damage and failure; increased livestock deaths; increased risk of wildfire	More widespread water stress	Increased risk of food and water shortage; increased risk of malnutrition; increased risk of water- and food- borne diseases	Water shortage for settlements, industry and societies; reduced hydropower generation potentials; potential for population migration

TABLE 5.3—CONT'D

| Intense tropical cyclone activity increases | Likely | Damage to crops; windthrow (uprooting) of trees; damage to coral reefs | Power outages causing disruption of public water supply | Increased risk of deaths, injuries, water- and food-borne diseases; post-traumatic stress disorders | Disruption by flood and high winds; withdrawal of risk coverage in vulnerable areas by private insurers; potential for population migrations; loss of property |
| Increased incidence of extreme high sea level (excludes tsunamis)[c] | Likely[d] | Salinisation of irrigation water, estuaries and fresh-water systems | Decreased fresh-water availability due to saltwater intrusion | Increased risk of deaths and injuries by drowning in floods; migration-related health effects | Costs of coastal protection versus costs of land-use relocation; potential for movement of populations and infrastructure; also see tropical cyclones above |

a) See Working Group I Table 3.7 for further details regarding definitions.
b) Warming of the most extreme days and nights each year.
c) Extreme high sea level depends on average sea level and on regional weather systems. It is defined as the highest 1% of hourly values of observed sea level at a station for a given reference period.
d) In all scenarios, the projected global average sea level at 2100 is higher than in the reference period. The effect of changes in regional weather systems on sea level extremes has not been assessed.

resources, food insecurity, trends in economic globalisation, conflict and incidence of diseases such as HIV/AIDS. *[4.2]*

Some planned adaptation to climate change is already occurring on a limited basis. Adaptation can reduce vulnerability, especially when it is embedded within broader sectoral initiatives (Table 5.4). There is *high confidence* that there are viable adaptation options that can be implemented in some sectors at low cost, and/or with high benefit-cost ratios. However, comprehensive estimates of global costs and benefits of adaptation are limited. *[4.2, Table 4.1]*

" Adaptive capacity is intimately connected to social and economic development but is unevenly distributed across and within societies. *[4.2]*

A range of barriers limits both the implementation and effectiveness of adaptation measures. The capacity to adapt is dynamic and is influenced by a society's productive base, including natural and man-made capital assets, social networks and entitlements, human capital and institutions, governance, national income, health and technology. Even societies with high adaptive capacity remain vulnerable to climate change, variability and extremes. *[4.2]*

" Both bottom-up and top-down studies indicate that there is *high agreement* and *much evidence* of substantial economic potential for the mitigation of global GHG emissions over the coming decades that could offset the projected growth of global emissions or reduce emissions below

Table 5.4

Selected examples of planned adaptation by sector. {Table 4.1}

Sector	Adaptation option/strategy	Underlying policy framework	Key constraints and opportunities to implementation (Normal font = constraints: italics = opportunities)
Water	Expanded rainwater harvesting; water storage and conservation techniques; water re-use; desalination; water-use and irrigation efficiency	National water policies and integrated water resources management; water-related hazards management	Financial, human resources and physical barriers; *integrated water resources management; synergies with other sectors*
Agriculture	Adjustment of planting dates and crop variety; crop relocation; improved land management, e.g. erosion control and soil protection through tree planting	R&D policies; institutional reform; land tenure and land reform; training; capacity building; crop insurance; financial incentives, e.g. subsidies and tax credits	Technological and financial constraints; access to new varieties; markets; *longer growing season in higher latitudes; revenues from 'new' products*
Infrastructure/ settlement (including coastal zones)	Relocation; seawalls and storm surge barriers; dune reinforcement; land acquisition and creation of marshlands/wetlands as buffer against sea level rise and flooding; protection of existing natural barriers	Standards and regulations that integrate climate change considerations into design; land-use policies; building codes; insurance	Financial and technological barriers; availability of relocation space; *integrated policies and management; synergies with sustainable development goals*
Human health	Heat-health action plans; emergency medical services; improved climate-sensitive disease surveillance and control; safe water and improved sanitation	Public health policies that recognise climate risk; strengthened health services; regional and international cooperation	Limits to human tolerance (vulnerable groups); knowledge limitations; financial capacity; *upgraded health services; improved quality of life*
Tourism	Diversification of tourism attractions and revenues; shifting ski slopes to higher altitudes and glaciers; artificial snow-making	Integrated planning (e.g. carrying capacity; linkages with other sectors); financial incentives, e.g. subsidies and tax credits	Appeal/marketing of new attractions; financial and logistical challenges; potential adverse impact on other sectors (e.g. artificial snow-making may increase energy use); *revenues from 'new' attractions; involvement of wider group of stakeholders*

Table 5.4

Selected examples of planned adaptation by sector. {Table 4.1}—cont'd

Sector	Adaptation option/strategy	Underlying policy framework	Key constraints and opportunities to implementation (Normal font = constraints: italics = opportunities)
Transport	Ralignment/relocation; design standards and planning for roads, rail and other infrastructure to cope with warming and drainage	Integrating climate change considerations into national transport policy; investment in R&D for special situations, e.g. permafrost areas	Financial and technological barriers; availability of less vulnerable routes; *improved technologies and integration* with key sectors (e.g. energy)
Energy	Strengthening of overhead transmission and distribution infrastructure; underground cabling for utilities; energy efficiency; use of renewable sources; reduced dependence on single sources of energy	National energy policies, regulations, and fiscal and financial incentives to encourage use of alternative sources; incorporating climate change in design standards	Access to viable alternatives; financial and technological barriers; acceptance of new technologies; *stimulation of new technologies; use of local resources*

Note:
Other examples from many sectors would include early warning systems.

current levels (Figures 5.9, 5.10).[15] While top-down and bottom-up studies are in line at the global level (Figure 5.9) there are considerable differences at the sectoral level. *{4.3}*

No single technology can provide all of the mitigation potential in any sector. The economic mitigation potential, which is generally greater than the market mitigation potential, can only be achieved when adequate policies are in place and barriers removed (Table 5.5). *{4.3}*

Bottom-up studies suggest that mitigation opportunities with net negative costs have the potential to reduce emissions by around 6 GtCO$_2$-eq/yr in 2030, realising which requires dealing with implementation barriers. *{4.3}*

Future energy infrastructure investment decisions, expected to exceed US$20 trillion[16] between 2005 and 2030, will have long-term impacts on GHG emissions, because of the long lifetimes of energy plants and other infrastructure capital stock. The widespread diffusion of low-carbon technologies may take many decades, even if early investments in these technologies

---

[15] The concept of **'mitigation potential'** has been developed to assess the scale of GHG reductions that could be made, relative to emission baselines, for a given level of carbon price (expressed in cost per unit of carbon dioxide equivalent emissions avoided or reduced). Mitigation potential is further differentiated in terms of 'market mitigation potential' and 'economic mitigation potential'.

Market mitigation potential is the mitigation potential based on private costs and private discount rates (reflecting the perspective of private consumers and companies), which might be expected to occur under forecast market conditions, including policies and measures currently in place, noting that barriers limit actual uptake.

Economic mitigation potential is the mitigation potential that takes into account social costs and benefits and social discount rates (reflecting the perspective of society; social discount rates are lower than those used by private investors), assuming that market efficiency is improved by policies and measures and barriers are removed.

Mitigation potential is estimated using different types of approaches. **Bottom-up studies** are based on assessment of mitigation options, emphasising specific technologies and regulations. They are typically sectoral studies taking the macro-economy as unchanged. **Top-down studies** assess the economy-wide potential of mitigation options. They use globally consistent frameworks and aggregated information about mitigation options and capture macro-economic and market feedbacks.

[16] 20 trillion = 20,000 billion = 20×10^{12}

CHAPTER 5 Energy and Environment

Comparison between global economic mitigation potential and projected emissions increase in 2030

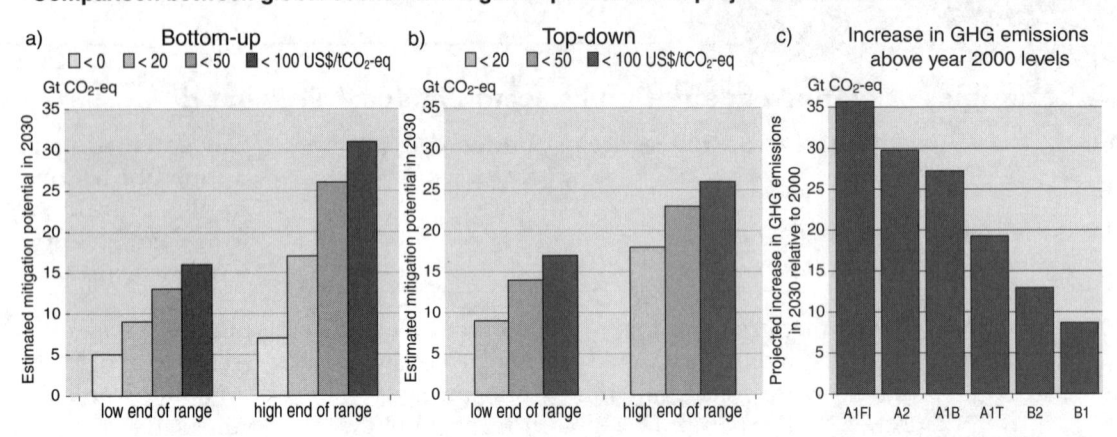

FIGURE 5.9 Global economic mitigation potential in 2030 estimated from bottom-up (Panel a) and top-down (Panel b) studies, compared with the projected emissions increases from SRES scenarios relative to year 2000 GHG emissions of 40.8 GtCO$_2$-eq (Panel c). Note: GHG emissions in 2000 are exclusive of emissions of decay of above ground biomass that remains after logging and deforestation and from peat fires and drained peat soils, to ensure consistency with the SRES emission results. {Figure 4.1}

Economic mitigation potentials by sector in 2030 estimated from bottom-up studies

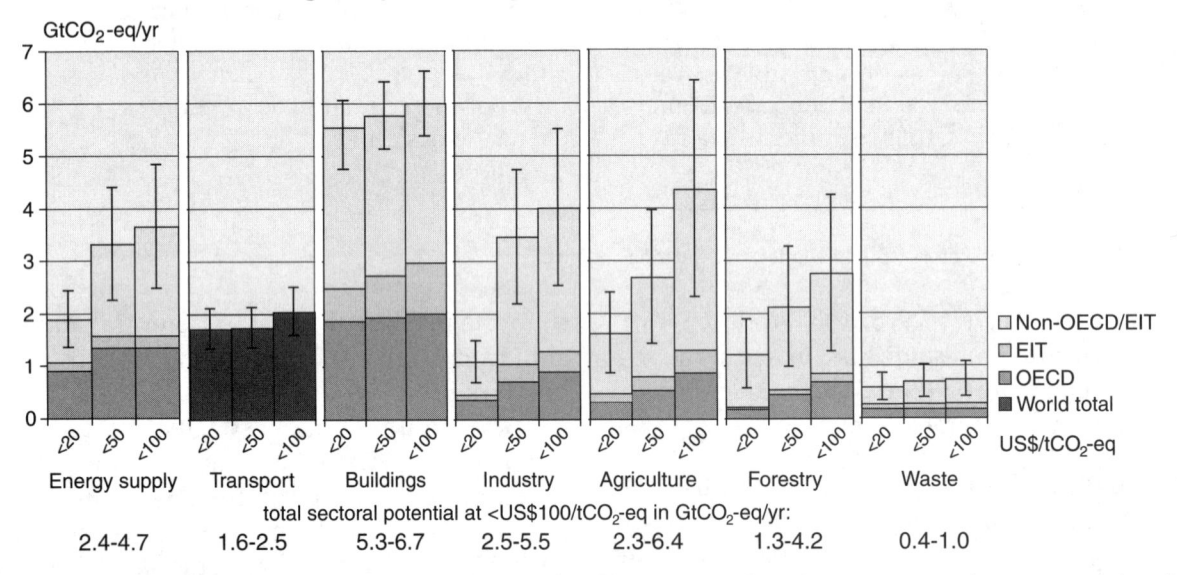

total sectoral potential at <US$100/tCO$_2$-eq in GtCO$_2$-eq/yr:
Energy supply 2.4–4.7; Transport 1.6–2.5; Buildings 5.3–6.7; Industry 2.5–5.5; Agriculture 2.3–6.4; Forestry 1.3–4.2; Waste 0.4–1.0

FIGURE 5.10 Estimated economic mitigation potential by sector in 2030 from bottom-up studies, compared to the respective baselines assumed in the sector assessments. The potentials do not include non-technical options such as lifestyle changes. (Figure 4.2}

Notes:
a) The ranges for global economic potentials as assessed in each sector are shown by vertical lines. The ranges are based on end-use allocations of emissions, meaning that emissions of electricity use are counted towards the end-use sectors and not to the energy supply sector.
b) The estimated potentials have been constrained by the availability of studies particularly at high carbon price levels.
c) Sectors used different baselines. For industry, the SRES B2 baseline was taken, for energy supply and transport, the World Energy Outlook (WEO) 2004 baseline was used; the building sector is based on a baseline in between SRES B2 and A1B; for waste, SRES A1B driving forces were used to construct a waste-specific baseline; agriculture and forestry used baselines that mostly used B2 driving forces.
d) Only global totals for transport are shown because international aviation is included.
e) Categories excluded are: non-CO$_2$ emissions in buildings and transport, part of material efficiency options, heat production and co-generation in energy supply, heavy duty vehicles, shipping and high-occupancy passenger transport, most high-cost options for buildings, wastewater treatment, emission reduction from coal mines and gas pipelines, and fluorinated gases from energy supply and transport. The underestimation of the total economic potential from these emissions is of the order of 10 to 15%.

TABLE 5.5

Selected examples of key sectoral mitigation technologies, policies and measures, constraints and opportunities. [Table 4.2]

Energy supply	Improved supply and distribution efficiency; fuel switching from coal to gas; nuclear power; renewable heat and power (hydropower, solar, wind, geothermal and bioenergy); combined heat and power; early applications of carbon dioxide capture and storage (CCS) (e.g. storage of removed CO_2 from natural gas); CCS for gas, biomass and coal-fired electricity generating facilities; advanced nuclear power; advanced renewable energy, including tidal and wave energy, concentrating solar, and solar photovoltaics	Reduction of fossil fuel subsidies; taxes or carbon charges on fossil fuels	Resistance by vested interests may make them difficult to implement
		Feed-in tariffs for renewable energy technologies; renewable energy obligations; producer subsidies	*May be appropriate to create markets for low-emissions technologies*
Transport	More fuel-efficient vehicles; hybrid vehicles; cleaner diesel vehicles; biofuels; modal shifts from road transport to rail and public transport systems; non-motorised transport (cycling, walking); land-use and transport planning; *second generation biofuels; higher efficiency aircraft; advanced electric and hybrid vehicles with more powerful and reliable batteries*	Mandatory fuel economy; biofuel blending and CO_2 standards for road transport	Partial coverage of vehicle fleet may limit effectiveness
		Taxes on vehicle purchase, registration, use and motor fuels; road and parking pricing	Effectiveness may drop with higher incomes
		Influence mobility needs through land-use regulations and infrastructure planning; investment in attractive public transport facilities and non-motorised forms of transport	*Particularly appropriate for countries that are building up their transportation systems*

continued

TABLE 5.5

Selected examples of key sectoral mitigation technologies, policies and measures, constraints and opportunities. [Table 4.2]—cont'd

Buildings	Efficient lighting and daylighting; more efficient electrical appliances and heating and cooling devices; improved cook stoves, improved insulation; passive and active solar design for heating and cooling; alternative refrigeration fluids, recovery and recycling of fluorinated gases; *integrated design of commercial buildings including technologies, such as intelligent meters that provide feedback and control; solar photovoltaics integrated in buildings*	Appliance standards and labelling	Periodic revision of standards needed
		Building codes and certification	*Attractive for new buildings.* Enforcement can be difficult
		Demand-side management programmes	Need for regulations so that utilities may profit
		Public sector leadership programmes, including procurement	Government purchasing can expand demand for energy-efficient products
		Incentives for energy service companies (ESCOs)	Success factor: Access to third party financing
Industry	More efficient end-use electrical equipment; heat and power recovery; material recycling and substitution; control of non-CO_2 gas emissions; and a wide array of process-specific technologies; *advanced energy efficiency; CCS for cement, ammonia, and iron manufacture; inert electrodes for aluminium manufacture*	Provision of benchmark information; performance standards; subsidies; tax credits	*May be appropriate to stimulate technology uptake.* Stability of national policy important in view of international competitiveness
		Tradable permits	Predictable allocation mechanisms and stable price signals important for investments
		Voluntary agreements	Success factors include: clear targets, a baseline scenario, third-party involvement in design and review and formal provisions of monitoring, close cooperation between government and industry

Selected examples of key sectoral mitigation technologies, policies and measures, constraints and opportunities. [Table 4.2]

Sector	Technologies/Practices	Policies and Measures	Constraints and Opportunities
Agriculture	Improved crop and grazing land management to increase soil carbon storage; restoration of cultivated peaty soils and degraded lands; improved rice cultivation techniques and livestock and manure management to reduce CH_4 emissions; improved nitrogen fertiliser application techniques to reduce N_2O emissions; dedicated energy crops to replace fossil fuel use; improved energy efficiency; improvements of crop yields	Financial incentives and regulations for improved land management; maintaining soil carbon content; efficient use of fertilisers and irrigation	*May encourage synergy with sustainable development and with reducing vulnerability to climate change, thereby overcoming barriers to implementation*
Forestry/forests	Afforestation; reforestation; forest management; reduced deforestation; harvested wood product management; use of forestry products for bioenergy to replace fossil fuel use; *tree species improvement to increase biomass productivity and carbon sequestration; improved remote sensing technologies for analysis of vegetation/soil carbon sequestration potential and mapping land-use change*	Financial incentives (national and international) to increase forest area, to reduce deforestation and to maintain and manage forests; land-use regulation and enforcement	Constraints include lack of investment capital and land tenure issues. *Can help poverty alleviation*
Waste	Landfill CH_4 recovery; waste incineration with energy recovery; composting of organic waste; controlled wastewater treatment; recycling and waste minimisation; *biocovers and biofilters to optimise CH_4 oxidation*	Financial incentives for improved waste and wastewater management Renewable energy incentives or obligations Waste management regulations	*May stimulate technology diffusion* Local availability of low-cost fuel Most effectively applied at national level with enforcement strategies

are made attractive. Initial estimates show that returning global energy-related CO_2 emissions to 2005 levels by 2030 would require a large shift in investment patterns, although the net additional investment required ranges from negligible to 5 to 10%. {4.3}

> A wide variety of policies and instruments are available to governments to create the incentives for mitigation action. Their applicability depends on national circumstances and sectoral context (Table 5.5). {4.3}

They include integrating climate policies in wider development policies, regulations and standards, taxes and charges, tradable permits, financial incentives, voluntary agreements, information instruments, and research, development and demonstration (RD&D). {4.3}

An effective carbon-price signal could realise significant mitigation potential in all sectors. Modelling studies show that global carbon prices rising to US$20-80/t$CO_2$-eq by 2030 are consistent with stabilisation at around 550ppm CO_2-eq by 2100. For the same stabilisation level, induced technological change may lower these price ranges to US$5-65/t$CO_2$-eq in 2030.[17] {4.3}

There is *high agreement* and *much evidence* that mitigation actions can result in near-term co-benefits (e.g. improved health due to reduced air pollution) that may offset a substantial fraction of mitigation costs. {4.3}

There is *high agreement* and *medium evidence* that Annex I countries' actions may affect the global economy and global emissions, although the scale of carbon leakage remains uncertain.[18] {4.3}

Fossil fuel exporting nations (in both Annex I and non-Annex I countries) may expect, as indicated in the TAR, lower demand and prices and lower GDP growth due to mitigation policies. The extent of this spillover depends strongly on assumptions related to policy decisions and oil market conditions. {4.3}

There is also *high agreement* and *medium evidence* that changes in lifestyle, behaviour patterns and management practices can contribute to climate change mitigation across all sectors. {4.3}

> Many options for reducing global GHG emissions through international cooperation exist. There is *high agreement* and *much evidence* that notable achievements of the UNFCCC and its Kyoto Protocol are the establishment of a global response to climate change, stimulation of an array of national policies, and the creation of an international carbon market and new institutional mechanisms that may provide the foundation for future mitigation efforts. Progress has also been made in addressing adaptation within the UNFCCC and additional international initiatives have been suggested. {4.5}

Greater cooperative efforts and expansion of market mechanisms will help to reduce global costs for achieving a given level of mitigation, or will improve environmental effectiveness. Efforts can include diverse elements such as emissions targets; sectoral, local, sub-national and regional actions; RD&D programmes; adopting common policies; implementing development-oriented actions; or expanding financing instruments. {4.5}

> In several sectors, climate response options can be implemented to realise synergies and avoid conflicts with other dimensions of sustainable development. Decisions about macro-economic and other non-climate policies can significantly affect emissions, adaptive capacity and vulnerability. {4.4, 5.8}

Making development more sustainable can enhance mitigative and adaptive capacities, reduce emissions and reduce vulnerability, but

---

[17] Studies on mitigation portfolios and macro-economic costs assessed in this report are based on top-down modelling. Most models use a global least-cost approach to mitigation portfolios, with universal emissions trading, assuming transparent markets, no transaction cost, and thus perfect implementation of mitigation measures throughout the 21st century. Costs are given for a specific point in time. Global modelled costs will increase if some regions, sectors (e.g. land use), options or gases are excluded. Global modelled costs will decrease with lower baselines, use of revenues from carbon taxes and auctioned permits, and if induced technological learning is included. These models do not consider climate benefits and generally also co-benefits of mitigation measures, or equity issues. Significant progress has been achieved in applying approaches based on induced technological change to stabilisation studies; however, conceptual issues remain. In the models that consider induced technological change, projected costs for a given stabilisation level are reduced; the reductions are greater at lower stabilisation level.

[18] Further details may be found in Topic 4 of this Synthesis Report.

there may be barriers to implementation. On the other hand, it is *very likely* that climate change can slow the pace of progress towards sustainable development. Over the next half-century, climate change could impede achievement of the Millennium Development Goals. *{5.8}*

5. THE LONG-TERM PERSPECTIVE

"Determining what constitutes "dangerous anthropogenic interference with the climate system" in relation to Article 2 of the UNFCCC involves value judgements. Science can support informed decisions on this issue, including by providing criteria for judging which vulnerabilities might be labelled 'key'. *{Box 'Key Vulnerabilities and Article 2 of the UNFCCC', Topic 5}*

Key vulnerabilities[19] may be associated with many climate-sensitive systems, including food supply, infrastructure, health, water resources, coastal systems, ecosystems, global biogeochemical cycles, ice sheets and modes of oceanic and atmospheric circulation. *{Box 'Key Vulnerabilities and Article 2 of the UNFCCC', Topic 5}*

"The five 'reasons for concern' identified in the TAR remain a viable framework to consider key vulnerabilities. These 'reasons' are assessed here to be stronger than in the TAR. Many risks are identified with higher confidence. Some risks are projected to be larger or to occur at lower increases in temperature. Understanding about the relationship between impacts (the basis for 'reasons for concern' in the TAR) and vulnerability (that includes the ability to adapt to impacts) has improved. *{5.2}*

This is due to more precise identification of the circumstances that make systems, sectors and regions especially vulnerable and growing evidence of the risks of very large impacts on multiple-century time scales. *{5.2}*

- ***Risks to unique and threatened systems.*** There is new and stronger evidence of observed impacts of climate change on unique and vulnerable systems (such as polar and high mountain communities and ecosystems), with increasing levels of adverse impacts as temperatures increase further. An increasing risk of species extinction and coral reef damage is projected with higher confidence than in the TAR as warming proceeds. There is *medium confidence* that approximately 20 to 30% of plant and animal species assessed so far are *likely* to be at increased risk of extinction if increases in global average temperature exceed 1.5 to 2.5°C over 1980-1999 levels. Confidence has increased that a 1 to 2°C increase in global mean temperature above 1990 levels (about 1.5 to 2.5°C above preindustrial) poses significant risks to many unique and threatened systems including many biodiversity hotspots. Corals are vulnerable to thermal stress and have low adaptive capacity. Increases in sea surface temperature of about 1 to 3°C are projected to result in more frequent coral bleaching events and widespread mortality, unless there is thermal adaptation or acclimatisation by corals. Increasing vulnerability of indigenous communities in the Arctic and small island communities to warming is projected. *{5.2}*

- ***Risks of extreme weather events.*** Responses to some recent extreme events reveal higher levels of vulnerability than the TAR. There is now higher confidence in the projected increases in droughts, heat waves and floods, as well as their adverse impacts. *{5.2}*

- ***Distribution of impacts and vulnerabilities.*** There are sharp differences across regions and those in the weakest economic position are often the most vulnerable to climate change. There is increasing evidence of greater vulnerability of specific groups such as the poor and elderly not only in developing but also in developed countries. Moreover, there is increased evidence that low-latitude and less developed areas generally face greater risk, for example in dry areas and megadeltas. *{5.2}*

- ***Aggregate impacts.*** Compared to the TAR, initial net market-based benefits from climate change are projected to peak at a lower magnitude of warming, while damages would be higher for larger magnitudes of warming. The net costs of impacts of increased warming are projected to increase over time. *{5.2}*

---

[19] Key vulnerabilities can be identified based on a number of criteria in the literature, including magnitude, timing, persistence/reversibility, the potential for adaptation, distributional aspects, likelihood and 'importance' of the impacts.

- **Risks of large-scale singularities.** There is *high confidence* that global warming over many centuries would lead to a sea level rise contribution from thermal expansion alone that is projected to be much larger than observed over the 20th century, with loss of coastal area and associated impacts. There is better understanding than in the TAR that the risk of additional contributions to sea level rise from both the Greenland and possibly Antarctic ice sheets may be larger than projected by ice sheet models and could occur on century time scales. This is because ice dynamical processes seen in recent observations but not fully included in ice sheet models assessed in the AR4 could increase the rate of ice loss. *{5.2}*

> There is *high confidence* that neither adaptation nor mitigation alone can avoid all climate change impacts; however, they can complement each other and together can significantly reduce the risks of climate change. *{5.3}*

Adaptation is necessary in the short and longer term to address impacts resulting from the warming that would occur even for the lowest stabilisation scenarios assessed. There are barriers, limits and costs, but these are not fully understood. Unmitigated climate change would, in the long term, be *likely* to exceed the capacity of natural, managed and human systems to adapt. The time at which such limits could be reached will vary between sectors and regions. Early mitigation actions would avoid further locking in carbon intensive infrastructure and reduce climate change and associated adaptation needs. *{5.2, 5.3}*

> Many impacts can be reduced, delayed or avoided by mitigation. Mitigation efforts and investments over the next two to three decades will have a large impact on opportunities to achieve lower stabilisation levels. Delayed emission reductions significantly constrain the opportunities to achieve lower stabilisation levels and increase the risk of more severe climate change impacts. *{5.3, 5.4, 5.7}*

In order to stabilise the concentration of GHGs in the atmosphere, emissions would need to peak and decline thereafter. The lower the stabilisation level, the more quickly this peak and decline would need to occur.[20] *{5.4}*

Table 5.6 and Figure 5.11 summarise the required emission levels for different groups of stabilisation concentrations and the resulting equilibrium global warming and long-term sea level rise due to thermal expansion only.[21] The timing and level of mitigation to reach a given temperature stabilisation level is earlier and more stringent if climate sensitivity is high than if it is low. *{5.4, 5.7}*

Sea level rise under warming is inevitable. Thermal expansion would continue for many centuries after GHG concentrations have stabilised, for any of the stabilisation levels assessed, causing an eventual sea level rise much larger than projected for the 21st century. The eventual contributions from Greenland ice sheet loss could be several metres, and larger than from thermal expansion, should warming in excess of 1.9 to 4.6°C above pre-industrial be sustained over many centuries. The long time scales of thermal expansion and ice sheet response to warming imply that stabilisation of GHG concentrations at or above present levels would not stabilise sea level for many centuries. *{5.3, 5.4}*

> There is *high agreement* and *much evidence* that all stabilisation levels assessed can be achieved by deployment of a portfolio of technologies that are either currently available or expected to be commercialised in coming decades, assuming appropriate and effective incentives are in place for their development, acquisition, deployment and diffusion and addressing related barriers. *{5.5}*

All assessed stabilisation scenarios indicate that 60 to 80% of the reductions would come from energy supply and use and industrial processes, with energy efficiency playing a key role in many scenarios. Including non-CO_2 and CO_2 land-use and forestry mitigation options provides greater flexibility and cost-effectiveness.

---

[20] For the lowest mitigation scenario category assessed, emissions would need to peak by 2015, and for the highest, by 2090 (see Table 5.6). Scenarios that use alternative emission pathways show substantial differences in the rate of global climate change.

[21] Estimates for the evolution of temperature over the course of this century are not available in the AR4 for the stabilisation scenarios. For most stabilisation levels, global average temperature is approaching the equilibrium level over a few centuries. For the much lower stabilisation scenarios (category I and II, Figure 5.11), the equilibrium temperature may be reached earlier.

TABLE 5.6

Characteristics of post-TAR stabilisation scenarios and resulting long-term equilibrium global average temperature and the sea level rise component from thermal expansion only.[a] {Table 5.1}

Category	CO_2 concentration at stabilisation (2005 = 379 ppm)[b]	CO_2-equivalent concentration at stabilisation including GHGs and aerosols (2005 = 375 ppm)[b]	Peaking year for CO_2 emissions[a,c]	Change in global CO_2 emissions in 2050 (percent of 2000 emissions)[a,c]	Global average temperature increase above pre-industrial, using 'best estimate' climate sensitivity[d,e]	Global average sea level rise above pre-industrial at equilibrium from thermal expansion only[f]	Number of assessed scenarios
	ppm	ppm	year	percent	°C	metres	
I	350–400	445–490	2000–2015	−85 to −50	2.0–2.4	0.4–1.4	6
II	400–440	490–535	2000–2020	−60 to −30	2.4–2.8	0.5–1.7	18
III	440–485	535–590	2010–2030	−30 to +5	2.8–3.2	0.6–1.9	21
IV	485–570	590–710	2020–2060	+10 to +60	3.2–4.0	0.6–2.4	118
V	570–660	710–855	2050–2080	+25 to +85	4.0–4.9	0.8–2.9	9
VI	660–790	855–1130	2060–2090	+90 to +140	4.9–6.1	1.0–3.7	5

Notes:
a) The emission reductions to meet a particular stabilisation level reported in the mitigation studies assessed here might be underestimated due to missing carbon cycle feedbacks (see also Topic 2.3).
b) Atmospheric CO_2 concentrations were 379ppm in 2005. The best estimate of total CO_2-eq concentration in 2005 for all long-lived GHGs is about 455ppm, while the corresponding value including the net effect of all anthropogenic forcing agents is 375ppm CO_2-eq.
c) Ranges correspond to the 15th to 85th percentile of the post-TAR scenario distribution. CO_2 emissions are shown so multi-gas scenarios can be compared with CO_2-only scenarios (see Figure 5.3).
d) The best estimate of climate sensitivity is 3°C.
e) Note that global average temperature at equilibrium is different from expected global average temperature at the time of stabilisation of GHG concentrations due to the inertia of the climate system. For the majority of scenarios assessed, stabilisation of GHG concentrations occurs between 2100 and 2150 (see also Footnote 21).
f) Equilibrium sea level rise is for the contribution from ocean thermal expansion only and does not reach equilibrium for at least many centuries. These values have been estimated using relatively simple climate models (one low-resolution AOGCM and several EMICs based on the best estimate of 3°C climate sensitivity) and do not include contributions from melting ice sheets, glaciers and ice caps. Long-term thermal expansion is projected to result in 0.2 to 0.6m per degree Celsius of global average warming above pre-industrial. (AOGCM refers to Atmosphere-Ocean General Circulation Model and EMICs to Earth System Models of Intermediate Complexity.)

Low stabilisation levels require early investments and substantially more rapid diffusion and commercialisation of advanced low-emissions technologies. *[5.5]*

Without substantial investment flows and effective technology transfer, it may be difficult to achieve emission reduction at a significant scale. Mobilising financing of incremental costs of low-carbon technologies is important. *[5.5]*

The macro-economic costs of mitigation generally rise with the stringency of the stabilisation target (Table 5.7). For specific countries and sectors, costs vary considerably from the global average.[22] *[5.6]*

In 2050, global average macro-economic costs for mitigation towards stabilisation between 710 and 445ppm CO_2-eq are between a 1% gain and 5.5% decrease of global GDP (Table 5.7). This corresponds to slowing average annual global GDP growth by less than 0.12 percentage points. *[5.6]*

---

[22] See Footnote 17 for more detail on cost estimates and model assumptions.

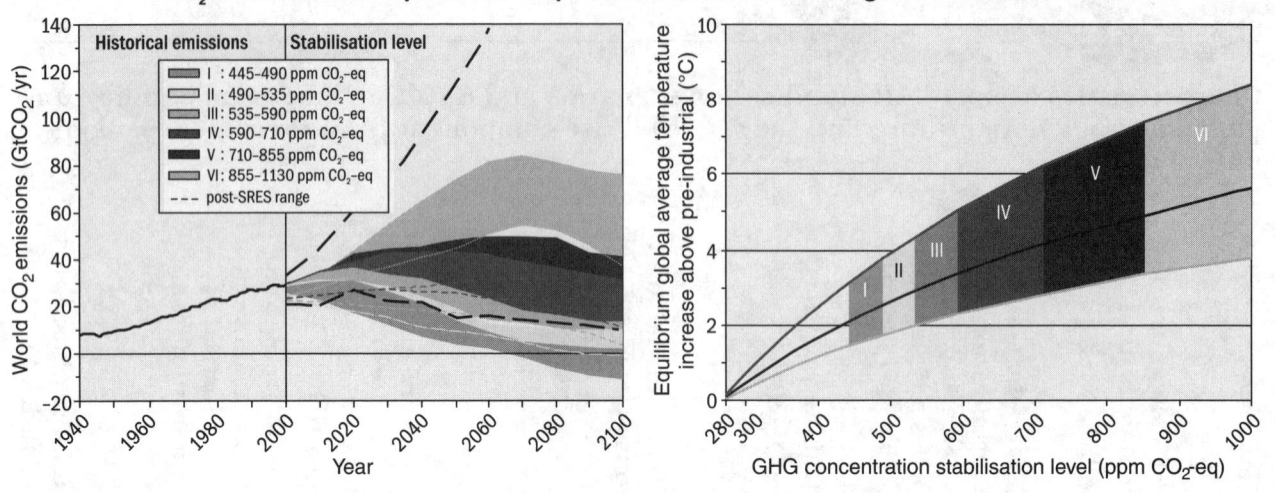

FIGURE 5.11 Global CO_2 emissions for 1940 to 2000 and emissions ranges for categories of stabilisation scenarios from 2000 to 2100 (left-hand panel); and the corresponding relationship between the stabilisation target and the likely equilibrium global average temperature increase above pre-industrial (right-hand panel). Approaching equilibrium can take several centuries, especially for scenarios with higher levels of stabilisation. Coloured shadings show stabilisation scenarios grouped according to different targets (stabilisation category I to VI). The right-hand panel shows ranges of global average temperature change above pre-industrial, using (i) 'best estimate' climate sensitivity of 3°C (black line in middle of shaded area), (ii) upper bound of likely range of climate sensitivity of 4.5°C (red line at top of shaded area) (iii) lower bound of likely range of climate sensitivity of 2°C (blue line at bottom of shaded area). Black dashed lines in the left panel give the emissions range of recent baseline scenarios published since the SRES (2000). Emissions ranges of the stabilisation scenarios comprise CO_2-only and multigas scenarios and correspond to the 10th to 90th percentile of the full scenario distribution. Note: CO_2 emissions in most models do not include emissions from decay of above ground biomass that remains after logging and deforestation, and from peat fires and drained peat soils. {Figure 5.1}

TABLE 5.7

Estimated global macro-economic costs in 2030 and 2050. Costs are relative to the baseline for least-cost trajectories towards different long-term stabilisation levels. {Table 5.2}

Stabilisation levels (ppm CO_2-eq)	Median GDP reduction[a] (%) 2030	2050	Range of GDP reduction[b] (%) 2030	2050	Reduction of average annual GDP growth rates) percentage points)[c,e] 2030	2050
445–535[d]	Not available		< 3	< 5.5	< 0.12	< 0.12
535–590	0.6	1.3	0.2 to 2.5	slightly negative to 4	< 0.1	< 0.1
590–710	0.2	0.5	−0.6 to 1.2	−1 to 2	< 0.06	< 0.05

Notes:
Values given in this table correspond to the full literature across all baselines and mitigation scenarios that provide GDP numbers.
a) Global GDP based on market exchange rates.
b) The 10th and 90th percentile range of the analysed data are given where applicable. Negative values indicate GDP gain. The first row (445-535ppm CO_2-eq) gives the upper bound estimate of the literature only.
c) The calculation of the reduction of the annual growth rate is based on the average reduction during the assessed period that would result in the indicated GDP decrease by 2030 and 2050 respectively.
d) The number of studies is relatively small and they generally use low baselines. High emissions baselines generally lead to higher costs.
e) The values correspond to the highest estimate for GDP reduction shown in column three.

> Responding to climate change involves an iterative risk management process that includes both adaptation and mitigation and takes into account climate change damages, co-benefits, sustainability, equity and attitudes to risk. *{5.1}*

Impacts of climate change are *very likely* to impose net annual costs, which will increase over time as global temperatures increase. Peer-reviewed estimates of the social cost of carbon[23] in 2005 average US$12 per tonne of CO_2, but the range from 100 estimates is large ($-$$3 to $95/$tCO_2$). This is due in large part to differences in assumptions regarding climate sensitivity, response lags, the treatment of risk and equity, economic and non-economic impacts, the inclusion of potentially catastrophic losses and discount rates.

Aggregate estimates of costs mask significant differences in impacts across sectors, regions and populations and *very likely* under-estimate damage costs because they cannot include many non-quantifiable impacts. *{5.7}*

Limited and early analytical results from integrated analyses of the costs and benefits of mitigation indicate that they are broadly comparable in magnitude, but do not as yet permit an unambiguous determination of an emissions pathway or stabilisation level where benefits exceed costs. *{5.7}*

Climate sensitivity is a key uncertainty for mitigation scenarios for specific temperature levels. *{5.4}*

Choices about the scale and timing of GHG mitigation involve balancing the economic costs of more rapid emission reductions now against the corresponding medium-term and long-term climate risks of delay. *{5.7}*

---

[23] Net economic costs of damages from climate change aggregated across the globe and discounted to the specified year.

Resolving the impasse in American energy policy: The case for a transformational R&D strategy at the U.S. Department of Energy

Benjamin K. Sovacool*

ABSTRACT

From its inception in 1977, the U.S. Department of Energy (DOE) has been responsible for maintaining the nation's nuclear stockpile, leading the country in terms of basic research, setting national energy goals, and managing thousands of individual programs. Despite these gains, however, the DOE research and development (R&D) model does not appear to offer the nation an optimal strategy for assessing long-term energy challenges. American energy policy continues to face constraints related to three 'I's": *inconsistency, incrementalism,* and *inadequacy*. An overly rigid management structure and loss of mission within the DOE continues to plague its programs and create *inconsistencies* in terms of a national energy policy. Various layers of stove-piping within and between the DOE and national laboratories continue to fracture collaboration between institutions and engender only slow, *incremental* progress on energy problems. And funding for energy research and development continues to remain *inadequate*, compromising the country's ability to address energy challenges. To address these concerns, an R&D organization dedicated to transformative, creative research is proposed.

1. Introduction

Imagine walking into a building where a hybrid, multi-functional solar-lighting system utilizes direct sunlight to provide part of its illumination and automatically switches on and off as you traverse down the hallway. Conceptualize a refinery that incorporates algae and other unconventional feed-stocks in its manufacturing of biofuel. Envision stepping into a fully automated personal land transit system that takes you effortlessly across town. Are each of these ideas eccentric and unconventional, perhaps even slightly far-fetched? Perhaps. But are they inherently *good* ideas? Are they even *possible*?

The U.S. Department of Energy (DOE) was created, in part, to answer basic questions concerning energy research and development (R&D). Established in 1977 to manage the nation's nuclear weapons complex, clean up the "environmental legacy" from the production and testing of nuclear weapons, and conduct R&D on energy and basic science, the DOE is a behemoth organization dedicated to an overwhelmingly complicated task: provide "the framework for a comprehensive and balanced national energy program." To meet its mission, the DOE controls a $23 billion budget, employs a workforce of 14,500 people and more than 100,000 contractors, and operates 50 major installations in 35 states. The DOE also directs a complex network of 24 national laboratories located in 14 states with an additional staff of 60,000 and a budget of $7.6 billion.[1]

---

[1] See U.S. National Science Foundation, *Federal Funds for Research and Development: Fiscal Year 2003–2005* (Washington, DC: NSF, 2005), p. 48; U.S. Department of Energy, *Protecting National, Energy, and Economic Security with Advanced Science and Technology and Ensuring Environmental Cleanup: The Department of Energy Strategic Plan*, August, 2003, available at http://www.nti.org/e_research/official_docs/doe/doe080603.pdf; and U.S. General Accounting Office, *Department of Energy: Fundamental Reassessment Needed to Address Major Mission, Structure, and Accountability Problems* (Washington, DC: GAO-02-51, December, 2001), p. 5.

"Resolving the impasse in American energy policy: The case for a transformational R&D strategy in the U.S. Department of Energy" by Benjamin K. Sovacool, from *Renewable and Sustainable Energy Reviews*, 13:8, pp. 346-361. Copyright © 2009 by Elsevier Science & Technology Journals. Reproduced with permission of Elsevier Science & Technology Journals in the format Textbook via Copyright Clearance Center.

Like all large institutions, the DOE has developed its own way of conducting research, and consequently its own research culture. The concept of culture has often taken specific institutional forms, such as the "national culture" of the state, the "market culture" of the economy, the "organizational culture" of the business firm, and the "medical culture" of doctors.[2] Indeed, Ludwig Fleck, Emile Durkheim, Thomas Kuhn, Derek de Sola Price, and Mary Douglas have long argued that different groups of scientists promote and believe in different cultural practices through "thought collectives," "paradigms," and "invisible colleges." For these authors, true solidarity is possible only to the extent that individuals share the categories of their thought, contradicting the basic axiom that sovereign actors always behave rationally.[3] Karin Knorr-Cetina notes that:

> Science and expert systems are obvious candidates for cultural division; they are pursued by groupings of specialists who are separated from other experts by institutional boundaries deeply entrenched in all levels of education, in most research organizations, in career choices, in our general systems of classification.[4]

It follows, then, that country's national laboratories have their own unique styles of research based on "external" or "non-scientific" factors such as the availability of financial and human resources, safety and security protocol, geography, the personalities of managers, and political support.[5]

But is the DOE model of R&D working, at least for the long-term? The DOE has been responsible for leading the country in terms of basic research and managing thousands of individual programs. Notable inventions within the past 10 years include the bio-mechanical pancreas (which uses a chemical glucose sensor to help patients manage diabetes), thin-film photovoltaic modules for roofs, and green solvents used for the bioremediation of toxic substances. In parallel, the past 30 years have seen incredible advances in energy technologies, ranging from more effective wind turbines, aero-derivative natural gas turbines, and bioelectric generators to hydrogen powered vehicles, co-generation units, clean coal systems and advanced nuclear reactors.

Yet, despite these gains, the DOE model does not appear to offer the nation an optimal strategy for assessing long-term, transformational risks that require creative, "out-of-the-box" thinking to handle them. An overly rigid management structure and loss of mission within the DOE continues to plague its programs and create inconsistencies in terms of a national energy policy. Various layers of stove-piping within and between the DOE and national laboratories continue to fracture collaboration between institutions and engender only slow, incremental progress on energy problems. Energy research and development continues to remain grossly under-funded in both the public and private sectors, greatly compromising the country's ability to address energy challenges and contributing to an overall loss of economic competitiveness. Each of these three trends—*inconsistent* short-term energy policies, *incrementalism* in the way the nation's scientists and engineers approach energy problems, and *inadequate* support of energy research and development—contributes directly to the country's energy *insecurity*, risking inflated energy prices, environmental degradation, and recurring energy crises.

To respond to these challenges, the country needs a new, independent organization within the DOE. The idea was first proposed in a 2006 National Academies report entitled *Rising Above the Gathering Storm*, which suggested that the DOE create an institution (called the Advanced Research Projects Agency-Energy, or ARPA-E) to sponsor transformational, creative research.[6] The proposal was drafted into legislation before the U.S. Senate (S. 2197—Protecting America's

---

[2] See Andrew Abbott, *The System of Professions: An Essay on the Division of Expert Labor* (Chicago: University of Chicago Press, 1988).

[3] See Mary Douglas, *How Institutions Think* (Syracuse: Syracuse University Press, 1986); Ludwig Fleck, *Genesis and Development of a Scientific Fact* (University of Chicago, 1979); Thomas S. Kuhn, *The Structure of Scientific Revolutions* (University of Chicago, 1962); Thomas S. Kuhn, *The Essential Tension: Selected Studies in Scientific Tradition and Change* (University of Chicago, 1977); and Derek de Sola Price and Donald Beaver, "Collaboration in an Invisible College," *American Psychologist* 21 (1966), p. 1011–1018.

[4] Karin Knorr-Cetina, *Epistemic Cultures: How the Sciences Make Knowledge* (Cambridge, MA: Harvard University Press, 1999), p. 2.

[5] See Hugh Gusterson, *Nuclear Rites: A Weapons Laboratory at the End of the Cold War* (University of California, 1996).

[6] National Academy of Sciences, *Rising Above the Storm: Energizing and Employing America for a Brighter Economic Future* (Washington, DC: National Academies Press, 2006).

Competitive Edge [PACE] Act—Energy), but failed to pass in March 2006. Based on similar organizations within the U.S. Department of Defense and the intelligence community, an ARPA-E like institution would need to conceptualize the R&D process differently than the DOE. It would have to be mission-oriented to focus on long-term, creative, transformational research and subscribe to an entirely different management philosophy.

The complete dependence of our modern culture on energy places it at a nexus of important concerns related to progress and modernity, nationalism, agriculture, industry, human needs and the environment. Yet while energy policy is indeed the primary focus of this investigation, do not be lulled into thinking that such an inquiry is just about energy. Assessing DOE research methods provides insight into how many of the country's best engineers and scientists conceptualize technology and innovation. Practitioners paint the national laboratories as a hot bed of innovation, where scientists and engineers rationally pursue the best scientific projects based on merit and fecundity.

Contrary to this view, social attitudes, interests, and values intricately shape DOE R&D agendas, which in turn mold technologies that profoundly shape society to better match those interests. The research system, as currently structured, not only condones small, incremental development but also actively encourages it. Program managers, more often than not, subtly prevent radical and progressive change, and innovative ideas regarding energy technologies are often subverted, or worse, ignored. In this way, the difficulties in motivating the DOE to conduct transformational research threaten to surface wherever large institutions attempt to produce knowledge, patronage complicates the R&D process, and the boundaries between science, technology, and society are being negotiated. The lessons here are not just for energy policymakers and research managers, but for anyone concerned with the difficulties of managing large, centralized networks of scientists and investigators, ranging from those working in the fields of aerospace and defense to biotechnology, pharmaceuticals, and telecommunications.

Ultimately, clashes over the optimal R&D pathway at the DOE and its national laboratories are preludes to a deeper clash about technological systems, or about what type of society we want to build. What seem on the surface to be merely technical debates over the different segments of an R&D strategy are also subtle and often invisible contests over social ideology. Donald MacKenzie reminds us that technological systems "should not be taken simply as given, as unproblematic features of the world; nor should the use of the term 'system' be taken to imply stability or lack of conflict. Systems are constructs and hold together only so long as the correct conditions prevail."[7] Therefore, the way that DOE research on energy technology redistributes social, political, and economic power is as important as how efficiently such technologies actually produce energy. It should come as no surprise, then, that the existing R&D pathways at the DOE surreptitiously impede radical change.

2. THE THREE "I'S" OF THE AMERICAN ENERGY IMPASSE
2.1. INCONSISTENCY

Contrary to a historical role as an incubator of energy technologies and a supporter of scientific research, the DOE and its national laboratories have been recently criticized for losing their sense of mission and ineffective management. DOE labs are said to be the most lacking in flexibility and cost effectiveness, resulting from an overly centralized, hierarchical and micromanaged resource allocation system.[8] Such criticism is usually based on three grounds: that the DOE's diverse mission creates an uncoordinated approach to energy problems; loss of mission is further compounded by a dysfunctional organizational structure; and as a result DOE research remains hindered by a weak culture of accountability.

As an example, the complicated nature of managing the nation's nuclear stockpile, cleaning up environmentally hazardous waste, and conducting basic and energy research have made programs within the DOE difficult to integrate. Separate energy, environmental, science, and

---

[7] Donald MacKenzie, "Missile Accuracy: A Case Study in the Social Process of Technological Change," In: Wiebe Bijker, Thomas P. Hughes, and Trevor Pinch (Eds.) *The Social Construction of Technological Systems: New Directions in the Sociology and History of Technology* (London: MIT Press, 1987), p. 197.

[8] Kenneth M. Brown, *Downsizing Science: Will the United States Pay a Price?* (Washington, DC: American Enterprise Institute Press, 1998).

national nuclear security staff tend to operate as isolated entities, each with their own operational styles and decision-making practices. This is affected partly by managerial style (some exercise strong central control over programmatic actions, others delegate responsibility) and partly by area of expertise (national security programs operate in secret, science programs attempt to be more open).[9] A 2003 Secretary of Energy task force assessing DOE science programs concluded that, as a result, "the mission of the Department of Energy is widely misunderstood and considered to be unclear and unstable" and the budgets of the national laboratories suffer from a historically poor reputation as "badly managed, excessively fragmented, and politically unresponsive."[10] Another influential report concluded that "there is neither an overarching strategic vision integrating and ensuring the comprehensiveness of the array of federal activities on energy research, development, and demonstration cooperation nor a mechanism for implementing such a vision in a coherent and efficient way."[11] Similarly, the Committee on Economic Development expressed concern about "mission creep in those sectors of the basic research establishment—particularly certain of the Department of Energy's national laboratories—that have completed or lost their mandates."[12] The lack of such vision only increases the likelihood that DOE grant solicitations will not match programmatic need.

Furthermore, the DOE suffers from an exceedingly complicated organizational structure connected to the sheer challenge of coordinating their vast network of field offices and national laboratories widely dispersed throughout the country. Within each individual organization, multiple levels of reporting exist vertically between management, group leaders, and research associates, and horizontally between the DOE, other laboratories, operations offices, and headquarters program offices. Unclear chains of command, weak integration of programs and functions, and confusion over staff roles remain common. In 1999, the Special Investigative Panel of the President's Foreign ntelligence Advisory Board noted that "convoluted, confusing, and often contradictory reporting channels have made the relationships between DOE headquarters and the laboratories, in particular, tense, internecine, and chaotic."[13]

The implications of this lack of coordination are manifold. Disharmony makes it difficult to detect inconsistencies within individual programs and almost impossible to coordinate the national laboratories to meet pressing nation-wide problems; programs instead tend to operate on a case-by-case basis. Applied research programs tend to be organized around fuel sources, such as coal, oil, nuclear, and natural gas, which increases the risk of isolating oil supply from transportation or fossil fuels from efficiency. Such isolation, in turn, promotes a tendency to focus on incremental or discrete technologies as opposed to systems that integrate research needs from supply to distribution to end use. Melanie Kenderline, Vice President for the Gas Technology Institute, argues that "in the final analysis, competition for funding from the same appropriation, bureaucratic separation, and different program cultures and performance measures ultimately work against optimum levels of cooperation and coordination across programs [at the DOE]."[14] Similarly, Jerome Hinkle recently told senators that "it is unlikely that a traditional federal agency structure could accomplish blending the necessary functions [to distribute promising technologies,] because they are often assigned to completely separate programs whose cooperation is incidental."[15]

Moreover, poor coordination makes it challenging to track and enforce laboratory reforms. A 2001 report from the National Resource

---

[9] U.S. General Accounting Office, *Department of Energy: Fundamental Reassessment Needed to Address Major Mission, Structure, and Accountability Problems* (Washington, DC: GAO-02-51, December, 2001).

[10] Secretary of Energy Advisory Board, *Critical Choices: Science, Energy, and Security* (Final Report of the Task Force on the Future of Science Programs at the Department of Energy), October 13, 2003, p. 12–15.

[11] John P. Holdren et al., *Powerful Partnerships: The Federal Role of International Cooperation on Energy Innovation* (Washington, DC: Office of Science and Technology Policy, 1999), p. ES-5.

[12] Committee on Economic Development, *America's Basic Research: Prosperity Through Discovery* (Washington, DC: CED, 1998), p. 2.

[13] Special Investigative Panel of the President's Foreign Intelligence Advisory Board, *Science At Its Best, Security At Its Worst: A Report on Security Problems at the U.S. Department of Energy*, 1999, available at http://www.hanford.gov/oci/maindocs/ci_r_docs/sciencebest.pdf.

[14] Melanie Kenderdine, "Should Congress Establish ARPA-E?" *Statement Before the Committee on Science, U.S. House of Representatives*, March 9, 2006, p. 4–5.

[15] Jerome Hinkle, "Assessing Progress in Advanced Technologies for Vehicles and Fuels," *Testimony Before the House Committee on Science*, June 5, 2006, p. 10–11.

Council assessing DOE research and development on energy technologies from 1978 to 2000 noted that "managers of both the energy efficiency and fossil energy research, development, and demonstration programs [at the Department of Energy] did not utilize a consistent methodology or framework for estimating and evaluating the benefits of the numerous projects within their programs."[16] Similarly, a 2000 report from the National Academies reviewing U.S. Department of Energy's renewable energy programs found that "Office of Power Technology's programs are not well integrated or coordinated but have operated as relatively separate groups with no common policy focus."[17] The 2000 National Academies report also accused DOE energy programs of having insufficient strategic planning and analysis, poor R&D project selection, inability to learn lessons from past failures, and weak coordination with other government agencies.[18] And a 1998 GAO report noted that the Department of Energy's national laboratories were "unfocused, micro-managed, and do not function as an integrated national research and development system."[19] The GAO accused the labs of duplicating private research, conducting programs that were fragmented and unrelated to the overall mission of the DOE, and an overall loss of coherence and effectiveness.

The aforementioned problems relating to loss of mission and confusing organizational structure have promoted a weak culture of accountability. Poorly performing contractors and staff are rarely held accountable for mistakes, and "mission creep" often complicates the termination of unsuccessful programs. For example, the Galvin Task Force was commissioned in 1995 by Secretary of Energy Hazel O'Leary to produce a 10-month study on the national laboratories. Their report concluded that "research culture at many of the laboratories has been influenced by their relative physical and intellectual isolation and by a sense of entitlement to research funds."[20] Because project managers tend only to work on their projects, they tend to self-perpetuating. As Ronald J. Sutherland and Jerry Taylor put it, "program goals are more likely to be technical than economic, and program managers are technical optimists about their own programs."[21]

A similar Brookings Institution study found that DOE managers are therefore more likely to be risk averse, and that the "overriding lesson" about the national laboratories is that they remain "so severely constrained by political forces that an effective, coherent national commercialization R&D program has never been put in place."[22] For instance, according to the GAO, the DOE has only once—at Brookhaven National Laboratory in 1997—fired a contractor for poor performance. Inflated staffing levels, in turn, complicate the ability to recruit and hire more qualified engineers and scientists. Prominent examples of programs that continued to receive funding long after they were determined technologically unfeasible include the Clinch River Breeder Reactor (a $2.5 billion demonstration liquid-metal fast breeder reactor plant), magnetohydrodynamics program (a $61 million fossil energy program attempting to use electromagnetic induction to produce electric power from coal), and the creation of the Synfuels Corporation (a $2.1 billion synthetic fuels program established in 1981 to develop alternatives to oil).[23]

2.2. INCREMENTALISM

In addition to promoting inconsistency, the DOE, and to a degree most American research institutions, "stove-pipes" research in at lease two ways: by relying on a linear, "assembly-line" model that segregates the stages of R&D; and by training scientists and engineers exclusively as "problem solvers," which contributes to them "working

---

[16] National Resource Council, *Energy Research at DOE: Was it Worth It? Energy Efficiency and Fossil Energy Research 1978–2000* (Washington, DC: National Academies Press, 2001), p. 7.

[17] Committee on Programmatic Review of the U.S. Department of Energy's Office of Power Technologies, *Renewable Power Pathways: A Review of the U.S. Department of Energy's Renewable Energy Programs* (Washington, DC: National Academies Press, 2000), p. 3.

[18] Ibid., p. 92–101.

[19] U.S. General Accounting Office, *Department of Energy: Uncertain Progress in Implementing National Laboratory Reforms* (Washington, DC: GAO/RCED-98-197, September, 1988), p. 1.

[20] Secretary of Energy Advisory Board, *Alternative Futures for the Department of Energy National Laboratories* (Washington, DC: Task Force on Alternative Futures for the Department of Energy National Laboratories, 1995), p. 41.

[21] Ronald J. Sutherland and Jerry Taylor, "Time to Overhaul Federal Energy R&D," *Policy Analysis* 424 (February 7, 2002), p. 7.

[22] Linda R. Cohen and Roger G. Noll, *The Technology Pork Barrel* (Washington, C: Brookings Institution, 1991), p. 378.

[23] Kelly Sims Gallagher, Robert Frosch, and John P. Holdren, "Management of Energy Technology Innovation Activities at the U.S. Department of Energy," *Report to the Belfer Center for Science and International Affairs*, September, 2004, available at http://bcsia.ksg.harvard.edu.

within the system" rather than challenging its fundamental assumptions.

Almost since the beginning of the 20th century, scientists, industrialists, researchers, managers, politicians, statisticians, and economists—along with universities, national laboratories, and organizations such as the National Science Foundation, National Research Council, and Organization for Economic Cooperation and Development—have subscribed to a linear, assembly line model of technological development. Such a model sharply divides research into stages, such as "basic" and "applied" research, "development," and "innovation." Whatever its name, the model has been "the very mechanism used for explaining innovation in the literature on technological change and innovation since the 1940s."[24]

The linear model of innovation gained popularity in the 1910s and 1920s, when academic and industrial natural scientists conceived of basic research as the source behind applied research and technology. It was during this phase that the ideal of pure science was articulated as a method of research performed without commercial or practical ends, a form of inquiry that benefits all of society and the good of humanity. Basic research was held to be distinct from applied science, a method directed towards practical or commercial gain, or the use of science to achieve some specific purpose or objective. Put another way, applied science is "pure science applied," or:

> The applied scientist as such is concerned with the task of discovering applications for pure theory. The technologist has a problem which lies a little nearer to practice. Both applied scientist and technologist employ experiment; but in the former case guided by hypotheses deduced from theory, while in the latter case employing trial and error or skilled approaches derived from concrete experience.[25]

Vannevar Bush subscribed to this type of thinking in his seminal *Science: The Endless Frontier*, where he equated college and university research as "basic" and industrial or government research as 'applied.' According to Bush:

> Basic research leads to new knowledge. It provides scientific capital. It creates the fund from which the practical applications of knowledge must be drawn. New products and new processes do not appear full-grown. They are founded on new principles and new conceptions, which in turn are painstakingly developed by research in the purest realms of science. Today, it is even truer that basic research is the pacemaker of technological progress.[26]

Such thinking develops a causal relationship between basic and applied research, placing the former as the foundation for scientific progress.

The notions of "development" and "innovation" were added to the linear model in the 1950s and 1960s. Business school researchers studying industrial management of R&D noted that "development" was often needed to take a new process or product from the laboratory to the stage where it was ready to manufacture on a large scale, or translating applied research findings into products and processes. Economists extended the three-phase model of basic research → applied research → development to production and diffusion under the concept of "innovation."[27]

In practice, such idyllic thinking compliments the way most DOE practitioners conceive of science, and is often used to justify rigid distinctions between basic research, applied research, and technological development.[28] Engineers and scientists working at the national laboratories often conclude that technology and technological

---

[24] Benoit Godin, "The Linear Model of Innovation: The Historical Construction of an Analytical Framework," *Science, Technology, & Human Values* 31(6) (November, 2006), p. 641.

[25] James K. Feibleman, "Pure Science, Applied Science, and Technology: An Attempt at Definitions," In: Carl Mitcham and Robert Mackey (Eds.) *Philosophy and Technology: Readings in the Philosophical Problems of Technology* (London: The Free Press, 1983), p. 36.

[26] In Edwin Layton, "Mirror-Image Twins: The Communities of Science and Technology in 19th-Century America," *Technology and Culture* 12(4) (October, 1971), p 563.

[27] See Benoit Godin, "The Linear Model of Innovation: The Historical Construction of an Analytical Framework," *Science, Technology, & Human Values* 31(6) (November, 2006), p. 639–667.

[28] For excellent investigations of the historical development of such distinctions between basic and applied science and the role of government in scientific research, see Bruce Smith, *American Science Policy Since World War II* (Washington, DC: Brookings Institution, 1990); A. Hunter Dupree, *Science in the Federal Government: A History of Policies and Activities* (Baltimore: Johns Hopkins University Press, 1986); Daniel Lee Kleinman, *Politics on the Endless Frontier: Postwar Research Policy in the United States* (London: Duke University Press, 1995); David M. Hart, *Forged Consensus: Science, Technology, and Economic Policy in the United States, 1921–1953* (Princeton, NJ: Princeton University Press, 2000); and Daniel J. Kevles, "The National Science Foundation and the Debate over Postwar Research Policy, 1942–1945," *ISIS* 68(241) (1977), p. 5–26.

development progress in a rational, ordered, and predictable manner. They see science and technology as an assembly line that begins with basic research, follows with development and marketing of a given technology, and ends with the product being purchased by consumers.[29] Such thinking structures technological development and diffusion into at least four separate levels: (1) a basic research phase; (2) an applied research or invention phase, in which other engineers actually create artifacts in laboratories, apply for patents, model the prototype, and test it; (3) a market phase, in which technology is then passed onto salespeople and managers; before (4) a consumption phase, in which technology is sold to the public, consumed, and perhaps modified by users. Put simply, the assembly line model suggests that engineers and scientists design technology, manufacturers produce it, salespeople sell it, and users use it.[30]

The "assembly-line model" of technical development holds immense appeal for scientists, engineers, managers, and policymakers for five reasons. First, it seems to explain the nature of technological development during World War II—where scientific research was conducted under the auspices of the military, and the diffusion of technology tended to occur along a linear pathway. Second, it served as a powerful rhetorical resource for various disciplinary groups attempting to establish, define, demarcate, or maintain their power over technological development. Scientists often referenced the model to justify financial support for projects; engineers to raise the status of their discipline; and industrialists to attract workers to their research organizations. Third, the model assuages a general wariness among scientists towards intrusive industrial policy, since the assembly-line model posits that technological diffusion is more or less automatic and unmanaged—and should thus be controlled by scientists rather than the state. Fourth, the model helps soften mainstream political fears of a loss of technological competitiveness, as it suggests a certain level of funding in "basic science" will always yield plentiful technological results.[31] And fifth, the model is attractive in its simplicity. Alternative models of diffusion—with their multiple feedback loops and triple helixes of knowledge dissemination—are perceived to be overly complicated, looking more like "modern artwork" or a "plate of spaghetti and meatballs" than useful descriptive frameworks.[32]

A research strategy for supporting novel energy technologies, the thinking goes, becomes relatively simple. Merely provide enough funding and support for basic research, and if a technology is truly possible, it can be developed by scientists and then diffused into the marketplace, where rational actors will seek to fully exploit its promise. Under this system, the role of the DOE is to support basic scientific research that industry will not. The model made perfect sense in an era characterized by mass production, expanding national markets, complicated but connected factory systems, and economies of scale. Susan Hockfield explains that "the corporations that dominated that economy were interested in incremental rather than radical innovation; technology was not intended to be, as we now put it, 'disruptive;' and we built great industry lab systems to support incremental innovation."[33]

Now, however, distinctions between basic and applied science have become so blurred that the model no longer makes sense.[34] The historical record seems to disprove any sharp distinction between basic and applied research. Otto Mayr argues that such boundaries remain incongruent because many "scientists" such as William

---

[29] Brian Elliott, "Introduction," In: Brian Elliott (Ed.) *Technology and Social Process* (Edinburgh: Edinburgh University Press, 1988), p. 3; George Wise, "Science and Technology," *Osiris* 1 (1985), p. 229.

[30] Wiebe Bijker, "The Social Construction of Fluorescent Lighting, or How an Artifact Was Invented in its Diffusion Stage," In: Wiebe Bijker and John Law (Eds.) *Shaping Technology/Building Society: Studies in Sociotechnical Change* (Cambridge, MA: MIT Press, 1992), p. 76.

[31] See David H. Guston, "Stabilizing the Boundary between US Politics and Science: The Role of the Office of Technology Transfer as a Boundary Organization," *Social Studies of Science* 29(1) (February, 1999), p. 87–111, especially 93–94.

[32] Benoit Godin, "The Linear Model of Innovation: The Historical Construction of an Analytical Framework," *Science, Technology, & Human Values* 31 (6) (November, 2006), p. 660.

[33] Susan Hockfield, "The University in the U.S. Innovation System," Presentation at the Bernard L. Schwartz Forum on U.S. Competitiveness in the 21st Century, Brookings Institution, Washington, DC, April 26, 2006, available at http://web.mit.edu/hockfield/speech-brookings.html.

[34] Everett Mendelsohn, "Science, Scientists, and the Military," In: John Krige and Dominique Pestre (Eds.) *Science in the Twentieth Century* (London: Harwood Academic Publishers, 1997), p. 176.

Thompson the Baron of Kelvin, Galileo Galilei, and Gottfried Leibniz became famous as contributors to technology, yet many "engineers" such as Leonardo da Vinci and James Watt became famous in science. Mayr suggests that:

> The words 'science' and 'technology' are useful precisely because they serve as vague umbrella terms that roughly and impressionistically suggest general areas of meaning without precisely defining their limits. Most successfully the words are used in conjunction; 'science and technology' together refer to an entity that actually exists in our civilization but which is impossible to divide into two parts, 'science' and 'technology.' Within this whole the two words only set accents, referring to two sets of general styles and approaches that are contrasting as well as complimentary.[35]

The only benefit of distinguishing between types of basic and applied research, Mayr concludes, is the strategic flexibility the terms offer in supporting each other.

Indeed, history is replete with instances of technologies that have emerged without preceding theoretical work in science. As one classic example, consider the work of D.S.L. Cardwell on 18th century power technologies. Cardwell argues that steam engines emerged as successful technologies more than a century before the science of thermodynamics became formulated.[36] David Nye notes that changes in barometric pressure in early coal mines were suspected before they could be explained scientifically.[37] Semiconductor electronics existed before the specifics of semiconductor physics were fully comprehended.[38] Thus, Derek De sola Price is quick to reject that technology is applied knowledge, stating that "inventions do not hang like fruits on a scientific tree."[39] Instead, technologies emerge in a nonlinear and unpredictable fashion that depends deeply on the way that a system challenges, rearranges, or supports social and technical arrangements.

Additionally, distinctions between the stages of R&D appear to be more a product of human interpretation rather than historical fact or natural law. In the 1960s the Department of Defense commissioned Project Hindsight in an attempt to better understand the technological R&D process. Project Hindsight took 8 years to complete and employed forty people to analyze some 700 contributions or "events" resulting from science and technology in an attempt to better distinguish basic research, applied research, and technology. Surprisingly, the study found that 91% of events were considered "technological," with only 9% classified as "science." And of that 9%, only 0.3% was considered "basic research."[40] Thus, the study suggests that the unidirectional relationship posited by the assembly line model is unable to fully explain the course of technological development and innovation.

Furthermore, a second form of "stove-piping" relates to how most scientists and engineers are trained to think as "problem solvers." The American engineering profession became formulated in an early context in which national progress had come to be measured in terms of the private-sector production of low cost goods for mass consumption.[41] As American engineering practices gained association with mass industrial production, practitioners continued to narrow the engineering field to focus only on core technical issues relating to science and technology.[42] The American response to Sputnik

---

[35] Otto Mayr, "The Science-Technology Relationship as a Historiographic Problem," *Technology and Culture* 17(4) (October, 1976), p. 668–669.

[36] D.S.L. Cardwell, "Power Technologies and the Advance of Science, 1700–1825," *Technology and Culture* 6(2) (Spring, 1965), p. 188–207.

[37] David Nye, *Consuming Power: A Social History of American Energies* (Cambridge, MA: MIT Press, 1999), p. 86.

[38] Susan Hockfield, "The University in the U.S. Innovation System," *Presentation at the Bernard L. Schwartz Forum on U.S. Competitiveness in the 21st Century*, Brookings Institution, Washington, DC, April 26, 2006, available at http://web.mit.edu/hockfield/speech-brookings.html.

[39] Derek J. de S. Price, "The Parallel Structures of Science and Technology," In: Barry Barnes and David Edge (Eds.) *Science in Context: Readings in the Sociology of Science* (London: Open University Press, 1982), p. 169–170.

[40] Edwin Layton, "Mirror-Image Twins: The Communities of Science and Technology in 19th-Century America," *Technology and Culture* 12(4) (October, 1971), p. 564.

[41] See Gary Downey, "Are Engineers Losing Control of Technology? From Problem Solving to Problem Definition and Solution in Engineering Education," *Chemical Engineering Research and Design* 83(6) (2005), p. 585; and Eda Kranakis, *Constructing a Bridge: An Exploration of Engineering Culture, Design, and Research in Nineteenth-Century France and America* (Cambridge, MA: MIT Press, 1997).

in 1960s and 1970s redefined this technical core to include science-based problem solving for society's needs. Everything else was relegated as a "soft skill" and set to the periphery.[43]

However, defining engineering in this way conditions engineers to become problem solvers but not problem definers. Gary Downey and Juan Lucena elaborate that:

> As students become transformed into engineering problem solvers, what gets weeded out is everything else. That is, engineering students experience a compelling demand to separate the work part of their lives from the non-work parts. Work is about rigorously applying the engineering method to gain control over technology and is simply not about any other stuff. Budding engineers can have the other stuff in their lives, but not in their practices as engineers.[44]

Problem solving is judged to be wholly technical (and thus within the exclusive field of engineering), whereas defining and assessing problems is said to be non-technical, and therefore unimportant.[45] As Ken Adler put it, "The immediate purview of engineering is technological design ... In this sense, engineering denies history. It has no sympathy with the conflict, compromise, and happenstance that brought the world to its present state."[46] In other words, engineers are trained to think in terms that bias the present, and presume that technological development is synonymous with progress.

Consequently, American engineers are supposed to respond to calls from society "much like a consultant responds to clients."[47] This disciplines them to a method that draws sharp boundaries between social problems and technical solutions. The result is that most engineers think narrowly in terms of their area of expertise; they think in incremental rather than progressive terms; and they solve problems that they are assigned, rather than thinking creatively and devising transformational research solutions, Joe Loper argues that since big, revolutionary projects at the DOE are structurally impossible, "only small things are doable, so you end up with a bunch of little doable policies that will result in no real impact."[48] Thomas Petersik, a former analyst for the U.S. Energy Information Administration, adds that American energy policy can best be characterized by "a series of baby steps in many directions, carefully avoiding any fundamental movements on anything."[49]

2.3. Inadequacy

In addition to inadvertently condoning inconsistency and incrementalism in its research, the federal government continues to under-fund energy and science R&D. The American Association for the Advancement of Science reports that federal funding of research in the physical sciences as a percentage of the country's gross domestic product (GDP) was 45% less in 2004 than in 1976.[50] A similar National Academies report noted that federal funding for environmental sciences, physical sciences, mathematics and engineering shrank from more than 15% (in real terms) from 1994 to 2003.[51] From 1985 to 1994, total U.S. expenditures

---

[42] See David Hounshell, *From the American System to Mass Production, 1800–1933: The Development of Manufacturing Technology in the United States* (Baltimore: Johns Hopkins University Press, 1984); David F. Noble, *Forces of Production: A Social History of Industrial Automation* (New York: Alfred Knopf, 1984); Thomas J. Misa, *A Nation of Steel: The Making of Modern America, 1865–1925* (Baltimore: Johns Hopkins University Press, 1995); and Gary Downey and Juan Lucena, "When Students Resist: Ethno-graphy of a Senior Design Experience in Engineering Education," *International Journal of Engineering Education* 19(1) (2003), p. 168–176.

[43] See, for instance, National Academy of Engineering, *The Engineer of 2020: Visions of Engineering in the New Century* (Washington, DC: National Academies Press, 2004), p. 43.

[44] Gary Lee Downey and Juan C. Lucena, "Engineering Selves: Hiring into a Contested Field of Education," In: G. L. Downey and J. Dumit (Eds.) *Cyborgs and Citadels: Interventions in Emerging Sciences and Technologies* (Sante Fe, NM: School of American Research Press, 1997), p. 128.

[45] See Gary Downey and Juan Lucena, "Are Globalization, Diversity, and Leadership Variations of the Same Problem? Moving Problem Definition to the Core," *Distinguished Lecture to the American Society for Engineering Education*, Chicago, Illinois, available at http:www.asee.org/chicago2006/.

[46] Ken Adler, *Engineering the Revolution: Arms and Enlightenment in France, 1763–1815* (Princeton, NJ: Princeton University Press, 1997), p. 15.

[47] Gary Downey, "Are Engineers Losing Control of Technology? From Problem Solving to Problem Definition and Solution in Engineering Education," *Chemical Engineering Research and Design* 83(6) (2005), p. 586.

[48] In Benjamin K. Sovacool, *The Power Production Paradox: Revealing the Socio-technical Impediments to Distributed Generation Technologies* (Blacks-burg, VA: Virginia Tech, Doctoral Dissertation, April 17, 2006), p. 164, available at http://scholar.lib.vt.edu/theses/available/etd-04202006-172936/, p. 260.

[49] Ibid, p. 289.

[50] American Association for the Advancement of Science, *Trends in the Federal Research by Discipline, FY 1976-2004*, available at http://www.aaas.org/spp/rd/discip04c.pdf.

on energy R&D decreased from $7 billion per year to $5 billion (in 1995 dollars). During that time, the federal government invested only approximately 3% of total R&D expenditures on energy, even though energy industries contribute more than 8% to the country's gross domestic product.[52] And while federal R&D in technology reached $132 billion in 2005, it continued to be concentrated in the fields of defense, homeland security, and the space program (See Fig. 1).[53]

Federal funding for R&D in efficiency measures, distributed generation, and renewable energy technologies, for instance, have declined as a portion of real gross domestic product by more than 70% over the past 10 years.[54] After funding for such technologies peaked in 1980 at $1.3 billion, it declined to $560 million in 1980 and just under $140 million in 1990, after which funding stabilized at around $200 million (see Figs. 2 and 3).

As Kurt Yeager, former president of the Electric Power Research Institute, remarked, "Today the United States invests at a lower rate than its major international competitors . . . Federal energy-related R&D has declined significantly."[55]

This decline in public support for energy research and development has continued even though multiple studies have shown that the benefits of R&D in the energy sector far outweigh its costs. For instance, Robert N. Schock et al. estimate just the *insurance* value of energy R&D per year (in 1999 dollars)—the contribution of research towards fighting climate change, minimizing oil price shocks, fighting urban air pollution, and minimizing energy disruptions—at more than $12 billion, even though it cost the government only $1.5 billion.[56]

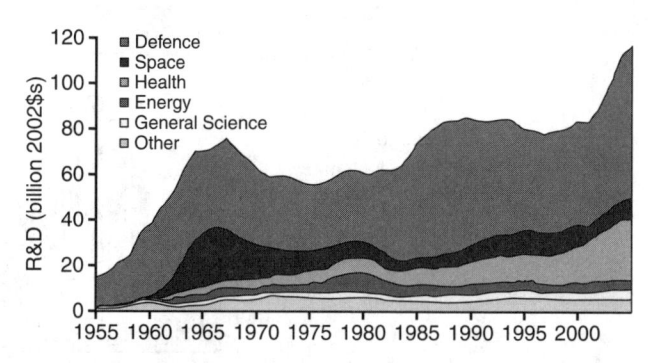

FIGURE 5.12 Fig. 1. U.S. Federal Research and Development, 1955–2004[93].

[93] *Source:* Robert M. Margolis and Daniel Kammen, "Underinvestment: The Energy Technology and R&D Policy Challenge," *Science* 285(5428), p. 690–692. Used with permission.

Recent events in the energy sector—such as the restructuring of the electric utility industry and increased competition—make it unlikely that the industry will be able to compensate for public underinvestment. Restructuring of the electric utility industry and the repeal of the Public Utilities Holding Company Act of 1935 (PUHCA) has only increased the incentive for companies and firms to invest in short-term technologies with rapid financial returns. A 1999 Office of Science and Technology Policy report cautioned that:

" Privatization, deregulation, and restructuring of energy industries . . . can lead to neglect of the ways the composition and operation of energy systems affect the wider public interest (including meeting the basic needs of the poor, as well as addressing other macroeconomic, environmental, and international security needs).[57]

A resulting gap between what the private sector does and what society's interests require continues to emerge.

As a result, energy R&D *intensity*—expenditures for energy R&D as a percentage of the utility's total sales for 1 year—among energy companies averages 0.3%, compared to an average industrial benchmark of 3.1%. The U.S. National Association of Regulatory Utility

---

[51] National Academies, *Engineering Research and America's Future: Meeting the Challenges of a Global Economy* (Washington, DC: National Academies Press, 2005).

[52] Robert N. Schock et al., "How Much is Energy Research & Development Worth as Insurance?" *Annual Review of Energy and Environment* 24 (1999), p.488.

[53] Adam Segal, "Is America Losing Its Edge? Innovation in a Globalized World," *Foreign Affairs* 83(6) (2004), p. 2–8.

[54] See Woodrow Clark and William Isherwood, "Distributed Generation: Remote Power Systems With Advanced Storage Technologies," *Energy Policy* 32 (2004), p. 1573–1589; S. Julio Friedman and Thomas Homer-Dixon, "Out of the Energy Box," *Foreign Affairs* 83(6) (2004), p. 72–83.

[55] Kurt E. Yeager, "Electricity Deregulation and Implications for R&D and Renewables," *Hearing Before the Subcommittee on Energy and Environment of the House Committee on Science*, March 31, 1998, p. 57.

[56] Robert N. Schock, William Fulkerson, Merwin Brown, Robert San martin. David Greene, and Jae Edmonds, "How Much is Energy Research & Development Worth as Insurance?" *Annual Review of Energy and Environment* 24 (1999), p. 487–512.

[57] John P. Holdren et al., *Powerful Partnerships: The Federal Role of International Cooperation on Energy Innovation* (Washington, DC: Office of Science and Technology Policy, 1999), p. ES-4.

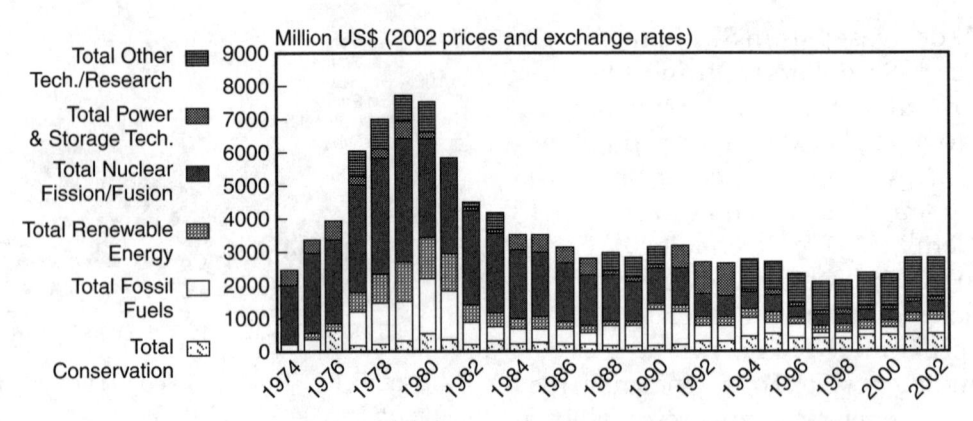

FIGURE 5.12 U.S. Government Research and Development on Energy Technologies, 1974–2002[94].

[94] Source: International Energy Agency, *Renewable Energy RD&D Priorities: Insights from IEA Technology Programs* (Paris: OECD Publishing, 2004), p. 646. Figure used with permission.

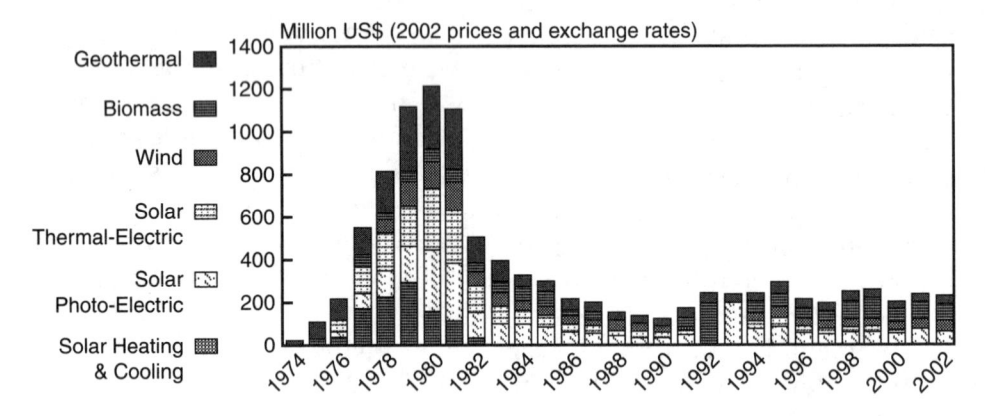

FIGURE 5.13 U.S. Government Research and Development on Renewable Energy, 1974–2002[95].

[95] Source: International Energy Agency, *Renewable Energy RD&D Priorities: Insights from IEA Technology Programs* (Paris: OECD Publishing, 2004), p. 646. Figure used with permission.

Commissioners has traditionally recommended that utilities devote at least 1.0% of their sales to energy R&D.[58] Yet increased competition means that companies are likely to make investments only in short-term products that have better discount rates, lower risk, and perceived better financial return to the company's investors. It also means that, in order to prepare for competition, many utilities cut investment in discretionary spending. Because restructuring generally attempts to eliminate rate of return regulation and integrated resource planning with price caps, it further decreases the incentive for utilities to conduct energy research and development.[59]

For instance, during the late 1990s, utilities drastically cut R&D spending on energy technologies to prepare for restructuring and impending competition. A 1998 study conducted by the U.S. Government Accountability Office (GAO) concluded that "increased competition from restructuring was cited as the primary reason for the biggest cutbacks in research to date by utilities in California, New York, and Florida."[60] The revocation of PUHCA could accelerate this trend, since the financial consolidation of utilities and holding companies will likely convince utilities to shift the

---

[58] JJ. Dooley, "Unintended Consequences: Energy R&D in a Deregulated Energy Market," *Energy Policy* 26(7) (1998), p. 547–555.

[59] See Benjamin K. Sovacool, "PUHCA Repeal: Higher Prices, Less R&D, and More Market Abuses?" *Electricity Journal* 19(1) (January/February, 2006), p. 85–89; Steve Nadel and Marty Kushler, "Public Benefits Funds: A Key Strategy for Advancing Energy Efficiency," *Electricity Journal* 13(10) (October, 2000), p. 76.

[60] In Victor S. Rezendes, "Electricity Deregulation and Implications for R&D and Renewables," *Hearing Before the Subcommittee on Energy and Environment of the House Committee on Science*, March 31, 1998, p. 97.

focus of their R&D from collaborative projects benefiting society to proprietary R&D giving their affiliates a competitive edge. Empirically, the GAO has noted that when utilities must consolidate, the result is "slowing technology development, sacrificing future prosperity to meet short-term goals, and failing to meet national energy goals."[61] Or, as Robert Margolis and Daniel Kammin put it succinctly, "the energy sector dangerously underinvests relative to other technology intensive sectors of the economy."[62] R&D investments made by all energy companies, for instance, have declined 50% between 1991 and 2003.[63]

Subsequently, indicators confirm that the nation's economic competitiveness is deteriorating. According to the U.S. National Science Foundation, in 2001 the country became a net importer of advanced technologies. The nation's trade balance in high technology products—computers, office equipment, chemicals, communication equipment, electronic components, instruments, and data processing services—shifted from a positive $54 billion in 1990 to negative $50 billion in 2001.[64] Furthermore, from June 2005 to June 2006, the United States suffered a trade deficit of approximately $814.7 billion.[65] Data from the Organization for Economic Cooperation and Development marked 2005 as the first year that Japan, Finland, and Sweden surpassed the United States as the world leader in terms of research and development intensity—the amount the country spends as a whole on research compared to GDP.[66] Richard M. Jones from the American Institute of Physics put it simply by noting that:

> As a result, Europe and Asia are threatening America's dominance in the physical sciences as measured by the number of patents won, articles submitted to scientific journals, degrees awarded, Nobel prizes won, or the percentage of GDP dedicated to research and development. Furthermore, test scores show that American youth, as they progress through the education system, fall further and further behind their counterparts in other counties, especially when it comes to math and science.[67]

This could be why the *New York Times* reported in 2004 that low-wage employers like Wal-Mart and McDonald's (who tend to pay unskilled workers $8 an hour) created 44% of the country's new jobs, whereas high-wage employers (who tend to pay educated workers more than $25 an hour) created only 29% of new jobs.[68] Robert Blecker, an economist at American University, summed it up concisely by stating that "in recent decades, the United States position has eroded on every front. The U.S. has clearly lost its unique dominance in the field of technological innovation."[69]

The collective result of diminishing private and public research is an inevitable crisis of economic competitiveness. Norman Augustine, former Chief Executive Officer of Lockheed Martin, told senators in 2005 that "it is the unanimous view of our committee that America today faces a serious and intensifying challenge with regard to its future competitiveness and standard of living. Further, we appear to be on a losing path."[70] The American Electronics Association reached a similar conclusion when they stated that:

> We are slipping. Yes, the United States still leads in nearly every way one can measure, but that does not change the fact that the foundation on which this lead was built is eroding. Our leadership in technology and innovation has benefited from an infrastructure created by 50 years of continual investment, education,

---

[61] Ibid, p. 94–107.

[62] Robert M. Margolis and Daniel Kammen, "Underinvestment: The Energy Technology and R&D Policy Challenge," *Science* 285(5428), p. 690–692.

[63] Daniel M. Kammen and Gregory F. Nemet, "Reversing the Incredible Shrinking Energy R&D Budget," *Issues in Science & Technology* (Fall, 2005), p. 84.

[64] National Science Board, *Science and Engineering Indicators 2004* (Arlington, VA: National Science Foundation, 2004), p. A6-5.

[65] *The Economist*, "Trade, Exchange Rates and Budgets," 380(8485) (July 8, 2006), p. 93.

[66] Organization for Economic Cooperation and Development, *Science, Technology, and Industry Scoreboard: 2005*, available at http://www.oecd.org/dataoecd/18/21/35471711.pdf.

[67] Richard M. Jones, "Building Support in the House for the DOE Office of Science," April 12, 2005, available at http://www.aip.org/fyi/2005/054.html.

[68] Steve Roach, "More Jobs, Worse Work," *New York Times*, July 22, 2004, p. A21.

[69] Robert A. Blecker, "The Trade Deficit and U.S. Competitiveness," In: Candace Howes and Ajit Singh (Eds.) *Competitiveness Matters: Industry and Economic Performance in the United States* (Ann Arbor, MI: University of Michigan Press, 2000), p. 53–54.

[70] Norman Augustine, "Rising Above the Gathering Storm," *Statement Before the Committee on Science, U.S. House of Representatives*, October 20, 2006, p. 2.

Table 5.8

Comparing incremental vs. transformative R&D

Incremental R&D	Transformational R&D
Emphasis on refining existing technology	Looks beyond existing technologies to tomorrow's needs and requirements
Operates within traditional programs and offices	Does not follow prescribed orthodoxy
Tends to alter processes and materials rather than systems	Tends to alter entire technological systems
Promotes incremental and cumulative change	Promotes radical and transformative change

and research. We are no longer maintaining this infrastructure.[71]

Correspondingly, the country faces an urgent need for high quality research and development in basic science and energy—two core areas of the DOE. The National Academy of Sciences (2005) recently concluded that "without high-quality, knowledge-intensive jobs and the innovative enterprises that lead to discovery and new technology, our economy will suffer and our people will face a lower standard of living."[72] Zalmay Khalilzad, the former American ambassador to Afghanistan, has argued that "to remain the preponderant world power, U.S. economic strength must be enhanced ... by generating and using superior science and technology."[73] And Wendy H. Schacht, senior researcher for the Congressional Research Service, has noted that "over the long run, enhanced technologies and manufacturing techniques can be very important for increasing productivity and economic growth."[74] In this way, inadequate funding of research and development on energy technologies greatly contributes to the deteriorating competitiveness of the U.S. economy.

3. Proposing a solution: the creation of ARPA-E

Collectively, inconsistent energy policies, incremental progress on energy technologies, and inadequate support of energy institutions have made the country increasingly susceptible to recurring energy crises. Rising energy demand yet stagnating supply, growing volatility of energy markets, increasing dependence on foreign supplies of fuel, a degrading electric transmission and distribution grid, and continually mounting environmental costs of energy production and consumption—demand a robust and sustained research strategy on energy technologies. As Stephen Chu, Director of the Lawrence Berkeley National Laboratory, succinctly stated, "The energy problem is *the single most important problem* that has to be solved by science and technology in the coming decades"[75]

One would think that the sheer magnitude of the energy problems facing society would spur quick, decisive action yielding profuse and ecumenical solutions. Instead, the problems with the current method of thinking merely recur. This is partly because, unlike the beginning of the Great Depression on October 29, 1929, the December 7, 1941 attack on Pearl Harbor, the Soviet launch of Sputnik on October 4, 1951, the explosion of the *Challenger* Space Shuttle on January 28, 1986, and the September 11, 2001 terrorist attacks on the World Trade Center and Pentagon, there is no "crisis like moment" to spur public sentiment and political action. Instead, we have what William A. Wulf, President of the National Academy of

---

[71] American Electronics Association, *Losing the Competitive Advantage? The Challenge for Science and Technology in the United States* (Washington, DC: AEA, 2005).

[72] National Academy of Sciences, *Rising Above the Storm: Energizing and Employing America for a Brighter Economic Future* (Washington, DC: National Academies Press, 2006), p. 3.

[73] Zalmay Khalilzad, "Losing the Moment? The United States and the World After the Cold War," *The Washington Quarterly* 18(2) (Spring, 1995), p. 84–102.

[74] Wendy H. Schacht, "Manufacturing, Technology, and Competitiveness," In: Wendy H. Schacht (Ed.) *Critical Technology* (New York: Penny Hill Press, 2000), p. 46.

[75] Stephen Chu, "Should Congress Establish ARPA-E?" *Statement Before the Committee on Science, U.S. House of Representatives*, March 9, 2006, p. 3.

Engineering, calls a "creeping crisis."[76] Like each of the "proverbial blind beggars" feeling an individual part of an elephant, the public and many federal offices hear about nuclear security, energy security, alternative energy sources, national laboratories, and big computers, but are left with no sense of an urgent, coherent mission to quickly integrate or synergize American energy research.[77]

To respond to these challenges, a new type of organization called the Advanced Research Projects Agency-Energy (ARPA-E) should be created. ARPA-E would fundamentally differ from any other existing organization conducting energy research in four ways: (1) it would focus exclusively on transformational R&D; (2) it would be mission-oriented to focus on broad technology challenges rather than narrow technological programs, thus escaping the technical "problem-solver" mentality of most engineers; (3) it would make no distinction between basic and applied research, instead promoting technologies until they are completely diffused into the marketplace; and (4) it would operate according to an innovative institutional structure to avoid many of the problems plaguing DOE research practices.

3.1. An exclusive focus on transformational R&D

The essential difference between energy R&D with radical/creative and traditional/conventional properties concerns a distinction between incremental and transformative research. *Incremental* R&D focuses on refining existing technology, fits neatly into established programs and offices, and tends to produce change at the process and material level, rather than the systems level. In contrast, *transformational* R&D focuses on looking beyond today's needs and requirements, challenges conventional program structure, and produces change at the systems level (see Table 1).

Philosophically, the same institution can conduct both incremental and transformational research. Admittedly, the national laboratories occasionally produce transformational breakthroughs in technological systems. However, in a world of limited resources and rigid institutional frameworks the two are mutually exclusive. Most program managers tend to choose an incremental research strategy because it is much safer: it can more easily appease sponsors, it is less risky, it fits into convention, and it promotes the existing R&D system of which the researchers are a part of.

The difference between incremental and transformational R&D parallels a debate in the 1970s between soft and hard energy paths. In his widely synthetic work, Amory Lovins commented that the dominant energy strategy for the country was "strength through exhaustion," or simply expanding supplies of energy to meet the extrapolated demands of a dynamic economy, treating those demands as homogeneous—as aggregated numbers representing total energy in a given year. Such a strategy, termed the *hard* path, utilized large, mammoth, centralized fossil-fuel and nuclear facilities to meet energy demand. The hard strategy was subscribed to by the federal government, energy companies, and energy think tanks such as the Edison Electric Institute and Electric Power Research Institute.[78]

Lovins argued that hard path suffered from a number of significant problems. Large generators cannot be mass produced. Their centralization requires costly distribution systems. They are inefficient, often not recycling excess thermal energy. They are much less reliable, unreliability being a graver fault that requires more and costlier reserve capacity. They take much longer to build, and are therefore exposed to escalated interest costs, mistimed demand forecasts, and wage pressure by unions. Ultimately, the hard energy path is woefully inefficient. To heat water to thousands of degrees to produce steam that turns a turbine, generates electricity, and transmits that electricity over a hundred miles only so that someone can boil water a few hundred degrees is "like cutting butter with a chainsaw—which is inelegant, expensive, messy, and dangerous."[79]

---

[76] William A. Wulf, "Remarks on Rising Above the Gathering Storm," *Statement Before the Committee on Science, U.S. House of Representatives*, October 20, 2005, p. 3.

[77] Secretary of Energy Advisory Board, *Critical Choices: Science, Energy, and Security* (Final Report of the Task Force on the Future of Science Programs at the Department of Energy), October 13, 2003, p. 12.

[78] See Amory Lovins, "Energy Strategy—The Road Not Taken?" *Foreign Affairs* 55 (1976–1977), p. 65–96; Amory Lovins, *Soft Energy Paths: Towards a Durable Peace* (New York: Harper Collins, 1979); and Amory Lovins, "A Target Critics Can't Seem to Get in Their Sights," In: Hugh Nash (Ed.) *The Energy Controversy: Soft Path Questions and Answers* (San Francisco: Friends of the Earth, 1979), p. 15–34.

[79] Amory Lovins, "A Target Critics Can't Seem to Get in Their Sights," In: Hugh Nash (Ed.) *The Energy Controversy: Soft Path Questions and Answers* (San Francisco: Friends of the Earth, 1979), p. 26.

In contrast, Lovins proposed a *soft* path promoting energy technologies that were (a) diverse, providing energy in smaller quantities from decentralized sources; (b) renewable, operating on non-depleteable fuels; (c) simple, or relatively easy to understand; (d) modular, or matched in scale to energy needs; and (e) qualitative, or matched in energy quality to end-use needs. Basically, a decision about the pursuit of hard versus soft energy paths boils down to a set of two questions: Do we want a small to medium scale, decentralized energy system that is more efficient, subject to local control by the same people who want the energy, operates with minimal disruption of ecological services, remains resilient to disruptions and terrorist assaults, is equally available to all future generations, highly beneficial to developing countries and truly renewable? Or do we want a plutonium or fossil fuel economy, centrally administered by a technical elite, sure to promote international proliferation and increase inequity and vulnerability, which increases the dependence of poor countries on rich countries, requires garrison-like security measures at many points in the fuel cycle, wastefully generates and distributes energy at too high a quality, must be uselessly degraded to fit the majority of end uses, and remains based on highly uncertain projections about fuel availability and capacity factors?

The point is that the true contest between hard and soft energy paths had little to do with the technologies themselves. It had much more to do with the way that energy policymakers *thought* about energy. In a theoretical sense, the soft and hard paths are both possible, and can be pursued simultaneously. One could conceivably integrate a soft energy technology—a collection 1 kW solar panels, for instance—with a hard energy technology—on the cooling tower of a 1000 MW nuclear facility. Yet while hard and soft paths may not be theoretically exclusive, they are still "culturally and institutionally antagonistic."[80] The tools required for each inhibit the availability of the other. "Soft and hard paths are culturally incompatible," Lovins concluded, since "each path entails a certain evolution of social values and perceptions that makes the other kind of world harder to imagine."[81]

Moreover, the choice between hard and soft paths also requires completely different orders of thinking. Two distinctions must be made—one between deciding whether to live off of natural capital or income; another between tactics and strategy. A policy based on depleting fossil fuels and polluting the environment more than just "different" than one utilizing non-depleting and non-polluting ones. Obviously, it will always be seemingly cheaper and easier to live off natural capital than income—for as long as our natural capital lasts, the economics of living off soft resources differs from depleting fossil fuels as chess differs from checkers. The very rules of the game are different, though the board on which the two games are played looks the same.

One game recognizes permanence and ecological discipline as rules restricting legitimate moves. The other game has no such rules. A good move in the checkers of hard-path geocapital consumption economics is not usually a good move in the soft-path chess of permanent renewable income economics. In checkers, all pieces are comparable; in chess, essential and qualitative differences exist. A definite decision must be made the about direction we move—renewable or fossil—before we decide about the rate at which we move in that direction.[82] One strategy is based on depleting natural capital, the other income; both strategies have their own tactics, but those tactics make sense if *only* one game is being played—not both.

Much like the distinction between hard and soft energy paths, the choice between incremental and transformational research strategies is about more than just conducting research. It is about how institutions conceive of the entire research and development process. Trying to do both at once—at least in terms of incremental or transformational pathways—is like playing chess and checkers simultaneously on the same board. The

---

[80] Hugh Nash, "Foreword," In: Hugh Nash (Ed.) *The Energy Controversy: Soft Path Questions and Answers* (San Francisco: Friends of the Earth, 1979), p. 1–6.

[81] Amory Lovins, "A Target Critics Can't Seem to Get in Their Sights," In: Hugh Nash (Ed.) *The Energy Controversy: Soft Path Questions and Answers* (San Francisco: Friends of the Earth, 1979), p. 30.

[82] For an excellent summary of this type of thinking, see Herman E. Daly, "On Thinking About Future Energy Requirements," In: Charles T. Unseld, Denton E. Morrison, David L. Sills, and C.P. Wolf (Eds.) *Sociopolitical Effects of Energy Use and Policy* (Washington, DC: National Academy of Sciences, 1979), p. 232–240.

intellectual, financial, and institutional resources required for each strategy limit the efficacy of the other. It remains unlikely that a single institution could effectively do both—especially when stovepipes among various programs prevent cooperation and minimize accountability.

To emphasize this apparent conundrum, consider that DOE research on advanced lighting tends to focus on three separate elements of a lighting system—the light source, fixtures, and controls. Improvements to lighting technologies, when they are made, tend to revolve around augmenting the luminance, chromacity (color), and quality of light bulbs; refining automatic controls; producing better ballasts; and so on. Lighting devices are still mostly controlled by humans (who turn the light "on" and "off"), rarely incorporate natural light, and are wasteful in the sense that in many forms (such as overhead lights) they tend to illuminate the entire room or hallway rather than the immediate space around the user. When solar energy is incorporated into lighting systems, it must be captured, converted and stored.[83] Such ideas ignore more novel, adaptive, multifunctional approaches to adapting sunlight to a host of end-use applications in buildings. They disregard that sunlight has many possible uses in buildings including direct use as interior lighting and radiant heating of occupants, and that solar energy can be easily converted into hot water and electricity.

In contrast, a more transformational research strategy aimed at lighting could center on the creation of anticipatory lighting systems that integrate multi-functional solar technologies.[84] Such systems could use vision-based sensing and scene analysis of information so that the lights interact with room occupants, other luminaries, building energy systems, and external sources of information, such as the real-time price of electricity or sudden increases in sunlight. Anticipatory lighting systems would require distributed decision-making based on approximate reasoning and anticipatory algorithms and adapting the spatial distribution, intensity, and chromaticity of light emerging from luminaries based on a host of input parameters to continually optimize system performance from a lighting quality and energy-efficiency perspective. To oversimplify, the incremental strategy—still undertaken by the DOE—focuses on improving light bulbs. A transformational strategy focusing on improving the entire lighting system rarely occurs.

As a second example, current research on biomass and biofuel feed-stocks is split between the U.S. Department of Agriculture (USDA) and the DOE, with further divisions between basic science on genetics and genomics and the deployment of biofuel technologies. The overall mission of the DOE's bioenergy program is to develop biomass feedstock production and conversion technologies capable of providing significant fractions of domestic demands for transportation fuels, electric power, heat, chemicals, and materials. Such a research strategy remains centered on (a) the use of traditional feedstocks such as switch grass, rapeseed, and corn in (b) open-air climates located in (c) areas that have fertile and semi-fertile sources of soil. The overall mission of the USDA is to increase the use of agricultural crops and forest resources, improve crop tolerance and disease resistance, create jobs, and enhance income in America's rural sector. Improvements on biofuels within these two paradigms have tried to meet both goals, focusing on genetically engineering plants to use fewer pesticides, finding alternative feedstocks, and searching for suitable areas of land on which these plants can grow.

Yet these tenets discount more transformative techniques such as the use of photo-bioreactors for biofuel production, where biofuels can be produced using nontraditional feedstocks in closed-air climates in areas with little sources of fertile soil. Photo-bioreactors use solar energy to grow biomass in a self-contained network of pipes. Solar troughs—which use mirrors to concentrate sunlight—are placed on top of pipes filled with algae. In open-air environments, the sheer intensity of sunlight prevents algae from harnessing more than around 5% of solar energy due to photosynthetic saturation. The photo-bioreactor, however, uses the solar troughs to simultaneously generate electricity from the infrared light the algae never users and reduces the intensity of light distributed to the algae, so that 1 m² of sunlight can fuel up to 20 m² of algae. Since the photo-bioreactor is solar-powered, closed-loop, and uses very little

---

[83] U.S. Department of Energy, Office of Science, "Basic Research for Solar Energy Utilization," Notice DE-FG02-06ER06-15, April 19, 2006, available at http:www.science.doe.gov/grants/FAPN06-15.html.

[84] See Jeff Muhs, "Identifying and Understanding Innovation Gaps in America's Energy R&D Portfolio," Oak Ridge National Laboratory (Unpublished Manuscript), 2006.

water, it could be used to produce biofuels in deserts and other unsuitable or untraditional crop areas, and would ensure that such feedstocks are self-contained and would have little to no disruption on current food supply.[85]

Think about transportation as a final example. Research on transportation is spit between the DOE and the Department of Transportation (DOT). The entire DOE strategy can be divided into three sections: improving automobile performance (through better engines, light weight materials, and hybridization), promoting alternative fuels, and introducing hydrogen fuel cells into the market. The DOT is more concerned with vehicle infrastructure integration, advanced vehicle control, driver assistance, dynamic signal timing on arterials, and lessoning the extent and severity of traffic accidents. Both visions remain rooted to the same assumptions: using human-driven, self-powered, wheeled vehicles traveling on dedicated roadways and interstates. This dominate method of transportation brings with it a multitude of problems including an overdependence on foreign oil, vulnerability to economy-damaging energy price shocks, unsustainable air pollution, an aging and expensive transportation highway infrastructure that requires significant land use, and a growing traffic congestion problem that affects the safety and productivity of the motoring public.

Contrast such incremental thinking with dual mode transportation systems consisting of a network of automated personal land transit vessels with an associated electric guide-way infrastructure. The intent would be to transition from interstate, state, and local highways to integrated, automated guide-ways. In addition to being fully automated, vehicles could interact with other vehicles, buildings, and infrastructure, and could

---
[85] Ibid.

Table 5.9

Examples of incremental vs. transformational R&D strategies

Known problem/need	Energy relevance	Incremental R&D strategy	Transformational R&D strategy
Need lights that consume less energy	Lighting consumes roughly 20% of all electricity generated in the U.S.	Design static electric lighting systems—such as compact fluorescent light bulbs and solid state lighting systems—designed for "worst-case" scenario needs	Anticipatory lighting systems that adapt spatially, temporally, and chromatically to maximize quality and efficiency
Need technologies that more effectively utilize solar energy	Solar energy provides around 0.2% of electricity in the U.S. meaning its relative abundance remains largely untapped	Improve the efficiency of thin-film photovoltaic cells	Multi-functional and end-use responsive solar systems using direct sunlight and energy conversion
Need new sources of fuel for bioenergy facilities	Alternative fuels help reduce U.S. dependence on foreign supplies of petroleum	Improve the energy density of bio-crops through genetic engineering	Photo-bioreactors that can efficiently produce bio-fuels anywhere from algae grown in pipes
Need automobiles with better fuel economy and less air pollution	Current mode of land transportation plays a significant role in oil dependence, air pollution, and congestion	Increase fuel economy standards and improve light-weight vehicle materials and vehicle hybridization	Dual-mode transportation system utilizing automated, electric guide-ways

platoon or couple together for maximum efficiency. If made to run predominately on electricity, such a system could be much safer, cleaner, and more efficient than the way we conceive of transportation currently.

In each case, potentially novel and creative energy R&D is discarded in favor of incremental, conventional research (see Table 2). It is clear that existing energy research institutions have difficulty doing both incremental and transformational research at once.

3.2. A MISSION-ORIENTED FOCUS ON BROAD TECHNOLOGY CHALLENGES

Instead of focusing on particular technologies or programs, ARPA-E should organize its R&D around technology *challenges*. The organization would need to be completely mission driven, much like the Defense Advanced Research Projects Agency (DARPA). DARPA was created in 1958 after the Russian launch of Sputnik provoked a U.S. military investigation that revealed bureaucratic infighting and an unwillingness to take risks within the National Aeronautics and Space Administration and parts of the Department of Defense. President Dwight Eisenhower ordered the creation of DARPA as a way to avoid the disconnected manner that space and defense programs typically undertook their R&D.

Rather than wed researchers and managers to specific technologies, DARPA is instead focused on achieving a single mission: to sponsor revolutionary, high-risk research that bridges the gap between scientific discovery and military use. Since its inception, DARPA has helped develop better command and control systems for nuclear missiles, improved semiconductor manufacturing techniques, laid the groundwork for the internet by devising massive parallel computer processing, built two radar evading "Stealth" aircraft (the F-117 and the B-2), and invented phased array radars, night-vision goggles, and key parts of unmanned aerial vehicles global positioning satellites.[86]

F. L. Fernandez, Director of DARPA from 1998 to 2001, commented that within all large institutions like the DOE, "organizational stove pipes develop and these stove pipes often have risk-averse, parochial views which can misjudge the potential for new, technologically enabled opportunities and threats, especially if the technology is high risk."[87] To foster creativity and enable managers to undertake risky energy projects, ARPA-E should operate similarly by ensuring that every project matches its fundamental mission of promoting transformational energy R&D.

3.3. A MORE NUANCED VIEW OF THE SCIENCE AND TECHNOLOGY R&D PROCESS

To minimize stove-piping, ARPA-E should promote all stages of research and development on energy technologies—from invention and design to commercial diffusion and marketing. Such a research model should avoid demarcating between research stages. Instead, it should fully develop energy technologies to match pressing energy challenges.

To respond to similar challenges regarding technological diffusion, In-Q-Tel was been created by the U.S. intelligence community to help bring radical R&D projects to the marketplace. In-Q-Tel was created for the U.S. Central Intelligence Agency (CIA) to respond to a perceived "intelligence deficit" in advanced technologies caused by a perceived movement of capital and talent to the commercial sector during the internet boom of the late 1990s. The CIA believed that the American intelligence community had somehow become disconnected to the creative forces that underpinned the digital economy and, of equal importance, that many in Silicon Valley and emerging technological firms knew or cared little about the CIA's needs.

In response, In-Q-Tel was created as a strategic venture capital firm that operates as an independent, non-profit, government funded institution that receives oversight from the CIA. In-Q-Tel performs manifold functions: it engages start ups, emerging and established companies, universities, and research laboratories to identify technology innovations and products that can solve the American intelligence community's most pressing problems. In-Q-Tel employs venture capital investments, often coupled with product development funding, to create innovative intelligence technologies. Any profits it makes—$15

---

[86] Defense Advanced Research Projects Agency, *DARPA: Bridging the Gap, Powered by Ideas* (Washington, DC: DARPA, February, 2005), p. 1–28.

[87] F. L. Fernandez, "Hearing on ARPA-E," *Statement Before the House Committee on Science, U.S. House of Representatives*, March 9, 2006, p. 1.

Table 5.10

Differences between Methods of Research at the DOE and ARPA-E

Current methods of R&D related to	U.S. Department of Energy	ARPA-E
Mission	To manage nuclear weapons; clean up environmental pollution; conduct research and development on energy and basic science	To design creative, risky, transformational energy technologies
Management structure	Hierarchical, with multiple vertical and horizontal layers between scientists and managers	Flat, with an emphasis on the program manager
Degree of risk	Low	High
Primary historical focus	On incremental improvements of existing technology	On radical changes to technological systems
Staff turnover	Indefinite	Fixed

million so far from 2001 to 2006—get funneled back into helping the firm meet its mission.

In-Q-Tel commonly uses three approaches to support technologies: (1) giving seed money (grants up to $300,000) to accelerate university research on ideas that are not quite ready for commercial diffusion; (2) performing a "matchmaking" function that helps academics license their discoveries with a company already working with In-Q-Tel; and (3) financing money to start-up companies to develop and manufacture products.[88] As Catherine Cotell, Vice President of Strategy for In-Q-Tel, explained, "In-Q-Tel fosters the development of strong companies which produce commercially viable technologies that at the same time solve critical intelligence community mission challenges."[89]

To date, In-Q-Tel has supported more than 50 companies which in turn, have developed advanced data-mining software, nanotechnology devices, internet security programs, searching and indexing technologies for open-source documents, and improved wireless network security technologies. They are what the *Scientific American* named "a high-powered, in-house technology incubator."[90] They have proven so successful that, in 2002, the U.S. Army established its own $25 million independent venture capital firm to promote promising military technologies, and National Aeronautics and Space Administration started its own $10 million venture capital firm in 2006.

34. AN INNOVATIVE INSTITUTIONAL STRUCTURE

DARPA and In-Q-Tel possess a research culture almost the exact opposite of the traditional centralized, peer reviewed and layered research process undertaken by federal organizations such as DOE, USDA, and DOT. Instead of relying on mammoth programs with hundreds of staff, small groups of program managers exercise extensive power in directing high-risk technological projects.[91] To respond to the institutional problems of incrementalism, ARPA-E could operate with a flat management structure and a quick staff turnover. ARPA-E could compliment government

---

[88] David Malakoff, "Technology Transfer: CIA. Looks to Universities for Cutting-Edge Tools," *Science* 304 (April 2, 2004), p. 30.

[89] Catherine Cotell, "The Need for ARPA-E?" *Statement Before the Science Committee of the United States House of Representatives*, March 9, 2006, p. 1–4, 6.

[90] Daniel G. Dupont, "The Company's Company: Venture Capitalism Becomes a New Mission for the Nation's Spymasters," *Scientific American* (August, 2001), p. 26.

[91] For more on these types of differences, see Stephen Chu, "Should Congress Establish ARPA-E?" *Statement Before the Committee on Science, U.S. House of Representatives*, March 9, 2006, p. 3–5; Melanie Kenderdine, "Should Congress Establish ARPA-E?" *Statement Before the Committee on Science, U.S. House of Representatives*, March 9, 2006, p. 1–6.

research on energy, but would fundamentally differ in its staffing procedures, strategy, and structure. ARPA-E would recruit and maintain personnel differently. It would seek excited, fresh, and energized individuals who possess a sense of mission relating to energy research.

Like DARPA and In-Q-Tel, ARPA-E should be as lean and streamlined as possible. In-Q-Tel, for instance, employs a small number of staff—only 45 individuals working in two offices—and turns them over on a 3–5-year basis.[92] DARPA rotates their scientists and engineers out of the organization every 3–5 years. In contrast to a DOE research system heavily centered on the same individual programs, ARPA-E would need to be supportive of transparent and accountable programs that are clearly defined and have precise objectives, capable of cancelling projects quickly and recognizing failures, and focused entirely on breakthrough, new ideas (Table 3).

4. Conclusion

First, while transformational R&D does occasionally occur within the present energy system, it is a product of circumstance rather than design. Engineers and scientists remained predominately concerned with changing processes and components rather than systems. Research is stove-piped in at least three ways: (a) because of rigid distinctions between science/technology and basic/applied research; (b) because most scientists and engineers are trained as problem solvers rather than problem definers; and (c) because channels of coordination between external organizations (such as the USDA and DOT) and within the DOE remain confusing and complicated. The national laboratories are sponsor driven rather than mission driven, R&D programs are poorly funded compared to other federal activities, and inconsistencies make it virtually impossible to sustain a coherent, long-term national energy policy.

Second, the diffuse and growing challenges facing the American energy sector demand a fundamental rethinking and radical redesign of the processes the country utilizes to produce energy technologies. Contemporary research methods are plagued by institutional self-interests, less interdisciplinary teaming, and perpetual incrementalism rather than radical innovation. With the way things stand, transformational research on multi-functional anticipatory lighting systems, photo-bioreactors for bio-diesel production in deserts, and a radical dual-mode land transportation system do not fit neatly into established federal departments, programs, or offices. The DOE and national laboratories were not designed to pursue transformational R&D projects, and program mangers and policymakers often lack the personal, organizational and political will bring them forward. Managers at the DOE national laboratories conform to rather than confront the conventional wisdom and paradigms of their federal sponsors because of programmatic and financial risks to their organization of nonconformity are too great. In turn, individual researchers seeking to keep themselves gainfully employed "follow the money" down predetermined R&D pathways rather than expending considerable time and energy challenging existing paradigms and process structures. The evidence suggests that America's risk tolerance for transformational energy R&D at the federal level is growing, but personal, programmatic, political, organizational, social, and socio-scientific attitudes and values threaten to disrupt systems-level innovation. Like the DOD's creation of DARPA and the intelligence community's establishment of In-Q-Tel, the DOE needs to create and fund an independent organization—ARPA-E—dedicated

Benjamin K. Sovacool is currently a Research Fellow at the Centre on Asia and Globalization at the Lee Kuan Yew School of Public Policy, National University of Singapore. He serves as a Senior Research Fellow for the Network for New Energy Choices in New York, where he assesses renewable energy policy, and is an Adjunct Assistant Professor at the Virginia Polytechnic Institute & State University in Blacksburg, VA. Dr. Sovacool recently completed work on a grant from the National Science Foundation's Electric Power Networks Efficiency and Security Program investigating the social impediments to distributed and renewable energy systems. His most recent book (co-edited with Marilyn Brown) is *Energy and American Society—Thirteen Myths*, published by Springer in 2007. bsovacool#canus.edu.sg.

---

[92] Wendy Molzahn, "The CIA's In-Q-Tel Model—Its Applicability," *Acquisition News Quarterly* (Winter, 2003), p. 47–61.

primarily towards conducting transformational energy R&D.

Third, the energy challenges facing the country will only grow more urgent with time—meaning that the sooner an ARPA-E like organization is created the better. If one accepts the idea that our current strategy of "strength through exhaustion" is simply depleting natural capital at a rate far faster than it can be replenished, then our society is squandering precious and increasingly finite natural resources to produce energy. Albert Einstein once said that the "significant problems we face today cannot be solved at the same level of thinking we were at when we created them." As a culture, we can choose either to proactively undertake a transformative energy research strategy now, or wait until the inescapable laws of nature force us to.

Water conservation policy alternatives for the Ogallala Aquifer in Texas

Jeff Johnson, Phillip No. Johnson, Eduardo Segarra and David Willis

ABSTRACT

Texas groundwater law is based on the rule of capture; however, recent legislation provides groundwater conservation districts with the authority to implement groundwater use rules to manage aquifers. The objective of this study was to develop optimization models to analyze effects of groundwater policies on the Ogallala Aquifer and evaluate economic impacts on the Southern High Plains of Texas. The results of this study indicate that a policy that restricts the quantity of groundwater pumped conserved more water over the 50-year time horizon than implementation of a water use fee, but at a higher cost to local economies.

1. INTRODUCTION

Water scarcity, intergenerational transfers, and regional economic downturns are issues facing water policy decision-makers in the Great Plains of the United States, especially those regions that are dependent on production agricultural and groundwater irrigation from the Ogallala Aquifer. In the southern portion of the aquifer, these conditions are magnified by low initial saturated thickness, low recharge rates, high water withdrawals, and water rights ownership. Texas policy makers at the state and regional groundwater district levels are working to develop policies that will conserve water in the aquifer while maintaining a healthy regional economy that is currently heavily dependent on irrigated agricultural. This study evaluated two types of conservation policies, a quota and a water pumpage free, and the impact of each on conservation of water in the aquifer and the economic impact on irrigators and on the region. This study evaluated both the results of optimization models that maximized net income to the producer and the results of an input/output model that calculated the effects on the regional economy. By combining the results of the two models, policy makers can more readily identify the competing interests that are involved in the region.

Within the Southern High Plains region of Texas (SHTP) and Eastern New Mexico, over 95% of the water extracted from the Ogallala Aquifer is used for irrigation, so any effort to conserve water in the aquifer must focus on water withdrawals for agricultural (HDR Engineering, Inc., 2001). A combination of low-cost energy, fertile soils, favorable climate and seemingly boundless supply of water resulted in expansion of irrigation beginning in the 1940s and 1950s for the production of cotton, feed grains, and wheat (High Plains Associates, 1982). As the level of irrigation increased over time, the aquifer was characterized as exhaustible due to high levels of withdrawals and low levels of recharge with recharge estimates varying from 0.2 to 1.8 centimeters per year across the region (Nativ, 1988; Stovall, 2001). Diverse interests within the SHPT region are concerned that, at current withdrawal rates, the Ogallala Aquifer will reach economic depletion in many areas, resulting in decreased crop yields and declining economic activity throughout the region (High Plains Underground Water Conservation District No. 1, 2004).

In Texas, surface landowners own the right to pump and use groundwater under their property for beneficial use. While Texas courts have upheld the rule of capture over the past 100 years, the courts have left the regulation of groundwater to the Legislature (Kaiser, 1998; Kaiser & Skillern, 2001). Groundwater management districts were established in 1949 (Templer, 1989; House Research Organization, 2000), and the Texas

Legislature confirmed in 1997 and 2002 that groundwater management districts are the preferred institutions for management of groundwater, providing authority for districts to manage groundwater withdrawals through alternative regulatory policies such as water pumpage fees and water pumping quotas (House Research Organization, 2000; Texas Joint Committee on Water Resources, 2002).

This study uses a dynamic optimization technique to evaluate the impacts of these proposed changes in water district rules. By using dynamic optimization rather than a current period or myopic decision rule, a key assumption is that water in the aquifer acts as a private property good rather than a common property good, and that long-term benefits of water conservation accrue to the water user. Although not a true private good, it can be argued that given the storability and transmissivity characteristics of the aquifer, this aquifer tends towards a private good more than a common good, Alley *et al.* (1999) discussed the difference in characteristics of aquifers, which at the extremes, are described as a bathtub or egg carton as a means to provide a visualization of the common and private property aspects of aquifers. They proposed that the Ogallala Aquifer tended to act as an egg carton more than a bathtub, therefore it could be considered more of a private good than a common good.

Gisser & Sanchez (1980) presented results that suggest that for a large aquifer with linear water demand functions, differences between the results of competitive decisions and optimal control were so small that they could be ignored. Other studies (Niewiadomy, 1985; Rubio & Casino, 2001; Koundouri, 2004) have reevaluated the Gisser-Sanchez effect (GSF) and found that it holds under given assumptions.

The optimal control approach was used for this study for three reasons. The first is that the Ogalalla Aquifer is a large aquifer, thereby fitting the large aquifer assumption made by Gisser & Sanchez (1980) when they concluded that differences between the results of competitive decisions and optimal control were so small that they could be ignored. Although the GSE is used to argue that optimal control with its costs of implementation is not preferred to competitive decision making, recent legislation is moving toward more centralized control of groundwater. The second reason, therefore, was that since recent legislation paved the way for movement away from exclusive owner control, the time was right to provide some analysis of the impacts of these proposed policies to illustrate that GSE is still in effect and that control policies come at a cost to water rights owners and society. The third reason for the optimal control approach is to provide results that can be compared to the many competitive, myopic rule studies that have been performed for the Ogallala Aquifer, thereby broadening the wealth of available literature.

Bredehoeft & Young (1970) noted that three policy tools can be used in aquifer management: centralized decision-making, assigned quotas or pumping rights, and extraction fees or taxes on withdrawals. Centralized decision-making is unlikely to be adopted and, in Texas, centralized decision-making in inconsistent with the intent of recent legislation of "protecting the groundwater resource while respecting landowners' property rights historically acknowledged to be associated with ownership of real property" (Texas Joint Committee on Water Resources, 2002, p.44). The instruments of pumping quotas and water pumpage fees are possible and within the authority given to ground water conservation districts by the Texas Legislature.

In this study, policies that conserve water in the aquifer are defined as those approaches that reduce the amount of water withdrawn from the aquifer at a given level of water application efficiency. This reduction in the amount of water pumped represents a reduction in water applied to crops and, consequently, results in either a reduction in the consumption use by the crops being irrigated or a reduction in the area irrigated. In other words, the reduction in pumpage results in a reduction in the total amount of water used thus conserving the water by maintaining it in the aquifer. The water conservation policy alternatives selected for evaluation in this study were: (1) a water pumpage fee of US $0.0008 per m^3 pumped ($1 per acre foot) and (2) a restriction on the drawdown of the aquifer over a 50-year planning horizon to 50% of the initial (current) saturated thickness (50/50 policy). The water pumpage fee was authorized by state legislation in 2002 but has yet to be implemented by any groundwater management district. The 50/50 policy was also authorized by state legislation and has been implemented by one groundwater conservation district in the northern counties of Texas and is being considered for implementation by other districts (Panhandle Groundwater District, 2006).

Several studies (Harman, 1966; Lansford et al., 1983; Feng, 1992; Terrell, 1998; Stovall, 2001) have shown that with continued use, the level of the aquifer will continue to decline toward economic depletion. Economic depletion is defined as the exhaustion of a resource to the point at which the cost of extraction is greater than the value of the extracted resource. In this case, economic depletion is encountered at the aquifer level at which the marginal value product of applied irrigation water equals the marginal input cost of applying the water to the crop. As pump lift increases, the marginal cost of pumping groundwater increases. It is likely that with the decline of the aquifer, agricultural practices will transition from irrigated to non-irrigated. Terrell (1998) showed that with the transition from irrigated to dryland production systems, the SHPT regional economy would suffer significantly due to the decline in total crop production and the associated decline in economic activity.

Groundwater conservation districts in the SHPT region are faced with evaluating and implementing new groundwater management policies to address declining aquifer levels. They must consider the effectiveness of possible policy alternatives in conserving water in the aquifer and the potential impacts on the agricultural and regional economy. The objective of this study was to analyze the impacts of the water pumpage fee and 50/50 water conservation policy alternatives on the aquifer and the economy of the Southern High Plains region of Texas.

2. METHODS AND PROCEDURES

The geographical study region included 19 counties of the SHPT as shown in Figure 1. Dynamic optimization models were developed for each of the 19 counties to estimate the economic life of the aquifer across the region under alternative water conservation policies. The direct policy impacts to production agriculture provided by the dynamic optimization models were used in an input—output model to estimate the regional economic impact of each water conservation policy.

2.1. SPECIFICATION OF THE DYNAMIC NON-LINEAR OPTIMIZATION MODEL

Rowse (1995) describes the value of using non-linear dynamic programming models for computing the optimal allocation of nature resources and illustrates the effectiveness of using a single computing environment rather than multiple path modeling procedures such as the current-period decision rule. Non-linear dynamic programming models were developed using the General Algebraic Modeling System (GAMS) to facilitate multiple runs of the model under different water conservation policies (Brooke et al., 2003).

The objective function of the optimization model for this study maximized the present value of annual net returns to land, management, groundwater stock, risk, and investment over a specified planning horizon. Annual net income per hectare was expressed as:

$$NI_t \quad \sum_c \sum_t \theta_{cit} \{P_c Y_{cit}(WP_{cit})) \quad C_{cit}(WP_{cit}, L_t, ST_t)\}$$

where NI_t represents net income per hectare in time t, c represents the crop grown, i represents irrigated or non-irrigated systems where $i = 1$ represents irrigated systems and $i = 0$ represents non-irrigated systems, t represents the time period θ_{cit} represents the percentage of crop c produced with irrigation system i in period t, P_c represents the price of crop c, Y_{cit} represents the yield per hectare of crop c produced with irrigation system i in period t, WP_{cit} represents the amount of water pumped in cubic meters (m³) to irrigate crop c through irrigation system i in period t, C_{cit} represents the cost of production per hectare of crop c produced with irrigation system i in period t, L_t represents the pump lift in meters in time t, and ST_t represents the saturated thickness of the aquifer in time t. Yield (Y_{cit}) was calculated using the crop production functions as discussed in Section 2.2 below.

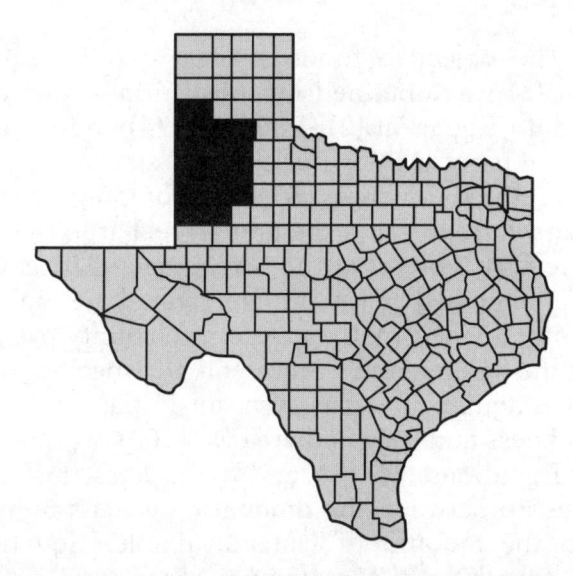

FIGURE 5.14 Southern High Plains Region of Texas.

The objective function was maximized for a 50-year planning horizon and was expressed as:

$$\text{Maximize PVNI} = \sum_{t=i}^{50} NI_t \, (1+r)^{-t}$$

where PVNI is the present value of net income and r represents the social discount rate of 3%. The dynamic optimization model can be represented as:

$$\text{Maximize PVNI} = \sum_t \sum_i \sum_c \theta_{cit}$$
$$\left\{ \left(P_c Y_{cu}(WP_{cit}) \right) - C_{cit}(WP_{cit}, L_t, ST_t) \right\} (1+r)^{-t}$$

Subject to:

$$ST_{t+1} = ST_t - \left[\left(\sum_\psi \sum_\tau \theta_{cit} WP_{cit} \right) - R_t \right] A / s$$

$$L_{t+1} = L_t + \left[\left(\sum_\psi \sum_\tau \theta_{cit} WP_{cit} \right) - R_t \right] A / s$$

$$GPC_t = (ST_t/IST)^2 \times (120 \times WY/AW)$$

$$WT_t = \sum_c \sum_t \theta_{cit} \times WP_{cit}$$

$WT_t \leq GPC_t$
$PC_{cit} \; 5 \; [[EF(L_t = 0.1 \times PRS)EP]/EFF] \times WP_{cit}$
$C_{cit} = VC_{ct} + PC_{cit} + HC_{cit} + MC_t + DP + LC_i$

$$\sum_c \theta_{it} \leq \text{Initial Irrigated Area}$$

$$\theta_{cit} \geq 0.9 \theta_{cit-1}$$

$$\sum_c \sum_t \theta_{ci} \leq 1 \text{ for all } t; \text{ and}$$

$$\theta_{cit} \geq 0$$

The objective function expressed in Equation (3) was obtained by substituting Equation (1) into Equation (2). Equations (4) and (5) are equations of motion for the two state variables of saturated thickness (ST_t) and pumping lift (L_t), where R_t represents the annual recharge rate in meters, A represents the percentage of irrigated area expressed as the initial irrigated area in the county divided by the area of the county overlying the aquifer, and s represents the specific yield of the aquifer. The base year for initial saturated thickness and irrigated area was 2001.

Equations (6), (7), and (8) express the relationship between the amount of water pumped and the amount of water available. Equation (6) calculates the maximum amount of water that can be pumped in each time period. Gross pumping capacity in period t (GPC_t), is a function of initial saturated thickness (IST), average initial well yield for a county (WY), and average number of wells per irrigated hectare for a county (AW) (Harman, 1966; Terrell, 1998; Texas Water Development Board 2001). The factor of 120 m³ per liter per minute is developed from the assumption of 2000 pumping hours in a growing season.[1] Equation (7) expresses the total amount of water pumped per hectare (WT_t) as the sum of water pumped on each crop. Equation 8 is a constraint requiring the amount of water pumped (WT_t) to be less than or equal to the amount of water available for pumping (GPC_t).

Equation (9) calculates the cost of pumping (PC_{cit}) for crop c produced by irrigation system i in period t, where EF represents the energy use factor for electricity, PRS represents the irrigation system operating pressure, EP represents energy price per unit of electricity, EFF represents pump engine efficiency, and the factor 0.1 m is the height of a column of water that will exert a pressure of 1 kilopascal (Terrell, 1998). Equation (10) expresses the cost of production (C_{cit}) for crop c produced by irrigation system i in period t, where VC_{ci} is the variable cost of production per hectare, HC_{cit} is the harvest costs per hectare, MC_i is the annual maintenance cost per hectare for the irrigation system, DP_t is the annual depreciation cost per hectare for the irrigation system, and LC_t is the irrigation labor cost per hectare for the irrigation system.

Equation (11) ensures that the irrigated area does not increase from the amount being irrigated at the beginning of the planning horizon. Equation (12) limits the annual change in the area of any crop to no more than 10% of the previous year's area. This limit on the rate of transition between crop enterprises controls the rate at which the model switches from one enterprise to another in order to replicate an orderly transition between crop enterprises. Both Equations (11) and (12) are used to capture unobserved constraints that impact irrigators' decisions but which are not replicated in the model. These equations are an attempt to ensure the model results mimic actual observations.

Equation (13) limits the sum of the percentage of area for all crops c produced by all irrigation systems i for each period t to be less than or

---

[1] From the assumption of 2,000 pumping hours, the following relationship was developed: [(2,000 hours) × (60 minutes/hour)]/ (1,000 liters/m³)] =120m³/liter per minute.

equal to 1. Equation (14) ensure that the values of the decision variables are non-negative.

WP$_{cit}$, representing the amount of water pumped in m^3 in Equations (3), (4), (5), (7), and (9), is a critical factor in determining costs of production. When the returns above specified costs for irrigated crops are less than the returns above specified costs for non-irrigated crops due to increasing pump lift, water is no longer pumped. When this happens, WP$_{cit}$ equals zero, thus reducing pumping costs and other irrigation-related costs to zero.

2.2. PARAMETERS FOR DYNAMIC NON-LINEAR OPTIMIZATION MODEL

Dynamic optimization models were developed for each of the 19 counties to estimate the optimal level of water extraction for irrigation and the resulting present value of net income from crop production over a planning horizon of 50 year. The models were used to establish a baseline scenario using current water policy and two conservation policy alternatives: (1) a water pumpage fee of US $0.0008 per m^3 pumped ($1 per acre foot)[2], and (2) a restriction on the drawdown of the aquifer over a 50-year planning horizon to 50% of the saturated thickness at the beginning of the study (50/50 policy).

The functional relationship between crop yield and applied irrigation water was estimated for the primary crops grown in the region. The Crop Production and Management Model (CROPMAN) was used to estimate the response of crop yields to applied irrigation water (Gerik et al., 2003). CROPMAN requires the designation of the crop, type of irrigation system, soil type, and weather data location. Production techniques and timing of cultural practices were held constant with only the amount of applied irrigation water varying. The irrigation timing was also held constant with the amount of irrigation water applied divided between the various dates of irrigation.

Production functions for irrigated crops were estimated for corn, cotton, grain sorghum, peanuts, and wheat using the results from CROPMAN. Yield response functions were estimated using a quadratic functional form with yield per hectare as the dependent variable and applied irrigation water as the independent variable. The quadratic function form was used to ensure that a global maximum would be achieved in the optimization model. The production functions were estimated using ordinary least squares regression techniques with the intercept set at the 3-year average yield for dryland production of each crop.

The two modeling assumptions of irrigation efficiency and recharge require additional discussion due to their importance as components of the model especially as projections are made for a relatively long planning horizon of 50 year. First, an irrigation efficiency of 90% was used for the model development. This is consistent with efficiencies found in improved center pivot irrigation systems and serves as a proxy for future irrigation technologies that may be adopted during the 50-year planning horizon. Currently, across the region, center pivot systems comprise 70% of the irrigation systems while furrow irrigation systems with efficiencies of approximately 75% comprise 30% of the irrigation systems. As improved irrigation technologies, such as subsurface drip irrigation with efficiency estimates of 98%, become more widely adopted, the average efficiencies across the region will approach the 90% level used in the model development (Texas Water Development Board, 2001).

Recharge values include both natural recharge and return flows (Stovall, 2001). As explained by Kendy et al. (2003). If improved efficiencies result in lower water withdrawals, the return flows to the aquifer will be reduced, thereby speeding the depletion of the aquifer. Two factors, however, influence the relative impact of reduced return flows in this region and support the assumption of constant total recharge values. Water levels of the Ogallala Aquifer in this region are relatively deep and infiltration rates are relatively slow resulting in a long lagged response of the aquifer level of changes in the level of return flows. The other factor reported by Peterson & Ding (2005), is the "water spreading" is common in the Ogallala region which is a result of improved technical efficiency of irrigation systems. This improvement in efficiency leads to more area being irrigated with the same amount of water thus resulting in no net water savings.

The county-level dynamic optimization models were solved using GAMS. County specific data for each model include total land area, land area overlying the Ogallala Aquifer, amount of annual recharge, specific yield for the aquifer, initial saturated thickness, initial pump lift, initial well yield, initial area per well, initial area per crop,

---
[3] An acre foot is a volumetric measure of water equal to 325,851 gallons or 1,233 m^3 and is the amount of water that will cover an acre at a depth of 1 foot.

and initial irrigated area. Crop specific data include commodity prices, variable costs of dryland crop production excluding harvest costs, added variable costs for irrigated crop production, and harvest costs per unit of production. Commodity prices used in the analysis were averages of monthly prices for 15 years from 1987 to 2001 as reported by the Texas Agricultural Statistics Services (various years). The variable costs for dryland crop production and the additional costs for irrigated production were taken from enterprise budgets developed by the Texas Cooperative Extension Service for Texas Extension District 2 (Texas Agricultural Extension Service, 2003).

Pumping costs were based on an energy use factor for electricity of 5.24×10^{-3} KWH per meter of lift per m^3, irrigation system operating pressure of 110 kPa, and energy price of $0.0633 per KWH. Other costs include the initial cost of the irrigation system of $692 per hectare, annual depreciation percentage of 5%, irrigation labor of 5 hours per hectare, and labor cost of $8 per hour. Annual maintenance cost was set at 8% of initial irrigation system cost, and a real discount rate of 3% was assumed (Terrell, 1998). Cost calculations included harvest costs, pumping costs and total costs of production for irrigated and dryland crops. The units for the resulting values were expressed in $/hectare.

2.3. INPUT—OUTPUT MODEL

The results of the dynamic nonlinear optimization models were imported into the input—output model, IMPLAN, to estimate the regional economic impact of the two water policy alternatives relative to the baseline scenario. The production levels for corn, cotton, grain sorghum, peanuts, and winter wheat under the two water alternative policies analyzed in 10-year increments resulted in five agricultural production "snapshots" for simulation years 10, 20, 30, 40, and 50 (Terrell et al., 2002). The impact of each water policy on regional economic activity relative to the baseline condition was estimated using IMPLAN. For each "snapshot" year the difference in agricultural gross revenue was calculated between the simulated water policy value and the simulated baseline level provided by the dynamic programming model.

The 1998 IMPLAN data set which included economic data for all counties in Texas was used to generate an input—output model for the 19-county region. A descriptive IMPLAN model was first developed for the baseline scenario, then a predictive model was developed using the Type SAM multipliers that consider direct, indirect, and induced effects from changes in output within specific sectors of the economy (Minnesota IMPLAN Group, Inc., 2000). The change in the predictive model was the calculated change in gross revenue between the baseline production levels for each commodity and their respective values under each water policy alternative.

3. RESULTS
3.1. REGIONAL RESULTS OF THE NON-LINEAR OPTIMIZATION MODELS

The simulated transition from irrigated to dryland cropland over the 50-year planning horizon for the region is presented in Table 1 for the baseline and two alternative water policies: water pumpage fee and 50/50 policies. The initial percentage or irrigated area for each county was reported by the Texas Agricultural Statistics Service for the year 2001 (Texas Agricultural Statistics Service, 2002). Irrigated area for subsequent years for each county was estimated using the dynamic programming model. Under the baseline scenario, the average percentage of irrigated area in the region decreased from approximately 52% to 23% over the planning horizon. The water pumpage fee policy showed little deviation from the baseline scenario, which was predictable due to the low water pumpage fee of $0.0008 per m^3 allowed current legislation compared to the average pumping costs for the region of approximately $0.04 per m^3. The 50/50 water conservation policy simulated a decrease in the average irrigated area from 52% to 17% of total cropland over the 50-year planning horizon. The 50/50 policy was more restrictive of groundwater withdrawals; therefore, a faster transition from irrigated to dryland production occurred under this policy.

Average aquifer saturated thickness across the region (weighted mean) under the baseline situation decreased approximately 38% from an initial level of approximately 21.4 m to 13.1 m by year 50 of the planning horizon as shown in Table 2. The decline in saturated thickness projected under the water pumpage fee policy is only slightly less than the decline in the baseline scenario with an average saturated thickness of

TABLE 5.11

Percent irrigated area within the region over the 50-year time horizon, by policy.

Period (year)	Baseline(%)	Water pumpage fee policy(%)	50/50 policy (%)
1	52.1	52.1	52.1
5	49.4	48.8	48.5
10	44.8	43.9	41.7
15	39.4	38.9	34.7
20	35.2	34.9	29.6
25	31.5	31.4	26.8
30	29.2	29.1	24.1
35	27.6	28.0	19.8
40	28.4	27.2	20.3
45	25.4	25.7	18.0
50	22.9	23.2	16.5

13.3 m by year 50, only 0.2m of saturated thickness greater than the baseline scenario. The average saturated thickness projected under the 50/50 policy declined by 30% from 21.4 m to 14.9 m by year 50 of the planning horizon.

Under the baseline conditions, the drawdown over 50 years did not exceed 50% of initial saturated thickness in 12 of the 19 counties, resulting in a smaller than expected drawdown of 30% across the region. Several factors contributed to these counties not reaching the 50% drawdown level. Of the 12 counties, seven maintained a constant level of irrigated area while five began an immediate decrease in irrigated area. The five counties that began the immediate decrease all had a relatively high percentage of irrigated area initially (>60%). Two of these counties had the greatest irrigated area in corn while two others had the greatest irrigated area in cotton. Three of these counties had pumping costs in the highest quartile (>$0.05/m^3) with medium to high well yields (2,500–3,500 1pm). All five of these counties had only medium level initial saturated thickness (20–24 m). The seven counties that maintained a steady level of irrigated area all had low to mid range pumping costs (<$0.04/m^3) and

TABLE 5.12

Average saturated thickness in meters over the 50-year time horizon, by policy.

Period (year)	Baseline (meters)	Water pumpage fee policy (meters)	50/50 policy (meters)
1	21.4	21.4	21.4
5	20.0	20.0	20.0
10	18.4	18.5	18.5
15	17.1	17.2	17.4
20	16.1	16.2	16.6
25	15.3	15.5	16.0
30	14.7	14.9	15.6
35	14.3	14.5	15.4
40	13.8	14.0	15.2
45	13.4	13.6	15.0
50	13.1	13.3	14.9

initial water withdrawals (<0.09 m³). These seven counties had the smallest irrigated area (< 50%) of the 19 counties.

Present values of net income from crop production for the 19-county region were calculated for the baseline and the two alternative water conservation policies over the 50-year period using a 3% discount rate. The total present value of net income for the region under the baseline scenario is $5,060 million, or $1191 per hectare. The water pumpage fee policy resulted in a 5.5% decrease in total present value of net income from the baseline to a value of $4,780 million, or $1124 per hectare. The 50/50 policy resulted in a decline from the baseline of 3.7% to a total present value of net income of $4,870 million, or $1147 per hectare. This many seem counter-intuitive that the policy that results in the least change in water use will cause the greater negative impact on net income. The water use fee is imposed on all water used while the 50/50 quota only affects the last unit of water used and only in those counties that used more that 50% of the water. The average net income across the region therefore was not impacted as severely by the 50/50 policy as by the water use fee.

The efficiency in reducing the decline of saturated thickness over the planning horizon can be measured for each policy as the ratio of the decrease in the present value of net income per hectare from the baseline scenario for the agricultural producer and the associated change in the level of saturated thickness under the alternative policy. The ratio estimates the average cost in foregone net income to maintain an additional meter of saturated thickness in the aquifer compared to the baseline scenario. The water pumpage fee conserved 0.24 m of the saturated thickness relative to the baseline at a present value cost of $66.72 per hectare, resulting in an efficiency ratio value of $278 per meter of saturated thickness saved. The 50/50 policy, on the other hand, conserved 1.8, of saturated thickness relative to the baseline at a present value cost of $44.50 per hectare, resulting in an efficiency ratio value of $25 per meter of saturated thickness saved. The ratio illustrates the interaction between water conserved in the aquifer and net income lost to the agricultural producer and the advantage of the increased flexibility available with the 50/50 policy. Under the water pumpage fee policy, the increased cost of production due to imposing the water use fee contributes to a greater cost in net income to agricultural producers, while the water savings are substantially less.

The analysis indicate that for the water pumpage fee to be effective in reducing the decline in saturated thickness, a higher fee would be required. Currently, the maximum allowed water use fee for agricultural uses is $0,0008 per m³ ($1 per acre foot). Table 3 shows the water pumpage fee per m³ of water pumped necessary to maintain the same level of conservation as the 50/50 policy for the seven counties that exceeded the 50% drawdown in 50 years under the baseline scenario. Examining the results from two counties shows the wide difference in the requirements for water pumpage fees. Specifically, Swisher County requires a fee of $0.032 per m³ of water pumped while Terry County requires a fee

TABLE 5.13

Water pumpage fee necessary to conserve water to the level of 50% drawdown in 50 years, for those counties that withdrew more than 50% in 50 years under the baseline scenario.

County	Water pumpage fee required to conserve water at 50% drawdown in 50 years ($/m³ × 10⁻²)
Deaf Smith	0.73
Floyd	1.22
Hale	2.11
Hockley	0.65
Lubbock	2.03
Swisher	3.16
Terry	0.41

of $0.004 per m³ of water pumped. The difference in these levels is the result of differences in initial saturated thickness, level of water withdrawals, and value of crops irrigated.

3.2. INPUT—OUTPUT MODEL

The regional economic impact of the alternative water conservation policies was developed using the IMPLAN input—out model. The values used in the IMPLAN model were the changes in regional gross revenue for the commodities of cotton, corn, grain sorghum, wheat, and peanuts from the baseline scenario for each of the two alternative policies. The changes in gross revenue from the baseline scenario were evaluated in 10-year increments for years 10, 20, 30, 40, and 50 of the planning horizon. The water pumpage fee policy exhibited the least change in gross revenues (direct economic output shown in Table 4) from the baseline scenario, ranging from $48 million below the baseline scenario in year 40 to $13 million above the baseline scenario in year 50. The 50/50 policy exhibited a decline in gross revenue through year 40 to a level $410 million below the baseline scenario then increased to $324 million below the baseline scenario in year 50. It is important to note that total gross revenue is the direct effect measure in the regional analysis while net income was the measure for the farm-level analysis. One of the key differences in the two measures is the water pumpage fee. In the farm-level analysis, the fee is included in the analysis while the fee is not considered in the regional analysis. The fee enters the local economy through the water districts' purchase of management, labor, and equipment.

The total regional economic impacts from the direct, indirect and induced effects are shown in Table 4. Direct impacts are derived directly from the change in gross revenue. Indirect impacts are defined as those effects that are related to producer purchases of goods and services from other industries, such as fertilizer, chemicals, equipment and fuel, and were found to be 53% of direct impacts. Induced effect are defined as those effects that are related to changes in household spending caused by changes in gross revenue and were found to be 16% of direct impacts.

The baseline scenario is considered to be the index with a value of zero and the differences between the results of the baseline and the two policies are the impacts on the regional economy. The water pumpage fee policy followed the path of the baseline with little change in regional impact as shown by the relatively small differences and exhibited a decrease in annual regional economic activity of $81 million from the baseline in year 40. The 50/50 policy exhibited a much greater economic impact as shown by the relatively larger values. The 50/50 policy did not follow the same path as the baseline with an early divergence due to a greater rate of decreasing

TABLE 5.14

Table 4. Change in regional economic output in dollars from baseline over the 50-year time horizon.

Period (years)	Direct ($ million)	Indirect ($ million)	Induced ($ million)	Total ($ million)
Water pumpage fee policy				
10	−34.6	−18.2	−5.5	−58.3
20	−11.9	−6.3	−1.9	−20.1
30	−4.7	−2.5	−0.7	−7.9
40	−48.4	−25.5	−7.8	−81.8
50	+13.1	+6.9	+2.1	+22.1
50/50 policy				
10	−169.1	−89.2	−26.8	−285.1
20	−248.9	−131.3	−39.8	−420.1
30	−224.5	−118.4	−36.0	−378.9
40	−410.2	−216.5	−65.6	−692.3
50	−324.2	−171.1	−51.8	−547.2

irrigated area in the early years of the study and exhibited a decline in annual regional economic activity to a level $547 million below the baseline scenario in year 50. The smaller difference in year 50 is a result of the baseline scenario beginning to converge to the low level of irrigated area of the 50/50 scenario.

The present value of gross revenue from each crop produced for each year of the planning horizon multiplied by the appropriate SAM multiplier from the IMPLAN model provided the present value of the total regional economic activity generated by the specified agricultural production for each policy. The water pumpage fee and 50/50 policies generated $624 million or $147 per cropland hectare and $9,368 million or $2206 per cropland hectare less regional economic activity compared to the baseline scenario, respectively.

When considering the efficiency measure of regional economic activity per meter of saturated thickness saved, the total economic cost of maintaining a meter of saturated thickness under the water pumpage fee policy was $244 per meter of saturated thickness ($0.45 per m^3 of water) and $496 per meter of saturated thickness ($0.81 per m^3 of water) under the 50/50 policy[3]. The evaluation found an opposite relationship compared to the ratio applied to the change in net income to agricultural producers. One of the key factors for this reversal is the use of water pumpage fee as an input into the economy rather than a direct effect. This illustrates the importance of defining the desired effects of proposed policies. In this case, the water use fee is the most efficient when considering regional economic impacts but the least efficient in terms of producer net income. Similarly, the 50/50 policy is most efficient when considering producer net income but least efficient when considering the regional economic impacts.

4. Policy implementation

The policies evaluated in this study have not been implemented by any of the water districts in the study area, although the Panhandle Groundwater Conservation District which is located north of the study area, has implemented the 50/50 policy across the district (Panhandle Groundwater Conservation District, 2006). The water use fee as currently defined would be assessed by the underground water district and be used locally in the district rather that at the state level. As shown, the $1 per acre foot of water use has very little impact on the amount of water pumped. Therefore, this fee becomes another method of collecting revenue for the water conservation district rather than being a conservation tool.

The first of two approaches to implementation of the 50/50 policy monitors wells to ensure that the saturated thickness does not decline more than the 50% level at any time during the 50 year period. An irrigator could possibly use the allotted 50% in less time than 50 years then stop pumping and stay within the stated guidelines. This is the approach evaluated in this study.

Another approach to implementation of the 50/50 policy is establishment of an annual quota that would result in no more than a 50% reduction in saturated thickness over the 50 year period. The most straightforward approach would be to establish an annual quota of 1% of the initial saturated thickness which would give a 50% drawdown over the 50 year period. Another approach would be to set the annual allowed drawdown at 1.25% of saturated thickness and recalculate the quota every 5 yeas based on the saturated thickness level at that time. This is the method adopted by the Panhandle Groundwater Conservation District (2006). The latter method allows more water use in the early years and rewards conservation efforts. The irrigator under the 1% alternative has no incentive to conserve because the allotted quota remains the same even if he is able to reduce pumpage over the 50 years. Although the advantage of the 1.25% per year alternative seems counter-intuitive because it allows more water to be used in the early years, the alternative provides the irrigator flexibility and incentive to reduce drawdown over the years.

5. Conclusions

Groundwater conservation districts in Texas have been identified by the Texas Legislature through Texas Senate Bills 1 (Brown et al., 1997) and 2 (Brown & Lewis, 2001) as the primary regulatory authorities to implement groundwater management policies to address the state's expanding water demand and declining aquifer levels. As groundwater conservation districts in the SHPT evaluate the implementation of new groundwater

---

[3] Saturated thickness of the aquifer was converted to cubic meters (m^3) of water using a storage coefficient of 15% per meter of saturated thickness.

management policies, they should consider the effectiveness of various policy alternatives in conserving water in the Ogallala Aquifer and the potential impacts on the agricultural and regional economy. The results of this study can be used in other regions to evaluate impacts on aquifers, producer net income, and regional economy due to policies that restrict water use.

This study evaluated the impacts of two alternative water management policies, a water pumpage fee and a 50/50 quota, on the saturated thickness of the Ogallala Aquifer, net income to agricultural producers, and the regional economy. The alternative policies were evaluated relative to a baseline scenario of the present water management policy in the region over a 50-year planning horizon. The alternative water management policies were chosen for evaluation because of their inclusion in recent legislation addressing water policy in Texas (water pumpage fee) or adoption by groundwater conservation districts as district policy (50/50 quota).

Under the baseline scenario, only 7 of the 19 counties showed declines in saturated thickness greater than 50% over the 50-year planning horizon. Across the SHPT, the average saturated thickness declined 38.8% and irrigated area declined from 52.1% to 22.9% of total cropland. The baseline scenario assumed that no new water management policies would be implemented over a 50-year planning horizon.

The comparison of the alternative water management policies to the baseline scenario indicated that a water pumpage fee of $0.0008 per m^3 was not effective in reducing the decline in the saturated thickness to any significant extent. Under the water fee policy, the reduction in the present value of net income to the agricultural producer was greatest due to the additional cost of the fee to irrigation users. Although water pumpage fees can be used in a management policy to enhance conservation, the low fee is essentially a revenue generating mechanism for the groundwater district with very little impact on water conservation. The analysis indicated that for the water pumpage fee to be effective in reducing the decline in saturated thickness, a higher fee would be required. The region should be divided into sub-regions with similar hydrology and water withdrawal patterns in order to maintain water pumpage fees that will be effective conservation tools. In addition, the water pumpage fee has a direct effect on net farm incomes because the fee in an added cost associated with irrigation.

The 50/50 quota policy showed the greatest effect on the decline in the regional average saturated thickness compared to the baseline scenario, reducing the regional drawdown in saturated thickness over the 50-year time horizon from 38.8% under the baseline scenario to 30.4% for the 50/50 policy. Net income was lower compared to the baseline, however, under the 50/50 policy the reduction in net income per meter of reduced drawdown in saturated thickness was much lower compared to the water pumpage fee policy. From a water management standpoint, the 50/50 quota policy appears to be the more effective and efficient of the two alternative water conservation policies evaluated.

The goal of reducing the drawdown in saturated thickness over time can only be reached by reducing total water withdrawals rather than improving irrigation efficiency. Within the models developed for this study, water conservation was accomplished by shifting toward crop enterprises that require less applied water or toward dryland production. The end result under each alternative policy was a reduced level of overall crop production, a lower level of net income to the agricultural sector, and a lower level of gross revenues contributed by the agricultural sector to the regional economy.

By combining the optimization analysis and regional economy analysis in this study, we are able to illustrate the opposing impacts on two sectors of the community. The water fee policy has virtually no impact on the regional economy but has a large negative impact on producers' net income. The 50/50 policy, on the other hand, did not reduce producers' net income as much as the water fee policy but the impact on the regional economy was dramatic due to the effect of the reduced irrigated area and the reduction in economic activity for input purchases. Although using both the optimization and input/output models adds complexity to the analysis, the results allow policy makers to understand the competing interests involved in the region.

Of the two alternative policies evaluated, the 50/50 quota policy was found to be the more effective in terms of the amount of water conserved and thus, maintaining a greater level of saturated thickness over the planning horizon. However, the 50/50 policy was only effective in those counties with high water withdrawals or low initial saturated thickness. In those counties with low water withdrawals and high initial saturated thickness, the policy had no effect on reducing water withdrawals, leading to distributional inequities across the region. Under the 50/50 quota policy, it was also found that the regional economy would be negatively impacted due to the reduced level of gross revenues contributed by the agricultural sector. For these reasons, groundwater conservation district policy makers should consider distributional inequities across the region due to the heterogeneity of the aquifer and of water withdrawal patterns, as well as the relative trade-offs between water conservation and economic impact when considering changes in current policies.

Discussion Questions

1. How clear is the concept of sustainable development? Can it be used effectively to describe the long-term goal of environmental policy? Does doing so help to build public understanding and support for environmental policy actions?
2. What is the current relationship between environmental science and environmental policy? What should the relationship be? Should scientists do more to help inform the public and policymakers on environmental issues? If so, what would be the best way to do so?
3. How do economic incentives affect individuals' behavior with respect to the environment, such as decisions to buy a car, home, or appliance? How might such incentives be altered to help promote more environmentally positive outcomes?
4. How would a broader societal commitment to an environmental ethic affect environmental policy decisions? What might be done to improve the public's understanding of environmental issues? What might be done to increase the saliency of those issues in people's daily lives?
5. Is it useful to think about environmental problems in terms of the risks they pose to human and ecological health? Given the controversies over risk assessment, to what extent do you think that public policy decisions should be based on scientific assessments of risk?

Sugested Readings

Brown, Lester R. 2008. *Plan B 3.0: Mobilizing to Save Civilization.* New York: W.W. Norton.

Fiorino, Daniel J. 2006. *The New Environmental Regulation.* Cambridge: MIT Press.

Friedman, Thomas L. 2008. *Hot, Flat, and Crowded: Why We Need a Green Revolution—and How It Can Renew America.* New York: Farrar, Straus, and Giroux.

O'Neill, Kate. 2009. *The Environment and International Relations.* New York: Cambridge University Press.

Speth, James Gustave. 2008. *The Bridge at the Edge of the World: Capitalism, the Environment, and Crossing from Crisis to Sustainability.* New Haven: Yale University

Vig, Norman J., and Michael E. Kraft, eds. 2010. *Environmental Policy: New Directions for the Twenty-First Century*, 7th ed. Washington, DC: CQ Press.

Endnotes

1. See, for example, N. Gregory Mankiw, "What If the Candidates Pandered to Economists?" *New York Times*, July 13, 2008, online edition.
2. Kendra Marr, "Can the Volt Jump-Start GM?" *Washington Post Week in Review*, March 23–29, 2009, 24. In August 2009, Nissan announced that it would market its fully electric car, the Leaf, in late 2010.
3. Clifford Krauss, "Gas Prices Send Surge of Riders to Mass Transit," *New York Times*, May 10, 2008, online edition.
4. Keith Bradsher, "China Far Outpaces U.S. in Building Cleaner Coal-Fired Plants," *New York Times*, May 11, 2009, 1, A3. China also is poised to pass the United States soon as the largest market in the world for wind power equipment, and it is building more nuclear power plants than all other nations in the world combined.
5. Keith Bradsher and David Barboza, "Pollution from Chinese Coal Casts a Global Shadow," *New York Times*, June 11, 2006. In early 2009 China was selling more cars and other vehicles

than the United States, but it announced in April 2009 that it was committed to making the country one of the leading producers of hybrid and all-electric vehicles within three years as well as staking out a leading role in solar energy technology. In addition, some 15 Chinese cities are building subway systems and a dozen others are planning to do so. See Keith Bradsher, "Digging a Hole Through China," *New York Times*, March 27, 2009, B1–5; Bradsher, "China Vies to Be World's Leader in Electric Cars," *New York Times*, April 1, 2009; and Bradsher, "China Races Ahead of U.S. in Drive to Go Solar," *New York Times*, August 25, 2009, 1, A3.

6. Lubchenco, a leading marine ecologist, was named by President Obama to head the National Oceanic and Atmospheric Administration and took office in early 2009.

7. See Ann Rappaport, "Campus Greening: Behind the Headlines," *Environment* 50(1) (January/February, 2008), 7–16. A national association promotes and reports on such activities: The Association for the Advancement of Sustainability in Higher Education (AASHE): www.aashe.org.

8. For an overview of issues related to the intersection of science and environmental policy, particularly efforts by scientists in recent decades to play a more central role in policymaking, see Keller (2009). The American Association for the Advancement of Science keeps a running tab on federal spending on scientific research, and details on environmental research spending can be found on its Web site: www.aaas.org. For a more recent statement on Lubchenco's views on the role of science and scientists in policymaking, see Cornelia Dean, "NOAA Chief Believes in Science as Social Contract," *New York Times*, March 24, 2009, D2.

9. Jeffrey Mervis, "Obama Courts a Smitten Audience at the National Academy," *Science* 324 (May 1): 576–77. See also Neil Munro, "Democratic Science," *National Journal*, March 7, 2009, 28–33; Eli Kintisch, "Science Wins $21 Billion Boost as Stimulus Package Becomes Law," *Science* 323 (February 20, 2009): 992–93; and Sheryl Gay Stolberg, "Obama Puts His Own Spin on the Mix of Science with Politics," *New York Times*, March 10, 2009, A15. For Holdren's views on the role of environmental science in public policy, see his AAAS presidential address, "Science and Technology for Sustainable Well-Being," *Science* 319 (January 25, 2008): 424–34.

10. For commentary on these kinds of conflicts over the role of science and scientists in policy decisions, see Martin Kady II, Mary Clare Jalonick, and Amol Sharma, "Science, Policy Mix Uneasily in Legislative Laboratory," *CQ Weekly*, March 20, 2004, 680–88; and Union of Concerned Scientists, "Scientific Integrity in Policymaking: An Investigation into the Bush Administration's Misuse of Science" (2004), available at the UCS Web site: www.ucsusa.org.

11. For example, see Leon M. Lederman and Shirley M. Malcolm, "The Next Campaign," *Science* 323 (March 6, 2009): 1265. Editorials in *Science* frequently call for improvements in the public's scientific literacy and often advocate increased involvement by scientists in public policy processes. Conflicts between the public's view of climate change and that of scientists can be seen in recent polls summarized in "An Inside/Outside View of U.S. Science," *Science* 325 (July 10, 2008), 132–33.

12. For commentary on the story, see Pam Belluck, "New England's Fishermen Fret for Industry's Future," *New York Times*, August 19, 2002, A9.

13. David M. Herszenhorn and Clifford Krauss, "Enthusiasm Builds for Helping a Shift to Fuel-Efficient Cars," *New Tork Times*, March 30, 2009, online edition; and Matthew L. Wald, "Cash Deal for 'Clunkers' So Popular That It's Broke," *New York Times*, July 31, 2009, B1, 6.

14. See Kirk Johnson, "City's Water-Quality Plan Working So Far, U.S. Finds," *New York Times*, June 1, 2002, A14.

15. Even by 2009, the IPCC forecasts released in 2007 were in need of updating, with newer estimates of accelerating climate change risks. See Eli Kintisch, "Projections of Climate Change Go From Bad to Worse, Scientists Report," *Science* 323 (March 20, 2009): 1546–47.

16. See Andrew C. Revkin, "New Climate Thriller: Scary, But Is It Science?" *New York Times*, December 14, 2004, D2.

17. For instance, a book published in 2002, a year after the terrorist attacks of September 11, 2001, highlighted public anxiety over unfamiliar, and highly publicized, risks; see David Ropeik and George Gray, *Risk: A Practical Guide for Deciding What's Really Safe and What's Really Dangerous in the World Around You* (Boston: Houghton Mifflin, 2002). The book sold briskly at the online sites for Amazon.com and Barnes and Noble.

18. One of the most thorough reviews of the disputes over the meaning of "rationality" in risk assessment and management and the implications for citizen participation in environmental policy is by the

philosopher K S. Shrader-Frechette (1991, 1993). See also Kraft (1994b, 1996) and Slovic (1993).

19. See the EPA's Web page on the subject: www.epa.gov/radon/.

20. Aside from being costly, the nuclear facilities cleanup relies heavily on private contractors rather than government personnel, and their work received a major boost from the Obama administration's economic stimulus program, $6 billion of which was dedicated to cleaning up 18 nuclear sites, twice the level of previous spending on the cleanup program. See Kimberly Kindy, "Rewarded Despite Errors," *Washington Post National Weekly Edition*, May 25–31, 2009, 34.

Acknowledgements

The authors gratefully acknowledge the financial assistance provide by the Texas Water Resources Institute and the Ogallala Aquifer Program, a consortium between USDA-Agricultural Research Service, Kansas State University, Texas AgriLife Research, Texas AgriLife Extension Service, Texas Teach University, and West Texas A&M University.

The authors also acknowledge the assistance of Ken Rainwater and Jeff Stovall of the Texas Water Resources Center, Texas Teach University, for technical assistance throughout the project. We thank Emmett Elam, Vernon Lansford, Erin Wheeler, and anonymous reviewers for their helpful comments.

References

Alley, W.M., Reilly, T.E. & Franke, O.L. (1999). *Sustainability of ground-water resources. USGS Circular 1186*. U.S. Geological Survey, Denver, CO.

Bredehoeft, J.D. & Young, R.A. (1970). The temporal allocation of ground water—a simulation approach. *Water Resources Research*, 6(1), 3–21.

Brooke, A., Kendrick, D., Meeraus, A. & Raman, R. (2003). *GAMS: A User's Guide,*, GAMS Development Corporation. Washington, DC.

Brown, J.E. & Lewis, R. (2001). *Texas Senate Bill 2—relating to the development and management of the water resources of the state*. 77th Texas Legislature, Regular Session, 2001. http:www.legis.state.tx.us/BillLookup/Text.aspx?LegSess=77 R&Bill=SB2

Brown, J.E., Lucio, E, & Wentworth, J. (1997). *Texas Senate Bill I—relating to the development and management of the water resources of the state*. 75th Texas Legislature, Regular Session, 1997, http://www.legis.state.tx.us/BillLookup/Text.aspx?LegSess=75R&Bill=SB1

Feng, Y. (1992). *Optimal intertemporal allocation of ground water for irrigation in the Texas High Plains*, Unpublished Doctoral Dissertation. Texas Teach University, Lubbock, TX.

Gerik, T., Harman, W., Williams, J., Francis, L., Griener, J., Magre, M., Meinardus, A. & Steglich, E, (2003). *User's Guide: CroPMan (Crop Production and Management Model)*. Blackland Research and Extension Center, Temple, TX.

Gisser, M, & Sanchez, D.A. (1980). Competition versus optimal control in groundwater pumping. *Water Resources Research*, 16(4), 638–642.

Harman, W.L. (1966). *An economic evaluation of irrigation water use over time on Texas High Plains forms with a rapidly diminishing water supply*. Unpublished Thesis, Texas A&M University, College Station, TX.

HDR Engineering, Inc. (2001). *Llano Estacado Regional Water Planning Area Regional Water Plan*. Prepared for Llano Estacado Water Planning Group. Lubbock, TX.

High Plains Associates (1982). *Six-state High Plains Ogallala Aquifer regional resources study. A report to the U.S. Department of Commerce and the High Plains Study Council*.

High Plains Underground Water Conservation District No. 1. (2004). *Llano Estacado Regional Water Planning Group, Information Paper*. http://www.hpwd.com/ogallala/llanogroup.asp (Last visited November 10, 2004).

House Research Organization (2000). *Management groundwater for Texas' future growth*. Texas House of Representatives Focus Report.

Kaiser, R.A. (1998). *A primer on Texas surface water law for the regional planning process*. Presented at Texas Water Law Conference, Austin, TX.

Kaiser, R.A. & Skillern, F.F. (2001). Deep trouble: options for managing the hidden threats of aquifer depletion in Texas. *Texas Teach Law Review*, 32(2), 249–304.

Kendy, E., Molden, D., Steenhuis, T., Liu, C. & Wang, J. (2003). *Policies drain the North China Plain: agricultural policies and groundwater depletion in Luancheng County, 1949–2000*. Research Report

71. International Water Management Institute, Colombo, Sri Lanka.

Koundouri, P. (2004). Potential for groundwater management: Gisser-Sanchez effect reconsidered. *Water Resources Research, 40,* W06S16 (doi:10.1029/2003WR002164).

Lansford, R.R., Gollehon, N.R., Mapel, C., Creel, B.J. & Ben-David, S. (1983). The on-farm economic impacts of the declining Ogallala Aquifer or the New Mexico High Plains, *Journal of American Society of Farm Managers and Rural Appraisers, 47,* 31–36.

Minnesota IMPLAN Group. Inc. (2000). *IMPLAN Professional, Version 2.0, Social Accounting & Impact Analysis Software.* Minnesota IMPLAN Group. Stillwater, MN.

Nativ, R. (1988). Hydrogeology and hydrochemistry of the Ogallala Aquifer, Southern High Plains, Texas Panhandle and Eastern New Mexico. *Report of Investigations No. 177.* Bureau of Economic Geology. Austin, TX.

Niewiadomy, M. (1985). The demand for irrigation water in the High Plains of Texas, 1957–80. *American Journal of Agricultural Economics, 67*(3), 619–626.

Panhandle Groundwater Conservation District (2006). *Rules of Panhandle Groundwater Conservation District.* http://www.panhandlegroundwater.org/

Peterson, J. M. & Ding, Y. (2005). Economic adjustment to groundwater depletion in the High Plains: do water-saving irrigation systems save water? *American Journal of Agricultural Economics, 87*(1), 147–159.

Rowse, J. (1995). Computing optimal allocations for discrete-time nonlinear natural resource models. *Natural Resource Modeling, 9*(2), 147–175.

Rubio, S. J. & Casino, B. (2001). Competitive versus efficient extraction of a common property resource: the groundwater case. *Journal of Economic Dynamic & Control, 25*(2001), 1117–1137.

Stovall, J.N. (2001). *Groundwater modeling for the Southern High Plains.* Unpublished Dissertation. Texas Teach University, Lubbock, TX.

Templer, O.W. (1989). Adjusting to groundwater depletion: the case of Texas and lessons for the future of the Southwest. In *Water and the Future of the Southwest,* Smith, Z.A. (ed). University of New Mexico Press. Albuquerque. (Chapter 14).

Terrell, B. (1998). *Economic impacts of the depletion of the Ogallala Aquifer: An application to the Texas High Plains.* Unpublished Masters Thesis. Texas Teach University. Lubbock, TX.

Terrell, B.L., Johnson, P.N. & Segarra, E, (2002). Ogallala Aquifer depletion: economic impact on the Texas High Plains. *Water Policy, 4,* 33–46.

Texas Agricultural Extension Service (2003). 2003 Texas Crop and Livestock Budgets. Texas A&M University, College Station, Texas. http://jenann.tamu.edu/budgets/district/1and2/2003/index.php (Last visited May 15, 2003).

Texas Agricultural Statistics Service (2002). *Texas Agricultural Statistics.* Austin, TX.

Texas Joint Committee on Water Resources (2002). *Interim Report to the 78th Legislature.* The Senate of the State of Texas, Austin, Texas.

Texas Water Development Board (2001). *Survey of irrigation in Texas,* Report 347. Texas Water Development Board, Austin, Texas.

chapter 6

Criminal Justice Policy

CRIMINAL JUSTICE POLICY

Christopher A. Simon

CHAPTER OVERVIEW

Criminal justice is one of the most visible confirmations of our liberal social contract—a commitment to the rule of law and due process. In recent years, the policy area has witnessed tremendous change. Many of the changes occurred prior to the terrorist acts of September 11, 2001, but a steady growth in national government influence in criminal justice has occurred over several decades. The events of September 11, however, accelerated change within criminal justice policy.

The specific goals for the chapter are:

- Discuss the major participants in criminal justice policy.
- Identify types of crime.
- Discuss causes of crime.
- Outline criminal procedure.
- Discuss perspectives on punishment.
- Discuss contemporary crime issues: hate crimes, child abduction, and racially biased policing.
- Discuss contemporary policing techniques and criminal justice issues
- Discuss the U.S.A. Patriot Act.

MAJOR PARTICIPANTS

COURTS

The lead officer in a criminal court is the judge. The judge plays the most significant role in making decisions that will protect an individual's right to a fair and speedy trial. The judge upholds policy (existing statutory and common law) and may create policy through common law decisions. Judges preside over the selection of fair and impartial juries, the actual trial process, and, if appropriate, determine punishment.

In terms of national criminal justice policy, district courts are the courts of original jurisdiction in criminal cases that involve federal law. Each state has at least one district court, but the exact number varies based on population factors. National courts become involved in criminal justice when: (1) an individual convicted of a state-level crime appeals his or her case to the national court system or (2) an individual is indicted by a federal grand jury on charges related to federal criminal law. (See Box 6.1, *Landmark Cases Related to Criminal Procedure*.)

ATTORNEYS

There are two major types of attorneys: **prosecuting attorneys** and **defense attorneys.** At the local level, prosecuting attorneys work within the district attorney's office. In national (or federal) criminal justice trials, the prosecuting attorneys are known as **assistant attorneys general** and work for the U.S. Department of Justice. Defense attorneys work either in private sector practice or are government-funded **public defenders,** representing defendants who are unable to afford representation.

ELECTED OFFICIALS

In the post-September 11 policy atmosphere, the presidency plays a much larger role in criminal justice policy. Although the president proposes policies, Congress crafts and introduces legislative bills. Legislation generally focuses on definitions of crime, criminal procedure, and programs designed to combat crime at the national, state, and local level. Criminal justice policy debates seek a balance between individual rights and freedoms, and the public good.

BUREAUCRACY

Criminal justice bureaucrats hold various titles. At the national level, criminal justice bureaucrats may be called federal agents or special agents. Federal or special agents work in agencies such as the Federal Bureau of Investigation (FBI) or Secret Service. At the state and local level, criminal justice bureaucrats include state troopers, sheriff's deputies, or police officers. Bureaucrats

---

"Criminal Justice Policy" from *Public Policy: Preferences and Outcomes, 2nd ed.*, by Christopher A. Simon, pp. 242-267. Copyright © 2010 by Pearson Education, Inc. Reprinted by permission.

BOX 6.1
LANDMARK CASES RELATED TO CRIMINAL PROCEDURE

A discussion of courts as actors in criminal justice; policy must not overlook the Supreme Court's role in formulating *criminal justice procedure*—the "methods that the government uses to detect, investigate, apprehend, prosecute, convict, and punish criminals.[10] Criminal procedure is outlined in the *Federal Rules of Criminal Procedure*, which serves as the basis for state and local government rules governing the method by which suspected offenders and convicted criminals are treated.

The Supreme Court has used a series of landmark court cases to delineate specific standards for criminal procedure.

Search & Seizure I *Wolf V. Colorado* 338 U.S. 25 (1949)

"... in a prosecution in a state court for a state crime, the Fourteenth Amendment does not forbid the admission of evidence obtained by an unreasonable search and seizure. The question whether Congress could validly enact legislation permitting the introduction in Federal courts of evidence seized in violation of the Fourth Amendment was left open."

Exclusionary Rule *Mapp V. Ohio* 367 U.S. 643 (1961)

Overturned *Wolf v. Colorado* (1961). "... it was held that, as a matter of due process, evidence obtained by a search and seizure in violation of the Fourth Amendments is inadmissible in a state court as it is in a federal court."

Search & Seizure II *Terry V. Ohio* 392 U.S. 1 (1967)

The Court offers a clearer definition of reasonable search. In the case of imminent danger (suspect is "armed and dangerous") the police can, in the course of an arrest, take the seized weapon as evidence that can be used as evidence in a trial. "... it was held that the search was a reasonable search under the Fourth Amendment, and that the revolver seized from the defendant was properly introduced in evidence, where the police officer reasonably concluded in the light of his experience that criminal activity might be afoot and that persons with whom he was dealing might be armed and presently dangerous," Emergent from the *Terry* case was the "*Terry* stop" and "*Terry* search." The Court found that in cases in which the police confront an armed and dangerous individual, they can enter and search private property for the promotion of community safety.

Self-Incrimination *Malloy V. Hogan* 378 U.S. 1 (1964)

"... it was held that (1) the Fourteenth Amendment makes the Fifth Amendment privilege against self-incrimination applicable to the states; (2) the privilege, if properly invoked in a state proceeding, is governed by federal standards, and (3) judged by those standards, the petitioner's claim of privilege should have upheld."

Assistance Of Counsel *Gideon V. Wainwright* 372 U.S. 335 (1963)

"... it was held that the Sixth Amendment's provision that in all criminal prosecutions the accused shall enjoy the right to have the assistance of counsel for his defense was made obligatory upon the states by the Fourteenth Amendment."

Confrontation Of Witness *Pointer V. Texas* 380 U.S. 400 (1965)

The defendant did not have counsel, yet was denied the right to cross-examine witnesses at his trial. "... it was held that (1) the Sixth Amendment's guaranty protecting an accused's right to confront the witnesses against him was made obligatory on the states by the Fourteenth Amendment."

Compulsion Of Witness *Washington V. Texas* 388 U.S. 14 (1967)

The defendant claimed to have been denied the right to have a convicted individual who was party to the crime testify on his behalf. "...it was held that an accused's. Sixth Amendment right to have compulsory process for obtaining witnesses in his favor was so fundamental that it could be considered incorporated in the due process clause of the Fourteenth Amendment and that the defendant was denied such right in the instant case."

continued

> **BOX 6.1—con'd**
>
> **LANDMARK CASES RELATED TO CRIMINAL PROCEDURE**
>
> **Speedy Trial** *Klopfer V. N. Carolina* **386 U.S. 213 (1967)**
>
> Juries failed to convict an individual on the same changes on two occasions. The prosecutor had been granted the opportunity to try the individual on the same changes at an unspecified future date when the prosecuting attorney had collected further evidence, ". . . it was held that (1) the Sixth Amendment's guaranty of an accused right to a speedy trial was rendered applicable to the states through the due process clause of the Fourteenth Amendment, and (2) this right was denied accused by the procedure applied in the instant case."
>
> **Cruel And Unusual Punishment** *Robinson V. California* **370 U.S. 660 (1962)**
>
> A drug addict was incarcerated under a California state law that makes drug addiction illegal. The Court overturned the conviction concluding that addiction is not a criminal offense; rather, addiction is an illness that requires medical treatment rather than punishment. ". . . it was held that the [California] statute inflicted] a cruel and unusual punishment in violation of the Eighth and Fourteenth Amendments."
>
> Through their decisions in the these landmark cases, the Court has defined and applied elements of the U.S. Constitution's Bill of Rights to national, state, and local criminal procedure. The Court's influence does not end here; the Court continues to define the constitutionality of criminal procedure through cases that come before the justices.

enforce criminal laws, criminal justice policies, and criminal procedures in a manner consistent with constitutional law and jurisdiction statutes.

Interest Groups

Interest groups abound in criminal justice policy. Although some groups support strong criminal justice policies and enforcement, other groups focus on the rights of the individual in relation to the power of the state to create and enforce laws. The latter groups tend to be vigilant and critical of expanded powers of the government and limitations on individual freedom.

Police unions represent the interests of law enforcement personnel. Unions seek to protect their members from liability as they do their jobs. Unions want processes to be clear cut so that officers, their members, can do their jobs with confidence. Unions support salary and benefit packages that are worthy of the law enforcement function.

The mission of the American Civil Liberties Union (ACLU) is to "Keep America safe and free."[1] More specifically, the ACLU seeks to restrain the application of the Fourth and Sixth Amendments—that is, the ACLU does not support expanded searches and seizure powers and wishes to restrain harsh sentences such as "three strikes and you're out" or capital punishment. Also, the ACLU sees the War on Terrorism as destructive to basic rights and liberties.

Types of Crime

There are two major types of crime: person-related crime and property-related crime. **Person-related crimes** involve the physical assault or threat of assault on another person's physical being or psyche or a crime against oneself with the intent to cause harm. Person-related crimes include: murder, assault, drug use or dealing, and domestic violence. Property crimes involve the taking, damaging, or destroying of property belonging to another individual or individuals. Property-related crimes include: burglary, forgery, vandalism, and arson.

Homicide and Other Violent Crimes

The homicide rate in the United States is higher than in other industrialized nations. In 1991, the homicide rate was 9.8 (crime rates are the number of crime events per 100,000 population), but that rate has been largely declining for more than a decade. In 2008, the homicide rate was 5.4—approximately 16,500 murders. (See Figure 6.1.)

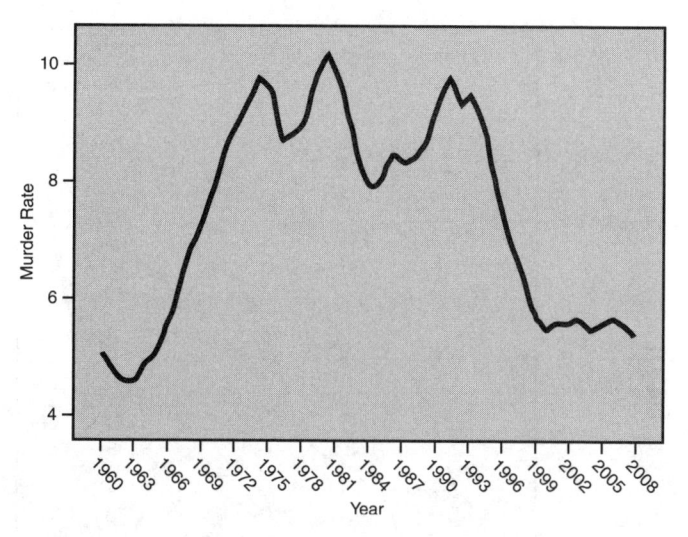

FIGURE 6.1 Murder rate (1960–2008).

Forcible rape rates steadily increased from 9.6 in 1960 to 42.8 in 1992. Since 1993, forcible rape rates have declined to 29.0 in 2008—more than 88,000 forcible rapes. Robbery rates have declined since 1991, the 2008 rate being 144.0—roughly, 440,000 robberies. Aggravated assault rates have declined to 272 in 2005 from a high of 441.8 in 1992. The 2008 aggravated assault rates are at their lowest level in 30+ years. (See Figures 6.2–6.4)

Property Crimes

Property-related crime involves the use or taking of property that belongs to someone other than the individual caught using or taking the property. The Bureau of Justice Statistics (BJS) has three major categories of property crime:

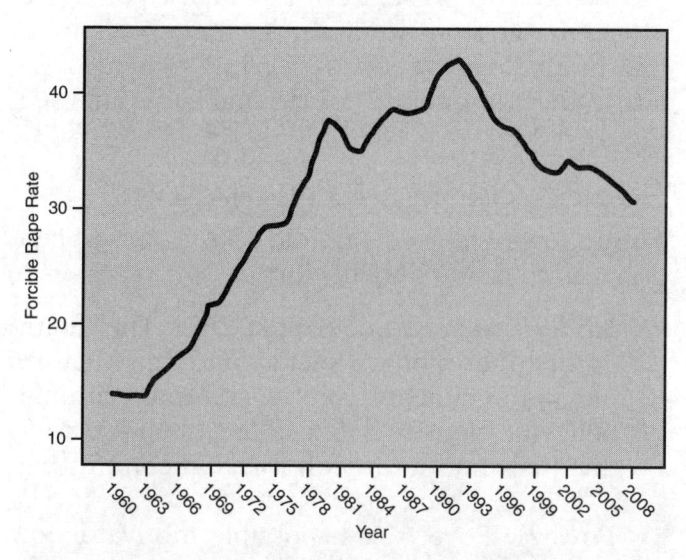

FIGURE 6.2 Forcible rape rate (1960–2008).

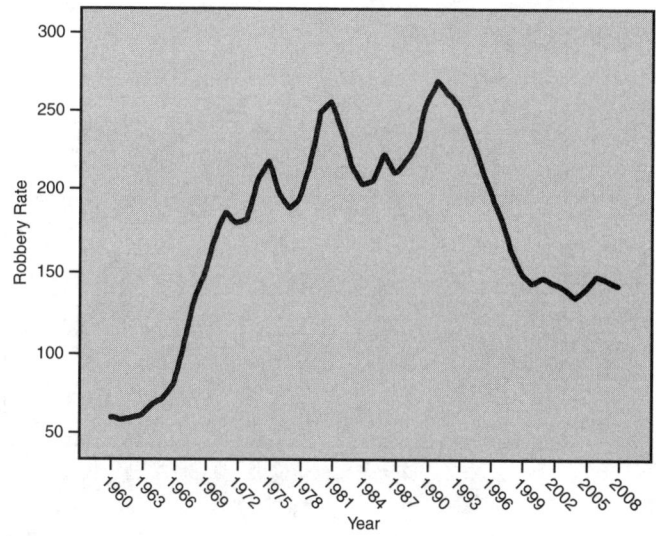

FIGURE 6.3 Robbery rate (1960–2008).

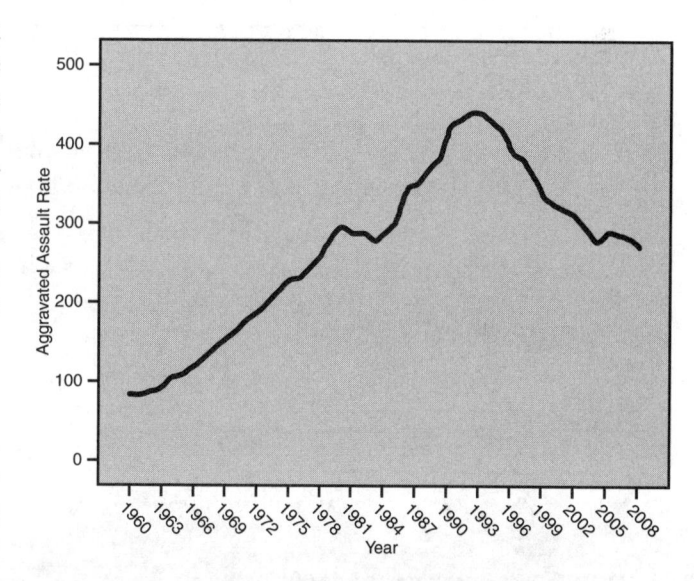

FIGURE 6.4 Aggravated assault rate (1960–2008).

burglary, auto theft, and larceny. Between 1960 and 1980, burglary rates increased by more than 200 percent, according to the BJS report drawn from the Uniform Crime Statistics (UCS) collected by the FBI. With some exceptions in the mid-1980s, the burglary rate in the United States has steadily declined between 1980 and 2008 and now stands at a rate not seen since the mid-1960s. (See Figures 6.5–6.7)

Drug Crimes

A four-year study of drug-related crime (1995–1998) found that arrests for the possession, manufacture, sale, or use of illegal drugs rose modestly during the late 1990s. In 1995, the arrest rate for drugs was 564.7. By 2000, however, the rate

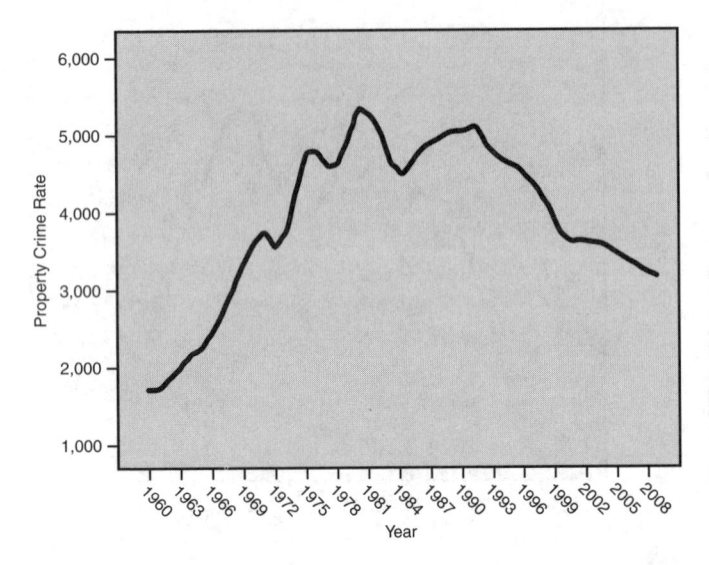

FIGURE 6.5 Property crime rate (1960–2008).

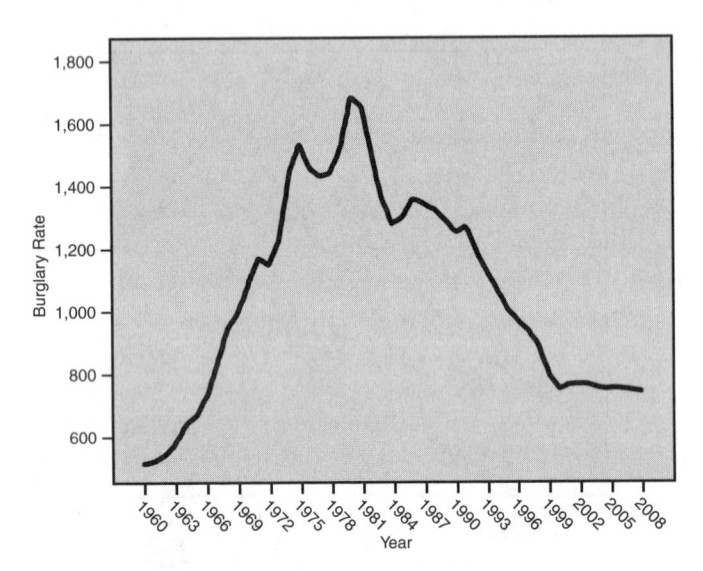

FIGURE 6.6 Burglary rate (1960–2008).

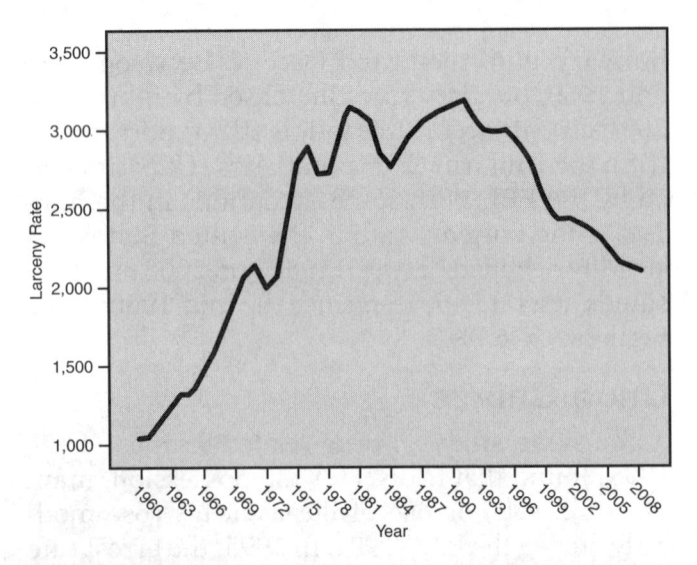

FIGURE 6.7 Larceny rate (1960–2008).

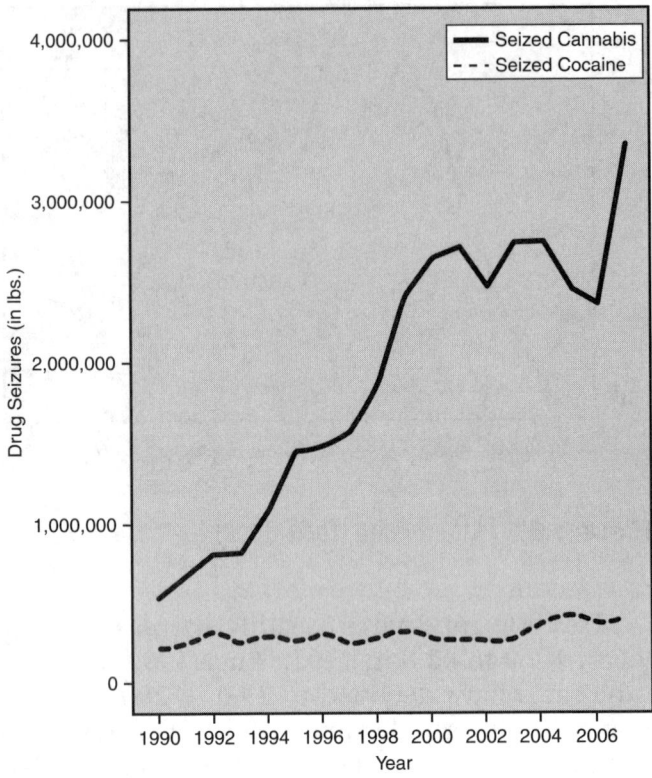

FIGURE 6.8 Drug seizures (lbs.) (1990–2007).

had risen to 587.1. Drug arrest rates have retreated moderately from the 2000 arrest rate. Drug seizures increased tremendously since 1990, with cannabis seizures rising at rate much greater than cocaine seizures. (See Figure 6.8.)

CAUSES OF CRIME

Causes of crime are really theories about criminal behavior—what it is, why it occurs, and what can be done to prevent crime. Theories of crime often emerge from studies of genetics, sociology, and psychology. Theories of crime may also relate to the "rationality" of criminal behavior. (See Figure 6.9.)

SOCIOECONOMIC EXPLANATIONS

The following socioeconomic factors have been ascribed to criminal behavior:

- **Modern society:** Sociologist Emile Durkheim argued that modern society and its structure plays a significant role in creating criminal behavior. Society defines illegal behavior; individuals find it difficult to avoid committing a "criminal" act.
- **Poverty:** Poverty is a possible motivator for certain property crimes, whereas the cul-

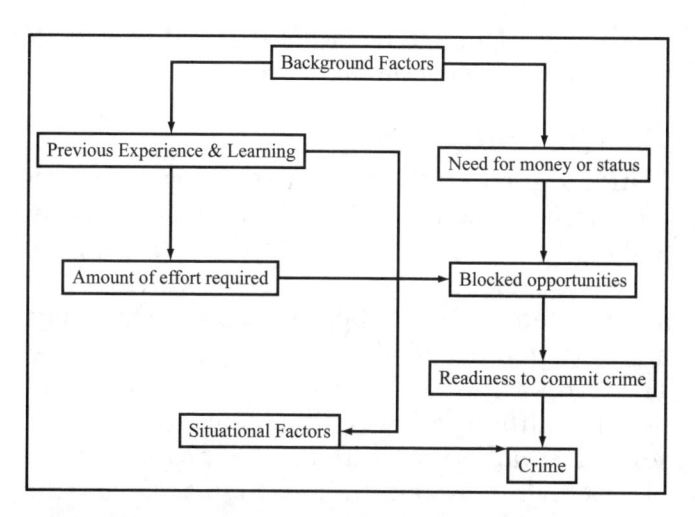

FIGURE 6.9 Theories of crime.
Source: Adapted from D. Cornish and R. Clarke, eds. 1986. *The Reasoning Criminal.* New York: Springer-Verlag.

ture of poverty is an explanation for violent crimes.
- **Education:** Crime theories argue that individuals with lower levels of education have a higher probability of committing criminal acts. The choice to reject formal education may be a "first step" in the development of antisocial attitudes, juvenile delinquency, or deviancy.
- **Race or ethnicity:** Theorists have long discussed subgroup characteristics in relation to general socioeconomic conditions and, more controversially, a subculture's tendency to use violence as an acceptable method of solving disputes or pursuing personal goals.

BIOLOGICAL THEORIES OF CRIME

Possibly the oldest theory of crime, it was once thought that criminals were physically and emotionally weakened individuals easily possessed and influenced by evil spirits. Many biological theories have fallen into disrepute. Contemporary biological theories consider two factors:

- **Genetic composition:** Often focuses on relationships between parental characteristics and predilection to engage in criminal behavior, relating the findings to offsprings' (and siblings') criminality.
- **Intelligence:** IQ tests and psychological profiles have been used to explain and predict the probability of criminal behavior. With some exceptions, criminals tend to have lower levels of intellectual and emotional intelligence.

CRIMES AND CRIMINAL PROCEDURE

The Federal Rules of Criminal Procedure outline six major elements of **criminal procedure:**

- *Preliminary proceedings:* Following the collection of evidence, the prosecuting attorney requests an arrest warrant from a judge. Law enforcement executes the arrest warrant, making an arrest. An exception to this rule is if law enforcement personnel witness a crime—criminal suspects can be arrested for community protection. Still, an arrest warrant is issued for the particular charge.

  The charges against a person (the defendant) are presented to a judge or magistrate during an initial appearance by the defendant. If the judge does not find probable cause for proceeding, the charges against the person are dropped. If the judge finds probable cause, the charges are presented to a grand jury.
- *Indictment:* Only the prosecuting attorney, judge, and grand jury are present. If the grand jury finds that the evidence is sufficient for a trial, there is an arraignment.[2]
- *Arraignment:* In an open courtroom, the charges against a defendant are made public and the defendant is asked to enter a plea of guilt or innocence. If the defendant pleads innocent, then a venue for trial must be determined. A defendant likely has chosen defense counsel at this point—private attorney or public defender.
- *Venue:* A trial date and location is chosen. The trial may occur in another jurisdiction to ensure fairness to the defendant.
- *Trial:* At trial, a defendant will be asked whether or not he or she wishes to be tried by jury. If a jury trial is chosen, then unbiased adult citizens (normally twelve individuals) must be chosen prior to the commencement of the trial. If the defendant is found guilty of the charges presented against him or her, then the judge establishes a date for sentencing.
- *Postconviction procedures:* Prior to sentencing, the victim or the victim's family are given an opportunity to speak in court to discuss the economic and emotional impact of the crime. The convicted person is also given an opportunity to speak prior to sentencing.

Perspectives on Punishment
Rehabilitation Versus Retribution

Proponents of rehabilitation believe that socioeconomic deprivation often contributes to criminal behavior, a condition that must be rectified by society. Proponents of rehabilitation tend to hold modern liberal perspectives of crime policy—the criminal is less advantaged in relation to other members of society. The impact of rehabilitation programs is unclear, possibly due to underfunding.

Proponents of retribution see crime as a rational choice—the prospective criminal considers the costs and benefits of crime. Punishment is one way of increasing potential costs, thereby discouraging crime. Proponents of retribution tend toward a classical liberal view of crime and punishment. The impact of retributive crime policy is publicly debated.

Three Strikes and You're Out

In the 1990s, ballot initiatives were passed in many states requiring life sentences for third-time felons—twenty-six states have provisions that qualify as "three strikes" policies. Proponents argue that by the third "strike," rehabilitation efforts have obviously not succeeded and society should exact retributive justice.

Community Corrections

Community corrections facilities are for low-security-risk prisoners who have committed lesser offenses. Inmates are taught decision-making skills, helping them return to "real life" in a free society. Community corrections intends for inmates to discover the benefits of crime-free life, reducing **recidivism.**

House Arrest and Electronic Surveillance

With more than 1.5 million individuals in federal and state prisons, policy experts seek alternative methods of punishment. Technology has made it possible to restrict individuals' movements and behavior in their own homes through electronic monitoring, often used for lesser offenses. Electronic bands are attached to the prisoner; if he or she wanders from proscribed boundaries or violates curfew restrictions, law enforcement locates and apprehends the individual. Proponents argue that the method is cheaper and effective, having the effect of reintegrating prisoners into free society. Opponents argue that it does not effectively punish criminals.

Death Penalty

Critics argue that the death penalty does not deter crime and is based in a false sense of moral justice. Life in prison without the possibility of parole is seen as having the equivalent effect on a convicted criminal. Death penalty critics also argue that the punishment is applied unfairly. The proportion of blacks receiving the death penalty, although lower than that of whites, is several times greater than the proportion of blacks living in the United States. Given the disadvantaged socioeconomic backgrounds of many black criminals, critics charge that it is a socially unjust punishment. Critics of the death penalty tend to be modern liberals.

Proponents see a moral element to the death penalty and support **retributive justice**—punishment should be a form of revenge for a criminal act against other parties to the social contract. Proponents claim that higher execution rates are related to decreases in violent crime. Proponents are not overly concerned with the racial composition of the condemned—punishment focuses solely on crime itself. Proponents are inclined to support the tenets of classical liberalism. (See Figure 6.10.)

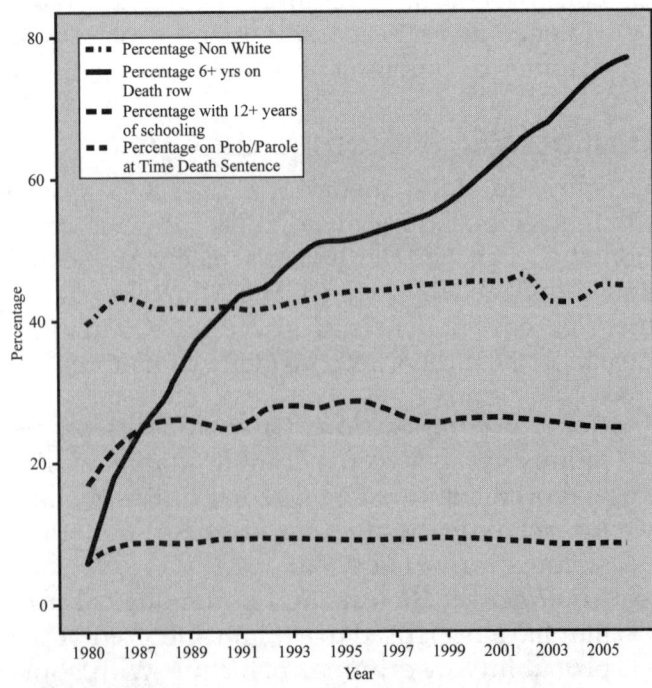

Figure 6.10 Characteristics of death row prisoners (1980–2006).

Incarceration Policy and Management

Punishment for criminal acts usually involves the loss of liberty through incarceration. When an individual is convicted of a crime and sentenced to prison or jail, the government assumes responsibility for protecting prisoners' rights and for providing for basic needs (e.g., food, shelter, and clothing). Government is also responsible for determining what it seeks to achieve for the prisoner, within the scope of the individual's rights—societal retribution or rehabilitation or a combination of both.

Control Model of Incarceration

The control model views incarceration as being both punishment leading to contrition and sense of social renewal. According to DiIulio (1987), the control model advocates that each prisoner should "do his [or her] own time," reflecting on past criminal choices. The validity of this approach is not supported by data—recidivism rates remain high.

Responsibility Model of Incarceration

The responsibility model downplays the symbols of authority that govern prisons. The model focuses attention on the variations in prisoner type, matching the prisoner to incarceration strategies. The responsibility model often rewards good behavior and self-discipline. Prisoners are offered some ability to learn new behaviors that will serve them well should they regain their freedom.

Consensual Model of Incarceration

Prison guards are expected to act professionally. But, unlike the control model, this approach can be viewed as a weak form of the responsibility model. Except for violent prisoners, the consensual model incorporates inmates into prison governance. The model often maintains prison security through nonviolent methods.

Hot Topic Crimes in the Twenty-First Century

Certain types of crime are of particular interest in the United States today. Three types of crime that are often discussed in media reports are **hate crimes, child abuse,** and **public corruption.**

Hate Crimes

In the early 1990s, the state of Wisconsin passed legislation implementing stronger penalties for violent crimes in which the victim had been selected on the basis of his or her race, gender, ethnicity, religion, or sexual preference. The law reflected model legislation developed by a public interest group known as the Anti-Defamation League (ADL). The legislation was supported by interest groups (e.g., National Organization for Women, gay rights advocacy groups, and groups representing various ethnic minority causes) as well as members of the broader community. The statute was challenged in *Wisconsin v. Mitchell* 508 U.S. 476 (1993), but the Supreme Court did not find the law unconstitutional. Although U.S. hate crimes law had already initiated a nationwide monitoring program (see Figures 6.11–6.15), the Court decision was key to effectively legitimizing legislation, to include:

- ***The Hate Crime Statistics Act of 1990 (28 U.S.C. 534)***
  The law required that from 1990 to 1994, the U.S. Department of Justice would collect annual data on violent or property-related crimes that showed evidence of prejudice in relation to the victim's race, ethnicity, religion, or sexual orientation.
- ***The Hate Crimes Sentencing Enhancement Act of 1994 (28 U.S.C. 534)***
  "This act requires the Department of Justice to collect data on hate crimes. Hate crimes are defined as 'manifest prejudice based on race, religion, sexual orientation, . . . ethnicity, [and disability]'."[3]
- ***The Violence Against Women Act of 1994 (42 U.S.C. 13981)***
  ". . . provides for . . . grants are 'to assist States, Indian tribal governments, and units of local government to develop and strengthen effective law enforcement and prosecution strategies to combat violent crimes against women, and to develop and strengthen victim services in cases involving violent crimes against women'" (Burt et al. 1996).
- ***The Church Arsons Prevention Act of 1996 (18 U.S.C. 247)***
  "This act created the National Church Arson Task Force (NCATF) in June 1996 to oversee the investigation and prosecution of arson at houses of worship around the country."[4]

FIGURE 6.11 Hate crimes involving religion (1995–2007).

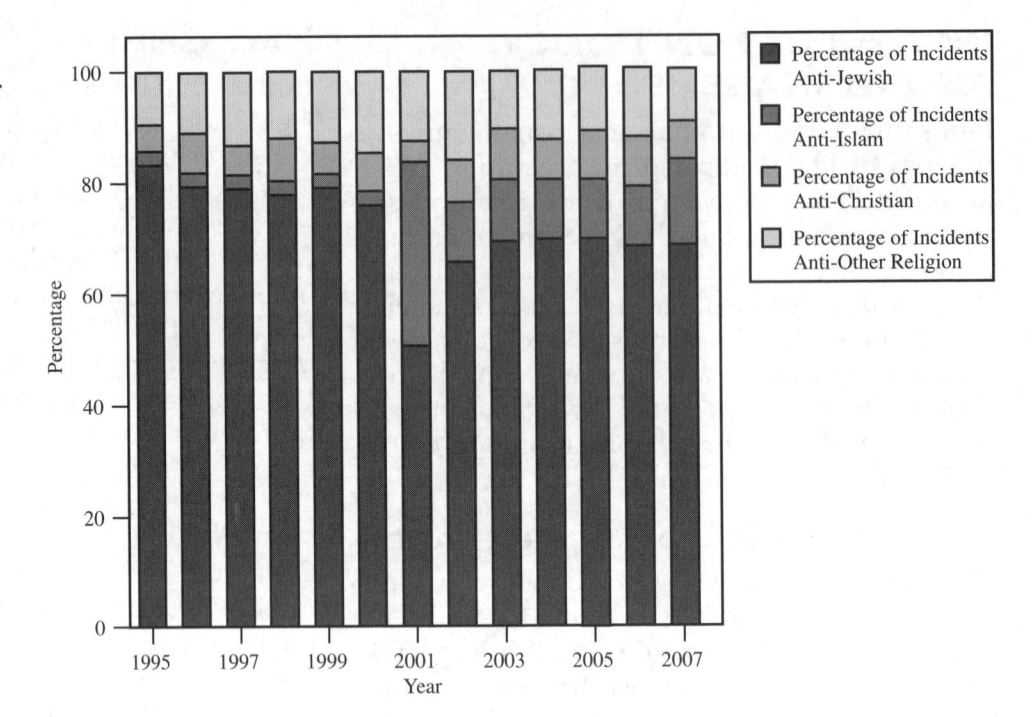

FIGURE 6.12 Hate crimes involving race (1995–2007).

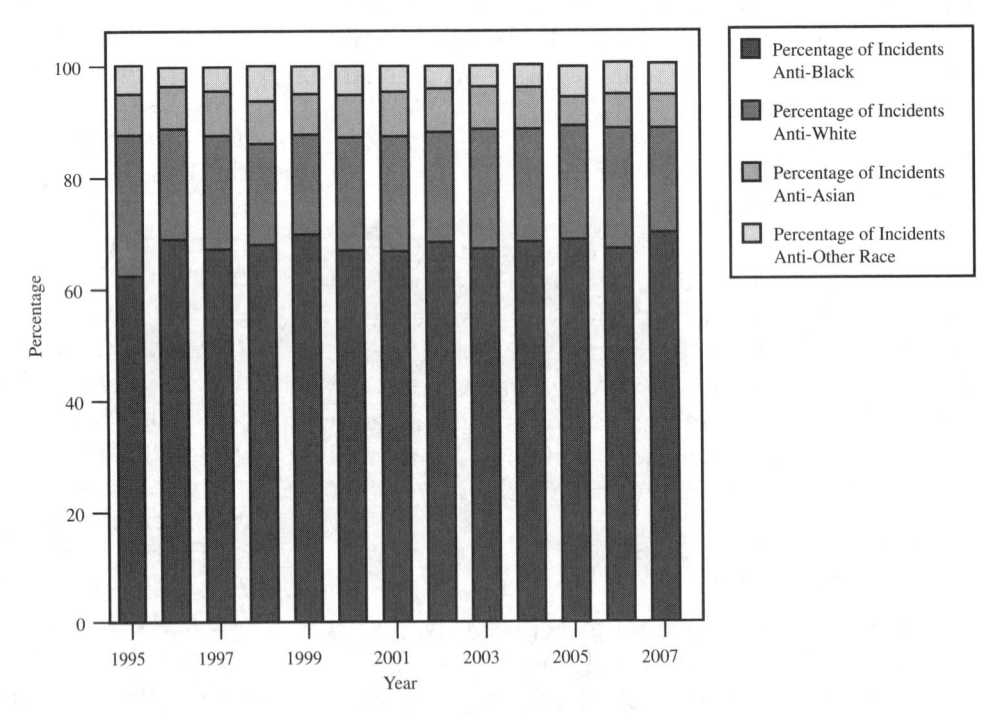

- **Hate Crimes Prevention Acts of 1998 and 1999**
  "... prohibits persons from interfering with an individual's Federal rights (voting or employment) by violence or threat of violence due to his or her race, color, religion, or national origin ... allows for more authority for the Federal government to investigate and prosecute hate crime offenders who committed their crime because of perceived sexual orientation, gender, or disability of the victim."[5]

In 1997 and 1998, the hate crime incidence rate declined marginally, but increased sharply from 1999 through 2001. The percentage of hate crimes that led to indictments is particularly high for cases involving race, ethnicity, gender or sexual preference, religion, and physical disability. Most religion-based hate crimes are directed against adherents of Judaism. Prior to September 11, anti-Islamic hate crimes reported were never greater than 3 percent of all religion-based hate crimes reported nationwide.

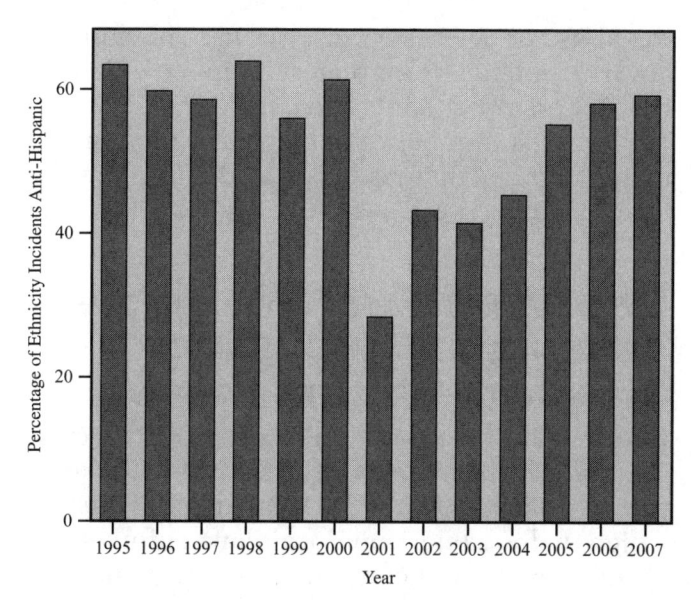

FIGURE 6.13 Hate crimes involving ethnicity: percentage anti-Hispanic (1995–2007).

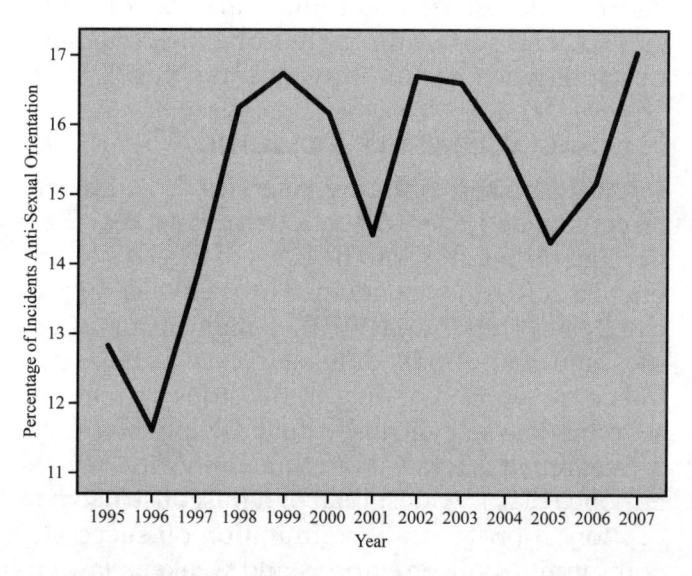

FIGURE 6.14 Hate crimes involving antisexual orientation (1995–2007).

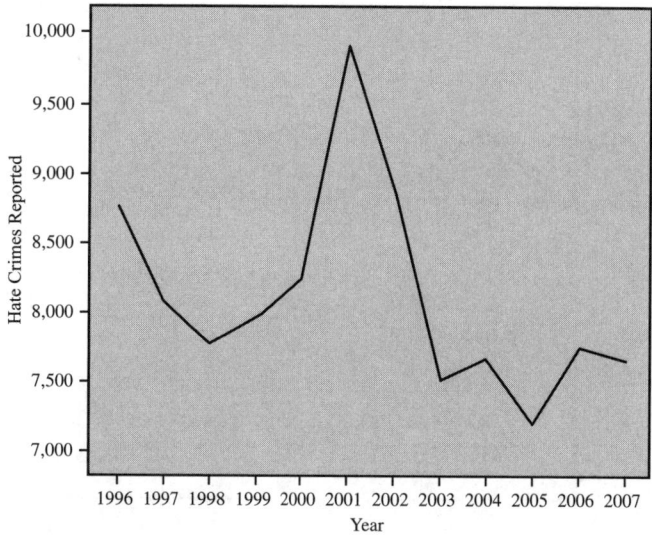

FIGURE 6.15 Hate crimes reported (1995–2007).

Since September 11, anti-Islam hate crimes have increased.

CHILD ABUSE

In the 1990s, child abductions, sexual assault, abuse, and murder became a highly visible part of criminal justice policy. The 1996 abduction and murder of Amber Hagerman in Texas led to the **Amber Alert** system, part of a nationwide effort to keep the public informed about abductions in local communities. The interstate or international transportation (e.g., Internet) of children or images for sexual exploitation is a violation of federal law.[6] The FBI and other law enforcement agencies enforce antiexploitation laws to protect children's rights.

The Violent Crime Control and Law Enforcement Act of 1996 (42 U.S.C. 14071) requires the registration of individuals convicted of crimes against children. Known as **Megan's Law,** the statute "arms the public with certain information on the whereabouts of dangerous sex offenders . . . . The law also authorizes local law enforcement to notify the public about high-risk and serious sex offenders who reside in, are employed in, or frequent the community. . . . The law is not intended to punish the offender and specifically prohibits using the information to harass or commit any crime against the offender."[7]

According to the Children's Bureau, Department of Health and Human Services, child maltreatment investigation rates have increased dramatically. Reported in the *Statistical Abstract of the United States*, there were approximately 900,000 child abuse cases in the United States in 2005. According to the Children's Bureau report cited here, the single most common perpetrator of child maltreatment is the child's mother acting alone. (See Figure 6.16 and Table 6.1.)

PUBLIC CORRUPTION

Public corruption refers to malfeasance on the part of government officials. Public corruption could involve using power and authority for personal gain or the misuse of government information or public funds. It might also involve

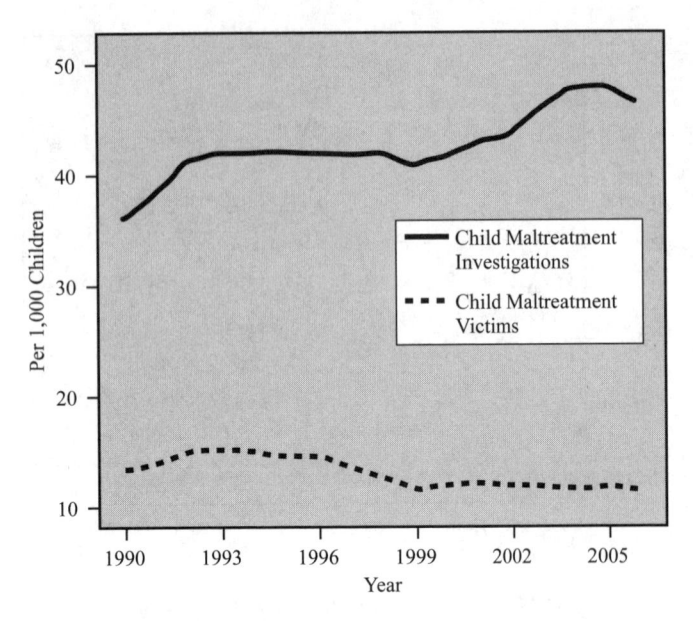

FIGURE 6.16 Child maltreatment rates (1990–2006).

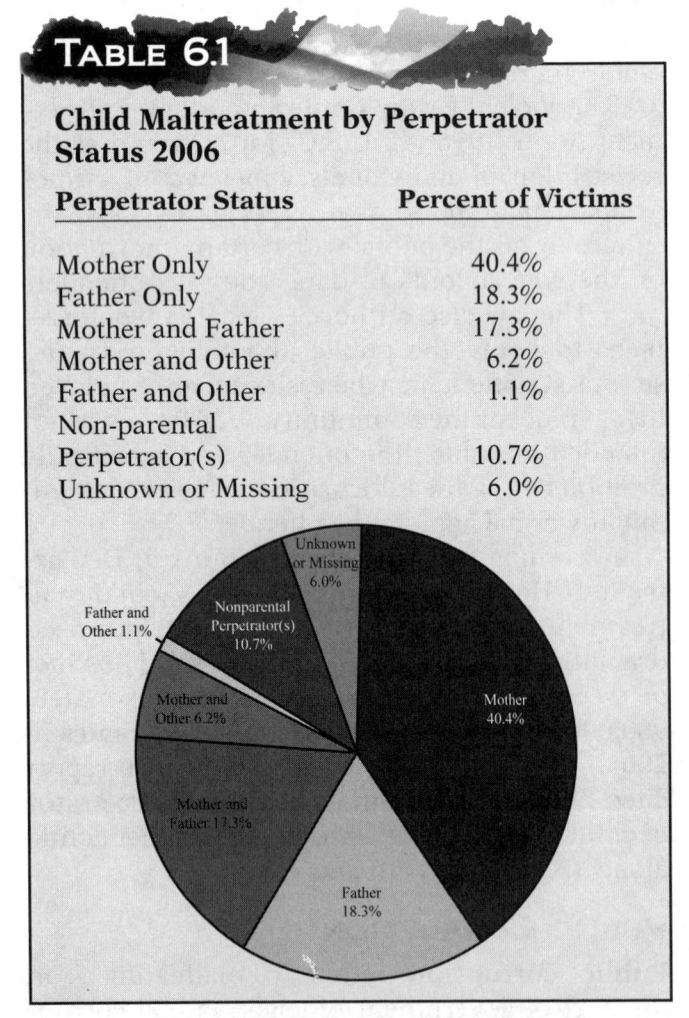

TABLE 6.1

Child Maltreatment by Perpetrator Status 2006

Perpetrator Status	Percent of Victims
Mother Only	40.4%
Father Only	18.3%
Mother and Father	17.3%
Mother and Other	6.2%
Father and Other	1.1%
Non-parental Perpetrator(s)	10.7%
Unknown or Missing	6.0%

Source: U.S. Department of Health and Human Services, Administration on Children, Youth and Families 2007. *Child Maltreatment 2005*. Washington, DC: US Government Printing Office.

the abuse of coworkers or citizens. The national government has the greatest number of public corruption indictments and convictions. The second greatest number of public corruption indictments and convictions occur at the local level—nearly 300 cases per year. (See Figure 6.17.)

CONTEMPORARY POLICING TECHNIQUES AND ISSUES

COMMUNITY-ORIENTED POLICING

Community-oriented policing (COP) represents a return to many of the historical principles of policing. The U.S. Department of Justice, which helps state and local law enforcement agencies build and continue to develop the COP programs, defines this contemporary policing paradigm as "a policing philosophy that promotes and supports organizational strategies to address the causes and reduce the fear of crime and social disorder through problem-solving tactics and police–community partnerships."[8]

RACIALLY BIASED POLICING

Racially biased policing refers to ". . . law enforcement activities (detentions, arrests, searches) that are initiated . . . on the basis of race."[9] According to a 2001 study conducted by the Police Executive Research Forum (PERF), a majority of minorities and white individuals surveyed believe that police frequently conduct traffic stops and initiate searches because the individual driving the car being searched is a racial or ethnic minority. Whether police bias is widespread or a misconstrued perception, it proves to be a limitation on successful community–police relations and weakens law enforcement capacity. Many police agencies conduct analyses of traffic stop and citizen–police interactions to determine whether racial bias is present. Additionally, police are reaching out to local communities to reestablish mutual trust.

U.S.A. PATRIOT ACT, ANTITERRORISM, AND CRIMINAL JUSTICE POLICY

The **U.S.A. Patriot Act** is a policy response to the events of 9/11. The Patriot Act broadens the powers of federal law enforcement in the following ways:

- Relaxes requirements for searches and seizures, particularly in the area of electronic transmission surveillance.

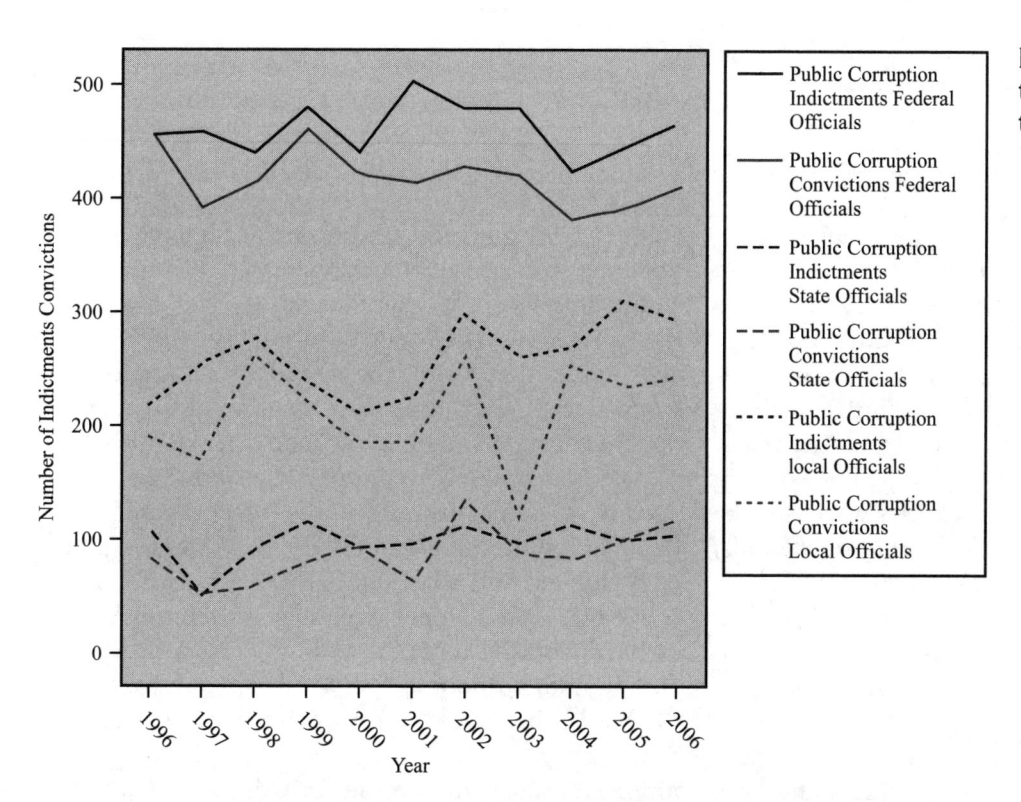

FIGURE 6.17 Public corruption: indictments and convictions (1996–2006).

- Relaxes *posse commitatus* restrictions—the U.S. military can now play a role in criminal apprehension within the United States. *Posse commitatus* laws were an attempt to keep military and domestic policy areas separate.
- Increases penalties for money laundering activities and requires private businesses involved in large business deals to file suspicious activity reports (SARs), documenting the exchange of money for goods and/or services that could conceivably be used for terrorist activities.
- Reduces controls on government monitoring activities and expands government's role in accounting for private financial transactions.
- Coordinates domestic and foreign intelligence efforts to construct a more complete view of terrorism worldwide in relation to U.S. security and criminal justice policy areas. (See Box 6.2, *Immigration and Identity Theft*.)

Explaining Criminal Justice Policy
Elite Theory

Criminal justice policy defines crime. At the national level, the presidency and Congress are composed of elected policy elites who make major decisions about criminal justice policy. President George W. Bush's antiterrorism initiative was the newest and largest addition to criminal justice policy, although Bush's approach is currently being reevaluated by the Obama administration.

Appointed elites—federal judges, Supreme Court justices, presidential appointees—and senior civil servants have visible roles in criminal justice policy. Judges and Supreme Court justices shape criminal justice policy through court judicial interpretations. Attorneys general, the secretary of Homeland Security, and the FBI director are examples of policy elites shaping policy formulation and implementation. Senior civil servants are administrative elites who shape policy decisions.

Elites are temporary actors in the policy process—elected officials win and lose elections. Judges and justices retire from office eventually. Civil servants finish their careers and leave their posts. Policy elites, therefore, are constantly changing. These changes eventually lead to changing policy priorities. Elites represent different notions of what government *ought* or *ought not* do, and their views directly impact policy priorities.

Group Theory

Pressure groups play a substantial role in shaping criminal justice policy in the United States. The criminalization of drugs is vigorously opposed by drug-legalization advocacy groups. Other groups actively support and lobby for even more stringent penalties for drug dealing, possession, and

BOX 6.2
IMMIGRATION AND IDENTITY THEFT

One of the more serious issues to emerge from illegal immigration is identity theft.[11] In order to gain employment, illegal immigrants often produce some form of fake identification indicating their legal status in the United States. In the past, employers often did not have the time nor the incentive to check the accuracy of those documents. In recent years, Homeland Security has begun to crack down on employers and illegal immigrant workers who use fake documents or steal the identity of other individuals, such as citizens' Social Security numbers.

Although one approach to the problem of identity theft by illegal immigrants is through law enforcement activities—that is, regulatory policy—President George W. Bush proposed an alternative solution—a distributive policy. Namely, Bush proposed registering illegal immigrants. His plan was that after illegal immigrants have identified themselves as illegal, they are to return to their native countries for a period of time before applying for documented status. After applying for documented status, immigrant workers would be given a criminal background check and assuming the result was acceptable, they would be given work permits to work in the United States for a period of time. Opponents of Bush's plan have called it "amnesty."

Public opinion of immigrants, however, has become more positive. Recently, the Pew Research Center[12] found that about one-third of opinion poll respondents felt that immigrants increased the crime rate. Increasingly, the public sees immigrants as hard-working individuals from close-knit families. Although opponents of Bush's plan have won the battle, an increasingly positive image of immigrants might lead to some form of official recognition of their status in the United States,[13] which in turn might contribute to a reduction in identity theft concerns.

use. The three strikes laws came into being due to pressure group advocacy leading to citizens' ballot initiative campaigns to create the policies. Death penalty advocates and opponents often work feverishly to ensure that an execution occurs, or to file legal papers to delay or stop an execution. Crime policy provokes sharp divisions about what government *ought* or *ought not* do.

INSTITUTIONALISM

The institutions of government that create and implement criminal justice policy play a substantial role in what these policies represent. Community-oriented policing and racial profiling illustrate the challenges institutions face when confronted with the need for change. Community-oriented policing challenges law enforcement officers to reconsider decades of development within policing practices. Racial profiling policy requires a reconsideration of the goal and method of achieving public safety. Law enforcement at the national, state, and local levels must establish new priorities and methods of fighting crime while preserving civil rights and liberties.

The most dangerous right

Dennis A. Henigan March 01, 2010

In its second landmark Second Amendment case in two years, the U.S. Supreme Court, in *McDonald v. City of Chicago,* considers whether the new right to possess guns in the home, declared in its 2008 ruling in *District of Columbia v. Heller,* is incorporated as a restraint against state and local law through the 14th Amendment.

As intriguing as the incorporation issue is as a matter of constitutional law, the ultimate significance of *McDonald* to ordinary Americans may turn on a different issue, not formally posed by the case but difficult to avoid as the Court considers the reach of the *Heller* right. The "hidden" issue in *McDonald* is this: To what extent is the right to keep and bear arms different in nature from the other guarantees in the Bill of Rights?

In terms of the incorporation issue, particularly under a due process clause analysis, the issue is whether the Second Amendment is as "fundamental," or as "implicit in the concept of ordered liberty," as other rights previously held incorporated under that test. But even if the Court decides that the *Heller* right meets the test for incorporation, other critical issues also will turn on whether the Second Amendment is properly analogous to other provisions of the Bill of Rights. For the future of gun control laws, the most important of these issues may be whether courts should closely scrutinize the considered judgments of state and local legislative bodies on gun control (similar to the standard of review in certain First Amendment cases) or whether they should be highly deferential to those judgments.

There is at least one respect in which the new right to have guns is vastly different than other rights. A wealth of empirical evidence shows that the exercise of the right to possess guns increases the risk of harm to individuals exercising the right, to their families and to the community at large. However the Court decides the incorporation question, its discussion of Second Amendment issues in *McDonald* and its future Second Amendment jurisprudence must recognize that the Second Amendment is, indisputably, the most dangerous right.

Although the *Heller* right is to possess a gun in the home for self-defense, there is, unfortunately, no way to guarantee that guns will be used only for that salutary purpose. In fact, the research shows that, for every time a gun in the home is used in a self-defense shooting, there are four unintentional shootings (often involving young children), seven criminal assaults (often involving domestic disputes) and 11 completed or attempted suicides.

It is unassailable that guns are simply more lethal than other weapons. Domestic assaults with firearms are more than 23 times as likely to be deadly than assaults with all other weapons or bodily force. It is hardly surprising, therefore, that the presence of a gun in the home is associated with a threefold increase in the risk of homicide and a fivefold increase in the risk of suicide. This is not to deny that guns are used in lawful self-defense of the home. The point is that gun possession, on balance, increases the risk of physical harm.

The increased risk also is borne by the community at large. As one study concluded, "an increase in gun prevalence causes an intensification of criminal violence — a shift toward greater lethality, and hence greater harm to the community." Indeed, states with the highest levels of gun ownership have 60% higher homicide rates than states with the lowest levels of gun ownership. The more Americans decide to exercise the *Heller* right, the more deadly violence becomes.

Of course, it is true that the exercise of free expression, for example, also can create a risk of violence or physical injury. If that risk becomes sufficiently great, the courts will deny the protection of the First Amendment altogether. But the core exercise of freedom of expression is unlikely to pose serious risks of physical harm, particularly

"The most dangerous right" by Dennis A. Henigan from *The National Law Journal.* Copyright © 2010. ALM Properties, LLC. All rights reserved. National Law Journal Online: http://www.nlj.com.

lethal harm. The same cannot be said about the Second Amendment right.

Indeed, the dangers necessarily posed by the widespread exercise of the right to possess guns were implicitly recognized in *Heller* itself. The Court went out of its way to offer reassurance about the continued constitutionality of other gun laws not as restrictive as the District of Columbia handgun ban at issue in *Heller*. "[N]othing in our opinion," the Court wrote, "should be taken to cast doubt on" the constitutionality of several broad categories of gun laws, including "laws imposing conditions and qualifications on the commercial sale of arms." The majority thus sent a strong signal to the lower courts that the Second Amendment was not to be applied to severely restrict the authority of our elected officials to ameliorate the danger posed by exercise of the new right.

Even if the Court decides to incorporate the *Heller* right, it should make explicit what was left implicit in *Heller* — that the unique risks associated with the exercise of the right to gun possession require that the courts show great deference to the elected representatives of the people in fashioning public policies to reduce those risks. Courts in states with their own constitutional guarantees of the personal right to be armed have reached a strong consensus that gun laws need only be a reasonable exercise of the police power to be upheld. If it applies the Second Amendment to the states, the McDonald Court should announce a similarly deferential standard of review.

It is unclear whether the high court will declare the Second Amendment right as "fundamental" as the other rights that have been applied to the states. But even if it does, it should confront the hard reality that this "fundamental" right is also the most dangerous right of all.

Dennis Henigan is vice president for law and policy at the Brady Center to Prevent Gun Violence, which filed briefs amicus curiae in the Heller *and* McDonald *cases. He also is the author of* Lethal Logic: Exploding the Myths that Paralyze American Gun Policy *(Potomac Books 2009).*

District of Columbia et al. v. Heller

certiorari to the united states court of appeals for the district of columbia circuit
Argued March 18, 2008–Decided June 26, No. 07–290. 2008

District of Columbia law bans handgun possession by making it a crime to carry an unregistered firearm and prohibiting the registration of handguns; provides separately that no person may carry an unlicensed handgun, but authorizes the police chief to issue 1-year licenses; and requires residents to keep lawfully owned firearms unloaded and dissembled or bound by a trigger lock or similar device. Respondent Heller, a D. C. special policeman, applied to register a handgun he wished to keep at home, but the District refused. He filed this suit seeking, on Second Amendment grounds, to enjoin the city from enforcing the bar on handgun registration, the licensing requirement insofar as it prohibits carrying an unlicensed firearm in the home, and the trigger-lock requirement insofar as it prohibits the use of functional firearms in the home. The District Court dismissed the suit, but the D. C. Circuit reversed, holding that the Second Amendment protects an individual's right to possess firearms and that the city's total ban on handguns, as well as its requirement that firearms in the home be kept nonfunctional even when necessary for self-defense, violated that right.

Held:

1. The Second Amendment protects an individual right to possess a firearm unconnected with service in a militia, and to use that arm for traditionally lawful purposes, such as self-defense within the home. Pp. 2–53.
    (a) The Amendment's prefatory clause announces a purpose, but does not limit or expand the scope of the second part, the operative clause. The operative clause's text and history demonstrate that it connotes an individual right to keep and bear arms. Pp. 2–22.
    (b) The prefatory clause comports with the Court's interpretation of the operative clause. The "militia" comprised all males physically capable of acting in concert for the common defense. The Antifederalists feared that the Federal Government would disarm the people in order to disable this citizens' militia, enabling a politicized standing army or a select militia to rule. The response was to deny Congress power to abridge the ancient right of individuals to keep and bear arms, so that the ideal of a citizens' militia would be preserved. Pp. 22–28.
    (c) The Court's interpretation is confirmed by analogous arms-bearing rights in state constitutions that preceded and immediately followed the Second Amendment. Pp. 28–30.
    (d) The Second Amendment's drafting history, while of dubious interpretive worth, reveals three state Second Amendment proposals that unequivocally referred to an individual right to bear arms. Pp. 30–32.
    (e) Interpretation of the Second Amendment by scholars, courts and legislators, from immediately after its ratification through the late 19th century also supports the Court's conclusion. Pp. 32–47.
    (f) None of the Court's precedents forecloses the Court's interpretation. Neither *United States v. Cruikshank*, 92 U. S. 542, 553, nor *Presser v. Illinois*, 116 U. S. 252, 264–265, refutes the individual-rights interpretation. *United States v. Miller*, 307 U. S. 174, does not limit the right to keep and bear arms to militia purposes, but rather limits the type of weapon to which the right applies to those used by the militia, *i.e.*, those in common use for lawful purposes. Pp. 47–54.
2. Like most rights, the Second Amendment right is not unlimited. It is not a right to keep

and carry any weapon whatsoever in any manner whatsoever and for whatever purpose: For example, concealed weapons prohibitions have been upheld under the Amendment or state analogues. The Court's opinion should not be taken to cast doubt on longstanding prohibitions on the possession of firearms by felons and the mentally ill, or laws forbidding the carrying of firearms in sensitive places such as schools and government buildings, or laws imposing conditions and qualifications on the commercial sale of arms. *Miller*'s holding that the sorts of weapons protected are those "in common use at the time" finds support in the historical tradition of prohibiting the carrying of dangerous and unusual weapons. Pp. 54–56.

3. The handgun ban and the trigger-lock requirement (as applied to self-defense) violate the Second Amendment. The District's total ban on handgun possession in the home amounts to a prohibition on an entire class of "arms" that Americans overwhelmingly choose for the lawful purpose of self-defense. Under any of the standards of scrutiny the Court has applied to enumerated constitutional rights, this prohibition–in the place where the importance of the lawful defense of self, family, and property is most acute–would fail constitutional muster. Similarly, the requirement that any lawful firearm in the home be disassembled or bound by a trigger lock makes it impossible for citizens to use arms for the core lawful purpose of self-defense and is hence unconstitutional. Because Heller conceded at oral argument that the D. C. licensing law is permissible if it is not enforced arbitrarily and capriciously, the Court assumes that a license will satisfy his prayer for relief and does not address the licensing requirement. Assuming he is not disqualified from exercising Second Amendment rights, the District must permit Heller to register his handgun and must issue him a license to carry it in the home. Pp. 56–64.

478 F. 3d 370, affirmed.

Scalia, J., delivered the opinion of the Court, in which *Roberts, C. J.,* and *Kennedy, Thomas,* and *Alito, JJ.,* joined. Stevens, J., filed a dissenting opinion, in which *Souter, Ginsburg,* and *Breyer, JJ.,* joined. Breyer, J., filed a dissenting opinion, in which *Stevens, Souter,* and *Ginsburg, JJ.,* joined.

DISTRICT OF COLUMBIA, *ET AL., PETITIONERS V.* DICK ANTHONY HELLER

on writ of certiorari to the united states court of appeals for the district of columbia circuit
[June 26, 2008]

Justice Scalia delivered the opinion of the Court.

We consider whether a District of Columbia prohibition on the possession of usable handguns in the home violates the Second Amendment to the Constitution.

I

The District of Columbia generally prohibits the possession of handguns. It is a crime to carry an unregistered firearm, and the registration of handguns is prohibited. See D. C. Code §§7–2501.01(12), 7–2502.01(a), 7–2502.02(a)(4) (2001). Wholly apart from that prohibition, no person may carry a handgun without a license, but the chief of police may issue licenses for 1-year periods. See §§22–4504(a), 22–4506. District of Columbia law also requires residents to keep their lawfully owned firearms, such as registered long guns, "unloaded and dissembled or bound by a trigger lock or similar device" unless they are located in a place of business or are being used for lawful recreational activities. See §7–2507.02.[1]

Respondent Dick Heller is a D. C. special police officer authorized to carry a handgun while on duty at the Federal Judicial Center. He applied for a registration certificate for a handgun that he wished to keep at home, but the District refused. He thereafter filed a lawsuit in the Federal District Court for the District of Columbia seeking, on Second Amendment grounds, to enjoin the city from enforcing the bar on the registration of handguns, the licensing requirement insofar as it prohibits the carrying of a firearm in the home without a license, and the trigger-lock requirement insofar as it prohibits the use of "functional firearms within the home." App. 59a. The District Court dismissed respondent's complaint, see *Parker* v. *District of Columbia*, 311 F. Supp. 2d 103, 109 (2004). The Court of Appeals for the District of Columbia

Circuit, construing his complaint as seeking the right to render a firearm operable and carry it about his home in that condition only when necessary for self-defense,[2] reversed, see *Parker v. District of Columbia*, 478 F. 3d 370, 401 (2007). It held that the Second Amendment protects an individual right to possess firearms and that the city's total ban on handguns, as well as its requirement that firearms in the home be kept nonfunctional even when necessary for self-defense, violated that right. See id., at 395, 399–401. The Court of Appeals directed the District Court to enter summary judgment for respondent.

We granted certiorari. 552 U. S. ___ (2007).

II

We turn first to the meaning of the Second Amendment.

A

The Second Amendment provides: "A well regulated Militia, being necessary to the security of a free State, the right of the people to keep and bear Arms, shall not be infringed." In interpreting this text, we are guided by the principle that "[t]he Constitution was written to be understood by the voters; its words and phrases were used in their normal and ordinary as distinguished from technical meaning." *United States* v. *Sprague*, 282 U. S. 716, 731 (1931); see also *Gibbons v. Ogden*, 9 Wheat. 1, 188 (1824). Normal meaning may of course include an idiomatic meaning, but it excludes secret or technical meanings that would not have been known to ordinary citizens in the founding generation.

The two sides in this case have set out very different interpretations of the Amendment. Petitioners and today's dissenting Justices believe that it protects only the right to possess and carry a firearm in connection with militia service. See Brief for Petitioners 11–12; *post*, at 1 *(Stevens, J., dissenting)*. Respondent argues that it protects an individual right to possess a firearm unconnected with service in a militia, and to use that arm for traditionally lawful purposes, such as self-defense within the home. See Brief for Respondent 2–4.

The Second Amendment is naturally divided into two parts: its prefatory clause and its operative clause. The former does not limit the latter grammatically, but rather announces a purpose. The Amendment could be rephrased, "Because a well regulated Militia is necessary to the security of a free State, the right of the people to keep and bear Arms shall not be infringed." See J. Tiffany, A Treatise on Government and Constitutional Law §585, p. 394 (1867); Brief for Professors of Linguistics and English as *Amici Curiae* 3 (hereinafter Linguists' Brief). Although this structure of the Second Amendment is unique in our Constitution, other legal documents of the founding era, particularly individual-rights provisions of state constitutions, commonly included a prefatory statement of purpose. See generally Volokh, The Commonplace Second Amendment, 73 N. Y. U. L. Rev. 793, 814–821 (1998).

Logic demands that there be a link between the stated purpose and the command. The Second Amendment would be nonsensical if it read, "A well regulated Militia, being necessary to the security of a free State, the right of the people to petition for redress of grievances shall not be infringed." That requirement of logical connection may cause a prefatory clause to resolve an ambiguity in the operative clause ("The separation of church and state being an important objective, the teachings of canons shall have no place in our jurisprudence." The preface makes clear that the operative clause refers not to canons of interpretation but to clergymen.) But apart from that clarifying function, a prefatory clause does not limit or expand the scope of the operative clause. See F. Dwarris, A General Treatise on Statutes 268–269 (P. Potter ed. 1871) (hereinafter Dwarris); T. Sedgwick, The Interpretation and Construction of Statutory and Constitutional Law 42–45 (2d ed. 1874).[3] " 'It is nothing unusual in acts ... for the enacting part to go beyond the preamble; the remedy often extends beyond the particular act or mischief which first suggested the necessity of the law.' " J. Bishop, Commentaries on Written Laws and Their Interpretation §51, p. 49 (1882) (quoting *Rex* v. *Marks*, 3 East, 157, 165 (K. B. 1802)). Therefore, while we will begin our textual analysis with the operative clause, we will return to the prefatory clause to ensure that our reading of the operative clause is consistent with the announced purpose.[4]

1. OPERATIVE CLAUSE.

a. "Right of the People." The first salient feature of the operative clause is that it codifies a "right of the people." The unamended Constitution and the Bill of Rights use the phrase "right of the people" two other times, in the First Amendment's

Assembly–and-Petition Clause and in the Fourth Amendment's Search-and-Seizure Clause. The Ninth Amendment uses very similar terminology ("The enumeration in the Constitution, of certain rights, shall not be construed to deny or disparage others retained by the people"). All three of these instances unambiguously refer to individual rights, not "collective" rights, or rights that may be exercised only through participation in some corporate body.[5]

Three provisions of the Constitution refer to "the people" in a context other than "rights"–the famous preamble ("We the people"), §2 of Article I (providing that "the people" will choose members of the House), and the Tenth Amendment (providing that those powers not given the Federal Government remain with "the States" or "the people"). Those provisions arguably refer to " the people" acting collectively–but they deal with the exercise or reservation of powers, not rights. Nowhere else in the Constitution does a "right" attributed to "the people" refer to anything other than an individual right.[6]

What is more, in all six other provisions of the Constitution that mention "the people," the term unambiguously refers to all members of the political community, not an unspecified subset. As we said in *United States* v. *Verdugo-Urquidez*, 494 U. S. 259, 265 (1990):

"'[T]he people' seems to have been a term of art employed in select parts of the Constitution.... [Its uses] sugges[t] that 'the people' protected by the Fourth Amendment, and by the First and Second Amendments, and to whom rights and powers are reserved in the Ninth and Tenth Amendments, refers to a class of persons who are part of a national community or who have otherwise developed sufficient connection with this country to be considered part of that community."

This contrasts markedly with the phrase "the militia" in the prefatory clause. As we will describe below, the "militia" in colonial America consisted of a subset of "the people"–those who were male, able bodied, and within a certain age range. Reading the Second Amendment as protecting only the right to "keep and bear Arms" in an organized militia therefore fits poorly with the operative clause's description of the holder of that right as "the people."

We start therefore with a strong presumption that the Second Amendment right is exercised individually and belongs to all Americans.

b. "Keep and bear Arms." We move now from the holder of the right–"the people"–to the substance of the right: "to keep and bear Arms."

Before addressing the verbs "keep" and "bear," we interpret their object: "Arms." The 18th-century meaning is no different from the meaning today. The 1773 edition of Samuel Johnson's dictionary defined "arms" as "weapons of offence, or armour of defence." 1 Dictionary of the English Language 107 (4th ed.) (hereinafter Johnson). Timothy Cunningham's important 1771 legal dictionary defined "arms" as "any thing that a man wears for his defence, or takes into his hands, or useth in wrath to cast at or strike another." 1 A New and Complete Law Dictionary (1771); see also N. Webster, American Dictionary of the English Language (1828) (reprinted 1989) (hereinafter Webster) (similar).

The term was applied, then as now, to weapons that were not specifically designed for military use and were not employed in a military capacity. For instance, Cunningham's legal dictionary gave as an example of usage: "Servants and labourers shall use bows and arrows on *Sundays*, &c. and not bear other arms." See also, *e.g.*, An Act for the trial of Negroes, 1797 Del. Laws ch. XLIII, §6, p. 104, in 1 First Laws of the State of Delaware 102, 104 (J. Cushing ed. 1981 (pt. 1)); see generally State v. *Duke*, 42 Tex. 455, 458 (1874) (citing decisions of state courts construing "arms"). Although one founding-era thesaurus limited "arms" (as opposed to "weapons") to "instruments of offence *generally* made use of in war," even that source stated that all firearms constituted "arms." 1 J. Trusler, The Distinction Between Words Esteemed Synonymous in the English Language 37 (1794) (emphasis added).

Some have made the argument, bordering on the frivolous, that only those arms in existence in the 18th century are protected by the Second Amendment. We do not interpret constitutional rights that way. Just as the First Amendment protects modern forms of communications, e.g., *Reno* v. *American Civil Liberties Union*, 521 U. S. 844, 849 (1997), and the Fourth Amendment applies to modern forms of search, *e.g.*, *Kyllo* v. *United States*, 533 U. S. 27, 35–36 (2001), the Second Amendment extends, prima facie, to all instruments that constitute bearable arms, even those that were not in existence at the time of the founding.

We turn to the phrases "keep arms" and "bear arms." Johnson defined "keep" as, most relevantly, "[t]o retain; not to lose," and "[t]o have in custody." Johnson 1095. Webster defined it as "[t]o hold; to retain in one's power or possession." No party has apprised us of an idiomatic meaning of "keep Arms." Thus, the most natural reading of "keep Arms" in the Second Amendment is to "have weapons."

The phrase "keep arms" was not prevalent in the written documents of the founding period that we have found, but there are a few examples, all of which favor viewing the right to "keep Arms" as an individual right unconnected with militia service. William Blackstone, for example, wrote that Catholics convicted of not attending service in the Church of England suffered certain penalties, one of which was that they were not permitted to "keep arms in their houses." 4 Commentaries on the Laws of England 55 (1769) (hereinafter Blackstone); see also 1 W. & M., c. 15, §4, in 3 Eng. Stat. at Large 422 (1689) ("[N]o Papist ... shall or may have or keep in his House ... any Arms ... "); 1 Hawkins, Treatise on the Pleas of the Crown 26 (1771) (similar). Petitioners point to militia laws of the founding period that required militia members to "keep" arms in connection with militia service, and they conclude from this that the phrase "keep Arms" has a militia-related connotation. See Brief for Petitioners 16–17 (citing laws of Delaware, New Jersey, and Virginia). This is rather like saying that, since there are many statutes that authorize aggrieved employees to "file complaints" with federal agencies, the phrase "file complaints" has an employment-related connotation. "Keep arms" was simply a common way of referring to possessing arms, for militiamen *and everyone else*.[7]

At the time of the founding, as now, to "bear" meant to "carry." See Johnson 161; Webster; T. Sheridan, A Complete Dictionary of the English Language (1796); 2 Oxford English Dictionary 20 (2d ed. 1989) (hereinafter Oxford). When used with "arms," however, the term has a meaning that refers to carrying for a particular purpose–confrontation. In *Muscarello* v. *United States*, 524 U. S. 125 (1998), in the course of analyzing the meaning of "carries a firearm" in a federal criminal statute, *Justice Ginsburg* wrote that "[s]urely a most familiar meaning is, as the Constitution's Second Amendment ... indicate[s]: 'wear, bear, or carry ... upon the person or in the clothing or in a pocket, for the purpose ... of being armed and ready for offensive or defensive action in a case of conflict with another person.' " *Id.*, at 143 (dissenting opinion) (quoting Black's Law Dictionary 214 (6th ed. 1998)). We think that *Justice Ginsburg* accurately captured the natural meaning of "bear arms." Although the phrase implies that the carrying of the weapon is for the purpose of "offensive or defensive action," it in no way connotes participation in a structured military organization.

From our review of founding-era sources, we conclude that this natural meaning was also the meaning that "bear arms" had in the 18th century. In numerous instances, "bear arms" was unambiguously used to refer to the carrying of weapons outside of an organized militia. The most prominent examples are those most relevant to the Second Amendment: Nine state constitutional provisions written in the 18th century or the first two decades of the 19th, which enshrined a right of citizens to "bear arms in defense of themselves and the state" or "bear arms in defense of himself and the state." [8] It is clear from those formulations that "bear arms" did not refer only to carrying a weapon in an organized military unit. Justice James Wilson interpreted the Pennsylvania Constitution's arms-bearing right, for example, as a recognition of the natural right of defense "of one's person or house"–what he called the law of "self preservation." 2 Collected Works of James Wilson 1142, and n. x (K. Hall & M. Hall eds. 2007) (citing Pa. Const., Art. IX, §21 (1790)); see also T. Walker, Introduction to American Law 198 (1837) ("Thus the right of self-defence [is] guaranteed by the [Ohio] constitution"); see also *id.*, at 157 (equating Second Amendment with that provision of the Ohio Constitution). That was also the interpretation of those state constitutional provisions adopted by pre-Civil War state courts.[9] These provisions demonstrate–again, in the most analogous linguistic context–that "bear arms" was not limited to the carrying of arms in a militia.

The phrase "bear Arms" also had at the time of the founding an idiomatic meaning that was significantly different from its natural meaning: "to serve as a soldier, do military service, fight" or "to wage war." See Linguists' Brief 18; post, at 11 (*Stevens*, J., dissenting). But it *unequivocally* bore that idiomatic meaning only when followed by the preposition "against," which was in turn followed by the target of the hostilities. See 2 Oxford 21. (That is how, for example, our Declaration of Independence ¶28, used the phrase: "He has constrained our fellow Citizens taken

Captive on the high Seas to bear Arms against their Country ... .") Every example given by petitioners' *amici* for the idiomatic meaning of "bear arms" from the founding period either includes the preposition "against" or is not clearly idiomatic. See Linguists' Brief 18–23. Without the preposition, "bear arms" normally meant (as it continues to mean today) what *Justice Ginsburg*'s opinion in *Muscarello* said.

In any event, the meaning of "bear arms" that petitioners and *Justice Stevens* propose is *not even* the (sometimes) idiomatic meaning. Rather, they manufacture a hybrid definition, whereby "bear arms" connotes the actual carrying of arms (and therefore is not really an idiom) but only in the service of an organized militia. No dictionary has ever adopted that definition, and we have been apprised of no source that indicates that it carried that meaning at the time of the founding. But it is easy to see why petitioners and the dissent are driven to the hybrid definition. Giving "bear Arms" its idiomatic meaning would cause the protected right to consist of the right to be a soldier or to wage war–an absurdity that no commentator has ever endorsed. See L. Levy, Origins of the Bill of Rights 135 (1999). Worse still, the phrase "keep and bear Arms" would be incoherent. The word "Arms" would have two different meanings at once: "weapons" (as the object of "keep") and (as the object of "bear") one-half of an idiom. It would be rather like saying "He filled and kicked the bucket" to mean "He filled the bucket and died." Grotesque.

Petitioners justify their limitation of "bear arms" to the military context by pointing out the unremarkable fact that it was often used in that context–the same mistake they made with respect to "keep arms." It is especially unremarkable that the phrase was often used in a military context in the federal legal sources (such as records of congressional debate) that have been the focus of petitioners' inquiry. Those sources would have had little occasion to use it *except* in discussions about the standing army and the militia. And the phrases used primarily in those military discussions include not only "bear arms" but also "carry arms," "possess arms," and "have arms"–though no one thinks that those *other* phrases also had special military meanings. See Barnett, Was the Right to Keep and Bear Arms Conditioned on Service in an Organized Militia?, 83 Tex. L. Rev. 237, 261 (2004). The common references to those "fit to bear arms" in congressional discussions about the militia are matched by use of the same phrase in the few nonmilitary federal contexts where the concept would be relevant. See, *e.g.*, 30 Journals of Continental Congress 349–351 (J. Fitzpatrick ed. 1934). Other legal sources frequently used "bear arms" in nonmilitary contexts.[10] Cunningham's legal dictionary, cited above, gave as an example of its usage a sentence unrelated to military affairs ("Servants and labourers shall use bows and arrows on *Sundays*, &c. and not bear other arms"). And if one looks beyond legal sources, "bear arms" was frequently used in nonmilitary contexts. See Cramer & Olson, What Did "Bear Arms" Mean in the Second Amendment?, 6 Georgetown J. L. & Pub. Pol'y (forthcoming Sept. 2008), online at http://papers.ssrn.com/abstract=1086176 (as visited June 24, 2008, and available in Clerk of Court's case file) (identifying numerous nonmilitary uses of "bear arms" from the founding period).

Justice Stevens points to a study by *amici* supposedly showing that the phrase "bear arms" was most frequently used in the military context. See *post*, at 12–13, n. 9; Linguists' Brief 24. Of course, as we have said, the fact that the phrase was commonly used in a particular context does not show that it is limited to that context, and, in any event, we have given many sources where the phrase was used in nonmilitary contexts. Moreover, the study's collection appears to include (who knows how many times) the idiomatic phrase "bear arms against," which is irrelevant. The *amici* also dismiss examples such as " 'bear arms ... for the purpose of killing game' " because those uses are "expressly qualified." Linguists' Brief 24. (*Justice Stevens* uses the same excuse for dismissing the state constitutional provisions analogous to the Second Amendment that identify private-use purposes for which the individual right can be asserted. See *post*, at 12.) That analysis is faulty. A purposive qualifying phrase that contradicts the word or phrase it modifies is unknown this side of the looking glass (except, apparently, in some courses on Linguistics). If "bear arms" means, as we think, simply the carrying of arms, a modifier can limit the purpose of the carriage ("for the purpose of self-defense" or "to make war against the King"). But if "bear arms" means, as the petitioners and the dissent think, the carrying of arms only for military purposes, one simply cannot add "for the purpose of killing game." The right "to carry arms in the militia for the purpose of killing game" is worthy of the mad hatter. Thus, these purposive qualifying phrases positively establish that "to bear arms" is not limited to military use.[11]

Justice Stevens places great weight on James Madison's inclusion of a conscientious-objector clause in his original draft of the Second Amendment: "but no person religiously scrupulous of bearing arms, shall be compelled to render military service in person." Creating the Bill of Rights 12 (H. Veit, K. Bowling, & C. Bickford eds. 1991) (hereinafter Veit). He argues that this clause establishes that the drafters of the Second Amendment intended "bear Arms" to refer only to military service. See *post*, at 26. It is always perilous to derive the meaning of an adopted provision from another provision deleted in the drafting process.[12] In any case, what *Justice Stevens* would conclude from the deleted provision does not follow. It was not meant to exempt from military service those who objected to going to war but had no scruples about personal gunfights. Quakers opposed the use of arms not just for militia service, but for any violent purpose whatsoever–so much so that Quaker frontiersmen were forbidden to use arms to defend their families, even though "[i]n such circumstances the temptation to seize a hunting rifle or knife in self-defense ... must sometimes have been almost overwhelming." P. Brock, Pacifism in the United States 359 (1968); see M. Hirst, The Quakers in Peace and War 336–339 (1923); 3 T. Clarkson, Portraiture of Quakerism 103–104 (3d ed. 1807). The Pennsylvania Militia Act of 1757 exempted from service those "*scrupling the use* of *arms*"–a phrase that no one contends had an idiomatic meaning. See 5 Stat. at Large of Pa. 613 (J. Mitchell & H. Flanders eds. 1898) (emphasis added). Thus, the most natural interpretation of Madison's deleted text is that those opposed to carrying weapons for potential violent confrontation would not be "compelled to render military service," in which such carrying would be required.[13]

Finally, *Justice Stevens* suggests that "keep and bear Arms" was some sort of term of art, presumably akin to "hue and cry" or "cease and desist." (This suggestion usefully evades the problem that there is no evidence whatsoever to support a military reading of "keep arms.") *Justice Stevens* believes that the unitary meaning of "keep and bear Arms" is established by the Second Amendment's calling it a "right" (singular) rather than "rights" (plural). See post, at 16. There is nothing to this.

State constitutions of the founding period routinely grouped multiple (related) guarantees under a singular "right," and the First Amendment protects the "right [singular] of the people peaceably to assemble, and to petition the Government for a redress of grievances." See, *e.g.*, Pa. Declaration of Rights §§IX, XII, XVI, in 5 Thorpe 3083–3084; Ohio Const., Arts. VIII, §§11, 19 (1802), in id., at 2910–2911.[14] And even if "keep and bear Arms" were a unitary phrase, we find no evidence that it bore a military meaning. Although the phrase was not at all common (which would be unusual for a term of art), we have found instances of its use with a clearly nonmilitary connotation. In a 1780 debate in the House of Lords, for example, Lord Richmond described an order to disarm private citizens (not militia members) as "a violation of the constitutional right of Protestant subjects to keep and bear arms for their own defense." 49 The London Magazine or Gentleman's Monthly Intelligencer 467 (1780). In response, another member of Parliament referred to "the right of bearing arms for personal defence," making clear that no special military meaning for "keep and bear arms" was intended in the discussion. *Id.*, at 467–468.[15]

c. Meaning of the Operative Clause. Putting all of these textual elements together, we find that they guarantee the individual right to possess and carry weapons in case of confrontation. This meaning is strongly confirmed by the historical background of the Second Amendment. We look to this because it has always been widely understood that the Second Amendment, like the First and Fourth Amendments, codified a *pre-existing* right. The very text of the Second Amendment implicitly recognizes the pre-existence of the right and declares only that it "shall not be infringed." As we said in *United States* v. *Cruikshank*, 92 U. S. 542, 553 (1876), "[t]his is not a right granted by the Constitution. Neither is it in any manner dependent upon that instrument for its existence. The Second amendment declares that it shall not be infringed ... ."[16]

Between the Restoration and the Glorious Revolution, the Stuart Kings Charles II and James II succeeded in using select militias loyal to them to suppress political dissidents, in part by disarming their opponents. See J. Malcolm, To Keep and Bear Arms 31–53 (1994) (hereinafter Malcolm); L. Schwoerer, The Declaration of Rights, 1689, p. 76 (1981). Under the auspices of the 1671 Game Act, for example, the Catholic James II had ordered general disarmaments of regions home to his Protestant enemies. See Malcolm 103–106. These experiences caused Englishmen to be extremely wary of concentrated military forces run by the state and to be jealous of their arms. They accordingly obtained an assurance from William and Mary, in the Declaration of Right (which was codified as the English Bill of Rights), that Protestants would never be disarmed: "That the subjects which are Protestants may have arms for their defense suitable to their conditions and as allowed by law." 1 W. & M., c. 2, §7, in 3 Eng. Stat. at Large 441 (1689). This right has long been understood to be the predecessor to our Second Amendment. See E. Dumbauld, The Bill of Rights and What It Means Today 51 (1957); W. Rawle, A View of the Constitution of the United States of America 122 (1825) (hereinafter Rawle). It was clearly an individual right, having nothing whatever to do with service in a militia. To be sure, it was an individual right not available to the whole population, given that it was restricted to Protestants, and like all written English rights it was held only against the Crown, not Parliament. See Schwoerer, To Hold and Bear Arms: The English Perspective, in Bogus 207, 218; but see 3 J. Story, Commentaries on the Constitution of the United States §1858 (1833) (hereinafter Story) (contending that the "right to bear arms" is a "limitatio[n] upon the power of parliament" as well). But it was secured to them as individuals, according to "libertarian political principles," not as members of a fighting force. Schwoerer, Declaration of Rights, at 283; see also *id.*, at 78; G. Jellinek, The Declaration of the Rights of Man and of Citizens 49, and n. 7 (1901) (reprinted 1979).

By the time of the founding, the right to have arms had become fundamental for English subjects. See Malcolm 122–134. Blackstone, whose works, we have said, "constituted the preeminent authority on English law for the founding generation," *Alden* v. *Maine*, 527 U. S. 706, 715 (1999), cited the arms provision of the Bill of Rights as one of the fundamental rights of Englishmen. See 1 Blackstone 136, 139–140 (1765). His description of it cannot possibly be thought to tie it to militia or military service. It was, he said, "the natural right of resistance and self-preservation," *id.*, at 139, and "the right of having and using arms for self-preservation and defence," *id.*, at 140; see also 3 *id.*, at 2–4 (1768). Other contemporary authorities concurred. See G. Sharp, Tracts, Concerning the Ancient and Only True Legal Means of National Defence, by a Free Militia 17–18, 27 (3d ed. 1782); 2 J. de Lolme, The Rise and Progress of the English Constitution 886–887 (1784) (A. Stephens ed. 1838); W. Blizard, Desultory Reflections on Police 59–60 (1785). Thus, the right secured in 1689 as a result of the Stuarts' abuses was by the time of the founding understood to be an individual right protecting against both public and private violence.

And, of course, what the Stuarts had tried to do to their political enemies, George III had tried to do to the colonists. In the tumultuous decades of the 1760's and 1770's, the Crown began to disarm the inhabitants of the most rebellious areas. That provoked polemical reactions by Americans invoking their rights as Englishmen to keep arms. A New York article of April 1769 said that "[i]t is a natural right which the people have reserved to themselves, confirmed by the Bill of Rights, to keep arms for their own defence." A Journal of the Times: Mar. 17, New York Journal, Supp. 1, Apr. 13, 1769, in Boston Under Military Rule 79 (O. Dickerson ed. 1936); see also, *e.g.*, Shippen, Boston Gazette, Jan. 30, 1769, in 1 The Writings of Samuel Adams 299 (H. Cushing ed. 1968). They understood the right to enable individuals to defend themselves. As the most important early American edition of Blackstone's Commentaries (by the law professor and former Antifederalist St. George Tucker) made clear in the notes to the description of the arms right, Americans understood the "right of self-preservation" as permitting a citizen to "repe[l] force by force" when "the intervention of society in his behalf, may be too late to prevent an injury." 1 Blackstone's Commentaries 145–146, n. 42 (1803) (hereinafter Tucker's Blackstone). See also W. Duer, Outlines of the Constitutional Jurisprudence of the United States 31–32 (1833).

There seems to us no doubt, on the basis of both text and history, that the Second Amendment conferred an individual right to keep and bear arms. Of course the right was not unlimited, just as the First Amendment's right of free speech was not, see, e.g., *United States* v. *Williams*, 553 U. S. ___ (2008). Thus, we do not read the Second Amendment to protect the right of citizens to carry arms for *any sort* of confrontation, just as we do not read the First Amendment to protect the right of citizens to speak for *any purpose*. Before turning to limitations upon the individual right, however, we must determine whether the prefatory clause of the Second Amendment comports with our interpretation of the operative clause.

2. Prefatory Clause.

The prefatory clause reads: "A well regulated Militia, being necessary to the security of a free State ... ."

a. "Well-Regulated Militia." In *United States v. Miller*, 307 U. S. 174, 179 (1939), we explained that "the Militia comprised all males physically capable of acting in concert for the common defense." That definition comports with founding-era sources. See, *e.g.*, Webster ("The militia of a country are the able bodied men organized into companies, regiments and brigades ... and required by law to attend military exercises on certain days only, but at other times left to pursue their usual occupations"); The Federalist No. 46, pp. 329, 334 (B. Wright ed. 1961) (J. Madison) ("near half a million of citizens with arms in their hands"); Letter to Destutt de Tracy (Jan. 26, 1811), in The Portable Thomas Jefferson 520, 524 (M. Peterson ed. 1975) ("[T]he militia of the State, that is to say, of every man in it able to bear arms").

Petitioners take a seemingly narrower view of the militia, stating that "[m]ilitias are the state- and congressionally-regulated military forces described in the Militia Clauses (art. I, §8, cls. 15–16)." Brief for Petitioners 12. Although we agree with petitioners' interpretive assumption that "militia" means the same thing in Article I and the Second Amendment, we believe that petitioners identify the wrong thing, namely, the organized militia. Unlike armies and navies, which Congress is given the power to create ("to raise ... Armies"; "to provide ... a Navy," Art. I, §8, cls. 12–13), the militia is assumed by Article I already to be *in existence*. Congress is given the power to "provide for calling forth the militia," §8, cl. 15; and the power not to create, but to "organiz[e]" it–and not to organize "a" militia, which is what one would expect if the militia were to be a federal creation, but to organize "the" militia, connoting a body already in existence, *ibid.*, cl. 16. This is fully consistent with the ordinary definition of the militia as all able-bodied men. From that pool, Congress has plenary power to organize the units that will make up an effective fighting force. That is what Congress did in the first militia Act, which specified that "each and every free able-bodied white male citizen of the respective states, resident therein, who is or shall be of the age of eighteen years, and under the age of forty-five years (except as is herein after excepted) shall severally and respectively be enrolled in the militia." Act of May 8, 1792, 1 Stat. 271. To be sure, Congress need not conscript every able-bodied man into the militia, because nothing in Article I suggests that in exercising its power to organize, discipline, and arm the militia, Congress must focus upon the entire body. Although the militia consists of all able-bodied men, the federally organized militia may consist of a subset of them.

Finally, the adjective "well-regulated" implies nothing more than the imposition of proper discipline and training. See Johnson 1619 ("Regulate": "To adjust by rule or method"); Rawle 121–122; cf. Va. Declaration of Rights §13 (1776), in 7 Thorpe 3812, 3814 (referring to "a well-regulated militia, composed of the body of the people, trained to arms").

b. "Security of a Free State." The phrase "security of a free state" meant "security of a free polity," not security of each of the several States as the dissent below argued, see 478 F. 3d, at 405, and n. 10. Joseph Story wrote in his treatise on the Constitution that "the word 'state' is used in various senses [and in] its most enlarged sense, it means the people composing a particular nation or community." 1 Story §208; see also 3 *id.*, §1890 (in reference to the Second Amendment's prefatory clause: "The militia is the natural defence of a free country"). It is true that the term "State" elsewhere in the Constitution refers to individual States, but the phrase "security of a free state" and close variations seem to have been terms of art in 18th-century political discourse, meaning a "'free country'" or free polity. See Volokh, "Necessary to the Security of a Free State," 83 Notre Dame L. Rev. 1, 5 (2007); see, *e.g.*, 4 Blackstone 151 (1769); Brutus Essay III (Nov. 15, 1787), in The Essential Antifederalist 251, 253 (W. Allen & G. Lloyd eds., 2d ed. 2002). Moreover, the other instances of "state" in the Constitution are typically accompanied by modifiers making clear that the reference is to the several States–"each state," "several states," "any state," "that state," "particular states," "one state," "no state." And the presence of the term "foreign state" in Article I and Article III shows that the word "state" did not have a single meaning in the Constitution.

There are many reasons why the militia was thought to be "necessary to the security of a free state." See 3 Story §1890. First, of course, it is useful in repelling invasions and suppressing insurrections. Second, it renders large standing armies unnecessary–an argument that Alexander Hamilton made in favor of federal control over the militia. The Federalist No. 29, pp. 226, *227* (B. Wright ed. 1961) (A. Hamilton). Third, when the able-bodied men of a nation are trained in arms and organized, they are better able to resist tyranny.

3. Relationship between Prefatory Clause and Operative Clause

We reach the question, then: Does the preface fit with an operative clause that creates an individual right to keep and bear arms? It fits perfectly, once one knows the history that the founding generation knew and that we have described above. That history showed that the way tyrants had eliminated a militia consisting of all the able-bodied men was not by banning the militia but simply by taking away the people's arms, enabling a select militia or standing army to suppress political opponents. This is what had occurred in England that prompted codification of the right to have arms in the English Bill of Rights.

The debate with respect to the right to keep and bear arms, as with other guarantees in the Bill of Rights, was not over whether it was desirable (all agreed that it was) but over whether it needed to be codified in the Constitution. During the 1788 ratification debates, the fear that the federal government would disarm the people in order to impose rule through a standing army or select militia was pervasive in Antifederalist rhetoric. See, *e.g.*, Letters from The Federal Farmer III (Oct. 10, 1787), in 2 The Complete Anti-Federalist 234, 242 (H. Storing ed. 1981). John Smilie, for example, worried not only that Congress's "command of the militia" could be used to create a "select militia," or to have "no militia at all," but also, as a separate concern, that "[w]hen a select militia is formed; the people in general may be disarmed." 2 Documentary History of the Ratification of the Constitution 508–509 (M. Jensen ed. 1976) (hereinafter Documentary Hist.). Federalists responded that because Congress was given no power to abridge the ancient right of individuals to keep and bear arms, such a force could never oppress the people. See, *e.g.*, A Pennsylvanian III (Feb. 20, 1788), in The Origin of the Second Amendment 275, 276 (D. Young ed., 2d ed. 2001) (hereinafter Young); White, To the Citizens of Virginia, Feb. 22, 1788, in *id.*, at 280, 281; A Citizen of America, (Oct. 10, 1787) in *id.*, at 38, 40; Remarks on the Amendments to the federal Constitution, Nov. 7, 1788, in *id.*, at 556. It was understood across the political spectrum that the right helped to secure the ideal of a citizen militia, which might be necessary to oppose an oppressive military force if the constitutional order broke down.

It is therefore entirely sensible that the Second Amendment's prefatory clause announces the purpose for which the right was codified: to prevent elimination of the militia. The prefatory clause does not suggest that preserving the militia was the only reason Americans valued the ancient right; most undoubtedly thought it even more important for self-defense and hunting. But the threat that the new Federal Government would destroy the citizens' militia by taking away their arms was the reason that right–unlike some other English rights–was codified in a written Constitution. *Justice Breyer*'s assertion that individual self-defense is merely a "subsidiary interest" of the right to keep and bear arms, see *post*, at 36, is profoundly mistaken. He bases that assertion solely upon the prologue–but that can only show that self-defense had little to do with the right's *codification*; it was the *central component* of the right itself.

Besides ignoring the historical reality that the Second Amendment was not intended to lay down a "novel principl[e]" but rather codified a right "inherited from our English ancestors," *Robertson v. Baldwin*, 165 U. S. 275, 281 (1897), petitioners' interpretation does not even achieve the narrower purpose that prompted codification of the right. If, as they believe, the Second Amendment right is no more than the right to keep and use weapons as a member of an organized militia, see Brief for Petitioners 8–if, that is, the *organized* militia is the sole institutional beneficiary of the Second Amendment's guarantee–it does not assure the existence of a "citizens' militia" as a safeguard against tyranny. For Congress retains plenary authority to organize the militia, which must include the authority to say who will belong to the organized force.[17] That is why the first Militia Act's requirement that only whites enroll caused States to amend their militia laws to exclude free blacks. See Siegel, The Federal Government's Power to Enact Color-Conscious Laws, 92 Nw. U. L. Rev. 477, 521–525 (1998). Thus, if petitioners are correct, the Second Amendment protects citizens' right to use a gun in an organization from which Congress has plenary authority to exclude them. It guarantees a select militia of the sort the Stuart kings found useful, but not the people's militia that was the concern of the founding generation.

B

Our interpretation is confirmed by analogous arms-bearing rights in state constitutions that preceded and immediately followed adoption of the Second Amendment. Four States adopted analogues to the Federal Second Amendment in the period between independence and the ratification of the Bill of Rights. Two of them–Pennsylvania and Vermont–clearly adopted individual rights unconnected to militia service. Pennsylvania's Declaration of Rights of 1776 said: "That the people have a right to bear arms *for the defence of themselves*, and the state ... ." §XIII, in 5 Thorpe 3082, 3083 (emphasis added). In 1777, Vermont adopted the identical provision, except for inconsequential differences in punctuation and capitalization. See Vt. Const., ch. 1, §15, in 6 *id.*, at 3741.

North Carolina also codified a right to bear arms in 1776: "That the people have a right to bear arms, for the defence of the State ... ." Declaration of Rights §XVII, in *id.*, at 2787, 2788. This could plausibly be read to support only a right to bear arms in a militia–but that is a peculiar way to make the point in a constitution that elsewhere repeatedly mentions the militia explicitly. See §§14, 18, 35, in 5 *id.*, 2789, 2791, 2793. Many colonial statutes required individual arms-bearing for public-safety reasons–such as the 1770 Georgia law that "for the security and *defence of this province* from internal dangers and insurrections" required those men who qualified for militia duty individually "to carry fire arms" "to places of public worship." 19 Colonial Records of the State of Georgia 137–139 (A. Candler ed. 1911 (pt. 2)) (emphasis added). That broad public-safety understanding was the connotation given to the North Carolina right by that State's Supreme Court in 1843. See *State* v. *Huntly*, 3 Ired. 418, 422–423.

The 1780 Massachusetts Constitution presented another variation on the theme: "The people have a right to keep and to bear arms for the common defence... ." Pt. First, Art. XVII, in 3 Thorpe 1888, 1892. Once again, if one gives narrow meaning to the phrase "common defence" this can be thought to limit the right to the bearing of arms in a state-organized military force. But once again the State's highest court thought otherwise. Writing for the court in an 1825 libel case, Chief Justice Parker wrote: "The liberty of the press was to be unrestrained, but he who used it was to be responsible in cases of its abuse; like the right to keep fire arms, which does not protect him who uses them for annoyance or destruction." *Commonwealth* v. *Blanding*, 20 Mass. 304, 313–314. The analogy makes no sense if firearms could not be used for any individual purpose at all. See also Kates, Handgun Prohibition and the Original Meaning of the Second Amendment, 82 Mich. L. Rev. 204, 244 (1983) (19th-century courts never read "common defence" to limit the use of weapons to militia service).

We therefore believe that the most likely reading of all four of these pre-Second Amendment state constitutional provisions is that they secured an individual right to bear arms for defensive purposes. Other States did not include rights to bear arms in their pre-1789 constitutions–although in Virginia a Second Amendment analogue was proposed (unsuccessfully) by Thomas Jefferson. (It read: "No freeman shall ever be debarred the use of arms [within his own lands or tenements]."[18] 1 The Papers of Thomas Jefferson 344 (J. Boyd ed. 1950)).

Between 1789 and 1820, nine States adopted Second Amendment analogues. Four of them–Kentucky, Ohio, Indiana, and Missouri–referred to the right of the people to "bear arms in defence of themselves and the State." See n. 8, *supra*. Another three States–Mississippi, Connecticut, and Alabama–used the even more individualistic phrasing that each citizen has the "right to bear arms in defence of himself and the State." See ibid. Finally, two States–Tennessee and Maine–used the "common defence" language of Massachusetts. See Tenn. Const., Art. XI, §26 (1796), in 6 Thorpe 3414, 3424; Me. Const., Art. I, §16 (1819), in 3 *id.*, at 1646, 1648. That of the nine state constitutional protections for the right to bear arms enacted immediately after 1789 at least seven unequivocally protected an individual citizen's right to self-defense is strong evidence that that is how the founding generation conceived of the right. And with one possible exception that we discuss in Part II-D-2, 19th-century courts and commentators interpreted these state constitutional provisions to protect an individual right to use arms for self-defense. See n. 9, supra; *Simpson* v. *State*, 5 Yer. 356, 360 (Tenn. 1833).

The historical narrative that petitioners must endorse would thus treat the Federal Second Amendment as an odd outlier, protecting a right unknown in state constitutions or at English common law, based on little more than an overreading of the prefatory clause.

C

Justice Stevens relies on the drafting history of the Second Amendment–the various proposals in the state conventions and the debates in Congress. It is dubious to rely on such history to interpret a text that was widely understood to codify a preexisting right, rather than to fashion a new one. But even assuming that this legislative history is relevant, *Justice Stevens* flatly misreads the historical record.

It is true, as *Justice Stevens* says, that there was concern that the Federal Government would abolish the institution of the state militia. See *post*, at 20. That concern found expression, however, not in the various Second Amendment precursors proposed in the State conventions, but in separate structural provisions that would have given the States concurrent and seemingly nonpre-emptible authority to organize, discipline, and arm the militia when the Federal Government failed to do so. See Veit 17, 20 (Virginia proposal); 4 J. Elliot, The Debates in the Several State Conventions on the Adoption of the Federal Constitution 244, 245 (2d ed. 1836) (reprinted 1941) (North Carolina proposal); see also 2 Documentary Hist. 624 (Pennsylvania minority's proposal). The Second Amendment precursors, by contrast, referred to the individual English right already codified in two (and probably four) State constitutions. The Federalist-dominated first Congress chose to reject virtually all major structural revisions favored by the Antifederalists, including the proposed militia amendments. Rather, it adopted primarily the popular and uncontroversial (though, in the Federalists' view, unnecessary) individual-rights amendments. The Second Amendment right, protecting only individuals' liberty to keep and carry arms, did nothing to assuage Antifederalists' concerns about federal control of the militia. See, *e.g.*, Centinel, Revived, No. XXIX, Philadelphia Independent Gazetteer, Sept. 9, 1789, in Young 711, 712.

Justice Stevens thinks it significant that the Virginia, New York, and North Carolina Second Amendment proposals were "embedded ... within a group of principles that are distinctly military in meaning," such as statements about the danger of standing armies. *Post*, at 22. But so was the highly influential minority proposal in Pennsylvania, yet that proposal, with its reference to hunting, plainly referred to an individual right. See 2 Documentary Hist. 624. Other than that erroneous point, *Justice Stevens* has brought forward absolutely no evidence that those proposals conferred only a right to carry arms in a militia. By contrast, New Hampshire's proposal, the Pennsylvania minority's proposal, and Samuel Adams' proposal in Massachusetts unequivocally referred to individual rights, as did two state constitutional provisions at the time. See Veit 16, 17 (New Hampshire proposal); 6 Documentary Hist. 1452, 1453 (J. Kaminski & G. Saladino eds. 2000) (Samuel Adams' proposal). *Justice Stevens'* view thus relies on the proposition, unsupported by any evidence, that different people of the founding period had vastly different conceptions of the right to keep and bear arms. That simply does not comport with our longstanding view that the Bill of Rights codified venerable, widely understood liberties.

D

We now address how the Second Amendment was interpreted from immediately after its ratification through the end of the 19th century. Before proceeding, however, we take issue with *Justice Stevens'* equating of these sources with postenactment legislative history, a comparison that betrays a fundamental misunderstanding of a court's interpretive task. See *post*, at 27, n. 28. "Legislative history," of course, refers to the pre-enactment statements of those who drafted or voted for a law; it is considered persuasive by some, not because they reflect the general understanding of the disputed terms, but because the legislators who heard or read those statements presumably voted with that understanding. Ibid. "Postenactment legislative history," *ibid.*, a deprecatory contradiction in terms, refers to statements of those who drafted or voted for the law that are made after its enactment and hence could have had no effect on the congressional vote. It most certainly does not refer to the examination of a variety of legal and other sources to determine *the public understanding* of a legal text in the period after its enactment or ratification. That sort of inquiry is a critical tool of constitutional interpretation. As we will show, virtually all interpreters of the Second Amendment in the century after its enactment interpreted the amendment as we do.

1. Post-ratification Commentary

Three important founding-era legal scholars interpreted the Second Amendment in published writings. All three understood it to protect an individual right unconnected with militia service.

St. George Tucker's version of Blackstone's Commentaries, as we explained above, conceived of the Blackstonian arms right as necessary for self-defense. He equated that right, absent the religious and class-based restrictions, with the Second Amendment. See 2 Tucker's Blackstone 143. In Note D, entitled, "View of the Constitution of the United States," Tucker elaborated on the Second Amendment: "This may be considered as the true palladium of liberty ... . The right to self-defence is the first law of nature: in most governments it has been the study of rulers to confine the right within the narrowest limits possible. Wherever standing armies are kept up, and the right of the people to keep and bear arms is, under any colour or pretext whatsoever, prohibited, liberty, if not already annihilated, is on the brink of destruction." 1 id., at App. 300 (ellipsis in original). He believed that the English game laws had abridged the right by prohibiting "keeping a gun or other engine for the destruction of game." Ibid; see also 2 id., at 143, and nn. 40 and 41. He later grouped the right with some of the individual rights included in the First Amendment and said that if "a law be passed by congress, prohibiting" any of those rights, it would "be the province of the judiciary to pronounce whether any such act were constitutional, or not; and if not, to acquit the accused ... ." 1 id., at App. 357. It is unlikely that Tucker was referring to a person's being "accused" of violating a law making it a crime to bear arms in a state militia.[19]

In 1825, William Rawle, a prominent lawyer who had been a member of the Pennsylvania Assembly that ratified the Bill of Rights, published an influential treatise, which analyzed the Second Amendment as follows:

"The first [principle] is a declaration that a well regulated militia is necessary to the security of a free state; a proposition from which few will dissent... .

"The corollary, from the first position is, that the right of the people to keep and bear arms shall not be infringed.

"The prohibition is general. No clause in the constitution could by any rule of construction be conceived to give to congress a power to disarm the people. Such a flagitious attempt could only be made under some general pretence by a state legislature. But if in any blind pursuit of inordinate power, either should attempt it, this amendment may be appealed to as a restraint on both." Rawle 121–122.[20]

Like Tucker, Rawle regarded the English game laws as violating the right codified in the Second Amendment. See id., 122–123. Rawle clearly differentiated between the people's right to bear arms and their service in a militia: "In a people permitted and accustomed to bear arms, we have the rudiments of a militia, which properly consists of armed citizens, divided into military bands, and instructed at least in part, in the use of arms for the purposes of war." Id., at 140. Rawle further said that the Second Amendment right ought not "be abused to the disturbance of the public peace," such as by assembling with other armed individuals "for an unlawful purpose"–statements that make no sense if the right does not extend to *any* individual purpose.

Joseph Story published his famous Commentaries on the Constitution of the United States in 1833. *Justice Stevens* suggests that "[t]here is not so much as a whisper" in Story's explanation of the Second Amendment that favors the individual-rights view. *Post*, at 34. That is wrong. Story explained that the English Bill of Rights had also included a "right to bear arms," a right that, as we have discussed, had nothing to do with militia service. 3 Story §1858. He then equated the English right with the Second Amendment:

"§1891. A similar provision [to the Second Amendment] in favour of protestants (for to them it is confined) is to be found in the bill of rights of 1688, it being declared, 'that the subjects, which are protestants, may have arms for their defence suitable to their condition, and as allowed by law.' But under various pretences the effect of this provision has been greatly narrowed; and it is at present in England more nominal than real, as a defensive privilege." (Footnotes omitted.)

This comparison to the Declaration of Right would not make sense if the Second Amendment right was the right to use a gun in a militia, which was plainly not what the English right protected. As the Tennessee Supreme Court recognized

38 years after Story wrote his Commentaries, "[t]he passage from Story, shows clearly that this right was intended ... and was guaranteed to, and to be exercised and enjoyed by the citizen as such, and not by him as a soldier, or in defense solely of his political rights." *Andrews v. State*, 50 Tenn. 165, 183 (1871). Story's Commentaries also cite as support Tucker and Rawle, both of whom clearly viewed the right as unconnected to militia service. See 3 Story §1890, n. 2; §1891, n. 3. In addition, in a shorter 1840 work Story wrote: "One of the ordinary modes, by which tyrants accomplish their purposes without resistance, is, by disarming the people, and making it an offence to keep arms, and by substituting a regular army in the stead of a resort to the militia." A Familiar Exposition of the Constitution of the United States §450 (reprinted in 1986).

Antislavery advocates routinely invoked the right to bear arms for self-defense. Joel Tiffany, for example, citing Blackstone's description of the right, wrote that "the right to keep and bear arms, also implies the right to use them if necessary in self defence; without this right to use the guaranty would have hardly been worth the paper it consumed." A Treatise on the Unconstitutionality of American Slavery 117–118 (1849); see also L. Spooner, The Unconstitutionality of Slavery 116 (1845) (right enables "personal defence"). In his famous Senate speech about the 1856 "Bleeding Kansas" conflict, Charles Sumner proclaimed:

"The rifle has ever been the companion of the pioneer and, under God, his tutelary protector against the red man and the beast of the forest. Never was this efficient weapon more needed in just self-defence, than now in Kansas, and at least one article in our National Constitution must be blotted out, before the complete right to it can in any way be impeached. And yet such is the madness of the hour, that, in defiance of the solemn guarantee, embodied in the Amendments to the Constitution, that 'the right of the people to keep and bear arms shall not be infringed,' the people of Kansas have been arraigned for keeping and bearing them, and the Senator from South Carolina has had the face to say openly, on this floor, that they should be disarmed–of course, that the fanatics of Slavery, his allies and constituents, may meet no impediment." The Crime Against Kansas, May 19–20, 1856, in American Speeches: Political Oratory from the Revolution to the Civil War 553, 606–607 (2006).

We have found only one early 19th-century commentator who clearly conditioned the right to keep and bear arms upon service in the militia–and he recognized that the prevailing view was to the contrary. "The provision of the constitution, declaring the right of the people to keep and bear arms, &c. was probably intended to apply to the right of the people to bear arms for such [militia-related] purposes only, and not to prevent congress or the legislatures of the different states from enacting laws to prevent the citizens from always going armed. A different construction however has been given to it." B. Oliver, The Rights of an American Citizen 177 (1832).

2. PRE-CIVIL WAR CASE LAW

The 19th-century cases that interpreted the Second Amendment universally support an individual right unconnected to militia service. In *Houston v. Moore*, 5 Wheat. 1, 24 (1820), this Court held that States have concurrent power over the militia, at least where not pre-empted by Congress. Agreeing in dissent that States could "organize, discipline, and arm" the militia in the absence of conflicting federal regulation, Justice Story said that the Second Amendment "may not, perhaps, be thought to have any important bearing on this point. If it have, it confirms and illustrates, rather than impugns the reasoning already suggested." *Id.*, at 51–53. Of course, if the Amendment simply "protect[ed] the right of the people of each of the several States to maintain a well-regulated militia," *post*, at 1 (Stevens, J., dissenting), it would have enormous and obvious bearing on the point. But the Court and Story derived the States' power over the militia from the nonexclusive nature of federal power, not from the Second Amendment, whose preamble merely "confirms and illustrates" the importance of the militia. Even clearer was Justice Baldwin. In the famous fugitive-slave case of *Johnson v. Tompkins*, 13 F. Cas. 840, 850, 852 (CC Pa. 1833), Baldwin, sitting as a circuit judge, cited both the Second Amendment and the Pennsylvania analogue for his conclusion that a citizen has "a right to carry arms in defence of his property or person, and to use them, if either were assailed with such force, numbers or violence as made it necessary for the protection or safety of either."

Many early 19th-century state cases indicated that the Second Amendment right to bear arms was an individual right unconnected to militia service, though subject to certain restrictions. A Virginia case in 1824 holding that the Constitution did not extend to free blacks explained that "numerous restrictions imposed on [blacks] in our Statute Book, many of which are inconsistent with the letter and spirit of the Constitution, both of this State and of the United States as respects the free whites, demonstrate, that, here, those instruments have not been considered to extend equally to both classes of our population. We will only instance the restriction upon the migration of free blacks into this State, and upon their right to bear arms." *Aldridge v. Commonwealth*, 2 Va. Cas. 447, 449 (Gen. Ct.). The claim was obviously not that blacks were prevented from carrying guns in the militia.[21] See also *Waters v. State*, 1 Gill 302, 309 (Md. 1843) (because free blacks were treated as a "dangerous population," "laws have been passed to prevent their migration into this State; to make it unlawful for them to bear arms; to guard even their religious assemblages with peculiar watchfulness"). An 1829 decision by the Supreme Court of Michigan said: "The constitution of the United States also grants to the citizen the right to keep and bear arms. But the grant of this privilege cannot be construed into the right in him who keeps a gun to destroy his neighbor. No rights are intended to be granted by the constitution for an unlawful or unjustifiable purpose." *United States v. Sheldon*, in 5 Transactions of the Supreme Court of the Territory of Michigan 337, 346 (W. Blume ed. 1940) (hereinafter Blume). It is not possible to read this as discussing anything other than an individual right unconnected to militia service. If it did have to do with militia service, the limitation upon it would not be any "unlawful or unjustifiable purpose," but any nonmilitary purpose whatsoever.

In *Nunn v. State*, 1 Ga. 243, 251 (1846), the Georgia Supreme Court construed the Second Amendment as protecting the "natural right of self-defence" and therefore struck down a ban on carrying pistols openly. Its opinion perfectly captured the way in which the operative clause of the Second Amendment furthers the purpose announced in the prefatory clause, in continuity with the English right:

"The right of the whole people, old and young, men, women and boys, and not militia only, to keep and bear *arms* of every description, and not such merely as are used by the *militia*, shall not be infringed, curtailed, or broken in upon, in the smallest degree; and all this for the important end to be attained: the rearing up and qualifying a well-regulated militia, so vitally necessary to the security of a free State. Our opinion is, that any law, State or Federal, is repugnant to the Constitution, and void, which contravenes this *right*, originally belonging to our forefathers, trampled under foot by Charles I. and his two wicked sons and successors, re-established by the revolution of 1688, conveyed to this land of liberty by the colonists, and finally incorporated conspicuously in our own Magna Charta!"

Likewise, in *State v. Chandler*, 5 La. Ann. 489, 490 (1850), the Louisiana Supreme Court held that citizens had a right to carry arms openly: "This is the right guaranteed by the Constitution of the United States, and which is calculated to incite men to a manly and noble defence of themselves, if necessary, and of their country, without any tendency to secret advantages and unmanly assassinations."

Those who believe that the Second Amendment preserves only a militia-centered right place great reliance on the Tennessee Supreme Court's 1840 decision in *Aymette v. State*, 21 Tenn. 154. The case does not stand for that broad proposition; in fact, the case does not mention the word "militia" at all, except in its quoting of the Second Amendment. *Aymette* held that the state constitutional guarantee of the right to "bear" arms did not prohibit the banning of concealed weapons. The opinion first recognized that both the state right and the federal right were descendents of the 1689 English right, but (erroneously, and contrary to virtually all other authorities) read that right to refer only to "protect[ion of] the public liberty" and "keep[ing] in awe those in power," *id.*, at 158. The court then adopted a sort of middle position, whereby citizens were permitted to carry arms openly, unconnected with any service in a formal militia, but were given the right to use them only for the military purpose of banding together to oppose tyranny. This odd reading of the right is, to be sure, not the one we adopt– but it is not petitioners' reading either. More importantly, seven years earlier the Tennessee Supreme Court had treated the state constitutional provision as conferring a right "of all the free citizens of the State to keep and bear arms for their defence," *Simpson*, 5 Yer., at 360; and 21 years later the court held that the "keep" portion of the state constitutional right included the right to personal self-defense: "[T]he right to keep arms involves, necessarily, the right to use such arms for all the ordinary purposes, and in all the ordinary modes usual in the country, and to which arms are adapted, limited by the duties of a good citizen in times of peace." *Andrews*, 50 Tenn., at 178; see also *ibid*. (equating state provision with Second Amendment).

3. POST-CIVIL WAR LEGISLATION.

In the aftermath of the Civil War, there was an outpouring of discussion of the Second Amendment in Congress and in public discourse, as people debated whether and how to secure constitutional rights for newly free slaves. See generally S. Halbrook, Freedmen, the Fourteenth Amendment, and the Right to Bear Arms, 1866–1876 (1998) (hereinafter Halbrook); Brief for Institute for Justice as *Amicus Curiae*. Since those discussions took place 75 years after the ratification of the Second Amendment, they do not provide as much insight into its original meaning as earlier sources. Yet those born and educated in the early 19th century faced a widespread effort to limit arms ownership by a large number of citizens; their understanding of the origins and continuing significance of the Amendment is instructive.

Blacks were routinely disarmed by Southern States after the Civil War. Those who opposed these injustices frequently stated that they infringed blacks' constitutional right to keep and bear arms. Needless to say, the claim was not that blacks were being prohibited from carrying arms in an organized state militia. A Report of the Commission of the Freedmen's Bureau in 1866 stated plainly: "[T]he civil law [of Kentucky] prohibits the colored man from bearing arms.... Their arms are taken from them by the civil authorities.... Thus, the right of the people to keep and bear arms as provided in the Constitution is *infringed*." H. R. Exec. Doc. No. 70, 39th Cong., 1st Sess., 233, 236. A joint congressional Report decried:

"in some parts of [South Carolina], armed parties are, without proper authority, engaged in seizing all fire-arms found in the hands of the freemen. Such conduct is in clear and direct violation of their personal rights as guaranteed by the Constitution of the United States, which declares that 'the right of the people to keep and bear arms shall not be infringed.' The freedmen of South Carolina have shown by their peaceful and orderly conduct that they can safely be trusted with fire-arms, and they need them to kill game for subsistence, and to protect their crops from destruction by birds and animals." Joint Comm. on Reconstruction, H. R. Rep. No. 30, 39th Cong., 1st Sess., pt. 2, p. 229 (1866) (Proposed Circular of Brigadier General R. Saxton).

The view expressed in these statements was widely reported and was apparently widely held. For example, an editorial in The Loyal Georgian (Augusta) on February 3, 1866, assured blacks that "[a]ll men, without distinction of color, have the right to keep and bear arms to defend their homes, families or themselves." Halbrook 19.

Congress enacted the Freedmen's Bureau Act on July 16, 1866. Section 14 stated:

"[T]he right ... to have full and equal benefit of all laws and proceedings concerning personal liberty, personal security, and the acquisition, enjoyment, and disposition of estate, real and personal, including the constitutional right to bear arms, shall be secured to and enjoyed by all the citizens ... without respect to race or color, or previous condition of slavery.... " 14 Stat. 176–177.

The understanding that the Second Amendment gave freed blacks the right to keep and bear arms was reflected in congressional discussion of the bill, with even an opponent of it saying that the founding generation "were for every man bearing his arms about him and keeping them in his house, his castle, for his own defense." Cong. Globe, 39th Cong., 1st Sess., 362, 371 (1866) (Sen. Davis).

Similar discussion attended the passage of the Civil Rights Act of 1871 and the Fourteenth Amendment. For example, Representative Butler said of the Act: "Section eight is intended to enforce the well-known constitutional provision guaranteeing the right of the citizen to 'keep and bear arms,' and provides that whoever shall take away, by force or violence, or by threats and intimidation, the arms and weapons which any person may have for his defense, shall be deemed guilty of larceny of the same." H. R. Rep. No. 37, 41st Cong., 3d Sess., pp. 7–8 (1871). With respect to the proposed Amendment, Senator Pomeroy described as one of the three "indispensable" "safeguards of liberty ... under the Constitution" a man's "right to bear arms for the defense of himself and family and his homestead." Cong. Globe, 39th Cong., 1st Sess., 1182 (1866). Representative Nye thought the Fourteenth Amendment unnecessary because "[a]s citizens of the United States [blacks] have equal right to protection, and to keep and bear arms for self-defense." *Id.*, at 1073 (1866).

It was plainly the understanding in the post-Civil War Congress that the Second Amendment protected an individual right to use arms for self-defense.

4. POST-CIVIL WAR COMMENTATORS.

Every late-19th-century legal scholar that we have read interpreted the Second Amendment to secure an individual right unconnected with militia service. The most famous was the judge and professor Thomas Cooley, who wrote a massively popular 1868 Treatise on Constitutional Limitations. Concerning the Second Amendment it said:

"Among the other defences to personal liberty should be mentioned the right of the people to keep and bear arms... . The alternative to a standing army is 'a well-regulated militia,' but this cannot exist unless the people are trained to bearing arms. How far it is in the power of the legislature to regulate this right, we shall not undertake to say, as happily there has been very little occasion to discuss that subject by the courts." *Id.*, at 350.

That Cooley understood the right not as connected to militia service, but as securing the militia by ensuring a populace familiar with arms, is made even clearer in his 1880 work, General Principles of Constitutional Law. The Second Amendment, he said, "was adopted with some modification and enlargement from the English Bill of Rights of 1688, where it stood as a protest against arbitrary action of the overturned dynasty in disarming the people." *Id.*, at 270. In a section entitled "The Right in General," he continued:

"It might be supposed from the phraseology of this provision that the right to keep and bear arms was only guaranteed to the militia; but this would be an interpretation not warranted by the intent. The militia, as has been elsewhere explained, consists of those persons who, under the law, are liable to the performance of military duty, and are officered and enrolled for service when called upon. But the law may make provision for the enrolment of all who are fit to perform military duty, or of a small number only, or it may wholly omit to make any provision at all; and if the right were limited to those enrolled, the purpose of this guaranty might be defeated altogether by the action or neglect to act of the government it was meant to hold in check. The meaning of the provision undoubtedly is, that the people, from whom the militia must be taken, shall have the right to keep and bear arms; and they need no permission or regulation of law for the purpose. But this enables government to have a well-regulated militia; for to bear arms implies something more than the mere keeping; it implies the learning to handle and use them in a way that makes those who keep them ready for their efficient use; in other words, it implies the right to meet for voluntary discipline in arms, observing in doing so the laws of public order." *Id.*, at 271.

All other post-Civil War 19th-century sources we have found concurred with Cooley. One example from each decade will convey the general flavor:

"[The purpose of the Second Amendment is] to secure a well-armed militia... . But a militia would be useless unless the citizens were enabled to exercise themselves in the use of warlike weapons. To preserve this privilege, and to secure to the people the ability to oppose themselves in military force against the usurpations of government, as well as against enemies from without, that government is forbidden by any law or proceeding to invade or destroy the right to keep and bear arms... . The clause is analogous to the one securing the freedom of speech and of the press. Freedom, not license, is secured; the fair use, not the libellous abuse, is protected." J. Pomeroy, An Introduction to the Constitutional Law of the United States 152–153 (1868) (hereinafter Pomeroy).

"As the Constitution of the United States, and the constitutions of several of the states, in terms more or less comprehensive, declare the right of the people to keep and bear arms, it has been a subject of grave discussion, in some of the state courts, whether a statute prohibiting persons, when not on a journey, or as travellers, from *wearing or carrying concealed weapons*, be constitutional. There has been a great difference of opinion on the question." 2 J. Kent, Commentaries on American Law *340, n. 2 (O. Holmes ed., 12th ed. 1873) (hereinafter Kent).

"Some general knowledge of firearms is important to the public welfare; because it would be impossible, in case of war, to organize promptly an efficient force of volunteers unless the people had some familiarity with weapons of war. The Constitution secures the right of the people to keep and bear arms. No doubt, a citizen who keeps a gun or pistol under judicious precautions, practices in safe places the use of it, and in due time teaches his sons to do the same, exercises his individual right. No doubt, a person whose residence or duties involve peculiar peril may keep a pistol for prudent self-defence." B. Abbott, Judge and Jury: A Popular Explanation of the Leading Topics in the Law of the Land 333 (1880) (hereinafter Abbott).

"The right to bear arms has always been the distinctive privilege of freemen. Aside from any necessity of self-protection to the person, it represents among all nations power coupled with the exercise of a certain jurisdiction. ... [I]t was not necessary that the right to bear arms should be granted in the Constitution, for it had always existed." J. Ordronaux, Constitutional Legislation in the United States 241–242 (1891).

E

We now ask whether any of our precedents forecloses the conclusions we have reached about the meaning of the Second Amendment.

United States v. Cruikshank, 92 U. S. 542, in the course of vacating the convictions of members of a white mob for depriving blacks of their right to keep and bear arms, held that the Second Amendment does not by its own force apply to anyone other than the Federal Government. The opinion explained that the right "is not a right granted by the Constitution [or] in any manner dependent upon that instrument for its existence. The second amendment ... means no more than that it shall not be infringed by Congress." 92 U. S., at 553. States, we said, were free to restrict or protect the right under their police powers. The limited discussion of the Second Amendment in *Cruikshank* supports, if anything, the *individual-rights* interpretation. There was no claim in *Cruikshank* that the victims had been deprived of their right to carry arms in a militia; indeed, the Governor had disbanded the local militia unit the year before the mob's attack, see C. Lane, The Day Freedom Died 62 (2008). We described the right protected by the Second Amendment as " 'bearing arms for a lawful purpose' "[22] and said that "the people [must] look for their protection against any violation by their fellow-citizens of the rights it recognizes" to the States' police power. 92 U. S., at 553. That discussion makes little sense if it is only a right to bear arms in a state militia.[23]

Presser v. Illinois, 116 U. S. 252 (1886), held that the right to keep and bear arms was not violated by a law that forbade "bodies of men to associate together as military organizations, or to drill or parade with arms in cities and towns unless authorized by law." *Id.*, at 264–265. This does not refute the individual-rights interpretation of the Amendment; no one supporting that interpretation has contended that States may not ban such groups. *Justice Stevens* presses *Presser* into service to support his view that the right to bear arms is limited to service in the militia by joining *Presser*'s brief discussion of the Second Amendment with a later portion of the opinion making the seemingly relevant (to the Second Amendment) point that the plaintiff was not a member of the state militia. Unfortunately for *Justice Stevens*' argument, that later portion deals with the *Fourteenth Amendment*; it was the *Fourteenth Amendment* to which the plaintiff's nonmembership in the militia was relevant. Thus, *Justice Stevens*' statement that *Presser* "suggested that... nothing in the Constitution protected the use of arms outside the context of a militia," *post*, at 40, is simply wrong. *Presser* said nothing about the Second Amendment's meaning or scope, beyond the fact that it does not prevent the prohibition of private paramilitary organizations.

Justice Stevens places overwhelming reliance upon this Court's decision in *United States* v. *Miller*, 307 U. S. 174 (1939). "[H]undreds of judges," we are told, "have relied on the view of the amendment we endorsed there," *post*, at 2, and "[e]ven if the textual and historical arguments on both side of the issue were evenly balanced, respect for the well-settled views of all of our predecessors on this Court, and for the rule of law itself ... would prevent most jurists from endorsing such a dramatic upheaval in the law," *post*, at 4. And what is, according to *Justice Stevens*, the holding of Miller that demands such obeisance? That the Second Amendment "protects the right to keep and bear arms for certain military purposes, but that it does not curtail the legislature's power to regulate the nonmilitary use and ownership of weapons." *Post*, at 2.

Nothing so clearly demonstrates the weakness of *Justice Stevens*' case. *Miller* did not hold that and cannot possibly be read to have held that. The judgment in the case upheld against a Second Amendment challenge two men's federal convictions for transporting an unregistered short-barreled shotgun in interstate commerce, in violation of the National Firearms Act, 48 Stat.

1236. It is entirely clear that the Court's basis for saying that the Second Amendment did not apply was not that the defendants were "bear[ing] arms" not "for ... military purposes" but for "nonmilitary use," *post*, at 2. Rather, it was that the *type of weapon at issue* was not eligible for Second Amendment protection: "In the absence of any evidence tending to show that the possession or use of a [short-barreled shotgun] at this time has some reasonable relationship to the preservation or efficiency of a well regulated militia, we cannot say that the Second Amendment guarantees the right to keep and bear *such an instrument*." 307 U. S., at 178 (emphasis added). "Certainly," the Court continued, "it is not within judicial notice that this weapon is any part of the ordinary military equipment or that its use could contribute to the common defense." *Ibid*. Beyond that, the opinion provided no explanation of the content of the right.

This holding is not only consistent with, but positively suggests, that the Second Amendment confers an individual right to keep and bear arms (though only arms that "have some reasonable relationship to the preservation or efficiency of a well regulated militia"). Had the Court believed that the Second Amendment protects only those serving in the militia, it would have been odd to examine the character of the weapon rather than simply note that the two crooks were not militiamen. *Justice Stevens* can say again and again that *Miller* did "not turn on the difference between muskets and sawed-off shotguns, it turned, rather, on the basic difference between the military and nonmilitary use and possession of guns," *post*, at 42–43, but the words of the opinion prove otherwise. The most *Justice Stevens* can plausibly claim for Miller is that it declined to decide the nature of the Second Amendment right, despite the Solicitor General's argument (made in the alternative) that the right was collective, see Brief for United States, O. T. 1938, No. 696, pp. 4–5. *Miller* stands only for the proposition that the Second Amendment right, whatever its nature, extends only to certain types of weapons.

It is particularly wrongheaded to read *Miller* for more than what it said, because the case did not even purport to be a thorough examination of the Second Amendment. *Justice Stevens* claims, *post*, at 42, that the opinion reached its conclusion "[a]fter reviewing many of the same sources that are discussed at greater length by the Court today." Not many, which was not entirely the Court's fault. The respondent made no appearance in the case, neither filing a brief nor appearing at oral argument; the Court heard from no one but the Government (reason enough, one would think, not to make that case the beginning and the end of this Court's consideration of the Second Amendment). See Frye, The Peculiar Story of *United States* v. *Miller*, 3 N. Y. U. J. L. & Liberty 48, 65–68 (2008). The Government's brief spent two pages discussing English legal sources, concluding "that at least the carrying of weapons without lawful occasion or excuse was always a crime" and that (because of the class-based restrictions and the prohibition on terrorizing people with dangerous or unusual weapons) "the early English law did not guarantee an unrestricted right to bear arms." Brief for United States, O. T. 1938, No. 696, at 9–11. It then went on to rely primarily on the discussion of the English right to bear arms in *Aymette* v. *State*, 21 Tenn. 154, for the proposition that the only uses of arms protected by the Second Amendment are those that relate to the militia, not self-defense. See Brief for United States, O. T. 1938, No. 696, at 12–18. The final section of the brief recognized that "some courts have said that the right to bear arms includes the right of the individual to have them for the protection of his person and property," and launched an alternative argument that "weapons which are commonly used by criminals," such as sawed-off shotguns, are not protected. See *id.*, at 18–21. The Government's *Miller* brief thus provided scant discussion of the history of the Second Amendment–and the Court was presented with no counterdiscussion. As for the text of the Court's opinion itself, that discusses *none* of the history of the Second Amendment. It assumes from the prologue that the Amendment was designed to preserve the militia, 307 U. S., at 178 (which we do not dispute), and then reviews some historical materials dealing with the nature of the militia, and in particular with the nature of the arms their members were expected to possess, id., at 178–182. Not a word (*not a word*) about the history of the Second Amendment. This is the mighty rock upon which the dissent rests its case.[24]

We may as well consider at this point (for we will have to consider eventually) *what* types of weapons *Miller* permits. Read in isolation, *Miller's* phrase "part of ordinary military equipment" could mean that only those weapons useful in warfare are protected. That would be a startling reading of the opinion, since it would mean that the National Firearms Act's restrictions on machineguns (not challenged in *Miller*) might be unconstitutional, machineguns being useful in warfare in 1939. We think that *Miller's* "ordinary military equipment" language must be read in tandem with what comes after: "[O]rdinarily when called for [militia] service [able-bodied] men were expected to appear bearing arms supplied by themselves and of the kind in common use at the time." 307 U. S., at 179. The traditional militia was formed from a pool of men bringing arms "in common use at the time" for lawful purposes like self-defense. "In the colonial and revolutionary war era, [small-arms] weapons used by militiamen and weapons used in defense of person and home were one and the same." *State* v. *Kessler*, 289 Ore. 359, 368, 614 P. 2d 94, 98 (1980) (citing G. Neumann, Swords and Blades of the American Revolution 6–15, 252–254 (1973)). Indeed, that is precisely the way in which the Second Amendment's operative clause furthers the purpose announced in its preface. We therefore read *Miller* to say only that the Second Amendment does not protect those weapons not typically possessed by law-abiding citizens for lawful purposes, such as short-barreled shotguns. That accords with the historical understanding of the scope of the right, see Part III, *infra*.[25]

We conclude that nothing in our precedents forecloses our adoption of the original understanding of the Second Amendment. It should be unsurprising that such a significant matter has been for so long judicially unresolved. For most of our history, the Bill of Rights was not thought applicable to the States, and the Federal Government did not significantly regulate the possession of firearms by law-abiding citizens. Other provisions of the Bill of Rights have similarly remained unilluminated for lengthy periods. This Court first held a law to violate the First Amendment's guarantee of freedom of speech in 1931, almost 150 years after the Amendment was ratified, see *Near* v. *Minnesota ex rel. Olson*, 283 U. S. 697 (1931), and it was not until after World War II that we held a law invalid under the Establishment Clause, see *Illinois ex rel. McCollum* v. *Board of Ed. of School Dist. No. 71, Champaign Cty.*, 333 U. S. 203 (1948). Even a question as basic as the scope of proscribable libel was not addressed by this Court until 1964, nearly two centuries after the founding. See *New York Times Co.* v. *Sullivan*, 376 U. S. 254 (1964). It is demonstrably not true that, as *Justice Stevens* claims, *post*, at 41–42, "for most of our history, the invalidity of Second-Amendment-based objections to firearms regulations has been well settled and uncontroversial." For most of our history the question did not present itself.

III

Like most rights, the right secured by the Second Amendment is not unlimited. From Blackstone through the 19th-century cases, commentators and courts routinely explained that the right was not a right to keep and carry any weapon whatsoever in any manner whatsoever and for whatever purpose. See, *e.g.*, *Sheldon*, in 5 Blume 346; Rawle 123; Pomeroy 152–153; Abbott 333. For example, the majority of the 19th-century courts to consider the question held that prohibitions on carrying concealed weapons were lawful under the Second Amendment or state analogues. See, *e.g.*, *State* v. *Chandler*, 5 La. Ann., at 489–490; *Nunn* v. *State*, 1 Ga., at 251; see generally 2 Kent *340, n. 2; The American Students' Blackstone 84, n. 11 (G. Chase ed. 1884). Although we do not undertake an exhaustive historical analysis today of the full scope of the Second Amendment, nothing in our opinion should be taken to cast doubt on longstanding prohibitions on the possession of firearms by felons and the mentally ill, or laws forbidding the carrying of firearms in sensitive places such as schools and government buildings, or laws imposing conditions and qualifications on the commercial sale of arms.[26]

We also recognize another important limitation on the right to keep and carry arms. *Miller* said, as we have explained, that the sorts of weapons protected were those "in common use at the time." 307 U. S., at 179. We think that limitation is fairly supported by the historical tradition of prohibiting the carrying of "dangerous and unusual weapons." See 4 Blackstone 148–149 (1769); 3 B. Wilson, Works of the Honourable James Wilson 79 (1804); J. Dunlap, The New-York Justice 8 (1815); C. Humphreys, A Compendium of the Common Law in Force in Kentucky 482 (1822); 1 W. Russell, A Treatise on Crimes and Indictable Misdemeanors 271–272 (1831); H. Stephen, Summary of the Criminal Law 48 (1840); E. Lewis, An Abridgment of the Criminal Law of the United States 64 (1847); F. Wharton, A Treatise on the

Criminal Law of the United States 726 (1852). See also *State v. Langford*, 10 N. C. 381, 383–384 (1824); *O'Neill v. State*, 16 Ala. 65, 67 (1849); *English v. State*, 35 Tex. 473, 476 (1871); *State v. Lanier*, 71 N. C. 288, 289 (1874).

It may be objected that if weapons that are most useful in military service—M—16 rifles and the like–may be banned, then the Second Amendment right is completely detached from the prefatory clause. But as we have said, the conception of the militia at the time of the Second Amendment's ratification was the body of all citizens capable of military service, who would bring the sorts of lawful weapons that they possessed at home to militia duty. It may well be true today that a militia, to be as effective as militias in the 18th century, would require sophisticated arms that are highly unusual in society at large. Indeed, it may be true that no amount of small arms could be useful against modern-day bombers and tanks. But the fact that modern developments have limited the degree of fit between the prefatory clause and the protected right cannot change our interpretation of the right.

IV

We turn finally to the law at issue here. As we have said, the law totally bans handgun possession in the home. It also requires that any lawful firearm in the home be disassembled or bound by a trigger lock at all times, rendering it inoperable.

As the quotations earlier in this opinion demonstrate, the inherent right of self-defense has been central to the Second Amendment right. The handgun ban amounts to a prohibition of an entire class of "arms" that is overwhelmingly chosen by American society for that lawful purpose. The prohibition extends, moreover, to the home, where the need for defense of self, family, and property is most acute. Under any of the standards of scrutiny that we have applied to enumerated constitutional rights,[27] banning from the home "the most preferred firearm in the nation to 'keep' and use for protection of one's home and family," 478 F. 3d, at 400, would fail constitutional muster.

Few laws in the history of our Nation have come close to the severe restriction of the District's handgun ban. And some of those few have been struck down. In *Nunn v. State*, the Georgia Supreme Court struck down a prohibition on carrying pistols openly (even though it upheld a prohibition on carrying concealed weapons). See 1 Ga., at 251. In *Andrews v. State*, the Tennessee Supreme Court likewise held that a statute that forbade openly carrying a pistol "publicly or privately, without regard to time or place, or circumstances," 50 Tenn., at 187, violated the state constitutional provision (which the court equated with the Second Amendment). That was so even though the statute did not restrict the carrying of long guns. *Ibid*. See also *State v. Reid*, 1 Ala. 612, 616–617 (1840) ("A statute which, under the pretence of regulating, amounts to a destruction of the right, or which requires arms to be so borne as to render them wholly useless for the purpose of defence, would be clearly unconstitutional").

It is no answer to say, as petitioners do, that it is permissible to ban the possession of handguns so long as the possession of other firearms (*i.e.*, long guns) is allowed. It is enough to note, as we have observed, that the American people have considered the handgun to be the quintessential self-defense weapon. There are many reasons that a citizen may prefer a handgun for home defense: It is easier to store in a location that is readily accessible in an emergency; it cannot easily be redirected or wrestled away by an attacker; it is easier to use for those without the upper-body strength to lift and aim a long gun; it can be pointed at a burglar with one hand while the other hand dials the police. Whatever the reason, handguns are the most popular weapon chosen by Americans for self-defense in the home, and a complete prohibition of their use is invalid.

We must also address the District's requirement (as applied to respondent's handgun) that firearms in the home be rendered and kept inoperable at all times. This makes it impossible for citizens to use them for the core lawful purpose of self-defense and is hence unconstitutional. The District argues that we should interpret this element of the statute to contain an exception for self-defense. See Brief for Petitioners 56–57. But we think that is precluded by the unequivocal text, and by the presence of certain other enumerated exceptions: "Except for law enforcement personnel ... , each registrant shall keep any firearm in his possession unloaded and disassembled or bound by a trigger lock or similar device unless such firearm is kept at his place of business, or while being used for lawful recreational purposes within the District of Columbia." D. C. Code §7–2507.02. The nonexistence of a self-defense exception is also suggested by the D. C. Court of Appeals' statement that the statute forbids residents to use firearms to stop intruders, see *McIntosh* v. *Washington*, 395 A. 2d 744, 755–756 (1978).[28]

Apart from his challenge to the handgun ban and the trigger-lock requirement respondent asked the District Court to enjoin petitioners from enforcing the separate licensing requirement "in such a manner as to forbid the carrying of a firearm within one's home or possessed land without a license." App. 59a. The Court of Appeals did not invalidate the licensing requirement, but held only that the District "may not prevent [a handgun] from being moved throughout one's house." 478 F. 3d, at 400. It then ordered the District Court to enter summary judgment "consistent with [respondent's] prayer for relief." *Id.*, at 401. Before this Court petitioners have stated that "if the handgun ban is struck down and respondent registers a handgun, he could obtain a license, assuming he is not otherwise disqualified," by which they apparently mean if he is not a felon and is not insane. Brief for Petitioners 58. Respondent conceded at oral argument that he does not "have a problem with ... licensing" and that the District's law is permissible so long as it is "not enforced in an arbitrary and capricious manner." Tr. of Oral Arg. 74–75. We therefore assume that petitioners' issuance of a license will satisfy respondent's prayer for relief and do not address the licensing requirement.

Justice Breyer has devoted most of his separate dissent to the handgun ban. He says that, even assuming the Second Amendment is a personal guarantee of the right to bear arms, the District's prohibition is valid. He first tries to establish this by founding-era historical precedent, pointing to various restrictive laws in the colonial period. These demonstrate, in his view, that the District's law "imposes a burden upon gun owners that seems proportionately no greater than restrictions in existence at the time the Second Amendment was adopted." *Post*, at 2. Of the laws he cites, only one offers even marginal support for his assertion. A 1783 Massachusetts law forbade the residents of Boston to "take into" or "receive into" "any Dwelling House, Stable, Barn, Out-house, Ware-house, Store, Shop or other Building" loaded firearms, and permitted the seizure of any loaded firearms that "shall be found" there. Act of Mar. 1, 1783, ch. 13, 1783 Mass. Acts p. 218. That statute's text and its prologue, which makes clear that the purpose of the prohibition was to eliminate the danger to firefighters posed by the "depositing of loaded Arms" in buildings, give reason to doubt that colonial Boston authorities would have enforced that general prohibition against someone who temporarily loaded a firearm to confront an intruder (despite the law's application in that case). In any case, we would not stake our interpretation of the Second Amendment upon a single law, in effect in a single city, that contradicts the overwhelming weight of other evidence regarding the right to keep and bear arms for defense of the home. The other laws *Justice Breyer* cites are gunpowder-storage laws that he concedes did not clearly prohibit loaded weapons, but required only that excess gunpowder be kept in a special container or on the top floor of the home. *Post*, at 6–7. Nothing about those fire-safety laws undermines our analysis; they do not remotely burden the right of self-defense as much as an absolute ban on handguns. Nor, correspondingly, does our analysis suggest the invalidity of laws regulating the storage of firearms to prevent accidents.

Justice Breyer points to other founding-era laws that he says "restricted the firing of guns within the city limits to at least some degree" in Boston, Philadelphia and New York. *Post*, at 4 (citing Churchill, Gun Regulation, the Police Power, and the Right to Keep Arms in Early America, 25 Law & Hist. Rev. 139, 162 (2007)). Those laws provide no support for the severe restriction in the present case. The New York law levied a fine of 20 shillings on anyone who fired a gun in certain places (including houses) on New Year's Eve and the first two days of January, and was aimed at preventing the "great Damages ... frequently done on [those days] by persons going House to House, with Guns and other Firearms and being often intoxicated with Liquor." 5 Colonial Laws of New York 244–246 (1894). It is inconceivable that this law would have been enforced against a person exercising his right to self-defense on New Year's Day against such drunken hooligans. The Pennsylvania law to which *Justice Breyer* refers levied a fine of 5 shillings on one who fired a gun or set off fireworks in Philadelphia without first obtaining a license from the governor. See Act of Aug. 26, 1721, §4, in 3 Stat. at Large 253–254. Given Justice Wilson's explanation that the right to self-defense with arms was protected by the Pennsylvania Constitution, it is unlikely that this law (which in any event amounted to at most a licensing regime) would have been enforced against a person who used firearms for self-defense. *Justice Breyer* cites a Rhode Island law that simply levied a 5-shilling fine on those who fired guns in *streets* and *taverns*, a law obviously inapplicable to this case. See An Act for preventing Mischief being done in the town of Newport, or in any other town in this Government, 1731, Rhode Island Session Laws. Finally, *Justice Breyer* points to a Massachusetts law similar to the Pennsylvania law, prohibiting "discharg[ing] any Gun or Pistol charged with Shot or Ball in the Town of *Boston*." Act of May 28, 1746, ch. X, Acts and Laws of Mass. Bay 208. It is again implausible that this would have been enforced against a citizen acting in self-defense, particularly given its preambulatory reference to "the *indiscreet* firing of Guns." *Ibid*. (preamble) (emphasis added).

A broader point about the laws that *Justice Breyer* cites: All of them punished the discharge (or loading) of guns with a small fine and forfeiture of the weapon (or in a few cases a very brief stay in the local jail), not with significant criminal penalties.[29] They are akin to modern penalties for minor public-safety infractions like speeding or jaywalking. And although such public-safety laws may not contain exceptions for self-defense, it is inconceivable that the threat of a jaywalking ticket would deter someone from disregarding a "Do Not Walk" sign in order to flee an attacker, or that the Government would enforce those laws under such circumstances. Likewise, we do not think that a law imposing a 5-shilling fine and forfeiture of the gun would have prevented a person in the founding era from using a gun to protect himself or his family from violence, or that if he did so the law would be enforced against him. The District law, by contrast, far from imposing a minor fine, threatens citizens with a year in prison (five years for a second violation) for even obtaining a gun in the first place. See D. C. Code §7–2507.06.

Justice Breyer moves on to make a broad jurisprudential point: He criticizes us for declining to establish a level of scrutiny for evaluating Second Amendment restrictions. He proposes, explicitly at least, none of the traditionally expressed levels (strict scrutiny, intermediate scrutiny, rational basis), but rather a judge-empowering "interest-balancing inquiry" that "asks whether the statute burdens a protected interest in a way or to an extent that is out of proportion to the statute's salutary effects upon other important governmental interests." Post, at 10. After an exhaustive discussion of the arguments for and against gun control, Justice Breyer arrives at his interest-balanced answer: because handgun violence is a problem, because the law is limited to an urban area, and because there were somewhat similar restrictions in the founding period (a false proposition that we have already discussed), the interest-balancing inquiry results in the constitutionality of the handgun ban. QED.

We know of no other enumerated constitutional right whose core protection has been subjected to a freestanding "interest-balancing" approach. The very enumeration of the right takes out of the hands of government–even the Third Branch of Government–the power to decide on a case-by-case basis whether the right is *really worth* insisting upon. A constitutional guarantee subject to future judges' assessments of its usefulness is no constitutional guarantee at all. Constitutional rights are enshrined with the scope they were understood to have when the people adopted them, whether or not future legislatures or (yes) even future judges think that scope too broad. We would not apply an "interest-balancing" approach to the prohibition of a peaceful neo-Nazi march through Skokie. See *National Socialist Party of America* v. *Skokie*, 432 U. S. 43 (1977) (*per curiam*). The First Amendment contains the freedom-of-speech guarantee that the people ratified, which included exceptions for obscenity, libel, and disclosure of state secrets, but not for the expression of extremely unpopular and wrong-headed views. The Second Amendment is no different. Like the First, it is the very *product* of an interest-balancing by the people–which *Justice Breyer* would now conduct for them anew. And whatever else it leaves to future evaluation, it surely elevates above all other interests the right of law-abiding, responsible citizens to use arms in defense of hearth and home.

Justice Breyer chides us for leaving so many applications of the right to keep and bear arms in doubt, and for not providing extensive historical justification for those regulations of the right that we describe as permissible. See *post*, at 42–43. But since this case represents this Court's first in-depth examination of the Second Amendment, one should not expect it to clarify the entire field, any more than *Reynolds* v. *United States*, 98 U. S. 145 (1879), our first in-depth Free Exercise

Clause case, left that area in a state of utter certainty. And there will be time enough to expound upon the historical justifications for the exceptions we have mentioned if and when those exceptions come before us.

In sum, we hold that the District's ban on handgun possession in the home violates the Second Amendment, as does its prohibition against rendering any lawful firearm in the home operable for the purpose of immediate self-defense. Assuming that Heller is not disqualified from the exercise of Second Amendment rights, the District must permit him to register his handgun and must issue him a license to carry it in the home.

We are aware of the problem of handgun violence in this country, and we take seriously the concerns raised by the many *amici* who believe that prohibition of handgun ownership is a solution. The Constitution leaves the District of Columbia a variety of tools for combating that problem, including some measures regulating handguns, see *supra*, at 54–55, and n. 26. But the enshrinement of constitutional rights necessarily takes certain policy choices off the table. These include the absolute prohibition of handguns held and used for self-defense in the home. Undoubtedly some think that the Second Amendment is outmoded in a society where our standing army is the pride of our Nation, where well-trained police forces provide personal security, and where gun violence is a serious problem. That is perhaps debatable, but what is not debatable is that it is not the role of this Court to pronounce the Second Amendment extinct.

We affirm the judgment of the Court of Appeals.

It is so ordered.

Justice Stevens, with whom *Justice Souter, Justice Ginsburg*, and *Justice Breyer* join, dissenting.

The question presented by this case is not whether the Second Amendment protects a "collective right" or an "individual right." Surely it protects a right that can be enforced by individuals. But a conclusion that the Second Amendment protects an individual right does not tell us anything about the scope of that right.

Guns are used to hunt, for self-defense, to commit crimes, for sporting activities, and to perform military duties. The Second Amendment plainly does not protect the right to use a gun to rob a bank; it is equally clear that it *does* encompass the right to use weapons for certain military purposes. Whether it also protects the right to possess and use guns for nonmilitary purposes like hunting and personal self-defense is the question presented by this case. The text of the Amendment, its history, and our decision in *United States* v. *Miller*, 307 U. S. 174 (1939), provide a clear answer to that question.

The Second Amendment was adopted to protect the right of the people of each of the several States to maintain a well-regulated militia. It was a response to concerns raised during the ratification of the Constitution that the power of Congress to disarm the state militias and create a national standing army posed an intolerable threat to the sovereignty of the several States. Neither the text of the Amendment nor the arguments advanced by its proponents evidenced the slightest interest in limiting any legislature's authority to regulate private civilian uses of firearms. Specifically, there is no indication that the Framers of the Amendment intended to enshrine the common-law right of self-defense in the Constitution.

DISTRICT OF COLUMBIA, *ET AL., PETITIONERS* V. DICK ANTHONY HELLER

on writ of certiorari to the united states court of appeals for the district of columbia circuit [June 26, 2008]

LESSONS LEARNED FROM CHAPTER 6
SPECIFICS

- There are two major types of crime: property-related and person-related
- There are three major theories of crime: biological theory, social inequity theory, and rational choice theory.
- Basic criminal procedure is uniform to ensure that the accused are afforded legal due process.
- Two major theories of punishment are rehabilitation and retribution.
- Contemporary criminal justice issues include: hate crimes, child abduction, and racially biased policing.

- Community-oriented policing is an innovative model for reinvigorating policy practices.
- The U.S.A. Patriot Act brought law enforcement and defense policy functions into closer proximity.

THE BIG PICTURE

Criminal justice is one of the central purposes of government. It is a highly complex function that exists at the national, state, and local levels. Criminal justice policy incorporates everything from identifying suspects to incarcerating convicted criminals to fighting the illegal trafficking in drugs to fighting the war against international terrorism. For the most part, we agree that crime is bad; however, our differing views of what crime entails, why it occurs, and what should be done about it often leads us to different views about what government *ought* or *ought not do*.

KEY TERMS

Amber Alert
assistant attorneys general
child abuse
community-oriented policing (COP)
criminal procedure
defense attorneys
hate crimes
Megan's Law
person-related crimes

property-related crime
prosecuting attorneys
public corruption
public defenders
racially biased policing
recidivism
retributive justice
U.S.A. Patriot Act

QUESTIONS FOR STUDY

1. What is criminal procedure? Outline the process. Discuss three major landmark court cases that have impacted our understanding of criminal procedure.
2. Identify and discuss two major theories of criminal behavior and two major theories of punishment.
3. In what ways does the U.S.A. Patriot Act impact criminal justice policy? Using three policy models, explain and describe the U.S.A. Patriot Act.

CASE STUDY

Senator Samuel D. Brownback Opening Comments During Death Penalty Hearing Senate Subcommittee on the Constitution, Washington, DC, December 1, 2006 "The Fifth and Fourteenth Amendments to the U.S. Constitution provide that no person may be deprived of life without due process of law. Yet the Eighth Amendment prohibits in undefined terms the use of cruel and unusual punishment. In subsequent decisions, the Supreme Court found what it deemed to be a popular consensus against use of the death penalty in cases involving mentally disabled or minor defendants. Reading these provisions together, it seems our founding document neither demands nor prohibits capital punishment. Instead, the Constitution generally permits the people to decide whether and when capital punishment is appropriate.

"So each generation may—and good citizens should—consider anew the law and facts involving this solemn judgment. I believe America must establish a culture of life. If use of the death penalty is contrary to promoting a culture of life, we need to have a national dialogue and hear both sides of the issue. All life is sacred, and our use of the death penalty in the American justice system must recognize this truth.

"I called this hearing in order to conduct a full and fair examination of the death penalty in the United States. I believe it is important for lawmakers and the public to be informed about a punishment which, because it is final and irreversible, stirs much debate. It is my intention to explore in this hearing the various aspects of capital punishment, from the statistics on deterrence to the views of crime victims. It is my hope that by carefully reflecting on America's experience with the death penalty, the people can make informed judgments worthy of the Constitution's faith in future generations."

COURTESY OF PROJECT VOTE SMART
WWW.VOTESMART.ORG
Thinking about what Senator Brownback said about the death penalty, is it something that we ought or ought not do? Why or why not? Based on the group viewpoints presented, develop a short recommendation for keeping or ending death penalty policies. If presenting your findings in a paper or class presentation, gather additional background information to make your case—for example, exploring the policy history of the death penalty, the events that led to its creation. Use three policy models to explain the death penalty as a policy.

BIBLIOGRAPHY

American Civil Liberties Union. 2007. "Safe and Free: Restore our Constitutional Rights," www.aclu.org/safefree/resources/17343res20031114.html (accessed August 17, 2007).

Burt, M., L. Newmark, M. Norris, D. Dyer, and A. Harrell. 1996. "The violence against women act of 1994: Evaluation of the STOP block grants to combat violence against women." www.urban.org/publications/306621.html (accessed August 17, 2007).

Cassel, E. 2007. *Criminal behavior*. Mahwah, NJ: L. Erlbaum Associates.

Cornish, D., and R. Clarke, eds. 1986. *The reasoning criminal*. New York Springer-Verlag.

Dilulio, J. 1987. *Governing prisons*. New York: Free Press.

Durkheim, E. 1982. *Règles de la Méthode Sociologique*. New York: Free Press.

Fridell, L., R. Lunney, D. Diamond, and B. Kabu. 2001. *Racially-biased policing. A principled approach*. Washington, DC: Police Executive Research Forum. Hall, N. 2005. *Hate crime*. Collumpton, Devon, UK: Willan.

Levin, J., and J. McDevitt. 1993. *Hate crimes: The rising tide of bigotry and bloodshed*. New York: Plenum Press.

Lippke, R. 2007. *Rethinking imprisonment*. New York: Oxford University Press. Lowi, T. 1969. *The end of liberalism*. New York: Norton.

National Criminal Justice Reference Service. 2005. "Hate Crime Resources—Legislation." www.ncjrs.org/hate_crimes/legislation.html (accessed January 31, 2005).

Office of the Attorney General. 2001. *Registered sex offenders (Megan's law)*. Sacramento, CA; Department of Justice, www.caag.state.ca.us/megan accessed January 31, 2005).

Samaha, J. 1999. *Criminal procedure*, 4th ed. Belmont, CA: West/Wadsworth.

Santos, M. 2006. *Inside: life behind bars in America*. New York: St. Martin's Press.

U.S. Department of Health and Human Services, Administration on Children, Youth and Families 2007. *Child Maltreatment 2005*. 'Washington, DC: U.S. Government Printing Office.

University of Texas. 2007. "Community Oriented Policing." www.utexas.edu/police/cops/ (accessed August 17, 2007).

Wilson, J. 1975. *Thinking about crime*. New York: Basic Books.

Wilson, J., and J. Petersilia. 2001. *Crime: Public policies for crime control*. Oakland: ICS Press.

Zimring, F., and G. Hawkins. 1989. *Capital punishment and the American agenda*. New York: Cambridge University Press.

COURT CASES

Gideon v. Wainwright 372 U.S. 335 (1963)
Klopfer v. N. Carolina 386 U.S. 213 (1967)
Malloy v. Hogan 378 U.S. 1 (1964)
Mapp v. Ohio 367 U.S. 643 (1961)
Pointer v. Texas 380 U.S. 400 (1965)

Robinson v. California 370 U.S. 660 (1962)
Teny v. Ohio 392 U.S. 1 (1967)
Washington v. Texas 388 U.S. 14 (1967)
Wisconsin v. Mitchell 508 U.S. 476 (1993)
Wolf v. Colorado 338 U.S. 25 (1949)

Endnotes

1. www.aclu.org/CriminalJustice/CriminalJusticeMain.cfm (accessed May 27, 2003).
2. A grand jury decision in favor of a trial does not mean that the defendant is guilty of the crime.
3. www.ncjrs.gov/spotlight/Hate_Crimes/Summary.html (accessed May 26, 2009).
4. www.ncjrs.gov/spotlight/Hate_Crimes/Summary.html (accessed May 26, 2009).
5. www.ncjrs.gov/spotlight/Hate_Crimes/Summary.htrnl (accessed May 26, 2009).
6. 18 U.S.C. 110, Section 2251.
7. www.caag.state.ca.us/megan (accessed June 5, 2003); more current link to Megan's Law information: www.meganslaw.ca.gov/ (accessed May 26, 2009).
8. www.cops.usdoj.gov/Default.asp?Item=36 (accessed January 31, 2005).
9. Fridell et al. 2001, 1.
10. Samaha. 1999, 48.
11. Stana, R. 2002. "Identity Fraud: Prevalence and Links to Alien Illegal Activities." Testimony before the Subcommittee on Crime, Terrorism, and Homeland Security, and the Subcommittee on Immigration, Border Security, and Claims, Committee on the Judiciary, House of Representatives, June 25. Washington, DC: GAO. GAO-02-830T.
12. Pew Research Center. 2006. "America's Immigration Quandary: Section IV—Views and Perceptions of Immigrants," www.people-press.org/reports/display.php3?PageID=1049 (accessed May 26, 2009).
13. According to the Pew study, 76 percent of Americans favor a government identification card for immigrants.

Review Questions

chapter 6

1. Discuss who makes criminal justice policy and how whether they are elected or not matters for the content of criminal justice policy.

2. Discuss the most important court cases in the area of criminal justice policy (at least four cases from the Supreme Court), and explain why the Supreme Court has been the most important player in this policy area?

3. What did the writer Dennis Henigan mean by the phrase, "the most dangerous right"?

4. Review the major constitutional provisions, court cases, and legislative acts that have made gun policy in the United States, and discuss how the recent *District of Columbia vs. Heller case* affected gun policy.

Welfare Policy

chapter 7

The Politics and Economics of Inequality

Charles L. Cochran and Eloise F. Malone

This chapter focuses on the oldest story in every society: the tension between the haves and have-nots. As Plutarch observed early in the first millennium, "An imbalance between rich and poor is the oldest and most fatal ailment of all republics." Throughout history, elites have boldly justified their special claim to wealth, power, and privilege through the development of national myths that legitimize their position at the expense of the masses. Democracy in its most narrow formal requirement of individual freedom of expression, regular elections with full citizen participation, and a responsive government, was not possible where an aristocracy only controlled all political power, but also had tight control over land, labor, and capital. Democracy, based on the fundamental principle of equality, sweeps aside all claims of privilege. As Supreme Court Justice Louis Brandeis said. "We can have democracy in this country or we can have great wealth concentrated in the hands of a few, but we cannot have both."[1] When great wealth is concentrated in relatively few hands that also control the institutions of governmental power, government will serve the interests of those elites first. Democratic government's stated primary purpose of serving "we the people" to "promote the general welfare" can become an illusion manipulated by the powerful to gain approval of the nonelites. Democracy is always threatened by the possible collusion between the rich to take control of government for their own benefit. When that effort succeeds, the institutions of democracy will continue to exist long after the political system has degenerated into an oligarchy.

The study of income distribution is concerned with an analysis of the way national income is divided among persons. There are several issues of normative and positive theory that crop up when examining income distribution. For economists such as Adam Smith, Thomas Malthus, David Ricardo, and Karl Marx, distribution was a central issue. At the end of the nineteenth and the beginning of the twentieth century, many policy analysts and economists were not significantly concerned with the distribution of wealth and income. The Great Depression and the theory of John Maynard Keynes renewed interest in the subject.

Major questions regarding the distribution of wealth and income include whether or not inequality is inevitable. If so, how much inequality is optimal? Is there a threshold beyond which inequality in wealth or income undermines political democracy? What kinds of public policies regarding inequalities would improve the quality of life for most citizens? Should there be a coordination of policies by democratic forms of government to reduce the variability of inequality in various nations?

The Promise of Equality in the First New Nation

Politics is often defined as the ongoing struggle over who gets what, when, and how. Throughout history much of the struggle was determined by the ability of a powerful actor, whether a warlord, a monarch, or an oligarch, to maintain his life of wealth and privilege at the expense of others. The eighteenth-century Enlightenment thinkers challenged the domination of society by a hereditary and tyrannical aristocracy. They believed that human reason was the indispensable weapon needed to battle ignorance, superstition, and tyranny and build a better world. Thinkers of the Enlightenment stressed individualism over community, and freedom replaced authority as a core value. Many Enlightenment thinkers were merchants who resented paying taxes to support a privileged aristocracy who contributed little of value to society. It was particularly galling that the aristocrats were unwilling to share power with the

"The Politics and Economics of Inequality" from *Public Policy: Perspectives and Choices, 3rd edition* by Charles L. Cochran and Eloise F. Malone. Copyright © 2005 by Lynne Rienner Publishers, Inc. Used with permission of the publisher.

merchants and manufacturers who actually created the national wealth.

The intellectual leaders of the American Revolution were captivated by the Enlightenment's opposition to unchecked privilege, since they hoped to build a democracy that would require tolerance, respect for evidence, and informed public opinion. Their notion of democracy was one in which government would make decisions on behalf of the "general welfare," not for the advantage of the privileged few. The concept of equality written into the Declaration of Independence, together with the concept of "human rights," which has become an essential part of U.S. culture, has been called our "civil religion."

These notions from the Enlightenment were not seen by early Americans as naive optimism, but as the promise of the **American Dream**—the widespread belief in an open, vigorous, and progressive community committed to equal opportunities for all in which life would improve for each generation. It includes the belief that the income and wealth the economy generated would become more evenly distributed.

The leaders of the American Revolution wanted to do more than free themselves from forced obedience to a monarch; they wanted to create a government that would offer greater freedom and dignity to the average citizen. Some went so far as to propose that all free white males be allowed to vote. Other influential members of the delegation in Philadelphia in 1787 were more dubious and proposed a government administered by gentlemen of property to maintain their life of privilege at the expense of others. The constitution that resulted from all the compromises provided a system of separation of powers between the president, Congress, and the judiciary. It specifically provided for a house of representatives to represent the interests of "the people." Congress, aware of the unprecedented grant of power to the people, used the words of Roman poet Virgil in the Great Seal of the United States—"a new age now begins."[2] The principle of checks and balances resulted from the inability of the framers of the Constitution to agree on precisely how power should be distributed among the branches. Although the commitment to hold all men as being created equal and endowed by their creator with inalienable rights to life, liberty, and the pursuit of happiness was not enforced, a war on inequality began immediately to force the government to live up to the promise. Property rights for voting were abolished, but it took a civil war to free slaves, and another century passed before civil rights legislation gave substance to that freedom.

EQUITY AND EQUALITY

To many of the leaders of the American Revolution, democracy was looked upon as the completion of the human struggle for freedom. The framers of the Constitution were well aware of the difficulty of reconciling individuality and liberty with democratic equality. James Madison expressed his concern over the inherent conflicts a democratic society would have to address when he wrote that the "most common and durable source of factions" in society is "the various and unequal distribution of property."

Thomas Jefferson's bias in favor of equality is well known. He believed that the innate differences between men were small:[3]

> I am conscious that an equal division of property is impracticable. But the consequences of this enormous inequality producing so much misery to the bulk of mankind, legislators cannot invent too many devices for subdividing property . . . Another means of silently lessening the inequality of property is to exempt all from taxation below a certain point, and to tax the higher portions of property in geometrical progression as they rise.[4]

He went on to say that the government should provide "that as few as possible shall be without a little portion of land" as the "small landholders are the most precious part of a state."[5]

Opponents of the trend toward equality used the vocabulary of the Enlightenment and Jeffersonian liberalism, but provided their own definitions to words like "individualism" and "progress." They even claimed support from those who were clearly concerned about the problem. For example, Charles Darwin expressed concern for the poor when he wrote, "If the misery of the poor be caused not by the laws of nature, but by our institutions, great is our sin."[6] Nevertheless, his theory of natural selection, which led to the theory of evolution, was revised by Herbert Spencer into "social Darwinism" and endorsed as a scientific finding that the destruction of the weak and the "survival of the fittest" constituted the essence of progress.

Americans have often boastfully quoted Alexis de Tocqueville's observation of "the equality of conditions" in the United States in the 1830s. U.S. culture has always emphasized equality rather than deference. Politicians, especially wealthy politicians, claim that they share the same social and cultural *values* of the average American, even if they do not share the same tax bracket. Indeed, de Tocqueville believed that the Americanization of the world in terms of the ever-increasing equality of conditions was inevitable. He realized that the creation of democratic forms of government was not the end of the struggle, but that it was a continuous process. And he believed that inevitably the rest of humanity would finally arrive at an almost complete equality of conditions. He sensed a growing "aristocracy of manufacturers" who had no sense of public responsibility and whose aim was to use the workers and then abandon them to public charity. He believed that the manufacturing aristocracy "is one of the harshest which ever existed in the world. . . . [T]he friends of democracy should keep their eyes anxiously fixed in this direction; for if ever a permanent inequality of conditions and aristocracy again penetrate into the world, it may be predicted that this is the channel by which they will enter."[7]

Writing a century later, Keynes pointed out that we could hardly expect business to act on behalf of the well-being of the workers, let alone the entire society. He noted that in democracies the government has the responsibility to protect the economic well-being of the nation. The main failure of capitalism, according to Keynes, is its "failure to provide for full employment and its arbitrary and inequitable distribution of wealth and incomes."[8] Keynes was not opposed to economic inequality. What was required, he said, was a collective management of the system that would be as efficient as possible without offending our notions of a satisfactory way of life. The problem then becomes, what is a socially optimal amount of economic inequality?

U.S. political institutions declare the equality of citizens. However, capitalism creates economic and social inequalities. The disparity between presumed equal rights and economic inequality creates tension between capitalism and the principles of democracy. Owners of capital may use money or their position of power in imperfect markets to deny others a minimum standard of living. Beginning in the Progressive era and reaching its high points during the administrations of Franklin Roosevelt and Lyndon Johnson, democratic institutions were used to keep market excesses within acceptable limits. During the 1930s, President Roosevelt inaugurated the New Deal. The Great Depression caused a national crisis that resulted in a third of the nation being ill-fed, ill-housed, and ill-clothed. The minimum wage, the eight-hour day, Social Security, trade union legislation, civil rights, women's rights, a progressive federal income tax, and civil service reform based on merit rather than a spoils system were all achieved over the vigorous opposition of business interests, which were concerned that such benefits to workers would reduce profits. The American Dream was reinforced by the notion that business prospers when workers are paid wages sufficient to allow them to buy what they produce. We prosper as "one nation, indivisible" when workers are paid wages that allowed a "middle-class" income. A broad middle class contributes to prosperity for all. Government responsibility to narrow the gap between rich and poor was largely accepted by liberals and conservatives alike after the New Deal. Others sought to preserve equality of opportunity by opposing any alliance between government and business elites. That effort, and the unsteady progress by reformers in advancing the American Dream of equality, was seriously challenged in the 1980s by a resurgence of conservatism under President Ronald Reagan. Supply-side economic thinking defended economic inequality as a source of productivity and economic growth.

The successive federal tax cuts proposed by the George W. Bush administration and enacted by Congress were for most Americans actually tax shifts that redistributed after-tax income from the bottom 99 percent to the top 1 percent, exacerbating the inequality between the rich and everybody else. The federal government has concentrated on eliminating estate taxes and reducing taxes especially for the wealthy, while ignoring social safety net policies for the poor, like raising the minimum wage, providing health care for the uninsured, or providing more funds for housing the poor.

Many of those most adversely affected by the economic changes did not respond with anger toward those primarily responsible for their economic decline. Rather than focusing their anger on the corporate and financial elite derided by Roosevelt as "economic royalists" and "malefactors of great wealth," they identified their antagonists as "liberals." Conservative strategists successfully cast the problem as "cultural" rather than "economic." These activists, with the support of conservative think tanks, pundits, lobbyists, ministers, and right-wing radio talk-show hosts, provided a smoke screen that shielded the dismantling of middle- and working-class protections while they added fuel to their anger against "liberals."

A recent study by Thomas Frank titled What's the Matter with Kansas? analyzes how many vulnerable Americans have been persuaded that cultural issues override economic issues, and therefore persuaded to vote against their economic and social interests.[9] Political liberals are portrayed as waging cultural warfare against a fundamentally Protestant Christian culture that is perceived as the basis of U.S. society. Conservatives argue that this is a battle to determine whether U.S. culture as we have known it can be saved. On issue after issue, they feel threatened: gay marriage, abortion rights, the Pledge of Allegiance, prayer in schools, the promiscuity portrayed in movies and television programming, to name just a few.

The economically disadvantaged segment of the U.S. population provided critical electoral support in the 2004 elections to politicians who acted against their economic interest by implementing policies that increased the gap between themselves and the affluent. Political campaigns increasingly rely on professional managers, constant polling, focus groups to test appeals to voters, and expensive television advertising. This has forced political fundraising to become increasingly dependent on large contributors. The wealthy are not surprisingly inclined to contribute money to politicians and organizations that endorse reductions in most government programs, including social welfare programs, taxes, and government regulation of business. They are very aware of the benefits of economic inequality for themselves and focus clearly on the goal of protecting their economic status when they contribute to political candidates. It is estimated that the richest 3 percent of the voting population accounts for 35 percent of all private campaign contributions during presidential elections.[10] The major corporate political action committees did not hedge their bets in the 2004 elections. They favored Republicans ten to one. Of 268 corporate political action committees that donated $1 million or more to presidential and congressional candidates from January 2003 through October 2004, 245 gave the majority of their contributions to Republicans.[11]

The nonelites are aware of the downside of economic inequality, but vote on the basis of noneconomic issues like crime, abortion, or immigration.[12] The poor are more cynical regarding government and are less likely to register and vote.[13] The federal government's response is to advance the economic interests of the wealthy and the noneconomic interests of the less affluent.

As labor organizer Oscan Ameringer observed, in such a scenario, politics becomes the art of winning votes from the poor and campaign contributions from the rich through promises "to defend each from the other."[14]

Elites' contributions give them greater political influence than less affluent voters. The process then results in economic policies that add to elites' share of total wealth and income, which is at variance with theories of democracy. The alliance between government and the rich (the U.S. equivalent of the aristocrats' relationship to King George III), so long feared by the reformers, has been realized.

INCOME DISTRIBUTION

It has long been known that extreme inequality is a major cause of political instability in many developing countries. Even in a wealthy country like the United States, economic inequality is associated with poverty, crime, political alienation, and social unrest. Great inequality in income and wealth is a social problem and therefore an issue for the policy agenda. Whether the government should reduce the great inequality between the rich and the poor is the focus of contention. Part of the uncertainty arises from the imperfect knowledge about the relationship between inequality and economic growth. It is often held that there is a tradeoff between equality and efficiency, suggesting that policies aimed at reducing inequality reduce economic growth.

The concept of liberty and egalitarianism has been a cornerstone of U.S. social and political culture. Liberty, protected by government as the pursuit of one's own self-interest, permits each to acquire material goods according to one's circumstances and abilities. The result has been a great disparity in income and wealth that undermines equality. We hear a great deal about political equality, which typically means that individuals are equal before the law, and that regardless of ability or income, each has the right to vote. There appears to be an assumption that this narrow technical political equality is *the* significant equality in the United States, and we disregard or minimize the fact of economic inequality. Most countries of the Western world have policies designed to *reduce* the differences between rich and poor. In those countries most concede that the role of government should not be to widen the gap between rich and poor, but rather to reduce it.

How Has U.S. Income Distribution Changed?

Between 1935 and 1945 there was a clear trend toward a more equal distribution of income in the United States, primarily because of four factors. (1) The end of the Great Depression and a wartime economy provided full employment, significantly raising the wages of labor. (2) During World War II a more progressive income tax and excess-profits taxes reduced the after-tax income of the rich more than that of the poor. (3) Labor scarcity during the war reduced discrimination against minorities and increased economic opportunities for them. (4) Union membership quadrupled and increased the relative income of labor.[15]

In the decade between 1945 and 1955, the trend toward greater equality continued, but at a much slower pace as unions began meeting more resistance after the war, and as continued prosperity meant continued employment and educational opportunities for minorities. From 1955 through about 1980 the distribution of income remained relatively constant, largely because governments at all levels imposed taxes that were less progressive than in former years. Since 1980, inequality in incomes has increased.

Factors Contributing to Greater Economic Inequality

The gap between pay for higher- and lower-paid workers has accelerated at least since 1980, particularly among men.[16] Between 1980 and 2003, real wages fell for those at the bottom of the income distribution, while they remained rather stagnant for those close to or just above the average and rose briskly for those at the top. Women's real wages on average grew about 1 percent faster annually during the same period.

The question is, why did wage inequality expand so rapidly in the past quarter century? A variety of factors contribute to wage differentials that exist between and within the same occupation. And not surprisingly, different scholars tend to focus on different explanations. Marvin Kosters and Murray Ross emphasize supply-side factors, such as the maturing baby boom generation and the growing role of women in the labor force.[17] Others emphasize demand-side factors, such as the shift from a manufacturing to a service-oriented economy.[18]

Several policies contributed to the reversal. Since the Reagan administration, enforcement of antitrust laws has been given a very low priority. Mergers of large corporations have become a method for concentrating wealth, undertaken because of the huge payouts received by chief executive officers and senior executives when two companies merge. Historically, an increase in worker productivity resulted in a similar increase in income for the average worker. But from 1973 to 2002, median family income grew only about one-third as fast as productivity.[19] The pay gap between more highly educated workers and less educated workers has indeed increased. Those with more human capital can demand more for their more highly skilled labor, which pushes up pay levels. Highly educated (or skilled) workers are often in a more inelastic supply position, and rising demand forces up their wage rate.

Globalization is increasingly put forward as an explanation for a growing income inequality. Undoubtedly, free trade does exert a downward pressure on U.S. wages, but some scholars are skeptical that it is a major cause of rising inequality.[20] Rising inequality also results from the decline in the number of middle-class jobs and the accompanying rise in the proportion of jobs in the service sector that pay lower wages.[21]

In 1983, the first year for which comparable statistics are available, 20.1 percent of the labor force belonged to a union; by 2003 the number of private sector union members had declined to 8.2 percent of the labor force. The minimum wage of $5.15 an hour was just 34 percent of the average hourly wage in 2003, down from about 45 percent of the average wage in the mid-1970s. The decline in their minimum wage relative to the average wage is clearly a relevant factor The coverage of workers with employer-provided pensions or health care has also declined for middle- and low-income workers over the past two decades.

Immigration policy is related to globalization. It increases the pool of labor and also exerts a greater downward pressure, particularly on middle- and low-wage workers. Many immigrants who enter the United States are attracted by the availability of jobs, even though they pay low wages by U.S. standards. But this is preferable to unemployment or even lower wages in their native countries. While they are a labor safety valve in their native countries, they clearly increase income inequality in the United States.

It is largely a matter of public choice as to how much inequality the society will permit. Growing inequality has become a politically charged topic in recent years, which raises the question, is there something public policy can or should do to reduce growing inequalities? Some conservatives have argued that significant differences in economic inequalities do not necessarily have policy implications. They argue that the wealthy are inclined to invest their money, creating jobs and contributing to faster economic growth. Conservatives accuse liberals of fomenting class warfare when they point to the growing inequality of income and wealth in society.

Others see the growing inequality as a serious threat to society's political, social, and economic well-being. They argue that income inequality causes spillover effects into the quality of life, even for those not necessarily in poverty. Wide economic disparities result in frustration, stress, and family discord, which increases the rate of crime, violence, and homicide. Robert Putnam has suggested that at the breakdown of social cohesion brought about by income inequality threatens the functioning of democracy. He found that low levels of civic trust spill over into a lack of confidence in government and low voter turnout at elections.[22] There is a serious concern that too much inequality could lead to a cycle in which lack of trust and civic engagement reinforce a public policy that does not result from the collective deliberation about the public interest, but merely reflects the success of campaign strategies. In a democracy, the electorate pick their representatives. However, members of Congress increasingly choose who can vote for them through gerrymandering. In the 2004 election fewer than 3 percent of the seats were competitive.[23]

Although the current intellectual climate is less supportive of an egalitarian position than a decade or two ago, it is still true that in most Western countries, including the United States, significant majorities believe that a bias in favor of equality to reduce a large income gap accords with a democratic approach.[24]

AMERICANS' BIAS IN FAVOR OF EQUALITY

While we may declare our sympathy for policies favoring equality, most of us would support inequality if it resulted from certain conditions:

1. *People would agree that inequality is justified if everyone has a fair (not necessarily equal) chance to get ahead.*[25] Not only would most people not object to inequality in the distribution of wealth or income if the race was run under fair conditions with no one handicapped at the start, but they would actively support it as well. However, the situation quickly becomes murky. Many people do try to compete for scarce highly paid jobs by attending college so their future incomes will be higher. Some may choose not to attend college, while others may have grown up in families who could not afford to send them to college or provide a background conducive to preparation for it. For those people, the resulting lower income is not voluntary.

  What parameters make conditions fair? Of particular concern is the fairness of inheritances. What of the genetic inheritance of talent? Much of our most important human capital is carried in our genes, with the ownership of productive resources just an accident of birth. Is it fair that some individuals through their genetic endowment, a factor beyond the control of the person so equipped, have high innate intelligence, the physical ability that allows them to become professional athletes, or the physical attributes that allow them to become highly paid models, while the genetic inheritance of others determines that they will be mentally or physically limited or even both? We usually do not worry too much over this kind of inheritance, but its effects are very real.

  What of the inheritance of gender? Studies make it plain that females born in the United States doing the same job as men receive approximately 70 percent of the pay received by a male. Is that fair? What about the inheritance of those who do not pick their parents wisely and grow up as an ethnic minority, in a culturally deprived family in a ghetto neighborhood, as opposed to a child born to a white privileged family who can afford the richest environment and best schools available for their children?

Then there is the income differential resulting from inherited wealth. Many of the super-rich in the United States got that way through merely inheriting large sums of money. That it should be possible to pass some wealth on from one generation to another is generally conceded, but the passing on of large fortunes virtually intact is frequently challenged. Classical conservatives tend to be most supportive of the theory of social Darwinism, which holds that society is a place of competition based on the principle of "survival of the fittest," in which those who are most fit win in the competition for material goods. Social Darwinists are opposed to the passing on of large inheritances from one generation to the next, because it nullifies the fairness of the competition. Someone who inherits a fortune may have mediocre ability, but does not have to "compete" with others and prove their ability through competition. As Barry Switzer famously said, "some people are born on third base and go through life thinking they hit a triple."[26] The wealthy who truly believe in the theory maintain their consistency by opposing the repeal of estate taxes. They are not a large group.

Any discussion of inheritances suggests the role of chance in income distribution. Chance operates not only in inheritances, but also in the wider region of income differentials. One individual hits a lottery jackpot, another finds a super-highway built adjacent to her farm, increasing its value several times, another unexpectedly finds oil on his land. On the other hand, a worker may find himself out of work for a prolonged period due to a recession beyond his control, or the victim of an expensive debilitating illness, or that a highly paid position she was trained for disappears.

2. *No one objects to inequality if it reflects individual choice.* If an individual decides to turn his back on the secular world, become a Franciscan, and take a vow of poverty, no one would object. If someone decides to take a job that offers financial incentives because of unpleasant or inconvenient working conditions, or because it is more dangerous, we will not object to her higher wages. The problem is that frequently these decisions do not result from free choices but are brought about by circumstances. A person raised in a ghetto with no opportunity to sacrifice *current* income to improve skills through education so that a *future* income will be higher, may not have the option of choosing to work in a highly paid profession.

3. *People accept inequality when it reflects merit.* Nearly everyone believes in the correctness of higher pay when we can show that it is justified by a different contribution to output.[27] Some people work longer hours than others, or work harder when on the job. This may result in income differences that are largely voluntary. Other workers acquire experience and technical skills over time that may result in their earning a higher wage. This is part of the justification for a wage differential based on seniority.

4. *People accept and even support inequality when we are persuaded that the inequality will benefit everyone.* Often the common good is thought to include an increase in the gross domestic product (GDP), since greater productivity typically means a brisk demand for labor, higher wages, and greater economic activity. Therefore, the argument is often made by some politicians and some economists that policies encouraging inequalities that benefit those with higher incomes are justified because they will lead to higher savings for the wealthy, which in turn will ultimately be translated into investments, which will create the jobs enriching the prospects of everyone else. The proposal for a lower capital gains tax is just such a suggestion. This is the trickle-down theory, which suggests that if the wealthy only had more money, they would be more highly motivated to invest more of it in the hope of making a profit, and these investments would then create more jobs, thus helping society in general.[28] These four general principles describe how the unequal distribution of income and wealth *is* defended. There is no suggestion that this is the way we *should* think about inequality.

THE FUNCTIONAL THEORY OF INEQUALITY

There is a theory that maintains that inequality is functionally imperative, because no stable system can long survive without it.[29] According to the **functional theory of inequality**, society must first distribute its members into the various jobs or roles defined by the society and then motivate them to perform their tasks efficiently. Some jobs are more important than others in the sense that successful performance of them is crucial to the welfare of the whole society.[30] Additionally, some tasks require skills that are either difficult or scarce because they require special training. To ensure that the most important jobs are performed competently, every society provides a system of unequal rewards to produce incentives to channel the most competent people into the most important and difficult jobs. This ensures the greatest efficiency in the performance of these jobs.

It should be emphasized that, according to this theory, "a position does not bring power and prestige because it draws a high income. Rather it draws a high income because it is functionally important and the available personnel is for one reason or another scarce."[31] So the population comes to understand that inequality is functional. The system of unequal rewards works to the advantage of the whole system by guaranteeing that jobs essential to society's welfare are performed efficiently and competently.[32]

Milton Friedman believes that the market is the most efficient way of filling the most important positions with the most capable people. Equality of opportunity is the principle that allows the market to select the most competent individuals: "No society can be stable unless there is a basic core of value judgments that are unthinkingly accepted by the great bulk of its members. I believe that payment in accordance with product has been, and in large measure still is, one of these accepted value judgments or institutions."[33] The functional theory of inequality is intuitively appealing, but it immediately raises several problems.

Tradeoffs Between Equality, Equity, and Efficiency

Equality of income and *equity* of income are not the same. Equality deals with incomes in terms of "the same amount," while equity refers to "fairness." Equality deals with what incomes *are* and variance from a standard, while equity is the normative question of what incomes *should be*.

The main argument against an equal distribution of income is based on efficiency. An unequal distribution does provide incentives. To illustrate the point, imagine the consequences if the society decided to achieve equality by taxing away all individual income and then dividing the taxes collected equally among the entire population. Realizing that harder work would no longer lead to a higher income would eliminate an important incentive. Any incentive to forgo current consumption to purchase capital goods would also be abolished, since there would be no chance of additional income. Since all rewards for harder work, investing, entrepreneurship, and taking risks by developing capital and acquiring land would disappear, the gross domestic product would decline dramatically. This suggests that policies that increase the amount of economic equality (or reduce inequality) may reduce economic efficiency—that is, lower the incentive to produce (thus lowering the GDP).

A second argument against an equal distribution of income or wealth is based on the concept of equity. As noted earlier, people with different natural abilities and who make unequal contributions to output should not receive the same income. An equal distribution is not equitable if individual contributions are unequal. U.S. society has been based on the idea of equality of opportunity rather than equality of results.

The case in favor of an equal distribution of income must include the argument that an unequal distribution leads to unequal opportunities. Some income differences arise because of differences in wealth. Many with income-producing assets such as stocks and bonds may receive sizable incomes from them. Not only are these individuals able to acquire additional income-producing assets such as land or capital investments (i.e., more stocks and bonds), but they are also more able to invest in human capital through training and education to increase even further the amount of income they can earn in the future. A person with less wealth is, by contrast, less able to invest in other productive factors such as land and capital, or in education. Therefore, an unequal distribution tends to be perpetuated and even increased because of the unequal market power of those who already have wealth, unless the government intervenes through taxes and transfers of income.

A second argument made by those in favor of a more equal income distribution is that a highly unequal distribution that provided a great deal for the few and little or nothing for the many creates political unrest and threatens the stability of the society. When 25 percent of the population live at the subsistence level and the top 10 percent who receive most of the income, also dominate the political and economic levers of power, the poor may be driven to rebel against the economic and political political elites.

Third, it may be argued that a highly unequal distribution of income can, contrary to the conservative view, inhibit investment in capital, which is crucial to economic growth. While it is true that investment usually comes from people with higher incomes, if relatively few members of a society have most of its income, the rest of the population cannot put significant demand into the economy to stimulate growth. With a lack of investment incentives, the wealthy may opt to use their incomes for personal consumption instead.

Liberals sometimes undermine their case for more equality by denying that their proposals will have any harmful effects on incentives. Conservatives, on the other hand, undermine their case against greater equality by making greatly exaggerated claims about the loss of efficiency that would arise.

Qualifications to the Theory

The functional theory of inequality is open to some criticisms that do not demolish it, but that significantly narrow the range of inequalities that can be justified as functionally imperative:

1. *It is relatively easy to determine which skills are in scarce supply, but difficult to tell which jobs are the most important to the welfare of a particular society.* Questions of comparable worth, for example, are notoriously complex problems. After agreement is reached regarding the extremes—for example, the importance of the cardiovascular surgeon compared to the street-sweeper—it becomes very difficult to determine the relative importance of jobs more at the "center," managing a corporation versus teaching young children, for instance, or working as an accountant versus being a dentist. How does one decide?

   Those supporting the functionalist approach usually shift from an assessment of the relative importance of any particular position to assessing its relative skill level and the scarcity of that skill in the society.

2. *Contrived scarcity can affect the supply of skilled personnel.* Once we shift attention from the importance of the job to the scarcity of talent, we must confront the reality that a critically located profession can control the supply of talent. Any profession tries to promote the economic interest of its members by increasing their income. Competitive conditions would attract more members, potentially developing a surplus and driving incomes down. So the profession will typically try to limit its membership through occupational licensing, creating a contrived scarcity. Many occupations require a state license. Frequently, the licensing process is very strongly influenced by the profession, whose members claim that they alone are competent to judge the criteria necessary for training and certification. Members justify their control by citing the need to exclude "quacks." But the certification, whether for architects, accountants, lawyers, or physicians, has substantial economic value. Frequently, the license is fundamentally a way to raise wages in a particular profession by limiting competition. Typically, licenses are granted by a panel of practitioners in the field, who determine how many are to be granted and to whom. The potential for conflicts of interest is apparent.[34] Restricting competition raises the income of the rent seekers. But if those who benefit can then buy more political influence, which further increases their share of income, it undermines the democratic notion of equality of competition.

   The point is that once the first criterion of the functionalists—the importance of a particular kind of job—recedes into the background, the functionalist interpretation of the second criterion—the scarcity of needed skills—becomes doubtful.

3. *Functionalists emphasize the positive side of their theory and ignore its negative aspects.* The theory does identify the value of talent and shows how rewarding various talents motivates those who possess them to work efficiently. However, it ignores the demotivating effects for those with fewer talents. Those at the higher end of the income stream can be motivated with the aspiration to bonuses, higher wages, life and health insurance benefits, promotions, and pension programs. But workers at the lower end of the income stream cannot be motivated by higher pay, for at least two main reasons. First, low income at this end of the pay scale must provide the differential to fill the higher positions with competent and conscientious workers. Second, the money needed to pay some people more must be taken from those who will be paid less. Thus, in functionalist theory, the workers on garbage trucks who are quick

and efficient cannot be rewarded by higher pay or bonuses, although they may be valued employees. As these individuals get older, and slower, they must continue to work because of the need to provide for their families, even under the most adverse conditions. Consequently, low income, unemployment, and the threat of unemployment are concentrated among those jobs where the skill levels are the lowest and the supply of people having the skills is the greatest. In sum, the carrot motivating those at the upper-income levels requires the stick to motivate those at the lower levels of income. Functionalist theory rarely mentions this.

4. *For the functionalist system of inequality to operate smoothly, the society as a whole must see it as working to benefit the entire population.* Most of the population must also believe that their tasks and their income levels reflect their skills and their relative contributions to the society. The stratified system will then rest on a consensus in which even those at the lower end of the income stream understand that their low wages and the threat of unemployment are necessary motivators to keep them working. Not surprisingly, those who wholeheartedly believe in the system tend to be found at the upper end of the income stream. Those at the lower levels cannot both believe in the system *and* have a sense of self-esteem.

TRENDS IN INCOME AND WEALTH INEQUALITY

There is no established theory of income distribution to guide us to an optimal amount of inequality. Anyone interested in studying the social structure of the United States must begin by examining the disparities of income and wealth. **Income** is defined as the total monetary return to a household over a set period, usually a year, from all sources of wages, rent, interest, and gifts. Income refers to the flow of dollars within a year. Labor earnings (wages) constitute an ever-larger component of total income as one moves down the income ladder. Income tends not to be as unequally distributed as wealth. **Wealth** refers to the monetary value of the assets of a household minus its liabilities (or debt), which is its net worth. Wealth includes the accumulation of unspent past income and is a source from which capital income is realized.

INCOME

From 2000 through 2004, average income fell for middle-income wage earners, largely due to weak demand for labor caused by the recession of 2001 and its slow recovery. At the end of 2004 the economy had not recovered all the jobs lost since the last employment peak. In addition, greater numbers of people were underemployed, that is, working at part-time jobs because full-time jobs were not available. Declines in health and pension programs eroded the income of workers, especially those in the middle- and lower-income brackets. Over the same period, executive compensation soared. From 1992 to 2003 the median chief executive officer received an 80.8 percent raise, while the median worker's average hourly wage rose 8.7 percent.[35] The unbalanced nature of the tax cuts during the George W. Bush administration has redistributed after-tax income from the bottom 99 percent to the top 1 percent.[36]

In 2003 the real median household income was $43,318, which means that half the households received more and half less. The upper income limit of the lowest 20 percent of households declined 1.9 percent between 2002 and 2003, from $18,326 to $17,984 At the other end, it took $85,941 to get into the top 20 percent in household income in 2002, which rose to $86,867 in 2003. The median earnings of men who worked full-time, year-round in 2003 was $40,668, the same as in 2002. Real earnings of women declined to $30,724 (0.6 percent) in 2003, the first decline since 1995.

Another way to look at the growth in inequality is to look at the change in real income in each quintile. The average income of households in the top quintile grew 34 percent, from $97,376 in 1980 (in 2003 dollars) to $147,078 in 2003 (see Table 7.1). During the same twenty-three-year period, the average income in the bottom quintile grew by only 6 percent, from $9,479 to $9,996. The significant gains made during the Clinton administration were only a memory and were still fading in 2004.

This unequal distribution is portrayed in Table 7.2, which reports the Gini indexes of the shares of aggregate income by each quintile. The **Gini index** provides a measure of income concentration by ranking households from the lowest to the highest based on income divided into groups of equal population size (20 percent each, or quintiles). The aggregate income of each group

Table 7.1

Mean Household Income by Quintile, 1980–2003 (constant 2003 dollars)

	Bottom Quintile	Second Quintile	Third Quintile	Fourth Quintile	Top Quintile
1980	9,479	22,876	37,652	55,439	97,376
1985	9,472	23,336	38,701	58,201	104,357
1990	9,819	24,606	40,644	61,279	118,920
1995	10,009	24,449	40,881	62,844	131,146
2000	10,849	27,090	45,113	70,130	151,969
2003	9,996	25,678	43,558	68,994	147,078

Source: Carmen DeNavas-Walt, Bernadette, Proctor, and Robert J. Mills,"Income, Poverty, and Health Insurance Coverage in the United States: 2003," *Current Population Reports* (Washington, D.C.: U.S. Census Bureau, August 2004) pp.35–36.

Table 7.2

Share of Aggregate Income Received by Household Quintile, 1980–2003 (constant 2003 dollars)

	Bottom Quintile	Second Quintile	Third Quintile	Fourth Quintile	Top Quintile	Gini Index
1980	4.3	10.3	16.9	24.9	43.7	0.403
1985	4.0	9.7	16.3	24.6	45.3	0.419
1990	3.9	9.6	15.9	24.0	46.6	0.428
1995	3.7	9.1	15.2	23.3	48.7	0.450
2000	3.6	8.9	14.8	23.0	49.8	0.462
2003	3.4	8.7	14.8	23.4	49.8	0.464
Change, 1980–2003	−0.9	−1.6	−2.1	−1.5	+6.1	

Source: Carmen DeNavas-Walt, Bernadette, Proctor, and Robert J. Mills,"Income, Poverty, and Health Insurance Coverage in the United States: 2003," *Current Population Reports* (Washington, D.C.: U.S. Census Bureau, August 2004), pp.36–37.

is then divided by the overall aggregate income to determine shares. The Gini index ranges from 0, indicating a perfect equality where everyone has an equal share, to 1, indicating a perfect inequality where all the income is received by one recipient or group of recipients. The data reveal that each of the quintiles from the lowest through the fourth declined in its share of aggregate income from 1980 to 2003, with the lowest losing the most ground and each successive fifth declining by a smaller percentage. The bottom quintile saw its share of aggregate income decline by 21 percent, while the second quintile declined by 16 percent, the third by 13 percent, and the fourth by 7 percent. Only the top fifth steadily increased its share of aggregate income over this period (by 13 percent). The top 5 percent actually increased its share of aggregate income by 34 percent. Since census data do not include capital gains, the total-income figures for those at the top are actually significantly higher.

Wealth

An examination of wealth provides a more complete picture of family economic well-being than does an examination of income. The richest man in the world is Bill Gates, who in his late forties is worth an estimated $46 billion, which is equal to the combined net worth of the bottom 40 percent of U.S. households.[37] Power also flows from wealth. Fortunes can be a source of political and social influence that goes beyond having a high income. Large holdings of wealth can also be transferred to succeeding generations, which includes the transmission of power and influence associated with it. There is a correlation, although not a strong one, between wealth and age, since older individuals typically have worked more years and have accumulated more assets. There is also a correlation between income and wealth in that those with high income generally have more wealth.[38]

Through the first three-quarters of the twentieth century, distinctions based on class became progressively less important, and opportunities for upward mobility expanded. This stopped during the 1970s, and since about 1980 both poverty and wealth have been increasing together, indicating that the distance between the rich and poor is widening.

The most recent study completed by the Federal Reserve, using data from a triennial survey of consumer finances based on data compiled from 1989 through 2001, found that wealth is highly concentrated, with the top 1 percent of the wealthiest households owning one-third (32.7 percent) of all household net worth in 2001, up from 30.3 percent in 1989 (see Table 7.3). Note that those in the bottom half saw their share of ownership of assets remain flat, while those in top half, from the fiftieth through the ninety-fourth percentile, saw their share of ownership declined somewhat. Only the top 5 percent increased their share of the nation's assets and wealth in this period, with the largest gains going to those in the top 1 percent. As the table indicates, half the families in the country have less than 3 percent of the nation's wealth to divide between them. Those in the top 1 percent have more wealth to divide between them (32.7 percent) than does the bottom 90 percent of the people (2.8 percent 1 27.4 percent). And the top 5 percent have a larger share of the wealth (57.7 percent) than 94 percent of the population combined.

The top 1 percent significantly increased their share of holdings in stocks, bonds, and business investments, including equity in commercial real estate holdings. The wealthiest 1 percent owned approximately $2.3 trillion in stocks in 2001, roughly 53 percent of all individually held shares. They also owned 64 percent of bonds and about 31 percent of all financial assets held by families (which includes cash, stocks, bonds, and other securities). For the bottom 90 percent of the households, homes (their largest investment) and automobiles were the most important assets. Mortgages were by far their major liability. Money held in checking accounts and the cash value of life insurance policies were a significant form of savings for this group. It is noteworthy that, with the significant increase in the stock market over the past several years, the share of stock and mutual funds owned by the bottom 90 percent declined between 1989 and 2001.

The effects of the Bush tax cuts are not included in Table 7.3, which includes data only through 2001. The cuts include a reduction in the top tax rate and the elimination of estate, capital gains, and dividend taxes, all of which favor the wealthy and have made money available for the stock market. While the stock market has rebounded, average real wages have continued to stagnate. Home values, which are not a major factor in the holdings of the ultra-rich, although they are the largest share of wealth for middle-income families, have surged in recent years. Interest rates could rebound with a stronger economy, sending real estate prices downward, however. President Bush's tax cut programs have especially benefited those at the top of the wealth pyramid, which will increase the gap between the affluent and the poor.

THE LORENZ CURVE AND INCOME AND WEALTH INEQUALITY

A **Lorenz curve** can be used to measure the degree of inequality in a given population by plotting a cumulative percentage of income against a cumulative percentage of population (see Figure 7.1). If every household had the same income and wealth, the distribution would follow the 45 degree line of complete equality. Any variance from equality will result in the graph falling below the line of equality. The shaded area shows the amount of income inequality. The larger this area, the more unequal is the distribution of income. If there were no government policies to transfer income from the rich to the poor, income inequality would be even greater.

HOW DOES THE UNITED STATES COMPARE WITH OTHER OECD COUNTRIES?

The United States consistently ranks as one of the most unequal countries when compared to other developed countries. However, since each country develops unique policy approaches for underwriting various social welfare programs,

TABLE 7.3

Changes in Concentration of Wealth 1989–2001 (percentage share of total)

Item	All Families 2001 ($ billions)	0–50% 1989	0–50% 2001	50–89% 1989	50–89% 2001	90–94% 1989	90–94% 2001	95–99% 1989	95–99% 2001	99–100% 1989	99–100% 2001
Assets	482,053	5.5	5.6	32.4	29.9	12.6	11.7	22.3	23.4	27.2	29.5
Liquid	2,380.6	6.1	6.0	32.1	32.7	13.3	13.3	21.4	21.9	27.2	26.2
Private, residence	13,063.6	9.9	12.3	55.5	50.6	12.8	12.2	15.2	16.0	6.6	9.0
Other residential real estate	2,256.5	2.6	1.9	30.4	26.8	19.9	11.7	27.9	30.5	19.3	29.1
Nonresidential real esteate	2,289.3	0	0.6	11.6	14.5	9.6	9.1	25.9	35.2	55.1	40.7
Stocks	4,378.9	1.3	.5	15.8	11.4	10.2	9.9	31.3	25.3	41.5	52.9
Bonds	924.1	.3	.3	7.8	4.0	11.0	8.8	29.1	22.7	51.8	64.3
Savings bonds	139.8	6.7	41.	47.6	45.5	19.1	10.1	19.3	21.9	7.3	18.5
RetQLiquid	5,720.3	6.0	3.3	37.9	36.4	15.1	17.6	26.3	29.1	14.8	13.6
Nonmutual	2,477.8	0.9	0.9	15.3	20.5	16.2	17.9	33.6	32.6	34.1	28.1
Othre managed accounts	628.8	0.4	0.3	13.3	13.0	11.4	12.1	29.4	28.3	45.5	46.2
Other financial assets	412.4	5.6	4.1	18.3	17.1	14.9	5.3	32.9	33.1	28.4	40.4
Businesses	8,148.5	0.5	0.4	8.8	9.9	10.2	6.6	27.1	24.9	53.4	58.3
Automobiles	1,656.2	25.6	27.9	48.7	48.3	9.5	9.5	10.4	9.3	5.8	9.0
Liabilities	3,429.2	25.5	5.9	49.9	47.9	9.7	.6	9.5	11.6	5.4	5.9
Private residential debt	4,370.8	21.2	3.5	57.3	51.7	9.9	.1	8.7	11.1	2.9	4.7
Installment debt	714.0	41.2	8.0	43.5	37.5	5.5	.2	6.1	5.2	3.7	3.6
Credit card debt	195.7	42.8	9.8	49.0	41.6	5.0	.2	2.8	4.9	0.3	0.5
Equity	11,348.1	1.6	1.4	20.7	21.7	11.7	14.4	29.6	29.0	36.4	33.6
Income	7,400.8	24.4	22.9	40.7	38.1	8.9	9.2	12.3	15.3	13.7	14.5
Net worth	42,389.2	2.7	2.8	29.9	27.4	13.0	12.1	24.1	25.0	30.3	32.7

Source: Adapted from Arthur B. Kennickell *Rolling Tide Changes the Distribution of Wealth in the U.S. 1989–2001.* Working Paper no. 393 (Washington: D.C.: Board of Governors of the Federal Reserve, 2003), pp. 17, 21.

Notes: Net worth = asset – liabilities. Financial assets = liquid cash = certificates of deposit + savings bonds + bonds + stocks + non-money market mutual funds + IRAs, Keogh accounts and other person accounts where withdrawals or loans may be taken + cash value of life insurance + equity holdings of annuities, trusts, and managed investment accounts + value of miscellaneous nonfinancial assets (e.g., antiques, artworks, etc.) Total = income: total income for the year preceding the survey year RetQLiquid. = IRAs, Keogh accounts, and other pension accounts where withdrwals or loans may be taken.

cross-country comparisons must be treated with some caution. For example, in some countries, like the United States, the poor may receive monetary benefits for housing, while in another country subsidized housing may be provided. Many countries provide a mix of goods (e.g., health care for everyone), largely paid for by tax receipts. Any given cross-national comparison based on income alone may over- or understate inequality relative to consumption. In developing countries and especially for lower-income families, income inequalities are very close to consumption inequalities.[39] Table 7.4 uses the Gini coefficient, the standard statistic, to measure income inequality in nineteen Organization for Economic Cooperation and Development (OECD) nations identified by the World Bank as "high-income" nations.

The data indicate that someone in the top quintile in Denmark received an income 4.3 times that of someone in the bottom quintile.

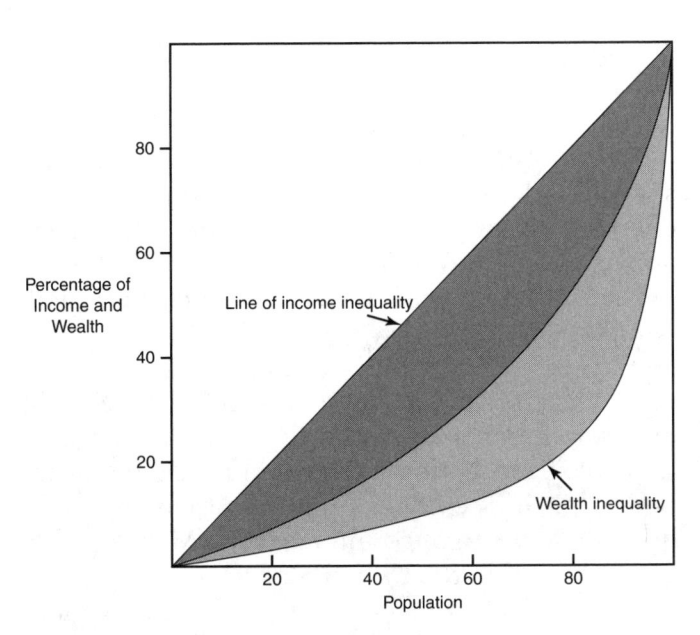

FIGURE 7.1 Lorenz Curve Showing Cumulative Percentage of Income and Wealth, 1995

If everyone had the same income and wealth the distribution would folow the 45 degree complete equality line. The darker shaded area shows the amount of income inequality. The lighter shaded area shows the inequality in the distribution of wealth. The larger the shaded area, the greater the inequality.

The average gap between the highest and lowest OECD quintiles is 4.8 to 1.0. By comparison in the United States the same income ratio was 8.4 to 1.0, or 40 percent greater. The proportional distance between the bottom and top quintiles is about twice as large in the United States as in Denmark, Japan, Sweden, Belgium, and Finland The household income ratio of the ninetieth percentile to the tenth percentile was 11.22 to 1.0.[40] In the United States, income inequality is much greater than in most OECD nations, and is more unequally distributed than in any other high-income OECD nation. The greater inequality cannot be said to have stimulated faster economic growth of GDP in the United States, which averaged 2 percent after inflation while the average growth rate of OECD countries was 2.4 percent.

The variation in the Gini index in each country is illustrative of the fact that the distribution of income is fundamentally the outcome of the political and economic choices made by decisionmakers. There has been a pattern of an increase in inequality throughout the OECD nations. However,

TABLE 7.4

Gini Index Comparison of High-Income OECD Nations, 2003.

	Average Annual Real Growth (% of GDP), 1990–2003	Gini Index	Percentage Share of Income or Consumption Lowest 20%	Highest 20%
Denmark	2.0	24.7	8.3	35.8
Japan	−0.5	24.9	10.6	35.7
Sweden	1.8	25.0	9.1	36.6
Belgium	1.8	25.0	8.3	37.3
Finland	2.0	26.9	9.6	40.2
Germany	1.6	28.3	8.5	36.9
Austria	1.7	30.0	8.1	38.5
Korea, Rep.	4.8	31.6	7.9	37.5
Spain	3.8	32.5	7.5	40.3
Netherlands	2.4	32.6	7.3	40.1
France	1.5	32.9	7.2	40.2
Canada	1.5	33.1	7.0	40.4
Switzerland	1.1	33.1	6.9	40.3
Australia	1.9	35.2	5.9	41.3
Greece	7.5	35.4	7.1	43.6
Italy	3.4	36.0	6.5	42.0
United Kingdom	2.8	36.0	6.1	44.0
New Zealand	1.6	36.2	6.4	43.8
United States	2.0	40.8	5.4	45.8

Source: World Bank, *World Development Report 2005* (New York: Oxford University Press, 2004), pp. 258–261.

the increase has been greatest those nations that emphasize a laissez-faire approach to capitalism, such as the United States and the United Kingdom.

Those OECD countries that have more corporate institutions, such as Belgium, Sweden, and Denmark, together with a greater tendency to intervene with social welfare programs, have experienced much smaller increases in inequality The resurgence of income inequality in U.S. society is abrupt enough to be called the "great U-turn" by Bennett Harrison and Barry Bluestone, who place the beginning of the increased inequality in the early 1970s.[41]

The most comprehensive analysis of income inequality has been developed by the Luxembourg Income Study project, which uses census survey data from OECD nations and finds that the most corporatist countries have a less unequal distribution of income. The study confirms that inequality generally declined throughout all the OECD countries until about 1974, after which inequality began to rise. Since that time "the living standards of the least well-off families tended to decline as overall inequality rose."[42] The study also finds evidence that the income shares of the middle classes have declined.

Child poverty is a particular concern of all governments, because children are not responsible for their life situation. It is also generally accepted that deprivation may limit cognitive and social development of children, limiting their life chances. As might be expected from the tables above, the highest child poverty rates are found in the United States, Turkey, Italy, and the United Kingdom, and the lowest are found in the Nordic countries and Belgium (see Table 7.5).

Children living in the richest U.S. households are by a large margin the most affluent of any industrialized country. Those children living in poor U.S. house-hold are poorer than the children of any other country except Mexico. The gap is greater in the United States largely because U.S. taxes and transfer programs are less generous than in other OECD countries. In the United States, taxes and transfers reduce the Gini coefficient by 23 percent (from 0.48 to 0.37).[43] If the United States redistributed as much income as do the other OECD countries, the dispersion of disposable incomes would be close to the middle range of the countries represented.

Through the beginning of the twenty-first century, actual market incomes in the United

TABLE 7.5

Variation in OECD Child Poverty Rates

	Child Poverty Rate	Single Parent, Working	Two Parents, One Worker	Two Parents, Both Working	Employment Rate (%)
Finland	2.1	3.0	3.5	1.5	67.7
Sweden	2.7	3.8	6.0	0.8	75.3
Denmark	3.4	10.0	3.6	0.4	75.9
Belgium	4.1	11.4	2.8	0.6	59.7
Norway	4.4	4.6	3.9	0.1	77.5
France	7.1	13.3	7.3	2.1	62.0
Netherlands	9.1	17.0	4.7	1.2	72.1
Germany	10.6	32.5	5.6	1.3	65.9
Australia	10.9	9.3	8.9	5.0	68.9
Greece	12.3	16.3	15.1	5.0	55.6
Canada	14.2	26.5	18.1	3.7	70.9
United Kingdom	18.6	26.3	19.3	3.3	71.3
Italy	18.8	24.9	12.2	6.1	54.9
Turkey	19.7	16.3	17.8	14.4	45.1
United States	23.2	38.6	30.5	7.3	73.1
OECD (15)	10.7	16.9	11.2	3.5	66.3

Source: Society at a Glance, OECD Social Indicators (Parts OECD, 2003), pp. 53, 31.
Note: Poverty is defined as the share of children living in households earning less than 50 percent of the median income.

CASE STUDY: GLOBAL INEQUALITIES

Not only are the gaps between rich and poor in the United States wider than in the past, but similar pressures that increase inequality are being felt world wide as well. United Nations (UN) surveys have concluded that the wealthiest and the poorest people—both within and among countries—are living in increasingly separate worlds. The UN's Human Development Report 2002 found that incomes are distributed more unequally across the world population (with a Gini's coefficient of 0.66) than in countries with the highest inequality (e.g., Brazil has a Gini coefficient of 0.61). The world population's richest 5 percent receive 114 times the income of the poorest 5 percent. The world's richest 1 percent receives as much as the poorest 57 percent. The wealthiest 25 million. Americans have as much income as almost 2 billion of the world's poorest combined.

The UN's *Human Development Report 1996* found that many of the most equitable societies are in Asia, where economic growth has been the fastest and division of national wealth has been the most equitable. Several economies in Asia, including. Japan Indonesia, Hong Kong, Malaysia, the Republic of Korea, and Singapore, have maintained rapid economic growth together with relatively low inequality. The report found that during the past three decades, "every country that was able to combine and sustain rapid growth did so by investing first in schools, skills and health while keeping the income gap from growing too wide."

A central theme of the UN's 2002 report is that, contrary to the conventional wisdom, income and wealth inequality are harmful to economic growth. "The new insight is that an equitable distribution of public and private resources can enhance the prospects for further growth."

The 2002 report also found that:

- The net worth of the world's richest 358 billionaires is equal to the combined annual incomes of the poorest 45 percent of the world's population (2.3 billion people).
- Eighty-nine countries are worse off economically than they were a decade ago. Seventy developing countries have lower incomes than they did twenty-five years ago. In nineteenth countries, per capita income is below the 1960 level.

Branko, Milanovic analyzed data on a global scale using household surveys and concluded that an important increase in inequality, from 1988 to 1993, was caused by slower growth of rural incomes in populous. Asian countries compared to OECD countries, as well as by rising urban-rural income differences in China and by falling incomes in transition countries. Xavier Sala-i-Martin produced a study based on aggregate income and estimates of within-country distributions of income between rich and poor, suggesting that income inequality was actually falling in the 1980s and 1990s.

Amartya Sen, a Nobel Prize-winning economist, replied to the debate regarding whether inequality is increasing or decreasing by noting.

> Even if the poor were to get just a little richer, this would not necessarily imply that the poor were getting a fair share of the potentially vast benefits of global economic interrelations. It is not adequate to ask whether international inequality is getting marginally larger or smaller. In the contemporary world—or to protest against the unfair sharing of benefits of global cooperation—it is not necessary to show that the massive inequality or distributional unfairness is also getting marginally larger. This is a separate issue altogether.

Sources: United Nations Development Programme. *Human Development Report 1996* (New York: Oxford University Press, 1996). United Nations Development Programme, *Human Development Report 2002* (New York: Oxford University Press, 2002), pp. 10. 19, 34; Branko Milanovic, "True World Income Distribution, 1988 and 1993, First Calculation Based on Household Surveys Alone." (New York: World Bank, 1999); Xavier Salai Martin. "The World Distribution Income" (estimated from individual country distributor) (New York: Columbia University Press, 2002); Amariya Sen, "How to Judge, Globalism," American Prospect, January, 2002.

States were very comparable to those in France or Germany. The reason for this anomaly is that although senior U.S. business executives receive much higher compensation than their counterparts elsewhere, other countries provide many more benefits for those who are unemployed. As a result of low government transfers to the unemployed in the United States, unemployment has more serious consequences than in most European nations. Since job loss is more disastrous in the United States, labor is more inclined to accept wage cuts than in Europe, where more generous public social expenditures make the prospect of losing a job altogether less severe. The compensation for employment for many Americans who work for low wages is not very large. Nonetheless, when the relatively high number of individuals with zero earnings are included in OECD national averages, the Gini coefficient for the United States is not too dissimilar from coefficients for other high-income countries. Since 1980, inequality has increased somewhat in all OECD countries. About half the countries have taken steps to prevent a significant increase in inequality. Actions taken in the United States and the United Kingdom have, as a whole, actually reduced the equalizing effects of taxes and transfers.[44]

What Is the Relationship Between Inequality and Economic Growth?

Simon Kuznets received the Nobel Prize in 1971 for research on economic growth and income distribution. He found that economic growth in poor countries increased the income gap between rich and poor people. However, once a threshold level of maturity was crossed in its transition from a rural to an industrial and urbanized society, economic growth would reduce income disparity. Thus Kuznets argued that income distribution follows a U-curve in which economic expansion makes poor people relatively poorer during the initial stage of a country's development. The concentration of workers in urban areas encourages both union and political organizations to press for worker rights, the regulation of business, progressive taxes, and public social expenditures, all of which reduce inequality. Kuznets presented historical data to show, for example, that income inequality in the United States peaked in the 1890s, and did not begin to decline until after World War I.[45] Later research by Robert Lampman on the distribution of wealth, as opposed to income, found a similar pattern of increasing inequality of wealth, with a decline in the gap occurring between the late 1920s and continuing through the next several decades.[46]

However, the United States is something of an anomaly since it is the richest OECD country and has the most inequality. But as Gary Burtless and Christopher Jencks point out, "If we eliminate the United States and look at the sixteen remaining big OECD countries, the richer ones have *less* inequality than the poorer ones, as the Kuznets model predicts."[47] Nevertheless, a model that would predict lower inequality in the United States, which is at variance with the facts, is inadequate.

Some investigators have found evidence of a cycle in which wealthy power elites wage a counteroffensive to reestablish their dominant control.[48] Noted economist John Galbraith suggests that there is struggle in which the elites, in defense of their social and economic advantage, must now persuade the majority of voters in a democracy that government must accommodate the needs of the haves.[49] The late Arthur Okun focused on ways in which economic inequality can affect growth. He noted that political institutions proclaim the equality of individuals and distribute rights and privileges universally.[50] Economic institutions inevitably create inequalities in material welfare. The political principles of democracy and the economic principles of capitalism create tensions. Whenever the market denies a worker a minimum standard of living or when the wealthy use their power and privilege to obtain more of the rights that are supposedly equally distributed, then "dollars transgress on rights," in Okun's expression.

Efforts to solve the problem involve a tradeoff in which greater equality has been achieved only at heavy costs in efficiency, while in other cases greater efficiency has been achieved only by severely restraining civil liberties. In Okun's view the U.S. system of mixed capitalism is a workable compromise in which the market has its place as long as democratic institutions are able to keep it within acceptable boundaries. He felt that the democratic concern for human dignity could be directed at reducing economic deprivation in the United States through progressive taxes and transfer payments, and removing certain barriers to capital.

Although there are many theories on the relationship between inequality and growth, the evidence regarding whether or not inequality reduces growth is inconclusive. There is some evidence that inequality can reduce growth by preventing the poor from providing an adequate health diet for their children, thereby limiting their potential. Many will have insufficient capital to invest in education or to launch a small business. If returns to these investments would have been high, their lack of availability will limit growth. Or the unequal economic status may breed strong social tensions that discourage productive capital investments.

How Does Economic Inequality Threaten Democratic Equality?

Aaron Bernstein wrote an article summarizing research indicating that social mobility has declined in recent decades.[51] Corporate strategies to control labor costs, such as hiring temporary employees, fighting unions, dismantling internal career ladders, reducing benefits, and outsourcing, are successful in restraining consumer prices. Unfortunately, these tactics trap about 34 million workers, over a quarter of the labor force, in low-wage and usually dead-end jobs. Many middle-income employees face fewer opportunities as work is shifted to temporary agencies and outsourced jobs overseas. The result, according to Bernstein, has been an erosion of one of the most cherished values in the United States: the ability to move up the economic ladder over one's lifetime.

The myth of income mobility has always exceeded the reality. But it is true that there has been considerable intergenerational mobility. One study cited by Bernstein shows, for example, that 23 percent of men from families in the bottom 25 percent of the economic ladder make it into the top 25 percent by the end of their working careers. Bernstein cites a new survey that finds that this number has dropped to only 10 percent. Fewer children of lower-class families are making it to even moderate affluence.

A study by the Federal Reserve Bank of Boston analyzed families' incomes over three decades and found that the number of people who stayed in the same income bracket—whether the bottom or the top—jumped to 53 percent in the 1990s, up from 36 percent in the 1970s. The income bracket persisted even after accounting for the major growth of two-earner families. For mobility to increase in relative terms, someone has to move down the pecking order to make room for another to move up. The new reality has a greater impact on those at the bottom, who tend to stay poor because of the creation of millions of jobs that pay rates at around the poverty-line wage of $8.70 an hour. A college degree remains out of reach for most students from low-income families. The number of poor students who get a degree—about 5 percent—has been stable for almost thirty years.

Business strategy is putting a lid on the intergenerational progress that has been a part of the American Dream, but public policy also plays a role, Paul Krugman speculates about what policies someone who controlled government and wanted to entrench the advantages of the haves over the have-nots might engage in.[52] One policy initiative would definitely be to get rid of the estate tax, to allow fortunes to be passed on to the next generation untouched. Other policies would include a reduction in tax rates on corporate profits and on unearned income such as dividends and capital gains. Tax rates would be reduced on people with high incomes, shifting the burden to the payroll tax and other revenue sources that bear most heavily on people with lower incomes. On the spending side, he suggests that one should cut back on health care for the poor and on federal aid for higher education, which would result in rising tuitions and make it more difficult for people with low incomes to acquire the education essential to upward mobility.

Current policies of closing off routes to upward mobility lead Thomas Piketty and Emmanuel Saez to conclude that current policies will eventually create "a class of rentiers in the U.S., whereby a small group of wealthy but untalented children controls vast segments of the U.S. economy and penniless, talented children simply can't compete."[53]

Economic Inequality and Life Expectancy

The United States is the wealthiest major country in the world in terms of per capita GDP (and second only to Luxembourg overall). Since longevity is associated with income, we might hypothesize that Americans would have a longer life expectancy than those living in other large industrialized and relatively wealthy OECD states. However, we find that life expectancy in the United States, at age sixty-five for both males and females, is just about in the middle of the thirty OECD countries. Throughout the twentieth century until about 1980, the United States was the leader in increases in life expectancy due to improvements in public health and medicine. Since then, life expectancy has increased more rapidly for citizens of all other industrial nations.

A higher GDP per capita would suggest that the United States has more resources that it can dedicate to education, medical care, and other services associated with longevity. However, while the average GDP per capita is high, those in the top quintiles receive a much larger share compared to other OECD nations. At the lower levels of the income distribution, U.S. incomes now fall in the middle of the OECD countries. Median family income growth has slowed dramatically since 1980, at the very time inequality in the distribution of income began to surge in the United States.

Richard Wilkinson's original research, focused on the relationship between overall levels of inequality (rather than individual income levels) and mortality across OECD countries, has inspired much of the subsequent research on the subject.[54] In a series of papers, Wilkinson found negative associations between inequality and mortality that persisted even after he controlled for cross-country differences in median income.[55] Several scholars have focused on the United States and have documented similar findings between mortality rates and inequality across states and metropolitan areas within the United States after controlling for income levels.[56] Metropolitan areas with low per capita incomes and low levels of income inequality have lower mortality rates than metropolitan areas with high median incomes and high levels of income inequality. Although many studies now show that inequality and health are linked in OECD countries, the reasons for the association are still debated in the United States, the United Kingdom, and Brazil.

Wilkinson and his colleagues suggest several reasons for the association. They suggest that the larger the income gap between the rich and the poor, the more reluctant the affluent are to pay taxes for public services they will likely never use or for which their payment in taxes will significantly exceed the benefit they expect to receive. A reduction in public expenditures on public health, hospitals, schools, or other basic services will be negligible on the life expectancies of the wealthy, but it will significantly impact poor people's life expectancies. Second, an income gap is inversely related to social cohesion (i.e., the larger the income inequality, the lower the social cohesion in society). Greater socioeconomic equality is associated with higher levels of social involvement. Social isolation, which increases with inequality, is a documented health risk factor.[57]

Various researchers have challenged Wilkinson's conclusions and insist that it is not clear that inequality is due to the rich getting richer rather than the poor getting poorer. They maintain that while it is demonstrable that the rich are getting richer, the poor, it is alleged, are not getting poorer in absolute terms, but only in "relative" terms. They concede that in theory the rich may be less inclined to support taxes for items that will not benefit themselves, or that the poor will find their concerns being crowded out by the demands of the affluent. But benefits may also result from positive externalities created by the wealthy, who may demand the development of more advanced medical technology or crime prevention.

Michael Marmot has written extensively on the study of social inequality and health and finds that diseases that are commonly thought of as diseases of affluence—like heart disease, associated with high-calorie and high-fat diets and lack of physical activity—are actually most prevalent among the least-affluent people in rich societies.[58] He claims that social inequality frequently shadows the more immediate cause of death, whether it is listed as heart disease, diabetes, accidental injury, or homicide. The lower one is in the socioeconomic hierarchy, the worse one's health and the shorter one's life is likely to be. Most of the top causes of death are not "equal opportunity killers." They tend to strike poor people at an earlier age than they do rich people, the less educated more than they do the highly educated, people of color more than they do white people—generally, those people lower rather than higher on the income ladder. A poor person with a health problem is about half as likely to see a physician as a high-income individual. Adults living in low-income areas are more than twice as likely to be hospitalized for a health problem that could have been treated with timely outpatient care, compared to adults living in high-income areas.[59]

Marmot's best-known research is a study of health among British civil servants. Since civil servants share similar office work environments and job security, he expected to find only very minor health differences among them. However, he found an unexpected significant increase in mortality with each step down the job hierarchy—including from the highest to the second highest grade. Over a decade, employees in the lowest grade were three times as likely to die as those in the highest grade. Those in the lower grades had a higher incidence of risk factors such as smoking, unhealthy diet, and lack of exercise. But even after controlling for these "lifestyle" risk factors, over half the mortality gap remained. Those at lower levels were less likely to express satisfaction with their work situation and were more likely to indicate they felt they had less "control over their working lives," while those at a higher level were likely to complain of working at a fast pace. Marmot concluded that psychosocial factors—the psychological costs of being lower in the hierarchy—played a significant role in the mortality gap.[60]

Research has definitely found a relation between economic inequality and life expectancy. Cross-country research clearly suggests that economic inequality may reduce life expectancy for lower-income workers. The reduction in life expectancy is difficult to calculate and projections are very tentative. Burtless and Jencks estimate that inequality reduces life expectancy for low-income individuals by about five months.[61] In this debate, poverty and inequality are closely related. Whether public policy focuses primarily on the elimination of poverty or on reduction of income inequality, neither goal is likely to be achieved without the other.

Economic Inequality and Justice

When Thomas Jefferson wrote that it was self-evident and that all men are created equal and are endowed by their creator with certain inalienable rights, and that government's purpose was to promote the "general" welfare, he was expressing principles of justice that are the essence of U.S. democracy. Politics would be the method by which average citizens would work out common problems through the instrument of government, whose function would be to promote the safety and happiness of the people. The American Revolution ushered in a democracy that gave hope to the exploited and downtrodden as the enemy of unchecked privilege.

This was not an empty idea, and Americans have made great strides toward equality in several areas. For example, Americans embrace the notions of equality before the law: one person, one vote; and equality of opportunity. As the income gap has increased, however, awareness that economic inequalities may undermine all the various forms of equality has increased.

The political system of democracy has a bias in favor of equality. The principle of individual freedom finds its expression for many in capitalism, which leads to vast economic inequalities and threatens to bring about an aristocracy of wealth. Power flows from wealth. And those who control vast amounts of money may translate their economic power to political power to increase their dominance.

As the functional theory of inequality suggests, inequality can perform a positive function in society by motivating individuals to produce more under the hope of financial reward. On the other hand, the functional theory must be qualified, since it assumes perfect market conditions and does not take into account the differences in inheritances, power, or economic rent seeking that occur in imperfect markets. That is, much of the inequality is not based on merit in that many members of society have no control over the conditions of the competition. Nor is it clear that the rewards for "winning" and the penalties for "losing" are fair. The conclusion is that we do not want perfect equality, or a society that is so equal as to be unjust. We are left to search for an optimal amount of inequality.

Many who argue in favor of a progressive income tax, an inheritance tax, or social welfare programs seldom emphasize Keynesian arguments based on economic theory.[62] They usually support increasing taxes on capital gains or other sources of income, because they believe the current level of income and wealth inequality is unfair. Although sound economic principles may be called on to support a national health insurance program, a higher minimum wage, or more college tuition assistance for low-income families, usually moral arguments are stressed. People should not be denied medical care or the ability to go to college because their parents cannot afford it. Such moral arguments are often supplemented by practical arguments that point out that investments in college subsidies for low-income individuals will allow them to become more productive and pay more in taxes. Raising the minimum wage helps keep families together and reduces welfare dependency. But these arguments often appear to be secondary. Egalitarians would probably favor national health care and a higher minimum wage even if it had no effect on longevity or did not reduce welfare dependency.

Those opposed to the proposals for less inequality do not defend large disparities in income as positive. Their economic arguments tend to be limited to concerns, expressed by Arthur Okun, that the transfer of resources from one group to another has inherent inefficiencies that exact a tradeoff between equity and efficiency. Their main contention tends to be that the market is fairer at distributing income than is the government. Empirical evidence that redistribution has fewer costs than they assumed is rarely persuasive. Like their egalitarian rivals, they argue from a moral perspective that emphasizes their belief that government interference unfairly punishes those who have been more successful in competing for money while it rewards dependent behavior.

Philosophers have debated the issue of justice and the distribution of income throughout history. John Rawl's answer to the problem of determining a fair distribution of goods states the egalitarian position well. He contends that the fairest distribution of goods is one that individuals would freely choose, or agree to, if they had no knowledge of their own ultimate position in society.[63] If individuals were behind a "veil of ignorance" and did not know their race, sex, social class, innate talents, and psychological propensities, they would only agree to those inequalities that benefited everyone, but especially the least advantaged. Such inequalities would be those required to call forth sufficient talent and effort in the production of social goods that would improve the lot of the least advantaged as much as the most advantaged. Rawls's attention to the least advantaged originates from a desire to protect against the worst outcome that we can imagine for ourselves. Since it is possible that we could find ourselves at the bottom of society, we would want to ensure that it is not a terrible place to be. His assumption is that most are risk-adverse and would want to avoid a very bad outcome even if that meant doing with less should we be fortunate to end up near the top.

Robert Nozick makes the opposite case, pointing out that most people may not be as risk-adverse as Rawls assumes.[64] Also, the process of redistributing income from the more to the less advantaged requires interfering with the basic liberties of those who happen to begin (whether for reasons of history, individual effort, or inheritance) with certain advantages. As long as the *process* is fair, everyone should be permitted to keep whatever they have.

John Kennedy lamented the practical problem for public policy when he said, "If a free society cannot help the many who are poor, it cannot save the few who are rich."[65] Distributive justice is basically an ethical problem. The National Conference of Catholic Bishops issued a statement that noted, "The moral measure of any economy is not simply the information shared, the wealth created, the trade encouraged, but how the lives and dignity of the poor and vulnerable, the hungry and destitute are protected and promoted."[66]

Policies to Reduce Poverty and Inequality

The fact that an economy is efficient says nothing about the distribution of income. Competitive markets may give rise to a very unequal distribution, which may leave some individuals with insufficient resources on which to live. One of the more important activities of democratic government is to reduce poverty and redistribute income. This is the express purpose of policies such as the Earned Income Tax Credit, Medicaid, and Social Security.

Conclusion

The American Revolution ushered in a new age of democracy. The democratic ideal, based on the fundamental principle of equality, sweeps aside all claims of special power and privilege. Democracy as a form of government is an ideal to be pursued rather than a goal fully achieved merely through recognition of the rights to free speech or the right to vote. The framers of the Constitution dedicated themselves to the proposition that all men are created equal, even though some were slaves and others without property were denied the right to vote. The United States became more democratic when it abolished ownership of property as a requirement to be a voting member of society. U.S. democracy advanced further when the Civil War abolished slavery, and when civil rights legislation a century later gave substance to the ideal of political equality.

Democracy, as the Constitution attests, is based on compromise between society's elites and nonelites. The elites, not surprisingly, resist with every means at their disposal any movement toward greater equality that challenges their interests. Control over the political institutions is always central to the struggle, since the elites can use the political institutions to influence the perceptions, values, and political preferences of the nonelites by their dominant position as opinion-makers in mass communication. Through money and organization, the elites more than make up for their small numbers, while the poor, lacking both resources and organization, are not as powerful a political group as their numbers might suggest.

In a capitalist society, power flows from money. The financially powerful naturally seek ways to leverage their wealth and status into political power. Through the late nineteenth and early twentieth century, theories of laissez-faire capitalism were put forward as justification for preventing the federal government from "interfering" in the economy, despite the fact that monopolistic and oligopolistic market power was clearly being used to increase the political power of those who ran the giant corporations. Government should not interfere in business, corporate leaders said, because government was not competent, and the interference was undemocratic in that it limited the freedoms of those who were creating the nation's wealth. The gap in income and wealth distribution grew in the 1920s.

The Great Depression encouraged a rethinking of economic theory. Keynesian theory showed that excessive economic inequality could not only hinder economic growth and stability, but also threaten the very survival of democratic systems. because the overwhelming majority of Americans also depend on employment for their economic security, Franklin Roosevelt embarked on a series of policies, such as adoption of a minimum wage, pro—labor union legislation, unemployment compensation, and Social Security, that worked to reduce economic inequality. Since about 1980, inequality in both income and wealth distribution has increased markedly. The increase, which has been greater in the United States than in other OECD countries, is due to a variety of factors, including globalization, oligopolistic power, and changes in tax and social welfare legislation designed to redistribute income toward those already at the top.

The functional theory of inequality holds that economic inequality has a beneficial effect in a capitalist society. The theory has several drawbacks, however, that justify government involvement to redress the power imbalance of dominant economic groups. Economic theory makes no claim that capitalism distributes income and wealth in a just fashion.

To the extent that the political apparatus becomes dependent on a financial elite, democracy is undermined. In the extreme case, the old hereditary aristocracy is merely traded for a financial aristocracy. An economic elite with inordinate political power moves the democratic ideal of meaningful political equality further from our grasp.

Let us be clear that some inequality is not only inevitable but also even necessary. However, a healthier democracy would result from less inequality than now exists. Policies that would reduce inequality would include raising the minimum wage, strengthening antipoverty programs such as the Earned Income Tax Credit, strengthening the social safety net to include health care, and increasing rather than decreasing progressiveness in the tax code. Some of these policies will be addressed more fully in the next chapter.

Personal Responsibility and Work Opportunity Reconciliation Act of 1996 Summary Of Provisions

National Association of Social Workers

Overview

The Personal Responsibility and Work Opportunity Reconciliation Act (PRWORA) replaces the Aid to Families with Dependent Children (AFDC) program with the Temporary Assistance for Needy Families (TANF) block grant and makes deep funding cuts in basic programs for low-income children, families, the elderly, people with disabilities, and immigrants. According to the Congressional Budget Office (CBO), the law cuts funding for low-income programs by approximately $55 billion over the next six years. Nearly all of the savings come from reductions in the Food Stamp program, the Supplemental Security Income (SSI) program for the elderly and disabled poor, and assistance to legal immigrants.

A summary of provisions follows.

TANF

- *Block Grant/Entitlement*. Replaces AFDC, emergency assistance, and the JOBS (Job Opportunities and Basic Skills) program with the Temporary Assistance for Needy Families (TANF) Block Grant.

    Funding: $16.4 billion each year from FY 1997–2002. States will receive the greatest of: (1) the average of their federal payment from FY 1992–1994; their federal payment in FY 1994; or (3) their federal payment in FY 1995. Effective date: July 1, 1997, but states may implement earlier. The entitlement ends September 30, 1996; the new funding system begins October 1, 1996.

    The block grant provides essentially fixed federal funding, which CBO estimates will fall $1.2 billion short of expenditures under previous law over the next six years.

    Under the block grant, there is no assurance that children or their parents will receive cash assistance even if they are poor and meet all state eligibility requirements. States have broad discretion to maintain, broaden or substantially curtail eligibility for income assistance for any poor family or category of poor families. For example, states can deny aid to families with teen parents or to two-parent families. In addition, if a state runs out of block grant funds for the year, they can place new applicants on a waiting list.

- *Contingency Fund*. Creates a contingency fund of $2 billion over five years for states which experience recessions.

    During the last, relatively mild recession between 1990 and 1992, federal AFDC funding increased $6 billion over just three years–triple the amount of the contingency fund for five years. In order to qualify for contingency funds, state Food Stamp caseloads must increase by at least 10 percent over their 1994 or 1995 level or their state unemployment rate must reach at least 6.5 percent and be at least one-tenth higher than the rate in the same months of either of the two prior years. In past recessions, many states experienced substantial increases in unemployment without reaching the 6.5 percent unemployment rate or experiencing a 10 percent increase in their Food Stamp caseloads.

- *Population Fund*. Creates a population adjustment fund of $800 million over four years, an amount equal to an increase in block grant funds of just one percent.

    National population is projected to grow at a rate of 4.6 percent–more than four times

---

"Personal Responsibility and Work Opportunity Reconciliation Act of 1996 (Public Law 104-193): Summary of Provisions, August 1996," from the National Association of Social Workers website, http://www.socialworkers.org/advocacy/welfare/legislation/summary.pdf. Copyrighted material reprinted with permission from the National Association of Social Workers, Inc.

greater than the funding allocated for population growth.
- *Program Administration*. Requires states to operate a welfare program in all political subdivisions, but the programs need not be uniform across the state. States have the option to contract with private charities, religious organizations, or other private entities to administer and provide services.
- *State Plan*. Requires states to make summaries of the state plan available to the public and the plan itself must include assurances that local governments and private sector organizations have been consulted so that services are "provided in a manner appropriate to local populations," and that those entities have had at least 45 days to submit comments on the plan.
- *Time Limits*. Institutes a five year lifetime time limit on cash assistance; and requires recipients to work after two years. In addition, unless states opt out, they must require parents receiving assistance to participate in community service after just two months. States may set shorter time limits and exempt 20 percent of their caseload from the five year limit.

  CBO estimates that between 2.5 million and 3.5 million children could be affected by the law's five year time limit when it is fully implemented, even after the 20 percent hardship exemption is taken into account. If states adopt shorter time limits, as some already have done, the number of affected children will be substantially greater. The U.S. Department of Health and Human Services (HHS) estimates that if all states were to adopt a two year time limit, 5.5 million children would be denied aid by 2006.

  Prohibits use of TANF block grant funds to provide vouchers for goods and services to children whose parents reach the time limit, but permits use of Social Services Block Grant (Title XX) funds for vouchers. Cuts Title XX funding by 15 percent.
- *State Maintenance of Effort*. Requires states to maintain funding at 75 percent of FY 1994 state expenditures for AFDC, Emergency Assistance, the JOBS Program, AFDC Child Care and At-Risk Child Care. Requires an 80 percent maintenance of effort for states who fail to meet work participation requirements and 100 percent to be eligible for contingency funds.

  If every state were to spend only what is required to receive its full block grant allocation, state funding over the next six years would fall nearly $32 billion below the level CBO projects states would have spent under the previous law. This would represent a 33 percent reduction in state resources devoted to these programs.
- *Funding Transfers*. Permits states to transfer up to 30 percent of TANF block grant funds into the reconstituted Child Care and Development Block Grant (CCDBG) or Social Services Block Grant (Title XX). No more than 10 percent can be transferred into Title XX.

  Services funded under Title XX include an array of politically popular services, many of which go to the elderly and to families with incomes well above the poverty line. Therefore, transfer of funds is likely in a number of states. Such a transfer would almost inevitably lead to fewer work slots being provided for very poor families, cuts in cash benefit levels for these families, still-shorter time limits, or some combination of such steps.

  Funds transferred from the TANF block grant to Title XX may be used only for services to children whose family incomes fall below 200 percent of the poverty line, but this provision is cosmetic. States can simply shift a portion of their existing Title XX funds from poor children to other populations at the same time they transfer funds from the TANF block grant and not violate the statute.
- *Work Requirements*. Requires states to have 50 percent of single-parents receiving cash assistance in work programs by FY 2002. The rate for two-parent families reaches 90 percent by 1999. Single-parent recipients will be required to work at least 30 hours per week by 2000 (20 hours per week for single parents with a child under age six). Two-parent families must work 35 hours per week.

  CBO estimates that funding falls $12 billion short of what will be needed over the next six years to meet the work requirements. In order to avoid some of the costs of meeting the requirements, states can reduce the number of people required to work simply by reducing the number of families eligible for assistance. States also may decide to accept the penalty for noncompliance: five percent reduction in TANF funding for first year, increasing by two percentage points a year, with a cap of 21 percent.

- *Work Activities*. Narrows the definition of work. Countable activities are limited to: unsubsidized or subsidized employment; on-the-job training; work experience; community service; 12 months of vocational training; or providing child care services to individuals participating in community service. Up to six weeks of job search (no more than four consecutive weeks) also count, as do teens attending secondary school. However, only 20 percent of those counting toward the work requirement can be participating in vocational training or be teens attending school.

    By narrowing the activities that count toward satisfying work participation rates, the law reduces state flexibility to permit or require parents to participate in education or training programs. In FY 1994, over half of the participants in the JOBS program were involved in some form of education or training activity–from remedial education to higher education.

    Since the overall single-parent work participation rate for states in FY 1997 is 25 percent and states cannot count more than 20 percent of adults participating in vocational training (including teens in school), the effective countable rate of adults in vocational training for FY 1997 is only five percent.
- *Individual Development Accounts*. Permits states to establish Individual Development Accounts (IDA) for recipients. IDA funds may be used for postsecondary education, purchase of a first home, or start-up of a business. Recipients may contribute "earned income" only, which may be matched by a not-for-profit organization or a state or local government.
- *Family Cap*. Permits, but does not require, states to impose a family cap–to deny cash benefits to children born into families already receiving assistance.
- *Teen Parents*. Requires unmarried parents under age 18 to live with an adult and stay in school in order to receive benefits.

    States are responsible for locating or assisting in locating an adult-supervised setting for teens, but there is no additional funding for establishing "second chance homes."
- *Teen Pregnancy*. Requires HHS to implement a strategy to prevent non-marital teen pregnancy and assure that at least 25 percent of communities have teen pregnancy prevention programs. Also requires the Justice Department to implement a program that provides research, education and training on the prevention and prosecution of statutory rape.
- *Out-of-Wedlock Births*. Establishes a bonus program for up to five states who demonstrate that the number of out-of-wedlock births that occurred in the state in the most recent two-year period decreased compared to the number of such births in the previous period without an increase in abortions. <u>Funding</u>: Approximately $1 billion in each year (1999–2002).
- *Domestic Violence*. Permits states to develop procedures to screen and identify recipients with a history of domestic violence, refer them to counseling and other support services, and waive program requirements, such as time limits, residency, family cap, and child support cooperation.
- *Drug Convictions*. Prohibits parents who have been convicted of felony drug offenses from receiving benefits under the TANF block grant or Food Stamp program for life. Pregnant women and individuals participating satisfactorily in drug treatment programs are exempted. States must pass a law if they wish to opt out of this requirement.
- *Research/Evaluations*. Requires HHS to conduct research on the benefits, effects, and costs of operating different state programs, including tracking child poverty rates. Beginning 90 days after enactment and yearly thereafter states must submit information on child poverty rates, and if the rate increases by five percent or more, must submit a plan for corrective action. <u>Funding</u>: $15 million for each year (1997–2002).

WAIVERS

- *Granted Prior to Enactment*. States which had waivers granted before August 22, 1996 have the option of continuing to operate their cash assistance programs under some or all of their waivers. However, states will still receive funding in a block grant. If the state opts to continue the waivers, provisions of the law which are "inconsistent with the waiver(s)" will not take effect until the waivers expire.
- *Submitted Prior to Enactment and Granted Prior to Implementation*. States which had waivers pending as of August 22, 1996 and that are approved prior to July 1, 1997, still

must comply with the law's work participation requirements, even if they are inconsistent with the waivers granted.
- *Submitted Following Implementation*. After July 1, 1997, the effective authority to grant waivers will be substantially curtailed.

The section on waivers is likely to require further guidance by HHS.

CHILD CARE

- *Block Grant/Entitlement*. Replaces the AFDC, Transitional, and At-Risk Child Care programs with a new fixed-sum block grant, which is combined with the existing Child Care and Development Block Grant (CCDBG). The reconstituted CCDBG consists of two funding streams: (1) $15 billion over seven years in a capped state entitlement (money guaranteed to the states), which requires a state match; and (2) $7 billion over seven years in discretionary funding for which Congress must appropriate specific amounts each year. Effective date: October 1, 1996.

  Eliminates entitlement to child care for parents receiving cash assistance and for those making the transition from welfare to work. Since these open-ended funding streams are capped under the new law, states have a limited amount of child care dollars. Due to the law's greatly expanded work requirements and the subsequent increased need for child care, CBO estimates that child care funding will fall $1.8 billion short of what is needed, even if Congress appropriates the full discretionary amount authorized.

- *Exemptions*. Prohibits states from sanctioning parents who cannot find child care for a child younger than age six, but requires states to count such parents in calculating work participation rates. States may exempt parents with children under age one from the work requirements and may exclude them in calculating participation.

  Parents who cannot participate in work or training because of a lack of child care may still reach a time limit and be cut off. Such a parent could be cut off without having had access to work preparation assistance.

  Parents with children under the age of one may use this exemption only once; they cannot use it again for subsequent children.

These parents also are still subject to the five year time limit for cash assistance.
- *Market Rates*. Eliminates previous language which required states to pay market rate for child care. States must assure that payment rates will be adequate to provide eligible children with equal access to child care as compared to those children not eligible for subsidies.
- *Administration*. Limits administrative costs to five percent, but defines a range of services as non-administrative, which means they are not counted in the limitation. They include: eligibility determination; participation in judicial hearings; recruitment; licensing; inspection; reviews and supervision of child care placements; rate setting; resource and referral services; training; and the establishment and maintenance of computerized child care information.
- *Quality Set-Aside*. Sets aside a minimum of four percent of total funding for improving quality, expanding supply and providing consumer education.

  This replaces a 25 percent set-aside in the original CCDBG which included approximately 19 percent for early childhood development and before and after school care, five percent for quality activities, and one percent for either.
- *Health and Safety*. Maintains existing state health and safety standards for child care providers in the areas of prevention and control of infectious diseases (including immunizations), building and physical premises, and minimum health and safety training.

CHILD WELFARE

- *Program Integrity*. Maintains current law and funding for all child welfare programs, including Title IV-B and IV-E training programs, by rejecting proposals to block grant any child welfare or protection programs.
- *For-Profit Providers*. Allows states to make Title IV-E foster care maintenance payments to for-profit as well as non-profit private child care institutions. Under current law, IV-E foster care payments only can be made to non-profit private or public child care institutions.
- *Kinship Care*. Requires states to consider giving preference to an adult relative over a non-related caregiver when determining a foster care placement for a child, provided

that the relative caregiver meets all relevant state child protection standards.
- *Research.* Establishes and funds at $6 million per year (1996–2002) a national random sample study of children who have been abused and neglected or are at risk of abuse or neglect. The study is to be longitudinal and assess the nature of the abuse or neglect, the involvement of the child and family with the public child protection agency, and the experiences with out-of-home care, including the duration of placements.

MEDICAID

- *Entitlement.* Maintains entitlement to Medicaid for currently-eligible AFDC recipients (as of July 1996) and those making the transition from welfare to work (for up to one year).
- *Sanctions.* Allows states to deny Medicaid to adults who lose cash assistance for failure to comply with work requirements. Children and pregnant women are exempt from this provision.
- *Relationship to SSI.* Fails to preserve Medicaid coverage for children losing SSI because of new rules (see below).

CBO estimates that 15 percent of those children who lose or are denied access to SSI also will lose eligibility for Medicaid.

SUPPLEMENTAL SECURITY INCOME (SSI)

- *Individual Functional Assessment.* Tightens eligibility, in part, by eliminating the Individual Functional Assessment (IFA) for children. Children only can qualify through the more restrictive medical listings. <u>Effective date</u>: day of enactment for new claims; July 1, 1997 for current recipients.

    In some instances, the same disability that qualifies an adult for SSI will not be sufficient to qualify a child. Among the children most likely to lose benefits are those suffering from multiple impairments, none of which is severe enough to meet the more stringent disability criteria established by the law, but the combined effect of which is substantial.

    The Social Security Administration (SSA) estimates that the following percentage of children, based on diagnosis, will lose access to SSI through elimination of the IFA: 49 percent of children with mood disorders; 38 percent with pulmonary tuberculosis; 33 percent with mental retardation; 29 percent with burns; 25 percent with intercranial injuries; 22 percent with schizophrenia; and 22 percent with arthritis.

- *Maladaptive Behavior.* Removes references in the medical listing to "maladaptive behavior" in evaluating personal/behavioral functioning for children with mental impairments.

    CBO estimates that over the next six years 48,000 children will lose access to benefits as a result of this change.

- *Disability Reviews.* Mandates continuing disability reviews every three years for all children except those whose conditions are not expected to improve. The child's representative payee will have to show evidence at the time of the review that the child is receiving treatment to the extent medically necessary and available for the qualifying condition.
- *Funding.* Reduces total benefits by more than $7 billion over the next six years.

    CBO estimates that by 2002, 315,000 low-income children who would have qualified under previous law will be denied SSI—or 22 percent of previously eligible children.

- *Research.* Requires a study by the General Accounting Office (GAO) on the impact of the new children's SSI provisions and the extra expenses incurred by families of receiving benefits that are not covered by other federal, state or local programs.

FOOD STAMPS

- *Block Grant.* Removes state option to block grant Food Stamps.
- *Funding.* Cuts funding by $28 billion over six years, including reductions in Food Stamp benefits for legal immigrants (see below).
Half of the law's spending reductions come from the Food Stamp program. When fully implemented, the law will slice benefits almost 20 percent, the equivalent of reducing the average Food Stamp benefit from its current level of 80 cents per person per meal to 66 cents per person per meal.

    Two-thirds of the benefit reductions will be borne by families with children. In 1998, nearly seven million families with children will lose an average of $435 in Food Stamp benefits. Working poor families—2.3 million–will lose an average of $355; and the poorest of the poor—those with incomes below half of the poverty line (below $6,250 for a family of three) will absorb 50 percent of the Food Stamp cuts in the law. In 1998, they will lose an average of $655 per year in benefits. In addition, 1.75 million low-income elderly households will lose about 20 percent of their Food Stamp benefits.

- *Single Adults*. Limits receipt of Food Stamp benefits to three months every three years to able-bodied single adults aged 18–50 who are unemployed. After three months, these individuals can continue receiving Food Stamps only if they are working at least half-time or are in a workfare training slot.

  The law provides no new money for workfare training lots, which are quite scarce in the Food Stamp program.

  CBO estimates that in a average month, one million jobless individuals who are willing to work and would take a work slot if one was available will be denied Food Stamps under this provision. Data from the U.S. Department of Agriculture (USDA) show that more than 40 percent of those who will be affected by this provision are women. Nearly one-third are over the age of 40, when individuals with limited skills often have great difficulty in finding jobs quickly.

  This provision can be suspended upon request of a state if the local unemployment rate surpasses 10 percent (a level few areas reach even during recessions) or with USDA approval for individuals who reside in an area that "does not have a sufficient number of jobs to provide employment for such individuals." It is not yet clear how such a determination will be made.

- *Outreach*. Eliminates federal matching funds for outreach.
- *Cash Out*. Allows states to "cash out" benefits to use as wage supplements.
- *Waivers*. Eliminates prior restriction forbidding USDA from granting waivers that would result in a reduction in Food Stamp benefits for any group of households. New waiver authority sweeps away that restriction and allows states to make major changes in their Food Stamp benefit structure.

CHILD NUTRITION

- *Funding*. Cuts $2.9 billion from child nutrition programs–more than 85 percent of which come from the Child and Adult Care Food Program (CACFP). The bulk of the reductions will result from reduced federal support for meals served in family day care homes that are not located in a low-income area or operated by a low-income provider.

  Child advocates predict that the reductions are likely to force CACFP sponsors serving hundreds of thousand of children to drop out of the program, reducing nutritional aid to poor children in day care.

IMMIGRANTS

- *Funding*. Benefits for legal immigrants are reduced by more than $22 billion. Undocumented immigrants already are ineligible for most major entitlement programs.
- *SSI and Food Stamps*. Denies benefits for most legal immigrants—both current and future—until they become U.S. citizens. Exceptions: refugees/asylees for first five years in U.S.; members of the Armed Forces; veterans; and individuals who have paid 40 quarters (10 years) of Social Security taxes.

  For many poor immigrants who are old or disabled and can neither work nor, given their age or physical or mental condition, learn all that is necessary to obtain citizenship, this is tantamount to a denial of benefits for the rest of their lives. Nearly half a million current elderly and disabled beneficiaries will lose their SSI benefits.

- *Medicaid*. Denies coverage for most legal immigrants entering the country for five years (with same exceptions as Food Stamps and SSI), with states having the option of extending the ban for a longer period and including current recipients. In addition, many current poor elderly and disabled individuals who receive Medicaid as a result of receiving SSI will lose their Medicaid coverage when they are terminated from SSI.

  CBO estimates that by 2002, approximately 260,000 elderly legal immigrants, 65,000 people with disabilities, 175,000 other adults, and 140,000 children who would be eligible for Medicaid under current law will be denied

it under the new law. Most of these individuals are likely to have no other health insurance.
- *TANF Block Grant*. Provisions are identical to those for Medicaid.
- *State and Local Programs*. Gives state and local governments broad authority to deny assistance to legal immigrants under state and local programs. Prohibits state and local governments from using their own funds to provide many kinds of assistance to undocumented immigrants and to some small categories of legal immigrants.
- *Sponsors*. Bans future immigrants from receiving benefits from most other federal means-tested programs for five years and imposes broad restrictions on the receipt of benefits after five years through new deeming rules and sponsorship requirements.

Programs exempted from five year limit include: emergency medical care; short-term disaster relief; school lunches; WIC/child nutrition; limited public health services for immunizations and communicable diseases; payments for foster care; nonprofit, in-kind community services such as shelters and soup kitchens; student assistance under the Higher Education Act and Public Health Service Act; means-tested elementary and secondary education programs; Head Start; and the Job Training Partnership Act (JTPA).

CHILD SUPPORT ENFORCEMENT

- *Federal Registry*. Establishes a federal case registry and national directory of new hires to track noncustodial parents across state lines.
- *State Registry*. Requires states to establish central registries of child support orders and centralized collection and disbursement units.
- *Income Withholding*. Expands income withholding by requiring all child support orders issued or modified before October 1, 1996 to become subject to income withholding without a hearing or advance notice if an arrearage occurs.
- *Health Care*. Requires all child support orders to include health care coverage. If the noncustodial parent changes jobs and the new employer provides health insurance, the child support agency must notify the employer and the notice enrolls the children in the new health plan unless the noncustodial parent contests the enrollment.
- *Enforcement*. Requires states to implement numerous new enforcement techniques, including the revocation of drivers, professional, occupational and recreational licenses for delinquent parents.
- *Paternity*. Streamlines the process for establishing paternity and expands the in-hospital voluntary paternity establishment program.
- *Visitation Grants*. Provides grants to states for access and visitation programs for noncustodial parents.

For more information contact: Cynthia Woodside, Office of Government Relations, National Association of Social Workers, 750 First Street, NE, Suite 700, Washington, DC 20002–4241, (800) 638–8799, x324 or e-mail address cwoodside@naswdc.org

Inside the Middle Class: Bad Times Hit the Good Life

Paul Taylor

Foreword

In the presidential campaign of 2008, candidates have risen and fallen; issues come and gone; and momentum shifted with the wind. But through it all, one character in the drama has never strayed far from center stage: the American middle class.

The overarching economic narrative of the 2008 campaign is the idea that life for the middle class has grown more difficult. There are Republican and Democratic variations on this theme, but very few dissenters from its core premise. If anything, the "middle class squeeze" has grown into a more insistent story line as the campaign season has progressed and economic news – rising fuel and food prices, falling house values, impending recession, turmoil in the financial and mortgage markets – has become more ominous.

This report sets out to present a comprehensive portrait of the middle class – its demography; its standard of living; its sense of progress and mobility; its economic behaviors; its anxieties and aspirations; and its social and political values. It portrays the middle class as it is in 2008, and it shows how it has changed since 1970. It does so by combining findings from a new national public opinion survey with new analyses of demographic and economic data from the Census Bureau and other sources.

At the outset, we should acknowledge that "middle class" is a term that is both universally familiar and devilishly difficult to pin down. It is both a social and economic construct, and because these domains don't always align, its borders are fuzzy. Is a $30,000-a-year resident in brain surgery lower class? Is a $100,000-a-year plumber upper-middle class? One way to sidestep riddles of this sort is to let people label themselves. That's what we did in our survey, and it produced a straightforward-seeming result: about half (53%) of all adults in America say they are middle class. But behind the reassuring simplicity of this number lies a nest of anomalies. For example, about four-in-ten (41%) adults with $100,000 or more in annual household income say they are middle class. So do nearly half (46%) of those whose household incomes are below $40,000. As for those in between, about a third say they're *not* in the middle class. If being middle income isn't the sole determinant of being middle class, what else is? Wealth? Debt? Homeownership? Consumption? Marital status? Age? Race and ethnicity? Education? Occupation? Values? Throughout the first section of this report, we present the public's verdict, gleaned from responses to survey questions on all these topics.

In addition to taking the public's pulse about what it means to be middle class, our report undertakes a parallel analysis – this one driven by economic and demographic data rather than by self-definition. Using Census Bureau reports, we divide Americans into three income tiers – low, middle and high. We define the middle tier as consisting of adults who live in a household where the annual income falls within 75% and 150% of the median. (The boundaries of this middle tier vary by household size; in 2006, they were about $45,000 to $90,000 for a family of three, which is close to the typical household size in the U.S.[1]) This analytical frame enables us to compare who is in the middle income tier now with who was in it in 1970. Has it gotten smaller or larger since then? Is it made up of different people, in different kinds of jobs, in different size homes and households, in different marital circumstances, in different phases of their lives, with different levels of educational attainment? Does the middle tier have higher inflation-adjusted income now than it did in 1970? More wealth? Different patterns of expenditures?

---

[1] 2006 is the last year for which Census Bureau data are available that allow for these comparisons by income tier. However, all dollar figures are inflated-adjusted to January 2008 dollars.

"Inside the Middle Class: Bad Times Hit the Good Life" A Social & Demographics Trend Report, published by the Pew Research Center for release April 9, 2008, Paul Taylor, Project Director. Copyright © 2008. Pew Research Center, Social & Demographic Trends project, http://pewsocialtrends.org/pubs/706/middle-class-poll. Reprinted by permission.

By bringing together these complementary frames of analysis, we hope to shed light on what the "middle class squeeze" means in the real lives of middle class Americans. Are they falling behind in life? Running faster just to stay in place? Moving ahead, but not as fast as the folks on the rungs above them? And as the middle class contemplates the squeeze, whom do they blame? The government? The price of oil? Foreign competition? Themselves?

ABOUT THE REPORT

This report is the work of the Social and Demographic Trends Project of the Pew Research Center. The Center is a nonpartisan "fact tank" that provides information on the issues, attitudes and trends shaping America and the world. It does so by conducting public opinion polling and social science research; by reporting news and analyzing news coverage; and by holding forums and briefings. It does not take positions on policy issues.

The public opinion survey findings that form the basis for the first section of the report comes from a telephone survey conducted from Jan. 24 through Feb. 19, 2008 among a nationally representative sample of 2,413 adults. The survey design included an over-sample of blacks and Hispanics, as well as a dual sample frame of respondents reached via landline (1,659) or cell (754) phone. All data are weighted to produce results from a representative sample of the full adult population. Margin of sampling error is plus or minus 2.5 percentage points for results based on the total sample at the 95% confidence level. The field work was performed by Princeton Survey Research Associates International. For more details, see the methodology section on Page 78.

This report was edited and the overview written by Paul Taylor, director of the Social and Demographic Trends Project and executive vice president of the Pew Research Center. In Section I, Chapter One on middle class self-definition and Chapter Three on middle class finances were written by Richard Morin, senior editor; Chapter Two on the middle class squeeze was written by Taylor; Chapter Four on middle class values was written D'Vera Cohn, senior writer; Chapter Five on middle class jobs was written by Stephen Rose, a project consultant; Chapter Six on middle class politics was written by April Clark, research associate. In Section II, Chapter Seven on the changing demography of income groups was written by Richard Fry, senior researcher; and Chapter Eight on trends in income, wealth and expenditures was written by Rakesh Kochhar, senior researcher. Morin and Clark led the team that created the survey questionnaire and analyzed its findings. Research assistant Felisa Gonzales helped with fact-checking and the preparation of charts. Other fact-checkers were provided by the Pew Research Center for the People & the Press. Pew Research Center Board Chairman Donald Kimelman, President Andrew Kohut and Director of Survey Research Scott Keeter all provided valuable counsel to this project. We are grateful for their assistance. We also thank the Pew Charitable Trusts, which funds the Pew Research Center.

OVERVIEW

Most Americans feel stuck in their tracks. A majority of adults in this country say that in the past five years they either haven't moved ahead in life or have fallen backwards. This is the most downbeat assessment of personal progress in nearly a half century of polling by the Pew Research Center and the Gallup Organization.

---

[2] U. S. Census Bureau, Historical Income Tables, Table H-6. In 1999, median household income was $51,910. In 2006, the last year for which these data are available, it was 50,811. All figures inflated-adjusted to January 2008 dollars.

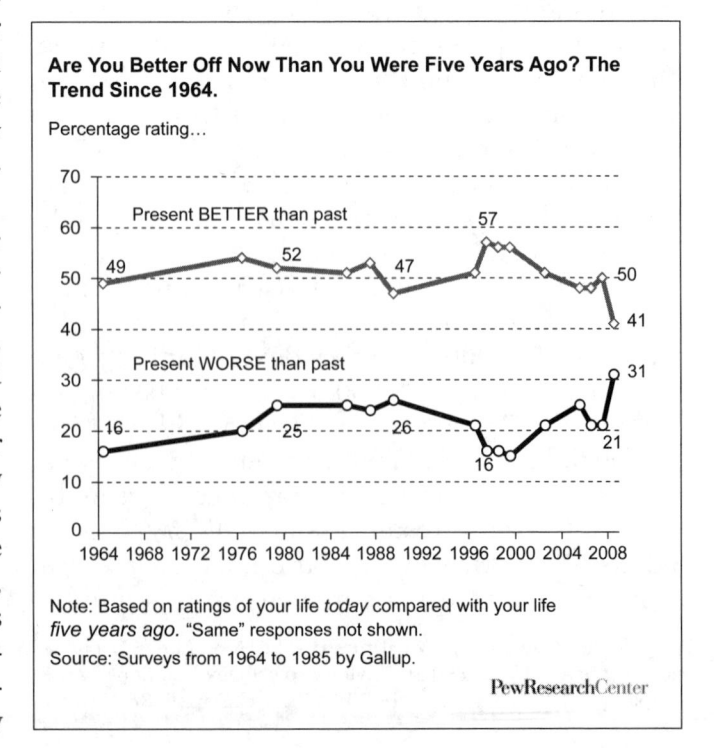

Are You Better Off Now Than You Were Five Years Ago? The Trend Since 1964.

Percentage rating...

Present BETTER than past: 49, 52, 47, 57, 50, 41
Present WORSE than past: 16, 25, 26, 16, 21, 31

Note: Based on ratings of your life *today* compared with your life *five years ago*. "Same" responses not shown.
Source: Surveys from 1964 to 1985 by Gallup.

PewResearchCenter

EXECUTIVE SUMMARY

Fewer Americans now than at any time in the past half century believe they're moving forward in life.

- Americans feel stuck in their tracks. A majority of survey respondents say that in the past five years, they either haven't moved forward in life (25%) or have fallen backward (31%). This is the most downbeat short-term assessment of personal progress in nearly half a century of polling by the Pew Research Center and the Gallup organization.
- When asked to measure their progress over a longer time frame, Americans are more upbeat. Nearly two-thirds say they have a higher standard of living than their parents had when their parents were their age.

For decades, middle income Americans had been making absolute progress while enduring relative decline. But since 1999, they have not made economic progress.

- As of 2006 (the last year for which trend data are available), real median annual household income had not yet returned to its 1999 peak, making this decade one of the longest downturns ever for this widely-accepted measure of the middle-class standard of living. Over a longer time period, the picture is much brighter; since 1970, median household income has risen by 41%.
- However, this long-term prosperity has not spread evenly. The upper income tier (households with annual incomes above 150% of the median) has outperformed the middle tier (households with annual incomes between 75% and 150% of the median) – not just in income gains, but also in wealth accumulation. From 1983 to 2004, the median net worth of upper income families grew by 123%, while the median net worth of middle income families grew by just 29%. In effect, those in the middle have been making progress in absolute terms while falling behind in relative terms.

About half of all Americans think of themselves as middle class. They are a varied lot.

- Some 53% of adults in America say they are middle class. On key measures of well-being–income, wealth, health, optimism about the future – they tend to fall between those who identify with classes above and below them. But within this self-defined middle class, there are notable economic and demographic differences. For example, four-in-ten Americans with incomes below $20,000 say they are middle class, as do a third of those with incomes above $150,000. And about the same percentages of blacks (50%), Hispanics (54%) and whites (53%) self-identify as middle class, even though members of minority groups who say they are middle class have far less income and wealth than do whites who say they are middle class.

For the past two decades middle income Americans have been spending more and borrowing more. Housing has been the key driver of both trends.

- A new single-family house is about 50% larger and existing houses are nearly 60% more expensive (in inflation adjusted dollars) now than in the mid 1980s. Goods and services that didn't exist a few decades ago – such as high definition television, high speed internet, and cable or satellite subscriptions – have become commonplace consumer items. And the costs of many of the anchors of a middle class lifestyle – not just housing, but medical care and college education – have risen more sharply than inflation.
- As expenses have risen, middle income Americans have taken on more debt, often borrowing against homes that, at least until recently, had been rising rapidly in value. The median debt-to-income ratio for middle income adults increased from 0.45 in 1983 to 1.19 in 2004. Ratios have also increased for upper and lower income adults, but not by as much.

(Continued)

> **EXECUTIVE SUMMARY—con'd**
>
> **At a time when these borrow-and-spend habits have spread, Americans say it has become harder to sustain a middle class lifestyle.**
>
> - Nearly eight-in-ten (79%) respondents in the Pew Research Center survey say it is more difficult now than five years ago for people in the middle class to maintain their standard of living. Back in 1986, just 65% of the public felt this way.
> - The current economic slowdown and uptick in prices are taking a bite out of the family budget. Slightly more than half of middle class respondents say they've had to tighten their belts in the last year. Roughly the same proportion expect to make more cutbacks in the year ahead, and a quarter say they expect to have trouble paying their bills. About a quarter of those who are employed worry they could lose their job.
> - Nonetheless, the American middle class is optimistic about the future. Most are confident that their quality of life in five years will be better than it is now. And, gazing farther ahead, most expect their children to do better in life than they themselves have done.
>
> **Economic, demographic, technological and sociological changes since 1970 have moved some groups up the income ladder and pushed others down.**
>
> - Winners include seniors (ages 65 and older), blacks, native-born Hispanics and married adults. The income status of all of these groups improved from 1970 to 2006. Losers include young adults (ages 18 to 29), the never-married, foreign-born Hispanics and people with a high school diploma or less. All of these groups have seen their relative income positions decline.
>
> **Most middle class adults agree with the old saw that the Republican Party favors the rich while the Democratic Party favors the middle class and the poor.**
>
> - Nearly six-in-ten (58%) middle class survey respondents say the Republican Party favors the rich, while nearly two-thirds say the Democratic Party favors the middle class (39%) or the poor (26%).

People feel this way for a reason. Median annual household income in the United States – arguably the best single measure of a middle class standard of living – is below the peak it reached in 1999, after adjusting for inflation.[2] This has been one of the longest slumps for this key indicator in modern U.S. history. And the pain has not been spread evenly. Those in the upper income tier have done better than those in the middle and lower tiers – not just during this decade's downturn, but through good times and bad stretching back to the early 1970s.

These two trends – a recent decline in standard of living, coming on top of a long-term rise in income inequality – have conspired to produce the economic malaise characterized by candidates and commentators alike during this presidential campaign season as "the middle class squeeze."

There's no denying that the phrase strikes a chord with the American public. According to a new Pew Research Center survey, about eight-in-ten (79%) adults say it is more difficult now than it was five years ago for middle class people to maintain their standard of living. Two decades ago, just 65% felt this way, according to a 1986 NEC/Wall Street Journal poll.

Nonetheless, these downbeat appraisals – both of personal progress and of middle class well-being in general – are not the public's only perspectives on this matter. Despite their short-term sense of stagnation, most Americans see in the sweep of their lives a long arc of progress. Nearly two-thirds (65%) say they have already exceeded the standard of living that their parents had at the age they are now. Most expect to face some belt-tightening – or worse – in the coming year, but a majority is confident that their quality of life in five years will be significantly better than it is now. And, gazing into a more distant future, most expect their children's standard of living to be better than their own.

In short, the public is beleaguered but unbowed. And its positive long-term perspective, like its negative short-term assessment, is in line with underlying economic realities. Despite the downturn of the current decade, median household income increased by 41% from 1970 to 2006 (the last year for which such data are available), after adjusting for inflation and changes in household size. To be sure, the rising tide favored some boats over others. The income gains over this period were greater for upper income adults than for middle or low income adults, and the wealth gains were *much* greater in the top income tiers than in the middle or at the bottom. So for those in the middle peering upward, absolute progress has gone hand in hand with relative decline.

All of these economic trends – stagnation in the short term, rising prosperity and rising inequality in the long term – provide a context for the nuances of public opinion on the subject of the "squeeze." When survey respondents say they haven't moved forward in recent years, the economic data say they're right. When respondents say they're doing better than their parents, the economic data say they're right. When respondents say it has become more difficult to maintain a middle class standard of living, the data once again say they're right – if what they mean is that it has become harder for people in the middle to keep pace with those above them.

Through the Looking Glass of Class

To examine the dynamics of public opinion through the prism of socioeconomic class, the survey asked respondents to place themselves into one of five groups – upper class, upper middle class, middle class, lower middle class and lower class. About half (53%) say they are middle class; some 19% percent say they are upper middle class and another 19% say they are lower middle class; 6% say they are lower class and 2% say they are upper class.[3]

One overarching finding from this exercise in self-identification is that class divides people far more by their economic experiences and characteristics than it does by their social values and life priorities, their demographic traits or their evaluations of their own quality of life and economic mobility.

For example, the percentage of people who say they "live comfortably" ranges from 66% of the self-defined upper class to 39% of the self-defined middle class to just 9% of the self-defined lower class. But the range is not nearly as wide when respondents are asked whether they're doing better in life than their parents; some 80% of the upper class say they are, compared with 67% of the middle class and 49% of the lower class. And the class disparities grow smaller on questions about life priorities. For example, 66% in the upper class say it is important to be wealthy, compared with 55% in the middle class and 51% in the lower class. On the demographic front, class disparities are fairly wide with regard to education and less wide with regard to homeownership and marriage.

On virtually every topic explored in this survey, responses of the middle class fall between those of the upper and lower classes – but sometimes the middle leans toward the bottom, and sometimes toward the top. This report will examine the attitudes, aspirations and anxieties of America's middle class in detail – and it will also explore the economic and demographic realities that underlie them. It will focus on changes in the middle class since 1970; on differences among the middle, lower and upper income groups; and

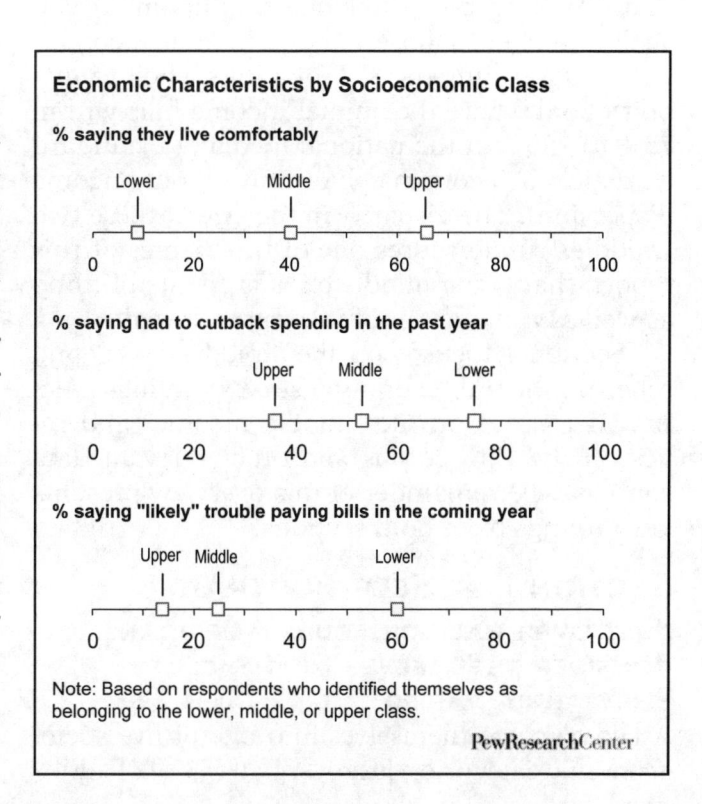

---

[3] Throughout this report, we combine respondents who say they are "upper" and "upper middle" into a single "upper class" category and we combine respondents who say they are "lower middle" and "lower" into a single "lower class" category.

Economic Characteristics by Socioeconomic Class

% saying they live comfortably

Lower ~9, Middle ~39, Upper ~66

% saying had to cutback spending in the past year

Upper ~40, Middle ~53, Upper ~75 (Lower)

% saying "likely" trouble paying bills in the coming year

Upper ~15, Middle ~22, Lower ~58

Note: Based on respondents who identified themselves as belonging to the lower, middle, or upper class.

PewResearchCenter

Priorities and Values by Socioeconomic Class

% saying "important" to be successful in a career

Lower, Middle, Upper all cluster near 90–95.

% saying "important" to be wealthy

Lower ~48, Middle ~52, Upper ~65.

% saying the rich are rich because of hard work

Lower ~33, Middle ~43, Upper ~58.

Note: Based on respondents who identified themselves as belonging to the lower, middle, or upper class.

PewResearchCenter

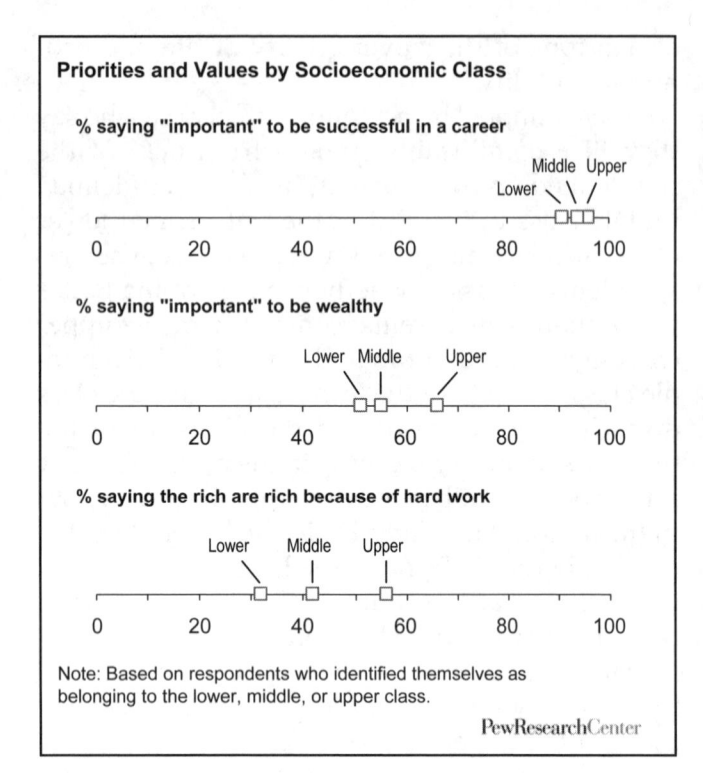

Half of Americans Say They're Middle Class

Percentage of Americans who identify themselves as . . .

	All
	%
Upper class (NET)	21
Upper	*2*
Upper-middle	*19*
Middle class	53
Lower class (NET)	25
Lower-middle	*19*
Lower	*6*
Don't know/Refused	1/100
Number of respondents	2413

PewResearchCenter

on the wide range of experiences, opinions and values within the middle class itself.

Before summarizing our findings, a note about terminology. Throughout the report, when we refer to the "middle class" we are describing the 53% of adults who identified themselves that way in response to a question in our survey. When we refer to those who are "middle income," we are describing the 35% of adults who live in a household where the annual income falls within 75% to 150% of the national median (a standard yardstick in economic literature about income dispersion). The disparity in the size of these two "middles" underscores one of the themes of this report: that being middle class is a state of mind as well as a statement of income and wealth.

Section I focuses on the "middle class" and relies on the public opinion survey findings. Section II focuses on the "middle income" and relies on the U.S. census and other relevant data sources. The remainder of this overview presents key findings from both sections.

SECTION I: A SELF-PORTRAIT

JUST OVER HALF OF ADULT AMERICANS CONSIDER THEMSELVES MIDDLE CLASS. THEY ARE A VARIED LOT.

Asked to place themselves into one of five socioeconomic categories, just over half (53%) of adults in our survey describe themselves as middle class, a finding that has varied very little over many decades of social science survey research.[4] On most key components of social and economic status – such as income, wealth, health, education, homeownership – the survey finds that the self-defined middle class is truly in the middle, positioned between those who identify with the classes above and below them. But even *within* this self-defined middle class, there are notable economic and demographic differences. For example, younger adults and older adults are both more likely than middle-aged adults to describe themselves as middle class, even though their income levels are lower. Meantime, middle-aged middle class adults are more likely than those who are younger and older to report financial stresses, even though they have more income. Also, roughly the same percentages of whites (53%), blacks (50%) and Hispanics (54%) self-identify as middle class, despite the fact that the income and wealth of blacks and Hispanics who say they are middle class is much lower than that of whites who say they are middle class.

---

[4] Over the years, other surveys have presented respondents with four categories of socioeconomic class rather than five: upper class, middle class, working class and lower class. Using those definitions, a 2006 survey by the *General Social Survey (GSS)* found that 46% of respondents identified as middle class and 45% as working class.

MIDDLE CLASS AMERICANS — AND ALL AMERICANS — FEEL LESS PROGRESS IN THEIR LIVES NOW THAN AT ANY TIME IN AT LEAST 44 YEARS.

On a scale of zero to ten, survey respondents were asked to give a numerical rating to their present quality of life, then to use the same scale to rate the life they led five years ago and finally to rate the life they expect to lead five years from now. More than half rate their life today either worse (31%) than their life five years ago or the same (25%). Just 41% say their life today is better. In the 44 years that these "ladder of life" questions have been asked in Pew and Gallup surveys, these are the most bearish ratings ever recorded. Not surprisingly, there is a class-based pattern to the public's judgments. The self-defined lower classes are the most discouraged about their recent progress (44% rate their life today below their life five years ago); the self-defined upper classes are the least discouraged (just 22% rate their life today below their life five years ago); while the self-defined middle class is situated between the two groups, but closer to the top than the bottom (28% rate their life today below their life five years ago).

MOST PEOPLE IN THE MIDDLE CLASS FEEL THEY'VE EXCEEDED THEIR PARENTS' STANDARD OF LIVING.

When the middle class lengthens its time horizons, it elevates its assessment of personal progress. Two-thirds (67%) say their standard of living is better than the one their parents had at the age they are now. Just 10% say their standard of living is worse. In these judgments, the middle class is less upbeat than those in the upper classes (80% of whom say they're doing better than their parents) and more upbeat than those in the lower classes (49% of whom say they're doing better than their parents). Many of these differences between the classes wash away when people are asked about their expectations for the next generation. Roughly half of respondents in all three classes say they expect their children's standard of living to exceed their own. However, a significantly larger share of those in the lower class (31%) than of those in the upper (17%) or middle (19%) classes say they think their children's lives will be *worse* than theirs. A greater share in the latter two groups say that they expect their children to do about the same in life as they themselves have done.

THE VAST MAJORITY OF MIDDLE CLASS ADULTS SAY IT HAS BECOME HARDER TO MAINTAIN A MIDDLE CLASS LIFESTYLE. BUT MOST OF THEM THINK THEY THEMSELVES ARE BEATING THE ODDS.

Just 28% of middle class respondents say they've fallen backward in life in the past five years. But a lopsided majority (78%) says it has become more difficult over the past five years for people who

Intergenerational Upward Mobility

	All	Upper class	Middle class	Lower class
My standard of living compared to my parents' is . . .	%	%	%	%
Much better	38	57	38	22
Somewhat better	27	23	29	27
About the same	19	13	21	19
Somewhat worse	9	5	7	17
Much worse	5	1	3	13
Don't know/Refused	2/100	1/100	2/100	2/100
Number of respondents	2413	522	1276	588

Question wording: Compared to your parents, when they were the age you are now, do you think your own standard of living now is much better, somewhat better, about the same, somewhat worse or much worse than theirs was?
Note: Based on respondents who identified themselves as belonging to the lower, middle, or upper class.

PewResearchCenter

The Middle Class Blues

Compared with five years ago, is it more or less difficult for middle class people to maintain their standard of living?

	All	Upper class	Middle class	Lower class
	%	%	%	%
More difficult	79	72	78	89
Less difficult	12	15	13	7
About the same (VOL.)	6	11	6	1
Don't know/ Refused	3/100	2/100	3/100	3/100
Number of respondents	2413	522	1276	588

Note: Based on respondents who identified themselves as belonging to the lower, middle, or upper class.

PewResearchCenter

are middle class to maintain their standard of living. These responses suggest that most middle class adults think of themselves as at least holding their own against daunting odds. The widespread perception that it is harder now than it was five years ago to maintain a middle class standard of living is not class-based. Large majorities of all three classes (72% upper; 78% middle; 89% lower) share this view.

THERE IS NOTHING APPROACHING A CONSENSUS ABOUT WHO OR WHAT IS RESPONSIBLE FOR THE MIDDLE CLASS SQUEEZE.

Nearly everyone agrees that it's become harder to maintain a middle class lifestyle, but there's no consensus about who or what is mostly to blame. Among middle class respondents, about a quarter (26%) blame the government, 15% blame the price of oil, 11% blame the people themselves, 8% blame foreign competition, 5% blame private corporations and the rest cite other factors or do not have an answer. Within the middle class, big differences on this question occur along partisan lines. Democrats are most likely to point the finger at government (35% do so) while Republicans divide blame among the people (17%), the government (16%)

Is Life More Difficult for the Middle Class? And Who is to Blame?

	All middle class	Rep/Lean Rep	DeM/Lean Dem	Ind/No Lean
	%	%	%	%
More difficult (NET)	78	73	85	67
The government	26	16	35	22
The price of oil	15	16	15	12
People themselves	11	17	8	8
Foreign competition	8	9	8	7
Private corporations	5	2	8	3
Combination of these things	3	1	3	4
Economy/Cost of living	1	*	2	*
President George Bush	1	0	1	0
Something else	2	5	1	2
DK/Refused	6	7	4	9
Less difficult (NET)	13	16	9	19
About the same	6	8	,3	8
DK/Refused	3/100	3/100	3/100	6/100
Number of respondents	1276	435	633	208

Note: Based on respondents who identified themselves as belonging to the middle class.

PewResearchCenter

and the price of oil (16%). There are also class divisions on this question, with the lower class nearly twice as likely as the upper class to blame the government (39% versus 21%).

WITHIN THE MIDDLE CLASS, THERE'S A WIDE RANGE OF FINANCIAL CIRCUMSTANCES AND ANXIETIES.

Fully four-in-ten Americans with family incomes below $20,000 say they are middle class, as do a third of those with incomes of $150,000 or more. Not surprisingly – given this broad range – some in the middle class (39%) report that they are financially comfortable, while 37% say they "have a little left over after meeting expenses" and 20% say they "just meet expenses." Only 3% say they can't meet expenses. Asked about their financial experiences in the past year, more than half of middle class adults report that they've had to tighten their belts. Half also expect that they will have to cut more spending in the year ahead. Among those in the middle class who are employed, about a quarter (25%) worry that they could be laid off, that their job could be outsourced, or that their employer could relocate in the coming year, and a bit more (26%) worry that they could suffer a cutback in salary or health benefits.

Who's Comfortably Middle Class, and Who's Not?

Which phrase best describes your financial situation?

	Live Comfortably	Meet expenses, some left	Just meet expenses	Don't meet expenses	DK/Ref
	%	%	%	%	%
All middle class	39	37	20	3	1=100
Gender					
Male	43	35	18	3	1=100
Female	36	38	21	4	1=100
Race/Ethnicity					
White, non-Hispanic	42	38	17	2	1=100
Black, non-Hispanic	43	32	17	7	1=100
Hispanic	24	39	30	7	*=100
Age					
18-29	45	33	16	6	*=100
30-49	34	43	20	2	1=100
50-64	38	34	24	3	1=100
65+	46	33	18	3	0=100
Education					
College grad	45	40	14	1	*=100
Some college	41	40	18	1	*=100
HS grad or less	36	33	24	6	1=100
Family income					
$100,000+	53	33	13	1	*=100
$50K-$99K	42	44	13	*	1=100
$30K-$49K	37	39	21	3	*=100
LT $30,000	28	33	30	9	=100

Note: Based on respondents who identified themselves as belonging to the middle class.

PewResearchCenter

KEEPING UP WITH THE JONESES: AMERICANS HAVE A FINELY CALIBRATED SENSE OF HOW MUCH MONEY IT TAKES TO LIVE A MIDDLE CLASS LIFESTYLE IN THEIR AREA. BUT THEY TEND TO OVERESTIMATE HOW MANY PEOPLE HAVE CERTAIN HIGH-END GOODS AND SERVICES.

When we asked respondents to estimate how much money it takes for a family of four to live a middle class lifestyle in their community, the median of all responses was $70,000 – uncannily close to the Center's national estimate, based on Census Bureau data, of $68,698 a year for a four-person household.[5] However, when we presented respondents with a list of high-end consumer goods and services, and asked whether they have them and whether they believe most other people have them, their tendency in some cases was to over-estimate what most other families have. For example, more than six-in-ten (62%) believe say that most families have a high definition television, whereas just 42% of all adults say that their family has one. Similarly, about a quarter (24%) of respondents believe that most people have a child in private school, though only 15% of parents with school age children report having a child in private school. Lopsided majorities also believe that most families have cable or satellite service, two or more cars, and high speed internet access. In these judgments, they are correct – a majority of families report that they do in fact have these goods and services.

EVERYTHING IS RELATIVE: PEOPLE'S ESTIMATES OF THE PRICE OF ADMISSION TO A MIDDLE CLASS LIFESTYLE RISES WITH THEIR OWN INCOME LEVELS AND WITH THE COST OF LIVING IN THEIR OWN COMMUNITIES.

There's a strong correlation between respondents' family income and their estimate of what it takes to lead a middle class lifestyle. The greater the income, the higher the estimate. Adults in families whose income is between $100,000 and $150,000 a year believe, on average, that it takes $80,000 to live a middle class life in their area. By contrast, adults in families whose income is less than $30,000 a year believe that a middle class lifestyle can be had for about $50,000 a year. Analyzing these estimates by the ZIP codes of the respondents yields a similar finding: that people who live in communities with a high cost of living think it takes, on average, about $15,000 more to be in the middle class than do people who live in communities with a low cost of living.

ASKED TO WEIGH THEIR PRIORITIES IN LIFE, THE MIDDLE CLASS PUTS TIME AHEAD OF WEALTH — AND EVERYTHING ELSE.

Some two-thirds (68%) of middle class respondents say that "having enough free time to do the things you want" is a very important priority in their lives. That's more than say the same about any other priority we asked about in this survey including having children (62% said that is very important), being successful in a career (59%), being married (55%), living a religious life (53%), doing volunteer work/donating to charity (52%); and being wealthy (12%). Upper and lower class respondents give essentially the same answers. The demographic groups most inclined to say they highly value free time are the ones least likely to have it – such as the employed, the middle-aged, and mothers of young children. In recent years, a number of public opinion surveys have documented Americans' growing sense of feeling rushed, and this perception tracks with the growth in the number of mothers who are

---

[5] This figure is for 2006 (the most recent year for which census data are available) but is inflation-adjusted to January 2008 dollars. See the appendix section "Adjusting for Household Size" for an explanation of how this calculation was made.

What I Have, What Most People Have

	Most families have	My family has
	%	%s
Cable or satellite service*	90	70
Two or more cars	88	70
High-speed Internet	86	66
High-def or flat screen TV	62	42
Child in private school**	24	15
Paid household help	21	16
A vacation home	10	10

Note: *Beyond the basic service. **Based on respondents with minor-age children.

PewResearchCenter

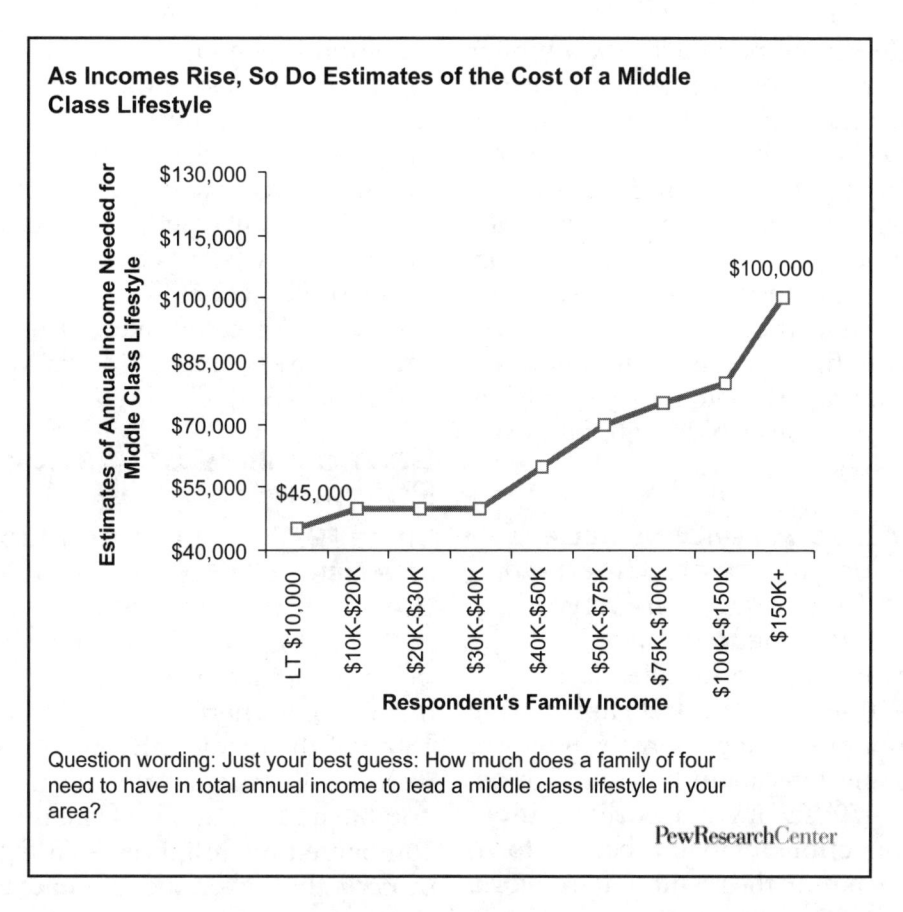

As Incomes Rise, So Do Estimates of the Cost of a Middle Class Lifestyle

Respondent's Family Income	Estimate
LT $10,000	$45,000
$10K–$20K	
$20K–$30K	
$30K–$40K	
$40K–$50K	
$50K–$75K	
$75K–$100K	
$100K–$150K	
$150K+	$100,000

Question wording: Just your best guess: How much does a family of four need to have in total annual income to lead a middle class lifestyle in your area?

PewResearchCenter

Life's Priorities: Time Over Money

% of middle class respondents saying this is "very important"

Having free time	68
Having children	62
Successful career	59
Being married	55
Living a religious life	53
Volunteer or charity work	52
Being wealthy	12

Note: Based on respondents who identified themselves as belonging to the middle class.

PewResearchCenter

employed outside the home and in the number of two-earner couples. However, recent research on whether Americans in fact have less leisure time has produced mixed findings. At least one major report, which relied on five decades of time use logs kept by different groups of survey respondents, found that no matter what most people may perceive, Americans today have more leisure time now than they did several decades ago.[6] Other reports find that many middle class families have maintained their lifestyle only by becoming two-earner households, with all the attendant time stresses.[7]

MOST MIDDLE CLASS AMERICANS BELIEVE THAT THE RICH JUST KEEP GETTING RICHER, BUT THEY DON'T HAVE A SETTLED VIEW ABOUT HOW THE RICH BECOME RICH.
Two thirds of people in the middle class agree with the proposition that the rich are getting richer and the poor are getting poorer. But they're split in their explanations about how the rich become rich. Some 47% say it's mainly the result of having good connections or being born into it, while 42% say it's mainly the result of hard work,

---

[6] Aguiar, Mark A. and Erik Hurst, 2007. "Measuring Trends in Leisure," *The Quarterly Journal of Economics*, vol. 122, no. 3: pp. 969-1006.

[7] Jacobs, Elizabeth, September, 2007. "The Politics of Economic Insecurity," The Brookings Institution, Issues in Governance Studies, no. 10, p. 4

ambition and education. Not surprisingly, those in the upper classes (56%) are more inclined to cite hard work, ambition and education than are those in the middle (42%) or lower (32%) classes. Class divisions also are apparent on a related question about whether success in life is determined by forces outside one's control. Majorities of all three classes disagree with that proposition, with a greater share of the upper class disagreeing (69%) than of the middle (62%) or lower (51%) classes.

SECTION II: A STATISTICAL PORTRAIT[8]

SINCE 1970, THE MIDDLE INCOME TIER IN AMERICA HAS SHRUNK BY ABOUT 5 PERCENTAGE POINTS.
In 1970, 40% of all adults in this country lived in a middle income household, with "middle" defined as one where the income falls within 75% to 150% of the median. By 2006, just 35% of adults were in the middle income tier. This small but notable hollowing out of the middle has been accompanied by an increase in the share of adults in *both* the lower income category and the upper income category. The rise in share has been greater over this time period for the upper group (to 32% in 2006 from 28% in 1970) than for the lower income tier (to 33% in 2006 from 31% in 1970). Looking at these changes by age group shows that the trends have been very different for the youngest and oldest adults. The 65 and

---

Does Wealth Come from Hard Work or Good Connections?

	All	Upper class	Middle class	Lower class
Main reason the rich are rich . . .	%	%	%	%
Hard work, ambition, or education	42	56	42	32
OR				
Knowing the right people or born into it	46	33	47	53
Neither/Both equally (VOL.)	8	9	7	9
Other (VOL.)	8	9	7	9
DK/Ref	4/100	2/100	4/100	5/100
Number of respondents	2413	522	1276	588

Question wording: Which of these statements comes closer to your own view - even if neither is exactly right. Most rich people today are wealthy mainly because of their own hard work, ambition, or education OR Most rich people today are wealthy mainly because they know the right people or were born into wealthy families.
Note: Based on respondents who identified themselves as belonging to the lower, middle, or upper class.

PewResearchCenter

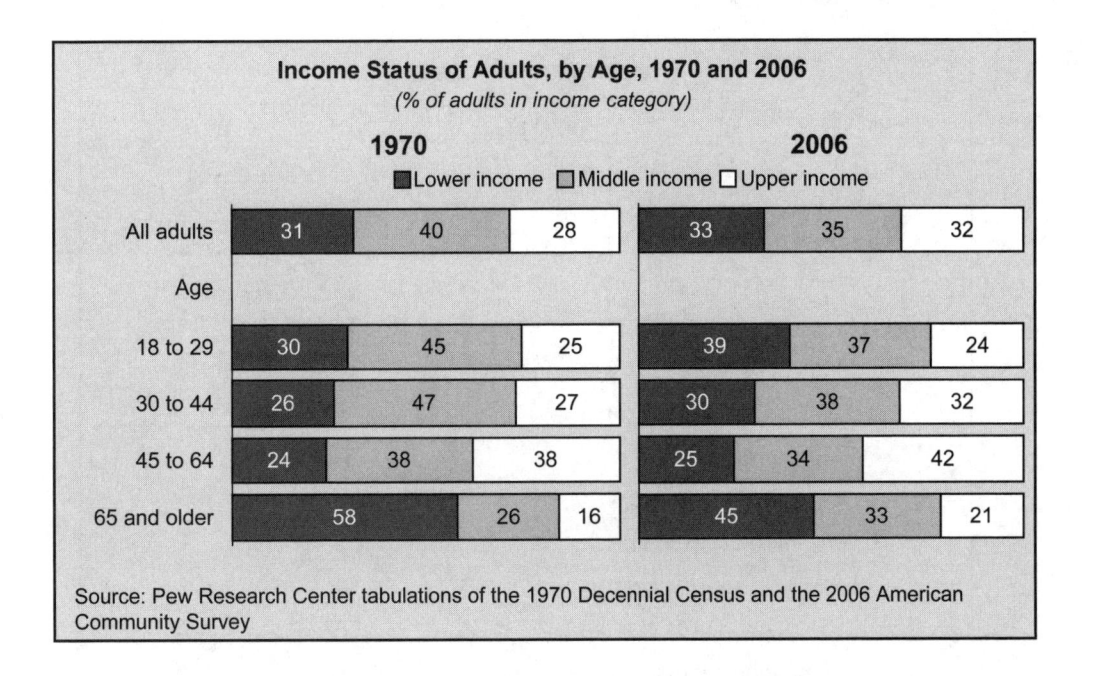

Income Status of Adults, by Age, 1970 and 2006
(% of adults in income category)

	1970 Lower	1970 Middle	1970 Upper	2006 Lower	2006 Middle	2006 Upper
All adults	31	40	28	33	35	32
Age						
18 to 29	30	45	25	39	37	24
30 to 44	26	47	27	30	38	32
45 to 64	24	38	38	25	34	42
65 and older	58	26	16	45	33	21

Source: Pew Research Center tabulations of the 1970 Decennial Census and the 2006 American Community Survey

older group has moved ahead during the past 36 years; the 18-to-29 year old group has fallen behind. Among the older group, just 45% were in the lower income tier in 2006, down from 58% in 1970. Among the younger group, 39% were lower income in 2006, up from 30% in 1970.

SOME DEMOGRAPHIC GROUPS HAVE IMPROVED THEIR INCOME STATUS SINCE 1970; OTHERS HAVE FALLEN BEHIND.

The period since 1970 has seen a distinct sorting of many different demographic groups into different income tiers. In addition to the elderly, the groups that have gained the most include blacks and native-born Hispanics. Married adults have also done well, while the never-married have fallen behind. On the gender front, men and women have moved in different directions, depending on marital and work status. Working husbands and working wives both have seen their income positions improve since 1970, but the gains have been greater for working husbands. Among those who are not married, the gender pattern is reversed: single working women's income position has improved since 1970, while single working men's income position has declined. Other groups that have not fared well are young adults, people in lower-skilled jobs, people with less educational attainment, and immigrant Hispanics. The decline for this last group is mainly the result of a heavy influx of low-skilled immigrants, rather than downward mobility among immigrants already in the U.S.

SINCE 1970, THE MIDDLE INCOME TIER HAS GOTTEN OLDER, BETTER EDUCATED, LESS LIKELY TO BE WHITE AND LESS LIKELY TO BE MARRIED.

Demographic changes in the middle income tier since 1970 are very similar to the changes in the U.S. adult population as a whole. The average age for middle income adults was 45 in 2006, up from 41 in 1970 (comparable figures for the full adult population are 46 in 2006 and 44 in 1970). In 1970, 88% of the middle income group was white; by 2006, just 71% was white (comparable figures for the full adult population are 86% in 1970 and 70% in 2006). The ethnic group that moved heavily into the middle income tier during this period was Hispanics: in 1970, they made up just 3% of the middle tier; by 2006, they were 13%. In 1970, more than three-quarters (76%) of the middle income group were married; by 2006, just 57% were married. But the biggest demographic change has come in levels of educational attainment. In 1970, just one-in-five middle income adults had at least some college education; by 2006, more than half did. As noted on the previous page, never married adults and those with less educational attainment have been among the groups suffering the biggest losses in income status over this period.

---

[8] Charts that appear in blue shading in this overview are not based on Pew Research Center survey data. The charts are based on data drawn from outside sources and analyzed by Pew Research Center staff.

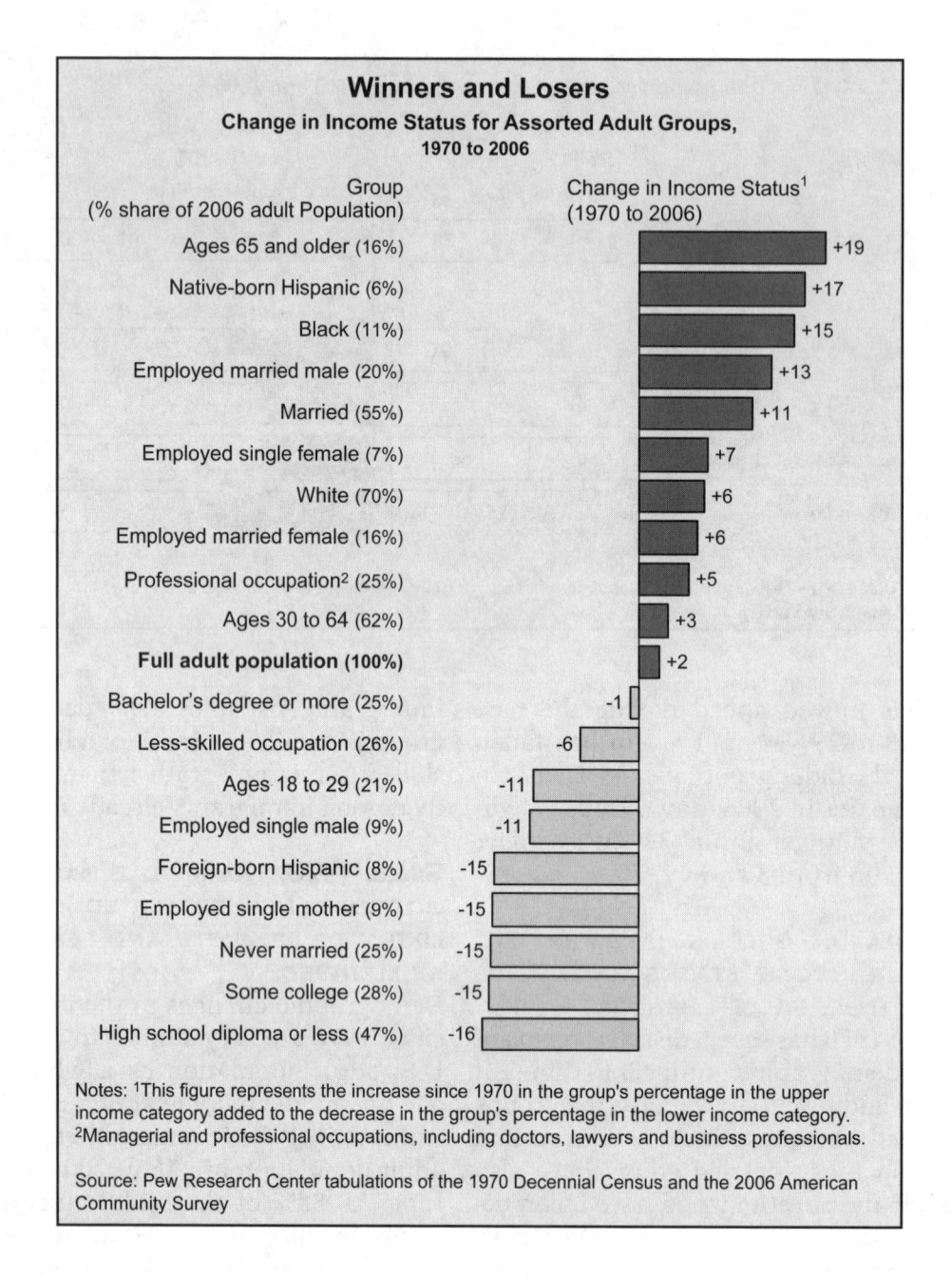

Winners and Losers
Change in Income Status for Assorted Adult Groups, 1970 to 2006

Group (% share of 2006 adult Population)	Change in Income Status[1] (1970 to 2006)
Ages 65 and older (16%)	+19
Native-born Hispanic (6%)	+17
Black (11%)	+15
Employed married male (20%)	+13
Married (55%)	+11
Employed single female (7%)	+7
White (70%)	+6
Employed married female (16%)	+6
Professional occupation[2] (25%)	+5
Ages 30 to 64 (62%)	+3
Full adult population (100%)	**+2**
Bachelor's degree or more (25%)	-1
Less-skilled occupation (26%)	-6
Ages 18 to 29 (21%)	-11
Employed single male (9%)	-11
Foreign-born Hispanic (8%)	-15
Employed single mother (9%)	-15
Never married (25%)	-15
Some college (28%)	-15
High school diploma or less (47%)	-16

Notes: [1]This figure represents the increase since 1970 in the group's percentage in the upper income category added to the decrease in the group's percentage in the lower income category.
[2]Managerial and professional occupations, including doctors, lawyers and business professionals.

Source: Pew Research Center tabulations of the 1970 Decennial Census and the 2006 American Community Survey

SINCE 1969, MEDIAN HOUSEHOLD INCOME HAS RISEN FOR ALL AMERICANS. BUT IT HAS NOT RISEN AS MUCH FOR THE MIDDLE INCOME GROUP AS FOR THE LOWER AND UPPER INCOME GROUPS.

From 1969 through 2006, median annual household income increased by 41%, after adjusting for the decline in household size.[9] However, the rise was greater for the upper income tier (50%) than for the middle (40%) or lower (42%) tier. By 2006, the median income of the upper group was $128,040, about double the $63,955 median income of the middle group and about five times the $25,201 median income of the lower group. This long-term increase in income inequality is more pronounced when one focuses on the top 1%, 5% or 10% of U.S. households. Each of these high-end groups has pulled farther away from the group just below it.[10]

---

[9] In 1970, the typical household had 3.1 people. In 2006, the typical household had just 2.5 people. This trend is the result of a decline in fertility (leading to smaller families) and a decline in the years that adults spend being married (leading to more single person households). Without making an adjustment for this change, the increase in median household income from 1970-2006 would be just 23%.

[10] Piketty, Thomas and Emmanuel Saez, January 2006. "The Evolution of Top Incomes: A Historical and International Perspective," NBER Working Paper No. 11955.

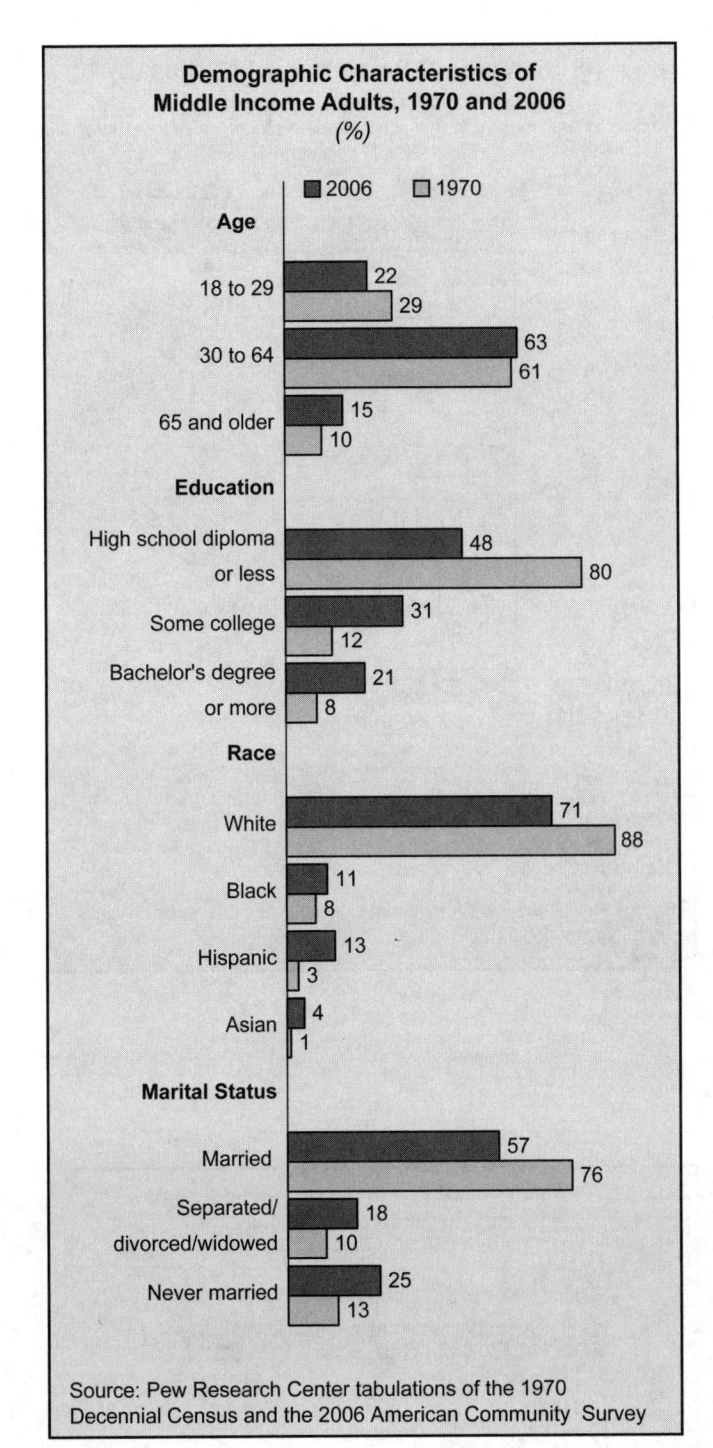

CHAPTER 7 Welfare Policy 361

Demographic Characteristics of Middle Income Adults, 1970 and 2006
(%)

■ 2006   □ 1970

Age
- 18 to 29: 22 / 29
- 30 to 64: 63 / 61
- 65 and older: 15 / 10

Education
- High school diploma or less: 48 / 80
- Some college: 31 / 12
- Bachelor's degree or more: 21 / 8

Race
- White: 71 / 88
- Black: 11 / 8
- Hispanic: 13 / 3
- Asian: 4 / 1

Marital Status
- Married: 57 / 76
- Separated/divorced/widowed: 18 / 10
- Never married: 25 / 13

Source: Pew Research Center tabulations of the 1970 Decennial Census and the 2006 American Community Survey

Median Household Income: 1970-2006
(January 2008 dollars)

- 1970: $41,318
- ~1973: $43,924
- ~1975: $41,430
- ~1978: $45,038
- ~1982: $42,358
- ~1989: $47,839
- ~1993: $45,250
- ~1999: $51,910
- ~2004: $49,885
- 2006: $50,811

Note: Periods of recession are shaded in gray. Estimates of income are derived from the Current Population Survey (March supplements).

Source: U.S. Census Bureau. "Income, Poverty, and Health Insurance Coverage in the United States: 2006," CPR P60-233 Table A-1 (August 2007)

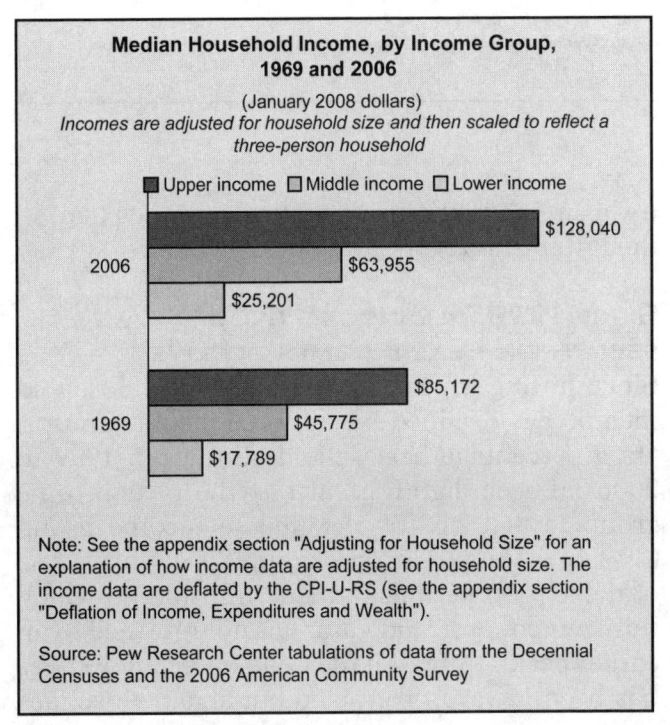

Median Household Income, by Income Group, 1969 and 2006
(January 2008 dollars)
Incomes are adjusted for household size and then scaled to reflect a three-person household

■ Upper income   ▨ Middle income   □ Lower income

2006:
- Upper income: $128,040
- Middle income: $63,955
- Lower income: $25,201

1969:
- Upper income: $85,172
- Middle income: $45,775
- Lower income: $17,789

Note: See the appendix section "Adjusting for Household Size" for an explanation of how income data are adjusted for household size. The income data are deflated by the CPI-U-RS (see the appendix section "Deflation of Income, Expenditures and Wealth").

Source: Pew Research Center tabulations of data from the Decennial Censuses and the 2006 American Community Survey

THE GROWTH IN MEDIAN FAMILY INCOME HAS BEEN SLOWER AND MORE SKEWED TO UPPER INCOME GROUPS SINCE 1973 THAN IT HAD BEEN IN EARLIER DECADES.

When looking at changes over time in the standard of living of the American public, economists often divide the past six decades into two eras. The period from 1947-73 was characterized by robust average annual increases for all income tiers, as well as a modest decline in income inequality.

The period since 1973 has been characterized by much slower growth for all groups, and also by an *increase* in income inequality. The chart to the right illustrates the divergent patterns during these two eras. In the first era, the average annual growth rate in family income exceeded 2.5% in all income quintiles – and the growth was slightly higher in the lower quintiles than in the upper quintiles. In the second era, the average annual growth rate was much lower for all quintiles, but

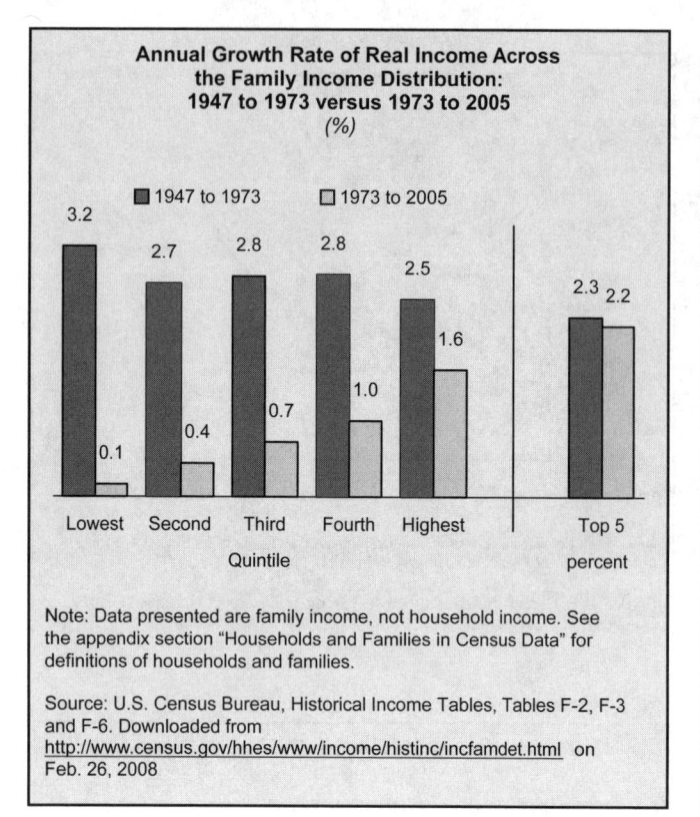

362 CHAPTER 7 Welfare Policy

Annual Growth Rate of Real Income Across the Family Income Distribution: 1947 to 1973 versus 1973 to 2005 (%)

■ 1947 to 1973   □ 1973 to 2005

Quintile	1947 to 1973	1973 to 2005
Lowest	3.2	0.1
Second	2.7	0.4
Third	2.8	0.7
Fourth	2.8	1.0
Highest	2.5	1.6
Top 5 percent	2.3	2.2

Note: Data presented are family income, not household income. See the appendix section "Households and Families in Census Data" for definitions of households and families.

Source: U.S. Census Bureau, Historical Income Tables, Tables F-2, F-3 and F-6. Downloaded from http://www.census.gov/hhes/www/income/histinc/incfamdet.html on Feb. 26, 2008

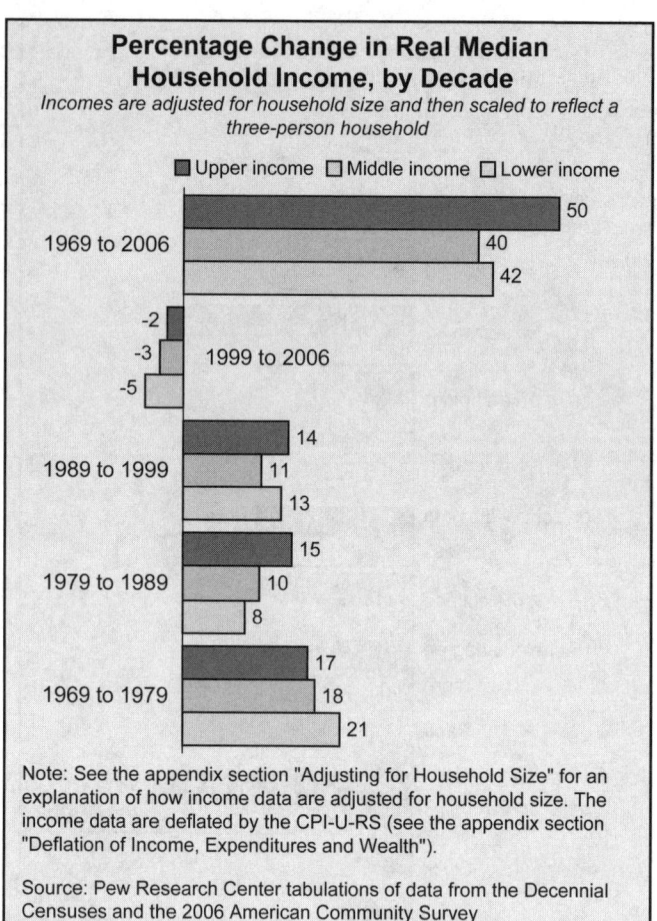

Percentage Change in Real Median Household Income, by Decade
Incomes are adjusted for household size and then scaled to reflect a three-person household

■ Upper income   □ Middle income   □ Lower income

Period	Upper	Middle	Lower
1969 to 2006	50	40	42
1999 to 2006	-2	-3	-5
1989 to 1999	14	11	13
1979 to 1989	15	10	8
1969 to 1979	17	18	21

Note: See the appendix section "Adjusting for Household Size" for an explanation of how income data are adjusted for household size. The income data are deflated by the CPI-U-RS (see the appendix section "Deflation of Income, Expenditures and Wealth").

Source: Pew Research Center tabulations of data from the Decennial Censuses and the 2006 American Community Survey

it was much higher in the upper quintiles than in the lower quintiles.

SINCE 1999, ALL INCOME GROUPS HAVE SEEN THEIR REAL INCOMES DECLINE.

Since hitting a peak in 1999, median household income has declined for all three income groups. On a percentage basis, the decline from 1999 to 2006 has been slightly greater for the lower income group (5%) than for the middle income group (3%) or the upper income group (2%). This is one of the longest periods in modern history in which this key economic indicator has not returned to an earlier peak – although the trend in recent decades has been toward protracted but shallow declines following periods of growth. Should the economy fall into a new recession – as many economists now predict – the current downturn would become the longest in modern history.

MEDIAN FAMILY WEALTH HAS GROWN IN RECENT DECADES. THE BIGGEST GAINS BY FAR HAVE BEEN MADE BY THOSE IN UPPER INCOME GROUPS.

The median net worth of families (all assets minus all debt) has risen by 50% over the past two decades, from $69,902 in 1983 to $104,645 in

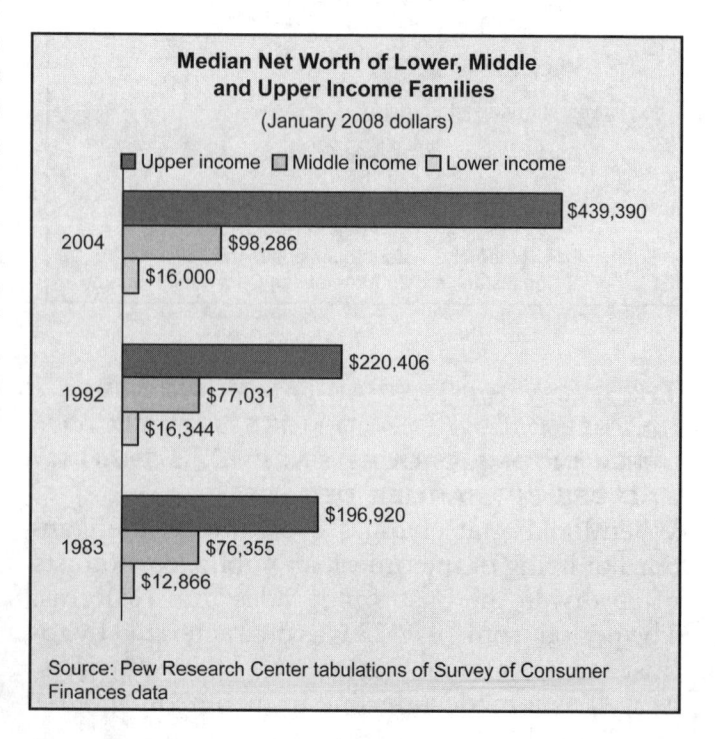

Median Net Worth of Lower, Middle and Upper Income Families
(January 2008 dollars)

■ Upper income   □ Middle income   □ Lower income

Year	Upper	Middle	Lower
2004	$439,390	$98,286	$16,000
1992	$220,406	$77,031	$16,344
1983	$196,920	$76,355	$12,866

Source: Pew Research Center tabulations of Survey of Consumer Finances data

2004 (all figures inflation-adjusted to 2008 dollars). But this growth has been spread unevenly through the income tiers. For the top income group, median family wealth has more than doubled during this time period, rising by 123% to $439,390 in 2004. For the middle income group, median wealth increased by only 29%, rising to $98,286 in 2004. For the lower income group, median wealth increased by just 24%, rising to $16,000 in 2004.

AS AMERICANS HAVE SEEN THE VALUES OF THEIR HOMES RISE OVER THE PAST TWO DECADES, THEY HAVE INCREASED THE SIZE OF THEIR DEBT. THIS IS ESPECIALLY TRUE FOR THOSE IN THE MIDDLE INCOME GROUP.
In every way that can be measured – size, value, source of wealth, collateral for debt – the American home bulks larger than ever in the economic life of the middle class (and the nation as whole). A new single-family home is about 50% bigger today than a new home was a generation ago.

The median sales price of existing single-family homes has risen in inflation-adjusted dollars from $142,578 in 1983 to $223,362 in 2007.[11] However, while homeowners have seen the value of their biggest asset rise sharply, they have also leveraged their homes to take out ever more debt. This is especially true for middle income families, whose overall debt-to-asset ratio rose from 0.25 in 1983 to 0.40 in 2004. Their increase in debt burden was much greater than that of the upper income group (it rose from 0.21 in 1983 to 0.27 in 2004) and slightly greater than that of the lower income group (for whom it rose from 0.29 in 1983 to 0.42 in 2004). For middle income families, 78% of their increase in debt between 1983 and 2004 was due to debt secured by their primary residence.

SINCE 1980, EXPENDITURE LEVELS HAVE RISEN FOR ALL THREE INCOME TIERS, BUT THEY HAVE RISEN THE MOST FOR THE UPPER TIER. FAMILIES IN ALL TIERS HAVE CHANGED THE MIX OF WHERE THEY SPEND THEIR MONEY.
As with income and wealth, consumer expenditures have risen for all three tiers from 1980 to 2006, but the growth in spending has been greater for the upper tier (32%) than for the middle (15%) or lower (16%) tiers. Looking just at the current decade, expenditures continued to rise for all three income tiers, while incomes have declined during this period (see page 23), suggesting that families have been financing their lifestyles in this decade by more borrowing or less saving, or both.

Patterns of expenditures have changed as well. Over the course of those two and a half decades, families in all three tiers are devoting proportionately more of their budgets to housing, pensions, medical care, and education; and less to recreation, transportation, food and clothing.

THERE IS A GREAT DEAL OF SHORT-TERM ECONOMIC MOBILITY AMONG INDIVIDUALS IN THE MIDDLE INCOME BRACKET.
A 2007 study by the U.S. Treasury Department found that about half of all taxpayers are in a different income quintile from the one they had been in a decade earlier. It also found that the highest levels of churn occur in the middle income brackets. The chart to the right illustrates,

The Median Debt-to-Asset Ratio

	2004	1992	1983
All families	0.34	0.28	0.25
Upper income families	0.27	0.25	0.21
Middle income families	0.40	0.30	0.25
Lower income families	0.42	0.29	0.29

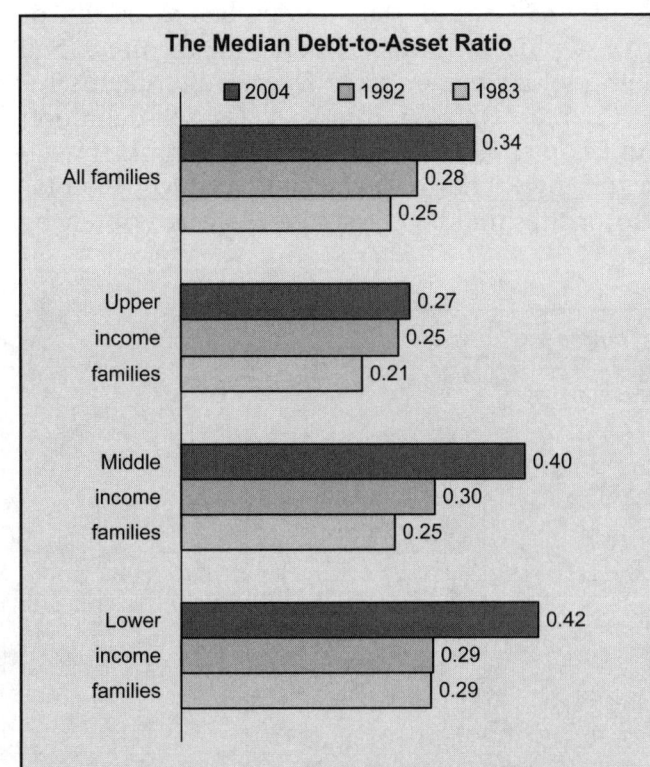

Note: The chart shows the median value of the ratio of total debt to assets computed for each family in the sample. The sample includes only families with positive levels of debt and income. Those families encompassed 69% of the sample in 1983, 72% in 1992 and 76% in 2004.

Source: Pew Research Center tabulations of Survey of Consumer Finances data

---

[11] The National Association of Realtors®, Median Sales Price of Existing Single-Family Homes.

Percentage Change in Real Median Family Expenditures

Expenditures are adjusted for family size and then scaled to reflect a three-person family

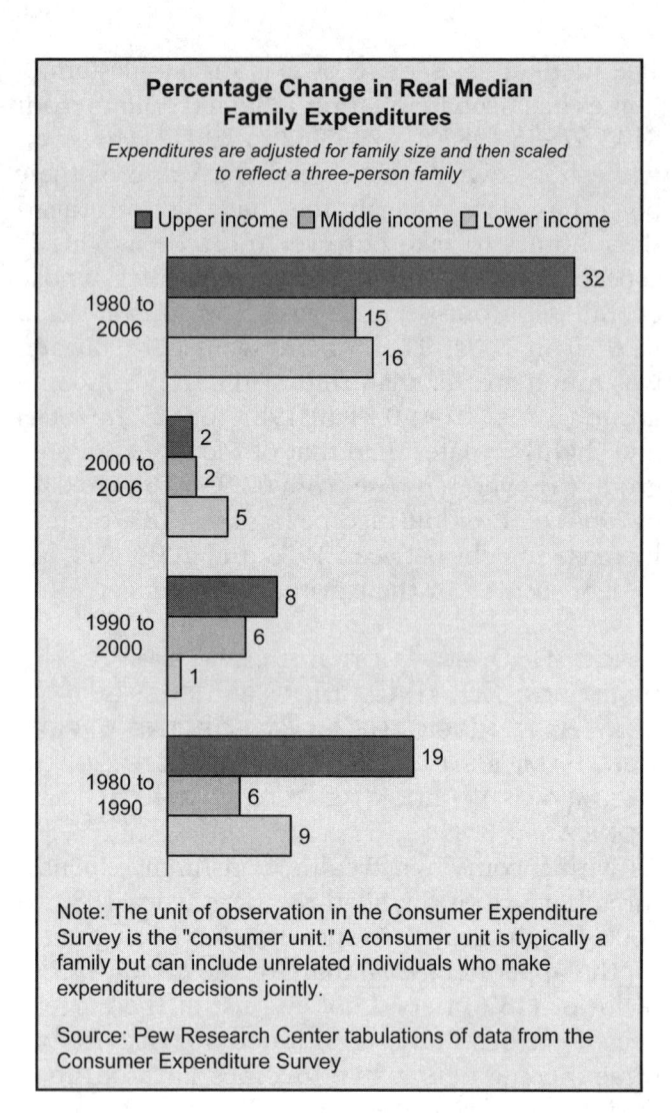

■ Upper income ☐ Middle income ☐ Lower income

Period	Upper	Middle	Lower
1980 to 2006	32	15	16
2000 to 2006	2	2	5
1990 to 2000	8	6	1
1980 to 1990	19	6	9

Note: The unit of observation in the Consumer Expenditure Survey is the "consumer unit." A consumer unit is typically a family but can include unrelated individuals who make expenditure decisions jointly.

Source: Pew Research Center tabulations of data from the Consumer Expenditure Survey

for two consecutive nine-year periods, where taxpayers who were in the middle income quintile at one point in time wound up nine years later. It shows that, in each time period, roughly two-thirds of the middle quintile taxpayers were in a different quintile after nine years. (It should be noted that the skew toward upward mobility reflected in this chart is due in part to a life cycle effect; at least through late middle age, adults tend to earn more as they age). The chart offers one explanation for the Pew survey finding that individuals with widely varying incomes identify themselves as being in the middle class. Unlike groups of people, individuals and families experience a good deal of variability from one year to the next in their annual incomes; these variances, however, do not necessarily cause them to change their affiliation with a socioeconomic class.

SECTION I – A SELF-PORTRAIT

This section is based on findings from a telephone survey conducted January 24 through February 19, 2008 among a nationally representative sample of 2,413 adults. The survey has a margin of error of plus or minus 2.5 percentage points. (See methodology box on page 78 for more details).

Chapter One on middle class self-definition and Chapter Three on middle class finances were written by Richard Morin, senior editor; Chapter Two on the middle class squeeze was written by

Percentage Point Change in Share of Expenditures on Major Consumer Items
All U.S. Families, 1980/81 to 2005/06

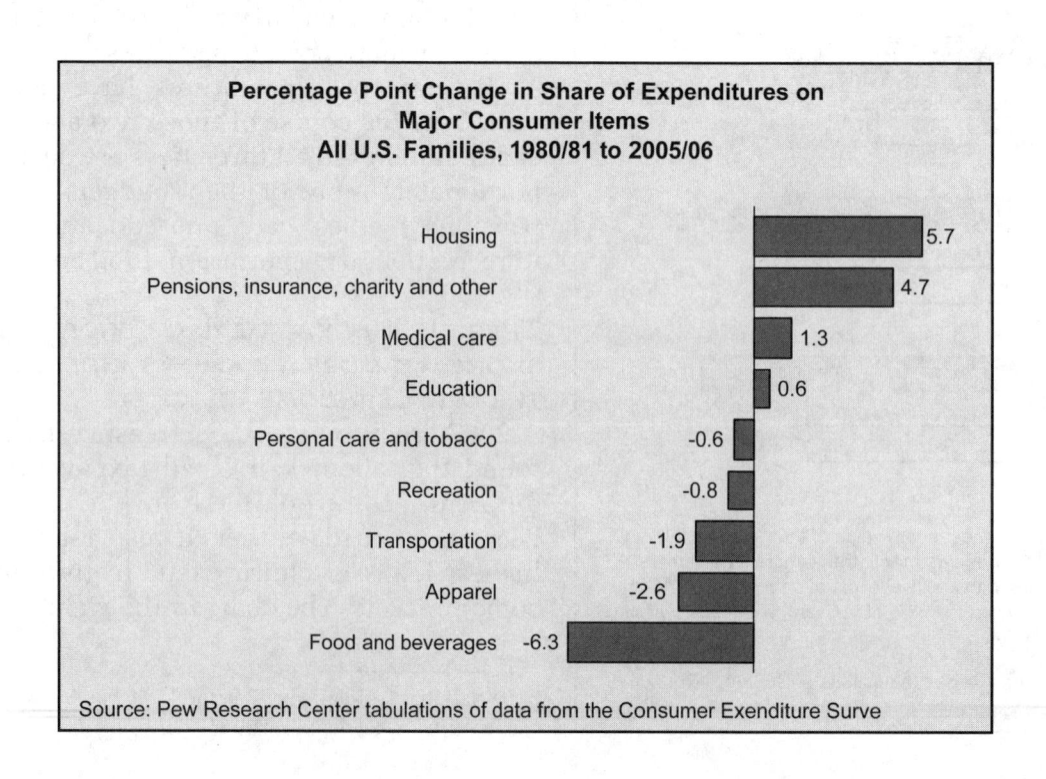

Item	Change
Housing	5.7
Pensions, insurance, charity and other	4.7
Medical care	1.3
Education	0.6
Personal care and tobacco	-0.6
Recreation	-0.8
Transportation	-1.9
Apparel	-2.6
Food and beverages	-6.3

Source: Pew Research Center tabulations of data from the Consumer Exenditure Surve

Income Mobility of Taxpayers in the Middle Quintile, 1987 to 1996 and 1996 to 2005

1996: Quintile distribution of taxpayers, by income (%)

Lowest	20.0
Second	20.0
Middle	20.0
Fourth	20.0
Highest	20.0

2005: Distribution of taxpayers from the 1996 middle quintile (%)

Lowest	5.9
Second	14.0
Middle	32.6
Fourth	31.1
Highest	16.3

1987: Quintile distribution of taxpayers, by income (%)

Lowest	20.0
Second	20.0
Middle	20.0
Fourth	20.0
Highest	20.0

1996: Distribution of taxpayers from the 1987 middle quintile (%)

Lowest	6.1
Second	17.4
Middle	33.9
Fourth	28.4
Highest	14.2

Source: Table 7 in U.S. Department of the Treasury. "Income Mobility in the U.S. From 1996 to 2005," (November 13, 2007)

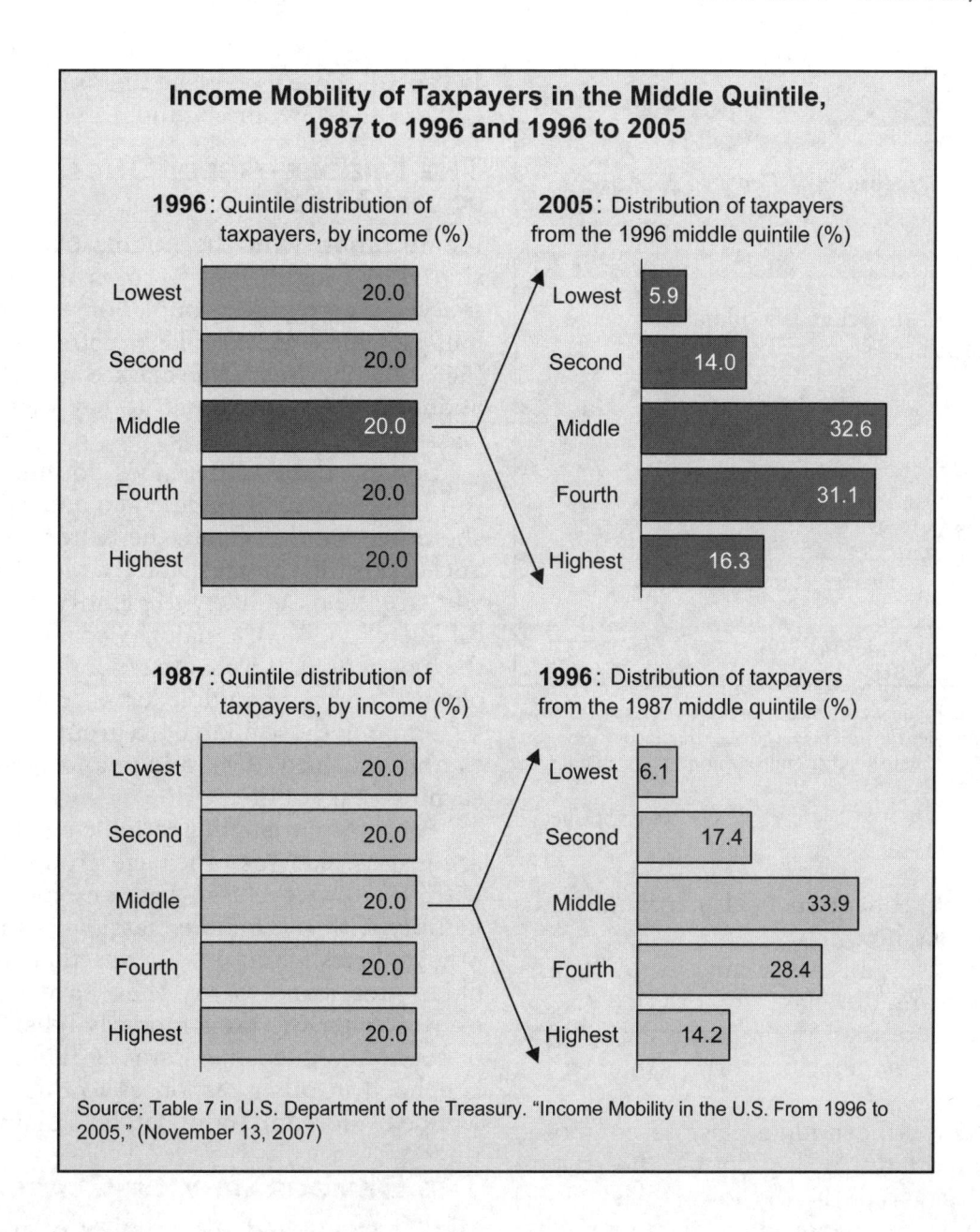

Paul Taylor, director of the Social and Demographic Trends project of the Pew Research Center; Chapter Four on middle class values was written by D'Vera Cohn, senior writer; Chapter Five on middle class jobs was written by Stephen Rose, a project consultant; and Chapter Six on middle class politics was written by April Clark, research associate. Morin and Clark led the team that created the survey questionnaire and analyzed its findings.

Chapter 1: The Middle Class Defines Itself

America is predominantly middle class—or most Americans say they are. When asked where they stand on the socioeconomic ladder, fully 53% of the public classifies itself as squarely in the middle class—a proportion that varies little by race, education, age and other key demographic characteristics. An additional 21% identify with the upper classes while slightly more (25%) say they are in the lower class,[12] according to the Pew survey.

On virtually every important measure of life, the middle class is truly in the middle, positioned between the upper and lower classes in terms of

---

[12] For purposes of this report, the proportion of Americans who are upper class include those who identify themselves as upper-middle (19%) or upper class (2%); the proportion who are lower class includes those who say they are lower middle (19%) or lower class (6%). The remaining 1% of survey respondents declined to answer the question or did not know.

Half of Americans Say They're Middle Class

Percentage of Americans who identify themselves as . . .	All
	%
Upper class (NET)	21
Upper	*2*
Upper-middle	*19*
Middle class	53
Lower class (NET)	25
Lower-middle	*19*
Lower	*6*
Don't know/Refused	1/100
Number of respondents	2413

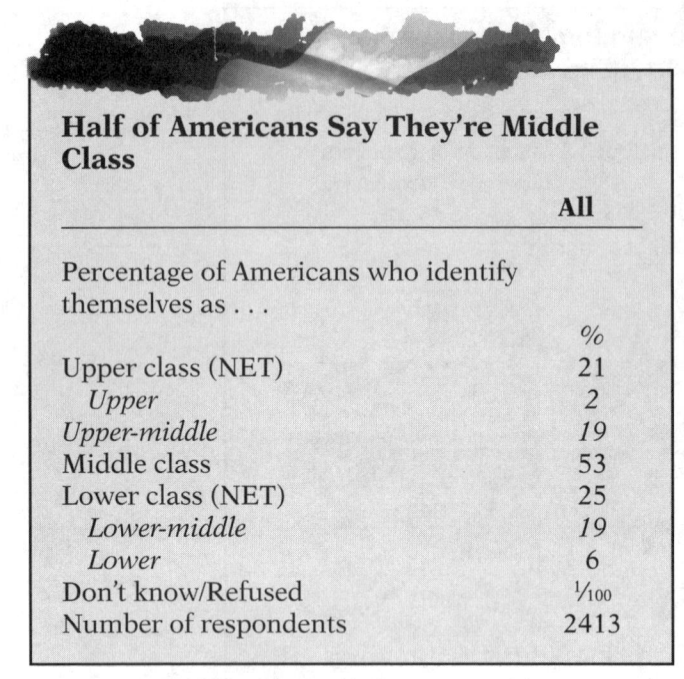

Question wording: If you were asked to use one of these commonly used names for the social classes, which would you say you belong in? The upper class, upper-middle class, middle class, lower-middle class, or lower class?

PewResearchCenter

income, wealth, education, health, marital status and homeownership.

About half of all Americans who identify themselves as middle class are married (52%), significantly more than in the lower class (37%) but a somewhat smaller proportion than in the upper class (59%).

A quarter of the middle class is composed of college graduates, nearly double the proportion of college grads in the lower class (14%) and about half the proportion in the upper class (48%). About two-thirds (68%) own their own home, compared with about three-quarters of the upper class (76%) and fewer than half of those who identify with the lower class. Three-in-ten eat out at least several times a week; that's less often than members of the upper class (42%) but more frequently than those who describe themselves as being in the lower class (22%). Three-quarters of the middle class fear they aren't saving enough, a concern they share with 69% of the upper class and 82% of the lower.

Even in terms of their physical health, the middle class is firmly in the middle. While most Americans report they are in good health, 29% of those who say they are middle class describe their health status as "excellent," compared with 18% of all those who place themselves in the lower class and 43% among those in the upper class.

THE MIDDLE-AGED: UNCOMFORTABLE IN THE MIDDLE

Identification with the middle class is broadly shared by roughly equal proportions of virtually every demographic group. For example, about half of whites (53%), blacks (50%) and Latinos (54%) say they're middle class. Similarly, men are about as likely as women to say they're middle class (51% vs. 55%).

Some notable differences do emerge. While it might seem as if middle-age and middle class should go hand-in-hand, the pattern is more nuanced: It is the youngest and the oldest Americans who are the most likely to identify themselves as middle class. A 54% majority of all adults under the age of 34 and 59% of respondents ages 65 or older say they're middle class, compared with 49% among those 45 to 64, a group that comprises about a third of all adults and is in the peak earning years of life.

Perhaps more telling, middle-aged Americans are just as likely as other age groups to identify with the lower class. And among those who identify with the middle class, adults in this age bracket are slightly more likely than younger or older Americans to say they have nothing left over after paying their monthly bills. This sense of economic uneasiness among the middle aged is echoed in other responses to this survey and will be explored in more detail in Chapter 3.

THE DEMOGRAPHY OF CLASS

Marital status and the number of workers per household correlate to some degree with self-identification of class. For example, married couples in which both are wage earners are about as likely to place themselves in the upper classes as are married couples with one wage earner. However, multi-earner couples are much less likely to be in the lower classes than are one-earner couples (13% versus 25%). Consequently, two-earner couples are much more likely than one-earner couples to be in the middle class (61% versus 45%). By contrast, households that do not include married adults tend to have lower incomes and hence don't self-identify much with the upper class; just 17% of those who say that they are living with a partner and working full- or part-time do so, along with just 18% of those who are neither married nor

Who Identifies with Which Class?

	All adults	Upper class	Middle class	Lower class	DK/ Ref
	%	%	%	%	%
Gender					
Male	48	21	51	26	2=100
Female	52	21	55	23	1=100
Race/Ethnicity					
White, non-Hispanic	70	23	53	23	1=100
Black, non-Hispanic	11	15	50	33	2=100
Hispanic	12	13	54	30	3=100
Age					
18-34	29	18	54	26	2=100
35-44	19	22	54	23	1=100
45-64	33	24	49	26	1=100
65+	16	19	59	21	1=100
Education					
College grad	27	37	49	12	2=100
Some college	24	17	58	24	1=100
HS grad or less	48	14	53	32	1=100
Neighborhood type					
Urban	36	23	49	27	1=100
Suburban	46	22	54	22	2=100
Rural	18	17	57	26	*=100
Generation					
First generation	11	13	56	28	3=100
Second generation	9	22	50	27	1=100
Third or later	79	22	53	24	1=100

Note: Based on respondents who identified themselves as belonging to the lower, middle, or upper class. Hispanics are of any race.

PewResearchCenter

cohabiting. About a third of both of these groups self-identify as being in the lower class.

There are also some geographic patterns to class identification, though they do not all conform to stereotypes. While many people equate suburbia with the middle class, nearly as many city dwellers (49%) as suburban residents (54%) identify themselves as members of the middle class. In rural America, nearly six-in-ten (57%) say they're firmly in the middle.

Also, immigrant status seems to have little effect on self-definition of middle class. About half of those Americans who are first generation (56%), second generation (50%) and third generation or later (53%) identify themselves as middle class—despite the fact that first-generation Americans (immigrants) have less income than those whose families have been in the country a generation or more.

While the middle class label may be broadly shared, other findings underscore longstanding inequalities between key demographic groups. For example, while similar proportions of blacks and whites say they're middle class, a third of African Americans identify themselves as lower class compared with only about a quarter of whites (23%) who do the same. At the same time, whites are significantly more likely than blacks to say they're members of the upper class (23% versus 15%). Similarly, nearly four-in-ten college graduates say they're in the upper class (37%), more than double the proportion of those whose

the enduring attraction of the middle class life to Americans.

INCOME DIFFERENCES IN THE MIDDLE CLASS

Middle class Americans share a class identity but live different lives. In important ways, the survey finds that members of the middle class are different not only from the upper or lower classes, but also from each other. Nowhere are these differences more apparent than in the vast range of incomes reported by key demographic groups within the middle class, suggesting that identification with the middle class is based on a complex mix of attitudes, behaviors and experiences, and not merely on income alone.

For example, the median family income for whites who say they are middle class is just over $56,000—nearly $10,000 more than for self-identified middle class blacks. Even bigger income disparities occur along generational lines: Adults between the ages of 30 and 49 who say they are in the middle class earn slightly more than $65,000, nearly double the median family income of those older than 65 and about $27,000 more than the median for those under the age of 30. Similarly large disparities exist between self-identified middle class college graduates (whose median family income exceeds $75,000) and those with only a high school education or less (whose median educational attainment is a high school diploma or less. Despite these clear differences, it is nonetheless notable how many Americans of all backgrounds identify with the middle class, a finding that at once reflects economic realities as well as

Median Incomes Vary Widely Within Middle Class

	Median family income
Total	$52,285
Gender	
Men	$58,102
Men under 50	$56,162
Men 50+	$61,017
Women	$47,334
Women under 50	$54,670
Women 50+	$41,614
Race/Ethnicity	
White, non-Hispanic	$56,295
Black, non-Hispanic	$46,849
Hispanic	$39,363
Age	
18-29	$38,493
30-49	$65,529
50-64	$61,542
65+	$34,512
Work status	
Retired	$38,455
Employed	$60,121
Networking	$38,919
Education	
College grad	$75,198
Some college	$57,083
HS grad or less	$39,765
Neighborhood type	
Urban	$52,205
Suburban	$54,945
Rural	$47,768
Region	
Northeast	$49,860
Midwest	$57,290
South	$49,280
West	$54,229

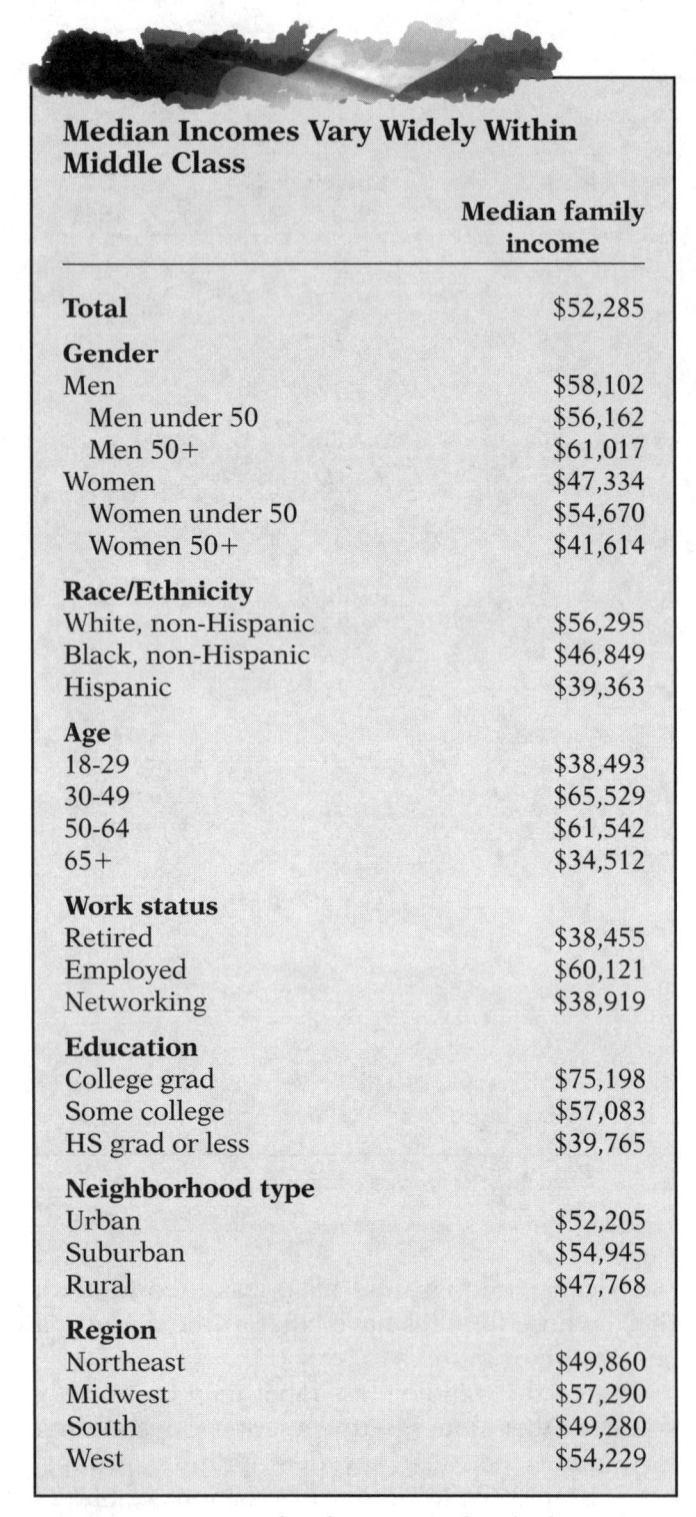

Note: Figures are grouped median estimates based only on respondents in each category who identified themselves as belonging to the middle class. Hispanics are of any race.

PewResearchCenter

Middle Class Incomes Percentage in each income group that identify as middle class

	% in Middle class
	%
Less than $19,999	41
$20,000-$29,999	49
$30,000-$39,999	50
$40,000-$49,999	59
$50,000-$74,999	68
$75,000-$99,999	63
$100,000-$149,999	47
$150,000 or more	33
Number of respondents	2413

PewResearchCenter

CHAPTER 7 Welfare Policy

Middle Class Incomes Percentage of middle class with family incomes of . . .

	Middle class
	%
Less than $19,999	12
$20,000-$29,999	9
$30,000-$39,999	9
$40,000-$49,999	11
$50,000-$74,999	18
$75,000-$99,999	14
$100,000-$149,999	8
$150,000 or more	4
Don't know/Refused	15/100
Number of respondents	1276

Note: Based on respondents who identified themselves as belonging to the middle class.

PewResearchCenter

The Price of Admission What Americans say a family must earn to be middle class

	%
Less than $40,000	11
$40,000-$59,999	24
$60,000-$79,999	27
$80,000-$99,999	14
$100,000-$149,999	16
$150,000 or more	8/100
Number of respondents	2005*

Question wording: Just your best guess: How much does a family of four need to have in total annual income to lead a middle-class lifestyle in your area?
Note: *Based on respondents who answered the question.

PewResearchCenter

income is just under $40,000 a year). Among the middle class, reported median family incomes are highest in the Midwest ($57,290) and West ($54,229), and lowest in the Northeast ($49,860) and South ($49,280).

The survey also finds that men who identify as middle class have median family incomes more than $10,000 higher than women who identify as middle class. A deeper look finds, however, that much of this difference is explained by the fact that people 65 or older with lower incomes are more likely to identify with the middle class, and this group is disproportionately composed of women. Among men and women under the age of 50, median family incomes are virtually identical ($56,162 versus $54,670), while older men report family incomes nearly $20,000 higher than that of older women.

LIVING THE MIDDLE CLASS LIFE ON $20,000 A YEAR?

Overall, the median family income of Americans who say they are middle class is about $52,000, and about half of respondents who identify as middle class earn between $30,000 and $100,000 annually. But about one-in-ten (9%) earn between $20,000 and $29,999 annually, and another 12% say they make under $20,000 annually. At the top end of the income scale, 12% of all middle class identifiers earn more than $100,000 a year. (The remaining 15% declined to answer the question.)

Analyzing these survey findings by income group dramatizes the breadth of identification with the middle class. About four-in-ten (41%) Americans with family incomes under $20,000 a year say they're middle class, as do a third of those earning $150,000 or more. Could it be that many lower and upper class Americans are inaccurately characterizing their socioeconomic class, either out of the desire to appear to be doing better than they are or because they are reluctant to acknowledge their advantaged status?

The answer appears to be no. Those who say they are middle class but have modest family incomes are disproportionately older Americans, retirees, college students, and younger adults — groups with relatively modest incomes but equally modest expenses. For example, about half of all students and retirees with family incomes under $30,000 a year say they're member of the middle class. At the other end of the income scale, those who say they are middle class but have six-figure family incomes tend to be married, own their home, have larger families and live in the northeast or in areas where it costs more to live. According to our analysis of respondents by their zip code and by local cost-of-living scales, people earning $100,000 a year are much more likely to describe themselves as upper class if they live in communities with a low cost of living than if they live in expensive communities.

WHAT IT COSTS TO BE MIDDLE CLASS

Collectively, the American public is spot-on with its estimate of what it costs to be middle class. Asked how much income a family of four in their community needs to lead a middle class life, respondents gave a median answer of about $70,000 a year – very close to the national median income of $68,698 for a household of four in 2006[13] (the most recent year for which such data are available).

But this "wisdom of the crowd" masks a wide range of individual estimates, with some respondents offering figures of $20,000 or less and others offering estimates of $200,000 or more. Overall, more than three-in-ten (35%) respondents say it takes less than $60,000 to be middle class where they live, while slightly more (38%) estimate a family needs 580,000 or more.

There is a clear correlation between respondents' incomes and their estimates of how much money it takes to be middle class. Americans with family incomes between $100,000 and $150,000 believe, on average, that families must earn $80,000 a year to be middle class in their area. In contrast, those earning less than $30,000 believe a family of four has to make about $50,000 to be middle class. Part of the reason for these differences is that people with higher incomes tend to live in large cities or adjacent suburbs— areas where it costs more to live a middle class life.

An analysis that combined federal government cost-of-living data and survey results confirms this view. Survey respondents living in areas that rank in the top third of the country in terms of local cost of living estimate that a family income of about $75,000 a year is needed to be middle class in their areas. That's about $15,000 higher than the median estimate of the third of the country that lives in places where costs are the lowest.

HOME OWNERSHIP AND THE MIDDLE CLASS

Homeownership has been in the news a lot lately, for all the wrong reasons: Housing prices are falling and foreclosure rates are rising. These are worrisome developments for middle class

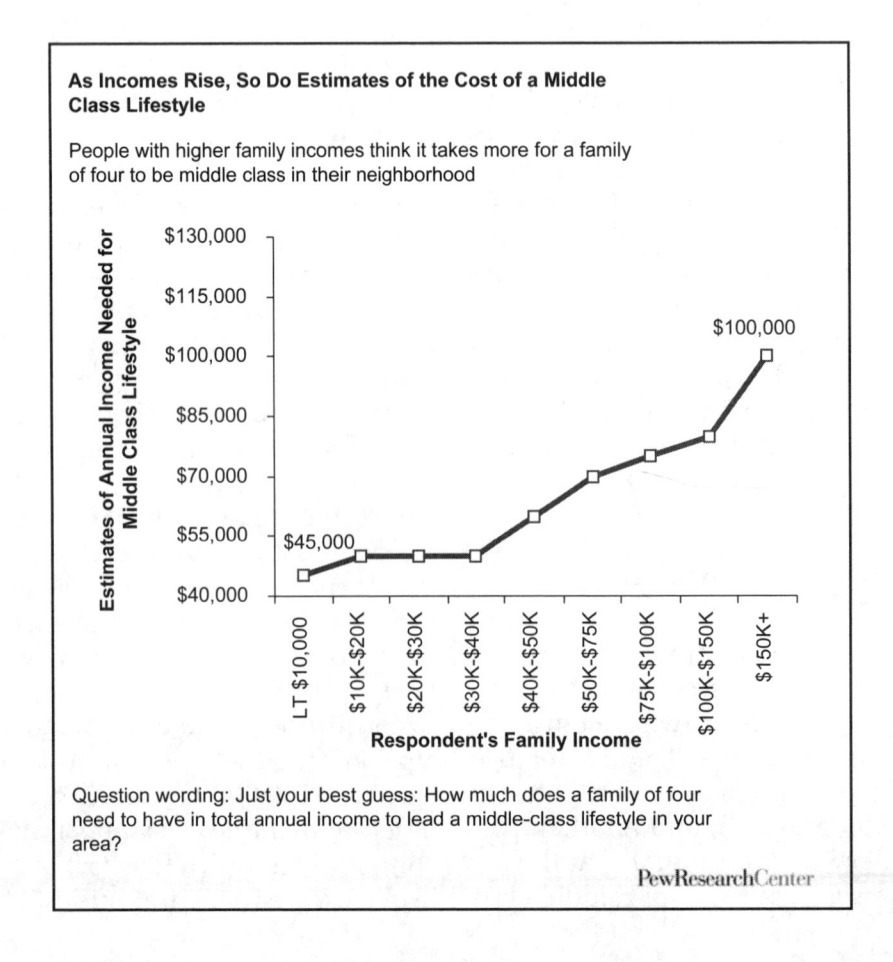

---

[13]This figure is for 2006 but is inflation-adjusted to January 2008 dollars. Income is also adjusted for household size and scaled to reflect a four-person household. See Appendix section "Adjusting for Household Size" for an explanation of the methodology.

As Incomes Rise, So Do Estimates of the Cost of a Middle Class Lifestyle

People with higher family incomes think it takes more for a family of four to be middle class in their neighborhood

Question wording: Just your best guess: How much does a family of four need to have in total annual income to lead a middle-class lifestyle in your area?

PewResearchCenter

Home Ownership, by Class

Class	Own home
	%
Upper class	76
Middle class	68
Lower class	46

Note: Based on respondents who identified themselves as belonging to the lower, middle, or upper class.

PewResearchCenter

Income and Homeownership
Based on middle class respondents

■ % Own home

Income	%
LT $10,000	28
$10,000–$19,999	40
$20,000–$29,999	57
$30,000–$39,999	54
$40,000–$49,999	70
$50,000–$74,999	79
$75,000–$99,999	86
$100,000–$149,999	83
$150,000+	90

PewResearchCenter

Americans, who regard their home as their most important asset and the anchor of their lifestyle.

Nearly seven-in-ten middle class Americans are homeowners. The median value of these homes, as reported by middle class survey respondents, is between $100,000 and $250,000. About one-in-five estimate that their homes are worth $100,000 or less. At the upper end of the scale, only 5% of middle class respondents say their homes are worth $500,000 or more.

Fewer than a third of middle class homeowners (30%) say they own their homes outright. A 40% plurality say they have paid off less than half of the money they owe on their home, while 27% say they have paid off half or more. Adults over the age of 50 are most likely to own a home free and clear.

Predictably, home ownership in the middle class is closely tied to family income and age, as well as to marital status and family size. More than eight-in-ten middle class Americans earning $100,000 or more own their own home, compared with barely half of those who make less than $50,000. Nearly nine-in-ten middle class married couples with minor children own their own homes, compared with about two-thirds of all single adults without children.

The survey finds that large numbers of middle class Americans who aren't very old or very affluent have bought a home. Nearly half of all adults between the ages of 25 and 29 say they are homeowners. By the time Americans turn 40, more than six-in-ten (63%) say they own a home. Home ownership peaks just before retirement; nearly nine-in-ten middle class adults ages 60 to 64 years are homeowners. At that point, home ownership begins to decline. In terms of income groups, more than four-in-ten (44%) middle class Americans with family incomes under $30,000 a year own their own home. That figure, however, is somewhat misleading because nearly half (44%) of this group is 65 or older, and many older adults have paid off their home.

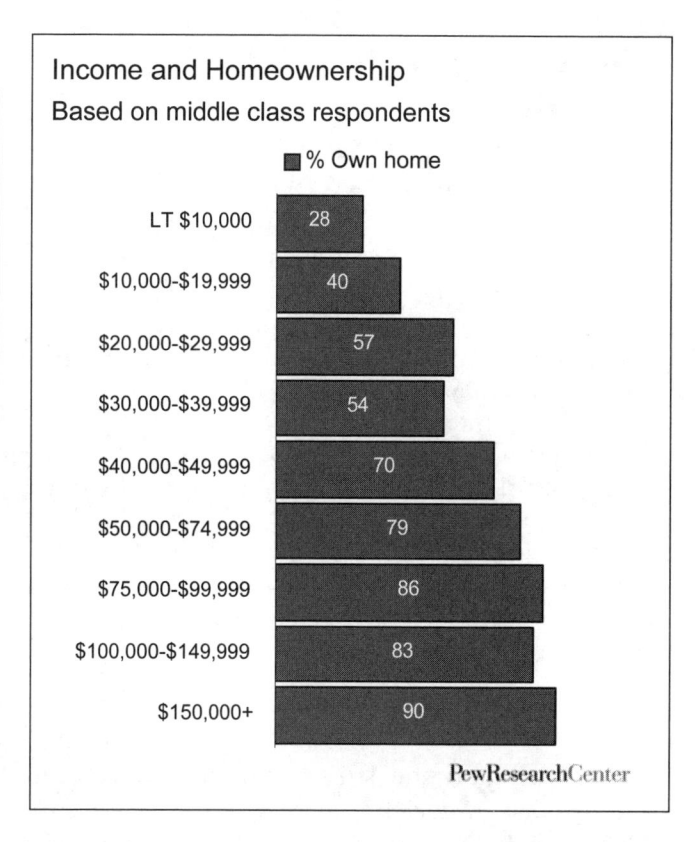

For the past several decades, median housing prices have risen much faster than median incomes. In 1970, the typical American house cost more than twice the typical American family's annual income. By 2005, that ratio had risen to nearly five-to-one. It's no surprise then, that in our survey, nearly two-thirds of middle class homeowners say that the value of their homes represents half or more of their total net worth.

WHAT THE MIDDLE CLASS OWNS

In addition to larger and more expensive homes, majorities or substantial minorities of middle class families own or use a wide range of goods and services, some of which until either didn't exist a decade ago, or until fairly recently may have been viewed as luxury items. Yet middle class Americans also tend to believe that most other families have even more of these items than they do.

What I Have, What Most People Have
Based on middle-class respondents

	Most families have	My family has
	%	%
Cable or satellite service*	91	71
Two or more cars	90	72
High-speed Internet	87	67
High-def or flat screen TV	63	42
Child in private school**	25	14
Paid household help	22	13
A vacation home	12	9

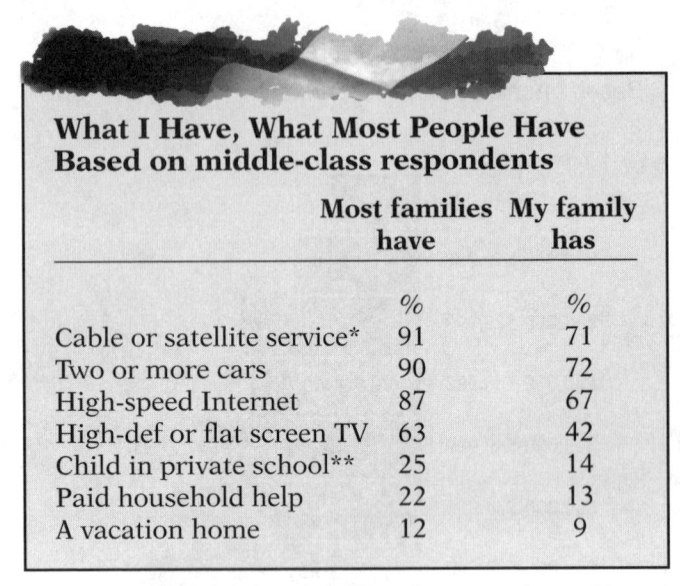

Note: *Beyond the basic service. **Based on respondents with minor age children.

PewResearchCenter

According to the survey, about seven-in-ten middle class Americans own two or more cars (72%) and have cable or satellite television service (71%). Two thirds have high speed internet access to surf the Web. About four-in-ten watch television using a flat-screen TV (42%). About 15% send their children to private schools, and a similar proportion has paid help to assist them with household chores.

Not surprisingly, middle class Americans with the largest family incomes also have the most luxuries: about two-thirds of all families making $100,000 or more owned at least four of the items or services included in the survey, nearly two and half times more than the proportion of families earning less than $50,000 (68% versus 26%). But perhaps less predictable is how widely distributed these goods are across income groups within the middle class. For example, 12% of all middle class adults with incomes below $50,000 have paid household help, compared with 10% of middle class adults who earn between $50,000 and $100,000 and 19% who earn more than $100,000.

THE "POSSESSIONS PERCEPTION GAP"

Middle class Americans are inclined to believe others have more of life's goodies than they do. On three of seven non-essential or quasi-luxury goods and services tested in the survey, the middle class does get it right: Substantial majorities believe most Americans have cable or satellite television service, own at least two cars and have high-speed Internet access. And in fact, most people surveyed say they do have these things.

But a substantial "possessions perception gap" emerges on other items tested in the survey. Well under half (42%) of all Americans have a flat screen television, though a substantial majority of the middle class (63%) believe most people own one. A more modest discrepancy occurs when the middle class is asked if "most families" send their children to private school. A quarter of the middle class thinks most people send their child to private school; in fact, only 15% of those respondents who have minor children say they

Haves and Have-Nots % that have

	All	Upper Class	Middle Class	Lower Class
	%	%	%	%
Cable or satellite service	70	80	71	62
Two or more cars	70	83	72	57
High-speed Internet	66	80	67	50
High-def or flat screen TV	42	59	42	28
Child in private school*	15	31	14	6
Paid household help	16	36	13	7
A vacation home	10	19	9	4

Note: *Based on respondents with minor age children.

PewResearchCenter

have a child in private school. Similarly, 22% of the middle class think most Americans have paid help around the home while 16% of the total sample report that they do.

CHAPTER 2: THE MIDDLE CLASS SQUEEZE

Back in 1980, Ronald Reagan framed his campaign for president around a simple but powerful question to the American public: "Are you better off now than you were four years ago?"

His timing was exquisite. In 1979, a public opinion survey had found a rise in the number of Americans who said their lives were getting worse, and the word "malaise" had worked its way into the American political lexicon.

Memo to John McCain, Barack Obama and Hillary Clinton: This new Pew Research Center survey finds that Americans are even more downbeat about their lives now than they were in 1979. In fact, the public's sense of personal stagnation is more prevalent today than at any time in the more than four decades that this ladder-of-life question has been asked by Pew and Gallup.

More than half of all Americans say they've either made no progress in life over the past five years (25%) or have actually fallen backward (31%). Just four in ten (41%) – a record low – rate their lives today as better than their lives fives years ago.

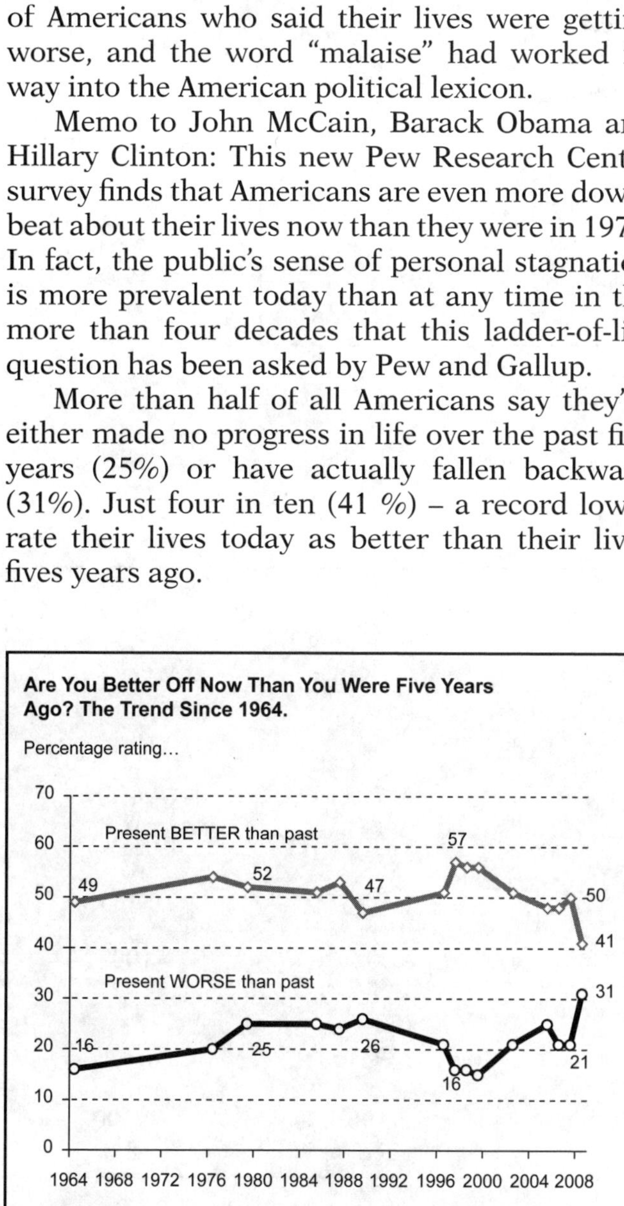

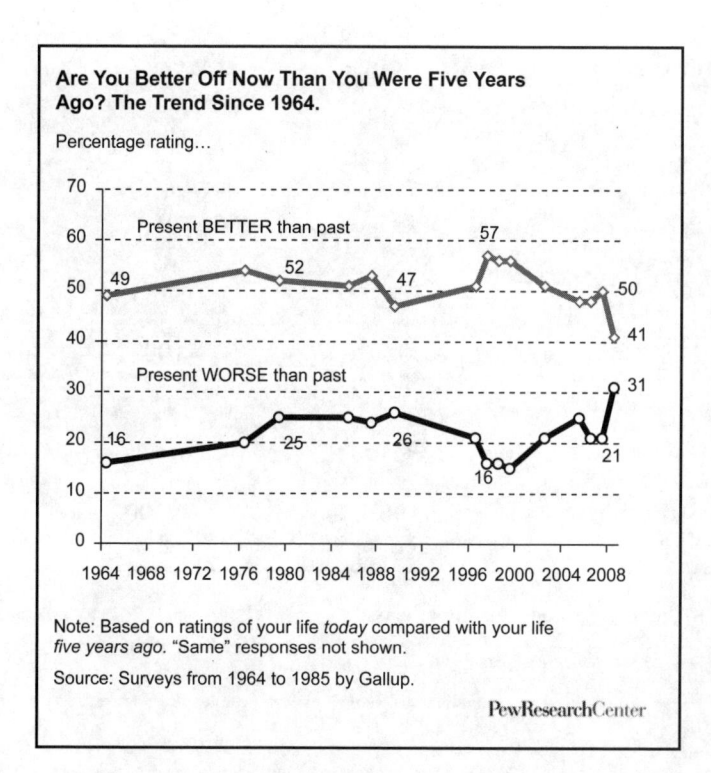

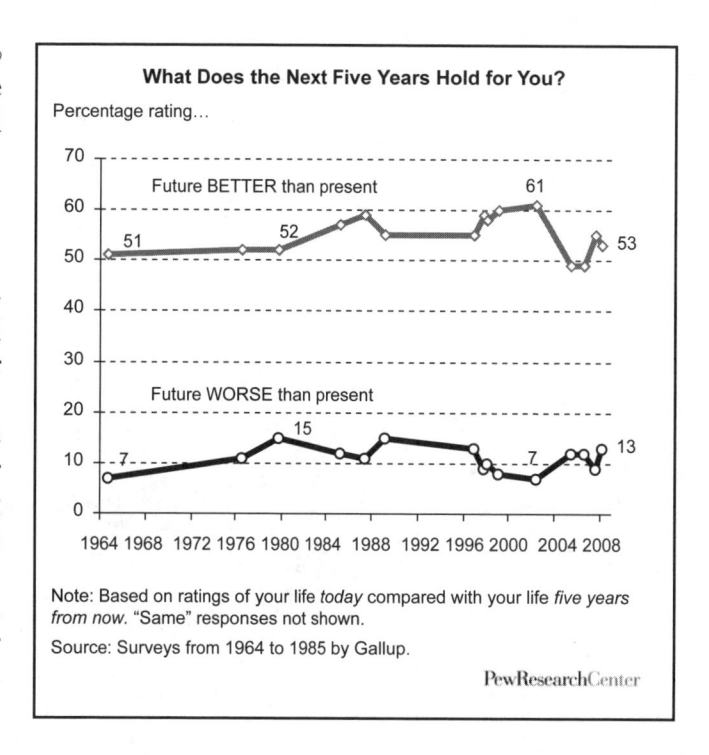

What Does the Next Five Years Hold for You?
Percentage rating...

[Line graph showing "Future BETTER than present" ranging from 51 (1964) to 52, 61 (2002), 53 (2008); and "Future WORSE than present" ranging from 7 to 15 (1980), 7, 13 (2008), years 1964-2008]

Note: Based on ratings of your life *today* compared with your life *five years from now*. "Same" responses not shown.
Source: Surveys from 1964 to 1985 by Gallup.

PewResearchCenter

Americans have always been great believers in the ethos of personal advancement, and throughout the history of this survey question, those who say they've moved forward in the past five years typically outnumber those who say they've fallen behind, by ratios ranging between nearly two-to-one peak of optimism in 1997, 57% of adults said they had moved forward in the previous five years and just 16% said they had fallen behind. That 41 percentage point difference has now sunk all the way down to just 10 percentage points.

The bright spot in this survey is that Americans' faith in their future remains largely undiminished. More than half (53%) expect their life will be better in five years, while just 13% think it will be worse. These percentages are in sync with long-term trends, though the share of adults who think their future will be better is down a bit from a recent peak of 61% in 2002. Also, in absolute terms, the average rating that adults give to their lives five years from now – 7.6 on a scale of zero to ten – is close to historical norms, though it has dropped sharply since 2007, when it was 8.2.

The ladder-of-life battery of questions employ what researchers call a "self-anchoring scale." Respondents are asked to give a numerical rating to their present quality of life, on a scale of zero to ten. Then, using the same scale, they are asked to rate what their life had been like five earlier, and what they expect it to be like five years from now.

Are You Better Off Now Than You Were Five Years Ago? The Trend Since 1964.
Percentage rating...

[Line graph showing "Present BETTER than past" ranging from 49 (1964), 52, 47, 57, 50, 41 (2008); and "Present WORSE than past" ranging from 16, 25, 26, 16, 21, 31 (2008), years 1964-2008]

Note: Based on ratings of your life *today* compared with your life *five years ago*. "Same" responses not shown.
Source: Surveys from 1964 to 1985 by Gallup.

PewResearchCenter

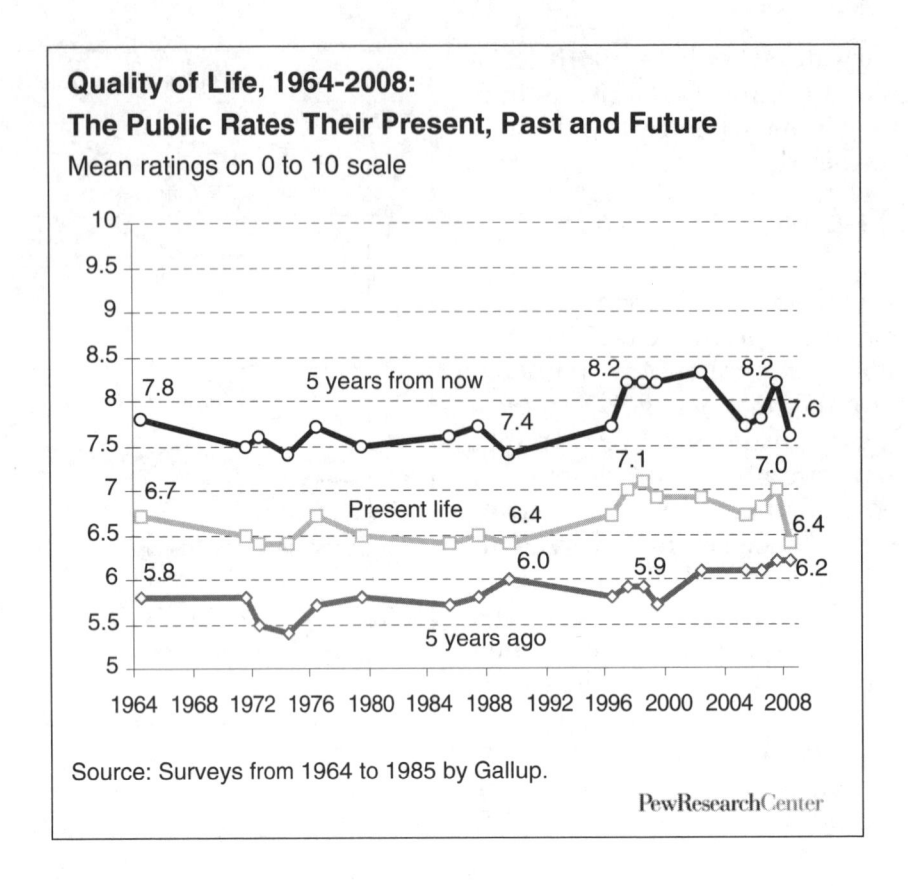

Quality of Life, 1964-2008:
The Public Rates Their Present, Past and Future

Mean ratings on 0 to 10 scale

5 years from now: 7.8, ..., 7.4, ..., 8.2, 8.2, 7.6
Present life: 6.7, ..., 6.4, ..., 7.1, 7.0, 6.4
5 years ago: 5.8, ..., 6.0, 5.9, 6.2

Source: Surveys from 1964 to 1985 by Gallup.

PewResearchCenter

Progress in Life, by Class

	All	Upper class	Middle class	Lower class
Mean rating (present)	6.4	7.3	6.7	5.2
	%	%	%	%
Present vs. Past				
Present better	41	51	42	30
Same	25	26	26	23
Present worse	31	22	28	44
Don't know/Refused	3	1	4	3
	100	100	100	100
Present vs. Future				
Future better	53	55	52	54
Same	23	30	24	16
Future worse	13	9	12	18
Don't know/Refused	11/100	6/100	12/100	12/100
Number of respondents	2413	522	1276	588

Note: Based on respondents who identified themselves as belonging to the lower, middle, or upper class.

PewResearchCenter

Americans in 2008 give their present life an average rating of 6.4 on the zero-to-ten scale. This is tied for the lowest mark on record for this question, and its falls well below the peak rating of 7.1 in 1998.

Today's respondents give their life five years ago an average rating of 6.2. This 0.2 point difference between today's current rating and today's five-years-ago rating is the smallest measure of progress ever recorded on this question. Looking ahead, today's respondents give the life they expect to be leading five years from now an average rating of 7.6. That is a bit below the historic norm, and the 1.2 point difference between the present and the future is about average.

DIFFERENCE BETWEEN THE CLASSES

Not surprisingly, the life ratings that people give themselves are closely correlated with the socioeconomic class they place themselves in. About half (49%) of those who say they are in the upper or upper middle class give their present life a high rating (8, 9 or 10 on the ten-point scale). Only a third (34%) of those who say they are middle class do the same, as do just 13% of those who say they are lower middle or lower class.

Those in the upper class are also more likely than those in the middle or lower classes to say their lives are better now than they were five years ago – 51% of the upper class say this, versus 42% of the middle class and 30% of the lower class. But when it comes to expectations for progress in the next five years, these differences disappear. Virtually identical shares of the upper (55%), middle (52%) and lower (54%) classes expect their lives will be better in five years. However, twice as many in the lower class (18%) as in the upper class (9%) think their lives will be worse, a view held by 12% of those in the middle. The remainder in all three classes think their lives will be the same, or they declined to answer.

DIFFERENCES WITHIN THE MIDDLE CLASS

Looking only at those who describe themselves as middle class – 53% of the public – one finds some demographic differences in the way people rate their quality of life, though these differences are relatively modest.

For example, those in the middle class who are ages 65 and above are more inclined than younger adults to give their lives one of the high ratings

How the Middle Class Sees Their Lives
How do you rate your present quality of life?

■ High (8-10) □ Medium (6-7) □ Low (0-5)

	High	Medium	Low
All middle class	34	36	28
Men	32	40	27
Women	37	32	29
White	36	37	26
Black	30	33	36
Hispanic	32	29	37
18-29	33	44	23
30-49	33	39	27
50-64	35	33	31
65+	40	24	32
Men, 18-49	27	46	25
Women, 18-49	38	36	26
Men, 50+	39	31	30
Women, 50+	36	28	33
College grad	40	41	18
Some college	35	40	25
HS grad or less	31	31	35
Family Income			
$100K+	47	36	17
$50K - $99K	32	45	23
$30K - $49K	32	38	29
Under $30K	31	27	40
Married	36	39	24
Not married	32	33	33

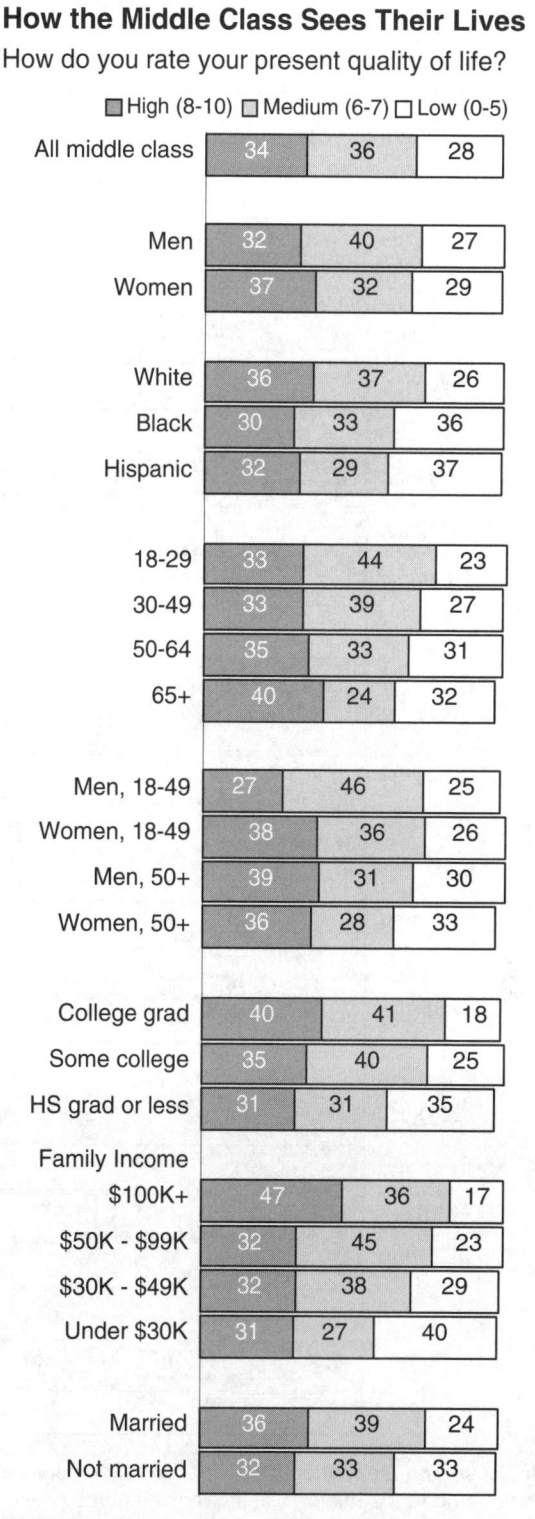

Note: Based on respondents who identified themselves as belonging to the middle class. Whites include only non-Hispanic whites. Blacks include only non-Hispanic blacks. Hispanics are of any race. Don't know responses are not shown.

PewResearchCenter

Moving Forward, Backward and Sideways
Compared with five years ago, my life is...

■ Better now □ Same □ Worse now

	Better	Same	Worse
All middle class	42	26	28
Men	43	28	26
Women	41	25	30
White	41	28	28
Black	48	22	28
Hispanic	39	21	33
18-29	55	17	25
30-49	49	23	25
50-64	39	30	30
65+	19	40	34
College grad	51	26	22
Some college	43	26	30
HS grad or less	37	27	30
Family Income $100K+	48	28	24
$50K - $99K	43	29	28
$30K - $49K	46	26	27
Under $30K	42	19	33
Married	43	30	25
Not married	42	23	31

Note: Based on respondents who identified themselves as belonging to the middle class. Whites include only non-Hispanic whites. Blacks include only non-Hispanic blacks. Hispanics are of any race. Don't know responses not shown.

PewResearchCenter

(40% do so). However, those in the 65 and over age group are also the most inclined to give their quality of life one of the lower ratings (32% rate their lives from 0 through 5), likely reflecting in part the health problems that come with old age.

Within the middle class, there is virtually no difference in life ratings between those who are married and those who are unmarried – with 36% and 32%, respectively, giving their lives one of the high ratings. On the educational front, those who have college or graduate degrees rate their lives somewhat better than do those with less educational attainment. Those with incomes above $100,000 give their lives higher marks than those with lower incomes. Fully 41% of the rural middle class gives their lives a top rating, compared with a just a third of the urban and suburban middle class. Finally, there is a difference on the gender front, especially between men and women under age 50. Some 38% of women in that age group give their lives one of the high ratings, compared with 27% of men.

Turning to the comparisons between life now and life five years ago, those in the middle class who are 18 to 49 years old are more inclined than those over 50 years old to see personal progress in this time frame. And older adults (ages 65 and above) are more likely than any other age group to say things are not as good now.

Another demographic difference on this measure of personal progress is related to race. More middle class blacks (48%) than whites (41%) or Hispanics (39%) say their lives have improved over the past five years.[14] Nevertheless, even with this more widespread sense of personal progress, middle class blacks still lag behind middle class whites in the ratings they give their current lives. These racial differences hold not just for middle class blacks and whites, but also for all blacks and whites. As for all Hispanics, they rate their present quality of life higher than blacks rate theirs, but lower than whites rate theirs.

When asked to envision their lives five years from now, middle class blacks once again stand out for their relative optimism. Two-thirds (67%) expect their lives to better than they are now; by contrast, only about half of the white and Hispanic middle class feels this way. The other big optimists

---

[14] Given the small sample size in this survey of blacks and Hispanics who self-identify as middle class, this finding falls short of statistical significance.

How the Middle Class Sees Their Lives

How do you rate your present quality of life?

■ High (8-10) ■ Medium (6-7) □ Low (0-5)

Group	High	Medium	Low
All middle class	34	36	28
Men	32	40	27
Women	37	32	29
White	36	37	26
Black	30	33	36
Hispanic	32	29	37
18-29	33	44	23
30-49	33	39	27
50-64	35	33	31
65+	40	24	32
Men, 18-49	27	46	25
Women, 18-49	38	36	26
Men, 50+	39	31	30
Women, 50+	36	28	33
College grad	40	41	18
Some college	35	40	25
HS grad or less	31	31	35
Family Income $100K+	47	36	17
$50K - $99K	32	45	23
$30K - $49K	32	38	29
Under $30K	31	27	40
Married	36	39	24
Not married	32	33	33

Note: Based on respondents who identified themselves as belonging to the middle class. Whites include only non-Hispanic whites. Blacks include only non-Hispanic blacks. Hispanics are of any race. Don't know responses are not shown.

PewResearchCenter

are the young. Almost three-quarters (74%) of 18-to-29 year olds who define themselves as middle class expect their lives to be better in five years. As people get older, this optimism steadily declines. Just four-in-ten members of the middle class who are ages 50-64 group think their lives will improve in five years, and fewer than one-in-five (19%) people ages 65 and above feel this way.

Within the self-defined middle class, differences in gender, marital status and region have little or no effect on the level of optimism about the progress in one's life over the next five years. However, those with at least some college education are more optimistic than those with a high school diploma or less.

WHO'S TURNED THE MOST SOUR ABOUT THEIR PERSONAL PROGRESS?

Americans in virtually every income level and demographic group have felt a sharp drop since the halcyon days of the late 1990s in their sense of personal progress. However, trend comparisons of responses from 1997 through 2008 show that those in the middle and upper income ranges register somewhat steeper declines than do those in the lower income group in their assessment of personal advancement today versus five years ago. During this same period, the ratings of the

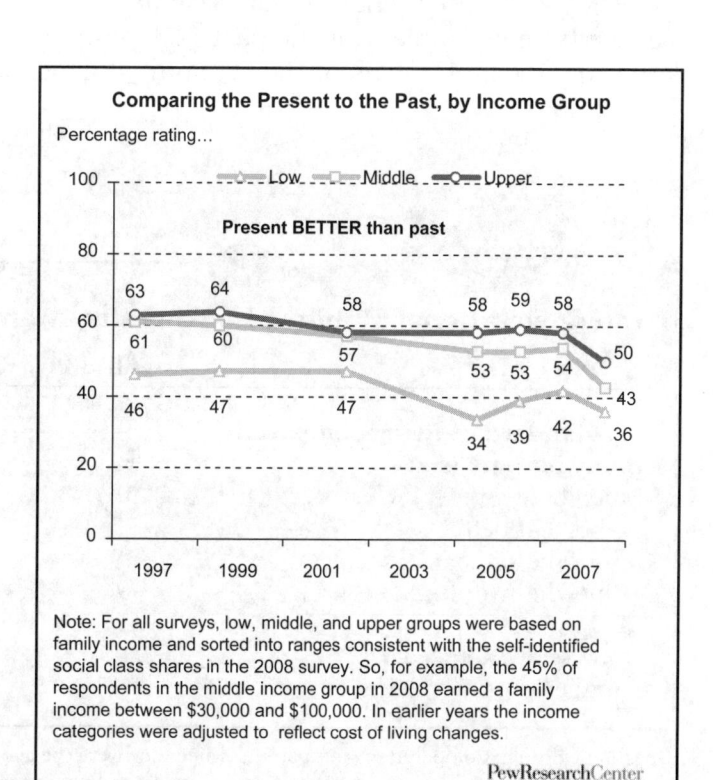

Comparing the Present to the Past, by Income Group

Percentage rating...

△ Low □ Middle ● Upper

Present BETTER than past

Year	Low	Middle	Upper
1997	46	61	63
1999	47	60	64
2001	47	57	58
2004	34	53	58
2005	39	53	59
2006	42	54	58
2007	36	43	50

Note: For all surveys, low, middle, and upper groups were based on family income and sorted into ranges consistent with the self-identified social class shares in the 2008 survey. So, for example, the 45% of respondents in the middle income group in 2008 earned a family income between $30,000 and $100,000. In earlier years the income categories were adjusted to reflect cost of living changes.

PewResearchCenter

present have fallen in roughly equal proportions among the lower, middle and upper groups.

DOING BETTER THAN MY PARENTS

Despite the stagnation that so many in the middle class feel about their lives in the past five years, their outlook is far more upbeat when they make judgments that encompass a longer time period.

Fully two-thirds of those in the middle class say their standard of living is better than the one their parents had when they were at the same stage of their lives. Moreover, just one-in ten say their standard of living is worse than their parents' was at the same stage of life.

The idea that each generation should outdo its parents' generation has always been one of the keystones of the American dream. In this Pew survey, even a plurality of those who say they are lower or lower-middle class see themselves as having made this journey. Nearly half (49%) of these respondents say they are doing better than their parents did at the same age, while 30% say they are doing worse. And, at the other end of the class rankings, fully 80% of those who describe themselves as upper or upper middle class say they're doing better than their parents, including 57% who say they are doing *much* better.

Looking at the full population, these assessments about inter-generational mobility have been extremely stable over the past 14 years, despite the ups and downs of the economy during this period.

WHAT ABOUT THE KIDS?

There *has* been some change, however, in a different measure of generational mobility—one that asks people to compare their own lives with the lives they expect their children to lead at the age they themselves are now.

The optimists outnumber the pessimists on this question, but not by nearly as lopsided a margin as they do on the question that asks people to rate their lives against their parents' lives. About half of the public (49%) say they expect their children to do better than them in life, while two-in-ten (21%) expect their children to do worse. The rest expect no difference or decline to answer. As recently as 2002, the public had been far more inclined to see their children besting them in life—61% felt this way, compared with just 10% who felt their children would do worse.

There are very few class differences on this question. Nearly identical shares of the self-defined upper, middle and lower class say they expect their children to best them in life. However, there is a difference by class in those who take a very dim view of their children's prospects. Fully 15% of the self-defined lower class say they expect their children to do *much* worse than them in life, a view shared by just 5% of those in the middle and upper class.

THE MIDDLE CLASS ASSESSES THE MIDDLE CLASS

There are several ways to look at how the middle class feels about the middle class standard of living. One is to ask them about their

Intergenerational Mobility: Looking Backward

My standard of living compared to my parents is ...	All	Upper class	Middle class	Lower class
	%	%	%	%
Much better	38	57	38	22
Somewhat better	27	23	29	27
About the same	19	13	21	19
Somewhat worse	9	5	7	17
Much worse	5	1	3	13
Don't know/Refused	2/100	1/100	2/100	2/100
Number of respondents	2413	522	1276	588

Question wording: Compared to your parents, when they were the age you are now, do you think your own standard of living now is much better, somewhat better, about the same, somewhat worse or much worse than theirs was?

PewResearchCenter

Intergenerational Mobility: Looking Forward

My children's standard of living compared to mine will be...	All	Upper class	Middle class	Lower class
	%	%	%	%
Much better	26	27	27	23
Somewhat better	23	25	24	22
About the same	20	25	20	14
Somewhat worse	14	12	14	16
Much worse	7	5	5	15
No children (VOL.)	5	4	5	4
Don't know/Refused	5/100	2/100	5/100	6/100
Number of respondents	2413	522	1276	588

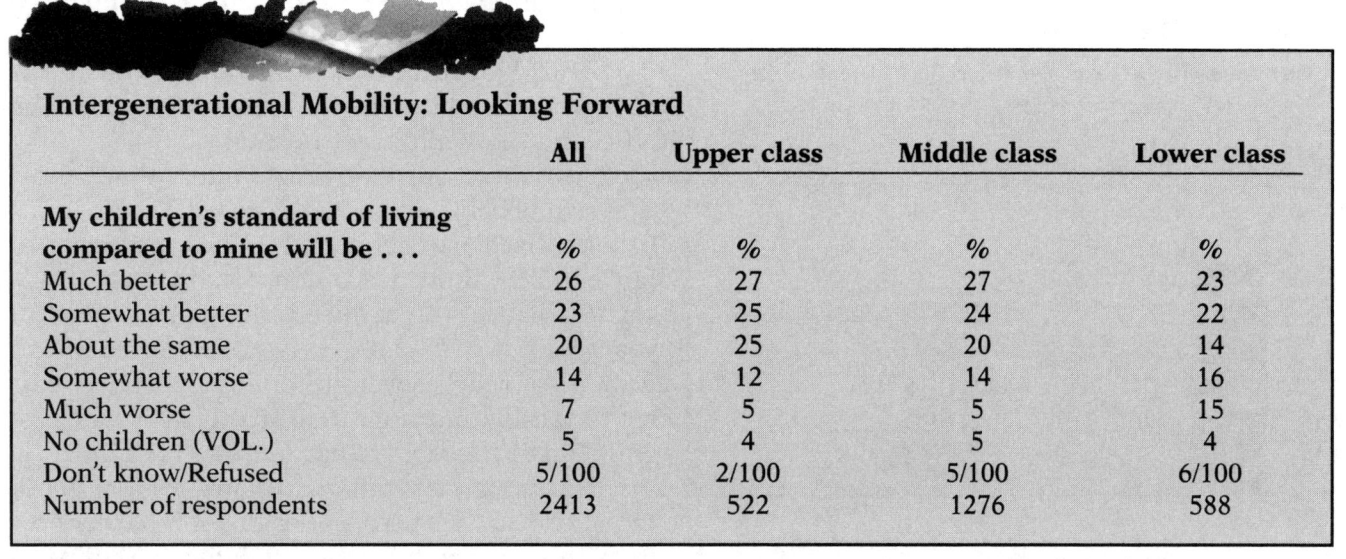

Question wording: When your children are at the age you are now, do you think their standard of living will be much better, somewhat better, about the same, somewhat worse, or much worse than yours is now?

PewResearchCenter

The Middle Class Blues

Compared with five years ago, is it more or less difficult for middle class people to maintain their standard of living?

	All	Upper class	Middle class	Lower class
	%	%	%	%
More difficult	79	72	78	89
Less difficult	12	15	13	7
About the same (VOL.)	6	11	6	1
Don't know/Refused	3/100	2/100	3/100	3/100
Number of respondents	2413	522	1276	588

Note: Based on resposndents who identified themselves as belonging to the lower, middle, or upper class.

PewResearchCenter

own lives. As we have shown in the preceding section, this line of inquiry yields a mixed verdict. Most people feel stagnant about their lives in the short term, but ahead of the game when they compare themselves with their parents.

But there is another perspective to consider. What happens when the middle class is asked to assess not their own lives, but the lives of the middle class?

Here, the responses turn broadly negative—to some degree, perhaps, reflecting the "I'm-okay-but-everyone-else-isn't" syndrome that has been familiar to social scientists since the dawn of public opinion survey research.

Fully 78% of those who describe themselves as middle class say it is more difficult now than five years ago for middle class people to maintain their standard of living. This view is so widely-held within the middle class that there are very few differences by demographic characteristic. However, middle class whites (81%) are a bit more inclined than middle class blacks (70%) or Hispanics (72%) to say that middle class life has grown more difficult. Also, 84% of those who are ages SO to 64 say life for the middle class has

The Middle Class Blues, 1986 and 2008

Compared with five years ago, is it more or less difficult for middle class people to maintain their standard of living?

■ More difficult   ☐ Less difficult   ☐ About the same (VOL)

	2008	1986
More difficult	79	65
Less difficult	12	22
About the same	6	9

Note: Don't know responses not shown.

PewResearchCenter

---

to maintain their standard of living is much more prevalent now than it was two decades ago. Today 79% of all adults say this, compared with the 65% who said the same thing in a 1986 survey by NBC and the Wall Street Journal.

The Pew survey also finds that most Americans believe that in the past 10 years it has become harder to get ahead in life, and easier to fall behind. About six-in-ten respondents (59%) say it is harder to get ahead today than it was 10 years ago; just 15% say it is easier to get ahead now. Also, nearly seven-in-ten (69%) say it is easier to fall behind now than it was 10 years ago, while just 11% say it is harder to fall behind.

The biggest class differences on questions about mobility deal with perceptions that it is harder now than 10 years ago to get ahead in life. Seven-in-ten of the self-described lower class feels this way, compared with 59% of the middle class and just 50% of the upper class. By contrast, on the question of whether it is easier to fall behind now than it was 10 years ago, there are virtually no differences by class; 71% of the lower class, 68% of the middle class and 68% of the upper class all agree.

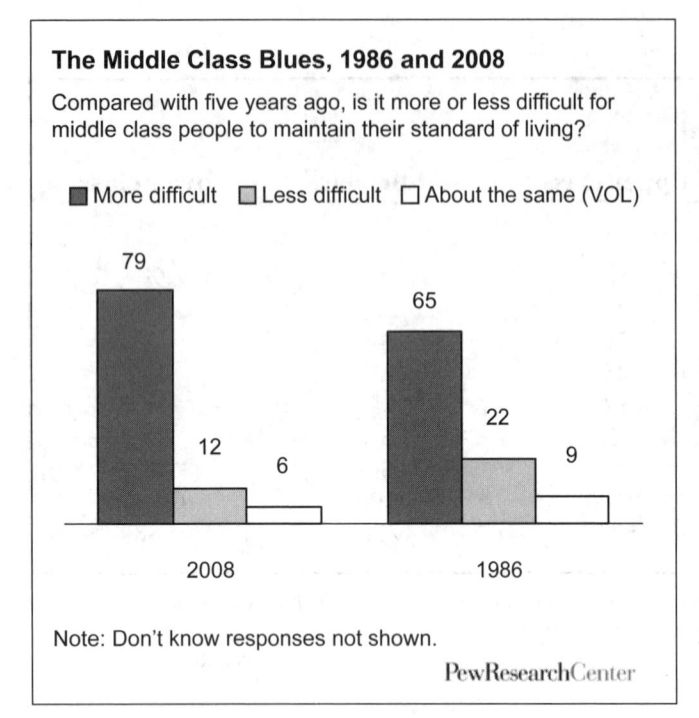

gotten more difficult—a slightly higher share than among younger or older adults who feel that way.

People who self-describe as upper and lower class also agree that life for the middle class has grown more difficult in the past five years. Nearly nine in ten (89%) of those who say they are lower or lower middle class say this, as do 72% of those who say they are upper or upper middle class.

Among the public as a whole, the view that it has become more difficult for middle class people

THE PUBLIC IS IN A SOUR MOOD ON MANY FRONTS

As this survey was in the field, much of the economic news agenda was devoted to reports about rising oil prices, falling housing prices, a turbu-

Easier to Fall Behind, Harder to Get Ahead

Compared with ten years ago, is it easier or harder today for people to . . .

	All	Upper class	Middle class	Lower class
	%	%	%	%
Get ahead				
Easier to get *ahead* today	15	15	16	11
Harder to get *ahead* today	59	50	59	70
Same as 10 years ago	24	33	23	17
Don't know/Refused	2/100	2/100	2/100	2/100
Fall behind				
Easier to fall *behind* today	69	68	68	71
Harder to fall *behind* today	11	7	10	16
Same as 10 years ago	18	23	19	11
Don't know/Refused	2/100	2/100	3/100	2/100
Number of respondents	2413	522	1276	588

PewResearchCenter

Public in a Sour Mood about Nation, Economy

	All	Upper class	Middle class	Lower class
	%	%	%	%
Satisfied with the way things are going in the country?				
Satisfied	30	38	32	17
Dissatisfied	62	58	60	72
Don't know/Refused	8/100	4/100	8/100	11/100
Describe state of the nation's economy				
Excellent	2	3	2	1
Good	21	29	23	12
Not so good	50	47	53	45
Poor	26	21	21	40
Don't know/Refused	1/100	*/100	1/100	2/100
Number of respondents	2413	522	1276	588

PewResearchCenter

lent mortgage market, and growing fears of a recession. Not surprisingly, the public's assessments about the state of the nation in general, and about the state of the national economy in particular, are quite downbeat.

Just three-in-ten Americans say they satisfied with the way things are going in the country, compared with 62% who are dissatisfied. Fully 72% of those in the lower-class say they are dissatisfied, compared with 60% in the middle class and 58% in the upper-class.

More than three-quarters of the public describes the economy as not so good (50%) or poor (26%). Here, too, there are some differences by class. Some 32% of the upper-class describes the economy as excellent or good, compared with 25% of the middle class and just 13% of the lower class.

What effect might these very negative assessments about the economy have on people's assessments of their own personal financial situation? If history is a guide, not much. As the chart to the right illustrates, the public's judgments about the national economy fluctuate widely in response to changing economic conditions, while their judgments about their own personal financial situation tend to be more stable.

Ratings for U.S. Economy and Own Financial Situation, 1992-2008

% of respondents saying "excellent or good"

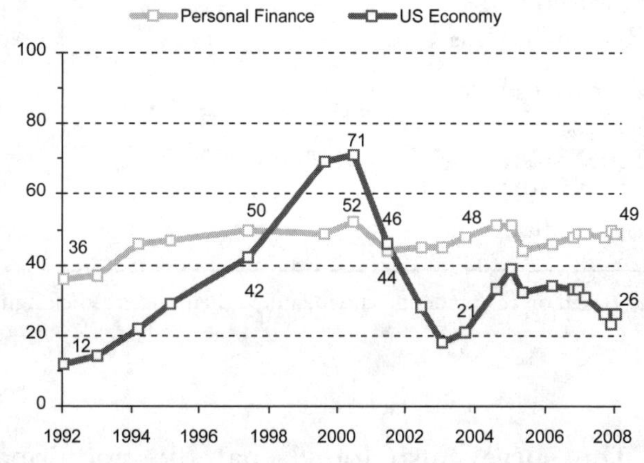

Question wording: How would you rate economic conditions in this country today as excellent, good, only fair, or poor? AND How would you rate your own personal financial situation? Would you say you are in excellent shape, good shape, only fair shape or poor shape financially? Source: Surveys on the US economy from 1992 to 2003 by Gallup; from 2004 to present by The Pew Research Center for the People and the Press. Personal finance data from 1992 and 1993 by U.S. News & World Report; from 1994 to present by the Pew Research Center for the People & the Press.

PewResearchCenter

Chapter 3: Middle Class Finances

The financial circumstances of the middle class range from comfortable and secure to stressed and uncertain. While most in the middle class report they have money to spend after the bills are paid, six-in-ten say that they faced at least some financial pressures in the past year—and about two-thirds expect to have problems in the year ahead.

Who's Comfortably Middle Class, and Who's Not?

Which phrase best describes your financial situation?

	Live Comfortably	Meet expenses, some left	Just meet expenses	Don't meet expenses	DK/Ref
	%	%	%	%	%
All middle class	39	37	20	3	1=100
Gender					
Male	43	35	18	3	1=100
Female	36	38	21	4	1=100
Race/Ethnicity					
White, non-Hispanic	42	38	17	2	1=100
Black, non-Hispanic	43	32	17	7	1=100
Hispanic	24	39	30	7	*=100
Age					
18-29	45	33	16	6	*=100
30-49	34	43	20	2	1=100
50-64	38	34	24	3	1=100
65+	46	33	18	3	0=100
Education					
College grad	45	40	14	1	*=100
Some college	41	40	18	1	*=100
HS grad or less	36	33	24	6	1=100
Family income					
$100,000+	53	33	13	1	*=100
$50K-$99K	42	44	13	*	1=100
$30K-$49K	37	39	21	3	*=100
LT $30,000	28	33	30	9	*=100

Note: Based on respondents who identified themselves as belonging to the middle class.

PewResearchCenter

The survey also found that the traditional relationship of home ownership and higher income remains particularly strong in the middle class. Still, many middle class homeowners also report feeling the strain: 21% say that they are living from paycheck to paycheck. That share is not appreciably different from other middle class Americans.

Overall, the survey finds that three-quarters of all middle class Americans say they either live comfortably (39%) or say they meet expenses with "a little left over" (3 7%). But for nearly a quarter of all middle class Americans, the monthly race to pay their bills ends, at best, in a dead heat, including 3% who say they don't meet expenses.

Hispanics and those with family incomes of less than $30,000 a year have the most trouble when it comes time to pay the bills: nearly four-in-ten of each group say they just meet their expenses or fall short. Notably, when asked to characterize their financial condition, similar proportions of middle class blacks (43%) and whites (42) describe their financial condition as "comfortable." The least financially pressured: the youngest and oldest. Nearly half of all middle class Americans ages 65 or over say they live comfortably (46%), and a third say they have a little extra left over each month. Similarly, a 45% plurality of those younger than 30 say they live comfortably while a third report having extra cash after their expenses are paid. Among those 30 to 64 years old about a third say they live comfortably.

THERE'S TROUBLE RIGHT HERE IN THE MIDDLE CLASS

To measure the extent to which the middle class is facing financial difficulties, survey respondents were asked if they had experienced each of five financial problems in the past year, ranging in severity from having to trim expenses to losing their job. An analysis of their responses suggests that, to some degree, financial strain is broadly felt throughout much of the middle class.

Predictably, the middle class faced fewer financial problems in the past year than the lower class but significantly more than those in the upper class. For example, about half of the middle class (53%) say they had to cut back on household spending in the past year, compared with 75% of those in the lower classes and just 36% of those who identify with the upper class. Also, one-in-ten middle class Americans say they lost their job in the past year, similar to the proportion of the upper class who say they were laid off or fired, but less than half the proportion of the lower class who say they lost their job (25%).

Middle class Americans also are less than half as likely as those in the lower class but nearly twice as likely as the upper class to have trouble paying housing expenses or to experience difficulties getting or paying for medical care.

Overall, six-in-ten middle class adults say they faced at least one of the five problems in the past year, and nearly a third (31%) report they had experienced two or more. Forty percent experienced none of the five problems, compared with just over half (56%) of all upper class Americans but only 15% of those who self-identified as lower class.

LOOKING AHEAD

Many in the middle class anticipate more economic problems in the year ahead. About half say it's likely that in the coming year they will have trouble saving money, while a similar proportion predict they will be forced to cut back on spending. A quarter predict they'll have trouble paying their bills. Two-in-ten say they probably will face all three problems.

Troubled Times...

Percentage who have experienced the following problems in the past year

	All	Upper	Middle	Lower
	%	%	%	%
Had to cut back on your household spending because money was tight	55	36	53	75
You or someone else in your household had to start working or take an extra job	24	10	21	42
Had trouble getting or paying for medical care	23	11	18	43
Had problems paying your rent or mortgage	16	5	12	33
Been laid off or lost your job	14	9	10	25

Percentage who experienced problems in the past year:

None of these things	37	56	40	15
One	27	28	29	22
Two or three	27	14	25	42
Four or more	9/100	2/100	6/100	21/100

Note: Based on respondents who identified themselves as belonging to the lower, middle, or upper class and also answered the five questions composing the index.

PewResearchCenter

...And More Trouble is Coming

Percentage who say it is likely they will experience the following in the coming year:

	All	Upper	Middle	Lower
	%	%	%	%
Have trouble paying your bills	31	14	25	60
Have trouble saving for the future	52	38	51	67
Have to cut back on household spending	54	37	50	77

Percentage that says it is likely they will experience problems in the coming year:

	All	Upper	Middle	Lower
	%	%	%	%
None of the problems	31	47	33	12
One	23	27	24	14
Two	22	16	23	27
All three	24	10	20	47

Note: Based on respondents who identified themselves as belonging to the lower, middle, or upper class and also answered the three questions composing the index.

PewResearchCenter

There is a predictable class division on most of these concerns. For example, 51% of the middle class say that in the coming year they will have trouble saving for the future, compared with 38% of the upper class and 67% of the lower class. A slightly different question produces a complementary result: Three-quarters of the middle class say they currently aren't saving as much money as they should—a finding confirmed by federal data which shows that the personal savings in this country has declined sharply in the past several decades.[15]

The survey also found that those who faced the most problems in the past year were the most likely to predict they'll have difficulties in the next 12 months. More than eight-in-ten middle class Americans who experienced at least three financial problems in the past year say they expected to face multiple financial challenges in the year ahead.

WHO'S HURTING?

The older, better educated and more affluent members of the middle class experienced relatively few financial problems in the past year. At the same time, minorities as well as those who are less financially well-off experienced comparatively more difficulties.

Fully half of all those with incomes of $100,000 or more experienced none of the five problems tested in the survey, compared with a third of whose family incomes are below $50,000. By contrast, a four-in-ten plurality of those in the middle class who earned the least experienced two or more problems.

Similarly, the better educated faced fewer problems than those with comparatively less schooling, in part because education and income are positively linked. Among college graduates, nearly half (46%) experienced none of the problems financial problems tested in the survey the previous year, compared with 23% of those who did not finish high school.

The differences by age apparent elsewhere in the survey are even more striking here. Middle class Americans who are ages 65 or older experienced remarkably few financial difficulties, large or small, in the past year: Fully two-thirds say they did not have to deal with any of the five problems tested in the survey. And seven-in-ten say they didn't have to trim expenses in the past 12 months, compared with less than half of all Americans.

HOME OWNERSHIP AND WEALTH

To help gauge the financial situation of America's middle class homeowners, our survey asked respondents if they owned a home, how much

---
[15] Federal Reserve Bank of San Francisco, *Economic Letter*, 2005-30, November 10, 2005.

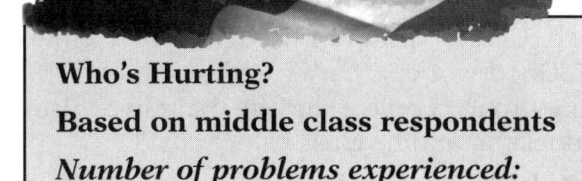

Who's Hurting?
Based on middle class respondents
Number of problems experienced:

	None	One	Two or More
Gender	%	%	%
Male	42	27	31
Under 50	*31*	*31*	*38*
50 or older	*58*	*20*	*22*
Female	38	31	31
Under 50	*30*	*31*	*39*
50 or older	*47*	*32*	*21*
Race/Ethnicity			
White, non-Hispanic	42	31	27
Black, non-Hispanic	35	25	40
Hispanic	25	27	48
Age			
18-29	30	28	42
30-49	31	33	36
50-64	41	30	29
65+	66	21	13
Retirement status			
Retired	60	26	14
Not retired	33	30	37
Education			
College grad+	46	30	24
Some college	38	29	33
High school grad	42	28	30
LT HS	23	30	47
Income			
Lt $50,000	34	25	41
50-100,000	39	34	27
100,000+	50	25	25

Note: Based on respondents who identified themselves as belonging to the middle class and also answered the five questions composing the index.

PewResearchCenter

Middle Class and Home Ownership

	Middle class
Values of One's Home	%
Less than $100,000	19
$100,000-$249,999	46
$250,000-$499,999	24
$500,000 or more	5
Don't know/Refused	6/100
Share of Mortgage Paid	
All	30
More than half	15
About half	12
Less than half	40
Don't know/Refused	3/100
Number of respondents	891

Note: Based on respondents who own a home and identified themselves as belonging to the middle class.

PewResearchCenter

of their home loans they had paid off, and what proportion of their total net worth was represented by the equity they had in their home. Almost one-in-five (19%) assesses their homes as being worth under $100,000. A plurality (46%) of middle class homeowners say that their homes are worth $100,000 to $250,000; 24 percent put this value as between $250,000 to $500,000; while 5 percent report their homes are worth $500,000 or more.

In terms of paying off their mortgages, 30 percent say they have paid them off in full. An additional 15 percent have paid off more than half their mortgages and 12 percent have paid off about one-half. That leaves 40 percent of the middle class homeowners with more than half of their mortgages still to be paid.

Nearly two-thirds of all middle class homeowners say their home represents at least half of their total assets, which includes business assets, savings, investments, and retirement accounts. More than a third (36%) say their home amounts to "about fifty percent" of their total holdings. An additional 29% estimate that the home equity is more than half of the total wealth while 27 percent say it is less than half.

Using these questions, we made a rough estimate of homeowners' total wealth holdings. Our median value of middle class home-owner wealth is $187,500 (which is very close to the 2004 Survey of Consumer Finances median net worth of homeowners of $185,000).

Using the median wealth estimate as a dividing line, we split all homeowners into a high-wealth group and a low-wealth group. The high-wealth homeowner group includes 30% of the middle class, and the low-wealth homeowner group includes about 29% of the middle class. The remainder of the middle class, 41%, consists of non homeowners and of homeowners who

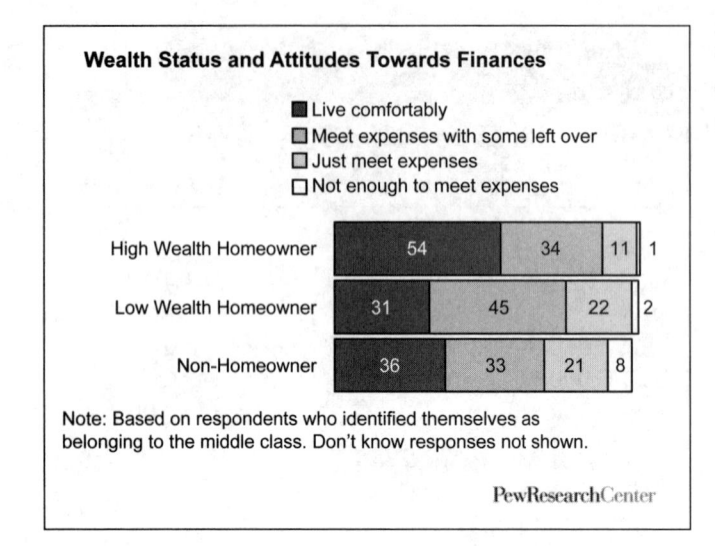

Wealth Status and Attitudes Towards Finances

- ■ Live comfortably
- ▨ Meet expenses with some left over
- ▥ Just meet expenses
- ☐ Not enough to meet expenses

Group	Live comfortably	Meet expenses with some left over	Just meet expenses	Not enough to meet expenses
High Wealth Homeowner	54	34	11	1
Low Wealth Homeowner	31	45	22	2
Non-Homeowner	36	33	21	8

Note: Based on respondents who identified themselves as belonging to the middle class. Don't know responses not shown.

PewResearchCenter

declined to answer questions about the value of their homes.[16]

These groups align reasonably closely with individuals' assessment of their own financial situation within the middle class. Among the high wealth group, more than half describe themselves as "living comfortably"; by contrast, only three-in-ten of the low wealth group say that about themselves.

Middle class non-homeowners are a more mixed group. Some 36 percent say that they live comfortably. This group is disproportionately young—41 percent are under 30 years old, compared with just 3 percent of the high-wealth group. Twenty-nine percent of this group has trouble meeting expenses, while 24% of low wealth homeowners and 12% of high wealth homeowners feel similarly stressed.

When comparing themselves to their parents at a similar age, both middle class home-owning groups are more likely than non-owners to say they live better than their parents did: 73 percent for the high wealth group, 69 percent for the low wealth group, and 61 percent for those who do not own their homes.

But more than half of the high-wealth group is more than 50 years of age, and many are past their peak earning years. Consequently, they are more likely than the other two groups to not expect their quality of life to rise in the next five years. Further, they are less likely to say that their quality of life is higher than five years earlier.

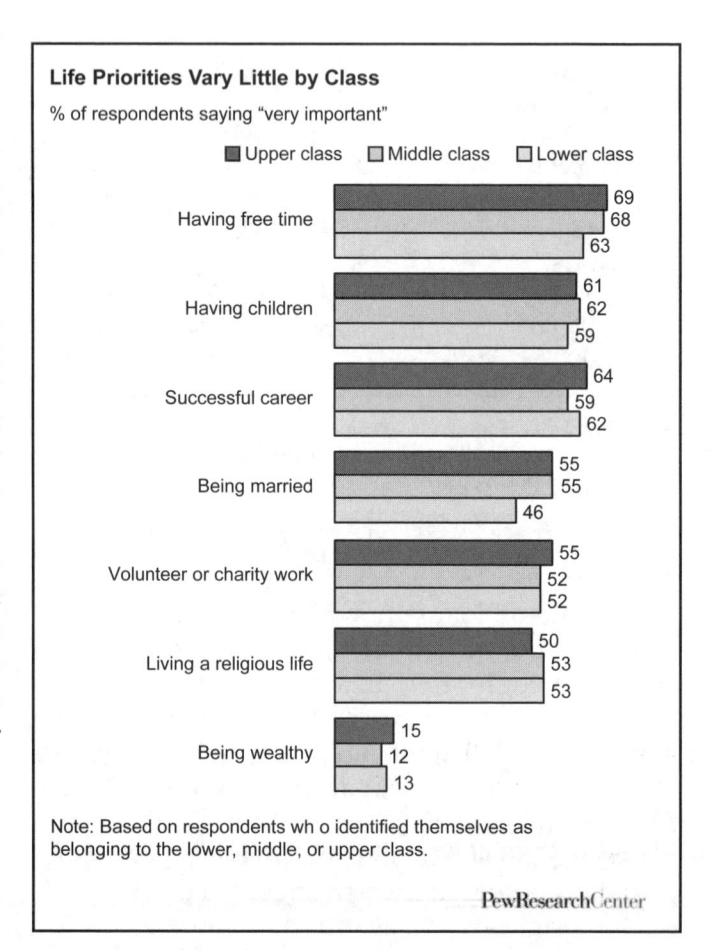

[16] About 10 percent of homeowners were included in the non-homeowner group because they declined to answer one of the three follow-up questions given to homeowners.

CHAPTER 4: MIDDLE CLASS PRIORITIES AND VALUES

Marriage. Career. Children. Religion. Free time. Wealth. Good works. That's a list of some of the big things that people value in their lives. But which does the middle class value most?

In a nation often portrayed as idealizing money and hard work, the answer given as "very important" most often among a list of seven items is free time—or as the Pew survey question puts it, "having enough time to do the things you want."

Some two-thirds (68%) of the self-identified middle class say that free time is very important to them. That's more than say the same about anything else on the list, including having children (62%), having a successful career (59%), being married (55%), living a religious life (53%), and donating to charity or doing volunteer work (52%). And having free time is many times more important than being wealthy, which was rated as very important by only 12% of the middle class.

When it comes to these life priorities, there is almost no class difference in the responses. Slightly higher shares of the middle class and upper class,

Life Priorities Vary Little by Class

% of respondents saying "very important"

■ Upper class   ▨ Middle class   ☐ Lower class

Priority	Upper	Middle	Lower
Having free time	69	68	63
Having children	61	62	59
Successful career	64	59	62
Being married	55	55	46
Volunteer or charity work	55	52	52
Living a religious life	50	53	53
Being wealthy	15	12	13

Note: Based on respondents who identified themselves as belonging to the lower, middle, or upper class.

PewResearchCenter

The Importance of Free Time by Age

% of middle class respondents saying "very important"

Free time

Age	%
18-29	71
30-49	75
50-64	64
65+	55

Note: Based on respondents who identified themselves as belonging to the middle class.

PewResearchCenter

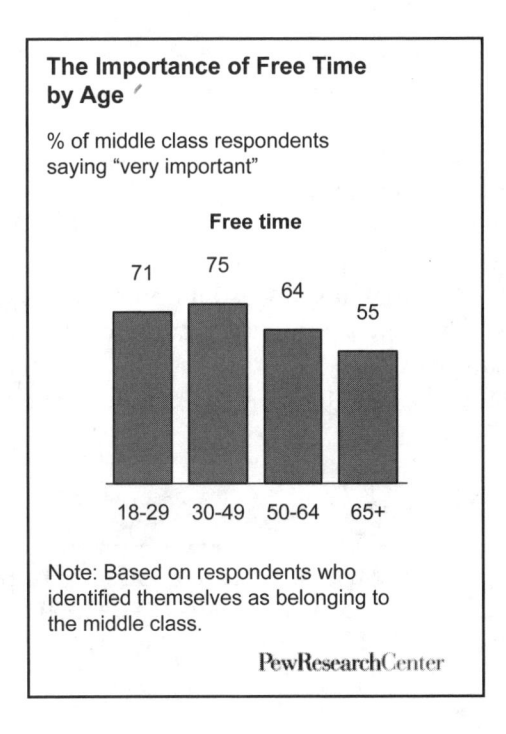

compared with the lower class, say that being married is very important to them. The upper class is slightly more likely than the middle and lower classes to say that being wealthy is very important. Other than that, the three classes respond to the questions about priorities in similar ways.

The finding about the widespread importance of free time raises intriguing questions. Is this a reaction to the stress of modern life? Is leisure-time shrinking for middle class Americans? And who values free time the most—those who already have it, or those who wish they did?

The last question is easiest to answer. Free time holds the most widespread appeal for those who are in demographic groups that would seem to have the least of it. Among the middle class, a greater share people who are employed (72%) than those who are not employed (66%) or are retired (57%) say that free time is very important to them. Similarly, 75% of adults who are in the busy middle years of life (ages 30 to 49) say that free time is very important to them, compared with just 55% of those who are ages 65 and older.

Using a broader measure of personal priorities, middle class mothers with children younger than 18 are slightly more likely to say that free time is somewhat or very important to them (98% do) than are fathers of minor children (91%). But what stands out more is that free time is so important to middle class Americans that there are few stark distinctions. Among all major demographic categories—by race or ethnicity, marital status and age—at least 90% say that free time is somewhat or very important.

The image of the American in a hurry has been a theme of literature and essays since the founding of the republic. It also has been a finding of social science surveys. In a 2004 General Social Survey, for example, 31% of Americans said they always feel rushed. That was significantly higher than the 25% who felt that way in 1982. The share of people who sometimes feel rushed stayed about the same (it was 54% in 2004). But the proportion that never feels rushed declined, from 22% in 1982 to 15% in 2004.

As for who feels most rushed, a 2005 Pew survey found that women are slightly more likely than men to say they are rushed. The gap is widest between working mothers of children younger than 18 (41%) and working fathers of children younger than 18 (26%).

However, this increased perception of being rushed comes as some recent findings from social science research indicate that Americans may have more free time now than they did several decades ago. Weekly leisure for men grew by at least six hours between 1965 and 2003, and for women by at least four hours, according to recent research by economists Mark Aguiar and Erik Hurst, who analyzed data from standardized time-use diaries kept over many decades by different people. Their work also found that the most educated Americans (those with college degrees) had the smallest gains in leisure time.

Not all researchers agree that leisure time has increased in recent decades; some cite other data indicating that Americans' work hours have expanded, reducing their free time. Even some of those who contend that free time has increased say that leisure time has become more fragmented or interrupted, and therefore less pleasant. For example, they point to a rise in multi-tasking and conclude that doing more than one activity at a time produces a more rushed leisure experience.

In short, there is no settled view from the academic community about whether Americans have more free time now than in the past. But no matter what the trends may show, a large majority of Americans today see free time as a major priority in their lives.

Questions for Discussion

1. Democracy is based on the principle of equality, while capitalism as an economic system inevitably leads to inequality. Are the two systems incompatible and destined to produce frustration or even cynicism? Will either capitalism or democracy dominate?
2. What are the strengths and weaknesses of the functional theory of inequality? Do the qualifications destroy the value of the theory? Why or why not?
3. Can you explain what public policy decisions were made throughout Europe and the OECD countries that have resulted in greater equality than is present in the United States?
4. If you were to recommend public policies to reduce inequality in the United States, what would you recommend? What are the negative consequences of your proposals?
5. Is there such a thing as an optimal amount of inequality? What criteria would you use to determine it?
6. Why is inequality increasing in the United States?

Useful Websites

Bureau of Labor Statistics, Consumer Expenditure Survey, http://stats.bls.gov/cex/home.htm

Census Bureau, http://www.census.gov/population/socdemo.

U.S. Office of Management and Budget, http://www.whitehouse.gove/omb/budget. World Trade Organization (WTO), http://www.wto.org.

Suggested Readings

Arjons, Maxime Ladaique, and Mark Pearson. *Growth, Inequality, and Social Protection*. Labor Market and Social Policy Occasional Paper no. 51. Paris: Organization for Economic Cooperation and Development, 2001.

Burtless, Gary. "Effects of Growing Wage Disparities and Changing Family Composition on the U.S. Income Distribution." *European Economic Review* 43 (May 1999).

Burtless, Gary, and Timothy Smeeding. "The Level, Trend, and Composition of Poverty." In Sheldon Danziger and Robert Haveman, eds., *Understanding Poverty: Progress and Problems*. Cambridge: Harvard University Press, 2001.

Danziger, Sheldon, and Jane Waldfogel, eds. *Securing the Future: Investing in Children from Birth to College*. New York: Russell Sage, 2000.

Forster, Michael, and Michele Pellizzari. *Trends and Driving Factors in Income Distribution and Poverty in the OECD Area*. Occasional Paper no. 42. Paris: Organization for Economic Cooperation and Development, 2000.

Gerreira, Francisco H.G. *Inequality and Economic Performance: A Brief Overview to Theories of Growth and Distribution*. Washington, D.C.: World Bank, 1999.

Kawachi, Ichiro, and Bruce P. Kennedy. *The Health of Nations: Why Inequality Is Harmful to Your Health*. New York: New Press, 2002.

Notes

1. *Labor Journal*, October 17, 1941, p. 18.
2. See Page Smith, *A New Age Now Begins* (New York: McGraw-Hill, 1976), for a detailed discussion of the importance of this idea.
3. Garry Wills develops the thesis that the idea of all men being created equal was more than just rhetoric. See Garry Wills, *Inventing America: Jefferson's Declaration of Independence* (New York: Doubleday, 1978).
4. Thomas Jefferson, *The Papers of Thomas Jefferson*, vol. 8, edited by Julian P. Boyd (Princeton: Princeton University Press, 1953), p. 682.
5. Ibid.
6. See http://www.quotegarden.com/poverty.html.
7. Alexis de Tocqueville, *Democracy in America*, cited in William Ebenstein and Alan Ebenstein, *Great Political Thinkers* (New York: Harcourt Brace, 1991), p. 641.

8. John Maynard Keynes, *The General Theory of Employment, Interest and Money* (London: Macmillan, 1936), p. 372.
9. Thomas Frank, *What's the Matter with Kansas? How Conservatives Won the Heart of America* (New York metropolitan Books, 2004).
10. Robert Putnam, "The Strange Disappearance of Civic America," American Prospect, Winter 1996, pp. 34–48. See also Sidney Verba, Kay Schlozman, and Henry Brady, Voice and Equality: Participation in American Politics (Cambridge: Harvard University Press, 1996).
11. Associated Press, "Corporate PAC's Backed Republicans 10 to 1," New York Times, November 26, 2004.
12. Gary Burtless and Christopher Jencks, "American Inequality and Its Consequences," in Henry J. Aaron, James M. Lindsay, and Pietro S. Nivola, eds., *Agenda for the Nation* (Washington, D.C.: Brookings Institution, 2003), p. 62.
13. The Pew Research Center for the People and the Press reports that 84 percent of those making $75,000 or more are registered to vote, compared to just 66 percent of those earning $20,000–$29,000, and only 60 percent of those earning less than $20,000. See Pew Research Center for the People and the Press, *Evenly Divided and Increasingly Polarized: 2004 Political Landscape* (Washington, D.C.: Pew Research Center for the People and the Press, November 5, 2003), pt. 6, "Cynicism, Trust, and Participation," p. 5.
14. See http://www.quotegarden.com/politics.html.
15. See James Willis, Martin Primack, and Richard Baltz, *Explorations in Economics*, 3rd ed. (Redding, Calif.: CAT, 1990), p. 43.
16. Martin Dooley and Peter Gottschalk, "Earnings Inequality Among Males in the United States: Trends and the Effects of Labor Force Growth," *Journal of Political Economy* 92, no. 1 (1984): 59–89. For women the annual increase in wages was about 1 percent faster than for men. The gap between high- and low-wage females is increasing as well, just not as rapidly as for men.
17. Marvin Kosters and Murray Ross, "The Influence of Employment Shifts and New Job Opportunities on the Growth and Distribution of Real Wages," in Phillip Cagan and Eduardo Somensatto, eds., *Deficits, Taxes, and Economic Adjustments* (Washington, D.C.: American Enterprise Institute, 1987).
18. See Barry Bluestone and Bennett Harrison, *The Great American Job Machine: The Proliferation of Low Wage Employment in the U.S. Economy*, Report to the Joint Economic Committee of the U.S. Congress, December 1986.
19. Jared Bernstein, "Facts and Figures: Income," in Jared Bernstein, *The State of Working America 2004/2005* (Washington, D.C.: Economic Policy Institute, 2005), http://www.epinet.org, p. 2.
20. See Gary Burtless, "International Trade and the Rise in Earnings Inequality," *Journal of Economic Literature* 33 (June 1995): 800–816.
21. For a time, there was debate among scholars over whether wage inequality was increasing, and whether real wages had declined in absolute terms. The trends and data are now clear, and there is general agreement that both trends are occurring. See especially Bennett Harrison, Barry Bluestone, and Chris Tilly, "Wage Inequality Takes a Great U-Turn," *Challenge* 29 (March-April 1986): 26–32. See also Bennett Harrison and Barry Bluestone, *The Great U-Turn: Corporate Restructuring and the Polarizing of America* (New York: Basic Books, 1988).
22. Robert Putnam, "Bowling Alone: America's Declining Social Capital," *Journal of Democracy* (January 1995): 34–35.
23. See http://www.cookpolitical.com/races/report_pdfs/2004_house_competitive_oct8.pdf.
24. See, for example, Pew Research Center for the People and the Press, *Evenly Divided*. See also http://www.trinity.edu/mkearl/equalize3.jpg; *U.S. News and World Report*, August 7, 1989, p. 29; and more recently, Marc Suhrcke, *Preferences for Inequality: East vs. West*, Working Paper no. 89 (Florence: Unesco Innocenti Center, October 2001).
25. See especially Robert Heilbroner and Lester Thurow, Economics Explained, rev. ed. (Englewood Cliffs, N.J.: Prentice-Hall, 1994), pp. 216–218. Our discussion on the bias in favor of equality relies heavily on this source.
26. See http://www.quotegarden.com/humility.html.
27. Economic discrimination occurs when duplicate factors of production receive different payments for equivalent contributions to output. This definition is difficult to test because of the difficulty of measuring all the relevant market characteristics. For example, the average female earns less than the average male. Women are less likely to have majored in a technical subject than are men. It might not be discrimination if a woman with a high school diploma receives a lower salary than a man with a college degree (although discrimination might help in explaining their educational achievements). It is too simplistic to try to

measure discrimination by merely comparing the typical incomes of different groups. The question is not, "Do women earn less than men?" but rather, "Do women earn less than men *with like market characteristics* (work experience, age, education, etc.)?"

28. We could achieve the same goal without yielding to inequality by financing the investment through taxation and government purchases (public investment) rather than through private investment through savings.

29. The functional theory of inequality is a variation on the **marginal productivity** theory (MPT) of distribution, which holds that the income of any factor will be determined by the contribution that each factor makes to the revenue of the endeavor. Its income will be higher or lower depending on the ability and willingness of the suppliers of land, labor, and capital to enter the market at different prices. But at each price, factors will earn amounts equal to the marginal revenue they produce. The result, in theory, is that there cannot be exploitation of any factor in a perfect market.

    The functional theory challenges the assumption of the MPT that a perfect market exists. If it does not, then the earnings of each factor may not reflect their contribution to output. The MPT cannot explain the variation of incomes due to nonmarket factors such as discrimination, imperfect markets, and other factors.

30. Kingsley Davis and Wilbert Moore, *Some Principles of Stratification*, Reprint Series in Social Science (New York: Columbia University Press, 1993).

31. Ibid, p. 37.

32. James Madison, in *The Federalist* no. 10, clearly states that it is a primary function of governments to protect individual freedom, which will lead to inequalities in income based on differing abilities and interests. He notes that this is the basis for factions, which he laments. The most common and enduring source of factions is the unequal distribution of property. This poses a major dilemma for governmental administration.

33. Milton Friedman, *Capitalism and Freedom* (Chicago: University of Chicago Press, 1962), p. 167.

34. See Doug Bandow, "Doctors Operate to Cut Out Competition," *Business and Society Review*, no. 58 (Summer 1986): 4–10. Bandow illustrates that entry into the medical profession is essentially controlled through the use of licensing arrangements, which increase health care costs and decrease the options available to patients.

35. Bernstein, "Facts and Figures: Income."

36. Jared Bernstein, "Facts and Figures: Inequality," in Bernstein, *State of Working America 2004/2005*.

37. Mary H. Cooper, "Income Inequality," *CQ Researcher*, April 17, 1998, p. 341. See also *Forbes*, 2004 list of world's richest people, http://www.forbes.com/lists/results.jhtml.

38. Edward N. Wolff, *Top Heavy: A Study of the Increasing Inequality of Wealth in America* (New York: Twentieth Century Fund, 1995), p. 6.

39. Timothy Smeeding, *Globalization, Inequality, and the Rich Countries of the G-20: Evidence from the Luxembourg Income Study* (Syracuse, NY: Maxwell School of Citizenship and Public Affairs, July 2002), p. 7.

40. Carmen DeNavas-Walt, Bernadette D. Proctor, and Robert J. Mills, "Income, Poverty, and Health Insurance Coverage in the United States: 2003," in U.S. Census Bureau, *Current Population Reports* (Washington, D.C.: U.S. Government Printing Office, August 2004), p. 36.

41. Harrison and Bluestone, *Great U-Turn*.

42. Francis Green, Andrew Henley, and Euclid Tsakalotos, *Income Inequality in Corporatist and Liberal Economies: A Comparison of Trends Within OECD Countries*, Studies in Economics (Canterbury, UK: University of Kent, November 1992), p.13.

43. Burtless and Jencks, "American Inequality," p. 77.

44. Ibid., p. 80.

45. Simon Kuznets, "Economic Growth and Income Inequality," *American Economic Review* 45, no. 1 (March 1955): 1–28.

46. Robert J. Lampman, *The Share of Top Wealth-Holders in National Wealth, 1922–1956* (Princeton: Princeton University Press, 1962). Other research confirmed the Kuznets-Lampman research in various countries. See Peter Lindert and Jeffrey Williamson, *Explorations in Economic History* 22 (1985): 341–377.

47. Burtless, "International Trade," pp. 80–81 (emphasis in original).

48. Kevin Phillips, *Arrogant Capital: Washington, Wall Street, and the Frustration of American Politics* (Boston: Little, Brown, 1994). Phillips continues the theme in *American Dynasty: Aristocracy, Fortune, and the Politics of Deceit in the House of Bush* (New York: Viking, 2004). William E. Simon's *A Time for Truth* (New York: Reader's Digest Press,

1978) is sometimes cited as a call to arms for U.S. business to recover the privileges it lost after 1929.

49. See John Kenneth Galbraith, *The Culture of Contentment* (New York: Houghton Mifflin, 1992).
50. Arthur M. Okun, *Equality and Efficiency: The Big Tradeoff* (Washington, D.C.: Brookings Institution, 1975).
51. Aaron Bernstein, "Waking Up from the American Dream," *Business Week*, December 1, 2003.
52. Paul Krugman, "The Death of Horatio Alger," *The Nation*, January 5, 2004, p. 16.
53. As quoted in ibid.
54. See especially Richard G. Wilkinson, *Unhealthy Societies: The Afflictions of Inequality* (London: Routledge, 1996). See also B. Kennedy, I. Kawachi, and D. Prothrow-Stith, "Income Distribution and Mortality: Cross Sectional Ecological Study of the Robin Hood Index in the United States," *British Medical Journal* 312 (1996): 1004–1007.
55. See Ichiro Kawachi, Bruce Kennedy, and Richard Wilkinson, eds., *The Society and Population Healthreader*, vol. 1, *Income Inequality and Health* (New York: New Press, 1999).
56. George Kaplan, E. Pamuk, J. W. Lynch, R. D. Cohen, and J. L. Balfour, "inequality in Income and Mortality in the United States: Analysis of Mortality and Potential Pathways," *British Medical Journal* 312 (1996) 999–1003. See also John Lynch, George Davey Smith, George Kaplan, and James House, "Income Inequality and Mortality: Importance to Health of Individual Income, Psychosocial Environment, or Material Conditions" *British Medical Journal* 320 (2000): 1200–1204.
57. See Thad Williamson, "Social Movements Are Good for Your Health," *Dollars and Sense*, May 2001, p. 7. See also Robert Putnam, *Bowling Alone: The Collapse and Revival of American Community* (New York: Simon and Schuster, 2000). Putnam analyzes the decline of social ties in the United States. He argues that social ties and strong communities are important to human well-being, particularly in the area of health.
58. Michael Marmot, "The Social Pattern of Health and Disease," in David Blane, Eric Brunner, and Richard Wilkinson, eds., *Health and Social Organization: Towards a Health Policy for the Twenty-First Century* (New York: Routledge, 1996).
59. Alejandro Reuss, "Cause of Death: Inequality—Mortality Statics Analysis, United States—Statistical Data Included," *Dollars and Sense*, May 2001.
60. Marmot, "Social Pattern."
61. Burtless and Jencks, "American Inequality," p. 95.
62. See ibid., pp. 98–102, for an excellent discussion of these issues.
63. John Rawls, *A Theory of Justice* (Cambridge: Harvard University Press, 1971).
64. Robert Nozick, *Anarchy, State, and Utopia* (New York: Basic Books, 1974).
65. Inaugural address, January 21, 1961.
66. U.S. Conference of Catholic Bishops, "Labor Day Statement" (Washington, D.C.: Office of Domestic Social Development, September 3).

Foreign Policy

chapter **8**

Models of International Relations and Foreign Policy

Ole R. Holsti

Universities and professional associations usually are organized in ways that tend to separate scholars in adjoining disciplines and perhaps even to promote stereotypes of each other and their scholarly endeavors. The seemingly natural areas of scholarly convergence between diplomatic historians and political scientists who focus on international relations have been underexploited, but there are also a few welcome signs that this may be changing. These include recent essays suggesting ways in which the two disciplines can contribute to each other; a number of prize-winning dissertations, later turned into books, by political scientists during the past decade that effectively combine political science theories and historical research and materials; collaborative efforts among scholars in the two disciplines; and the appearance of such interdisciplinary journals as *International Security* that provide an outlet for historians and political scientists with common interests.[1]

This essay is an effort to contribute further to an exchange of ideas between the two disciplines by describing some of the theories, approaches, and "models" that political scientists have used in their research on international relations during recent decades. A brief essay cannot do justice to the entire range of models that may be found in the current literature, if only because the period has witnessed a proliferation of approaches. But perhaps the models described here, when combined with citations to some representative works, will provide diplomatic historians with a useful, if sketchy, road map toward some of the more prominent landmarks in a neighboring discipline. Because "classical realism" is the most venerable and persisting model of international relations, it provides a good starting point and baseline for comparison with competing models. Robert Gilpin may have been engaging in hyperbole when he questioned whether our understanding of international relations has advanced significantly since Thucydides, but one must acknowledge that the latters analysis of the Peloponnesian War includes concepts that are not foreign to contemporary students of balance-of-power politics.[2]

Following a discussion of classical realism, an examination of "modern realism" will identify the continuities and differences between the two approaches. The essay then turns to several models that challenge one or more core premises of both classical and modern realism. The first two challengers focus on the system level: Global-Society/Complex-Interdependence models and Marxist/World-System/Dependency models. Subsequent sections discuss several "decision-making" models, all of which share a skepticism about the adequacy of theories that focus on the structure of the international system while neglecting political processes within units that comprise the system.

Three limitations should be stated at the outset. Each of the three systemic and three decision-making approaches described below is a composite of several models; limitations of space have made it necessary to focus on the common denominators rather than on subtle differences among them. This discussion will also avoid purely methodological issues and debates; for example, what Stanley Hoffmann calls "the battle of the literates versus the numerates."[3] Finally, efforts of some political scientists to develop "formal" or mathematical approaches to international relations are neglected here; such abstract, often ahistorical models are likely to be of limited interest to historians.[4] With these caveats, let me turn now to classical realism, the first of the systemic models to be discussed in this essay.

There have always been Americans, such as Alexander Hamilton, who viewed international relations from a realist perspective, but its contemporary intellectual roots are largely European.

Three important figures of the interwar period probably had the greatest impact on American scholarship: the historian E. H. Carr, the geographer Nicholas Spykman, and the political theorist Hans J. Morgenthau. Other Europeans who have contributed significantly to realist thought include John Herz, Hedley Bull, Raymond Aron, and Martin Wight, while notable Americans of this school include scholars Arnold Wolfers and Norman Graebner, as well as diplomat George F. Kennan, journalist Walter Lippmann, and theologian Reinhold Niebuhr.[5]

Although realists do not constitute a homogeneous school—any more than do any of the others discussed in this essay—most of them share at least five core premises about international relations. To begin with, they view as central questions the causes of war and the conditions of peace. They also regard the structure of the international system as a necessary if not always sufficient explanation for many aspects of international relations. According to classical realists, "structural anarchy," or the absence of a central authority to settle disputes, is the essential feature of the contemporary system, and it gives rise to the "security dilemma": in a self-help system one nation's search for security often leaves its current and potential adversaries insecure, any nation that strives for absolute security leaves all others in the system absolutely insecure, and it can provide a powerful incentive for arms races and other types of hostile interactions. Consequently, the question of *relative* capabilities is a crucial factor. Efforts to deal with this central element of the international system constitute the driving force behind the relations of units within the system; those that fail to cope will not survive. Thus, unlike "idealists" or "liberal internationalists," classical realists view conflict as a natural state of affairs rather than a consequence that can be attributed to historical circumstances, evil leaders, flawed sociopolitical systems, or inadequate international understanding and education.[6]

A third premise that unites classical realists is their focus on geographically based groups as the central actors in the international system. During other periods the major entities may have been city states or empires, but at least since the Treaties of Westphalia (1648), states have been the dominant units. Classical realists also agree that state behavior is rational. The assumption behind this fourth premise is that states are guided by the logic of the "national interest," usually defined in terms of survival, security, power, and relative capabilities. To Morgenthau, for example, "rational foreign policy minimizes risks and maximizes benefits." Although the national interest may vary according to specific circumstances, the similarity of motives among nations permits the analyst to reconstruct the logic of policymakers in their pursuit of national interests—what Morgenthau called the "rational hypothesis"—and to avoid the fallacies of "concern with motives and concern with ideological preferences."[7]

Finally, the nation-state can also be conceptualized as a *unitary* actor. Because the central problems for states are starkly defined by the nature of the international system, their actions are primarily a response to external rather than domestic political forces. At best, the latter provide very weak explanations for external policy. According to Stephen Krasner, for example, the state "can be treated as an autonomous actor pursuing goals associated with power and the general interest of the society."[8] However, classical realists sometimes use domestic politics as a residual category to explain deviations from rational policies.

Realism has been the dominant model of international relations during at least the past five decades, perhaps in part because it seemed to provide a useful framework for understanding World War II and the Cold War. Nevertheless, the classical versions articulated by Morgenthau and others have received a good deal of critical scrutiny. The critics have included scholars who accept the basic premises of realism but who found that in at least four important respects these theories lacked sufficient precision and rigor.

Classical realism usually has been grounded in a pessimistic theory of human nature, either a theological version (e.g., St. Augustine and Reinhold Niebuhr), or a secular one (e.g., Machiavelli, Hobbes, and Morgenthau). Egoism and self-interested behavior are not limited to a few evil or misguided leaders, as the idealists would have it, but are basic to *homo politicus* and thus are at the core of a realist theory. But according to its critics, because human nature, if it means anything, is a constant rather than a variable, it is an unsatisfactory explanation for the full range of international relations. If human nature explains war and conflict, what accounts for peace and cooperation? In order to avoid this problem, most modern realists have turned their attention from human nature to the structure of the international system to explain state behavior.

In addition, critics have noted a lack of precision and even contradictions in the way classical realists use such concepts as "power," "national interest," and "balance of power."[9] They also see possible contradictions between the central descriptive and prescriptive elements of classical realism. On the one hand, nations and their leaders "think and act in terms of interests defined as power," but, on the other, statesmen are urged to exercise prudence and self-restraint, as well as to recognize the legitimate national interests of other nations.[10] Power plays a central role in classical realism, but the correlation between the relative power balance and political outcomes is often less than compelling, suggesting the need to enrich analyses with other variables. Moreover, the distinction between "power as capabilities" and "useable options" is especially important in the nuclear age.

While classical realists have typically looked to history and political science for insights and evidence, the search for greater precision has led many modern realists to look elsewhere for appropriate models, analogies, metaphors, and insights. The discipline of choice is often economics, from which modern realists have borrowed a number of tools and concepts, including rational choice, expected utility, theories of firms and markets, bargaining theory, and game theory. Contrary to the assertion of some critics, however, modern realists *share* rather than reject the core premises of their classical predecessors.[11]

The quest for precision has yielded a rich harvest of theories and models, and a somewhat less bountiful crop of supporting empirical applications. Drawing in part on game theory, Morton Kaplan described several types of international systems—for example, balance-of-power, loose bipolar, tight bipolar, universal, hierarchical, and a unit-veto system in which any action requires the unanimous approval of all its members. He then outlined the essential rules that constitute these systems. For example, the rules for a balance-of-power system are: "(1) increase capabilities, but negotiate rather than fight; (2) fight rather than fail to increase capabilities; (3) stop fighting rather than eliminate an essential actor; (4) oppose any coalition or single actor that tends to assume a position of predominance within the system; (5) constrain actors who subscribe to supranational organizational principles; and (6) permit defeated or constrained essential actors to re-enter the system."[12] Richard Rosecrance, J. David Singer, Karl Deutsch, Bruce Russett, and many others, although not necessarily realists, also have developed models which seek to understand international relations by virtue of system-level explanations. Andrew M. Scott's survey of the literature, which yielded a catalogue of propositions about the international system, also illustrates the quest for greater precision in systemic models.[13]

Kenneth Waltz's *Theory of International Politics*, the most prominent effort to develop a rigorous and parsimonious model of "modern" or "structural" realism, has tended to define the terms of a vigorous debate during the past decade. It follows and builds upon another enormously influential book in which Waltz developed the Rousseauian position that a theory of war must include the system level (what he called the "third image") and not just first (theories of human nature) or second (state attributes) images. Why war? Because there is nothing in the system to prevent it.[14]

Theory of International Relations is grounded in analogies from microeconomics; international politics and foreign policy are analogous to markets and firms. Oligopoly theory is used to illuminate the dynamics of interdependent choice in a self-help anarchical system. Waltz explicitly limits his attention to a structural theory of international systems, eschewing the task of linking it to a theory of foreign policy. Indeed, he doubts that the two can be joined in a single theory and he is highly critical of many system-level analysts, including Morton Kaplan, Stanley Hoffmann, Richard Rosecrance, Karl Deutsch and J. David Singer, and others, charging them with various errors, including "reductionism"; that is, defining the system in terms of the attributes or interactions of the units.

In order to avoid reductionism and to gain rigor and parsimony, Waltz erects his theory on the foundations of three core propositions that define the structure of the international system. The first concentrates on the principles by which the system is ordered. The contemporary system is anarchic and decentralized rather than hierarchical; although they differ in many respects, each unit is formally equal.[15] A second defining proposition is the character of the units. An anarchic system is composed of similar sovereign units and therefore the functions that they perform are also similar rather than different; for example, all have the task of providing for their own security. In contrast, a hierarchical system would be characterized by some type of division of labor, as is the case in domestic politics. Finally, there is a distribution of capabilities among units in the system. Although capabilities are a unit-level attribute, the distribution of capabilities is a system-level concept.[16]

A change in any of these elements constitutes a change in system structure. The first element of structure as defined by Waltz is a quasi-constant because the ordering principle rarely changes, and the second element drops out of the analysis because the functions of units are similar as long as the system remains anarchic. Thus, the last of the three attributes, the distribution of capabilities, plays the central role in Waltz's model.

Waltz uses his theory to deduce the central characteristics of international relations. These include some non-obvious propositions about the contemporary international system. For example, with respect to system stability (defined as maintenance of its anarchic character and no consequential variation in the number of major actors) he concludes that: because the present bipolar system reduces uncertainty, it is more stable than alternative structures; interdependence has declined rather than increased during the twentieth century, a tendency that has actually contributed to stability; and the proliferation of nuclear weapons may contribute to rather than erode system stability.[17]

Unlike some system-level models, Waltz's effort to bring rigor and parsimony to realism has stimulated a good deal of further research, but it has not escaped controversy and criticism.[18] Leaving aside highly charged polemics—for example, that Waltz and his supporters are guilty of engaging in a "totalitarian project of global proportions"—most of the vigorous debate has centered on four alleged deficiencies relating to interests and preferences, system change, misallocation of variables between the system and unit levels, and an inability to explain outcomes.[19]

Specifically, a spare structural approach suffers from an inability to identify completely the nature and sources of interests and preferences because these are unlikely to derive solely from the structure of the system. Ideology or domestic considerations may often be at least as important. Consequently, the model is also unable to specify adequately how interests and preferences may change. The three defining characteristics of system structure are too general, moreover, and thus they are not sufficiently sensitive to specify the sources and dynamics of system change. The critics buttress their claim that the model is too static by pointing to Waltz's assertion that there has only been a single structural change in the international system during the past three centuries.

Another drawback is the restrictive definition of system properties, which leads Waltz to misplace, and therefore neglect, elements of international relations that properly belong at the system level. Critics have focused on his treatment of the destructiveness of nuclear weapons and interdependence. Waltz labels these as unit-level properties, whereas some of his critics assert that they are in fact attributes of the system.

Finally, the distribution of capabilities explains outcomes in international affairs only in the most general way, falling short of answering the questions that are of central interest to many analysts. For example, the distribution of power at the end of World War II would have enabled one to predict the rivalry that emerged between the United States and the Soviet Union, but it would have been inadequate for explaining the pattern of relations between these two nations—the Cold War rather than withdrawal into isolationism by either or both, a division of the world into spheres of influence, or World War III.[20] In order to do so, it is necessary to explore political processes *within* states—at minimum within the United States and the USSR—as well as *between* them.

Robert Gilpin shares with Waltz the core assumptions of modern realism, but his study of *War and Change in World Politics* also attempts to cope with some of the criticism leveled at Waltz's theory by focusing on the dynamics of system change. Drawing upon both economic and sociological theory, his model is based on five core propositions. The first is that the international system is stable—in a state equilibrium—if no state believes that it is profitable to attempt to change it. Second, a state will attempt to change the status quo of the international system if the expected benefits outweigh the costs; that is, if there is an expected net gain for the revisionist state. Related to this is the proposition that a state will seek change through territorial, political, and economic expansion until the marginal costs of further change equal or exceed the marginal benefits. Moreover, when an equilibrium between the costs and benefits of further change and expansion is reached, the economic costs of maintaining the status quo (expenditures for military forces, support for allies, etc.) tend to rise faster than the resources needed to do so. An equilibrium exists when no powerful state believes that a change in the system would yield additional net benefits. Finally, if the resulting disequilibrium between the existing governance of the international system and the redistribution of power is not resolved, the system will be changed and a new equilibrium reflecting the distribution of relative capabilities will be established.[21]

Unlike Waltz, Gilpin includes state-level processes in order to explain change. Differential economic growth rates among nations—a structural-systemic level variable—play a vital role in his explanation for the rise and decline of great powers, but his model also includes propositions about the law of diminishing returns on investments, the impact of affluence on martial spirits and on the ratio of consumption to investment, and structural change in the economy.[22] Table 8.1 summarizes some key elements of realism. It also contrasts them to two other system-level models of international relations—the Global-Society/Complex-Interdependence and the Marxist/World-System/Dependency models, to which we now turn our attention.

Just as there are variants of realism, there are several Global Society/Complex-Interdependence (GS/CI) models, but this discussion focuses on two common denominators; they all challenge the first and third core propositions of realism identified earlier, asserting that inordinate attention to the war/peace issue and the nation-state renders it an increasingly anachronistic model of global relations.[23] The agenda of critical problems confronting states has been vastly expanded during the twentieth century. Attention to the issues of war and peace is by no means misdirected, according to proponents of a GS/CI perspective, but concerns for welfare, modernization, the environment, and the like are today no less potent sources of motivation and action. The diffusion of knowledge and technology, combined with the globalization of communications, has vastly increased popular expectations. The resulting demands have outstripped resources and the ability of existing institutions—notably the sovereign nation-state—to cope effectively with them. Interdependence arises from an inability of even the most powerful states to cope, or to do so unilaterally or at acceptable levels of cost and risk, with issues ranging from trade to AIDS, and immigration to environmental threats.

Paralleling the widening agenda of critical issues is the expansion of actors whose behavior can have a significant impact beyond national boundaries; indeed, the cumulative effects of their actions can have profound consequences for the international system. Thus, although nation-states continue to be important international actors, they possess a declining ability to control their own destinies. The aggregate effect of actions by multitudes of non-state actors can have potent effects that transcend political boundaries. These may include such powerful or highly visible non-state organizations as Exxon, the Organization of Petroleum Exporting Countries, or the Palestine Liberation Organization. On the other hand, the cumulative effects of decisions by less powerful or less visible actors may also have profound international consequences. For example, decisions by thousands of individuals, mutual funds, banks, pension funds, and other financial institutions to sell securities on 19 October 1987 not only resulted in an unprecedented "crash" on Wall Street, but also within hours its consequences were felt throughout the entire global financial system. Governments might take such actions as loosening credit or even closing exchanges, but they were largely unable to contain the effects of the panic.

The widening agenda of critical issues, most of which lack a purely national solution, has also led to creation of new actors that transcend political boundaries; for example, international organizations, transnational organizations, non-government organizations, multinational corporations, and the like. Thus, not only does an exclusive focus on the war/peace issue fail to capture the complexities of contemporary international life but it also blinds the analyst to the institutions, processes, and norms that permit cooperation and significantly mitigate some features of an anarchic system. In short, according to GS/CI perspectives, an adequate understanding of the emergent global system must recognize that no single model is likely to be sufficient for all issues, and that if it restricts attention to the manner in which states deal with traditional

TABLE 8.1

Three Models of the International System

	Realism	Global Society	Marxism
Type of model	Classical: descriptive and normative Modern: deductive	Descriptive and normative	Descriptive and normative
Central problems	Causes of war Conditions of peace	Broad agenda of social, economic, and environmental issues arising from gap between demands and resources	Inequality of exploitation Uneven development
Conception of current international system	Structural anarchy	Global society Complex interdependence (structure varies by issue-area)	World capitalist system
Key actors	Geographically based units (tribes, city-states, nation-states, etc.)	Highly permeable nation-states *plus* a broad range of onstate actors, including IOs, IGOs, NGOs, and individuals	Classes and their agents
Central motivations	National interest Security Power	Human needs and wants	Class interests
Loyalties	To geographically based groups (from tribes to nation-states)	Loyalties to nation-state declining To emerging global values and institutions that transcend those of the nation-state and/or to sub-national groups	To class values and interests that transcend those of the nation-state
Central processes	Search for security and survival	Aggregate effects of decisions by national and nonnational actors How units (not limited to nation-states) cope with a growing agenda of threats and opportunities arising from human wants	Modes of production and exchange International division of labor in a world capitalist system
Likelihood of system transformation	Low (basic structural element of system have revealed an ability to persist despite many other kinds of changes)	High in the direction of the model (owing to the rapid pace of technological change, etc.)	High in the direction of the model (owing to inherent contradiction within the world capitalist system)
Sources of theory, insights, and evidence	Politics History Economics (especially 'modern' realists)	Broad range of social sciences Natural and technological sciences	Marxist-Leninist theory (several variants)

security concerns, it is more likely to obfuscate than clarify the realities of contemporary world affairs.

The GS/CI models have several important virtues. They recognize that international behavior and outcomes arise from a multiplicity of motives, not merely security, at least if security is defined solely in military or strategic terms. They also alert us to the fact that important international processes and conditions originate not only in the actions of nation-states but also in the aggregated behavior of other actors. These models not only enable the analyst to deal with a broader agenda of critical issues but, more importantly, they force one to contemplate a much richer menu of demands, processes, and outcomes than would be derived from power-centered realist models. Stated differently, GS/CI models are more sensitive to the possibility that politics of trade, currency, immigration, health, the environment, and the like may significantly and systematically differ from those typically associated with security issues.

On the other hand, some GS/CI analysts underestimate the potency of nationalism and the durability of the nation-state. Two decades ago one of them wrote that "the nation is declining in its importance as a political unit to which allegiances are attached."[24] Objectively, nationalism may be an anachronism but, for better or worse, powerful loyalties are still attached to nation-states. The suggestion that, because even some well-established nations have experienced independence movements among ethnic, cultural, or religious minorities, the sovereign territorial state may be in decline is not wholly persuasive. Indeed, that evidence perhaps points to precisely the opposite conclusion: In virtually every region of the world there are groups which seek to create or restore geographically based entities in which its members may enjoy the status and privileges associated with sovereign territorial statehood. Evidence from Poland to Palestine, Spain to Sri Lanka, Estonia to Eritrea, Armenia to Afghanistan, and elsewhere seems to indicate that obituaries for nationalism may be somewhat premature.

The notion that such powerful non-national actors as major multinational corporations (MNC) will soon transcend the nation-state seems equally premature. International drug rings do appear capable of dominating such states as Colombia and Panama. However, the pattern of outcomes in confrontations between MNCs and states, including cases involving major expropriations of corporate properties, indicate that even relatively weak nations are not always the hapless pawns of the MNCs. Case studies by Joseph Grieco and Gary Gereffi, among others, indicate that MNC-state relations yield a wide variety of outcomes.[25]

Underlying the GS/CI critique of realist models is the view that the latter are too wedded to the past and are thus incapable of dealing adequately with change. At least for the present, however, even if global dynamics arise from multiple sources (including non-state actors), the actions of nation-states and their agents would appear to remain the major sources of change in the international system. However, the last group of systemic models to be considered, the Marxist/World-System/Dependency (M/WS/D) models, downplays the role of the nation-state even further.

As in other parts of this essay, many of the distinctions among M/WS/D models are lost by treating them together and by focusing on their common features, but in the brief description possible here only common denominators will be presented. These models challenge both the war/peace and state-centered features of realism, but they do so in ways that differ sharply from challenges of GS/CI models.[26] Rather than focusing on war and peace, these models direct attention to quite different issues, including uneven development, poverty, and exploitation within and between nations. These conditions, arising from the dynamics of the modes of production and exchange, are basic and they must be incorporated into any analysis of intra- and inter-nation conflict.

At a superficial level, according to adherents of these models, what exists today may be described as an international system—a system of nation-states. More fundamentally, however, the key groups within and between nations are classes and their agents: As Immanuel Wallerstein put it, "in the nineteenth and twentieth centuries there *has* been only one world system in existence, the world capitalist world-economy."[27] The "world capitalist system" is characterized by a highly unequal division of labor between the periphery and core. Those at the periphery are essentially the drawers of water and the hewers of wood, whereas the latter appropriate the surplus of the entire world economy. This critical feature of the world system not only gives rise to and perpetuates a widening rather than narrowing gap between the wealthy core and poor periphery but also to a dependency relationship from which the latter are unable to break loose. Moreover, the class structure within the core, characterized by a growing gap between capital and labor, is faithfully reproduced in the periphery so that elites there share with their counterparts in the core an interest in perpetuating the system. Thus, in contrast to realist theories, M/WS/D models encompass and integrate theories of both the global and domestic arenas.

M/WS/D models have been subjected to trenchant critiques.[28] The state, nationalism, security dilemmas, and related concerns essentially drop out of these analyses; they are at the theoretical periphery rather than at the core: "Capitalism was from the beginning an affair of the world-economy" Wallerstein asserts, "not of nation-states."[29] A virtue of many M/WS/D models is that they take a long historical perspective on world affairs rather than merely focusing on contemporary issues. However, by neglecting nation-states and the dynamics arising from their efforts to deal with security in an anarchical system—or at best relegating these actors and motivations to a minor role—M/WS/D models lose much of their appeal. Models of world affairs during the past few centuries that fail to give the nation-state a central role seem as deficient as analyses of *Hamlet* that neglect the central character and his motivations.

Second, the concept of "world capitalist system" is central to these models, but its relevance for the late twentieth century can be questioned. Whether this term accurately describes the world of the 1880s could be debated, but its declining analytical utility or even descriptive accuracy for international affairs of the 1980s seems clear. Thus, one can question Wallerstein's assertion that "there are today no socialist systems in the world economy any more than there are feudal systems because there is only *one world system*. It is a world-economy and it is *by definition capitalist* in form."[30] Where within a system so defined do we locate the USSR or Eastern Europe? This area includes enough "rich" industrial nations that it hardly seems to belong in the periphery. Yet to place these states in the core of a "world capitalist system" would require terminological and conceptual gymnastics of a high order. Does it increase our analytical capabilities to describe the USSR and East European countries as "state capitalists?" Where do we locate China in this conception of the system? How do we explain dynamics within the "periphery," or the differences between rapid-growth Asian nations such as South Korea, Taiwan, or Singapore, and their slow-growth neighbors in Bangladesh, North Korea, and the Philippines? The inclusion of a third structural position—the "semi-periphery"—does not wholly answer these questions.

Third, M/WS/D models have considerable difficulty in explaining relations between non-capitalist nations—for example, between the USSR and its East European neighbors or China—much less outright conflict between them. Indeed, advocates of these models usually have restricted their attention to West-South relations, eschewing analyses of East-East or East-South relations. Does one gain greater and more general analytical power by using the lenses and language of Marxism or of realism to describe relations between dominant and lesser nations; for example, the USSR and Eastern Europe, the USSR and India or other Third World nations, China and Vietnam, India and Sri Lanka, or Vietnam and Kampuchea? Are these relationships better described and understood in terms of such M/WS/D categories as "class" or such realist ones as "relative capabilities?"

Finally, the earlier observations about the persistence of nationalism as an element of international relations seem equally appropriate here. Perhaps national loyalties can be dismissed as prime examples of "false consciousness," but even in areas that have experienced almost two generations of one-party Communist rule, as in Poland, evidence that feelings of solidarity with workers in the Soviet Union or other nations have replaced nationalist sentiments among Polish workers is in short supply.

Many advocates of realism recognize that it cannot offer fine-grained analyses of foreign policy behavior and, as noted earlier, Waltz denies that it is desirable or even possible to combine theories of international relations and foreign policy. Decision-making models challenge the premises that it is fruitful to conceptualize the nation as a unitary rational actor whose behavior can adequately be explained by reference to the system structure—the second, fourth, and fifth realist propositions identified earlier—because individuals, groups, and organizations acting in the name of the state are also sensitive to pressures and constraints other than international ones, including elite maintenance, electoral politics, public opinion, pressure group activities, ideological preferences, and bureaucratic politics. Such core concepts as "the national interest" are not defined solely by the international system, much less by its structure alone, but they are also likely to reflect elements within the domestic political arena. Thus, rather than assuming with the realists that the state can be conceptualized as a "black box"— that the domestic political processes are both hard to comprehend and quite unnecessary for explaining its external behavior—decision-making analysts believe one must indeed take these internal processes into account, with special attention directed at decision-makers and their "definitions of the situation."[31] To reconstruct how nations deal with each other, it is necessary to view the situation through the eyes of those who act in the name of the nation-state: decision makers, and the group and bureaucratic-organizational contexts within which they act. Table 8.2 provides an overview of three major types of decision-making models that form the subject for the remainder of this essay, beginning with bureaucratic-organizational models.[32]

Traditional models of complex organizations and bureaucracy emphasized the positive contributions to be expected from a division of labor, hierarchy, and centralization, coupled with expertise, rationality, and obedience. Such models assumed that clear boundaries should be maintained between politics and decision making, on the one hand, and administration and implementation on the other. Following pioneering works by Chester I. Barnard, Herbert Simon, James G. March and Simon, and others, more recent theories depict organizations quite differently.[33] The central premise is that decision making in bureaucratic organizations is not constrained only by the legal and formal norms that are intended to enhance the rational and eliminate the capricious aspects of bureaucratic behavior. Rather, all (or most) complex organizations are seen as generating serious "information pathologies."[34] There is an *emphasis* upon rather than a denial of the political character of bureaucracies, as well as on other "informal" aspects of organizational behavior. Complex organizations are composed of individuals and units with conflicting perceptions, values, and interests that may arise from parochial self-interest ("what is best for my bureau is also best for my career"), and also from different perceptions of issues arising ineluctably from a division of labor ("where you stand depends on where you sit"). Organizational norms and memories, prior policy commitments, normal organizational inertia routines, and standard operating procedures may shape and perhaps distort the structuring of problems, channeling of information, use of expertise, and implementation of executive decisions. The consequences of bureaucratic politics within the executive branch or within the government as a whole may significantly constrain the manner in which issues are defined, the range of options that may be considered, and the manner in which executive decisions are implemented by subordinates. Consequently, organizational decision making is essentially political in character, dominated by bargaining for resources, roles and missions, and by compromise rather than analysis.[35]

Perhaps owing to the dominant position of the realist perspective, most students of foreign policy have only recently incorporated bureaucratic-organizational models and insights into their analyses. An ample literature of case studies on budgeting, weapons acquisitions, military doctrine, and similar situations confirms that foreign and defense policy bureaucracies rarely conform to the Weberian "ideal type" of rational organization.[36] Some analysts assert that crises may provide the motivation and means for reducing some of the non-rational aspects of bureaucratic behavior: crises are likely to push decisions to the top of the organization where a higher quality of intelligence is available; information is more likely to enter the top of the hierarchy directly, reducing the distorting effects of information processing through several levels of the organization; and broader, less parochial values may be invoked. Short decision time in crises reduces the opportunities for decision making by bargaining, logrolling, incrementalism, lowest-common-denominator values, "muddling through," and the like.[37]

However, even studies of international crises from a bureaucratic-organizational perspective are not uniformly sanguine about decision making in such circumstances. Graham T. Allisons analysis of the Cuban missile crisis identified several critical bureaucratic malfunctions concerning dispersal of American aircraft in Florida, the location of the naval blockade, and

Table 8.2

Three Models of Decision Making

	Bureaucratic politics	Group dynamics	Individual decision making
Conceptualization of decision making	Decision making as the result of bargaining within bureaucratic organizations	Decision making as the product of group interaction	Decision making as the result of individual choice
Premises	Central organizational values are imperfectly internalized Organizational behavior is political behavior Structure and SOPs affect substance and quality of decisions	Most decisions are made by small elite groups Group is different than the sum of its members Group dynamics affect substance and quality of decisions	Importance of subjective appraisal (definition of the situation) and cognative processes (information processing, etc.)
Constraints on rational decision making	Imperfect information, resulting from: centralization, hierarchy, and specialization Organizational inertia Conflict between individual and organizational utilities Bureaucratic politics and bargaining dominate decision making and implementation of decisions	Groups may be more effective for some tasks, less for others Pressures for conformity Risk-taking propensity of groups (controversial) Quality of leadership "Groupthink"	Cognitive limits on rationality Information processing distorted by cognitive consistency dynamics (unmotivated biases) Systematic and motivated biases in causal analysis Individual differences in abilities related to decision making (e.g., problem-solving ability, tolerance of ambiguity, defensiveness and anxiety, information seeking, etc.)
Sources of theory, insights, and evidence	Organization theory Sociology of bureaucracies Bureaucratic politics	Social psychology Sociology of small groups	Cognitive dissonance Cognitive psychology Dynamic psychology

grounding of weather reconnaissance flights from Alaska that might stray over the Soviet Union. Richard Neustadt's study of two crises involving the United States and Great Britain revealed significant misperceptions of each other's interests and policy processes. And an examination of three American nuclear alerts found substantial gaps in understanding and communication between policymakers and the military leaders who were responsible for implementing the alerts.[38]

Critics of some organizational-bureaucratic models and the studies employing them have directed their attention to several points.[39] They point out, for instance, that the emphasis on bureaucratic bargaining fails to differentiate adequately between the positions of the participants. In the American system, the president is not just another player in a complex bureaucratic game. Not only must he ultimately decide but he also selects who the other players will be, a process that may be crucial in shaping the ultimate decisions. If General Matthew Ridgway and Attorney General Robert Kennedy played key roles in the American decisions not to intervene in Indochina in 1954 or not to bomb Cuba in 1962, it was because Presidents Eisenhower and Kennedy chose to accept their advice rather than that of other officials. Also, the conception of bureaucratic bargaining tends to emphasize its non-rational elements to the exclusion of genuine intellectual differences diat may be rooted in broader concerns—including disagreements on what national interests, if any, are at stake in a situation—rather than narrow parochial interests. Indeed, properly managed, decision processes that promote and legitimize "multiple advocacy" among officials may facilitate high-quality decisions.[40]

These models may be especially useful for understanding the slippage between executive decisions and foreign policy actions that may arise during implementation, but they may be less valuable for explaining the decisions themselves. Allisons study of the Cuban missile crisis does not indicate an especially strong correlation between bureaucratic roles and evaluations of the situation or policy recommendations, as predicted by his "Model III" (bureaucratic politics), and recently published transcripts of deliberations during the crisis do not offer more supporting evidence for that model.[41] On the other hand, Allison does present some compelling evidence concerning policy implementation that casts considerable doubt on the adequacy of "Model I" (the traditional realist conception of the unitary rational actor).

Another decision-making model used by some political scientists supplements bureaucratic-organizational models by narrowing the field of view to top policymakers. This approach lends itself well to investigations of foreign policy decisions, which are usually made in a small-group context. Some analysts have drawn upon sociology and social psychology to assess the impact of various types of group dynamics on decision making.[42] Underlying these models are the premises that the group is not merely the sum of its members (thus decisions emerging from the group are likely to be different than what a simple aggregation of individual preference and abilities might suggest), and that group dynamics, the interactions among its members, can have a significant impact on the substance and quality of decisions.

Groups often perform better than individuals in coping with complex tasks owing to diverse perspectives and talents, an effective division of labor, and high-quality debates centering on evaluations of the situation and policy recommendations for dealing with it. Groups may also provide decision makers with emotional and other types of support that may facilitate coping with complex problems. On the other hand, they may exert pressures for conformity to group norms, thereby inhibiting the search for information and policy options or cutting it off prematurely, ruling out the legitimacy of some options, curtailing independent evaluation, and suppressing some forms of intragroup conflict that might serve to clarify goals, values, and options. Classic experiments by the psychologist Solomon Asch revealed the extent to which group members will suppress their beliefs and judgments when faced with a majority adhering to the contrary view, even a counterfactual one.[43]

Drawing upon a series of historical case studies, social psychologist Irving L. Janis has identified a different variant of group dynamics, which he labels "groupthink" to distinguish it from the more familiar type of conformity pressure on "deviant" members of the group.[44] Janis challenges the conventional wisdom that strong cohesion among the members of a group invariably enhances performance. Under certain conditions, strong cohesion can markedly degrade the group's performance in decision making. Thus, the members of a cohesive group may, as a means of dealing with the stresses of having to cope with consequential problems and in order to bolster self-esteem, increase the frequency and intensity of face-to-face interaction. This results in a greater identification with the group and less competition within it. The group dynamics of what Janis calls "concurrence seeking" may displace or erode reality testing and sound information processing and judgment. As a consequence, groups may be afflicted by unwarranted feelings of optimism and invulnerability, stereotyped images of adversaries, and inattention to warnings. Janis's analyses of both "successful" (the Marshall Plan, the Cuban missile crisis) and "unsuccessful" (Munich Conference of 1938, Pearl Harbor, the Bay of Pigs invasion) cases indicate that "groupthink" or other decision-making pathologies are not inevitable, and he develops some guidelines for avoiding them.[45]

Still other decision-making analysts focus on the individual. Many approaches to the policymaker emphasize the gap between the demands of the classical model of rational decision making and the substantial body of theory and evidence about various constraints that come into play in even relatively simple choice situations.[46] The more recent perspectives, drawing upon cognitive psychology, go well beyond some of the earlier formulations that drew upon psychodynamic theories to identify various types of psychopathologies among political leaders: paranoia, authoritarianism, the displacement of private motives on public objects, etc.[47] These more recent efforts to include information-processing behavior of the individual decision maker in foreign policy analyses have been directed at the cognitive and motivational constraints that, in varying degrees, affect the decision-making performance of "normal" rather than pathological subjects. Thus, attention is directed to all leaders, not merely those, such as Hitler or Stalin, who display evidence of clinical abnormalities.

The major challenges to the classical model have focused in various ways on limited human capabilities for performing the tasks required by objectively rational decision making. The cognitive constraints on rationality include limits on the individual's capacity to receive, process, and assimilate information about the situation; an inability to identify the entire set of policy alternatives; fragmentary knowledge about the consequences of each option; and an inability to order preferences on a single utility scale.[48] These have given rise to several competing conceptions of the decision maker and his or her strategies for dealing with complexity, uncertainty, incomplete or contradictory information, and, paradoxically, information overload. They variously characterize the decision maker as a problem solver, naive or intuitive scientist, cognitive balancer, dissonance avoider, information seeker, cybernetic information processor, and reluctant decision maker.

Three of these conceptions seem especially relevant for foreign policy analysis. The first views the decision maker as a "bounded rationalist" who seeks satisfactory rather than optimal solutions. As Herbert Simon has put it, "the capacity of the human mind for formulating and solving complex problems is very small compared with the size of the problem whose solution is required for objectively rational behavior in the real world—or even a reasonable approximation of such objective rationality."[49] Moreover, it is not practical for the decision maker to seek optimal choices; for example, because of the costs of searching for information. Related to this is the more recent concept of the individual as a "cognitive miser," one who seeks to simplify complex problems and to find shortcuts to problem solving and decision making.

Another approach is to look at the decision maker as an "error prone intuitive scientist" who is likely to commit a broad range of inferential mistakes. Thus, rather than emphasizing the limits on search, information processing, and the like, this conception views the decision maker as the victim of flawed heuristics or decision rules who uses data poorly. There are tendencies to underuse rate data in making judgments, believe in the "law of small numbers," underuse diagnostic information, overweight low probabilities and underweight high ones, and violate other requirements of consistency and coherence. These deviations from classical decision theory are traced to the psychological principles that govern perceptions of problems and evaluations of options.[50]

The final perspective I will mention emphasizes the forces that dominate the policymaker, forces that will not or cannot be controlled.[51] Decision makers are not merely rational calculators; important decisions generate conflict, and a reluctance to make irrevocable choices often results in behavior that reduces the quality of decisions. These models direct the analyst's attention to policymakers' belief systems, images of relevant actors, perceptions, information-processing strategies, heuristics, certain personality traits (ability to tolerate ambiguity, cognitive complexity, etc.), and their impact on decision-making performance.

Despite this diversity of perspectives and the difficulty of choosing between cognitive and motivational models, there has been some convergence on several types of constraints that may affect decision processes.[52] One involves the consequences of efforts to achieve cognitive consistency on perceptions and information processing. Several kinds of systematic bias have been identified in both experimental and historical studies. Policymakers have a propensity to assimilate and interpret information in ways that conform to rather than challenge existing beliefs, preferences, hopes, and expectations. Frequently they deny the need to confront tradeoffs between values by persuading themselves that an option will satisfy all of them. And, finally, they indulge in rationalizations to bolster the selected option while denigrating those that were not selected.

An extensive literature on styles of attribution has revealed several types of systematic bias in causal analysis. Perhaps the most important for foreign policy analysis is the basic attribution error—a tendency to explain the adversary's behavior in terms of his characteristics (for example, inherent aggressiveness or hostility) rather than in terms of the context or situation, while attributing one's own behavior to the latter (for example, legitimate security needs arising from a dangerous and uncertain environment) rather than to the former. A somewhat related type of double standard has been noted by George Kennan: "Now is it our view that we should take account only of their [Soviet] capabilities, disregarding their intentions, but we should expect them to take account only for our supposed intentions, disregarding our capabilities?"[53]

Analysts also have illustrated the important effect on decisions of policymakers' assumptions about order and predictability in the environment. Whereas a policymaker may have an acute appreciation of the disorderly environment in which he or she operates (arising, for example, from domestic political processes), there is a tendency to assume that others, especially adversaries, are free of such constraints. Graham T. Allison, Robert Jervis, and others have demonstrated that decision makers tend to believe that the realist "unitary rational actor" is the appropriate representation of the opponent's decision processes and, thus, whatever happens is the direct result of deliberate choices. For example, the hypothesis that the Soviet destruction of KAL flight 007 may have resulted from intelligence failures or bureaucratic foulups, rather than from a calculated decision to murder civilian passengers, was either not given serious consideration or it was suppressed for strategic reasons.[54]

Drawing upon a very substantial experimental literature, several models linking crisis-induced stress to decision processes have been developed and used in foreign policy studies.[55] Irving L. Janis and Leon Mann have developed a more general conflict-theory model which conceives of man as a "reluctant decision-maker" and focuses upon "when, how and why psychological stress generated by decisional conflict imposes limitations on the rationality of a person's decisions."[56] One may employ five strategies for coping with a situation requiring a decision: unconflicted adherence to existing policy, unconflicted change, defensive avoidance, hypervigilance, and vigilant decision making. The first four strategies are likely to yield low-quality decisions owing to an incomplete search for information, appraisal of the situation and options, and contingency planning, whereas the vigilant decision making characterized by a more adequate performance of vital tasks is more likely to result in a high-quality choice. The factors that will affect the employment of decision styles are information about risks, expectations of finding a better option, and time for adequate search and deliberation.

A final approach we should consider attempts to show the impact of personal traits on decision making. There is no shortage of typologies that are intended to link leadership traits to decision-making behavior, but systematic research demonstrating such links is in much shorter supply. Still, some efforts have borne fruit. Margaret G. Hermann has developed a scheme for analyzing leaders' public statements of unquestioned authorship for eight variables: nationalism, belief in one's ability to control the environment, need for power, need for affiliation, ability to differentiate environments, distrust of others, self-confidence, and task emphasis. The scheme has been tested with impressive results on a broad range of contemporary leaders.[57] Alexander L. George has reformulated Nathan Leites's concept of "operational code" into five philosophical and five instrumental beliefs that are intended to describe politically relevant core beliefs, stimulating a number of empirical studies and, more recently, further significant conceptual revisions.[58] Finally, several psychologists have developed and tested the concept of "integrative complexity," defined as the ability to make subtle distinction along multiple dimensions, flexibility, and the integration of large amounts of diverse information to make coherent judgments.[59] A standard content-analysis technique has been used for research on documentary materials generated by top decision makers in a wide range of international crises, including World War I, Cuba (1962), Morocco (1911), Berlin (1948–49 and 1961), Korea, and the Middle East wars of 1948, 1956, 1967, and 1973.[60]

Decision-making approaches clearly permit the analyst to overcome many limitations of the systemic models described earlier, but not without costs. The three decision-making models described here impose increasingly heavy data burdens on the analyst. Moreover, there is a danger that adding levels of analysis may result in an undisciplined proliferation of categories and variables with at least two adverse consequences: it may become increasingly difficult to determine which are more or less important; and ad hoc explanations for individual cases erode the possibilities for broader generalizations across cases. However, several well-designed, multicase, decision-making studies indicate that these and other traps are not unavoidable.[61]

The study of international relations and foreign policy has always been a somewhat eclectic undertaking, with extensive borrowing from disciplines other than political science and history.[62] At the most general level, the primary differences today tend to be between two broad approaches. Analysts of the first school focus on the structure of the international system, often borrowing from economics for models, analogies, insights, and metaphors, with an emphasis on *rational preferences and strategy* and how these tend to be shaped and constrained by the structure of the international system. Decision-making analysts, meanwhile, display a concern for domestic political processes and tend to borrow from social psychology and psychology in order to understand better the *limits and barriers* to information processing and rational choice.

At the risk of ending on a platitude, it seems clear that for many purposes both approaches are necessary and neither is sufficient. Neglect of the system structure and its constraints may result in analyses that depict policymakers as relatively free agents with an almost unrestricted menu of choices, limited only by the scope of their ambitions and the resources at their disposal. At worst, this type of analysis can degenerate into Manichean explanations that depict foreign policies of the "bad guys" as the external manifestation of inherently flawed leaders or domestic structures, whereas the "good guys" only react from necessity. Radical right explanations of the Cold War often depict Soviet foreign policies as driven by inherently aggressive totalitarian communism and the United States as its blameless victim; radical left explanations tend to be structurally similar, with the roles of aggressor and victim reversed.[63]

Conversely, neglect of foreign policy decision making not only leaves one unable to explain the dynamics of international relations, but many important aspects of a nation's external behavior will be inexplicable. Advocates of the realist model have often argued its superiority for understanding the "high" politics of deterrence, containment, alliances, crises, and wars, if not necessarily for "low" politics. But there are several rejoinders to this line of reasoning. First, the low politics of trade, currencies, and other issues that are almost always highly sensitive to domestic pressures are becoming an increasingly important element of international relations. Second, the growing literature on the putative domain *par excellence* of realism, including deterrence, crises, and wars, raises substantial doubts about the universal validity of the realist model even for these issues.[64] Finally, exclusive reliance on realist models and their assumptions of rationality may lead to unwarranted complacency about dangers in the international system. Nuclear weapons and other features of the system have no doubt contributed to the "long peace" between major powers.[65] At the same time, however, a narrow focus on power balances, "correlations of forces," and other features of the international system will result in neglect of dangers—for example, the command, communication, control, intelligence problem, or inadequate information processing—that can only be identified and analyzed by a decision-making perspective.[66]

At a very general level, this conclusion parallels that drawn three decades ago by the foremost contemporary proponent of modern realism: the "third image" (system structure) is necessary for understanding the context of international behavior, whereas the first and second images (decision makers and domestic political processes) are needed to understand dynamics within the system.[67] But to acknowledge the existence of various levels of analysis is not enough. *What the investigator wants to explain and the level of specificity and comprehensiveness to be sought* should determine which level(s) of analysis are relevant and necessary. In this connection, it is essential to distinguish two different dependent variables: foreign policy decisions by states, on the one hand, and the outcomes of policy and interactions between two or more states, on the other. If the goal is to understand the former—foreign policy decisions—Harold and Margaret Sprout's notion of "psychological milieu" is relevant and sufficient; that is, the objective structural variables influence the decisions via the decision makers perception and evaluation of those "outside" variables.[68] However, if the goal is to explain outcomes, the "psychological milieu" is quite inadequate; the objective factors, if misperceived or misjudged by the decision maker, will influence the outcome. Political scientists studying international relations are increasingly disciplining their use of multiple levels of analysis in studying outcomes that cannot be adequately explained via only a single level of analysis.[69]

Which of these models and approaches are likely to be of interest and utility to the diplomatic historian? Clearly there is no one answer; political scientists are unable to agree on a single multilevel approach to international relations and foreign policy; thus they are hardly in a position to offer a single recommendation to historians. In the absence of the often-sought but always-elusive unified theory of human behavior that could provide a model for all seasons and all reasons, one must ask at least one further question: A model for what purpose? For example, in some circumstances, such as research on major international crises, it may be important to obtain systematic evidence on the beliefs and other intellectual baggage that key policymakers bring to their deliberations. Some of the approaches described above should prove very helpful in this respect. Conversely, there are many other research problems for which the historian would quite properly decide that this type of analysis requires far more effort than could possibly be justified by the benefits to be gained.

Of the systemic approaches described here, little needs to be said about classical realism because its main features, as well as its strengths and weaknesses, are familiar to most diplomatic historians. Those who focus on security issues can hardly neglect its central premises and concepts. On the other hand, modern or structural realism of the Waltz variety is likely to have rather limited appeal to historians, especially if they take seriously his doubts about being able to incorporate foreign policy into it. It may perhaps serve to raise consciousness about the importance of the systemic context within which international relations take place, but that may not be a major gain—after all, such concepts as "balance of power" have long been a standard part of the diplomatic historians vocabulary. Gilpin's richer approach, which employs both system- and state-level variables to explain international dynamics, may well have greater appeal. It has already been noted that there are some interesting parallels between Gilpin's *War and Change in World Politics* and Paul Kennedy's recent *The Rise and Fall of the Great Powers*.

The Global-Society/Complex-Interdependence models will be helpful to historians with an interest in evolution of the international system and with the growing disjuncture between demands on states and their ability to meet them—the "sovereignty gap." One need not be very venturesome to predict that this gap will grow rather than narrow in the future. Historians of all kinds of international and transnational organizations are also likely to find useful concepts and insights in these models.

It is much less clear that the Marxist/World-System/Dependency models will provide useful new insights to historians. They will no doubt continue to be employed, but for reasons other than demonstrated empirical utility. If one has difficulty in accepting certain assumptions as *true by definition*—for example, that there has been and is today a single "world capitalist system"—then the kinds of analyses that follow are likely to seem seriously flawed. Most diplomatic historians also would have difficulty in accepting models that relegate the state to a secondary role. Until proponents of these models demonstrate a greater willingness to test them against a broader range of cases, including East-South and East-East relations, their applicability would appear to be limited at best. Finally, whereas proponents of GS/CI models can point with considerable justification to current events and trends that would appear to make them more rather than less relevant in the future, supporters of the M/WS/D models have a much more difficult task in this respect.

Although the three decision-making models sometimes include jargon that may be jarring to the historian, many of the underlying concepts are familiar. Much of diplomatic history has traditionally focused on the decisions, actions, and interactions of national leaders who operate in group contexts, such as cabinets or ad hoc advisory groups, and who draw upon the resources of such bureaucracies as foreign and defense ministries or the armed forces. The three types of models described above typically draw heavily upon psychology, social psychology, organizational theory, and other social sciences; thus for the historian they open some important windows to highly relevant developments in these fields. For example, theories and concepts of "information processing" by individuals, groups, and organizations should prove very useful to diplomatic historians.

Decision-making models may also appeal to diplomatic historians for another important reason. Political scientists who are accustomed to working with fairly accessible information such as figures on gross national products, defense budgets, battle casualties, alliance commitments, United Nations votes, trade and investments, and the like, often feel that the data requirements of decision-making models are excessive. This is precisely the area in which the historian has a decided comparative advantage, for the relevant data are usually to be found in the paper trails—more recently, also in the electronic trails—left by policymakers, and they are most likely to be unearthed by archival research. Thus, perhaps the appropriate point on which to conclude this essay is to reverse the question posed earlier: Ask not only what can the political scientist contribute to the diplomatic historian but ask also what can the diplomatic historian contribute to the political scientist. At the very least political scientists could learn a great deal about the validity of their own models if historians would use them and offer critical assessments of their strengths and limitations.

A Moral Core for U.S. Foreign Policy: Is Idealism Dead?

By Derek Chollet and Tod Lindberg

Is idealism dead? Should the promotion of American values of liberalism, democracy, human rights, and rule of law be a core element of U.S. foreign policy? Where to strike the balance between principles and interests is—one of the most enduring debates about America's role in the world. But since September 11, this question has become intensely contested and deeply controversial. It has emerged as one of the central divides between the political right and left—in large part because of the history of the past seven years, the Bush administration's rhetoric, its strong association with the "freedom agenda," and its actions justified at least in part by democracy promotion (namely the war in Iraq). Yet it is also becoming a sharper division *within* each end of the political spectrum.

Of course, the choice between realism and idealism is a false one: U.S. foreign policy must be firmly rooted in both national interests and values. But now, after two successive presidents of opposite political parties (Bill Clinton and George W. Bush) have argued that spreading American values is itself a vital interest, there is growing skepticism in many quarters about whether trying to do so is worth significant costs, or even a true interest of the United States at all. Facts matter, and after several difficult years of pursuing a foreign policy framed as a fight for American values, more are wondering whether the sacrifice is worth it. In the view of many policymakers, politicians, analysts, and average citizens, the time has come to have a more realistic foreign policy—scaling back the United States' global ambitions, respecting the limits to America's capabilities and will, recognizing and embracing the constraints of the international system, and maintaining a healthy skepticism about the broad applicability of American values.

But if the values agenda has been discredited among many on both the left and the right and a greater realism is the preferred alternative, what would such a strategy look like? Moving beyond the slogans, would a truly values-free foreign policy really secure U.S. interests, strengthen U.S. power, and draw the sustained support of the American people? We think not. American values are an indispensable component of the U.S. role in the world—they are a key part of what unites the United States to allies in Europe and elsewhere and distinguishes the United States from countries like China. Instead of dividing conservatives and liberals, American values in foreign policy can in fact translate into a moral core that both sides can rally around. In the current political environment, as we approach the first post-9/11, post-Bush election, building such a policy bridge will be difficult. But given the stakes, it is imperative.

Skepticism on the Left

The emphasis placed on promoting liberal values internationally has drawn increasing hostility among traditional liberals and within the Democratic Party. Many of those who once embraced the proud liberal tradition of Woodrow Wilson, Franklin D. Roosevelt, and John F. Kennedy find themselves questioning their assumptions. And for those liberals who still embrace the importance of values, their numbers are fewer. According to a June 2006 poll commissioned by the German Marshall Fund of the United States, only 35 percent of Democrats said that the United States should "help establish democracy in other countries"—whereas 64 percent of Republicans responded favorably.[1]

This skepticism is driven by several factors. First, and most fundamental, is the fact that this approach is so closely identified with President Bush and his administration's policies. In the wake of 9/11, Bush tapped into many common (and bipartisan) themes about the enduring importance of American values, but his vision is infused with a religiosity that leaves many liberals nervous. Yet even when he got his rhetoric right—for example, many liberals admired statements like his November 2003 speech at the National Endowment for Democracy—the means he chose to implement policies, such as the war in Iraq, have proven very costly. The result now is that for many on the left, efforts to pursue policies largely rooted in values, especially democracy promotion, have become discredited and are increasingly unpopular politically.

For some liberals, the political difficulty of supporting a values-based foreign policy stems from a second factor: the structural incentives of the current political environment. Because an unpopular president has so closely identified his policies with the promotion of values, liberals are driven to oppose him. In fact, the president's leadership style has offered very little in return, even to those liberals who might agree with him. So for many on the left, if Bush is for it, they must be against it—even if this means embracing the cognitive dissonance of turning away from long-held beliefs and traditions. For many liberals, it has become politically incorrect to admit it when Bush has actually gotten something right. With Democrats in control of the U.S. Congress these incentives of opposition are now also institutional. This creates a dynamic similar to that of the aftermath of the 1994 congressional elections, when the new Republican majority turned increasingly inward in opposition to the internationalism of the Clinton administration. Whereas the Bush team came into office in 2001 with an "ABC" policy—anything but Clinton—the Democratic Congress today, and a possible Democratic president in 2009, will be tempted to do exactly the same: anything but Bush.

But liberal skepticism is more than structural or institutional—it is also internal to the debates among different camps within liberal politics. The history of the past seven years—and the consequences of a policy perceived as driven more by values than interest—has been sobering for a number of left-leaning members of the foreign policy establishment. Many supported the 2003 invasion of Iraq for the same reasons that they supported confronting Saddam Hussein during the Clinton years. And many applauded President Bush when he talked about the importance of democracy promotion. Yet now that the costs of such policies are apparent—whether in terms of political capital, U.S. global prestige, or blood and treasure—many in the foreign policy elite have become more cautious, scaling back ambitions and endorsing more realistic goals. For many mainstream foreign policy liberals, the downfall of Britain's Tony Blair—who championed values-based concepts like "humanitarian intervention" during the late 1990s—is a stark warning about the costs of embracing such policies too tightly.

The intellectual and political disconnect between the liberal establishment and the liberal grassroots activists is growing, especially over U.S. foreign policy and the purpose and use of American power. The convulsions within the political left that began in the late 1990s—illustrated by the rise of the antiglobalization movement and division over the Clinton administration's military interventions in Bosnia, Kosovo, and its 1998 air strikes against Iraq—have only become more severe and divisive. To be sure, this reflects anger with President Bush But it is more than that. When it comes to national security issues, the left has become splintered in a way not seen since the 1970s, when Vietnam split the Democratic party and ruined the post-World War II liberal establishment. A similar dynamic is at work today as a new generation of liberal activists (fueled by the power of the blogosphere) rages not just against Bush, but against a Democratic foreign policy establishment they perceive as aiding and abetting the Bush agenda—central to which is the promotion of American values. If this divide deepens, it will become very difficult for Democratic leaders to embrace explicitly values-centered policies even if they want to.

WARINESS ON THE RIGHT

The growing discomfort with the promotion of American values in foreign policy is felt not only by those on the left. Increasingly, conservatives are having second thoughts about the extent to which U.S. foreign policy should be driven by ideology and the promotion of values ahead of interests. Since the Bush administration still dominates conservative politics, the right remains more strongly identified with the values agenda, and the wariness among conservatives is more muted than among liberals. But the recent rise of "realists"—as illustrated by the personnel changes at the Defense Department and the U.S. Mission to the United Nations, greater pragmatism at the State Department, and the return to prominence of figures like former Secretary of State James Baker and Brent Scowcroft—has been heralded as rebalancing away from what many argue were the ideological excesses of the presidents first four years in office. Like liberals, conservatives are contemplating their future beyond the Bush presidency—and this debate will only intensify as the focus turns from the current administration to the one that will take office in January 2009.

In several respects, the factors driving conservatives' frustrations with the values agenda mirror the frustrations on the left. The first issue is a practical one: The American people's deepening disillusionment with the Bush administration's policies is raising the political costs of supporting the Bush agenda. Bush's unpopularity makes supporting his policies risky Put another way, the presidents success at branding his administrations actions as part of a values-based policy is directly related to the political efficacy of supporting it. When it was seen as working, the bandwagon was enthusiastic and big, but the more it is perceived as a failure, many of the president's political allies are more than happy to let him ride alone.

Like liberals, conservatives also face a structural challenge that will only increase as the 2008 election draws closer. Any Republican presidential nominee will seek to differentiate himself from his predecessor. And since more conservatives are reading the Bush years as a caution against an ambitious, values-based foreign policy, stressing realism might be the way to distinguish oneself. In this sense, one can foresee a replay of the early 1990s, when the lesson drawn from George H. W. Bush's electoral defeat in 1992—that his presidency was too focused on foreign affairs at the expense of domestic issues—caused many conservatives to move away not only from a values-based policy but from internationalism itself.

Moreover, the events of the past several years, especially the war in Iraq, have thrown much of the conservative foreign policy establishment into a crisis of confidence. Like many establishment liberals, conservatives in and out of government are questioning not only the capabilities required to implement values-promoting policies (and whether the United States can ever develop such capabilities), but the underlying assumptions of the policy itself. Such self-doubt is especially acute because many of the officials so closely identified with these policies were once heralded for their national security experience and acumen. Expectations were high, so the results of their time in office—a major crisis for America's role in the world—have been sobering.

The neoconservatives, those most closely identified with a foreign policy based on promoting American values and bold interventionism—have come in for the most criticism, and not just from the left. The internal split reemerging within conservatism over ideals is the fourth driver of wariness. During the 1990s, neoconservatives saw themselves as insurgents, agitating against both the creeping isolationism within the Republican party and what they considered the feckless policies of the Clinton team (even if most neoconservatives agreed on actions like intervention in the Balkans). But for several years after 9/11, their agenda wielded great influence over the direction of the Bush administration's policy, especially its focus on spreading American values. Six years later, neoconservatives again find themselves largely on the outside looking in as many mainstream Republicans seek a return to the kinds of policies then-Governor Bush articulated during the 2000 presidential campaign: a foreign policy based on humility, skepticism about the United States' interests in "nation-building," and the limited applicability of American values to regions like the Middle East.

So for political and intellectual reasons, the role of values in foreign policy is now in retreat domestically—liberals are increasingly skeptical, and conservatives have deep doubts. One must also note the suspicion (or worse) with which many in other countries view a values-based U.S. foreign policy. In the first place, many around the world are disinclined to take Americans at their word on the principles they claim to be promoting. They hear rhetoric of principle as nothing more than a cover for the raw assertion of American power. Some world leaders hear the rhetoric of democracy promotion and take it seriously and for that very reason regard it as dangerous, a threat to their own claims of legitimacy. One could probably break this category down further, into those hostile to any threat to their personal prerogatives on the one hand and, on the other, those generally sympathetic to liberalization but worried that too-hasty movement in that direction might tear their societies apart.

Finally, the promotion of American values opens the United States to charges of hypocrisy:

Does American conduct actually live up to the values America espouses? Many have found the United States's actions wanting in areas ranging from Guantanamo and Abu Ghraib to the U.S. relationship with Pakistan and the House of Saud and would urge that the United States tone down its complaints about others until it removes the log in its own eye. By these lights, 'the promotion of American values should begin at home (a view that also has purchase both on the left side of American public opinion and, to a degree, on the libertarian right).

THE "ACIREMA" WORLD

But if a foreign policy that promotes American values is the problem, what is the solution? In considering this question, it might be helpful to ask: What would U.S. foreign policy actually look like if it were somehow stripped of its "values" component? It's worth trying to conjure such a vision, not only as an intellectual exercise, but also because there is no quicker way to see exactly why such a policy would be a nonstarter for the United States.

As a point of departure, we might look to the assumptions about the character of the international system embraced by scholars in the "neorealist" school of international relations, on the grounds that neorealists regard such considerations as morality as largely epiphenomenal in explaining the behavior of states. Since one key neorealist assumption is that the internal characteristics of states don't matter (or matter much), we find a more or less explicit attempt to write moral considerations out of the rules of statecraft. What they posit, then, is an anarchical international system—no authority higher than the state. Each state wishes to be entirely free to make its own judgments about the conduct of its internal affairs. These judgments, insofar as they implicate events outside the state's territory and thus beyond its uncontested authority, yield a set of national interests in relation to other states. Because any state's supreme vital interest is self-preservation, each state's first priority is to ensure its security. The only means of achieving security is self-help. Unfortunately, the actions states take in pursuit of their own security and national interests tend to bring them into conflict with other states. Some structural configurations of the international system are more conducive to peace and stability than others, but no structure is impervious to internal stresses that may cause it to collapse or change convulsively as states act in pursuit of security under shifting perceptions of national interest.

How might this abstract description of state action in the international system translate into policy choices for a state in the position in which the United States finds itself today? For purposes of our investigation, we will call this state "Acirema," which is "America" spelled backwards. We do this for two reasons. First, by speculating in accordance with this "values-free" scenario, we do not want to be taken to be proposing what follows as a genuine alternative to U.S. policy; on the contrary, the speculation shows how far removed from the realm of possibility and desirability such a neorealist scenario would be. Second, "Acirema" strikes us as capturing just how radical an inversion of American priorities and traditions the pursuit of such a values-free policy would be.

In the first place, Acirema is the dominant military power in the world, and it would certainly make sense to try to maintain that dominance. This is not a judgment alien to existing U.S. policy: The Bush administrations 2002 National Security Strategy (NSS) pledged not to allow a "peer competitor" to its military power to emerge. The Bush NSS, however, justified this policy as a way to encourage peaceful relations among states. State-on-state conflict—for example, the attempt to conquer territory by force—would be discouraged by overwhelming U.S. power. But it is by no means clear, from a values-free perspective, why Acirema should be attached to a principle of peaceful relations among states and the illegitimacy of aggressive war or conquest. True, Acirema does not want to be attacked and would seek to maintain sufficient power to deter and if necessary defeat any potential aggressor. But why Acirema would care if Iran attacked Iraq, or China attacked Russia, or France attacked Germany is entirely a question of whether Acirema's aims would best be served by peace or war between any given two states.

Acirema would pursue an overall strategy of maintaining its dominance. Again, this is not foreign to current U.S. grand strategy. But the United States has welcomed and encouraged modernization, economic growth, and globalization not only in order to enrich Americans, but also according to a theory that greater trade flows and economic interdependence make for a more peaceful international environment and are good in themselves. Neither of the latter two justifications would matter to Acirema.

There is danger in an Aciteman policy that encourages other states to become rich: With riches comes the capacity to develop military power that in turn might challenge Acirema, or covertly to fund challenges and challengers. Aciteman policymakers would want to examine the trade-off between the economic benefits of an open trading system and the potential danger in allowing others to enrich themselves, thus potentially increasing their power. An Asian economic flu might be a bad thing, but it might also be a good thing.

China's modernization might yield cheap goods, but if the price is a more formidable military challenge to Acirema, the price might be too high. The best way to deal with China's self-professed desire for a "peaceful rise" might be to disregard the rhetoric of peaceability and act to prevent the rise. Acirema might want to identify potential vulnerabilities in the Chinese economy and try to exploit them to undermine Chinese economic growth. The collapse of central authority in China would be destabilizing—but primarily for the Chinese, who might then be too preoccupied with their internal turmoil to pose a threat.

More generally, the stability Acirema would seek would be the stability of its own position. The stability of other states and relations among other states is of concern only insofar as it impinges on the stability of the Aciteman position. Indeed, a subsidiary strategy of preserving dominance might be to maintain a *fragile* international stability, one in which all other states felt themselves to be constantly at *risk* from instability without actually sliding into it with a potentially adverse effect on Acirema.

Under this scenario, one would have to reject engagement in the Middle East, except with regard to securing Aciteman energy needs. To the extent that support for Israel arouses hostility from Israel's neighbors, Acirema should cease such support unless Israel is capable of providing a benefit to Acirema sufficient to offset the damage—a tall order. Meanwhile, however, it is not solely Aciteman support for Israel that antagonizes certain elements in the Middle East, and to the extent that funding for these elements comes from governments that have grown wealthy from oil revenues, it may be best to go directly to the source and deprive the hinders of the revenue. Acirema might seize and hold sufficient oil fields to see to its needs and then destroy the capacity of others to exploit the resources on their territory.

In the event that the negative repercussions of such a move might be deemed too costly, then Aciteman disengagement from the region might work—provide accompanied by an unambiguous warning from Acirema to states in the region about the unacceptability of funding terrorists, their ideological supporters, and their sympathizers. Acirema would have to make clear that regime elimination awaits any states that fail to accept that their continued oil revenue depends on their refraining from harboring, funding, or supporting anti-Aciteman terrorism. The credibility of such a policy would likely require a demonstration. A policy of regime elimination would differ from "regime change" in its rejection of Colin Powell's "Pottery Barn" principle: You break it, you own it. On the contrary, any state foolish enough to provoke Acirema to forcibly remove its regime, with all the risk and expense that would entail for Aciremans, would be on its own to sort out what comes next. Acirema wouldn't care, though it would certainly hope that whatever regime emerged had learned a lesson from the experience of the toppling of its predecessor.

The policy of Acirema toward Israel is a specific case of what would be a more general revision in alliance policy. The essential question for Acirema with regard to any ally is whether Aciteman security is improved, on net, as a result of the alliance. The notion of an alliance as an all-purpose mechanism for securing the cooperation of others in mutual pursuit of security objectives would need to be reassessed. What, specifically, is the value of "cooperation"? Needless to say, Acirema will harbor no prejudice in favor of cooperation or multilateralism, instead asking whether cooperative or multilateral means would bring a benefit that Acirema cannot obtain on its own. Acirema need not be especially concerned with the opinions of states that lack the capacity to make a difference. There will be no free-riding on the provision of security, because Acirema will not enter into alliance relationships except with partners whose tangible assets improve Aciteman security.

Needless to say, any assistance Acirema would choose to provide to other states would be tightly tied to the tangible benefit received, either economically or in terms of security. The notion of "humanitarian" aid or "humanitarian" intervention of any kind is self-evidently meaningless to a foreign policy free of moral consideration. Acirema might have a concern with averting refugee flows toward its shores, but only if the cost of action abroad to prevent the flows exceeds the cost of turning away those attempting to enter.

Local disputes in faraway places would not necessarily bother Acirema. There is nothing historically unusual about violent contests for power within states, and Acirema would not worry overmuch about the outbreak of such conflicts. They have disadvantages in terms of disrupting commerce, but they have advantages as well in that those engaged in fierce local conflict are unlikely to have the surplus capacity to threaten Acireman national interests. Even intense local conflict, with civilian deaths running to hundreds of thousands, would have to be assessed through the prism of whether it poses any sort of threat to Acirema that might warrant intervention.

It is difficult to see what gain Acirema might get from raising the issue of "human rights" with other states. Doing so would come at the cost of pressing other, more useful demands upon weaker states and would needlessly complicate relations with stronger states. There might be advantages to be gained from fomenting internal dissension and rebellion within stronger states in accordance with a general strategy of fragile stability, and this provocation might be couched in terms of "human rights" in the event that doing so would be efficacious. But the use of "human rights" would be entirely instrumental, and Acirema would have to refrain from establishing any sentimental bonds with those it was encouraging, since the likelihood is that the state in which they are rebelling will move to crush them if the crisis becomes serious, and of course Acirema would have no reason to assist them at that point.

The strongest states will be those with nuclear weapons, and the impulse of states to acquire them would undoubtedly be very strong Needless to say, Acirema would have to be very wary of states already possessing substantial nuclear arsenals. Freedom of action against Russia, China, Great Britain, France, and Israel would accordingly be constrained. As for those newly seeking to acquire the technology of atomic weapons, Acirema might choose to acquiesce, provided it was confident that its own arsenal was deterring any aggression against Acirema. This might be true of some but not all states. On the other hand, possession of a nuclear deterrent by another state might embolden that state to act against the national interests of Acirema. It might be necessary to take preemptive action to establish that mere possession of a few nuclear weapons is not sufficient to deter or coerce Acirema. Acirema might have to launch a nuclear attack first. Of course, there would be some risk of nuclear counterattack if the other state had the means to deliver its nuclear weapons. On the other hand, Acirema could withstand such a small strike, whereas its antagonist would be obliterated.

Yes, we have wandered into the bizarro territory of Dr. Strangelove, and the scenario described above is both monstrous to contemplate and impossible to envision actually coming to pass. But why is that? In the first place, an anyone—liberal or conservative—plausibly imagine the United States electing a president on such a callous "Acirema First" platform? Patrick Buchanan tried a slightly attenuated version of the Acirema project and was unable to win the Republican nomination, let alone seriously contest the general election. During the 2000 election, the platform of Ralph Nader's Green Party shared many aspects of the Acireman program but garnered little support (yet just enough to help determine the outcome). The closest a Democratic presidential nominee has ever come to the Acirema agenda is probably George McGoverns disastrous 1972 campaign, in which his slogan "Come home, America" was taken as a call for broad-based disengagement and dramatic reduction of defense spending, not just an immediate end to the Vietnam War.

Disband, NATO abandon Israel, destabilize China, welcome wars when useful, disregard genocide, and wage preemptive nuclear war? While such views are consistently found in certain small segments of the political spectrum, there is, thankfully, no plausible passageway from America to Acirema.

Some have claimed—and the 2002 National Security Strategy and other statements of President Bush flirt with—the notion that U.S. values and interests are quite closely aligned or can be so. Such an argument effectively dodges the question of which should take precedence. And indeed, it may be that "failed states" are something the United States should take action to prevent because of the potential for danger where no one is adequately in charge. We disagree on the relative magnitude of the danger there.[2] We agree, however, that U.S. action to prevent the failure of states is morally good. The point is that without the moral frame of reference, one could imagine having a debate about whether the collapse of a state into civil war, warlordism, and genocide is good or bad for the United States—and that such a debate would remain imaginary, because it can never occur in the real world.

Moreover, it is a conceit that this "values-free" *machtpolitik* or *realpolitik* is truly free of moral considerations. Even the proposition "look out for No.1" has a moral aspect. Why should you look out for No. 1? Because you place a value on No. 1 and think it is morally good to seek the benefit of No. 1. Indeed, there may have been a time in human history—perhaps in Hobbes's state of nature, the "war of all against all"—when moral considerations, though hardly absent, involved calculations no more complicated than this.

But the United States was founded not as a "values-free" rational calculator of what's good for No. 1, but as a nation embodying certain values or principles that justified rebellion against its lawful sovereign. While, to this day, the United States has been accused (often with justification) of failing to live up to the values of the Declaration of Independence, the United States has never been able to or seriously attempted to expunge those values from all consideration in the conduct of domestic or foreign policy. This seems unlikely to change. And rightly or wrongly, Americans demand consideration for those principles not simply because they are "ours"—and no one has the right to interfere in our affairs by telling us anything different—but because of our belief that they are true.

TOWARD A NEW CONSENSUS ON PRINCIPLES

While the place of American values in foreign policy endures, questions remain about how such policies should be implemented and how the inevitable trade-offs should be managed, especially in the current political environment. The Bush legacy casts a long shadow. During the past several years, intellectuals and policy analysts have offered numerous grand strategies as a corrective to Bush, rebalancing foreign policy between realism and idealism. Some stress one perspective more than the other, and they usually combine some version of both words in their titles:

Francis Fukuyama offers "Realistic Wilsonianism," Robert Wright proposes "Progressive Realism," John Human and Anatol Lieven describe "Ethical Realism," Charles Krauthammer espouses "Democratic Realism," James Baker explains "Pragmatic Idealism" and John Ikenberry and Charles Kupchan outline "Liberal Realism" (we could go on).

Instead of adding yet another grand strategy slogan into the mix, we believe that it is more important to describe a set of principles and priorities that should guide U.S. foreign relations in the challenging years ahead. Below we outline six principles, each rooted in American ideals and serving American interests. This is not an exhaustive list, yet it shows that it is possible to construct a common agenda between liberals and conservatives that is firmly built upon a commitment to uphold—and promote—values.

Standing against the conquest of territory by force. The United States must continue to uphold one of tie most basic norms of international relations: preventing and, when necessary, reversing the conquest of territory across an international border by military force. While support for this principle may seem self-evident—after all, it is at the heart of the UN Charter and the underlying rationale of the worlds most important security organization, NATO—it is in fact a value that the United States must choose to defend. As made clear by the alternative Acirema world described earlier, a great power like the United States could decide that upholding this norm is too costly or outside the bounds of its core national interests. We believe that since preventing territorial conquest by force remains a keystone of the international system and a driver of its enduring stability, this must remain a core value of U.S. foreign policy.

Such a commitment entails certain responsibilities around the world and, fundamentally, demands an interventionist foreign policy—preferably as an active partner through international institutions, but if necessary alone. The means that are required will depend on the specific situation and the other U.S. interests at stake, such as alliance or other security or political relationships and the potential for wider violence. Yet the full range of tools—from diplomacy to sanctions and political isolation to military force—must always be available.

Sometimes this might require active diplomacy to prevent one state from threatening another with force, such as the United States' repeated efforts in recent years to reduce tensions between India and Pakistan. Other instances will require U.S. leadership to try to negotiate an end to conflicts after they have broken out. For example, this is what the Clinton administration did when it hammered out the Dayton Peace Accords in 1995, reversing Slobodan Milosevic's aggression against the newly independent Bosnia. And on some (and hopefully rare) occasions, the United States will have to use military force to reverse aggression, as George H. W. Bush did in 1991 when he created and led a UN-sanctioned international coalition to kick Iraq out of Kuwait. Today, looking into the future and the probability of a smaller American presence in Iraq, the commitment to territorial integrity will be critical insurance against potential incursions by neighbors such as Iran.

Of course, another way of describing this is that by valuing the protection of territorial integrity from threats of force, we are valuing the defense of sovereignty. That's correct to an extent, but we do recognize that under certain circumstances this value can be trumped by other values, such as the responsibility to defend the rights and lives of people living within another state's territory. We discuss this in greater detail below, but suffice it to say that the United States should not allow any leader to hide behind one value (the right not to be invaded) in order to violate another (his people's right not to be brutalized).

Defending liberal regimes. The United States should be prepared and willing to help any and all democratic governments that come under challenge internationally or from internal antidemocratic elements seeking to overturn liberal political and social order and the rule of law. This is a basic principle of *democratic solidarity*, according to which the most secure, established, and stable liberal democracies, the United States above all, should acknowledge a responsibility to come to the assistance of democratic governments that are threatened, that have yet to become fully consolidated and mature, or are subject to forces of internal instability.

Liberal democracy, in the view of most of those who govern themselves according to its principles, is not merely a matter of sovereign choice—just one among many options. Rather, citizens of democracies tend to regard their form of government as the *right* or best choice, at least for them; they would not consider trading their form of government for autocratic or totalitarian or theocratic government and would rightly consider any force in favor of such a change in governance as a serious threat, one to be challenged and defeated—*not* by whatever means necessary, such as abandonment of liberal principles for the sake of security, but by any means legitimate *within* the horizon of liberal principles.

If citizens of democracies view their system as the right or best choice for themselves, those citizens and that state ought to be willing to acknowledge the rightness of the choice of liberal democracy among the citizens of other states. They have a stake not only in their own domestic political arrangements, but in their view of the rightness of liberal democracy, which does not end at their borders. A threat to liberal democracy elsewhere is accordingly a challenge and one to which any democratic states with the means to do so should be willing to meet head on.

The United States has a number of alliances with democratic states, including several with allies that were not democratic when the alliance relationship began but became so, perhaps partly as a result of the security provided by the United States. These alliance commitments remain fully in force, but they are only a beginning. The United States must recogzise that it will not sit idly by as nondemocratic states try to undermine or even overturn democracies or fragile liberalizing states. On the contrary, the United States should step up, together with other democratic states, to provide all the support or assistance possible.

The correct response when a powerful nondemocratic state tries to coerce a weaker democratic state—as Russia has tried with Ukraine and especially Georgia—is not to temporize out of deference to the power of the strong but to speak up unequivocally in defense of democracy under threat. To stand aloof or to appease the stronger power would be to embolden antidemocratic forces, and not just locally. Some argued that extending the NATO alliance to the Baltic States was foolish because of the military difficulty of defending Estonia, Latvia, and Lithuania against attack and because extending the Atlantic Alliance onto the territory of the former Soviet Union would unnecessarily antagonize Russia. We strongly disagreed at the time and believe we were correct. In our view, the newly won freedom of the Baltic nations and the establishment of liberal democratic governments there *already* created obligations for the United States and NATO countries. NATO accession did not create but ratified and codified that obligation toward these peoples. The process was exemplary in warding off any urge to interfere with and disrupt democratic development and consolidation there—and elsewhere in Central and Eastern Europe, in our view.

A principle of democratic solidarity is not only good in itself; it makes external threats to democratic governments less likely by demonstrating that making such threats will have adverse *global* consequences for anyone inclined to pursue such a course. It would be a mistake to view the principle of democratic solidarity as a military doctrine; its main components are political, diplomatic, and social.

There are some instances in which democratic solidarity comes with conditions. For example, U.S. willingness to defend Taiwan against Chinese attack depends on Taipei's not taking the provocative step of a declaration of independence—to which China would respond militarily, according to Beijing's declaratory policy. This is a reasonable codicil given local circumstances. There may be others (though Taiwan is arguably the most neuralgia of such at present). An absolute *military* doctrine of democratic solidarity would create moral hazard, since a state might conclude it could act as provocatively as it wished in response to local circumstances and still receive the backing of the United States and other democratic states. That is not the deal. Such a state, by taking action other democratic states would regard as unreasonable, would itself be breaking from democratic solidarity. But with such nuances always in mind, a principle of democratic solidarity should guide U.S. policy, and the United States should encourage other democratic states to embrace it.

Promoting liberal governance. If a principle of democratic solidarity makes sense at the level of state-to-state relations, it also makes sense for the United States in relation to people working toward liberalization and democracy in their own societies. This is not likely to be especially controversial as a matter of principle among democratic allies. Opinion surveys in Europe, for example, show large majorities in favor of promotion of democracy by peaceful means.[3] And it seems likely that a substantial part of the lingering opposition is a product of concern that democracy will not be liberal, but rather will bring to power illiberal elements. Our discussion should be understood to refer to the promotion of liberal democracy, in which the two components are a liberal social order based on principles of freedom and minority rights as well as popularly elected governments followed by peaceful transfer of power.

Nevertheless, it cannot be denied that a principle of democratic solidarity—even if broadly accepted by and among, and in application to, democratic states facing external threats or internal challenge, and even if accepted as the rightness of supporting development of liberal democracy in principle—will surely be controversial when considered in application to supporters of democracy in nondemocratic states.

We think that the United States should, as far as possible, provide whatever help aspiring democrats and liberalizers seek. The United States should also encourage similar support among fellow democratic states—an extension of democratic solidarity. But considerations of prudence, national interests (such as access to energy resources), and *force majeure* will inevitably weigh into such decisions.

What we propose is the imperative of *balancing prudential considerations and principle*. It is not enough to take note of Saudi oil fields and declare, therefore, that Saudi Arabia is off limits for criticism and promotion of reform of its extraordinarily repressive regime. Similarly, China is big, powerful, rising—and undemocratic (indeed, increasingly openly antidemocratic). We must deal with the fact that China is a vast and increasingly powerful country; it would be madness to try to deny it. But we must also deal with the fact that China is undemocratic.

The United States can and must pursue dual-track policies in such cases, as Francis Fukuyama and Michael McFaul argue.[4] One track will address exigency, the other the moral case. On the moral track, rather than a one-size-fits-all model of democracy promotion, we propose a method, a way of thinking about and acting on the problem that does not pretend to a greater degree of generality than is appropriate. The objective, in each country in which liberal democracy has yet to take hold or take hold fully, is to identify *next steps*. What is the next plausible step for the expansion of the liberal and democratic space? Conversely, what is the next plausible step for the constriction of the space in which authoritarians or antidemocratic elements operate? The United States should then work vigorously to promote the next step, applying pressure for reform against the authoritarian element (typically, the government) and assistance to the democratic element to help achieve measurable progress. Once the next-step objective has been achieved, the United States must immediately move on to the *next* next step. Pressure and assistance must not let up following interim successes; on the contrary, it should increase.

We agree that the key failure of the Bush administration's democracy promotion policy in Egypt, for example, was overeagerness to claim credit for progress in response to small positive steps. Yes, it was consequential that the Mubarak government decided to allow other parties to compete in a presidential election. But it was hardly the birth of liberal democracy on the Nile Delta. Mubarak deserved congratulations for taking the step he took—followed without pause by the demand that he take the next step of moving toward a free and fair election.

With this next-step policy of constant pressure to expand the liberal space while contracting the authoritarian space, the United States will be in a position to say it is keeping faith with the forces of democracy and liberalization in every country, even in the face of inevitable practical constraints.

Enforcing the "responsibility to protect." Liberal democracy, in which people choose their leaders in free and fair elections and in which political and human rights are secure, including for minorities, stands at the pinnacle of human political achievement. For some states, such as the United States, the most urgent political task lies in helping others achieve this great end while being ever mindful of and seeking to address the imperfections of its own governance. For others, the consolidation of transition to democratic governance is the key political task, and it can often be one of life and death, as the assassination of reformist Serbian Prime Minister Zoran Djindjic or the dioxin poisoning of Orange Revolution leader Viktor Yushchenko in Ukraine both demonstrate. For still others, the political challenge is to pry open any space at all for the opposition in an authoritarian country.

But for the worst off of all, such as the Tutsi minority in Rwanda or the Curds of Saddam Hussein's Iraq, the essential political challenge is survival—against the wishes of the government or the mob in whose midst they have the misfortune to live. Surely, it cannot be right to embrace a principle of democratic solidarity and democracy promotion for those relatively high on the social ladder while offering nothing to those in greatest peril of losing the most basic human right: the right to live.

At the United Nations' 2005 World Summit in New York, the world's leaders embraced for the first time the doctrine of the "responsibility to protect." It holds, briefly, that with sovereign rights come sovereign responsibility, and the primary responsibility of a government is to protect the people who live within its territory. In the event that a government is unable or unwilling to provide protection for its people from would-be perpetrators of genocide or mass killing and ethnic cleansing—or worse, is complicit in such crimes against humanity—the international community must take upon itself the responsibility to protect. No government that fails to protect its people may legitimately assert a right to noninterference in its internal affairs.

The responsibility to protect is a transformational concept in international relations. Previously, the victims of the worst sort of war crimes and human rights abuses on a mass scale had no recourse, trapped as they were behind a curtain of sovereign right. The adoption of the responsibility to protect grants them an appeal to the international community.

This is often construed solely through the prism of military intervention, and in some cases, the only way to stop determined genocidaires may be by force. But it is wrong to think that military means are the first or main recourse. The international community needs to take active measures in terms of monitoring and applying diplomatic and other forms of pressure (such as sanctions, diplomatic isolation, and negotiations) to avert mass killings and ethnic cleansing whenever possible.

Of course, there is much dispute over how the "international community" may act. We agree that the United Nations Security Council is the best venue, not because we think that the United Nations is the only path to legality and legitimacy, but because so many other states take this view, and their wishes deserve respect. However, in the event the Security Council fails to take timely and effective action as a human rights catastrophe unfolds, the United States must not stand on the sidelines. In the case of Kosovo, when the Security Council was blocked, NATO stepped up to take decisive action, thereby preventing a genocide.

Some still question the legality of that action. We take the concern seriously coming from those who were willing to act; we do not take it seriously coming from those who were prepared to let hundreds of thousands fall prey to ethnic cleansing and genocide. When necessary, the United States must lead or be willing to join others to mobilize an effective response to mass killing and widespread repression.

Addressing global hardship. As the worlds most powerful country, the United States has the capability to help address the challenges stemming from poverty, hunger, disease, and lack of opportunity for billions of people in the developing world. We believe that leadership in these areas is not just something the United States can do—it is what the United States *must* do.

While these issues were once only considered "humanitarian" or "soft"—implying that they are always elective or secondary—there are instrumental reasons why the United States s' should focus on them. If one accepts the argument" (and we do) that threats emanating from weak or failed states can endanger U.S. national security, then it is in America's interest to help these states stabilize. Some describe this as part of "draining the swamp" of desperation and hardship that radical jihadists and other extremists thrive in by reducing extreme poverty and replacing the extreme fundamentalism taught in some madrassas with basic education. As evidence of the growing consensus on the relationship between these issues and national security, the Bush administration justifies many of its efforts along these lines—and when it is criticized, it is usually for not doing enough.

But U.S. leadership in these areas is about more than protecting security. America's actions in the world are a powerful demonstration of what it wants to accomplish with its power and the values it wishes to uphold. In this sense, the United States should embrace humanitarianism and not consider it optional or of minor importance. To do so is both the smart and the morally right thing to do for our security.

This is also an area where there is significant common ground between the political right and left. Liberals have long argued that addressing issues like poverty and disease need to be a core part of U.S. foreign policy. Many conservatives have as well, especially among the evangelical community (as exemplified by the work of Franklin Graham and Rick Warren). Spurred in part by evangelical advocates, the Bush administration has made positive strides in this direction, increasing assistance to Africa by 67 percent and boosting spending for programs to fight HIV/AIDS. Meanwhile, three of the major Democratic candidates for president have talked about the importance of fighting global poverty and making a major push to improve education throughout the developing world.

Looking ahead, both conservatives and liberals should embrace an agenda centered on stronger American leadership in these areas—in fact, one valid criticism of recent U.S. policy is that it too often cedes the initiative to others. For example, greater resources should be put behind combating poverty and disease, and there should be a broad recognition that free trade is critical to helping the developing world advance economically. And we should consider fundamental reforms in the way the U.S. government is organized to implement such policies, including ideas like establishing a Department of Global Development (along the lines of that in the United Kingdom) and replacing the Foreign Assistance Act.

Strengthening alliances and institutions. Any discussion of implementing the principles outlined above begs a fundamental question about means: How should the United States work with other countries? Throughout American history, the subject of whether the United States should tie itself to the fate of others abroad—or work with others to solve problems—has been hotly contested. This has been especially true since the end of tine Cold War and the apogee of U.S. primacy, when we really didn't *need* others to solve a lot of problems. While this tugging between unilateralism and multilateralism is often seen as concerned solely with efficacy and instrumentality—sometimes it is better for us to share the burden, sometimes not—we believe that it is in fact a debate about what kind of global power America should be and what kind of international system we should support. It is not about instruments; it is about principles.

As Ivo Daalder and Robert Kagan argue, it is important for U.S. policies to be seen as legitimate both in the eyes of the American people and in the eyes of the the world.[5] That is a value that other countries—certainly Acirema—might not necessarily care about. America does and should. But the question is how best to uphold this value and what institutions (whether existing or new) or multilateral arrangements are the best means to do so.

As discussed earlier, when it comes to implementing values-based policies like defending liberal regimes or enforcing the responsibility to protect, working through alliances and international institutions should be as important to the United States (at least as something to aspire to) as it is to others.

The challenge has been that for many conservatives and liberals, the unilateral vs. multilateral discourse has framed these ideas as an either/or choice. The right has focused too much on the constraints of multilateralism and maintaining U.S. freedom of action. We agree that the United States always reserves the right to act alone if the circumstances require, but this should not be the preferred option. In this sense, the Bush administrations substance and style—exemplified by its "with us or against us" statements or rhetoric about preemption—have prompted international skepticism about whether the United States genuinely wants institutions like the United Nations to function or even exist at all.

Yet too many liberals slide into the opposite problem; upholding multilateralism for its own sake. This has only intensified during the Bush years, when support for the United States around the world has reached alarming lows. If the United States is unpopular, some believe that it must be solely our fault and make no judgment about the behavior of our allies. The remedy among many on the left seems to us to be overly simplistic: defer at all times to the collective decisions of institutions. This confuses the reality that international organizations are stages, not actors. They are simply groupings of other sovereign states, and while organizations can help facilitate decisions for states, they cannot make choices for them. They can neither prevent internal disagreements nor force free riders and buck passers to act.

Recently we've seen signs of greater nuance in the unilateral/multilateral debate between left and right. For example, in his second term President Bush began working through institutions like the UN Security Council to deal with problems like Iran and Darfur, and with an ad hoc coalition to negotiate with North Korea. Even his rhetoric is softening: when asked recently what he has learned from his European partners, he said, "I have come to realize that other countries do rely upon the United Nations, and I respect that a lot. So there's an area, for example, where I have been taught a lesson by my allies and friends."[6] And among liberals, there is greater recognition that the multilateral route often can frustrate rather than facilitate action. For example, the longer the Security Councils divisions prevent strong action to end the genocide in Darfur, the louder the calls become for a NATO response or even unilateral U.S. military intervention.

This bolsters our belief that a new concensus can be formed in support of seeking the broadest possible coalition to pursue U.S. foreign policy goals. This means working through alliances and institutions, but also ensuring that these organizations work. The United States should have high expectations of its alliances, and in turn it should have high expectations of its allies. It should be an active and energetic partner, recognizing that getting something done through a coalition often requires the same land of daily politicking, strong-arming, logrolling, and hand-holding used every day in working with the U.S. Congress. And while the United States should seek to make existing institutions like the United Nations and NATO stronger and more effective, it should also work to build other organizations like the Alliance of Democracies.

THE MORAL CORE

The conclusion we come to is that while an idealistic foreign policy has become harder to defend politically, it is possible to construct a forward-looking, values-based agenda that both liberals and conservatives can support. In fact, such an approach should garner more than just passive support—the policies presented above can actually serve as part of the foundation for U.S. foreign policy in the years ahead. Neither sentimental nor coldly aloof, these values comprise the core of the rules-based, liberal international order that the United States should aspire to achieve. This is about more than what we want; it is about who we are.

Yet because the political incentives against an approach to foreign policy that promotes American values remain so powerful, as we described at the outset, such a policy will not emerge on its own. Even with greater clarity about what values we want to uphold and promote, difficult questions will remain about how to do so. There will always be debates about acceptable costs and the trade-offs involved. So success will require sustained attention and steadfast leadership. With both, the American people will rise to the challenge.

WHAT SHOULD THIS FIGHT BE CALLED?

Metaphors of Counterterrorism and Their Implications
Arie W. Kruglanski,[1] Martha Crenshaw,[2] Jerrold M. Post,[3] and Jeff Victoroff[4]
[1]Department of Psychology, University of Maryland, College Park; [2]Center for International Security and Cooperation, Stanford University; [3]Elliot School for International Affairs, The George Washington University; and [4]Departments of Clinical Neurology and Psychiatry, University of Southern California Keck School of Medicine

SUMMARY

This monograph examines from a psychological perspective the use of metaphors in framing counterterrorism. Four major Counterterrorism metaphors are considered, namely those of war, law enforcement, containment of a social epidemic, and a process of prejudice reduction.

The war metaphor is as follows: Wars are fought by states; the enemy is thus an identifiable entity whose interests fundamentally oppose your own. The conflict is zero-sum—the outcome will be victory for one side or the other—and there is no compromise. The war metaphor is totalistic and extreme. Arguably, it was adopted in light of the immensity of damage and national hurt produced by the 9/11 attack. It has insinuated itself into the public discourse about Counterterrorism, and it has guided policy, but it has also met challenges because of lack of fit and the availability of counteranalogies with different lessons of history.

Some of the drawbacks of the war metaphor are addressable in the law enforcement metaphor of Counterterrorism. Unlike war's special status and circumscribed duration, law enforcement is an ongoing concern that must compete for resources with other societal needs. A major advantage of law enforcement over warfare is its focused nature—targeting the actual terrorists, with less likelihood of injuring innocent parties. Yet despite its advantages, the law enforcement metaphor exhibits a partial mismatch with the realities of terrorism. Its complete and uncritical adoption may temporarily hamper terrorists' ability to launch attacks without substantially altering their motivation to do so.

The public health epidemiological model was usefully applied to the epidemic of terror that followed the 9/11 attacks. It utilizes a partition between (a) an external agent, (b) a susceptible host, (c) an environment that brings them together, and (d) the vector that enables transmission of the disease. In the specific application to jihadist terrorism, the agent refers to the militant Islamist ideology, the susceptible host refers to radicalizable Muslim populations, the environment refers to conditions that promote the readiness to embrace such ideology, and the vectors are conduits whereby the ideology is propagated. The epidemiological metaphor has its own advantages over the war and law enforcement metaphors, but also limitations. Whereas the latter metaphors neglect the long-range process of ideological conversion and radicalization that creates terrorists, the epidemiological metaphor neglects the "here and now" of Counterterrorism and the value of resolute strikes and intelligence-gathering activities needed to counter terrorists' concrete schemes and capabilities.

Framing Counterterrorism as the process of prejudice reduction addresses the interaction between two communities whose conflict may breed terrorism. This

"What Should This Fight Be Called? Metaphors of Counterterrorism and Their Implications" by Arie W. Kruglanski, Martha Crenshaw, Jerrold M. Post, and Jeff Victoroff, from *Psychological Science in the Public Interest* (Vol. 8, No. 3), pp. 97-133. Copyright © 2007 Association for Psychological Science. Reprinted by permission of SAGE Publications.

framing shifts the focus from a unilateral to a bilateral concern and acknowledges the contribution to intergroup tensions that the party targeted by terrorists may make. A major tool of prejudice reduction is the creation of positive contact between members of the conflicted groups. Efforts at prejudice reduction via positive contact need to take place in the context of a larger set of policies, such as those concerning immigration laws, educational programs, and foreign policy initiatives designed to augment the good-will-generating efforts of optimal-contact programs. For all its benefits, the prejudice-reduction framework is also not without its drawbacks. Specifically, the positive-contact notion highlights the benefits of mere human interaction; it disregards differences in ideological beliefs between the interacting parties, thereby neglecting an element that appears essential to producing their estrangement and reciprocal animosity. Too, like the epidemiological metaphor, the prejudice-reduction framing takes the long view, thereby neglecting the "here and now" of terrorism and the need to counter specific terrorist threats.

Thus, each of the foregoing frameworks captures some aspects of counterterrorism's effects while neglecting others. Accordingly, an integrated approach to counterterrorism is called for, one that exploits the insights of each metaphor and avoids its pitfalls. Such an approach would maximize the likelihood of enlightened decision making concerning contemplated counterterrorist moves given the complex tradeoffs that each such move typically entails.

INTRODUCTION

Though modern terrorism has captured the world's attention intermittently since the late 19th century (Rapoport, 2004), its contemporary forms pose a particularly acute danger to orderly societies. The coordinated 2001 attacks on the World Trade Center in New York and the Pentagon in Washington, DC, symbolic pillars of American economic and military might; the March 4, 2004 bombing of the Madrid train station; the London transit bombing of July 5, 2005; the daily suicide bombings in Iraq and Afghanistan; the political ascendancy of fundamentalist terrorism-using groups, such as Hamas and Hezbollah; the emergence of the global Salafi Jihad movement inspired by al-Qaeda; and the specter of the acquisition and use of weapons of mass destruction by terrorists have made the task of opposing terrorism as difficult as it is pressing. As one commentator put it, "international terrorism [is] the most serious strategic threat to global peace and safety" (Ganor, 2005, p. 293).

As a form of intelligible human behavior, terrorism has fundamental psychological aspects. It rests on its own subjective rationality (Crenshaw, 1990/1998); Post, 1990) and is anchored in terrorists' ideologically based beliefs about its utility and ethical justifiability (Kruglanski & Fishman, 2006). It is driven by goals it is presumed to serve for groups and individuals. It is enabled by mechanisms of moral disengagement (Bandura, 1998). And it is heavily dependent on processes of communication, persuasion, leadership, and group dynamics (Post, 1986). These varied psychological factors need to be taken into account in devising effective strategies for undermining terrorism and reducing its appeal for sympathizers and potential recruits.

As is the case with any systematic initiative, policies aimed at opposing terrorism require a guiding conception that affords a plan of action and forecasts its likely consequences. Perhaps because terrorism is refractory to a broadly accepted definition[1] (e.g., Schmid & Jongman, 1988), it has been often understood metaphorically, as has counterterrorism. In the present monograph, we review several major metaphors of counterterrorism and assess their likely psychological impacts and policy implications. Specifically, we seek to identify the complex tradeoffs, intricate ramifications, and unintended outcomes that adopting a given counterterrorism metaphor may promote.

Webster's dictionary (1986, p. 746) defines *metaphor* as "a figure of speech in which a word or a phrase literally denoting one kind of object

---

[1] Throughout the present article, the term *terrorism* is meant to refer to violence perpetrated by non-state actors against noncombatants in order to advance ideological objectives via fear. Our analysis pertains primarily to the contemporary Islamist brand of terrorism, rather than to other varieties.

or idea is used in place of another to suggest a likeness or analogy between them." In the present context we use the term loosely to denote a framing or a conceptual paradigm invoked to pinpoint the putative essence of effective counterterrorism. The use of metaphor is commonplace in the construction of new knowledge. It involves an assimilation of a relatively unfamiliar and poorly understood phenomenon (such as terrorism) to a well-known concept embedded in a different domain (Gentner & Jeziorski, 1995, p. 448). Metaphors are ways of understanding complex situations (Gelfand & McCusker, 2002). They structure thought in application to particular events. They constitute ways of simplifying complex realities, and they induce a sense of familiarity and comprehension. Metaphors enable problem setting and the generation of proposed solutions (Shon, 1993). These advantages may be offset by potential oversimplification, stereotyping, and judgmental error. In other words, the "mapping" of one experiential domain onto another may be inaccurate. As Lakoff (1990) has argued, understanding a thing in terms of a particular metaphorical concept necessarily conceals other aspects of that thing that may be inconsistent with the metaphor. Metaphors can thus hide aspects of experience from our perception.

Shimko (2004) highlighted the differences between metaphors and analogies. Both are based on comparisons, but analogies apply to "within-domain" comparisons, whereas metaphors apply to "cross-domain" comparisons. In terms of impact, analogies provide specific policy guidance, whereas metaphors frame or represent problems. Our view is that metaphors of counterterrorism construct a conceptual framework within which historical analogies can be evoked. For instance, without the "war" metaphor of counterterrorism (considered subsequently), the historical analogies to specific wars would not enter the debate.

As is the case with flawed theories generally, flawed metaphors may be abandoned when confronted with inconsistent facts. However, a strong motivational commitment to a particular metaphor may lead to a selective perception of the facts. Such commitment may be augmented by individuals' prior investment in the metaphor's implications (e.g., policymakers' investment in strategic activities implied by a metaphor) and/or by the degree to which such implications serve the user's ulterior agendas or specific interests (Kruglanski, 1996; Kunda, 1990). Adoption of a metaphor can lead to "top-down processing," in which actors' perceptions are biased by the metaphor rather than faithfully reflecting the realities at hand. Such biases are particularly likely when the facts are ambiguous (Hsee, 1993; Kruglanski, 1996; Kunda, 1990), as they often are in the realm of terrorism and counterterrorism.

In the present monograph, co-authored by a political scientist (M.C.), a psychiatrist (J.P.), a neuropsychiatrist (J.V.) and a social/cognitive psychologist (A.K.), we first outline our assumptions regarding the possible psychological objectives of counterterrorism. We then describe four major metaphoric frameworks in which terms counterterrorism has been characterized and consider their implications for pertinent strategies and tactics of counterterrorism. The closing discussion compares the various ways to conceptualize counterterrorism in terms of their potential contributions for controlling terrorism, as well as their pitfalls and pratfalls. Though consistent with known facts and psychological theory, our analysis is primarily conceptual rather than grounded in rigorous empirical findings. Indeed, it is one of our aims to encourage the collection of pertinent psychological data concerning various facets of terrorism and counterterrorism. Nonetheless, we feel that a comparative analysis of counterterrorism framings of the kind attempted here will be useful in focusing policymakers' and researchers' attention on the complexities of the counterterrorism effort and on the potential costs of neglecting these complexities.

PSYCHOLOGICAL OBJECTIVES OF COUNTERTERRORISM

We assume that counterterrorism has short-term and long-term objectives. In the short term, its objective is to thwart specific terrorist attacks. In the long term, it is to minimize their occurrence. From a psychological perspective, such minimization amounts to reducing a party's motivation to pursue terrorism. If the motivation to engage in terrorism persists, attempts at thwarting, however successful, may have merely temporary effects. They may hamper terrorists' *ability* to carry out attacks in given circumstances, yet, sooner or later, motivated actors may find other ways and means of doing so. Targeted assassinations of leaders may prompt the ascendance of fresh operatives to leadership positions (Kaplan, Mintz, Mishal, & Samban, 2005), physical barriers and fences may be surmounted by rocket technology, detection of metal explosives may encourage the use of liquid explosives, protection of symbolic targets may put ordinary targets at risk, and so on.

In contrast, absent the motivation to engage in terrorism, there may be nothing to thwart, hence no need to invest costly resources in interminable "cat and mouse games" with terrorists. In this sense, an approach that promises to reduce groups' and individuals' motivation to pursue violence and to discourage potential recruits from joining terrorism-using groups in the first place may seem superior in the long run to an approach that aims to foil plans for specific acts of violence. But how does one reduce terrorists' motivation?

Recent analyses of terrorism (Atran, 2003; Bloom, 2005; Pedahzur, 2005; Post, 2005, Sageman, 2004; Speckhard & Akhmedova, 2005; Stern, 2003) imply that the heterogeneous motives underlying terrorists' activities around the globe may be subsumed within three broad motivational categories: (a) terrorists' personal traumas or humiliations, (b) the ideologies they subscribe to, and (c) the social influence of their peers and revered authorities. These motivational categories may often function in concert and address different aspects of the process that pushes individuals toward terrorism.

Empirical research suggests that ideological themes (of religious or ethno-nationalist varieties) are ubiquitous in terrorists' narratives (Atran, 2003; Fishman, Orehek, Dechesne, Chen, & Kruglanski, 2007; Hafez, 2007; Kruglanski, Chen, Dechesne, Fishman, & Orehek, in press; Post, 2007; Smith, 2004) and that such themes likely constitute important conscious reasons for individuals' commitment to militancy. Yet, personal traumas and frustrations may create the emotional push to "buy into" those ideologies. In other words, personal frustrations and pain that one is powerless to undo (having a loved one killed by an occupying force, experiencing alienation and discrimination by a majority culture, suffering ostracism from one's community in response to one's normative infractions) may translate into embracing a terrorism-justifying ideology that identifies a collective grievance said to be rectifiable via militancy (Kruglanski et al., in press; Post, 2007; Speckhard & Akhmedova, 2005). Finally, the social influence by members of one's group (e.g., pressure from peers, comrades, and venerated leaders) may instill in an individual the motivation to accept the ideological contents *they* subscribe to as true and valid.

Based on this account, long-term counterterrorism efforts may attempt (a) to alleviate as much as possible the frustrations that prompt individuals to embrace terrorist ideologies; and (b) to invalidate those ideologies, for instance by arguments that the collective-grievance claim is false, that terrorism *is not* an efficient means of addressing the grievance (if it is real), and/or that terrorism is incompatible with other important objectives and moral values. Such invalidation may be carried out by (c) a social-influence process involving communicators or "epistemic authorities" (Kruglanski et al., 2005) that the terrorists and/or their sympathizers find credible. The various counterterrorism framings discussed subsequently may be assessed in reference to these objectives.

In this paper, we describe four major metaphors in which terms counterterrorism has been characterized:

- Counterterrorism as *war* (as in the "global war on terrorism")
- Counterterrorism as *law enforcement*
- Counterterrorism as *containment of a social epidemic*
- Counterterrorism as a program of *prejudice reduction*

We now proceed to describe each in turn.

COUNTERTERRORISM AS WAR

Framing post-9/11 counterterrorist policy as a "global war on terrorism" or a "war on terror" represents a conceptual construction, a metaphor reinforced by historical examples or analogies (Shimko, 2004) that helps define the American perception of the threat of terrorism. In speeches and writings of U.S. officials, the metaphor of war is strengthened and made more concrete by references to specific past wars, such as the Second World War or the Cold War. Such references evoke distinct narratives and have an emotional and cultural resonance with the public. This dramatic framing of the threat is a departure from its portrayal by past administrations, although the United States had previously "gone to war" against social problems such as drugs and crime and earlier U.S. administrations had employed military force against terrorists, albeit in limited fashion (the Reagan administration's actions in Libya in 1986, the Clinton administration's actions in Afghanistan and Sudan in 1998). Furthermore, what might initially have seemed an abstraction or a rhetorical flourish—the idea of a "war" as an all-out effort against some evil—became real and literal with the wars in Afghanistan in October of 2001 and, especially, in Iraq in 2003. Whether or not the war in Iraq is part and parcel of the war on terrorism is a subject of political dispute, and critics of the Iraq war themselves appeal to a different historical analogy: Vietnam.

One question that is often raised is whether or not powerful metaphors and analogies are adopted for public consumption only, rather than actually guiding decision-making. In a study of the 1965 decisions during the Vietnam War, Khong (1992) found that the private deliberations of policymakers mirrored their public stance. American leaders were genuinely influenced by their choice of analogy (in this case, the Korean War was the dominant historical analogy). As Vertzberger (1990, p. 306) noted, "argumentation by reference to history is a vital component of policy formulation and serves as a means of persuading both the self and others." Holmes (2006) similarly sees the Bush administration as guided by the same references that are presented to the public. In short, metaphors and historical analogies are relevant to policies. They can increase the intensity of motivation for a particular action, or remove inhibitions. They legitimize particular policies, and lend them force. In short, they exert a clear and present influence on world affairs.

The Break From the Past

The idea of a war on terrorism represents a departure from the conceptions of past U.S. administrations in regard to this problem. After all, terrorism against the United States is not a new phenomenon. It has threatened American interests since the mid 1960s, so that in 1972 the U.S. government saw fit to establish a Cabinet Committee to Combat Terrorism.

The Nixon administration faced Palestinian terrorism abroad and violence at home accompanying the student protest movement against the Vietnam War. President Nixon tended to prefer a disease metaphor and interpreted the two phenomena as the same threat: Palestinian hijackings and a bombing at the University of Wisconsin were thus described as symptoms of the "same cancerous disease" (Nixon 1970). (The disease analogue is central to the social epidemic metaphor considered later in this monograph.) Nixon expressed fears that society would accept such violence and permissiveness and that it would be, in effect, contagious. The disease metaphor wasn't exclusive of other negative metaphors and epithets in which terms Nixon depicted terrorists. They were defined as "international outlaws" (Nixon, 1972a, 1973; recalling the law enforcement metaphor considered later) and terrorism was said to threaten "the very principles on which nations are founded" (Nixon, 1972b).

The Carter administration had to deal with the Iran hostage crisis. The president frequently expressed a fear of anarchy and of rules being abandoned. He described terrorism as a threat to civilization, the rule of law, and human decency. The Iranian hostage crisis, in his somewhat introspective view, was a test for America. Carter brought a religious dimension to his perspective that "220 million people [are] brought to their knees not in submission but in prayer" (Carter, 1980) for the hostages' release. Moreover, he stressed that American concern for the hostages showed that it was a moral nation with character, strength, and greatness. His speeches contained frequent references to Iranian government support of "mob violence and terrorism" (Carter 1979a) and referred to "an irresponsible attempt at blackmail . . . supported by Iranian officials" (Carter, 1979b). His focus was on unity at home, American vulnerability to foreign oil supplies, and the need to protect human rights.

Reagan came to power believing that Carter's response to the hostage crisis was unacceptably weak. He referred to "swift and effective retribution" (Reagan, 1981) at the welcoming ceremony for the returning hostages in January of 1981. His consistent theme was the need for firmness: Terrorism would not be tolerated, the United States would not be intimidated, and its resolve would not be shaken. National pride, not national security, was at stake. Terrorism was defined as an attack on democracy, freedom, and even civilization itself. It was described as a form of surrogate warfare, which linked it to states—particularly the Soviet Union and its allies. Reagan warned that sponsors would be held responsible, and he put these words into practice in 1986 when the

United States bombed Libyan targets (the capital, Tripoli, and the Benghazi region) in retaliation for its involvement in a terrorist attack in Germany. Terrorism was said to blur the distinction between peace and war. Like Nixon, Reagan favored the disease metaphor: "If we permit terrorism to succeed anywhere, it will spread like cancer" (Reagan, 1985); the world needs to come to grips with "the plague of terrorism" (Reagan, 1986).

Reagan's rhetoric tended toward the imaginative and extravagant: At different times he called terrorists fanatical, cowardly, cynical, madmen, skulking barbarians, vicious, ruthless, savage, criminals, thugs, despicable, repulsive, pitiless, crude, indiscriminate, evil, contemptible, and abhorrent. Terrorism was described as senseless, ugly, wanton, grisly, intolerable, and heinous. It was denned as an atrocity and an affront to humanity.

Clinton entered office determined to tone down the government's rhetoric and avoid any suggestion of a "clash of civilizations" (Huntington, 1998). His general themes were the pursuit of justice, law enforcement, and international cooperation. Terrorism was compared to other intractable global problems such as drugs, crime, the environment, and disease. These common dangers were defined as boundary-crossing threats prevalent in the post-Cold War world, part of an environment characterized by modernity, open societies, open borders, technological advance, and access to information. Terrorism was often discussed in the context of nuclear proliferation and ethnic and nationalist conflict. (Clinton was particularly concerned with the threat of chemical and biological terrorism.) Even though the Clinton administration acknowledged that Osama bin Laden had declared war against the United States, and even though Clinton used military force to retaliate against terrorism-linked targets in Sudan and Afghanistan after the 1998 embassy bombings, Clinton did not adopt the war metaphor but employed more moderate—if somewhat combative—language, such as "[not letting] the terrorists . . . have the victory" (Clinton, 1996a), "battling terrorism" (Clinton, 2000), and "[taking] the fight to terrorists" (Clinton, 1996b).

In his farewell address to the nation in January, 2001, Clinton remained temperate about terrorism in providing his thoughts for the future:

> [B]ecause the world is more connected every day, in every way, America's security and prosperity require us to continue to lead in the world. At this remarkable moment in history, more people live in freedom than ever before. Our alliances are stronger than ever. People around the world look to America to be a force for peace and prosperity, freedom and security.
>
> The global economy is giving more of our own people and billions around the world the chance to work and live and raise their families with dignity. But the forces of integration that have created these good opportunities also make us more subject to global forces of destruction, to terrorism, organized crime and narcotrafficking, the spread of deadly weapons and disease, the degradation of the global environment. (Clinton, 2001)

Terrorism is thus only one of several "forces of destruction." The question of agency—who the responsible perpetrators are—is left out.

THE WAR METAPHOR

After he came to office, President Bush initially spoke of terrorism as one of a number of "new and different threats, sometimes hard to define and defend against, threats such as terrorism, information warfare, the spread of weapons of mass destruction" (Bush, 2001a). However, on September 11, 2001, this changed. Bush adopted the war construct immediately, in the heat of the moment, according to Woodward (2002), although Suskind (2006, p. 19) recounts that in the period between September 11 and September 20, when the "war" was first declared, the meaning of the term drifted and several "facsimiles" were floated. Woodward (2002, pp. 30-31) reports that Bush's chief speechwriter, Michael Gerson, included the sentence "This is an act of war" in the first draft of the President's brief speech to the nation on the evening of 9/11, and that other assistants (communications director Dan Bartlett, for example) supported the declaration, but that the President ordered it taken out (and stuck to his decision) because he wanted to reassure the public. However, on the morning of September 12, after a meeting of the National Security Council, the President told reporters "The deliberate and deadly attacks which were carried out yesterday against our country were more than acts of terror. They were acts of war" (Woodward, 2002, p. 45; Woodward describes this as a deliberate escalation of public rhetoric).

It is understandable that the enormity of the destructiveness of the 9/11 attacks would lead the president to reach for a comparison with the worst threat that could be imagined. Certainly the attack itself seemed to meet the requirements of an "act of war." Had it been committed by a state, the U.N. Charter certainly would have permitted the United States to use force in self-defense. Furthermore, being a "wartime President" seemed to suit Bush's personality; Suskind (2006) comments that he liked to call himself by this role (p. 72). His swift decision-making style also seemed appropriate for a crisis situation, whereas prior to 9/11 it might have been a liability. The President liked to hear "tales of combat" when he was briefed by the intelligence community and was apparently deeply interested in individual al-Qaeda leaders. Suskind recounts in the early days much boasting about putting their heads on sticks or bringing their heads back in boxes (p. 21).

Essentials of the War Metaphor

The war metaphor is as follows. Wars are fought by states.[2] The enemy is thus an identifiable national entity whose interests fundamentally oppose those of one's own nation. The stakes could not be higher, since the national security, indeed the very existence, of each side is threatened. The conflict is zero-sum—the outcome will be victory for one side or the other. The enemy necessarily wishes to destroy you, the defender, typically by conquering or destroying your territory. (Thus the frequent admonition with regard to Iraq, "if we weren't fighting them there, we would be fighting them here"; wars are about defending the homeland.) By "war," we understand the Clausewitzian sense of "total war," in which there is no compromise.

Being in a state of war has other connotations for domestic politics. National unity is required, and the population must be mobilized in support of the cause. Dissent is thus easily interpreted as unpatriotic—or even as giving aid and comfort to the enemy. Going to war calls up the values of solidarity, heroism, valor, and sacrifice. And in war, of course, God is always on one's own side. The moral dimension is clear.

The prescriptive part of the war metaphor is also straightforward. Nations do not go to war without using military force. The solution to the problem as diagnosed has to be military. Thus, necessarily, the U.S. Department of Defense (DOD) must play a lead role in the war on terror (and the DOD began planning the invasion of Afghanistan in November 2001, although early on the CIA took the lead role in the fight against al-Qaeda in Afghanistan and around the world).

Furthermore, if the struggle against terrorism is a war, the President's role as Commander in Chief must dominate his other roles. In wartime, leaders are given extraordinary powers. Measures that would not be acceptable in peacetime (restrictions on civil liberties, brutal interrogation practices, etc.) are now necessary. Thus an expansion of executive power accompanies the war metaphor.

Issues of Fit

The fit of the generic war metaphor to combating terrorism is problematic at the outset. First, there is the question of who the enemy is. The entity that attacked the United States in 2001 was not a state. It was an organization, al-Qaeda, with a territorial base within the weak "failed state" of Afghanistan, whose ruling Taliban regime was not internationally recognized. The regime in partial control of that state, which had harbored al-Qaeda, was quickly overthrown (although the Taliban still exist and are now resurgent). However, since 2001, as a result of pressures that are due only in part to the war in Afghanistan, the threat of terrorism has been transformed into something much more amorphous and diffuse. The agency behind the threat thus has even fewer of the qualities of a state adversary than it did prior to the war in Afghanistan. Moreover, even prior to the invasion of Afghanistan by the United States and its allies, al-Qaeda lacked the capacity to defeat or destroy the United States (nor is it even certain that bin Laden had the intent to do so). It posed little threat to the U.S. armed forces. It could not conquer the United States nor deprive it of vital resources.

Suskind (2006) refers to the war in Afghanistan as a "bridge" between the old and the new modes of the struggle against terrorism (p. 53) and as a prelude to Iraq (p. 79). It also seemed to end in clear-cut victory (although as time has passed the outcome appears less certain). The threat from

---

[2] We also have the concept of civil war, which involves a government fighting an army of its citizens for control of the country. But since the threat in the current instance issues from outside the nation's boundaries, the basic concept of interstate war is the relevant one.

Iraq fit the war metaphor even more easily, and it too was an effective bridge between conventional war and war on terrorism. The initial rationale for war was that Iraq was hostile to U.S. interests, that it possessed weapons of mass destruction, and that it might give those weapons to terrorists who had already demonstrated their harmful intent. Iraq had also conquered one neighbor and threatened others, in line with traditional state expansionism. Thus, linking Iraq to terrorists and going to war with that nation on those grounds could be seen as a way of making the reality of counterterrorism fit the abstraction of the war metaphor.

The Bush administration used the "counterterrorism as war" construct to argue that the post-2003 war in Iraq is an integral and necessary part of counterterrorism, but for many the connection weakened as the war progressed.[3] While most observers agreed that the 2001 war in Afghanistan was essential to diminishing the threat of al-Qaeda, whether or not they accepted the war metaphor for counterterrorism policy, the issue of Iraq provoked fierce debate both within and outside the United States. Critics of U.S. policy argue that the war in Iraq is a distraction from the struggle against terrorism. They contend that the war in Iraq actually increases the threat of terrorism and makes the United States less secure. The war gives the "violent extremists" against whom the United States is fighting both valuable experience and a popular cause: defending Islam against Western military incursions. Public opinion polls by *The New York Times* and *CBS News* in August of 2006 showed that a bare majority (55%) of those surveyed approved of the President's handling of the campaign against terrorism (this figure was up slightly from the previous week). Also, 51% of the sample thought that the war in Iraq was independent of the war on terrorism, an increase of 10 percentage points since June of that year (Hulse & Connelly, 2006).

War Against What?

Over the 5 years since 2001, the general perception of the terrorist enemy has shifted somewhat from an entity or entities of some sort (so-called "terrorist organizations") to an *ideology* that aspires to world domination. Despite Iraq—or perhaps because it was revealed that Saddam Hussein did not have connections with al-Qaeda—it has not been easy to develop a clear conception of what or who the enemy is. The 2006 National Strategy for Combating Terrorism (White House, 2006b) defines the enemy as having a "murderous ideology" (p. 3), a movement united by an "ideology of oppression, violence, and hate" (p. 4), that wishes to establish totalitarian rule over a world empire. (It thus combines elements of the criminal and the state foe.) This enemy threatens "global peace, international security and prosperity, the rising tide of democracy, and the right of all people to live without fear of indiscriminate violence" (p.6). David Brooks, writing in *The New York Times* on September 21, 2006, expressed frustration:

> The definition of the threat determines the remedies we select to combat it, and yet what we have now is a clash of incongruous definitions and an enemy that is chaos theory in human form—an ever-shifting array of state and non-state actors who cooperate, coagulate, divide, feud, and feed on one another without end (Brooks, 2006a, p. 31).

The Detainee Issue

Further political complications were created by the issue of how to treat captured members of enemy forces. Strict application of the war metaphor would require that they be considered prisoners of war and thus subject to the provisions of international law embodied in the Geneva Conventions. Because the Bush administration did not wish to accord its prisoners these rights, it devised the awkward category of *unlawful enemy combatants*. The treatment of detainees continues to be politically controversial, damaging to the country's moral claims, and subject to legal challenge.

Criteria for Victory

Beyond the issue of defining the enemy, a second question is what victory in a war on terrorism would mean. How will we know when we have won? An ideal-type real war would end in the capitulation of the enemy (although real wars sometimes end in messy stalemates on the ground

---

[3]But see Gershkoff and Kushner (2005), who argue that the war in Iraq initially received public support because it was successfully framed as an extension of the global war on terror. They also note the absence of public debate over the war framing based on their analysis of Bush's speeches from September 11, 2001, to May 1, 2003. The 2006 elections indicate, however, declining support for this formulation.

with no formal treaty to terminate the conflict), but the proponents of a war on terrorism do not expect al-Qaeda to issue a formal surrender. *The National Strategy for Combating Terrorism 2003* (White House, 2003) described victory as "a world in which our children can live free from fear and where the threat of terrorist attacks does not define our daily lives" (p. 12) and the national goal sees the United States and its allies as eliminating "terrorism as a threat to the our way of life" (p. 29). In 2006, the revised strategy defined its goal as being to "bring an end to the scourge of terrorism" (White House, 2006b, p. 3) and to bring about the "defeat of violent extremism" (p. 7) around the world. It will be difficult to tell when these objectives—eradicating a method of violence and a way of thinking—have been met.

Another problem with employing the war metaphor is that it structures expectations about victory (despite administration warnings from the start that the war would be long). At the least, it leads opinion pollsters to ask whether their respondents think the government is winning the war. Thus, according to a survey by *Foreign Policy* and the Center for American Progress in the summer of 2006, most of the experts who were surveyed (a bipartisan majority of 84%) did not think that the United States was winning the war on terrorism (Center for American Progress & *Foreign Policy*, 2006, p.49-55). Almost 80% of the over 100 experts who were questioned had worked in the American government. Asked if they thought the world was becoming safer or more dangerous for the United States and the American people, 86% thought that the world was much or somewhat more dangerous.

On the other hand, the journalist and political commentator James Fallows (2006) thinks that the United States is succeeding and that it is time to declare victory. He claims that the 60-odd experts he interviewed are quite positive about the outcome of the war on terrorism (although they disapprove of the war in Iraq). In his view, al-Qaeda "Central" has been defeated, and a second 9/11 is highly unlikely. In Fallows' opinion, the United States is its own worst enemy by responding clumsily to provocations. To him the answer is simply to declare that we have won the global war on terror. Maintaining a standing state of war indefinitely offers no advantages; instead, he says, it "cheapens the concept of war, making the word a synonym for *effort or goal*" (p.71).

An ongoing state of war predisposes a nation to overreaction and maintaining a permanent state of emergency, encourages fear by raising public anxieties, and (as we would expect from the effects of a metaphor) blinds people to possibilities other than military force—such as more effective diplomacy. Fallows also argues that an open-ended war is an invitation to defeat because more terrorist attacks are bound to happen. A victory declaration could thus be a means of escaping the metaphor trap that the Bush administration set for itself.

ANALOGIES AND THE LESSONS OF HISTORY

The generic and abstract war metaphor has been reinforced by concrete historical analogies to World War II and to the Cold War, including both the "war's" conduct and its ending. In the context of the Second World War, two events stand out in collective memory: Munich and Pearl Harbor. These are sources of transgenerational analogies, in that they influence both the generation that lived through them and later generations who did not have the same formative experience. Both events have deep meaning in the American view of history. They are available, vivid, and persistent myths with enormous affective power, resistant to disconfirmation by new information (see Vertzberger, 1990, p. 329). In the post-2003 debate over the Iraq war, critics of the Bush administration increasingly refer to a more recent counter-analogy, the war in Vietnam. It suggests a much more negative policy outcome.

President Bush also made unfortunate allusions to the Crusades in the early post 9/11 period. Here it was probably the case that he meant the reference as a general metaphor to imply a "moral crusade" against evil rather than as a specific comparison of American policy to the Western assaults on Muslims during the Middle Ages, which is the sense in which Osama bin Laden invokes the idea of a crusade when he refers to his enemy as "Jews and Crusaders" (bin Laden, 1998a).[4] It is easy to misjudge the emotional

---

[4] But see Graham, Keenan, and Dowd (2004), who compare the President's remarks on returning to the White House on September 16, 2001 (Bush 2001b) to that of Pope Urban II in 1095 to the Council of Clermont (Krey, 23), which launched the Crusades, calling both speeches "'call to arms' texts" (p. 200). We are indebted to Joanna Scott for drawing this article to our attention.

effect of an analogy on an unfamiliar audience. Misplaced analogies can backfire and be politically dangerous. In this specific case they may feed negative images of the United States and fuel anti-American sentiments among Muslims.

Pearl Harbor

Woodward (2002, p. 37) reports that President Bush wrote in his diary on the night of September 11: "The Pearl Harbor of the 21st century took place today." The Pearl Harbor analogy may be an intuitive one for trying to understand the events of 9/11, since that attack also was a deadly surprise attack from the air. The Pearl Harbor analogy supports the war metaphor because Pearl Harbor led to war against Japan. It also supports the concept of the enemy as an entity that wishes to establish totalitarian rule over a world empire (as per the 2006 strategy statement; White House, 2006a). The analogy does not fit the current adversary or even pre-2001 al-Qaeda very well, of course, as Japan was a major military and economic power fully embarked on expansionist policies in Asia. It was already an empire. Furthermore, the Japanese attack was on an American military target, not on civilians in the U.S. homeland. Yet the Pearl Harbor analogy also implies a conclusion about how a war following an unjustified and devastating surprise attack will end: victory, unconditional surrender of the adversary, occupation of the enemy's homeland, and restoration of that enemy to the ranks of civilized nations by transforming it into a democracy. If the war in Iraq is part of the war on terrorism, then the lessons of history are clear.

The Pearl Harbor analogy may also contribute to the assumption not just that the proper response is war but also that preemption is essential to a defensive military strategy. If one is at risk of a devastating surprise attack and cannot prevent it, then (as Roberta Wohlstetter's classic 1962 study of the Pearl Harbor attack advises, since intelligence services cannot distinguish between signals and noise) the best strategy is to preempt the adversary. Preemption (which shaded easily into preventive war) was a hallmark of the 2002 National Security Strategy (White House, 2002), although it was less prominent in the 2006 version (White House, 2006b). The idea of preemption helped justify war in Iraq. If the claim, that Saddam Hussein possessed weapons of mass destruction had been true, then he could have been capable of a more horrifying surprise attack than 9/11 or even Pearl Harbor. (It is interesting that what Ramzi Yousef, a planner of the 1993 World Trade Center bombing, bin Laden, and others invoke with regard to their critiques of the Pacific war is the American use of atomic weapons against Japan (bin Laden, 2005; Bird & Sherwin, 2005; "Excerpts From Statements in Court," 1998). Woodward (2002, pp. 22-23, also p. 283) reports that surprise was one of Donald Rumsfeld's major themes when he became secretary of defense. According to Woodward, Rumsfeld handed out copies of Wohlstetter's book on Pearl Harbor to his subordinates.

The comparison between 9/11 and Pearl Harbor remained a main theme in the Bush administration's discourse on the struggle against terrorism. For example, in December 2005, on the anniversary of Pearl Harbor, President Bush have a speech emphasizing the continuities between the two events to the Council on Foreign Relations in Washington:

> Like generations before us, we're taking the fight to those who attacked us—and those who share their murderous vision for future attacks. Like generations before us, we've faced setbacks on the path to victory—yet we will fight this war without wavering. And like the generations before us, we will prevail (Bush, 2005c).

Munich

The Munich analogy has been arguably even more salient to American policymakers than the Pearl Harbor analogy. It is pervasive and persistent in American political commentary and historical analysis. Its lesson is that any concession to an adversary is fatal; "appeasement" is the worst option to choose when confronted by an aggressor. Chamberlain's sincere attempt to avoid war by accepting what appeared to be minor, even justifiable, demands on Hitler's behalf only made war more likely.[5] Restraint and patience only encouraged aggression. The enemy, as in the Japanese case, was a totalitarian empire that aspired to

---

[5] In fact, David Brooks (2006b) referred to one wing of the conservative foreign policy camp as "Churchillians." Churchillians "know that occasionally civilization is confronted by enemies so ideologically extreme and so greedy for domination that decent nations must use military power to confront and defeat them" (p. 413).

world domination. Germany was also a deceptive enemy, pretending to be satisfied with small gains while hiding a desire for world conquest. Victory required unconditional surrender, military occupation, and democratization, as in Japan. In both cases, the long-term outcome was highly positive: a stable and democratic ally. But if success in Iraq is defined as success in the war on terrorism, then the analogy is prescriptive.

Fascism

The reference to an "axis of evil" in the January 2002 State of the Union speech (Bush, 2002) also recalled the Axis powers of the second world war. Thus states labeled as supporters of terrorism (Iran and Syria primarily) become the equivalent of 1930s and 40s Germany and Italy. In addition, the general World War II framing surely contributed to the use of the labels "Islamofascism" and "Islamic fascists," terms used by President Bush in 2005 (Bush, 2005a) and 2006.[6] Although the use of the label appears to date at least back to 1990 (Ruthven, 1990), well before the war on terrorism, the President's references provoked a storm of controversy.

These analogies contribute to a view of the global jihadist movement,[7] which was characterized by the 2006 National Intelligence Estimate" as "Al Qaeda, affiliated and independent terrorist groups, and emerging networks and cells" and as "decentralized, lacking a coherent global strategy, and increasingly diffuse" (Office of the Director of National Intelligence, 2006), as being, instead, a monolithic and powerful enemy. Likening jihadism to interwar fascism makes this diverse and dispersed movement appear as a genuine, unified mass movement capable of capturing state power rather than as an ideology with limited appeal.

The NIE finds that the jihadist idea of governance (a state ruled by Islam and waging relentless war—i.e., jihad—against unbelievers) is unpopular with the vast majority of Muslims. In the view of the intelligence community, then, actual jihadism does not resemble the historical examples of National Socialism in Germany or fascism in Italy.

The Cold War

The war on terrorism is also compared to the Cold War. This analogy predicts that the war will be long, a "generational struggle" according to the strategy statements, rather than conclude in a matter of years as World War II did. It also predicts that the opponent will eventually collapse if sufficient military power is exerted. Holmes (2006) gleans from Francis Fukuyama's (2006) analysis of the Bush Administration's Iraq decisions that the administration misunderstood the causes of the collapse of the Soviet Union, attributing it to the pressure of American military power. In thinking that an adversary can be completely destroyed by superior force, administration policymakers have apparently forgotten that the strength of the Soviet Union was consistently overestimated. The Cold War required a state of permanent crisis, with the nation constantly under mortal threat, and this perception of the world carried over to the post-Cold War world. Furthermore, the Cold War analogy has encouraged the use of tropes from that period, such as charging opponents of one's policy with being "soft" on Communism/terrorism. Holmes contends:

> Under such conditions, a counterterrorism policy that aims at extirpating the terrorist threat is bound to be delusional. Promoted by an unsound analogy with the end of the Soviet Union, such Utopian impatience can also be profoundly self-defeating, especially if it prompts policy-makers to focus irrationally on the wrong part of the threat—for example, on a minor danger that happens to lend itself to definitive obliteration. Saddam Hussein comes to mind. (Holmes, 2006, p. 1)

The Vietnam War

The war metaphor also permits critics of the war in Iraq to call up a hotly contested competing analogy: the Vietnam War. As early as May 2004, the Strategic Studies Institute of the U.S. Army War College issued a report arguing that the

---

[6] "Islamofascism" was first used by President Bush in a speech to the National Endowment for Democracy, October 6, 2005 (Bush, 2005a). On May 25, 2006, in a news conference with Prime Minister Tony Blair, Bush referred to al-Qaeda using the phrase "Islamic fascism" (Bush, 2006). See Pollitt (2006) and, for the other side of the debate, see Kramer (2006).

[7] Jihadism has been defined as "a revolutionary program whose ideology promises radical social change in the Muslim world. It displays a coherent set of beliefs and behaviours, which . . . give a central role to jihad as an armed political struggle to overthrow 'apostate' regimes, to expel their infidel allies, and thus to restore Muslim lands to governance by Islamic principles" (Charters, 2007). "The jihadism that adopts terrorism as its most recent military strategy is only one branch of Islamism. This jihadism presents a new pattern for warfare, one that is no longer waged between organized state armies" (Tibi. 2007).

military dimensions of the two wars could not be compared (and referring to a host of press articles making the comparison; Record & Terrill, 2004). They conclude, however, that "reasoning by historical analogy is an inherently risky business" (p. 61). Policymakers' knowledge of history is often poor, they said, and they are predisposed to choose analogies that suit a preferred policy. Thus proponents of the Iraq war embraced the Munich analogy, and opponents cited Vietnam. The authors of the report acknowledge that, as in Vietnam in 1965, U.S. power and prestige have been massively committed. "Under no circumstances *other than the descent of Iraq into civil war* should the U.S. abandon Iraq as it did Vietnam in 1975" (Record & Terrill, 2004, p. 55; italics added), and we should not underestimate the insurgents in Iraq, as we did the Vietcong. The authors recommend that policymakers consider two instructive dimensions of the analogy: the need for effective state-building, on the one hand, and the need for domestic public support, on the other. Furthermore, policymakers should note that Iran might come to play the role of North Vietnam.

In December 2005, President Bush, answering a reporter's question regarding Howard Dean, Chairman of the Democratic National Committee, who was making an analogy of Iraq to Vietnam, replied "there's pessimists, you know, and politicians who try to score points" (Bush, 2005b). In the spring of 2006, Stephen Biddle, a senior fellow at the Council on Foreign Relations, denied the relevance of the Iraq-Vietnam analogy: "Vietnam was a Maoist peoples' war, Iraq is a communal civil war" (Biddle, 2006 p. 10). Despite this, he argued, the administration is actually following the same policies. While advocating a policy change, Biddle admits that changing policy will require replacing "a Manichaean narrative featuring evil insurgents and a noble government with a complicated story of multiparty interethnic intrigue" (Biddle, 2006, p.12).

> Understanding the contested nature of the Vietnam analogy may help explain why the administration resisted the charge that Iraq was slipping into civil war (see Sambanis, 2006) and why former secretary of defense Donald Rumsfeld dismissed the term "insurgents" in favor of "enemies of the legitimate Iraqi government" (see Milbank, 2005).

CONCLUDING COMMENTS: PSYCHOLOGICAL ASPECTS OF THE WAR METAPHOR

Why does the Bush administration's conception of counterterrorism policy as a "war" matter? It seems clear that the metaphorical and analogical reasoning underlying this framing is a genuine reflection of key policymakers' views, not just a way of framing the issue in order to mobilize the public behind a new policy that is potentially more risky and costly than past responses to terrorism. The war metaphor is totalistic and extreme in its demands. Arguably, it was adopted in light of the immensity of damage and national hurt produced by the 9/11 attack. In addition, it might have suited the beliefs, policy objectives, and personal styles of key decision makers and was useful in implementing policy interests that entered with the Bush administration. It has insinuated itself into the public discourse about counterterrorism, and it has guided policy, but it has also met challenges because of lack of fit and the availability of counteranalogies with different lessons of history.

Suskind (2006) offers a motivational explanation for the relatively unchallenged development of the war metaphor and its acceptance in the early days after 9/11:

> 9/11 allowed for preparation to meet opportunity. The result: potent, wartime authority was granted to those guiding the ship of state. A final, customary check in wartime—demonstrable evidence of troop movements or casualties, of divisions on the move, with correspondents filing dispatches—was also missing once the Afghanistan engagement ended. In the wide, diffuse "war on terror," so much of it occurring in the shadows—with no transparency and only perfunctory oversight—the administration could say anything it wanted to say and the public was motivated to accept its interpretation in order to escape the ambiguity, and attain cognitive clarity and closure. (pp. 98–99)

The war metaphor of counterterrorism focuses on an actor who employs violence as a tactic and is defined as the enemy. The psychological rationale of war in its general sense is to bring the enemy to its knees and convince it, and its support base, that its objectives are unattainable. In this sense, the logic of warfare in its application to terrorism is to address that part of the terrorists' belief system that sees terrorism as effective, and to demonstrate compellingly that it is not (Kruglanski & Fishman, 2006).

Does this logic work? Cumulative experience (in Chechnya, Afghanistan, Iraq, Ireland, or Palestine) suggests that the use of military force to "prove" the inefficacy of terrorism may have limited success. Often, military strikes against terrorist targets may have short-term effects involving temporary interference with terrorists' ability to launch their operations but might not undermine terrorists' motivation (Kaplan et al., 2005), because of the enmity that foreign occupation typically engenders and the injustice and excesses that the waging of war typically entails. In this connection, Anthony Cordesman (2006), a strategy expert at the Center for Strategic and International Studies in Washington, DC, stated that the "US . . . needs to give avoiding unnecessary civilian casualties and collateral damage *the same priority* as directly destroying the enemy" (p. 15, emphasis added). A 2007 news item (Tang, 2007) states that more Afghan civilians were killed by U.S. or NATO forces (203 from January 1 to June 23, 2007) than were killed in attacks by the Taliban (178). In response, Afghan president Hamid Karzai "directed . . . his anger at foreign forces for being careless and viewing Afghan life as cheap" (Tang, 2007). Evoking such anger is a seemingly unavoidable (if unintended) consequence of waging massive military operations (i.e., "war") against terrorists and the result of conflating the "war on terrorism" with more limited interventions in insurgencies.

The perpetrators of terrorism have often claimed considerable staying power, as well as numerous achievements on the ground. Hezbollah boasts having forced the withdrawal from Lebanon of the French, the Italians and the Americans in 1984, and of the Israelis in 2000. Hamas credits its waves of suicidal terrorism for the Israeli disengagement from Gaza in 2005 (see Prusher & Mitnick, 2005). The destabilization in Iraq, perpetrated by terrorist attacks with partial involvement of al-Qaeda, highlights the considerable difficulty of defeating terrorism by military force alone. The apparent staying power of various terrorist organizations and their survival of massive assaults by superior military powers—in a war that they themselves declared on the United States in 1996—feeds the belief that the West is vulnerable and tends to run out of steam, so that despite momentary setbacks (like that in Afghanistan), insurgency will prove effective and, ultimately, successful.

Nor is the war concept sufficiently attuned to the sources of terrorists' motivation. By framing the issue squarely in terms of "good" versus "evil" (a framing often invoked to justify a massive effort such as war) it minimizes attempts to appreciate the other side's concerns or address the frustrations and grievances that may have fostered terrorism, as well as the belief systems (jihadism) that may have lent it ideological sustenance.

Finally, framing counterterrorism as war may exact considerable costs from society. It threatens to corrupt its values, disrupt its orderly functioning, and reshuffle its priorities. We have already commented on war's all-encompassing nature. It calls for the disproportionate investment of a nation's resources, with correspondingly less left for other concerns such as the economy, health, welfare, or education (McCauley, 2007). For a nation at war, security is the overriding goal, and it trumps (or renders less psychologically accessible) alternative national objectives or ethical values. As a consequence, putative means to security become liberated from constraints usually dictated by alternative objectives (Kruglanski et al., 2002). "Collateral damage," ethnic profiling, overly harsh interrogation tactics, unlimited internment of suspects, etc., may all be condoned given the centrality of security concerns and excused by the uniqueness of circumstances the war concept implies.

Most problematic is the difficulty with war termination. Despite the Bush administration's cautions concerning a "long war" and the attempts to redefine "victory," well remembered in the public's mind is the surrender ceremony on the deck of the USS Missouri, marking the unconditional surrender of the adversary and cessation of conflict. Imprisoned by the metaphor, as long as terrorist bombs keep exploding, the war is not over, and the United States must remain on a war footing.

COUNTERTERRORISM AS LAW ENFORCEMENT
MAGNITUDE OF THE CHALLENGE TO STATE AUTHORITY

Some of the drawbacks of the war metaphor are addressable in the law enforcement metaphor of counterterrorism. One thing war and law enforcement have in common is that they both constitute major ways in which states are geared to protect their citizens from harm. The choice between them will often depend on the perceived magnitude of the challenge—law enforcement constituting the response to a relatively restricted challenge to the state's authority, and war to a massive one. For instance, on February 16, 1993, Ramzi Yousef and his co-conspirators placed a truck bomb in the parking garage of the World Trade Center that resulted in six deaths, hundreds of injuries, and property damage not exceeding half a billion dollars (McCauley, 2007). The response to this event was entirely in terms of law enforcement, including extensive police work, prosecution, trials, and convictions. Compare this with the devastating attack on the same structure on September 11, 2001 that caused close to 3,000 deaths and untold tens of billions in damage. The response to that attack was war. The implicit attributional logic of such differential responding could be that a high-magnitude effect requires a cause of a comparable magnitude (Kelley, 1971), elimination of which requires a commensurately powerful response, in turn.

Qualitative Differences Between War and Law Enforcement

Beyond the difference in response magnitude, the war and the law enforcement metaphors have qualitatively distinct implications for how terrorism is understood and reacted to. Whereas the war metaphor is focused on an actor defined as the enemy, the law enforcement metaphor is focused on the act (the "crime") deemed unacceptable and unlawful. In support of the law enforcement approach. Shibley Telhami (2004), a political scientist and Mideast expert, argued that an emphasis on the (criminal) terrorist activities would be more efficient than "waging war" on the terrorists and their supporters. Specifically:

> if American efforts focus on defeating 'terrorist means' defined as the deliberate targeting of civilians, the United States would have a better chance of succeeding. [This would involve rallying] the international community to apply the principle universally . . . In this way a deliberate attack on civilian targets in one state would become an attack on all. (p. 10)

Similarly, Senator John Kerry, in a presidential candidates' debate in South Carolina in 2004, stated that, although counterterrorism will be "occasionally military," it should be "primarily an intelligence and law enforcement operation that requires cooperation around the world" (Will, 2006). The United Nations has never been able to agree on a definition of terrorism, but it has developed several articles prohibiting particular acts—such as airline hijacking and violence against diplomatic persons—consistent with a law enforcement framing.

Beginnings and Endings

In a recent chapter, McCauley (2007) systematically compared the law enforcement metaphor of counterterrorism to the war metaphor, and identified a number of major differences between them. Unlike wars that typically have clear-cut beginnings and endings, law enforcement is a continual enterprise. Law enforcement begins with a clear infraction of a criminal code. War is defined less clearly and is determined by "a declaration from one government to another that a state of war exists between them" (McCauley, 2007, p. 58). Unlike criminal investigation that requires investigation or discovery, war requires neither, and "an attack or ultimatum is typically the clear occasion of war" (p. 58).

Thus, in a videotaped conference that took place on May 26th, 1998, bin Laden formally declared war on the United States (bin Laden, 1998b). CNN recovered the tape in 2002 and Nic Robertson reported its content: ' "By God's grace,' bin Laden says on the tape, 'we have formed with many other Islamic groups and organizations in the Islamic world a front called the International Islamic Front to do jihad against the crusaders and Jews" ' (Robertson, 2002). And President Bush, in a speech to the joint session of Congress on September 20, 2001, labeled the 9/11 attack as an act of war: "On September the 11th, enemies of freedom committed an act of war against our country" (Bush, 2001c).

In contrast to the state of war, the extraordinary nature of which requires a special declaration by a nation's leadership, law enforcement is an ongoing concern, as the potential for crime is ever-present in orderly societies; it arguably serves an important function for society (Durkheim, 1947), and presumably it will even exist "in a society of saints" (Erickson, 1966,

p. 4). Whereas war's special nature and presumed circumscribed duration justify pumping extraordinary resources into the war effort, law enforcement, as an ongoing concern, must compete for resources with education, jobs, housing, and welfare policy. Taking issue with the terrorism-as-war framework, General Wesley Clark and Kal Raustalia (Clark & Raustalia, 2007) argue in an opinion piece that terrorists should be viewed as criminals, and "ought to be pursued, tried and convicted in the courts" (p. A19).

COMPATIBILITY WITH ALTERNATIVE SOCIETAL CONCERNS

Because it forms part of a comprehensive network of arrangements designed to address society's varied needs, the law enforcement approach is less likely than the war approach to collide with alternative values and rights similarly protected under such arrangements. McCauley (2007) puts it as follows: "In time of war, talk about money cost or opportunity cost or human rights cost is unpatriotic; in the criminal justice system, these costs can be counted in the balance of competing values and priorities" (p. 62).

Perceived violations of human rights resulting from the war approach to counterterrorism have evoked considerable criticism both in the United States and abroad. Washington has not been unresponsive to these concerns. Specifically,

> The U.S. Supreme Court rejected the Bush administration's attempts to exclude Guantánamo U.S. legal protections or to prosecute alleged terrorists before military commissions that violate the Geneva Conventions. The U.S. Congress rejected a Bush administration claim that the prohibition of cruel, inhuman or degrading treatment does not protect non-Americans held by U.S. forces outside the United States. These developments, coupled with revelations of the CIA's secret detention centers and growing public pressure, led President Bush to close those secret prisons, at least for the moment. Uniformed members of the U.S. military, successfully resisting pressure from their civilian superiors, have reaffirmed rules against the abusive techniques that those superiors had authorized. (Roth, 2004)

A major advantage of the law enforcement approach to counterterrorism is its focused nature. If one conceives of terrorists themselves as an apex of a pyramid whose base is made up of sympathizers who support the terrorists' goals even if they aren't themselves prepared to engage in terrorist attacks, law enforcement is much more likely to target the apex and avoid the base. The law enforcement metaphor suggests precision of counterterrorist initiatives and minimization of possible over-reactions to terrorist strikes, which constitute major problems or the war-on-terrorism framing.

MINIMIZATION OF COSTLY MISTAKES

McCauley (2007) points out that the costs of mistakes incurred in the course of counterterrorist operations are considerably smaller when such operations are conducted as law enforcement than they are when they are conducted as war. Civilian casualties, nearly unavoidable in bombing raids of terrorist targets when implementing the war metaphor, are unlikely under law enforcement policies. As already noted, such casualties ("collateral damage") could represent a major factor fueling anger and increasing support for terrorist organizations (Kaplan et al., 2005). As an Irish Republican Army member remarked, "the British security forces are the best recruitin' officer we have" (Geraghty 2000, p. 36).

"The criminal justice system also makes mistakes, but these mistakes are more likely to lead to imprisoning the wrong people than killing the wrong people" (McCauley, 2007, pp. 62–63). In this vein, the criminologists LaFree & Hendrickson (2007) note that "The supreme penalty—execution—is used rarely in criminal justice, even in democracies such as the United States that have not banned its use" (p. 9). In contrast, the killing of innocents in war is seen as inevitable and morally acceptable, even if sad and regrettable. As Onkar Ghate (2003) of the Ayn Rand Institute put it, "The moral principle is: the responsibility for all deaths in war lies with the aggressor who initiates force, not with those who defend themselves" (p. 1); in so far as each side in a war tends to view the other as aggressor, each side treats the killing of innocents on the other side as excusable.

FOCUS ON THE ACT

Another advantage of the law enforcement metaphor is its focus on the criminal act, rather than on the actor vaguely defined as the enemy. This reduces the tendency of those who combat the terrorists to stereotype them and to discriminate against (innocent) members of the broad social categories to which they may belong (e.g., Muslims, Saudi Arabians, Middle Easterners; McCauley, 2007).

TERRORISM AS CRIME

LaFree & Dugan (2004) enumerated several major features that terrorism and crime share in common: "Terrorism, like common crime, is disproportionately committed by young males" (p. 56); "sustained levels of terrorism, like sustained levels of crime, undermine social trust" (p. 56.); and "terrorism is . . . closely related to breaking of laws" (p. 53). As Osama bin Laden expressed it, "let history be a witness that I am a criminal" (Rahimullah, 1999).

Indeed, terrorists often engage in crime as it is conventionally defined. And "while terrorist activities typically constitute multiple crimes (e.g., murder, kidnapping, extortion), for many nations a specific crime of terrorism does not exist" (LaFree & Dugan, 2004, p. 57). Accordingly,

> suspected terrorists in the United States are typically prosecuted for a variety of criminal offenses rather than terrorism . . . in a study of federal prosecution of terrorists in the U.S. from 1982 to 1989, Smith & Orvis (1993, p. 669) show that the most common subjects of terrorist prosecutions have been racketeering (30.2% of the total), machine guns, destructive devices and other firearms (16.7%), and conspiracy (9.3%). This situation began to change in the United States after the mid 1990s, and especially after the terrorist attack of September 11, 2001. Nevertheless, even today, most persons suspected of terrorism in the U.S. are being prosecuted not for terrorism per se, but for a range of crimes commonly associated with terrorism . . . (LaFree & Dugan, 2004, p. 57)

Though terrorist activities per se are often classifiable as criminal, terrorists often engage in additional criminal activities—such as drug trafficking, bank robberies, extortion, kidnapping for ransom, and smuggling—aimed at financing terrorist operations. For instance, in 1994, Jawed Naqvi, writing in the *News India-Times*, quoted Interpol's chief drugs officer, Iqbal Hussain Rizvi, as saying that "Drugs have taken over as the chief means of financing terrorism" (Naqvi, 1994, p. 30). Because the law enforcement system is oriented and equipped to cope with criminality in its varied forms, it is ipso facto equipped to cope with those aspects of the terrorists' operation that are criminal in the conventional sense of the term.

POLICE WORK

But the efficacy of law enforcement as an approach to counterterrorism extends even farther. Experience of the Israelis and the British suggests that effective counterterrorism often resembles painstaking police work more than it resembles war. McCauley (2007) notes that

> Effective police work requires understanding a local culture, knowing the details of social and physical geography in a local area, developing local relationships and cultivating local sources of information . . . [The] modern army . . . is ill prepared for police work or the kind of economic and community development work that can support effective police work. At a minimum, effective police work requires speaking the local language, but learning foreign languages is not typically a high priority in military training. (p. 61)

International cooperation in counterterrorism is also more likely under the law enforcement metaphor than under the war approach. According to Senator John Kerry's comment (as paraphrased in a 2004 *New York Times Magazine* article), cooperation between law enforcement agencies has shown that "many of the interdiction tactics that cripple drug lords, including governments working jointly to share intelligence, patrol borders, and force banks to identify suspicious customers, can also be some of the most useful tools in the war on terror" (Bai, 2004, p. 45). McCauley (2007) states in this connection that

> International cooperation is crucial for fighting international terrorists. International police cooperation is a better model of this kind of sharing than international military cooperation; police and security services are more likely than the military to have useful information about terrorist individuals and terrorist groups. (p. 61)

INTERNATIONAL COOPERATION

Whereas the international community is basically in favor of law and order, and hence likely to support international law enforcement treaties aimed at stopping terrorism, the war metaphor might be too committing and demanding for numerous states to embrace; it might encourage sitting-on-the-fence neutrality in the struggle against the terrorist enemy.

For instance, even in 2003, when political tensions between the United States and France ran strong because of France's opposition to the Iraq war, there was still highly effective cooperation between American and French law enforcement that had dated to the post-9/11 period. Thus, a joint American–French investigation brought Richard Reid, the would-be shoe bomber, to justice. Similarly, France and the United States shared evidence in the case of Zacarias Moussaoui, who was allegedly involved in the 9/11 attacks. International cooperation in law enforcement resulted in the apprehension and trials of suspected terrorists in the United Kingdom, Spain, Italy, Germany, the Netherlands, Turkey, and other European countries (Nacos, 2003). Nonetheless, as observed ruefully by the Secretary General of Interpol Raymond E. Kendall, one of the impediments to sharing information through the international police organization is that states supporting terrorism also belong to Interpol—in particular Iran, Iraq, Syria, and Libya (personal communication, interview with R.E. Kendall, by Jerrold Post in 1986).

Concluding Comments: Psychological Implications of the Law Enforcement Metaphor

The law enforcement metaphor of counterterrorism offers appreciable advantages over the war metaphor. It affords an approach to counterterrorism that is focused on the actual perpetrators and that balances security needs with human rights concerns. Thus, it may minimize the outrage (and support for terrorism) that civilian casualties, human rights abuses, or stereotyping and discrimination commonly inspire. Moreover, it encourages international cooperation that transcends shifting political contingencies. In view of these obvious advantages, McCauley (2007) asserted that "Criminal justice can be a treatment of choice for a chronic terrorist threat" (p. 22).

Nonetheless, careful scrutiny suggests that the law enforcement approach to terrorism also has limitations. A main issue is that terrorism, unlike typical crime, is ideologically inspired (e.g., by religious, ethno-nationalist, or political beliefs). As LaFree & Dugan (2004, pp. 59–60) noted,

> criminals often have selfish, personal motivations and their actions are not intended to have consequences or create psychological repercussions beyond the criminal act. By contrast, the fundamental aim of terrorists is often a political motivation to overthrow or change the dominant political system ... few criminals see their crimes as altruistic behavior. By contrast, many terrorists see themselves as altruistic. In this vein, Hoffman (1998, p. 43) claims that terrorists frequently believe that they are serving a cause that will achieve a greater good for some wider constituency ...

In a similar vein, Pape (2005) concluded from his research that "altruistic motives . . . play an important role [in terrorism]" (p. 187). Gunaratna (2007) similarly noted that "what actually motivates Al Qaeda is not power, wealth or fame but an ideological belief" (p. 29). And Atran (2004) observed that terrorists "are motivated not by personal comfort or immediate gain but rather by religious or ideological conviction and zeal" (pp. 68–69).

These differences between crime and terrorism have far-reaching implications for counterterrorism. Because of their ideological commitments and collective motivations, terrorists often inspire admiration and respect on the part of the larger communities in which they are embedded. The "cult of the suicide bomber" is widespread in the West Bank and Gaza, for example. During much of the second intifada, public opinion polls conducted among the Palestinians have revealed support for suicide attacks against Israelis to be at the 70–80% level (Atran, 2004). Thus, in the recent past, terrorist activities in Palestine and other locations were anchored in a solid base of community support.

The reason this matters is that effective police work requires extensive community support, including the collection of background information and its transmittal to law enforcement agents (Siegel & Senna, 2004). As the economists Akerlof & Yellen (1994) remarked, "the major deterrent to crime is not an active police presence but rather the presence of knowledgeable civilians, prepared to report crimes and cooperate in police investigations" (p. 174). In a larger sense, effective police work requires driving a wedge between a community and the criminals living within it, and the same applies to psychological and physical separation of insurgents or terrorists from their communities. In this vein, David Ucko (2007, p. 63), a security expert at King's College, London, comments on the successful campaign of the British and Commonwealth forces against the insurgent Malayan Races Liberation Army (MRLA) from 1948 to 1960. Specifically,

> the construction of New Villages built as progressive communities where the Chinese villagers could own land, work, engage in local politics and move freely ... effectively minimized the incidence of 'collateral damage'—an inflammatory and counterproductive feature of most counter-insurgency campaigns ... [Too] the separation of combatants and civilians made the MRLA more desperate and therefore easier to spot. Denied access to the civilian population, the MRLA found it increasingly difficult to attract fresh recruits, particularly as the political and economic opportunities afforded to the inhabitants of the New Villages had removed the primary incentive to join the guerilla ranks. Gaining information from the wider population [required] the provision of security, of services and of a political strategy deemed largely legitimate by the populace and as worthy of support. (Ucko, 2007, p. 66)

On the flip side of the coin, community cooperation with law enforcement may be difficult to secure if terrorists' activities *are* supported by their communities, as they often are. Where this is the case, collaboration with law enforcement is often seen as treason to the cause. For instance, according to a recent account, in the West Bank, approximately one person a day is killed having been accused of collaborating with the Israeli security forces (B'tselem, n.d.). Thus, despite the Israelis' apparent successes in information gathering, arrests of suspected terrorists, targeted assassinations, etc., their law enforcement efforts are a daily struggle against community resistance.

Law enforcement efforts against terrorism may also be countered by a community's perception that law is sometimes devised and followed hypocritically. For example, (a) many Palestinians would argue that the United States's refusal to hold Israel to U.N. resolutions is at odds with international law; (b) the U.S. definition of terrorism carefully excludes state actors from any culpability; and (c) the U.S. refusal to submit to the legal oversight of the World Court diminishes the credibility of American claims of pursuing justice through law.

Finally, despite considerable policing efforts against terrorism-using organizations in various world locations, attempts to quell terrorist activities have often been unsuccessful in the long run. Various ethnonationalist movements (e.g., in Algiers, Israel, or Kenya) have used terrorism successfully to attain national independence for their peoples. The research literature on human goals (see Kruglanski et al., 2002 for a review) suggests that the higher the importance of a goal, the greater the number and variety of means to the goal that people are likely to generate. Terrorists' ideological commitment, particularly if supported by their broader community, indicates the supreme importance that they attach to their goals.

Law enforcement operations, however successful, may be countered by terrorists' creativity in finding effective countermeasures to counterterrorism initiatives (Kruglanski et al., in press). Difficulties of finding escape routes and the costs involved in keeping an intricate network of safe houses may prompt the "invention" of suicide terrorism. Hard-to-penetrate boundaries may lead to increased use of rocket technology that overcomes distance and barriers (Sharvit, 2005). Indeed, as compared to typical criminals, terrorists have been often credited with considerable inventiveness (LaFree & Dugan, 2004).

Ultimately, despite several advantages, the law enforcement framing of counterterrorism and the approach it implies exhibits a partial mismatch with the realities of terrorism. Especially, law enforcement methods might temporarily hamper terrorists' *ability* to launch attacks without substantially undermining their *motivation* to do so. For example, although the Israeli West Bank barrier and military initiatives are credited with substantial reduction in Palestinian suicide terrorism from the West Bank (Israeli West Bank barrier, n.d.), in 2007 there were hundreds of Qassam rocket and mortar attacks each month launched from the Gaza strip against Israeli towns (Chehab, 2007). This suggests that terrorism is often a part and parcel of a broader, ideologically based social movement, and in this sense it is distinct from mere crime in significant ways.

Counterterrorism as Containment of a Social Epidemic

Partitioning the Ingredients of Jihadist Terrorism

Both the war and the law enforcement metaphors of counterterrorism deal with the violent manifestations of terrorism rather than with the constellation of factors that may have engendered terrorism in the first place. These latter factors are addressed by the epidemiological metaphor of terrorism we now consider.

The epidemic spread of ideas has long been a subject of study. In his 1843 work *Extraordinary Popular Delusions and the Madness of Crowds* (Mackay, 1967), Charles Mackay wrote of the tulip mania that consumed the Netherlands in the first part of the 17th century. In 1636 and 1637, a speculative frenzy overtook the tulip market, with vast fortunes being spent for a single tulip bulb. Indeed, the term "tulipomania" was applied to the so-called dot.com bubble of 1995 to 2001 (Wallace, 2001). Gustav Le Bon's *The Crowd: A Study of the Popular Mind* (Le Bon, 1896) addressed herd behavior and crowd psychology, emphasizing the role of the media in spreading ideas. In *Crowds and Power*, the Nobel Prize-winning writer Elias Canetti likened the spread of the psychology of mass hatred to a forest fire or a flood (Canetti, 1984).

The public health epidemiological model has been applied to the phenomenon of terrorism. This model utilizes the *epidemiologic triad*, consisting of (a) an external agent, (b) a susceptible host, and (c) an environment that brings them together. An important element of the environment is what is known as the vector. So, for example, for a malaria epidemic, such as that which almost brought the Panama Canal project to a halt, the pathogen (or agent) was the protozoan *Plasmodium falciparum*; the vulnerable host was the nonimmune population; and the environment was the tropical jungle with standing water that fostered the breeding of the vector, the Anopheles mosquito. A major contribution to countering the epidemic was preventive methods, such as spraying the ponds of stagnant water in which the mosquitoes bred, wearing protective clothing, and using screens and mosquito nets; chemoprophyllaxis is currently employed to protect susceptible individuals who travel or work in areas where malaria is endemic.

The public health epidemiological model has been applied to the phenomenon of terrorism in two distinct senses: (a) to the targeted populations' psychological reactions to terrorist attacks, and (b) to the spread of terrorist ideology in societies potentially susceptible to such ideologies. In regards to the first sense, the Committee on Responding to the Psychological Consequences of Terrorism, formed by the National Academy of Sciences under the Institute of Medicine, characterized the violent terrorist act or threat as the agent; affected individuals and populations as the host; the way terror is propagated, including the role of the media, as the vector or vehicle; and characteristics of both the physical and the social environment as the environment (Butler, Panzer & Goldfrank, 2003, p. 29).

In the second sense, and of greater relevance to counterterrorism, the epidemiological metaphor was used in a recent paper by Stares and Yacoubian of the United States Institute of Peace (Stares & Yacoubian, 2006). The authors note the several practical advantages that the epidemiological approach to the strategic struggle against terrorism may afford. First, it guides intelligible questions as to "the origins, geographical and social contours of an outbreak, where is the disease concentrated, how is it transmitted, who is most at risk or 'susceptible' to infection, as well as why some portions of society may be less susceptible or immune" (Stares & Yacoubian, 2006, p. 88). Second, "epidemiologists recognize that diseases emerge and evolve as a result of a complex interactive process between people, pathogens and the environment in which they live" (p. 88). Third and relatedly, "just as epidemiologists view disease as a complex, multifaceted phenomenon so public health officials have come to recognize that success in controlling and rolling back an epidemic typically results from a carefully orchestrated systematic, prioritized multi pronged effort to address each of its constituent elements" (p. 88).

Stares and Yacoubian (2006) classify the factors involved in an epidemic into four separate categories of host, agent, environment, and vector. In their scheme, "The agent refers to the pathogen (e.g., a virus, or bacterium) that causes disease, the host refers to a person infected by the disease ("infective"), while the environment refers to a variety of external factors that affect both agent and host [and] the vectors [are] the key pathways or conduits that help propagate the disease" (p. 89).

In Stares & Yacoubian's (2006) specific application of the epidemiological metaphor to jihadist terrorism, the agent refers to the militant

Islamist ideology,[8] the environment "refers to key factors specific to the Muslim world that promote exposure to Islamist militancy—conflict, political repression, economic stagnation, and social alienation. Vectors . . . refer to a variety of known conduits . . . used to propagate the ideology and associated action agendas such as mosques, prisons, madrassas, the Internet, satellite television and diasporic networks" (Stares & Yacoubian, 2006, p. 90). It is important to emphasize in this context that the pathogenic ideology identified by Stares and Yacoubian (2006) is *militant Islamism*, an ideology that may be adhered to by a group significantly larger than the terrorists per se (as in the pyramid model described earlier). Thus a broader population may approve of what the terrorists are doing, as well as gratefully accept the terrorist organizations' (e.g., Hamas' or Hezbollah's) financial and logistical aid to the community at large without taking the leap to killing in the name of God. Nonetheless, this larger supportive "sentiment pool" is not irrelevant to counterteirorism, as it constitutes the population whose members may be particularly prone to move to active militancy—prompted, for example, by the death of a close friend or a relative.

In specifying the epidemiologic elements of agent, host, vector, and environment, the epidemiological metaphor usefully focuses the challenges of counterterrorism on these essential ingredients, which we now discuss individually.

Ideology

It is interesting to consider more fully the psychological ingredients that make up the concept of "agent" in this model—the terrorism-justifying ideology—and that lend that agent motivating force.[9] Basically, the key elements include (a) a depiction of some sort of *collective grievance*, (b) attribution of responsibility for the grievance to some actor (e.g., a state, a regime, or a form of governance) identified as a *culprit*, (c) portrayal of terrorism as a morally justifiable as well as an efficient *tool* for redressing the grievance (Kruglanski & Fishman, 2006), and (d) the bestowal of status and prestige on those willing to risk or sacrifice their lives for the cause by engaging in terrorist activities. Those elements may exist in any terrorism-justifying ideology, whether social, nationalist, or religious.

The ideology articulated by a charismatic leader provides a sense-making device for the group, and in identifying an external cause for the members' frustration and alienation it helps promote a potent "us versus them" social psychology, setting in motion powerful group dynamics centered on the ideology. Indeed, a principal conclusion of the Committee on the Psychological Roots of Terrorism, which developed a consensus document for the March 2005 International Summit on Democracy, Terrorism and Security, was that group, organizational, and social psychology placing particular emphasis on collective identity provided the greatest analytic power in understanding terrorism and its spread (Post, 2005).

Post, Sprinzak, and Denny (2003) carried out extensive interviews with 35 Middle Eastern terrorists incarcerated in Israeli and Palestinian prisons. The contents of these interviews afford glimpses into central facets of terrorists' ideological reasoning. The following excerpt from one of the interviews contains references to three of the four ideological ingredients mentioned earlier, namely the grievance, the culprit, and the tool of terrorism for redressing the grievance:

> You Israelis are Nazis in your souls and in your conduct. In your occupation you never distinguish between men and women, or between old people and children. You adopted methods of collective punishment; you uprooted people from their homeland and from their homes and chased them into exile. You fired live ammunition at women and children. You smashed the stalls of defenseless civilians. You set up detention camps for thousands of people in subhuman conditions. You destroyed homes and turned children into orphans. You prevented people from making a living, you stole their property, you trampled on their honor. Given that kind of conduct, there is no choice but to strike at you without mercy in every possible way. (Post, Sprinzak, & Denny, 2003, p. 178)

---

[8] Islamism has been defined as "a religious ideology with a holistic interpretation of Islam whose final aim is the conquest of the world by all means. This definition is composed of four interrelated elements. The first is a religious ideology, the second a holistic interpretation of Islam, the third conquest of the world, and finally the fourth and the last element is the use of all means in the search for the final objective" (Mozaffari, 2007).

[9] Thus, Stares and Yacoubian (2006, p. 89) distinguish "two primary strains [of Islamist militant ideology:] (1) a transnational Salafist/jihadist ideology as espoused by Al Qaeda, and (2) a nationalist/insurgent Islamist militant ideology as espoused by groups such as the Hezbollah, Hamas, and some of the Kashmiri militant groups."

An ideology constitutes a belief system, and belief systems are typically anchored in a shared reality defining a worldview of a given group (Hardin & Higgins, 1996). The scope of such a group can range from a limited network of close friends and associates (Sageman, 2004) to a broader community of identity.

Relevant in this connection is the observation that group dynamics differ considerably between social-revolutionary and nationalist-separatist types of terrorists (Post, 1986). To join a social revolutionary group may mean to go underground and isolate oneself from the broader society whose workings one is attempting to alter. It is a fundamental decision, which the German Red Army Faction terrorists called *Der Sprung* ("the leap"), an act that in a certain sense may be seen as rebellion against the parents' generation that is loyal to the regime. This is the opposite of the generational dynamics of nationalist-separatist groups who are carrying on the mission of their parents' generation, which itself is dissident and disloyal to the (foreign or imposed) regime. Members of such groups are often well known and respected in the surrounding community, as they are in fact expressing its values.

Not unlike the latter, the jihadist groups are also based on a set of wider cultural values that they are expressing in practice. These are the values of radical Islamist ideology that has been growing in popularity over the last several decades (Moaddel, 2005) and that generates a continuing supply of recruits to terrorism, including suicide terrorism—an ideology that, according to Israeli terrorism expert Ariel Merari, has fostered a veritable "suicide bomber production line" (A. Merari, personal communication, January 12, 2004). To counter the growing threat of Islamist terrorism, it is imperative to understand and address the broader ideological context from which it emerges.

Scope of the Support

Major theoretical analyses of terrorism (e.g., Gurr, 1990/1998) have highlighted the broad base of support that terrorist activities require. The foundation of the "pyramid" (McCauley, 2004) consists of sympathizers with the terrorist cause who may not be prepared themselves to launch terrorist activities. This is the "sentiment pool" on whose support terrorists may count in times of need. The apex of the pyramid consists of individuals who actually engage in terrorist operations. According to Silke (2003), "even 'popular' terrorist groups . . . represent a violent and extreme minority within the immediate social group that shares the terrorists' beliefs and backgrounds. While the terrorist . . . may be largely tolerated within their communities, the number of individuals actively involved in the campaign of violence is always relatively low" (p. 30).

Gurr (1990/1998) comments that the "erosion of political support is not an immediate cause of decline in terrorist campaigns but an underlying one" (p. 94). For instance, the decline in the 1970s of the Front de Liberation du Quebec (FLQ) may be attributed to the decline of political support for its activities by the separatist Parti Quebecois. Similarly, the decline of the Weather Underground in the United States has been attributed to a withdrawal of public support from the deadly violence it perpetrated in the early 1970s. According to Gurr, "The general public's reaction to the rhetoric, disorder, and violence of this era crystallized in . . . widespread opposition to the advocacy of radical social change and sharp resentment against groups making extreme demands or using disruptive or violent tactics" (Gurr, 1990/1998, p. 97).

Although minority groups that espouse terrorism can maintain worldviews at odds with those of the majority (Asch, 1946; Moscovici, 1980), this may require considerably greater effort than the maintenance of popular, broadly supported opinions. Maintenance of discrepant views may require isolation of the minority from majority influence and the maintenance of a strictly controlled opinion environment that assures consensus around the group's ideology.

Presumed Efficacy of Terrorism

An important component of terrorists' ideological belief system is that the violence they perpetrate will advance their cause. To interviewees of Post et al. (2003), armed attacks seemed essential to the operation of the organization. One interviewee stated:

> You have to understand that armed attacks are an integral part of the organization's struggle against the Zionist occupier. There is no other way to redeem the land of Palestine and expel the occupier. Our goals can only be achieved through force, but force is the means, not the end. History shows that without force it will be

impossible to achieve independence. The more an attack hurls the enemy, the more important it is. That is the measure. The mass killings, especially the "Martyrdom Operations", were the biggest threat to the Israeli public and so the most effort was devoted to these. The extent of the damage and the number of casualties are of primary importance. (Post et al., 2003, p. 179)

Another interviewee remarked:

> I regarded armed actions to be essential, it is the very basis of my organization and I am sure that was the case in the other Palestinian organizations. An armed action proclaims that I am here, I exist, I am strong, I am in control, I am in the field, I am on the map. (Post et al., 2003, p. 183)

Explicit emphasis on the efficacy of terrorism is apparent in an interviewee's comment that "the various armed actions (stabbing, collaborators, martyrdom operations, attacks on Israeli soldiers) all had different ratings. An armed action that caused casualties was rated highly . . . An armed action without casualties was not rated" (Post et al., 2003, p. 183).

Terrorists' concern with the efficacy of their activities is attested directly by recent data reported by Benmelech and Berrebi (2007). These investigators find that, in the Palestinian context, older and better-educated individuals are assigned more important missions (indexed by the size of the population centers attacked and the civilian vs. military nature of the targets[10]) than younger and less educated individuals are. Specifically, the age of the suicide bomber was found to be significantly and positively associated with the attack being carried out in a big city, and the education of the suicide bomber was significantly and positively associated with the attack being carried out against a civilian (vs. a military) target. The tactical decisions of terrorist organizations to assign more important missions to older and better-educated operatives seem to be warranted by outcomes: Benmelech and Berrebi (2007) report that "older and educated suicide bombers kill more people in their suicide attacks when assigned to important targets . . . also older and educated suicide bombers are less likely to fail or to be caught when they attack" (p. 16).

If belief in the efficacy of terrorist attacks is an essential moderator of their use, one reason why people may desist from terrorism is a loss of faith in its ability to advance their cause. In an interview with the author and journalist Alison Jamieson, Adriana Faranda, a former member of the Italian Red Brigades who later disengaged from the movement, talked about questioning of "Marxism, [and] violence . . . [as] a way of working out problems," implying a loss of faith in terrorism as a tactic (Horgan, 2005, p. 148).

In summary, there is evidence that the belief systems of members of terrorist organizations include as essential ingredients the notions of grievance (e.g., humiliation of one's nation or one's religion), culprit (the party deemed responsible for the grievance), and method for addressing the grievance (i.e., portraying terrorism as an efficient tactic for attaining the terrorists' objectives). Of considerable importance is the fact that, as with any ideology or belief system, a terrorism-supporting belief system is grounded in a shared social reality (Festinger, 1950; Hardin & Higgins, 1996)—that is, in a consensual support for the ideology within one's relevant reference group, whether it is a small cluster of intimates or one's broader community.

The Vectors of Terrorism

Mosques. Post et al. (2003) report that the mosque was consistently cited as the place where most members were initially introduced to the Palestinian cause. Authority figures from the mosque were prominent in all conversations with group members, and most dramatically so for members of the Islamist organizations (versus members of secular militant groups). The unquestioning reverence of Allah and other authorities appears to be instilled in Palestinian Muslims at a young age and it continues to be evident in the individual members' subservience to the larger organization. The preconditioning of absolute acceptance of authority seems to be most explicit among members of the Islamist groups such as Hamas and Islamic Jihad. One Islamist interviewee stated:

> My initial political awareness came during the prayers at the mosque. That's where I was also asked to join religious classes. In the context of

---

[10] Benmelech and Berrebi (2007) present evidence that larger population centers and civilian target were perceived by terrorist organizations as being more significant than smaller centers and/or military targets.

these studies, the sheik used to inject some historical background in which he would tell us how we were effectively evicted from Palestine. The sheik also used to explain to us the significance of the fact that there was an IDF military outpost in the heart of the camp. He compared it to a cancer in the human body, which was threatening its very existence. At the age of 16 I developed an interest in religion. I was exposed to the Moslem Brotherhood and I began to pray in a mosque and to study Islam. The Koran and my religious studies were the tools that shaped my political consciousness. The mosque and the religious clerics in my village provided the focal point of my social life. (Post et al., 2003, p. 177)

Madrassas. Do the madrassas, Muslim religious schools, (e.g., in Pakistan, Indonesia, or Saudi Arabia) constitute breeding grounds for terrorism, and should they, therefore, be subject to tight governmental supervision and control? Different views have been expressed on this topic with little hard evidence brought in their support. The emerging consensus among experts seems to be that (a) there do exist radical madrassas that preach extremist views and that encourage jihadism, although many madrassas focus squarely on religious teachings and eschew politics; (b) if anything, the radical madrassas impart the jihadist ideology and foment a positive attitude toward jihad as opposed to providing actual training in the tactics of terrorism and insurgency; and (c) attending the madrassas isn't a necessary condition for recruitment to, or embarkation upon, terrorism.

In a *New York Times* article titled "The Madrassa Myth," journalists Bergen and Pandey (2005) examined the educational background of 75 terrorists involved in some of the major anti-Western attacks. They concluded that madrassas are not an important source of recruits to terrorism:

> While madrassas may breed fundamentalists ... such schools do not teach the technical or linguistic skills to be an effective terrorist. Indeed, there is little or no evidence that madrassas produce terrorists capable of attacking the West.... We found that a majority of them are college educated, often in technical subjects like engineering ... Of the 75 terrorists ... only nine attended madrassas, and all of those played a role in one attack—the Bali bombing. Even in this instance, however, five college educated 'masterminds'—including two university lecturers—helped to shape the Bali plot. (Bergen & Pandey, 2005, p. A23)

Self-Recruitment. In a recent report, Rik Coolsaet, a professor of international relations at Ghent University in Belgium (2005), describes evidence from European security agencies for a "growing tendency of self-radicalization and self-recruitment of individuals [so that] self recruitment now appears to have become a more important source of jihadi recruitment than any organised international network of recruiters" (p.6). Coolsaet (2005) characterizes self-recruitment as

> the result of an individual track of self-radicalization outside usual meeting places such as mosques. It more often than not involves individuals with college education (Bergen & Pandey, 2005) ... It mixes a psychological process of personal *reidentification* ... implying searching (through chat rooms, prisons, backroom meetings) for others with a similar world view ... In this process groupthink gradually eliminates alternative views, simplifies reality and dehumanizes all who are not subscribing to their extreme views. (pp. 6–7)

Indeed, it is now estimated that some 80% of new recruits to the global Salafi jihad emerge from the diaspora—sons and daughters of Muslim émigrés to Western Europe who emigrated for a better life. Not having found acceptance within the host society, they have become radicalized within radical mosques in Great Britain, Germany, France, Belgium, The Netherlands, Spain, etc. (Post & Sheffer, 2007).

Experts agree that the Internet now plays an important role in the radicalization and self-recruitment process into terrorist groups; in epidemiologic terms, it constitutes a major vector affording the spread of extremist ideologies. It targets potential recruits' "soft spots" and inflames their imaginations. Army Brigadier General John Custer, head of intelligence at central command, responsible for Iraq and Afghanistan, stated on *60 Minutes* in 2007 that "Without doubt, the Internet is the single most important venue for the radicalization of Islamic youth" (Pelley, 2007), The *60 Minutes* segment with Custer further stated that

"The number of [jihadi] Internet sites has exploded since 9/11. It is estimated that there are over 5,000 today."

To illustrate the role of the Internet as a conduit of terrorists' tactical planning, consider the following message that appeared on an al-Qaeda Web site 4 months before the Madrid train station bombing of March, 2004.

> In order to force the Spanish government to withdraw from Iraq, the resistance should deal painful blows to its forces . . . It is necessary to make the utmost use of the upcoming general election in March next year. We think that the Spanish government could not tolerate more than two, maximum three blows, after which it will have to withdraw as a result of popular pressure. If its troops remain in Iraq after these blows, the victory of the Socialist Party is almost secured, and the withdrawal of the Spanish forces will be on its electoral program. (Lia & Hegghammer, 2004)

With the increasing role of the Internet in the socialization of youth, there is a growing hazard of extremist ideas propagated on the Internet contributing to a virtual community of hatred (Post, 2007). Well aware of efforts to counter this vector, al-Qaeda has provided the following counsel to Muslim Internet professionals:

> Due to the advances of modern technology, it is easy to spread news, information, articles and other information over the Internet. We strongly urge Muslim Internet professionals to spread and disseminate news and information about the Jihad through e-mail lists, discussion groups, and their own websites. If you fail to do this, and our site closes down before you have done this, you may hold you to account before Allah on the Day of Judgment . . . This way, even if oursites are closed down, the material will live on with the Grace of Allah. (Azzam Publications, 2001)

Gabriel Weinman, a political scientist at Haifa University in Israel (2004) conducted a 6-year study of terrorists' use of the Internet. In commenting on the role it plays in recruitment and mobilization, he wrote,

> In addition to seeking converts by using the full panoply of website technologies (audio, digital video, etc.) to enhance the presentation of their message, terrorist organizations capture information about the users who browse their websites. Users who seem most interested in the organization's cause or well suited to carrying out its work are then contacted. Recruiters may also use more interactive Internet technology to roam online chat rooms and cyber-cafes, looking for receptive members of the public, particularly young people. Electronic bulletin boards and user nets (issue-specific chat rooms and bulletins) can also serve as vehicles for reaching out to potential recruits. [Furthermore] some would-be recruits use the Internet to advertise themselves to terrorist organizations. . . . More typically, however, terrorist organizations go looking for recruits rather than waiting for them to present themselves.

The SITE Institute, a Washington, D.C.-based terrorism research group that monitors al Qaeda's Internet communications, has provided chilling details of a high-tech recruitment drive launched in 2003 to recruit fighters to travel to Iraq and attack U.S. and coalition forces there. Potential recruits are bombarded with religious decrees and anti-American propaganda, provided with training manuals on how to be a terrorist, and—as they are led through a maze of secret chat rooms—given specific instructions on how to make the journey to Iraq. (p. 8)

Although the Internet may be an invaluable tool in the recruitment of terrorist operatives, it is unlikely to constitute a sufficient medium for recruitment. Before they become a part of potential recruits' world view, sufficiently crystallized to stir them to action, the notions espoused on terrorists' Web sites need to be integrated into their shared reality, evolved through intensive discussion with trusted friends and members of their inner circle (Hardin & Higgins, 1996). In a recent report on the recruitment of Islamist terrorists in Europe, Taarnby (2005) writes that

> While there have been examples of top-down recruitment the general trend both before and after 11 September 2001 is largely a bottom-up process. While many European Muslims were sensitized to current issues on the Internet and developed a sense of collective social identity through it, none went straight from interacting

on the Internet to Jihad. Personal acquaintances are still required, (p. 50)

In the same vein, Sageman's (2004) work on terrorist networks finds that face-to-face interaction among friends was a major ingredient in the formation of action-oriented cells such as those involved in the March '04 Madrid or the July '05 London bombings.

Counterterrorism on the Internet

The Internet affords significant possibilities for counterterrorism as well. Two seem of particular interest, related to information gathering about terrorist activities and Counterterrorism argumentation respectively. Information-gathering activities may include efforts to infiltrate the most heavily secured terrorist Web sites and chat rooms in the guise of potential recruits for terrorist missions. For instance, the SITE (Search for International Terrorist Entities) Institute, "through [its] continuous and intensive examination of extremist websites, public records, and international media reports, as well as through undercover work on both sides of the Atlantic . . . locates links among terrorist entities and their supporters" (SITE Institute, 2007). According to the *Christian Science Monitor*, "information on the SITE website was used within hours of posting to prevent a terrorist attack in Iraq, demonstrating that third party analysis has become a key component of intelligence" (Katz, 2007). Furthermore, "the SITE institute has provided intelligence to foreign governments that has aided in preventing jihadists from leaving European countries to join jihadists in foreign countries to attack coalition forces . . . The European governments determined that the intelligence was indeed actionable and promptly detained the individuals" (Katz, 2007).

Counterterrorism argumentation on the Internet is exemplified by the Saudi *Al-Sakinah*. ("Tranquility") campaign, an "independent initiative for online dialogue with Islamists in order to prevent the spread of extremist views via the internet" (Yehoshua, 2006). In this project "some 40 ulema [Islamic clerics] and propagators of Islam who have Internet skills enter extremist websites and forums and converse with the participants in order to bring them to renounce their extremist ideas" (Yehoshua, 2006). This initiative, assisted by psychological and sociological experts in addition to Sunni clerics, is claimed by the organizers to have been "successful in persuading extremists to renounce their views" (Yehoshua, 2006).

In summary, the vector component of the epidemiological metaphor focuses attention on several potentially important conduits of terrorist rhetoric: radical mosques, madrassas, 24/7 cable channels such as al Jazeera, and increasingly extremist Web sites on the Internet.[11] Though possibly insufficient in and of itself to effect conversion to a terrorism-justifying ideology or recruitment for terrorist missions, exposure to such a rhetoric might be necessary to provide the guiding conceptual frame within which embarkation on a terrorism project is carried out.

Susceptible Populations and Contributing Situations Socialization.

The epidemiological metaphor highlights the importance of susceptibility to terrorist rhetoric and its determinants. It is possible to distinguish two general categories of such determinants: (a) early socialization to a terrorism-justifying ideology producing the susceptible "host" category of the metaphor, and (b) current personal circumstances that render such ideology appealing, paralleling the "environment" category. Post (2005) writes about cases in which ideological education into a terrorism-glorifying ideology was established early in the socialization process, so that "hatred [was] bred in the bone" (Post, 2005, p. 615).

Young children's mentality is especially malleable and vulnerable to persuasion by adults, who constitute revered "epistemic authorities" for their targets (cf. Kruglanski et al., 2005). According to an Intelligence and Terrorism Information Center report, children in the Hezbollah Shi'ite youth movement known as the Imam al-Mahdi Scouts range in age from 8 to 16, number in the tens of thousands, and are indoctrinated with the ideology of radical Iranian Islam ("Hezbollah's Shi'ite Youth Movement," 2006). The report quotes *Ruz al Yusuf*, an Egyptian newspaper, as saying that the group's objective is "to train [a] high caliber Islamic generation of children who would be will-

---

[11] Besides serving as a recruitment tool, the numerous Web sites used by terrorist organizations convey operational knowledge regarding the production of explosives and the construction of rockets, constitute an avenue of communication between command centers and operational infrastructures, and accomplish important fund-raising functions.

ing to sacrifice themselves for the sake of Allah" ("Hezbollah's Shi'ite Youth Movement," 2006). Kindergarten children are an important target audience for the educational efforts of Hamas. On May 31, 2007, the Hamas Al-Aqsa satellite TV channel featured an end-of-the-year party for kindergarten members of the Al-Mujamma" al-Islami society (a Muslim Brotherhood Society operating in the Gaza Strip). The children paraded in camouflage suits, carried plastic rifles, and demonstrated various military exercises. Then one of the children posed a series of questions that were answered in the unison by the group: "Who is your model?" "The prophet Muhammad." "What is your path?" "Jihad." "What is your greatest aspiration?" "To die for the sake of Allah!" (Intelligence & Terrorism Information Center, 2007). In brief, then, the adoption of ideological goals (such as jihad) can represent a shared reality deliberately engineered by an organization and inculcated in its members from an early age.

Personal Circumstances. Personal suffering and frustrations can render individuals particularly vulnerable to terrorism-justifying ideologies. Many of the interviewees of Post et al. (2003) reported growing up or currently living in repressed or limited socioeconomic conditions. Their ability to work was regulated, their ability to travel freely was severely restricted, and they report having felt unable to advance economically. There was a common theme of having been "unjustly evicted" from their land, of being relegated to refugee status, or living in refugee camps in a land that was once considered theirs. Many of the interviewees expressed a sense of despair about the future under Israeli rule. Few of the interviewees were able to identify personal goals that were separate from those of the organization to which they belonged. Most interviewees reported that the families of fallen or incarcerated members enjoyed enhanced social status. Success within the community was defined as fighting for "the cause"—liberation and religious freedom were the values that defined success, not necessarily academic or economic accomplishment. As the young men adopted this view of success, their own self-image became more intimately intertwined with the success of the organization. With no other means to achieve status and success, the organization's success become central to individual identity and provided a "reason for living."

In a recent analysis of terrorists' motivations, Kruglanski et al. (in press) suggested that personal traumas stemming from having a relative or friend killed by the enemy, humiliation and shame delivered at the hands of one's fellow group members, and alienation and estrangement felt by Muslim minorities in European diasporas (Sageman, 2004) may all produce a sense of significance loss, prompting the quest for significance restoration through the adoption of collectivistic causes.

Speckhard & Akhmedova (2005) carried out an extensive study of Chechen suicide terrorists via interviews with their family members and close associates and with hostages who spoke with the terrorists during the 3-days siege in Moscow's Dubrovka theater in October, 2002. All of the interviewees mentioned traumatic events that appeared to alter the course of the fallen terrorists' lives. Accordingly, the authors concluded: "[W]hen we looked for the primary motivation in our sample of terrorists we would have to say that it was *trauma* in every case" (Speckhard & Akhmedova, 2005, p. 25). Of particular interest was Speckhard and Akhmedova's (2005) observation that suicide terrorists sought out ideological inspiration in response to their personal traumas. Specifically,

> In the interviews concerning the accomplished suicide terrorists, eighty-two percent (28/34) were secular Muslims prior to their experiences of trauma. Of these, twenty-seven had no prior relationship to fundamental militant groups but sought out the Wah-habists radical groups in direct reaction to the traumas they had endured, knowing full well of the groups' beliefs and terroristic practices (p. 22).

It appears then that personal trauma, feelings of alienation, and disenfranchisement may spur a quest for significance that,in cases of a severe intergroup conflict, may be afforded by a terrorism-justifying ideology.

In summary, personal suffering and frustrations represent a significance loss, motivating the quest for significance restoration. Where the direct restoration of one's lost sense of personal significance seems impossible, the individual may seek to accomplish this restoration indirectly through alternative means, including an identification with a collective loss (one's group's relative deprivation) that affords a clear path to renewed significance via participation in militancy and terrorism. Thus, through a kind of "collectivistic shift"—or fusion of one's personal identity with that of the group—individual powerlessness may be overcome by an empowering collectivistic ideology in which name terrorist acts are carried out (Post et al., 2003). Adoption of ideologically based means (terrorism in this instance) may constitute a substitute vehicle for significance restoration if individual means for doing so are thwarted (Kruglanski et al., 2002). The ideologies elucidate what a significance gain according to one's group consists of, and they afford a way of preventing a significance loss through adherence to these ideological dictates.

The notion of population susceptibility inherent in the epidemiological metaphor draws attention to the motivational bases of participation in terrorism. These include (a) ideological frames that identify collectivistic goals for individuals and that portray terrorism as an effective and morally warranted means to achieve these goals, and (b) personal circumstances that affect individuals' readiness to subscribe to these ideological frames. By implication, *immunization* of the susceptible population can occur when there are alternate pathways for success within society, when bright educated individuals can succeed and do well within their culture rather than being driven to strike out in despair.

Concluding Comments: Psychological Implications of the Epidemiological Metaphor

In its fourfold partition between ingredients of terrorism (including the "agent"/ideology, the "vector"/communication sources, the "host"/susceptible populations, and the "environment"/predisposing situational factors), the epidemiological metaphor is more comprehensive than either the war or the law enforcement metaphors. It addresses at once the individual level of analysis represented in the focus on the susceptible population, the social/organizational level represented in the focus on the vector that accomplishes recruitment and indoctrination of potential terrorists (e.g., via the Internet, mosques, or radical madrassas), and the cognitive level of analysis represented in the focus on the ideological "virus" (radical beliefs and terrorism-justifying arguments). Thus, it implies a varied array of efforts meant to counteract and discourage the development of attitudes and beliefs likely to translate into terrorism: Individual disaffections may need to be ameliorated in order to reduce people's readiness to buy into terrorism-warranting ideologies, and the ideologies themselves may need to be countered by credible authorities presenting cogent counterarguments to the extremist rhetoric—especially countering the extremist messages found on radical Web sites and sermons of radical imams preached in the mosques.

More than an alternative metaphoric framing of the counterterrorism effort, the epidemiological metaphor implies the need to focus particular attention on the ideological struggle against jihadist extremists, with the aim of winning the hearts and minds of potential recruits to jihadism. Indeed, in 2007 al-Qaeda intensified its propaganda efforts, releasing a video every 3 days aimed to generate substantially more recruits and support for its cause. (Gunaratna, 2007).

In an attempt to counteract this "virulent" lobbying enterprise, moderate Muslim communities and governments in states with substantial Muslim populations (e.g., in Singapore., Saudi Arabia, Egypt, Jordan, Afghanistan, Indonesia, and Pakistan) have initiated systematic deradicalization programs designed to "cure" detainees suspected of terrorism of adherence to their ideology and to "immunize" youths who might find it appealing against such ideology. We have already mentioned the on-line dialogue with jihadists by moderate clerics and jurists supported by the Saudi interior ministry. In addition, there exists a program carried out in Saudi prisons in which moderate Muslim clerics, abetted by psychologists and sociologists, attempt to dissuade the detainees from their ideology and incite them to abandon their radical beliefs (Boucek, 2007).

A particularly comprehensive deradicalization effort directed at Al-Jemmah Al-Islamiya detainees in Singapore was launched in 2003 by the Religious Rehabilitation Group, a Muslim organization based in the Khadija Mosque of that city. In addition, the Taman Bacaan, or "After Care" organization (bin Kader, 2007), attends to the needs of the detainees' families and organizes educational and media events (workshops, lectures, artistic performances) for Singaporean youths (Muslim as well as non-Muslim) designed to carry an ideological antidote to jihadism.

What is uniquely impressive about the Singaporean deradicalization efforts is their psychological comprehensiveness. Specifically, they target not only the minds (i.e., ideological beliefs) of the detainees and potential recruits to terrorism but also their hearts (i.e., feelings and desires). Just as the anger at the West (fueled by the al-Qaeda propaganda machine through messages and videos portraying the suffering of Muslims in the hands of their enemies) may increase Muslims' readiness to open up to vengeful interpretations of Islam, so assuaging the detainees' anger and frustrations by showing authentic concern for their families, actually funding their children's education (through private donations), and offering professional training for their wives may increase their readiness to open up to moderate religious interpretations and to accept the notion that jihadism is contrary to the humane principles on which Islam is founded. Similarly, the twin efforts to address the concerns of the detainees and those of their communities (and families) supports the classic psychological principle that changing an individual's belief systems (ideology in this case) requires changing the norms of the group to which the individual belongs (Lewin, 1947). Though such deradicalization efforts are promising and constructive, their actual socio-psychological impact is in need of careful evaluation. Assessment of these programs poses, therefore, an important challenge for psychological researchers.

Finally, it is noteworthy that whereas the war and the law enforcement metaphors address the proximal "here and now" of terrorist activities, the epidemiological metaphor highlights the long-term motivational, cognitive, and social/organizational processes that increase the likelihood of terrorism. Nonetheless, all three metaphors approach terrorism as an *external* problem in need of treatment via action against its actual and/or potential perpetrators. In contrast, the analysis considered next views terrorism as a "two way street," focused on the social relations between terrorists and their potential targets.

COUNTERTERRORISM AS PREJUDICE REDUCTION

Framing counterterrorism in terms of prejudice reduction maintains the focus on terrorism's broad base of support while adding a dimension largely absent from the metaphoric frames we discussed previously. Instead of focusing exclusively on the perpetrators of terrorism, it addresses the interaction between two communities whose intergroup conflict may breed terrorism. This shifts the focus from a unilateral to a bilateral concern and acknowledges the contribution to intergroup tensions that the party targeted by terrorists may make. The main premise of the prejudice-reduction framing is that terrorists represent a subset of a group of people who have an unfavorable attitude toward another group of people. Interviews with non-state terrorists, trial transcripts, terrorist writings, public pronouncements, and Internet communications suggest that terrorists typically harbor highly negative sentiments toward those they target for attacks (Alexander 2002; Cordes, 2001; Oliver & Steinberg 2005). Hence, terrorism could be viewed as one expression of tense and deteriorating intergroup relations. A particularly poignant example of a deteriorating interaction between groups, potentially prompting radicalization and extremism, concerns the relations between Muslim immigrants in Europe and the (ethnically) native European populations. We begin the discussion with the story of the perpetrators of the infamous attacks of September 11, 2001 on New York and Washington.

INTERGROUP RELATIONS IN WESTERN EUROPE

On that fateful date, three young Muslims—Mohamed Atta, Marwan al Shehhi, and Ziad Jarrah—each piloted an airplane in a spectacular strike on a monument of American military or economic power. Atta is thought to have been the tactical leader of the 9/11 plot. Ramzi Binalshibh, who shared an apartment with the first two, probably facilitated the plot. All four were apparently radicalized while living in Hamburg, Germany, and were probably influenced, at least in part, by cleric Mohammed Haydar Zammar at the Quds Mosque (National Commission on Terrorist Attacks on the United States, 2004). One of the most important discoveries of the 9/11 investigation was that young Muslims who had spent substantial time living and working in Western Europe could become principals in the most infamous anti-Western terrorist act in history.

The story of the 9/11 cell is hardly unique. Since then, a series of attacks, interrupted attacks, or plots has been linked to other young Muslims from European backgrounds: On December 22, 2001, Bromely-born Richard Reid attempted to blow up an American Airlines flight en route from London to Miami. He had apparently converted to Islam while incarcerated in Feltham young offenders' institution and is thought to have become radicalized while attending the Brixton Mosque in south London (BBC News, 2001).

On November 2, 2004, Dutch filmmaker Theo van Gogh was murdered by a 26-year-old Amsterdam-born Mohammed Bouyeri, who apparently became radicalized in 2003, perhaps influenced by visits to the El Tawheed Mosque in Amsterdam (BBC News, 2005). Also in 2004, Operation Crevice by the British Metropolitan and local police led to discovery of a 1,300-pound cache of ammonium nitrate, used in making explosives, and the arrest of seven young British Muslim men, including 24-year-old Omar Khyam, accused of plotting to bomb targets including a shopping mall and a nightclub (Rotella, 2006a). In late 2005, French police arrested 35-year-old Safe Bourada and 31-year-old Oussani Cherifi; both were of Algerian descent, both grew up in the tough suburbs of Paris, and both were accused of organizing multiple bloody plots for the Salafist Group for Call and Combat (known by its French initials GSPC; Rotella, 2006b).

The life stories of the Madrid train bombers of March 11, 2004; of the London transport bombers of July 7, 2005; and of those suspected in a U.K. plot publicly revealed in August 2006 to blow up airlines en route to the United States have also been documented. Most recently, eight Muslim doctors or doctors-in-training working in British hospitals were arrested in connection with two attempts to explode car bombs in downtown London on June 29, 2007 and an attempt on the subsequent day to ram a flaming Jeep into the main entrance of Glasgow airport. All of the known perpetrators and suspects in these varied incidents were young Muslim men who had either been born and raised in, or lived and worked for extended periods of time in, Western Europe. In terms of McCauley's (1991) pyramid model, these individuals represent the tiny apex of a much larger group: the disaffected Muslim diaspora population of Western Europe.

The size of the Muslim population in Europe and its increasing proportionality in European societies can be explained by two factors: (a) the considerably greater natural growth of the Muslim population than that of Europe's ethnically native populations[12] (the United Kingdom's National Intelligence Council predicts that Europe's Muslim population will double by 2025; Hunter, 2002; Nielsen, 1999; Pauly, 2004); and (b) the unprecedented migration of people from underdeveloped, often politically oppressed Muslim states into Europe. The actual Muslim population of most European nations is unknown due to restrictions on gathering religion data, but estimates put the current number of Muslims in Europe between 15 and 20 million, or 4 to 5% percent of Europe's total population.

The problem is that Muslims and non-Muslim Europeans are failing to integrate. Data confirm the development of highly negative attitudes on both sides of the divide, defining an EU-wide apartheid reminiscent in many ways of the state of relations between Blacks and Whites in the mid-20th-century United States. Several factors might be contributing to this problem: cultural differences in values and world views separating Muslim and non-Muslim Europeans (Huntington, 1998); the sheer size of the immigrant population, affording newcomers a coherent shared reality (Hardin & Higgins, 1996) distinct from that of the host countries and reducing their psychological need to integrate (Kosic, Kruglanski, Pierro, & Mannetti, 2004); and a lack of consistent immigration policies in EU countries, breeding uncertainty and intergroup tension (Kosic et al., 2004).[13]

Attitudes of the Muslim Diaspora Community

In a 2006 telephone survey by the Pew Global Attitudes Project, Muslims in Great Britain, France, Germany, and Spain were asked, "What do you consider yourself first? A citizen of your coun-

---

[12] Between 1965 and 1990, the world's population rose from 3.3 to 5.3 billion, with an overall annual growth rate of 1.85%. Muslim societies, however, exhibited growth rates from 2 to 3% (United Nations Population Division, 1993). Meanwhile, the European Union's ethnically native population has not even been replacing itself since 1973, when, for the first time, the fertility rate fell below the critical replacement rate of 2.1. That rate has continued to plunge and currently stands at just 1.5 (Euroslat, 2006). Huntington (1998) noted that, in part as a result of this differential growth rate, in 1900 Muslims made up just 4% of the world's population but by 2025 they are predicted to make up 19%.

[13] Generally, member countries of the European Union have tended to adopt an assimilationist policy toward immigrants (exceptions being the Netherlands, Sweden and England, which support multiculturalism). Italy, for instance, initially pursued an assimilation policy, but in recent years concepts of multiculturalism and cultural diversity have been articulated with some frequency by policymakers, occasionally prompting specific initiatives for the promotion of multiculturalism.

try or a Muslim?" With the exception of Spain, where the percentage of religious (46%) versus national (42%) identifications was about equal, the overwhelming majority of these European Muslims embraced their religious identity ahead of their national identity (81% vs. 7% in the United Kingdom, 69% vs. 3% in France, and 66% vs. 13% in Germany). Strikingly, the religious identification of European Muslims was higher than that reported by Muslims in Egypt, Turkey, or Indonesia. For comparison purposes, 59% of Christians in Great Britain, 83% in France, 59% in Germany, and 60% in Spain put their national identity first (Pew Global Attitudes Project, 2006a).

These data tell us that European Muslims tend to hold strikingly different identity attitudes than do non-Muslim Europeans. The typical young Muslim living in Western Europe identifies him- or herself as belonging to a separate community—a religious collectivity not bound by geography or temporal limits—consistent with a stereotype about European Muslims held by many non-Muslim Europeans. In this vein, Roy (2004) writes of the recent emergence of Islamic Neofundamentalism, "a view of Islam that rejects the national and statist dimension in favor of the *ummah*, the universal community of all Muslims, based on sharia [Islamic law]" (p. 1). According to Roy, "Neofundamentalism has gained ground among rootless Muslim youth, particularly among second- and third-generation migrants in the West. These Muslims experience a deter-ritorialization of Islam" (p. 2).

The 2006 Pew Global Attitudes Project reveals that about half of British, German, French, and Spanish Muslims regard Western people as selfish, arrogant, greedy, immoral, and violent. There is general agreement on both sides that relations are bad between Muslims and Western people but sharp disagreement about who is to blame: Between 58% and 70% of both Muslims and non-Muslims in Great Britain, France, and Germany say that intergroup relations are bad, with large proportions of the Muslims explicitly blaming Westerners for the poor quality of the relationship and vice-versa (Pew Global Attitudes Project, 2006b).

Such attitudes are potential harbingers of violent intergroup conflict. For example, 24% of British Muslims and 35% of French Muslims endorse the statement that violence against civilian targets is sometimes or rarely justified in the service of Islam. Averaging the respondents' attitudes toward native Europeans and their support for terrorism, it appears that roughly 44% of European Muslims in the countries surveyed hold very negative views of Westerners and 24.25% are actually sympathetic to terrorism. Multiplying by the mean estimate of their total population (17.5 million), one might conclude that about 7.7 million Muslims living in Europe dislike Westerners and more than 4.2 million are sympathetic to terrorism. These could serve as substantial pools from which active terrorists might be drawn.

Islamophobia

Europeans feel threatened, angered, and rejecting toward their new Muslim neighbors. There are variations within this trend. Citizens of some nations express more tolerance than others. Younger, better-educated, and urban citizens are more tolerant on average than older, less educated, rural citizens (European Monitoring Center on Racism and Xenophobia, 2005; Marsh & Sahin-Dikmen, 2002). And (although one must exercise caution in generalizing U.S. research data to European populations) one U.S. study reports that certain individual traits—including racism, social-dominance orientation, right-wing authoritarianism, and religious fundamentalism—predict stronger anti-Muslim sentiments (Rowatt, Franklin, & Cotton, 2005).

Research indicates that by the mid-90s there was much blatant prejudice but even more subtle prejudice by Europeans against Turks, Asians, and North Africans. Furthermore, beginning in the early 1990s, right-wing political movements emerged in response to the perceived threat (Pettigrew, 1998b).

Anti-immigrant sentiments are not equally distributed throughout the EU, nor have they remained stable over time. According to results from the 1997 Eurobarometer attitudes survey, Denmark had the highest level of racial prejudice among the 15 surveyed European nations: 83% of the respondents openly admitted to harboring racist views and 43% admitted to being "very racist" or "quite racist" (European Commission, 1997). Since then, there has been an increase in the proportion of Europeans who wish to place limits on multiculturalism (International Helsinki Federation for Human Rights, 2005; Widdop, 2007). By late 2001, the Vienna-based European Monitoring Center on Racism and Xenophobia had documented a significant increase in violent assaults against Muslims (European Monitoring Center on Racism and Xenophobia, 2005). A 2002 survey by the Policy Studies Institute of London found that ethnic or racial discrimination was the most frequently observed form of prejudice throughout Europe (Marsh & Sahin-Dikmen, 2002). Distrust and hostility have become widespread and anger at Muslims is very high (Harrison, Law, & Phillips, 2005). One measure of these sentiments, the European Social Survey, Round 2, determined that a large proportion of residents of many European nations agree with the statement "If a country wants to reduce tension it should stop immigration" (Widdop, 2007).

In its most recent surveys, the Pew Global Attitudes Project has developed a more detailed profile of anti-Muslim feelings. For example, many non-Muslim Europeans tend to hold that Muslims are fanatical, violent, and disrespectful of women. And, after *Jyllands-Posten*, Denmark's largest newspaper, published cartoons depicting Mohammed in September, 2005, solid majorities of British, French, German, and Spanish people attributed the resulting outrage and violence to Muslim intolerance (Pew Global Attitudes Project, 2006b).

Most (77% of British, 76% of French, 82% of Germans, and 66% of Spaniards) are very or somewhat concerned about the rise of Islamic extremism in their own countries. And, consistent with the impression of self-imposed isolation and the data on religious rather than nationalist identities, most non-Muslim Europeans (64% of British, 53% of French, 76% of Germans, and 66% of Spaniards) perceive Muslim immigrants as wishing to remain separate from their host societies (Pew Global Attitudes Project, 2006b). This suite of attitudes, opinions, and fears has been referred to as Islamophobia.

Islamophobia in Europe contains multiple elements. Exclusion from full political participation; discrimination in housing, employment, and services; and prejudice in multiple aspects of everyday life have combined to create a lower caste overtly or covertly denied political equality. In addition to these formal manifestations, Islamophobia reveals itself in the simple day-today interactions through which people ordinarily express belonging to the same society. There is prejudice—on both sides—against patronizing the same stores, entertainment venues, clubs, and sporting activities. There is, more profoundly, an almost total mutual prejudice against intermarriage. The broad psychological impact of such tensions results in a situation wherein Muslims in Europe largely see themselves as isolated from the mainstream of non-Muslim society and living instead as part of a global *ummah*—a widely-dispersed community with shared identity, interests, and destiny (Coolsaet, 2005; Hunter, 2002; Jordan & Boix, 2004; Nielsen 1999; Roy, 2004).

The failure of Muslims to integrate into European societies, or intergroup tensions as such, may not constitute the sufficient conditions for terrorism, but they may instill the readiness to buy into a terrorism-justifying ideology if one is offered. Such an ideology is offered abundantly these days, on thousands of jihadist Web sites, in radical mosques or madrassas, in the writings of extremist clerics, etc. To the degree that European Muslim communities see themselves as alienated from their host societies, at war with the West, subject to local perceived discrimination, and steeped in feelings of rage stoked by fundamentalist *imams*, young European Muslims—like the members of the 9/11cell—are potential recruits to terrorism.

European Efforts to Enhance Integration

Multiple initiatives to enhance integration and reduce friction between Muslims and non-Muslims in Europe are currently underway. Some initiatives involve efforts to document discriminatory behavior or civil rights violations, such as the work of the International Helsinki Federation for Human Rights (2005), the European Monitoring Centre on Racism and Xenophobia (including the Danish Documentation and Advisory Centre on Racial Discrimination), or Sweden's Health and Discrimination project (Racism and Xenophobia in Sweden, 2004). Other efforts strive to promote dialogue, such as the Council of Europe's Expert Colloquies and Intercultural Dialogue and Conflict Prevention Project (e.g., Etienne, 2002).

Yet other initiatives involve legislation to punish discriminatory behaviors in employment, housing, or banking. Some efforts are intra-national—for example, a number of programs in Germany to improve relations with the large Turkish minority, or the community introduction programs in Swedish municipalities. More ambitious projects are being evaluated for possible international adoption—for example, the Council of Europe's "Shared Cities" program (Wilson, 2003) or the proposals currently being formulated by

The European Dilemma, an eight-nation research consortium at the Center for Multiethnic Research at Uppsala University that is committed to an examination of discrimination and exclusion in both labor markets and educational systems and is meant to offer antixenophobia strategies on the EU, local, and national levels (Center for Multiethnic Research, 2003).

In short, there are in place considerable social-engineering efforts aimed at ameliorating charged intergroup relations between Muslims and non-Muslims in Europe. Yet, once again, one vital element is surprisingly rare in this mix: an attempt to evaluate what works. As a result, expenditures of money, time, and human resources take place with no persuasive evidence that they will achieve the desired outcomes—enhancement of social integration, acceptance of multiculturalism, pluralism, and the reduction of inter-group tensions. Yet, there exists considerable social-psychological research pertinent to these concerns. We now briefly address this work and its implications.

Prejudice Reduction

Prejudice and discrimination have been among the most intensively studied social-psychological phenomena. Since the publication of Gordon Allport's classic book, *The Nature of Prejudice* (1954/1979), a massive body of empirical work examining what prejudice is and what can be done about it has been compiled. Obviously, psychological efforts at prejudice reduction alone do not overcome gross disparities in income and legal inequalities, or remove intergroup competition for scarce resources. In fact, prejudice is strongly related to measures of objective disparities and conflicts and is augmented by a sense of injustice, humiliation, and competition. For that reason, psychological efforts at attitude change and prejudice reduction may work best if combined with credible policies aimed at the elimination of objective inequalities.

It is also true, however, that prejudice contains strong elements of *misperception*: It tends (a) to generalize to individual group members the traits and attitudes that are perceived to characterize the group as an aggregate (Fiske, 1998; Macrae, Stangor, & Hewstone, 1996; Schneider, 2004), and (b) to generalize from some perceived negative traits to other, evaluatively consistent negative traits, producing a "halo effect" for which there may be little if any objective evidence (Nisbett & Wilson, 1977).

The promise of prejudice-reduction efforts is that they may eliminate those misperceptions and, under proper conditions, may help build a common identity. The less that people regard others as competing, threatening, alien out-group members and the more they come to see others as supportive in-group members with shared goals, the lower the impetus for discriminatory behavior and the higher the impetus for social cooperation (Dovidio & Gaertner, 1986; Gaertner & Dovidio, 2000). Fifty years of research suggests that prejudice reduction is an essential step toward successful integration. And in the long run, integration may prove to be an effective strategy of counterterrorism. Just as the 50-year desegregation battle in the United States was primed by early prejudice-reduction experiments, successful integration in the EU could be primed by forward-thinking social science devoted to understanding the most effective ways to increase intercultural harmony.

Origin and Evolution of the Contact Hypothesis

Until the end of WWII, the United States largely ignored the problem of racial prejudice. African Americans were technically freed and even enfranchised to vote, yet they were subjected to systematic prejudice, discrimination, and outright oppression. By the early 1950s, pioneering social scientists were finally turning their attention to the pernicious problem of prejudice. Gordon Allport's seminal 1954 text created a watershed moment in the history of social psychology. In his book, Allport laid out the emotional, developmental, cognitive, and cultural roots of prejudice. He also described the fitful first efforts to resolve the problem or at least reduce its magnitude. Hinting at the direction that efforts to reduce prejudice may take, Allport cited a commentary by Lee and Humphrey regarding the Bloody Monday race riots in Detroit in 1943: "People who had become neighbors did not riot against each other. The students of Wayne University—white and black—went to their classes in peace throughout Bloody Monday. And there were no disorders between white and black workers in the war plants" (Allport, 1954/1979, p. 261).

Allport's mam point was that contact between rival groups may initially lead to anxiety and competition but that this often gives way to accommodation and eventually to integration. Based on his review of different programs for prejudice reduction, Allport arrived at what later became known as the contact hypothesis:

> Prejudice (unless deeply rooted in the character structure of the individual) may be reduced by equal status contact between majority and minority groups in the pursuit of common goals. The effect is greatly enhanced if this contact is sanctioned by institutional supports (i.e., by law, custom or local atmosphere), and provided it is of a sort that leads to the perception of common interests and common humanity between members of the two groups. (Allport, 1954/1979, p. 281)

According to Allport, optimal intergroup contact contains a number of essential elements:

- *Equal status* of members of the separate groups that are brought into contact with each other
- *Pursuit of common goals*—that is, adoption of superordinate objectives that members of the separate groups may share
- *Institutional sanction* by respected societal authorities
- *Positive outcome*—that is, a realization by members of the separate groups that contact produced desirable results

By the mid-1990s, it became apparent that prejudice reduction required a second look. Allport had explained how to reduce prejudice, but not why contact should work. Some scholars (e.g., Brewer, Manzi, & Shaw, 1993) attributed successful prejudice reduction to personal contact between individuals leading to *personalization*, or the breakdown of arbitrary judgments based on social categories. Critics asked how the development of personal friendships through contact would generalize to all members of a stereotyped category (Hewstone, 1996). Some scholars suggested that positive intergroup contact worked so long as participants maintained identity with their own in-group (Hewstone and Brown, 1986). Others advised that maintenance of in-group identity was exactly wrong; the success of prejudicereduction interventions depended on the development of a shared group identity (Dovidio & Gaertner, 1986; Gaertner & Dovidio, 2000).

Pettigrew (1998a) offered an important reformulation of the contact hypothesis, in which contact is described as a process of change taking place over time. This process is assumed to consist of three stages. In Pettigrew's model, initial contact provokes anxiety, but positive personal contact with someone from the other group serves to reduce anxiety and allows liking to take place—albeit liking for that one person, not for her or his group as a whole. Over time, the liking can be extended to other members of the out-group, perhaps in accordance with Heider's (1958) balance-theoretic logic whereby the friends of a friend are one's friends as well. This may occur even though the in-group member is still very much aware of her or his own group membership and identity—consistent with Hewstone and Brown's (1986) theory. Finally, when the established contact is optimal, a shift in identity may take place as superordinate goals supercede the old in-group/out-group differentiation, and—as predicted by Gaertner and Dovidio (2000)—a common ingroup identity may emerge and optimal prejudice reduction may occur. According to Pettigrew (1998a), many groups fail to achieve the final step. The crucial question is, what is the best way to optimize the chances of success?

Fifty years after Allport, a wealth of experimental literature testing ways to reduce intergroup prejudice has appeared (Lemmer & Wagner, 2006; Pettigrew & Tropp, 2006). Multiple methods, varying the duration, frequency, and type of intergroup contact, have been examined. Some methods have involved school-based experiences, others community- or employment-based encounter groups, yet others recreational groups or groups of fellow travelers. This body of work has led to several conclusions.

Perhaps the most significant conclusion is that contact seems to work. In a meta-analytic review of 515 studies involving 713 population samples and 1,383 tests, there was a significant negative correlation between contact and prejudice. While the mean correlation of $r = -.21$ might be considered modest, the correlation was actually higher among the most rigorously conducted projects and was most robust when measured by direct observation of intergroup contact as opposed to self-report measures. Numerous observations conducted in laboratories, schools, residential settings, recreational activities, or travel contexts yielded evidence of benefits.

Second, some types of interventions appear to work better than others. Generally speaking, incidental contact or travel excursions seem to yield little positive effect (mean $r = -.113$).

Residential interaction appears to fare somewhat better ($r = -.202$). Educational and work-based settings seem better yet ($r = -.213$ and $-.224$). The best effects were seen in studies carried out in recreational contexts ($r = -.299$).

Third, there was some support for Allport's suggestions for optimal contact conditions of equality, authority sanction, and cooperation. However, it appears that Allport's conditions do not assure beneficial effects, nor are they absolutely required for beneficial outcomes. The single most important factor appears to be institutional support: When authorities sanction the contact, it predicts success better than any other factor (Pettigrew & Tropp, 2006). It may also be essential that the groups achieve success in their cooperative endeavors (the positive-outcome condition in Allport's list), for failure enhances bias and scapegoating (Worchel, Andreoli, & Folger, 1977).

Fourth, there was strong support for the so-called "extended contact" effect. That is, reduction of prejudice was typically generalized not only to nonparticipant members of the out-group (for example, to all Blacks when participants were White) but to other out-groups as well (for example, to the disabled or the intellectually impaired). Overall, the authors concluded, "There is little need to demonstrate further contact's general ability to lessen prejudice" (Pettigrew & Tropp, 2006, p. 768).

It must be acknowledged that prejudicial attitudes are by no means the only explanation for aggression toward the out-group that may translate to terrorism. Some scholars have claimed that the relationship between prejudice, discrimination, and overt aggression is weak and theorized that other factors may be more important than prejudice in determining discriminatory acts and actual physical aggression (e.g., Dovidio, Brigham, Johnson, & Gaertner, 1996; Struch & Schwartz, 1989). In regard to the 2006 U.K. mass airline-bombing plot, for example, Elliot (2006) writes,

> Nor can it be easily argued that social deprivation or ethnic discrimination breeds radicalism; many of those arrested were from middle class homes—the sort that send their children to university—in standard British multicultural neighborhoods, where Muslims, white Britons and more recent immigrants from Eastern Europe live together, (p. 29)

Indeed, prejudicial attitudes need not derive from personal experience of deprivation or discrimination but may be stoked by inflammatory rhetoric in mosques or Web sites or shaped by events far afield—such as the war in Iraq—as they are depreneted in the media. In the same vein, individual poverty was not a factor motivating al-Qaeda's 9/11 bombers (Krueger & Maleckova, 2003; National Commission on Terrorist Attacks on the United States, 2004). Still, the *facts* of poverty, of income discrepancy, or discrimination in the work-place may translate into widespread perceptions and prejudicial attitudes fueling the readiness to embrace extremist rhetoric and to support political violence. Overcoming such prejudice would probably require a coordinated set of measures, including media campaigns, enforcement of strict anti-discriminatory norms and policies, etc., as well as the creation of opportunities for optimal contact between members of the Muslim and non-Muslim communities.

Concluding Comments: Psychological Implications of the Prejudice-Reduction Frame

The unique aspect of the prejudice-reduction frame is its explicitly bilateral character. Admittedly, the war, law enforcement, and epidemiological metaphors did hint that some counterterrorist tactics employed by the targets of terrorism (e.g., those likely to produce the killing of innocents, destruction of property, and spawning of a refugee problem) may augment rather than reduce terrorism; yet their primary focus has been on the psyche of the terrorists and their supporters. By contrast, the prejudice-reduction approach recognizes that terrorism involves a recursive interplay of two types of mentality, that of the terrorists and that of their targets. For instance, the perceived otherness of Muslim immigrants for European hosts, and vice versa, as well as the aversion that otherness often evokes, may feed mutually negative stereotypes that motivate actions that may, in turn, augment and polarize the stereotypes (via an expectancy-confirmation mechanism)—and hence exacerbate intergroup tensions.

A major social-psychological intervention to reduce prejudice is the creation of positive contact between members of the conflicted groups (Pettigrew & Tropp, 2006). Research suggests that the creation of optimal contact, particularly if carried at an early enough age, may contribute to the development of positive attitudes toward members of the out-group. However, positive contact in unique and isolated settings (e.g., a certain school or recreational facility) may be counteracted by events, initiatives, and rhetorics external to that context, such as depictions in the media and discussions in one's community. To the extent that such depictions portray aggressive, humiliating, or discriminatory activities perpetrated by one group against the other, they might well damage the positive will engendered in the restricted, positive-contact settings. Thus, efforts at prejudice reduction via positive contact need to be pursued in the context of a larger set of policies—for example those concerning immigration laws, educational programs, and foreign policy initiatives designed to augment the good-will-generating efforts of optimal-contact programs.

GENERAL DISCUSSION

The four ways of thinking about counterterrorism considered in the preceding pages roughly define a continuum. The continuum ranges from a totalistic and undiscriminating war metaphor (inherent in the "global war on terrorism" concept) that condemns the enemy group as "evil" and pulls out all stops in order to defeat it; through a more nuanced law enforcement metaphor that seeks to precisely target the actual perpetrators of terrorism and separate them from their potential base of community support; through the epidemiological metaphor that addresses the sources of such support as they derive from the ideological belief system that justifies terrorism and the mechanisms of persuasion and indoctrination that spread the ideology in the pool of potential supporters; and finally to the prejudicereduction framing that highlights the dynamic interplay of perceptions that conflicted groups may have of each other and the spiral of alienation and increasing psychological distance (Liberman, Trope, & Stephen, 2007) that need to be broken on both sides of the divide.

THE WAR METAPHOR

Each of the perspectives discussed in this monograph addresses a specific psychological piece of the "counterterrorism puzzle" (Ganor, 2005); each has vulnerabilities as well as points of strength. The flaws of the war metaphor include the massive overcommitment to counterterrorism at the expense of major alternative concerns including the humanitarian value of protecting lives and ensuring the enlightened treatment of prisoners. Much has been written about the outrage in affected communities evoked by killing of innocents, destruction of property, and dislocation of families. All these may create a "boomerang effect" based on a defiance motivation (LaFree & Dugan, 2007), potentially boosting the stock of recruits to terrorism (Kaplan et al., 2005).

An additional drawback of the war metaphor, related to overcommitment of resources that the war concept implies, is the arousal of unreasonable expectations as to the counterterrorism effort's required duration. In case of asymmetrical struggle against insurgents or terrorists, such expectations often involve serious underestimates, breeding general disappointment with the results and a public outcry to discontinue the effort and bring the troops home. Finally, the war metaphor may evoke conflicting and inconsistent expectations derived from the divergent war analogies one may envision (e.g., the Second World War, the Cold War, or the Vietnam War). These may forestall the formulation of a coherent counterterrorism policy and give rise to unhelpful debates based on questionable historical similes.

Undermining Terrorists' Capability

These drawbacks notwithstanding, the war metaphor isn't totally devoid of utility. As Ganor (2005) noted, "the military component should not be discounted as a legitimate and effective means for eliminating terrorist attacks, reducing their damage, and hurting terrorist organizations" (p. 40). Primarily, military measures, if properly executed, may hamper terrorists' ability to carry out attacks. In a recent paper, LaFree & Dugan (2007) used a continuous-time survival analysis based on Cox's (1972) proportional-hazard models (see Dugan, LaFree, & Piquero, 2005) to analyze the impact of military measures carried out by the British in Northern Ireland. LaFree & Dugan (2007) These authors have shown that a massive military intervention by the British, referred to as the Motorman Operation in 1972 (that involved the participation of 30,000 troops, the use of heavy armor, etc.), appeared to reduce over the long term the incidence of subsequent terrorist attacks, whereas more restricted military interventions (namely, the Falls Curfew, the Loughall and the Gibraltar incidents) appeared to significantly increase it. Similarly, Chen, Fishman, & Kruglanski (2007), using proportional-hazard models, found that a massive occupation by the Israeli military of West Bank towns in 2002, referred to as Operation Defensive Shield, and the construction of the defensive fence by Israel decreased the incidence of suicide bombing by Hamas militants, whereas a more restricted 2004 operation in Gaza lasting 2 weeks, called Operation Days of Penitence, actually increased their incidence.

Eppright (1997) concluded that Israel's massive 1996 incursion into Lebanon significantly reduced the amount of Hezbollah's rocket attacks on Israel, and Greener-Barcham (2002) reported that the liberation of hostages in the Entebbe airport by Israeli commandos in 1976 markedly reduced the number of airline hijackings against Israeli targets and the seizure of hostages. At least in the short term, then, successful military operations might reduce terrorist organizations' operational capability, and in that sense reduce the threat that their intentions may pose. However, it is often suggested that, in the long run, terrorism—at least if it enjoys a broad base of popular support—has no ready military solution (Ganor, 2005, p. 39).

Motivational Effects

Mention was already made of the potential of military operations to evoke outrage and elevate terrorists' defiance motivation (LaFree & Dugan, 2007). Indeed according to Ganor (2005), one of the dilemmas of counterterrorism is the fact that "the more successful one is in carrying out actions that damage the terrorists organizations' ability to perpetrate attacks, the more ... their motivation will only increase" (p. 41). From this perspective, former Prime Minister Ariel Sharon remarked that counterterrorism military activities undertaken by Israel were "successes for periods of time [gaining] breathing space for certain periods of time" (Ganor, 2005, p. 292).

These insights notwithstanding, it also seems possible that sustained military pressure would ultimately gnaw at terrorists' motivations and deflate their morale. Palestinians have repeatedly complained about the Israeli policy of targeted killings and demanded that it be stopped. It also appears that this particular policy instilled a measure of fear in militants' leaders, forcing them to go "partially underground, turning off their cell phones, avoiding official vehicles and restricting their movements" (El Deeb, 2007).

Furthermore, sustained military pressure might induce in members of a terrorist group the motivation to disengage from terrorism under some conditions. Ironically, such motivation may arise from the increased "group-centrism" (Kruglanski, Pierro, Mannetti, & DeGrada, 2006) that external pressures may create. Horgan (2005) cites in this connection the reflections of Michael Bauman, who disengaged from the German June 2nd movement of which he was member. In Bauman's words, "The group becomes increasingly closed. The greater the pressure from the outside, the more you stick together, the more mistakes you make, the more pressure is turned inward.... [T]hose are ...the things that come together horribly at the end" (as cited in Horgan, 2005, p. 14).

The extensive "group centrism" that external (e.g., military) pressures encourage may come at the expense of one's individualistic objectives. To the extent that the latter are important to the individual, this may induce a growing desire to disengage from the terrorist organization. The relevant motivational considerations are apparent in Adriana Faranda's reflections on her dissociation from the Red Brigades (as cited in Horgan, 2005):

> Choosing to enter the Red Brigades—to become clandestine and ... to break off relations with your family, is a choice so total that it involves your entire life ... It means choosing to occupy yourself from morning till night with problems of politics, or organization, and fighting; and no longer with normal life—culture, cinema, babies, the education of your children, with all the things that fill other people's lives ... [W]hen you remove yourself from society ... you become sad because a whole area of life is missing, because you are aware that life is more than politics and political work. (p. 148)

The individualistically motivated wish to disengage from the group might usher in a rationalization in form of a disenchantment with the group's ideology or with the degree to which the group is living up to its ideological commitments. In Faranda's words, the process of ideological disenchantment encompassed "everything ... It [involved] the revolution itself; Marxism, violence, the logic of enmity, of conflict, of one's relationship with authority, a way of working out problems, of confronting reality and of facing the future" (cited in Horgan, 2005, p. 148).

In summary, relentless military pressure on a terrorist organization may generate a complex field of opposing psychological forces acting upon its members, including the motivation to strengthen one's commitment to the cause, fomenting one's resolve and defiance in face of the enemy, as well as yearnings to liberate oneself from excessive group centrism and to regain the freedom to pursue one's individualistic objectives. Which of these forces may prevail may partially depend on the degree to which the group enjoys a wide degree of support in the larger society in which it is embedded. Members of groups whose world views and shared realities are discrepant from the society at large (as may be the case with urban terrorist organizations such as the Bader Meinhoff group or the Italian Red Brigades) may be aware of general societal values and objectives, even if they suppress them for a time. Under external pressure, the members' dependence on the group may turn into an insufferable psychological burden fostering the motivation to disengage from the group, and allowing the suppressed societal values (e.g. concerns with individual freedom and happiness) to rebound.

Unlike members of those latter groups for whom a reintegration in the larger society and the embrace of its values constitutes a potentially viable alternative,[14] for members of groups whose ideological objectives coincide with values of their community (e.g., Hamas or Hezbollah) such an alternative is less available. For the latter individuals, disengagement from the terrorist organization implies to some extent betrayal of one's society, leaving them with little psychological choice. Unless the ideological climate in the society shifts, members of such groups might, therefore, respond with defiance rather than acquiescence to military pressures exerted on their organization.

THE LAW ENFORCEMENT METAPHOR

Like the war metaphor, the law enforcement metaphor has some advantages but also potential disadvantages. One of its main advantages is its targeting precision in focusing on actual perpetrators/conspirators who are in violation of the legal code. Such an approach avoids the sense of injustice and attendant outrage that indiscriminate war-related destruction may invite. Relatedly, the targeting precision of law enforcement may allow a separation of the apex of the terrorism pyramid (i.e., actual perpetrators) from its support base (i.e., individuals whose attitudes may be aligned with those of the terrorists but whose actions are in conformity with the law). Such separation may constitute a precondition for driving a wedge between terrorists and their broader community; an obvious advantage of this is the potential for obtaining invaluable human intelligence needed to thwart impending terrorist schemes.

The law enforcement metaphor also has possible disadvantages. Police forces are limited, for example, in their ability to launch the massive strikes that may be occasionally required to cripple terrorists' capability (even if temporarily) and reduce the damage that such capability might afford. Additionally, massive commitment of force communicates resolve and determination, an asset in the battle of wills that counterterrorism typically involves.

A further limitation of the strict law enforcement metaphor is that it neglects the ideological basis of terrorists' struggle. It is that feature of terrorism, after all, that distinguishes it from ordinary crime. In this sense, the rational cost—benefit analysis that decision to collaborate with the police versus the gangs, say, may involve (Akerlof & Yellen, 1994) doesn't fully apply to terrorism.[15] Especially in those cases where a strong ideological bond exists between large segments of the broader society and the militant organization (a bond that may exist between the Palestinian population and Hamas, the Southern Lebanese population and Hezbollah, or the Tamil population and the Liberation Tigers of Tamil

---

[14] For instance, in 1979 and 1982 the Italian government enacted repentance laws meant to facilitate an exit from terrorism and a reintegration into society. The laws "promised substantial leniency if terrorists collaborate with the police and judicial authorities and a lesser degree of leniency if they only separate themselves from the terrorist group" (Ferracuti, 1998, p. 62). These legal initiatives are generally credited with dismantling of the Red Brigades movement in the 1980s.

[15] In this connection, Krueger & Maleckova (2002, pp. 31–32) remark that "The standard economic model of crime suggests that those with the lowest value of time should engage in criminal activity. But . . . in most cases terrorism is less like property crime and more like a violent form of political engagement . . ."

Eilam [LTTE]), it may be rather difficult to drive a wedge between the community and the militants without addressing the ideological underpinnings of their collaboration. The latter enterprise may necessitate a "struggle of ideas" in attempts to persuade the broader community that terrorism is (a) ineffectual and/or (b) immoral, (c) that there exist alternative superior means (e.g., negotiations, diplomacy) to achieve the goals currently pursued via terrorism,[16] or (d) that those goals (e.g., the dream of a global *ummah*) are unattainable and in need of adjustment (for discussion, see Kruglanski & Fishman, 2006).

THE EPIDEMIOLOGICAL METAPHOR

An advantage of the epidemiological metaphor (Stares & Yacoubian, 2006) is the linkage of the terrorism problem to the ideological bases of terrorist commitments (the "virus"), their modes of transmission (the "vector"), and the vulnerability factors present in certain segments of society (the "susceptible populations") that fuel people's readiness to buy into terrorism-warranting ideologies. In this sense, the epidemiological metaphor explicitly recognizes the wide-ranging efforts needed to combat certain (strongly ideologically entrenched) types of terrorist activity as well as the likely protracted nature of the process that might be needed to eradicate it.

Despite its several advantages, the epidemiological metaphor has limitations as well. Whereas the war and law enforcement metaphors that focus on the immediate threat neglect the longrange process of ideological conversion and radicalization, the epidemiological metaphor, focused on the wider picture, neglects the "here and now" of counterterrorism and the value of resolute strikes and intelligence gathering activities needed to counter terrorists' concrete schemes and capabilities.

The epidemiological metaphor may also be faulted for its unilateral emphasis on the perpetrators of terrorism and its neglect of the targeted side's policies and their possible part in offending the Muslim population and fueling its resonance to the terrorist rhetoric.[17] As part of the issue, the negative language of the metaphor that likens the Islamist ideology to a malignant "virus" (as well as the disease metaphor as a whole) might be offensive to adherents of the Islamist ideology, hence inducing resistance to campaigns designed to change their hearts and minds.

THE PREJUDICE-REDUCTION FRAME

The danger of offending groups that use terrorism is avoided by the prejudice-reduction frame, which explicitly locates the terrorism problem at the interface of two communities troubled by deteriorating relations. One advantage of this approach is its appreciation of the dynamic character of intergroup relations and of the potential for a spiraling enmity that leads intergroup communication to break down (Deulsch, 1973), for mutual blame placing, and for the entrenchment of positions behind pernicious stereotypes.

Another advantage of the prejudice-reduction approach is provision of a specific intervention technique that is grounded in the notion of optimal intergroup contact. If applied broadly, such a prejudice-reduction technique might make an appreciable contribution to the lessening of tensions between groups and the opening of minds to more constructive reciprocal approaches (Kruglanski, 2004; Kruglanski, Dechesne, & Erb, 2006). In particular, the possibility of applying the technique to children in school settings at a relatively early age might afford an opportunity to psychologically "immunize" individuals' attitudes (McGuire, 1961) against subsequent conflict-promoting communications.

---

[16] In recent years, several terrorism-using organizations seem to have reverted to political means, in recognition that the armed struggle has failed to advance their strategic means. The cases in point are the Irish Republican Army (IRA) following the Good Friday agreement on April 10, 1998; the ETA organization (Basque Fatherland and Liberty) in Spain, which declared a permanent ceasefire in 2006; and similar ceasefire announcements by the Kurdish Workers' Party (PKK) in Turkey, the Revolutionary Armed Forces of Columbia (FARC), the Front Islamic du Salut (FIS) in Algeria, the al-Jihad and Gam'at al Islamiyya in Egypt, and the LTTE (Liberation Tigers of Tamil Eilam) in Sri Lanka (see also Karmon, 2002).

[17] In a recent public opinion survey conducted in Morocco, Egypt, Pakistan, and Indonesia by the National Center for the Study of Terrorism and the Response to Terrorism (START) at the University of Maryland, only minorities of the populations surveyed endorsed support for the killing of civilians. Given the overall sizes of the populations involved, however, these minorities translate into millions of terrorism supporters. Thus, in Morocco the 8% minority of terrorism supporters translates into the figure of 2,600,000 people, in Egypt the 15% minority translates into 12,000,000 people, in Pakistan the 5% minority translates into 8,000,000 people, and in Indonesia the 4% minority translates into 20,000,000 people. (National Center for the Study of Terrorism and the Response to Terrorism, 2007).

In fact, some "optimal contact" programs are already under way—for instance, the School Linking Project in Bradford, West Yorkshire, where teenaged students from different backgrounds are brought together for multiple contact experiences in which they work cooperatively on learning projects. This project, which has been underway since 2000 and other similar ones merit careful psychological assessment as to how effective they are at promoting positive intergroup attitudes, how persistent they are, and how resistant they are to radical rhetoric. Substantial evidence that carefully designed prejudice-reduction interventions yield measurable short-term improvement in intergroup relations exists. However, a major gap appears in the literature of applied social psychology: It has yet to be demonstrated that such interventions produce long-term enhancement in intergroup relations and reduction in intergroup violence. Given the current worldwide tensions between Muslims and non-Muslims, rigorous research in this area is urgently needed.

For all its benefits, the prejudice-reduction framework, like the previously considered metaphors, captures a particular aspect of the terrorism problem, however important, and inevitably neglects other aspects: First, it is vulnerable to being overridden by other powerful influences, including policies of states (e.g., Britain's involvement in Iraq and Afghanistan, the U.S. support for Israel) that may be readily interpreted as anti-Muslim. Thus, even if a positive-contact program manages to instill positive attitudes toward specific members of an out-group, large-scale events on the social and political levels might undermine their generalization to the out-group as a whole.

Second, in context of the positive-contact notion, the prejudice-reduction framework is free of ideological contents. It is mediated by cooperative activities on neutral tasks, such as the jigsaw classroom (Aronson & Bridgman, 1979), and it fails to address the ideological element (radical Islamism and jihadism) that appears essential to the process of radicalization.

Finally, like the epidemiological metaphor, the prejudicereduction concept cannot address the "here and now" of terrorism and the need to counter specific terrorist schemes and protect societies from the immediate threats that these entail. Thus, the prejudice framework offers a potential long-term solution to one important driver of the psychology of grievance, but it neglects the short-term challenges posed by terrorism; it does not resolve substantive political issues and grievances, does not disable terrorists' methods for addressing such issues, and may only influence the communication channels for disseminating ideological arguments and a radicalized belief system after considerable delay.

Concluding Comments: Paradoxes of Counterterrorism

The counterterrorism metaphors examined in this paper beam a search light (to use a metaphor!) onto diverse aspects of the problem, each illuminating some of its aspects while leaving others in darkness. Jointly, however, they manage to convey the considerable complexity that systematic counterterrorism efforts must encounter.

In part, the complexity stems from the fact that counterterrorist activities that may appear desirable from the standpoint of a given framing of the problem may contradict goals implicit in another metaphor. For instance, the use of military force suggested by the war metaphor might convey one's resolve and determination, cripple a terrorist organization's ability to function, and apply psychological pressure on its members. Yet at the same time it might fuel the outrage of the population affected by the military activity and undermine the objective of reducing their support for terrorists, which are desirable goals from the perspective of the law enforcement metaphor. The same may be said of tough interrogation tactics, ethnic profiling, and discriminatory immigration policies that are compatible with the war metaphor but rather incompatible with the law enforcement metaphor or the long-term goal of reducing prejudice. Negotiating with terrorists may communicate that there are alternative means to their goals outside of terrorism—consistent with the goal of countering the virulent terrorism-encouraging ideology, as suggested by the epidemiological metaphor. Yet negotiating with terrorists also conveys that terrorism is an efficient tactic for the attainment of strategic objectives, thereby encouraging its future use. This is consistent with the terrorist-promoting ideology and inconsistent with implications of the epidemiological approach to counterterrorism. Attempting to treat all varieties of terrorism as crime, suggested by the law enforcement metaphor, may encourage international cooperation in the fight against terrorism but may also contribute to a collaboration between terrorist organizations and forego possible alliances with militant organizations whose activities are consistent with one's own strategic interests—an approach suggested by the war metaphor.[18]

As is typically the case with metaphors (Lakoff, 1990), each counterterrorism framing described earlier affords a restricted understanding of the phenomenon. Hence, its unlimited adoption may impose blinders on decision makers' vision, leading to potential pitfalls and producing unintended consequences. From this perspective, a comprehensive approach is called for, based on appreciation of the complex trade-offs that each move in the counterterrorism enterprise may entail. At present, such an integrated counterterrorism policy seems to be lacking in most nations' dealings with terrorism,[19] Ideally, military, law enforcement, and area experts should collaborate and utilize data from social scientists in pertinent disciplines that may contribute to the tactical and strategic decision-making process by highlighting the likely psychological, political, or sociological impact of various counterterrorism initiatives.

Admittedly, setting up of such a collaboration may not be easy. The difficulties of coordination and information sharing between the different intelligence-gathering and law enforcement agencies in the United States received ample commentary and led, in 2005, to establishment of the office of director of National Intelligence, the effectiveness of which has yet to be determined. No less problematic is utilization by government of academic knowledge. Ariel Merari, an Israeli terrorism expert, noted in 1991 that "For a variety of reasons including resistance to external influences in general and suspicion of academia in particular, government officials have failed to utilize even sound knowledge and competent professional advice of academics" (Merari, 1991, p. 88).

Sixteen years later, in 2007, the situation is somewhat different. There seems at least the will (if not exactly the way) on part of government to draw on pertinent academic knowledge in regards to terrorism. The Homeland Security Act of 2002 wrote into law the establishment of the University Programs under the Division of Science and Technology at the U.S. Department of Homeland Security (DHS). This initiative has led to the establishment of several centers of excellence (COEs) at different U.S. universities, addressing different aspects of terrorism—including its social and behavioral aspects, investigated at The Center for the Study of Terrorism and the Response to Terrorism (START). Thus, an important formal step toward establishing a communication channel between academic research in the behavioral and social sciences and a government agency entrusted with national security has been made. The common task of the COEs and the DHS is to develop ways in which each is continually kept abreast of the other's concerns, questions, and pertinent findings. To be sure, the incorporation of long-term considerations may seem at odds with, or tangential to, current security needs as seen by the government.[20] Indeed, the appreciation of their essential relevance to policy may require a climate change and cultivation of new cadres of security experts whose outlook would be formed through an educational process in which social and psychological aspects of terrorism and counterterrorism constitute an inseparable part and parcel. Training such cadres is a major task confronting the security community these days.

---

[18] For instance, Israel started supporting Hamas in the late 1970s, seeing that organization as an ally against the PLO. Similarly, During most of the 1980s, the CIA secretly sent billions of dollars of military aid to Afghanistan to support the Mujahedeen—or "holy warriors"—against the Soviet Union, which had invaded in 1979. And writing in July 10, 2007, in the *New York Sun*, Daniel Pipes recommends "unleashing" against the Iranian regime the Iranian opposition group known as the Mujahedeen-e Khalq or MEK, despite it being accused of constituting a Marxist-Islamist terrorist cult (Pipes, 2007, p.7).

[19] Ganor (2005), for instance, states that "Most Israeli policymakers who were interviewed . . . were in complete agreement that Israel does not have—nor did it ever have a written, structured and unambiguous counterterrorism policy" (p. 288).

[20] In commenting on the Israeli approach to counterterrorism, Ganor (2005) writes that "The most prominent disappointment of Israel's counterterrorism activities has been the failure to understand the phenomenon as morale-psychological warfare . . . [hence] almost no morale psychological considerations are taken into account in choosing the counter-terrorism actions that Israel undertakes' (p. 292).

Notes

1. See, for example, John Lewis Gaddis, "Expanding the Data Base: Historians, Political Scientists, and the Enrichment of Security Studies," *International Security* 12 (Summer 1987): 3–21; John English, "The Second Time Around: Political Scientists Writing History," *Canadian Historical Review* 57 (March 1986): 1–16; Jack S. Levy, "Domestic Politics and War," *Journal of Interdisciplinary History* 18 (Spring 1988): 653–73; Joseph S. Nye, Jr., "International Security Studies," in *American Defense Annual*, 1988–1989, ed. Joseph Kruzel (Lexington, MA, 1988), 231–43; Deborah Larson, *Origins of Containment: A Psychological Explanation* (Princeton, 1985); Timothy Lomperis, *The War Everyone Lost-And Won: America's Intervention in Viet Nam's Twin Struggles* (Washington, 1987); Barry Posen, *The Sources of Military Doctrine: France, Britain, and Germany between the World Wars* (Ithaca, 1984); Paul Gordon Lauren, ed., *Diplomacy: New Approaches to History, Theory, and Policy* (New York, 1979); and Richard R. Neustadt and Ernest R. May, *Thinking in Time: The Use of History for Decision-Makers* (New York, 1986). Many other examples could be cited.
2. Robert Gilpin, *Change and War in World Politics* (Cambridge, England, 1981).
3. Stanley Hoffmann, "An American Social Science: International Relations," *Daedalus* 106 (Summer 1977): 54.
4. The British meteorologist Lewis Fry Richardson is generally regarded as the pioneer of mathematical approaches to international relations. See his *Statistics of Deadly Quarrels* (Pittsburgh, 1960); and his *Arms and Insecurity: A Mathematical Study of the Causes and Origins of War* (Chicago, 1960). These are summarized for nonmathematicians in Anatol Rapport, "L. F. Richardson's Mathematical Theory of War," *Journal of Conflict Resolution* 1 (September 1957): 249–99. For a more recent effort see Bruce Bueno de Mesquita, *The War Trap* (New Haven, 1981); and idem, "The War Trap Revisited: A Revised Expected Utility Model," *American Political Science Review* 79 (March 1985): 156–77.
5. Among the works that best represent their realist perspectives are E. H. Carr, *Twenty fears' Crisis* (London, 1939); Nicholas Spykman, *America's Strategy in World Politics: The United States and Balance of Power* (New York, 1942); Hans J. Morgenthau, *Politics among Nations: The Struggle for Power and Peace*, 5th ed. (New York, 1973); John Herz, *International Politics in the Atomic Age* (New York, 1959); Hedley Bull, *The Anarchical Society: A Study of Order in World Politics* (London, 1977); Raymond Aron, *Peace and War* (Garden City, NY, 1966); Martin Wight, "The Balance of Power and International Order," in *The Bases of International Order: Essays in Honor of C. A. W. Manning*, ed. Alan James (London, 1973); Arnold Wolfers, *Discord and Collaboration* (Baltimore, 1962); Norman A. Graebner, *America as a World Power: A Realist Appraisal from Wilson to Reagan* (Wilmington, DE, 1984); George F. Kennan, *American Diplomacy, 1900–1950* (Chicago, 1951); Walter Lippmann, *U.S. Foreign Policy: Shield of the Republic* (Boston, 1943); and Reinhold Niebuhr, *The Children of Light and the Children of Darkness* (New York, 1945).
6. For useful comparisons of realism and liberalism see Joseph Grieco, "Anarchy and the Limits of Cooperation: A Realist Critique of the Newest Liberal Institutionalism," *International Organization* 42 (Summer 1988): 485–507; and Joseph S. Nye, Jr., "Neorealism and Neoliberalism," *World Politics* 40 (January 1988): 235–51.
7. Morgenthau, *Politics*, 7, 5.
8. Stephen D. Krasner, *Defending the National Interest: Raw Materials Investment and U.S. Foreign Policy* (Princeton, 1978), 33. Krasner's study compares realist, interest-group liberal, and Marxist theories.
9. Inis L. Claude, *Power and International Relations* (New York, 1962); James S. Rosenau, "National Interest," *International Encyclopedia of the Social Sciences*, vol. 11 (New York, 1968), 34–40; Alexander L. George and Robert Keohane, "The Concept of National Interests: Uses and Limitations," in *Presidential Decision-Making in Foreign Policy: The Effective Use of Information and Advice*, ed. Alexander George (Boulder, 1980); Ernst B. Haas, "The Balance of Power: Prescription, Concept, or Propaganda?" *World Politics* 5 (July 1953): 442–77; Dina A. Zinnes, "An Analytical Study of the Balance of Power," *Journal of Peace Research* 4, no. 3 (1967): 270–88.
10. Morgenthau, *Politics*, 5.
11. Richard K. Ashley, "The Poverty of Neorealism," *International Organization* 38 (Spring 1984): 225–86.
12. Morton Kaplan, *System and Process in International Politics* (New York, 1957).
13. Richard Rosecrance, *Action and Reaction in International Politics* (Boston, 1963); idem,

"Bipolarity, Multipolarity, and the Future," *Journal of Conflict Resolution* 10 (September 1966): 314–27; Kenneth Waltz, "The Stability of a Bipolar World," *Daedalus* 93 (Summer 1964): 881–909; J. David Singer, "Inter-Nation Influence: A Formal Model," *American Political Science Review* 57 (June 1963): 420–30; Bruce M. Russett, "Toward a Model of Competitive International Politics," *Journal of Politics* 25 (May 1963): 226–47; Karl W. Deutsch and J. David Singer, "Multipolar Power Systems and International Stability," *World Politics* 16 (April 1964): 390–406; Andrew Scott, *The Functioning of the International Political System* (New York, 1967).

14. Kenneth Waltz, *Theory of International Politics* (Reading, MA, 1979); idem, *Man, the State, and War* (New York, 1959).
15. Because Waltz strives for a universal theory that is not limited to any era, he uses the term "unit" to refer to the constituent members of the system. In the contemporary system these are states, but in order to reflect Waltz's intent more faithfully, the term "unit" is used here.
16. Waltz, *Theory*, 82–101.
17. Waltz, "The Myth of National Interdependence," in *The International Corporation*, ed. Charles P. Kindleberger (Cambridge, MA, 1970); Waltz, "The Spread of Nuclear Weapons: More May Be Better," *Adelphi Papers*, no. 171 (1981).
18. Joseph M. Grieco, *Cooperation Among Nations: Europe, America, and Non-Tariff Barriers to Trade* (Ithaca: Cornell University Press, 1990); Stephen M. Walt, *The Origin of Alliances* (Ithaca, 1987). The best single source for the various dimensions of the debate is Robert Keohane, ed., *Neorealism and Its Critics* (New York, 1986).
19. Ashley, "Poverty," 228.
20. I am grateful to Alexander George for this example.
21. Gilpin, *War and Change*, 10–11.
22. *Ibid.*, Chap. 4. Gilpin's thesis appears similar in a number of respects to Paul Kennedy, *The Rise and Fall of the Great Powers: Economic Change and Military Conflict from 1500 to 2000* (New York, 1987).
23. Robert Keohane and Joseph S. Nye, Jr., *Power and Interdependence: World Politics in Transition* (Boston, 1977); Edward Morse, *Modernization and the Transformation of International Relations* (New York, 1967); James N. Rosenau, *The Study of Global Interdependence* (London, 1980); Richard Mansbach and John Vasquez, *In Search of Theory: A New Paradigm for Global Politics* (New York, 1981); Andrew M. Scott, *The Dynamics of Interdependence* (Chapel Hill, 1982); James N. Rosenau, *Turbulence in World Politics: A Theory of Change and Continuity* (Princeton: Princeton University Press, 1990).
24. Rosenau, "National Interest," 39. A more recent statement of this view may be found in Richard Rosecrance, *The Rise of the Trading State* (New York, 1986). See also John H. Herz, "The Rise and Demise of the Territorial State," *World Politics* 9 (July 1957): 473–93; and his reconsideration in "The Territorial State Revisited: Reflections on the Future of the Nation-State," *Polity* 1 (Fall 1968): 12–34.
25. Joseph Grieco, *Between Dependence and Autonomy: India's Experience with the International Computer Industry* (Berkeley, 1984); Gary Gereffi, *The Pharmaceutical Industry and Dependency in the Third World* (Princeton, 1983).
26. John Galtung, "A Structural Theory of Imperialism," *Journal of Peace Research* 8, no. 2 (1971): 81–117; James Cockroft, André Gunder Frank, and Dale L. Johnson, *Dependence and Under-Development* (New York, 1972); Immanuel Wallerstein, *The Modern World-System* (New York, 1974); idem, "The Rise and Future Demise of the World Capitalist System: Concepts for Comparative Analysis," *Comparative Studies in Society and History* 16 (September 1974): 387–415; Christopher Chase-Dunn, "Comparative Research on World System Characteristics," *International Studies Quarterly* 23 (December 1979): 601–23; idem, "Interstate System and Capitalist World Economy: One Logic or Two?" *ibid*. 25 (March 1981): 19–42; J. Kubalkova and A. A. Cruickshank, *Marxism and International Relations* (Oxford, 1985). Debates among advocates of these models are illustrated in Robert A. Denemark and Kenneth O. Thomas, "The Brenner-Wallerstein Debates," *International Studies Quarterly* 32 (March 1988): 47–66.
27. Wallerstein, "Rise and Future Demise," 390.
28. Tony Smith, "The Underdevelopment of Development Literature: The Case of Dependency Theory," *World Politics* 31 (January 1979): 247–88; Aristide R. Zolberg, "Origins of the Modern World System," *ibid*. 33 (January 1981): 253–81.
29. Wallerstein, "Rise and Future Demise," 401.
30. *Ibid.*, 412 (emphasis added).
31. Richard C. Snyder, H. W. Bruck, and Burton Sapin, eds., *Foreign Policy Decision-Making* (New York, 1962).

32. There are also models that link types of polities with foreign policy. Two of the more prominent twentieth-century versions – the Leninist and Wilsonian – have been effectively criticized by Waltz in *Man, the State, and War*. Although space limitations preclude a discussion here, for some recent and interesting research along these lines see, among others, Rudolph J. Rummel, "Libertarianism and International Violence," *Journal of Conflict Resolution* 27 (March 1983): 27–71; Michael Doyle, "Liberalism and World Politics," *American Political Science Review* 80 (December 1986): 1151–70; and Doyle, "Kant, Liberal Legacies, and Foreign Affairs," *Philosophy and Public Affairs* 12 (Winter 1983): 205–35.

33. Chester Barnard, *Functions of the Executive* (Cambridge, MA, 1938); Herbert Simon, *Administrative Behavior: A Study of Decision-Making Processes in Administrative Organization* (New York, 1957); James G. March and Herbert Simon, *Organizations* (New York, 1958).

34. Harold Wilensky, *Organizational Intelligence: Knowledge and Policy in Government and Industry* (New York, 1967).

35. Henry A. Kissinger, "Domestic Structure and Foreign Policy," *Daedalus* 95 (Spring 1966): 503–29; Graham T. Allison, *Essence of Decision: Explaining the Cuban Missile Crisis* (Boston, 1971); Graham T. Allison and Morton Halperin, "Bureaucratic Politics: A Paradigm and Some Policy Implications," *World Politics* 24 (Supplement 1972): 40–79; Morton Halperin, *Bureaucratic Politics and Foreign Policy* (Washington, 1974).

36. The literature is huge. See, for example, Samuel R. Williamson, Jr., *The Politics of Grand Strategy: Britain and France Prepare for War, 1904–1914* (Cambridge, MA, 1969); Paul Gordon Lauren, *Diplomats and Bureaucrats: The First Institutional Responses to Twentieth-Century Diplomacy in France and Germany* (Stanford, 1975); and Posen, *Sources of Military Doctrine*.

37. Wilensky, *Organizational Intelligence*; Theodore J. Lowi, *The End of Liberalism: Ideology, Policy, and the Crisis of Public Authority* (New York, 1969); Sidney Verba, "Assumptions of Rationality and Non-Rationality in Models of the International System," *World Politics* 14 (October 1961): 93–117.

38. Charles F. Hermann, "Some Consequences of Crises which Limit the Viability of Organizations," *Administrative Science Quarterly* 8 (June 1963): 61–82; Allison, *Essence*; Richard Neustadt, *Alliance Politics* (New York, 1970); Scott Sagan, "Nuclear Alerts and Crisis Management," *International Security* 9 (Spring 1985): 99–139.

39. Robert Rothstein, *Planning, Prediction, and Policy-Making in Foreign Affairs: Theory and Practice* (Boston, 1972); Stephen D. Krasner, "Are Bureaucracies Important? (Or Allison Wonderland)" *Foreign Policy* 7 (Summer 1972): 159–70; Robert J. Art, "Bureaucratic Politics and American Foreign Policy: A Critique," *Policy Sciences* 4 (December 1973): 467–90; Desmond J. Ball, "The Blind Men and the Elephant: A Critique of Bureaucratic Politics Theory," *Australian Outlook* 28 (April 1974): 71–92; Amos Perlmutter, "Presidential Political Center and Foreign Policy: A Critique of the Revisionist and Bureaucratic-Political Orientations," *World Politics* 27 (October 1974): 87–106.

40. Alexander L. George, "The Case for Multiple Advocacy in Making Foreign Policy," *American Political Science Review* 66 (September 1972): 751–85, 791–95.

41. David A. Welch and James G. Blight, "The Eleventh Hour of the Cuban Missile Crisis: An Introduction to the ExComm Transcripts," *International Security* 12 (Winter 1987/88): 5–29; McGeorge Bundy and James G. Blight, "October 27, 1962: Transcripts of the Meetings of the ExComm," *ibid.*, 30–92.

42. Joseph de Rivera, *The Psychological Dimension of Foreign Policy* (Columbus, OH, 1968); Glenn D. Paige, *The Korean Decision, June 24–30, 1950* (New York, 1968); Irving L. Janis, *Victims of Groupthink: A Psychological Study of Foreign Policy Decisions and Fiascos* (Boston, 1972); idem, *Groupthink: Psychological Studies of Policy Decisions and Fiascos* (Boston, 1982); Margaret G. Hermann, Charles F. Hermann, and Joe D. Hagan, "How Decision Units Shape Foreign Policy Behavior," in *New Directions in the Study of Foreign Policy*, ed. Charles F. Hermann, Charles W. Kegley, and James N. Rosenau (London, 1987); Charles F. Hermann and Margaret Hermann, "Who Makes Foreign Policy Decisions and How: An Initial Test of a Model" (Paper presented at the annual meeting of the American Political Science Association, Chicago, 1987); Philip D. Stewart, Margaret G. Hermann, and Charles F. Hermann, "The Politburo and Foreign Policy: Toward a Model of Soviet Decision Making" (Paper presented at the annual meeting of the International Society of Political Psychology, Amsterdam, 1986).

43. Leon Festinger, "A Theory of Social Comparison Processes," and Solomon Asch, "Opinions and Social Pressure," in *Small Groups: Studies in*

Social Interaction, ed. A. Paul Hare, Edgar F. Borgatta, and Robert F. Bales (New York, 1965); Asch, "Effects of Group Pressures upon Modification and Distortion of Judgment," in *Group Dynamics: Research and Theory*, ed. Dorwin Cartwright and A. Zander (Evanston, IL, 1953).

44. Janis, *Victims;* idem, *Groupthink*. See also Philip Tetlock, "Identifying Victims of Groupthink from Public Statements of Decision Makers," *Journal of Personality and Social Psychology* 37 (August 1979): 1314–24; and the critique in Lloyd Etheredge, *Can Governments Learn? American Foreign Policy and Central American Revolutions* (New York, 1985), 112–14.

45. Janis, *Groupthink*, 260–76.

46. For a review of the vast literature see Robert Abelson and A. Levi, "Decision Making and Decision Theory," in *Handbook of Social Psychology*, 3d ed., vol. 1, ed. Gardner Lindzey and Elliot Aronson (New York, 1985). The relevance of psychological models and evidence for international relations is most fully discussed in Robert Jervis, *Perception and Misperception in International Politics* (Princeton, 1976); John Steinbruner, *The Cybernetic Theory of Decision: New Dimensions of Political Analysis* (Princeton, 1974); and Robert Axelrod, ed., *The Structure of Decision: The Cognitive Maps of Political Elites* (Princeton, 1976).

47. See, for example, Harold Lasswell, *Psychopathology and Politics* (Chicago, 1931).

48. March and Simon, *Organizations*, 113.

49. Simon, *Administrative Behavior*, 198.

50. Amos Tversky and Daniel Kahneman, "The Framing of Decisions and the Psychology of Choice," *Science* 211 (30 January 1981): 453–58; Kahneman and Tversky, "On the Psychology of Prediction," *Psychological Review* 80 (July 1973): 237–51; Kahneman, Paul Slovic, and Tversky, *Judgment under Uncertainty: Heuristics and Biases* (Cambridge, England, 1982).

51. Irving L. Janis and Leon Mann, *Decision Making: A Psychological Analysis of Conflict, Choice, and Commitment* (New York, 1977); Miriam Steiner, "The Search for Order in a Disorderly World: Worldviews and Prescriptive Decision Paradigms," *International Organization* 37 (Summer 1983): 373–414; Richard Ned Lebow, *Between Peace and War* (Baltimore, 1981).

52. Donald Kinder and J. R. Weiss, "In Lieu of Rationality: Psychological Perspectives on Foreign Policy," *Journal of Conflict Resolution* 22 (December 1978): 707–35; Ole R. Holsti, "Foreign Policy Formation Viewed Cognitively," in Axelrod, *Structure of Decision*.

53. George F. Kennan, *The Cloud of Danger: Current Realities of American Foreign Policy* (Boston, 1978), 87–88.

54. Allison, *Essence;* Jervis, *Perception;* Seymour M. Hersh, *The Target Is Destroyed: What Really Happened to Flight 007 and What America Knew about It* (New York, 1986).

55. Charles F. Hermann, International Crises: Insights from Behavioral Research (New York, 1972); Margaret G. Hermann and Charles F. Hermann, "Maintaining the Quality of Decision-Making in Foreign Policy Crises," in Report of the Commission on the Organization of the Government for the Conduct of Foreign Policy, vol. 2 (Washington, 1975); Margaret G. Hermann, "Indicators of Stress in Policy-Makers during Foreign Policy Crises," *Political Psychology* 1 (March 1979): 27–46; Ole R. Holsti, Crisis, *Escalation, War* (Montreal, 1972); Ole R. Holsti and Alexander L. George, "The Effects of Stress on the Performance of Foreign Policy-Makers," *Political Science Annual*, vol. 6 (Indianapolis, 1975); Lebow, *Between Peace and War*.

56. Janis and Mann, *Decision Making*, 3.

57. Margaret G. Hermann, "Explaining Foreign Policy Behavior Using Personal Characteristics of Political Leaders," *International Studies Quarterly* 24 (March 1980): 7–46; idem, "Personality and Foreign Policy Decision Making," in *Perceptions, Beliefs, and Foreign Policy Decision Making*, ed. Donald Sylvan and Steve Chan (New York, 1984).

58. Nathan Leites, *The Operational Code of the Politburo* (New York, 1951); Alexander L. George, "'The 'Operational Code': A Neglected Approach to the Study of Political Leaders and Decision-Making," *International Studies Quarterly* 13 (June 1969): 190–222; Stephen G. Walker, "The Interface between Beliefs and Behavior: Henry Kissinger's Operational Code and the Vietnam War," *Journal of Conflict Resolution* 21 (March 1977): 129–68; idem, "The Motivational Foundations of Political Belief Systems: A Re-Analysis of the Operational Code Construct," *International Studies Quarterly* 27 (June 1983): 179–202; idem, "Parts and Wholes: American Foreign Policy Makers as 'Structured' Individuals" (Paper presented at the annual meeting of the International Society of Political Psychology, Secaucus, New Jersey, 1988).

59. Integrative simplicity, on the other hand, is characterized by simple responses, gross distinctions, rigidity, and restricted information usage.

60. Peter Suedfeld and Philip Tetlock, "Integrative Complexity of Communications in International Crises," *Journal of Conflict Resolution* 21 (March 1977): 169–86; Suedfeld, Tetlock, and C. Romirez, "War, Peace, and Integrative Complexity: UN Speeches on the Middle East Problem, 1947–1976," ibid. (September 1977): 427–42; Theodore D. Raphael, "Integrative Complexity Theory and Forecasting International Crises: Berlin 1946–1962," ibid. 26 (September 1982): 423–50; Tetlock, "Integrative Complexity of American and Soviet Foreign Policy Rhetoric: A Time Series Analysis," *Journal of Personality and Social Psychology* 49 (December 1985): 1565–85.

61. Alexander L. George and Richard Smoke, *Deterrence in American Foreign Policy: Theory and Practice* (New York, 1974); Smoke, *Escalation* (Cambridge, MA, 1977); Glenn H. Snyder and Paul Diesing, *Conflict among Nations: Bargaining, Decision Making, and System Structure in International Crises* (Princeton, 1977); Michael Brecher and Barbara Geist, *Decisions in Crisis: Israel, 1967 and 1973* (Berkeley, 1980); Lebow, *Between Peace and War*. Useful discussions on conducting theoretically relevant case studies may be found in Harry Eckstein, "Case Study and Theory in Political Science," in *Handbook of Political Science*, ed. Fred I. Greenstein and Nelson W. Polsby (Reading, MA, 1975), 7: 79–138; and Alexander L. George, "Case Studies and Theory Development; The Method of Structured, Focused Comparison," in *Diplomacy: New Approaches in History, Theory, and Policy*, ed. Paul Gordon Lauren (New York, 1979), 43–68.

62. The classic overview of the field and the disciplines that have contributed to it is Quincy Wright, *The Study of International Relations* (New York, 1955).

63. Ole R. Holsti, "The Study of International Politics Makes Strange Bedfellows: Theories of the Radical Right and the Radical Left," *American Political Science Review* 68 (March 1974): 217–42.

64. In addition to the literature on war, crises, and deterrence already cited see Richard Betts, *Nuclear Blackmail and Nuclear Balance* (Washington, 1987); Robert Jervis, Richard Ned Lebow, and Janice G. Stein, *Psychology and Deterrence* (Baltimore, 1985); Lebow, *Nuclear Crisis Management: A Dangerous Illusion* (Ithaca, 1987); and Ole R. Holsti, "Crisis Decision-Making," and Jack S. Levy, "The Causes of War: A Review of Theories and Evidence," in *Behavior, Society, and Nuclear War*, vol. 1, ed. Philip E. Tetlock et al. (New York, 1989).

65. John Lewis Gaddis, "The Long Peace: Elements of Stability in the Postwar International System," *International Security* 10 (Spring 1986): 99–142.

66. Paul Bracken, *Command and Control of Nuclear Forces* (New Haven, 1983); Bruce Blair, *Strategic Command and Control: Redefining the Nuclear Threat* (Washington, 1985); John D. Steinbruner, "Nuclear Decapitation," *Foreign Policy* 45 (Winter 1981–82): 16–28; Sagan, "Nuclear Alerts"; Alexander L. George, *Presidential Decision-Making in Foreign Policy: The Effective Use of Information and Advice* (Boulder, 1980).

67. Waltz, *Man, the State, and War*, 238.

68. Harold and Margaret Sprout, "Environmental Factors in the Study of International Politics," *Journal of Conflict Resolution* 1 (December 1957): 309–28.

69. See, for example, David B. Yoffie, *Power and Protectionism: Strategies of the Newly Industrializing Countries* (New York, 1983); John Odell, *U. S. International Monetary Policy: Markets, Power, and Ideas as Sources of Change* (Princeton, 1982); Jack Snyder, *The Ideology of the Offensive: Military Decision Making and the Disaster of 1914* (Ithaca, 1984); Vinod K. Aggarwal, *Liberal Protectionism: The International Politics of Organized Textile Trade* (Berkeley, 1985); Larson, Origins of Containment; Posen, Sources of Military Doctrine; and Walt, *Alliances*.

Notes

1. *Transatlantic Trends 2006*. German Marshall Fund of the United States (2006), 16.
2. Lindberg tends to the view that failed states pose a problem mainly for those directly affected, who have their hands full trying to survive the local crisis. Chollet is more concerned about spillover effects and broader destabilization.
3. *Transatlantic Trends* 2006, German Marshall Fund of the United States.
4. Francis Fukuyama and Michael McFaul, "Should Democracy Be Promoted or Demoted?" in Derek Chollet, Tod Lindberg, and David Shorr, eds., *Bridging the Foreign Policy Divide* (Routledge 2007), Chap. 9.
5. Ivo Daalder and Robert Kagan, "America and the Use of Force: Sources of Legitimacy," in Chollet et al., *Bridging trie Foreign Policy Divide*, Chap. 1.
6. See Bush press conference with German Chancellor Angela Merkel (January 4, 2007).

REFERENCES

Akerlof, G., & Yellen, J.L. (1994). Gang behavior, law enforcement, and community values. In T.E. Mann, H.J. Aaron, & T. Taylor (Eds.), *Values and public policy* (pp. 173–209). Washington, DC: Brookings Institution Press.

Alexander, Y. (2002). *Palestinian religious terrorism: Hamas and Islamic Jihad*. Ardsley, NY: Translational Publishers.

Allport, G.W. (1979). *The nature of prejudice*. Cambridge, MA: Addison-Wesley Publishing Company. (Original work published 1954)

Aronson, E., & Bridgeman, D. (1979). Jigsaw groups and the desegregated classroom: In pursuit of common goals. *Personality and Social Psychology Bulletin, 5*, 438–446.

Asch, S.E. (1946). Forming impressions on personality. *Journal of Abnormal and Social Psychology, 41*, 258–290.

Atran, S. (2003). The genesis of suicide terrorism. *Science, 299*, 1534–1540.

Atran, S. (2004). Mishandling suicide terrorism. *Washington Quarterly, 27*, 67–90.

Azzam Publications. (2001). Farewell message from Azzam Publications. Retrieved May 30, 2008, from http://dc.indymedia.org/ newswire/display/15909/index.php

Bai, M. (2004, October 10). Kerry's undeclared war. *New York Times Magazine, 38–45*, 52, 68, 70.

Bandura, A. (1998). Mechanisms of moral disengagement. In W. Reich (Ed.), *Origins of terrorism: Psychologies, ideologies, theologies, stales of mind* (pp. 161–191). Washington, DC: Woodrow Wilson Center Press.

BBC News. (2001, December 28). *Who is Richard Reid?* Retrieved September 1, 2006, from http://news.bbe.co.uk/1/hi/uk/1731568.stm

BBC News. (2005, July 11). *Van Gogh suspect refuses defence*. Retrieved September 1, 2006, from http://news.bbc.co.uk/1/hi/world/ europe/4670535.stm

Benmelech, E., & Berrebi, C. (2007, February). *Attack assignments in terror organizations and the productivity of suicide bombers* (Working Paper No. 12910). Cambridge, MA: National Bureau of Economic Research.

Bergen, P., & Pandey, S. (2005, June 14). The madrassa myth. *The New York Times*, p. A23.

Biddle, S. (2006). Seeing Baghdad, thinking Saigon. *Foreign Affairs, 85*, 2–14.

bin Kader, A.H. (2007). *Fighting terrorism: The Singapore perspective*. Singapore: Taman Bacaan.

bin Laden, O. (1998a, February 23). Fatwa urging Jihad against Americans. Retrieved May 30, 2008, from http://www.mideastweb.org/osamabinladen2.htm

bin Laden, 0. (1998b, May 26). Videotaped news conference. Retrieved May 20, 2008, from http://www.cnn.com/2002/US/08/19/terror. tape.main/index.html

bin Laden, O. (2005). Letter to the Americans, October 6, 2002. In B. Lawrence (Ed.), *Messages to the world: The statements of Osama Bin Laden* (pp. 160–172). London: Verso.

Bird, K., & Sherwin, M.J. (2005, April 25). Bin Laden's nuclear connection. *The Nation*, pp. 3–4.

Bloom, M. (2005). *Dying to kill: The allure of suicide terror*. New York: Columbia University Press.

Boucek, C. (2007). Extremist reeducation and rehabilitation in Saudi Arabia. *Terrorism Monitor, 5(16)*. Retrieved October 26, 2007, from http://www.jameslown.org/terrorism/news/article.php?issue_id=4213

Brewer, M.B., Manzi, J., & Shaw, J. (1993). Ingroup identification as a function of depersonalization, distinctiveness, and status. *Psychological Science, 4*, 88–92.

Brooks, D. (2006a, September 21). Lessons from UN week [Op-Ed]. *The New York Times*, p.31.

Brooks, D. (2006b, July 23). Onward cautious soldiers [Op-Ed]. *New York Times*, pp. 4, 13.

B'Tselem. (n.d.). *Harm to Palestinians suspected of collaboration with Israel*. Retrieved September 1, 2006, from http://www.btselem.org/English/Collaboration/Index.asp

Bush, G.W. (2001a, March 20). Remarks to Central Intelligence Agency employees in Langley, Virginia. In J.T. Woolley & G. Peters (Eds.), *The American Presidency Project [online]*. Santa Barbara, CA: University of California (hosted), Gerhard Peters (database). Retrieved June 3, 2008, from http://www.presidency.ucsb.edu/ws/index.php?pid=45788

Bush, G.W. (2001b, September 16). Remarks on the arrival at the White House and an exchange with reporters. In J.T. Woolley & G. Peters (Eds.), *The American Presidency Project [online]*. Santa Barbara, CA: University of California (hosted), Gerhard Peters (database). Retrieved June 3, 2008 from http://www.presidency.ucsb.edu/ws/index.php?pid=64346

Bush, G.W. (2001c, September 20). Speech presented to the joint session of Congress, House of Representatives, Washington, DC. In J.T. Woolley & G. Peters (Eds.), *The American Presidency Project* [online]. Santa Barbara, CA: University of California (hosted), Gerhard Peters (database). Retrieved June 3, 2008 from http://www.presidency, ucsb.edu/ws/index.php?pid=64731

Bush, G.W. (2002, January 29). Address presented to the joint session of Congress, House of Representatives, Washington, DC. In J.T. Woolley & G. Peters (Eds.), *The American Presidency Project [online]*. Santa Barbara, CA: University of California (hosted), Gerhard Peters (database). Retrieved June 3, 2008 from http://www.presidency.ucsb.edu/ws/index.php?pid=29644

Bush, G.W. (2005a, October 6). Remarks to the National Endowment for Democracy. In J.T. Woolley & G. Peters (Eds.), *The American Presidency Project [online]*. Santa Barbara, CA: University of California (hosted), Gerhard Peters (database). Retrieved June 3, 2008, from http://www.presidency.ucsb.edu/ws/index.php?pid=73821

Bush, G.W. (2005b, December 6). Remarks following a meeting with Director-General Lee Jong-Wook of the World Health Organization and an exchange with reporters. In J.T. Woolley & G. Peters (Eds.), *The American Presidency Project [online]*. Santa Barbara, CA: University of California (hosted), Gerhard Peters (database). Retrieved June 3, 2008 from http://www.presidency.ucsb.edu/ws/index.php?pid=65242

Bush, G.W. (2005c, December 7). Speech presented to the Council on Foreign Relations, Omni Shoreham Hotel, Washington, DC. In J.T. Woolley & G. Peters (Eds.), *The American Presidency Project [online]*. Santa Barbara, CA: University of California (hosted), Gerhard Peters (database). Retrieved June 3. 2008, from http://www.presidency.ucsb.edu/ws/index.php?pid=65072

Bush, G.W. (2006, May 25). The President's news conference with Prime Minister Tony Blair of the United Kingdom. In J.T. Woolley & G. Peters (Eds.), *The American Presidency Project [online]*. Santa Barbara, CA: University of California (hosted), Gerhard Peters (database). Retrieved June 3, 2008 from: http://www.presidency. ucsb.edu/ws/index.php?pid=46

Butler, A.S., Panzer, A.M., & Goldfrank, L.R. (2003). *Preparing for the psychological consequences of terrorism: A public health strategy*. Washington, DC: National Academy of Sciences.

Canetti, E. (1984). *Crowds and power* (C. Stewart, Trans.). New York: Farrar, Straus and Giroux.

Carter, J. (1979a, November 28). The President's news conference of November 29, 1979. In J.T. Woolley & G. Peters (Eds.), *The American Presidency Project [online]*. Santa Barbara, CA: University of California (hosted), Gerhard Peters (database). Retrieved June 3, 2008, from http://www.presidency.ucsb.edu/ws/index.php?pid=31752

Carter, J. (1979b, December 21). International economic sanctions against Iran remarks announcing intention to seek United Nations action. In J.T. Woolley & G. Peters (Eds.), *The American Presidency Project [online]*. Santa Barbara, CA: University of California (hosted), Gerhard Peters (database). Retrieved June 3, 2008, from http://www.presidency.ucsb.edu/ws/index.php?pid=31865

Carter, J. (1980, July 19). Carter/Mondale Presidential campaign remarks at a White House reception for delegates to the Democratic National Convention. In J.T. Woolley & G. Peters (Eds.), *The American Presidency project [online]*. Santa Barbara, CA: University of California (hosted), Gerhard Peters (database). Retrieved June 3, 2008, from http://www.presidency.ucsb.edu/ws/index.php?pid=44779

Center for American Progress & *Foreign Policy* (2006). The terrorism index. *Foreign Policy, 155*, 48–55.

Center for Multiethnic Research, Uppsala University. (2003). *The European dilemma: Institutional patterns of 'racial' discrimination*. Retrieved August 29, 2007, from http://www.multietn.uu.se/research/eu_dilemma/project_owerview.pdf

Charters, D.A. (2007). Something old, something new . . . ? Al Qaeda, jihadism and fascism. *Terrorism and Political Violence, 19*,65–93. Chehab, Z. (2007, May 28). Gaza: The jailed state. *New Statesman, 136*(4846), 24–25.

Chen, X., Fishman, S., & Kruglanski, A.W. (2007). Unpublished data, University of Maryland, College Park.

Clark, W.K., & Raustalia, K. (2007, August 8). Why terrorists aren't soldiers [Op-Ed]. *The New York Times*, p. A19.

Clinton, W.J. (1996a, March 11). Remarks on receiving the Irish-American of the Year Award in New York City. In J.T. Woolley & G. Peters (Eds.), *The American Presidency Project [online]*. Santa Barbara, CA: University of California (hosted), Gerhard Peters (database). Retrieved June 3, 2008, from http://www.presidency.ucsb.edu/ws/index.php?pid=52527

Clinton, W.J. (1996b, January 26). Statement on Senate ratification of the START II nuclear arms reduction treaty with Russia. In J.T. Woolley & G. Peters (Eds.), *The American Presidency Project [online]*. Santa Barbara, CA: University of California (hosted), Gerhard Peters (database). Retrieved June 3, 2008, from http://www.presidency.ucsh.edu/ws/?pid=53236

Clinton, W.J. (2000, September 22). Remarks on the dedication of the Harry S. Truman Building. In J.T. Woolley & G. Peters (Eds.), *The American Presidency Project [online]*. Santa Barbara, CA: University of California (hosted), Gerhard Peters (database). Retrieved June 3, 2008, from http://www.presidency.ucsb.edu/ws/index.php?pid=1324

Clinton, W.J. (2001, Janaury 18). Farewell address to the Nation. In J.T. Woolley & G. Peters (Eds.), *The American Presidency Project [online]*. Santa Barbara, CA: University of California (hosted), Gerhard Peters (database). Retrieved June 3, 2008, from http:// www.presidency.ucsh.edu/ws/?pid=63777

Coolsaet, R. (2005). *Between al-Andalus and a failing integration: Europe's pursuit of a long-term counterterrorism strategy in the post-al Qaeda era*. Egmont Paper 5. Brussels: Royal Institute for International Relations (IRRI-KIB).

Cordes, B. (2001). When terrorists do the talking: Reflections on terrorist literature. In D.C. Rapoport (Ed.), *Inside terrorist organizations* (pp. 130–171). London: Frank Cass.

Cordesman, A.H. (2006). *Preliminary lessons of the Israeli-Hezbollah war*. Washington, DC: Center for Strategic and International Studies.

Cox, D.R. (1972). Regression models and life tables (with discussion). *Journal of the Royal Statistical Society, Series B, 34*, 187–220.

Crenshaw, M. (1998). The logic of terrorism: Terrorist behavior as a product of strategic choice. In W. Reich (Ed.), *Origins of terrorism: Psychologies, ideologies, theologies, states of mind* (pp. 7–24). Baltimore, MD: Johns Hopkins University Press. (Original work published 1990).

Deutsch, M. (1973). *The resolution of conflict*. New Haven, CT: Yale University Press.

Dovidio, J.F., Brigham, J.C., Johnson, B.T., & Gaertner, S.L. (1996). Stereotyping, prejudice, and discrimination: Another look. In C.N. Macrae, C. Stangor, & M. Hewstone (Eds.), *Stereotypes and stereotyping* (pp. 276–319). New York: Guilford Press.

Dovidio, J.F., & Gaertner, S.L. (Eds). (1986). *Prejudice, discrimination, and racism*. New York: Academic Press.

Dugan, L., LaFree, G., & Piquero, A.R. (2005). Testing a rational choice model of airline hijacking. *Criminology, 43*, 1031–1065.

Durkheim, E. (1947). *The division of labor in society*. (G. Simpson,Trans.). New York: The Free Press.

El Deeb, S. (2007, May 22). Israel hints it may target Hamas political leaders. *Deseret News* (Salt Lake City). Retrieved May 30, 2008, from http:// findarticles.com/p/articles/mi_qn4188/is_20070522/ai_n19166785/pg_1

Elliot, M. (2006, August 21). Such lovely lads. *Time*, 28–29.

Eppright, C.T. (1997). "Counter terrorism" and conventional military force: The relationship between political effect and utility. *Studies in Conflict and Terrorism, 20*, 333–344.

Erickson, K.T. (1966). *Wayward puritans: A study in the sociology of deviance*. Boston: Allyn and Bacon.

Etienne, B. (2002, October). *Establishing links between religious communities*. Paper presented to the Council of Europe Steering Committee for Culture, Intercultural Dialogue and Conflict Prevention Project, Strasbourg, France. Retrieved July 21, 2008, from http://www.coe.int/t/dg4/cultureheritage/Source/Completed/Dialogue/DGIV_CULT_PREV_ICIR(2002)3_Etienne_E.pdf

European Commission. (1997). *Central and Eastern Eurobarometer (CEEB) survey series*. Retrieved August 29, 2007, from http://ec.europa.eu/public_opinion/archives/ceeb_en.htm

European Monitoring Center on Racism and Xenophobia. (2005). *Attitudes toward migrants and minorities in Europe* (Media Release No. 194–03-05-01-EN). Vienna: Author.

Eurostat. (2006). *EU integration seen through statistics: Key facts of 18 policy areas*. Luxembourg: Office for Official Publications of the European Communities. Retrieved August 22, 2006, from http://epp.eurostat.ec.europa.eu/cache/ITY_OFFPUB/KS-71-05-691/EN/KS-71-05-691-EN.pdf

Excerpts from Statements in Court. (1998, January 9). *The New York Times*, p. 2.

Fallows, J. (2006, September). Declaring victory. *The Atlantic Monthly*, 60–73.

Ferracuti, F. (1998). Ideology and repentance: Terrorism in Italy. In W. Reich (Ed.). *Origins of terrorism: Psychologies, ideologies, theologies, slates of mind* (pp. 59–64). Washington, DC: Woodrow Wilson Center Press.

Festinger, L. (1950). Informal social communication. *Psychological Review, 57*, 271–282.

Fishman, S., Orehek, E., Dechesne, M., Chen, X., & Kruglanski, A.W. (2007). *The role of individualistic and collectivistic goals in support for terrorist attacks*. Manuscript submitted for publication.

Fiske, S.T. (1998). Stereotyping, prejudice, and discrimination. In D.T. Gilbert, S.T. Fiske, & G. Lindzey (Eds.), *The handbook of social psychology* (4th edition, Vol. 2, pp. 357–4111). New York: McGraw-Hill.

Fukuyama, F. (2006). *America at the crossroads: Democracy, Power, and the Neoconservative Legacy*. New Haven, CT: Yale University Press.

Gaertner, S.L., & Dovidio, J.F. (2000). *Reducing intergroup bias: The common ingroup identity model*. Philadelphia, PA: Psychology Press.

Ganor, B. (2005). *The counter-terrorism puzzle: A guide for decision makers*. Herzlia, Israel: The Interdisciplinary Center for Herzliya Projects.

Gelfand, M.J., & McCusker, C. (2002). Metaphor and the cultural construction of negotiation: A paradigm for theory and research. In M. Gannon & K.L. Newman (Eds.), *Handbook of cross-cultural management* (pp. 292–314). New York, NY: Blackwell.

Gentner, D., & Jeziorski, M. (1995). The shift from metaphor to analogy in western science. In A. Ortony (Ed.), *Metaphor and thought* (2nd ed., pp. 447–480). Cambridge, United Kingdom: Cambridge University Press.

Geraghty, T. (2000). *The Irish war*. Baltimore, MD: The Johns Hopkins University Press.

Gershkoff, A., & Kushner, S. (2005). The 9/11-Iraq connection in the Bush administration's rhetoric. *Perspectives on Politics, 3*, 525–537.

Ghate, 0. (2003, March 7). Innocents in war. *Capitalism Magazine*. Retrieved October 29, 2006, from http://www.capmag.com/article.asp?id=2547

Graham, P., Keenan, T., & Dowd, A.M. (2004). A call to arms at the end of history: A discourse-historical analysis of George W. Bush's declaration of war on terror. *Discourse & Society, 15*, 199–221.

Greener-Barcham, B.K. (2002). Before September: A history of counterterrorism in New Zealand. *Australian Journal of Political Science, 37*, 509–524.

Gunaratna, R (2007). Ideology in. terrorism and counter terrorism: Lessons from combating al Qaeda and al Jemaah Islamiyah in Southeast Asia. In A. Aldis & G.P. Herd (Eds.), *The ideological war on terror: Worldwide strategies for counter-terrorism* (pp. 33–75). New York: Routledge.

Gurr, T.R. (1998). Terrorism in democracies: Its social and political bases. In W. Reich (Ed), *Origins of terrorism: Psychologies, ideologies, theologies, slates of mind* (pp. 103–130). Baltimore, MD: Johns Hopkins University Press. (Original work published 1990).

Hafez, M.M. (2007). Martyrdom mythology in Iraq: How Jihadists frame suicide terrorism in videos and biographies. *Terrorism and Political Violence, 19*, 95–115.

Hardin, C.D., & Higgins, E.T. (1996). Shared reality: How social verification makes the subjective objective. In R.M. Sorrentino & E.T. Higgins (Eds.), *Handbook of motivation and cognition* (pp. 28–84). New York: Guilford Press.

Harrison, M., Law, I., & Phillips, D. (2005). Migrants, minorities and housing: Exclusion, discrimination and anti-discrimination in 15 member states of the European Union. European Monitoring Centre on Racism and Xenophobia. Retrieved July 21, 2006, from http://www.eumc.europa.eu/eumc/index.php

Heider, F. (1958). *The psychology of interpersonal relations*. New York: Wiley.

Hewstone, M. (1996). Contact and categorization: Social psychological interventions to change intergroup relations. In C.N. Macrae, C. Stangor, & M. Hewstone (Eds.), *Stereotypes and stereotyping* (pp. 323–368). New York: Guilford Press.

Hewstone, M., & Brown, R. (1986). Contact is not enough: An intergroup perspective on the "contact hypothesis.". In M. Hewstone & R. Brown. *Contact and conflict in intergroup encounters* (pp. 1–44). Oxford, England: Basil Blackwell.

Hoffman, B. (1998). *Inside terrorism*. New York: Columbia University Press.

Holmes, S. (2006). Neo-con futurology [Review of *After the neocons: America al the crossroads* by Francis Fukuyama]. London Review of Books. Retrieved October 29, 2007, from http://www.lrb.co.uk/v28/nl9/holm01_html

Horgan, J. (2005). *The psychology of terrorism*. London: Routledge.

Hsee (1993). Elastic justification: Affective influences on monetary decision-making. *Dissertation Abstracts International, 54*, 3388.

Hulse, C., & Connelly, M. (2006, August 23). Poll shows a shift in opinion on war in Iraq. *The New York Times*. A16.

Hunter, S.T. (Ed.). (2002). *Islam, Europe's second religion: The new social, cultural, and political landscape*. Westport, CT: Praeger.

Huntington, S.P. (1998). *The clash of civilizations and the remaking of world order*. New York: Simon & Schuster.

Intelligence & Terrorism Information Center, Israel Intelligence Heritage & Commemoration Center. (2006, September 11).

Hezbollah's Shi'ile youth movement, "The Imam al-Mahdi Scouts" . . . Retrieved July 18, 2008, from http://www.terrorisminfo.org.il/malam_multimedia/English/eng_n/html/hezbollah scouts_e.htm

Intelligence & Terrorism Information Center, Israel Intelligence Heritage & Commemoration Center. (2007, June 6). *Inculcating kindergarten children with radical Islamic ideology and the culture of anti-Israel terrorism*. Retrieved May 27, 2007, from www.terrorism-info.org.il/malam_multimedia/English/eng_n/pdf/kindergarten_gaza060607.pdf

International Helsinki Federation for Human Rights (2005). *Intolerance and discrimination against Muslims in the EU: Developments since September 11*. Vienna: International Helsinki Federation for Human Rights and IHF Foundation.

Israeli West Bank barrier, (n.d.). Retrieved July 18, 2008, from Wikipedia: http://en.wikipedia.org/wiki/Israeli_West_Bank_barrier

Jamieson, A. (1989). *The heart attacked: Terrorism and conflict in the Italian stale*. London: Marian Boyars.

Jordan, J., & Boix, L. (2004). Al-Qaeda and western Islam. *Terrorism and Political Violence, 16*, 1–17.

Kaplan, E.H., Mintz, A., Mishal, S., & Samban, C. (2005). What happened to suicide bombings in Israel? Insights from a terror stock model. *Studies in Conflict & Terrorism, 28*, 225–235.

Karmon, E. (2002). The role of intelligence in counter-terrorism. *The Korean Journal of Defense Analysis, 19*, 119–139.

Katz, R. (2007). The online jihadist threat: Testimony before the subcommittee on Terrorism, Unconventional Threats, and Capabilities, of the House Armed Services Committee, 110th Cong. (2007). Retrieved October 26, 2007, from http://armedservices.house. gov/pdfs/TUTC021407/Katz_Testimony021407.pdf

Kelley, H. (1971). Moral evaluation. *American Psychologist, 26*, 293–300.

Khong, Y. (1992). *Analogies at war: Korea, Munich, Dien Bien Phu, and the Vietnam decisions of 1965*. Princeton, NJ: Princeton University Press.

Kosic, A., Kruglanski, A.W., Pierro, A., & Mannetti, L. (2004). Social cognition of immigrants acculturation: Effects of the need for closure and the reference group at entry. *Journal of Personality and Social Psychology, 86*, 796–813.

Kramer, M. (2006, September 20). Islamism and fascism: Dare to compare. Downloaded May 26, 2008, from http://www.geocities.com/martinkramerorg/2006_09_20.htm

Krey, A.C. (1921). *The First Crusade: The accounts of eyewitnesses and participants* (pp. 23–36). Princeton, NJ: Princeton University Press.

Krueger, A.B., & Maleckova, J. (2002). *Education, poverty and terrorism: Is there a causal connection?* (Working Paper 9074). Cambridge, MA: National Bureau of Economic Research.

Krueger, A.B., & Maleckova, J. (2003). Education, poverty and terrorism: Is there a causal connection? *Journal of Economic Perspectives, 17*, 119–144.

Kruglanski, A.W. (1996). Goals as knowledge structures. In P.M. Goll- witzer & J.A. Bargh (Eds.), *The psychology of action: Linking cognition and motivation to behavior* (pp. 599–618). New York: Guilford Press.

Kruglanski, A.W. (2004). The quest for the gist: On challenges of going abstract in social and personality psychology. *Personality and Social Psychology Review, 8*, 156–163.

Kruglanski, A.W, Chen, X., Dechesne, M., Fishman, S., & Orehek, E. (in press). Fully committed: Suicide bombers' motivation and the quest for personal significance. *Political Psychology*.

Kruglanski, A.W, Dechesne, M., & Erb, H.P. (2006). Modes, systems and sirens of specificity: The issues in gist. *Psychological Inquiry, 17*, 256–264.

Kruglanski, A.W, & Fishman, S. (2006). The psychology of terrorism: "Syndrome" versus "tool" perspectives. *Journal of Terrorism and Political Violence, 18*, 69–82.

Kruglanski, A.W, Pierro, A., Mannelti, L., & DeGrada, E. (2006). Groups as epistemic providers: Need for closure and the unfolding of group-centrism. *Psychological Review, 113*, 84–100.

Kruglanski, A.W, Raviv, A., Bar-Tal, D., Raviv, A., Sharvil, K., & Ellis, S. et al. (2005). In M.P. Zanna (Ed.), *Advances in experimental social psychology, 34*, 345–392.

Kruglanski, A.W, Shah, J., Fishbach, A., Friedman, R., Chun, W.Y., & Sleeth-Keppler, D. (2002). A theory of goal systems. In M.P. Zanna (Ed.), *Advances in experimental social psychology, 34*, 331–378.

Kunda, Z. (1990). The case for motivated reasoning. *Psychological Bulletin, 108*, 480–498.

LaFree, G., & Dugan, L. (2004). How does studying terrorism compare to studying crime? *Terrorism and Counter-Terrorism*: Criminological Perspectives. *Sociology of Crime,*

Law and Deviance, 15, 53–75. LaFree, G., & Dugan, L. (2007). *Deterrence and defiance models of terrorist violence in northern Ireland, 1969 to 1992*. Manuscript submitted for publication.

LaFree, G., & Hendrickson, J. (2007). Build a criminal justice policy for terrorism. *Criminology & Public Policy, 6*, 781–790.

Lakoff, G. (1990). Metaphor and war. Retrieved October 26, 2006, from http://philosophy.uoregon.edu/metaphor/lakoff-l.htm

Le Bon, G. (1896). *The crowd: A study of the popular mind*. London: Unwin.

Lemmer, G., & Wagner, U. (2006). *The effectiveness of prejudice prevention programs: A meta-analysis*. Poster presented at the annual meeting of the International Society for Political Psychology, Barcelona.

Lewin, K. (1947). Group decision and social change. In T.M. Newcomb & E.L. Hartley (Eds.) *Readings in social psychology*. New York: Holt, Reinhart and Winston.

Lia, B., & Hegghammer, T. (2004). FFI explains al-Qaida document. Retrieved May 30, 2008, from http://www.mil.no/felles/ffi/start/ article.jhtml?articleID=71589

Liberman, N., Trope, Y., & Stephan, E. (2007). Psychological distance. In A.W. Kruglanski & E.T. Higgins (Eds.), *Social psychology: Handbook of basic principles* (2nd ed., pp. 353–381). New York: Guilford Press.

Marsh, A., & Sahin-Dikmen, M. (2002). *Discrimination in Europe* (Report B). London: Policy Studies Institute.

Mackay, C. (1967). *Extraordinary Popular Delusions and the Madness of Crowds*. Wells, VT: Fraser. (Original work published 1843)

Macrae, C.N., Stangor, C., & Hewslone, M. (Eds.). (1996). *Stereotypes and stereotyping*. New York: Guilford Press.

McCauley, C. (1991). Terrorism, research and public policy: An overview. In C. McCauley (Ed.) *Terrorism, research and public policy* (pp. 126–145). New York: Frank Cass.

McCauley, C. (2004). Psychological issues in understanding terrorism and the response to terrorism. In C. Stout (Ed.), *The Psychology of Terrorism: Theoretical Understandings and Perspectives, condensed ed* (pp. 3–30). Westport, CT: Praeger.

McCauley, C. (2007). War versus justice in response to terrorist attacks: Competing frames and their implications. In B. Bongar, L.M. Brown, L.E. Beutler, J.N. Brackenridge, & P.G. Zimbardo (Eds.), *Psychology of terrorism*. New York: Oxford University Press.

McGuire, WJ. (1961). The effectiveness of supportive and refutational defenses in immunizing and restoring beliefs against persuasion. *Sociometry, 24*, 184–197.

Merari, A. (1991). Academic research and government policy on terrorism. In C. McCauley (1991). *Terrorism, research and public policy* (pp. 88–102). New York: Frank Cass.

Milbank, D. (2005, November 30). Rumsfeld's War on 'Insurgents.' *Washington Post*, p. A18.

Moaddel, M. (2005). *Islamic modernism, nationalism, and fundamentalism: Episode and Discourse*. Chicago: University of Chicago Press.

Moscovici, S. (1980). Toward a theory of conversion behavior. In L. Berkowitz (Ed.), *Advances in Experimental Social Psychology* (Vol. 13, pp. 209–239). New York: Academic Press.

Mozaffari, M. (2007). What is Islamism? History and definition of a concept. *Totalitarian Movements and Political Religions, 8*, 17–33.

Nacos, B.L. (2003). International cooperation in law enforcement and intelligence translates into the most effective strikes against international terrorists. *NY Cop Online Magazine*. Retrieved October 26, 2006, from http://www.nycop.com/Summer2003/LAW_ENFORCEMENT_AND_TERRORISM/ody_law_enforcement_and_terrorism.html

Naqvi, J. (1994, December 23). Drug trafficking second most lucrative business. *News India—Times, 24*(51), p. 30.

National Center for the Study of Terrorism and the Response to Terrorism (START). (2007). [Public opinion survey on the killing of civilians]. Unpublished raw data.

National Commission on Terrorist Attacks on the United States. (2004). *The 9/11 commission report*. New York: Norton.

Nielsen, J.S. (1999). *Toward a European Islam*. Migration, minorities and citizenship series. Houndmills, Basingstoke, Hampshire: Macmillan.

Nisbett, R.E., & Wilson, T.D. (1977). The halo effect: Evidence for unconscious alteration of judgements. *Journal of Personality and Social Psychology, 35*, 250–256.

Nixon, R.M. (1970, September 16). Address in the Alfred M. Landon lecture series at Kansas State University. In J.T. Woolley & G. Peters (Eds.), *The American Presidency Project* [online]. Santa Barbara, CA: University of California (hosted), Gerhard Peters (database). Retrieved June 3, 2008, from http://www.presidency.ucsb.edu/ws/index.php?pid=2663

Nixon, R.M. (1972a, September 5). Remarks to reporters about the assault on Israeli athletes at the Olympic Games in Munich, Germany. In J.T. Woolley & G. Peters (Eds.), *The American Presidency Project* [online]. Santa Barbara, CA: University of California (hosted), Gerhard Peters (database). Retrieved June 3, 2008, from http//:www.presidency.ucsb.edu/ws/index.php?pid= 3560

Nixon, R.M. (1972b, September 27). Statement about action to combat terrorism. In J.T. Woolley & G. Peters (Eds.), *The American Presidency Project* [online], Santa Barbara, CA: University of California (hosted), Gerhard Peters (database). Retrieved June 3, 2008, from http://www.presidency.ucsb.edu/ws/index.php?pid=3602

Nixon, R.M. (1973, March 6). Remarks at a ceremony honoring slain Foreign Service Officers. In J.T. Woolley & G. Peters (Eds.), *The American Presidency Project* [online]. Santa Barbara, CA: University of California (hosted), Gerhard Peters (database). Retrieved June 3, 2008, from http://www.presidency.ucsb.edu/ws/index. php?pid=4132

Oliver, A.M., & Sleinberg, P. (2005). *The road to martyrs' square: A journey into the world of the suicide bomber*. Oxford, England: Oxford University Press.

Office of the Director of National Intelligence. (2006, September 26). Declassified key judgments of the National Intelligence Estimate "Trends in Global Terrorism: Implications for the United Stales" dated April 2006 [Press Release]. Retrieved May 26, 2008, from http://www.dni.gov/press_releases/Declassified_NIE_Key_Judgments.pdf

Pape, R. (2005). *Dying to win: The strategic logic of suicide terrorism*. New York: Random House.

Pauly, RJ. (2004). *Islam in Europe: Integration or marginalization?* London: Ashgale.

Pedahzur, A. (2005). *Suicide terrorism*. Cambridge: Polity Press. Pelley, S. (Reporter). (2007, March 4). Terrorists take recruitment efforts online. *60 Minutes* [Television series]. New York: CBS News.

Pettigrew, T.F. (1998a). Intergroup contact theory. *Annual Review of Psychology, 49*, 65–85.

Pettigrew, T.F. (1998b). Reactions toward the new minorities of Western Europe. *Annual Review of Sociology, 24*, 77–103.

Pettigrew, T.F., & Tropp, L.R. (2006). A meta-analytic test of intergroup contact theory. *Journal of Personality and Social Psychology, 90*, 751–783.

Pew Global Attitudes Project (2006a, July 6). *Few signs of backlash from Western Europeans*. Washington, DC. Retrieved September 1, 2006, from http://pewglobal.org/reports/pdf/254.pdf

Pew Global Attitudes Project (2006b, June 22). *The great divide: How Westerners and Muslims view each other*. Washington, DC: author. Pipes, D. (2007, July 10). To terrify Tehran, unleash the Iranian opposition. *The New York Sun*, p. 7.

Pollitt, K. (2006, September 11). Wrong war, wrong word. *The. Nation*. Retrieved October 26, 2006, from http://www.thenation.com/doc/ 20060911/pollitt

Post, J.M. (1986). Hostilité, conformité, fraternité: The group dynamics of terrorist behavior. *International Journal of Group Psychotherapy, 36*, 211–224.

Post, J.M. (1990). Terrorist psychologic: Terrorist behavior as a product of psychological forces. In W. Reich (Ed). *Origins of terrorism: Psychologies, ideologies, theologies, states of mind* (pp. 25–40). Washington, DC: Woodrow Wilson Center Press.

Post, J.M. (2005). When hatred is bred in the bone: Psycho-cultural foundations of contemporary terrorism. *Political Psychology, 26*, 615–636.

Post, J.M. (2007). Deterrence in an age of asymmetric rivals. In S.A. Renshon & P. Suedfeld (Eds.), *Understanding the Bush Doctrine: Psychology and strategy in an age of terrorism* (pp. 153–174). New York: Routledge/Taylor & Francis Group.

Post, J.M., & Sheffer, G. (2007). The risk of radicalization and terrorism in U.S. Muslim communities. *Brown Journal of World Affairs, 13*.

Post, J.M., Sprinzak, E., & Denny, L.M. (2003). The terrorists in their own words: Interviews with 35 incarcerated Middle Eastern terrorists. *Terrorism and Political Violence, 15*, 171–184.

Prusher, I.R., & Mitnick, J. (2005, September 30). West Bank vote to gauge Hamas: Thursday's local election amid new attacks is seen as a barometer of Palestinian politics after the Gaza pullout. *Christian Science Monitor, 67*(216), 6.

Racism and Xenophobia in Sweden. (2004). Retrieved August 8, 2006 from http://www.integrationsverket.se

Rahimullah, Y. (1999, January 11). Conversation with terror. *Time*. Retrieved April 30, 2007, from http://www.time.com/time/ magazine/article/0,9171,989958,00.html

Rapoport, D.C. (2004). Modern terror: The four waves. In A.K. Cronin & J. M. Ludes (Eds.), *Attacking terrorism: Elements of a grand strategy* (pp. 46–73). Washington, DC: Georgetown University Press.

Reagan, R. (1981, January 27). Remarks at the welcoming ceremony for the freed American hostages. In J.T. Woolley & G. Peters (Eds.), *The American Presidency Project* [online]. Santa Barbara, CA: University of California (hosted), Gerhard Peters (database). Retrieved June 3, 2008, from http://www.presidency.ucsb.edu/ws/index.php?pid=43879

Reagan, R. (1985, June 28). Remarks to citizens in Chicago Heights, Illinois. In J.T. Woolley & G. Peters (Eds.), *The American Presidency Project* [online]. Santa Barbara, CA: University of California (hosted), Gerhard Peters (database). Retrieved June 3, 2008, from http://www.presidency.ucsb.edu/ws/index.php?pid=38838

Reagan, R. (1986, Mary 31). Radio address to the nation on terrorism. In J.T. Woolley & G. Peters (Eds.), *The American Presidency Project* [online]. Santa Barbara, CA: University of California (hosted), Gerhard Peters (database). Retrieved June 3,

2008, from http://www.presidency.ucsb.edu/ws/index.php?pid=37376

Record, J., & Terrill, W.A. (2004). *Iraq and Vietnam: Differences, similarities and insights*. Strategic Studies Institute, U.S. Army War College, Carlisle, PA. Retrieved October 29, 2006, from http://www.strategicstudiesinstitute.army.mil

Robertson, N. (2002, August 20). Previously unseen tape shows bin Laden's declaration of war. Retrieved May 20, 2008, from http://64.233.169.104/search?q=cache:_biJzbQAlRYJ:www.cnn.com/2002/US/08/19/terror.tape.main/index.html

Rowatt, W.C., Franklin, L.M., & Cotton, M. (2005). Patterns of personality correlates of implicit and explicit attitudes toward Christians and Muslims. *Journal for the Scientific Study of Religion, 44*, 29–43.

Rotella, S. (2006a, September 1). British terrorism case parallels others. *Los Angeles Times*, p. A7.

Rotella, S. (2006b, September 5). The enemies in their midst: Europe confronts terrorists home-grown an inspired abroad. *Los Angeles Times*, p. Al.

Roth, K. (2004, January–February). The law of war in the war on terror. *Foreign Affairs, 83*, 2–7.

Roy, O. (2004). *Globalized Islam: The search for a new ummah*. New York: Columbia University Press.

Ruthven, M. (1990). Constructing Islam as a language. *The Independent*, p. 8.

Sageman, M. (2004). *Understanding terror networks*. Philadelphia, PA: University of Pennsylvania Press.

Sambanis, N. (2006, July 23). It's official: There is now a civil war in Iraq. *The New York Times*, pp. 4, 13.

Schmid, A., & Jongman, AJ. (1988). *Political terrorism* (rev. ed.). Somerset, NJ: Transaction Publishers.

Schneider, DJ. (Ed.). (2004). *The psychology of stereotyping*. New York: Guilford Press.

Sharvit, M. (2005). The military and security implications of Israel's disengagement from the Gaza strip. *Strategic Assessment, 8(3)*. Retrieved October 26, 2006, from http://www.tau.ac.il/jcss/sa/v8n3p9Sharvit.html

Shimko, K.L. (2004). The Power of metaphors and the metaphors of power: The United States in the Cold War and after. In F.A. Beer & C. de Landtsheer (Eds.), *Metaphorical world politics* (pp. 199–215). Lansing: Michigan State University Press.

Shon, D.A. (1993). Generative metaphor: A perspective on problem setting in social policy. In A. Ortony (Ed.), *Metaphor and thought* (2nd ed., pp. 137–163). Cambridge, England: Cambridge University Press.

Siegel, L.J., & Senna, JJ. (2004). *Introduction to criminal justice*. New York: Thompson Wadsworth.

Silke, A. (2003). Becoming a terrorist. In A. Silke (Ed.). *Terrorists, victims and society: Psychological perspectives on terrorism and its consequences* (pp. 29–53). West Sussex, England: John Wiley & Sons Ltd.

SITE (Search for International Terrorist Entities) Institute. (2007). Mission Statement. Retrieved October 26, 2007 from http://siteinstitute.org/mission.html. (Institute has been disbanded and site no longer functions)

Smith, A.G. (2004). From words to action: Exploring the relationship between a group's value references and its likelihood of engaging in terrorism. *Studies in Conflict and Terrorism, 27*, 409–137.

Smith, B.L., & Orvis, G.P. (1993). America's response to terrorism: An empirical analysis of federal intervention strategies during the 1980s. *Justice Quarterly, 10*, 661–678.

Speckhard, A., & Akhmedova, K. (2005). Talking to terrorists. *Journal of Psychohistory, 33*, 125–156.

Stares, P.B., & Yacoubian, M. (2006). Unconventional approaches to an unconventional threat: A counter-epidemic strategy. In K.M. Campbell & W. Darsie (Eds.), *Mapping the jihadist threat: The war on terror since 9/11. A report of the Aspen Strategy Group* (pp. 85–98). Queenstown, MD: The Aspen Institute.

Stern, J. (2003). *Why religious militants kill: Terror in the name of God*. New York: HarperCollins.

Struch, N., & Schwartz, S.H. (1989). Intergroup aggression: Its predictors and distinctness from in-group bias. *Journal of Personality and Social Psychology, 56*, 364–373.

Suskind, R. (2006). *The one percent doctrine: Deep inside America's pursuit of its enemies since 9/11*. New York: Simon & Schuster. Taarnby, M. (2005). Recruitment of Islamist terrorists in Europe: Trends and perspectives. Research Report Funded by the Danish Ministry of Justice. Retrieved October 26, 2006, from http://www.investigativeproject.org/documents/testimony/58.pdf

Tang, A. (2007, June 25). Civilian deaths in Afghanistan causing alarm. *Army Times*. Retrieved July 20, 2008, from http://www.armytimes.com/news/2007/06/ap_afghandeaths_070624/

Telhami, S. (2004). *The slakes – America and the Middle East: The consequences of power and the choice for peace*. Boulder, CO: Westview Press.

Tibi, B. (2007). The totalitarianism of jihadist Islamism and its challenge to Europe and to Islam. *Totalitarian Movements and Political Religions, 8*, 35–54.

Ucko, D. (2007). Countering insurgents through distributed operations: Insights from Malaya 1948–1960. *The Journal of Strategic Studies, 30*, 47–72.

United Nations Population Division. (1993). *World population prospects: 1992 revision*. New York: Author.

Vertzberger, Y. (1990). *The world in their minds: Information processing, cognition, and perception in foreign policy decision making*. Stanford, CA: Stanford University Press.

Wallace, J. (2001, January). The Internet bubble. *The Ethical Spectator*. Retrieved on May 30, 2008, from http://www.spectacle.org/0101/ bubble.html

Webster's Ninth New Collegiate Dictionary. (1986). Springfield, MA: Merriam-Webster, Inc.

Weinman, G. (2004). How modern terrorism uses the Internet. United States Institute of Peace. Special Report No. 116.

White House. (2002). *National security strategy of the United States of America*. Washington, DC: Author. Retrieved May 23, 2008, from http://www.whitehouse.gov/nsc/nss/2002/nss.pdf

White House. (2003). *National strategy for combating terrorism*. Washington, DC: Author. Retrieved May 29, 2008, from http:// www.whitehouse.gov/news/releases/2003/02/counter_terrorism/ counter_terrorism_strategy.pdf

White House. (2006a). *National security strategy of the United States of America*. Washington, DC: Author. Retrieved May 23, 2008, from http://www.whitehouse.gov/nsc/nss/2006/nss2006.pdf

White House. (2006b). *National strategy for combating terrorism*. Washington, DC: Author. Retrieved May 29, 2008, from http:// www.whitehouse.gov/nsc/nsct/2006/nsct2006.pdf

Widdop, S.E. (2007). *European Social Survey Codebook: Round 1 and Round 2*. London: Centre for Comparative Social Surveys.

Will, G.F. (2006, August 15). The triumph of unrealism. *Washington Post*, p. A13.

Wilson, R. (2003). *A city for all our citizens: Reflections on shared cities*. Council of Europe. Retrieved August 8, 2006 from http://www.coe.int/t/dg4/cultureheritage/Source/Completed/Dialogue/DGIV_CULT_PREV_SHARED_CITIES(2003)2_Wilson_E.PDF#xml=http://www.search.coe.int/texis/search/pdfhi.txt?query=shared+ cities&pr=Internet_D2&prox=page&rorder=500&rprox=750&rdfreq= 500&rwfreq=500&rlead=500&rdepth=250&sufs=l&order=r&mode= &opts=&cq=&sr=&id=484b34ebl8

Wohlstetter, R. (1962). *Pearl Harbor: Warning and decision*. Stanford, CA: Stanford University Press.

Woodward, B. (2002). *Bush at war*. New York: Simon & Schuster.

Worchel, S., Andreoli, V.A., & Folger, R. (1977). Intergroup cooperation and intergroup attraction: The effect of previous interaction and outcome of combined effort. *Journal of Experimental Social Psychology, 13*, 131–140.

Yehoshua, Y. (2006, January 18). Reeducation of extremists in Saudi Arabia. MEMRI: The Middle East Research Institute (Inquiry & Analysis Series, No. 260). Retrieved August 15, 2007, from http:// memri.org/bin/articles.cgi?Page=archives&Area=ia&lD=lA26006

Index

Page numbers followed by n indicate Notes.

A

Ability-to-pay principle, 46–48
Accelerator effect, 68
Acirema, 421–424
ACLU. *See* American Civil Liberties Union (ACLU)
Adler, Ken, 246
Administrative agency, 144
Advanced lighting, 253
Advanced Research Projects Agency-Energy (ARPA-E), 239, 251, 255–257
Afghanistan, 436n
Agenda setting, 4
Aggravated assault rates, 281
Agreement on policy, 18
Aguiar, Mark, 393
AIHEC, 156
al-Qaeda, 436, 453
al Shehhi, Marwan al, 457
ALF-CIO, 142
Allison, Graham T., 410, 412, 414
Allport, Gordon, 461, 462
AMA. *See* American Medical Association (AMA)
Amber alert, 287
American Arbitration Association, 144
American Civil Liberties Union (ACLU), 280
American Dream, 325, 326
American Indian Higher Education Consortium (AIHEC), 156
American Medical Association (AMA), 90, 91, 102
American nuclear alerts, 411
American Recovery and Reinvestment Act (ARRA), 58, 61, 77
American Revolution, 324–325, 344
Ameringer, Oscan, 327
Analogy, 432
Antarctic ice sheet, 219
Anthropogenic warming, 219, 223
Anticipatory lighting system, 253
Antipoverty movement, 91
Antitax sentiment, 42
Antiterrorism, 288–289
Applied science, 243–245
Aquifer management, 260. *See also* Ogallala Aquifer
Arbitration, 144
Aron, Raymond, 403
ARPA-E. *See* Advanced Research Projects Agency-Energy (ARPA-E)
ARRA. *See* American Recovery and Reinvestment Act (ARRA)
Arraignment, 283
Arrest warrant, 283
Asch, Solomon, 412
Assembly-line model of technical development, 244–245
Assistance of counsel, 279
Assistant attorney general, 278
Atta, Mohamed, 457
Attorneys, 278
Attribution error, 414
Augustine, Norman, 249
Axis of evil, 440

B

Bacaan, Taman, 456
Bader Meinhoff group, 466
Bailouts, 61
Baker, Dean, 55
Baker, James, 420, 424
Balance-of-power system, 404
Bandwagon effects (elections), 31
Barnard, Chester I., 410
Baron of Kelvin, 244–245
Bartlett, Michael, 435
Basic attribution error, 414
Basic research, 243–245
Bauman, Michael, 465
Beach, William W., 80
Belief system, 450
Belton, Ethel, 159
Belton v. Gebhart, 158
Benefit principle, 45–46
Bernstein, Aaron, 341
Bernstein, Jared, 78
Bernstein, Lenny, 211
Biddle, Stephen, 441
Bilingual education, 137
Bill-John City, 32
bin Laden, Osama, 435, 438, 439, 443, 445
Binalshibh, Ramzi, 457

Biomass/biofuel feed-stocks, 253–254
Bishop, Gardner, 159
Bivens, Josh, 58
Black liquor, 113
Blahous, Charles, 55
Blecker, Robert, 249
Bloody Monday race riots (Detroit), 461
Blue Cross/Blue Shield, 93
Bluestone, Barry, 338
Bolling, Spottswood, 159
Bolling v. C. Melvin Sharpe, 159
Borick, Christopher P., 134
Borrowing, 74–75
Bosch, Peter, 211
Bositis, David, 149
Boston Public Latin Grammar School, 137
Bottom-up studies, 227n
Bourada, Safe, 458
Bouyeri, Mohammed, 458
Brandeis, Louis, 324
Briggs, Harry, Sr., 159
Briggs v. Elliot, 159
Brookings Institution, 242
Brooks, David, 437
Brown, Marilyn, 257
Brown, Oliver, 159
Brown v. Board of Education, 135–136, 158–159
Brownback, Samuel D., 317
Brundtland Commission, 196
Buchanan, James, 9, 153
Buchanan, Patrick, 423
Budget deficit, 58–77
  bailouts, 61
  borrowing, 74–75
  causes of current deficits, 59–61
  debt-to-GDP ratio, 61–63
  defined, 59
  deflation, 69–71
  foreign indebtedness, 72–73
  future projections, 62–64
  generation fairness, 71–73
  inflation, 68–69
  interest rates, 66–68
  Recovery Act, 61
  stimulus packages, 75–79
  trade deficit, 73–74

481

Budget deficit/surplus (1961–2004), 50
Budget projections, 41
Bulah, Shirley, 159
Bulah v. Gebhart, 158
Bull, Hedley, 403
Bureaucratic bargaining, 411–412
Bureaucratic/organizational models, 410–412
Burglary rates, 281, 282
Burnett, McKinley, 159
Burtless, Gary, 340
Bush, George H. W., 42, 420, 425
Bush, George W., 42, 48, 50–51, 52, 55, 104, 149, 290, 326, 333, 418, 419, 423, 429, 435–441
Bush, Vannevar, 243
Bush tax cuts, 50–51
Busing, 139

C
CACFP. *See* Child and Adult Care Food Program (CACFP)
Campbell, Karen, 78
Canetti, Elias, 448
Cannon, Michael F., 116
Canziani, Osvaldo, 211
Capacity utilization rate, 70
Capital punishment, 284, 317–318
Capitalist society, 345
Car allowance rebate system, 200
Carbon dioxide, 214
Cardwell, D. S. L., 245
Carr, E. H., 403
Carter, Jimmy, 434
Catton, William, 201
Causes of death, 342
CCDBG. *See* Child Care and Development Block Grant (CCDBG)
CEA. *See* Council of Economic Advisors (CEA)
Center of excellence (COE), 469
Chamberlain, Neville, 439
Chechen suicide terrorists, 455
Chen, Zhenlin, 211
Cherifi, Oussani, 458
Chess *vs.* checkers, 252
"Chicken," game of, 10, 11
Child abuse, 287, 288
Child and Adult Care Food Program (CACFP), 351
Child care, 349
Child Care and Development Block Grant (CCDBG), 349

Child maltreatment rates, 288
Child nutrition, 351
Child poverty, 338
Child support enforcement, 352
Child welfare, 349–350
Chollet, Derek, 418
Christ, Renate, 211
Chu, Stephen, 199, 250
Church Arsons Prevention Act, 285
Churchillians, 439n
Civil war, 436n
Clark, April, 354, 371
Clark, Wesley, 444
Class. *See* Middle class
CLASS Act, 114
Classical model (economic policy), 39
Classical realism, 403–404, 416
Climate change. *See* Intergovernmental Panel on Climate Change (IPCC)
Clinch River Breeder Reactor, 242
Clinician licensing laws, 122
Clinton, Bill, 38, 42, 50, 101, 418, 435
Clinton, Hilary, 194
Cochran, Charles L., 38, 324
Cochrane, John H., 124
COE, 469
Cohn, D'Vera, 354, 371
Cold War analogy, 440
Collective action problems, 31
Collective bargaining, 143, 145
Common problems, 30–31
Common school movement, 138
Community, 28–30
Community corrections, 284
Community health centers, 109
Community Living Assistance Services and Supports (CLASS) program, 114
Community mental health centers, 111
Community-oriented policing (COP), 288
Complex organization, 410
Compulsion of witness, 279
Compulsory arbitration, 144
Conceptual models. *See* Models for policy analysis
Conciliation, 143
Concurrence seeking, 412
Conflict of interest, 146
Confrontation of witness, 279
Consensual model of incarceration, 285

Constitution
 appropriation of money, 41
 First Amendment, 137
 Fourteenth Amendment, 135
 key structural components, 3
 promote general welfare, 38
 supreme law of the land, 3
 taxes, 43
Consumer price index, 69, 70
Contact hypothesis, 461–463
Contractionary policy, 66
Control model of incarceration, 285
Controlled-choice (public school choice), 147
Coolsaet, Rik, 452
Cooperation, 32
COP. *See* Community-oriented policing (COP)
Cordesman, Anthony, 442
Cotell, Catherine, 256
Council of Economic Advisors (CEA), 39
Counterterrorism, 430–469
 epidemiological metaphor. *See* Public health epidemiological model
 executive summary, 430–431
 Internet, 454. *See also* Internet
 law enforcement. *See* Law enforcement metaphor
 paradoxes, 468–469
 prejudice reduction. *See* Prejudice-reduction framework
 psychological objectives, 432–433
 war metaphor. *See* War metaphor
Courts, 278
Craft, Michael E., 194
Crenshaw, Martha, 430
Crichton, Michael, 206
Criminal justice policy, 277–322
 antiterrorism, 288–289
 biological theories, 283
 causes of crime, 282–283
 child abuse, 287, 288
 community corrections, 284
 COP, 288
 death penalty, 284, 317–318
 District of Columbia v. Heller, 293–316
 elite theory, 289
 group theory, 289–290
 gun policy, 291–316

Egalitarianism, 327
1890 land-grants, 152, 155
Eisenhower, Dwight, 255, 412
Elam, Emmett, 272
Elderly persons, 53–57
Electronic surveillance, 284
Elementary and Secondary Education Reauthorization Act, 156
Elite model, 8
Elite theory, 8–9, 289
Employee Retirement Income Security Act (ERISA), 94
Employment Act of 1946, 38, 39
Employment-to-population ratio, 69, 70
Energy and American Society — Thirteen Myths (Sovacool/Brown), 257
Energy and environment, 183–276
    ARPA-E, 239, 251, 255–257
    assembly-line model of technical development, 244–245
    basic research *vs.* applied science, 243–245
    Brundtland Commission, 196
    chess *vs.* checkers, 252
    climate change. *See* Intergovernmental Panel on Climate Change (IPCC)
    Craft, Michael, 194–210
    defining environmental policy, 203–205
    DOE, 238
    Earth Summit, 195
    economics and incentives, 200–201
    funding, 246–250
    hard *vs.* soft energy path, 251–252
    In-Q-Tel/DARPA-like institutional structure, 255–257
    inadequacy, 246–250
    inconsistency, 240–242
    incrementalism, 242–246, 250
    IPCC. *See* Intergovernmental Panel on Climate Change (IPCC)
    linear model of innovation, 243
    ocean acidification, 219, 223
    Ogallala Aquifer. *See* Ogallala Aquifer
    problem solving v. problem defining, 245–246
    public policy, 205, 209–210
    risk assessment, 206–209
    scientific knowledge and its use, 199–200
    Sovacool, Benjamin, 238–258
    stove-piping, 239, 242, 245, 253, 255, 257
    sustainable development, 197
    tragedy of the commons, 200
    transformation R&D strategy, 250–255
    values and ethics, 201–202
Enlightenment, 324
Entebbe airport rescue operation, 465
Environmental policy, 203
Environmental risks, 206–209
Environmental values and ethics, 201
Epidemiological metaphor. *See* Public health epidemiological model
ERISA. *See* Employee Retirement Income Security Act (ERISA)
Establishment clause, 136
ETA organization, 467n
Ethical realism, 424
European Dilemma, 461
Evans-Allen program, 155
Excise tax, 44
Exclusionary rule, 279
Executive branch, 40
Expansion policy, 66
Extended contact effect, 463
Externalities, 9
Extraordinary Popular Delusions and the Madness of the Crowds (Mackay), 448

F
Fact finding, 143–144
Fads, 31
Fallows, James, 438
Faranda, Adriana, 451, 465
FARC. *See* Revolutionary Armed Forces of Columbia (FARC)
Fascism, 440
Federal debt, 61
Federal deficit. *See* Budget deficit
Federal funds rate (1973–2009), 76
Federal government receipts (2004), 44
Federal Mediation and Conciliation Service (FMCS), 144
Federal Reserve, 41
Federal revenues, 59
Federal Rules of Criminal Procedure, 279
Federal spending, 59
Federal tax progressivity, 48
Federalism, 3
Fernandez, F. L., 255
50/50 quota policy, 264–270
First Amendment, 137
FIS. *See* Front Islamic du Salut (FIS)
Fiscal policy, 66
Flat tax, 47
Fleck, Ludwig, 239
Flight to safety, 68
FLQ. *See* Front de Liberation du Quebec (FLQ)
FMCS. *See* Federal Mediation and Conciliation Service (FMCS)
Food stamps, 350–351
Forcible rape rate, 280–281
Foreign indebtedness, 72–73
Foreign policy, 401–486
    Acirema, 421–424
    addressing global hardship, 428
    bureaucratic/organizational models, 410–412
    Chollet/Lindberg, 418–429
    counterterrorism. *See* Counterterrorism
    decision-making models, 410–415, 416–417
    defending liberal regimes, 425–426
    enforcing the "responsibility to protect," 427–428
    group dynamics, 411, 412–413
    GS/CI models, 406–408, 416
    Holsti, Ole, 402–417
    idealism, 418–429
    individual decision making, 411, 413
    Kruglanski et al., 430–469
    M/WS/D models, 407, 408–409, 416
    nationalism, 409–410
    promoting liberal governance, 426–427
    promotion of American values, 418–419
    realism, 403–406, 407, 416
    standing against conquest of territory by force, 424–425
    strengthening alliances/institutions, 428–429

Foster, J. D., 80
Fourteenth Amendment, 135
Frank, Thomas, 327
Friedman, Milton, 148, 149, 331
Friendships, 33
Front de Liberation du Quebec (FLQ), 450
Front Islamic du Salut (FIS), 467n
Fry, Richard, 354
Fuchs, Victor, 117
Fukuyama, Francis, 424, 426, 440
Full Employment and Balanced Growth Act, 38, 57
Full employment budget, 40
Functional theory of inequality, 330–333

G

Gale, William, 48, 52
Galilei, Galileo, 245
Galvin Task Force, 242
Game of "chicken," 10, 11
Game theory, 10–11
Gates, Bill, 334
General algebraic modeling system, 261, 263
Generational fairness, 71–73
Generic drugs, 112
George, Alexander L., 414, 471
Gereffi, Gary, 408
Gerson, Michael, 435
Ghate, Onkar, 444
G.I. Bill, 138
Gideon v. Wainwright, 279
Gilder, George, 47
Gilpin, Robert, 402, 405–406, 416
Gingrich, Newt, 103
Gini index, 333–334, 337
Gisser-Sanchez effect, 260
Global inequalities, 336–340
Global jihadist movement, 440
Global Society/Complex-Interdependence (GS/CI) models, 406–408, 416
Globalization, 328
Goldhill, David, 117
Gonzales, Felisa, 354
"Good" policy, testing of, 17–18
Graebner, Norman, 403
Graham, Franklin, 428
Graig, Laurene, 96
Great Depression, 39, 324, 326, 345
Great U-turn, 338
Greenhouse gases, 214, 215
Greenland ice sheet, 219
Greenspan, Alan, 54
Grieco, Joseph, 408
Grievance, 145–146
Groundwater conservation. *See* Ogallala Aquifer
Group-centrism, 465
Group dynamics, 411, 412–413
Group Health Cooperative, 123
Group theory, 6–8, 289–290
Groups, 33
Groupthink, 412, 413
GS/CI models, 406–408, 416
GSPC (Salafist Group for Call and Combat), 458
Gun policy, 291–316

H

Hadden, Susan, 207
Hagerman, Amber, 287
Halo effect, 461
Hamilton, Alexander, 402
Hanford Nuclear Reservation, 208
Hansen, Alicia, 489
Hard energy path, 251
Hardin, Garrett, 200
Hare, William, 211
Harrison, Bennett, 338
Hatch Act, 152, 155
Hate Crime Statistics Act, 285
Hate crimes, 285–287
Hate Crimes Prevention Acts, 286
Hate Crimes Sentencing Enhancement Act, 285
Hayek, Frederick, 148
Health care costs, 94–97, 117
Health care policy, 89–132
  access problem, 97–99
  Cannon, Michael, 116–125
  choice of doctors and health plans, 121–124
  cost problem, 94–97, 117
  free market, 116–125
  health insurance, 93–94
  Health Security Act, 101–103
  HMOs, 93–94, 95
  improved health status over time, 100–101
  infant mortality rates, 100, 101
  Kennedy-Kesselbaum Act, 103–104
  life expectancy, 100, 101
  Medicare. *See* Medicare/Medicaid
  Medicare Modernization Act, 104
  monopolistic clinician licensing, 122
  monopolistic insurance licensing, 121–122
  needy, helping the, 124
  Obama's proposal. *See* President's health care proposal (2010)
  PPOs, 94
  quality issue, 99–100
  regulatory federalism, 121–123
  taxes, 113, 114, 118–120
  underinsured, 98
  uninsured, 97–98
  websites, 125
  Wilson, Carter, 90–105
Health insurance, 93–94
  licensing, 121–122
Health maintenance organization (HMO), 93–94, 95
Health of Nations: An International Perspective on U.S. Health Care Reform, 96
Health Security Act, 101–103
Henigan, Dennis A., 291
Heritage Foundation, 80
Hermann, Margaret G., 414
Herring, Bradley, 124
Herz, John, 403
Hezbollah Shi'ite youth movement, 454
HI tax, 113
Hill-Burton Act, 90
Hinkle, Jerome, 241
Hitch, Charles, 14
HMO. *See* Health maintenance organization (HMO)
Hobbes, Thomas, 403
Hockfield, Susan, 244
Hoffman, Stanley, 402, 404
Holdren, John, 199
Holmes, S., 440
Holsti, Ole R., 402
Home ownership, 376–377, 390–392
Homeland Security Act, 469
Homicide rate, 280, 281
Homo economicus, 9
Homo politicus, 9
Horizontal equity, 47
Hospital Survey and Construction Act, 90
House arrest, 284
Household income (1980–2003), 334
Houston, Charles H., 158
Human, John, 424
Huq, Saleemul, 211
Hurst, Erik, 393
Hussein, Saddam, 439

I

Ice sheet, 219, 223
IDA. *See* Individual Development Account (IDA)
Ideas, 36
Identity theft, 290
Ideology, 450
IFA. *See* Individual functional assessment (IFA)
Ikenberry, John, 424
Imam al-Mahdi Scouts, 454
Immigration backlash movements, 29
Immigration/immigrants, 290, 328, 351–352
Impasse, 143
Impasse resolution, 143–144
IMPLAN input-output model, 264
In-Q-Tel, 255–256
Incarceration, 285
Income, 333
    distribution, 328
    equality, 333–334, 337–338
    mobility, 341
    status, 365–366
Incremental model, 6
Incremental R&D strategy, 242–246, 250, 251, 254
Incrementalism, 5–6, 242–246, 250
Indictment, 283
Individual Development Account (IDA), 348
Individual functional assessment (IFA), 350
Infant mortality rates, 100, 101
Inflation, 68–69
Influence, 31–32
Information, 33–34
Institutionalism, 2–3, 290
Instrumental argument (public school choice), 147
Insurance, 29
Integrative complexity, 414
Integrative simplicity, 473
Interdistrict model (public school choice), 147
Interest rates, 66–68
Intergenerational mobility, 359, 384–385
Intergovernmental Panel on Climate Change (IPCC), 206, 211–237
    adaptation and mitigation options, 223–233
    causes of change, 214–216
    long-term perspective, 233–237
    observed changes in climate, 211–214
    ocean acidification, 219, 223
    projected climate change, 216–225
    projected regional impacts, 221–222
International relations. *See* Foreign policy
Internet
    counterterrorism, 454
    self-recruitment (terrorism), 452
    terrorists' tactical planning, 453
Internet websites. *See* Websites
IPCC. *See* Intergovernmental Panel on Climate Change (IPCC)
IRA. *See* Irish Republican Army (IRA)
Iran hostage crisis, 434
Irish Republican Army (IRA), 467n
Islamism, 449n
Islamofascism, 440
Islamophobia, 459–460
Israel/Palestine, 446, 447, 469n
Italian Red Brigades, 466

J

Jamieson, Alison, 451
Janis, Irving L., 412, 414
Jarrah, Ziad, 457
Jefferson, Thomas, 9, 325, 343
Jencks, Christopher, 340
Jervis, Robert, 414
Jihadism, 440
Jihadist terrorism, 448–456. *See also* Public health epidemiological model
Jim Crow, 134
Johns, Barbara, 159
Johnson, Jeff, 259
Johnson, Lyndon, 38, 49, 54, 91, 326
Johnson, Phillip, 259
Joint Economic Committee (Congress), 39
Jones, Richard M., 249
Judge, 278

K

Kagan, Robert, 428
Kaiser Permanente, 123
KAL flight 007, 414
Kammin, Daniel, 249
Kaplan, Morton, 404
Karoly, David, 211
Karzai, Hamid, 442
Kattsov, Vladimir, 211
Katzenbach, Nicholas, 134
Keeping up with the Joneses, 362
Keeter, Scott, 354
Kendall, Raymond E., 446
Kenderline, Melanie, 241
Kennan, George F., 403, 414
Kennedy, Edward, 103
Kennedy, John, 49, 54, 134, 344, 412, 418
Kennedy, Paul, 416
Kennedy, Robert, 412
Kennedy-Kesselbaum Act, 103–104
Kerr-Mills Act, 91
Kerry, John, 443, 445
Kessebaum, Nancy, 103
Keynes, John Maynard, 38, 40, 57, 324, 326
Khalilzad, Zalmay, 250
Khyam, Omar, 458
Kimelman, Donald, 354
Klopfer V. N. Carolina, 280
Knorr-Cetina, Karin, 239
Kochhar, Rakesh, 354
Kohut, Andrew, 354
Kosters, Marvin, 328
Kozol, Jonathan, 141
Krauthammer, Charles, 424
Kruglanski, Arie W., 430
Krugman, Paul, 341
Kuhn, Thomas, 239
Kundzewicz, Zbigniew, 211
Kupchan, Charles, 424
Kurdish Workers' Party (PKK), 467n
Kuznets, Simon, 340
Kyoto Protocol, 204

L

Labor relations, 142–146
Lampman, Robert, 340
Land ethic, 201
Land-grant college, 152
Land-grants, 152–157
    of 1890, 152, 155
    of 1994, 152
Lansford, Vernon, 272
Larceny rate, 282
Latent group, 7
Lau v. Nichols, 137
Law enforcement metaphor, 430, 442–447, 466–467
    advantages/limitations, 466–467
    compatibility with alternative societal concerns, 444

focus on criminal act, 444–445
international cooperation, 445–446
minimization of costly mistakes, 444
police work, 445
psychological implications, 446–447
terrorism as crime, 445
Laws of matter, 34
Laws of paradox, 34
Laws of passion, 34
Le Bon, Gustav, 448
LeBow, Robert, 95, 96
Leibniz, Gottfried, 245
Leisure time, 362–364
Leites, Nathan, 414
Lemon v. Kurtzman, 160–185
Leopold, Aldo, 201
Lethal Logic: Exploding the Myths that Paralyze American Gun Policy (Henigan), 292
Liberal democracy, 425, 426
Liberal realism, 424
Liberation Tigers of Tamil Eilam (LTTE), 467n
Liberty, 327
Lieberthal, Robert, 121
Lieven, Anatol, 424
Life expectancy, 100, 101, 341–342, 343
Lighting system, 253
Limbaugh, Rush, 206
Lincoln, Abraham, 153
Lindberg, Tod, 418
Lindblom, Charles E., 5, 13
Linear model of innovation, 243
Lippmann, Walter, 403
Liu, Jian, 211
Loanable funds market, 66–68
Lock-step pay scale, 146
Locke, John, 9
Lohmann, Ulrike, 211
Long, David G., 141
Loper, Joe, 246
Lorenz curve, 335, 337
Lorraine, Anne, 98
Lotteries, 49
Lovins, Amory, 251, 252
Loyalty, 32–33
LTTE (Liberation Tigers of Tamil Eilam), 467n
Lubchenko, Jane, 196, 199
Lucena, Juan, 246
Luxembourg Income Study project, 338
Luxury tax, 44

M

M/WS/D models, 407, 408–409, 416
Machiavelli, Niccolo, 403
Mackay, Charles, 448
MacKenzie, Donald, 240
Madison, James, 325
Madrassa, 452
"Madrassa Myth, The" (Bergen/Pandey), 452
Magnet school, 142
Magnetohydrodynamics program, 242
Malaria epidemic, 448
Malayan Races Liberation Army (MRLA), 447
Malloy v. Hogan, 279
Malone, Eloise F., 38, 324
Malthus, Thomas, 38, 324
Mann, Dean, 205
Mann, Horace, 138
Manning, Martin, 211
Mapp v. Ohio, 279
March, James G., 410
Marginal productivity theory (MPT), 396
Margolis, Robert, 249
Market and the polis, 28–37
common problems, 30–31
community, 28–30
cooperation, 32
groups, 33
influence, 31–32
information, 33–34
loyalty, 32–33
market model/poli model, compared, 36
passion, 34–35
polis, characteristics of, 35
power, 35–37
public interest, 30
Market mitigation potential, 227n
Marmot, Michael, 342
Marquis, Susan, 121
Marshall, Thurgood, 134–136, 158
Marx, Karl, 324
Marxist/World System/Dependency (M/WS/D) models, 407, 408–409, 416
Matsuno, Taroh, 211
Mayr, Otto, 244–245
MCA. *See* Medical savings account (MCA)
MCCA. *See* Medicare Catastrophic Coverage Act (MCCA)
McCain, John, 194
McCormick, Mary, 98

McDonald v. City of Chicago, 291
McFaul, Michael, 426
McGovern, George, 423
Means-ends relationship, 17
Median family wealth, 368–369
Mediation, 143
Medicaid prescription drug profiling, 111
Medical savings account (MCA), 104
Medicare Advantage, 111–113
Medicare Catastrophic Coverage Act (MCCA), 92, 93
Medicare HI tax, 113
Medicare/Medicaid
changes to, 93
costs, 95
"donut hole," 108
fraud, 111, 112
HMOs, 93–94
holes in safety net, 98–99
immigrants, 351–352
overview, 91–92
President's proposal (2010), 111–113
PRWORA, 350
reform, 104
Medicare Modernization Act, 104, 112
Medicare Part A, 92
Medicare Part B, 92
Medicare Part C, 92
Medicare Part D, 92
Medicare Plus Choice, 92
Medigap, 92
Megan's law, 287
Membership, 29
Menne, Bettina, 211
Merari, Ariel, 450, 469
Meridional overturning circulation (MOC), 223
Metaphor, 431–432
Methane, 214
Metz, Bert, 211
Middle class, 353–393
children's standard of living, 384
demographic characteristics, 365, 367
economic mobility, 367, 369–370
executive summary, 355–356
financial circumstances and anxieties, 361, 387–392
home ownership, 376–377, 390–392
income differences, 374–375

keeping up with the Joneses, 362
leisure time, 362–364
living comfortably, 361
overview, 354–370
ownership of?, 377–378
parents' standard of living, 359, 384
possessions perception gap, 378–379
priorities/values, 392–393
self-definition, 371–379
terminology, 358
what it costs, 376
Milanovic, Branko, 339
Militant Islamism, 449
Mill, John Stuart, 148
Miller, Matthew, 146
Mirza, Monirul, 211
Mission creep, 242
Missouri v. Jenkins, 142
Mitigation potential, 227n
MNC-state relations, 408
Mobs, 31
MOC. *See* Meridional overturning circulation (MOC)
Model, 2
Models for policy analysis
  are they working?, 11–12
  elite theory, 8–9
  game theory, 10–11
  group theory, 6–8
  incrementalism, 5–6
  institutionalism, 2–3
  objectives, 2
  process model, 3–4
  public choice theory, 9–10
  rationalism, 4–5
Modern realism, 404–406, 416
Moe, Terry M., 149
Monetary policy, 41, 66
Monopolistic licensing, 121–122
Moore, Michael, 118
Morgenthau, Hans J., 403
Morin, Richard, 354, 370
Morrill, Justin Smith, 152, 154
Morrill Act, 152, 154, 155
Mosque, 451–452
Motorman Operation, 464
Moussaoui, Zacarias, 446
MPT. *See* Marginal productivity theory (MPT)
MRLA. *See* Malayan Races Liberation Army (MRLA)
Mubarak, Hosni, 427
Muddling through. *See* Science of "muddling through"

Multinational corporation (MNC), 408
Munich analogy, 439–440
Murder rate, 281
Muslim diaspora community, 458–459
Mutual adjustment, 19
Mutual aid societies, 29

N
Nader, Ralph, 423
Nagourney, Adam, 149
Naqvi, Jawed, 445
NASULGC, 156–157
National Association of Social Workers, 346
National Association of State Universities and Land-Grant Colleges (NASULGC), 156–157
National Conference of Catholic Bishops, 344
National courts, 278
National Federation of Independent Business (NFIB), 103
National Strategy for Combating Terrorism 2003, The, 438
Nationalism, 409–410
Nature of Prejudice, The (Allport), 461
Navarro, Vicente, 98
Nazi concentration camps, 32
Neal, Terry M., 149
Nelson Amendment (Morrill Act), 152
Neoclassical model (economic policy), 39–40
Neustadt, Richard, 411
New Deal, 39, 57, 326
NFIB. *See* National Federation of Independent Business (NFIB)
Nicholls, Neville, 211
Niebuhr, Reinhold, 403
9/11 terrorist attacks, 435–436
9/11 terrorist cell, 457
1994 land-grants, 152
Nitrous oxide, 214
Nixon, Richard, 434
No Child Left Behind Act, 139
No Name Coalition, 103
Noblesse oblige, 9
Non-linear dynamic programming models, 261–264
Nozick, Robert, 344
Nurse, Leonard, 211
Nye, David, 245

O
Obama, Barack, 62, 116, 121, 124, 125, 194, 199. *See also* President's health care proposal (2010)
Ocean acidification, 219, 223
OECD child poverty rates, 338
Office of Management and Budget (OMB), 40
Ogallala Aquifer, 259–270
  dynamic non-linear optimization model, 261–264
  executive summary, 259
  50/50 quota policy, 264–270
  IMPLAN input-output model, 264
  possible policy tools, 260
  results, 264–268
  water pumpage fee, 264–269
Okun, Arthur, 340, 344
O'Leary, Hazel, 242
Oligopoly theory, 404
OMB. *See* Office of Management and Budget (OMB)
Operation Crevice, 458
Operation Days of Penitence, 465
Operation Defensive Shield, 465
Operational code, 414
Optimal contact programs, 468
Organizational-bureaucratic models, 410–412
Original intent, 135
Orzag, Peter, 52, 56–57, 118
Our Common Future, 196
Our Liberty (Mill), 148
Overlapping group membership, 7

P
Pachauri, Rajendra, 211
Paehlke, Robert, 201
Paine, Thomas, 137, 148
Palestine/Israel, 446, 447, 469n
Palestinian Muslims, 451
Palutifkok, Jean, 211
Panhandle Groundwater Conservation District, 268
Panics, 31
Parente, Stephen, 123
Parry, Martin, 211
Passion, 34–35
Patriot Act, 288–289
Pauly, Mark, 121, 124
Pay-for-delay, 112
Payroll tax, 43
Pearl Harbor analogy, 439
Peloponnesian War, 402

Person-related crimes, 280
Personal Responsibility and Work Opportunity Reconciliation Act (PRWORA), 346–352
   child care, 349
   child nutrition, 351
   child support enforcement, 352
   child welfare, 349–350
   food stamps, 350–351
   further information, 352
   immigrants, 351–352
   Medicaid, 350
   SSI, 350
   TANF, 346–348
   waivers, 348–349
Petersik, Thomas, 246
Peterson, Mark, 94
Pew Research Center, 353–393, 354
PHNP. *See* Physicians for a National Health Program (PHNP)
Photo-bioreactor, 253
Physicians for a National Health Program (PHNP), 102
Piketty, Thomas, 341
PKK. *See* Kurdish Workers' Party (PKK)
Plato, 47
Plessy v. Ferguson, 134–135
Plutarch, 37, 324
Pointer v. Texas, 279
Police
   corruption of, 287–288, 289
   unions, 280
Policies, 4
Policy elites, 289
Policy models. *See* Models for policy analysis
Polis, 35. *See also* Market and the polis
Political community, 29
Political conflict, 37
Political economic policy, 39
Political entrepreneurs, 42, 49
Political equality, 327
Politics, 324
Pollock v. Farmers' Loan and Trust Co., 43
Pope, Alexander, 137
Pork-barrel policies, 204
Posse commitatus, 289
Possessions perception gap, 378–379
Post, Jerrold M., 430
Postconviction procedures, 283

Power, 35–37, 334
PPO. *See* Preferred provider organization (PPO)
PPS. *See* Prospective payment system (PPS)
Pragmatic idealism, 424
Precedent, 34
Preferred provider organization (PPO), 93
Prejudice-reduction framework, 430–431, 457–464, 467–468
   advantages/limitations, 467–468
   contact hypothesis, 461–463
   enhancing integration, 460–461
   Islamophobia, 459–460
   Muslim diaspora community, 458–459
   prejudice reduction, 461
   psychological implications, 463–464
President's health care proposal (2010), 107–115
   affordability/accountability, 107–110
   CLASS Act, 114
   community health centers, 109
   community mental health centers, 111
   consumer protections, 109
   costs/fiscal sustainability, 112–114
   employer responsibility, 110
   federal funding, 114
   generic drugs, 112
   Medicare Advantage, 112–113
   Medicare HI tax, 113
   other policy improvements, 114–115
   overview, 107
   rate review, 109
   simplify income definitions, 114
   Social Security Trust Funds, 115
   tax loopholes, 113–114
   UPNs, 111
   waste, fraud, abuse, 110–112
   website for further information, 114
Price, Derek de Sola, 239, 245
Price indexing, 55
Principled argument (public school choice), 147
Probable cause, 283
Problem identification, 4

Problem solving v. problem defining, 245–246
Process model, 3–4
Progress in life, 380
Progressive realism, 424
Progressive tax, 47
Project Hindsight, 245
Property-related crime, 281, 282
Property tax, 44, 140, 141
Proportional tax, 47
Proposition 187 (California), 29
Prosecuting attorney, 278
Prospective payment system (PPS), 97
PRWORA. *See* Personal Responsibility and Work Opportunity Reconciliation Act (PRWORA)
Public choice theory, 9–10
Public defender, 278
Public goods, 9
Public health epidemiological model, 430, 448–457, 467
   advantages/limitations, 467
   ideology, 449–450
   presumed efficacy of terrorism, 450–451
   psychological implications, 456–457
   scope of support, 450
   self-recruitment, 452–454
   susceptible populations/contributing situations socialization, 454–456
   vectors of terrorism, 451
Public interest, 30
Public policy, 203
Public school choice, 147
Public Utilities Holding Company Act (PUHCA), repeal of, 247, 248
Pure commercial relationship, 33
Putnam, Robert, 329

Q
Qin, Dahe, 211
Quality to life, 380, 381

R
Racial desegregation, 134–136, 158–159
Racially biased policing, 288
Radon, 207–208
RADV. *See* Risk adjustment data validation (RADV)
Rainwater, Ken, 272

RAND Health Insurance Experiment, 120
Rational comprehensive method, 15
Rational hypothesis, 403
Rational policy, 4
Rationalism, 4–5
Raustalia, Kal, 444
Ravindranath, Nijavalli, 211
Rawl, John, 344
Reagan, Ronald, 41, 49, 198, 326, 379, 434–435
Reagan revolution, 148
Real income, 368
Realism, 403–406, 407, 416
Realistic Wilsonianism, 424
Recovery Act, 58, 61, 77
Redding, Louis, 159
Reducing Risk: Setting Priorities and Strategies for Environmental Protection, 209
Reductionism, 404
Regressive tax, 47
Regulatory federalism, 121–123
Regulatory policies, 204
Reid, Richard, 446, 457
Reisinger, Andy, 211
Relevance and realism, 18–19
Religion and education, 160–185
Religious Rehabilitation Group, 456
Remediation of hazardous waste, 208
Ren, Jiawen, 211
Republic, The (Plato), 47
Responsibility model of incarceration, 285
Retributive justice, 284
Revolutionary Armed Forces of Columbia (FARC), 467n
Riahi, Keywan, 211
Ricardo, David, 324
Richardson, Lewis Fry, 470
Ridgway, Matthew, 412
Rights of Man, The (Paine), 148
Rio-Plus-10 summit, 195
Rise and Fall of the Great Powers, The (Kennedy), 416
Rising Above the Gathering Storm, 239
Risk adjustment data validation (RADV), 111
Rizvi, Iqbal Hussain, 445
Robbery rates, 281
Robertson, Nic, 443

Robinson Crusoe society, 28
Robinson v. California, 280
Romer, Christina, 78
Romer-Bernstein report, 78
Roosevelt, Franklin, 38, 39, 326, 418
Rose, Stephen, 354, 371
Rosecrance, Richard, 404
Rosenberg, Bella, 147
Rosenzweig, Cynthia, 211
Ross, Murray, 328
Rumsfeld, Donald, 439
Russett, Bruce, 404
Rusticucci, Matilde, 211

S
Saez, Emmanuel, 341
Salafist Group for Call and Combat (GSPC), 458
Sala-i-Martin, Xavier, 339
Salazar, Ken, 204
Sales tax, 44
San Antonio Independent School District v. Rodriguez, 140, 142
Sand County Almanac, A (Leopold), 201
Saudi *Al-Sakinah* campaign, 454
Savage Inequalities (Kozol), 141
Schacht, Wendy H., 250
Schattschneider, E. E., 32
Schneider, Stephen, 211
Schock, Robert N., 247
School board, 139
Schools. *See also* Education policy
    choices, 147–150
    districts, 139
    funding, 139–142
    taxes, 140
    vouchers for, 147–150
School District of Abington Township v. Schemp, 136
School Linking Project, 468
Science: The Endless Frontier (Bush), 243
Science of "muddling through," 13–22
    achieving degree of comprehensiveness, 19–20
    evaluation and empirical analysis, 15–17
    non-comprehensive analysis, 18
    relations between means and ends, 17
    relevance and realism, 18–19
    by root or by branch, 14–15

succession comparison as a system, 21–22
succession of comparisons, 20–21
test of "good" policy, 17–18
theorists and practitioners, 21
Scott, Andrew M., 404
Scowcroft, Brent, 420
Search & seizure, 279
Segarra, Eduardo, 259
Self-anchoring scale, 379
Self-incrimination, 279
Sen, Amartya, 339
September 11 terrorist attacks, 435–436, 457
Serrano v. Priest, 140
Shafritz, Jay M., 134
Sharing burdens and bounty, 29
Sharon, Ariel, 465
Shock absorbers, 67
Shop steward, 146
SHTP. *See* Southern High Plains region of Texas (SHTP)
Sicko (Moore), 118
Simon, Christopher A., 278
Simon, Herbert, 410, 413
Sin tax, 44
Singer, J. David, 404
SITE Institute, 453, 454
Smith, Adam, 148, 324
Smith-Lever Act, 152, 155
Social Darwinism, 325, 330
Social revolutionary group, 450
Social Security, 53–57
Social Security Commission Plan, 55
Social Security tax, 48
Social Security Trust Funds, 115
Social welfare policy, 38
Socioeconomic class. *See* Middle class
Socioeconomic indicators. *See* Welfare policy
Soft energy path, 252
Sokoma, Youba, 211
Solar troughs, 253
Solidarity Forever, 145
Solomon, Susan, 211
Sonar, 91
Southern High Plains region of Texas (SHTP), 259, 261
Sovacool, Benjamin K., 238
Special district, 138–139
Special Report on Emissions Scenarios (SRES), 216
Spencer, Herbert, 325

Sponsored gambling, 49
Sprout, Harold and Margaret, 416
Spykman, Nicholas, 403
SRES, 216
SSI. *See* Supplemental security income (SSI)
St. Augustine, 403
State health insurance licensing, 121–122
State of Fear (Crichton), 206
Statewide choice (public school choice), 147
Stern, Sol, 143
Stimulus spending, 75–79
Stone, Deborah, 28
Stott, Peter, 211
Stouffer, Ronald, 211
Stovall, Jeff, 272
Stove-piping, 239, 242, 245, 253, 255, 257
Strike, 144
Strong, Maurice, 195
Structural anarchy, 403
Structural deficit, 53
Structural realism, 404
Succession of comparisons, 20–21
Successive limited comparisons, 15, 21
Sugiyama, Taishi, 211
Suicide terrorists, 446, 455
Summers, Larry, 117
Supplemental security income (SSI), 350
Supply-side economic thinking, 326
Sustainable development, 197
Sutherland, Ronald J., 242
Swart, Rob, 211
Switzer, Barry, 330
Synfuels Corporation, 242
Systematic bias, 413–414

T
TANF. *See* Temporary Assistance for Needy Families (TANF)
TAR. *See* Third Assessment Report (TAR)
TARP. *See* Troubled Assets Relief Program (TARP)
Taxes
 on consumption, 44
 cuts, 49–53, 75
 efficiency of, 44–48
 expenditures, 45, 46
 fairness of, 45–48
 health care, 113, 114, 118–120
 incidence, 47
 on income, 43–44
 loopholes in, 48, 113–114
 Medicare HI tax, 113
 progressive *vs.* regressive tax, 47
 on property and wealth, 44
 revenue as percentage of GDP, 43
Tax-exempt bonds, 83
Taylor, Jerry, 242
Taylor, Paul, 353, 354, 371
Technical rationality, 207
Telhami, Shibley, 443
Temporary Assistance for Needy Families (TANF), 346–348
Terrorism, 431, 433. *See also* Counterterrorism
Terry v. Ohio, 279
Test for "best" policy, 18
Theorists and practitioners, 21
Theory of International Politics (Waltz), 404
Third Assessment Report (TAR), 211
Thompson, William (Baron of Kelvin), 244–245
Three Is of the American Energy Impasse, 240–250
Three strikes policy, 284
Thucydides, 402
Tirpak, Dennis, 211
Top-down studies, 227n
Trade deficit, 73–74
Tragedy of the commons, 200
Transformation R&D strategy, 250–255
Transportation, 254
Trial, 283
Trickle-down theory, 330
Troubled Assets Relief Program (TARP), 61
Truman, David, 7
Tulipmania, 448
Turner, Jonathan Baldwin, 153, 154

U
Ucko, David, 447
Underinsured, 98
Unfinished Business: A Comparative Assessment of Environmental Problems, 209
Uninsured, 97–98
Unions, 142–146
United States Department of Agriculture (USDA), 153, 155
Universal product number (UPN), 111
U.S.A. Patriot Act, 288–289
USDA. *See* United States Department of Agriculture (USDA)

V
Values-based foreign policy, 418–429
van Gogh, Theo, 458
Vector, 448
Vertical equity, 47
Victoroff, Jeff, 430
Vietnam War, 440–441
Violence Against Women Act, 285
Virgil, 325
Vogel, Coleen, 211
Voucher programs, 147–150

W
Wage indexing, 55
Waivers, 348–349
Wallerstein, Immanuel, 408
Waltz, Kenneth, 404, 409
War and Change in World Politics (Gilpin), 405, 416
War metaphor, 430, 433–442, 464–466
 Cold War analogy, 440
 detainee issue, 437
 fascism, 440
 historical overview, 434–435
 issues of fit, 436–437
 motivational effects, 465–466
 Munich analogy, 439–440
 9/11 terrorist attacks, 435–436
 Pearl Harbor analogy, 439
 psychological aspects, 441–442
 undermining terrorists' capability, 464–465
 Vietnam War, 440–441
Warren, Earl, 135
Warren, Rick, 428
Washington v. Texas, 279
Water conservation policy. *See* Ogallala Aquifer
Water pumpage fee, 264–269
Watt, James, 245
Wealth, 333
Wealth inequality, 334–335, 336
Wealth of Nations (Smith), 148
Weather Underground, 450
Websites
 economic policy, 82
 education policy, 187

health care policy, 125
politics and the policy process, 23
President's health care proposal, 115
welfare policy, 394
Weingarten rule, 146
Weinman, Gabriel, 453
Weisbrot, Mark, 55
Welfare economies, 38
Welfare policy, 323–400
    child care, 349
    child nutrition, 351
    child support enforcement, 352
    child welfare, 349–350
    class. *See* Middle class
    Cochran/Malone, 324–345
    debt-to-asset ratio, 369
    democratic equality, 341–344
    economic growth, 340–341
    economic inequality, 341–344
    equity and equality, 325–327
    expenditure levels, 369
    factors contributing to inequality, 328–329
    food stamps, 350–351
    functional theory of inequality, 330–333
    Gini index, 333–334, 337
    global inequalities, 336–340
    income distribution, 328
    income equality, 333–334, 337–338
    Lorenz curve, 335, 337
    median family wealth, 368–369
    Pew Research Center, 353–393
    policies to reduce inequality, 344
    progress in life, 380
    PRWORA. *See* Personal Responsibility and Work Opportunity Reconciliation Act (PRWORA)
    quality to life, 380, 381
    real income, 368
    sour mood, 386–387
    SSI, 350
    support for inequality, 329–330
    TANF, 346–348
    tradeoffs, 331–332
    wealth inequality, 334–335, 336
    websites, 394
Welfare state, 38
West Virginia University Extension Service, 152
"What's the Matter with Kansas?" (Frank), 327

Wheeler, Erin, 272
White flight, 148
Wight, Martin, 403
Wilkinson, Richard, 342
Will, George, 150
Williams, Juan, 134
Willis, David, 259
Wilson, Carter A., 90
Wilson, Charles E., 146
Wilson, Woodrow, 418
Winfree, Paul, 78
Wohlstetter, Roberta, 439
Wolf v. Colorado, 279
Wolfers, Arnold, 403
World capitalist system, 408, 409
World Trade Center bombing (1993), 443
Wright, Robert, 424
Wulf, William A., 250

Y
Yeager, Kurt, 247
Yohe, Gary, 211
Yousef, Ramzi, 439, 443
Yushchenko, Viktor, 427

Z
Zammar, Mohammed Haydar, 457
Zandi, Mark, 52
Zelman v. Simmons-Harris, 149
Zoning, 139